THE PSYCHOLOGY *of* ABNORMALITY

THE PSYCHOLOGY
of ABNORMALITY

Christopher Peterson

University of Michigan, Ann Arbor

HARCOURT BRACE COLLEGE PUBLISHERS

Fort Worth   Philadelphia   San Diego   New York   Orlando   Austin   San Antonio
Toronto   Montreal   London   Sydney   Tokyo

Publisher	*Ted Buchholz*
Editor in Chief	*Christopher P. Klein*
Senior Developmental Editor	*Sarah Helyar Smith*
Senior Project Editor	*Angela Williams*
Senior Production Manager	*Kenneth A. Dunaway*
Art Directors	*Nick Welch / Melinda Welch*

ABOUT THE ARTIST

Born in 1949 in Detroit, Michigan, Kevin Tolman attended classes at the Detroit Institute and Cass Tech. He is a graduate of the Art School of the Society of Arts & Crafts, where he studied with Brenda Goodman.

Tolman left Detroit for Ireland in 1977. But, before moving to the Ramah Navajo Reservation in New Mexico in 1981, he lived in Fort Worth and Dallas, Texas; Los Angeles, California; and Lawrence, Kansas. The artist settled in the Duranes area of Albuquerque in 1987, building an adobe house and studio. In 1990, he spent a year painting in Arraiolos, a small hill town in Central Portugal.

Tolman works in a variety of media—drawing in pencil and caran d'ache on paper, painting in both acrylic and oil on canvas and wood, and collage. The drawings and paintings are primarily landscape-based abstractions offering intimate views of New Mexico. Indeed, the orchards seen out the artist's studio window serve as the basis for the "birds in a tree" series. Many other pieces reflect views found along the Rio Grande River near his home or in the high mesa country near Ramah and Zuni.

Several of Tolman's drawings have been used on book jackets, in magazines, and on album covers. His work is also included in the book *Twelve New Mexican Landscape Painters,* published in the spring of 1994.

Requests for permission to make copies of any part of the work should be mailed to:
Permissions Department, Harcourt Brace & Company, 6277 Sea Harbor Drive, Orlando, FL 32887-6777.

Address for Editorial Correspondence
Harcourt Brace College Publishers, 301 Commerce Street, Suite 3700, Fort Worth, TX 76102

Address for Orders
Harcourt Brace & Company, 6277 Sea Harbor Drive, Orlando, FL 32887
1-800-782-4479, or 1-800-433-0001 (in Florida)

Copyright acknowledgments begin on page 545.

ISBN: 0-15-500092-6

Library of Congress Catalogue Number: 94-74222

Printed in the United States of America

5 6 7 8 9 0 1 2 3 4   032   10 9 8 7 6 5 4 3 2 1

PREFACE

The Psychology of Abnormality is a comprehensive yet efficient textbook on psychological disorders. Containing only 15 chapters, it is designed to fit readily within a typical academic term. Theoretically balanced, it includes DSM-IV criteria and up-to-date coverage; it places psychopathology in its multiple contexts (historical, social, and cultural); it stresses the continuity between normality and abnormality; and it attends to human diversity more than the typical textbook. This book systematically features numerous, evocative case examples, as well as parallel figures and charts across chapters. The single voice with which this book is written makes the reading consistent and lively.

BACKGROUND

Abnormal psychology is an extremely popular course at most colleges and universities. Students invariably find the subject matter intellectually and personally intriguing. The task of the instructor (and the textbook author) is to tap this interest by providing compelling, up-to-date information and by encouraging critical thinking.

In addition to being trained as a clinical psychologist and experimental psychopathologist, I studied social psychology and personality. These perspectives have intermingled in both my research and teaching, causing me to emphasize the continuity between normality and abnormality and allowing me to place the problems of individuals in their multiple contexts. Students respond very well to this broad perspective, as shown by their naming my abnormal psychology course the "outstanding university course" at the University of Michigan. *The Psychology of Abnormality* grows directly out of this course.

The subject matter of psychology is *all* people, and throughout the book I have discussed topics in terms of their interpersonal, cultural, and historical contexts. People share much in common, including psychological problems, but there exist important differences along lines of gender, ethnicity, socioeconomic status, age, and cohort. *The Psychology of Abnormality* represents a significant step toward a perspective that is becoming increasingly compelling. Diversity is addressed both in the text and in the focus sections of each chapter.

I have tried to be scientifically honest, identifying what is *not* known as well as what *is* known, and I have tried to cover the range of theoretical perspectives that compete within the field. If I have a bias, it is in favor of attempts that pull perspectives together.

ORGANIZATION

The first four chapters provide a general introduction, after which the book moves to the discussion of specific disorders. In other words, *The Psychology of Abnormality* gets to the "interesting stuff" more quickly than most other textbooks but not at the expense of the basic ideas.

The specific placement of two chapters is different from other textbooks in this field. Chapter 5 addresses substance abuse and, for the most part, alcohol abuse. I chose to cover these topics in the first disorder chapter because it allows me to establish the introductory ideas from Chapters 1 through 4 while discussing a topic of great importance and interest to students. Chapter 5 is an extended and explicit example, hence its title, "The Case of Substance Abuse." I have attempted to establish the connections with earlier ideas very clearly so that students themselves can follow this model in subsequent chapters. Most abnormal psychology textbooks present substance abuse later in the book in the vicinity of sexual disorders and personality disorders, but I believe the pedagogical value of this chapter in its early location outweighs any inconvenience created by its placement.

Chapter 6 addresses organic disorders. There is no typical placement of this sort of chapter in other textbooks, but it is rarely encountered near the beginning; some books even relegate it to an appendix. I decided to place it early in the book because I find that some students need an overview of the nervous system. The concepts presented here show up in every subsequent chapter.

The remaining chapters move from relatively common and circumscribed problems (for example, fears and phobias in Chapter 7) to relatively severe and pervasive disorders (for example, schizophrenia in Chapter 12 and personality disorders in Chapter 13). These chapters have been further ordered to allow for appropriate transitions. Thus, Chapter 7 (Fear and

Anxiety Disorders) leads readily to Chapter 8 (Somatoform and Dissociative Disorders) because the disorders covered in each entail anxiety. Chapter 9 (Mood Disorders) then follows because of the comorbidity of anxiety and depression, as well as the obvious comparisons and contrasts that can be drawn. Chapter 10 (Mind–Body Disorders) comes next because anxiety and depression are among the presumed mechanisms of psychosomatic problems. Chapter 11 (Sexual Disorders) appears next as a special case of mind–body problems. Chapter 12 (Schizophrenic Disorders) precedes Chapter 13 (Personality Disorders) because some of the interesting speculation regarding personality disorders concerns their link with schizophrenia. Finally, Chapter 14 (Disorders of Childhood and Adolescence) completes the disorder chapters and represents a different perspective—developmental psychopathology—from the earlier chapters. *The Psychology of Abnormality* concludes with Chapter 15, a discussion of the social context of abnormality, in particular the community and the legal system.

CASE EXAMPLES

Numerous case studies provide clear, evocative examples of given psychological disorders. Drawn from actual cases—that is, from my own work as well as from other published sources—the subjects both exemplify and reflect the contextual emphasis of the book.

FOCUS SECTIONS

Within each chapter, a focus section looks closely at one particular example of the given disorder in its larger context. The topics range from ethnic differences in substance abuse, to mania and creativity in mood disorders, to sexuality among Sambian males, and finally to sex differences in personality disorders.

PEDAGOGY

Key terms, shown in boldface in the text, are defined within the sentence where they first appear and are listed at the end of each chapter. A glossary at the back of the book collects all of the terms for easy reference. A point-by-point chapter summary encapsulates the important ideas from each major section.

ANCILLARIES

Textbook authors often do not write ancillaries for their own books, a practice that can create inconsistencies that puzzle students and instructors alike. Another strength of *The Psychology of Abnormality* is a set of ancillary materials that I prepared myself.

The Study Guide is based on the material I make available to my own students. Each chapter, which reinforces the pedagogy of the textbook, contains the following elements: learning objectives; a summary of each section; a review of the key terms, theorists, and dates; connections to other chapters; a multiple-choice practice test (25–35 items); critical-thinking questions that encourage students to synthesize information from throughout the chapter (these questions also make good topics for research papers); and suggestions for further reading.

The Instructor's Manual begins by recommending several themes by which to structure the course. It then closely follows the textbook and the Study Guide by providing the following elements in each chapter: learning objectives, an annotated chapter outline that addresses both the key topics and the key terms in each section, general references, suggestions for how to discuss each case study, suggestions for activities and exercises, and a list of films and videotapes.

The Test Bank, which is available in both print and computerized forms, features more than 1700 items (an average of over 110 test items per chapter). Each item is categorized according to whether it is factual, conceptual, or applied. Most of the items have been tested in the classes from which the textbook grew.

ACKNOWLEDGMENTS

Many individuals helped me in the five years that I spent writing *The Psychology of Abnormality*. Instructors at other colleges and universities reviewed drafts of individual chapters. I took something helpful from every review, and *The Psychology of Abnormality* is a much better book because of this advice. Thanks to Jack R. Adams-Webber, Brock University; Gordon Atlas, Alfred University; John S. Baer, University of Washington; Marna Barrett, Indiana University of Pennsylvania; Larry Bernard, Loyola Marymount University; Mia Biran, Miami University; Robert Bornstein, Gettysburg University; Melissa M. Brown, State University of New York, Brockport; M. Lynne Cooper, State University of New York, Buffalo; Phil Cowan, University of California, Berkeley; James H. Dalton, Jr., Bloomsburg University; William Davidson, Michigan State University; Roland Engelhart, University of Windsor; Peter R. Finn, Indiana University; Victoria M. Follette, University of Nevada; John Foust, Parkland College; Stan Friedman, Southwest Texas State University; William Rick Fry, Youngstown State University; John Gabrieli, Stanford University; Perilou Goddard, Northern Kentucky University; John Grossberg, San Diego State University; William Haley, University of Alabama; Laurie Heatherington,

Williams College; T. Ken Ishida, California State University, Bakersfield; Kenneth E. Leonard, Research Institute on Alcoholism; Elissa Lewis, Southwest Missouri State University; Steve Lopez, University of California, Los Angeles; Joseph Lowman, University of North Carolina, Chapel Hill; Justin Douglas McDonald, University of North Dakota; Dudley McGlynn, Auburn University; Janet Matthews, Loyola University; David Mostovsky, Boston University; Greg J. Niemeyer, University of Florida; Susan Nolen-Hoeksema, Stanford University; Paul Olczak, State University of New York, Geneseo; Les Parrott, Seattle Pacific University; Richard Pasewark, University of Wyoming; Max Rardin, University of Wyoming; Beth Rienzi, California State University, Bakersfield; Caton Roberts, State University of New York, Buffalo; David Santogrossi, Purdue University; Sandra Sigmon, University of Maine, Orono; Jacob Sines, University of Iowa; Jerome Small, Youngstown State University; Timothy Strauman, University of Wisconsin, Madison; Yolanda Suárez, Jacksonville State University; Douglas Ullman, Bowling Green State University; Norris Vestre, Arizona State University; Richard M. Wenzlaff, University of Texas, San Antonio; and Michael Wierzbicki, Marquette University.

Among the staff at Harcourt Brace, acquisitions editors Rick Roehrich, Marcus Boggs, and Eve Howard have been supportive of my writing. Senior developmental editor Sarah Helyar Smith worked closely with me through more drafts than I can count, and I always appreciated her gentleness and humor. Marketing manager Susan Kindel adeptly marketed the book, and senior project editor Angela Williams skillfully shepherded the book through production. Photo editor Susan Holtz researched the photo program, art directors Nick Welch and Melinda Welch created the handsome design, and senior production manager Ken Dunaway coordinated a varying schedule.

Library staff members at the University of Michigan were always prompt and helpful when I needed to track down an elusive fact or reference. My friends at Kinko's in Ann Arbor duplicated drafts rapidly and flawlessly, time after time. The waitstaff at the Cottage Inn in Ann Arbor never shooed me away as I sat in a booth for hours and edited my chapters.

I also am grateful to my students and teaching assistants at the University of Michigan. My abnormal psychology course evolved as my writing proceeded, and vice versa, and the input of my students and teaching assistants made this development possible.

Finally, I could not have written this book without the encouragement and assistance of Lisa M. Bossio. From comments about the big picture to reminders about the small details, she helped me write a coherent book. Thanks, Lisa, as usual.

To Lisa, with all of my love.

ABOUT THE AUTHOR

Christopher Peterson attended the University of Illinois as a National Merit Scholar, graduating with a major in psychology and a minor in mathematics. He then enrolled in the social/personality graduate program at the University of Colorado, Boulder, where he received his Ph.D. in 1976. Wishing to expand his work in psychology, he went to the University of Pennsylvania for postdoctoral respecialization in clinical psychology and experimental psychopathology.

Professor Peterson is an award-winning teacher. His abnormal psychology course was voted by students as the "outstanding university course" at the University of Michigan, Ann Arbor, where he is professor of psychology in the Clinical Psychology and Personality Graduate Programs. Prior to teaching at the University of Michigan, he taught at Virginia Tech and at Hamilton and Kirkland Colleges.

Dr. Peterson's research interests include cognitive influences on achievement, depression, and physical well-being. He has written numerous articles for and has been on the editorial boards of the *Journal of Abnormal Psychology, Journal of Personality and Social Psychology,* and *Psychological Bulletin.* He is also a member of the American Psychological Association Media Referral Service.

BRIEF CONTENTS

CONTENTS

The Psychology *of* Abnormality

What Is Abnormality?

1 SUPPOSE YOU ARE HAVING A CONVERSATION with a friend. Most of the time you probably talk about the meaning of life or how to improve the world for future generations. But you may occasionally stoop to talking about other people, gossiping about strange things you have seen or heard about. In the course of such a conversation you might say, "Hey, that's crazy! Somebody ought to do something about that." When you do so, you are discussing the subject matter of this textbook: psychological abnormality.

Here are paraphrased versions of actual stories that my students have told me over the years. They

2

always start by saying, "I have a friend . . ." Most of their stories are poignant, and what they share in common is the question about whether the friend described should be called *abnormal*.

I invite you to eavesdrop and come up with an opinion in each case. Which of these people strike you as crazy? In which cases should somebody—parents, counselors, friends, teachers—intervene and do something?

✦ *I have a friend who barely eats anything. She's very skinny, but she insists she looks chubby. She wants to lose 5 more pounds, but I'm afraid she'll make herself sick.*

✦ *I have a friend who drinks every Friday and Saturday night. He says he's okay because he doesn't drink during the week and that his grades are good. He says he likes to relax, and that I have a problem because I'm judgmental.*

✦ *I have a friend who broke up with his girlfriend a few months ago. He sleeps all the time now, and never wants to do anything. His grades have slipped. Yesterday he said that he saw no reason to keep living.*

Is a college student who drinks only on the weekends or vacations psychologically abnormal?

◆ *I have a friend who is an incredible procrastinator. He's always putting off his school projects. His teachers think he's smart—I guess because he really is—and they cut him a lot of slack. But I think it's all going to come crashing down someday.*

◆ *I have a friend who has the strangest habit when she eats. She counts the number of times that she chews each mouthful of food, and she tells me that she tries to chew an even number of times. I can't talk to her at dinner anymore, because she doesn't pay attention to what I'm saying. She's too busy counting.*

◆ *I have a friend who shaved his head and wears only black leather. I think the clothes are okay, but he's also started to wear an earring shaped like an Iron Cross. That really gets to me, because my grandparents died in a concentration camp.*

◆ *I have a friend whose goal in life seems to be to go to bed with as many people as possible. At this point everybody is laughing behind her back. And I'm worried she'll get AIDS. Then what?*

Are members of hate groups psychologically abnormal?

In this book, you will learn about the psychological problems that people experience. There are several important points to keep in mind throughout this discussion of how psychology approaches the topic of abnormality. First, the study of abnormality by psychologists is a subset of general psychology, which means you should approach the topic with a scientific attitude. Because abnormality is often so interesting in its own right, it is easy to lose track of psychology's goal of explaining how problems come about and devising means of preventing and treating them.

Second, there is a tendency for us to d–i–s–t–a–n–c–e ourselves from people with severe problems. Often we can see ourselves in them and their difficulties, and this makes us feel uncomfortable. When you are tempted to think of people with problems as "those kinds of people," stop and appreciate how in many ways we are all those people.

Third, there is sometimes a tendency to romanticize abnormality, to think that people with strange problems are somehow charismatic and creative. They march to a different drummer, somehow more true than our own. As you will see, this is not exactly the case. Choice has little to do with psychological abnormality. The people described in this book are not to be envied. By definition, they have problems with life. We should try to understand them and be sympathetic to them, but they are not heroes.

Fourth, many problems exist in degrees, which means that you should not panic simply because part of what you experience in your life is similar to the striking cases of psychological abnormality described throughout the book. Indeed, sadness and worry, obstinacy and error, confusion and hurt are all part of the human condition. If you occasionally experience a symptom of some disorder, that in itself is normal.

DEFINING ABNORMALITY

Defining psychological abnormality is no easy task, which is why I would like to start by discussing what is involved. I offer no simple or firm conclusions. Instead, I raise issues that will recur throughout the text. Any judgment of abnormality has two parts: a *label* placed on some action by a person ("that's crazy") and a *recommendation*, explicit or implicit, that an *intervention* be undertaken ("somebody ought to do something about that").

An important difference between you and mental health professionals is that they have a socially sanctioned role that allows them to make these judgments. Professionals have special expertise and are paid for offering such opinions, and their judgments may have considerable consequences. But the point remains that they are doing much of what you are doing.

Think back to the stories my students have told me. Which of these people are abnormal? In which cases should an authority intervene? Most of you labeled at least some of these people as abnormal. You probably had a reasonable explanation for each of your judgments. But consider two points. First, few of these stories lead to a consensus. In each case, some of you think the person is behaving in an abnormal fashion, whereas others think not. Second, even when people agree about what is abnormal and normal, the rationales behind their judgments often differ. The same holds true for professionals trained to make judgments of abnormality. They may show great disagreement. Judgments of abnormality are fuzzy. The very meaning of abnormality cannot be precisely expressed.

RESEARCH DEFINITIONS OF ABNORMALITY

I can further illustrate the imprecision inherent in the definition of abnormality by looking at the different ways researchers have tried to get a handle on what is and is not abnormal (Scott, 1958). Consider common operational definitions used by psychologists and psychiatrists in their investigations of abnormality (see Figure 1.1). An **operational definition** specifies in concrete terms how to measure some concept (Chapter 4), so we can expect these definitions to be as exact as any we could find. All of these operational definitions have seen frequent use in well respected research. However, none is fully satisfactory. Although certainly capturing part of what is meant by abnormality, in each case there are some mistakes.

Exposure to psychiatric or psychological treatment One operationalization of abnormality common to survey research simply asks if a person has ever been in therapy (e.g., Klein, Behnke, & Peterson, 1993). If so, then the individual is classified as abnormal. If not, then she is considered normal. ·

On the whole, people in therapy have more difficulties than people who are not. But a moment's thought convinces us that this definition does not always identify the right people. There will be individuals in therapy who are not particularly troubled and other individuals out of therapy who are profoundly distressed (see Figure 1.2). Many people enter therapy when they have begun to lose hope in the face of some particular problem. But if they have lost too much hope, they will be fatalistic about therapy as well. Also, people may enter therapy at the urging of friends or family members, but a socially-isolated individual—despite serious problems—may lack this encouragement.

Furthermore, whether or not people are in treatment reflects not just problems they may have but whether they are able to pay for treatment. Therapists usually receive fees for their services. In many cases, these fees are so high ($90 to $125 per hour) that only some people are able to afford them. Relying on this definition of abnormality drags in the confound of economics, and we would not want this to be part of what we mean by abnormality.

Diagnosis of abnormality   A second operationalization that is often used does not require the person in question actually to seek treatment for a problem, but merely to receive a diagnosis from somebody in a position to make one (e.g., Kessler et al., 1994). A *diagnosis* is a label placed on a person that says he or she has one of the possible psychological problems that people experience, and it usually results from a standardized interview with a trained diagnostician (Chapter 2). This is one of the most common ways of ascertaining abnormality. In subsequent chapters, when I describe investigations of particular disorders, you will see how research participants are selected (or not) based on the diagnoses they warrant.

In several ways, this operational definition improves on the previous one. By this definition, a person

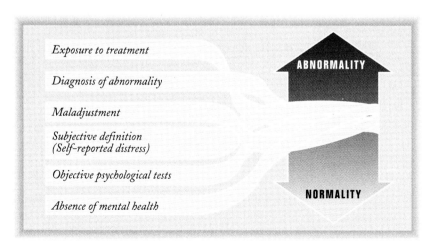

Exposure to treatment

Diagnosis of abnormality

Maladjustment

*Subjective definition
(Self-reported distress)*

Objective psychological tests

Absence of mental health

ABNORMALITY

NORMALITY

FIGURE 1.1

RESEARCH DEFINITIONS OF ABNORMALITY   *Several definitions of abnormality have seen wide use by researchers. These definitions are often useful, but they are not foolproof. They do not always identify the same individuals as abnormal.*
SOURCE: FROM "RESEARCH DEFINITIONS OF MENTAL HEALTH AND MENTAL ILLNESS," BY W. A. SCOTT, 1958, *Psychological Bulletin, 55,* PP. 1–45.

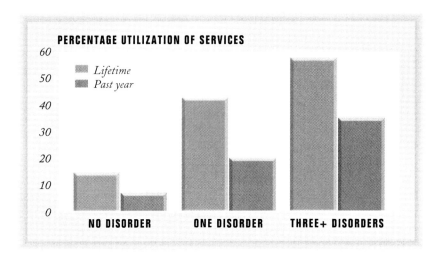

FIGURE 1.2

PEOPLE IN TREATMENT　　*R. C. Kessler and colleagues surveyed a random sample of American adults, administering a diagnostic interview to determine the presence of serious psychological difficulties during the past year and during their entire life. These researchers also asked respondents whether they had ever received treatment. Utilization of mental health services was more likely as people's problems increased. However, some people without serious problems had been in treatment, whereas many with diagnosable disorders had never been in treatment.*

SOURCE: "LIFETIME AND 12-MONTH PREVALENCE OF DSM-III-R PSYCHIATRIC DIAGNOSES IN THE UNITED STATES," BY R. C. KESSLER, K. A. McGONAGLE, S. ZHAO, C. B. NELSON, M. HUGHES, S. ESHLEMAN, H.-U. WITTCHEN, AND K. S. KENDLER, 1994, *Archives of General Psychiatry, 51,* PP. *8–19.*

who cannot afford therapy can still be considered abnormal. And a person pursuing treatment for reasons other than psychological distress would not warrant such a label. But problems remain. One is posed by

Access to the mental health system is controlled by gatekeepers such as police officers. An individual who does not enter the system cannot be diagnosed as abnormal, despite the existence of serious psychological problems.

gatekeepers: those who control access to the mental health system and thus to those who actually make diagnoses. Diagnoses are only made when people come into the presence of mental health professionals, and there are usually several steps before people are ever in this position.

Suppose Ms. Bazzetti is taken off the street by a police officer. She is dazed and disheveled. What happens to her? The police officer—one important keeper of the gate—makes a decision. Maybe she will be taken to jail to sleep off what looks like a hangover. Maybe she will be left on the sidewalk with what looks like a case of the flu. Maybe she will be released into the care of a friend. Maybe she will be referred to a hospital. Suppose she goes to a hospital. There Ms. Bazzetti faces various options, again under the sway of whoever happens to first see her—yet another gatekeeper. She may be sent to internal medicine or neurology or psychiatry. Only in the latter case do we know that a diagnosis of psychological abnormality will be considered.

A less extreme example is Mr. Hart. He has a problem and wants to talk to someone about it. If Mr. Hart rings up a friend on the phone, he does not receive a diagnosis. If he visits a clergyman, again he does not receive a diagnosis. But if he talks to a clinical psychologist, he may well receive a diagnosis. In other words, according to this operational definition, Mr. Hart's "abnormality" depends on the person he seeks out, which is why this particular approach is far from foolproof.

More insidiously, there is a well documented social class bias in the offering of diagnoses (Garfield, 1986). Lower-class individuals are more likely than those of the upper class to receive labels that suggest serious problems in living (Hollingshead & Redlich, 1958). The question of whether people of different social classes actually are more likely to suffer particular problems is a legitimate one, but at least part of this difference represents a bias in the mind of the diagnostician.

Maladjustment   Yet another common operational definition of abnormality is whether people are maladjusted—failing to meet the demands of the world in which they find themselves. In the extreme, this is a very reasonable definition. Consider that problems like depression or schizophrenia often lead to suicide. Taking your own life certainly qualifies as a failure to adjust to the world. Other problems such as substance abuse or anxiety take a clear toll on social and occupational satisfaction.

But matters are not always so clear because we must ask about *which* demand of the world a person is failing to satisfy. In a country like the United States, there is no single standard of adjustment. What looks like poor adjustment for one person might be reasonable adjustment for another. Standards differ, and there is considerable danger in using a monolithic standard to judge adjustment in a pluralistic society like our own.

For example, the Strange Situation Test is a procedure for judging whether children are securely attached to their parents (Ainsworth & Wittig, 1969). A mother brings her child to a researcher's lab where they are briefly separated, then reunited. How does the child respond to this strange situation? If the child is anxious upon separation and relieved upon being reunited, then this is judged to be a securely attached pattern—healthy and normal. But if the child is indifferent about the separation, then this is thought to show an insecure attachment, and is presumably cause for alarm.

Children in day care sometimes show the "insecure" pattern of adjustment, leading some psychologists to suggest that day care in America is disrupting the attachment of parents and children (Belsky, 1988). But realize that a child in day care is an old hand at the very essence of the Strange Situation Test, being

How children respond to separation from their caretakers is sometimes used to gauge their attachment. A typical response—presumably a sign of a secure attachment—is distress upon separation. However, some children who are securely attached take separation in stride and should not be considered abnormal.

separated and reunited with his mother. In other words, it is a familiar situation, and his reaction may actually be a quite reasonable one, granted his social reality (cf. Zigler & Frank, 1988).

It is difficult to apply the same standard of adjustment to people who live in different parts of the social world, in this case children where both parents work versus children in the mother-stays-at-home kind of family. The same point must be made when we are talking about the social adjustment of males versus females, the young versus the old, people from different families, people from different ethnic groups, people of different occupational and economic groups, and so on. What makes sense in one social context may be abnormal in another.

Subjective definition   Another common research definition of abnormality relies on self-report about the person's own state of affairs. Typically, an individual is given a questionnaire like the one in Table 1.1, which asks the individual to indicate the presence or absence in recent weeks of a number of possible symptoms of distress. A relatively high score means the respondent is abnormal, and a relatively low score indicates that he is normal (e.g., Peterson & Seligman, 1984). This definition is reasonable in that those who report many symptoms are on the whole more likely to have problems than those who report few. People may occasionally be mistaken, confused, or defensive, however—which means that once again we have an operationalization of abnormality that is often useful but still less than ideal. Consider people who engage in *denial,* failing to acknowledge consciously anything negative about themselves. By the subjective definition, they would be considered normal (Shedler, Mayman, & Manis, 1993). But part and parcel of many psychological problems is precisely the fact that people do not admit, even to themselves, that anything is wrong.

Of course, not all problems involve denial. Many highly anxious or depressed people have their feelings front and center. They can and will tell a psychologist exactly how they are feeling. But other people with problems like alcoholism or eating disorders often deny that anything is wrong, particularly when confronted with an impersonal questionnaire like the one shown in Table 1.1.

Another difficulty occasionally encountered with this operationalization comes when people exaggerate

TABLE 1.1

A SYMPTOM QUESTIONNAIRE *Here is an example of a questionnaire that asks the respondent about a variety of negative feelings that may indicate problems in living. The more negative feelings that an individual reports, the greater his or her problem is assumed to be.*

Instructions: Below is a list of feelings that people have. In each case, write the number in the blank space that best describes how you have been feeling during the past week:

1 = not at all
2 = somewhat
3 = moderately
4 = a great deal
5 = extremely

_____ anxious	_____ irritable
_____ angry	_____ sad
_____ bitter	_____ sluggish
_____ confused	_____ sorry
_____ forgetful	_____ tired
_____ frightened	_____ uncertain
_____ hopeless	_____ unhappy

their problems, possibly out of a mistaken view that abnormality is romantic or exciting. For instance, "No one understands me" is a frequent adolescent complaint (Raimy, 1976). These adolescents believe they are experiencing feelings and emotions that no one has ever before experienced. In most cases, of course, little is occurring except the stirrings of puberty. Almost everyone who has gone through puberty has had the exact same feelings, but adolescents often decide that they have become abnormal.

Objective psychological tests   One of the major activities of clinical psychologists is administering objective psychological tests. These tests aid professionals in making particular diagnoses (Chapter 2). Hence, they include guidelines about how to identify abnormality. Can we turn to these tests to *define* abnormality? Unfortunately, the answer is no. Although the tests were created to distinguish normal from abnormal people, how did the original researchers know who was normal and abnormal in the first place? They could not rely on the tests to provide the definition. Objective tests are only as reasonable as the definition on which they are based, and this definition must originate somewhere other than the tests themselves.

Absence of mental health   We sometimes encounter yet one more research definition of abnormality in the literature: People are abnormal to the degree that they *lack* mental health. We can see immediately that this is not a satisfactory definition because we first have to define what mental health is, which leads us through a tangle analogous to the present one. Defining health can be as elusive as defining its absence (Peterson & Bossio, 1991).

Interestingly, health and illness are not always the simple opposites that we usually make them out to be. We can force them to be opposite, by rating people on a scale that runs from abnormal to normal—choose one and only one answer. But when psychological "health" and "illness" are allowed to range independently of one another, they are often found to coexist.

A study of patients with AIDS illustrates this point (Chuang, Devins, Hunsley, & Gill, 1989). The subjects reported various symptoms of depression and anxiety, but at the same time they also reported sources of pleasure and happiness. They were more upset than other people, but beyond their feelings of distress, they at times were also just as happy. This study reminds us that we should not glibly define the one concept in terms of the other.

ABNORMALITY AS A SOCIAL JUDGMENT

I hope you have not been convinced that the definition of abnormality is impossible. Difficult yes, impossible no. We can take a step back from all these research definitions and conclude that none of them is completely off base; each captures part of what is meant by abnormality, but another part is missed. Perhaps the generic problem with these and similar research definitions of abnormality is that they assume there is something objective that resides in a person to which we can point and identify as psychological abnormality ("Hey, that's crazy!"). These definitions by and large neglect what necessarily is common to all judgments of abnormality: To have a person or action called abnormal, there must be another person who offers that judgment. Diagnoses of abnormality take place within a social context, which means that they must be examined and defined in these terms. What is deemed abnormal is what another person finds distressing, unusual, shocking, bizarre, wrong, and/or ignorant. When the person making the judgment is trained and empowered to offer a diagnosis, then what we have is psychological abnormality.

This analysis is similar to the approach for understanding deviance called *labeling theory* (Ericson, 1975). By this view, there is no such thing as deviance per se until a majority group places a deviant label on a minority group. The minority group might well be engaging in what is normative within its group; this does not matter if the behavior in question is upsetting to the group with the power to call it deviant.

Abnormality is not solely in the eye of the beholder, however, and it is not simply a matter of semantics. In other words, it is not just the label that distinguishes normal behavior from abnormal behavior. Labels may have a life of their own, but at the same time, they are applied to something. They may be handed out unfairly—remember the example mentioned earlier of the social class bias in how problems are diagnosed—but they are not handed out randomly. Banishing the label is not going to banish abnormality any more than removing offensive words from our language will make everyone act kindly.

The deviant or abnormal person is *not* simply unusual. This person may well be suffering a great deal and might even pose a danger to himself or to others. When you encounter schizophrenia later in the text, you will be disabused of the notion that the voices schizophrenic individuals sometimes hear are like an internal Walkman playing their favorite tunes. Instead, hallucinated voices are often accusatory, calling the people names and urging them to do something hazardous. Along these lines, many abnormal people are socially estranged. Their abnormal behavior obviously strains social relationships. Acquaintances and family members keep their distance. People with serious problems are not happy; this is what it means to have a problem.

THE FUZZINESS OF ABNORMALITY

I have suggested that abnormality is an imprecise concept that must be placed in its social context. My examples have illustrated abnormality, but they have not conveyed its full meaning. How can we define an imprecise notion such as abnormality? One strategy is to turn to the branch of philosophy concerned with ordinary language (Rundle, 1990). Many concepts used in everyday conversation lack necessary and sufficient conditions. This means that they are *not* characterized by attributes that all examples of the concept have *(necessary conditions)* and only examples of this concept have *(sufficient conditions)*.

Even if there are no necessary or sufficient conditions, there still are attributes or features that *tend* to cut across examples of a concept. Ludwig Wittgenstein (1953) referred to the set of pertinent attributes as a **family resemblance.** Just as members of a family tend to resemble each other on a set of characteristics, so do examples of a concept. The resemblance is defined by a set of pertinent attributes, not a single feature.

Tom and Dick are brothers who share the same shaggy hair. Dick looks like another brother, Harry, because they both have freckles. Harry in turn resembles Tom, because they are both angular and bony. Do Tom, Dick, and Harry look alike? Yes. Do they share any one feature? No. So it goes for ordinary language concepts.

Wittgenstein's ideas were brought into psychology by Eleanor Rosch, who demonstrated that his ideas are generally true about concepts used in ordinary language (e.g., Rosch & Mervis, 1975). Psychologists nowadays refer to these fuzzy concepts as *natural categories,* to convey the idea that this is the typical state of affairs. In contrast, the handful of concepts with necessary and sufficient conditions are termed *artificial categories,* because they usually have meaning within a scientific or mathematical system that people artificially create (e.g., triangles are necessarily and sufficiently defined by having three and only three sides).

Rosch has shown in her research that people agree on good (and bad) examples of natural concepts. Robins are "good" examples of birds. Apples are "good" examples of fruits. Kiwis are "bad" examples, of birds and fruits. Why? Good examples possess a number of the pertinent attributes that comprise the family resemblance. Bad examples, although still acknowledged as instances of the concept in question, do not have as many pertinent attributes, and they tend to share attributes with other concepts. Something may be an example, however bad, of several different concepts.

I think you see where this is leading. Abnormality is an imprecise concept, as used by everyday people as well as mental health professionals. Imprecise as well are specific categories of abnormality like substance abuse, anxiety, depression, and schizophrenia. We should expect definition via necessary and sufficient conditions to fail, because the boundaries of abnormality constantly shift. Note that an operational definition is an attempt to force a concept to be an artificial category by putting imprecise pegs into precise holes.

There are excellent examples of abnormality as well as poor examples. If we look to the excellent examples, we can begin to identify the attributes that comprise the family resemblance of abnormality. Here are factors that cut across many excellent examples of abnormality (Rosenhan & Seligman, 1984):

◆ suffering

◆ maladaptiveness

◆ violation of societal standards

◆ unusualness

◆ loss of control

◆ rigidity

Was the well publicized standoff between David Koresh and authorities a legal phenomenon, a moral one, or a psychological/psychiatric one? These domains may overlap, which muddies definition and thus understanding in all areas.

And so on. The different research definitions of abnormality overlap with some of these attributes, which is why these definitions are somewhat useful. But none of them embodies all of them.

This analysis pertains to global judgments of abnormality and to the specific judgments that enter into making distinctions among particular types of abnormality. For instance, consider the sexual problem known as *inhibited orgasm,* defined as the failure to achieve orgasm after sexual activity deemed "adequate" in focus, duration, and intensity (Chapter 11). There are obviously several difficult judgments that enter into this diagnosis.

This analysis also helps explain the occasional confusion encountered concerning professional jurisdiction over problematic people. Consider David Koresh and his well publicized standoff with authorities in 1993. Something was amiss, but we did not know if we were seeing a legal phenomenon, a religious one, or a psychological/psychiatric one. These domains of judgment overlap. We can find instances that fall unambiguously into one and only one category, but we can also find examples that seem to straddle the border of two or more.

The family resemblance approach to defining abnormality is persuasive up to a point (Cantor, Smith, French, & Mezzich, 1980), but it is nonetheless unsatisfactory to many who concern themselves with abnormality. It is completely relativistic. It provides no clear answer about what is abnormal. It may well be that no clear answer exists, but the mental health system is not set up on a fuzzy basis. People cannot receive a fuzzy diagnosis, fuzzy treatment, or a fuzzy disability pension. They cannot be "kind of" insane.

If abnormality is an imprecise concept reflecting social judgment, then we are in effect saying that people "vote" on what is normal or not. In point of fact, citizens at large do *not* have an equal voice in deciding what is normal or not. What really happens is that mental health professionals vote, and whatever biases they bring to bear will influence what is and is not deemed abnormal.

Maybe there is something objective at the base of at least some types of abnormality. Over the years, there has been great interest in finding biological causes for a variety of problems. If it can be determined, let us say, that some large number of people with problem X have a defect in their brain or endocrine system, their problem presumably is more objective than a social judgment. The tension between the fuzzy concept perspective and those who think nature has a deeper structure is an ongoing one which we will encounter throughout this book.

TAKING STOCK

Here are the major points of this section. First and quite obviously, *a firm definition of abnormality cannot be proposed,* at least at the present time. Stating this in another way, *there is an imprecise line between normality and abnormality.* We can speak therefore of abnormality being continuous, reflecting differences in degrees but not always in kind. The fuzzier the line, the more continuity can be assumed.

Consider depression, which refers to both a transient emotional reaction to disappointment ("I'm depressed; I missed my favorite cartoon show") and a chronic and pervasive state that might lead an individual to attempt suicide ("I'm depressed; I have no reason to keep on going"). Obviously, the former instance of depression is trivial and the latter profound. Where do we draw the line between the two? Perhaps in no particular place.

Second, despite the imprecision in the definition, *extreme examples of abnormality are easy to recognize and agree upon.* By and large, the particular problems that I consider in subsequent chapters of this text are excellent examples of abnormality.

Consider the case of a woman who drank herself to death. I brand this an unambiguous instance of abnormality. Wait, you say. Perhaps alcohol consumption made sense in her subculture. Perhaps she had an unrecognized enzyme problem. Perhaps she was 97 years old and had lived this long because drinking reduced her anxieties.

No, this woman drank herself to death with water. Apparently she believed she had intestinal cancer, despite assurances from numerous physicians to the contrary. She was convinced that she had a tumor and that the way to deal with it was to flush it from her system, like we would flush something down a drain. Thus, she undertook to drink water, gallons per day. This is not healthy, because it upsets the body's electrolyte balance, eventually causing a heart attack (Mook, 1987). All of this ensued. She drank herself to death.

None would disagree that this is an excellent example of what we mean by abnormality, but when we leave the textbook and such examples behind, we find much more uncertainty. Practicing psychologists and psychiatrists should always keep in mind the imprecise borders of abnormality. So too should you as a student and citizen of the world. When discussing particular problems, I will remind you just where the ambiguity exists. One way to do this is to take a view across history and culture. Considerable variation exists in terms of just what and why something is considered abnormal.

Extreme examples of abnormality are easy to recognize and agree upon. This homeless woman collects only red things, a habit that most people would regard as highly unusual.

The third point is that *the social context of abnormality must never be forgotten.* Many definitions of abnormality seem to locate problems solely within the individual—but the individual lives within a family within a community within a time and place. The social setting of abnormality is the context within which we offer conclusions and qualifications. The study of abnormal psychology is necessarily the study of us, and we live in a social world shaped by history and culture (see Focus on Cross-Cultural Psychopathology).

THE HISTORY OF ABNORMALITY

I now turn to *why* people are abnormal and how we might help them. Explanations often suggest interventions, and so these matters are linked. Adding to the difficulty of defining abnormality in the present is the fact that a historical view shows considerable diversity in how abnormality has been conceived. Further, later perspectives on abnormality build on earlier ones. As we progress through time we find ever more complicated views. Two constants remain: the attempt to explain abnormality and the use of these explanations as the rationale for interventions.

In the Western world, we can distinguish three perspectives on abnormality. I cover them in order of their appearance and dominance. First, we have *magical* explanations. According to these notions, people act in unusual or bizarre fashion because of evil forces. This mode of explanation, which implicates causes transcending the mundane world of nature, stands in contrast to the other ways of conceptualizing abnormality. The *somatic* view argues that abnormality reflects the malfunction of a person's body; in other

FOCUS ON

Cross-Cultural

Psychopathology

CULTURE REFERS TO THE shared knowledge transmitted from one generation to another. It is represented externally in terms of roles and institutions, as well as internally in terms of values and beliefs. If people's problems are located in a social context, then it is obvious that the culture in which they exist demands scrutiny. The field that specifically investigates problems in their cultural context is **cross-cultural psychopathology.**

Over the years, cross-cultural psychopathology has oscillated between two extremes (Marsella, 1988). On one hand, some theorists have expressed the opinion that culture does not matter; all disorders at their basis are the same regardless of the culture in which they occur. On the other hand, different theorists have espoused total relativism; all disorders are unique to a particular time and place. Today, a middle ground is occupied by most cross-cultural psychopathologists. Many of the broad categories of abnormality—anxiety, depression, schizophrenia, and substance abuse—seem to have a certain universality, perhaps because they have a basis in biology and/or common environmental demands. But culture nonetheless shapes many of these disorders—how they manifest themselves and to whom they occur.

For example, cross-cultural studies of depression show that virtually every culture recognizes behaviors reflecting despondency, fatigue, and diminished sexual interest (Kleinman & Good, 1985; Marsella, 1980). These are central depressive symptoms in the contemporary United States. At the same time, a closer look reveals important differences. In Nigeria, "depression"

as a syndrome is not recognized, although its component symptoms are. In many Asian cultures such as China, the core symptoms of depression tend not to be accompanied by guilt and self-deprecation as they are in Western cultures.

Nonetheless, we must be aware of what is termed the *category fallacy*, taking a diagnostic category from one culture and expecting it to exist in all other cultures without establishing that it actually does (Rogler, 1989). There exist disorders in some cultures that have no clear counterpart in other cultures (Chapter 2). Related to the category fallacy is the notion that disorders are entities existing in pure forms that may be disguised by culture (Kleinman, 1977). So, we can presumably strip away culture to find "true" psychopathology underneath. This line of reasoning is faulty because culture affects behavior—normal or abnormal—in a multitude of ways, not simply by adding a layer to basic human nature (Rogler, 1989). For troubled individuals, culture provides the context for their problems, not a disguise.

In referring to cross-cultural differences, I do not mean simply variations around the globe. I am also talking about those differences that exist *within* a multicultural society, like our own. There exist a variety of ethnic and cultural groups in the United States. How do disorders compare and contrast across these? Blacks, for example, appear to be more at risk for hypertension than whites (Gillum, 1979). What is the significance of this difference? And different socioeconomic classes may show variations in abnormality as well.

Where does this leave us? Mental health professionals should be aware of the culture in which they are working. Rogler (1989) describes culturally sensitive work as a constant checking back and forth between one's approach and the culture in which it is used. This, of course, is what occurs in any scientific endeavor—an attempt to make procedures valid.

words, abnormality is conceived as an injury or illness. The third perspective is the *psychogenic* view, which argues that abnormality reflects a problem with a person's psychological makeup.

It is customary to place these perspectives in their own eras, but that implies that they are more distinct than is really the case. In fact, these explanations have intermingled over the years, and it is not always easy to say when one ends and another begins.

MAGICAL EXPLANATIONS

Our distant ancestors are described as believing in the supernatural. However, this description does not allow us to step inside their heads. "Supernatural" only means something to those who have a "natural" to juxtapose with it. By natural, I mean a scientific, deterministic, materialistic explanation of the world and its entities, including abnormality. To say that a belief system is supernatural is to say that it is *not* natural in this sense, but this does not tell us what it actually is.

I take a different tack here by drawing on Frazer's (1922) descriptions of societies that believed in magic. "Magic" describes what once was a common belief system in a variety of cultures around the world. Frazer's anthropological and historical studies suggest that certain beliefs were widespread, specifically:

1. There exist powerful forces in nature that can be directed by divine interventions and/or liberated by special arts called **magic.**

2. The mechanisms of magic include certain words or spells, certain substances, and/or certain symbols.

3. People and their environments are continuous, exerting mutual influence on one another.

4. People can influence one another by telepathy.

5. The future can be predicted.

Try to imagine living in a society in which these beliefs are universally accepted. Suppose you see one of your friends acting in an unusual way ("Hey, that's crazy!"). To explain his behavior, you draw on your magical beliefs, because these are available to you. You assume his actions have something to do with the forces in the universe, because everything in the world reflects them. Perhaps your friend has been sent over the edge through divine intervention or because somebody has directed a magical spell at him. In these terms, consider examples of early instances of how abnormality was explained and treated (see Figure 1.3).

Trephination   One example is reflected in the existence of skulls from the Stone Age (ca. 3000 B.C.),

found all over the globe (Australia, Europe, Central America, South America, Africa), in which holes have been drilled. We know that these holes were not immediately fatal, because at least some of the bone had grown back in 90% of the cases. This practice is called **trephination,** and one interpretation is that it was supposed to allow evil spirits to escape from the skull (Velasco-Suarez, Bautista Martinez, Garcia Oliveros, & Weinstein, 1992).

But it might also be that these operations were done to alleviate swelling of the brain. Most trephined skulls have the hole drilled on the left side, implying that the procedure was undertaken to relieve a pain specifically on that side. Perhaps these pains resulted from being struck in combat. Most often the blow would be struck by a weapon held in an opponent's right hand, and hence the injury would be on the left side.

Shamanism   In many cultures in the world, there exists a special role filled by a person called a **shaman, witch doctor,** or **medicine man** (Turner, 1992). Such an individual is regarded as particularly sensitive to the forces found in nature and well versed in the arts of magic. Someone experiencing distress seeks out a shaman, who goes into a spell and thereby brings relief to the person. Presumably, he has redirected the evil forces causing the problem. Note the parallels between the shaman and mental health professionals (Bromberg, 1975; Torrey, 1986). Both play a socially sanctioned role as they attempt to heal people in distress. Both rely on the status of their role. Both may show specialization, dealing with some problems but not others. In drawing these parallels, do not forget that the underlying rationales are quite different. The shaman thinks in terms of magical forces. The psychiatrist or psychologist thinks in terms of science. Some modern writers dismiss shamanism as "just" suggestion,

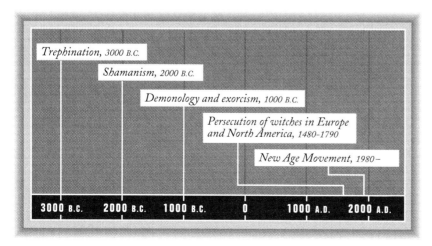

FIGURE 1.3

THE HISTORY OF MAGICAL EXPLANATIONS OF ABNORMALITY   *Explanations of abnormality in terms of immaterial forces date back thousands of years. This chart shows the beginnings of several important examples of magical explanations. In many cases, these explanations are still influential today.*

Trephination, 3000 B.C.

Shamanism, 2000 B.C.

Demonology and exorcism, 1000 B.C.

Persecution of witches in Europe and North America, 1480-1790

New Age Movement, 1980–

| 3000 B.C. | 2000 B.C. | 1000 B.C. | 0 | 1000 A.D. | 2000 A.D. |

Shamanism has existed in many groups around the world, including the Nootka, a Native American tribe. This Nootka shaman's headdress was a badge of her office as well as a symbol of power.

subsuming it under their own view of things. Appreciate that the shaman could just as easily reinterpret modern approaches like behavior therapy.

Demonology   The notion of possession figures in magical accounts of abnormality (Kemp, 1990). According to the beliefs of many cultures, people may be "taken over" by a spirit or deity, which causes them to act in unusual ways. This idea is sometimes called **demonology,** and we find mention of it in ancient Babylonia, China, Egypt, and Greece. In Homer's writings, for instance, accounts are common of how the Greek gods and goddesses would take over people and influence their actions. Among the ancient Hebrews as well we encounter the idea that a person may act in an unusual way because she has been possessed by evil spirits, who would enter her body if and when God removed his protection.

If abnormality is viewed in these terms, various treatment strategies are implied. One is **exorcism,** inducing the demon to leave. This can be done with prayers, or sometimes may be accomplished by making the body inhospitable for the demon. Loud noises

might suffice, or the person might be asked to drink foul-tasting substances. He might also be beaten or tortured or starved or even burned at the stake. From our vantage point, most of these examples seem cruel and malicious. Try to step inside the worldview of those involved. Exorcists were sincere in trying to help the person, and indeed to help the most important part of the person—his soul or spirit. The body was not as important, and if it was damaged or even destroyed during exorcism, then that was acceptable, so long as the demon left.

Witchcraft   In the Middle Ages, in Europe, deviance and abnormality fell under the province of the Catholic Church. In monasteries, people found care and help if they were ailing, either physically or mentally. The monks attempted to help people by praying for them, giving them potions to drink, and touching them with holy relics. In the first thousand years of its existence, the Catholic Church did not concern itself much with supposed **witches:** people, usually women, who had presumably made a pact with the devil. But this state of affairs began to change in the 1300s, occasioned by theological and social changes. Theologically, we see an increasing emphasis on the devil as an equal opponent to God, not simply a minor player on the divine stage. Societally, we see Europe greatly disrupted by social unrest, plagues, and famine. The Black Death—presumably bubonic plague— swept Europe on several occasions, killing off one third of the entire population (Mee, 1990).

In seeking explanations for these events, both the Catholic Church and ordinary people turned to the devil as a plausible source. Witchcraft represented a tangible link to the devil and soon became the essence of heresy against God. The Inquisition undertaken by the Catholic Church to root out those who disagreed with standard teachings thus focused in particular on witches. These people had supposedly sealed their pact with the devil through sexual intercourse with him. They were thereby granted powers, which allowed them to work mischief and worse—like causing crops to fail, bringing illness and death, and making men sexually impotent.

Pope Innocent VIII, in the 1400s, issued a proclamation that the clergy in Europe should spare no efforts in seeking out and destroying witches. Two Dominican monks were inspired and wrote a "manual"—the *Malleus Maleficarum* (or *Witches' Hammer*)— detailing exactly how a witch could be recognized (Kraemer & Sprenger, 1486). This book came to be the classic text on identifying witches, specifying such signs as birthmarks or insensitivity to pain and such behaviors as insatiable lust. The *Malleus Maleficarum* also told inquisitors how to win a confession of witch-

In the Middle Ages, several hundred thousand individuals, mostly women, were accused of witchcraft and put to death. Many were burned at the stake in order to drive away the demons and devils that presumably inhabited their bodies. In this picture, you can see a monstrous creature hovering near the woman being burned.

craft from the accused and also what to do with them whether they did or did not confess.

Although exact figures are hard to come by, perhaps as many as several hundred thousand men, women, and even children were accused of witchcraft, tortured, and then killed during this period. Persecution of suspected witches started to come to a halt in the 1600s, when various church officials grew skeptical of "confessions" obtained by torture. Witchcraft trials ended. The last accused witch executed in Europe died in Switzerland in 1782.

The most famous accusations of witchcraft in the United States occurred in colonial Salem, Massachusetts, in 1692. For example, Bridget Bishop was an elderly woman, poor and socially isolated (Chandler, 1970). She was charged with practicing sorcery against several individuals and brought to trial. Testimony by her victims included the following charges:

> *The shape of the prisoner sometimes very grievously pinched, choaked [sic], bit and afflicted them; urging them to write their names in a book, which the said spectre called "ours." (p. 98)*

Signing this book would seal a pact with the devil. Other testimony reported that a ghost with her appearance would suddenly appear and disappear, that animals she raised and sold were uncontrollable, and that the health of any children with whom she came in contact suffered. One man described how Miss Bishop sent a goblin—with the body of a monkey, the feet of a chicken, and the face of a man—to threaten him.

The court ordered her body to be examined for possible signs of witchcraft. An extra nipple was supposedly identified and interpreted as the way she nursed supernatural creatures. The fact that the nipple was not evident upon a second examination counted strongly against Miss Bishop; by her magical powers, she had made it vanish.

Throughout the trial, she maintained her innocence, stating that she had always been on poor terms with her neighbors, who were now blaming her for all their misfortunes. The court was not swayed, and Miss Bishop was found guilty of witchcraft. She was executed June 10, 1692, by hanging.

At one time, historians interested in abnormal psychology believed that the people identified as witches in the Middle Ages would be the people identified today as psychologically abnormal—that is, they were schizophrenic, manic-depressive, or hysterical (Zilboorg & Henry, 1941). Consider the confessions of accused witches, filled with mention of having intercourse with the devil, changing into animals, and flying through the sky. Delusions are common symptoms of severe abnormality. Also, insensitivity to pain, one of the tests for witchcraft, is a possible symptom of several psychological problems.

In light of new scholarship, however, current opinion is not so unanimous that yesterday's witches would have been today's mental patients (Kemp, 1985, 1990; Schoenman, 1982, 1984; Spanos, 1978). First of all, many of the victims of witchcraft were single women—and persecutions of these women can be seen as profound misogyny by a culture that distrusted and feared sexuality (Anderson & Gordon, 1978). By this view, the sin or abnormality of the women was simply that they were women. Contributing as well to the persecution of specific individuals was the fact that their property was seized following an accusation. Furthermore, we can interpret "signs" of witchcraft—like delusional confessions—as the result of torture, not the cause of it. And finally, other information from the Middle Ages shows that there were people regarded as "mad" who were separated from those regarded as possessed. As early as the 13th century, trials in England were conducted to determine an individual's sanity. Neugebauer (1979) examined the records of these trials, and found reference to possession in only one case. When experts offered explanations of insanity in these hearings, they usually made reference to injury or illness (the somatic model) or emotional trauma (the psychogenic model).

But at least some of the accused witches experienced problems that allowed them to be subsumed under a magical perspective, to be diagnosed and treated, as it were. To make sense of witchcraft and its relationship to abnormality, we need a sophisticated view that recognizes the simultaneous existence of several perspectives on abnormality that compete with respect to individual cases.

Magical explanations today　　　Although the examples I have so far discussed come from history, it would be a mistake to conclude that such perspectives are things of the past. Shamanism is still practiced today in many parts of the world (e.g., Neki, Joinet, Ndosi, & Kilonzo, 1986).

Consider the informal mental health system represented by the curanderas *found in some Mexican American communities (Torrey, 1986). These people fill several overlapping roles, including the diagnosis and treatment of abnormality. The* curanderas *show specialization. Some rely on herbs for cures. Others combine herbs with spiritual treatment. Some use only holy water. Some treat only certain disorders. Most of the* curanderas *are female. They learn their profession through an apprenticeship. The major characteristic of the* curanderas *is their acknowledged religiosity. All have a pronounced religious demeanor. Most accept only a small fee for their services, regarding their gift of healing as coming directly from God.*

The existence and importance of the curanderas *are denied in many quarters, due to fear of connotations of superstition as well as of the Internal Revenue Service. However, a study in a southwestern city of the United States found that as many as 20% of Mexican American*

women had visited a curandera *(Martinez & Martin, 1966). This compares almost exactly to the utilization of conventional mental health services by contemporary Anglos.*

One of the problems for which a person might seek out a curandera *is called* susto, *known as the "fright disease" because it is presumably caused by a traumatic experience, either natural (like an auto accident) or supernatural (like a ghost). Its symptoms include fatigue, restlessness, decreased appetite, decreased interest, weakness, loss of interest in customary activities, withdrawal, and sadness. The symptoms of* susto *overlap considerably with those of depression (Chapter 9). Contemporary people who believe in* susto *are not simply superstitious. Rather, they have a point of view about matters, and they are engaged in the effort to explain and ultimately treat problems.*

Note that a worldview ends up affecting the very nature of problems. To believe that fatigue is due to an encounter with a ghost is to give a different significance to your symptom than if you believe it is due to poor diet or overwork.

Another example of how magical explanations are still with us today comes from the rough grouping of ideas and practices called the *New Age Movement* (cf. Ferguson, 1980). In its most flamboyant manifestations, we see references to reincarnation, telepathy, extraterrestrials, and channeling (i.e., speaking with spirits long gone or far away). New Agers have opinions about health and illness, physical and mental, and regard abnormality as due to imbalances in the spiritual realm (Fuller, 1988). These imbalances can be corrected in various ways, as by thinking positive thoughts, applying healing crystals, sitting under a pyramid, or getting advice through a channeler.

John Mack is a Harvard psychiatrist who has attracted a great deal of attention with his claims that UFO abductions are real (Willwerth, 1994). Mack hypnotizes people, who then report similar stories about being taken aboard spaceships against their will by aliens. The aliens are invariably described as human-like, but very small in size and with huge, dark eyes. Often some sort of sexual encounter ensues between the aliens and those they abduct. According to Mack, the aliens are attempting to establish an intergalactic breeding program. Critics of Mack and his approach point out that hypnotism may create memories as much as retrieve them. Mack counters that "we have lost the faculties to know other realities. . . . We've lost all that ability to know a world beyond the physical. . . . I am a bridge between those two worlds" (p. 75).

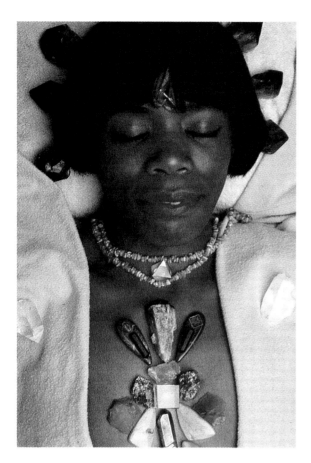

Some followers of the New Age Movement believe that contact with crystals can promote healing by restoring spiritual balance.

At the fringes of the New Age Movement we find what many ridicule about southern California (or Cambridge, Massachusetts, for that matter). At the same time, true to the theme of this section, not everything the New Age advocates is so unreasonable. New Agers believe in holistic medicine, which points to the interdependence of the mind and body. Most of us find that highly persuasive. They also believe in ecology, which points to the interdependence of people and their environments. Most of us find that highly persuasive as well. And they worry about nutrition and toxins and stress. We should *all* worry about these matters. Again we see supernatural and natural explanations intermingled.

SOMATIC EXPLANATIONS

Another popular account of abnormality suggests that people act in unusual fashion because something is wrong with their bodies. These somatic explanations have also been around a long time (see Figure 1.4), and some examples are presented here.

Humours   A well known approach to the bodily causes of abnormality comes from the Greek physician Hippocrates (ca. 460–377 B.C.). Hippocrates is considered the father of modern medicine, and contemporary physicians still take a vow called the Hippocratic Oath. He was explicit that medicine was distinct from theology, that the causes of illness were not to be confused with possession by gods and goddesses. Even mental disturbances were due to mundane "natural causes" and were to be treated as such. He wrote to the effect that "no god would ever befoul a human body." The causes of abnormality must be sought elsewhere. Foreshadowing modern opinion, Hippocrates believed that the brain was the center of mental activity, and he conducted experimental research on animals.

Hippocrates drew on prevailing theories to offer his own explanation of abnormality. Popular then was the notion of **humoural theory.** The body was thought to contain four important humours (i.e., bodily fluids): blood, black bile, yellow bile, and phlegm. A healthy

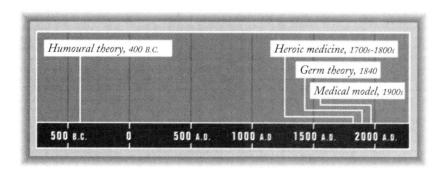

FIGURE 1.4

THE HISTORY OF SOMATIC EXPLANATIONS OF ABNORMALITY   *As shown in this chart, explanation of abnormality in terms of bodily disease or defect first appeared many centuries ago and continues in popularity. Humoural theory influenced medical practice well into the 19th century, where it provided the rationale for heroic medicine.*

According to the humoural theory, there are four basic bodily fluids, each associated with a basic personality type (i.e., melancholic = sad; phlegmatic = impassive; choleric = angry; and sanguine = cheerful) and characteristic psychological and physical difficulties.

person's humours were in balance with one another. Even today, we speak of an individual being in "good humor" when doing well, and this expression literally goes back thousands of years.

It was thought that an imbalance of humours produced illness—physical or emotional as the case may be (Chapter 10). Too much black bile resulted in a state known as *melancholia* (*melan* means black), what we nowadays call depression. Melancholia is still a synonym for depression. Too much yellow bile made a person feel anxious. Too much blood made him moody and irritable. And too much phlegm made him act sluggish.

Humoural theory is much more complicated than I have so far conveyed. It derived from a view of the entire universe, and each humour had a counterpart in a basic element: earth, air, fire, and water. A balance of these defines the world, and so we find in each person a microcosm.

In other writings by Hippocrates, we can recognize people who suffered from epilepsy, stroke, alcohol delusion, paranoia, depression, and mania. His somatic approach was taken up by such luminaries as Galen (130–200). These ideas were then passed on to the Romans, and from there, we can trace the steady existence of the idea that mental illness has physical causes.

The somatic view took a back seat during the Middle Ages, called the Dark Ages by many historians because the teachings of Greece and Rome were shelved as the Catholic Church grew in its influence. Renewed somatic theorizing about abnormality began with the waning of the Middle Ages, when people began to believe that human beings were subject to mundane physical laws. Theologians in western Europe started to regard God as a watchmaker who created the universe, wound it up, and let it tick away without any direct supervision of day-to-day matters. The weight of church authority was thrown off, and people began to test theories against evidence. And thus modern science began to take form.

Heroic medicine   But modern science did not instantly displace the older ideas. For instance, humoural theory persisted well into the 1800s, where it influ-

During the era of heroic medicine, bleeding was a common technique of restoring balance among bodily humours, as shown in this 1804 woodcut. In retrospect, we see that bleeding was more harmful than beneficial, particularly for a physically ill individual.

enced everyday medical practice (Chapter 10). The humoural doctrine was obviously proposed without much knowledge of the way the body works, but it was still widely accepted by many physicians in the 19th century. This period is sometimes called the era of **heroic medicine** (Weil, 1988). During this era, most doctors believed that all illnesses were progressive (Duffy, 1979). In other words, once something was wrong with you, you would inevitably die unless something drastic was done. To believe that illness could be self-limiting was to assume that the body could heal itself, and this struck 19th century doctors as mystical.

Doctors undertook extreme interventions in the case of illness, which is why they are called heroic. The balance among humours had to be restored to effect a cure, and thus we saw bleeding to reduce the amount of "bad" blood in the body. Drugs were also used, such as calomel (a mercury extract), that produced copious and uncontrollable salivation.

According to historians, George Washington may well have died because of heroic treatment:

> *On December 14, 1799, the former President came down with a severe sore throat. It was inflamed and gave him some difficulty in breathing. His overseer removed a pint of blood, but it provided no relief. A physician was called, who soon after his arrival . . . let another pint of blood. At three o'clock in the afternoon, two other doctors came to consult with the first one, and by a vote of two to one, they decided to let more blood, removing a quart at that time . . . By then the President was dehydrated, and it would seem that the doctors must have had to squeeze out the final drops of blood. Washington died sometime between ten and eleven that same night. (Kaufman, 1971, pp. 7–9).*

The mentally disturbed were similarly treated with heroic means, intended to restore the balance among their humours. Some of the treatments popular in the 1800s included the careful choosing of food and drink and abstinence from sexual activity. Immersion in cold water was a common tactic, and so too was spinning a person around rapidly. Frightening patients was another presumed way to help them, and so they were routinely told that they would soon die.

Several discoveries in the 1700s and 1800s gave the somatic view of abnormality a big boost. First, we see the development of the **germ theory** of illness in the 1800s by Louis Pasteur and others (Maher & Maher, 1979). This theoretical model proposed that germs were necessary and sufficient causes of illness, with different illnesses caused by different germs. The

germ model provided an overall theory of disease that proved highly useful for several related reasons.

- ✦ It replaced the untenable notion that there was but one disease state (bodily humours out of balance).
- ✦ It forced attention on to the classification of illnesses, and so scientists began to make distinctions among types of disease.
- ✦ It suggested treatments: Remove the germs.
- ✦ It proposed that people could be protected against illnesses through inoculation: Expose them to small amounts of a germ so they build up immunity to its effects.

Discoveries about the way the nervous system worked led to the creation in the 1800s of a new field of medicine, **neurology,** which dealt with people who behaved in unusual ways. They were termed "neurotics" because presumably there was something wrong with their nervous systems. Heretofore these individuals might have been seen as malingerers or possessed, but now they were seen as ill.

General paresis   Finally, there was the discovery that a complex condition known as **general paresis** was due to a physical cause. This condition involved progressive paralysis and loss of intellectual ability. At one time, general paresis was responsible for as many as 20% of all admissions to mental hospitals in the United States (Dale, 1980). Tens of thousands of people suffered from this condition. Theorists knew that general paresis was more common among men than women, so some theorists looked for its cause in terms of being a male. They also knew that general paresis was more common among those who used tobacco and alcohol, so other theorists proposed that it was due to overindulgence. And they knew that this condition was more common among sailors than the general population, so some theorists suggested that general paresis was due to stress and/or exposure to salty air.

There was also considerable suspicion that general paresis had something to do with sexual activity, and a link between early promiscuity and later paresis was proposed by yet other theorists. Some hypothesized a specific link between syphilis, contracted early in life, and general paresis, which showed up later in life. Patients with the condition sometimes reported that they had years before contracted syphilis, although others had no such memory. It was not clear what to make of these reports, granted the problems with memory that characterize general paresis. The stigma that surrounded syphilis also made direct questioning a suspect research strategy.

In 1897, Richard von Krafft-Ebing undertook a bold experiment to see if general paresis was the result of untreated syphilis. Relying on the logic of germ theory, he knew that people who had once contracted syphilis could not do so again. Accordingly, those with general paresis should be immune to syphilis. He therefore injected pus from syphilitic sores into the bodies of nine patients with general paresis and waited to see what would happen.

The answer was nothing, not in a single case, and in this experiment Krafft-Ebing was able to confirm what the "epidemiological" information had suggested but not proved. All these people previously had syphilis. Soon after, a treatment for syphilis became available, eventually to be replaced by penicillin, which could arrest even advanced cases of general paresis, now recognized as the late effects of syphilis.

There are several things to note about Krafft-Ebing's work. First, this experiment is far from what we would nowadays call an ethical study. He did not obtain permission from the subjects. Second, his study is at the same time considered a classic. It has greatly benefited people, because general paresis is almost never encountered anymore in the United States.

But Krafft-Ebing's research is only a classic because it worked. Had it not worked, he would have had nine patients on his hands with general paresis *and* syphilis. There is an important lesson here about the dynamic between the good of the research subject and the potential good of society. There is never an

easy answer. One of the themes you will see throughout this discussion of abnormality is that desperate problems often demand desperate attempts at cure, and not all of these result in success (Valenstein, 1986).

The medical model   The demonstration that general paresis was due to a physical cause—untreated syphilis—inspired other physicians to look within the body for analogous causes of other forms of abnormality. Their attempts took them into the nooks and crannies of the body, as they sought out injuries, illnesses, or defects responsible for people's problems. Collectively, these attempts are referred to as the **medical model.** As Bursten (1979, p. 662) put it, "Whenever you see mental illness, look to biology for the significant etiological data." The medical model is the modern descendant of the somatic view, and it is represented today in the field of biological psychiatry. This medical field treats problems by looking to biology for an explanation and a target for intervention. Currently popular are neurotransmitter excesses and deficiencies, structural abnormalities in the brain, and hormonal irregularities. Although this model does not demand that problems have a genetic basis, this too is an interest of those who currently advocate a somatic approach. If it can be shown that a given problem is heritable, then this obviously is further support for the notion that it must have a biological basis.

Various biological treatments reside in the repertoire of biological psychiatrists—notably medications, electroconvulsive shock, and surgery. I cover the details of these approaches in subsequent chapters. There exist as well treatments such as diet, massage, hemodialysis (i.e., filtering the blood), sleep induction or deprivation, exercise, and exposure to sunlight. What they share is the assumption that problems have a biological basis and hence should respond to biological treatment.

Criticism of the somatic view   The success of the medical model is not uniform. The example of general paresis remains one of the most straight-forward explanations of abnormality in somatic terms. There are contemporary examples as well, like bipolar depression. But not all forms of abnormality fit the somatic formula. Substance abuse, for instance, which I consider in detail in Chapter 5, is not well conceptualized in strictly biological terms, nor is it well treated. Many forms of depression and anxiety do not conform well to somatic theorizing either.

In a famous critique, Thomas Szasz (1961) dismissed what he termed the **myth of mental illness.** According to Szasz, the medical model—as applied to psychological abnormality—is highly misleading. It encourages us to interpret problems in living as if they

In 1897, Richard von Krafft-Ebing (1840–1902) conducted an important experiment showing that general paresis was the result of untreated syphilis.

were literal illnesses. Unhappiness, spitefulness, and worry are lumped together with chicken pox and the flu, despite the fact that there is no good evidence that anyone's underlying tissue is diseased or injured. What kind of illnesses are these? There is a twofold danger in calling something an illness when it really is not. We absolve the individual from any responsibility in bringing about or solving her problems and embark on treatments that may be inappropriate.

You will encounter the myth of mental illness throughout the book, whenever I criticize attempts to explain abnormality in solely biological terms. Perhaps the best way to take into account Szasz's ideas is on a case-by-case basis. There seems to be no doubt that he is correct in dismissing some attempts to "medicalize" our problems in living. Think back to the "I have a friend" stories told to me by my students. How many of these behaviors strike you as illnesses? But in other cases, Szasz calls for a restrictive view that is simply wrong, because biological factors often do contribute to people's psychological problems.

PSYCHOGENIC EXPLANATIONS

The idea that abnormality has psychological causes, as opposed to a magical or somatic basis, has been a highly influential notion during the 20th century. If the supernatural approach conceives abnormality as something done to a person, if medical explanations see it as something that a person has, then psychological explanations see abnormality as something that a person displays because of his or her psychological makeup. This book is about the *psychology* of abnormality, written for the most part from this particular perspective. At the same time, psychological explanations intermingle with the others. They have been around for thousands of years, despite their relatively recent prominence (see Figure 1.5).

Early examples   Plato (ca. 427–347 B.C.), for instance, was a forerunner of the psychogenic model of abnormality. He stressed the importance of a person's ideas, holding that the mind was the true reality. Reason was therefore the most valued of the human faculties. People could lose their reason, often because it was overpowered by emotions. Then we had cases of abnormality, due to clearly psychological reasons. The conflict between thought and emotion is still alive today, particularly in psychoanalytic theories. One reason for having a problem was ignorance, particularly ignorance of oneself—what modern scholars call *self-deception* (Starek & Keating, 1991).

As you saw in the case of magical and somatic explanations, the bottom line of a psychogenic view of abnormality is that it guides our attempts to help in a psychological direction. We can look through the writing of the early Greeks for suggestions about how to help people with problems, and we can find many references to what are very much psychological interventions.

Dream interpretation, which we associate with psychoanalytic therapy, dates back at least to this time (Mora, 1980). At one point in Greek culture, dreams were apparently regarded as real events. Then somewhat later they were interpreted in magical terms, as the voices of the gods or as prophecies. But eventually there was a class of dreams recognized simply as the product of the dreamer, revealing the workings of his or her mind. That dreams could take on wholly opposite meanings than what the dreamer intended or wanted was widely recognized, foreshadowing psychoanalytic notions of unconscious defenses.

Another example of an early psychological therapy is the notion that words could heal. In Homer's poems, for instance, we find reference to three sorts of words said when a person was ill: prayers, magical spells, and suggestions. Socratic dialogues, in which a teacher and

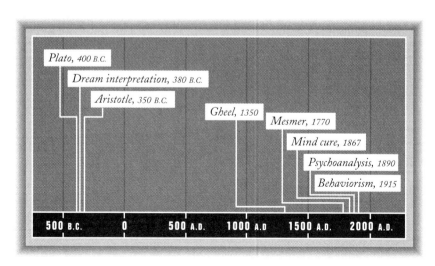

FIGURE 1.5

THE HISTORY OF PSYCHOGENIC EXPLANATIONS OF ABNORMALITY
Explanations of abnormality in psychological terms were first proposed by Greek thinkers such as Plato and Aristotle. This perspective has enjoyed particular prominence in the 20th century.

student go back and forth in a systematic method of doubt and questioning, were seen not simply as a way to instruct but as a way to achieve harmony between body and soul.

In Aristotle's *Rhetoric,* we find a lengthy discussion of how words could be used to persuade (in other words, to change) a person. Aristotle (384–322 B.C.) anticipated what is now considered a truism in psychotherapy. Words per se do not heal; it is the character of the person who utters them that gives them the ability to effect change (Chapter 4). The speaker should have prestige, expertise, integrity, and wisdom. Aristotle recognized that certain messages would have a cathartic effect, bringing about profound emotional reactions and subsequent relief. In fact, Aristotle coined the term **catharsis,** which Freud would later use to describe the beneficial effects of speaking about long repressed conflicts (Chapter 3).

Plutarch (ca. 46–120) mentions that Antiphon in Corinth had a doorplate saying that he was qualified to heal by words those who suffered from grief and melancholy. Perhaps Antiphon was the first psychotherapist. Certainly, he was the first to advertise. The Greeks, by the way, explicitly contrasted the power of words to heal with the power of drugs, anticipating a debate that still goes on today between psychogenic and somatic therapists.

A psychogenic perspective shows up throughout history. For instance, in Belgium is a small town called Gheel that has functioned as a retreat for the insane since the Middle Ages (Carty & Breault, 1967). Originally the site of a supposed miracle, the mad sought out Gheel for a cure. They were hospitably received by the residents of the town. They were shown great kindness, gentleness, and unflagging courtesy. They lived in the homes of the Gheel natives, who treated them as guests. Gheel illustrates a psychological approach to those with problems, and it foreshadowed client-centered therapy of today (Chapter 3).

Mesmer   Perhaps the single most important figure in winning acceptance for the psychogenic view was Sigmund Freud, but to appreciate fully Freud's contribution it is necessary to start a bit earlier (Ellenberger, 1970). Franz Anton Mesmer (1734–1815), a colorful and creative individual, is counted among the central figures in the history of abnormality, despite being dismissed as a charlatan in his own time.

Mesmer was a physician, a native of Austria, who proposed a complex view of the universe to explain illnesses, psychological and physical. He believed that the universe was filled with an invisible fluid known as *animal magnetism.* Illnesses resulted when a person's fluid was out of kilter, depleted, or obstructed. Mesmer thought, therefore, that the way to cure illness was

to redistribute the animal magnetism in an afflicted person's body.

To this end, a variety of techniques were available. You could touch the person. You could hold hands. You could use large magnets. Mesmer felt that he himself was the best way to redistribute animal magnetism, and he often could bring relief to people simply by bringing his own body into contact with them while speaking. Regardless of the particular technique, Mesmer would induce a trance in his patients and thereby bring relief to them (Podmore, 1963). These techniques for redistributing animal magnetism became known as **mesmerism.** And as you know, the word "*mesmerize*" still survives in our language.

Mesmer's cures attracted much attention, and many were carefully chronicled by writers of his era.

> *Mesmer's first big success with magnets was with a young woman of twenty-nine, Franzl Oesterline, and it was through her that his name was first brought to the public's attention. Fraulein Oesterline . . . for several years . . . had been the victim of a convulsive malady, "the most troublesome symptoms of which were that the blood rushed to her head and there set up the most cruel toothache and earache, followed by delirium, rage, vomiting and swooning." . . . On July 28, 1774, after his patient had a renewal of her usual attacks, Mesmer applied three magnets . . . to the lady's stomach and legs. Shortly, his patient experienced some extraordinary sensations and the symptoms of the attack ceased. He applied the same*

An 18th-century mesmerist attempts to redistribute a woman's animal magnetism and cure her ailments.

treatment the following day, with similar success. With the help of the magnets he had produced an artificial flow [of animal magnetism] in the patient's body. (Wyckoff, 1975, pp. 35–36)

Mesmer published a description of the case, arguing that he had discovered a new cure for nervous conditions based on his theory of animal magnetism.

Another well known case was Mesmer's treatment in 1777 of Maria Theresa von Paradis, a talented pianist who had been blind since age 4 (Wyckoff, 1975). She was idolized in Vienna for being so accomplished a musician despite her blindness. Mozart took an interest in her career and even composed a concerto especially for her. Mesmer met Fraulein von Paradis and began to treat her. She would gaze at a mirror while he would wave a magnetized wand in front of her eyes. After 3 weeks of daily treatments, she began to discern the movements of the wand. Eventually her sight was restored, along with her sense of smell, which had also been lost since she was a small girl.

However, Fraulein von Paradis could no longer play the piano as well as she once had, because now she looked at her fingers on the keyboard and became tentative while performing. Her career as a pianist suffered, and her parents demanded that Mesmer cease his treatment. A violent scene took place between Mesmer and the woman's family. Afterwards, Maria Theresa von Paradis was again unable to see.

When he became better known, Mesmer moved to Paris to find a more appreciative clientele than was available in his native Vienna. Once he moved, his cures attracted even more attention, so much so that the established physicians of his time became a bit worried. Political pressure was brought to bear, and the Royal Academy appointed a board of distinguished scientists—including Benjamin Franklin, then the United States ambassador to France—to investigate his claims. They concluded that the theory of animal magnetism was groundless. Interestingly, they did not dispute the fact of Mesmer's cures, arguing that they were due to suggestion.

If we had to classify Mesmer's theory, it would be a somatic theory because he believed animal magnetism to be a tangible thing. He used it to treat, among others, *hysterics*—chiefly women who suffered a host of puzzling physical inabilities including blindness or deafness or inability to move (Chapter 8). Hysteria in Mesmer's day was widely thought to be a physical condition, due to something wrong with a woman's womb. (*Hysterus* is the Latin word for uterus.) But Mesmer's techniques for cure were psychological

ones, at least in retrospect. They passed into medical use under the rubric of hypnotism, and were widely employed among French physicians to treat hysteria and other forms of abnormality.

Mind cure   I now jump to the relatively recent past to illustrate further the psychogenic model. Appearing in the late 1800s and early 1900s was an approach known as **mind cure.** Popularized by various writers and lecturers—including Mary Baker Eddy (1821–1910), the founder of Christian Science—this approach was based on the premise that the mind was preeminent. *Everything* was possible if a person simply believed in it. Among the Christian Scientists, physical illness and even death were regarded as illusory, the product of incorrect thinking.

Mental disorders were similarly regarded as the product of wrong thinking, and a person could be cured simply by thinking the right thoughts. Part of this thinking involved religious beliefs, and another part involved boosting his self-esteem and sense of what was possible. Particularly in the United States, mind cure proved to be highly popular.

In the 1800s, a commonly blamed cause of mental distress was the hustle and bustle of America, particularly as manifest in its large cities. The solution was to think differently about things (Meyer, 1980). In one celebrated mind cure approach, the person was to say to herself repeatedly, "Day by day, in every way, I am getting better and better" (Starker, 1989). Correct thinking was also held out as the route to material success, and so mind cure was linked to a number of rags-to-riches schemes. Mind cure authors provided readers with lists of things to do, which means their formulations went beyond thoughts to include behaviors as well (e.g., Carnegie, 1936).

By and large, mind cure was opposed by professionals, but as it swept the general public, it legitimized the psychogenic view that psychologically oriented professionals would eventually endorse. Several factors explain its popularity. The general public was fed up with heroic medicine, which it suspected—correctly—of killing more patients than it helped (Weil, 1988). If mind cure was at best innocuous, it still was preferable to the medical alternative. Also, mind cure resonated with dominant intellectual and social trends in the United States: Protestantism, laissez-faire capitalism, the American Dream, and the celebration of the individual.

Sigmund Freud   I now move forward once more, back to Austria, and encounter the young neurologist Sigmund Freud (1856–1939), who was soon to make a large contribution to the world of psychology and to the whole of Western thought. Freud originally planned a research career (Gay, 1988). He published an influential treatise on aphasia. He was one of the first to discover the analgesic properties of cocaine. And he also discovered inadvertently that it was an addictive substance that could lead to serious withdrawal, a lesson rediscovered in the 1980s (Chapter 5).

Freud's research career might well have continued in this vein if he had not fallen in love with Martha Bernays. He soon concluded that his meager research salary would not support the two of them and the family they planned. He reluctantly turned to the practice of medicine to make more money.

Many of Freud's patients were the hysterics just encountered. Freud spent a year in France, where he was influenced by Jean Charcot (1825–1893), the leading neurologist of his time who was particularly interested in hysteria. Freud learned techniques of hypnosis from the French psychiatrists with whom he studied, and came to the opinion that hysteria was a psychological problem. Hypnosis was effective not because it did something to a patient's body but because it affected her mind. Upon his return to Vienna, Freud delivered a paper arguing that males could be hysterical, too. His proposal was greeted at first with disagreement, but it nonetheless marked the beginnings of his thinking about the psychological cause of problems.

Freud began to collaborate with an older physician named Joseph Breuer, who also treated hysterics. From Breuer, he learned the technique of catharsis: how to bring unconscious conflicts to light through hypnotism

and thereby alleviate hysterical symptoms (Breuer & Freud, 1895). Freud eventually abandoned hypnosis, relying on a technique that he called **free association** to unearth material hidden from a person's awareness. In free association, people say whatever comes to mind without censorship. The train of associations is an emotional one, and eventually leads them back to unconscious conflicts.

The first patient treated in this way is usually identified as Anna O. Her real name was Bertha Pappenheim, a pioneer social worker and an important figure in the women's movement in Germany of the 1920s. As a young woman, she suffered a variety of hysterical symptoms:

> *[She] spoke in half or broken sentences and complained that "black snakes" and "death's heads" were present in her room. [Her] mother reported to Breuer that most of the time [she] did not appear to hear what was being said to her. She appeared very weak and sickly and refused to eat. (Rosenbaum, 1984, p. 2)*

She had difficulty swallowing, and her right arm was paralyzed. She coughed constantly. Breuer began to treat her in 1880, putting her into a hypnotic trance and encouraging her to speak of what troubled her. Anna O. apparently suggested to Breuer that this strategy be followed, and she referred to it as "chimney-sweeping."

One at a time, her physical symptoms vanished, often after speaking about events that bore a symbolic relationship to the symptom in question. For example, Anna O. was able to swallow again after describing an incident in which her governess allowed a dog to drink from her glass, something that had greatly disgusted Anna O.

Although Breuer and Freud (1895) described the treatment of Anna O. as a success, a different reading of the case is possible (Rosenbaum, 1984). Breuer ceased treatment of Anna O. when he found her in an agitated state, believing she was about to give birth to a child fathered by Breuer. Breuer's wife was pregnant at the time, and Anna O. was highly attached to Breuer. Her phantom pregnancy seemed to be an attempt to solidify her relationship with Breuer. Many of her hysterical symptoms returned. She was then treated in a hospital exclusively with drugs and became addicted to morphine. Eventually, however, she recovered and went on to become a highly honored member of her society.

Viennese neurologist Sigmund Freud (1856–1939) created psychoanalysis.

It is impossible to give a simple overview of Freud's theory, which he called **psychoanalysis.** I spend more time with it in Chapter 3 and elsewhere in the book. Here are its key aspects:

1. People's problems are due to conflicts.

2. These conflicts are hidden from a person's conscious mind.

3. Indeed, the mind actively defends itself against conflicts.

4. Many conflicts are sexual in nature, and many date back to childhood.

5. Problems represent the tying up of psychological energy in conflicts and their defense, making it otherwise unavailable.

6. Therapy consists of freeing this energy, and to this end a host of techniques are available, including free association but also dream interpretation and working through transference—how the patient treats the therapist.

Freud's importance cannot be overestimated. He devised a general theory of psychopathology, but also one of normal personality and of history, society, and the arts. He developed a therapy to help people, and many of the techniques he devised have been incorporated into the standard procedures of all psychotherapists. He inspired both followers and critics. His influence on psychiatry and psychology has been mammoth. Many of his terms—such as *the unconscious, defense mechanisms, libido,* and *sexual symbolism*—are now part of our everyday language and culture.

In the present context, Freud is important because he provided a thoroughly psychological account of abnormality. Ironically, this may not have been Freud's original wish. As a neurologist, he phrased his theories, at least metaphorically, in the language of neurology. In one of his famous papers, written early in his career (the "Project for a Scientific Psychology"), he left no doubt that his intent was to describe abnormality in somatic terms (Freud, 1950). He often acknowledged constitutional (i.e., somatic) contributions to abnormality, particularly in his early writing. But Freud's greatest impact was on psychological theorizing.

Neo-Freudians   Among those inspired by Freud were a group of theorists that we nowadays call the **neo-Freudians** (Brown, 1964). They extended even further Freud's psychological as opposed to his somatic emphases. They were as apt to be trained as social scientists as physicians. They saw the conflicts from which people suffered as social in nature. The neo-Freudians also took account of cross-cultural evidence like that gathered by Margaret Mead (1928), challenging the universality of certain of Freud's pronouncements. If the antecedents of abnormality vary from culture to culture, then abnormality must be something we learn. The neo-Freudians were responsible for

Among the important neo-Freudians was Karen Horney (1885–1952), who emphasized the social aspects of people's conflicts and insecurities.

spreading Freud's psychogenic view of abnormality *without* bringing along its somatic overtones.

Among the important neo-Freudians were Erich Fromm, Karen Horney, and Harry Stack Sullivan, theorists familiar to you if you have studied the psychology of personality (Peterson, 1992). Another well known individual in this tradition was Erik Erikson. Erikson (1950) proposed an influential theory of development, from birth to death, that emphasizes the *social* conflicts people must confront and resolve at different points in life.

Behaviorism   The approach to psychology known as **behaviorism** provided yet another boost for the psychogenic model. According to the first behaviorist John Watson (1913), psychology should study overt behavior: what people (and animals) actually do. Watson called psychology's attention to the theories of learning that had recently been proposed by the Russian physiologist Pavlov, suggesting that these could provide a general explanation of behavior. Behaviorists soon brought to bear these theories of learning on both normal and abnormal behavior.

One of Watson's studies is particularly important for the psychogenic view of abnormality. Using an infant known to history only as Little Albert, Watson and his collaborator Rosalie Rayner demonstrated how a fear could be acquired through mundane learning.

By the report of Watson and Rayner (1920), Albert was a cheerful, placid baby. They took him to their laboratory and gave him—what else?—a white rat to handle. He enjoyed playing with the creature. One of the researchers then came up behind Little Albert while he was playing with the rat and made a loud noise by striking a metal bar with a hammer. Albert jumped and whimpered. The experience was repeated several times. Soon Albert started to cry and act afraid of the rat, even without any loud noises.

You recognize what happened to Albert as an instance of Pavlovian (classical) conditioning. An unconditioned stimulus (the loud noise) was paired with a previously neutral stimulus (the white rat), after which the neutral stimulus in its own right could evoke an emotional response (crying). Albert also became afraid of other white and furry things, like rabbits and even Professor Watson when he donned a Santa Claus mask.[1]

If you were to see only the end product of the conditioning, you might conclude that something was profoundly wrong with Albert. Perhaps there was something amiss with his nervous system. Perhaps he had an unresolved conflict surrounding toilet training or breast feeding. Perhaps he was possessed by the Grinch. But you know the rest of the story, the fact that Albert's fear of the white rat and associated objects was brought about by mundane associative learning. This is why the demonstration is important.

American psychologist John B. Watson (1878–1958) was the first behaviorist.

And what about other instances of abnormality we may encounter? Knowing nothing except the end product of unknown processes, we may seek magical or somatic explanations. Watson and Rayner would have us look for a psychogenic explanation that stresses learning and hence draws our attention to the abnormal individual's environment. Further, if problems can be learned, then they can be unlearned, again through changes in an individual's environment.

Behavior and cognitive therapies   Here is the rationale for an influential approach to therapy known as **behavior therapy,** which uses principles of learning to treat people's problems in living (cf. Jones, 1924). Behavior therapy has been one of the success stories of modern psychology, and there are hundreds of tech-

niques that qualify as behavior therapy (Bellack & Hersen, 1985). It is customary to group them under the type of learning that they embody. So, we have techniques based on classical conditioning, on operant conditioning, and on vicarious conditioning (or modeling). I discuss particular behavior therapy techniques throughout the book.

In recent decades, behavior therapists have increasingly acknowledged the importance of people's thoughts and beliefs in learning processes (e.g., Bandura, 1986; Mahoney, 1974; Meichenbaum, 1977). Several therapy techniques therefore directly target these beliefs. Nowadays, it is common to speak of cognitive-behavioral approaches to problems as essentially one approach, so intermingled have behavior therapy and cognitive techniques become.

Other psychogenic approaches   Behavioral and psychoanalytic approaches to abnormality have enjoyed great popularity, but there also exist other psychogenic approaches. Indeed, several of these arose in response to the popularity of behavioral and psychoanalytic theories and their common assumption that people's actions are totally determined, either by external events or internal conflicts. **Humanism** stresses the goals for which people strive, their conscious awareness of this striving, the importance of their own choices, and their rationality. **Existentialism** emphasizes the

[1] Historians of psychology do not know what happened to Little Albert (Samelson, 1980). According to Watson and Rayner's original research report, the infant's mother removed him from the study before its intended conclusion, which was to eradicate his acquired fear. Like the Krafft-Ebing experiment described earlier, there are some obvious ethical questions that can be raised about this study.

primacy of a person's experience. **Phenomenology** attempts to describe a person's conscious experience in terms that are coherent to that individual. These theories are described in detail in Chapter 3—along with still other conceptions that explicitly locate problems in their interpersonal context, often within the family. The point here is the variety of psychogenic approaches that exist today.

HOSPITAL TREATMENT OF ABNORMALITY

I close this discussion by looking at how abnormality has been treated within the institutions known as hospitals. You may think of hospitals as purely somatic in approach, but this is not what a historical view reveals (see Figure 1.6). Instead, we see a blending of perspectives. One more time, we find that explanations of psychological abnormality and its treatment are complex.

It was not until people began to settle in one place that we had institutionalized reactions to abnormality and other forms of social deviance (Mora, 1980). Before then, throughout much of human existence, people wandered about the world in small bands, hunting and gathering. If an individual did not fit in and resisted care, he was ostracized from the group. He either perished, lived as a nomad, or joined another group. There was no organized social response to abnormality.

The first hospitals   As the population grew, wandering ceased. The population put down roots in one place. Religious groups began to offer asylum to the troubled. In many cases, these asylums were regarded as holy places, which means that cures were expected, at least for some people. These shrines represent the earliest versions of hospitals, and of course they embodied a magical point of view on abnormality.

Much more recently, but still hundreds of years ago, cities and states started to run their own hospitals. These were created to house all sorts of people who did not fit within "civilized" society: the unemployed, the feeble, the abandoned, the ill, and of course the mad (Foucault, 1965). Distinctions were not made among the various inmates. For instance, the Hôpital Général was founded in Paris in 1656 as a place to house "undesirable" individuals—that is, those not gainfully employed. The government took it upon itself to provide shelter and food to people who heretofore had roamed the streets begging. Within 4 years of its founding, the Hôpital Général housed 1% of the entire population of Paris.

Similar institutions sprung up throughout the rest of Europe, lumping together poor people, insane people, ill people, old people, and criminals. These hospitals were often used as workhouses, coinciding with the rise of industrialization. The inmates, who usually were forcibly taken to them and kept there against their will, were required to provide labor. They were paid a fraction of what people on the outside would earn for the same efforts.

Within the hospitals, distinctions eventually began to be made by those who ran them. Those with psychological abnormality were usually singled out for particularly harsh treatment, in part because they could not or would not work. They were often chained in tiny cells deep in dungeons. If they were treated at all, it was in terms of the heroic medicine of the time.

I can again observe that from our vantage, this treatment looks cruel and unusual, but there was a rationale. It was believed that the mad had lost their power of reason. Stripped of this faculty, they became like animals. And to restore their reason, they had to be controlled. The best way to control an animal was

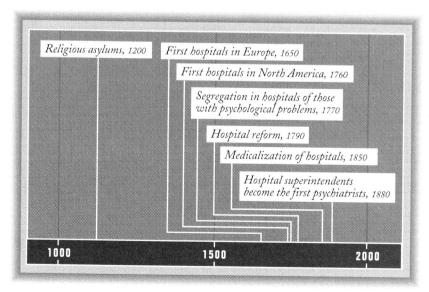

FIGURE 1.6

THE HISTORY OF HOSPITAL TREATMENT OF ABNORMALITY
Hospitals have long housed those suffering from psychological problems. Treatment strategies have changed over the centuries in accordance with prevailing explanations of abnormality.

(Figure labels: *Religious asylums, 1200* · *First hospitals in Europe, 1650* · *First hospitals in North America, 1760* · *Segregation in hospitals of those with psychological problems, 1770* · *Hospital reform, 1790* · *Medicalization of hospitals, 1850* · *Hospital superintendents become the first psychiatrists, 1880* · 1000 · 1500 · 2000)

Patients in mental hospitals in the 19th century were often singled out for harsh and unusual treatment, as shown in this 1889 woodcut depicting "therapy" in Salpêtrière, a Paris hospital.

with fear, so the reasoning went, and the ostensibly cruel treatments followed.

An example of this approach comes from descriptions of how King George III of England (1738–1820) was treated. King George ruled during the time of the American Revolution, and as is well documented, he suffered from periods of insanity:

> *Sometimes King George declared himself in love with Lady Pembroke, a grandmother well over fifty, and on other occasions said that the institution of marriage would soon be abolished. . . . He declared he could see Hanover through . . . [a] telescope; he thought London had been flooded and expressed anxiety about a valuable manuscript he had left there; he issued apparently sensible orders but applying them to people who did not exist. . . . By 19 November he had a fortnight's growth of beard; he allowed one side of his face to be shaved, but then refused to let the barber continue. (Clarke, 1972, p. 137)*

Just exactly why King George acted this way is a source of continuing historical debate. But to help him, his doctors immobilized him by tying him to a stake. He was beaten and starved, threatened and cursed. He was bled and purged constantly.

Hospital reform   Reform came to hospitals in the 1700s and 1800s. The mad had their chains removed.

They were allowed freedom of movement, and given fresh air and good food. It is tempting to regard these reforms as simply a decision to be decent to the patients, but that would be too simple an explanation of the reforms (Foucault, 1965). Rather, they were theoretically motivated. It was thought that previous treatments should be abandoned—not because they were cruel, but because they were ineffective. Perhaps treating patients in different ways would lead to better results.

In 1792, during the French Revolution, Philippe Pinel (1745–1826) decided to strike the chains of the patients in the Hôpital Général, remove them from dungeons, and let them move about the hospital grounds. Liberty and equality were not his motive so much as the notion that effective control had to be psychological in nature rather than physical (Zilboorg & Henry, 1941). He believed that the mad had lost their reason. He ascribed to a somatic theory of problems and believed that the mad should be incarcerated. But he felt that effective treatment had to proceed in a different way, one which today we would call psychological in nature—despite his somatic rationale.

Pinel had his counterparts in other countries. In England, William Tuke (1732–1819) was greatly distressed when one of his friends—Hannah Mills—died under mysterious circumstances at the Lunatick Asylum at York. Tuke suspected that her treatment there had something to do with why she died. He urged the Yorkshire Society of Friends (Quakers) to establish a

King George III (1738–1820) of England suffered from periods of insanity and was treated with the heroic techniques then in fashion.

more humane refuge for the insane. The Retreat at York was thus founded in 1796.

In the United States, other Quaker groups, inspired by the York Retreat, founded similar refuges. The Bloomingdale Asylum, for instance, was founded in 1821; it stood where Columbia University is now located. McLean Hospital, near Boston, was opened in 1818 and still exists today. In the United States, these reforms were collectively referred to as **moral treatment,** because they assumed that relief could be brought to the troubled by treating them in a humane fashion. Just how effective moral treatment really was in alleviating people's problems is not clear, except in comparison to the way that patients had been treated in hospitals prior to these reforms. Earlier treatments, however intended, could only have exacerbated the problems of the inmates.

An important figure in the United States was physician Benjamin Rush (1745–1813), regarded as the founder of American psychiatry. He was associated with Pennsylvania Hospital (in Philadelphia) and was the first American to teach a course in psychiatry. He also wrote the first book on psychiatry in America. Although an adherent to heroic medicine, Rush also advocated the humane treatment of psychiatric patients.

Another important figure in hospital reform in the United States was Dorothea Dix (1802–1887). During the middle 1800s, she tirelessly campaigned on behalf of more humane treatment of those with psychological problems. Dix is credited with the establishment of dozens of hospitals in the United States as well as in Canada and Scotland (Zilboorg & Henry, 1941).

It is ironic that the immediate impact of these hospital reforms and the ensuing moral treatment was the medicalization of hospitals. Although the reforms appeared psychological, physicians were hired in their wake. Influenced by the medical model and later by the biological aspects of psychoanalytic theory, they applied a somatic perspective to abnormality. Subtle

Dorothea Dix (1802–1887) was an important figure in hospital reform in the United States, as well as in Canada and Scotland.

distinctions among types of disorders started to be made. Hospitals became more specialized, and soon some became solely devoted to the care of the mentally ill. These were called insane asylums, and the superintendents of these asylums were usually medical doctors.

These superintendents became the doctors we now call psychiatrists. In the United States, for instance, the first professional organization of insane asylum superintendents was the Association of Medical Superintendents for the Insane. In 1892, this organization changed its name to the American Medico-Psychological Association. Finally, in 1921, this group became the American Psychiatric Association, today a thriving and influential professional group.

Upon the direction of Philippe Pinel (1745–1826) at the time of the French Revolution, mental patients were no longer chained.

FOCUS ON

Clinical

Psychology Today

AT THE PRESENT TIME, WE find a variety of professionals who specialize in people's psychological problems. Social workers may be therapists. So too may nurses, members of the clergy, and educators. Among the most familiar mental health professionals are *psychiatrists,* who have medical degrees and training in medicine, and *clinical psychologists,* who have psychology degrees and training in psychology.

The psychogenic perspective is represented most clearly today by clinical psychologists. These people have received their degrees—usually Ph.D. or Psy.D. degrees—from graduate programs emphasizing not only therapy but also research and expertise in general psychology. Perhaps 30,000 people today are clinical psychologists, and the majority of them ascribe to one or more of the various psychological approaches to abnormality and its treatment: psychoanalytic therapies, behavior therapies, cognitive therapies, group and family therapies, and various others (Chapter 3).

The professional organization representing psychologists is the American Psychological Association (APA). The APA was founded about 100 years ago, as a group for academic psychologists (Hilgard, 1987).

Over the years, it has grown and specialized. In the 1920s, the APA took clinical psychology under its wing. In recent decades, it has been responsible for accrediting graduate programs in clinical psychology and providing ethical guidelines for clinical practice (Chapter 15). The power of clinical psychologists within the APA has steadily grown, in large part due to their sheer numbers, and now an increasing amount of the time and money of the APA is spent on professional issues as opposed to strictly academic and scientific ones.

Often these professional issues involve the APA squaring off with the American Psychiatric Association (the "other" APA). Debate takes place on scientific grounds (which profession is better able to conceptualize and treat psychological abnormality) as well as more crass grounds (who shall have the bigger share of the mental health dollar). Psychologists who work in hospitals are pushing for the privilege of admitting patients and prescribing medications to them (e.g., Boswell & Litwin, 1992).

As you have seen, there is no good answer about which approach—psychogenic or somatic—is superior. These two views have coexisted for thousands of years, and the debates about their relative merits will not be resolved in the near future. If anything, we can expect combinations of psychogenic and somatic approaches, which ideally would find psychologists and psychiatrists working together, contributing their respective expertise.

Psychiatric hospitals still exist today, although fewer patients are to be found in them than in the 1950s and 1960s. The introduction of drugs to treat severe symptoms of schizophrenia and other disorders, coupled with societal disenchantment with institutionalization, led to a dramatic reduction of patients hospitalized for psychological reasons. An unintended consequence of this trend has been a vast increase in the number of homeless individuals with severe psychological problems. We can expect yet further changes in hospital practices and procedures.

This historical view of the hospital treatment of abnormality parallels our more general history of abnormality. A magical view pervaded the very first hospitals, which often were religious shrines. Hospitals eventually came to embrace a more scientific view of psychological problems. Today a somatic view dominates in hospitals, but this may not always prevail. Clinical psychologists are increasingly apt to work in

hospitals, to which they of course bring their own perspective. Considerable practical importance hangs in the balance. Suffice it to say that the study of abnormality must—as I have been saying—be examined within its social context (see Focus on Clinical Psychology Today).

Summary

DEFINING ABNORMALITY

✦   Any judgment of abnormality consists of a label placed on some action by a person and a recommendation, explicit or implicit, that an intervention be undertaken. Although judgments of abnormality are applied frequently in a wide range of situations, there is often disagreement about where to draw the line. Further, even when people's judgments are in agreement, the underlying rationales may differ from person to person.

◆ Several operational definitions of abnormality can be found in the research literature: exposure to psychological or psychiatric treatment; diagnosis of abnormality; maladjustment; subjective definition; objective psychological tests; and the absence of mental health. Although each of these definitions captures part of what we mean by abnormality, none is perfect.

◆ A precise definition of abnormality proves elusive because it is inherently a social judgment. Abnormality must be defined not simply in terms of what the "abnormal" person is doing but also by taking into account the perspective of the person making the judgment.

◆ As we currently use the term, abnormality is a fuzzy concept, in that it does not have necessary and sufficient conditions. Instead, abnormality is captured by a family resemblance of pertinent—but not critical—attributes. Viewing abnormality as a fuzzy social judgment is not fully satisfactory, and attempts continue to characterize abnormality more precisely. Although an unambiguous definition of abnormality is not currently available, extreme examples of abnormality are nonetheless easy to recognize and agree upon.

THE HISTORY OF ABNORMALITY

◆ History reveals three major perspectives on abnormality. Magical explanations view abnormality in terms of the operation of evil forces. The somatic view explains abnormality in terms of bodily malfunction. The psychogenic view proposes that abnormality reflects a problem with a person's psychological makeup. These perspectives have each enjoyed a period of dominance, but all have been present for thousands of years, during which time they have intermingled. Regardless, each perspective points to particular causes of abnormality as well as particular treatments.

◆ "Magic" refers to a set of beliefs about the existence and operation of powerful forces in the universe. Magical explanations of abnormality can be seen throughout history in such examples as trephination, shamanism, demonology, and witchcraft—as well as today.

◆ Somatic explanations also occur through history, from humours to heroic medicine to general paresis. Today, the attempt to explain abnormality in somatic terms is called the medical model. The medical model has been strongly criticized by Thomas Szasz, who brands the notion of mental "illness" a myth.

◆ Psychogenic explanations of abnormality date at least to the writings of Socrates, Plato, Aristotle, Homer, and Plutarch. In the 1700s, Mesmer popular-

ized treatment techniques that we nowadays refer to as hypnotism. In the 1800s, the popular approach of mind cure legitimized to the general public a psychogenic view of abnormality.

◆ The single most important figure in winning acceptance for the psychogenic view of abnormality was neurologist Sigmund Freud, whose psychoanalytic theory proposed that people's problems were due to unconscious conflicts. The neo-Freudians were theorists who followed Freud and extended even further his psychological emphasis.

◆ Psychology itself became interested in abnormality through the efforts of behaviorists at the beginning of the 20th century. John Watson showed that "abnormality" could be produced by mundane processes of learning. Following from this view was the notion that principles of learning could be used to treat problems, an approach known as behavior therapy.

◆ Other psychological therapies developed in the 20th century target a person's thoughts and beliefs for change.

◆ The history of hospital treatment parallels the general history of abnormality. Hospitals began as religious shrines. Then they housed people who were not gainfully employed, including those with psychological abnormality. The mad were subjected to particularly harsh treatment under the assumption that this would help restore to them their power of reason. Around 1800, reforms came to hospitals, and the insane were treated in more humane fashion. Only at this time were physicians put in charge of hospitals. Hospitals specializing in the treatment of the insane came into existence, and the directors of these hospitals were the very first psychiatrists.

Key Terms

behavior therapy
behaviorism
catharsis
cross-cultural
  psychopathology
curanderas
demonology
existentialism
exorcism
family resemblance
free association
general paresis
germ theory
heroic medicine
humanism
humoural theory

magic
medical model
mesmerism
mind cure
moral treatment
myth of mental illness
neo-Freudians
neurology
operational definition
phenomenology
psychoanalysis
shaman; witch doctor;
  medicine man
trephination
witches

Diagnosis and Assessment

2 IN THE LAST CHAPTER, I DISCUSSED HOW abnormality might be defined as well as how it has been conceived over the years. Here I consider the judgment about exactly what sort of problem a person may have. Two topics are of concern. **Diagnosis** refers to the categorization of people's problems, and **assessment** is the process of gathering specific information about a person in order to make a diagnosis and to understand the particulars of his or her given problem. Even though I address these topics separately, diagnosis and assessment go hand in hand.

DIAGNOSIS

The term *diagnosis* literally means to distinguish or differentiate, and in Chapter 1, I noted a great deal of interest in one aspect of diagnosis: distinguishing those with problems from those without. Another sense in which diagnosis involves distinctions is *within* the group of people who have problems. Remember the trend sketched within medicine as a whole: a movement from the notion that there is but one disease state to the assumption that there are many different diseases. The same trend can be found in the field of abnormality: a proliferation of suggested types of abnormality, and a concomitant attempt to discern exactly what type of problem a person may have.

IDEAL DIAGNOSTIC SYSTEMS

A *diagnostic system* is a set of possible types of abnormality and the rules for recognizing them. Theorists have attempted to specify the properties of an ideal diagnostic system. Here are the characteristics of one popular vision of such a system (Robins & Helzer, 1986). First, an ideal diagnostic system is one in which the categories are *mutually exclusive*. In other words, the categories do not overlap. If you assign an entity to one category, then it does not at the same time belong to another category.

An ideal diagnostic system also has categories that are *jointly exhaustive*. They encompass the entire range of categories into which we sort things so that there is nothing left over. When I try to pair up my socks after washing them, my goal is to have a large number of meaningful categories, each with two matching socks in it. I am usually forced to create a meaningless pile for socks that do not match, and there have been wash days when this miscellaneous pile is larger than any other pile. My "system" does not work well because its categories are not jointly exhaustive.

Finally, an ideal diagnostic system is one in which category membership is defined by *features that are either present or absent*. The criteria by which we assign entities to categories must allow us to make either-or decisions. Consider how the United States decides if citizens can vote: how old they are. Eighteen or over, they can vote. Under 18, they cannot.

We can evaluate a diagnostic system by how closely it approaches these ideal criteria. Consider a system with which we are all familiar, that for classifying vertebrate species. A typical way of sorting out the species that have spinal columns is into the categories called fish, amphibians, reptiles, birds, and mammals. By and large, this is a useful system because we can apply dichotomous rules (e.g., it breathes in water; it has feathers) to assign most species to one and only one category.

At the same time, there are problems with this system, at least in terms of being an ideal classification. The debate over where dinosaurs fit is illustrative (Krishtalka, 1989). Although they have traditionally been classified with reptiles, some contemporary theorists argue that dinosaurs should instead be classified with birds. Here we see a problem with the defining features used to place a species in one category or another. With dinosaurs, these features disagree. So, dinosaurs had scales (like reptiles), but many were warm-blooded (like birds).

This example of classifying vertebrates is forced, because modern biologists classify species based on their theorized evolutionary lineage. Dinosaurs are classified with birds because they presumably arose from a common ancestor some 120 million years ago. Because we have an alternative basis for classifying these species, we can see the pitfalls of a diagnostic system based on a classification that looks solely at their surface features.

And this is why I have talked about vertebrates and socks before I address the real topic of the chapter: diagnosing psychological abnormality. Unlike vertebrates or socks, we do not at the present time have a system for classifying problems based on their inherent structure. Our diagnostic systems are based on surface features, and sometimes these do not allow fully satisfactory classification of people's problems. Any classification system can tolerate a handful of failures. The problem is when there are many failures relative to the number of successes.

A HISTORY OF DIAGNOSTIC SYSTEMS

I have talked about diagnostic systems in the plural, because there is no single way to classify people's problems. Today, we have several systems competing for professional attention around the world. A view across history reveals an incredible array of such systems. Indeed, diagnostic systems have existed for thousands of years (Menninger, 1963). Although it is difficult to generalize across all of these different systems, one trend is toward systems with ever more categories.

Early diagnostic systems   Hippocrates, for instance, described a mere handful of disorders: epilepsy, psychosis, transvestism, hysteria, depression, and phobia. Aristotle, Galen, and others from the Greek and Roman era had similarly simple classification systems. As already noted, the prevailing belief for many hundreds of years was that there was but one underlying state of illness, physical or mental, and there was little need to proliferate distinctions among its manifestations.

THE FAR SIDE   By GARY LARSON

"Yes, they're all fools, gentlemen ... But the question remains, 'What KIND of fools are they?'"

The Far Side cartoon by Gary Larson is reprinted by permission of Chronicle Features, San Francisco, CA. All rights reserved.

This view started to change in more recent centuries. Notable here is the English physician Thomas Sydenham (1624–1689), who was one of the first to argue that each illness had its own cause. He believed that each disease had a uniform presentation—that is, it produced exactly the same symptoms from person to person (Kendell, 1975). If symptoms differed, even to a small degree, then illnesses necessarily differed.

The germ model of illness, when generalized to psychological abnormality, encouraged diagnostic theorists to propose more elaborate systems. Different problems presumably had different underlying causes. According to the germ model, the correct identification of the underlying cause of a problem was possible if the problem were carefully described.

Another boost to the growing complexity of diagnostic systems was the rise of psychiatric hospitals, which brought together large numbers of people with problems under the observing eyes of physicians who wished to distinguish one type of problem from another. However, many systems were still rather simple. Philippe Pinel, the French physician who worked at the Hôpital Général, proposed that there were but four major problems: mania (intense excitement or fury), melancholia (depression), dementia (lack of cohesion in ideas), and idiocy (mental retardation). Pinel saw these four problems in turn as due to something wrong with the nervous system.

Emil Kraepelin Current diagnostic systems are usually quite complex, and many can be traced to Emil Kraepelin (1856–1926), a German physician widely regarded as the founding father of modern diagnosis. Kraepelin was an astute observer as well as a theorist. In a series of influential textbooks at the turn of the century, he synthesized what was then known about psychological abnormality. In distinguishing 13 major disorders, he provided the structure that still characterizes contemporary diagnostic systems. Today's systems differ from Kraepelin's (1899) view mainly by adding subcategories of his major divisions.

Kraepelin subscribed to a medical view of disorders, viewing all of them as having biological determinants. His hope in classifying disorders was to allow researchers to work backwards from the classifications to discover their underlying causes. In this one sense, then, Kraepelin's system can be regarded as psychologi-

cal in approach because of his advocacy of a careful description of a patient's behavior (Blashfield, 1984).

Diagnostic systems in the United States Whatever the intrinsic validity of his system, Kraepelin was undoubtedly helped by the fact that he was a clear and interesting writer. Striking examples from his clinical work appeared in his books, adding to their popularity. His texts were frequently translated, and English-language versions became widely available in the United States in the early years of the 20th century.

Previously, the only diagnostic system that could be regarded as an "official" one was the set of categories used in the United States Census (Spitzer & Williams, 1980). Starting with the 1840 census, an attempt was made to ascertain the number of people in the country with psychological abnormality. At first, only one category—"idiocy"—was used, and it grouped together both the psychologically disturbed and the retarded. In subsequent census systems, there was a steady increase in the number of categories, and by the 20th century, Kraepelin's system started to have an influence.

In 1935, the American Psychiatric Association contributed a Kraepelin-based diagnostic system to the American Medical Association for inclusion in its *Standard Classified Nomenclature of Disease*. This system sufficed until World War II, when weaknesses became apparent. The Kraepelin system was developed for hospitalized patients, many of whom suffered chronic disorders, yet World War II saw a great increase in acute conditions among soldiers in combat. They had no ready place within the existing system.

Another problem with the existing system was that it did not take psychoanalytic theory into account, which was at that time becoming popular in the United States. Psychoanalytic theory was concerned mainly with differentiating various "neurotic" disorders, but the prevailing diagnostic system did not allow such theoretical distinctions to be made in practice.

Faced with the inadequacy of the existing system, the U.S. Army hospitals, the U.S. Navy hospitals, and the Veterans Administration hospitals each developed classification systems, which were sometimes at odds with one another and thus made communication between and among them difficult. In 1951 the United States Public Health Service commissioned representatives from the American Psychiatric Association to standardize the diagnostic systems used in the United States (Grob, 1991).

The resulting document was published in 1952 as the first edition of the *Diagnostic and Statistical Manual of Mental Disorders* (or *DSM-I*). By the way, the word *statistical* in DSM-I and its subsequent editions refers to the fact that each type of abnormality listed has an associated code number, allowing the

Many current diagnostic systems, including DSM-IV, can be traced to the work of German physician Emil Kraepelin (1856–1926), who wrote a series of influential textbooks at the turn of the century.

particular abnormality to be briefly identified, as on an insurance reimbursement claim. These numbers need not concern us. What we should note is that DSM-I reflected prevailing concerns. Many problems were described as "reactions" (e.g., schizophrenic reaction), in keeping with the notion that environmental conditions could precipitate problems. Also, the then-current acceptance of psychoanalytic theory was evident, as shown in the use of "defense mechanisms" to define and explain disorders. DSM-I described 108 separate disorders, contrasted with the 13 major disorders in Kraepelin's system—illustrating the trend toward complexity of diagnostic systems.

The American Psychiatric Association eventually decided to issue a new edition of the manual, and in 1968 *DSM-II* was published. DSM-II differed from its predecessor by eliminating the term *reaction* and with it the implication that disorders are necessarily responses to life's circumstances. It specified 182 different disorders.

At the time of DSM-II, researchers started to take seriously the need to ascertain the reliability of diagnostic systems, and DSM-II was found to be lacking. Many of its symptoms were vaguely defined. Even when symptoms were more clearly defined, cutoff points were not provided for the diagnostician to decide how many symptoms needed to be present before a given diagnosis was to be made. Schizophrenia could be indicated by a dozen different symptoms. What about the individual who displayed 10 or 11 of these? Was she to be given a diagnosis?

Research using the DSM-II classification system was difficult, with solid evidence bearing on its validity precluded. In 1972, psychiatrist John Feighner and his colleagues described what they called **research diagnostic criteria,** explicit rules to be used in diagnosing patients for inclusion (and exclusion) in research studies. For many disorders, these criteria resulted in more reliable diagnoses than those in DSM-I and DSM-II (Helzer et al., 1977). One important consequence of improved reliability is more valid research, which in turn leads to more useful diagnostic systems (Chapter 4).

When the American Psychiatric Association in 1980 published the third edition of its *Diagnostic and Statistical Manual (DSM-III),* it based its guidelines on the Feighner research diagnostic criteria. Unlike its immediate predecessors, DSM-III described symptoms in explicit fashion, provided cutoffs for making diagnoses, and also specified considerations that precluded other diagnoses. It listed 265 separate disorders.

Several other things should be stressed about DSM-III. It did away with a great deal of psychoanalytic terminology, in an attempt to be more neutral theoretically. DSM-III also introduced what is called

multiaxial classification: the description of people and their problems in several different ways simultaneously. Finally, the reliability of DSM-III was tested in actual clinical practice prior to its publication. In 1987, DSM-III was slightly revised, resulting in a diagnostic manual referred to as *DSM-III-R.*

DSM-IV

Diagnosticians in many countries outside the United States describe people's medical and psychological problems using a system sponsored by the World Health Organization called the **International Classification of Diseases,** or **ICD** (World Health Organization, 1990). Due to a treaty obligation with the World Health Organization, the United States needed to make DSM terminology consistent with the most recent edition of the ICD (Hohenshil, 1992; Kendell, 1991). Thus, another revision of DSM appeared in 1994, giving us the fourth edition of the American Psychiatric Association's diagnostic manual: **DSM-IV.**

Like its immediate predecessors, DSM-IV uses multiaxial classification, describing disorders in terms of five different axes; a full diagnosis contains information on each axis. Axis I describes an individual's **clinical syndrome:** the acute problem that brings the person into treatment. Clinical syndromes include such familiar difficulties as alcohol abuse, depression, phobia, schizophrenia, and the like. See Table 2.1 for sketches of the clinical syndromes described in DSM-IV.

Diagnosed on Axis II[1] are **personality disorders,** defined as pervasive styles of dysfunctional behavior. For example, a person may be excessively dependent, or self-dramatizing, or timid. Personality disorders can exacerbate a clinical syndrome as well as be problems in their own right.

On Axis III, the diagnostician notes any physical illnesses or medical conditions pertinent to the individual's clinical syndrome. Suppose an individual has thyroid disease. Among the possible consequences of such a condition are mood changes, and we would want to take this into account in judging whether this person warrants an Axis I diagnosis of depression.

Our understanding of abnormal behavior is increased when we take into account the setting where it occurs. Axis IV of DSM-IV captures an important situational characteristic: existing problems like unemployment or divorce (see Table 2.2). A physical illness might well be coded here as well as on Axis III, if the illness creates stress that contributes to a clinical syndrome. Imagine having a serious kidney disease that

---

[1] Also diagnosed on Axis II is *mental retardation* (Chapter 14).

TABLE 2.1

MAJOR CLASSES OF DSM-IV CLINICAL SYNDROMES

The hundreds of specific disorders described in DSM-IV are classified under the major headings listed here.
SOURCE: *DSM-IV DRAFT CRITERIA*, 1993, WASHINGTON, DC: AMERICAN PSYCHIATRIC ASSOCIATION.

◆ **disorders usually first diagnosed in infancy, childhood, or adolescence:** problems that usually show themselves before adulthood, such as conduct disorder and infantile autism (Chapter 14)

◆ **delirium, dementia, amnestic, and other cognitive disorders:** problems associated with impairment of the brain by illness or injury, such as difficulties in thinking brought on by chronic exposure to toxic substances (Chapter 6)

◆ **substance-related disorders:** psychological and social problems resulting from the ingestion of substances like alcohol, narcotics, and cocaine (Chapter 5)

◆ **schizophrenia and other psychotic disorders:** problems involving deterioration of self-care, work, and social relations, as well as profound disturbances in thought, language, and communication (Chapter 12)

◆ **mood disorders:** problems characterized by extreme and inappropriate sadness and/or elation, such as depression or bipolar disorder (Chapter 9)

◆ **anxiety disorders:** problems characterized by excessive worry and apprehension, such as phobia, panic disorder, and post-traumatic stress disorder (Chapter 7)

◆ **somatoform disorders:** problems with physical symptoms that have no organic cause, such as hysteria (Chapter 8)

◆ **factitious disorders:** physical or psychological "problems" that are deliberately produced or faked

◆ **dissociative disorders:** problems marked by a splitting of consciousness, memory, and/or identity, such as psychogenic amnesia and multiple personality (Chapter 8)

◆ **sexual and gender identity disorders:** problems involving sexuality, either the orientation toward inappropriate sexual objects or the inability to perform sexually, or cross-gender identification such as transsexualism (Chapter 11)

◆ **eating disorders:** problems involving unusual patterns of food consumption, such as anorexia and bulimia (Chapter 14)

◆ **sleep disorders:** problems in which the normal process of sleep is disturbed or unusual events like nightmares or sleepwalking take place

◆ **impulse-control disorders:** problems characterized by an inability to refrain from performing acts harmful to the self or others, such as kleptomania (stealing), pyromania (fire-starting), or compulsive gambling

◆ **adjustment disorders:** problems involving a maladaptive reaction to an identifiable stressor, like divorce or unemployment

◆ **psychological factors affecting physical condition:** problems in which physical illnesses are caused or exacerbated by psychological factors, such as tension headaches, gastric ulcers, and obesity (Chapter 10)

Existing problems like unemployment are coded on Axis IV of DSM-IV.

necessitates dialysis. Above and beyond the physical aspects of your disease and its treatment is the associated psychological significance.

Finally, Axis V is a global assessment of how well or poorly a person functions in social and occupational spheres (see Table 2.3). Usually this rating is made in terms of an individual's present situation, to quantify the degree to which his or her problems have been disruptive. But a diagnostician may also wish to make this global assessment in terms of a person's past functioning. It is often important to know how an individual coped before his clinical syndrome developed, because this information allows a plausible goal for therapy to be specified. An individual's level of functioning in the past provides a reasonable clue about his potential level in the future.

Here is an example of a full DSM-IV diagnosis. I once treated Mr. Williams, a 35-year-old man who was depressed and also a heavy drinker. On Axis I, he was given a diagnosis of major depressive episode, *as well as* alcohol dependence. *On Axis II, he was described as having a* dependent personality disorder, *because he relied excessively on other people to make decisions for him. He did not require an Axis III description, according to examining physicians, although his drinking suggested that his physical condition should be closely monitored. Because he was unemployed, he was described on Axis IV as having* occupational problems. *Finally, in terms of Axis V, he showed* serious impairment *at the time I saw him, most obviously because of his thoughts of suicide.*

Although this is only a brief sketch of Mr. Williams, you have a much better sense of what his problems were all about than if he were simply described in terms of his clinical syndromes.

TABLE 2.2

DSM-IV PSYCHOSOCIAL AND ENVIRONMENTAL PROBLEMS *According to DSM-IV, psychosocial and environmental problems include life events, environmental difficulties, interpersonal stresses, and deficits in social support. Any problem should be noted that provides the context in which an individual's psychological difficulties arose. The following categories of problems are suggested.* SOURCE: *DSM-IV DRAFT CRITERIA*, 1993, WASHINGTON, DC: AMERICAN PSYCHIATRIC ASSOCIATION.

✦ **problems with primary support group:** e.g., death of a family member, health problems in the family, sexual or physical abuse

✦ **problems related to the social environment:** e.g., death or loss of a friend, social isolation, difficulty with acculturation

✦ **educational problems:** e.g., illiteracy, inadequate school environment

✦ **occupational problems:** e.g., unemployment, threat of job loss, job dissatisfaction

✦ **housing problems:** e.g., homelessness, unsafe neighborhood

✦ **economic problems:** e.g., extreme poverty, insufficient welfare support

✦ **problems with access to health care services:** e.g., inadequate health care, inadequate health insurance

✦ **problems related to interaction with the legal system/crime:** e.g., arrest, victim of crime

✦ **other psychosocial problems:** e.g., exposure to natural disasters, war, other hostilities

TABLE 2.3

DSM-IV GLOBAL ASSESSMENT OF FUNCTIONING SCALE *Consider psychological, social, and occupational functioning on a hypothetical continuum of mental health versus illness. Do not include impairment in functioning due to physical (or environmental) limitations.*

Note: Use intermediate codes when appropriate (e.g., 45, 68, 72).

SOURCE: *DSM-IV DRAFT CRITERIA*, 1993, WASHINGTON, DC: AMERICAN PSYCHIATRIC ASSOCIATION.

CODE

100 – 91	Superior functioning in a wide range of activities, life's problems never seem to get out of hand, is sought out by others because of his many positive qualities. No symptoms.
90 – 81	Absent or minimal symptoms (e.g., mild anxiety before an exam); good functioning in all areas, interested and involved in a wide range of activities, socially effective, generally satisfied with life, no more than everyday problems or concerns (e.g., an occasional argument with family members).
80 – 71	If symptoms are present, they are transient and expectable reactions to psychosocial stressors (e.g., difficulty concentrating after family argument); no more than slight impairment in social, occupational, or school functioning (e.g., temporarily falling behind in school work).
70 – 61	Some mild symptoms (e.g., depressed mood and mild insomnia) OR some difficulty in social, occupational, or school functioning (e.g., occasional truancy, or theft within the household), but generally functioning pretty well, has some meaningful interpersonal relationships.
60 – 51	Moderate symptoms (e.g., flat affect and circumstantial speech, occasional panic attacks) OR moderate difficulty in social, occupational, or school functioning (e.g., few friends, conflicts with fellow workers).
50 – 41	Serious symptoms (e.g., suicidal ideation, severe obsessional rituals, frequent shoplifting) OR any serious impairment in social, occupational, or school functioning (e.g., no friends, unable to keep a job).
40 – 31	Some impairment in reality testing or communication (e.g., speech is at times illogical, obscure, or irrelevant) OR major impairment in several areas, such as work or school, family relations, judgment, thinking, or mood (e.g., depressed man avoids friends, neglects family, and is unable to work; child frequently beats up younger children, is defiant at home, and is failing at school).
30 – 21	Behavior is considerably influenced by delusions or hallucinations OR serious impairment in communication or judgment (e.g., sometimes incoherent, acts grossly inappropriately, suicidal preoccupation) OR inability to function in almost all areas (e.g., stays in bed all day; no job, home, or friends).
20 – 11	Some danger of hurting self or others (e.g., suicide attempts without clear expectation of death, frequently violent, manic excitement) OR occasionally fails to maintain minimal personal hygiene (e.g., smears feces) OR gross impairment in communication (e.g., largely incoherent or mute).
10 – 1	Persistent danger of severely hurting self or others (e.g., recurrent violence) OR persistent inability to maintain minimal personal hygiene OR serious suicidal act with clear expectation of death.

THE ADVANTAGES OF DIAGNOSING ABNORMALITY

What can we conclude about the value of diagnosis? Simply put, a system for classifying psychological abnormality is useful to the degree that the benefits of diagnosis outweigh the costs. I start with the benefits and then move on to the costs, after which I turn a critical eye to DSM-IV.

Communication　　　On the positive side, a correctly made diagnosis greatly facilitates communication among mental health professionals.

To say that Mr. Smith has a panic disorder with agoraphobia *is to include a great deal of information into a brief phrase. We know from this diagnosis that Mr. Smith experiences episodes of fear and apprehension and that he is apt to avoid crowded stores and public transportation (Chapter 7). Without the diagnostic label, we could still describe the nature of Mr. Smith's problem, but the diagnosis makes communication more efficient. Further, it gives us an idea about other sorts of symptoms that he might evidence. Feelings of depression may well be present, and we are reminded to ask Mr. Smith about such feelings.*

Etiology　　　Another positive aspect of diagnosis is that it can provide suggestions about the **etiology** of a particular problem—that is, the factors that have led up to it.

Suppose Ms. Jones well satisfies the criteria for bipolar disorder. *She experiences alternating periods of inappropriate elation and inappropriate depression (Chapter 9). Research suggests that there is a genetic predisposition to this problem; therefore, the diagnosis of bipolar depression tells us something very important:* why *Ms. Jones has the problem that she does. And this information may lead us to some useful strategies for helping her or even to interventions that will prevent her offspring from developing the problem in the first place.*

Treatment　　　I have a third positive thing to say about diagnoses: they may suggest useful treatments for given problems. Mental health professionals have at their disposal a variety of treatment options. In any given case, there are simply too many to be used on a trial-and-error basis. Diagnoses point therapists in the direction of the treatments with which they might most reasonably start. Let us return to Ms. Jones. Granted her diagnosis of bipolar disorder, the drug *lithium* is the treatment of choice (Schou, 1988). Odds are that it will help her stay on a more even keel, avoiding both mania and depression.

Prognosis　　　Finally, a diagnosis can provide important information about the **prognosis** of a particu-

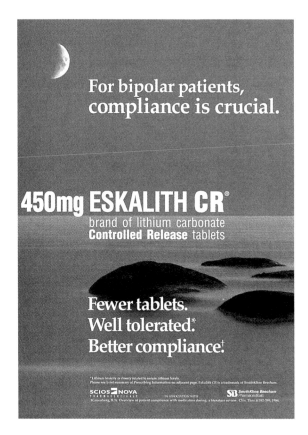

Drugs are used to treat a variety of psychological disorders. For example, lithium carbonate is a popular treatment for bipolar disorder (see Chapter 9).

lar problem—what the likely course of events will be. Will the person get better, get worse, or stay the same? What time course can be expected? For instance, we know that many people suffering an episode of depression are apt to improve in 3 to 6 months (Chapter 9). I have relied on this useful information in my own work as a therapist, as something hopeful to tell a depressed individual. A person who is depressed often feels hopeless, about life in general and her depression in particular (Beck, 1967). It is bolstering to be assured that bad feelings will probably pass. At the same time, we also know that many of the people who come out of a depressed episode will have another one, so this information alerts us to that future possibility (Perris, 1968). The risk of recurrence is greatest in the immediate 6 months following recovery.

In sum, diagnoses may have several notable virtues. They provide an efficient means of communicating about people's problems. Some diagnoses suggest the likely causes of a problem, the treatments that may be effective, and what will happen to the person with the problem in the future. These are considerable strengths, and a diagnostic system that possesses them is said to have **validity,** identifying coherent problems.

THE DISADVANTAGES OF DIAGNOSING ABNORMALITY

The most obvious problem with a diagnosis, of course, is that it might be wrong. The virtues I have enumerated for diagnoses all vanish if the label placed on a person's problem describes a problem that the person does not have. Not only are we *un*informed about etiology, treatment, and prognosis, we are *mis*informed; consequences may be severe if we act on a wrong diagnosis.

Occasionally, a dramatic story appears in which some patient who has lingered for years on the back wards of a mental hospital is suddenly discovered not to be suffering from any psychological problem. Once the person's history is reconstructed, his initial admission is seen as a mistake and his continued stay as unnecessary. This is a striking example of what happens when a judgment of "abnormality" is incorrectly made.

Consider the case of Amos Jefferson, who was institutionalized for five decades with a diagnosis of mental retardation (Niemiec, 1991, p. 1):

> *Jefferson rebelled from the beginning. He wildly waved his hands, wrote notes that people could read but not understand and made loud noises that scared other residents. His calm, when he achieved it, was always temporary.*
>
> *In April 1992 Jefferson threw a chair in a crowded workshop room, which prompted a review of his medical records. It was then discovered that he had never been mentally retarded. Rather, he was deaf, a fact unknown to those charged with his care. When administered IQ tests decades ago, Mr. Jefferson had scored within normal ranges. He could read and write, and he knew American Sign Language.*
>
> *For reasons that remain a mystery, he was admitted to a state institution in 1942, when he was a teenager. He was given the diagnosis of mental retardation and remained institutionalized for the next 50 years, unable to communicate with anyone. His gestures were not seen as language but rather as the signs of agitation that sometimes are observed among those with mental retardation. Once he encountered someone who knew American Sign Language, he was able to tell his story and win release from the state institution.*

Misdiagnosis   There are other examples of wrong diagnoses that can be cited, less dramatic but more common and in some cases just as dire in their results. I am referring to cases where the person actually has a problem but is misdiagnosed.

Amos Jefferson was institutionalized for five decades with a diagnosis of mental retardation. He was released in 1992, when it was discovered that he was really deaf, not retarded.

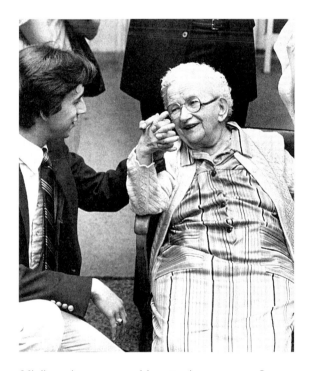

Misdiagnosis can occur and have tragic consequences. In 1985, Gladys Tyler Burr settled a suit against the state of Connecticut charging that she had been wrongfully kept in an institution for the retarded for 42 years.

When I worked in a hospital, one of the patients on our ward behaved in a strange fashion. He sat for long periods of time without moving or talking. When he did talk, he made little sense. He was disheveled. The diagnosis given to this patient was schizophrenia, *and the doctors prescribed a medication often helpful for people with this problem. Then a staff member brought up yet another concern. Mr. S. had extremely dry skin, she observed, and above and beyond all his other problems, we should be sure to give him hand lotion, because he seems to spend all his time sitting in a chair rubbing his thumbs against the tips of his fingers. With that statement, several physicians yelled, "He does what?" And the person who had made this observation, which had eluded everyone else, demonstrated the specific movements that the patient made.*

There is a term for these movements:—pill-rolling—because it is as if the person is rolling a pill between his thumb and his fingertips. Pill-rolling is a sign not of schizophrenia but of Parkinson's disease, *a progressive neurological disorder (Chapter 6). Perhaps Mr. S. had been misdiagnosed. And this was a grievous error, because the medication prescribed for him would exacerbate his Parkinson's disease. These drugs certainly could not help him with the "schizophrenia" from which he did not suffer. The diagnosis of Parkinson's disease was confirmed, and appropriate treatment on a neurology ward was undertaken. I cannot add that Mr. S. lived happily ever after, because Parkinson's disease can be highly debilitating. But he certainly lived longer and more comfortably than he would have if the misdiagnosis had not been corrected.*

The lesson of this case is *not* that diagnosis as such is bad. Eventually giving Mr. S. the diagnosis of Parkinson's disease proved beneficial. Instead, the lesson is that wrong diagnosis is bad, and the process of making diagnoses is hardly foolproof. The diagnostician should consider a label as a hypothesis—that is, a working assumption constantly to be scrutinized critically and evaluated against the evidence.

Assumption of discontinuity Besides the possibility of misdiagnosis, what other drawbacks can I point to about the use of diagnoses? As discussed earlier, "diagnosis" often involves putting people into mutually exclusive categories according to their problems, using either-or features. However, "abnormality" does not refer to a discrete category or set of categories. Present-absent features are another way to talk about necessary and sufficient conditions, and abnormality does not have necessary and sufficient conditions (Chapter 1). Stated another way, many diagnostic systems assume discontinuity between normality

and abnormality as well as between different types of abnormality, and this is often an unreasonable assumption (Kendell, 1975).

There are many people whose difficulties represent clear examples of abnormality, and for them, the assumption of discontinuity does not impede what mental health professionals do to help. The problem ensues when we encounter people who "kind of" have a difficulty, who are somewhat depressed or somewhat anxious. Because we have no single place to put them in typical diagnostic systems, our conclusions about etiology, treatment, and prognosis are necessarily qualified.

Embodiment of medical model From the viewpoint of many psychologists, typical diagnostic systems are additionally problematic because they are based on the medical approach to abnormality (Eysenck, 1986), as described in Chapter 1. Often these systems are derived from the germ theory. They assume that we should describe overt symptoms with a goal of seeing how they cohere into particular patterns called **syndromes**. These syndromes in turn are thought to reflect the operation of an underlying biological cause (i.e., a germ).

This is useful to the degree that symptoms comprise syndromes and that these syndromes have underlying causes. In some cases, this is a reasonable way to look at problems. Note that many of the examples on which I drew for explaining the benefits of diagnosis had biological causes and/or treatments. But in other cases, this is a wrong-headed way of looking at problems. When we speak of symptoms, we assume that there is something more to the problem than what meets the eye. But according to some theorists, people's symptoms might simply be their problem. There is nothing else going on. Swollen glands may be a sign of an infection, for instance, but sad feelings may not signify anything else but sadness. Perhaps sadness *is* the problem in its own right and not a symptom. Perhaps there is no underlying syndrome that shows itself as sadness, just people who are sad to varying degrees. The general issue is whether people's problems as expressed in their thoughts, feelings, and actions are sufficiently described in these terms, or whether we should go further and regard observable behavior as symptomatic of some underlying physical problem.

Typical diagnostic systems are useful insofar as the medical model is relevant, and problematic when this is not the case. As already mentioned, the diagnostic system most widely used in the United States is a product of the American Psychiatric Association; DSM-IV is a medical document (Wilson, 1993). Psychologists have not come up with their own system of describing problems that has caught on to the same degree that the psychiatric document has (Millon, 1986a), and so psychologists find themselves using a diagnostic system that may be at odds with their own conceptions of problems (Carson, 1991; Schact & Nathan, 1977).

Questionable reliability   Even if a diagnostic system is a sensible one, it is only as useful as the way it is actually employed in practice. I turn therefore from this discussion of the validity of diagnostic systems to a discussion of their **reliability**—the degree to which different diagnosticians using a particular system arrive at the same diagnosis for an individual.

Suppose an individual comes to a clinic, where he is interviewed by a diagnostician. Two questions are of interest. First, does the person have a problem? Second, if the answer is yes, what kind of problem does the person have? If the same person talks to more than one diagnostician, we can find out the degree to which the diagnosticians agree in their answers to these questions.

Perfect agreement of course is the goal, but this is unreasonable to expect. Instead, we see how closely the diagnosticians approach the goal of perfect agreement. Several generalizations can be made about diagnostic reliability. As already noted, past diagnostic systems used in the United States had unsatisfactory reliability. Different diagnosticians could not agree very well on what kind of problem a person had (e.g., Ash, 1949; Beck, 1962; Masserman & Carmichael, 1938) or even if he or she had a problem in the first place (Temerlin, 1968). We can attribute this poor reliability to the imprecision of defining features (Ward, Beck, Mendelson, Mock, & Erbaugh, 1962).

Another generalization is that current diagnostic systems are much more satisfactory in terms of reliability (e.g., Fogelson, Nuechterlein, Asarnow, Subotnik, & Talovic, 1991; Skre, Onstad, Torgersen, & Kringlen, 1991; Spitzer, Forman, & Nee, 1979; Williams et al., 1992). Diagnosticians have become aware of the need to make diagnosis more reliable, and impressive strides have been made by making the criteria for diagnosis as precise as possible. There is sometimes a tendency to refer to clinical judgment as intuition or art. While I do not deny the role played by these processes, it is dangerous to talk in these terms if they are used to rationalize a failure to articulate just what is behind a particular judgment made by a diagnostician.

Finally, despite the strides that have been made, the reliability of currently diagnosing some disorders is much less satisfactory than others (e.g., Mellsop, Varghese, Joshua, & Hicks, 1982). Perhaps the problem lies in the respective criteria utilized in the diagnostic system. Or perhaps it lies in the nature of the particular disorder. Some psychological difficulties lend themselves to reliable diagnosis in terms of a categorical system and all that it implies, whereas others are too ambiguous, too embedded in a social context to admit so easily to a simple label.

Labeling   When we categorize our socks or creatures like dinosaurs, we do not affect the entities we are sorting. Matters are different when we sort human beings into categories, precisely because people think and react to the labels placed on themselves and others. We cannot escape labels and categories in our social lives, so a radical critique of labeling will not be attempted here. Instead, I suggest careful consideration of the power of the labels placed on people. To diagnose individuals is to identify them as abnormal, and those who are abnormal might be stigmatized (Monahan, 1977; Scheff, 1966). Does anyone want a "former mental patient" living next door?

A diagnostic label can take on a life of its own, even when it is incorrect. David Rosenhan (1973) reported a provocative study in his article titled "On Being Sane in Insane Places." Rosenhan and seven other researchers went individually to mental hospitals and told the examining physician that they heard voices saying "empty, dull, or thud." Aside from this, they answered all questions truthfully. Based on this one symptom, most were given the diagnosis of schizophrenia and admitted to the hospitals. Length of hospitalization varied from 7 to 52 days, with an average stay of 19 days. Only in one case was the presence of one of these **pseudopatients** *known in advance to hospital administrators. In all other cases, the pseudopatients were told that they were on their own. Their task was to win discharge by convincing the staff that they were sane.*

Although they acted in a perfectly normal fashion following their admission to the various hospital wards, **not in a single case** *did a member of the professional staff suspect that they were anything other than what the initial diagnosis indicated. Instead, the label was used to interpret what the pseudopatients did. For example, Rosenhan and the others took notes while they were there on the wards. At first, they disguised what they were doing, fearing that they would be detected. Then they realized that they could take notes openly because the nurses and doctors saw this as another manifestation of their presumed illness. One nurse duly recorded in a chart, "Patient engages in writing behavior."*

Do you see how this description strips away the meaning of what the person was actually doing? When you take notes in class, are you "engaged in writing behavior"? Of course not. You are taking notes, a mean-

ingful activity chosen by a healthy individual. But if you are diagnosed as schizophrenic, then the same activity becomes a sign of your problem.

Two more points about the study are important. The real patients on the wards often detected the sanity of the pseudopatients, asking them if they were journalists or professors. This may mean that the professionals were more blinded by their labels than were the other people who came into contact with the pseudopatients. It may also mean that the time professionals spend with hospitalized patients is often incredibly brief (Rosenhan, 1973).

When the pseudopatients were eventually discharged, they were given a diagnosis of schizophrenia in remission—*meaning that schizophrenia was still present within them, although not currently active. Here we see the consequences of regarding symptoms as signs of an underlying problem. The signs may go away, but the underlying illness lingers.*

In Rosenhan's study, we know that the pseudopatients had no problems, yet the label alone was enough to set all sorts of processes into action. This is a serious drawback of the entire business of diagnosing people. We can criticize the study, of course, for putting the staff members of the hospitals in a difficult and perhaps impossible position (Spitzer, 1975). After all, they were deliberately misled. Can we fault them for erring on the side of caution when faced with what seemed to be a serious symptom of psychological abnormality? That they made a mistake in the case of pseudopatients does *not* mean that comparable mistakes are common when professionals work with actual patients. Most individuals who enter a psychiatric hospital have some sort of problem. Nonetheless, the study illustrates that labels can have considerable power.

In sum, diagnosis has both benefits and costs. So too does not making a diagnosis. Whether diagnosticians should be lenient or stringent reflects a judgment of what is to be gained or lost in specific cases.

A CRITICAL LOOK AT THE MODERN DSM APPROACH

Let us look in particular at DSM-IV and its immediate predecessors. Although certainly an improvement over earlier diagnostic systems, the modern DSM approach is not a final product. Critics argue that DSM-IV followed too closely on the heels of its previous versions (e.g., Zimmerman, Jampala, Sierles, & Taylor, 1991). Appreciate, however, that I will be relying on this

system in the rest of the book, not exclusively but still substantially. DSM-IV provides much of the language used in the mental health system of the United States (e.g., Jampala, Zimmerman, Sierles, & Taylor, 1992; Setterberg et al., 1991) and other parts of the world (Maser, Kaelber, & Weise, 1991; Mezzich, Fabrega, Mezzich, & Coffman, 1985). We must be of two minds about it: conversant with its details yet skeptical of its thrust.

A system of disorders or just a heap?   One overarching question must be raised about the modern DSM approach: Why these disorders as opposed to others? The system is very much a mixed metaphor. Schact and Nathan (1977) call the DSM systems a symphony composed by a committee. The clinical syndromes are not described at the same level of abstraction (again see Table 2.1). Some disorders are described on the basis of a dominant symptom (e.g., mood disorders), whereas others are described in terms of the sphere of impaired functioning (e.g., sexual disorders). Some disorders are described in terms of when they appear in the lifespan (e.g., disorders usually first apparent in infancy, childhood, or adolescence). Still others are described in terms of their etiology (e.g., delirium, dementia, amnestic, and other cognitive disorders). There is little coherent organization here. What we might have instead is just a heap of troubles.

There have been attempts to provide an overall structure to diagnostic systems. Remember the humoural theory described in Chapter 1. This was an explicit statement, not only of the problems that people experienced, but how they were produced. Most basically, there were four sorts of problems, respectively due to a preponderance of one humour rather than another. But the humoural theory did not stand the test of time.

A more contemporary attempt to systematize the disorders is in the distinction between neurotic disorders and psychotic disorders. DSM-II was based on this division. **Psychotic disorders,** exemplified by *schizophrenia* and *bipolar disorder,* are those in which a person's ability to test reality is impaired. In contrast, **neurotic disorders** are problems where the person's reality testing is intact. Examples include fear disorders such as a *phobia.* The power of this distinction derived from its reliance on psychoanalytic theory and the notion of a person defending against unconscious conflicts. In psychotic disorders, the person's defenses have failed, and they have become overwhelmed by instinctive drives. In neurotic disorders, the person's defenses are more than adequate to keep conflicts hidden. Indeed, neurotic symptoms can be understood as exaggerated defenses.

This distinction survives in our language. *Psychotic* and *neurotic* are still widely used adjectives for describing people and their problematic behavior. However, the distinction between psychotic and neurotic disorders has not proved as neat as once hoped. First, the popularity of psychoanalytic reasoning waned in the face of challenges from biomedical findings on the one hand and cognitive-behavioral ones on the other. Second, it was recognized that many "neurotic" disorders involve unusual ways of thinking that distort reality. Depressed people, for instance, systematically distort their perceptions and memories in negative ways, finding the cloud around every silver lining (Peterson, 1983). Although the schizophrenic is more estranged from the facts of the world than the depressive, the difference seems to be one of degree rather than kind. And third, even people suffering from the most clear examples of psychotic disorders rarely show constant impairment of reality testing.

Validity   Like its immediate predecessors, DSM-IV was created by a committee of mental health professionals. Decisions about what to include or not to include were usually made on the basis of the coherence of disorders by referring to the relevant research. Many disorders are valid ones; they involve problems with clear symptoms, causes, treatments, and prognoses. But this is not always the case. In some cases, people lobbied for and against inclusion of their "favorite" disorders, and inherent validity was not always the overriding criterion for including them in DSM-IV.

An instructive example is *homosexuality*. As I explain in Chapter 11, the early DSM systems included homosexual orientation as a mental disorder in its own right. The more recent versions of DSM do not. Part of the reason for deleting homosexuality was research evidence arguing against its designation as abnormal, but another part was explicitly political (Bayer, 1987). We can applaud this attempt, however belated, to destigmatize a large group of people. But there are, doubtlessly, other diagnostic categories remaining in DSM-IV that reflect unstated moral judgments more than they do bona fide psychological disturbance.

The authors of DSM-IV recognize the controversial nature of certain diagnostic categories and the implications of including or excluding them. In a lengthy appendix to the manual, possible diagnostic categories deserving "further study" are described. They are not formally considered mental disorders. In many cases, what is lacking is simply information about their coherence. But in other cases, if we read between the lines, what is lacking is a full discussion of the political consequences of considering a pattern of behavior as abnormal. Consider *premenstrual dysphoric disorder*, a suggested disorder involving symptoms of depression and anxiety that may occur for women during the last week of the luteal phase in the menstrual cycle. Psychological changes associated with menstruation are common for many women, but it is not at all clear that these produce marked distress or debilitation. The formal inclusion of this disorder in a DSM system, if and when it occurs, might legitimize discrimination against women simply because they are women.

By one view, DSM-IV already includes too many disorders of questionable validity to justify their inclusion, but they are nonetheless to be found in this diagnostic system (Zimmerman, 1988). Goodwin and Guze (1989) offered a strong statement when they wrote that "only about a dozen diagnostic entities in adult psychiatry have been sufficiently studied to be useful" (p. viii). Perhaps the almost 300 categories in DSM-IV result from overly fine distinctions (Pincus, Frances, Davis, First, & Widiger, 1992).

Although DSM-IV may well have too many categories, in another sense it has too few. Remember that an ideal diagnostic system specifies categories that allow all possible entities to be classified. Another term for the exhaustiveness of a classification system is *coverage*, and DSM-IV fails at full coverage. Large numbers of people who have problems in living are poorly described with its available diagnoses. People with work problems, or school difficulties, or religious crises may be shoehorned into one or more of DSM-IV's miscellaneous categories, but this is far from satisfactory (see Focus on Culture-Bound Syndromes, pp. 46–47). Neglected in particular are problems that exist in the context of a marriage or family.

Reliability   What about the reliability of the modern systems? Reliability is a prerequisite for studies and conclusions about the validity of any classification system. As mentioned earlier, DSM-III and DSM-IV can be praised relative to their predecessors for having undertaken studies of reliability (Robins & Helzer, 1986). Still, these studies were only preliminary. Not all axes have been subjected to the same scrutiny with respect to reliability (cf. Goldman, Skodol, & Lave, 1992). What we have are mainly studies of Axis I and Axis II, and the results, while encouraging, imply that further work is needed.

The typical way to ascertain reliability is to have the same two diagnosticians independently assess the same large group of potential patients. The diagnosticians make their respective diagnoses, and then we compare them on a case-by-case basis to see how well they agree. When studies of diagnostic reliability were first undertaken, agreement was calculated simply as the percentage of agreement between two diagnosticians.

However, so-called *simple agreement* is a misleading criterion of reliability because it is biased by

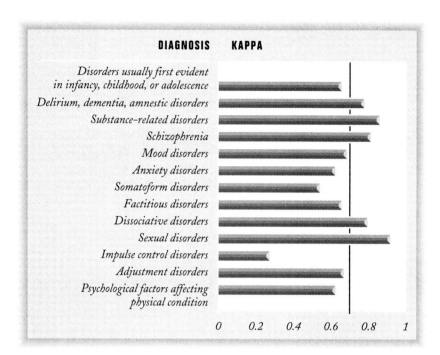

FIGURE **2.1**

AXIS I DIAGNOSIS
RELIABILITY   *In a study of
339 patients, the agreement of
diagnosticians with respect to
several major classes of DSM-III
clinical syndromes was
determined, using the kappa
statistic as explained in the text.
There exist slight differences in
terminology between DSM-III
and DSM-IV. For consistency
with our chapter, this figure uses
the more current terms, although
this study was conducted with the
DSM-III diagnostic system.*
SOURCE: *Diagnostic and Statistical Manual
of Mental Disorders* (3d ED., P. 470),
1980, WASHINGTON, DC: AMERICAN
PSYCHIATRIC ASSOCIATION.

the rates with which particular diagnoses are made. Suppose our two diagnosticians each tend to diagnose 90% of all the potential patients they see as schizophrenic. By chance alone, they are going to "agree" that 81% of the patients they see are schizophrenic (i.e., .90 × .90) and that 1% of them are not (i.e., .10 × .10). Their simple agreement of 82% (i.e., 81% + 1%) seems impressive until we realize that it is an artifact of the high likelihood of diagnosing schizophrenia.

We need to correct for chance agreement, and with the **kappa** statistic[2] we have a way to do this (Cohen, 1960). Kappa can be as high as 1.00, which corresponds to perfect agreement. When kappa is 0.00, this means that the two diagnosticians are operating in complete independence of one another. Finally, when kappa takes on a negative value, this means that the two diagnosticians, for some reason, are systematically disagreeing.

It is not possible to say exactly what absolute value of kappa is satisfactory for diagnosing psychological abnormality, because we have to take into account the

costs and benefits of agreements and disagreements. But conventionally, a kappa of at least .70 is considered "good" (Spitzer, Forman, & Nee, 1979). Figure 2.1 presents the kappas for various classes of DSM-III Axis I disorders, from a study conducted by those who compiled the manual. (The reliability studies described in Figures 2.1 and 2.2 were done with DSM-III, but this system is similar enough to DSM-IV that the conclusions apply to both.)

Several things are important to note about these figures. First, about half of the diagnoses have "good" reliability or better. Second, several of the diagnoses have far less satisfactory reliability. Third, the agreement is for general *classes* of diagnoses. Remember that DSM-IV specifies several hundred disorders, yet studies of diagnostic reliability rarely take such a fine-grained look.

Figure 2.2 presents the kappas from a study of DSM-III Axis II personality disorders. As you can see, none of these is satisfactory. Even the most general agreement—does this individual have a personality disorder or not, regardless of type?—had a kappa of only .41, which leaves us with serious doubts concerning reliability and hence validity in diagnosing personality disorders (Chapter 13).

THE FUTURE OF DIAGNOSIS

What can we expect of diagnosis in the future? No matter how its systems and applications evolve, most certainly we will not abandon diagnosis. Psychologists

---

[2] Here is the formula for kappa:

$$\text{kappa} = \frac{P_o - P_c}{1 - P_c}$$

P_o is the percent of observed agreement between two diagnosticians with respect to a given diagnosis, which I have referred to as simple agreement. P_c is the percent of agreement we would expect by chance, given the frequency with which the diagnosticians make the diagnosis.

FOCUS ON

Culture-Bound

Syndromes

AS DISCUSSED IN CHAPTER 1, *culture* refers to the shared knowledge transmitted from one generation to another. It is represented externally in terms of roles and institutions, as well as internally in terms of values and beliefs. If people's problems are located in a social context, then it is obvious that the culture in which they exist demands scrutiny. Indeed, there are some psychological disorders that occur only within specific cultures. For obvious reasons, such problems are called **culture-bound syndromes.** A number of these have attracted the attention of theorists and researchers (Akhtar, 1988; Jilek & Jilek-Aall, 1985; Littlewood, 1990; Mikhail, 1973; Prince & Tcheng-Laroche, 1987; Westermeyer, 1985). Their importance here lies in the reminder that people's problems do not exist apart from larger social factors.

Latah   This syndrome occurs only among females in Malaysia and Indonesia. *Latah* refers to an exaggerated startle response to minimal stimulation, such as mild tickling. Frequently accompanying this startle response are sexual obscenities. Sometimes *latah* is characterized by a heightened suggestibility and/or the tendency to mimic others in the immediate vicinity.

Taijinkyofusho   Seen chiefly among Asian males, *taijinkyofusho* (sometimes called *anthropophobia* in English) involves heightened anxiety over face-to-face contact with another person. It is marked as well by easy blushing and fear of rejection. The individual with *taijinkyofusho* imagines that he suffers a variety of shortcomings and deficiencies, such as an offensive facial expression or unpleasant body odors.

Amok   When we speak of a person running *amok*, killing people indiscriminately, we are using a Malaysian word that refers to a widely recognized syndrome seen among young males in the Malay culture. *Amok* consists of a sudden mass assault on others, usually with a sword or ax, sometimes resulting in numerous deaths. The *amok* individual may then kill himself as well. If he does not die, he typically has no memory of the episode (Schmidt, Hill, & Guthrie, 1977).

Grisi siknis   The syndrome of *grisi siknis* is encountered among the Miskito, a group living near the Atlantic Ocean in Honduras and Nicaragua. This syndrome is marked by anxiety, headaches, irrational anger at others, and aimless running around and falling down.

Koro   *Koro* is observed among males in a variety of Asian cultures and occasionally in Europe and the United States. *Koro* consists of the fear that the penis is retracting into the abdomen, eventually to cause death. Occasionally *koro* epidemics have been reported, in which hundreds of men in the same region experience its symptoms (Tseng et al., 1988, 1992).

Bebainin   This syndrome is observed only among the Bali, typically the women there. *Bebainin* includes abdominal pain, headache, ringing in the ears, impaired vision, screaming, weeping, and convulsions. Its onset is sudden, and its duration is brief. After an episode, the person is usually exhausted and has no memory of what ensued.

Dhat   Among young and sexually inexperienced males in India, the syndrome of *dhat* may occur (Chadda & Ahuja, 1990). The individual believes that his semen is being depleted because it is mingling with urine and thereby passing from his body. Accompanying *dhat* are anxiety, irritability, weakness, pain, impotence, and failure to meet social obligations. The individual with this syndrome also voices a host of somatic complaints.

Bulimia   This syndrome occurs among middle- and upper-class young women in the United States and western Europe; *bulimia* has not been described in other parts of the world. It is characterized by episodes of food binging, in which large amounts of high calorie food are consumed, followed by self-induced purging, as through vomiting. Feelings of depression often accompany *bulimia.*

Many more culture-bound syndromes could be described, but let me pause to draw some conclusions. First, culture-bound syndromes must necessarily be interpreted in terms of the particular culture in which they occur. They become sensible when we see that given syndromes have shared meanings within a cultural group. *Latah* can be interpreted as a way for Malay females, who are often psychologically and socially oppressed, to free themselves—however temporarily—from their restraints (Kenny, 1978). Along these same lines, despite looking like a random behavioral explosion, *amok* conforms to a societal script in Malaysia that recognizes the syndrome as a possible reaction to insult or jealousy (Carr & Tan, 1976; Tan & Carr, 1977). *Koro* occurs in a culture that uses the metaphor of a tree to describe the penis; a tree has a root that is vulnerable to unseeable attacks (Chowdhury, 1991). *Dhat* is consistent with the tenet of traditional Indian medicine that good health depends on the maintenance of vital bodily fluids (Paris, 1992).

Second, were these particular syndromes to occur in other cultures, most would still be considered problematic ways of behaving. Violence against others, excessive fear and anxiety, inaccurate somatic complaints, memory loss, and the like would be deemed "abnormal" in virtually any setting. The particular constellations of symptoms obviously may vary dramatically across cultures, yet the symptoms themselves appear to have greater universality.

Third, when Western researchers study culture-bound syndromes, they are usually drawn to faraway places.[3] It is doubtlessly easier to recognize a contextualized form of abnormality in a culture other than one's own. I deliberately included *bulimia* in my list of culture-bound syndromes to provoke your thinking on this point. It is rarely described as a culture-bound syndrome, although it perfectly fits the definition. Western researchers are probably guilty of looking too much within the bulimic individual for the causes of her problem and not enough at the larger cultural context that makes eating disorders so prevalent in the contemporary United States and Europe (McCarthy, 1990). We should look beyond the intrinsic interest of culture-bound syndromes, and see that *all* psychological problems, even those found widely around the world, occur in a cultural context.

[3] Under the influence of psychoanalytic theory, researchers have been drawn as well to syndromes involving sexuality.

and psychiatrists in North America will continue to use versions of DSM-whatever to describe people's problems. But several possibilities seem likely.

Increasing complexity of diagnostic systems   We can expect future diagnostic systems to describe problems with ever-increasing complexity as finer distinctions are made among the sorts of difficulties that people have. We should also expect the exact categories to change. One reason for this is the introduction of modern statistical techniques, made possible by computers, to the task of classifying symptom patterns (Blashfield, 1984).

Since the time of Hippocrates, diagnosticians have grouped symptoms into syndromes based on observation. We thus talk about depression as a syndrome because we observe that symptoms of sadness, appetite loss, sleep disturbance, low self-esteem, and suicidal

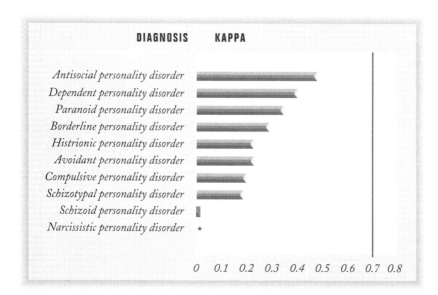

DIAGNOSIS   KAPPA

Antisocial personality disorder
Dependent personality disorder
Paranoid personality disorder
Borderline personality disorder
Histrionic personality disorder
Avoidant personality disorder
Compulsive personality disorder
Schizotypal personality disorder
Schizoid personality disorder
Narcissistic personality disorder   *

0   0.1   0.2   0.3   0.4   0.5   0.6   0.7   0.8

FIGURE 2.2

AXIS II DIAGNOSIS RELIABILITY   *In a study of 77 patients, the agreement of diagnosticians with respect to the DSM-III personality disorders was determined, using the kappa statistic as explained in the text. The label for a particular personality disorder describes the central characteristic of this dysfunctional style. Chapter 13 discusses these disorders in detail.*

*Note: This diagnosis was not made within this sample of patients.
SOURCE: "THE RELIABILITY OF AXIS II OF DSM-III," BY G. MELLSOP, F. VARGHESE, S. JOSHUA, AND A. HICKS, 1982, *American Journal of Psychiatry, 139,* P. 1361.

thoughts go together, co-occurring in different individuals. In many cases, the observations of diagnosticians over the centuries have been accurate, and the patterns discerned are present in the symptoms of the people being observed. But research by cognitive psychologists leaves no doubt that people's ability to detect complex patterns can be severely limited (Nisbett & Ross, 1980). We are biased in terms of noticing positive correlations as opposed to negative ones. We make mistakes in estimating the strength of correlations, particularly those in the direction of our expectations. Theories provide powerful expectations about which symptoms do and do not occur together; consequently, diagnostic theorists might see syndromes in part because they expect to see them.

At present, there is no need to rely on an unaided observer, subject to limitations and biases, when it is possible to have a computer detect patterns. In recent research, there has been an attempt to arrive at a more objective grouping of symptoms into disorders (e.g., Gara, Rosenberg, & Goldberg, 1992; Grove & Andreasen, 1986). Patients report on the presence or absence of many possible symptoms, and researchers feed these reports into computers programmed to find so-called *clusters*. Here we have an empirical basis for deciding that particular syndromes cohere (Mezzich & Solomon, 1980).

The future may also see a category that merges depression and anxiety because these often prove quite difficult to distinguish (Clark & Watson, 1991). You cannot easily find depressed people who are not at least somewhat anxious, and you cannot easily find anxious people who are not at least somewhat depressed (Dobson, 1985). There may also be a new category that merges bipolar disorder and schizophrenia. And perhaps other syndromes now recognized may be split into two or more distinct problems (e.g., Andreasen & Grove, 1982).

More profoundly, we might additionally see the introduction of **dimensional classification**, describing people's problems along continuous dimensions, in "how much" terms rather than "either-or" terms (Eysenck, 1986). So far, this chapter has described diagnosis in terms of placing people into categories, because this has been the customary practice. But I have also raised questions about this approach because it is at odds with the view of abnormality as continuous with normality. Dimensional classification is compatible with the view of abnormality I presented in Chapter 1.

We see dimensional classification already in Axis V of DSM-IV, which quantifies how a person is functioning in the world. This type of classification could also be extended to the sorts of problems described on Axis I and Axis II (Frances, 1982). Depression would no longer be described as a syndrome that some people display and other people do not, but as a dimension along which all people can be placed. This approach is typically championed by those who espouse a cognitive-behavioral view of abnormality and opposed by those who favor a medical one.

Etiological classification   At some point in the future, we can expect to see diagnostic systems based on the etiology of problems (Vaillant, 1984). This is already the case in many fields of medicine, where we group together problems not in terms of their symptoms but rather in terms of their causes. Imagine lumping together all problems that involve a sore throat—like a cold, cancer of the mouth, and laryngitis. The thought is ludicrous, of course, but only because we know that these different cases of a sore throat have drastically different causes and demand drastically different treatments.

At the present, however, we deal with psychological abnormality by lumping together problems based on their symptoms, treating all cases of anxiety or depression or schizophrenia as if they were the same. But suppose there are various causes of these disorders. It would be useful to subdivide these classes of disorders according to their specific causes. For instance, Abramson, Metalsky, and Alloy (1989) speculated that there is a subtype of depression that is caused by a negative style of viewing the self and the world. This can be called a cognitive depression, distinct from other types of depression, like those caused by biochemical anomalies. Along these same lines, Sheehan (1984) has suggested that anxiety disorders be classified according to the degree of biochemical involvement.

Changes in jurisdiction   We can expect that the disorders currently falling under the jurisdiction of clinical psychologists and psychiatrists will change, depending on breakthroughs in our knowledge about causes and treatments. For instance, when a disorder is found to have an unambiguous neurological basis—like general paresis as discussed in Chapter 1—it is usually moved out of psychiatry and psychology and into neurology (Goodwin & Guze, 1989). Perhaps other disorders might similarly be switched into neurology or other fields of health care. Alternatively, perhaps certain disorders will be switched into psychiatry and psychology, as psychological factors are found relevant to their etiology or treatment.

ASSESSMENT

How does the diagnostician go about the specific business of gathering information concerning individuals

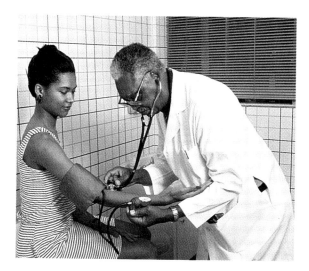

The future may see clinical psychologists increasingly involved in the treatment of physical illness, such as cardiovascular diseases.

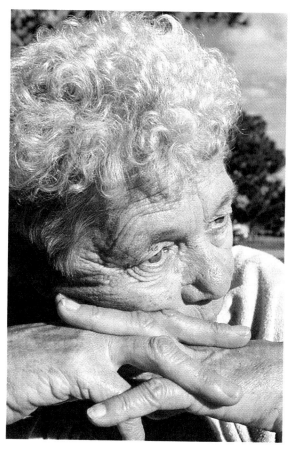

The dexamethasone suppression test (DST) was at one time thought to be a strong diagnostic test for depression. However, its early promise was not supported by further research. At present, there are no strong diagnostic tests for psychological abnormality.

and their problems in order to make these diagnoses? The diagnostician wants to arrive at not only a DSM-IV description of a person's problem but also a sense of the etiology of the problem, a treatment recommendation, and a prognosis. I stress again the link between assessment and treatment. Assessment always includes specific recommendations about treatment. We must consider these tentative, subject to revision as more information becomes available. But treatment recommendations provide the therapist with a place to start in the attempt to help.

Mental health professionals have often searched for **strong diagnostic tests,** simple procedures that unambiguously identify an individual as having a certain sort of problem or not. In medicine, we are familiar with such tests (e.g., throat cultures that tell if a patient has strep). At present, we have no such strong tests in the field of abnormal psychology, and it is not clear that they will ever exist, granted the way we currently conceive abnormality. How can an imprecise phenomenon have a single unambiguous sign?

On the other hand, perhaps the existence of strong tests would lead us to reconceptualize the nature of abnormality. A person has a given problem if, and only if, a strong diagnostic test indicates so. In the 1970s, there was hope that such a sign had been found for severe depression (Carroll, Curtis, & Mendels, 1976a, 1976b). The *dexamethasone suppression test* (or *DST*) determines the body's response to the introduction of a synthetic cortisol called dexamethasone. This chemical temporarily disrupts a hormonal feedback system involving the hypothalamus, pituitary, and adrenal glands, a process that can be tracked with blood tests.

Some people with severe depression evidence a different return to normalization following the administration of dexamethasone than do nondepressed people. At first it was thought that these individuals had a biologically based depression particularly amenable to treatment by biological means, like antidepressant medication. The DST promised to be a strong diagnostic test, but it eventually fell short (American Psychiatric Association Task Force, 1987). People who clearly were not depressed sometimes showed the "depressive" pattern. And people who clearly were depressed sometimes did not show the pattern. The DST remains nonetheless a good example of the continuing search for strong diagnostic tests (Nierenberg & Feinstein, 1988).

In the absence of strong tests, diagnosticians must make diagnoses by painstakingly gathering a great deal of information about people and then drawing inferences from what they have learned. They gather information in a variety of ways: by talking to their clients, observing them as they offer responses, administering various psychological tests, and speaking to their friends and family members.

Recent years have seen heightened awareness on the part of diagnosticians that assessment must be sensitive to the larger context of an individual's life. Clients from different groups need to be approached in ways that do justice to their particular culture. Problems may differ across cultural groups, and the diagnostician of course wishes to avoid misinterpretations. An assessment strategy developed for one group of people cannot automatically be generalized to another (see Table 2-4).

Along these lines, children present their own assessment challenges. As explained in Chapter 14, children have their own sorts of problems not readily recognized if they are considered miniature adults. Diagnosticians need to be familiar with the details of normal development in order to ascertain departures from it. They also need to be sensitive to the ways that children express themselves and how they respond to various tasks and questions (Hodges, 1993). The task of diagnosticians becomes even more daunting when their clients are children from culturally diverse groups (Canino & Spurlock, 1994).

DIAGNOSTIC INTERVIEWS

Virtually all diagnoses involve talking to an individual with a problem in an attempt to gather pertinent information (MacKinnon, 1980b). In a **diagnostic interview,** the diagnostician pays attention not just to *what* a person says but also to *how* he or she says it. Diagnostic interviews vary in their degree of structure. To what extent do diagnosticians simply talk, following leads in one direction or another like an investigative reporter, or adhere to prescribed questions? In either case, the interview must be organized into a beginning, middle, and end.

When a diagnostician first encounters a client, rapport must be established between the two, and the purpose of the interview must be made explicit. The interviewer begins to obtain routine information from the client. What is his name, age, sex, ethnic background, occupation, education, and so on? Why did he come to the hospital or clinic? Even in the beginning of an interview, the diagnostician is on the lookout for answers that might suggest the sort of problem from which the individual suffers.

"What brings you here today?" was a question I routinely asked when I worked at a clinic and interviewed patients for the first time. Usually, their response was a description of some problem in life. But sometimes the person would say "A taxi" or "My brother-in-law drove me."

Although technically an answer to the question about what brought them to the clinic, the response was too literal. In responding this way, perhaps these individuals were manifesting some problem involving concrete thinking, such as brain damage. Or maybe not. Perhaps they had a sense of humor. Because of the traffic jams outside the clinic, perhaps they believed that I was genuinely curious about their method of transportation. Regardless, a diagnostic possibility had been raised, and further questioning was needed.

TABLE **2.4**

GUIDELINES FOR PROVIDERS OF SERVICES TO DIVERSE POPULATIONS *The American Psychological Association has issued the following guidelines for those who provide psychological services—including in particular diagnosis and assessment—to individuals from ethnically, linguistically, and culturally diverse populations.* SOURCE: "GUIDELINES FOR THE PROVIDERS OF PSYCHOLOGICAL SERVICES," FROM THE OFFICE OF ETHNIC MINORITY AFFAIRS, 1993, *AMERICAN PSYCHOLOGIST, 48,* PP. 45–48.

1. Psychologists should educate their clients about the process of psychological intervention, including goals and expectations as well as the legal limits of confidentiality. The orientation of a psychologist should be explained.

2. Psychologists should be aware of research pertinent to the population they are serving.

3. Psychologists should recognize ethnicity and culture as important aspects of psychological processes.

4. Psychologists should respect the roles of family members and community structures as they exist within the client's culture.

5. Psychologists should respect their clients' religious and spiritual beliefs and values.

6. Psychologists should interact in the language requested by the client. If this is not possible, psychologists should refer the client to someone who can.

7. Psychologists should take into account adverse social, environmental, and political factors in assessing problems and planning interventions.

8. Psychologists should be aware of, and work to eliminate, biases, prejudice, and discrimination.

9. Psychologists who work with diverse populations should document in their records such culturally relevant factors as:
   a. number of generations in the country
   b. number of years in the country
   c. fluency in English
   d. extent of family support
   e. community resources
   f. level of education
   g. change in social status as a result of being an immigrant or refugee
   h. level of stress associated with acculturation

The middle of the interview is devoted to gaining a detailed sense of the client's current problem, his or her personality, and relevant events from the past. At the end of the interview, the diagnostician should attempt to answer any questions the client might have.

Sometimes diagnostic interviews take place over several different sessions. Often they can be completed in one sitting. What should result is a description of the client's problem—often phrased in the language of DSM-IV—as well as a notion of its etiology, possible treatment, and prognosis.

During the interview, the diagnostician attempts to gauge the individual's present psychological state, conducting a **mental status exam.** The ideal mental status exam describes all the aspects of psychological functioning that can be disturbed by one or more types of abnormality, including thoughts, feelings, and actions. The diagnostician faces a daunting task in obtaining and organizing this information (see Table 2.5).

As already noted, diagnostic interviews vary in terms of how structured they are. Mental status exams can be administered in a relatively casual way, varying particular questions from client to client and pursuing some areas of functioning more than others. But these interviews can also be highly structured. In recent years, we see an increasing trend toward specifying exactly the sorts of questions that should be asked (Matarazzo, 1983).

One example of a structured interview is the *Schedule of Affective Disorders and Schizophrenia* (or *SADS*), a series of questions that allows the diagnostician to make DSM diagnoses of depression and schizophrenia (Endicott & Spitzer, 1978). This interview specifies in great detail the questions to be asked of an individual, and how to proceed granted certain responses.

Research reveals that structured interviews typically produce more reliable diagnoses than do unstructured ones (e.g., Widiger & Frances, 1987). Prospective diagnosticians are usually trained in how to use a particular structured interview. They observe a set of standardized interviews on videotape, make diagnoses, and then check the diagnoses against those of experts who have seen the same tapes. These procedures allow the standardization of diagnoses across different diagnosticians in different places. Structured interviews have also made possible large-scale studies of the prevalence of different disorders (see Figure 2.3).

Even the most reliable diagnostic interviews are not without potential problems that limit their validity. Remember the pitfalls I discussed in Chapter 1 about relying on an individual's self-reported problems (or their absence). It would be desirable to verify with other means everything that a client says in an interview, but you can see that this is not always feasible.

Also, a diagnostician may inadvertently impose a bias on an interview, exploring some topics more than others, interpreting responses out of their appropriate context, or making incorrect presuppositions based on the individual's age, gender, and ethnicity. More profoundly, the interview itself, even if highly structured, may not provide a sufficient range of questions and diagnostic options (see Focus on DSM-IV's Approach to the Context of Disorder).

One of the ideas currently explored by diagnosticians is how to computerize interviews (e.g., Levitan, Blouin, Navarro, & Hill, 1991; Moreno & Plant, 1993;

TABLE 2.5

MENTAL STATUS EXAM *One possible way of systematizing the information obtained in a mental status exam is provided here. The diagnostician need not ask directly about each of these areas of functioning. Many of these can be evaluated simply by observing how the client responds to other questions.*
SOURCE: FROM "PSYCHIATRIC HISTORY AND MENTAL STATUS EXAM," BY R. A. MACKINNON, 1980. IN H. I. KAPLAN, A. M. FREEDMAN, AND B. J. SADOCK (EDS.), *COMPREHENSIVE TEXTBOOK OF PSYCHIATRY* (VOL. 1, 3D ED., PP. 916–919), BALTIMORE: WILLIAMS & WILKINS.

- **general description:** What is the person's physical appearance, general style and level of activity, and his attitude toward the diagnostician?

- **speech:** Does the person show any impairment of language, such as strange associations or neologisms?

- **mood and feelings:** What is the person's dominant mood? Are a range of feelings expressed? How appropriate are his emotional expressions?

- **perception:** Does the person report hallucinations or illusions? Does he feel depersonalized, as if he were a spectator to his own behavior?

- **thought process:** Are there disturbances in the content or process of thinking? Is the person capable of abstract thought? How good is his concentration? What is his store of general knowledge? How intelligent does he seem to be?

- **consciousness:** What is the person's awareness of the surrounding environment? Is he sleepy, demented, delirious, and/or intoxicated?

- **orientation:** Does the person know the date and the place? Does he know who he is?

- **judgment:** Does the individual display capacity for social judgment? Does he understand the likely consequences of different behaviors?

- **insight:** What is the individual's understanding of any difficulties he may be experiencing? Is he open to new ideas?

- **reliability:** How consistent is the person in answering questions?

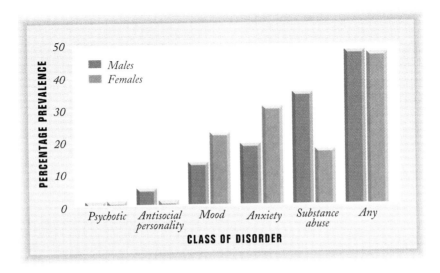

FIGURE 2.3

LIFETIME PREVALENCE OF CLINICAL SYNDROMES   *R. C. Kessler and colleagues administered a structured diagnostic interview to a random sample of American adults. These are the proportions of individuals interviewed who warranted given classes of diagnoses at some time during their life.*
SOURCE: "LIFETIME AND 12-MONTH PREVALENCE OF DSM-III-R PSYCHIATRIC DIAGNOSES IN THE UNITED STATES," BY R. C. KESSLER, K. A. McGONAGLE, S. ZHAO, C. B. NELSON, M. HUGHES, S. ESHLEMAN, H.-U. WITTCHEN, AND K. S. KENDLER, 1994, *Archives of General Psychiatry, 51,* PP. 8–19.

Roca-Bennasar, Garcia-Mas, Llaneras, & Blat, 1991). The basic principle is sound, because a computer is more capable of keeping track of information than any individual diagnostician and of applying this information in a completely consistent fashion (Schuler & Tinger, 1991). Computers do not become bored or fatigued. They are cost effective (Siddall & Keogh, 1993). And in some cases, clients may prefer the ostensible anonymity of a computer.

There are two approaches to computerizing diagnostic interviews (Morelli, Bronzino, & Goethe, 1987; Warzecha, 1991). In one, the client directly answers questions posed by the computer by typing on the terminal's keyboard. This may not work if the person has problems that interfere with being able to follow the computer's directions. So in the other approach, a diagnostician obtains information through an interview with the client and then enters it herself into the computer.

ASSESSMENT TRADITIONS

Besides interviewing their clients, diagnosticians usually gather further information, relying on specialized procedures. I describe these procedures in terms of the general assessment strategy they reflect, of which several exist (see Table 2.6). Each embodies a particular theoretical orientation.

TABLE 2.6

ASSESSMENT TRADITIONS *As described in the text, there exist a number of assessment traditions. Each reflects a theoretically motivated goal about the best way to describe people and their psychological problems.*

TRADITION	GOAL: TO DESCRIBE PEOPLE AND THEIR PROBLEMS
personological	in rich and complex ways: e.g., projective tests
psychometric	along carefully defined dimensions using standardized questionnaires; e.g., MMPI, intelligence tests
behavioral	in terms of actual behavior and the situations in which it occurs
cognitive	in terms of the contents and styles of thinking that create or maintain difficulties; e.g., thought monitoring
psychophysiological	in terms of physical systems; e.g., polygraph
neuropsychological	in terms of the brain and nervous system; e.g., neuropsychological batteries, imaging techniques
family assessment	in the context of marriage or family; e.g., FACES

FOCUS ON

DSM-IV's

Approach to the

Social Context

of Disorder

DSM-IV EMBODIES A MEDical approach, but at the same time it tries to recognize that problems exist within people who in turn exist within a society and a culture (see Mezzich, Fabrega, & Kleinman, 1992). This is in marked contrast to earlier versions of the DSM system, which either ignored culture altogether or made minimal reference to it (Lopez & Nunez, 1987). In several ways, DSM-IV is quite explicit in reminding the diagnostician to approach the individual in terms of his or her social context. The highly specific criteria for diagnoses cannot be used as rigid rules, because in so doing, a diagnostician loses track of individuals and their social context.

In its introduction, DSM-IV grapples with the meaning of *mental disorder* (i.e., psychological abnormality), and its authors note that the term conveys an unfortunate dichotomy between mind and body. Granted present knowledge, this is a difficult dichotomy to justify and maintain (Chapter 10). DSM-IV goes on to acknowledge that the term *mental disorder* lacks precise boundaries and thus proves difficult to define consistently.

DSM-IV abstractly characterizes a mental disorder as a behavioral or psychological pattern occurring in an individual and associated with present distress or disability. In making concrete diagnostic judgments, it is necessary to be knowledgeable about a given person's social setting. If a way of behaving is expected and sanctioned within a culture, then it cannot be regarded as a mental disorder, no matter how much distress or disability it seems to involve. The point is explicit that disorders are to be diagnosed, not individuals per se and certainly not entire societies or cultures.

Consider that all social groups have accepted ways of grieving and that these may differ markedly (Rosenblatt, Walsh, & Jackson, 1976). A diagnostician from one culture must beware of misinterpreting grief exhibited by an individual from a different culture as a mental disorder. In some societies, bereaved individuals report that they have heard or seen their dead relative. By definition, these are *not* hallucinations or delusions because these experiences are regarded as valid within such societies.

Along these same lines, DSM-IV cautions the diagnostician not to misinterpret a conflict that an individual may have with larger social institutions as a mental disorder unless the conflict is clearly the result of something problematic within the person (as opposed to within the society). Political dissent, even if it is unpopular or ill-advised, cannot be considered a sign of a mental disorder insofar as it is in response to prevailing policies. Relatedly, a client's religious beliefs, even when they differ from those of the diagnostician, cannot be interpreted in terms of a mental disorder (see Lukoff, Lu, & Turner, 1992; Post, 1992). These sorts of judgments require that the diagnostician be thoroughly conversant with the details of an individual's social and cultural context.

Finally, in its discussion of clinical syndromes, DSM-IV attempts where possible to explain how a problem manifests itself in different cultures. Idiomatic expressions used in given settings for describing anxiety or depression, for example, are provided. Various culture-bound syndromes are also described.

As you will see throughout the textbook, a great deal of the newest knowledge about psychological abnormality pertains to the biological processes underlying people's difficulties. Nonetheless, there is an increasing recognition—even by those theorists most intrigued by the biological aspects of abnormality—that this new information makes most sense when interpreted in light of an individual's social and cultural context.

Personological assessment   **Personological assessment** is the attempt "to describe the particular person in as full, multifaceted, and multilevel a way as possible" (Korchin & Schuldberg, 1981, p. 1147). This strategy reflects a conception of people and their problems as complex and idiosyncratic. The diagnostician places her clients in unconstrained situations and observes their responses. She relies on her own intuition about the person's meanings, motives, and meanderings.

Personological assessment often relies on **projective tests,** which ask clients to respond to ambiguous stimuli. Because the stimuli themselves do not demand particular reactions, everything the clients do in

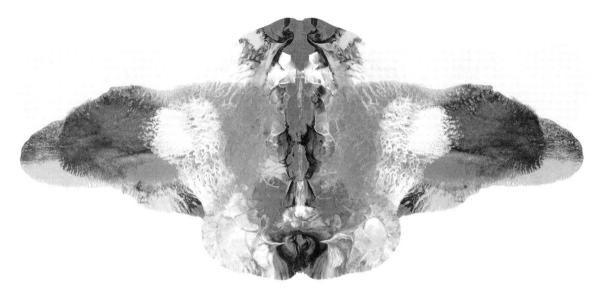

FIGURE 2.4

RORSCHACH-LIKE CARD   *In the Rorschach Inkblot Test, individuals are shown ambiguous inkblots such as this one and are asked to describe what they see. This is called a "projective" test because individuals are thought to project their own needs and conflicts onto the inkblot.*

Diagnostic interviews and tests are now being computerized. In contrast to human diagnosticians, computers are more capable of keeping track of information and applying it in a consistent manner to arrive at a diagnosis.

response to them reveals the workings of their personality. Projective tests allow the client to "project" his or her own drives and desires onto the test stimuli.

Hermann Rorschach's (1942) inkblots, referred to as the **Rorschach Inkblot Test,** are a well known projective procedure. This test presents clients with a series of ten symmetric inkblots (see Figure 2.4), asking them what each blot looks like and why. Their responses are scored in terms of what they see as well as their explanations of their perceptions. Detailed scoring systems exist for quantifying the responses of clients along numerous dimensions (e.g., Exner, 1974, 1978).

For instance, exactly where on the card is the perception located? Does the client see humans or animals in the inkblots? Are these figures moving? Are particular responses common or rare? An attempt is often made to relate particular Rorschach scores to particular psychological problems and to general personality styles. Studies have found, for instance, that individuals at risk for suicide may respond differently to the Rorschach inkblots than do those not at risk (e.g., Exner & Wylie, 1977).

Another well known projective test is Christiana Morgan and Henry Murray's (1935) **Thematic Apperception Test** (or **TAT**). The TAT is a series of ambiguous pictures (see Figure 2.5). Clients are shown the pictures one at a time and asked to tell a story

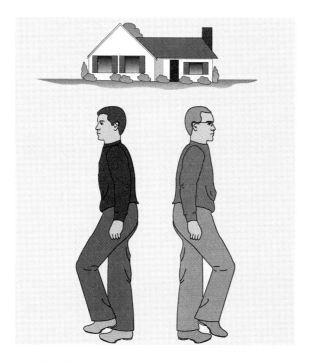

FIGURE 2.5

TAT-LIKE CARD   *Like the Rorschach, the TAT is a projective test. Respondents are shown an ambiguous picture like this one and are asked to tell a story about it.*

about each one. No constraints are placed on the client except that she must describe what the characters are doing, in a story format with a beginning, middle, and ending. An examiner may also request that the client describe the thoughts and feelings of the characters in each picture (Tomkins, 1947).

The TAT has been extensively used in personality research to measure the presence and strength of such motives as achievement, power, and affiliation (e.g., McClelland, 1989). For this purpose, detailed scoring systems have been devised. However, the diagnostic use of the TAT tends not to rely on these scoring systems. Despite the popularity of the TAT as an assessment device, there is no generally accepted approach for interpreting TAT responses in order to make a diagnosis (Dana, 1985). Diagnosticians instead use the TAT in a more intuitive way, looking for themes in the stories that have counterparts in the client's own life.

Here is a TAT story told in response to a picture about a boy sitting at a desk with a violin in front of him:

> *This looks like [he] either wants to learn how to play the violin or he's frustrated. . . . I can see in his eyes he doesn't*

hate it—or it could have belonged to someone who was very dear to him. (Dana, 1985, p. 111)

This story suggests, perhaps, that the client thinks in either-or terms, rapidly changing her train of thought. She may be particularly concerned with her family, because she mentioned that the violin perhaps belonged to someone dear. She might have found her own attempts at achievement to be frustrating.

Many other projective tests exist as well. Individuals are asked to offer associations to words, to complete sentences, or to draw pictures of themselves and their families. The goal of all these techniques is the same: to reveal something about the workings of the person's mind.

Projective tests are frequently criticized on grounds of reliability and validity, although recent investigations are much more attentive to these issues (e.g., Acklin, McDowell, & Orndoff, 1992; Burstein, 1989). To some degree, these criticisms are to be expected. Even the brief descriptions of the Rorschach and TAT provided here convey the complexity of these tests. Complex tests are difficult to score reliably, and poor reliability limits the validity of any diagnostic procedure; that is, an unreliable measure cannot possibly be valid.

Projective tests continue to be used by diagnosticians who favor personological assessment because of the richness of the information they provide. The assumption is that this rich information can suggest hypotheses about the client that would otherwise be elusive.

Psychometric assessment   In contrast to personological assessment, **psychometric assessment** embodies a relatively simple and quantitative view of people

Standardized questionnaires see frequent use within the tradition of psychometric assessment. Respondents are compared and contrasted along carefully defined dimensions.

and their problems (Meehl, 1954, 1957). Those who favor this strategy try to locate people along carefully defined dimensions by using their responses to standardized questionnaires. Comparisons and contrasts among people result. The goal of psychometric assessment is to maximize objectivity while minimizing subjective judgment and inference. Test reliability and validity take on central importance here. This approach to assessment well serves the goals of those who favor dimensional classification.

Psychometric assessment relies greatly on **objective tests,** measures of individual differences where scores are assigned according to explicit rules (as opposed to the subjective judgments that characterize the projective tests used in personological assessment). Among frequently used objective tests are **personality inventories,** sets of objective tests that attempt to measure the range of important individual differences. Perhaps the best known personality inventory is the **Minnesota Multiphasic Personality Inventory** (or **MMPI**), created in the 1940s at the University of Minnesota (Hathaway & McKinley, 1943). A revised and restandardized version—MMPI-2—appeared in the late 1980s (Butcher, Dahlstrom, Graham, Tellegen, & Kaemmer, 1989).

The original purpose of the MMPI was to aid diagnosis. Hundreds of items were assembled, all of which were to be answered either true or false. For example:

> Evil spirits possess me at times.
>
> I go to church almost every week.
>
> I sweat very easily even on cool days.
>
> I think Lincoln was greater than Washington.

Individuals with known diagnoses (given by clinicians on the basis of diagnostic interviews) answered these questions, and researchers determined which patterns of responses successfully distinguished respondents with a particular diagnosis from those without that diagnosis.

Over the decades, hundreds of thousands of individuals have taken the MMPI, and it has been successful in identifying clients who fit particular diagnoses (Gilberstadt & Duker, 1965). Efforts have been made to describe the MMPI responses of individuals from diverse social groups, enhancing the utility of this test in diagnostic practice (e.g., Dahlstrom, Lachar, & Dahlstrom, 1986). Although diagnosticians do not make a diagnosis solely on the basis of MMPI scores, they take these scores seriously and go against their recommendation only when there exists a reason for doing so.

The MMPI was developed by the *known-groups method* of ascertaining validity; that is, items were chosen for MMPI subscales only if responses to them successfully distinguished between respondents in two groups known to differ with respect to whatever characteristic the scale intended to measure, like depression or anxiety. The items have no necessary *face validity*, which means that it can be difficult to look at a particular question and decide what it is measuring.

The MMPI does not have a fixed number of subscales, because researchers are continually devising new configurations to predict characteristics not envisioned by those who originally devised it. However, there is a set of characteristics typically scored from MMPI responses, as shown in Table 2.7.

TABLE 2.7

MMPI SCALES *The following scales are among those conventionally scored from the MMPI. The validity scales tell the diagnostician whether an individual's responses are likely to be valid ones. Assuming that a person's scores on the validity scales fall within acceptable limits, the clinical scales—individually or in combination—are used to identify potential problems.*

VALIDITY SCALES	MEASURES THE DEGREE TO WHICH RESPONDENT . . .
cannot say (?)	does not answer items
lie (L)	tries to present an impossibly favorable image
infrequency (F)	falsely claims psychological problems
defensiveness (K)	is defensive or evasive

CLINICAL SCALES	MEASURES THE DEGREE TO WHICH RESPONDENT . . .
hypochondriasis (Hs)	has physical concerns and complaints
depression (D)	shows symptoms of depression
hysteria (HY)	develops physical symptoms under stress
psychopathic deviate (Pd)	shows antisocial tendencies
masculinity-femininity (Mf)	is stereotypically "masculine" or "feminine"
paranoia (Pa)	is suspicious and distrustful
psychasthenia (Pt)	is anxious and obsessive
schizophrenia (Sc)	has bizarre thoughts
hypomania (Ma)	is impulsive and excitable
social introversion (Si)	is shy and withdrawn

Graham (1990) provides an example of how the MMPI can be used diagnostically. Jane was a 35-year-old teacher who went to a hospital clinic specializing in chronic pain disorders (Chapter 8). She had been in an automobile accident several years before and afterwards complained of pain and discomfort in her neck and back. Neurologists who examined her could find no adequate physical basis for her symptoms. She was administered the MMPI-2, and her scores on the various scales are depicted in Figure 2-6.

The validity scales, on the far left of the profile, indicated that her scores fell within acceptable ranges. She did not omit items; she was neither too defensive nor too self-critical. Hence, her profile could be used further to understand her possible problems. The first and third clinical scales, measuring hypochondriasis and hysteria, respectively, were much higher than typical, a pattern indicating that she saw herself as having a medical problem needing medical treatment.

This so-called 1-3 code type further suggested to Graham (1990, p. 230) that Jane

> tends to be immature, egocentric, and selfish. She has strong needs for attention, affection, and sympathy, and is very demanding in relationships. She is a very dependent person, but she is not comfortable with the dependency and experiences conflict because of it. Although she may be involved with other people, her relationships are likely

to be quite superficial. She tends to exploit relationships to satisfy her own needs. She may use her physical symptoms as a way of justifying her demands for attention and support.

This interpretation is a set of tentative hypotheses to be explored. Other individuals with a 1-3 code type tend to have the characteristics Graham attributed to Jane. Even so, Graham's interpretation of her profile must be confirmed through further assessment. Assuming the utility of the interpretation, Jane is probably a poor candidate for traditional talking therapy, because she is unwilling to acknowledge any psychological basis to her symptoms. However, Graham believed that treatment could proceed to the degree that it focused on activities and exercises suggested by the therapist with no explicit suggestion that her pain was due to psychological factors.

Also part of the repertoire of diagnosticians who favor psychometric assessment are various intelligence tests. We show our *intelligence* when we act in adaptive and purposive ways (Sternberg & Salter, 1982), and to the degree that an intelligence test measures the adaptiveness and purposiveness of behavior, the information it provides is of obvious interest to a diagnostician.

Intelligence tests have been controversial throughout their history (Gould, 1981). Even today, there are

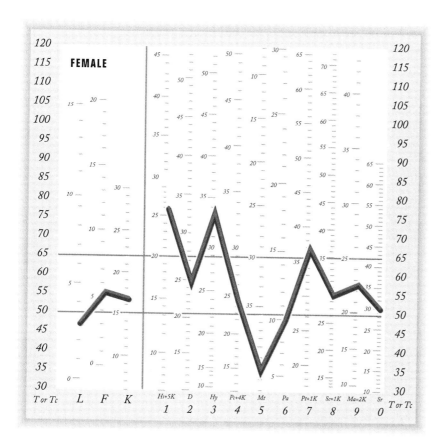

FIGURE 2.6

EXAMPLE OF MMPI PROFILE   *An individual's responses to the MMPI are compared to those of other individuals with known diagnoses. If the profile closely matches a given profile, the diagnostician has good reason to suspect that the individual may have a similar psychological problem.*

SOURCE: *MMPI-2: Assessing Personality and Psychopathology* (P. 228), BY J. R. GRAHAM, 1990, NEW YORK: OXFORD.

serious questions raised about the possibility that these tests are not equally valid across different social groups, particularly those defined by ethnicity. Helms (1992) observed that intelligence tests may fail to be equivalent across groups not just in obvious ways, such as the content of particular items, but also in more subtle ways, such as the sorts of cognitive skills emphasized. Probably the least controversial thing that can be said about intelligence tests developed to date is that they are fairly accurate in predicting how well or poorly students will do in *traditional* schools (Anastasi, 1982). Nonetheless, diagnosticians have several reasons for administering such tests to their clients.

One reason is historical. Intelligence tests were the first assessment devices developed by psychologists that won wide acceptance. At the turn of the century, the French psychologist Alfred Binet (1857–1911) created tests to administer to students in the public school system of Paris. His intent was to find a way to distinguish students who could profit from education from those who could not. He devised tasks highly similar to the actual skills that students needed to succeed in school (e.g., Binet & Simon, 1913). These were arranged in order of difficulty, and the more items a student could "pass" successfully, the greater the student's *mental age.* Eventually, psychologists divided a student's mental age by his or her chronological age, forming a quotient that has come to be called the **intelligence quotient** (or **IQ**). By convention, the average IQ was set at 100, and deviations from 100 marked the student as being above or below average in intelligence.

Binet's test was translated into English by Lewis Terman (1916) of Stanford University, and this translation is thus identified as the **Stanford-Binet Intelligence Scale.** It has gone through several revisions and is still widely used today. Two revisions in particular should be noted (Thorndike, Hagan, & Sattler, 1986). First, IQ is no longer calculated as a quotient of mental age and chronological age. Instead, it is defined with reference to the population of people taking the test. An IQ of 100 is still average; an IQ of 85 indicates that the individual scores higher than 16% of the people who take the test; an IQ of 115 indicates that the person scores higher than 84%; and so on.

Second, whereas the early versions of the Stanford-Binet yielded one overall IQ score, the most recent version of the test yields separate scores for different aspects of intelligence, such as verbal reasoning, quantitative reasoning, and short-term memory. This makes the Stanford-Binet more useful to diagnosticians who may wish to know the profile of an individual's skills.

In moving to this format, the Stanford-Binet followed the lead of another set of frequently used intelligence tests, the Wechsler scales. These tests were developed by David Wechsler (1939), who was concerned that the Stanford-Binet test available at that time did not seem suitable for individuals for whom English was not their native language. The Stanford-Binet relies greatly on verbal expression, and so Wechsler developed two different subtests, one group requiring verbal responses and the other nonverbal responses. These latter tests are often called performance subtests.

Another innovation by Wechsler was to develop intelligence tests appropriate for individuals of different ages. There are Wechsler scales suitable for children, called the **Wechsler Intelligence Scale for Children** (or **WISC**), and scales for adults, called the **Wechsler Adult Intelligence Scale** (or **WAIS**). There is even a Wechsler scale for extremely young children: the **Wechsler Preschool and Primary Scale of Intelligence** (or **WPPSI**). Like the Stanford-Binet, the Wechsler tests have gone through several revisions over the years (Wechsler, 1981). Regardless, they have always yielded a profile of scores, making them particularly useful for diagnosticians.

What can intelligence tests like the Wechsler scales tell a diagnostician? First, the general impairment of intelligence is a consequence of many disorders, and so the overall score can serve as an immediate clue that something is wrong. Because many people

The Wechsler intelligence scales are frequently used. Here a second grader responds to questions on the WISC.

have had intelligence tests administered throughout their lives, if a diagnostician can obtain past test scores, he can note any decline. Barring the availability of past scores, the diagnostician can at least use educational attainment as a rough way of gauging past intelligence (Matarazzo, 1980). What can we say of a university graduate who scores well below average on an intelligence test? Possibly that his intelligence has fallen off since his time in school and that psychological problems are responsible.

Second, because modern intelligence tests yield separate scores for aptitudes, the diagnostician can look for discrepancies across subscales. Usually, a person's scores on different subscales are comparable. Marked discrepancies point the diagnostician's attention to particular problems. For instance, suppose a person does generally well on an intelligence test, but poorly on a particular task that requires him to repeat back a series of digits after hearing them. This could mean that the person has a problem with attention (Zimmerman & Woo-Sam, 1973), which is an indication that he may have an anxiety or mood disorder.

Third, information about a client's intelligence can provide some clues about the suitability of certain forms of therapy. A person who is limited in her verbal skills would probably not be a good candidate for therapy that relied on talking. Or an individual with a memory impairment may need special help in remembering the tasks and goals of therapy.

Fourth, tested intelligence can give the diagnostician expectations about reasonable treatment goals for an individual. As one of the most extensively administered and normed tests, intelligence tests yield valuable information about what can be expected of a person in school and by implication at work.

Fifth, it is not simply people's scores that are of interest but how they went about attaining those scores. Test administrators watch carefully how clients respond to items. Are they nervous or indecisive? Problems may be particularly likely to appear under stress, and intelligence tests are a stressful experience for many people.

Behavioral assessment   More recently, we have seen the advent of **behavioral assessment,** yet another approach to gathering information about people and their problems. Behavioral assessment describes what a person actually does in particular circumstances, usually with the goal of identifying prevailing rewards and punishments influencing the behavior that a person does or does not display (Barlow, 1981).

Here is an example from a psychological clinic where I once worked. Katarina was an 8-year-old girl brought

In behavioral assessment, the individual's behavior in actual settings is observed to discover the environmental events that influence what a person does or does not do.

to our clinic by her father because her elementary school teacher said she had problems with discipline. The situation was potentially quite complicated. The family had recently moved to the United States from eastern Europe, so that the father could attend graduate school. After just a few weeks, the mother returned to their home country to care for an ill relative, taking with her the two younger children in the family. This is when Katarina began to have problems in school.

We could have spoken at length with her about her feelings of rejection and abandonment (personological assessment). We could have administered objective tests to see how she compared with her American peers with respect to intelligence, self-control, and social skills (psychometric assessment). Instead, because we were not quite sure what "problems with discipline" meant, we followed Katarina to school and observed how she behaved and the consequences that followed from her actions. We discovered that the little girl was excluded from games during recess because she did not understand how to play them. She rarely talked to the other students because they made fun of her accent. The only time anyone took Katarina seriously during the entire school day was when the teacher noticed her fidgeting.

In light of this information, we recommended that the school give her remedial instruction in schoolyard games as well as special help with her diction. The teacher caught the spirit of our suggestions and went further, devoting an entire week of class to life in other countries, which made Katarina the center of attention, this time because she had a positive contribution to make.

Behavioral assessment can be much more sophisticated than the example just provided. Diagnosticians may use carefully devised systems for describing particular behaviors and the situations in which they occur. Permanent recordings of behavior may be made with videocameras. The reliability of these descriptions may be ascertained by using multiple observers and calculating kappa coefficients, as discussed earlier. The information obtained not only allows a careful description of the behaviors of interest but also provides a basis of comparison for subsequent interventions.

Cognitive assessment   Even more recently we have seen the beginnings of yet another assessment tradition: **cognitive assessment.** Here the goal is to ascertain a person's characteristic way of thinking about matters, particularly those thoughts and styles that maintain problems (Merluzzi, Glass, & Genest, 1981). Remember from Chapter 1 how behavioral and cognitive approaches to abnormality are converging, and this is happening with behavioral and cognitive assessment as well. Diagnosticians who favor one approach often favor the other (Kendall & Hollon, 1981; Zarb, 1992).

Sometimes cognitive assessment relies on questionnaires, asking clients to indicate beliefs they habitually entertain. Another technique of cognitive assessment is called *thought monitoring* and requires clients to keep track of their thoughts in particular situations. An individual who frequently experiences negative emotions writes down the thoughts that accompany his feelings. With the help of a therapist, he then tries to challenge the basis for these thoughts.

Cognitive assessment may also focus on the process of thought (see Craske & Barlow, 1991; Hollon & Shelton, 1991). How do individuals interpret ambiguous information? People with anxiety disorders tend to see a wide range of events as potentially threatening (Chapter 7). How do individuals recall past events? People with depressive disorders tend to remember more negative than positive occurrences (Chapter 9). How do individuals deploy their attention? People with schizophrenia may be unable to ignore extraneous stimuli (Chapter 12). Any information that sheds light on an individual's style of thinking is useful to a therapist trying to explain interventions to a client.

Psychophysiological assessment   So far I have discussed assessment traditions that look at purely psychological factors. But the body is also involved in behavior, both normal and abnormal. Consider **psychophysiological assessment,** in which a person's bodily state is assessed with various high-tech devices (Ray, Cole, & Raczynski, 1983). Diagnosticians are often interested in bodily indexes of emotional response, such as heart rate, perspiration, blood pressure, pupil dilation, and the like.

For instance, the **polygraph,** popularly called a lie detector, simultaneously records such physiological reactions as heartbeat, blood pressure, breathing, and galvanic skin response. The polygraph has proved controversial for the purpose of detecting lying, because what it really measures is emotional arousal. But the ability of the polygraph to detect arousal can be quite useful to a diagnostician. Sensitive issues can be determined, even if the client is not aware of them, by interviewing the person while a polygraph records his or her reactions. Perhaps interpersonal problems are associated with high arousal. Perhaps plans for the future make the polygraph flutter.

Neuropsychological assessment   When a diagnostician suspects that an individual's psychological

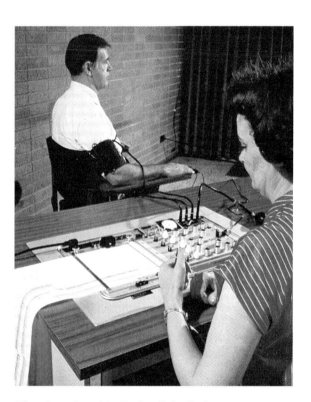

The polygraph—misleadingly called a lie detector—measures physiological reactions reflecting emotional arousal and thus can provide useful information to a diagnostician about sensitive areas in a person's life.

difficulties stem directly from problems with his nervous system—injuries, illnesses, or defects—she may well embark on **neuropsychological assessment:** strategies for identifying particular neurological problems responsible for abnormality (Lezak, 1976).

Neuropsychological assessment often uses tests and procedures associated with other diagnostic traditions, but the purpose is different. Psychometric diagnosticians, for instance, may administer the WAIS to clients to gauge their relative intelligence and make recommendations about the sorts of treatment to which they might respond. Neuropsychological diagnosticians might administer the WAIS as well, but they are interested in what this test reveals about the brain and nervous system. As discussed, intelligence tests typically give people a variety of tasks to perform. What does it mean when a person does well on a task requiring manual dexterity, whereas she does extremely poorly at a task requiring verbal skills? One possibility is that a lesion exists in the part of the brain responsible for language.

Another frequently used neuropsychological assessment strategy is the procedure developed by Lauretta Bender (1938) called the **Bender Gestalt Test.** Clients are presented with abstract symbols on a series of cards (see the left side of Figure 2.7). First they are asked to copy the symbols while looking at them. Then they are asked to copy them from memory. Discrepancies may indicate brain damage (Canter, 1985).

Consider J., a 70-year-old woman who volunteered to participate in a research study of memory and aging (Lacks, 1984). J. was a high school graduate who had retired after a career as a bookkeeper. For the past 5 years, she had experienced poor concentration and other cognitive difficulties. Her initial copies of the Bender Gestalt symbols are shown on the right side of Figure 2.7. Appreciate that she was looking at the symbols while reproducing them and that it took her 13 minutes to do so. As you can see, J. made a number of mistakes: rotating symbols, simplifying them, redrawing them, colliding them, and so on. This protocol strongly indicates the presence of an **organic brain disorder,** *a possibility further strengthened by her reported difficulties with thinking (Chapter 6).*

Often the neuropsychological assessment approach includes giving a person a battery of tests to ascertain the range of what can possibly go wrong. One commonly used battery is the **Halstead-Reitan Neuropsychological Battery** (Reitan & Wolfson, 1985), which takes some 8 hours to administer in its entirety (see Table 2.8). Another battery in widespread use is the **Luria-Nebraska Neuropsychological Battery** (Golden, Hammeke, & Purisch, 1980). Although there are differences in these two neuropsychological batteries, both share the common goal of determining first if brain damage is present

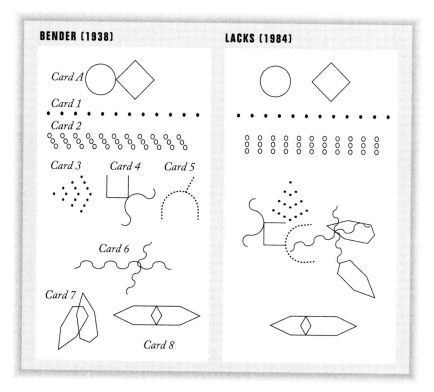

FIGURE 2.7

BENDER GESTALT TEST AND EXAMPLE   *The Bender Gestalt Test is used to test for organically based disorders. An individual is shown abstract symbols and asked to copy them. Discrepancies indicate problems.*
SOURCE OF TEST: *A Visual Motor Gestalt Test and Its Clinical Use,* BY L. BENDER, 1938, AMERICAN ORTHOPSYCHIATRIC RESEARCH MONOGRAPHS NO. 3.
SOURCE OF EXAMPLE: *Bender Gestalt Screening for Brain Dysfunction* (P. 150), BY P. LACKS, 1984, NEW YORK: WILEY.

and second if the affected part of the brain can be located.

If there is anything close to a strong test of abnormality, it is to be found in the realm of neuropsychological assessment, because this strategy aims at identifying the actual physical causes of problems. If we include the host of imaging techniques now available—like **CAT scans** (short for **computerized axial tomography**), which give three-dimensional X-ray pictures, **PET scans** (short for **positron emission tomography**), which reveal patterns of metabolic activity, and **magnetic resonance imaging** (**MRI**), which assesses both neurological structure and function— then neuropsychological assessment provides an almost unique vantage on possible causes of abnormality (see Figure 2.8), at least to the degree that biological factors play a role (Sochurek, 1987).

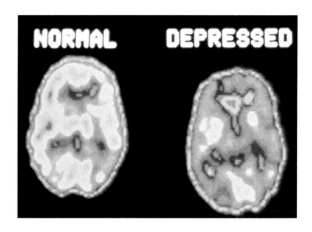

FIGURE 2.8

PET SCAN EXAMPLE   *PET scans use an imaging technique that allows the diagnostician to see patterns of metabolic activity in the brains of individuals with disorders. Too much or too little activity in a given brain structure suggests the involvement of that structure in the disorder of interest.*

TABLE 2.8

HALSTEAD-REITAN TESTS *Here are descriptions of some of the tests included in the Halstead-Reitan Battery, along with the psychological processes that each is thought to reflect.*

TEST	PSYCHOLOGICAL PROCESSES
category test: Can the individual pick the correct stimuli out of a set according to some principle?	abstraction; problem-solving
finger-tapping test: How rapidly can the individual push a lever on a counter with the index finger of each hand?	motor speed
rhythm test: Can the individual recognize various auditory stimuli with a beat as the same or different?	memory; attention
speech-sounds perception test: Can the individual match the correct written alternative to a nonsense word played on a tape recorder?	receptive language; attention
tactual performance (time): Can the individual while blindfolded replace forms into a formboard?	tactile speed; problem-solving
tactual performance (memory): Can the individual draw from memory the forms handled in the above test, along with their locations in the formboard?	incidental memory

At the same time, we should not overestimate the present value of these imaging techniques. Many instances of abnormality do *not* have their causes in structural or metabolic abnormality, and for these, CAT scans, PET scans, and MRIs reveal nothing unusual. There also are problems with biological bases not detected by these imaging techniques. Furthermore, these techniques can be extremely expensive to use, so there is an understandable reluctance on the part of diagnosticians to order them on a routine basis. Many studies using them have been plagued by small sample sizes, and results can be difficult to interpret. But they represent exciting future possibilities.

Family assessment   DSM-IV locates problems in individuals, but there are other ways to look at abnormality (Horton & Retzlaff, 1991). Some problems are better located not within an individual person but instead between or among people. We all know perfectly wonderful individuals who have a horrid marriage. Or we know families that do not mesh. Some psychologists prefer to approach these difficulties not as individual problems but as interpersonal ones. The marriage or the family per se becomes the "client" in therapy. Accordingly, the diagnostician needs to describe the problem at the level of the couple or the family. This is called **family assessment,** the description of couples or families and their problems as a whole (Filsinger, 1983).

Different strategies are available within this general approach. The diagnostician might interview the family members, separately or together, and talk about

In family assessment, the family is considered as a whole, under the assumption that problems reside not within individuals but within their styles of interaction.

the family and how they see it. If the interview is with a family as a whole, then the diagnostician can see how the family interacts. What does it mean if one member of the family, say the father, answers all the questions directed at other family members?

I once watched a videotape of a family being interviewed by a psychologist. The Katz family consisted of a wife, her husband, and three small children. The person showing the tape turned off the sound and told me just to watch the family. Soon, I saw his point. The children were all very active, running around and exploring the room but never once did they touch their parents. No crawling on them. No touching them. Although the children talked to their parents, they never ventured closer than a few feet away. This family was in treatment because Mr. and Mrs. Katz were physically abusive to their children, and even without hearing any conversation, I could see that something was amiss in their interaction.

Sometimes family assessment uses a more structured approach. A wife and her husband may be given a task to complete together as a couple, like planning a vacation or an afternoon of leisure. The diagnostician watches how they divide the task, how they resolve disagreements, and the like.

In some cases, family assessment relies on questionnaires (Fredman & Sherman, 1987). Typically, these are completed by each member of the family independently. A frequently used questionnaire is called the *FACES*, an acronym for *Family Adaptability and Cohesion Evaluation Scales*, that asks each family member to report on the flexibility of the family and the degree of emotional bonding among its members (Olson, Portner, & Lavee, 1985). We know that family members often disagree about how they see things, and one person's report on the family may reveal more about that individual than the family per se. When the diagnostician considers these reports jointly, expecting discrepancies, this becomes information in its own right, and it applies at the level of the family. The therapist can use such information to plan ways of helping the family change its style.

The different assessment traditions described here reflect a diagnostician's theoretical assumptions about the nature of abnormality and its causes. If the diagnostician believes that abnormality is due to a particular cause, then assessment is most concerned with factors related to that cause. This echoes the point of the first section of the chapter that diagnosis is a theoretical endeavor. I continue these ideas in the next chapter, in which I take a detailed look at theories of abnormality.

Summary

✦ Diagnosis refers to placing people in categories according to their problems. Assessment is the process of gathering specific information about a person in order to make a diagnosis.

DIAGNOSIS

✦   An ideal diagnostic scheme is one in which categories are mutually exclusive, jointly exhaustive, and defined by features that are either present or absent. No existing diagnostic system of abnormality is ideal.

✦   Diagnostic systems have a long history. One trend over the years has been toward increasing complexity. The father of modern diagnosis was the German physician, Emil Kraepelin, whose distinctions among types of disorders provide the model for many of today's diagnostic systems.

✦   During the 20th century, the American Psychiatric Association has published a series of *Diagnostic and Statistical Manuals* that have enjoyed widespread use in the United States for diagnosing abnormality. The current manual is the fourth edition, referred to as DSM-IV. It is notable because it attempts to describe symptoms in explicit fashion and to provide clear rules for making diagnoses. DSM-IV describes people and their problems in five different domains called axes. Axis I describes clinical syndromes (acute problems that bring people into treatment). Axis II describes personality disorders. Axis III specifies pertinent physical illnesses or conditions. Axis IV notes problems in an individual's life like divorce or unemployment. Axis V requires a global judgment about how well or poorly the person functions.

✦   Diagnosis is useful in part because it facilitates communication. Further, diagnoses may provide helpful information about the causes of problems, the treatments likely to help, and their probable consequences. Diagnosis is also problematic for several reasons, including the possibility of misdiagnosis, the doubtful assumption of discontinuity, the embodiment of the medical model, the questionable reliability of some diagnoses, and the stigma and self-fulfilling nature of labels imposed on people.

✦   Although an improvement over its predecessors, DSM-IV can still be criticized on several grounds. There is no overall structure to the disorders it includes. The validity of many of its diagnostic categories has not been investigated. The reliability of some diagnoses is poor.

✦   The future will see continued development of diagnostic systems. These will probably continue the historical trend toward greater complexity, and may begin to classify problems in terms of causes rather than symptoms. We may also see some problems switched out of psychiatry and psychology and into general medicine, and vice versa.

ASSESSMENT

✦   In the concrete activity of assessment, diagnosticians attempt to describe an individual's problem, understand its etiology, recommend a treatment, and forecast its prognosis.

✦   Common to almost all assessment approaches is the diagnostic interview, in which the diagnostician gathers pertinent information from a client by talking to him or her. Part of a diagnostic interview is the mental status exam, a description of an individual's present psychological state. In recent years, we can see a trend toward ever greater structure in diagnostic interviews.

✦   Several different assessment traditions exist. Each takes a particular stance on the nature of people and their problems.

✦   Personological assessment regards people as complex and idiosyncratic. Here the diagnostician tries to describe people in rich detail, often preferring projective tests such as the Rorschach Inkblot Test and the Thematic Apperception Test.

✦   Psychometric assessment, in contrast, embodies a simple and quantitative view of people. In this tradition, the diagnostician tries to locate people along carefully defined dimensions by administering objective tests such as the MMPI or various measures of intelligence.

✦   Behavioral assessment assumes that people are responsive to the rewards and punishments that prevail in the environment. Diagnosticians in this tradition describe what people actually do in particular circumstances.

✦   In cognitive assessment, the goal is to identify thoughts and beliefs that create or maintain people's problems.

✦   Psychophysiological assessment encompasses a variety of procedures for measuring a person's bodily state. Often the attention of diagnosticians in this tradition is drawn to indexes of emotional response.

✦   Neuropsychological assessment assumes that certain problems may stem from injuries, illnesses, or defects in an individual's nervous system. Tests such as the Bender Gestalt attempt to ascertain neurological abnormalities. The wide array of neuropsychological tests include the Halstead-Reitan Battery and the Luria-Nebraska Battery. Imaging techniques such as CAT scans, PET scans, and MRIs may also reveal neurological problems.

◆ Family assessment starts with the premise that some problems are best regarded as interpersonal and thus need to be described in the context of the marriage or family.

Key Terms

assessment

behavioral assessment

Bender Gestalt Test

CAT scan; computerized axial tomography

clinical syndrome

cognitive assessment

culture-bound syndrome

diagnosis

diagnostic interview

dimensional classification

DSM-IV (*Diagnostic and Statistical Manual of Mental Disorders,* Fourth Edition)

etiology

family assessment

Halstead-Reitan Neuropsychological Battery

intelligence quotient; IQ

International Classification of Diseases; ICD

kappa

Luria-Nebraska Neuropsychological Battery

magnetic resonance imaging; MRI

mental status exam

Minnesota Multiphasic Personality Inventory; MMPI

multiaxial classification

neuropsychological assessment

neurotic disorder

objective test

personality disorder

personality inventory

personological assessment

PET scan; positron emission tomography

polygraph

prognosis

projective test

psychometric assessment

psychophysiological assessment

psychotic disorder

reliability (of a diagnostic system)

research diagnostic criteria

Rorschach Inkblot Test

Stanford-Binet Intelligence Scale

strong diagnostic test

syndrome

Thematic Apperception Test; TAT

validity (of a diagnostic system)

Wechsler Adult Intelligence Scale; WAIS

Wechsler Intelligence Scale for Children; WISC

Wechsler Preschool and Primary Scale of Intelligence; WPPSI

Models of Abnormality: Explanations and Treatments

3 MOST OF YOU HAVE TAKEN AN INTRODUCtory psychology course, where you heard repeatedly that psychology is a science, regarding explanations as tentative and attempting to check them against evidence. Because the field of abnormal psychology is part of general psychology, it is also a scientific endeavor. In this chapter, I discuss theories of abnormality, focusing on how they explain psychological disorders and the treatments to which they give rise. I also cover the related topic of how to prevent problems in the first place. Chapter 4 continues these discussions in terms of how researchers evaluate theories.

MODELS OF ABNORMALITY

Theories concerning the causes of abnormality address two general issues. First, what are the **risk factors** for various disorders (events and characteristics making specific problems more likely)? Second, what are the **mechanisms** (or causal processes) by which these risk factors translate into disorders? Questions about mechanisms are usually more difficult to answer than those about risk factors, but we need to know about both to achieve a full understanding of abnormality. Consider that poverty is among the risk factors for schizophrenia (Clark, 1948). This may be important information about the origins of the disorder, but it is not sufficient. We also need to know *how* a person's economic state leads to the hallucinations, delusions, and other symptoms that characterize schizophrenia. Are poor people more likely to experience stressful events that trigger episodes of schizophrenia? Are they more likely to receive poor medical care during early childhood, resulting in neurological abnormalities? Are they more likely to be exposed to toxins in the environment?

The history of theoretical perspectives on abnormality parallels that of general psychology. These perspectives began to take clear shape a century ago in such fields as medicine, learning theory, and psychoanalysis (Boring, 1950). Soon after, the psychology of abnormality branched into so-called great schools of thought. Each of these schools proposed a consistent point of view about abnormality and then applied it to any and all instances.

We can describe these perspectives as **scientific models,** deliberately simplified versions of some phenomenon intended to capture its important characteristics while deleting its unimportant ones. Models are *not* literal replicas of whatever they are trying to represent. They intend only to capture some of its features, presumably those that are essential. The virtue of having a model available is that it can facilitate scientific theorizing and research. A scientist is less encumbered by irrelevancies and can focus on just those features that matter. For example, psychologists interested in trial-and-error learning have often studied how rats learn to run through mazes for a food reward. The intent is to capture the essence of trial-and-error learning by placing a simple creature in a simple situation.

The drawback of a model is that it may be useless. It might include inessential details—or worse, it might leave out crucial characteristics. To continue the example, perhaps the investigation of rats running mazes omits something important about trial-and-error learning, particularly as it occurs among people.

No model can represent a phenomenon perfectly, of course, but models vary in their usefulness. In the case of abnormality, we start with an acknowledged upper limit to the utility of any model. Abnormality is an imprecise concept that has pertinent characteristics but no critical ones. In surveying models of abnormality, we should not be surprised that different theorists arrive at very different emphases.

All useful models of abnormality share a common form. At the core of each is a set of assumptions about human nature. Specifically, each model takes a stance on the nature of behavior *(general psychology)*, on how behavior can go awry *(psychopathology)*, and on how abnormality can be prevented and/or corrected *(intervention)*.

Adopting a model of abnormality can put blinders on the therapist, leading her to look at problems and their treatment in but one way, when other perspectives might be profitable. Indeed, altogether different professional traditions have arisen to address biological versus psychological causes and treatments (Chapter 1). However, psychologically caused problems can sometimes be helped with biological interventions, and vice versa.

How do we choose among the models of abnormality? There are many specific questions we want to ask about abnormality. Each model provides its own answers, which may suggest a basis for choosing among them for given purposes. Research proves critical in making these choices (Chapter 4). If a theoretical model is impossible to test, then it is not useful. If a model can be tested, however, then the evidence tells us how to regard it.

Here are some common questions of concern about abnormality (Peterson & Seligman, 1985):

1. **WHAT IS BEING EXPLAINED?** Many forms of abnormality—like depression, anxiety, schizophrenia, or substance abuse—are described with terms having diverse meanings. A model of abnormality must be explicit about the type of abnormality it attempts to explain. Does it apply to all forms of depression or only to certain types? If it tries to explain all the instances of a particular problem, it must explain when and how these types are similar as well as when and how they are different. If it is more limited, it must explain why the boundaries have been drawn so tightly.

2. **ARE MILD FORMS AND SEVERE FORMS OF ABNORMALITY DIFFERENT IN DEGREE OR IN KIND?** This question is closely related to the previous one. I have already discussed the issue of continuity between normality and abnormality (Chapter 1). A given model might not be able to resolve this issue to the satisfaction of all, but it must at least take a position with respect to the debate.

3. **WHY DO THE VARIOUS SYMPTOMS OF A DISORDER CO-OCCUR?** Disorders are typically described as a complex of various symptoms. One view sees these as cohering into discrete *syndromes;* another view sees these symptoms as less coherent but nonetheless apt to co-occur. In either case, a model of abnormality must explain why particular symptoms fit together as they do. This can be daunting because many types of abnormality show up in a variety of spheres of functioning: physical, emotional, cognitive, behavioral, interpersonal, and so on. Theorists need somehow to integrate these spheres, to explain why given problems show up at so many levels.

4. **WHAT ARE THE BASIC FORMS OF ABNORMALITY?** Different diagnostic systems have been proposed throughout history (Chapter 2). All of these are theoretically driven in that they assume particular types of problems. Sometimes the role of theory in a typology is not explicit. However, a model often suggests its own typology in straightforward fashion, and it can be judged by how well it makes sense of the range of problems from which people suffer.

5. **WHAT IS THE LIKELIHOOD OF DIFFERENT TYPES OF ABNORMALITY?** The **prevalence** of a disorder refers to the percentage of people in a population who have that disorder at a particular time. The **incidence** of a disorder is the rate of new cases of that disorder in a given period of time for a particular population. Prevalence and incidence are related, but they provide somewhat different information about the likelihood of abnormality. Those problems that have a high prevalence usually have a high incidence, but not always. Do you see why? Suppose that when a person has a disorder, it stays with him or her forever; it could have a relatively low incidence but a relatively high prevalence. Regardless, a model of abnormality must explain the prevalence and incidence of different disorders. Why is depression a common problem and multiple personality disorder a rare one? An interesting version of this question is why the frequency of certain disorders apparently has changed throughout history (Gruenberg, 1980). Hysteria at one time was much more common than it currently is. And anorexia and bulimia, the eating disorders, are apparently much more common now than they were at the turn of the century.

6. **WHEN DO DEVELOPMENTAL DIFFERENCES EXIST?** For years, theorists assumed that they could explain the psychological difficulties of children by generalizing down the explanations available for adult disorders (Achenbach, 1986). This is now seen as an oversimplification. The problems of children are not scaled-down versions of adult problems. Models of abnormality must be grounded in what is known about developmental psychology and its assumption that development is a lifelong process (Chapter 14).

7. WHAT DIFFERENCES IN ABNORMALITY EXIST BETWEEN MEN AND WOMEN? Many disorders show different prevalences in men versus women. Women, for example, are more likely than men to be diagnosed as depressed (Nolen-Hoeksema, 1990). And men, for another example, are more likely than women to show antisocial behavior (Cadoret, 1986). One explanation for such sex differences may be that they are biologically based, but a moment's reflection shows us that women and men differ not only anatomically but also in the lives they lead. They find themselves in different social environments, and sex differences in disorders might reflect the differences in these settings.

8. WHY IS ABNORMALITY SOMETIMES EPISODIC? Many forms of abnormality admit to a quite simple treatment: the passage of time. Problems such as depression can be self-limiting; they may go away without any professional intervention (see Schachter, 1982). This is good news for the individual who happens to suffer from a problem, but it poses a challenge for a model of abnormality to explain why "spontaneous" recovery takes place when it does.

9. WHY DOES ABNORMALITY SOMETIMES RETURN? At the same time, spontaneous recovery does not mean that all people who once had a problem are thereafter immune. Some number of individuals will again encounter the same difficulty. Indeed, a good generalization is that one of the strongest risk factors for *any* particular problem is having suffered from that problem in the past. A useful model of abnormality must explain this characteristic, specifying who is at risk for recurrence following apparent recovery and who is not.

TREATMENT

As mentioned, each of the popular models of abnormality concerns itself with how psychological problems can be treated (Garfield & Bergin, 1986). My discussion of these models details interventions stemming from them. But before going any further, I should clarify some terms. I use *treatment, therapy,* and *intervention* interchangeably to refer to procedures undertaken by a practitioner in order to reduce or remove another individual's problem.

Therapy is an umbrella term. Treatments can be divided into **biomedical therapies,** which intervene biologically, and **psychotherapies,** which intervene psychologically as directed by one of the psychological models of abnormality. To some degree this is an artificial distinction, because it is yet one more version of a strict mind-body dichotomy that can be misleading in particular cases. In systematic desensitiza-tion, a person is taught to relax and imagine frightening images. This is regarded as psychotherapy, but suppose the person is given a drug to help him relax. Does this make it a biomedical therapy?

Perhaps we should classify treatments according to their rationales, which means that we need to be open to the possibility that research might call into question a given rationale and necessitate reclassification. Some psychoanalytic theorists once believed that electroconvulsive shock therapy (ECT) for depression satisfied the depressed person's supposed need to be punished (Kalinowsky, 1980). By this view, the biological effects of ECT on the brain are not relevant. This rationale in terms of punishment is no longer accepted, although ECT continues to be used with success (Chapter 9). However, this example illustrates how it is possible to interpret the same treatment in different ways.

There are different mental health professionals who are trained to provide therapy. Social workers may be therapists and in fact provide the most hours of therapy in the United States today. Nurses, members of the clergy, and educators may also be therapists, as well as those with expertise in massage, nutrition, or physical fitness.

Among the most familiar therapists are **clinical psychologists,** who have psychology degrees and training in psychology, and **psychiatrists,** who have medical degrees and training in medicine. Many clinical psychologists subscribe to one of the psychological models of abnormality, whereas many psychiatrists subscribe to the biomedical model. It is important to note that there are exceptions. One of the important influences on my career was a psychiatrist well known for his contributions to the behavioral approach.

A **psychoanalyst** has received training in a given field such as psychology or psychiatry as well as additional education at an institute that specializes in the teaching of psychoanalysis. Needless to say, a psychoanalyst adheres to the psychoanalytic model of abnormality.

I need to address one more question of terminology. What do we call the person receiving therapy? Throughout the book I will use the terms *patient* and *client*. Here are the rules I try to employ. The recipients of biomedical treatment are called **patients.** Those receiving such treatments while in the hospital are often referred to as *inpatients;* those receiving biomedical treatments while not in the hospital are often called *outpatients.* The term **client** refers to the recipient of psychotherapy. Many clinical psychologists react strongly to the use of the word *patient*, because to them it implies an acceptance of the biomedical model of abnormality and its conception of human nature. They prefer the term *client* because it implies that the person is a psychological being, an active agent as opposed to a physical body. Finally, individuals who receive psychoanalytic treatment are sometimes called **analysands.**

Regardless of what we call those involved in treatment, we can make several generalizations about the endeavor. Most importantly, there is no such thing as generic treatment. No one practices therapy without first establishing a theoretical position about human nature and the causes of people's problems. There are biomedical approaches to treatment, psychoanalytic approaches, cognitive-behavioral approaches, and so on. Besides providing particular treatment strategies, the different models provide different conceptions of psychological health.

Obviously, various treatments have survived because they each have something to offer. Is there thus some way to combine treatments and reap these benefits simultaneously? Many therapists describe themselves as **eclectic therapists,** which means they subscribe to no specific approach to treatment but try to take something useful from several of them. This is not always possible because different models may make diametrically opposed assumptions about problems and their treatments. A common ground can only be found where it is theoretically sensible.

Most models of abnormality acknowledge that people are both biological and psychological beings. So, common today are interventions that combine drugs and psychotherapy: minor tranquilizers *and* exposure to fearful images for anxiety disorders, antidepressants *and* cognitive therapy for depression, and so on. A combination is often superior to either alone, and eclectic treatment is thereby supported (e.g., Fairburn, 1988; Hyland, 1991; Krull, 1990; Muskin, 1990; Weiss & Mirin, 1990).

It is important to emphasize that the treatment of psychological abnormality can be expensive. Drugs may be costly, and psychotherapy takes place over weeks, months, or even years. Psychotherapists must obviously be compensated for their work, either directly by clients or indirectly by insurance companies or government agencies. The high cost of health care in the United States is currently of great concern, and any changes in policy will have a profound impact on how psychological problems are treated. We can expect time-limited therapies of proven effectiveness to become increasingly popular (Chapter 4). We can also expect therapy to become part of a *managed care* package in which those who pay for treatment—insurance companies hired by employers—become more involved in providing and regulating therapy options for individuals (e.g., Schreter, 1993; Winegar, 1993).

Another point to make about currently available forms of treatment is that they tend to be conservative.

They almost always involve helping the person adjust to the status quo, rather than changing the status quo to fit the person. Environmental conditions can influence or even cause many problems, but by and large, treatment focuses on the individual and how to help him or her adjust to such conditions. Of course, there are exceptions. Behavior therapy tries to change the person's situation, but it is usually the immediate environment on focus, not the entire world (cf. Skinner, 1986). This is still conservative: Leave a particular building if it is on fire, but do not enact laws requiring that all buildings must be fireproof.

In the United States, a major exception is the *community mental health movement,* in which larger social conditions are targeted, with the goal of being able to prevent or alleviate those problems caused by the status quo (Chapter 15). Another major exception is the development of *feminist therapy,* which starts with the explicit recognition that many of women's problems result from their disadvantaged position in contemporary society (see Focus on Feminist Therapy).

A number of models of abnormality have been popular, and you will encounter these models throughout the text. For the time being, I sketch the most important of their assumptions about general psychology, psychopathology, and intervention in Table 3.1.

BIOMEDICAL MODEL

The **biomedical model** is the current manifestation of the somatic approach that has long been popular in explaining abnormality (Chapter 1). Many who approach diagnosis in psychophysiological or neuropsychological terms adhere to this approach. At its essence, the biomedical model assumes that people are physical systems and must be understood in physical terms. Among the most important things we can know about people are their physiological states and the characteristics of their nervous system.

PSYCHOPATHOLOGY

The biomedical model proposes that the problems we encounter result from bodily defects, injuries, or illnesses, usually affecting the brain (Bursten, 1979). I described an excellent example of this formula in Chapter 1, in the link between untreated syphilis and general paresis. Particular lesions and tumors in the brain can lead to a host of psychological difficulties. Recent research hints that problems like schizophrenia and obsessive-compulsive disorder might also have their basis in abnormal brain structure and/or function.

Biomedical theorists today are particularly interested in **neurotransmitters,** the chemicals secreted by neurons that allow communication with other neurons. Hundreds of neurotransmitters exist, and different ones have been linked to particular disorders. Depression is thought by some theorists to be associated with unusually low activity of norepinephrine and serotonin (McNeal & Cimbolic, 1986). Schizophrenia is thought to be associated with unusually high activity of the neurotransmitter dopamine (Matthysse, 1977).

TABLE 3.1

MODELS OF ABNORMALITY *A model of abnormality consists of a set of related assumptions about human nature, psychological health, problems, and effective treatments.*

ASSUMPTIONS	MODEL
	Biomedical
human nature	people are physical systems
view of health	normal biological functioning
problems	bodily injury, illness, or defect
treatment	intervene with drugs, shock, or surgery
	Psychoanalytic
human nature	people are energy systems
view of health	availability of psychological energy
problems	investment of energy in symptoms
treatment	encourage insight
	Cognitive-Behavioral
human nature	people are information-processing systems
view of health	adaptive cognitive and behavioral habits
problems	inappropriate learning
treatment	change the environment and/or thoughts
	Humanistic-Existential-Phenomenological
human nature	people choose and define their own mode of existence
view of health	authentic living; congruence between self and world
problems	thwarting of self-actualization
treatment	choose to live authentically
	Family Systems
human nature	people are family products
view of health	healthy homeostasis within family
problems	family disturbances
treatment	change the status quo in the family
	Sociocultural
human nature	people are societal and cultural products
view of health	absence of stressful social conditions
problems	stressful life events; stigma
treatment	change societal conditions

Another aspect of the biomedical model is viewing people as products of evolution. Because the theory of evolution provides the unifying perspective for the whole of biology, it should also help explain problems that have a biological basis (Peterson, 1991a). Our characteristics—physical and psychological—exist as they do because they have contributed to the survival of our ancestors. How can a problem have a basis in evolution? Perhaps characteristics that at one time contributed to fitness no longer serve their original purpose.

When we take an evolutionary perspective, we become interested in the contribution of genetics to abnormality. Several strategies for studying genetic influence are available. Researchers can do *family studies,* looking to see if particular disorders run through families. Studies like this might be ambiguous, however, because the resemblance of family members might reflect a similar environment just as plausibly as a similar biology. One way around this problem is through *adoption studies,* which compare adopted children to the parents who conceived them versus those who raised them.

More compelling are *twin studies,* in which researchers compare the co-occurrence of problems in identical versus fraternal twins. If the co-occurrence of disorders is higher in identical twins (who share identical genes and a common environment) than

Twin studies are used to infer the possible contribution of genetics to abnormality. The similarity with respect to a psychological problem of identical versus fraternal twins is compared to tease apart the influences of biology and environment.

FOCUS ON

Feminist Therapy

NEW APPROACHES TO TREAT-ment and prevention appear with regularity, and one of the most notable in recent decades is **feminist therapy,** an intervention informed by feminist philosophy (Enns, 1993). According to this perspective, the psychological problems that women experience can only be understood in terms of the positions they occupy in society. Women do not have the same political and economic power that men do, and our society is structured in such a way that this gender-based hierarchy maintains itself.

In many ways, feminist therapy exemplifies an intervention that attempts to be sensitive to those in a given social group (see Sue & Sue, 1990). Its special characteristic is the explicit reminder that social groups in the United States (and elsewhere) typically reside in a hierarchy of power and status that must be taken into account when we explain and treat people's problems. Many approaches to psychological disorders ignore the important context represented by this hierarchy.

According to feminist therapists, traditional mental health approaches contribute to the societal status quo. Women's problems are often regarded as characteristics of individual women and not of the social and historical forces that have shaped them. That physical and sexual abuse contribute importantly to the distress of many women is not seen as a societal issue. Women who conform too much or too little to society's gender-role prescriptions run the risk of being diagnosed as abnormal. And according to many theories, women are to blame for the psychological problems of their children (Surrey, 1990).

Feminist therapy arose in the 1970s out of the experience of women in consciousness-raising groups. As women in the company of one another gave voice to their criticisms of societal institutions, psychotherapy became an easy target. In an influential critique,

Chesler (1972) argued that it involved the bending of the client's will to that of the therapist. Because the majority of clients were women, and the majority of therapists were men, typical psychotherapy was just one more example of women's subordination to men.

Some believed that women should not participate at all in traditional psychotherapy but instead should rely on self-help groups (Tennov, 1973). Others argued instead that therapy could be refashioned to benefit women, and from their efforts came feminist therapy (Enns, 1993). What changes were needed? Most importantly, therapy should not place the therapist above the client in status or privilege (Gilbert, 1980). Its goal should be to empower the client, not bring her into line.

A feminist approach has often been incorporated into existing strategies of psychotherapy (Enns, 1993). Although many of Freud's pronouncements are at odds with feminist thought, some feminist therapists have been able to work within the psychodynamic tradition (Chodorow, 1989). These therapists have also been attracted to family systems approaches (Goldner, 1985) and have expanded the basic premises to apply in particular to families in which abuse occurs as well as to nontraditional family units (Goodrich, Rampage, Ellman, & Halstead, 1988).

Feminist therapy has been highly influential in challenging long-held assumptions in the mental health professions. The possibility of gender bias in diagnosis is now recognized by many. More profoundly, the possibility that our very conceptions of normality and abnormality embody assumptions based on gender is also being considered. For example, Brown (1992) has suggested that post-traumatic stress "disorder" that follows assault or abuse be relabeled as a normal reaction to these events and treated accordingly (Chapter 7).

Feminist therapy can be criticized for being political in nature, but I find this criticism misguided (cf. Lazerson, 1992). It has an obvious political underpinning that guides its practitioners, but the same is true for any approach to treatment. Indeed, it can be lauded for making its political asssumptions quite explicit.

among fraternal twins (who do not share identical genes but do share a common environment), then we can be more certain that genetics play a role. The most elegant way of studying twins is within an adoption study format, because here the influences of biology and environment can best be teased apart (see Figure 3.1, p. 73).

Even more powerful in arguing that genetic factors are involved in abnormality are *genetic linkage studies.* Here researchers attempt to link the occurrence

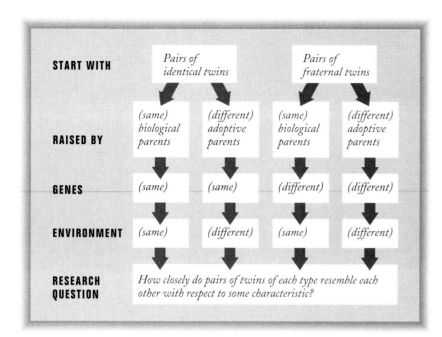

FIGURE **3.1**

DESIGN OF TWIN-ADOPTION
STUDIES   *Researchers are
sometimes able to compare the
resemblance with respect to some
characteristic of twins who are
identical versus fraternal and who
were raised together or raised
apart. This allows them to
estimate the separate influences of
genetics and environment. To the
degree that resemblance is high for
twins with the same genes,
regardless of environment, then
the characteristic is influenced by
genetics. To the degree that
resemblance is high for twins with
the same environment, regardless
of genes, then the characteristic is
influenced by learning and
socialization.*

in families of certain psychological disorders with physical characteristics known to be genetically determined, such as color blindness or blood type. If the disorders appear whenever the physical characteristic does, and not otherwise, then there may be a link between the biological basis of the problem and the biological basis of the physical characteristic.

Finally, the most persuasive studies would be those that find *actual genes* associated with disorders—but at present, there are few if any such investigations that are widely accepted. In any event, it is important to see that studies finding a genetic basis for disorders document only a risk factor. They do not tell us about the mechanism that leads from genetics to psychological difficulties.

Genes are only codes, directions for the body to follow in creating and maintaining itself. We are far from understanding how genetic information is used. Said another way, genetics represent a risk factor for many forms of psychopathology, but it is the physical expression of a person's genetic makeup that constitutes the relevant mechanism. How genes express themselves necessarily reflects the influence of the environment.

Studies of genetic influences on abnormality do not show that problems are inherited as a whole. The technical term for what such studies detect is the **heritability** of problems, which means that the *variation* across people in their behavior is correlated with the *variation* across their genes. In other words, people differ—in their tendency to be anxious or depressed, for example—in part because their genetic makeup differs. Formulas exist for calculating the degree to which a characteristic is heritable from information about the resemblance of family members with respect to this characteristic. We can thus conclude that characteristics are heritable without knowing what the relevant genes might be or how they contribute to problems that develop.

It is important to realize that characteristics with high heritability may well reflect the influence of the environment and socialization (Peterson, 1991a). For example, intelligence is heritable but at the same time influenced by educational opportunities. Similarly, certain physical illnesses—such as types of cancer—are demonstrably heritable but at the same time influenced by environmental factors and/or habits.

INTERVENTION

Biomedical treatments include any and all approaches to problems that involve physical interventions. They share the attempt to remove or undo the presumed physical causes of abnormality, return the body to normal functioning, and keep it there. The best known biomedical interventions—drugs, ECT, and surgery—are undertaken by physicians, because these are medical procedures and limited by law in most United States jurisdictions to those who are licensed to practice medicine.

Many drugs prove to be effective treatments for different disorders. Most work (presumably) by affecting neurotransmitter activity in the brain, and they tend to be explained by theories proposing that a given disorder is brought about by something amiss with the neurotransmitter in question. To the degree that the drugs work, this constitutes additional support for the neurotransmitter hypothesis. Appreciate, however, that treatments may be effective for reasons other than undoing the original causes of a problem. We cannot automatically infer etiology from treatment effectiveness.

We know that neurotransmitters can be amiss for various reasons. Too much or too little of the transmitter substance may be produced. Or too many or too few neurons may secrete the substance, or receive it. Or neurons might be too sensitive, or not sensitive enough. Or there might be other substances in the brain that inhibit the neurotransmitter, or destroy it, or make it linger. This is all played out on a microscopic level, impossible to study directly, and so we can only make inferences about the processes involved.

All drugs have side effects. Indeed, all treatments—including psychological ones—have effects that might not be intended (e.g., R. C. Erickson, 1987; Foa & Emmelkamp, 1983; Strupp, Hadley, & Gomes-Schwartz, 1977). This means we must be realistic when evaluating drugs. We cannot dismiss a treatment simply because it produces undesired effects. We must ask, in any given case, whether the side effects of a treatment are outweighed by its benefits. The greater the imbalance, in one direction or the other, the easier it is to decide whether to continue that particular treatment.

Some years ago, while working on a psychiatric ward in a hospital, I observed an excellent example of drug treatment and how side effects of medication can be minimized. Mr. Wotzkowski was a 50-year-old man hospitalized for severe depression. Among the matters that troubled him were several health problems, including extremely high blood pressure and the associated risk of a stroke or heart attack.

The head psychiatrist, who was also trained as a cardiologist, prescribed antidepressant medication for the patient and at the same time discontinued the drugs he took to combat his hypertension. This may seem like a rash strategy, but as it happens, one of the possible side effects of antidepressant medication is **low** *blood pressure. Mr. Wotzkowski's cardiac status was monitored carefully, and the hoped-for effects ensued. Not only did his depression decrease, but so did his blood pressure. Because the number of drugs Mr. Wotzkowski had to take was reduced, this intervention lowered the potential hazard of drug interactions. His case turned out well; free of depression, he was able to exercise more and change his diet, which further reduced his blood pressure.*

Other well known biomedical treatments include the use of electroconvulsive shock to treat unipolar depression (Chapter 9) and psychosurgery, such as lobotomies, at one time used to treat schizophrenia (Chapter 12). We no longer see much use of lobotomies, but this does not mean that there is no place for psychosurgery in the treatment of problems. You learn in Chapter 11 about the controversial surgical procedures used to deal with people who commit criminal sexual acts. Surgery can reduce their sex drive in general, which means that their criminal sexual conduct decreases as well. Psychosurgery is also used to treat intractable epilepsy (Chapter 6) and severe cases of obsessive-compulsive disorder (Chapter 7). Less controversial are surgical procedures that undo tumors and lesions in the brain, which may produce one or more of the organic disorders discussed in Chapter 6. I also touch on neural grafting, now being explored as a treatment for Parkinson's disease, in which healthy tissue is taken from adrenal glands and moved to the part of the brain that is deficient.

PSYCHOANALYTIC MODEL

The **psychoanalytic model** is the point of view originally espoused in Sigmund Freud's influential approach to abnormality. At its core, this model implies that people are closed energy systems. Freud (1950) seemed to regard psychological energy (or *libido*, to use his term) as an actual thing, eventually to be discovered by neurologists. Subsequent versions of psychoanalytic theory use the notion of energy in a more metaphorical way, but common to all these theories are assumptions stemming from the view of people as engaged in the transformation and redirection of psychological energy (Sulloway, 1979).

One of the overarching concepts of psychoanalytic theorizing is that of **overdetermined behavior,** meaning that even the most simple of our actions has numerous causes. The assumption of overdetermined behavior helps explain why the psychoanalytic model has been controversial. On the positive side, psychoanalytic theorizing about abnormality does justice to the complexity of the subject. On the negative side, because so many theoretical notions must be brought to bear in a single psychoanalytic explanation, the process may become unwieldy and appear arbitrary (Rapaport, 1959).

Another important aspect of the psychoanalytic model is that it takes a developmental approach to abnormality, stressing events and occurrences early in life that affect adult functioning. This emphasis stems from Freud's original medical training in neurology, where it is a truism that early structures form the

An impressionable moment in the childhood of Buffalo Bill.

foundation on which later structures are built. Put another way, the behavioral styles that a child develops early in life become the ingredients of his or her adult personality.

Freud believed that children develop by passing through a fixed sequence of **psychosexual stages,** discrete periods defined by the part of the body that provides gratification of the sexual drive (see Figure 3.2). The child who passes through these stages—oral, anal, phallic, latency, and genital—in satisfactory fashion becomes a normal adult. But frustration or indulgence at any stage may leave the child with a **fixation** at that stage, which influences his adult character. An orally fixated person, for example, might drink too much or eat too much as an adult, creating such problems as alcoholism or obesity.

Yet another noteworthy psychoanalytic idea is that of the dynamic **unconscious.** According to Freud and subsequent psychoanalytic theorists, there exists important mental activity of which we are not aware (see Figure 3.3). The unconscious is not just a deficit in knowledge but an active process in which we are motivated to keep threatening material from our conscious minds. Chief among these threatening contents are the sexual and aggressive motives that underlie our every action.

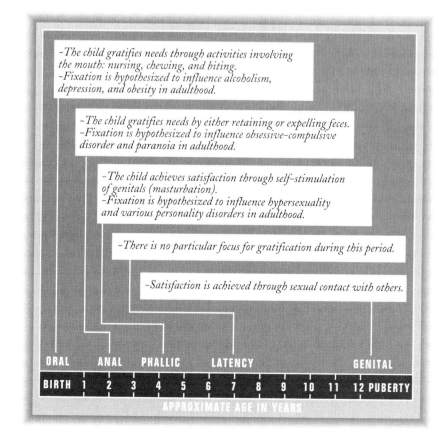

FIGURE 3.2

STAGES OF PSYCHOSEXUAL DEVELOPMENT *According to Freud, all children pass through stages defined by the part of the body that provides gratification. Failure to satisfactorily pass through a stage is thought to produce a fixation at that stage, which influences adult behavior.*

FIGURE 3.3

FREUD'S METAPHOR OF THE MIND   *Freud's conceptualization of the mind can be depicted as an iceberg. Only the tip of the iceberg shows above the surface of consciousness.*

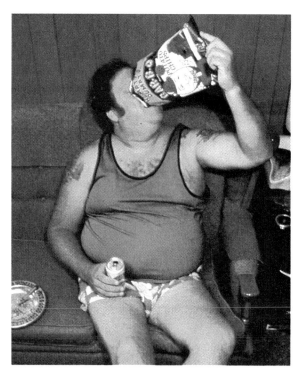

An orally fixated person may eat or drink too much. According to psychoanalytic theory, an individual's apparent symptoms reflect underlying conflicts.

Where does psychological energy originate? Freud's answer is that we have certain innate drives, in particular sexuality and aggression, that demand discharge. The term for the sexual drive is *Eros* (after the Greek god of love, a.k.a. Cupid). Eros is manifest not just in the narrow sense of genital activity culminating in orgasm, but also more broadly, in any and all activities that involve bodily pleasure. The aggressive drive is sometimes called *Thanatos* (after the Greek god of death). This drive is presumably behind the destructive acts we direct against ourselves and others: suicide, drug abuse, murder, and war.

Freud was a provocative writer, and he portrayed the interplay of these forces in vivid terms. In any given individual, Eros and Thanatos, the forces of life versus death, struggle for dominance. Of course, all of us eventually die, but Eros is behind much of what we do along the way.

These ideas stem from psychoanalytic theory's emphasis on energy. As a 19th-century intellectual, Freud was greatly influenced by the theoretical break-throughs in physics being made at that time. The *first law of thermodynamics*—that energy can neither be created nor destroyed—inspired his notion of a fixed amount of libido in each individual. The *second law of thermodynamics*—that all energy systems gradually run down—inspired his notion of Thanatos.

Another important concern is the struggle between the individual and his drives and the larger social group to which he belongs and its restrictions. According to Freud (1930), civilization would not be possible if people directly satisfied all sexual and aggressive drives as they arose. Who would raise the

According to Freud, in the course of socialization, children are transformed from bundles of drives into creatures capable of modifying their impulses or holding them in check.

children, harvest the crops, or pay the taxes? For society to exist, people's drives must be curbed.

Freud held that drives could not be eliminated. But people could be induced to compromise, either to delay their gratification or to find indirect or symbolic means of satisfying them. In the course of socialization, children are transformed from bundles of drives—literally wild animals—into creatures capable of modifying their impulses or holding them in check. Socialization is never fully achieved, and it produces casualties: people who never learn to control their drives as well as those who overdo it.

When infants are born, the only mental structure present is what Freud termed the **id,** responsible for our irrational and emotional aspects. The id operates according to the *pleasure principle:* gratification without delay. In the course of socialization, the infant develops an **ego,** mental structure that operates according to the *reality principle:* adaptation to external constraints. The internalization of parental dictates—mainly "thou shalt nots"—is accomplished by the development of yet a third structure, the **superego.** In the adult, these three systems, the id, ego, and superego, interact continually. Their dynamic balance determines an individual's personality in general and his or her problems in particular.

How does the mind defend itself? One of Freud's most important contributions to psychological thought is the notion of **defense mechanisms** (see Table 3.2). These are mostly unconscious strategies that the ego uses to protect itself from anxiety. Other theorists and writers have of course described the ways that people may rationalize, intellectualize, or deny events, but Freud brought all of these under the same explanatory umbrella. His daughter Anna Freud (1937) is well known for elaborating her father's ideas about defense mechanisms.

All people presumably use defense mechanisms, but they show considerable variation in those they habitually favor (Vaillant, 1977). Some people rely mainly on primitive defenses that distort or deny reality, such as denial or repression. Other people use more subtle ones, such as humor or sublimation. People with severe problems tend to use particularly immature or exaggerated defenses. Indeed, the psychoanalytic model gives us a rich vocabulary for describing various disorders in terms of the defense mechanisms that people typically use. Paranoid individuals use projection. Phobic individuals use displacement. And so on.

PSYCHOPATHOLOGY

Generally speaking, psychoanalytic theorists see problems as resulting from defects in the transformation

TABLE 3.2

DEFENSE MECHANISMS *According to the psychoanalytic model, defense mechanisms are strategies used to keep threatening thoughts and impulses out of consciousness. If taken to an extreme, a defense mechanism can become a problem in its own right.*

DEFENSE MECHANISM	CHARACTERIZATION AND EXAMPLE
compensation	investing energies in some activity to offset difficulties in another area; for example, working out or studying after a disappointing date
denial	acting as if something bad did not happen; for example, continuing to attend classes after flunking out of school
displacement	directing impulses toward a substitute object or person; for example, kicking the dog or yelling at the children after a difficult day at work
fantasy	engaging in wishful thinking or daydreaming when feeling stressed; for example, fantasizing about winning the lottery while taking final examinations
humor	seeing the amusing side of difficulties; for example, joking during a life-threatening crisis
intellectualization	discussing a traumatic event without experiencing any emotions, as when a patient with a serious illness calmly discusses the chances of survival
projection	attributing unacceptable characteristics of one's own to others; for example, a hostile person who sees everyone else as belligerent
rationalization	rewriting history after a disappointment, like the fox in Aesop's fables who decided that the grapes he couldn't have were probably sour anyway
reaction formation	replacing one impulse with its opposite; for example, acting hatefully toward a person one finds attractive
regression	acting like an infant or child in stressful circumstances; for example, throwing a tantrum during an argument
repression	forcing a threatening memory from awareness, as might happen when a person "forgets" the details of an assault
sublimation	channeling undesirable impulses into socially acceptable activities; for example, an aggressive individual who becomes a firefighter or a police officer

and use of psychological energy. A person may invest too much energy in defenses, thus having less available energy for more gratifying activities. Or another person may not invest enough energy in defenses, and as a result becomes overwhelmed by his drives.

"Defenses" can end up being problems in their own right. Consider *multiple personality disorder,* the existence within the same individual of discrete personalities with little awareness of one another (Chapter 8). Research implicates sexual or physical abuse in the childhood of most people with this disorder (Putnam, Guroff, Silberman, Barban, & Post, 1986). One interpretation is that as children, individuals who later develop multiple personality disorder create an alternative personality as a defense against abuse.[1] It is a way to escape an intolerable situation, psychologically if not physically. This strategy, although useful at the time, creates obvious problems for those who continue its use.

INTERVENTION

The first modern "talking cure" was Freud's psychoanalysis, and subsequent psychological therapies have often used it as a model. Even psychotherapists who take issue with psychoanalysis have been influenced by it. Many believe that talking about problems in a special way is curative, that insight into the source of one's own problems is a critical ingredient in improvement, and that a nonjudgmental relationship between client and therapist is crucial. For these reasons, psychoanalysis deserves its place in history.

Psychoanalytic treatment usually involves releasing energy, freeing it from investments in unhealthy purposes so that it is available for use elsewhere. The process by which energy is freed is termed *catharsis,* and it is accompanied by sudden emotional relief (Chapter 1).

As noted, a major strategy in this kind of intervention is attaining **insight:** the bringing of conflicts and motives into conscious awareness. If a person becomes conscious of ideas and impulses heretofore repressed, he has taken a major step toward helping himself because psychological energy is made available for pursuits more gratifying than the maintenance of defenses.

Psychoanalysts have developed a host of strategies for revealing unconscious conflicts. The technique of *free association* is one example. Here the person is instructed and encouraged to say anything that comes to his or her mind, one idea leading to another and

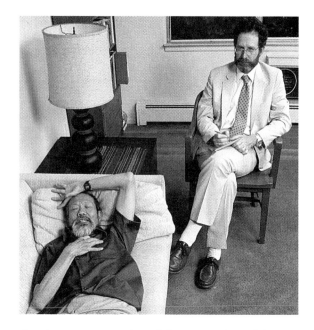

A major strategy in psychoanalytic treatment is attaining insight, achieved by bringing repressed material into consciousness. One way this is done is to ask the individual to free associate, saying anything and everything that comes to mind. The train of associations will lead eventually back to unconscious memories.

then another. The hope is that the train of associations will lead eventually back to unconscious memories.

Dream interpretation is another strategy for accomplishing the same purpose. According to Freud (1900), dreams are "the royal road to the unconscious," and he theorized extensively about how dreams may represent disguises of our unconscious wishes and fears via symbolism. If these disguises can be stripped away, then we might gain insight.

Another strategy emerging from psychoanalytic theory is the analysis of the *transference* relationship between therapist and client. By this view, the client in therapy inevitably reacts to the therapist as he reacted earlier to those people with whom his conflicts originated. If the therapist and client can recreate these conflicts, then they have a clue about how conflicts operated in the past. Again, insight is the goal. To help this process along, the therapist deliberately cultivates a pose of neutrality, a so-called blank screen.

It is quite difficult to say, fully one century after Freud first began to treat hysterical patients by asking them to free associate, that this type of treatment is effective. Neither can we say that it is ineffective. Its terms are ambiguous, the duration of psychoanalytic therapy is typically years, the clients are highly select, and there is a reticence on the part of some psychoanalytic therapists to subject their efforts to scientific investigation (but see Masling & Bornstein, 1993). Few

---

[1] Multiple personality disorder is not an inevitable result of childhood abuse, because the vast majority of abused children do *not* later develop this particular problem.

if any methodologically sound investigations of psychoanalysis have been conducted (Luborsky & Spence, 1978).

Psychodynamic Theories and Interventions

Throughout his long and productive career, Freud attracted a number of followers. Many of these individuals proposed their own versions of psychoanalysis, and what we have today is a large number of such approaches, each with somewhat different emphases. It is customary to refer to Freud's original theory as psychoanalysis, and the family of related approaches as **psychodynamic theories,** because they are concerned with the workings of the mind—their dynamics, as it were (Westen, 1990a). These theories assume that people's problems result from inner conflicts, which produce anxiety that overwhelms their defenses.

Contemporary psychodynamic theorists often follow the lead of Alfred Adler (1927), Carl Jung (1924), and the **neo-Freudians** (such as Erich Fromm, 1947; Karen Horney, 1937; Harry Stack Sullivan, 1947; Erik Erikson, 1963) by placing less emphasis on the purely biological or sexual aspects of personality. They are more likely to be interested in social determinants. Along these lines, they tend to downplay or even eliminate reference to psychological energy and drives.

Contemporary psychodynamic theorists have also followed the lead of the **ego psychologists** (such as Anna Freud, 1937; Heinz Hartmann, 1939; Robert White, 1959) by placing less emphasis on the conflict between id and superego and more stress on the ego as an active—not reactive—agent. Sometimes these theorists refer to defense mechanisms as *coping mechanisms,* to emphasize their active nature.

Many psychodynamic theorists today are particularly interested in the mental representations that people have of themselves and others. These representations are called **object relations** (Greenberg & Mitchell, 1983). "Object" was Freud's term for people or things, and the term "relations" refers to the perceived link between these objects and the individual. In one sense, the emphasis on object relations reflects the trend in recent decades for psychology to be more interested in cognition (Gardner, 1985). But object relations theories maintain the traditional psychoanalytic emphases on unconscious and emotional processes. Silbert (1992) studied how adult women who were sexually abused as children thought and felt about other people. Not surprisingly, these survivors of childhood abuse saw the social world as potentially dangerous and malicious.

Finally, psychoanalytic therapy itself has been modified. Traditional psychoanalysis typically lasted

Anna Freud (1895–1982), shown here in 1920, elaborated her father's ideas about defense mechanisms. She was also well known because of her work with children and their psychological problems.

for 3 to 5 years, sometimes longer. Psychodynamic therapists today still have the eventual goal of insight on the part of their client, but they try to achieve it in a more efficient and direct fashion. Therapy tends to be time-limited, more focused on symptom relief, and used in combination with other approaches, including medication (Luborsky, 1984).

Throughout the book I note problems for which psychodynamic approaches can be useful, including the dissociative disorders (Chapter 8) and unipolar depression (Chapter 9). The causes of these problems, not surprisingly, often include emotional conflicts and lack of acknowledgment of one's own motives. To the degree that these causes can be undone, then we can expect the client to be helped.

COGNITIVE-BEHAVIORAL MODEL

A third perspective on abnormality combines approaches that emphasize cognition on the one hand and processes of learning on the other. As explained in Chapter 1, theories of learning stemmed from behaviorism and thus made no use of cognitive explanations. Indeed, throughout most of the 20th century, learning theories and cognitive theories were clearly distinct and often antagonistic. Although some contemporary therapists regard themselves as strictly behavioral or strictly cognitive, recent years have seen many other therapists successfully combine these approaches (Peterson, 1992). The resulting **cognitive-behavioral model** of abnormality views people as information-processing systems, attempting to predict and understand events in the world with the goal of maximizing pleasure and minimizing pain. Said another way, the cognitive-behavioral model regards people as thinking hedonists.

Explicit in the cognitive-behavioral view of human nature is the assumption that people constantly interact with the world. Albert Bandura (1986) terms this give-and-take between a person and the world **reciprocal determinism.** Each of us is influenced by prevailing patterns of rewards and punishments in the environment, and our actions in turn influence these patterns. Furthermore, this transaction is mediated cognitively. We react to the world in terms of how we interpret events. The "reality" in which our behavior takes place is a *perceived* reality.

FORMS OF LEARNING

Cognitive-behavioral theorists emphasize several psychological processes. Chief among them are basic forms of learning. As you may recall from your introductory psychology course, there are different types of

learning. **Classical conditioning**—remember Pavlov's salivating dogs?—is the process by which people come to associate particular emotional reactions to previously neutral stimuli (see Figure 3.4). Imagine a person who has had a series of traumatic experiences with dogs, or airplane travel, or sexual relations. He may well develop a fear or aversion to these.

Operant conditioning is the process by which we come to associate responses with their consequences. If the consequences are reinforcing, we are more likely to repeat the actions that preceded them. Children might throw tantrums and act like hellions when this is the only way they can get attention from their parents or teachers. If the consequences of responses are painful, then we tend to refrain from repeating these actions.

Modeling—or vicarious conditioning—is the process by which we learn new behaviors by watching others perform them. If the person we watch, called

Do those who view violent models themselves act violently? If so, then perhaps children should not watch violent movies. Certainly, your family dog should not see "Man's Best Friend."

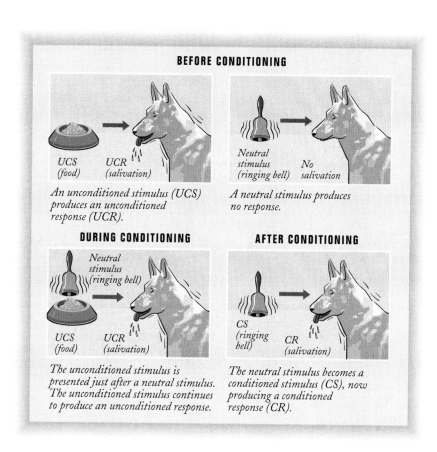

FIGURE 3.4

CLASSICAL CONDITIONING
An originally neutral stimulus comes to produce a response after being paired repeatedly with another stimulus that produces the response.

a *model*, meets with reward, then we are more likely to follow her example, even in problematic directions. Fears and phobias can be produced by modeling. Modeling also provides a theoretical rationale for worrying about how children are affected by the violence on television. Perhaps the cartoons that children see will lead them to carry out the same activities.

COGNITIVE CONTENTS AND PROCESSES

Cognitive-behavioral theorists believe that all of these types of learning (classical conditioning, operant conditioning, and modeling) must be placed in a cognitive context. Learning does not automatically occur just because certain environmental events take place. It occurs most readily for a thinking organism. Even the simplest examples of learning may reflect the influence of expectations (Schwartz, 1984). Theorists have accordingly introduced a host of cognitive constructs. One way to bring some order to cognitive theorizing is by distinguishing the content of thought from its process. *Cognitive contents* are mental representations: particular thoughts and beliefs. We transform and utilize these representations by using *cognitive processes:* judging, decision making, and problem solving.

Our cognitive contents are not simply a jumble of miscellaneous notions. They are organized. A **schema** refers to an organized set of beliefs about some subject—for example, your sense of who you are: your strengths, weaknesses, hopes, dreams, and fears. The key characteristic of a schema is that it has a structure.

Various principles have been suggested as a way of describing the organization of our different schemas (Taylor, 1981). One guiding principle is *consistency* (Festinger, 1957). People often seek out balance and harmony in their thoughts (Heider, 1958). They want their ideas to be consistent with one another. This can take an insidious turn if an individual happens to have a negative view of himself. Consistency may lead him to notice only events that confirm his negative view and ignore disconfirming ones (Mischel, Ebbesen, & Zeiss, 1973). Another guiding principle is *accuracy.* People try to understand the facts of the world. In particular, they notice very quickly what makes them feel good or bad. A third guiding principle is *self-aggrandizement.* Many individuals put a positive spin on their experiences whenever possible (Taylor, 1989). Depression is a notable exception (Chapter 9).

The needs for consistency, accuracy, and self-aggrandizement influence our thoughts, and they may each push us in different directions. What we think is always a compromise among them. Sometimes consistency or self-aggrandizement wins out, in which case we change our perceptions of reality to fit how we think. Other times accuracy wins out, and we change how we think to fit the available evidence.

Psychopathology

According to the cognitive-behavioral model, people's problems are not intrinsically different from their normal behavior; rather, all actions are produced by the same processes of learning and thinking. People encounter difficulties either when they are placed in situations that encourage problems or when they happen to be ignorant, confused, or wrong.

Sex therapists often stress that many people are ignorant of the basic operating principles of their bodies. They might be confused about how arousal and orgasm take place. As their own sexual experiences depart from incorrect expectations, they become anxious or depressed. These negative feelings can create further sexual difficulties.

Intervention

To treat problems from the cognitive-behavioral view, the therapist encourages adaptive habits, behavioral and/or cognitive. Clients are helped to see the world more accurately and to solve problems more efficiently. Therapists equate their treatment with education, because they conceive it as learning or relearning.

In the last few decades, a host of cognitive-behavior therapies have been developed. First we had **behavior therapy,** which applied ideas of classical conditioning and operant conditioning to people's problems. Joseph Wolpe's (1958) *systematic desensitization* was one of the first such therapies to be widely used. A person is asked to imagine a series of increasingly disturbing images while deeply relaxed. This is repeated until the images no longer elicit fear. Systematic desensitization continues to this day to be one of the most effective treatments for specific phobias (Chapter 7).

A behavioral strategy for helping children with problems is to teach their parents how to reward desirable behavior and not to reward undesirable behavior (Ollendick, 1986). This is called *parent training,* but appreciate that the point is to help children by changing their worlds—which in this case are made up of their parents and how the parents respond to what their children do.

Yet another behavioral approach is to teach people how to attain rewards when they lack the skills necessary to do so. Many people with problems may be deficient at winning friends and influencing people (Phillips, 1978). They lack the knowledge and ability to reap the benefits of living with others. *Social skills training* is thereby initiated, and clients are instructed in the basics of social life.

Then we saw the development of strategies based on modeling (Bandura, 1969), which advanced the notion that behavior change need not occur through trial and error. Sometimes people can shed old habits and acquire new ones by watching other individuals behave in adaptive ways. A person who is afraid of spiders or snakes is helped by watching someone else approach them without fear.

At the same time, therapies appeared assuming that people's problems are brought about by the thoughts and beliefs they entertain. An effective way to treat problems would thus involve changing these thoughts and beliefs. These cognitive interventions were foreshadowed by the approaches of George Kelly (1955), whose *fixed-role therapy* encouraged people to try out specific roles in order to experience the perspectives that went along with them, and Albert Ellis (1962), whose *rational-emotive therapy* identified and challenged people's irrational beliefs, chiefly those that are rigid and absolutist ("I must make $125,000 per year in order to be happy").

Today, one of the best known cognitive approaches to therapy was created by Aaron Beck. **Cognitive therapy** for depression targets for change the negative thoughts that depressed people hold about themselves (Beck, Rush, Shaw, & Emery, 1979). They are encouraged to evaluate their ideas against relevant evidence, testing the "reality" of their beliefs (Chapter 9). Cognitive therapy has also been used to treat anxiety disorders characterized by exaggerated beliefs about vulnerability (Chapter 7).

In cognitive therapy, a client may be told to carry out experiments that allow him to gather pertinent evidence:

> *You think you're a loser? Maybe yes, maybe no. Find out by asking ten people to have a cup of coffee with you. And tell me right now how many would need to say yes in order for you not to be considered a loser.*

Of course, if a therapist suggests such experiments, he or she must not make them overly stringent, because the experiments may boomerang and confirm the client's negative views. If there is a good reason to suspect that ten people out of ten will refuse to have coffee with the client, this experiment is best left on the drawing board. Maybe the person should be instructed on **how** *to ask somebody to have a cup of coffee.*

In this example, you see how cognitive treatment slides into behavioral treatment, hence the growing trend to combine these approaches to abnormality and its remediation. This is called **cognitive-behavior therapy.** Indeed, one of the good ways to change how people think is to change how they behave, and vice versa (Bandura, 1986).

Today it makes sense to speak of a cognitive-behavioral model of abnormality, and to subsume the various techniques of behavior therapy and cognitive therapy under this umbrella and call them cognitive-behavior therapy (Mahoney, 1974; Meichenbaum, 1977). Many "behavioral" techniques pay attention to mental occurrences; even the epitome of behavior therapy, systematic desensitization, employs mental images to bring about behavioral change. And many cognitive therapies take into account rewards and punishments.

Cognitive-behavioral techniques have been used with a variety of problems, often with very good success. In some cases, like infantile autism or organic brain disorder, the problem is not eradicated so much as the individual is helped to compensate or cope with it. In other cases, such as a specific phobia or sexual dysfunction, the problem indeed goes away. Once again, the general interpretation is straightforward. These techniques are effective in eliminating problems if they can undo basic causes. They may also be effective in helping an individual cope by providing an alternative way of reaching some goal.

Cognitive-behavioral approaches have their share of problems. They seem to work best when problems fit their formula—that is, when they are circumscribed, behavioral, and/or associated with immediately accessible thoughts. When problems do not readily fit this framework, cognitive-behavior therapy is apt to be misdirected.

To be more complete, the cognitive-behavioral approach should acknowledge the role of emotional influences on cognition, not just vice versa (Zajonc, 1984), and the possibility that some of the cognitive influences on behavior are unconscious (Kihlstrom, 1990). It is interesting that approaches so long regarded as diametrically opposed may be more compatible than had been thought originally. There have been several attempts to integrate behavioral and psychodynamic ideas, starting as early as Dollard and Miller (1950) and continuing to the present (e.g., Ryle, 1982; Wachtel, 1977).

Some advocates regard cognitive-behavioral approaches as superior to drug-based therapies because they effect long-lasting changes in behavior and/or cognition, as opposed to temporary changes in biochemistry (e.g., Rush, Beck, Kovacs, & Hollon, 1977). But the facts do not support the conclusion that cognitive-behavioral changes are always permanent. In many cases, they are not. Nor are they as general across situations as we might want.

This represents not only a practical problem but also a theoretical one. Part of the rationale for cogni-tive-behavioral approaches is the assumption that people have problems because they have not learned appropriate ways of being happy and winning reward. Therapy facilitates this new learning. The person without social skills should find a whole new world opened up to her once these skills have been acquired. Depression or anxiety stemming from this lack of knowledge about social skills should be permanently precluded. But this is not always so. Short-term benefits are simply that.

Why do the new skills not lead to a dramatically different life? One possible answer is that her environment did not change, and thus it cannot sustain the changes in her behavior. If a person lives in an objectively depressing or distressing world, any therapy, no matter how successful in changing her, is likely to appear ineffective when she returns home. Treatment cannot make her oblivious to the world.

Another possible answer is that the changes brought about by cognitive-behavior therapy are not always sufficiently deep. If these changes take place only on a superficial level, they can be dislodged. This points, perhaps, to the need for these approaches to address the physiological, emotional, and/or unconscious levels of problems.

HUMANISTIC-EXISTENTIAL-PHENOMENOLOGICAL MODELS

Biomedical, psychoanalytic, and cognitive-behavioral models all try to specify the causes of problems. Their approach to behavior very much characterizes 20th-century psychology, especially in the United States. But there are voices of dissent that have given rise to several important strands of thought. These dissenting traditions regard human behavior as freely chosen and inappropriately explained in cause-effect terms. These traditions also have something to say about the nature of abnormality and its treatment.

Humanism is the doctrine that the needs and values of human beings take precedence over material things—and further, that people cannot be studied simply as part of the material world. Humanists argue that psychologists may miss what is most important about people by focusing on the supposed causes of behavior, as if people were simply billiard balls, doing poorly or well depending on whatever happens to ricochet into them. Many psychologists are in turn impatient with humanistic theories because they seem vague and impossible to test.

Well known psychologists within the humanistic tradition include Abraham Maslow (1970) and Carl Rogers (1961). Both emphasized that people strive to make the most of their potential in a process called

self-actualization. Self-actualization can be thwarted by various conditions, but if these conditions are changed, then the potential within each individual will necessarily unfold.

This is a very different way of thinking about human nature, stressing the goals for which people strive, their conscious awareness of this striving, the importance of their own choices, and their rationality. The focus is thereby directed away from mechanical causes and toward fundamental questions about existence and meaning.

The humanistic models often overlap with another viewpoint that is termed **existentialism.** The critical idea of existentialism is that a person's experience is primary. To understand any individual is to understand him or her subjectively, from the inside out. Again, see that this perspective is at odds with the other models of abnormality I have been discussing.

Existentialists see people as products of their own choices, which are freely undertaken. To use their phrase, existence precedes essence, with *essence* understood to mean a person's particular characteristics. They also stress that there is no fixed human nature, only the sort of person that each unique individual becomes by the way she chooses to define herself.

As applied specifically to psychology, these humanistic and existential viewpoints have several emphases (Urban, 1983):

- the significance of the individual

- the complex organization of the individual

- the capacity for change inherent in the individual

- the significance of conscious experience

- the self-regulatory nature of human activity

Implicit here is a criticism of scientific psychology as typically conducted, because it does not deal with what is most important about people (Maslow, 1966).

Humanists and existential theorists believe that psychologists must pay more attention to an individual's way of seeing the world, and here they join ranks with yet another intellectual movement, namely **phenomenology,** which attempts to describe a person's conscious experience in terms meaningful for that individual. Phenomenology has a superficial resemblance to cognitive approaches, in that both are concerned with thoughts and thinking, but this is a misleading similarity. Cognitive approaches start by specifying the terms with which to describe "cognition" and then use this theoretical language to describe the thoughts of all people. In contrast, phenomenologists start with the experience of a specific individual and then attempt to describe it.

Carl Rogers (1902–1987) was an important contributor to the humanistic tradition in psychology. He developed a popular form of treatment, client-centered therapy.

Many models of abnormality are antithetical to the phenomenological goal of describing experience, because the theoretical terms introduced by these models turn people into objects, denying them—by implication—any experience. Scottish psychiatrist Ronald D. Laing (1959) eloquently phrased this critique. He pointed out that psychologists and psychiatrists describe schizophrenic symptoms with colorful terms like *word salad, loose associations,* and *poverty of speech,* which make schizophrenic individuals seem like broken machines (Chapter 12). Laing counsels us to listen to what "abnormal" people communicate, because their experience—even when at odds with our own—is still their defining characteristic, just as our own experience defines us.

Laing (1959) recounts the case of Peter, a young man diagnosed as schizophrenic. Among his symptoms was smelling something rotten, which no one else could detect. We could simply call this an olfactory hallucination and be done with it, but Laing delved into Peter's experience. He discovered that Peter had been raised in a family where he was not abused but rather ignored—in a profound way. His parents fed him and clothed him, but otherwise paid him absolutely no heed. They went about their business in their small apartment as if their son did not exist.

Peter came to experience the world in a highly idiosyncratic way. He never developed a sense of intersubjective reality: the convention that certain experiences are "public" because other people treat them as real, whereas other experiences are "private" because other people do not acknowledge them. Contrast cars and trucks whizzing by on the highway with the unspoken hopes and dreams we entertain about the future. For almost all of us, cars and trucks are public, and hopes and dreams are private. But Peter never regarded his experiences as public versus private, because his parents never validated or invalidated any of them. So what if other people did not experience smells in the way that Peter did? None of his experiences had intersubjective reality. To call his experience a "hallucination" is to disregard its significance.

Nowhere does Laing claim that the way Peter's parents treated him caused his schizophrenia. That is not the point of his phenomenological analysis. Rather, the way Peter was raised led him to experience the world in a certain way, and we cannot make sense of him until we know his experiences. According to Laing, simply diagnosing Peter as a schizophrenic is inadequate if our goal is to understand and eventually help another human being.

PSYCHOPATHOLOGY

Humanistic, existential, and phenomenological psychologists are not much concerned with traditional diagnosis. Although they certainly recognize that people have problems, their view of them is quite different. Problems ensue when people experience a discrepancy between their sense of who they are and the way the world treats them. Sometimes the world is to blame, in the sense of creating circumstances that lead them to doubt their own choices (Rogers, 1942). And sometimes people make poor choices by not declaring to themselves their true intentions. Simply put, problems are seen as derailments along the way to self-actualization.

People have a central fear, according to many theorists in this tradition, and this fear is one of nonexistence—death. Needless to say, all of us will die, but many of us fail to confront this eventuality. In denying death, we fail to live in an authentic way, and we fall short of actualizing our potential. Fear of death and our failure to deal with this fear may figure in a variety of psychological problems, notably anxiety disorders (Chapter 7) and depression (Chapter 9).

INTERVENTION

The first psychotherapies to appear after psychoanalysis were humanistic-existential approaches. Most of these were proposed by therapists originally trained in the psychoanalytic tradition. Disenchanted with it, these therapists articulated their own views of human nature, problems, and treatments. The humanistic-

Volunteer work may cultivate self-understanding and provide meaning to the volunteer's life. In the existential therapy technique of dereflection, troubled individuals are encouraged to turn from their own problems to those of others.

existential-phenomenological approach describes people's problems with terms like *angst, despair, crisis,* and *failure to take responsibility.* These are hardly DSM-IV categories, nor are they biochemical anomalies, unconscious conflicts, or bad habits. Instead, they are aspects of the human experience, and they can only be changed by encouraging the person to confront them and choose to act more forthrightly.

Viktor Frankl (1975), a well known existential theorist and therapist, devised strategies that nicely illustrate this point. In *dereflection,* people are encouraged to turn from their own problems to those of others. An insecure and depressed individual might be told to do volunteer work in a hospice. An aggressive and hostile person might be asked to undertake relief work for victims of famine. The intent of dereflection is not to distract, but rather to cultivate self-understanding and to provide meaning to one's own life.

Frankl (1963) provided the following example of how the ability to find meaning in misfortune transforms the individual:

> *An elderly general practitioner consulted me because of his severe depression. He could not overcome the loss of his wife who had died two years before and whom he had loved more than anyone else. Now how could I help him? What should I tell him? Well, I refrained from telling him anything but instead confronted him with the question, "What would have happened, Doctor, if you had died first, and your wife would have had to survive without you?" "Oh," he said, "for her this would have been terrible; how she would have suffered!" Whereupon I replied, "You see, Doctor, such a suffering has been*

spared her, and it was you who have spared her this suffering; but now, you have to pay for it by surviving and mourning her." He said no word but shook my hand and calmly left my office. Suffering ceases to be suffering in some way at the moment it finds a meaning, such as the meaning of a sacrifice.

Of course, this was no therapy in the proper sense since, first, his despair was no disease; and second, I could not change his fate, I could not revive his wife. But in that moment I did succeed in changing his attitude *toward his unalterable fate inasmuch as from that time on he could at least see a meaning in his suffering. (pp. 114–115)*

Among the best known humanistic therapies is **client-centered therapy** as developed by Carl Rogers (1951). Although he was originally trained in psychoanalytic therapy, he found it less than useful for many of the problems he encountered among his clients. He proposed his own view of human nature, one in which people know their own problems and how to solve them, if they could be placed in a setting that encouraged their natural wisdom. And thus his therapy took form, emphasizing the creation of a supportive atmosphere, one characterized by genuineness, empathy, and unconditional positive regard. As in psychoanalysis, there is an emphasis on the characteristics of the therapist, but in contrast to a carefully cultivated neutrality, we see warmth and concern stressed.

The therapist tries not to judge or evaluate what the client says. Rather, she repeats it back to him in order to convey her understanding and positive regard for him. When he can speak openly and without hesitation about his problems, then solutions may follow.

Unlike many humanistic and existential therapists, Rogers believed that the effectiveness of therapy was an open question that could be investigated scientifically. He conducted pioneering investigations of psychotherapy effectiveness (Chapter 4). Several conclusions emerged from his studies (Beutler, Crago, & Arizmendi, 1986). First, personal qualities of the therapist such as warmth, genuineness, and empathy are important ingredients in effective therapy, but in themselves they are not enough. Second, therapy works to the extent that people's perceptions of themselves become more congruent. Third, client-centered therapy is effective with milder forms of anxiety and depressive disorders, in which problems with self-esteem and self-perception predominate, but it is of more limited use when problems are more severe. Rogers conducted a well known investigation of client-centered therapy with schizophrenia, but he found little evidence for its effectiveness (Rogers, Gendlin, Kiesler, & Truax, 1967).

Another example of therapy within this general framework is **gestalt therapy** as pioneered by Frederick (Fritz) Perls (1969a, 1969b). Perls, like Rogers, was trained originally as a psychoanalyst. Among those who influenced him were Wilhelm Reich and Karen Horney, two of the most important of the psychodynamic theorists and therapists. As did Rogers, he became disenchanted with classical psychoanalysis. He adopted the stance that people were innately good, and that their problems resulted when they denied their inner nature. His treatment was a matter of encouraging—or even demanding—that people express their needs and desires, their feelings and fears.

Gestalt therapy became part of the once-popular *encounter group movement* that coalesced at the Esalen Institute in Big Sur in the 1960s and 1970s. In groups, people expressed all their feelings, including negative ones. They might scream at one another, or wrestle, or throw things. A person might be put on what was called the *hot seat* and find himself subjected to goading by those present until he became honest and expressive.

This kind of therapy is dramatic, an unusual approach to treatment. It attracts some people precisely because of this, and repels others. There is no extensive research literature, because those who adhere to this approach often distrust such evaluations. They point instead to striking case examples of its effectiveness. Critics point to case examples of the casualties of these dramatic encounters, concluding that they can be hazardous for the emotionally unstable (e.g., Glass, Kirsch, & Parris, 1977; Kufferle, 1988). Needless to say, there is cause for caution if people seeking help for their problems are particularly vulnerable.

Is the middle path the most reasonable? We can imagine that the short-term benefits of open expression can be exhilarating, but we should not confuse short-term with long-term effects. If a person needs to be nudged out of a rut, then gestalt therapy is an effective kick (Sulzbacher, Wong, McKeen, Glock, & MacDonald, 1981). Otherwise, if the rut is too deep, the person is bound to sink back into it once therapy is complete (Tyson & Range, 1987).

One final note before I move on. I will not make much explicit mention of these approaches throughout the book, for several reasons. One is that these approaches tend to be antidiagnostic. Existential and humanistic approaches often see problems as variations on the same basic themes, so it is not clear that they have that much to say specifically about diagnostic categories like schizophrenia.

FAMILY SYSTEMS MODEL

In Chapter 2, I introduced the idea that some problems can be described as existing between and among people. This perspective is embodied in the **family**

systems model, which takes the position that most problems—depression, anxiety, and substance abuse—are manifestations of disturbances in the family (Jacobson & Bussod, 1983). Family systems theories usually agree on several key points (e.g., Haley, 1976; Minuchin, 1974; Stanton, 1981).

Most basically, individuals must be located in their immediate social context, and usually this means their family. Each family has a unique style or character that shows itself in repetitive patterns of interactions among family members. Also, each family is regarded as a complex system, with every family member's behavior simultaneously a cause and an effect of everyone else's behavior. It is therefore difficult, if not impossible, to specify simple cause-effect relationships within the family. This model instead focuses on the factors existing among family members that maintain the behavioral status quo. This status quo is called *homeostasis:* balance among the behaviors of the family members. Conflicts in one aspect of the system are counteracted by changes elsewhere in an attempt to restore homeostasis.

PSYCHOPATHOLOGY

In a healthy family, the status quo represented by homeostasis is one in which the individuals can thrive as individuals as well as family members. But in other families, the status quo is achieved at a cost. An individual might develop "symptoms" as a way of compensating for problems elsewhere in the family. Family systems theorists call the family member with symptoms the **identified patient,** making the point that this person is merely the one who shows family problems most blatantly.

Stanton (1981) provided the following example of how a disturbed family takes its obvious toll on one family member:

> *Spouse A is driving and Spouse B is in a hurry to get to their destination. . . . A accelerates through a yellow light, B . . . criticizes A, who retorts and steps on the gas. B protests more loudly, A shouts back, and the child, C, starts to cry. At this point the argument stops, while B attends to C and A slows down. (p. 364)*

If this pattern repeats itself over and over, then the child, C, runs the risk of being seen as having an emotional problem, although the child's "problem" obviously serves a purpose. It reduces the tension between the parents and restores homeostasis.

The family systems approach often places great emphasis on triangles like the one just described, regarding these as the basic unit of family interaction (e.g., Zuk, 1971). When there is tension between two people in the family, a third person will often diffuse or eliminate it. Appreciate the complexity involved here, because all sorts of possible triangles exist even within a small family.

Families have their own styles or characters. According to the family systems model, ostensibly individual problems must be located in the context provided by family style.

INTERVENTION

Family systems theorists, not surprisingly, feel that problems are best dealt with by treating the family as a whole. **Couples therapy** (sometimes called **marital therapy** when the individuals are married) or **family therapy** accordingly is undertaken. The goal of the therapist is to intervene so that a new equilibrium can be established in the couple or the family, one without victims.

David Treadway (1985) is a family therapist who described his treatment of George and Betsy Hammerly, a couple married for 25 years. They regarded their marriage as basically good except that George would periodically disappear for several days at a time on a drinking binge. They came to therapy immediately after one of George's binges; he had promised Betsy that "this time things would be different" (p. 157), and she had asked him to prove it to her by entering therapy.

Dr. Treadway used the metaphor of a dance to capture the Hammerly family style. His task was two-fold: learn the dance and then change some of the steps. At first he just listened and observed. George did not work steadily. Because he had an independent source of income, this did not create financial hardships for the family, but George nonetheless expressed a desire to establish a career. George was a very dominant man, and Betsy in turn was very aloof and distant. The only time Betsy became emotionally involved with George was after he returned from a binge, contrite and ashamed.

The Hammerly family dance revolved around the symptom of his drinking, and it had the following rhythms and counter-rhythms:

✦ *George's dominance of Betsy was counteracted by his designation as an alcoholic.*

✦ *Betsy's distance from George was justified by both of them on the same grounds: He was an alcoholic.*

✦ *George and Betsy were closest to one another after he returned from a drinking binge.*

✦ *George explained the failure of his career on his alcoholism.*

✦ *Because George was always "recovering" from his drinking, he could not begin a real job.*

✦ *His periodic binges proved to him that he was not recovered.*

Although George certainly had a problem that involved drinking, he was not physically dependent on alcohol. He could readily abstain. What seemed to draw him to drink was his need to connect with Betsy.

Once he had the Hammerly family dance in mind, Dr. Treadway added several new steps to it. When George went on a binge, as he did several times during therapy, the therapist took the blame for it, saying he was pushing too hard for change because he was inexperienced. George always excused him, offering advice about how one must stick with what one wants to do in order to learn it. This allowed George to dominate the therapy session without his wife being the target. George was encouraged to create a detailed genealogy of his family for use in therapy. This information was perhaps useful in its own right, but it also gave George something to do other than not *embark on a work career he neither needed nor really wanted.*

In what Dr. Treadway admitted was a risky intervention, he subtly suggested to Betsy that she react to George's disappearances as she really felt. So when he next disappeared on a binge, Betsy went away herself, on a vacation to visit her sister in Florida, after asking people not to tell George where she was. He returned to an empty house. Betsy eventually came back, and therapy resumed. Dr. Treadway congratulated Betsy for finally showing George how much she loved him. After all, her previous acceptance of his drinking binges showed that she did not really care, right?

Therapy proceeded well and quickly after this event. George became less dominant, and Betsy became less withdrawn. They related much better to one another, feeling closer than they had in years. After almost 2 years, therapy ended on a note to which it was much easier for the Hammerlys to dance.

The idea of homeostasis leads the family systems therapist to expect resistance by the family to change. The family's style of relating, however unhealthy, is the status quo, and it maintains itself. Therefore, the family therapist must be a strategist, planning treatments that create change (Haley, 1973). One way of conducting this strategic form of therapy is with **reframing interventions:** techniques that encourage a more benign interpretation of what is going on. This is what Dr. Treadway did for the Hammerlys when he congratulated Betsy for leaving home unannounced.

Also part of the repertoire of family therapists are **paradoxical interventions,** suggestions that subtly communicate the message "Don't change!" In resisting these sorts of interventions, the family ends up changing (Haley, 1973, 1987).

If everyone in the O'Connell family yells at older brother Fred, a therapy session might be devoted to everyone trying to voice their complaints to him as loudly as possible. Compensatory processes may develop, for example, if someone in the family says, "Why are we picking on Fred? He's done a lot of good things for us. He shovels the walk in the winter and mows the grass in the summer. He takes care of our recycling. And his girlfriend is the nicest person we know." That of course is what the therapist wants to happen, but merely asking the O'Connells to say nice things about brother Fred is not likely to meet with much success.

Couples therapy   Within the general strategy of couples therapy, there are different approaches (Sundberg, Taplin, & Tyler, 1983). Therapies might emphasize the recognition that marriages, like any relationship, necessarily have a developmental history. They change over time, and what was sensible and comfortable at one point may be less so at another point. Therapies might emphasize communication, helping the couple send and receive messages more skillfully. Or therapies might be behavioral in nature, emphasizing the costs and benefits involved in a relationship, and trying to make this social exchange more explicit and equitable.

On the average, couples who go through couples therapy fare better than those who do not, tending to resolve conflicts more satisfactorily and staying together longer (Cookerly, 1980; Gurman, Kniskern, & Pinsof, 1986; Hazelrigg, Cooper, & Borduin, 1987). It seems to work better for younger couples and for those who have not begun divorce proceedings. In any event, this kind of therapy proves more effective in solving marital problems than does individual therapy undertaken with only one spouse.

Couples therapy can also be of help as a treatment for ostensibly "individual" problems, including depression, substance abuse, and obesity (e.g., Black, Gleser, & Kooyers, 1990; Jacobson, Holtzworth-Munroe, & Schmaling, 1989; O'Farrell, 1989). Although each of these problems has numerous determinants, among the important influences may be interpersonal processes that couples therapy can address.

Family therapy   As already mentioned, the "client" in family therapy is the family as a whole. The therapist attempts to establish a healthy equilibrium within the family, one without psychological casualties. Studies show that this kind of therapy is effective for reducing conflicts and resolving specific problems such as bulimia (Cox & Merkel, 1989). It sometimes exceeds individual therapy in effectiveness (DeWitt, 1978). As an adjunct to individual treatment of problems like substance abuse, bipolar disorder, and schizophrenia, family therapy also has proven to be of value (e.g., Kaufman, 1985; Lam, 1991; Miklowitz & Goldstein, 1990; Schooler, 1986; Steinglass, 1987; Tarrier & Barrowclough, 1990). This kind of therapy

can also help individuals and their families adjust to life-threatening and chronic physical illnesses, such as cancer, AIDS, or Alzheimer's disease (Sholevar & Perkel, 1990).

SOCIOCULTURAL MODEL

One more perspective on abnormality should be introduced, the **sociocultural model,** which emphasizes the larger societal context in which abnormality occurs (Triandis & Draguns, 1980). Like the other models, this one has a vision of human nature. People are seen as members of a particular society and participants in a given culture. Within their group, they play certain roles prescribed by norms.

PSYCHOPATHOLOGY

Problems, from this perspective, are produced by social conditions and shaped by culture. Poverty, crime, lack of education, unemployment, and discrimination may combine to deny people the skills and abilities to meet the demands that society places on them. Some people may find themselves at odds with a society's dominant culture. Psychological abnormality reflects the strain felt by these individuals, and it is a mistake, according to the sociocultural model, to regard these as simply "individual" problems. As with the family systems perspective, people are often influenced by factors outside themselves, such as stressful life events (Dohrenwend & Dohrenwend, 1974, 1981).

Most modern societies are stratified, which means that the different roles people play are arranged in a hierarchy of status and power. In the contemporary United States, we refer to these levels of stratification as *socioeconomic classes.* We casually think of socioeconomic status (SES) as simply how much money a person makes, but it has a "richer" meaning. Indeed, when researchers calculate SES, income may not enter into the formula at all (Hollingshead & Redlich, 1958). Instead, SES reflects the degree to which a person has advanced education and a high-status job. Education and occupation are of course correlated with salaries, but the point is that members of the various social classes differ not just in terms of income but also in terms of their lifestyles, the opportunities and expectations they have, and the specific norms to which they adhere.

A number of studies have compared the relative likelihood of problems across socioeconomic classes (e.g., Liem & Liem, 1978). In the United States, schizophrenia is more common among those in the lower class than those in the middle and upper classes (Chapter 12). The eating disorders of anorexia and bulimia, on the other hand, are more common among those in the middle and upper classes than those in the lower class (Chapter 14). Sociocultural theorists interpret such differences in terms of the contrasting experiences of people in different social classes (e.g., Kessler, 1979).

Another key idea of the sociocultural approach is **social support.** People differ in the supportiveness of their relationships with others (Cohen & Syme, 1985). This variation reflects not only skills that they possess in garnering such support but also their social circumstances. In times of societal upheaval and transition, social support is apt to be lean. At any rate, social support helps people cope with stress and misfortune. Those with numerous and/or solid friendships do better in life. Brown and Harris (1978), for example, found that having a close confidant worked against the development of depression among women in trying circumstances.

A final emphasis of this approach to abnormality is that socially prescribed roles, along with associated attitudes and values, may contribute to psychopathology. As I discuss in Chapter 7, women are more likely than men to experience fear and anxiety disorders. Perhaps the traditionally "feminine" role and its demand that women be passive and unassertive is a risk factor for such disorders. Similarly, the fact that men in our society are more likely than women to suffer cardiac problems may be caused in part by the traditionally "masculine" role that demands men to be stoic and unexpressive (Chapter 10).

INTERVENTION

Treatment from a sociocultural perspective stresses the need to appreciate the particular social roles played by an individual. In the United States, clients and

Childhood losses may leave a person vulnerable to depression as an adult (Chapter 9). However, social support may buffer individuals against the negative effects of stressful events.

therapists with some frequency find themselves to be of different genders, ethnic groups, and socioeconomic classes. If nothing else, mismatching of client and therapist can result in early termination of therapy, before much improvement has occurred (Beutler, Crago, & Arizmendi, 1986). More profoundly, mismatching can result in a deep misunderstanding of the client's problems on the one hand and the therapist's treatment strategy on the other.

Cultural diversity   In recent years, clinical psychologists have become increasingly sensitive to the need to acknowledge the diversity of the cultural groups to which their clients belong (Jenkins & Hunter, 1983). The therapist possesses his or her own ethnicity and of course cannot change it in accordance with that of a given client. Nonetheless, increased awareness of what is typical and valued within various social groups is a critical starting point for all treatment (see Lopez et al., 1989).

At the same time, a little knowledge about a certain culture can be dangerous if the therapist fails to take into account the individual differences that invariably exist within any group. Sue and Zane (1987) described the following example:

> [*We attended*] *a case conference ... concerning a Chinese-American client. The person presenting the case contrasted Chinese and American cultures and proceeded to apply the contrast to the client in a literal and stereotypic fashion, despite the fact that the client was a fourth-generation American. (p. 38)*

The more general point is that treatment needs to proceed by understanding the identity of the *specific* client and how this client sees matters. This may often be influenced by the individual's ethnicity, but any use of such information must be tailored to the client when treatment goals and strategies are devised (Lopez et al., 1989; Sue & Zane, 1987). Therapy, even from a sociocultural perspective, is not simply applied anthropology.

Betancourt and Lopez (1993) elaborated this idea in their critique of how psychologists have typically studied culture, ethnicity, and race. Often these social contrasts are treated as sufficient explanations in their own right, as in research that shows behavioral differences between citizens of different nations or members of different ethnic groups without attempting to specify the psychological mechanisms responsible for such differences.

Group therapy   Another important implication of the sociocultural model is that many problems can be effectively treated in the context of an interacting social group. In **group therapy,** members of a therapeutic group are typically strangers united by the fact that they share a similar problem, such as schizophrenia, or a similar challenge, such as a recent divorce or bereavement. Group therapy is typically less expensive than individual therapy, and participants benefit from learning that they are not alone in having problems.

I was once asked by a local police department to lead a group for experienced officers on stress and coping. Eight middle-aged male police officers attended weekly meetings over a 2-month period. I presented information on stress and coping, so in one way our meetings constituted an informational workshop. But by far the most beneficial part of the meetings was group discussions in which the officers listened to each other speak about the frustrations of their work. Each talked about being cursed by children and teenagers, insulted by automobile drivers, and distrusted by the people they were trying to help. Each officer admitted that he was afraid of being disabled or killed on the job. Who would take care of his family? And each expressed worries about growing older and becoming less alert and effective.

Even though these men had worked together for years and in many ways knew each other quite well, the thoughts and feelings each expressed came as revelations to the others, not because they were surprising but because they were so personally familiar. "I thought I was the only one . . ." was the invariant response, so frequently voiced that it became the slogan for our group. The only active role I ever took in these discussions was to deflect mere complaining and focus instead on how given incidents might best be handled. I never offered a solution but instead asked the group members to share effective approaches from their own experiences.

There are a variety of approaches to group therapy, depending on its particular purpose (Yalom, 1970, 1975, 1985). These can range from instilling hope and building camaraderie, to encouraging active problem solving, to creating social bonds, to raising consciousness. The group leader accomplishes one or more of these objectives by leading the discussion in such a way that they are achieved. Comments on the *group process* (patterns and styles of communication) may be more important than comments on the actual content of a discussion. "How does everyone feel when Neil is so hostile about political topics?" Presumably, the group members gain insight into how they relate to one another, the goal being to take this insight from the group session into everyday life.

The varied purposes of group therapy make it difficult to evaluate its overall effectiveness. However, if we simply look at the ability of group treatment to resolve interpersonal problems, it appears to be successful in a variety of spheres, often more so than individual therapy (Kaul & Bednar, 1986; Stravynski & Shahar, 1983). Adolescents might be best helped by groups, children least (Tillitski, 1990). Again, we have a reminder of the importance of locating individuals in their developmental contexts before we can understand their problems and know how to help them (Chapter 14).

Changing social conditions   Perhaps the most important contribution of the sociocultural perspective to intervention lies in prevention, which I discuss in detail in the final section of this chapter. The rationale is clear about how problems can be prevented in the first place: Change the social conditions that make certain difficulties more likely. Once the risk factors are known, the mechanism leading from these to actual disorders can be dislodged.

Zigler, Taussig, and Black (1992) surveyed research showing that early childhood intervention programs, intended to prevent school failure, pay the added dividend years later of reducing delinquency and related problems. Why? They suggested that these intervention programs target risk factors in a variety of domains—physical, intellectual, and interpersonal. Small changes in these different areas mutually strengthen one another and eventually "snowball" into large changes.

Relevant to the sociocultural perspective is the field of **community psychology,** which attempts to prevent problems by applying psychological knowledge in community settings (Munoz, Snowden, & Kelly, 1979). It differs from traditional psychotherapy because its interventions are preventive in nature and are usually deployed outside the clinic or hospital—in schools, work sites, churches and temples, voluntary associations, or government agencies (Shinn, 1987). Community psychology is covered in more detail in Chapter 15.

CONTEMPORARY EXPLANATIONS OF ABNORMALITY

I have discussed six perspectives on abnormality in terms of the models that embody them. Psychologists have long hoped for one approach that would answer all the questions we might pose about each and every disorder. This hope has not been realized for any of the existing models. As you will see in subsequent chapters, each model has what Kelly (1955) terms a *focus of convenience,* a domain of the world (in this case abnormality) where it works particularly well. Each model also encounters aspects of abnormality where it falls short. Hence, there is no "best" model of abnormality.

Indeed, it may be impossible to evaluate any of these models as a whole, much less to compare them across-the-board. The task of the theorist and the practitioner is to identify those purposes for which a given model is best suited. For a given disorder, which model best accounts for its risk factors and mechanisms? And again for a given disorder, which model generates the most demonstrably effective treatments?

MIDRANGE THEORIES

A common explanatory strategy narrows the intended focus of a theory to one type of disorder or even just one aspect of a disorder. What results are **midrange theories,** explanations that do not claim to be generally applicable, but rather apply—let us say—only to obsessive-compulsive disorder, or to a particular subtype of schizophrenia, or to a particular class of depressive symptoms. Midrange theories usually stem from one of the popular models of abnormality. Despite the failure of the biomedical approach to explain all forms of abnormality, it nonetheless does well for some disorders. The psychodynamic model is called on to explain other disorders; the cognitive-behavioral for still others; and so forth.

The growing popularity of midrange theories means that the psychology of abnormality has become a much more complicated endeavor—theoretically—than it used to be. In the era of great schools, a psychologist could simply choose a model that seemed sensible and apply its general formula to any and all instances of abnormality. Now a psychologist must be conversant with several models, their relative strengths and weaknesses.

THE SEARCH FOR INTEGRATED MODELS

The existence of midrange theories inevitably creates the need to make sense of all these circumscribed accounts. We call this a search for *integrated models,* points of view that identify what is useful about each of the traditional models and then combine this information into a single perspective. A number of theorists have called for an integrated model—but most attempts have been abstract, circular assertions that previous models all have something true to say, so we must somehow use them all. The real task is making this vision concrete. As noted earlier, models sometimes contradict each other with respect to their basic assumptions, which means that we cannot simply stir them all together and expect a useful result.

George Engel (1980) urged the mental health professions to adopt what he calls a **biopsychosocial model,** a perspective that acknowledges the role played by biological, psychological, and social factors. Attempts to apply this perspective to particular problems have often been little more than successive comments using the language of different models (e.g., Vasile et al., 1987). A true integration of biological, psychological, and social factors is just now beginning to occur, as you will see in subsequent chapters.

The current approach that most successfully integrates different perspectives is the **diathesis-stress model,** perhaps familiar to you because it is used to explain physical illnesses such as cancer (Chapter 10). By this view, problems result from a preexisting vulnerability of the person (the *diathesis*) coupled with an environmental event (the *stress*). Neither the diathesis alone nor the stress alone is sufficient for the problem to occur; it is their combination that produces difficulties (Monroe & Simons, 1991). For cancer, a genetic predisposition to develop tumors may exist for some people yet only manifest itself when carcinogens are present.

Applied to psychological abnormality, the diathesis-stress model is best supported for problems such as schizophrenia (Chapter 12) and bipolar disorder (Chapter 9), in which a genetic basis of these problems (i.e., the diathesis) is arguably present. There is nothing in the model that requires the diathesis to be biological; it could also be psychological. Ways of thinking encouraged early in life might create no problems for individuals until they experience a loss later in life (Peterson & Seligman, 1984). As I review different disorders in subsequent chapters, you will encounter a number of psychological difficulties for which a diathesis-stress conception proves useful.

PREVENTION

Prevention—as opposed to treatment—seems a more efficient way for the mental health professions to proceed, saving time and money, and of course avoiding human anguish (Albee, 1982). All of the problems I discuss in this book affect not only those who warrant diagnoses but also their friends, families, and the larger society. At the same time, there are barriers to mounting effective campaigns to prevent psychological abnormality. A simple way to prevent a problem is to reduce or neutralize a known cause identified by one of the popular models of abnormality. General paresis, discussed in Chapter 1, was a leading cause of psychiatric hospitalizations before its cause was identified (syphilis), and ways to neutralize it were devised and deployed (e.g., antibiotics). As a result, the number of cases of general paresis decreased dramatically.

But not all problems fit this formula. Often we do not have a good understanding of what the relevant causes might be, as in Alzheimer's disease, transsexualism, infantile autism, and anorexia nervosa, or we have learned that there are numerous causes that combine, as in anxiety disorders, depression, and schizophrenia. If a cause is unknown, it cannot be undone. When there are numerous causes, a campaign to target them all is likely to be diffuse, particularly because our state of knowledge usually does not allow us to say which is the most important, and which the least.

PRIMARY PREVENTION

Sometimes distinctions are made among types of prevention that intervene at different stages in the development of a problem. In **primary prevention,** the goal is to eliminate the basic causes of problems. As just noted, not all problems have single causes. Nonetheless, there are enough problems of this sort that we need not abandon the goal of primary prevention. In 1962, the American Public Health Association identified several types of psychological disturbance that can be readily prevented because each involves a known biological etiology: poisoning, infections, genetic diseases, nutritional deficiencies, physical or bodily injuries, and systemic disorders. We can also identify as preventable, at least in principle, problems that begin with behavior, such as substance abuse and those mind-body disorders to which lifestyle contributes.

We have seen a number of educational campaigns that provide information about the causes of such problems, in the hope that people will take steps to avoid them. In the United States, there is a great deal of information available about the hazards of alcohol use and the ways in which AIDS is transmitted.

Mental health education is an attempt to do exactly what its name implies: make available to the general public basic information about psychological problems—their causes, treatments, and preventions. It is not to be confused with clinical services (i.e., it is not therapy) but rather is informational and educational in nature. People are alerted to the psychological difficulties that can accompany certain life stages and crises. They are taught to recognize the warning signs of impending problems. They are informed about available clinical services and what realistically to expect from them. Programs in some of our schools try to impart information about social skills, for example, or how to raise children.

Shure and Spivack (1988) devised a program that is effective in reducing psychological disorders among youths. The premise of their program is that one of the *reasons children develop problematic ways of acting and feeling is that they do not know how to solve the interpersonal problems that arise in the course of life. They do not readily think of alternative solutions, and they do not foresee the consequences of their actions. In their program of* interpersonal cognitive problem solving, *Shure and Spivack spent 4 months teaching preschool children how to generate alternative solutions to problems and then how to evaluate them in terms of their likely results. Children were presented with scenarios and asked to create as many solutions to them as possible. Research showed that these lessons generalized outside the program and paid benefits years later.*

Do mental health education and other strategies of primary prevention work? This is too broad a question for a simple answer. Studies of messages about smoking, nutrition, safer sex, and the like have an effect on people's attitudes. Going from attitudes to behaviors, however, is not automatic. Some people are

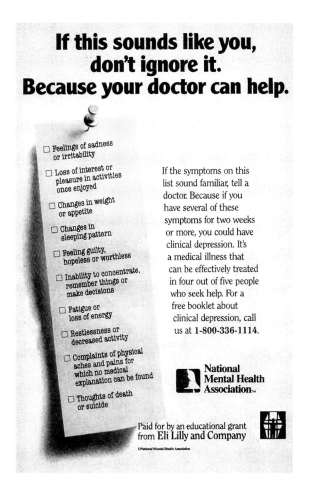

By providing basic information about psychological disorders to the general public, mental health education is a good example of primary prevention.

influenced by messages, whereas others are not. Future work must determine who is moved, and how to target messages accordingly. We know that information per se is not sufficient to resolve most psychological problems. Despite demonstrable reductions, many people still smoke, drink, and engage in unsafe sexual practices. On the other hand, we need not eradicate a problem entirely in order for prevention attempts to be worthwhile. Even if the prevalence of a disorder were to be reduced only a fraction, it would represent a considerable savings when we consider the sheer number of people involved.

SECONDARY PREVENTION

In **secondary prevention,** the goal is to control problems before they become more serious. This is sometimes referred to as **containment.** Typically, a group of individuals at high risk for a given problem is identified, and then steps are undertaken to help them. In Chapter 14, I discuss Operation Head Start, which fits this definition because it targets children who, by virtue of living in poverty, are at increased risk for academic and intellectual difficulties once they begin school. Another example, to be encountered in Chapter 9, is a suicide hotline, which makes available a resource for people contemplating suicide.

Secondary prevention is often guided by *crisis theory,* a perspective dating to an influential paper written by Lindemann (1944) that provided the rudiments of **crisis intervention,** a strategy for containing problems that follow in the wake of life crises.

Lindemann was a psychiatrist called on to provide services to the survivors of the 1942 Cocoanut Grove fire in Boston that left 493 individuals dead. Because of the emergency situation, only the briefest intervention was possible. Lindemann noted considerable uniformity in the initial response to the crisis: somatic symptoms, characterized by anxiety, that were rekindled by reminders of the crisis. People experienced ongoing events as unreal and felt guilt about surviving. Their social relationships suffered, and they became preoccupied with the losses associated with the fire. Gradually the survivors returned to their normal level of functioning. Lindemann believed that those who took the longest were those who did not express the intense emotions that they were experiencing. He felt that his efforts should be directed at helping people express their grief. What followed was a series of brief therapy sessions focusing on the expression of grief.

Lindemann's ideas have since been elaborated into crisis intervention (e.g., Baldwin, 1979). The goal, of

Crisis theory was developed from the attempt to help survivors of the famous Cocoanut Grove fire in Boston in 1942.

course, is to prevent a crisis from triggering chronic problems. Psychologists nowadays routinely offer their assistance to victims of natural disasters such as hurricanes and earthquakes (see Allen, 1992). They offer their assistance to victims of crime, or illness, or unemployment. What marks crisis theory is a focus on the immediate problems associated with loss, as opposed to an emphasis on the history of problems. Intervention is time-limited. The individual is given concrete assistance. His or her life resources are identified, and the person is encouraged to use them.

It can be difficult to evaluate this sort of intervention (Stein & Lambert, 1984). People who avail themselves of crisis services are not always the ones who most need them. There is also considerable worry about the staffing of these centers. Many people are unpaid volunteers, and they may lack information or skills needed to help (Bleach & Claiborn, 1974).

Yet another example of secondary prevention is the recent movement toward *self-help groups* for people facing life challenges (Rootes & Aanes, 1992; Schubert & Borkman, 1991). Unlike the therapeutic groups already discussed, these do not consist of an "expert" therapist coordinating group activities. Rather, self-help groups are conducted by peers, those confronting the same issues. They provide information and support. They sometimes organize for political action (Emerick, 1991; Hatfield, 1991). Their goal is to empower members so that they can cope without relying on traditional mental health services.

Self-help groups are available for those with medical problems as well as psychological conditions. Alcoholics Anonymous is one of the best-known examples (Chapter 5). Other self-help groups are available for parents, children, and siblings of those with difficulties. Frequently encountered are groups for people who must care for others, such as those with Alzheimer's disease, terminal cancer, or AIDS (Monahan, Greene, & Coleman, 1992). In many communities, teenage mothers have support groups, as do students, adoptive parents, children from divorced families, the homeless, and victims of accidents and injuries. Professionals, including psychotherapists, may also join self-help groups. There are even self-help groups for those who have had troubling experiences with the traditional mental health system.

TERTIARY PREVENTION

In **tertiary prevention,** the goal is to prevent relapse. Many people with problems can be helped, but at the same time, many of them are likely to develop the problem again. If the frequency of recurrence can be reduced, then we have in effect reduced the overall prevalence of a problem. Tertiary prevention provides services to individuals following formal treatment. Such *aftercare* assumes various forms, from merely maintaining contact with a therapist to participating in formal programs.

Halfway houses are places where patients live during their transition from the hospital to a completely independent life outside the mental health system. Research suggests that people who participate in these halfway houses may do better than those who do not (e.g., Paul & Lentz, 1977). However, they differ in their success (Brown, 1980). If a halfway house is simply a place to warehouse former patients, then it is not useful.

One of the most successful examples of tertiary prevention is the Lodge, established by George Fairweather as an aftercare facility for recently discharged schizophrenic patients (Fairweather, Sanders, Cressler, & Maynard, 1969). Former patients lived at the Lodge, where they assumed responsibility for running the household and seeking outside employment. Follow-up studies over several years compared these residents to patients given more routine aftercare options following discharge (Fairweather, 1979). Residents were more likely to remain free from hospitalization and much more likely to have found employment. This kind of aftercare seems an important addition to the way schizophrenia is usually treated (Chapter 12).

Tertiary care also takes as one of its goals the reduction of the stigma associated with being under mental health care. In this way, it starts to make contact with mental health education. Attempts are made to humanize mental patients, to reduce the discrepancy between them and us, to applaud people who have sought out help rather than fear and ridicule them.

The psychology of abnormality is part of general psychology, and so theories are of obvious importance. My discussion of theories has revealed considerable variety in the perspectives psychologists bring to bear on abnormality. Theories are informed by research, and in the next chapter, I cover research methods.

Summary

MODELS OF ABNORMALITY

✦ Psychological theories of abnormality must address questions about risk factors and mechanisms.

Theorists concerned with abnormality rely on scientific models: deliberately simplified accounts of human nature, problems, and treatment. Various models of abnormality have been and still are popular.

TREATMENT

✦ Various professions treat people with psychological problems. Clinical psychologists bring a psychological perspective to their work, and psychiatrists bring a medical perspective. Treatments can be roughly classified into biomedical therapies, which intervene biologically, and psychotherapies, which intervene psychologically. There is no such thing as generic treatment: all therapy is undertaken from a specific theoretical position.

BIOMEDICAL MODEL

✦ The biomedical model assumes that people are physical systems. Problems result from bodily injury, illness, or defect. Treatment consists of biological interventions such as drugs or surgery.

PSYCHOANALYTIC MODEL

✦ The psychoanalytic model assumes that people are energy systems. People have problems to the degree that their energy is tied up in unproductive defenses and symptoms. Psychoanalytic therapy aims at freeing energy by bringing motives and conflicts into awareness.

COGNITIVE-BEHAVIORAL MODEL

✦ The cognitive-behavioral model views people as information-processing systems, attempting to predict and understand events in the world in order to maximize pleasure and minimize pain. Proponents of this model see people's problems as learned and treatment as akin to education.

HUMANISTIC-EXISTENTIAL-PHENOMENOLOGICAL MODELS

✦ Humanistic, existential, and phenomenological approaches take issue with scientific psychology's goal of specifying the causes of people's problems. Instead, they emphasize the individual's conscious experience, ability to make free choices, and tendency to actualize an inner potential.

FAMILY SYSTEMS MODEL

✦ The family systems model assumes that individuals are inherently social, and that their problems are manifestations of disturbances within the family. Therapy from this perspective aims at establishing healthier patterns of family interaction.

SOCIOCULTURAL MODEL

✦ The sociocultural model looks at people in terms of their larger society and culture. Problems result from stressful life events, lack of social support, and socially prescribed roles. Therapy stresses the need to understand the cultural diversity of clients. Treatment in the context of interacting social groups may be undertaken, as well as attempts to undo the social conditions that produce problems in the first place.

CONTEMPORARY EXPLANATIONS OF ABNORMALITY

✦ No model answers all the questions we wish to pose about abnormality. One response to this realization is to propose midrange theories—explanations that do not attempt to be broadly applicable.

✦ Another response to the failure of individual models of abnormality is to search for perspectives that integrate insights of the traditional theories. An example is the diathesis-stress model, which explains abnormality in terms of preexisting states of the individual coupled with environmental events.

PREVENTION

✦ Prevention of psychological problems is obviously preferable to treatment of problems once they develop. Nonetheless, there are barriers to effective prevention, not least of which is knowing just how to go about it.

✦ Different strategies of prevention have achieved some success. In primary prevention, the goal is to eliminate the basic causes of problems. In secondary prevention, the goal is to control problems before they become more serious. In tertiary prevention, the goal is to prevent the recurrence of problems.

Key Terms

analysand

behavior therapy

biomedical model

biomedical therapy

biopsychosocial model

classical conditioning

client

client-centered therapy

clinical psychologist

cognitive-behavior
 therapy

cognitive-behavioral
 model

cognitive therapy

community psychology

couples therapy; marital
 therapy

crisis intervention

defense mechanism

diathesis-stress model

eclectic therapist

ego

ego psychologists

existentialism

family systems model

family therapy

feminist therapy

fixation

gestalt therapy

group therapy

heritability

humanism

id

identified patient

incidence

insight

mechanism

midrange theory

modeling

neo-Freudians

neurotransmitter

object relations

operant conditioning

overdetermined behavior

paradoxical intervention

patient

phenomenology

prevalence

primary prevention

psychiatrist

psychoanalyst

psychoanalytic model

psychodynamic theories

psychosexual stages

psychotherapy

reciprocal determinism

reframing intervention

risk factor

schema

scientific model

secondary prevention;
 containment

self-actualization

social support

sociocultural model

superego

tertiary prevention

unconscious

Research

4 In Chapter 3, I discussed the questions that psychologists interested in abnormality want to answer, and the general perspectives they bring to bear on them. In this chapter, I discuss how psychologists evaluate theories. The chapter concludes with a discussion of how researchers have investigated the effectiveness of psychotherapy.

METHODS

What makes the psychology of abnormality scientific is the attempt to test theories against evidence. This

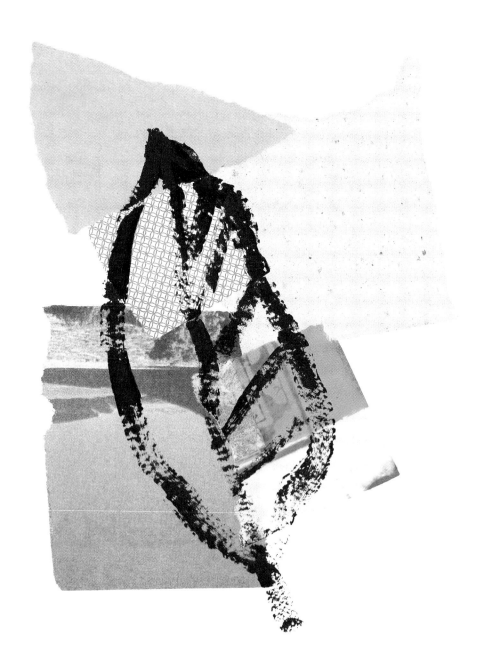

is always done in the concrete, by exerting control over the specific conditions of observation. This is the essence of the *scientific method*. Researchers often derive a specific hypothesis or question from a more general theoretical notion, then devise and carry out a specific study that tests this hypothesis, and finally evaluate the hypothesis in light of the evidence—and revise the theory if necessary.

Researchers use a great variety of procedures, such as case studies, correlational investigations, and experiments. None is best for all purposes. Rather, researchers choose a specific strategy in accordance with the specific hypothesis they wish to evaluate. It should be stressed that the entire psychology of abnormality is based on information provided by these research methods. Any conclusions about the causes of disorders and their possible remedies are only as valid as the underlying research.

GENERAL CONCERNS OF RESEARCHERS

I first cover topics that concern all researchers, then move to a discussion of some of the particular research methods commonly favored by those who investigate abnormality.

Sampling   Regardless of the general strategy that a researcher uses, he or she must first decide who is to be studied. There are billions of people on the planet, and any given investigation can include but a minuscule proportion of them. Researchers use the term **population** to describe the larger group of people to which the conclusions of a given study are intended to apply: middle-aged adults, children, those with severe depression, and so on. In contrast, the term **sample** refers to the actual individuals included in a given study: 54 volunteers from an office building in Fort Worth, 17 sixth graders from the local middle school, 32 individuals prescribed antidepressants at the Philadelphia Veterans Administration Medical Center, and so on.

In an ideal investigation, the sample is representative of the larger population of interest, resembling it in essential ways. The more representative, the more likely conclusions are to be generally applicable. The best way to achieve a representative sample is to ensure that every individual in the population of interest has an equal chance of being included in the study that is conducted. In other words, a sample should be randomly chosen from the population of concern. Random sampling almost always guarantees representativeness, even if the sample is small in size compared to the population.

The closest we get to random sampling in any sort of research are political polls and consumer surveys that start with the entire population of a state or nation and then try to select potential respondents at random. The well known Gallup Poll is highly accurate in forecasting the outcome of presidential elections, even though it usually samples only about 1,500 individuals per poll (Gallup, 1972). The accuracy derives from the success of its random sampling.

Investigations of psychological abnormality typically fall far short of the standard of representativeness set by the Gallup Poll. Individual researchers rarely have the resources (i.e., time and money) to choose a truly random sample. This becomes a particular problem when the goal of a study is to estimate the prevalence of given disorders among people in general. Such *epidemiological studies* are only as useful as their initial sample. Throughout the text, whenever I mention prevalence figures, I am relying on such epidemiological information.

How are these studies conducted? One strategy is simply to enumerate those who enter the mental health system for treatment and then to calculate the proportion of the population that they represent. You know from Chapter 1 that this is not an ideal approach because many people with problems do not seek treatment. Another strategy is to start with a circumscribed geographical area and then try to obtain a representative sample from among those within this region. This becomes questionable in light of the likely possibility that given problems are not distributed evenly across different regions. And even if they were, bias may be introduced by the way the sample is chosen. Epidemiological researchers usually sample randomly available telephone numbers and/or addresses, but not everyone may answer the phone, read the mail, or answer a knock on the door.

More profoundly, not everyone has a phone, a mailbox, or a permanent address. We need only think of the well documented problems encountered by the 1990 United States Census in simply counting how many people live in this country. The census takers had more resources, publicity, and credibility than any epidemiological researcher will ever have, yet the widespread suspicion is that their resulting count was off by literally millions of individuals. When we look at prevalence estimates from epidemiological studies, we must be similarly skeptical about their accuracy.

In Chapter 1, I mentioned a recent survey of American adults that estimated the prevalence of different psychological disorders and the utilization of mental health services (Kessler et al., 1994). This study is virtually unique in the psychopathology literature because it attempted to study a random sample of all American adults. But even this notable survey is flawed with respect to representativeness. The researchers interviewed individ-

uals on the telephone, but not everyone has a phone or is willing or able to talk on it. Those with unlisted numbers escaped the sample, and the homeless were obviously not included. Neither were those hospitalized because of psychological or medical problems, those in prison, or those serving in the armed forces. The researchers who conducted this survey tried to take these limitations into account by adjusting their estimates based on other information available about such excluded groups, but the point remains that it is all but impossible to obtain a completely representative sample.

The more typical practice in psychopathology research is the use of *convenience samples,* research participants who are studied simply because they are available to the researcher. These are often composed of individuals chosen because they are in treatment for a given disorder at a clinic or hospital to which the researcher has access. The hope is that a convenience sample is also a representative one, but we should always be skeptical. We know that many people with bona fide disorders are *not* in treatment. We also know that given clinics or hospitals have particular biases about who is admitted and treated.

With Robert Silverman, I conducted a study comparing depressed patients and schizophrenic patients with respect to certain cognitive characteristics (Silverman & Peterson, 1993). We were working in New York, but even in this huge city, it proved impossible for us to obtain sufficient numbers of research participants of both types at the same hospital. We found depressed individuals mostly at private hospitals, which required insurance reimbursement. We found schizophrenic individuals mostly at city and state hospitals, which did not have such a requirement. The bias here was the result of the economic realities associated with these two disorders. Depressed patients tend to have a more steady work history than schizophrenic patients, and thus they are more likely to have employer-provided health insurance. I believe our study had certain methodological virtues, but representative sampling was not among them.

In this book, I mention hundreds of studies. Space does not permit much detail about the particular samples used. The generic criticism of these studies—expressed here quite forcefully—is that the generality of their conclusions to larger populations remains an open question. Although psychologists have become increasingly aware of the possibility that problems differ importantly across gender, age, ethnicity, culture, and socioeconomic status, researchers to date have rarely explored these differences systematically.

Statistical significance   Aside from the issue of representativeness, researchers are also concerned with the question of how well their conclusions apply to the samples they actually studied. Investigations usually include a number of individuals. Characteristics of interest are ascertained, and the researchers then summarize these characteristics, often by calculating mean (or average) scores for given groups. These mean scores may then be compared to one another.

You will read in a later chapter that depressed people are more likely than nondepressed people to harbor thoughts of suicide. This is a good generalization, but appreciate that it does not apply to each and every individual. Some proportion of those who are depressed are not suicidal. Some proportion of those who are suicidal are not depressed. Any generalization that is offered about psychopathology has important exceptions. The intent of the researcher in offering general conclusions is simply to describe an overall pattern of results.

Patterns differ in their consistency, and researchers have the most confidence when speaking about those that are highly consistent. A typical way of judging the consistency of summarized research results is by using *inferential statistics*. These are techniques that allow an investigator to estimate how likely it is that given findings did not result from chance. No one would want to base a conclusion about the causes or treatments of disorders on patterns of data that reflect random fluctuations. Regardless of the particular inferential statistic calculated, a common rule of thumb is that results have **statistical significance**—that is, are not apt to be due to chance—if there is no more than one possibility out of twenty that this could have happened by chance granted the variability in the sample of the characteristics of concern. Most of the conclusions cited in this book are based on the results of studies that satisfy this criterion of statistical significance. Let me repeat the important point here: Statistically significant results are not invariant rules, just decent generalizations.

Along these lines, given research results may be statistically significant without being of much practical importance because their patterns are weak. The likelihood of statistically significant results increases as the sample size increases. A relatively large sample may yield statistically significant results that nonetheless are of trivial magnitude (i.e., they are not very useful in understanding or treating disorders).

For example, left-handed people are more likely than right-handed people to be given the diagnosis of schizophrenia. Among individuals with schizophrenia, approximately 20% are left-handed versus 10% to 12% of those in the general population (e.g., Green, Satz,

Smith, & Nelson, 1989; Nelson, Satz, Green, & Cicchetti, 1993). This is a relatively weak trend based on large sample studies. The result is intriguing on theoretical grounds (Chapter 6), although left-handedness is unlikely to ever be more than a tiny ingredient in any etiological theory of schizophrenia. We would not want to regard left-handedness as an informative risk factor for this disorder. Nor would we want to regard it as a diagnostic test or criterion. The exceptions are far too numerous.

Researchers therefore might calculate an additional statistic that estimates the so-called *magnitude* of research results (how robust or strong the patterns are). Later in the chapter, when I discuss investigations of psychotherapy effectiveness, I talk about the magnitude of the relevant research results. As you will see, the effectiveness of therapy is of sufficient magnitude to be taken seriously.

To summarize, researchers want to know that the conclusions they offer are reasonable descriptions of the samples they have studied. Inferential statistics are used to bolster conclusions, but even the best descriptions of results remain summaries, not guarantees. When describing research results in this book, I often use probabilistic qualifications (e.g., people with this disorder *tend* to think, feel, or act in these ways; they are *likely* to be helped by this treatment; their prognosis is *apt* to be good or bad). Do not interpret these qualifications as due to a lack of information. Instead, they reflect the nature of psychological abnormality and our ability to offer conclusions about it. Indeed, I should use such qualifications in all of my statements, but I trust you can provide them even when they are not explicit.

A related point concerns my use of specific examples of disorders and treatments. I provide a number of examples in the book because they are interesting and informative. However, do not regard any of them as an invariant rule concerning the topic being discussed. If I describe a depressed male, do not conclude that only males experience depression. If I describe a successful treatment using systematic desensitization, do not conclude that this procedure works all the time. Examples are simply examples.

Operational definitions   In order to do research, a psychologist must define and measure the concepts of concern. Suppose a researcher is interested in depression. A decision must then be made about how to identify its presence. A concrete measure of an abstract concept is called an **operational definition,** which specifies exactly how a researcher goes about the process of measurement (Chapter 1). An operational definition of depression might be the number of symptoms that a research participant reports she experiences "frequently" when asked about them on a questionnaire or in an interview.

Despite being explicit, no operational definition is foolproof. We can always raise the question of whether a specific measure operationalizes the intended concept, or whether it reflects some irrelevant factor. Measures that indeed capture the intended concepts possess **validity.** Those that yield the same results on different occasions have **reliability.**

Over the years, psychologists have used a variety of measures to operationalize abnormality. Some are not particularly rigorous, such as identifying "abnormal" research participants solely on the basis of responses to a self-report questionnaire. The risk with this approach is that the associated reliability and validity might be quite low. Single measures of any psychological construct are suspect (Campbell & Fiske, 1959), and in recent years researchers have become more careful about choosing their operationalizations.

One simple procedure now popular with researchers who use questionnaire measures of abnormality is to administer them at two different points in time. A research participant must have an extreme score on both occasions before she is deemed abnormal. That a person may score in the "anxious" range of a questionnaire one day but in the "nonanxious" range the following week underscores the wisdom of this approach.

Another procedure increasingly followed by researchers is the use of explicit **research diagnostic criteria**— assigning research participants to particular diagnostic categories only if they clearly exemplify schizophrenia, depression, or whatever. Recall from Chapter 2 that the criteria for research diagnoses proposed by Feighner and colleagues (1972) inspired DSM-III and its subsequent revisions. Research diag-

Researchers sometimes identify "abnormal" individuals on the basis of their responses to a self-report questionnaire. This operationalization may be suspect, and researchers often administer questionnaires on several occasions and/or supplement them with other procedures.

noses tend to be more strict than diagnoses given to patients in therapy because a researcher can throw out ambiguous cases whereas a therapist could not and would not want to do that. The point of explicit criteria is to be sure that conclusions about a given type of abnormality are based on relatively unambiguous instances.

Research design   So far I have discussed important elements in research studies. But an investigation is not simply a heap of research participants, measures, and statistical summaries. Rather, the elements of a study are assembled in a deliberate way to give the researcher the information that is of interest. The overall structure of a study and its elements is referred to as its **research design.** The obvious characteristics of a research design are what the study includes, but just as important are what it does not include. Only certain research participants are studied; others must be passed over. Only certain variables are measured; others must be excluded. Only some aspects of the results are summarized; others must be ignored.

A researcher's hypotheses, logic, common sense, and lessons from prior investigations dictate the details of a given research design. Will the study as structured answer the questions of interest while minimizing alternative explanations?

Suppose you conduct an investigation of people with an animal phobia, and you proceed by comparing them with "normal" individuals (those without a disorder of any kind). You find that people with a fear of cats or dogs are more likely than those without such fears to have parents who treated them inconsistently. You are tempted to conclude that inconsistent socialization during childhood puts a person at risk for animal phobias.

But stop and think about a more precise way of describing your findings. Keep in mind that you studied only two groups of people: those with animal phobias and those without phobias or any other problem. You may only have discovered that people treated inconsistently grow up to have problems, including animal phobias but not necessarily limited to them. Before you offer a specific conclusion about animal phobias, you had better study people with different problems as well.

This point is far from generally appreciated by researchers, who often fail to include in their studies individuals with a problem other than the one they wish to explain. The issue gets played out in a slightly different way when researchers look at the consequences of a particular disorder, which often includes one behavioral deficit or another. Suppose a researcher finds out that those with an eating disorder perform poorly at Task A. Does this mean that whatever specific skill Task A involves is an important characteristic of eating disorders? Maybe yes, maybe no. A researcher needs to include other tasks tapping different skills to see if deficits are specific or general.

Consider anorexia nervosa, *which puzzles everyday people and psychologists alike because food is the substance of life (Chapter 14). What would impel an individual not to eat? One possible answer points to a problem with how she perceives size and weight. Perhaps she literally sees these differently than others do. Researchers have tested this hypothesis in laboratory studies by comparing those with anorexia to "normal" individuals in the ability to judge bodily dimensions (e.g., Slade & Russell, 1973). Anorectics prove deficient when judging their own dimensions but not when judging those of others. Thus, the perceptual difficulties that characterize this disorder are* not *general deficits.*

The actual methods that psychologists use to study abnormality can be described in terms of three general strategies: case studies, correlational investigations, and experiments (see Table 4.1). Each strategy has its own inherent strengths and weaknesses, and a scientist's theoretical purpose of course influences his or her choice (see Focus on the Context of Psychopathology Research).

CASE STUDIES

I start with **case studies:** intensive investigations of a single individual. These have long been used to study abnormality. Freud considered case studies *the* preferred way of investigating psychoanalytic claims because they allowed access to the rich details about a person's life necessary for testing hypotheses.

Freud's case studies   What follow are thumbnail sketches of two of Freud's most famous case studies. Appreciate that the original reports are hundreds of pages long, filled with numerous details fleshing out the arguments that he wished to make.

A terrifying obsession brought a patient into therapy with Freud (1909b). The Rat Man had once been told of a torture that involved strapping a metal pot to the bare buttocks of a victim. In the pot was a hungry rat, who sooner or later would gnaw the victim ever so slowly to a horrible death. All of us are disturbed by this scenario, but we can eventually put it out of our minds. The Rat Man

was unable to do so. In fact, he elaborated the torture, imagining it being perpetrated on people he loved, specifically his fiancee and his father. He could not banish these thoughts from his consciousness, and thus experienced great difficulty in going about the business of life.

Other details in the case led Freud to the conclusion that the Rat Man felt ambivalence toward both his father and his fiancee, hating and loving them at the same time. The rat torture represented a frightful punishment, to be sure, but one with an erotic tinge. In Freud's formulation, then, the patient's obsession symbolized his underlying ambivalence.

Another of Freud's (1911) well known case studies did not involve a patient that he saw in therapy, but instead the author of a book that Freud read with great interest.

TABLE **4.1**

RESEARCH STRATEGIES *Each of the popular research strategies used by those who investigate abnormality has characteristic strengths and weaknesses.*

case study: intensive investigation of a single individual

strengths:	provides rich details about a person's life
	can demonstrate what is (or is not) possible
	may be the best way to investigate rare disorders
	may suggest hypotheses for study with other strategies
weaknesses:	may have problems with validity of information
	cannot establish what is generally true
	cannot establish casual links

correlational investigation: study of the relationship between two variables in a sample of research subjects

strengths:	allows generalization to other people
	allows study of topics impossible, unwieldy, and/or unethical to investigate with other strategies
weaknesses:	cannot establish casual links

experiment: investigation in which certain events are deliberately manipulated (independent variables) and the effects of these manipulations on other events (dependent variables) are measured

strengths:	can identify causal links
	allows efficient investigation of some topics
weaknesses:	may be artificial
	cannot be used to study some topics

FOCUS ON

The Context of

Psychopathology

Research

I HAVE STRESSED THAT PEOple's problems must be placed in their social and cultural context. So too must theories and research. Those who concern themselves with psychopathology are people necessarily shaped by their own specific environments. Historians of science refer to the influence of a given historical era as the **Zeitgeist,** literally "spirit of the times." The corresponding influence of a given culture is referred to as the **Ortgeist,** literally "spirit of the place." The prevailing Zeitgeist and Ortgeist dictate the topics of concern to a specific researcher, how he or she phrases questions and explanations concerning these topics, and the specific methods of investigation that are used.

I mentioned, for example, that Freud's work was influenced by then-prevailing ideas in physics. More generally, the fact that Freud lived in Victorian Europe, a time and place characterized by a pervasive denial of sexuality, drew his attention precisely to the importance of sexuality and the possible hazards of its repression (Gay, 1988). Most of his psychoanalytic patients were women, and women were more apt than men to encounter problems with the expression of their sexuality (Shorter, 1992).

As a practicing clinician, Freud was concerned with specific individuals and their problems, and his use of the case study approach readily followed. The less-than-objective nature of his case studies can be explained because in effect he was inventing this research approach as he went along (Peterson, 1992). Some historians have argued that Freud's theories and methods are culturally and historically bounded, that they provide a particularly good fit for his cultural era but not necessarily for other places and times (Ellenberger, 1970).

Along these lines, it is probably no coincidence that existential thinking became widespread in Europe around the time of World Wars I and II, which drew everyone's attention to basic questions about existence and the meaning of life. And consider that cognitive-behavioral approaches have flourished in the contemporary United States, where individual fulfillment and satisfaction are emphasized. Behavior therapy, after all, is a set of techniques that help people achieve the

bumper sticker slogan "Be Your Own Best Friend." These approaches appeal to the optimism inherent in the United States culture (Peterson, Maier, & Seligman, 1993).

One of behaviorist John Watson's best known declarations is the following:

> Give me a dozen healthy infants, well-formed, and my own specified world to bring them up in, and I'll guarantee to take any one at random and train him to become any type of specialist I might select—doctor, lawyer, artist, merchant-chief, and yes even beggar-man and thief, regardless of his talents, penchants, activities, vocations and race of his ancestors. (1930, p. 65)

If people are products of their environments, then so too are their problems and of course the solutions to these problems. Contrast this vision of the human condition with the pessimism inherent in many psychoanalytic theories.

Many cognitive-behavioral theorists have been academic psychologists with strong grounding in a research tradition that values experimentation. Accordingly, cognitive-behavioral theories are often investigated experimentally, and cognitive-behavioral researchers have been at the forefront of investigations of therapy effectiveness.

In the United States, recent years have seen a great interest in the biomedical approach to abnormality. You will see in subsequent chapters that many of the newest discoveries about psychopathology concern its biological underpinnings. Why the current interest? Whatever the biological bases of disorders might be, they have been there all along.

Cross-cultural studies may shed light on the ethnic strife that characterizes so many parts of the modern world. These individuals are mourning the death of a relative who was killed in a mortar attack in Sarajevo.

In recent years, the federal government has funded more biomedical research than sociocultural research. For example, although it seems clear that poverty like that which characterizes this South Bronx neighborhood takes a toll on psychological well-being, we do not know nearly enough about how this takes place and how the process can be reversed or prevented in the first place.

But the rise of conservatism during the 1980s influenced the way societal resources were used to support scientific research. Most scientists would agree that during the 1980s, biomedical investigations were more generously funded by the federal government than sociocultural ones. This reflects directly the political stance of Presidents Ronald Reagan[1] and George Bush (and the citizens who elected them). Political conservatives wish to preserve the societal status quo, not hold it responsible for creating psychological problems.

I do not know the degree to which the political pendulum is now swinging in the opposite direction, but there has been renewed interest in the field of *cross-cultural psychopathology*, which compares and contrasts psychological difficulties in cultures around the world. Perhaps the recent explosion of ethnic conflicts between and within nations has contributed to this renewed interest, which may become evident in the increased use of correlational approaches to understanding abnormality.

[1] As he left office, President Reagan signed a bill declaring the 1990s the Decade of the Brain (Goldstein, 1990; Judd, 1990).

Daniel Paul Schreber was a German judge who published his autobiography under the title Memoirs of My Nervous Illness. *In this book, he recounted the story of a psychotic episode during which he was flagrantly paranoid, believing that other people wanted to harm him. Even God had some strange intentions. By divine intervention, Schreber would be turned into a woman whom God would impregnate. Schreber would bear God many children, the start of a new race to populate the earth.*

To say the least, these are unusual beliefs, but Freud tried to delve below their surface meaning. From the details in the autobiography, Freud hypothesized that Schreber felt sexual desire for his own father as well as other men. These homosexual impulses were reprehensible to his conscious mind, so he disguised them with elaborate distortions. It was not Schreber who wanted to have sex with other men; it was other men who wanted to have sex with him—the defense mechanism of projection. *And it was not love that drove these people, but hate—the defense mechanism of* reaction formation.

But even these transformations did not allay Schreber's anxiety, so he took the process one step further by believing that God had designs on him. With this version of his paranoia, Schreber was able to justify his homosexual impulses, effectively removing the associated guilt. If a person is going to harbor embarrassing sexual desires, it helps if they are reciprocated by a divine partner. At any rate, the general proposal resulting from this case has been influential within psychoanalytic circles: paranoia = repressed homosexuality.

Freud's case studies are important because they introduced a number of hypotheses about the origins of particular disorders. Although they are not widely accepted today, these specific hypotheses mark the beginning of the psychoanalytic model of abnormality. As judged from the vantage of modern science, most of Freud's case histories qualify at best as borderline instances of good research (Peterson, 1992). They relied too much on Freud's unaided reporting of events that occurred during his psychotherapy sessions. We have no way of checking the original data of his case studies: the thoughts, feelings, and actions of his patients during psychoanalysis.

Contemporary case studies   For this reason, contemporary versions of the case study approach rely on more public procedures. A researcher may tape-record a therapy session, for instance, and then transcribe the tape for later content analysis of what was said. Lester Luborsky (1964) used this strategy to study the tendency of therapy clients to suddenly forget what they were about to say. By psychoanalytic reasoning, sudden forgetting signifies the introduction of a threatening topic.

Luborsky confirmed this hypothesis by finding numerous examples of sudden forgetting by a single client in therapy and working backward to learn what events had preceded them. He found that the client usually experienced sudden forgetting just as he was about to touch on themes of rejection. Comparison incidents, when sudden forgetting did not occur, were less likely to involve this kind of discussion.

Case studies cannot establish what is true about people and their problems in general. A long-standing criticism of the psychoanalytic model is that it rests too much on studies of a handful of people in Victorian Europe, a time and place in which people had particular difficulties acknowledging sexuality (Gay, 1984). The counterargument is that a case study can at least demonstrate what is possible, thereby suggesting ideas for further research with other methods.

Along these lines, Runyan (1981) suggested that the value of this approach can be increased if the researcher uses it to choose explicitly among alternative explanations. Given the evidence provided by a particular case, some explanations are more plausible than others and deserve further study. Other explanations prove implausible. The key is to entertain a variety of possible explanations—sound scientific procedure regardless of the research strategy.

As an example, Runyan (1981) examined a well known historical event: artist Vincent van Gogh cutting off his ear on December 23, 1888, and giving it to a prostitute. This event may seem too unusual and too distant in the past to explain, but over the years, historians and psychologists have suggested dozens of possibilities. For example:

✦ *He was frustrated by the engagement of his brother.*

✦ *He was frustrated by his inability to establish a working relationship with Paul Gauguin.*

✦ *The prostitute had previously teased van Gogh about his large ears.*

✦ *He was following the example of a victorious matador presenting the severed ear of a bull to his favorite lady.*

✦ *He was imitating the exploits of Jack the Ripper, who killed and mutilated prostitutes, in some cases cutting off their ears.*

✦ *He experienced hallucinations and thus thought that his ears were diseased.*

Some of these hypotheses lack any supporting evidence and can be dismissed. There is no record that the prostitute ever teased van Gogh about his ears. And there is no evidence that van Gogh had even heard of Jack the Ripper. But other hypotheses appear more reasonable. The artist's fragile relationship with his brother is well documented; he exhibited an extreme reaction whenever it was threatened.

Another problem with case studies is that they do not readily allow the researcher to discern causal links between the various events in a person's life. Which events were critical, which superfluous? Many of the questions we want to answer concerning abnormality involve causes and effects, yet case studies are ambiguous precisely in this regard. One partial solution to this difficulty is to look for repeated associations between supposed causes and effects, as illustrated in Luborsky's (1964) research on sudden forgetting. Consistent associations do not prove a causal link, but they are at least compatible with one, particularly as their number increases. And of course, inconsistent associations argue strongly against a causal sequence.

Why did Vincent van Gogh (1853–1890) cut off his ear? A definitive answer may not be available, but evidence can be used to narrow the range of possibilities.

I do not wish to leave you with the impression that case studies are used only to investigate psychoanalytic hypotheses. Although there is compatability between the psychoanalytic model and the case study strategy, case studies are used to evaluate hypotheses derived from a variety of models. One frequently encounters case studies of individuals with specific types of brain damage. I discuss several of these in Chapter 6. Other examples of case studies are found in Chapter 11, where they shed light on unusual sexual disorders. Case studies also see frequent use in the attempt to place a person's problems in their sociocultural context. Information about a person's ethnicity and how it *specifically* impacts on his or her problem can prove invaluable in devising treatments (Chapter 3).

Investigations of behavior therapy may also utilize case studies. One strategy here is to show on repeated occasions that a given behavioral intervention reduces a person's problem and that removal of the intervention is followed by increases in the problem (see Figure 4.1). Again we see that consistent patterns are compatible with causal conclusions, though they do not prove them conclusively.

Some object to describing such investigations of behavior therapy as *case studies* because they usually involve experimental manipulations (discussed later). The term *single-subject experiments* is therefore preferred. Accordingly, case studies are generally defined as investigations of individuals in treatment who do *not* receive any interventions beyond what happens in the course of therapy. Case studies and single-subject experiments nonetheless share a focus on a single individual.

Evaluation   The strengths of case studies are several. They provide rich details about their subject matter. They suggest what may or may not be possible concerning people and their problems. They narrow the range of possible explanations. And they are the best way to investigate rare disorders. On the negative side, case studies may have problems with validity of information, generalization of conclusions, and identification of causes.

CORRELATIONAL INVESTIGATIONS

A different strategy for testing hypotheses about abnormality is a **correlational investigation,** in which a researcher determines the relationship between two variables in a sample of research participants. Do these

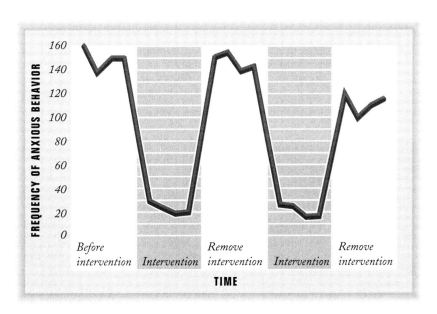

FIGURE 4.1

INVESTIGATING THE EFFECTIVENESS OF BEHAVIOR THERAPY   *If a person's problem is reduced when a behavioral intervention is introduced and increased when it is removed, this argues in favor of the intervention's effectiveness. This example is an abstraction of a study by Neisworth, Madle, and Goecke, who investigated what happened when the reappearance of a child's mother was used to reinforce nonanxious behavior on the part of the child.*
SOURCE: SEE "'ERRORLESS' ELIMINATION OF SEPARATION ANXIETY: A CASE STUDY," BY J. T. NEISWORTH, R. A. MADLE, AND K. K. GOECKE, 1975, *Journal of Behavior Therapy and Experimental Psychiatry, 6,* PP. 79–82.

factors show any association at all? If so, how strong is the association? A strong relationship allows the researcher to predict one factor from the other with some certainty. A weak relationship makes such a prediction much more tentative.

Correlation coefficients   The strength of the association between two variables is usually quantified with a statistic known as a **correlation coefficient.** Correlation coefficients range from -1.00 through 0.00 to $+1.00$. The larger the absolute magnitude of the correlation coefficient (i.e., the farther it is from 0), the more closely the association between the two variables approaches a perfectly straight line (see Figure 4.2).

Positive correlations describe relationships in which increases in one variable are associated with increases in the other variable. In contrast, *negative correlations* describe relationships in which increases in one variable are associated with decreases in the other variable. Finally, *zero correlations* describe independent relationships between two variables.

A study by Loewenthal and Goldblatt (1993) illustrates correlation coefficients. Here is some background. As you will read in Chapter 9, one of the apparent risk factors for depression among women is the presence at home of a large number of young children (e.g., Brown & Harris, 1978). This finding makes sense because such a household is apt to be stressful and can take a toll on the individual responsible for it. Loewenthal and Goldblatt did not contest this conclusion for most women, but they suspected that there were cultural boundaries to its generality. In particular, they hypothesized that among cultural groups that value large families, the presence of a large number of small children would not be linked with increased depression among women. Indeed, perhaps the relationship would be just the opposite.

In London, Loewenthal and Goldblatt studied Orthodox Jews, a group that places a high value on a large family. Fifty-six married women completed questionnaires measuring the following variables:

- ◆ *the number of dependent children (the range in this sample was from 0 to 12)*
- ◆ *the extent of current depressive symptoms*
- ◆ *the number of recent stressful events*
- ◆ *the degree of religious orthodoxy*

Then the researchers calculated correlation coefficients between all possible pairs of variables.

As hypothesized, the number of children at home was negatively correlated with depression. In other words, the more children, the lower the depression score; the fewer children, the higher the depression score. Similarly, religious orthodoxy was negatively correlated with depression. Family size and religious orthodoxy were positively correlated with one another; that is, those high on orthodoxy had large families, those low on orthodoxy had small families. Stressful life events showed a positive correlation with family size but a zero correlation with religiosity—that is, no association at all. And stressful life events were positively correlated with depression.

This is a complicated set of findings but nonetheless coherent (see Figure 4.3). Loewenthal and Goldblatt showed that family size per se is not always a direct risk factor for depression. A large family may contribute indirectly to depression because of its link with stress, but in this sample, such an indirect influence appears counterbalanced by its association with religiosity.

Note how easily my interpretation slipped into causal language—but correlation coefficients like these do not compel causal conclusions. They describe patterns—important and informative, we hope—but not causes and effects. Remember that Loewenthal and Goldblatt administered all their measures at the same time. A depressed mood may have affected the perception of life events as stressful. It may have affected how one regards one's faith. And so on.

Correlational investigations typically use a large sample of research participants, thus reducing prob-

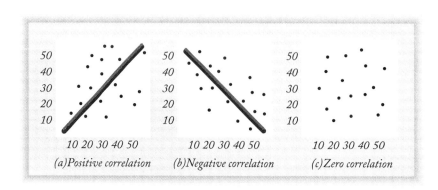

(a)Positive correlation (b)Negative correlation (c)Zero correlation

FIGURE 4.2

EXAMPLES OF CORRELATIONS   *Correlation coefficients describe how closely two variables fall along a straight line.*

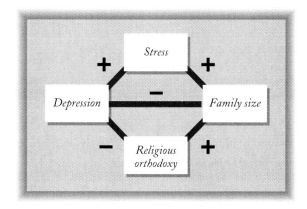

FIGURE 4.3

CORRELATIONS BETWEEN VARIABLES *Positive and negative correlations are indicated by plus (+) and minus (−) signs, respectively. There is a zero correlation between stress and religious orthodoxy.*
SOURCE: SEE "FAMILY SIZE AND DEPRESSIVE SYMPTOMS IN ORTHODOX JEWISH WOMEN," BY K. M. LOEWENTHAL AND V. GOLDBLATT, 1993, *Journal of Psychiatric Research, 27,* PP. 3–10.

lems with the generality of conclusions. So, a researcher might interview several hundred adults chosen at random from a community, some of whom warrant a diagnosis of depression and some of whom do not. What factors correlate with the diagnosis? If it can be argued that these factors occurred before depression did, a researcher might conclude that they are risk factors.

One straightforward way to find out whether supposed risk factors occurred before a disorder is to conduct the correlational investigation over time, first measuring possible risk factors and later determining the presence of the disorder. This is a **longitudinal design,** and it allows stronger conclusions about the direction of possible effects than an investigation that measures all variables simultaneously.

Correlational studies can be used to investigate the claims of most models of abnormality. In Chapter 3, I discussed how biomedical psychologists use family studies to investigate the possible genetic basis of disorders. In these investigations, a psychologist correlates the diagnosis of a particular individual (yes = 1; no = 0) with the number of his immediate relatives with the same diagnosis. If this correlation is positive, she has evidence that the disorder runs through families. Perhaps she also has evidence for a genetic basis, although other explanations must be considered as well, in particular the possibility that family members share common environmental characteristics that somehow predispose the disorder. This research strategy has been used to document the family basis of schizophrenia and other disorders (Rosenthal, 1970).

Psychodynamic formulations of depression emphasize how childhood losses leave a person vulnerable to profound disappointment as an adult. You can see how this might be studied with a correlational procedure: correlate the presence or absence of adult depression with the extent of early loss.

One study that did exactly this found a positive correlation for females but not for males (McLeod, 1987). The result for women is consistent with the psychodynamic hypothesis, but it does not prove it conclusively because third variables—not measured in the study—may be responsible for the observed correlation. These unmeasured third variables are often called confounds. *In other words, perhaps loss per se is not the critical factor. Perhaps early loss is associated with decreased family income, which in turn limits educational and career opportunities, which in turn prove critical in producing depression. Early loss appears to be a risk factor only because it tends to occur among poor families; the real risk factor is poverty. Or perhaps not. Specific third variables can of course be tested and ruled out, but a researcher can always think of additional ones. This is why correlational investigations remain ambiguous on the matter of causality.*

Multiple regression Contemporary correlational investigations often take into account a number of variables and hence are called *multivariate studies.* The examples I have used so far represent simple cases where a researcher is interested in the correlation between two variables and perhaps the confounding role of a third. But many theories of abnormality propose that several different variables may be simultaneous risk factors for given disorders.

The multivariate version of a correlational investigation makes use of a related statistical procedure termed **multiple regression,** which allows the researcher to investigate simultaneously the associations between several variables and some other variable of interest. The relative strength of these different associations can be estimated as well as their independence from one another. Multiple regression also allows the influence of possible confounds to be held constant.

In a study investigating some of the factors that predict the long-term outcome of those with depression, Swindle, Cronkite, and Moos (1989) found that stressful life events, lack of social support, and poor problem solving each correlated with the number of depressive symptoms reported by research participants and did so independently of one another. Said another way, none of these individual associations was confounded by any of the other measured variables. A particularly strong relationship was found between lack of social support and depressive symptoms. This implies that of the several factors maintaining depression, interpersonal ones play a notable role. These results held even when the initial level of depression—a likely third variable—was held constant. However, our conclusions about the direct influence of interpersonal factors on depression remains tentative because other variables, less obvious and thus unmeasured, may account for the observed results.

When coupled with a longitudinal design, multiple regression can provide very sophisticated information about psychopathology. While remaining a correlational strategy, these approaches can be used to decide whether certain patterns of associations are more compatible or less compatible with given causal hypotheses (Kenny, 1979).

Long, Chamberlain, and Vincent (1994) described a study of the possible effects of the 1991 Persian Gulf War on Vietnam veterans. They hypothesized that the widespread media coverage of the events of the more recent war would rekindle memories of the earlier war, which in turn would produce increased distress among those veterans who had experienced **post-traumatic stress disorder (PTSD)** *following their service in Vietnam (Chapter 7). An alternative hypothesis reverses this prediction; attention to the media and the rekindling of memories are the result of distress due solely to the lingering effects of the previous distress.*

Their research was done longitudinally; questionnaires were completed by 88 New Zealand veterans[2] immediately before and immediately after the Persian Gulf War. The initial questionnaire asked the research participants about the extent of their PTSD symptoms. The second questionnaire asked again about their PTSD symptoms as well as how closely they followed media coverage of the Persian Gulf War and the degree to which this coverage brought back thoughts and feelings they had experienced in Vietnam.

Correlating positively with the extent of PTSD symptoms following the Persian Gulf War were initial levels of PTSD symptoms **and** *the extent of revived memories. Attention to the media showed a zero correlation with subsequent PTSD symptoms, although it was positively correlated with the extent of revived memories. These correlations are consistent with the causal diagram shown at the top of Figure 4.4. They are inconsistent with the causal diagram shown at the bottom of this figure because there was no direct correlation between subsequent PTSD and attention to media coverage.*

These conclusions are important because clinicians have often suspected but rarely demonstrated with any certainty that reminders of a traumatic event can rekindle PTSD symptoms. Needless to say, a number of other causal possibilites exist with which the data are consistent or inconsistent, but the point is that correlational investigations can often be used to narrow the range of likely causal explanations.

[2] Approximately 3,000 New Zealand soldiers fought in the Vietnam War on the side of South Vietnam and the United States.

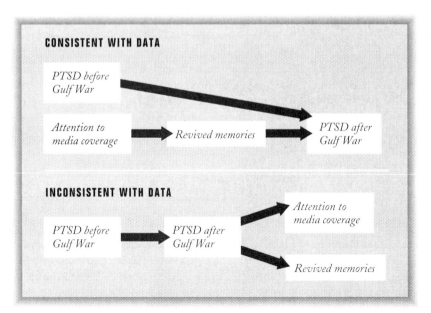

FIGURE 4.4

CAUSAL PATHS   *Although correlations do not conclusively prove causal influences, sometimes the pattern of correlations among variables can be used to narrow the range of causal possibilities. The correlations calculated by Long, Chamberlain, and Vincent in their study of post-traumatic stress disorder (see text) are consistent with the causal paths shown at the top of the figure and inconsistent with those shown at the bottom.* SOURCE: SEE "EFFECT OF THE GULF WAR ON REACTIVATION OF ADVERSE COMBAT-RELATED MEMORIES IN VIETNAM VETERANS," BY N. LONG, K. CHAMBERLAIN, AND C. VINCENT, 1994, *Journal of Clinical Psychology, 50,* PP. 138–144.

Evaluation   Like case studies, correlational investigations have inherent strengths and weaknesses. On the positive side, conclusions based on them can be generalized to other people. Correlational investigations provide access to topics impossible, unwieldy, and/or unethical to investigate with other strategies. Suppose a psychologist is interested in gender differences. Why are women more depressed than men? A case study of a particularly depressed woman does not really address this question. What the researcher needs is a comparison of men and women—that is, a correlational investigation looking at the relationship between gender on the one hand and depression on the other (Nolen-Hoeksema, 1990). Correlational investigations can further be used to elucidate the mechanism by which gender (or any other social contrast, for that matter) is related to abnormality (cf. Betancourt & Lopez, 1993).

The major drawback of a correlational investigation is that it does not allow conclusions about causes and effects. An association can be documented, but its direction remains unclear. Because the variables of interest are not controlled by the researcher, other factors may be entwined with them. He or she can never rule out all of these third variables, and so conclusions about causes remain inherently tentative. The best he or she can do is to make a reasoned argument in favor of a given interpretation and to remain open to the possibility that other ways of making sense of correlational patterns may exist. This caution is important to keep in mind while reading about the results of correlational studies throughout this book. In most cases, likely third variables have been examined and ruled out as confounds, but such examinations can never be exhaustive.

EXPERIMENTS

Some researchers investigate abnormality experimentally, thus exploiting the virtues of the experimental method to learn more about particular disorders. In an **experiment,** the researcher deliberately manipulates certain events and measures the effects of these manipulations on other events. An *independent variable* is the factor manipulated by the researcher; it is the potential cause she wishes to investigate. A *dependent variable* is the factor assessed by the researcher following the manipulation; it is the potential effect of concern.

In a study of the effects of stress on problem solving, an experimenter might manipulate the amount of time allowed research participants to solve long division problems. The independent variable is the amount of time allowed to participants, and the dependent variable is their subsequent performance.

Experiments are often more sophisticated in their design, manipulating not just one independent variable but several simultaneously. This way, *interactions* between and among independent variables can be investigated. In other words, is the dependent variable influenced by the joint operation of two or more independent variables?

Outcome research   Experiments are often used to investigate the effectiveness of biomedical or psychotherapeutic treatment. This is called **outcome research.**

A representative example was reported by Fisher and Thompson (1994). These investigators were interested in how to help individuals who express anxiety and depression concerning the appearance of their body. Body image dissatisfaction *is a problem in its own right as well as a possible symptom of various eating disorders. Previous studies had showed that body image dissatisfaction can be reduced by cognitive-behavior therapy in which individuals undergo systematic desensitization with regard to their body coupled with challenges to self-deprecating thoughts about their appearance. But how does the effectiveness of this kind of therapy compare to a program emphasizing aerobic exercise? Theorists have suggested that an exercise program might reduce body image dissatisfaction, but this hypothesis had not been put to an empirical test.*

From an initial sample of 500 female undergraduates, Fisher and Thompson chose 54 young women who expressed extreme dissatisfaction with the appearance of their body on several questionnaires typically used to measure this variable. Research participants were included only if they were physically healthy, of normal weight, nonpsychotic, nonsuicidal, and not receiving any psychotherapy. These women were then randomly *assigned to one of three groups; there were 18 women per group. As would be expected due to this randomization, the participants in the groups were highly comparable with respect to body image dissatisfaction, age, race, weight, and so on.*

The first group received 6 weeks of cognitive-behavior therapy, meeting once per week. The second group received a comparable amount of training and practice in aerobic exercise. The third group served as a comparison and received neither cognitive-behavior therapy nor exercise training. After the 6-week period, research participants in all three groups again completed the questionnaire measures of body image dissatisfaction originally used to select them for the study.

The design of this experiment is shown in Figure 4.5. There were two independent variables: *the group to which the research participants were assigned*

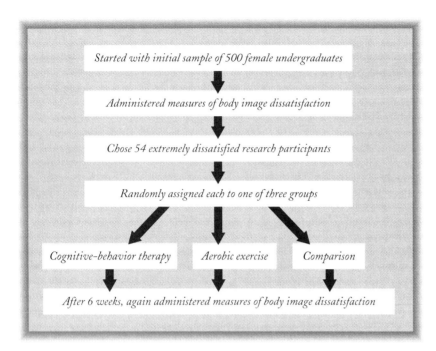

FIGURE **4.5**

**DESIGN OF
EXPERIMENT**   *What defines
an experiment is the* random
assignment *of research participants
to different conditions. In this
example of the experiment
described in the text, participants
were randomly assigned to one of
three groups, a process that
controls for preexisting differences.*
SOURCE: SEE "A COMPARATIVE
EVALUATION OF COGNITIVE-
BEHAVIORAL THERAPY (CBT) VERSUS
EXERCISE THERAPY (ET) FOR THE
TREATMENT OF BODY IMAGE
DISTURBANCE," BY E. FISHER AND J. K.
THOMPSON, 1994, *Behavior Modification,
18,* PP. 171–185.

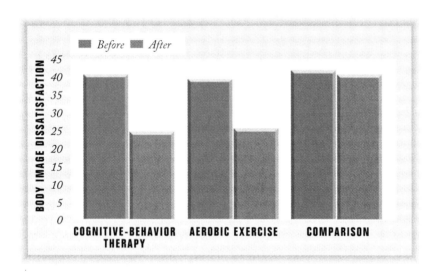

FIGURE **4.6**

**RESULTS OF
EXPERIMENT**   *In an
experiment, we can draw strong
conclusions about causes. In this
experiment by Fisher and Thompson,
differences in body image dissatisfaction
emerged after psychotherapy, which
means that something about
treatment* caused *improvement.*
SOURCE: SEE "A COMPARATIVE
EVALUATION OF COGNITIVE-BEHAVIORAL
THERAPY (CBT) VERSUS EXERCISE
THERAPY (ET) FOR THE TREATMENT OF
BODY IMAGE DISTURBANCE," BY E. FISHER
AND J. K. THOMPSON, 1994, *Behavior
Modification, 18,* PP. 171–185.

(cognitive-behavior therapy, aerobic exercise, and comparison) and the passage of time (i.e., before and after
the 6-week period). The **dependent** variables *were their
scores on the various measures of body image dissatisfaction at the second time period.*

Let us look at the effects of the manipulations on a
composite summary of these dependent variables. The
results are shown in Figure 4.6; higher scores indicate
greater dissatisfaction. There was a statistically significant **interaction** *between the group to which research
participants were assigned and the passage of time. As
you can see, the women in the cognitive-behavior therapy
group and the aerobic exercise group showed decreased*

scores over time, and the decreases in both cases were
comparable. Those in the comparison group remained
dissatisfied with their body image, showing that the mere
passage of time did nothing to remedy this problem. We
can conclude that something about treatment **caused** the
observed changes.

Experimental psychopathology   A common strategy of conducting experimental studies of abnormality
is sometimes called **experimental psychopathology.**
A researcher studies two groups of individuals—one
with a disorder and one without—and then assigns
them to various experimental conditions. How do they

solve problems, make judgments, and/or respond to stimuli that the experimenter presents to them?

Two versions of this strategy exist. In the first, researchers do not manipulate the disorder in which they are interested. Instead, they start with research participants who already have a particular problem or characteristic, and then they manipulate aspects of the experimental situation. Note that this procedure may introduce third variables, just as you saw in correlational investigations. Any comparison of how schizophrenic versus nonschizophrenic individuals solve various problems might end up being a social class comparison as well. We can draw strong causal conclusions about the factors actually manipulated in the experiment, but not about the disorder per se, because it was not manipulated.

With the second strategy of experimental psychopathology, researchers actually create via their manipulations phenomena analogous to disorders. This is called **analogue research.** A useful analogue of abnormality allows the researcher to manipulate it at will among research participants, avoiding third variables as well as the ethical and practical problems of creating actual problems in living.

The immediate objection to analogue research is that it is artificial, but artificiality can actually be a strength when the research captures the essentials of a phenomenon. We must always examine analogues individually. Some are better than others because they in fact isolate critical factors of a disorder while ignoring irrelevant ones.

The use of analogues is common in fields other than abnormal psychology. Medical researchers, for instance, frequently study monkeys or rats or mice because some of their illnesses can be analogous to our own. And—at least in years past—the cosmetics industry was a great consumer of rabbits. Rabbit eyes are analogous to human eyes insofar as what irritates them.

In psychopathology, numerous analogues have been proposed, in both animals and humans (Maser & Seligman, 1977; McKinney, 1988).

For example, psychologists have noted that people's prolonged use of amphetamines produces thoughts, feelings, and actions that are difficult to distinguish from the symptoms of schizophrenia (Snyder, 1974). Perhaps **amphetamines** *produce in animals a state biochemically analogous to that of schizophrenia in humans (Chapter 12). Because researchers can map out the biochemical pathways of amphetamine action within rat brains more efficiently and ethically than they can within human brains, we may have an intriguing analogue of schizophrenia in animals (e.g., Gambill & Kornetsky, 1976).*

For another example, consider **learned helplessness:** *the disruptions in learning, motivation, and mood that follow experience with uncontrollable events, such as loud noises that cannot be avoided or problems that cannot be solved. These disruptions prove of interest in their own right to some researchers, but other investigators have been intrigued by Seligman's (1974, 1975) hypothesis that learned helplessness is an analogue of depression (Chapter 9). Studies of learned helplessness therefore are often intended as analogue investigations of depression. College students in a laboratory are exposed to uncontrollable events, and their subsequent behavior is then compared to that of other individuals without this experience (Peterson, Maier, & Seligman, 1993). Do any differences that occur shed light on depression? Studies like these show that "helpless" people develop a host of short-term cognitive deficits, and these findings support recent conceptualizations of depression in cognitive terms.*

Analogue research can never be an end in itself because its conclusions must ultimately be judged in terms of their applicability to the actual disorder of concern, just as cancer treatment and eyeliner must be generalized from animals to humans. Some analogues pass this test. Others do not.

When first created, the drug LSD was termed **psychomimetic** *because it presumably mimicked the psychotic episodes characteristic of schizophrenia (Claridge, 1978). Researchers were excited at the prospect of being able to randomly assign some research participants to a "schizophrenic" condition in an experiment (by administering*

Researchers at one time believed that LSD mimicked the psychotic episodes that characterize schizophrenia. Critical differences are now recognized (see Chapters 5 and 12).

an LSD pill) and others to a "normal" condition (by administering an inert sugar pill). A number of studies embodying these assumptions were conducted (Lehmann, 1980), but it soon became clear that the LSD experience resembled schizophrenia only superficially (Chapters 5 and 12).

Evaluation   The considerable strength of experimentation as a research strategy is that it allows us to draw conclusions about causes and effects. Experiments are a powerful way to investigate the possible effects of psychotherapy and psychological mechanisms hypothesized to underlie abnormality. At the same time, they have their drawbacks. Certain topics cannot be investigated experimentally for reasons of ethics or practicality. Also, experimental manipulations are not foolproof. Investigators might manipulate factors in addition to the intended ones, thereby clouding the conclusions.

In the experiment described earlier of the effects of cognitive-behavior treatment and aerobic exercise on body image dissatisfaction, the apparent implication is that the details of these procedures proved critical in producing changes. But it could be argued instead that the research participants in these two treatment groups benefited simply because someone took an interest in them and spent considerable time interacting with them. Perhaps a similar benefit would result from participating in a weekly discussion of current events. In other words, third variables can plague experiments just as they do correlational investigations.

DOES PSYCHOTHERAPY WORK?

It may be a bit surprising to hear that the effectiveness of psychotherapy has not always been clear. This section will attempt to shed light on the issue by presenting historical details (see Figure 4.7) that illustrate some of the general points raised earlier in this chapter about research methods. You will see that psychotherapy *is* effective. Beyond that, we have much to learn.

THE FIRST PSYCHOTHERAPY

In the early decades of the 20th century, psychotherapy meant only one thing: psychoanalysis. When psychoanalysts first began to treat patients with psychological means, the effectiveness (or not) of treatment was judged by simple observation. The first psychotherapy patients were hysterics, with bizarre alterations in their physical functioning (Chapter 1). Some were blind or deaf. Others could not feel or walk or swallow. Following an intervention, such as hypnosis, their symptoms often vanished. There seemed little doubt that a cure had taken place, because both the therapist and the patient observed an apparently sudden and dramatic change unlikely to have occurred without intervention.

As psychoanalysis began to be used with a greater variety of patients, and as other forms of therapy came into being, no one seemed to question its effectiveness. Therapists and patients continued to believe that beneficial changes were taking place. However, with the continued growth of psychotherapy, there was increasingly less objective evidence to believe that it worked.

Patients were typically termed neurotic, which means they were defined not by their overt symptoms but by presumed underlying processes (Chapter 2). How can change be assessed when unconscious conflicts rather than overt symptoms are of interest? Furthermore, change for many patients occurs only gradually. Therapy can take years, during which other life events occur that might better explain any change that does occur. Finally, the most compelling research evidence for the effectiveness of therapy were case studies. As you have seen, case studies cannot be used

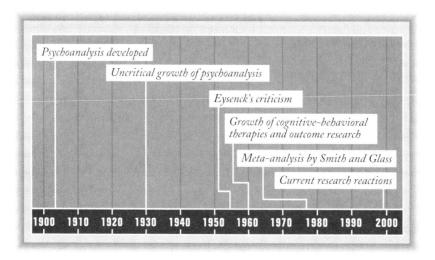

FIGURE 4.7

HISTORY OF PSYCHOTHERAPY RESEARCH   *At first, the effectiveness of psychotherapy was uncritically accepted. Skepticism arose in the 1950s but was later resolved by the meta-analysis of Smith and Glass. We now know that psychotherapy is effective, and researchers have turned their attention to more specific questions.*

The first psychotherapy patients suffered from hysteria, as shown in this sketch of one of the patients of Jean Charcot (1825–1893).

to establish what is generally the case, nor can they isolate operative causes.

DOUBTS ABOUT EFFECTIVENESS

As psychotherapy grew in use, criticisms eventually began to surface. In 1952, psychologist Hans Eysenck published a critical attack on psychotherapy. He assembled data from several investigations. From 5 studies of the effects of psychoanalytic therapy, he estimated that 44% of neurotic patients showed improvement (as judged by their therapist). And from 19 studies of "eclectic" therapy, he estimated that 64% of neurotic patients improved (again, as judged by their therapist).

Next he estimated how many people with problems like those of therapy clients improved without therapy. He chose two comparison groups. The first group consisted of patients with anxiety or depressive disorders discharged from state mental hospitals because they improved (even though they received only custodial care). The second group included individuals who filed disability claims for psychological reasons with insurance companies who then returned to work within 2 years. In both cases, 72% of the people apparently improved without therapy. This figure obviously exceeds the average improvement rate following psychotherapy.

Although Eysenck pointed out that further research would be a good idea, he drew the strong conclusion that psychotherapy was a failure and should be abandoned. His conclusion did not convince everybody, though, because his data were not as compelling as he thought them to be. His approach was correlational because patients were not randomly assigned to receive therapy or not, and unknown factors may have confounded the comparisons. Further, as you probably noticed, different criteria were used to operationalize improvement: therapist judgment on the one hand versus hospital discharge or returning to work on the other. The use of different operational definitions obviously precludes any strong conclusions.

Still, Eysenck's study was widely cited. It became commonplace to read the statement that therapy did not work. But as already noted, this conclusion is *not* compelled by what Eysenck reported.

INVESTIGATIONS OF EFFECTIVENESS

Although flawed, Eysenck's conclusions forcefully reminded psychotherapists that proof of their endeavor was not readily at hand. Appreciate that it is difficult to determine whether psychotherapy works. I can point to a number of reasons. The first experimental attempts to determine if treatment reduced psychological problems examined drug therapies. Drug research lends itself readily to simple experimental designs: Give one group of patients the drug of interest and withhold it from a second group. Researchers refined this basic procedure when they recognized that expectations on the part of the patient or the doctor can lead to a beneficial change, at least in the short run, even though the drug, in a pharmacological sense, is not helpful. Sometimes this is referred to as a **placebo effect.**

Placebo effects We rule out a placebo effect by administering an inert substance—called a placebo—packaged and prescribed in the same way as the drug of interest. "Real" cures are those that outperform the placebo effects. In **double-blind designs,** both the patient and the doctor are kept in the dark as to who is given the real medication and who receives the placebo. (Of course somebody must know this information, but it is withheld from the people in the study.) When drugs prove effective in this stringent design, we can conclude with considerable confidence that they work because of their pharmacological properties.

When researchers began to ask about the effectiveness of psychological treatment, they tried to make their studies fit the formula already developed for drug research. On the one hand, this makes sense. Treatment—whether pharmacological or psychological—became the independent variable in an experiment, and symptom relief, cure, and/or progress, however operationalized, the dependent variable. But on the other hand, the analogy begins to break down when we consider the confounding role played by expectations.

Can psychotherapy be confounded with placebo effects—that is, by an expectation that change is likely to occur? Yes and no. It might well be that any form of therapy—even something as nonsensical as reading aloud from a telephone book—could bring relief to some individuals. We would want to dismiss this possibility because no existing model provides a ready rationale for its effectiveness.

But we could argue that what makes psychotherapy effective is the kindling of hope (Frank, 1974, 1978). Perhaps hope is more important than any particular technique, which means that we should not glibly dismiss expectation-driven benefits. We can even go back and argue that placebo effects in drug therapy may be "real" because they work through psychological mechanisms.

I once treated a highly depressed 40-year-old man who was reluctant to discuss the personal issues that might have played a role in his problem. I discovered, however, that Mr. Faulkner was greatly interested in nutrition and its relationship to well-being. We spent a great deal of time during therapy sessions discussing his diet and how he might improve it. I requested that Mr. Faulkner keep track of the vegetables and fruits he consumed and try to have several servings of each every day. In particular, I asked him to note which combinations made him feel less depressed on the following day. Oranges coupled with fresh greens turned out to be the most satisfying diet, so I suggested that he should consume these every day, in large quantities. He did, and his depression lifted.

Do I believe that his diet had a direct effect on his mood? Not really. But I think my intervention helped because it made Mr. Faulkner feel in control of his feelings. My intervention also made him feel like an expert because he did a great deal of reading about nutrition, and I always asked him to share what he had learned. Finally, my intervention required that he be active; he awakened early every morning to walk to the neighborhood fresh produce store. There he made several friends with the clerks and the suppliers. He quit his job as a construction worker, which frustrated him, and began a much more satisfying career managing an organic restaurant. I have heard from Mr. Faulkner occasionally over the years, and he continues to eat well and be happy. When I think of him, I modify the cliche "you are what you eat" to proclaim "you are what you think you eat."

I made use of Mr. Faulkner's expectations in treatment, but his "cure" was not an illusion. So what can we conclude about the status of placebo effects in psychotherapy? The issue is complex, and a lively debate has surrounded it (e.g., O'Leary & Borkovec, 1978; Schumaker, 1991; Shepherd & Sartorius, 1989). I will not try to work through all the arguments but simply note that placebo effects can make the evaluation of psychotherapy effectiveness more challenging than the evaluation of drug effectiveness. Drug treatment is based on a clear assumption that the mechanism of action is pharmacological, not expectational, which means that a placebo effect casts doubt on the rationale of a drug treatment. A placebo effect does not cast the same degree of doubt on the apparent effectiveness of a psychological intervention, at least insofar as psychotherapy acknowledges the positive contribution of expectations.

We are confronted by a dilemma with regard to how a researcher chooses an appropriate comparison group for psychotherapy outcome studies. A double-blind design is difficult if not impossible. While a client might be told that a supposed neutral treatment is real, it is hard to envision psychotherapists being blind to whether or not what they are doing is real therapy.

Further complicating the matter is the fact that most psychological treatments take place over considerable time—weeks, months, or even years. Again, as a result, it is difficult to choose an appropriate comparison against which to gauge effectiveness. People with psychological problems who are not in therapy are one obvious choice, of course, but they will not sit still for years, content to be in a comparison group. They will do something in order to feel better, and as a result, some will experience **spontaneous recovery** (or **spontaneous remission**). This refers to improvement without professional intervention. The term is a misnomer because their improvement does not come about by chance but rather because they undertook something helpful on their own (cf. Schachter, 1982).

Trends making outcome research possible   In the decades since Eysenck's (1952) attack on therapy effectiveness, researchers have devised better ways to investigate the question, surmounting some of the problems just described. What follows are some relatively recent trends that make it possible to conduct more definitive investigations of therapy effectiveness.

First and perhaps foremost, the field has seen the growth of behavioral and cognitive therapies. Prior to World War II, psychologists were usually not psychotherapists (Hilgard, 1987). Their involvement with the mental health system was for the most part limited to diagnosis and assessment. World War II and the psychological problems it produced demanded that the ranks of practicing therapists be increased, and psychologists were tapped to fill this need. After the war, they continued to be involved in psychotherapy. Their presence in the field brought an interest in behavioral approaches to change and some years thereafter an interest in cognitive ones as well. A related consequence was an enhanced interest in objectively conducted outcome research.

The conceptualization of problems and their remedies thereby changed. According to the cognitive-behavioral perspective, improvement is defined in terms of relatively unambiguous criteria. So, a person with a fear of venturing outside is improved to the degree that she goes to crowded stores. Or a person with depression is improved to the degree that he no longer reports that he is constantly unhappy. Contrast these objective and measurable criteria of improvement with the vague "character change" that psychoanalysts take as their goal. Needless to say, social judgment enters into the use of all criteria for change, because a researcher must decide the degree of change needed to deem the intervention a success. But cognitive-behavioral criteria are at least readily operationalized.

Here began a trend for outcome researchers of all persuasions to use "hard" measures of improvement like observation of actual behaviors, as opposed to "soft" measures like therapist or client opinions. For example, the effectiveness of treatment for specific phobias can be measured by asking the client to touch a snake or lizard, *not* by asking the therapist (or client) if therapy has been successful or satisfactory. It must be pointed out, however, that outcome research still depends a great deal on unverified verbal reports by the client or therapist, a strategy open to question (Chapter 1).

Another change that has occurred in recent decades is that time limits are placed on therapy—often, ten or fifteen weekly sessions. This minimizes the problem of spontaneous recovery that threatens studies of psychoanalytic therapy, which can last for many months or even years. Along these lines, time-limited therapy has also solved in part the problem of an appropriate comparison group: Use individuals on a waiting list to receive therapy. Uncontrolled variations in spontaneous recovery are better controlled because there is less time elapsed during which they can occur.

As explained earlier in the chapter, researchers have recognized the need of ensuring that the people classified as having a given problem are really similar. This recognition has affected not only research into abnormality but also research into therapy effectiveness. Subjects in therapy outcome studies typically receive research diagnoses, particularly stringent diagnoses of their problems.

Yet another refinement of therapy research is the use of **therapy manuals,** explicit scripts describing what a therapist should do in particular sessions (Luborsky & DeRubeis, 1984). When therapists identify what they are doing as psychoanalytic therapy, or cognitive therapy, or behavior therapy, there is no guarantee that this is exactly what they are doing (cf. Fiedler, 1950, 1951). Therapy manuals guarantee that all clients receive the same intervention, a requirement if we want to say something about the effectiveness of a given therapy. Audiotapes or videotapes of sessions can be used to check the therapist's fidelity in following the manual.

Finally, recent decades have also seen the legitimization of therapy analogue research: studying people with circumscribed and specific problems (like test anxiety). Although these problems are usually not as profound as those of most individuals in actual therapy, they are thought to resemble them in relevant ways. And it is typically much easier to study interventions for these analogue problems, precisely because they are more circumscribed and specific.

Meta-analysis of psychotherapy effectiveness   All these innovations have improved psychotherapy research, and in recent decades researchers have conducted literally hundreds of sound investigations of psychotherapy effectiveness. An important review of early literature in this area was reported in 1977 by Mary Smith and Gene Glass. They surveyed 375 separate studies of therapy outcome, which together included 25,000 subjects. The sheer magnitude of the research summarized is not the only reason why this literature review is noteworthy. Rather, Smith and Glass (1977) surmounted a problem faced by all who struggle with how to summarize the general thrust of separate investigations: what to do when some studies point to one conclusion, other studies to the opposite conclusion, and still others to no conclusion at all.

They provided one resolution in the statistical technique of **meta-analysis.** This procedure combines quantitatively the results of separate experimental studies into an overall estimate of the magnitude of an experimental effect (in this case, therapy). Meta-analysis treats each research conclusion as a datum in its own right, and then asks how best to summarize all these findings.

Meta-analysis is an exciting development, but like any research strategy, it can be criticized. The meta-analyst can only work with available research results. Flawed studies obviously result in a flawed meta-analysis. Indeed, in treating all research results as equally informative, meta-analyses impose a bias that is rarely justified.

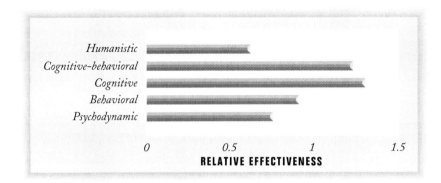

FIGURE 4.8

Effectiveness of Different Psychotherapies   *Smith, Glass, and Miller provided the following estimates of the relative effectiveness of different approaches to psychotherapy. Note: Although these figures may look different, none is significantly different from any other.*
Source: See *The Benefits of Psychotherapy,* by M. L. Smith, G. V. Glass, and T. I. Miller, 1980, Baltimore: Johns Hopkins University Press.

In an otherwise laudatory review of the procedure, Schmidt (1992) observed that those who do meta-analyses in a given area tend *not* to be the same investigators who do substantive studies on the topic of concern. The required statistical sophistication may be one reason for this division of labor, and the fact that any given researcher has a finite amount of time available may be another. Meta-analyses are so time-consuming that they often represent the major research endeavor of an individual. The point, though, is that those who conduct meta-analyses may not be as attuned to the nuances of research as those who actually do the research, which exacerbates the mistaken tendency to treat all results as equally valid.

In any event, Smith and Glass used meta-analysis to answer two questions. First, is therapy more effective than no therapy? Second, are some forms of therapy more effective than others? Here is their conclusion:

> The results ... demonstrate the beneficial effects of counseling and psychotherapy. [Yet] despite volumes devoted to the theoretical differences among different schools of psychotherapy, the results of research demonstrate negligible differences in the effects produced by different therapy types. Unconditional judgments of superiority of one type of therapy or another, and all that these claims imply about treatment and training policy, are unjustified. (1977, p. 760)

In other words, therapy works, but all forms empirically studied[3] work with the same effectiveness (see Figure 4.8).

[3] As mentioned in Chapter 3, not all approaches to treatment have received equal research attention. The burden of proof seems to lie with

Assuming that therapy—on the average—is more effective than no therapy, just how strong is this effect? One way to understand how effective therapy can be is to ask what proportion of people in therapy show greater improvement than the average person with the same problem not in therapy. According to Smith and Glass (1977), 80% of people in therapy do better than the average person not in therapy (see Figure 4.9). Remember the earlier discussion of the magnitude of research results. The estimate of the magnitude of psychotherapy effectiveness provided by Smith and Glass is not a trivial one. At the same time, there is no basis for assuming that psychotherapy is invariably effective. Remember also the earlier point that conclusions about research results are summaries, not guarantees.

Lipsey and Wilson (1993) recently summarized meta-analyses of treatment, locating more than 300 different reviews. The conclusion of Smith and Glass (1977) has been repeatedly confirmed: Psychotherapy on the average is effective. Indeed, the magnitude of the effect of psychotherapy is comparable to the effect of many well established medical treatments, including bypass surgery for blocked arteries, AZT for AIDS, and chemotherapy for breast cancer.

the practitioners of given treatments, particularly in light of a court decision—*Osheroff v. Chestnut Lodge*—holding that therapists should not treat an individual using a strategy not known to be effective when there exists another strategy of demonstrated effectiveness (Klerman, 1990). The implications of this decision have yet to filter through the whole of the mental health system, but if and when they do, treatments for which there is a good basis in outcome research will necessarily see even wider use.

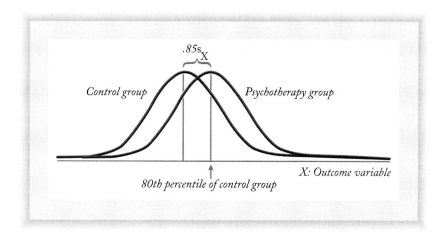

FIGURE **4.9**

EFFECT SIZE IN PSYCHOTHERAPY *According to Smith, Glass, and Miller, the typical individual in psychotherapy does better than 80% of individuals with the same problem not in psychotherapy.* SOURCE: FROM *The Benefits of Psychotherapy* (P. 88), BY M. L. SMITH, G. V. GLASS, AND T. I. MILLER, 1980, BALTIMORE: JOHNS HOPKINS UNIVERSITY PRESS. REPRINTED WITH PERMISSION.

In light of the drastically different assumptions on which different therapies are based, why are they apparently all equally effective? Researchers are currently taking an even more detailed look at psychotherapy in an attempt to understand why.

CURRENT ISSUES

There are several research reactions to the Smith and Glass review. As you will see, their goals are not incompatible. A full understanding of how psychotherapy is effective will include the contributions from all these lines of inquiry.

Matching models   The first research response has been an attempt to identify which therapies work best for which problems. This is sometimes described as a search for **matching models,** the approach that characterizes contemporary medicine. Depending on a person's particular problem, a therapist should try to treat it in the most effective manner; there is no reason to assume that given treatments are uniformly effective for all problems. Appreciate that this often is not the way psychotherapy has been conducted. Traditionally, all problems were approached in a similar way, depending on the theoretical orientation (model) of the therapist and the type of training he or she received.

Imagine that every sore throat was treated the same way—regardless of whether it was due to an infection, cancer, an obstructed windpipe, or a bullet wound. This would be absurd, of course, but this is often the case with psychotherapy. Many of the studies reviewed by Smith and Glass did not look for interactions between the problem and the treatment, and so it is not surprising that we do not know much about problem-treatment specificity. Everything has been mushed together, like all the sore throats in the world,

making it all the more striking that therapy really does prove effective.

I use the matching model approach in this textbook when I present treatments for each of the problems under discussion. I offer educated guesses, based on the relevant outcome research, that a given approach is effective for a specific problem. However, most of the research does not lend itself to a firm conclusion about the match. While we know something about what does work, we do not necessarily know in given cases if other treatments do not.

Because psychotherapy research is done by real people who have to provide concrete answers to practical questions, this is how our knowledge has evolved. A therapist feels a need to evaluate whether a procedure is effective, which means that she formulates her best hypothesis about what will work and then tests it. Often these hypotheses are good hunches. There is not much practical reward in showing that a given approach is ineffective. Researchers rarely undertake studies in which a given treatment is expected to fail, unless they are taking issue with exaggerated and/or potentially harmful claims. In Chapter 14, you will see how skeptical researchers challenged claims about the effectiveness of dietary treatments of hyperactivity. They were reacting in part to extravagant claims in the popular media.

Unpacking psychotherapy   A second response to the conclusions of Smith and Glass is an attempt to identify critical ingredients in therapy responsible for its effectiveness. As I described in Chapter 3, a given psychotherapeutic approach is a complex package of specific interventions. Are some important, and others irrelevant? Researchers therefore "unpack" therapeutic interventions, deleting one intervention at a time or in combination to see what drives therapeutic effectiveness.

It has often been assumed that psychotherapy effectiveness derives in part from the *professional* relationship between therapist and client. Friends after all do not function as therapists for one another, so perhaps the fact that therapists are paid for their services is an important ingredient in the success of the endeavor. Research does not bear this out. Neither the amount of money exchanging hands nor the fact that there is any exchange at all is important (e.g., Yoken & Berman, 1987). The conclusion is not that psychotherapists should be unpaid, merely that they need not be paid in order to help their clients.

Nonspecific factors   The third general research reaction to the conclusions of Smith and Glass is to believe that therapies work with the same effectiveness because they really are doing much the same thing. The differences to which theorists attach so much importance may not really be critical. We thus see a search for **nonspecific factors** that make therapy effective. They are nonspecific in the sense that they adhere to no given approach to therapy.

A number of such factors have been identified. Some are characteristics of the individual with the

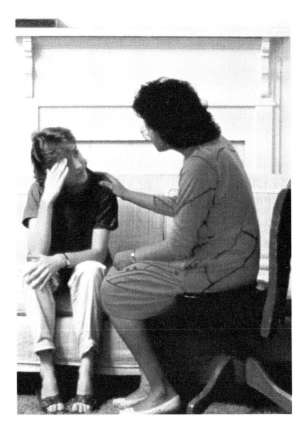

Warmth, genuineness, and empathy on the part of a therapist are associated with successful treatment.

problem (Garfield, 1986). Not surprisingly, the less entrenched the problem and the more resources a person has—intellectual, economic, social, and so on—the more likely therapy will be successful.

Other common ingredients are characteristics of the therapist (Beutler, Crago, & Arizmendi, 1986). As already implied, the theoretical orientation of the therapist is not particularly important. Neither—perhaps surprisingly—is his or her advanced training. And broad personality traits bear no consistent relationship to success, although the more specific qualities of warmth, genuineness, and empathy do seem to predict effectiveness.

In a provocative investigation, Strupp and Hadley (1979) compared the effectiveness of trained therapists with that of college professors (not psychologists) recruited because they were known to be good at establishing relationships with students. The therapy for each group was more effective than no therapy at all, and neither superior to the other. The point is *not* that anyone can be an effective therapist—the college professors were a select group. But advanced training and the specific therapy techniques imparted by such training may not be determining factors for therapy success.

Therapist age, sex, and ethnicity do not relate strongly to outcome either, although they may exert an indirect influence (Beutler, Crago, & Arizmendi, 1986). If the therapist and client are similar, this works against premature termination of therapy. If therapy does not continue, then there is obviously no way it can be effective.

One more set of common factors involves qualities that pertain to the relationship between therapist and client (Peterson, 1991b). Therapists have long believed that there is something special about the relationship between themselves and their clients. Consider, for example, the psychoanalytic notions of *transference* (on the part of the client) and *countertransference* (on the part of the therapist). They refer to unconscious modes of interaction that are driven by past conflicts in the lives of the client or therapist, respectively.

Thinking about the client-therapist relationship is even richer. The **real relationship** between the client and the therapist refers to the fact that the whole endeavor takes place between real people, who have appointments to keep, bills to pay, personal likes and dislikes, and idiosyncrasies. These factors exert an important influence on what goes on in therapy.

I am reminded of a disagreement I witnessed between two therapists about what to make of a client who had called several times to cancel therapy sessions because her car would not start. One therapist did not accept her excuse, arguing that she was resisting treatment. The other therapist took what she said at face value. The fact that the first therapist drove a new car that never failed to start, whereas the second therapist drove a jalopy that was frequently in the shop, is possibly relevant here. In both cases, the personal view of the therapist might have colored his interpretation of the client's excuse—whether or not it was valid—and the way therapy would thereby be conducted.

A number of therapists emphasize yet another aspect of the relationship between themselves and their clients, which goes by various names, including **helping alliance** (Bordin, 1979). The therapist and client work best together when they see each other as working in synchrony. Studies show that a good helping alliance is critical for success in therapy (C. H. Patterson, 1986). It includes such ingredients as agreement on the goals and tasks of therapy, the encouragement of hope, and the meeting of expectations (see Horvath & Greenberg, 1989; Luborsky, 1983, 1985; Marmor, 1975; Tichenor & Hill, 1989).

Recall my earlier example of Mr. Faulkner and my placebo treatment of his depression in terms of his diet. We had an effective helping alliance. I was sincerely interested in his well-being and how to enhance it, and he recognized it. I would bring him articles to read on health and nutrition. I would study the records he kept of his diet and mood. I would listen attentively as he summarized what he was learning about these subjects. We enjoyed working together, and treatment proceeded well.

Nonspecific factors appear to have considerable generality, characterizing not just psychotherapy but a variety of approaches to helping people with problems. In *Persuasion and Healing,* Jerome Frank (1974) reported a cross-cultural and cross-historical comparison of different strategies for alleviating distress and suffering. He identified four factors common to all forms of healing:

◆ a particular relationship between the healer and client, in which the client has faith in the healer's competence and his or her desire to be of help

◆ a locale for treatment that is designated by society as a place of healing

◆ a rationale for the treatment that includes an explanation of illness and health

◆ a task or procedure prescribed by the rationale

According to Frank's analysis, healing strategies, including psychotherapy, are successful to the degree that they enhance the individual's sense of mastery and reduce his or her alienation from others.

You might be tempted to conclude from the results of the meta-analysis by Smith and Glass that specific tasks in therapy are unnecessary, but Frank's study implies otherwise. It may not matter exactly what a therapist asks his or her client to do, but some specific task—whatever form it may take—is an essential part of helping others.

The notions of matching models, critical ingredients, and nonspecific factors need not be incompatible, although they reside at different conceptual levels. We can readily imagine that the common ingredients set the stage for specific interventions that work well granted given problems.

Psychotherapy process   Another line of current investigation looks into the *process* of therapy, not simply the endpoints, with the goal of discovering critical factors for success or failure, turning points, and so on (Orlinsky & Howard, 1986). For example, Lester Luborsky and his colleagues have devised a way to measure the existence of transference in psychotherapy sessions by analyzing the similarity between conflicts a client expresses concerning the therapist and those expressed concerning significant others (e.g., Fried, Crits-Christoph, & Luborsky, 1992; Luborsky, Crits-Christoph, & Mellon, 1986). This method allows researchers to study how conflicts change over the course of therapy. Clients indeed have similar conflicts with their therapists and other people, which is consistent with the psychoanalytic premise of transference.

Future research of psychotherapy process will be able to investigate the hypothesis that resolution of conflicts with the therapist leads to resolution of conflicts with others. More generally, process research like this can be used to investigate the claims of all approaches to psychotherapy about the relevant mechanisms of change. For example, do therapeutic benefits occur because a client's beliefs and experiences become congruent (as client-centered therapy assumes), because thoughts become realistic (as cognitive therapy assumes), or because interpersonal expectations become more explicit (as couples therapy assumes)?

Long-term outcomes   One more line of research studies long-term outcomes (e.g., Woody, McLellan,

Luborsky, & O'Brien, 1987). Maybe all therapies work in the same manner in the short run—that is, people improve in similar ways up to the point of their discharge from treatment—but perhaps we can distinguish among therapies by how the person fares *after* treatment is completed. Do people relapse, coming back to treatment with the same or other problems? Or has something been imparted that allows them to live a life where problems are less numerous or at least easier to solve?

This chapter concerned itself with the methods psychologists use to test hypotheses derived from their various theoretical perspectives. One especially important use of research has been to evaluate the effectiveness of psychotherapy. Empirical findings figure prominently in the rest of this book, which details what psychologists have discovered over the years about abnormality. As methods have become more sophisticated, so too have the theories that rest on their results.

Summary

METHODS

✦ Researchers are concerned with several general issues. One of these is how representative their sample is of the more general population to which they wish their conclusions to apply.

✦ Another important issue for researchers is how to offer sound conclusions about the samples they actually studied. Findings that are statistically significant—not likely to have occurred by chance—are given the most emphasis, but even in these cases researchers must judge the practical significance of their results.

✦ A basic decision that researchers must make concerns the type of abnormality to be studied and the way it is to be measured.

✦ Research design refers to the overall structure of an investigation. It should allow conclusions about the question of interest, while minimizing alternative interpretations.

✦ There are several research strategies for studying abnormality, each with characteristic strengths and weaknesses. Case studies provide rich details but have problems with fidelity of information, generalization of conclusions, and identification of causes. Correlational investigations lead to more general conclusions

but do not allow causes to be specified with certainty. With experiments, a researcher can identify operative causes, although experiments may sometimes prove unwieldy or unethical.

DOES PSYCHOTHERAPY WORK?

✦ The effectiveness of treatment has long been unclear. Psychotherapy in particular has proved difficult to evaluate. The very first psychotherapy was psychoanalysis. It was effective when used with hysterical patients. However, as psychoanalysis began to be applied to other problems, its effectiveness became more uncertain. In 1952, Hans Eysenck leveled the charge that psychoanalytic treatment did not work. Indeed, he argued that it was worse than no treatment at all. Although Eysenck's criticisms were not well supported by the research he cited, they were nonetheless influential. For years, it was believed that psychotherapy did not help people with problems.

✦ The development of behavioral and cognitive therapies, coupled with greater sophistication about how to evaluate therapy effectiveness, led to a renewed interest in psychotherapy outcome research. In 1977, Mary Smith and Gene Glass reviewed the relevant literature and concluded that psychotherapy after all was effective. They found no evidence that any given approach to psychotherapy was, in general, superior to any other.

✦ Current research into psychotherapy attempts to match problems with the most effective treatments, to discover critical ingredients in psychotherapy, to identify factors common to all successful forms of treatment, to study the process of psychotherapy, and to investigate long-term outcomes.

Key Terms

analogue research

case study

confound

correlation coefficient

correlational investigation

double-blind design

experiment

experimental psychopathology

helping alliance

longitudinal design

matching models

meta-analysis

multiple regression

nonspecific factor

operational definition

Ortgeist

outcome research

placebo effect

population

real relationship

reliability

research design

research diagnostic
  criteria

sample

spontaneous recovery;
  spontaneous remission

statistical significance

therapy manual

validity

Zeitgeist

The Case of
Substance
Abuse

5 Most of us think of F. Scott Fitzgerald (1896–1940) as the distinguished author of such novels as This Side of Paradise, The Great Gatsby, and Tender is the Night, who lived a lavish life. Long before anyone had the notion of Beautiful People, F. Scott and his wife Zelda were precisely that, celebrated from Paris to New York for being conspicuously outrageous. Fitzgerald's behavior at dinner parties was the stuff of legends. He would crawl under the table, cut his tie off with his dinner knife, and eat soup with a fork. He was also a severe abuser of alcohol. Despite repeated attempts to stop or moderate his drinking, he constantly

F. Scott Fitzgerald, shown here with his wife Zelda and their daughter Scottie, was a severe alcohol abuser.

drank to the point of grotesque excess. He was drunk more than he was sober during his entire adult life. His health began to suffer in his 20s, and he died at the age of 44 after his second heart attack.

Fitzgerald's alcoholism colored not only his flamboyant lifestyle but his writing as well. His first book contains one of the most vivid descriptions in literature of a drinking binge. It was autobiographical, based on his reaction at age 23 to Zelda's initial refusal to marry him because he made too little money (Goodwin, 1970). Once his novels and stories became popular, money followed, along with Zelda, and Fitzgerald went on a spree from which only death rescued him.

By all accounts, Fitzgerald was handsome, intelligent, gentle, and charming. He was a writer of obvious talent. What was behind his drinking? Why did he follow such a clearly destructive course? Could anything have been done to help him? Questions like these confront psychologists who concern themselves with one of the enduring problems from which people suffer—substance abuse. Alcohol is one of the most frequently abused substances, but there is an incredible variety of drugs that people use and abuse, including nicotine, heroin, tranquilizers, barbiturates, amphetamine, and cocaine.

Fitzgerald intrigues us because he is famous. Some even have suggested that his fame derived in part from his tragic alcoholism, because the public is always fascinated by flawed celebrities (Goodwin, 1970). But ordinary people drink, smoke, or snort their lives away as well. Indeed, people have long found ways to deliberately alter consciousness, changing their perception, mood, and behaviors, leaving behind undesired states for those that promise to be pleasurable, exciting, interesting, or profound. The most common way of altering consciousness is through the ingestion of **psychoactive drugs:** chemicals that affect brain activity and thereby the nature of consciousness.

The alteration in consciousness following ingestion of a psychoactive drug is called **intoxication.** Depending on the drug, the effects of intoxication range from euphoria to depression. Another alteration in consciousness follows the cessation or reduction of drug use. This is called **withdrawal.** Again, the nature of withdrawal depends on the drug in question, but it usually has the opposite effects of intoxication. It is invariably unpleasant. Common to most psychoactive drugs is the phenomenon of **tolerance** with increased use: the need to take more and more of a drug in order to produce the same effect.

How do psychologists define, explain, and finally treat substance abuse? I discuss these questions in the present chapter. So far, I have covered some rather abstract ideas about the psychology of abnormality. Now I begin to use these ideas to make sense of particular problems. Substance abuse is a good place to start.

ALCOHOL USE AND ABUSE

In the first part of this chapter, alcohol will provide most of the examples of substance abuse. It is one of the most abused drugs in the present day. It is one of the most familiar to us. It is the drug most studied by psychologists. Finally, it is a legal drug, which means that my discussion is not confounded by considerations of criminality. In the second part of the chapter, I cover other drugs that people abuse. Before I proceed, look at Table 5.1, which contains a quiz about alcohol. Ascertain your beliefs about alcohol use and abuse, and keep your answers in mind as I discuss what psychologists have learned.

The active ingredient in all alcoholic drinks—beer, wine, and liquor—is **ethyl alcohol,** a substance produced when organic material is fermented or distilled. The difference among alcoholic beverages is not the nature of this active ingredient but rather its concentration. In beer, the volume of ethyl alcohol is usually 4% to 6%. In wine, the figure is usually 10%

TABLE 5.1

QUIZ ON ALCOHOL

Answer "true" or "false" to each of the following statements.

true	false	1.	Alcohol abuse is less of a problem in the contemporary United States than heroin abuse.
true	false	2.	Alcohol abuse is less of a problem in the contemporary United States than cocaine and crack abuse.
true	false	3.	Alcohol abuse is mainly a 20th-century problem.
true	false	4.	The active ingredients differ in beer, wine, and liquor.
true	false	5.	There are three discrete groups of people: teetotalers, moderate drinkers, and alcoholics.
true	false	6.	Alcohol abuse is a problem of equal magnitude in all contemporary cultures.
true	false	7.	Only those physically dependent on alcohol have problems.
true	false	8.	The notion that alcoholism is a disease is new.
true	false	9.	Prohibition was brought about for reasons of public health.
true	false	10.	There is no good reason to believe that alcoholism has a genetic basis.
true	false	11.	Alcoholism is a progressive disease.
true	false	12.	Chronic alcohol abuse is reinforcing.
true	false	13.	Abstinence is the only reasonable goal for alcohol abusers.
true	false	14.	People who abuse alcohol and other drugs have an addictive personality.
true	false	15.	People who abuse alcohol and other drugs uniformly have underlying emotional problems.
true	false	16.	Contrary to appearances, people don't really enjoy being intoxicated.
true	false	17.	People who drink not at all are healthier than those who drink moderately.
true	false	18.	The number of alcoholics in the United States is on the rise.
true	false	19.	There are no effective treatments for alcohol abuse.
true	false	20.	We know more about alcohol use and abuse than we know about the use and abuse of other drugs.

NOTE: *Although there might be some disagreement, the consensus among psychologists seems to be that statements 1 through 19 are false; the only true statement is 20.*

In our society, alcohol is one of the most abused drugs. For some college students, spring break is as much about getting drunk as it is going to the beach.

to 13%. In liquor, the volume of ethyl alcohol usually ranges from 40% to 50% (figures that, when doubled, yield the so-called *proof* of the liquor). These are just rough guidelines, but there is essentially the same

amount of alcohol in a can of beer, a glass of wine, and a cocktail. If a person drinks them at the same rate, he or she will feel the same effect.

Light beer saves calories by cutting the volume of alcohol compared to that of typical beer. In contrast, malt liquor is a strong version of beer, just as muscatel, sherry, and port are strong versions of wine. Certain brands of rum or tequila may be as potent as 150 proof (75% ethyl alcohol).

When an individual drinks alcohol, it is absorbed mainly through the small intestine. Once in the blood, it is broken down into water and carbon dioxide. The rate of alcohol metabolism is fixed, and can readily be exceeded by the rate of ingestion, which means that alcohol circulates in the blood until it can be broken down. Hence, a person's **blood alcohol content** (or **BAC**) is a more exact index of the degree of intoxication than the amount of alcohol consumed. Many states define legal intoxication as a BAC of .10%, and sometimes .08%. Starting sober, if a person consumes three or four drinks in about an hour, he or she usually becomes legally intoxicated, although body size and sex determine the precise number (see Figure 5.1). Please note that considerable individual variation exists.

Alcohol depresses the functioning of the nervous system, but because it initially affects brain centers that are inhibitory, the drinker may at first experience alcohol intoxication as energizing. Another effect of alcohol is to impair the drinker's judgment and reduce conflicts so that his actions become more extreme (Steele & Josephs, 1990). Aggression and sexual activity not otherwise typical for the individual may ensue (Steele & Southwick, 1985).

As time passes and more alcohol is consumed and metabolized, the drinker begins to have difficulty

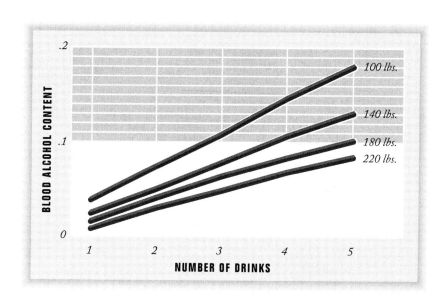

FIGURE 5.1

BLOOD ALCOHOL CONTENT (BAC) AS A FUNCTION OF NUMBER OF DRINKS AND BODY WEIGHT *Drink-for-drink and pound-for-pound, the BAC of a female is slightly higher than that of a male (see text). A BAC of .10 or more is considered legally intoxicated in most states.*

thinking, speaking, walking, and/or seeing. He might become withdrawn and sullen. In larger amounts, alcohol induces sleep. In still larger amounts, it can lead to a coma and even death.

The long-term effects of alcohol abuse are ubiquitous. Here is a list of consequences for the person who comes to tolerate alcohol and then to depend on it: Lesions in the brain develop, producing dementia and amnesia. Risk of heart failure increases. Hypertension is common, as is capillary rupture. Alcohol contains calories but no nutrients, and so abusers are often malnourished because they do not want food. Liver tissue is destroyed as cirrhosis develops. Curtailing alcohol use can bring on seizures. And drinking while pregnant can harm the developing fetus.

Because alcohol abuse is so widespread in our society, such effects on the individual, when multiplied over the entire population, consume a staggering amount of our nation's resources. Alcohol may be involved in as many as 50% of all auto fatalities, murders, suicides, and hospital admissions in the United States today (Gorsky, Schwartz, & Dennis, 1988).

HISTORICAL CONSIDERATIONS

In order to understand current approaches to alcohol use and abuse, consider the historical background of this drug. Historians estimate that beer and wine may date back more than 10,000 years (e.g., Johnson, 1989). Large accumulations of grape seeds have been found in archaeological sites in Turkey, Syria, and Lebanon, suggesting that they were discarded in the deliberate process of making wine. Cultivated grapes apparently made their appearance in the Republic of Georgia about 8,000 years ago.

Our distant ancestors had obviously discovered that a mash of fruits, grapes, berries, or honey would ferment when airborne yeasts acted on the sugar they contain, converting it to alcohol and carbon dioxide. Grains would similarly ferment when their starch turns to sugar, which happens—for instance—simply by adding saliva.

In Chapter 1, I discussed the history of abnormality: Three general perspectives were distinguished in terms of conceiving abnormality: as a magical, somatic, or psychological phenomenon. Frequently these views have coexisted and intermingled.

Alcohol abuse as a magical/moral phenomenon   Our ancestors who first drank ale or wine and experienced its effects must have been flabbergasted. "In a life that was nasty, brutish, and short, those who first felt the effects of alcohol believed that they were being given a preview of paradise" (Johnson, 1989, p. 10). This is not hyperbole. Alcohol was interpreted in magical

terms. It was incorporated in many religious ceremonies, and used in particular by shamans to achieve the trance state in which the immaterial forces of nature could be divined and directed.

Thousands of years ago, the ancient Greeks had their own god of wine, Dionysus (*also called* Bacchus). *They believed that when a person drank wine, he literally drank the god. Once inside the person, Dionysus would banish worries and cares. The parallel between this belief and the more recent Christian Eucharist is certainly no coincidence. In many religions, red wine symbolizes blood, and hence life.*

Dionysus was celebrated at festivals throughout the year. These involved worship of wine, to be sure, but also sexuality, which pertains in rather obvious ways to birth and renewal. These celebrations were called bacchanals, *and from our vantage point we would term them drunken orgies. Men dressed as satyrs and wore exaggerated phalluses made of leather. Women dressed as maenads to be pursued by the satyrs. The familiar masks of comedy and tragedy date from these celebrations, as the satyr's leer gave rise to the mask of comedy, and the maenad's alarm gave rise to the mask of tragedy. The term* comedy *is derived from the Greek word* komos, *a giant phallic figure around which the celebrants of Dionysus danced.*

So, alcohol use during the Greek era was given an explicit interpretation in terms of a magical view of

This drinking cup from 540 B.C. is decorated with a picture of Dionysus, the god of wine, traveling in a boat. Note the grapevine that entwines the boat's mast.

the world. People who were intoxicated were literally possessed by Dionysus, and the acts they would commit were attributed to the power of the god, not to their own volition. Those who worshipped Dionysus were wanton and violent. Being intoxicated meant going on rampages yet not being held responsible for so doing.

In early Judaism, wine was part of all important ceremonies. Because the consumption of alcohol was coupled with an attitude of reverence, acute intoxication was inappropriate and met with disapproval. Even today, the prevalence of problem drinkers among Jews is notably low (Flasher & Maisto, 1984; Keller, 1970; Yeung & Greenwald, 1992). The Koran condemns wine, and so Muslims also tend to eschew alcohol; Buddhists and many Hindus abstain as well (Cochrane & Bal, 1990).

The interpretation of drug use and abuse in magical terms has certainly not fallen off over the centuries if we include moral interpretations under this heading. The relatively recent history of the United States provides an excellent illustration of how alcohol use and abuse have been regarded as manifestations of evil. The social groups that brought about *prohibition* were morally opposed to alcohol.

The roots of prohibition extend to the early 1800s, when intense religious revivalism swept the United States. People should strive to be perfect, said the principle behind the movement, and this meant living without alcohol. The legal prohibition of alcohol was enacted on local and state levels throughout the 1800s. At the turn of the 20th century, there were calls for prohibition at the national level, on religious grounds as well as for social and economic reasons. There is no doubt that alcohol consumption was harming the well-being of many Americans, particularly those of Irish and English ancestry, whose cultural norms produced problematic drinking (Sournia, 1990). A large proportion of the population—mostly lower-class males—drank a great deal. Physical and emotional abuse of women and children followed in the wake of this alcohol abuse.

Spearheading the call for prohibition was the *women's temperance movement,* which urged temperance in all matters, but particularly alcohol consumption. Public drunkenness was strongly opposed. The movement attracted both moderates and extremists—such as Carry A. Nation, famed for laying waste to saloons with a hatchet. The women's temperance movement was grounded in religion. Those who drank were possessed by the devil. And thus alcohol abuse was regarded as a sign of moral depravity. People had to be rescued from their weakness, forcibly if need be.

Prohibitionist Carry A. Nation (1846–1911) won fame for destroying saloons with a hatchet.

The women's temperance movement was eventually joined in its fight for prohibition by the country's industrial leaders. Industrialists were motivated by more pragmatic concerns (Levine, 1984). Intoxicated workers were inefficient, particularly when asked to work on assembly lines and run complicated machinery. The temporary Wartime Prohibition Act during World War I, enacted to save grain for food, implied that national prohibition was feasible. And so in 1920, with prohibition already the law in 33 states, the 18th Amendment went into effect, prohibiting alcohol across the United States.

Prohibition was effective in the sense of decreasing the nation's overall alcohol consumption, but it certainly did not bring alcohol use and abuse to a halt. The enforcement of the ban on alcohol was uneven, and the new law created its own set of problems.[1] The production and sale of alcohol became the business of organized crime. Alcohol was no longer consumed in homes or taverns but in speakeasies, which existed for the sole purpose of getting people as drunk as possible in as short a time as possible.

---

[1] The point has been made that legal prohibition of *any* drug is ineffective in curtailing its abuse (Nadelmann, 1989). Although it is unlikely that we will see a relaxing of drug laws in the United States in the near future, the possibility that drug laws create their own share of problems must be considered. Today's jails and prisons are filled with drug offenders serving mandatory sentences, so much so that violent prisoners are often paroled well before their time has been served.

Bootlegger Al Capone (1899–1947), shown here on his way to prison in 1932, made millions of dollars selling illegal liquor during prohibition.

In view of the problems created by prohibition, people in the United States became disenchanted. In 1932, the Democratic party ran on a platform calling for its repeal. Their election victories assured the removal of the 18th Amendment the following year.

The temperance movement has its more modern equivalents. Former First Lady Nancy Reagan's "Just Say No" slogan has gained some currency as an incantation that youngsters can use to withstand the beckoning of drugs (Peele, 1989). This slogan makes substance abuse a moral issue and minimizes other important factors. If we counsel a young person to simply say no to drugs, while ignoring the biological, psychological, and social forces that might encourage him or her to say yes, then we are assuming that will power alone is sufficient. We do not tell people to just say no to cancer or heart disease. Nor do we tell them to just say no to bad habits or inappropriate expectations. But if we tell them to just say no to drugs, we are somehow treating substance abuse as different.

Alcohol abuse as a somatic phenomenon   The second historical perspective regards abnormality as a medical phenomenon. When applied to alcohol abuse, this view casts it in disease terms. Alcohol abuse as a

disease is associated with excessive consumption—but from the somatic perspective alcohol consumption itself is a sign or symptom of an underlying disease. Although this view has taken hold recently, and seems to be widespread among professionals and everyday citizens alike (Peele, 1989), it is a perspective that has been around a long time (Keller, 1976).

In the 1st century, the Roman philosopher Seneca distinguished between those who were intoxicated and those who were out of control of their drinking. The latter individuals had a problem that the former individuals did not. Similarly, the Talmud (completed around 500 A.D.) suggested that habitual drinkers should not be held responsible for crimes they might commit, even if the crimes took place when they were sober. In other words, the condition that produced alcohol abuse characterized the person whether or not he was intoxicated at any given moment.

So far I have used terms like *alcoholism* and *alcoholic* somewhat loosely, as synonyms of alcohol abuse and alcohol abuser, respectively. However, among those who view alcohol abuse in disease terms, more precise usage is needed. From this perspective, **alcoholism** is the disease that leads people to abuse alcohol; an **alcoholic** is an individual with the disease of alcoholism. Drinking is only a *possible* sign of alcoholism. A person can be an alcoholic and not drink; he or she can drink and not be an alcoholic.

The modern notion of alcoholism as a disease was phrased most influentially by Elvin Jellinek (1960), who described one type of alcohol abuse as a progressive disease. In other words, it runs an insidious course, eventually ending in the death of the alcoholic. Jellinek distinguished stages of this disease, from bad to worse, and he hypothesized that alcoholics moved steadily and inevitably through them.

While not necessarily equating alcohol abuse with a disease, other theorists have speculated that alcohol problems are predisposed by physiological characteristics of the alcohol abuser. At one time, alcoholism was thought to be caused by an allergy to alcohol (Randolph, 1956). Other theories suggested that it was due to a nutritional deficiency (Mardones, 1951). Still other hypotheses attributed it to metabolic irregularities (Dent, 1941), brain pathology (Little & McAvoy, 1952), or endocrine imbalances (Tintera & Lovell, 1949). Research investigating these possibilities has been hampered by the fact that chronic alcohol use produces a host of somatic changes; investigators must distinguish the effects of alcoholism from its possible causes (Vaillant, 1983).

Impressed with the idea that alcohol abuse runs through families, theorists have long attempted to explain why (Cotton, 1979). What heritable characteristics might predispose the incipient alcoholic to develop problems (Newlin & Thomson, 1990)? Perhaps alcoholics experience intoxication as particularly enjoyable. Perhaps they are less sensitive to hangovers.

If alcoholism has a somatic basis, then it can presumably be treated in somatic terms. Indeed, such an approach is widespread today, particularly in hospitals and clinics. Alcohol itself must be removed from the body and kept out of it. Abstinence is thus the preferred goal of most who view alcohol abuse in biomedical terms. When the disease notion of alcoholism became popular in the 20th century, organized efforts to "treat" it took form. To the extent possible, whatever physical characteristics predispose alcoholism should be targeted for change.

The view of alcoholism as a disease is shared by members of **Alcoholics Anonymous** (or **AA**), the popular self-help group for recovering alcohol abusers. AA members regard themselves as "powerless in the face of alcohol" because they suffer from an incurable disease. The goal of AA members is abstinence, but they never regard themselves as rid of their problem. A member will introduce himself by saying, "My name is Bill, and I am an alcoholic. I haven't had a drink in 10 years."

Regarding alcoholism as a disease is probably preferable to regarding it as a moral failure. Alcoholism brings with it enough problems; we gain nothing by adding to the guilt that the alcoholic experiences. We do not typically blame people for their illnesses (cf. Sontag, 1979). These fall outside the realm of moral responsibility. So why should we blame people for having the problem of alcoholism?

Alcohol abuse as a psychological phenomenon   The third perspective on abnormality regards it as a psychological phenomenon, something that a person has learned to do. In contrast to the magical and somatic views, the psychological approach sees the problem with alcohol as stemming from its consumption. Alcoholism is neither a bewitchment nor a disease, but a learned habit (Blume, 1984). Like any bad habit, alcohol abuse is rewarding on one level while problematic on another. I have already mentioned many of the physical and social problems that follow in the wake of excessive drinking. Where are the rewards? Several possibilities exist.

First, alcohol intoxication may simply be fun. There seems to be a taboo in popular antidrug campaigns against acknowledging that the changes in consciousness brought about by psychoactive substances are enjoyable (Weil, 1972). Televised beer commercials would have us believe that the decision to drink is driven by considerations of taste and/or calories. However, it is much more plausible that people consume alcohol because they enjoy the sensation of being

Beer advertisements rarely acknowledge that people drink because they enjoy being intoxicated.

People may drink in response to underlying problems, and treatment must address these problems as well as those brought about by alcohol abuse per se.

intoxicated. And beer commercials certainly *imply* that drinking is fun, even if they do not actually say so.

Second, alcohol may provide temporary relief for the person suffering from stress (Sher, 1987). Alcohol and anxiety do not easily coexist, and it has long been proposed that people drink in order to reduce tension (Conger, 1951, 1956). Research shows that for at least some drinkers, alcohol reduces their physiological response to stress (e.g., Finn, Zeitouni, & Pihl, 1990). In fact, tranquilizers such as Librium and Valium, frequently prescribed for anxiety disorders (Chapter 7), are highly similar in their effects to alcohol. Along these same lines, alcohol intoxication may provide temporary relief from an overly harsh conscience (McFadden, 1988).

Third, people might drink because of social reinforcement, direct as well as indirect. An adolescent's drug use or abstinence can be readily predicted on the basis of drug use or abstinence by his or her peers. The critical factor appears to be whether individuals perceive their peers as approving or disapproving (e.g., Jessor, Chase, & Donovan, 1980).

So far I have been discussing alcohol as if it has similar effects on all drinkers, but a number of studies show that expectancies about drinking and its consequences importantly influence what ensues (Goldman, Brown, & Christiansen, 1987). As their expectancies differ, so too do the ways people behave when intoxicated. No one proposes that the effects of alcohol use are due only to expectations, but this research reveals important psychological aspects of substance use and abuse.

Proponents of the psychological view tend to see normal behavior and abnormal behavior as continuous; they avoid drawing a firm line between alcohol use and alcohol abuse. Abuse exists to the degree that the costs of drinking accrue. In any case, it is presumably under the sway of the same environmental determinants as alcohol use, with the same behavioral and cognitive processes operative.

According to the psychological view, just how does one stop drinking? A straightforward strategy is based on principles of learning: Associate alcohol consumption with an aversive experience. Through conditioning, then, the person will develop an aversion to drinking. Examples of this behavior therapy technique appear in the form of advice throughout history. Put something disgusting in the drink of the alcohol abuser in order to create an aversion—owl eggs, frogs, earwax, urine, or sparrow dung (Keller, 1976).

Attempts to treat alcohol abuse with conditioning procedures are part of the contemporary scene as well.

According to studies in the contemporary United States, large groups—particularly of women—facilitate drinking.

Although medical doctors administer it, the drug **disulfiram** (or **Antabuse**) is a treatment that depends on psychological principles.

Mr. Kennedy is given a dose of disulfiram. He is told what happens when the drug and alcohol are combined, and he may be shown a film illustrating the results: nausea, vomiting, pounding of the heart, and the feeling of impending death. Disulfiram is then prescribed on a daily basis, and to the degree that Mr. Kennedy follows the prescription, he will be reluctant to drink.

The procedure just described attempts to eliminate drinking altogether. A different strategy, also in keeping with the view of alcoholism as a psychological phenomenon, aims not at abstinence but at moderation. The alcohol abuser is seen as a person who has not learned the right way to drink. The solution is to teach him how to drink so that he can avoid negative consequences. This approach is called **controlled drinking,** and it instructs the individual to drink low-proof beverages, to sip rather than gulp, and to regulate the total amount of alcohol he consumes at one sitting (Sobell & Sobell, 1978). He is also taught to identify the situations associated with excessive drinking and to approach them differently.

Sobell and Sobell described the case of Mr. J. A., an individual instructed in the details of controlled drinking:

> *Approximately 1 month subsequent to discharge . . . [he] was able to analyze an experienced desire to drink as resulting from the fact that his brother was living in his house, free-loading off of him, and attempting to seduce his wife. J. A. then generated a number of possible responses to this situation, including migrating to Chicago. After analyzing the various alternatives in terms of long-range consequences, he decided to confront his brother and demand that he move out of the house. To J. A.'s amazement, his brother did move out, and J. A.'s marital relationship improved considerably thereafter. (1973, p. 69)*

In this case, controlled drinking not only helped Mr. J. A. deal with his problem involving alcohol but paid dividends elsewhere.

This treatment strategy has proven controversial (Marlatt, 1983; Peele, 1987). Its premise is at odds with the widely held notion that abstinence is the only realistic goal for the alcohol abuser. An early study of controlled drinking produced highly encouraging

with other problems involving compulsive behavior. Orford (1985) describes the extremes of drinking, drug taking, eating, gambling, and sexuality as excessive appetites, and recommends that they be explained (and treated) similarly. Pop psychology books, such as *Women Who Love Too Much* (Norwood, 1985), sometimes draw explicit parallels between substance abuse on the one hand and maladaptive approaches to human relationships on the other. These analogies encourage a broad perspective, but they may at the same time lead to a superficial view.

DSM-IV   Remember from Chapter 2 that the American Psychiatric Association's (1994) DSM-IV is the diagnostic system most widely used in the United States. While recognizing that other diagnostic approaches to substance abuse exist, I focus here on how DSM-IV handles the matter.

Demonstrable impairments of the brain and nervous system brought about by the use of alcohol and other psychoactive drugs and resulting in persistent disturbances in consciousness and cognition are described as **substance-induced cognitive disorders.** The behavioral problems associated with the use of alcohol and other psychoactive substances are separately described as **substance-related disorders.**

DSM-IV classifies alcohol along with several other psychoactive substances that may be abused. Eleven different drugs are named (see Table 5-2). These particular drugs are included because individuals may respond to them with symptoms reflecting

substance dependence: a cluster of cognitive, behavioral, and physiological symptoms that indicate severe impairment and distress due to drug use.

These symptoms are described in Table 5.3. If a person shows three or more of them for at least a month, the DSM-IV diagnosis of substance dependence follows. DSM-IV thus embodies the idea that problematic substance use is best defined in terms of several simultaneous criteria. It directs the diagnostician to note whether substance dependence involves tolerance or withdrawal. If so, then the drug-dependent person is deemed *physiologically dependent.* However, physiological dependence is not necessary for the diagnosis of substance dependence. For example, only minimal signs of withdrawal characterize drugs such as LSD or marijuana, but a person can still be deemed dependent if other symptoms are present.

DSM-IV provides another diagnostic label for drug-using individuals who do not fully meet the criteria for a diagnosis of dependence but still evidence circumscribed impairment or distress due to drug use: **substance abuse.** Here individuals encounter problems at work, school, or home; find themselves in hazardous situations; run afoul of the law; and/or continue to use drugs despite the problems that are

TABLE 5.2

PSYCHOACTIVE DRUGS
SOURCE: *DSM-IV DRAFT CRITERIA*, 1993, WASHINGTON, DC: AMERICAN PSYCHIATRIC ASSOCIATION.

DSM-IV specifies 11 drugs subject to abuse and dependence:

alcohol

amphetamine ("speed")

caffeine

cannabis (marijuana)

cocaine

hallucinogens (e.g., LSD)

inhalants (e.g., glue, gasoline)

nicotine (tobacco)

opioids (e.g., opium, morphine, heroin)

phencyclidine (PCP or "angel dust")

sedatives (e.g., tranquilizers, barbiturates)

TABLE 5.3

DSM-IV CRITERIA FOR PSYCHOACTIVE SUBSTANCE DEPENDENCE
SOURCE: *DSM-IV DRAFT CRITERIA*, 1993, WASHINGTON, DC: AMERICAN PSYCHIATRIC ASSOCIATION.

A person is dependent on a psychoactive substance to the degree that he or she shows the following:

◆ tolerance
  – the need for increasing amounts of the drug to achieve its desired effect; and/or
  – decreased effect with continued use of the same amount of the drug

◆ withdrawal
  – characteristic withdrawal symptoms from the drug; and/or
  – use of the drug to relieve these symptoms

◆ drug use in larger amounts or over a longer period of time than intended

◆ a persistent desire for the drug or unsuccessful attempts to decrease or control its use

◆ a great deal of time devoted to obtaining or using the drug

◆ curtailing of other activities in order to use the drug

◆ continued use of the drug despite knowledge of its harmful effects

In 1994, Hall of Fame baseball player Mickey Mantle publicly acknowledged a long-standing problem with alcohol abuse.

produced or exacerbated by doing so. Consider people who repeatedly drive when impaired, or drink alcohol despite an ulcer, or buy cocaine rather than repay loans.

Although eleven different drugs are included in DSM-IV, several of them can be grouped together on the basis of common features: alcohol and sedatives; amphetamine and cocaine; the hallucinogens and phencyclidine. Within these categories, intoxication and withdrawal are similar, as are patterns of dependence and abuse.

Assessment   DSM-IV criteria for substance dependence and abuse are clear enough in the abstract, but the diagnostician faces a problem when he or she tries to apply them in concrete situations. Consider some of the complications involved in interviewing a person and trying to decide on the basis of her answers whether she has a problem with drugs and, if so, just what the nature of that problem is. In the heights of intoxication or the depths of withdrawal, she may be incoherent, uncooperative, or untrustworthy. When sober, she may consciously or unconsciously deny the details of her drug use.

Hall of Fame baseball player Mickey Mantle announced that he had recognized and sought treatment for a decades-long problem with alcohol abuse:

> *I began some of my mornings the past 10 years with the "breakfast of champions"—a big glass filled with a shot or more of brandy, some Kahlua and cream. Billy Martin and I used to drink them all the time, and I named the*

drink after us. Sometimes when I was in New York with nothing to do, and Billy and I were together, we would stop into my restaurant on Central Park South at around 10 in the morning, and the bartender would dump all of the ingredients into a blender and stir it right up. It tasted real good.

> *Unfortunately for everybody else around me, one "breakfast of champions" and they could kiss the day goodbye. After one drink, I was off and running. And unless I had a business engagement, I'd often keep on drinking until I couldn't drink anymore.*

> *Drinking had become an all-too-frequent routine for me. If I had a drink to start the day, I'd go out for lunch and go through three or four bottles of wine in the course of an afternoon. White wine. Red wine. It didn't matter, and I didn't care about the quality either. . . .*

> *Over the years I drank so much of it that I didn't care anymore.*

One effect of his constant alcohol abuse is that Mantle was unable to remember most of what he did, including his drinking. He reported that the last 10 years of his life were a blur, and this contributed to his not recognizing the extent of his problem with alcohol. In 1995, Mantle received a well-publicized liver transplant, but died soon after of cancer.

In light of the unreliability of the problem drinker, diagnosticians may turn to informants—friends and family members—to get a better picture of an individual's substance use, but this is not foolproof either (Vaillant, 1983). Informants may exaggerate the details of substance abuse, or they may minimize them. Substance use and abuse can have dire interpersonal consequences, and the friends and family members of an abuser might have difficulty playing the role of an unbiased reporter. Mickey Mantle was so popular with the general public that strangers literally lined up to buy him drinks; none of them regarded this as contributing to Mantle's problems, although of course it did.

Estimates of the prevalence of alcohol dependence and abuse have yet to be discussed because such figures depend greatly on the specific criteria employed. A study by Boyd, Weissman, Thompson, and Myers (1983) illustrates this point. These researchers administered a structured diagnostic interview to 510 adult residents of an urban community in the United States. A number of questions about past and present alcohol use were included. Their responses were then scored according to seven different definitions of alcoholism popular in the research literature, including DSM criteria for alcohol dependence. Different definitions yielded different estimates of the current prevalence of severe alcohol abuse, from 1.6% of the sample to 2.4%, as well as past prevalence at some time in life, from 3.1% to 6.3%. (By the way, the DSM figures were 2.2% and 5.3%, respectively.) These are not trivial differences, because if we were to use them to gauge the prevalence of alcoholism in the entire United States, with its population of 250 million people, our estimates would vary by millions of individuals.

When the popular media report statistics about the incidence and prevalence of drug abuse, the pertinent numbers are rarely based on diagnostic interviews (Kandel, 1991; Kozel, 1990). They usually reflect responses to brief surveys that ask respondents about the frequency and amount of their substance use (see Figure 5.2). A decision is then made about where to place a cutoff between use and abuse, and the number of people who fall on the abuse side of the line is reported. This information certainly has value by allowing comparisons across time and place about drug *use*. But it does not permit firm conclusions about the extent of drug *dependence* or *abuse*.

THEORIES AND RESEARCH

How might we explain substance abuse? How might we treat or prevent it? Numerous theories have been proposed. Lettieri, Sayers, and Pearson (1980) catalogued no fewer than 43 different accounts of drug abuse. Some order can be brought to this vast literature by organizing it in terms of the models of abnormality introduced in Chapter 3. Consistent with the general conclusion offered there, you will see that each model of abnormality explains some aspects of substance abuse but not others. A full account of substance abuse is one that integrates the insights of the different models.

Biomedical approach   As already discussed, biomedical explanations of substance abuse focus on a person's bodily processes. Substance abuse is thought to require medical treatment. Thus, biomedical treatment begins with **detoxification:** letting the substance clear the person's body. Because alcohol withdrawal symptoms may be quite severe and even life-threatening, detoxification is typically undertaken in a hospital. Following detoxification, the patient may be administered Antabuse and encouraged to join AA. In any case, abstinence is the goal of treatment. For psychoactive drugs such as morphine and heroin, there exist chemicals that block the drug effects. These are called **antagonists,** and they obviously have some role in treating abuse. No antagonists currently exist for alcohol.

What is useful about the biomedical approach? For starters, substance abuse involves the body in an obvious way. The phenomena of tolerance and withdrawal show that substance abuse alters physiological functioning, so that the person continues to seek out and use the drug in question, in ever-increasing amounts.

Studies point to the conclusion that some types of alcoholism are heritable for males. Several investigations have found that sons separated from their parents shortly after birth and raised in a foster home resemble their biological parents with respect to alcoholism (Murray, Clifford, & Gurling, 1983). In a study in Copenhagen, Goodwin and colleagues (1974) found that adopted boys with an alcohol abuser as a biological parent were *four times more likely* than other adopted boys to themselves abuse alcohol as adults. Twin studies also demonstrate that alcohol problems are heritable among males (e.g., McGue, Pickens, & Svikis, 1992). The evidence is more mixed concerning the heritability of alcohol abuse for females (e.g., Goodwin, Schulsinger, Knop, Mednick, & Guze, 1977; Kendler, Heath, Neale, Kessler, & Eaves, 1992).

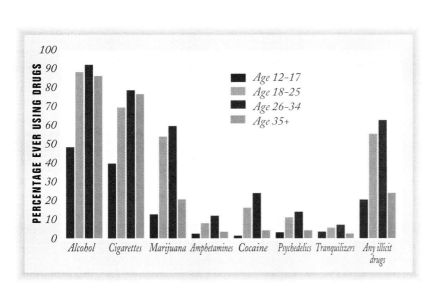

FIGURE 5.2

LIFETIME PREVALENCE RATES OF DRUG USE, 1990
Drug use of some sort is highly prevalent among those in the United States, particularly young adults.
SOURCE: *National Household Survey on Drug Abuse,* 1990, ROCKVILLE, MD: NATIONAL INSTITUTE ON DRUG ABUSE.

The biological mechanism by which alcohol abuse is predisposed has not been identified. I have discussed the long-standing attempt to find physical differences between alcoholics and nonalcoholics, noting that this search can be confounded by the biological effects of alcohol use. One way around this dilemma is to compare the children of alcoholics to the children of nonalcoholics, prior to the development of substance abuse by those in either group (Sher, 1991). The adult sons of alcoholics show more sensitivity to the effects of alcohol as BAC level increases yet less sensitivity as BAC level decreases (Newlin & Thomson, 1990). So, while becoming intoxicated, males with a family history of alcoholism experience more pleasure than those without; while withdrawing, they experience less pain.

Where does the biomedical approach fall short? Although it can account for the continued abuse of drugs by a physically addicted person, it fails to explain so readily a person's initial drug use. It fails to explain why many individuals who become dependent at one point in life may later taper their use to moderate levels (Vaillant, 1983). Substance abuse is not always a progressive problem. This approach also fails to account for the sensitivity of drug use and abuse to situational demands or life events.

Psychoanalytic approach   Whereas the biomedical approach sees substance abuse as the sign of an underlying physical problem, the psychoanalytic approach attributes it to an underlying emotional conflict (Smaldino, 1991). One clue to the nature of this conflict is found in the particular substance chosen for abuse. The two are thought to bear a symbolic relationship to one another. So, psychoanalytic theorists hypothesize that alcoholics have conflicts surrounding dependency (Rado, 1926, 1933). Because of a fixation at the oral stage of psychosexual development, they wish to be symbolically nursed. Alcoholics therefore "suck down" one drink after another. What about narcotics abusers who use a syringe to inject drugs into their veins? Mainlining is thought to reflect an indirect way of dealing with sexual or aggressive conflicts (Freedman, 1980; Khantzian, 1980).

Psychoanalytic theorists expect substance abusers to be troubled individuals with difficulties preceding their abuse. Such hypotheses draw our attention to personality traits that lead to abuse. The notion of an **addictive personality** captures this idea—a constellation of traits such as emotional immaturity, low self-esteem, and loneliness that leads people to overindulge their appetites when anxious. In its extreme, drug abuse may be a manifestation of the death instinct. Treatment from the psychoanalytic perspective is insight-oriented, focused on the underlying conflicts that lead an individual to abuse drugs in the first place.

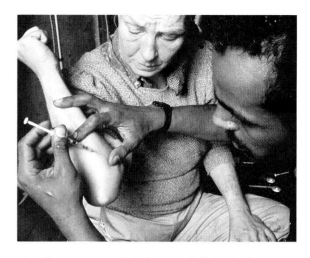

According to psychoanalytic theory, mainlining heroin— injecting it directly into one's veins—is an indirect way of dealing with sexual conflicts.

What is useful about the psychoanalytic approach to substance abuse? It focuses on the motives of the abuser, an issue on which the biomedical approach is conspicuously silent. People use and abuse drugs for reasons that cohere with the rest of their psychological makeup. The psychoanalytic approach can thus explain initial drug use, as well as its self-destructive aspects.

Where does the psychoanalytic approach fall short? There is little evidence of an addictive personality style. There is little evidence that people choose substances to abuse that symbolize conflicts lingering from childhood. Indeed, many substance abusers are quite broad in their preferences, using and abusing a variety of psychoactive drugs, which implies that access may be more important than symbolism (Clayton, 1986). This model also fails to explain the fact that psychological problems such as depression and anxiety are more likely to result from substance abuse than to precede it (Vaillant, 1983).

Some personality differences exist between those who abuse drugs and those who do not, although demonstrating that these differences precede substance abuse can be difficult. They may well be the *result* of substance abuse. Longitudinal studies suggest that future substance abusers differ from their nonabusing counterparts in terms of a history of antisocial behavior: nonconformity, acting out, and impulsivity (Cox, 1985; Nathan, 1988; Vaillant, 1983; Zucker & Gomberg, 1986). Those who use and abuse drugs tend to score high on measures of sensation seeking (Pedersen, 1991). Note that these differences are *not* the ones predicted by psychoanalytic theorists.

Cognitive-behavioral approach   The cognitive-behavioral approach to substance abuse regards it as something that a person has learned to do. People use drugs because the benefits outweigh the costs; they should stop using drugs as the costs mount. Treatment from this perspective encourages the person to learn other ways of behaving in order to gain rewards. You have already encountered the basics of the cognitive-behavioral approach in the earlier discussion of alcoholism as a psychological phenomenon, so let me just draw out some of its implications here.

Researchers using animals as subjects have shown that many of the phenomena of substance abuse are amenable to classical conditioning (Wikler, 1973). Suppose intoxication with a drug such as alcohol or heroin is repeatedly paired with a neutral stimulus. This stimulus is eventually able to elicit on its own at least part of the intoxication response (Chen, 1968). That is, a physically addicted animal will respond to the conditioned stimulus as if to the drug. Or suppose drug withdrawal is repeatedly paired with a neutral stimulus. This stimulus is eventually able to elicit on its own craving for the drug (Kaplan et al., 1985).

The importance of these demonstrations is that they place drug use and abuse in their environmental context. Encountering stimuli associated with past drug abuse may hinder the person who is trying to gain control over his or her consumption. Part of the common-sense advice to the person trying to stop drinking or smoking is to stay away from settings in which these habits have been indulged.

As described earlier, expectancies about alcohol are important cognitive determinants of its use and abuse. Expectancies can be studied with a laboratory procedure in which research subjects are given a beverage to drink. Half the time the beverage contains alcohol, and half the time it does not. Expectations are then manipulated by telling half of the subjects that they are drinking alcohol and the other half that they are not. Note that this procedure creates four different groups of subjects, defined by the combinations of the actual contents of the beverage (alcohol versus no alcohol) and the expectations about the contents (alcohol versus no alcohol). Results show that the belief that one has consumed alcohol can matter as much as whether one actually has (Leigh, 1989; Leigh & Stacy, 1991).

In a well known experiment along these lines, Merry (1966) studied hospitalized alcoholics who believed that they lost control after but a single drink. Each morning they were given a mixture of orange syrup and water identified as a "vitamin" drink. On alternate days, 1 ounce of vodka was added to the drink. Later each day, the subjects were asked to indicate the degree to which they experienced cravings for alcohol. There were no differences in the ratings between the days when subjects had been given alcohol and the days when they had not. Merry concluded that alcoholics lost control over their drinking when they expected to do so, not because alcohol automatically triggered the process.

Other studies show that subjects become more sexually aroused, more aggressive, and more relaxed if they believe they have consumed alcohol, whether or not they actually have (e.g., Lang, Goeckner, Adesso, & Marlatt, 1975; Wilson & Abrams, 1977; Wilson & Lawson, 1976). Interestingly, when individuals believe they are drinking alcohol, they are also likely to drink more, whether or not their beverages actually contain alcohol (Marlatt, Demming, & Reid, 1973).

Those who hold positive expectancies about alcohol use drink more than those who do not. Consider these expectancies about alcohol use:

♦ Drinking makes the future seem brighter.

♦ A few drinks make a person more sexual.

♦ When I drink, I can express my feelings better.

The more a person endorses such beliefs, the more apt he or she is to use and abuse alcohol (e.g., Brown, Goldman, Inn, & Anderson, 1980).

What is useful about the cognitive-behavioral approach? It emphasizes that drug use and abuse are responsive to the immediate environment, and that the mechanisms of this response are mundane: conditioning, expectancies, and the like. This approach also allows substance use and abuse to be explained in the same general terms as all other behaviors, normal and abnormal.

Where does the cognitive-behavioral approach fall short? Most basically, it neglects the biological realities of substance abuse. Once a person is physically addicted to a drug such as alcohol, continued drinking takes on a life of its own, even in the face of escalating troubles. Although intoxication may be rewarding in the short run, it cannot be argued that people chronically abuse drugs because they are reinforced for doing so. Anxiety and depression follow drug abuse, as does social estrangement (Vaillant, 1983).

Humanistic-existential-phenomenological approaches
As I discussed in Chapter 3, humanistic, existential, and phenomenological theories share an emphasis on a person's experience. When applied to substance use and abuse, they draw our attention to the drug experience. These approaches do more than characterize intoxication as pleasurable; they conceive it as a state of consciousness qualitatively different from our normal waking state.

Writing several decades ago, Andrew Weil (1972) proposed that people have an innate desire to experience altered states, particularly those similar to what William James (1890) described as a *mystical experience:*

✦   a feeling of oneness with the universe

✦   a sense of truth

✦   an inability to express experience in words

✦   vividness and a sense of clarity of sensations and perceptions

Because intoxication overlaps with the mystical experience, people may be inclined to use drugs. Indeed, Weil regarded drug use as natural, a way to facilitate access to alternative states. People who seek out drugs are actualizing themselves. A similar view of intoxication, via hallucinogenic drugs, was proposed by Aldous Huxley (1954) in *The Doors of Perception.* Huxley described his personal experimentation with the drug mescaline, hypothesizing that it stripped away an individual's interpretations of experience and opened a door to experience per se.

The views of Weil and Huxley are enthusiastic ones, standing in sharp contrast to the negative depictions of substance abuse so far presented. Keep in mind that these theorists wrote at a more innocent time, when the dangers of substance abuse were not fully realized. I can remember the widespread belief in the

1960s that the only harmful drugs were alcohol and tobacco. Drugs like mescaline or LSD were hailed by some as mind-expanding or consciousness-raising (e.g., Leary, 1964).

More recently, theorists have seen substance abuse as a roadblock on the way to self-actualization, not a route. Greaves (1980) proposed that altered states of consciousness are desirable for many people, but that drugs represent an immature attempt to achieve them. Those who use them are unable to attain transcendence and fulfillment in other ways. Treatment consists of helping people find healthier ways of actualizing themselves.

What is useful about the humanistic-existential-phenomenological approaches? The statement that drug use and abuse involve characteristic *experiences* with considerable significance is not to be found in other models of abnormality. To understand drug abuse, one must include a view from the inside. These approaches are consistent with the finding already mentioned that the trait of sensation seeking is associated with increased drug use (Zuckerman, 1979). These approaches also help explain why drug use has been part of religious ceremonies throughout recorded history.

I earlier discussed the use of alcohol and other psychoactive drugs as "self-medication" for depression and anxiety. Drugs may also be used to deal with the anguish of existence—feelings of being alone and fears of death. They allow people to let go of their inhibitions and, however briefly, to lead a life of grandeur and excitement. That these experiences may prove inauthentic does not detract from their appeal.

Where do these approaches to drug abuse fall short? It is ironic that for all their concern with describing how people experience reality, these approaches ignore many of the biological, psychological, and social realities of substance abuse. Demonstrable risk factors exist. People do not simply choose to indulge or abstain.

Family systems approach   The family systems model regards ostensibly individual problems as manifestations of problems within a family as a whole. Treatment targets styles of family interaction (McCrady et al., 1986). When applied to substance abuse, this approach looks at the abuse of one family member in terms of the dynamics among all family members. In some families, substance abuse by one or more family members is an organizing theme for the entire family (Steinglass, 1985). Somehow the abuse is instrumental in maintaining a homeostasis within the family, allowing some problems to be solved while creating others.

Perhaps an alcohol abuser functions as a scapegoat within his family. His difficulties draw attention away from other problems. His family members therefore

Jim Morrison was the lead singer of the Doors. The group's name is an allusion to mescaline, taken from Aldous Huxley's book about the drug. Morrison himself died of cirrhosis brought on by alcohol abuse.

act in ways to guarantee his continued abuse. Perhaps he provides a ready excuse for his family members wishing to shirk their social or occupational obligations: "I'm sorry I can't help you out at your garage sale next weekend; I never know if Tom will be sober or not, so it's best not to plan ahead." Or perhaps intoxication is so entwined with family patterns that they cannot be comfortably carried out any other way (Steinglass, 1981).

In my own clinical work several years ago, I encountered a married couple in their sixties who during 40 years of marriage had never had sexual intercourse unless both of them were drunk. They believed that they had a satisfactory sexual relationship, but they could not recount any details except the alcoholic haze that surrounded their lovemaking. Husband and wife were both unambiguous alcoholics, and it would not have made much sense to deal with the substance abuse of one without also considering the substance abuse of the other.

In a prospective study of alcohol use and abuse, Vaillant (1983) found that men who abused alcohol and later tapered their use to moderate levels were those who had something to gain by doing so. Typically, this was the continuation of a supportive relationship with another person. I want to underscore this finding, because the family's role has so far been discussed in strictly negative terms. But family influence can cut both ways, and people like Vaillant's recovered alcoholics stayed sober in order to maintain social homeostasis.

The concept of **codependency** makes sense within the family systems approach (Beattie, 1987). According to this pop psychology notion, the substance abuser maintains his abuse because of the tacit aid of another person, often a family member, who may base her identity on the ensuing enmeshment (Cermak, 1986). Let us say he abuses alcohol, and she abstains altogether. She may still be implicated in the abuse. By this view, substance dependence is an interpersonal problem, not simply an individual one (Mulry, 1987).

A colleague told me about a woman he saw in therapy who had a long history of alcohol abuse. Treatment proceeded well for Mrs. Tsoi, and she abstained from drinking for exactly 1 year. Her friends and family members were proud of her, and many marked the occasion with cards and presents. Mr. Tsoi cooked a special meal for her and upon serving it, took out an expensive bottle of wine he had purchased. He poured a glass for each of them and proposed a toast to her and her 1 year of sobriety! I would like to report that Mrs. Tsoi refused the drink, with laughter or anger or both—but she did

not. She drank it, and another, and yet another. And so it went. My colleague suggested to Mrs. Tsoi that her husband join her in therapy.

What is useful about the family systems approach? Most basically, it locates substance abuse in a social context. In addition to any genetic component to alcohol abuse, alcoholism is passed across the generations through socialization (Vaillant, 1983). Children enact what they see their parents do. Substance abuse is a "style" that certain families adopt, and children may carry this style with them when they become adults and start their own families. The same is true for drinking in moderation.

Where does the family systems approach fall short? As you saw with the other models, it can be difficult to separate the causes of abuse from its effects. Families in which particular members abuse drugs have other problems as well (Moos & Billings, 1982), but did those problems precede the substance abuse, as the family systems approach proposes, or follow it (Vaillant, 1983)?

Furthermore, a family systems approach can be circular. It starts with the assumption that a "symptom" satisfies some function within a family. But sometimes the only evidence for this role is the existence of the alcohol abuse. Along these same lines, notions such as codependency may lead us to blame the spouses of alcoholics for contributing to the problem rather than to view them as victims of it (Asher & Brissett, 1988).

Sociocultural approach   Sociocultural theories view substance use and abuse from the vantage of the larger culture (Heath, 1984). I have already discussed how a person's particular culture influences the manner in which alcohol is consumed. We can also make sense of variations within a culture by taking into account such characteristics as sex, age, and occupation. In the United States, males are much more likely to abuse alcohol than females, although the gap appears to be closing (Sournia, 1990). Alcohol consumption is greatest between the ages of 20 and 35. And those within certain occupations—such as sailors, railroad workers, bartenders, and waiters—are overrepresented among the ranks of alcohol abusers.

Sometimes a given drug pervades an entire culture. For example, in contemporary Yemen, the vast majority of individuals chew a bitter-tasting leaf called qat *that produces an intoxicated state characterized by a jittery hyperalertness (Hundley, 1992). Men, women, and children alike chew* qat, *and by some estimates, the typical family spends 35% of its entire income on the drug. It is usually chewed daily, in the afternoon, and a person may spend up to 5 or 6 hours intoxicated.*

Sometimes drug use marks an entire culture. In contemporary Yemen, the majority of individuals chew a bitter-tasting leaf called qat. *It produces a jittery hyperalertness.*

As mentioned earlier in the chapter, Muslims usually avoid alcohol, but qat *is not forbidden in the Koran, and so the Yemenites chew it. The drug has existed for centuries, but it was only in the late 1960s that its use became near universal in the country. Prior to that time, those in the upper classes opposed the drug, but after the 1967 revolution in Yemen, upper-class values were held in contempt. The drug spread quickly.* Qat *is not considered a dangerous drug, although the incredible amount of time devoted to its consumption is recognized by some as problematic. In any event, the use and abuse of* qat *in Yemen can only be understood in terms of the larger culture.*

The problem posed by substance abuse is attacked by the sociocultural model on two fronts. First are attempts to prevent abuse in the first place, through school or community programs and public service announcements. The effectiveness of these interventions is unclear (Marlatt, Baer, Donovan, & Kivlahan, 1988). Second is the deliberate creation of subcultures in which substance abuse is not tolerated. Alcoholics Anonymous, a self-help group, is the best known example of this kind of sociocultural therapy. For other drugs, there are parallel approaches, such as Narcotics Anonymous for narcotics abusers.

AA was founded in 1935 by recovering alcohol abusers. AA chapters exist in most United States cities and in 100 other countries. They hold frequent meetings, a time for members to tell their story and to hear the stories of others. The goal of AA is to prevent relapse into drinking, and so members seek out meetings and each other when they are tempted to drink. Although it has a high dropout rate (Ogborne, 1989), AA is effective for those who stay with the program (Smart, Mann, & Anglin, 1989). Why does it work? Perhaps it helps those who remain involved because it requires a lifetime commitment from them and hence a lifestyle change. Plus, it provides them with an explicit belief system (see Table 5.4) and a social group that supports abstinence.

TABLE **5.4**

THE TWELVE STEPS OF ALCOHOLICS ANONYMOUS
Members of Alcoholics Anonymous are provided with an explicit set of beliefs about alcohol and its abuse. The Twelve Steps shown here are a particularly well known example of this belief system.
SOURCE: ALCOHOLICS ANONYMOUS.*

1. We admitted that we were powerless over alcohol . . . that our lives had become unmanageable.

2. Came to believe that a Power greater than ourselves could restore us to sanity.

3. Made a decision to turn our will and our lives over to the care of God as we understood Him.

4. Made a searching and fearless moral inventory of ourselves.

5. Admitted to God, to ourselves, and to another human being the exact nature of our wrongs.

6. Were entirely ready to have God remove all these defects of character.

7. Humbly asked Him to remove our shortcomings.

8. Made a list of all persons we had harmed and became willing to make amends to them all.

9. Made direct amends to such people wherever possible, except when to do so would injure them or others.

10. Continued to take personal inventory and when we were wrong, promptly admitted it.

11. Sought through prayer and meditation to improve our conscious contact with God as we understood Him, praying only for a knowledge of His will for us and the power to carry that out.

12. Having had a spiritual awakening as the result of these steps, we tried to carry this message to alcoholics, and to practice these principles in all our affairs.

The Twelve Steps are reprinted with permission of Alcoholics Anonymous World Services Inc. Permission to reprint this material does not mean that AA has reviewed or approved the contents of this publication, nor that AA agrees with the views expressed herein. AA is a program of recovery from alcoholism only. Use of the Twelve Steps in connection with programs and activities which are patterned after AA, but which address other problems, does not imply otherwise.

What is useful about the sociocultural approach? It makes sense of broad patterns of substance use and abuse. A person's culture and his or her role within it are among the determinants of abuse on the one hand versus moderation or abstinence on the other. The lesson of AA—that the treatment of substance abuse should be approached in terms of an individual's subculture—is a wise one.

Where does the sociocultural approach fall short? Although it accounts for broad patterns, it does not explain particular instances of abuse. A young adult male of Irish ancestry who works as a waiter is at an increased risk for developing a drinking problem, but in any given case, he probably will not. The sociocultural model cannot say anything about the exceptions to its generalizations, and these are numerous. Relatedly, the model is silent about the mechanisms by which its risk factors translate themselves into problems.

An integrated approach   In my discussion of what is useful about the different models of abnormality as they are applied to alcohol abuse, you see illustrated two of the important points from Chapter 3. First, each model makes a contribution to our understanding of the causes and treatments of abnormality. Second, no individual model tells us all that we would want to know. We need to combine the insights of the different models (Cloninger, 1987; Marlatt et al., 1988; Nathan, 1990; Sher, 1991; Zucker & Gomberg, 1986).

Figure 5.3 presents one possible integration of the risk factors identified by the various models of abnormality. The most general influences on alcohol use and abuse are a person's culture, which provides roles and norms relevant to alcohol consumption, and his genetic makeup, which shapes his physiological response to intoxication and withdrawal. These in turn

influence a cascade of more immediate influences, which lead eventually to the person using and abusing alcohol, or not.

The process is more complex than Figure 5.3 implies. Reciprocal influence exists between many of the risk factors. And the psychological and physical consequences of alcohol consumption determine future consumption. Additionally, Figure 5.3 does not take into account the possibility of different types of alcohol abuse (e.g., Cooper, Russell, Skinner, & Windle, 1992). Nor does it grapple with the possibility that risk factors differ for men and women. A further complication is introduced by realizing that substance abuse is a problem with a beginning, a middle, and an end. At each stage, different influences may predominate (Zucker, 1987). Nonetheless, whatever its oversimplifications, Figure 5.3 at least shows that some of the important ingredients of an integrated perspective can be specified.

TREATMENT

Every model of abnormality suggests its own approach to the prevention or treatment of alcohol abuse (see Table 5.5), and I have sketched the basic strategies of each. At the present, we know very little about what helps alcohol abusers and why. Some good news is that a number of abusers improve without professional intervention (Vaillant, 1983). Some more good news is that a variety of treatment approaches, such as cognitive-behavior therapy, are effective, at least in the short run (Miller & Hester, 1986). But we cannot say that any given approach is superior to any other (Marlatt et al., 1988). And some programs, no matter how successful they might eventually prove to be, are too expensive to be practical on a large-scale basis. Other than knowing that social stability predicts good

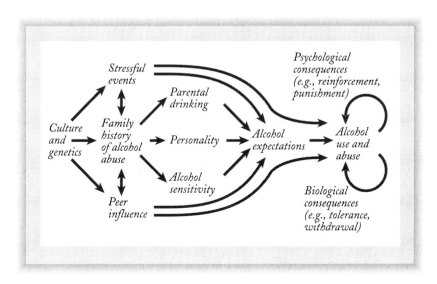

FIGURE 5.3

AN INTEGRATED MODEL OF ALCOHOL USE AND ABUSE   *A full explanation of alcohol use and abuse must take into account numerous influences and their relationships to one another.*

TABLE 5.5

ALCOHOL TREATMENT *Each of the popular models of abnormality suggests its own treatment strategy for those who abuse alcohol.*

MODEL	TREATMENT
biomedical	detoxify; encourage abstinence
psychoanalytic	resolve underlying conflicts
cognitive-behavioral	punish abuse; reward nonabuse; change expectancies; teach controlled drinking
humanistic-existential-phenomenological	encourage alternative ways of attaining self-actualization
family systems	change family patterns that maintain abuse and dependence
sociocultural	undertake prevention; provide social support (e.g., Alcoholics Anonymous)

prognosis, we cannot say with certainty who is most likely to benefit from treatment. Relapse is a real possibility for anyone who appears to have been successfully treated for alcohol abuse (Riley, Sobell, Leo, Sobell, & Klajner, 1987). Perhaps the multiplicity of influences on alcohol consumption makes this fact unsurprising.

There is a growing recognition that treatment of alcohol abuse should not end simply because a person has returned to a sober state. **Relapse prevention** is based on the assumption that a person successfully treated for alcohol problems is at risk for relapse whenever she encounters the circumstances associated with abuse in the first place (Marlatt & Gordon, 1985). The focus of relapse prevention is helping the person to identify these circumstances and devise responses to them other than drinking. The greater the range of possible risk factors with which she can successfully cope, the less likely she is to relapse (Myers & Brown, 1990). The most practical implication of any integrated perspective is that relapse prevention (and initial treatment) should be approached on several levels simultaneously.

Hodgson and Rankin (1982) described their treatment of Mr. M., a 43-year-old manual laborer in England. Mr. M. had been an extremely heavy drinker for over two decades. He consumed more than 2 quarts of vodka per day, usually drinking until he passed out. When he awakened, he would start to drink again. He even kept a bottle of vodka in bed with him, and he was intoxicated virtually around the clock.

Mr. M. wished to stop his drinking altogether, but his attempts to do so had proved fruitless. He had been hospitalized repeatedly for detoxification, but upon discharge he would immediately resume his previous level of consumption. It was at this point that Hodgson and Rankin entered the treatment scene and proposed a new strategy. Rather than just admonishing Mr. M. to be abstinent, they decided to teach him how to better control his impulse to drink to excess. They tried to identify the situational cues associated with his loss of control, and the most obvious trigger was the taste of alcohol. So, while Mr. M. was in the hospital, they provided him with the experience of stopping after a single drink:

> *Some drink will be given to you during your stay ... and ... your aim is to stop after a certain amount when you feel like continuing. In this way we believe you will gradually break the compulsion to continue and will develop your willpower. This should have two effects when you leave. ... First, when you attempt to drink, your experience of resisting temptation in the hospital will give you greater control. Second, if you do drink you will find it easier to pull out before you explode into a heavy-drinking binge. ... Although we are teaching you to have greater control, we are not advising a goal of controlled drinking. ... You should aim for greater abstinence. (p. 213)*

Mr. M. was given one drink at a time and encouraged to monitor his craving for another. He learned that the one drink increased his desire for another but that if he waited an hour, the desire decreased.

Hodgson and Rankin interpreted their approach in cognitive-behavioral terms, suggesting that each time Mr. M. resisted his impulse to drink further, the impulse was extinguished and his perceived control over drinking was increased. Most substance abuse experts would consider this treatment extremely hazardous, but it was successful for Mr. M in that over the next 5 years, his drinking subsided. The number of days he spent intoxicated was greatly reduced, as were his hospital stays. When binges occurred, they were no longer as extensive because Mr. M. was better able to stop. He still had a severe problem with alcohol, but he had gained a modicum of control over his drinking. Compared to his condition before this unusual version of relapse prevention, he was doing much better.

THE USE AND ABUSE OF OTHER DRUGS

Following are brief discussions of other psychoactive substances that people may abuse. I introduce these with some general points about recent trends in substance abuse in the United States. First, the phenomenon of **polysubstance dependence** is being increasingly recognized. Many drug abusers are quite broad in their tastes, using a variety of substances—successively or simultaneously (Clayton, 1986; McBride, Inciardi, Chitwood, & McCoy, 1992; Suwaki et al., 1992). The psychology of substance abuse has traditionally been drug specific, theoretically and therapeutically. This may well have to change.

Second, complicating matters further is the fact that many street drugs are incorrectly identified. Users believing they are buying one drug may in actuality be buying one or more other drugs (Ratcliffe, 1973). It is virtually impossible to obtain "heroin" or "cocaine" that is not adulterated with other psychoactive drugs (Gomez & Rodriguez, 1989). Relatedly, new drugs subject to abuse are being developed all the time. By intent, *designer drugs* have specific chemical structures *not* illegal at the time of their creation (Beebe & Walley, 1991; Ruttenber, 1991; Sternbach & Varon, 1992); hence, they can be freely sold and used until the legal system adds them to the list of forbidden substances.

Third, drug abuse in recent history has often been the province of males. This is changing, as women in increasing numbers join men in the tendency to use and abuse drugs (Harrison, 1989). Whether theories and treatments developed mainly with respect to males will generalize to females remains to be seen (Toneatto, Sobell, & Sobell, 1992).

And finally, although there seems to be an overall waning in the use of many drugs,[3] those individuals who do begin to use them are doing so at a younger age (Harrison, 1992; O'Malley, Bachman, & Johnston, 1988; Robins & Przybeck, 1985; Smart & Adlaf, 1986). Again, whether theories and treatment developed for adults will apply to children or adolescents is unclear. One well publicized example of this trend is former child actress Drew Barrymore, who drank alcohol at age 9, smoked pot at age 10, and snorted cocaine at age 12 (Peele, 1989). Before she was a teenager, she had already gone through drug rehabilitation.

NARCOTICS

You might encounter the term *narcotics* in two ways. In a legal sense, narcotics are drugs that are restricted because they are physically addictive. The problem with this definition is that many psychoactive drugs lead to addiction, yet are not classified by the legal

In 1987, after years of saying yes, actress Drew Barrymore pledged her support to Nancy Reagan's "Just Say No" campaign.

system as narcotics. Here, I use **narcotics** to describe opium and its derivatives, such as morphine and heroin; synonyms for narcotics in this sense are **opiates** and **opioids.**

To the observer, the narcotics user seems stuporous while intoxicated. Withdrawal from the drug, in contrast, is characterized by increased activity. His nose may run, and his eyes may tear. He might become restless and experience an intense desire to use the drug again. Withdrawal sometimes involves diarrhea and vomiting, as well as headaches and insomnia. Another dose of the drug banishes withdrawal, and the cycle of addiction may thus be entered. Although withdrawal from narcotics is far from pleasant, it resembles the flu more than the tortured agony of popular stereotypes.

Several decades ago, I met a man named Ted who had been recently discharged from the army. Ted told me that he had used heroin on a daily basis during his last 3 months of duty in Vietnam. Potent doses were readily available, and he used the drug with enthusiasm, at first snorting it and then injecting it. Once back in the United States, he experienced little withdrawal and virtually no craving. Ted enjoyed talking about his past drug use, but he apparently never used heroin again.

Other users do not have such a circumscribed experience. A more recent acquaintance of mine, whom I will call

---

[3] A survey completed in 1993 reported an *increase* in illicit drug use among American college students (Smolowe, 1993). We will have to wait and see whether this is a minor exception to recent trends or the sign of larger changes.

Alex, first tried heroin while visiting Thailand. Again, this is a place where the drug can be easily obtained, even by an American tourist speaking only English. Upon returning to the United States, Alex immediately sought out heroin on a daily basis, and soon the habit started to dominate his life. He lost his job and became estranged from his friends and family. Venturing into unfamiliar parts of Detroit to buy heroin, Alex was robbed at gunpoint several times. As of this writing, he is in treatment for his problem.

Opium   Like alcohol, the use of opiates has a long history. We find mention of the poppy, from which **opium** and all other narcotics are eventually derived, as early as 8,000 years ago. That this flower was originally described as "the plant of joy" implies that our ancestors knew well its psychoactive properties. Juice from the poppy creates relaxation, produces sleep, and kills pain. Tension and anxiety are obviously relieved. The individual using opium or one of its derivatives experiences intoxication initially as an intense rush of pleasure and then as a state of bliss that may linger for hours. Comedian John Belushi, one of the casualties of heroin, said that intoxication was "like kissing God" (Woodward, 1985).

Early physicians such as Galen included opium in their repertoire. It was particularly useful as a treatment for dysentery, but it was also prescribed for psychological difficulties such as depression. The non-medical use of opium spread through Asia. It became particularly popular in China, where at the turn of the 20th century there were reportedly 15 million opium smokers (Kolb, 1962).

Opium came to this country in the middle 1800s, when Chinese laborers were imported en masse to help lay railroad track. Fear of the cheap labor represented by the Chinese immigrants as well as racial prejudice created great concern in some quarters of the United States about the perils of opium use.

Morphine   Ironically, at this same time, narcotics abuse was running rampant in other segments of the United States population. Two scientific discoveries paved the way. First, in 1805, one of the active ingredients of opium was isolated; this new drug was named **morphine** (after Morpheus, the Greek god of sleep) because it proved to be a particularly powerful sedative and analgesic. Second, around the time of the Civil War, the hypodermic syringe was invented, making it possible to inject drugs directly into the blood.

Morphine was widely given to Civil War soldiers, with no appreciation that it was addictive. Upon discharge, soldiers were given free morphine and syringes. Simultaneously, the United States saw a boom in non-prescription *patent medicines,* so named because their ingredients were kept secret. They were sold as tonics that would cure any and all maladies. We now know that many of these medicines contained opium or morphine. So popular were these patent medicines that the typical narcotics addict during the 1800s was precisely the person to whom the patent medicines were marketed: a middle-class white woman who lived in the South, attended church, and was a pillar of her community (Kolb, 1962).

Heroin   Toward the end of the 1800s, the addictive nature of morphine was recognized. At this

Opium den in New York's Chinatown during the 1920s.

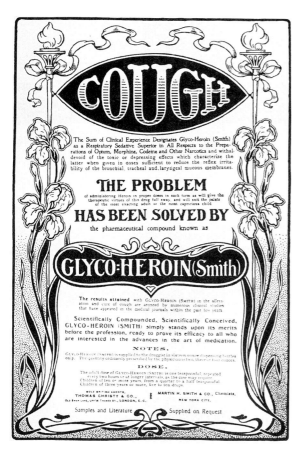

At the turn of the century in the United States, patent medicines often contained narcotics.

time, **heroin**, a derivative of morphine, was discovered. Heroin had the same sedating and pain-killing properties as its forerunners, but it was regarded as completely safe. It was therefore presented as a nonaddicting sub-

stitute for morphine. Heroin was added to patent medicines and prescribed to medical patients. All of this proved to be a grievous error, of course, and heroin soon became the most frequently abused narcotic, a distinction it still holds today.

In 1906, the Pure Food and Drugs Act forced the manufacturers of patent medicines to identify products that contained narcotics. In 1914, the nonprescription use of narcotics was banned. It says something about the significance of alcohol within the United States that the banning of narcotics required only Congressional action whereas the banning of alcohol required an amendment to the Constitution (Freedman, 1980).

Making narcotics illegal had several related consequences. Most generally, narcotics use and abuse ceased being a medical concern and became the province of law enforcement. Clinics for the treatment of narcotics dependence were closed down by the 1920s, and an exclusively punitive approach was taken. Criminalized, narcotics use was driven underground, becoming popular mainly among the most disenfranchised of society. Abusers tended increasingly to be black males leading a checkered existence in large cities.

In the 1960s, narcotics use moved from the Black ghettos to the White suburbs. The United States government responded by instituting educational programs aimed at prevention, increased treatment opportunities, and a tough stance against drug trafficking. Exact figures prove elusive, but everyone agrees that narcotics abuse skyrocketed throughout the 1960s until the middle 1970s (Kozel, 1990). Since then, we have seen a leveling off and perhaps an actual decrease in the number of individuals dependent on narcotics (see Figure 5.4). At present, however, several million Americans still abuse one or another of the opiates.

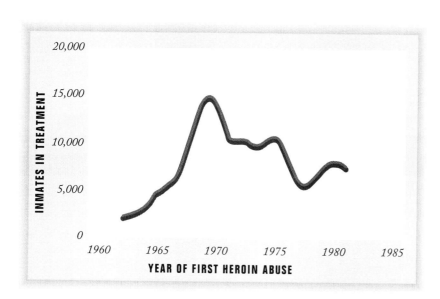

YEAR OF FIRST HEROIN ABUSE

FIGURE 5.4

FREQUENCY OF NARCOTICS USE   *Heroin use in the United States, as estimated by the number of individuals in treatment in federally funded programs, has decreased in recent decades.*

SOURCE: "EPIDEMIOLOGY OF DRUG ABUSE IN THE UNITED STATES: A SUMMARY OF METHODS AND FINDINGS," BY N. J. KOZEL, 1990, *Bulletin of the Pan American Health Organization, 24* (1), P. 57. REPRINTED WITH PERMISSION.

Smits (1980) described the path into heroin use followed by a young Canadian man:

> *John ... was in his early twenties when he first tried heroin. At nineteen, he was discharged from the armed services ... [and took a job] as a groom at a local racetrack. A fellow employee suggested that he and John move into an apartment together. John agreed since he had just arrived in the city and knew no one. One weekend he and his roommate attended a party at which several people used heroin, including John's roommate.*
>
> *According to John, "everyone was having a good time," and they did not seem adversely affected by the use of heroin. John did not try heroin that night but, rather, asked his roommate about it.... The next time John and his roommate went to a party where there was heroin, John tried it. When asked what made him decide to do so, he said that he was feeling socially awkward and thought the heroin might loosen him up. However, [his] initial reaction was not a pleasant one. He spent most of the night vomiting and feeling very sick. Despite this reaction to the drug, John tried it again the next weekend without any adverse effects.... John continued to use heroin on a weekend basis for more than two years before he began using it regularly, that is, about once every two or three days. (p. 20)*

Note that John's heroin use began in a social setting but eventually took on a life of its own.

It is ironic that narcotics use per se is not particularly dangerous to the user, at least when compared to the consequences of alcohol use. The risk with narcotics is the context in which its use takes place, and here we find problems galore. Narcotics are expensive, and addicts may turn to robbery or prostitution to pay for their habits. Heroin bought on the street is invariably "cut" (diluted) with other substances, which themselves can be dangerous. The abuser accustomed to a given potency might accidentally overdose when encountering a relatively uncut dose.

Addicts who use syringes often share their needles, not just carelessly but in a deliberate ritual signifying friendship (Klee, 1992). Diseases such as hepatitis or AIDS can be spread this way. Indeed, AIDS is rapidly afflicting narcotics addicts. Almost 60% of the intravenous drug users in the United States test HIV-positive (Des Jarlais et al., 1989). If addicts are also prostitutes, we have a blueprint for the continuation of the AIDS epidemic.

Treatment   Narcotics dependence has been treated in several ways, psychologically and biologically. None of these treatments works consistently.

However, each has achieved modest success with at least some abusers. Following detoxification, some abusers respond well to individual psychotherapy targeting emotional problems contributing to their use and abuse of narcotics (McLellan, Luborsky, Woody, O'Brien, & Druley, 1983). There is a paradox inherent in psychological treatments of addiction. To the degree that substance abuse is discussed during therapy, and of course it must be, the client is confronted with constant reminders of drugs. These may elicit craving and contribute to relapse.

Other abusers have been helped by medical approaches. In **substitution therapy,** an addict is given an oral dose of an opiate which is longer lasting and more gradual in its effects than heroin or morphine. This slows down the intoxication-withdrawal cycle. **Methadone** is the drug usually used in such therapy, and studies have found that methadone maintenance reduces the use of other narcotics, criminal activity, and needle sharing (Ball, Corty, Bond, Myers, & Tommasello, 1988). Needless to say, the individual taking methadone is still dependent on drugs. It has become a street drug in its own right, which is not surprising because it is—after all—an opiate.

As you may remember from your introductory psychology course, the brain produces its own form of opiates called **endorphins,** which play an important role in the body's attempts to relieve pain. Research into endorphins has shed some light on the possible biological processes involved in narcotics abuse. Narcotics may suppress the normal production of opiates by the brain, leaving a person without natural defenses against pain. Continued use of narcotics follows.

Drugs such as *naloxone* and *naltrexone,* which block the activity of endorphins, also function as antagonists to narcotics. In other words, these medications block the effects of narcotics, giving us yet another possible treatment for opiate abuse (Kosten, Morgan, & Kleber, 1991). If an individual can be encouraged to use naloxone or naltrexone, then narcotics of necessity have no appeal. Because the individual is required to be highly motivated, this treatment approach is not widely used (Gonzalez & Brogden, 1988).

Because narcotics use is illegal in the United States, treatments try to find some substitute—psychological or chemical—for the abused substance. In countries such as England, we see a very different approach. The government runs clinics that administer a daily dose of heroin to addicts at no cost. This obviously separates narcotics dependence from criminal activity. For some participants, long-term social stability is achieved (Wille, 1981). Other participants are not so successful.

Some in the United States have called for the legalization of all drugs, including narcotics. Government-run clinics such as we find in England would presumably be needed to serve addicted individuals. Or would these be franchised and run privately for profit? Either alternative seems unlikely in the current political climate.

STIMULANTS

Stimulants are drugs that stimulate the nervous system. They increase arousal and spur both mental and physical activity. Stimulants increase alertness and elevate mood. They may also produce agitation and insomnia.

Caffeine   The most widely used stimulant is **caffeine,** which originates in many botanical sources, and is available in coffee, tea, chocolate, and many soft drinks (see Figure 5.5). Caffeine is often used in over-the-counter preparations like NoDoz, to help people stay awake, as well as in headache medications like Anacin and Excedrin. Caffeine has been produced and sold for at least 1,000 years—and thoughout its history, its use has been debated, invoking magical, somatic, and psychological arguments. It has even been banned in various times and places. For example, the women's temperance movement grouped coffee and tea with alcohol (Greden, 1980).

Billions of pounds of caffeine-containing substances are consumed every year, and most of you are familiar with its effects. After just one or two cups of coffee or their equivalent, bodily processes noticeably speed up: metabolism, temperature, blood pressure, and urine production. Appetite may be suppressed; tremors may be experienced. In larger amounts, about five or more cups of coffee per day, *caffeinism* begins to occur—a constellation of symptoms including anxiety, hyperactivity, irritability, and insomnia. Withdrawal symptoms in the form of headaches and lethargy will then appear (Silverman, Evans, Strain, & Griffiths, 1992).

Unlike its immediate predecessors, DSM-IV includes caffeine as a substance associated with dependence or abuse (cf. Hughes, Oliveto, Helzer, Higgins, & Bickel, 1992). The rationale is clear. In large doses, it may create or exacerbate medical conditions involving cardiac, renal, or gastrointestinal functioning; however, the research results are mixed (see Chou, 1992; Stavric, 1992). People with peptic ulcers are routinely counseled to avoid caffeine. In extremely large doses, caffeine can be lethal, but it is almost impossible to ingest a fatal amount via coffee beverages. The danger lies in caffeine-containing tablets, but even in this case, dozens of these would need to be taken before life is jeopardized.

Because caffeine is not widely considered a dangerous substance in the present day, we know very little about how to treat those dependent on it. Physician John Greden (1980) estimated that among those individuals who try to curtail their caffeine intake, about one third can do so with little difficulty; the remaining individuals eventually resume their initial level of consumption.

Nicotine   Another familiar stimulant is **nicotine,** the active ingredient in tobacco. Nicotine is usually taken into the body by smoking cigarettes, cigars, or pipes, but it can also be consumed in "smokeless" form as snuff or chewing tobacco. Tobacco was first

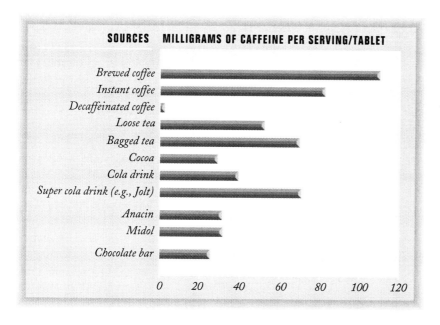

FIGURE 5.5

COMMON SOURCES OF CAFFEINE   *Caffeine is found in a variety of familiar products, from coffee to chocolate bars.*

cultivated by Native Americans, who regarded it as a gift from the gods. Its use spread through Europe following colonization of the Americas.

Tens of millions of Americans smoke cigarettes, despite its well documented physical dangers. In 1964, the Surgeon General of the United States declared that smoking was a medical hazard. There is hardly a system in the body not affected adversely by smoking[4] (e.g., Grady & Ernster, 1992; Lakier, 1992; Pomerleau, 1992), but in particular, it increases the chances of cancer and heart disease. Cigarette smoking is associated as well with anxiety, depression, and schizophrenia, although the reasons for these links remain unclear (Breslau, Kilbey, & Andreski, 1993a, 1993b; Glassman, 1993; Hughes & Boland, 1992; Lohr & Flynn, 1992). The annual cost of health care for cigarette-related illnesses in the United States is about $30 billion. On the average, chronic smokers reduce their life expectancy by 8 years.

Since 1965, health warnings on cigarette containers have been mandated. In 1970, cigarette advertising was banned from television and radio. We are currently seeing a flurry of ordinances prohibiting smoking in public places, from restaurants to supermarkets to airports. In 1994, we began to hear a nationwide call for nicotine to be branded an illegal drug. Still, people continue to smoke. Epidemiological studies show that the overall number of smokers in the United States has decreased in recent years, from a high in 1964 of 40% of adults to about 25% today (Fiore, 1992). However, across this time period, smoking by females and teenagers has increased.

Nicotine is clearly an abused drug. It produces a characteristic intoxication that is pleasurable. It leads to tolerance as well as withdrawal. The tribulations of the smoker without a cigarette are well known, and they include irritability, restlessness, headaches, sleep disturbances, anxiety, and a strong nicotine craving. Although the majority of people who smoke try repeatedly to curtail their consumption, relapse is extremely common (Garvey, Bliss, Hitchcock, Heinold, & Rosner, 1992).

Even so, there are more than 30 million ex-smokers in this country, which means that a person can overcome this addiction. Perhaps 95% of ex-smokers quit on their own without professional intervention, but they rarely succeed the first time they try. Indeed, the important lesson from ex-smokers is that they must usually make repeated attempts to quit before success is finally achieved (Hughes, Gulliver, et al., 1992).

What do the mental health professions offer to the nicotine dependent individual? From a biomedical approach, smokers may be given *nicotine gum* or a *nicotine patch* as a substitute for cigarettes. These satisfy part of the bodily need for nicotine while avoiding the dangers associated with smoking. Eventually, the individual gives up the nicotine source. This approach helps some smokers, but it is far from an across-the-board success (e.g., Jarvis, Raw, Russell, & Feyerabend, 1982; Johnson, Stevens, Hollis, & Woodson, 1992; McKenna & Cox, 1992). Some people become dependent on the alternative source of nicotine. Others suffer physical side effects and medical complications.

Behaviorally oriented therapists have devised therapies such as the *rapid smoking technique,* which directs a smoker to find a poorly ventilated room and smoke a cigarette taking deep and rapid puffs. Even addicted smokers become nauseated, and the aversion thereby conditioned may help them give up smoking (Lichtenstein, Harris, Birchler, Wahl, & Schmahl, 1973). Again, rapid smoking is helpful to some smokers but hardly a treatment for all.

Many believe that the real secret in combating nicotine abuse is to keep people from smoking in the first place (Tobler, 1986). Part of the population is already getting the message about the dangers of smoking, and the rest can perhaps be reached through programs directed at school children who have yet to begin smoking (Bruvold, 1993; Flynn et al., 1992). Because the tobacco industry generates tens of billions of dollars every year in the United States, tacit opposition to these programs will likely continue.

Amphetamine   Also classified as a stimulant is **amphetamine** ("speed"), a synthetic drug introduced in 1932 in the Benzedrine inhaler. This medication was sold for the purpose of increasing people's energy and capacity for work. Amphetamine pills followed shortly thereafter, and the American public literally ate them up. By the 1970s, the annual production of amphetamine pills had jumped to 10 billion units, and this estimate reflects only those that were legally produced (Grinspoon & Bakalar, 1980).

Amphetamines can be inhaled, swallowed, or injected directly into a user's veins. They heighten wakefulness and suppress appetite. An individual typically experiences intoxication as pleasant—feeling euphoric, alert, and energetic. Physicians may recommend amphetamines for weight loss and depression. Everyday people use them to stay awake. During World War II, soldiers on both sides frequently used amphetamines. The Japanese *kamikaze* pilots reportedly used them in preparation for their suicidal missions.

---

[4] More recent studies have documented diverse medical hazards of *secondhand smoke,* an individual's exposure to smoke from cigarettes smoked by others (see Boyle, 1993; Forastiere et al., 1992; Lesmes & Donofrio, 1992; Smith, Sears, Walker, & DeLuca, 1992; Steenland, 1992).

In large doses, this drug produces high blood pressure, cardiac and respiratory problems, tremors, convulsions, even coma and death. A chronic user may experience anxiety, restlessness, and insomnia. Malnutrition is a danger as well. In some cases, **amphetamine psychosis** develops (Connell, 1958; Kalant, 1966), a condition difficult to distinguish from paranoid schizophrenia (Chapter 12). The individual is irritable and suspicious. She experiences hallucinations and believes that others intend to persecute her. In most cases, these psychotic symptoms occur only while the amphetamine user is intoxicated. In a few cases, however, they persist beyond the intoxicated state.

Amphetamines are associated with rapid tolerance and a high degree of dependence. Withdrawal is quite unpleasant, characterized by lethargy, fatigue, and terrifying nightmares. Depression may surface, lasting from a few days to several weeks. Suicide is a threat during this time. The individual may be impelled to use the drug again in order to relieve her depression, which maintains the vicious cycle of intoxication and withdrawal.

Because amphetamines can be readily synthesized, new versions constantly appear on the street. Designer drugs such as *ecstasy* (Dowling, McDonough, & Bost, 1987) and *ice* (Holden, 1989) are just two examples. They hold the same appeal and pose the same dangers as the traditional amphetamines.

Cocaine   The final stimulant to be discussed is **cocaine,** which is derived from the leaves of the coca plant, native to Bolivia and Peru. South American natives knew about its stimulating properties and have chewed these leaves for centuries. Cocaine itself is the active ingredient, and chemists isolated it in 1860. It enjoyed brief medical use in the late 1800s as the first local anesthetic. Psychoanalyst Sigmund Freud was one of the physicians who pioneered this application (Byck, 1975). Shortly thereafter, the psychoactive properties of cocaine became evident to the medical community, and the drug was widely prescribed as a stimulant and antidepressant. In 1914, the United States government moved to restrict its use, classifying it with heroin and morphine as a narcotic.

Throughout most of the 20th century, cocaine has been expensive, and little was known about its use or abuse, except that cocaine intoxication is rapid, intense, and typically brief. Like amphetamine, it increases a person's sense of well-being and alertness. It enhances sexual desire. It deadens the experience of pain. For years, experts believed that the negative consequences of cocaine were minimal. As recently as 1980, it was regarded as a milder and more subtle version of amphetamine: "Studies of recreational users [of cocaine] suggest that, for the great majority, unde-

sired effects are rare and not serious" (Grinspoon & Bakalar, 1980, p. 1621). To this point, physical dependence had not been documented.

All of this changed in the 1980s. Users began to isolate the more potent ingredients of cocaine with a procedure known as *free-basing.* Cocaine was combined with ether and then heated. What resulted was a much stronger drug, which is typically smoked to produce an extremely brief yet intense high. A form of freebase cocaine called **crack** began to be sold in small and thus affordable amounts, and a new drug problem was born. Where before cocaine was a "champagne" drug, available only to the wealthy, now it was readily available on the street, in a highly potent form.

With more and more people using cocaine, it became evident that the drug was not so benign. If smoked, respiratory damage might take place (Itkonen, Schnoll, & Glassroth, 1984). Psychosis might accompany intoxication (Manschreck et al., 1988). Death by heart attack might also occur, as in the well publicized case of all-American basketball player Len Bias, who died in 1986 shortly after being drafted by the Boston Celtics. Physical dependence on the drug readily develops, and withdrawal reactions are severe. The crash from cocaine includes depression, confusion, and strong craving. Addicts may turn to crime to support their drug habit. So much money exchanges hands in the cocaine business that it has become an international concern, with governments literally rising and falling because of it.

Cocaine is one of the few illicit drugs whose use in the United States increased through the 1980s. Although the overall prevalence of cocaine use in the general population seems to be decreasing in the

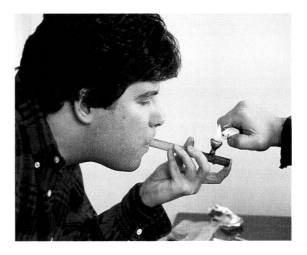

Crack cocaine is usually smoked, producing a brief yet intense intoxication. Because of its low cost and its high potential for addiction, crack is one of the few drugs that has seen increasing use in the United States during the last decade.

1990s, deaths due to this drug continue to increase (Kandel, 1991).

DEPRESSANTS

In terms of their effects on consciousness, **depressants** are the opposite of stimulants. They reduce a person's awareness of external stimuli and slow down his bodily functions. In small amounts, depressants create a relaxed state that frees the user from anxiety and inhibition. In large amounts, they lead to sedation and sleep, even coma and death. Alcohol is the most commonly used depressant, and I have already discussed its abuse in detail.

Tranquilizers   First synthesized in the 1950s, and widely prescribed for anxiety disorders (Chapter 7), **tranquilizers** such as Valium and Librium are subject to abuse. Perhaps because these drugs are so commonplace, their potential for misuse is not universally recognized. It is nonetheless clear that dependence can take place. Tolerance certainly develops, and when their use is curtailed, withdrawal symptoms may occur: insomnia, agitation, appetite loss, and sometimes convulsions. Tranquilizers and alcohol show what is known as **cross-tolerance,** meaning that the use of one increases tolerance to the other. Thus, alcohol abuse and tranquilizer abuse may exacerbate one another.

Barbiturates and methaqualone   **Barbiturates** ("downers") such as phenobarbital are yet another type of depressant. Although not technically a barbiturate, the sedative **methaqualone** (quaalude) is highly similar in its effects. These drugs work by slowing down activity in the entire nervous system. Barbiturates have been prescribed since the turn of the 20th century to aid sleep and to combat anxiety and seizures. Both barbiturates and methaqualone can be highly dangerous, whether obtained legally from a physician or illegally from a pusher on the street.

Tolerance readily develops, but the lethal dose does not appreciably change with chronic use (Grinspoon & Bakalar, 1980). In other words, as users escalate the dose in order to produce the same intoxication, accidental death is increasingly likely. Mild intoxication resembles alcohol intoxication, and some number of individuals combine barbiturates or methaqualone with alcohol. This can be particularly dangerous for several reasons. Barbiturates and alcohol are *synergistic,* meaning that each increases the effects of the other. People might depress their physical functioning so much that they simply cease to live. Or they might become nauseated, throw up, and then choke on their own vomit because their physical coordination has been compromised. Withdrawal from barbiturates

Inhalant abuse such as sniffing glue is limited almost exclusively to young males. This youngster, a street child in São Paulo, Brazil, is inhaling glue from a bag, which concentrates its fumes and maximizes his intoxication.

or methaqualone is not merely unpleasant but potentially life-threatening. A chronic user may experience convulsions if and when the drugs are suddenly stopped.

Inhalants   Those of you who have painted in an enclosed area know that breathing volatile substances such as paint can make you feel woozy. Paint is just one of several **inhalants** whose fumes may be deliberately inhaled to produce an intoxication characterized by dizziness, euphoria, excitement, and a breakdown of inhibitions (Chalmers, 1991). Other abused inhalants include glue, gasoline, solvents, aerosol can propellants, and even typewriter correction fluid (King, Smialek, & Troutman, 1985).

The inhalants depress central nervous system activity. Intoxication lasts from 15 minutes to several hours and may produce a sense of reckless abandon. Hallucinations sometimes occur. Afterwards, the individual may have amnesia for events that took place while he was high. Although the abuse of inhalants has been reported for at least a century, it seems to have increased in prevalence only during the past few decades (Westermeyer, 1987). Inhalant abuse is limited almost exclusively to young males—children and early adolescents—who often use these drugs in a group (Oliver & Watson, 1977). Abusers have been described as antisocial and immature (Dinwiddie, Zorumski, & Rubin, 1987), but this could be an effect of chronic use as well as a cause.

Watson (1986) described the following case of inhalant abuse in Scotland:

> *A 14-year-old boy was admitted to an assessment centre because of a variety of anti-social activities. After admission, it was discovered that he had been sniffing glue*

fumes for two years. He had started along with other boys in his area and they had continued to indulge in the practice for about six months. When the others had stopped sniffing, he had carried on because, in the first place, he liked it, and because he felt better when sniffing than at any other time. As time passed, he found that he required more solvents to achieve the intoxicated effect that he desired . . . By the time of his admission to the assessment centre, he was using about four pints of adhesive every day. (p. 80)

The boy eventually stopped sniffing glue but became a heavy drinker. His delinquent activities continued.

Inhalant use is quite hazardous to health. Fumes from volatile substances destroy bone marrow, brain tissue, the liver, and the kidneys. Damage may be irreversible. The intoxicated individual's judgment is markedly impaired, which can lead to needless risk taking. Finally, overdoses can be fatal, either because the heart stops or because the individual becomes nauseated, vomits, and chokes (Anderson, Dick, Macnair, Palmer, & Ramsey, 1982).

PSYCHEDELICS

The **psychedelics** are drugs touted by their users as consciousness-expanding, which means that intoxication closely resembles the mystical experiences described earlier in the chapter. Although psychedelics have a long history, their use proliferated in the 1960s and 1970s. They became entwined with the counterculture and constituted a political statement on the part of many. Cultural heroes such as the Beatles, Ken Kesey, and Timothy Leary conducted well publicized experiments with psychedelics. During this era, at least occasional use of these drugs was widespread among young people.

Hallucinogens The epitome of the psychedelics are **hallucinogens,** drugs that produce hallucinations. Most of the time, these hallucinations are visual. Other sensations and perceptions may be influenced as well, notably the sense of time. These drugs have varying effects on mood. In some cases, euphoria results. In other cases, the consequence is fear. Perhaps hallucinogens exaggerate the user's present mood, for better or for worse.

Some hallucinogens are derived from botanic material. **Mescaline** is the active ingredient in the peyote cactus. **Psilocybin** is found in a particular species of mushroom. Others are synthesized; a particularly well known example is **LSD** (or **lysergic acid diethylamide**), first created in the 1930s by a Swiss chemist named Albert Hofmann.

Hofmann took the first LSD "trip" in the 1940s when he accidentally swallowed a small amount of the drug. In his own words:

I had a great difficulty in speaking coherently, my field of vision swayed before me, and objects appeared distorted like images in curved mirrors. The faces of those around me appeared as grotesque, colored masks. . . . Everything seemed to sway and the proportions were distorted like the reflections in the surface of moving water. . . . Objects appeared in unpleasant, constantly changing colors, the predominant shades being sickly green and blue. When I closed my eyes, an unending series of colorful, very realistic and fantastic images surged in on me. (Hofmann, 1968, pp. 185-186)

Effects last from 8 to 12 hours. LSD became popular among those interested in such experiences in their own right or for their apparent spiritual significance.

A great deal of debate occurred in the 1960s and 1970s about the effects of hallucinogens. Critics argued that these drugs produced schizophrenia and chromosome damage (Cohen & Shiloh, 1977-1978). They pointed to the fact that some users spontaneously reexperienced the state of intoxication without ingesting the drug—*flashbacks*—as proof that their biochemistry was permanently affected. Advocates argued not only that hallucinogens were harmless but also that they enhanced creativity (Janiger & Dobkin de Rios, 1989). LSD was even urged as a treatment for mental disorders (Neill, 1987).

As hallucinogens became less popular, a moderate view emerged (Grinspoon & Bakalar, 1980). On the one hand, these drugs do not make a person more creative; neither do they hold therapeutic value. On the other hand, they are not particularly dangerous for most people. Chromosome damage does not result. "Bad trips" usually end when the drugs wear off. Those users who experience more lasting psychotic symptoms probably had preexisting problems of which they were unaware. Flashbacks are rarely unpleasant, and they may simply represent vivid memories. The biggest threat associated with hallucinogen use by most individuals is that drugs sold as mescaline or LSD may in actuality be something else truly hazardous.

Phencyclidine Frequently sold as a hallucinogen is another psychedelic known as **phencyclidine** (or **PCP**). This drug was first manufactured in the 1950s as a surgical anesthetic and analgesic, but its use was quickly discontinued when patients became disoriented, agitated, and delirious. PCP was then used only by veterinarians until the 1960s, when it appeared in San Francisco as a street drug. PCP impressed its users as a cross between a hallucinogen and a sedative. It proved remarkably easy to synthesize in home laboratories, and a small investment in chemicals could produce an incredible profit. The Hell's Angels motorcycle gang reportedly cornered the PCP market, which explains one of its street names: *angel dust.*

Although PCP may be ingested in a variety of ways, it is usually mixed with mint, parsley, or marijuana and then smoked. Intoxication begins with feelings of bodily warmth and tingling, followed shortly by visual hallucinations. Distortions of body image may occur; the user's hands and feet seem shrunken and distant. The drug often produces euphoria, but the user might also become anxious and irritable. Sometimes paranoia results. The person might act belligerently and even violently, although it is not clear if these are direct consequences of intoxication or secondary to the fear and confusion that PCP produces. Death by overdose can occur.

Marijuana   **Marijuana** can be classified as a hallucinogen, although some contest this designation because marijuana produces distortions of perception only in high doses. The more typical effects of the drug are euphoria, increased sensitivity to external stimuli, and increased appetite. It comes from the leaves and flowers of the hemp plant, long used as a source of rope. The psychoactive properties of marijuana have long been recognized as well. The Greeks believed that hemp plants lined the roads to heaven *and* to hell. **Hashish** is a more potent version of marijuana, derived from the resin exuding from the hemp plant.

The active ingredient in marijuana is **delta-9-tetrahydrocannabinol,** usually called **THC.** Marijuana is usually smoked, although it is also sometimes swallowed. The concentration of THC determines the nature of intoxication. Since the 1970s, the marijuana

sold in the United States has increased in potency as much as tenfold, which makes comparisons across time problematic. The drug has literally changed.

Decades ago, when marijuana was most widely used, it was regarded by many people as harmless. Today, both adverse psychological and physical consequences are recognized (Selden, Clark, & Curry, 1990). Whether these effects were present all along or are the result of the more potent strains of marijuana now available is not clear. At any rate, both short-term and long-term use may impair memory and other intellectual processes as well as interfere with psychomotor coordination. Among males and females, chronic use may reduce fertility. The most obvious damage due to smoking marijuana is to the lungs, because a user typically inhales deeply and holds in the smoke as long as possible (Tashkin, 1990). Chronic use can lead to problems with the teeth and gums as well (Darling & Arendorf, 1992).

In the 1960s and 1970s, marijuana use was normative among high school and college students (National Institute on Drug Abuse, 1986). A longitudinal study by Shedler and Block (1990) found that those young people who *abstained* from its use during this time were more likely to be maladjusted than those who occasionally experimented with it. "The picture of the abstainer that emerges is of a relatively tense, overcontrolled, emotionally constricted individual who is somewhat socially isolated and lacking in interpersonal skills" (p. 618).

These are striking findings, reminding us that drug use must be located in its societal and historical context. These researchers do not suggest that drug use per se is beneficial, but they also do not suggest that those who abstain are inherently healthy. In a context that legitimizes drug experimentation, the typical individual will experiment. Simply put, drug use need not become drug abuse, and it is thus a mistake to treat all instances of use as pathological.

A major purpose of the present chapter was to illustrate abstract ideas discussed in earlier chapters. My consideration here of alcohol use and abuse showed that the definition of abnormality can be difficult, that problems can be better understood by placing them in their social and historical context, that a variety of theoretical perspectives can be brought to bear on problems, and that an integrated perspective is probably the most plausible. Besides alcohol, people use and abuse other drugs. The points illustrated by the extended discussion of alcohol could also have been made with respect to each of these other drugs. Indeed, you will see in subsequent chapters that these general ideas recur when we investigate the other sorts of problems that people encounter.

The Hell's Angels motorcycle gang reportedly cornered the PCP market, hence one street name of the drug: angel dust.

Summary

✦ Psychoactive drugs affect brain activity and thus the nature of a person's consciousness. In seeking intoxication via psychoactive drugs, people may end up abusing these drugs.

ALCOHOL USE AND ABUSE

✦ The most frequently abused drug in the United States today is certainly ethyl alcohol, the active ingredient in beer, wine, and liquor. Alcohol has a host of negative physiological and psychological effects on the individual, and alcohol abuse exacts an incredible toll on society's resources.

✦ Alcohol has been available for 10,000 years, and over this period we see its use and abuse conceived in magical, somatic, and psychological terms.

✦ Alcohol abuse proves difficult to define precisely, because people do not fall into discrete groups of users versus abusers. Relevant in judging abuse are such criteria as the amount of alcohol consumed, the pattern of use, physical consequences, social consequences, and loss of control over drinking.

✦ The diagnosis of drug problems involves several general issues concerning classification. What substances can be abused? Are there different types of substance abuse? DSM-IV distinguishes between substance dependence, in which an individual experiences a variety of problems associated with drug use, and substance abuse, in which an individual experiences more circumscribed difficulties due to drug use. According to DSM-IV, eleven different drugs—including alcohol—may be associated with substance dependence and abuse. Assessment is made difficult by the possible unreliability of information provided by drug users.

✦ Each of the popular models of abnormality has been applied to substance use and abuse. Each suggests its own view of the causes of substance abuse and how best to treat it. Because each approach explains some aspects of it but not others, an integrated perspective is needed.

THE USE AND ABUSE OF OTHER DRUGS

✦ People use and abuse a variety of drugs besides alcohol.

✦ Narcotics refer to opium and its derivatives, such as morphine and heroin. These drugs produce an intense rush of pleasure followed by a lingering state of bliss. Illegal in the United States since 1914, narcotics are among the more commonly abused illicit drugs. Narcotics addiction is sometimes treated with substitution therapy, providing the individual with an opiate such as methadone which is longer-lasting and more gradual in its effects than heroin or morphine.

✦ Stimulants are drugs that stimulate the nervous system, increasing arousal and spurring mental and physical activity. Caffeine, nicotine, amphetamine, and cocaine are included among the stimulants. The abuse of an extremely potent yet inexpensive form of cocaine known as crack increased greatly throughout the 1980s.

✦ Depressants slow down the nervous system, creating a state of relaxation and temporarily ridding an individual of anxiety. The depressants include alcohol, tranquilizers, barbiturates, methaqualone, and inhalants such as glue, gasoline, and paint.

✦ Psychedelics are drugs touted by their users as "consciousness-expanding," and include hallucinogens (e.g., mescaline, psilocybin, and LSD), phencyclidine (PCP), and marijuana.

Key Terms

addiction
addictive personality
alcoholic
Alcoholics Anonymous; AA
alcoholism
amphetamine
amphetamine psychosis
antagonists
barbiturates
blood alcohol content; BAC
caffeine
cocaine
codependency
controlled drinking
crack
cross-tolerance
delirium tremens; DTs
depressants
detoxification
Dionysus; Bacchus
disulfiram; Antabuse
endorphins
ethnic group
ethyl alcohol
hallucinogens
hashish
heroin
inhalants
intoxication

LSD (lysergic acid diethylamide)
marijuana
mescaline
methadone
methaqualone
morphine
narcotics; opiates; opioids
nicotine
opium
phencyclidine; PCP
polysubstance dependence
psilocybin
psychedelics
psychoactive drugs
relapse prevention
stimulants
substance abuse
substance dependence
substance-induced cognitive disorders
substance-related disorders
substitution therapy
THC (delta-9-tetrahydrocannabinol)
tolerance
tranquilizers
withdrawal

Organic
Disorders

6 *WE OFTEN TAKE OUR BODIES FOR GRANTED until something goes wrong with them. Then we are aware that we are biological beings. Physical problems invariably have psychological consequences. For example, consider the case of Christina. Neurologist Oliver Sacks (1985b) described this 27-year old woman as happy and healthy, living an active life, until she developed gallstones and was told she needed to have her gallbladder removed. Shortly thereafter, she found herself unable to hold objects or to stand without swaying.*

A psychiatrist was consulted, who diagnosed her as having a conversion disorder, *a problem that looks*

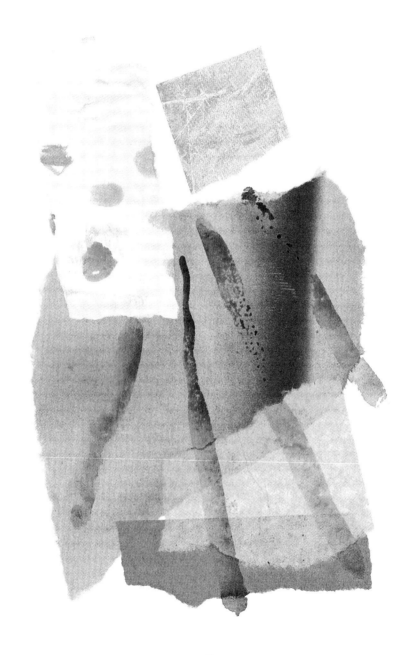

biological in nature but in actuality is not (Chapter 8). Christina presumably suffered from an unconscious emotional conflict. According to the psychiatrist, having to undergo a fairly serious operation triggered her symptoms. However, the diagnosis of conversion disorder failed to satisfy all of the physicians who attended Christina. For one thing, the particular inabilities that she displayed were unlike those usually seen with this type of disorder. In the typical case, one or another bodily system seems not to work—movement or touch or hearing or sight. But in the case of Christina, it was as if her entire muscle tone had collapsed. She could barely sit up. Her face was expressionless. Her voice was flat. These were highly unusual symptoms, granted the diagnosis.

And for another thing, Christina was greatly upset about what was happening. One of the striking aspects of conversion disorder is an indifference to the apparent loss of functioning. Christina's reaction was hardly one of indifference; she was quite distraught:

> "Something awful's happened," she mouthed, in a ghostly flat voice. "I can't feel my body. I feel weird—disembodied." (p. 44)

Oliver Sacks was one of Christina's physicians, and he decided to take her symptoms at face value, and then work backwards to try and understand what might be occurring within her nervous system to produce them. He concluded that her brain was not receiving any sensory information from her muscles and joints. A neurological examination fine-tuned this inference. Christina remained sensitive to touch, temperature, and pain. She was able to move her muscles, although awkwardly. What she was not able to do was get a sense of the position of her body and its limbs. What is referred to as her proprioceptive sense was profoundly absent.

A spinal tap then revealed that Christina was suffering from a form of polyneuritis (nerve inflammation) affecting only those neurons that carried proprioceptive information from the muscles and joints to the brain. Stripped of this information, her bodily movements became increasingly awkward. It was as if she no longer "owned" her own body. For obvious reasons, Christina's gallbladder operation was postponed, and eventually her polyneuritis subsided. However, the damage done to her proprioceptive nerves remained. She was like a rag doll, constantly "losing" her limbs. She would think that her arm was in one position, only to find it in another.

Where did this leave Christina? As Sacks tells the story, she had an indomitable spirit and decided that she would somehow have to compensate for what the polyneuritis had taken from her. She began to rely on her visual sense to tell her about her bodily position and posture. At first this was a deliberate and self-conscious process. Later it became more automatic, and at least to the observer, Christina's movements appeared graceful and smooth.

She learned to modulate her voice by listening to how it sounded. For those of us with an intact proprioceptive sense, we need not hear ourselves for our voices to be normal. We rely on the "feel" of our voice to judge its intonations. But Christina had to listen quite literally to how she sounded in order to be able to depart from her monotone. She ended up creating a theatrical voice, as if she were projecting what she said to an audience.

Christina resumed a normal life, yet she was not exactly normal. She had to be more vigilant than other people. Certain activities, if she did not pay attention to them, broke down. She could not talk and eat at the same time, for instance, because she had to give full attention to whichever activity she pursued. More generally, she experienced a loss of her sense of self. Our bodies are part of our selves, and Christina was denied her body. She sometimes raged that she felt unreal. She could not even remember what it was like to move as other people did.

Christina's case introduces us to the subject of the present chapter—**organic disorders:** psychological problems associated with physical injury, illness, or defect. Often when we discuss psychological abnormality, the underlying causes are a source of mystery and/or debate. We have no such problem with organic disorders, because part of their definition is their cause. So, organic disorders are an example of etiological classification because they are defined in terms of their cause.

I start this chapter with an overview of the nervous system. This will help you understand not only organic disorders but also the other disorders covered in this textbook. Many of the newest discoveries in the field of abnormal psychology involve the biological underpinnings of abnormality; a grasp of the nervous system is critical in appreciating these findings. The emphasis

here is placed less on the myriad of names for the structures of the nervous system and more on its operating principles. I conclude the chapter with a survey of organic disorders.

AN OVERVIEW OF THE NERVOUS SYSTEM

When we refer to the **nervous system,** we include the brain as well as the network of nerve cells throughout the entire body. It is composed of numerous individual neurons, perhaps in excess of 100 billion (Hubel, 1979). This system of neurons performs several related functions (Peterson, 1991a). It receives information from the world. It then coordinates this information, taking into account prevailing psychological and physical conditions. Finally, it reacts on the basis of this co-ordination.

The nervous system sets the parameters for our behavior, determining how we can and cannot think, feel, and act. Appreciate the complexity here, because thoughts, feelings, and actions can in turn influence the nervous system (Chapter 10). If we are fortunate, the physical constraints we face do not compromise the life we choose to lead. Often we can devalue or ignore those things we are unable to do. But if an individual faces constraints that are too severe, too sweeping, or too central, then difficulties ensue. Organic disorders exemplify such problems.

If we are fortunate, physical constraints do not compromise the life we choose to lead. Rehabilitation helps individuals compensate for physical difficulties.

Organic disorders are psychological problems associated with physical injury, illness, or defect.

THE STRUCTURE AND FUNCTION OF THE NERVOUS SYSTEM

It is customary to describe the nervous system in terms of the following distinctions (see Figure 6.1). The **central nervous system** is composed of the brain and spinal cord, and the **peripheral nervous system** is made up of the neurons in all the other parts of the body. The role of the peripheral nervous system is to carry impulses to and from the central nervous system, thereby communicating with all of our muscles, glands, and sense organs. Christina had a problem with her peripheral nervous system.

The peripheral nervous system is subdivided into the **somatic nervous system,** which controls the skeletal muscles and sense organs, and the **autonomic nervous system,** which controls the heart, lungs, and digestive organs. The autonomic nervous system is further divided into the **sympathetic nervous system,** which produces arousal, and the **parasympathetic nervous system,** which counteracts arousal. Usually, the sympathetic and parasympathetic nervous systems work in good coordination. But in fear and anxiety disorders, individuals experience overly frequent and/or intense arousal of their sympathetic nervous system, giving rise to such somatic symptoms as perspiration, shallow breathing, feelings of choking, "butterflies" in the stomach, and muscular tension (Chapter 7). Tranquilizers work by stimulating the parasympathetic nervous system, which then reduces sympathetic arousal (Shephard, 1986; Tallman & Gallager, 1985).

Neurons   The basic component of the nervous system is the **neuron.** Figure 6.2 shows a representative neuron, and identifies its major structures:

In fear and anxiety, individuals experience arousal of their sympathetic nervous system. The parasympathetic nervous system counteracts this arousal.

✦ the cell body, which contains the cell nucleus and the cell's largest concentration of mass

✦ dendrites, which *receive* messages from other neurons

✦ axons, which *send* messages to other neurons

✦ terminal buttons, which secrete chemicals that constitute the actual messages sent between neurons

About half the neurons of an adult are covered with a white, fatty substance called **myelin.** Myelin is

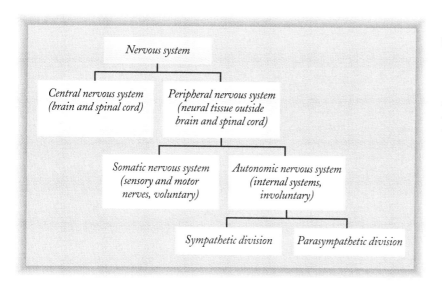

FIGURE 6.1

DIVISIONS OF THE NERVOUS SYSTEM   *Although the nervous system typically works as a whole, it is customary to make these broad distinctions among its different parts.*

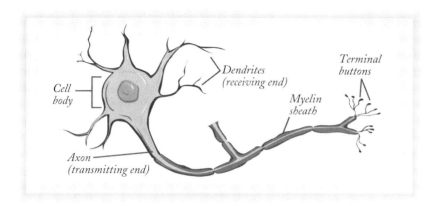

FIGURE **6.2**

A REPRESENTATIVE
NEURON   *Neurons take on a
variety of shapes and sizes, but
this figure is representative,
showing the important parts.*

an insulator, protecting neurons and allowing them to send their messages more rapidly. At birth, the neurons of an infant are not covered with myelin to the degree that an adult's are, which is one of the reasons why infants cannot move in the coordinated fashion of children or adults. They can only begin to crawl, then walk, and finally run when their nervous system develops enough to let them do so.

Neurons are not directly connected to one another; they communicate by secreting chemicals— **neurotransmitters**—from the terminal buttons on the axon of one neuron to stimulate the dendrites of another neuron. The space between two neurons is called a *synapse,* and it is tiny— about .0002 millimeter across (Carlson, 1986). When stimulated, a chemical reaction takes place within a neuron that changes the electrical charge of the inside of the neuron from negative to positive. This positive charge travels down the neuron to trigger further secretion of neurotransmitters at the other end, and the process takes place all over again. In some cases, as just described, one neuron stimulates another. But in other cases, the process starts when external energy stimulates sense organs. Light or sound or pressure stimulates the appropriate *receptor,* which is a neuron sensitive to this type of stimulation, which then sends this message on to other nerve cells. And in still other cases, the process ends at a muscle or gland, which is stimulated into action by a neural message as well.

We can describe messages as being sent, but appreciate that nothing concrete is transmitted along a neuron. It is an electrical impulse that is sent. Neural messages are more like FAX messages than letters or postcards.

When neurons induce other neurons to fire, this process is called **excitation.** But this is only one possible influence. Another process may occur, in which one neuron makes it less likely for a second neuron to fire. This is called **inhibition.** The mechanism for inhibition again is electrochemical, as the inside of a

neuron becomes even more negative than usual in its electrical charge and thus less susceptible to excitation. What results is a nervous system of compromise, delicate balances between excitation and inhibition. **Seizures** like those characterizing epilepsy occur when large numbers of neurons in the brain are excited in an uncontrolled, disorganized fashion. A wave of neural activity sweeps the brain, often resulting in the person losing consciousness and displaying frenzied motor movement. Most seizures are brief, because the nervous system quickly restores a coordinated balance between excitatory and inhibitory processes.

In a seizure, large numbers of neurons in the brain are excited in an uncontrolled and disorganized fashion.

Matters would be simple if there were but two neurotransmitters, one excitatory and the other inhibitory, but there are hundreds of different neurotransmitters (Panksepp, 1986). Some are exclusively excitatory and others exclusively inhibitory, and still others play both roles, depending on the synapse into which they happen to be secreted.

For the most part, individual neurons either fire or not. There is no in-between state. This is referred to as the *all-or-none principle*. The gradations in our sensory experience or movement are not produced by variations in the degree to which an individual neuron is stimulated. Instead, gradations reflect the number of different neurons in operation and/or the frequency with which they fire. Here the coordinated and integrated character of the nervous system becomes clear. Even when individual neurons function perfectly well, the individual is nonetheless impaired if there is a problem in coordinating the information they contain into psychologically meaningful terms.

Consider the case of another patient described by Oliver Sacks (1985b). Dr. P. was a music professor with a bizarre visual problem, due to a brain malfunction. He could see only parts, not wholes. For example, in a neurological examination, Sacks asked him to describe a picture in a **National Geographic** *magazine. Dr. P. noted only small details—colors and shapes—and not the entire scene. Sacks likened what his patient was doing to spotting blips on a radar screen.*

Sacks once showed the professor a glove and asked him what it was:

> *"A continuous surface," he announced at last, "infolded on itself. It appears to have"—he hesitated—"five outpouchings, if this is the word."*
>
> *"Yes . . . you have given me a description. Now tell me what it is."*
>
> *"A container of some sort?"*
>
> *"Yes . . . and what would it contain?"*
>
> *"It would contain its contents!" said Dr. P. with a laugh. "There are many possibilities. It could be a change-purse, for example, for coins of five sizes." (p. 15)*

Eventually, Dr. P. exclaimed "My God, it's a glove!" He had to infer what the object was, rather than simply observe it.

The brain   The human brain is about the size of a grapefruit and contains the largest number and most dense concentration of neurons in the body (see Figure 6.3). The complexity of interconnections among the neurons there is virtually beyond comprehension.

One approach to understanding the brain is to appreciate how it evolved (Jerison, 1973; Kaas, 1987).

Almost all multicelled animals have a nervous system composed of neurons that work according to the general principles just described. The nervous system thus appeared quite early in evolution, because of the obvious advantage enjoyed by organisms whose body parts could communicate with one another. Try, if you can, to imagine people whose right hands do not know what their left hands are doing, or vice versa. This is exactly what happens when neural connections are severed by illness or injury, like in a spinal cord injury. Fortunately, other systems can sometimes take over. But if not, survival is threatened.

As organisms became more complex, neurons began to clump together into groups called *ganglia,* and the ganglia became arranged in a hierarchy, so that some controlled others. Among those animals that became elongated, the most important neurons were those that ran down their entire length; the most important ganglia were those that existed at one end (or the other) of these animals. These later became the brain.

As evolution continued, the brain became an ever more complicated organ by the addition of new layers. Ornstein and Thompson (1984) described the evolution of the brain with the metaphor of a ramshackle house originally built for a small family but then added to repeatedly as subsequent family members needed shelter. We can approach the human brain, therefore, in terms of its major layers, which presumably reflect evolutionary history.

Appreciate that as the brain evolved, layers were not simply attached like Post-it notes, but instead were integrated with those already present. The brain acts as a whole, despite the fact that particular structures

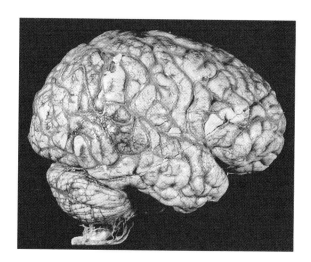

FIGURE **6.3**

A NORMAL ADULT BRAIN   *This photo shows a normal adult brain as seen from the right side.*

may be more involved or less involved with given psychological functions.

Figure 6.4 depicts the layers of the brain. The **hindbrain** exists at the very base of the brain, which is connected directly to the spinal cord. It is the oldest part of the brain and is involved in basic biological functions: the regulation of our respiration and cardiac function and the coordination of our motor movement. The structures of the hindbrain also play an important role as relay stations, sending neural messages from the spinal cord to the higher layers of the brain, and vice versa.

Boxers who have taken too many punches to the head may suffer in particular from damage to the hindbrain. Their speech becomes slurred because the muscles that control the lips, mouth, and tongue are no longer synchronized. They stagger when they walk, and tremble when they move. This phenomenon used to be called being *punch-drunk.*

Muhammad Ali may have suffered brain damage from the many blows he received during his long boxing career.

Consider Muhammad Ali, who in his prime was perhaps the most charismatic boxer the world has ever known (Boyle & Ames, 1983). Current observers frequently comment on his slurred speech and rambling monologues, which suggest the presence of Parkinson's disease. I have no privileged information, but it seems possible that Ali suffered brain damage during his long career in the ring—61 professional fights over 21 years. He was famous for his ability to "take" a punch, but short-term resilience does not mean that no damage occurred.

The **midbrain** exists in the middle of the brain, and its most important role is one of coordination of bodily systems. Particularly notable is its control over a person's general level of arousal and state of consciousness—awake, asleep, and so on. Damage to the midbrain can result in a **coma:** complete loss of consciousness and responsiveness to environmental stimuli. The lower the damage reaches into the brain stem, the worse the prognosis of the patient, because bodily functions necessary for life are more likely to be impaired (Weisberg, Strub, & Garcia, 1989).

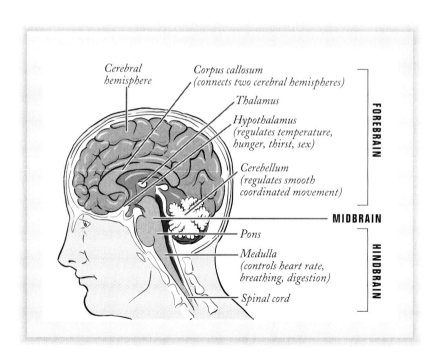

FIGURE **6.4**

THE LAYERS OF THE BRAIN   *The layers of the brain, from bottom to top, reflect the order in which these structures appeared in the course of evolution.*

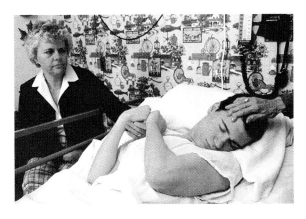

A coma is a complete loss of consciousness and responsiveness to environmental stimuli. One possible cause of a coma is damage to the midbrain.

The **forebrain** is the most recent structure to evolve, and it is found at the top of the brain. It contains a number of structures, and they tend to be responsible for the characteristically human functions: language, abstract thought, emotional expression, and memory. The forebrain also controls the activities of lower layers of the brain, sorting out their messages, coordinating them, and relaying them to the appropriate destinations. Damage here results in an incredible array of problems, from circumscribed to highly general, depending on the specific nature of the damage. As I go on to discuss different organic disorders, I will mention many of the particular structures of the forebrain, as well as those of the midbrain and hindbrain. For the time being, appreciate the layered structure of the brain, and the fact that these layers exist in a hierarchy.

Function   The nervous system works by a system of checks and balances. As already discussed, given neurons and neural structures may excite or inhibit one another. "Normal" functioning is characterized by a balance, a *homeostasis* if you will. The nervous system strives to maintain homeostasis. Disturbances in one direction give rise to processes that try to counteract them. Such self-correcting responses are referred to as *feedback systems,* and a familiar analogy is the thermostat that controls the temperature in your house. When the temperature falls too low, the thermostat turns on the furnace. When the temperature rises to an acceptable level, the furnace is turned off. If your house is equipped as well with an air conditioner, then the thermostat is more complicated, because it now also turns the air conditioner on when the temperature is too high. The checks and balances that take place within the brain work the same, but with much more complexity.

Particular problems with our nervous system—such as an injury or illness—do not simply break its parts; they also throw its operation out of kilter, and the effects may be far-reaching as the nervous system tries to restore equilibrium. If this equilibrium is impossible to restore, then death follows. For example, the chemical *strychnine,* the active ingredient in rat poison, prevents neurons from inhibiting one another. Strychnine unleashes—and this is exactly the right word—uncontrollable activity of the nervous system: twitches, spasms, and eventually convulsions that lead to death.

In other cases, an equilibrium can be restored, but it differs from the one that existed prior to the injury or illness. You saw this in the case of Christina, who suffered an acute inflammation of part of her nervous system, which quickly subsided but left permanent damage. As she accommodated herself to the damage, she became a somewhat different person.

The symptoms of organic brain disorders are sometimes described as positive versus negative. *Positive symptoms* represent excesses; the person does something she did not do before; these symptoms are due to increased activity in the nervous system. Epileptic seizures are a good example. *Negative symptoms* represent deficits; the person stops doing something she did before; these symptoms are due to decreased activity in the nervous system. A coma is a good example.

At this point in time, we know something about the neural structures involved in certain problems. We do not yet know exactly how they give rise to the problems. For example, depression involves problems with the neurotransmitters **norepinephrine** and **serotonin.** It has been proposed that depression occurs when these chemicals exist at overly low levels in certain parts of the brain (e.g., Schildkraut, 1965). In treatment, we try to boost their levels. But this is a static view of the problem and of the nervous system. The brain is not an automobile engine that simply needs to have its fluids maintained at certain levels. Instead, it is a dynamic mechanism that constantly changes as it maintains equilibrium.

A more contemporary view of neurotransmitters and the brain sees them as responsible for regulating and organizing physiological rhythms: sleep, appetite, activity, and mood (Tuomisto & Mannisto, 1985). What happens in depression, perhaps, is that the person gets out of synch (Healy & Williams, 1988). In treatment, we try to resynchronize bodily rhythms.

THE ORGANIZATION OF THE NERVOUS SYSTEM

One striking aspect of the nervous system is that it is organized in a multitude of ways (Rozin, 1984). For one, it is characterized by a *spatial organization,* meaning that neurons close to one another are apt to be involved in the same psychological functions. An injury to one part of the brain may therefore be highly specific in its most immediate psychological effects. Consider **aphasia,** which is actually a host of problems stemming from brain damage and involving the inability to express or comprehend speech or writing. All possible forms of aphasia seem to exist, forms in which people can read but not write, write but not speak, and so on (Albert & Helm-Estabrooks, 1988a, 1988b; Caramazza, 1988).

The nervous system is characterized as well by a *biochemical organization,* which means that different neurons are sensitive to different neurotransmitters. For example, the neurons in the brain triggered by **dopamine** can be regarded as a whole; this dopamine system is thought to play some role in schizophrenia (Andreasen et al., 1988; Reynolds, 1989), perhaps because its neurons have an excess of dopamine receptors (Owen, Crow, & Poulter, 1987).

The nervous system is also characterized by a *top-to-bottom organization;* its structures and functions exist on different levels, some higher and some lower.[1] As a rule of thumb, the higher structures tend to be those that are located near the top of the brain, and they play a role in directing the structures located lower in the brain. Such human abilities as language and abstract thought are made possible by these higher structures. They are most vulnerable to injury, granted their location, and this is why a person with a head injury might show considerable difficulty thinking and speaking, yet continue as usual with her breathing, digesting, and so on.

The nervous system is additionally characterized by a *front-to-back organization* of the brain structures responsible for certain functions. For example, the part of the brain responsible for voluntary motor movements is in front of the part that receives sensory input from the muscles and skin. Sometimes when the head has been struck, brain damage occurs in two places: at the point where the blow occurred as well as at the opposite point where the brain bounced against the skull. Sets of symptoms may thus appear in pairs, a fact that diagnosticians use in pinpointing the nature of brain damage.

Finally, the nervous system is characterized by a *lateral organization;* it is structured on a left-right basis. The outermost outer layer of the brain—the **cerebral cortex**—consists of two symmetric structures, the **cerebral hemispheres.** The left hemisphere controls the nerves on the right side of the body, whereas the right hemisphere controls the nerves on the left side. Diagnosticians use this fact to identify the source of brain damage responsible for symptoms such as weakness or loss of feeling on one side of the body but not the other; the opposite cerebral hemisphere is implicated.

Remember the earlier discussion of Christina. Her inability to feel her body showed no left-right difference. While she could have suffered the identical damage to both the left and right parts of her brain, thus producing the same deficits on both sides of her body, it was much more likely that her problem was peripheral—in the actual proprioceptive nerve cells.

The nervous system is not only integrated within itself, it is also intimately connected to other biological systems. For instance, it is linked to the **endocrine system**—which consists of the various glands that secrete hormones. Hormones influence our thoughts, feelings, and actions. The **hypothalamus** is a brain structure that is considered part of both the nervous system *and* the endocrine system. It secretes hormones that particularly influence the **pituitary gland.** This is sometimes called the *master gland* because its secretions direct the operation of so many other glands, such as the thyroid, the adrenals, the testes, and the ovaries.

Recent evidence shows that the nervous system is linked as well to the **immune system,** the part of the body that identifies and fights off foreign material such as germs (Chapter 10). In fact, a new field has taken form, dubbed **psychoneuroimmunology,** which studies the interrelations among psychological factors, the nervous system, and the immune system (Ader & Cohen, 1981). It now appears as if the immune system can be considered a bodily sense, much as our eyes or ears.

In sum, the nervous system directly influences psychological processes by setting parameters for them and determining just how they take place. And the nervous system also influences behavior through its interactions with the endocrine system and the immune system. Whether we are talking about learning, emotions, consciousness, memory, thinking, or motor movement, whatever we say must be based on what we know about the nervous system.

CONCEPTUALIZING ORGANIC DISORDERS

Having discussed the structure and function of the nervous system, I can now start to consider specific organic disorders (see Focus on Left-Handedness). Christina's case illustrates several generalizations about these problems. First, the part of the body implicated in these disorders is usually the central nervous system.

---

[1] Cognitive psychologists sometimes use terms like *higher* versus *lower* to refer to the degree to which psychological processes transform incoming information (Craik & Lockhart, 1972). These meanings differ from those in the present context.

Most often part of the brain is compromised, but sometimes—as with Christina—more peripheral parts of the nervous system are damaged.

Second, organic disorders can be broadly psychological in their impact, just as much as they are specifically biological in their causes. Christina's polyneuritis affected not simply her nervous system and her bodily movements but also her thoughts and emotions and her very sense of self. There is a tendency to separate mind and body into discrete realms, and thus to dismiss Christina's problem as "just" a neurological one, but this is not the way human beings are constituted. Minds and bodies interlock and interact, and so her problem was as fully psychological as it was biological.

Third, although one of the strong suits of the *neuropsychologists* who study organic disorders is diagnosis—pinpointing the exact causes of these problems—diagnosis is not foolproof. Brain imaging techniques and neuropsychological tests provide helpful diagnostic data (Chapter 2), but often the definitive causes can be determined only by an autopsy after death (e.g., Bennett & Evans, 1992; Koller, 1992; Lang, 1992). Furthermore, because diagnosticians usually interview their patients, the organic disorders represent a particular challenge if they show themselves in terms of confusion or incoherence. DSM-IV also reminds diagnosticians of another consideration:

> Cultural and educational background should be taken into consideration [in diagnosing organic disorders]. . . . Individuals . . . may not be familiar with the information used in certain tests of general knowledge (e.g., names of presidents, geographical knowledge), memory (e.g., date of birth in cultures that do not routinely celebrate birthdays), and orientation (e.g., sense of placement and location may be conceptualized differently in some cultures). (American Psychiatric Association, 1994, pp. 125–126)

To this end, investigators have devised diagnostic interviews suitable for people from varying social groups (e.g., Brayne, Day, & Gill, 1992; Molgaard et al., 1990).

A fourth general point about organic disorders is that even when we can specify causes, actual cures may not be possible. The tissue of the central nervous system, once destroyed, cannot be restored. In some cases, another part of the nervous system can take over for the damaged part—most readily for individuals who are young. If the brain hemisphere responsible for language is damaged during infancy, for example, the opposite hemisphere takes over (Lenneberg, 1967). But the identical damage later in life might leave the individual unable to speak.

Finally, even if literal cures are not possible, the person can still learn to compensate for the loss of

Sometimes an individual can compensate for the loss of certain abilities by learning new ones. Here a patient works to improve his hand-eye coordination.

certain abilities by developing new ones. These therapeutic efforts are collectively called **rehabilitation.** For instance, if an individual has experienced a spinal cord injury and can no longer walk, rehabilitation usually takes the form of showing him how to get around in a wheelchair. There is an increasing recognition that rehabilitation must be broad, focusing not just on specific losses but also on the person who has experienced them, and to involve the patient's family in the program (e.g., Tettenborn & Kramer, 1992).

THE APPROACH OF DSM-IV

The predecessors to DSM-IV included organic disorders as a separate category, defining them as problems caused by a brain dysfunction that resulted in an alteration of consciousness. In some cases, the brain dysfunction was known to be caused by a specific illness, injury, or defect. In other cases, it was inferred from characteristic symptoms. Regardless, organic disorders so defined were contrasted with **functional disorders,** problems due to "abnormal" experience superimposed on a "normal" nervous system. Depression following the unexpected loss of a job is a typical example of a functional disorder.

DSM-IV has dispensed with a separate category for organic disorders. It still groups together problems involving alterations in thought and consciousness to which such biological factors as illness or injury contribute, calling them **cognitive disorders.** Why the change? The authors of DSM-IV wished to avoid the implication that organic disorders are the only psychological problems with biological causes. With the growing popularity of a biopsychosocial approach to many disorders, it has become increasingly less tenable to propose that only some disorders have brain

FOCUS ON

Left-Handedness

THIS CHAPTER HAS CONcerned itself with psychological problems resulting from physical causes: illness, injury, or bodily defect. In a sense, left-handedness satisfies this definition of an organic disorder. This is a deliberately provocative conclusion, so let me examine what researchers have discovered about the causes and consequences of left-handedness (Coren, 1990, 1992).

Researchers speak of people's *lateral preference,* which refers to the side of the body used for common activities. Individuals show a lateral preference not simply for one hand or the other, but also for their eyes, ears, and feet. Most show a consistent right-sided lateral preference, which means that the typical person is not only right-handed but also right-eyed, right-eared, and right-footed. Some people depart from this consistent right-sided lateral preference, showing a left-sided preference instead. These departures are not usually consistent, which means that people fall into two groups: those with a consistently right-sided lateral preference versus those with a mixed lateral preference.

These distinctions are important because most studies of handedness do *not* take them into account. Research participants are simply asked with which hand they prefer to write, and their answers are used to divide them into right-handed versus left-handed groups. The full sense of lateral preference is not captured by this procedure, which means that research results based on it must be regarded with a fair amount of caution.

Here are some findings, starting with the demographics of left-handedness. In our current society, about 10% to 12% of individuals are left-handed. Those who are young and male are most likely to be left-handed. Throughout the 20th century, the proportion of left-handers in the United States has increased. There are cross-cultural differences in the prevalence of left-handedness as well. Countries with liberal educational systems (such as Sweden) have more left-handers than those with more conservative schools (such as Taiwan).

I now turn to some of the correlates of left-handedness. According to one study or another, left-handedness may be associated with any of the following:

- alcoholism (Chapter 5)
- allergies (Chapter 10)
- autism (Chapter 14)
- criminality (Chapter 13)
- depression (Chapter 9)
- epilepsy (Chapter 6)
- immune disorders (Chapter 10)
- juvenile delinquency (Chapter 14)
- mental retardation (Chapter 14)
- neuroticism (Chapter 7)
- reading disabilities (Chapter 14)
- schizophrenia (Chapter 12)

So, left-handed individuals are more likely than right-handed individuals to suffer from a variety of difficulties. This is a broad generalization, however, and should *not* be interpreted as saying that no right-handed individuals have these problems or that all left-handed individuals do. These findings are not particularly robust (Chapter 4). Furthermore, appreciate that these are correlational results and do *not* compel the conclusion that left-handedness causes any of these problems.

Perhaps the most striking correlate of being left-handed, according to one study, is a person's expected lifespan (Coren & Halpern, 1991). Among the research subjects, right-handed females had a life expectancy of 78 years; left-handed females had a life expectancy of 73 years. Among men, the corresponding figures were 72 years for right-handers and 62 years for left-handers. Another study has questioned these findings, noting the tendency among older individuals to have had their hand preference switched from left to right during childhood (Hugdahl, Satz, Mitrushina, & Miller, 1993). The fact that there are relatively few elderly left-handers might simply mean that decades ago, naturally left-handed individuals "became" right-handed.

Is there anything desirable associated with left-handedness? Researchers have found in various studies a correlation between left-handedness and artistic accomplishment, musical ability, mathematical skill, prowess at board games like chess and Go, and athletic achievement in sports requiring spatial ability, such as tennis and fencing. Again, appreciate that these are generalizations to which there are many exceptions.

I have not yet addressed why people are left-handed or not, and here we encounter the rationale for concluding that left-handedness may be an organic disorder. Most theorists trying to explain lateral preference have looked to biology for possible causes. Left-handedness runs in families, although it appears *not* to follow any pattern implicating a genetic basis. For example, although twins are more apt to be left-handed than non-twins, identical twins show no greater concordance for left-handedness than do fraternal twins.

Some theorists have thus suggested that left-handedness results from unusual prenatal events and experiences. According to one such theory, it occurs when a fetus is exposed to excessive testosterone. This slows the development of the left cerebral hemisphere, thereby allowing the right cerebral hemisphere to become more dominant. A non-right-sided lateral preference results, along with "right hemisphere" abilities such as art and music. Another effect of exposure to excess testosterone during prenatal development is that the thymus gland—critical in the function of the immune system—is suppressed, which may account for the preponderance of immunological illnesses and dysfunctions seen among left-handers.

This theory is elegant, making sense of a number of the correlates of left-handedness, but it is far from generally accepted. It does not explain why there sometimes is excess testosterone during prenatal develop-

ment. It does not explain why left-handed people typically have their language center in the "usual" place—the left hemisphere. It does not explain why so many left-handed people—the great majority in fact—are healthy.

At present, we do not know enough to say left-handedness truly is or is not an organic disorder. In any event, it is simply a risk factor for certain problems; the mechanisms involved are not agreed upon. I can nonetheless make an important point about left-handedness, which applies as well to the organic disorders described in this chapter: Whatever its biological basis left-handedness must be placed in its social and historical context. There has long been a considerable stigma surrounding it. In many cultures, left-handedness has been associated with evil or deficiency.

Left-handed individuals have been feared, criticized, and even persecuted throughout the ages. This is an important context in which to locate left-handedness and its correlates. Problems inherent in being left-handed have been exacerbated by its stigma. Even in our present society, where left-handedness is rarely seen as evil, inadvertent discrimination remains because our technological world is designed for right-handed people. Perhaps the reduced life expectancy of left-handers has less to do with their immune systems and more to do with automobile and industrial accidents to which they are prone.

dysfunction as a contributing cause. Even the best examples of functional disorders have some biological aspect to them. Depression may have an external trigger, such as a loss, but it nonetheless involves a biological disruption.

These ideas obviously blur the distinction between organic disorders and functional disorders and explain why DSM-IV uses the more neutral term *cognitive disorders* to describe problems once labeled as organic. We can still regard "organic" disorders versus "functional" disorders as the endpoints of a continuum defined by the *relative* contributions of biological causes. Accordingly, I will continue to use the term *organic disorder* in this chapter, with the aforementioned qualifications understood.

ORGANIC SYNDROMES

When one talks about organic disorders, certain terms prove useful because they capture common constellations of psychological symptoms that result from neurological damage or dysfunction. These are **organic syndromes** (American Psychiatric Association, 1987, 1994). After characterizing the most common of these, I move to a discussion of actual disorders.

Delirium   The syndrome of **delirium** refers to a global impairment of thinking. More specifically, the delirious individual evidences the following:

✦   reduced ability to pay attention to external stimuli and events

- ✦ problems shifting attention from one stimulus to another

- ✦ disorganized thinking, as shown by rambling or incoherent speech

- ✦ reduced level of consciousness, ranging from drowsiness to stupor

- ✦ sensory misperceptions, such as mistaking one stimulus for another (e.g., hearing a slammed door as a pistol shot)

- ✦ disturbances of the normal sleep-wake cycle

- ✦ restlessness and hyperactivity on the one hand versus sluggishness on the other, and rapid changes back and forth

- ✦ disorientation with respect to time, place, and person; in other words, the individual may not know the time or date, where he happens to be, or even who he is

- ✦ impaired memory

Imagine, if you will, being able to hear only some of the words in a phone conversation, or watching a television show in which the picture and sound come and go independently of one another, or having the person with whom you are talking suddenly start to use a language you do not understand. This is how the delirious person experiences the world.

Delirium usually has a sudden onset and a fluctuating course. Indeed, fluctuation of symptoms is a hallmark of this syndrome. Stable symptoms suggest that delirium is not the appropriate diagnosis. It tends not to last very long, usually just a few days and rarely more than a month. Children and the elderly are most at risk.

Delirium has a variety of causes. For one, infectious illnesses can bring it about. Many of us have been at least a bit delirious when we have run a high fever for an extended period of time. Metabolic disorders frequently produce delirium, and so too can kidney and liver disease, thiamine deficiency, and lesions in particular locations in the cortex. Cardiopulmonary insufficiency can make a person delirious as well, as can the side effects of some medications.

Drug intoxication and/or withdrawal can also lead to this syndrome. As described in Chapter 5, withdrawal from alcohol can produce the state known as **delirium tremens** (or **DTs**).

One of the best known depictions of delirium tremens comes from Mark Twain's (1885/1961) novel The Adventures of Huckleberry Finn, *in which Huck described his father withdrawing from alcohol:*

After supper pap took the jug, and said he had enough whiskey there for two drunks and one delirium tremens. That was always his word. I judged he would be blind drunk in about an hour. . . .

All of a sudden there was an awful scream and I was up. There was pap looking wild, and skipping about every which way and yelling about snakes. He said they was crawling up his legs, and then he would give a jump and scream, and say one had bit him on the cheek—but I couldn't see no snakes. He started and run round and round the cabin, hollering, "Take him off! take him off! he's biting me on the neck!" I never see a man look so wild in the eyes. Pretty soon he was all fagged out, and fell down panting; then he rolled over and over wonderful fast, kicking things every which way, and striking and grabbing at the air with his hands, and screaming and saying there was devils a-hold of him. . . .

He chased me round and round the place with a clasp knife, calling me the Angel of Death, and saying he would kill me, and then I could come for him no more. I begged, and told him I was only Huck; but he laughed such a screechy laugh, and roared and cussed, and kept on chasing me. (pp. 14–15)

Besides alcohol, there are a number of drugs that can make people delirious, including those prescribed by a physician. Prescription drugs can create particular problems for the elderly, because older persons might be overly sensitive to their effects as well as susceptible to accidental overdose.

Delirium represents a serious condition, whatever its causes. The delirious person is incapacitated. Injuries are common as he blunders about the world of which he is so oblivious. Relatedly, he is not able to cooperate with his treatment or even to report exactly what is going on.

Treatment takes two forms. Either we wait out the problem, as in some cases of acute intoxication, in hopes that whatever agent is attacking the nervous system clears the body. Or we intervene more energetically, trying to identify the causal agents, and removing or neutralizing them. Unfortunately, the fatality rates associated with severe delirium can be as high as 40% (Francis, Martin, & Kapoor, 1990; Rabins & Folstein, 1982).

Dementia   Like delirium, **dementia** refers to a global impairment of a person's cognitive functioning, including memory. However, there is an important distinction. In the case of delirium, the assumption is that an imposition has been made on an otherwise intact nervous system. In the case of dementia, the nervous system as a whole has been compromised. Contrast an otherwise healthy individual who has a cold with somebody who has obstructive lung disease. Both have problems breathing, but the person with the cold has normally functioning lungs, whereas the person with lung disease obviously does not. This difference is analogous to the one between delirium and dementia, respectively.

In dementia, both short-term *and* long-term memory can be affected. The person with dementia also evidences difficulties with her abstract thinking and judgment. More generally, her overall personality may change. In some cases, she becomes apathetic or withdrawn, in other cases slovenly and unconcerned about her appearance. The personality change may also involve an exaggeration of her previously existing personality traits. If she is extraverted, she may become impulsive; if cautious, paranoid; and so on.

The exact course of this syndrome varies according to its specific cause. There was a time when the term *dementia* was reserved exclusively for progressive conditions—those that invariably worsened over time. Today, we use the term more descriptively to refer to symptoms as they presently exist. However, I can still offer some generalizations. It is most likely to occur among the elderly—the result of a neurological disease. The more pervasive the dementia, the less likely it is to be arrested or reversed.

Intervention can help the person compensate for memory losses (e.g., Zencius, Wesolowski, & Burke, 1990). For example, people in the early stages of Alzheimer's disease may find it helpful if large signs are posted around their house reminding them of things to do. Routines can be kept the same to avoid the confusion that arises from novel demands. These are simple extensions of what all of us can do to jog our memory.

A more involved example is provided by Grafman (1984), who treated Ms. S., a 24-year-old woman who suffered brain damage following an assault. She had been strangled, and the temporary loss of oxygen to her brain destroyed neural tissue. She was left with mild paralysis as well as several perceptual and language difficulties. Ms. S. was often unable to remember newly presented information, either visual or verbal, particularly when it was complex. She did not recognize that she had a memory problem, but she cooperated with Dr. Grafman in the attempt to rehabilitate her memory.

She was taught several strategies that helped her better organize information in her memory, thereby facilitating its later recall. When presented with a list of items or actions, she was told to use **mental imagery** *to link these together. For instance, she could remember what she needed to buy at the grocery store by picturing the meals she wished to prepare from her purchases. She*

was also taught to use **verbal mediation** *to link items together, creating a story in which the items figured. Finally, she was instructed in the* **PQRSTP** *strategy for organizing text material.*

PQRSTP is an acronym for the following steps to be used when encountering written information for the first time:

- ✦ *PREVIEW the material by focusing on major headings and topic sentences.*

- ✦ *Transform the material by asking summary QUESTIONS about it, which are then written out.*

- ✦ *REREAD the material in order to answer these questions, writing out the answers.*

- ✦ *STUDY the written questions and answers.*

- ✦ *TEST by posing the questions and providing answers.*

- ✦ *PROBE for information not contained in the questions or answers but able to be inferred from them.*

If this strategy strikes you as a good way to study a textbook like the present one, then you are right. Educational psychologists have documented its effectiveness in boosting a student's comprehension and recall of textbook information (Thomas & Robinson, 1972).

Ms. S. practiced the PQRSTP strategy with simple stories from magazines, then progressed to more complex material like that encountered in school or at work. As long as she continued to practice the strategies she was taught, she showed marked improvement in her memory. She eventually passed her GED examination and was able to live on her own.

In some cases, such as following a blow to the head, the onset of dementia is sudden. In other cases, as with a neurological disease, the onset is gradual, and the person is aware of her loss of cognitive abilities. Here depression is a common consequence, as the individual reacts to the loss of her intellect just as she would react to the loss of a job or a loved one. This is another reason why "neurological" problems cannot be approached on just a neurological level. Depression of this sort clearly has a psychological etiology, brought about by the individual's thoughts and beliefs about her neurological condition and where it may lead her.

Amnestic syndrome   Organically caused memory impairment that is *not* associated with problems in attention or with general difficulties in thinking and judgment comprises the **amnestic syndrome,** also known as **organic amnesia.** Amnesia can also result from psychological causes, such as a severe emotional trauma that leads a person to repress its occurrence and all other memories associated with it; in this case, we speak of **dissociative amnesia** (Chapter 8). It differs from organic amnesia in several characteristic ways (see Table 6.1). However, matters are not always so clear-cut because sometimes physical and emotional trauma coexist.

For instance, colleagues have told me a chilling story of a woman who was brutally assaulted and raped. In the course of the attack, she was beaten about the head and repeatedly strangled. She suffered considerable brain damage, as documented by the appropriate neurological tests. But the experience was also psychologically traumatic. In the aftermath of the attack, the woman showed cognitive and emotional problems, including memory loss and depression. She also evidenced many of the signs of post-traumatic stress disorder (Chapter 7). Sorting these problems out as to organic versus psychogenic etiology was obviously difficult.

To return to simpler cases of amnestic syndrome, the common causes are head trauma, loss of oxygen to the brain, infections (as may occasionally occur with herpes simplex), and cerebral **stroke**—that is, bursting or blocking of the arteries that supply blood to the forebrain (Chapter 10). Other common causes of this syndrome include thiamine deficiency and chronic alcohol use.

TABLE 6.1

ORGANIC AMNESIA VERSUS DISSOCIATIVE AMNESIA
Although both organic amnesia and dissociative amnesia are characterized by memory loss, they differ in several critical ways.

	ORGANIC AMNESIA	DISSOCIATIVE AMNESIA
typical cause	blow to the head	psychological trauma
extent of memory loss	recent and remote past	recent past
personal identity	not lost	lost
loss of memory for events since onset of amnesia	yes	no
return of memory	gradually if at all	suddenly

Organic personality syndrome   Sometimes the most salient consequence of neurological damage is a persistent change in the individual's personality; this is often referred to as **organic personality syndrome,** and is shown by one or more of the following symptoms:

✦ instability of moods, including rapid shifts from a normal state into depression, anxiety, or irritability

✦ outbursts of aggression or rage, out of proportion to whatever situations precipitated them

✦ grossly impaired social judgment in such domains as spending money or engaging in sexual activity

✦ apathy and indifference

✦ suspicion and paranoia

Particular symptoms in any given case depend on the extent and location of the neurological damage.

Frequently associated with organic personality syndrome is cognitive impairment. Some of its defining features can be derived straightforwardly from the particular cognitive problems. The person unable to plan ahead is bound to make errors in social judgment. Similarly, the person who has memory difficulties may end up being overly suspicious, as he tries to make sense of events that seem puzzling to him because of what he does not remember.

For example, a colleague described to me a patient with organic personality syndrome who was not able to remember that his wife had a job. As a result, he became highly agitated every morning when she left the house. He thought she was having an affair. Along these lines, the patient became suspicious of my colleague because he would telephone the patient's wife at home to confirm appointments and the like. "Who was on the phone?" the patient would ask, and when his wife said that it was the doctor, the patient would accuse her of planning trysts with him. He drew no connection between his treatment and the phone calls, interpreting them instead as indications of his wife's supposed infidelity.

As with the other organic syndromes, different causes exist for this problem. Most commonly, it is brought about by some damage to the structure of the brain, such as a tumor pressing on neural tissue, head trauma, or circulatory disease. Some people with epilepsy develop a personality style that exemplifies this syndrome. Less common causes include endocrine disorders and the ingestion of psychoactive substances.

When I discussed dementia, I noted that personality changes could be part of it. The difference is one of relative predominance: memory versus personality disturbance. Sometimes as a neurological disease progresses, the description must be changed from organic personality syndrome to dementia, as intellectual functions are increasingly compromised.

A person with organic personality syndrome not only has problems with his own life but creates problems for those who associate with him (Lezak, 1978). He usually looks completely normal. He can work and maintain social relationships. But outbursts of anger, mood fluctuations, and impaired judgment make it difficult for those in his vicinity, especially if they do not fully appreciate the organic basis of the syndrome. Caretakers of these individuals, chiefly parents, or spouses, may become depressed (Brooks, 1984). Marital problems are frequent, as you might imagine (Panting & Merry, 1972). Children are quite vulnerable to the debilitating effects of living with an unpredictable and uncontrollable parent, especially if they are too young to understand the notion of neurological damage (Hansell, 1990).

Intervention is often educational in nature, as the person with this disorder is instructed about the behavioral tendencies that will create havoc in his life. Needless to say, if his judgment is markedly compromised, then there is an upper limit to how much insight there can be. Family members, friends, and fellow workers can and should be educated as well to attribute difficult personal interactions not simply to obstinacy on the individual's part but to neurological damage (Sanguinetti & Catanzaro, 1987).

Intoxication and withdrawal   I have already discussed the phenomena of intoxication and withdrawal in Chapter 5, so I mention them only briefly here. We can regard these psychological states as organic syndromes because they are due to an underlying biological cause: an alteration in brain function brought about by drug use—**intoxication**—or the cessation of drug use—**withdrawal.** The change in brain function affects a spectrum of thoughts, moods, and actions. Different drugs have characteristic patterns of intoxication and withdrawal, and for any given drug, these usually take opposite forms. Both states are self-limiting; as the substance clears the body, the syndromes cease. In some cases, drug use damages or destroys brain tissue, and it thus has much more lasting effects. Such enduring effects are then classified as delirium, dementia, amnesia, and so on—whatever description is appropriate.

NEUROLOGICAL PROBLEMS WITH PSYCHOLOGICAL CONSEQUENCES

As is evident from the previous discussion of organic syndromes, there are numerous ways in which biological functioning can be compromised so that psychological abnormality results, including the following:

✦ infections of the brain, such as meningitis, encephalitis, and syphilis

✦ degenerative diseases of neural tissue

✦ genetically predisposed malfunctioning of the brain

✦ poisoning by toxic substances, including prescription drugs taken in excess

✦ physical damage to the brain

✦ tumors of the brain

✦ brain hemorrhages

✦ obstructed blood flow to the brain

✦ problems with the endocrine system, particularly the thyroid gland

✦ malnutrition and vitamin deficiency, as often accompanies chronic alcohol abuse

On the positive side, humans are highly resilient. Granted the complexity of the nervous system and the subtlety of its organization, it is little short of amazing that there are not more instances of neurological damage.

In this section, I discuss a host of physical problems—chiefly neurological—that have psychological consequences (see Table 6.2). These problems are often helped by psychological interventions. Despite the focus here on neurological disorders, it should be noted that virtually all physical problems, including cancer and heart disease, have psychological impacts.

HUNTINGTON'S CHOREA

Huntington's chorea was first described in 1872 by an American physician, George Huntington. "Chorea" refers to the bizarre bodily movements that typically accompany the disease. (The word comes from a Latin term meaning *dance,* the source of the word *choreograph.*) The person's limbs and facial muscles go through irregular spasms. He has a jerky gait, impaired speech, and difficulty swallowing.

Psychologically, Huntington's chorea is marked by progressive dementia. Its early signs include failing memory and difficulties with attention. It eventually progresses to a total loss of cognitive abilities. Death is inevitable, usually about 10 to 20 years after the original diagnosis.

When the diagnosis of Huntington's chorea is confirmed, or even suspected, the individual may become extremely depressed, knowing what the future holds. Suicide is therefore a grim consequence, occurring in almost 7% of cases. This is roughly four times the suicide rate in the general population (Farrer, 1986).

Thomas "Skip" Hayes was a middle-aged pastor in Alabama (Breu, 1990). In his late thirties, he showed the first signs of Huntington's chorea. He was in the car with his wife, arguing over the family's finances. Skip, always a calm and caring man, lost his temper and threw a punch at his wife. He missed her, but he shattered the car's windshield. This action was so out of character that he suspected something was amiss with his body. Indeed, Hungtington's chorea was common in his family.

As other symptoms became apparent, and the diagnosis confirmed, Skip at first became overwhelmed and depressed. He knew what he faced. His grandfather, an aunt, and an uncle died from the disease, and his mother was confined to a nursing home because of it. Because his wife and his congregation were supportive, he eventually

TABLE 6.2

SPECIFIC ORGANIC DISORDERS *A variety of organic problems produce psychological disturbances.*

DISORDER	SYMPTOMS/CAUSE/TREATMENT	DISORDER	SYMPTOMS/CAUSE/TREATMENT
Huntington's chorea	progressive dementia; movement difficulties	Tourette's syndrome	multiple tics involving motor movement and the voice
	caused by degeneration of brain cells in cortex and basal ganglia		caused by acetylcholine and/or dopamine imbalance
	no treatment at present		helped by Haldol
Parkinson's disease	tremor; rigidity; expressionless face; social withdrawal; loss of intellectual abilities	AIDS dementia complex	cognitive impairment; loss of fine motor coordination
	caused by dopamine deficiency		caused by AIDS
	helped by L-dopa; perhaps neural grafting		helped by AZT
multiple sclerosis	unsteady gait; weakness; spasms and/or spasticity of legs; loss of intellectual abilities	Korsakoff's syndrome	memory loss; problems with attention and perception
	caused by myelin loss		caused by damage to thalamus and perhaps hypothalamus due to alcoholism and nutritional deficiency
	helped by beta interferon		helped by correcting nutritional deficiencies
Alzheimer's disease	progressive dementia	general paresis	cognitive impairment
	caused by loss of neurons in hippocampus, particularly those secreting acetylcholine		caused by frontal lobe damage due to syphilis
	no cure at present; perhaps helped by tacrine		helped by antibiotics
multi-infarct dementia	dementia	epilepsy	seizures of various forms
	caused by a series of strokes		caused by diverse factors
	helped by restoration of blood flow to brain and prevention of further strokes		helped by anticonvulsive medications, surgery, and behavior therapy
brain injury	diverse symptoms	migraine	pulsating headache characterized by nausea and diverse other symptoms
	damage to the brain by a blow		caused by diverse factors
	helped by resolving physical injuries		helped by drugs and biofeedback

regained his composure. However, the disease continued to progress.

Etiology   The immediate cause of the disease is a degeneration of brain cells, particularly those in the cortex and the basal ganglia. The loss of these cells produces both the motor movement disturbance and the symptoms of dementia, presumably because the loss of nerve cells throws various neurotransmitter systems out of balance. Some drugs that affect the implicated neurotransmitters can reduce the severity of symptoms, but this effect is short-lived and in no way a cure.

Huntington's chorea is rare, afflicting perhaps 6 people out of every 100,000 of European ancestry; it apparently is even less frequent among other groups (Harper, 1992). It has received widespread attention on two scores. First, it is the disease from which folksinger Woody Guthrie died in 1967. Guthrie wrote such songs as "This Land is Your Land." He was also the father of another well known folksinger, Arlo Guthrie, whose ballad "Alice's Restaurant" was one of the anthems of the counterculture during the 1960s. Second, the disease is hereditary, transmitted by a single dominant gene. This means that if you inherit the gene, you will develop Huntington's chorea— period. A child of a parent with the disease therefore has a fifty-fifty chance of getting it. Because its onset is during middle adulthood, between the ages of 30 and 50, future victims may well have begun their families before they know they carry the gene.

In recent years, the exact gene causing Huntington's chorea has been located, the result of work in San Luis, Venezuela, where as many as 5% of its residents carry the gene (Gusella et al., 1983). And procedures have been developed that can determine the presence of this gene before the disease develops (Bird, 1985). These genetic screens allow a person to know, with some degree of confidence, that he is or is not at risk (Gusella et al., 1984).

Treatment   The availability of genetic screening is a mixed blessing (Craufurd & Harris, 1986). Although anyone with a family history of Huntington's chorea would want to know that he or she is *not* carrying the gene, what would it be like to know, when you are 20 years of age, that some 10 to 20 years later you will definitely develop a progressive and fatal neurological condition (Terrenoire, 1992)? On the one hand, this information allows the individual to plan his or her life more carefully than might otherwise be the case. But on the other hand, some fear that considerable distress would be precipitated by this knowledge (Brandt, Quaid, & Folstein, 1989; Lam et al., 1988). There is also the fear of what is termed *genetic discrimination*—employers and/or insurance companies refusing to deal with people who are genetically at risk for certain debilitating and expensive diseases (Kolata, 1986; Nash, 1990; Nelkin & Tancredi, 1989).

As it happens, at-risk individuals have not turned out in large numbers for genetic screening (Quaid & Morris, 1993). Arlo Guthrie, for example, has chosen not to be tested for the presence of the Huntington's gene. The children of Skip Hayes will be allowed to take the test, if they choose, once they become 18 years old.

PARKINSON'S DISEASE

Another well known neurological disorder is **Parkinson's disease,** first described in 1817 by an English physician, James Parkinson. At least in mild forms, this disease afflicts perhaps 10% of the population aged 50 and older. It is marked by a tremor, rigidity, and an expressionless face. A person also shows characteristic psychological symptoms, including social withdrawal and an increasing inability to cope flexibly with problems (Gannon & Murphy, 1992). Dementia occurs in about 25% of the cases, particularly when the individual becomes older and the disease progresses (Stern, Marder, Tang, & Mayeux, 1993). In almost half the cases, depression accompanies Parkinson's disease (Cummings, 1992). There is debate whether these psychological symptoms are due directly to the disease or represent the individual's reaction to its physical symptoms.

Etiology   The current belief is that Parkinson's disease is characterized by a deficiency in the brain of the neurotransmitter dopamine. Remember the point mentioned earlier that schizophrenia possibly involves a problem with excess dopamine activity in the brain? What this means is that in some ways, Parkinson's disease and schizophrenia are neurochemical opposites. Indeed, the drugs used to treat schizophrenic symptoms sometimes have the side effect of producing a condition very much like Parkinson's disease. And the drugs used to treat Parkinson's disease sometimes produce a condition very much like schizophrenia. The tendency of the body to counteract disequilibrium is well illustrated here. Adding (or subtracting) a neurotransmitter from the brain may end up overshooting (or undershooting) in effect. Clearly, such treatments are far from an exact science.

What causes the brain of a Parkinson's patient to be deficient in dopamine? We do not fully know the answer, and so work here continues. However, there is an answer for some individuals, because one form of the disease appeared in the aftermath of a viral encephalitis outbreak of epidemic proportions in the 1920s (Sacks, 1974). (This was the epidemic giving rise to the patients featured in the film "Awakenings.")

Treatment   There exist drugs that increase available dopamine—notably *L-dopa,* a chemical precursor of dopamine—and these medications improve the functioning of Parkinson's patients (Coleman, 1992; Robertson & George, 1990). L-dopa does not cure the disease, because it must continue to be taken and eventually its effects wear off (Hardie, 1989). However, such drugs represent substantial benefit, at least for some period of time (Rajput, 1992).

Another treatment currently receiving much publicity is *neural grafting:* taking healthy neurological tissue and transplanting it to the part of the brain affected by the disease, usually the midbrain (Melamed, 1988). Research with animals suffering from an analogue of Parkinson's disease shows that they are helped by this procedure, and in a few cases with human subjects, similar success has been reported (Kimble, 1990). Sometimes the tissue transplanted comes from part of the subject's own body, such as the adrenal glands. In other cases, the tissue comes from another individual, and sometimes even another species.

Most transplanted tissues, such as hearts and lungs, tend to be rejected by the immune system of the host body, which identifies them as foreign material and mounts an attack. Transplants are therefore accompanied by massive (and hazardous) doses of drugs that suppress immune functioning. But neural grafting typically takes place without such drugs, and the rate of successful transplants is surprisingly high. Just why neural tissues are so amenable to transplanting is not yet known (see Mason, Charlton, Jones, Parry, & Simmonds, 1985).

Once a neural graft has taken place, it can benefit the individual in several ways. First, the grafted tissue can take over for damaged or deficient neural tissue, producing—for example—neurotransmitters that the unhealthy tissue cannot. Second, it can stimulate the damaged tissue to do its job. Third, it can serve as a bridge between parts of the nervous system that have been out of synchrony because of the illness or injury. Although we should not overestimate our current state of knowledge, it is obvious that neural grafting is an exciting avenue for the future treatment of Parkinson's disease and perhaps other neurological conditions as well.

MULTIPLE SCLEROSIS

Multiple sclerosis (MS) is a neurological disease characterized by the loss of myelin around nerves. It is a progressive disease, which means that the individual gradually becomes impaired as neural messages are increasingly delayed or blocked. Gait becomes unsteady, weakness is common, and the person may experience spasms and spasticity of the legs. Her intellectual functioning can also be affected, and she often experiences fatigue and depression (Devins & Seland, 1987; Mahler, 1992). The course of MS can be highly variable, often marked by remissions and relapses. In fact, early on, she may show improvement.

Etiology   The exact cause of this disease is not known. There is no solid evidence that it is genetically transmitted or contagious. Speculation exists that MS represents the influence of an environmental toxin (Schwyzer, 1992) and/or an immunological dysfunction (Barker & Larner, 1992). There are geographical variations in its prevalence, which may or may not provide clues about the origins of the disease (Lauer & Firnhaber, 1992). It is most commonly encountered in Northern Europe, and somewhat less frequently in North America. In these regions, perhaps 50 out of 100,000 individuals have MS. The disease is quite rare in Japan and tropical regions. Females are somewhat more likely to have MS than males, and it progresses more rapidly for them as well.

Treatment   Until recently, there was no specific treatment for MS other than attempting to provide symptom relief and encouraging the individual to lead an active life for as long as possible (Rudick, Goodkin, & Ransohoff, 1992). But in 1993, the FDA approved the use of *beta interferon* as a treatment for the disease, following a study showing that patients given this drug experienced fewer and less severe symptoms than patients in a control group (see Paty & Li, 1993). Beta interferon presumably works by slowing down the body's destruction of its own myelin.

ALZHEIMER'S DISEASE

Alzheimer's disease is a form of dementia. It is a progressive and eventually fatal disease characterized by forgetfulness, confusion, and loss of ability to care for oneself. Often its first signs are psychological in nature: a mild impairment of memory and knowledge of words. The individual is aware that something is amiss, and tries to compensate for these cognitive changes. The course of the disease is marked by a steady deterioration of her cognitive abilities. As her intellectual abilities are lost, depression and grief may enter the picture. Suicide is a possibility among some with the disease, who would rather die quickly than see it through to its inevitable end (Crow et al., 1984; Pearlson et al., 1990).

Alzheimer's disease is a progressive and eventually fatal form of dementia. Most common among the elderly, its prevalence in the United States is increasing as people live long enough to develop the disease.

One of the first individuals to seek Dr. Jack Kevorkian's help in committing suicide was Janet Adkins, a 57-year-old woman who had been diagnosed with Alzheimer's disease 1 year before (Johnson, Greenwalt, & Hauser, 1990). The earliest signs of her disease had appeared several years prior to the diagnosis. She had been a lifelong musician, but she could no longer read sheet music. An excellent tennis player, she could no longer keep score while playing. Ms. Adkins decided to end her life while she was still capable of making the decision. She did not want to linger on while others needed to dress her and take her to the bathroom. After saying good-bye to her friends and family, she died on June 4, 1990.

Etiology   What is going on in the nervous system of the Alzheimer's patient? In 1906, German neurologist Alois Alzheimer first described the disease that bears his name following an autopsy he performed on the brain of a patient with dementia. Throughout her brain, and particularly in the **hippocampus** in the forebrain, he saw scattered tangles of neural tissue, eventually identified as axons and dendrites of neurons that had died. The hippocampus is thought to be involved in the processing of memories, which explains why Alzheimer's disease results in dementia. He also found collections of degenerated neurons that coalesced around a starchy core. The most striking loss of neurons comprised those that communicate by secreting the neurotransmitter **acetylcholine.**

These changes are microscopic, to be sure, but they add up to a large-scale problem with many psychological ramifications. Alzheimer's disease is becoming more common simply because people now live long enough to develop it. Few cases occur before age 50, but as the person becomes older, the disease is a steadily increasing risk (see Figure 6.5). It is estimated that about 4 million people in the United States currently have Alzheimer's disease. By the year 2020, projecting current trends in life expectancy, more than 10 million Americans will probably suffer from it.

Treatment   In most cases, the person dies 5 to 7 years after the first appearance of the disease. Some individuals have survived for as long as 15 years following the initial diagnosis (Gruetzner, 1988). At the present time, there is no cure or effective treatment, although the recently approved drug tacrine (marketed under the name Cognex) can slow the progress of the disease in some cases (Knapp et al., 1994). Cures may

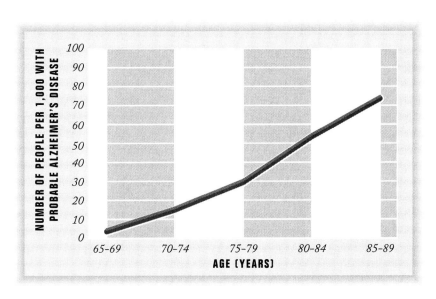

AGE (YEARS)

FIGURE 6.5

Likelihood of Alzheimer's Disease as a Function of Age   *In the United States, at each age women outnumber men, probably because of women's greater life expectancy.*
Source: Data are from "Incidence of Dementia and Probable Alzheimer's Disease in a General Population: The Framingham Study," by D. L. Bachman et al., 1993, *Neurology, 43,* pp. 515–519.

appear in the near future as researchers investigate the underlying causes. They appear on the verge of discovering why some people but not others develop Alzheimer's disease. Possible causes include genetic predispositions, contamination by trace metals like aluminum, and viral infections (Kraus & Forbes, 1992). Part of the Alzheimer's puzzle is the fact that about half the individuals with *Down syndrome*—a form of mental retardation caused by chromosomal abnormalities (Chapter 14)—develop the disease by middle age, and in some cases as early as adolescence.

Alzheimer's disease creates problems not only for the individuals with the illness but also for those responsible for their care—often spouses or children. Anxiety and depression are common reactions to the burden of round-the-clock caregiving and to the recognition of insidious changes in their loved ones (Scott, Roberto, & Hutton, 1986). Psychologists provide services to caregivers, and self-help groups are also available (Chapter 3).

MULTI-INFARCT DEMENTIA

Multi-infarct (MI) dementia, which DSM-IV calls **vascular dementia,** is caused by multiple strokes occurring over time. The effect of a stroke can range from trivial to profound, depending on its extent and location. A single, massive stroke can wipe out a particular mental function, such as speech or memory, but it tends not to produce a diffuse state of dementia. Instead, dementia usually follows in the wake of a series of strokes in different parts of the brain.

The most common cause of a stroke is hypertension. Diet can also contribute, not just to the presence of high blood pressure and thus an increased likelihood of a stroke, but also to the buildup of fatty deposits on the inner walls of a person's arteries. These desposits restrict and eventually block blood flow. Alcohol abuse, cigarette smoking, diabetes, and the use of oral contraceptives may also lead to strokes. Finally, the person might have a genetic predisposition to strokes, because the tendency to have them, or not, runs through families (Howard et al., 1990).

Let me contrast vascular dementia with dementia caused by Alzheimer's disease (Lechner & Bertha, 1991). The former appears to be less common,[2] and

---

[2] It can be difficult to distinguish multi-infarct dementia from Alzheimer's disease (Lang, 1992; Nussbaum, Treves, & Korczyn, 1992), which means that prevalence estimates for both are somewhat tentative. Indeed, some recent studies suggest that multi-infarct dementia is much more common than typically believed (e.g., Folstein, Bassett, Anthony, Romanoski, & Nestadt, 1991). Adding to the diagnostic complexity here is the possibility that an individual may suffer from both disorders.

it typically occurs earlier in life. Unlike Alzheimer's disease, which is somewhat more likely to occur among women than men, multi-infarct dementia is more common among men (because men are at greater risk for strokes). It can occur abruptly, and the person's cognitive impairment is patchy, with marked deficits existing side by side with perfectly normal cognitive functions. The course of this disorder is variable, depending on the degree to which the blood flow to and through the brain can be restored and future strokes can be prevented.

BRAIN INJURIES

In contrast to other species, humans have large heads quite vulnerable to damage. And when the head receives a blow, so too does the brain. Sometimes the head does not even need to be struck directly for brain damage to occur. In a whiplash injury, for example, the body is rapidly moved, and the head follows, unwillingly. When the body stops moving suddenly, the head continues to move until it is jerked to a stop; then the brain bounces against the skull, thereby causing injury.

Etiology   Health care professionals make the following distinctions among types of brain injuries (Weisberg, Strub, & Garcia, 1989):

✦ *concussion:* a transient state that changes the physical condition of the brain without damaging its structure

✦ *contusion:* damage to the microscopic structure of the brain, such as the rupturing of small blood vessels

✦ *laceration:* the destruction of large structures of the brain

The particular effects of brain injuries depend on a host of factors, such as the exact site of the damage, its extent, and the general health of the person suffering the injury. On the average, younger people fare better than older people, because their nervous system is still developing, and it can reorganize itself to compensate for injury to one of its parts.

Damage to different parts of the brain can produce drastically different patterns of symptoms. For example, damage to the **frontal lobes,** at the very front of the cortex, interferes specifically with a person's ability to plan ahead and anticipate the consequences of his or her actions (Goldstein, 1944). The ability to conduct a complicated sequence of acts is thus impaired by any frontal lobe damage.

One of the best known neurological cases is that of Phineas Gage, a workman who was injured in 1848 when an explosion blew an iron bar literally through his head (and of course his brain) (Bigelow, 1850). It entered through his jaw and came out the top of his head, obliterating much of his frontal lobes in the process (see Figure 6.6). Perhaps most amazing is the fact that he survived. In fact, Gage was able to resume his normal life. However, he was changed strikingly as a result of the accident. Where before he had been a modest and controlled individual, after the accident he was loud and profane. He was irresponsible and impetuous. And he was unable to plan ahead or carry out his intentions. We recognize this now as a typical response to frontal lobe damage (Bowen, 1989).

Injuries elsewhere produce other sorts of impairments with speaking, hearing, writing, or reading (McAllister, 1992). Brain injury can often produce problems with memory and abstract reasoning. Sometimes a person's mood is affected as well. The person becomes depressed and withdrawn, less frequently euphoric and exuberant.

Here is one generalization that I can offer. The extent of brain damage can be estimated by either the amount of time a person loses consciousness following

FIGURE 6.6

PHINEAS GAGE: A CAST OF HIS HEAD AND HIS SKULL *The skull of Phineas Gage is exhibited at the Harvard Medical School Museum. Injury to the brain's frontal lobes, such as that sustained by Phineas Gage, can result in drastic changes in personality and behavior.*

a head injury or the extent of the amnesia following such an injury. The greater either of these, the more reason there is to expect extensive damage (Siegel, Rivkind, Dalal, & Goodarzi, 1990).

Who suffers brain injuries? In modern societies, about two thirds of the victims are males, usually teenagers or young adults, simply because they are more apt to be involved in the sorts of things that result in brain injury: sports mishaps, fights and assaults, falls, and car and motorcycle accidents (Colohan & Oyesiku, 1992; Tiret et al., 1990). To the degree that these events can be decreased, the number of brain injuries is decreased as well (Jagger, 1992).

Treatment Treatment of brain injury is multifold. Obviously, an immediately threatening physical problem, such as hemorrhaging, requires rapid attention, so that further brain damage does not occur. Once the person's medical condition has stabilized, rehabilitation is undertaken. His or her specific difficulties must be ascertained, and then the therapist attempts to restore the skills compromised by the brain injury (McGlynn, 1990).

We must beware of too neat a distinction between organic and functional difficulties. A person who experiences changes in thoughts, feelings, or actions following a brain injury may do so as a direct biological consequence of damaged neural tissue, but he additionally may be reacting in a psychological way to the injury and its aftermath. In many cases, both biological and psychological processes are occurring (Prigatano, 1992).

How a person responds to a brain injury is influenced by his *premorbid makeup*—how he was getting along in the world before the injury. Those who suffer brain injuries are not a random sample of the world's population. They bring certain characteristics with them to their unfortunate accident, and it is difficult to sort out what existed when. An individual who was impetuous and explosive before a brain injury may well be impetuous and explosive afterwards, so it is obviously not reasonable to attribute these behaviors to the brain injury itself.

Prognosis following a brain injury does not have a one-to-one relationship with the nature and extent of the physical damage the person has suffered (Stambrook, Moore, Peters, Deviaene, & Hawryluk, 1990). Two people with the apparently same injury often respond quite differently. This is why we have reason to suspect the role of preexisting personality and intellectual characteristics. Remember the case of Christina in the beginning of the chapter. She brought considerable skills to the business of coping with her neurological deficit. There is also reason to suspect that the quality of the person's social environment following the injury is important. If a person finds herself in a supportive setting, with friends and family members helping her deal with the aftermath of her injury, then her prognosis is better than if she is ignored or treated with disdain.

Much of what I have covered here concerning brain injuries applies as well to brain tumors, which can create the same sorts of psychological effects by damaging or destroying neural tissue (McLeod & Lance, 1989). Medical treatment of brain tumors of course takes a different direction: the removal or shrinking of the tumor. If it is detected early and treated effectively, then the prognosis is good, and the damage might be reversible.

TOURETTE'S SYNDROME

A **tic** is a movement that occurs irresistably at frequent intervals, usually in an abrupt, rapid, and repetitive fashion. Tics are often highly stereotyped (performed in the exact same manner). They can be voluntarily suppressed, but the individual feels growing tension while doing so, as if the tic were waiting to burst forth. Interestingly, tics usually subside while the person is asleep.

One of the most striking and complex disorders involving tics is the syndrome named after French physician Gilles de la Tourette, who in 1885 argued for the existence of a complex of behavioral problems surrounding chronic multiple tics (Woodrow, 1974). **Tourette's syndrome** usually begins before the age of 14, in the form of a single tic that involves the eye. Then other tics develop, involving both motor movement and the voice.

These tics can be disquieting. Fully 60% of the individuals with Tourette's syndrome evidence **coprolalia**— blurting out obscene words. And sometimes the individual finds himself gesturing in obscene ways. Needless to say, these manifestations of Tourette's syndrome are highly disturbing to the individual as well as to those around him. As if all of this were not bad enough, sometimes the tics involve imitating other people in the immediate environment, exaggerating their mannerisms and habits. Although the person with this disorder does not show intellectual deterioration, other problems may occur: depression, sleep disturbance, obsessive-compulsive behaviors, and inappropriate sexual activity (Grossman, Mostofsky, & Harrison, 1986).

Oliver Sacks (1985b) vividly described a man with whom he worked who suffered from an extreme case of this syndrome:

Ray . . . was 24 years old, and almost incapacitated by multiple tics of extreme violence coming in volleys every few seconds. He had been subject to these since the age of four and severely stigmatized by the attention they aroused. . . . [He] had been fired from a dozen jobs— always because of tics, never for incompetence. . . . [He] found his marriage threatened by involuntary cries of "Fuck!" "Shit!" . . . which would burst from him at times of sexual excitement. (p. 92)

By Sacks's description, Ray was witty, intelligent, and kind, though Tourette's syndrome made it difficult for others to appreciate these qualities.

Sports fans may recognize Tourette's syndrome as the neurological problem of baseball player Jim Eisenreich and basketball player Mahmoud Abdul-Rauf. Both players struggled early in their lives before the condition was correctly diagnosed and treated.

This syndrome is rare, estimated to occur at about the rate of 1 to 5 cases per 10,000 individuals in the United States. It develops much more commonly

Baseball player Jim Eisenreich suffers from Tourette's syndrome. At one time, his symptoms were so severe that he discontinued his baseball career. Here he is shown hitting a home run in the 1993 World Series.

among men than women, at a ratio of about three to one. The disorder also tends to run in families, although not in a way to suggest any simple mode of genetic transmission (Nee, Caine, Polinsky, Eldridge, & Ebert, 1980). Unlike most tics, those associated with Tourette's syndrome persist for years.

As just noted, Tourette's syndrome may be associated with obsessive behavior. For example, Abdul-Rauf has a strong compulsion to repeat actions until they seem just right (Reilly, 1993):

> *He cannot help himself. The stove burner is hot. He reaches out his right hand, feels the heat rising up from the burner and—flick—touches it. And again. And again. He will not stop until the touch feels perfect.*
>
> *He cannot stop himself. He has been tying his shoes for ten minutes now. One shoelace must not touch the other before it is time. Can't have that. He is frustrated from doing it over and over again. There were times as a boy when he would be in tears over this. It's not his choice. It's the way it must be. His laces must feel* perfect.
>
> *He cannot understand himself. He has been trying to leave the gym floor for the last 45 minutes. He is exhausted. He is gasping for breath. There are two more practice sessions tomorrow, but still he keeps on. He must swish 10 straight shots before he leaves. And not just any swish. The net must snap* perfectly. *If even one doesn't swish to his absolute satisfaction, he must start over. He will shoot until they all feel* perfect. *(p. 81)*

Etiology   Granted the sexual content of the symptoms, early explanations of the disorder attempted to make sense of it solely in psychodynamic terms, as a result of an individual's unconscious conflicts (Flinn & Bazzell, 1983). Thinking has since shifted to the nervous system, although the lesson remains that symptoms of an organic disorder can have symbolic significance. Although autopsies of individuals who suffered from Tourette's syndrome reveal no structural abnormality of the nervous system, it is now agreed that the problem resides in a neurotransmitter imbalance. There is debate whether the neurotransmitter involved is acetylcholine or dopamine, and just what the nature of the imbalance might be (Barbeau, 1980).

Treatment   Regardless, many cases of Tourette's syndrome can be successfully treated with Haldol (Cohen, Riddle, & Leckman, 1992; Shapiro, Shapiro, & Wayne, 1973), one of the drugs used to treat schizophrenia. Most if not all of the symptoms of the syndrome are suppressed with this drug, and over time, ever smaller doses are required. The symptoms may

Mahmoud Abdul-Rauf has been a highly successful college and professional basketball player despite having Tourette's syndrome. Medication controls his symptoms but has not eradicated them. Here, Abdul-Rauf is showing his compulsion to touch the burner on a stove to test its temperature.

recur under stress, however, which means that the dose must be temporarily increased in accord with the person's life situation.

AIDS

Most of us are well aware of acquired immune deficiency syndrome—AIDS. First described in 1981, this disease is a shutdown of the body's immune system and hence its ability to fight off diseases. Forms of infection and types of cancer that almost never occur among people with an intact immune system are common among those with AIDS, at present a condition impossible to immunize against or cure.

Because one of the chief ways in which AIDS is spread is through sexual contact, its existence has exerted a powerful influence on contemporary sexual attitudes and behaviors. But the relevance of AIDS in the present context is that one of the few direct consequences of the disease—as opposed to indirect consequences through its effect on the immune system—is a syndrome of intellectual impairment dubbed **AIDS dementia complex.** Occurring in about 5% to 10% of those with AIDS, this form of dementia shows itself in difficulties with language, memory, fine motor coordination, and problem solving (Bridge & Ingraham, 1990; Egan, 1992).

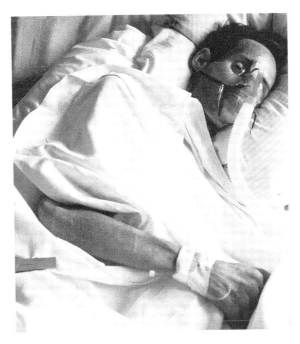

Among the consequences of AIDS is a syndrome of intellectual impairment, shown by 5 % to 10 % of those with the disease.

Obviously, dementia makes it difficult for the AIDS patient to conduct his life in a reasonable fashion. Following diagnosis, the amount of time a person survives varies dramatically. Perhaps behavioral habits play a role, if they help the person avoid infectious diseases. More speculatively, perhaps social support from others extends life. Regardless, the intellectual impairment associated with AIDS dementia complex undercuts these buffering influences.

There is no agreement about the part of the brain attacked by AIDS, but some speculation has centered on areas below the cortex, perhaps the same regions affected by Parkinson's disease. It appears that the drug AZT, which slows the progress of AIDS, also has the effect of delaying or even reversing symptoms of AIDS dementia (Brew, 1992; Perry, 1990b).

KORSAKOFF'S SYNDROME

I mentioned in Chapter 5 that chronic alcohol abuse affects virtually every system of the body. The nervous system is no exception, and one of the consequences was first described in 1887 by Sergei Korsakoff, a Russian neurologist. **Korsakoff's syndrome** is chiefly a loss of memory, usually of recent events. The person also has problems with attention and perception. It results from damage to the thalamus and perhaps the hypothalamus.

One of the striking aspects of Korsakoff's syndrome is the phenomenon of **confabulation,** which refers to the person filling in memory gaps with imaginary events.

Rather than saying he does not know the answer to a question, the person answers readily, often with absurd content:

> *He told involved, morbid, fictional tales in response to questions about his family, previous life, and illness. . . . [He] related that during WW II, he surprised a teenage German girl who shot him three times in the head, killing him, but that surgery had brought him back to life. When asked about his family, he had at various times described how they had died in his arms, or been killed before his eyes, or would relate in lurid detail his sexual experiences with his daughters. (Stuss, Alexander, Lieberman, & Levine, 1978, p. 1169)*

It is not clear how best to interpret confabulation. A patient's answers are not simply random, because he is aware of which questions require responses and which do not (Lechtenberg, 1982). That is, confabulators do not answer rhetorical questions. And they usually confabulate when they do not know the right answer.

This problem has something to do with memory loss, obviously, but it is not that simple. Individuals with organic amnestic syndrome do not usually confabulate. Perhaps confabulation is a result of an individual's attempt to deny at some level his memory loss (Joseph, 1986). We are all familiar with this phenomenon. Consider how we fill in the blanks when we meet somebody we have not seen in years and pretend to recall the last time we saw them. The difference, though, is that we know we are making something up, whereas the person with Korsakoff's syndrome apparently does not (Whitlock, 1981).

This syndrome occurs more frequently among men than women, reflecting their greater likelihood of being chronic alcohol abusers. The estimated prevalence is about 5 per 10,000, but there is nothing fixed about this figure. We should expect it to rise or fall in accordance with the future prevalence of severe alcoholism.

Although alcohol may have a direct effect on the brain and produce Korsakoff's syndrome—which is what Korsakoff himself believed—the more likely cause is a combination of alcohol and nutritional deficiency, which frequently accompanies severe alcoholism. More specifically, this syndrome is associated with a deficiency of *thiamine,* one of the B vitamins (Adams, 1969). If the nutritional deficiencies are corrected, then Korsakoff's syndrome can be arrested. Reversal of its effects, however, is rare.

Syphilis

In Chapter 1, I mentioned **general paresis,** the psychological disorder that results from untreated syphilis. My focus here is on the specific effects of syphilis on the nervous system.

Etiology   The disease itself is caused by a large bacterium called a *spirochete,* which is typically spread through sexual contact with an infected individual. The first reaction to a syphilitic infection is the development of a sore called a *chancre* that appears several weeks after initial contact, at the point of the body where the spirochete first entered. Usually, this is on or about the genitals. A fever and a rash then follow a few weeks later. The syphilitic sore, fever, and rash subside, and thereafter there may be no overt signs that the person has contracted syphilis.

The spirochete is still present in the body, though, where it lies dormant for a period ranging from 5 years to two or even three decades. Then it becomes active again and invades other parts of the body. One of the popular sites at this point is the central nervous system. If the spirochete invades the brain, the membranes that surround it become inflamed. Nerve cells progressively deteriorate, especially those in the frontal lobes. As syphilis progresses into its final stage, other parts of the brain become involved, and we see wide-ranging problems.

Treatment   With the advent of antibiotics, particularly penicillin, it became possible to treat syphilis, even in the late stages of infection, and thus arrest its effects. If antibiotics are not used, the person will die, usually within 3 years of the onset of the final stage. The earlier the disease is treated, the more likely we are to see a complete recovery.

Along with many other sexually transmitted diseases, syphilis has been increasing in recent years (Buckley, 1992). Even more alarming, people are reportedly not as likely to seek treatment as they once were. General paresis, at one time almost eradicated in the United States, may therefore be on the rise again in years to come.

Epilepsy

Epilepsy refers to a group of neurological disorders, all characterized by periodic bursts of neural discharge leading to seizures. Different forms of epilepsy are often classified according to the sort of seizure that is involved. **Generalized seizures** are those that disrupt the functioning of the entire brain. **Focal seizures** (or **partial seizures**) disrupt only limited regions of the brain. The line between the two can be fuzzy, and in fact both types of seizures can occur in the same person.

One form of generalized epilepsy is **petit mal epilepsy** (or **generalized nonconvulsive epilepsy**), which usually begins in childhood and can be outgrown by adulthood (Seidenberg & Berent, 1992). A petit mal seizure, also known as an *absence attack,* involves an interrupted consciousness and a blank stare lasting from several seconds to a few minutes. During such a seizure, the person is unresponsive. Ongoing activities cease, but the person does not fall to the ground. When he regains consciousness, he resumes his activities where they were left off. The frequency of these seizures varies greatly, from many times each day to only a few times in a person's lifetime. A person experiencing a petit mal seizure may be unaware that anything has happened. Along these lines, those interacting with the person experiencing a petit mal seizure may misinterpret what is going on, regarding him as merely not paying attention. In and of itself, this form of epilepsy is associated with no other neurological problems. However, to the degree that the seizures occur with some frequency, the person's life is of course upset (Hermann & Whitman, 1992). Demoralization and depression often follow.

Another form of generalized epilepsy is **grand mal epilepsy** (or **generalized convulsive epilepsy**), which is accompanied by much more severe seizures. In these, there is an abrupt loss of consciousness, followed by a stiffening of the body and an involuntary cry. The person then trembles for several minutes, followed by a period of alternating stiffening and relaxing. Upon regaining consciousness following the seizure, the person is typically confused and drowsy. He might complain of a headache. And he often falls asleep.

People about to experience a grand mal seizure sometimes experience signs that one is imminent. These signs are called an **aura,** and can range from a simple sense of discomfort and tingling in the extremities to an unambiguously altered state of consciousness marked by a sense of depersonalization and unreality as well as vivid hallucinations. The person does not remember the seizure itself, although the aura is often recalled.

The immediate danger to a person with this type of epilepsy is the risk of injury during seizures, from hitting his head while falling or thrashing about to biting his tongue. More generally, it creates numerous problems, particularly when the seizures occur at an appreciable frequency. A person's life is profoundly disturbed. Because most people develop epilepsy during childhood, their normal development can be hindered.

Grand mal epilepsy has been described since antiquity (Novelly, 1992). In ancient Greece, the disorder was regarded as a sacred disease, based on the assumption that the gods themselves visited the person during a seizure. The seizure took on different forms depending on the particular god involved. Throughout history, there have been many well known people who have suffered from this form of epilepsy, including Julius Caesar, Fyodor Dostoyevsky, Peter the Great, and Vincent van Gogh.

Let me move from generalized seizures to focal ones. A well known example here is **temporal-lobe epilepsy** (or **psychomotor epilepsy**). This disorder is characterized by seizures in which a person does not lose complete control of his motor behavior. He experiences a sort of trance and carries out movements in a repetitive and automatized fashion, such as smacking his lips or buttoning and unbuttoning his clothes. These seizures typically last several minutes. Temporal-lobe epilepsy is so named because it is thought to involve problems with the temporal lobe of the forebrain (located right behind the temple). It rarely occurs among children. And it is frequently confused with other psychological problems, such as schizophrenia or conversion disorder. There is some controversy whether this reflects mistakes on the part of diagnosticians or an actual co-occurrence of temporal lobe epilepsy with these other disorders (Bear & Fedio, 1977).

Etiology   Regardless of the particular type of epilepsy, the immediate cause of a seizure is a massive and disorganized discharge of neurons in the brain, which some liken to an electrical storm. An *electroencephalograph (EEG)* is used to record brain waves and categorize seizures by their type (see Figure 6.7). Seizures are typically self-limiting, because the neurons that discharge include inhibitory ones— which means that a seizure eventually turns itself off.

But this is just a description of the immediate trigger for a seizure. What are the root causes? What dictates their frequency? Once again, we find considerable controversy. At present, the best we can say is that epilepsy appears to have several contributing causes, from actual damage to parts of the brain, perhaps resulting from head injuries or brain infections, to genetic predispositions. Stressful events are sometimes, but not always, associated with the onset of seizures as well (Antebi & Bird, 1992).

Treatment   Three approaches to the treatment of epilepsy have emerged. The most common is the use of medication to reduce the frequency and severity of seizures. Drugs like Dilantin and phenobarbital are among the most familiar of the anticonvulsive medications. They are not foolproof, of course, because people respond to them in idiosyncratic ways. And they tend not to be effective for temporal-lobe epilepsy. Like all drugs, they have side effects, leading some not to take them at all. But for other individuals, medication represents a satisfactory solution to the problems of epilepsy.

Surgery is a second way to treat epilepsy. This is not an intervention that is chosen lightly, because the brain is so complicated that unforeseen consequences might follow. But if people do not respond to medication and if their seizures are so severe and frequent that their lives are profoundly upset, then they might consider it. The neurosurgeon attempts to determine from the EEG patterns which part of the brain is involved. If it is accessible, she undertakes surgery, removing the part of the brain where seizures originate.

FIGURE 6.7

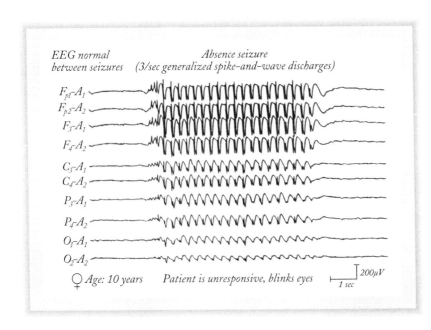

EEG RECORDINGS OF SEIZURES   *During a seizure, uncontrollable electrical activity sweeps over the brain, as shown in these EEG recordings made during a seizure.*

Pat was a 25-year old woman who worked part-time while attending graduate school (Backman, 1989). She had experienced petit mal seizures since she was 15 years old, following a case of meningitis. For years, the seizures were not problematic because they were completely controlled by drugs. However, without consulting her doctor, Pat decided to take herself off medication by the time she finished college. The week of her graduation, she had her first grand mal seizure. These continued, even when she resumed taking her medication. She became despondent and began to drink heavily. She contemplated suicide and made a serious attempt to end her life.

Her seizures embarrassed her, particularly when they occurred in the presence of strangers. She feared hurting herself. She was athletic, but her physician counseled against the strenuous sports she loved. Pat eventually decided to have surgery, which only partially alleviated her seizure disorder. More helpful was the support group she joined for those with epilepsy. From older individuals, Pat learned that she could adjust to her problem and still lead a rewarding life.

In some cases, surgery is more successful than it was for Pat. You probably remember from your introductory psychology course the famous split-brain patients, who had the connection between their cerebral hemispheres severed, creating two different brains that in some ways operate independently (Springer & Deutsch, 1985). Perhaps lost in the descriptions of these fascinating individuals was the fact that the split-brain operations were performed in the first place to alleviate otherwise intractable seizure conditions.

A third treatment is psychological in nature and takes several different forms (Gillham, 1990). Individuals are helped to conduct their lives in such a way as to minimize stress; then perhaps the frequency of seizures can be reduced. Some attempts have been made to use behavior therapy to reduce the frequency of seizures, by rewarding individuals who do not have them (e.g., Dahl, Melin, & Leissner, 1988; Ramani & Gumnit, 1982; Tan & Bruni, 1986), but results here are equivocal. Seizures may not be the sort of "behavior" that is responsive to reward and punishment. However, some people can use the aura's warning to behave in ways that prevent or minimize the impending seizure (e.g., Efron, 1957).

More generally, even if seizures cannot be reduced in frequency or severity, individuals are helped to cope with the problems that epilepsy can create in their lives. When psychologists work with individuals with epilepsy, such counseling is usually their main focus.

Not the least of the problems associated with epilepsy is the stigma that still surrounds it. Until

relatively recently, people with epilepsy were subject to widespread legal and occupational discrimination, based on society's misunderstanding of the disorder. The Epilepsy Foundation of America has long struggled to educate us all (McLin, 1992). Thus, part of the psychological "treatment" of epilepsy targets not the epileptic individual, but his or her world, changing attitudes and laws.

MIGRAINE

Among the most common of physical problems with psychological consequences is a **migraine,** an umbrella term for periodic headaches characterized by nausea and other symptoms of a dazzling variety (Sacks, 1985a): flushed face; bloodshot eyes; abdominal pain; constipation or diarrhea; dizziness; sensitivity to light; mood changes; and so on. Not all of these symptoms occur in all patients with a migraine. Typically, a person experiences some idiosyncratic combination of a handful of them. The frequency of migraines varies greatly, as do their regularity. Sometimes people use

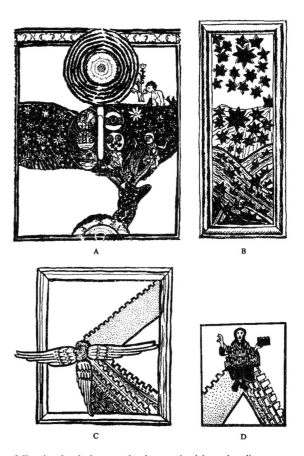

A   B

C   D

Migraine headaches may be characterized by a dazzling variety of symptoms, including visual hallucinations like those shown in these drawings by a woman who suffered migraines.

Supreme Court Justice William O. Douglas (1898–1980), shown here in 1970, suffered from migraines so severe that they threatened his ability to work. They eventually responded to treatment, allowing Douglas to remain on the bench for a distinguished career.

Particularly striking about migraines is that some people experience an **aura** before an attack, just as in grand mal epilepsy (Kaufman & Solomon, 1992). Such an aura includes mood changes as well as hallucinations. Some people show characteristic alterations of vision, seeing the world as if through a tunnel, or seeing it as a fractured mosaic, or seeing only part of the visual field. Less frequently, distortions and hallucinations involving other sensory systems are involved.

Etiology   The causes of a migraine are probably as numerous as its manifestations (Adams, Feuerstein, & Fowler, 1980). They run through families, although it is not clear if this suggests a genetic basis or common environmental conditions (Merikangas, Risch, Merikangas, Weissman, & Kidd, 1988). Theories variously implicate vascular contraction or dilation, neurotransmitter changes, or patterns of electrical discharge like those in an epileptic seizure (Silberstein, 1992). The problem with these theories, taken individually, is that each fails to account for the full range of migraine symptoms. They also fail to grapple fully with the fact that migraines may be triggered by specific environmental events, such as particular odors, high altitude, and glaring lights (Blau, 1992).

Some theorists have suggested that there is a personality style that predisposes migraines; at-risk individuals are perfectionistic and compulsive (Brandt, Celentano, Stewart, Linet, & Folstein, 1990).

the term *migraine* to describe any severe headache, but the term should probably be reserved for headaches of a particular quality: throbbing and pulsating pain localized on one side of the head, or the front (Rapoport, 1992). And as already noted, migraines are accompanied by nausea and various other symptoms. The common headache is not.

Headaches are a familiar bodily complaint, among the leading reasons why people in the United States see a doctor. They usually are *not* the result of serious disease but instead result from muscle contractions, changes in circulation of the blood to the brain, and/or pressure by fluid in the sinus cavities of the face.

An individual who experiences serious or frequent migraines may find his life greatly compromised, because he cannot do anything else except give way to the migraine. For example, Supreme Court Justice William O. Douglas, famed as a strong advocate of civil liberties, suffered from migraines so severe they threatened his career (Douglas, 1974). Had they not eventually responded to treatment, history might well have been different, because at one time he was on the verge of stepping down from the bench.

I once knew somebody subject to migraines. John tried to keep his life in perfect order. I remember seeing his bookshelves, and as I am likely to do, I scanned the books. I quickly discovered that his books were arranged not only in alphabetical order but also by color and by height. "Surely," I asked my friend, "you must have books that don't fit this scheme." "Oh yes," John said. Then he showed me, shoved behind his desk, box after box of books that did not fit, fully ten times as many as graced his shelves.

But does a perfectionistic style predispose migraine headaches or result from them? Perhaps the individual is trying to create an order to his life that will somehow mitigate stress (Ellertsen, Troland, & Klove, 1987).

Treatment   Migraines can be treated in several ways (Blanchard, 1992; Schulman & Silberstein, 1992). Sometimes they are simply tolerated, and sometimes they are outgrown. Some drugs, such as imipramine and Dilantin, when taken on a daily basis, can prevent migraines from occurring in the first place for some patients. (Elser & Woody, 1990; Millichap, 1978). Other drugs can relieve pain by constricting arteries in the scalp. Analgesics such as aspirin or anti-emetics may help with pain or nausea. Tranquilizers can take the edge off an attack. And caffeine helps.

The foregoing are physiological interventions. Psychological interventions are also useful—particularly **biofeedback,** a version of operant conditioning in which a person learns to control abnormal bodily responses (Turner & Chapman, 1982). The migraine sufferer is hooked up to a machine that monitors his blood flow and "feeds back" this information to him in a way he can discern (see Figure 6.8). He can then learn to control the feedback. The hope is that this will also undo the migraine. Because there is no consensus at the present time as to the actual causes of migraines, it is not clear which bodily responses should be modified with biofeedback (Fentress, Masek, Mehegan, & Benson, 1986). But at least for some people, biofeedback helps (Aubuchon, Haber, & Adams, 1985).

In this chapter, I have discussed how the nervous system sets parameters for our behavior. Our physical makeup dictates our behavior, normal and abnormal. The nervous system is one of the chief sources of physical problems with psychological consequences, and these may include difficulties with thinking, feeling, or just moving about. Different organic disorders exist, and although all have biological causes, they can be helped with both biological *and* psychological interventions. Rehabilitative efforts help a person restore or compensate for the abilities that have been lost.

FIGURE 6.8

BIOFEEDBACK SETUP   *In biofeedback, bodily processes are monitored and "fed back" to the individual so that she can change them.*

With respect to neurological disorders that lead to problems with attention, or memory, or judgment, there is debate whether rehabilitation restores an individual's original capacity to do things, or simply provides her with alternative skills. Suppose a person is no longer able to remember certain items of information as well as she once was. As described earlier, she can be taught cognitive techniques, such as visual imagery, that let her bring information more readily to mind. But what has changed—her capacity for recall or the particular way she goes about doing so?

This is not an idle debate, because it affects the direction of future therapeutic efforts. All things being equal, restored capacity is probably preferred. But in some cases this might be a wild-goose chase. Consider the example of spinal cord injuries. Should researchers spend their time and energy trying to figure out how to reconnect a severed spinal cord, or attempting to come up with better ways for individuals to compensate for their lack of movement and sensation? At present, there is no way to reconnect a spinal cord so that it works, and some feel this possibility is so far off in the future that money spent right now on this endeavor is a waste. Others disagree.

Summary

✦   Organic disorders are psychological problems associated with physical injury, illness, or defect. Often the part of the body involved in organic disorders is the nervous system.

AN OVERVIEW OF THE NERVOUS SYSTEM

✦   The nervous system includes the brain as well as the network of nerve cells throughout the body. It sets the parameters for behavior. The basic components of the nervous system are neurons, which communicate with one another by secreting chemicals called neurotransmitters. Neurons either excite other neurons to fire, or inhibit them. The brain contains the largest number and most dense concentration of neurons in the body. It consists of integrated layers; those near the top of the brain tend to regulate and direct those near the bottom of the brain.

✦   The nervous system is organized in multiple ways: spatially, biochemically, top-to-bottom, front-to-back, and laterally. The nervous system is integrated not only within itself but also with the endocrine system and the immune system.

CONCEPTUALIZING ORGANIC DISORDERS

◆   Unlike its predecessors, DSM-IV does not include organic disorders as a separate diagnostic category. However, it lists several cognitive impairment disorders with organic causes.

◆   Organic mental syndromes are common constellations of psychological symptoms resulting from neurological damage or dysfunction. They include delirium (global impairment of attention), dementia (global impairment of cognitive functions), amnestic syndrome (memory loss *not* associated with general cognitive problems), organic personality syndrome (changes in personality), and intoxication and withdrawal (changes in brain function brought about by drug use or the cessation of drug use, respectively).

NEUROLOGICAL PROBLEMS WITH PSYCHOLOGICAL CONSEQUENCES

◆   Among the progressive neurological diseases are Huntington's chorea, Parkinson's disease, multiple sclerosis, and Alzheimer's disease.

◆   Multi-infarct dementia is a form of dementia caused by multiple strokes over time.

◆   Brain injuries caused by blows to the head can result in a variety of psychological difficulties. Tumors of the brain may similarly compromise normal functioning.

◆   Tourette's syndrome is a neurological problem characterized by complex tics.

◆   One of the direct consequences of AIDS is a form of dementia called AIDS dementia complex.

◆   Korsakoff's syndrome is a form of memory loss that accompanies severe alcoholism.

◆   Untreated syphilis can result in a neurological condition known as general paresis that is marked by a host of cognitive difficulties.

◆   Epilepsy refers to a group of neurological disorders in which periodic bursts of neural discharge occur leading to seizures.

◆   Migraines are periodic headaches characterized by nausea and a variety of other symptoms.

Key Terms

acetylcholine

AIDS dementia complex

Alzheimer's disease

amnestic syndrome; organic amnesia

aphasia

aura (preceding a migraine)

aura (preceding a seizure)

autonomic nervous system

biofeedback

central nervous system

cerebral cortex

cerebral hemispheres

cognitive disorder

coma

confabulation

coprolalia

delirium

delirium tremens; DTs

dementia

dissociative amnesia

dopamine

endocrine system

epilepsy

excitation

focal seizure; partial seizure

forebrain

frontal lobes

functional disorder

general paresis

generalized seizure

grand mal epilepsy; generalized convulsive epilepsy

hindbrain

hippocampus

Huntington's chorea

hypothalamus

immune system

inhibition

intoxication

Korsakoff's syndrome

midbrain

migraine

multi-infarct (MI) dementia; vascular dementia

multiple sclerosis; MS

myelin

nervous system

neuron

neurotransmitter

norepinephrine

organic disorder

organic personality syndrome

organic syndrome

parasympathetic nervous system

Parkinson's disease

peripheral nervous system

petit mal epilepsy;
  generalized
    nonconvulsive epilepsy

pituitary gland

psychoneuroimmunology

rehabilitation

seizure

serotonin

somatic nervous system

stroke

sympathetic nervous
  system

temporal-lobe epilepsy;
  psychomotor epilepsy

tic

Tourette's syndrome

withdrawal

Fear and Anxiety Disorders

7 Wayne Gretzky is probably the greatest hockey player who has ever lived. In his autobiography, Gretzky (1990) described the whirlwind of his childhood. He could skate at age 2. He was known to hockey fans throughout Canada at age 6. He gave autographs at age 10. He was featured in magazine articles at age 11. He was the subject of television shows at age 15. He turned pro while still attending high school, and he subsequently set every scoring record imaginable (Swift, 1982). If ever an athlete symbolized his or her entire sport, Wayne Gretzky did so (Reilly, 1989).

At one point in his career, hockey player Wayne Gretzky suffered from a severe phobia concerning airplane travel.

It is hard to believe that anything could have stopped him from continuing his storied career. But Gretzky was afraid to fly. In his own words, he "was one of the worst fliers in the history of pro sports" (Gretzky, 1990, p. 84). His fear began when he was only 15, playing junior hockey, and flying with his team on rickety DC-3s. He was involved in a series of mishaps. One time, there was the threat of an emergency water landing. Another time, the plane in which he was flying hit some trees at the end of a runway. And yet another time, his plane narrowly missed hitting another plane in midair. These experiences made him understandably wary of flying.

Then matters became even worse when he joined the Edmonton Oilers. Flights to and from games were even longer and more frequent. He usually sat next to Edmonton announcer Rod Phillips, a white-knuckle flier himself. His obvious distress only exacerbated Gretzky's.

Gretzky's fear reached a peak in 1985. About to board a plane, he had a full-blown panic attack.

> Nothing was going to get me on that plane. I just freaked, started sweating and getting jumpy and mumbling things. (Gretzky, 1990, p. 85)

He began to find reasons not to fly, and he considered retiring from hockey, because there was no way he could avoid flying while still playing.

He saw a therapist who hypnotized him in an attempt to reduce his fear, but this proved unsuccessful.

What really helped him solve his problem was the assist-
ance of a friendly pilot.

> *Finally, on one flight, [he] ... snuck me into the cockpit*
> *to show me all the buttons and gears and exactly how it*
> *all worked. For some reason, that really helped me feel*
> *safer. (Gretzky, 1990, p. 86)*

He continues to sit in the cockpit whenever pilots will
let him. And today he reports that he is not afraid
of flying.

Wayne Gretzky's fear of flying introduces the subject of the present chapter: disorders characterized by
excessive fear and anxiety. His is just one example, yet
it well illustrates some of the generalizations I can
offer about these disorders.

First, fear and anxiety disorders exist in degrees.
You saw in Gretzky's case that his fear of flying took
different forms—from mild to moderate to severe.
The point stressed throughout this book about the
ambiguous boundaries of abnormality is readily apparent in the case of fears (Hodiamont, 1991). A touch of
apprehension is doubtlessly normal—even desirable—
whenever we travel. Fear leads us to follow safety
procedures such as buckling our seat belts. But when
our apprehension no longer reflects the danger that a
situation actually poses, then we label it abnormal.
When fear compromises the life we lead, then it is a
problem in need of a solution.

Second, disorders involving fear and anxiety show
themselves in all spheres of behavior. We may glibly
think of fear and anxiety as simply feelings, but they
do not exist in isolation from other aspects of what a
person does. They are reflected in a person's thoughts,
as expectations of harm. They are reflected in a person's
bodily responses, as excitation of the sympathetic nervous system. And they are reflected in a person's actions,
as avoidance of particular situations.

Third, fear and anxiety may result from particular
experiences, either direct or symbolic. Gretzky's fear
of flying followed several close calls in airplanes. Add
to that the in-flight terror of announcer Rod Phillips,
and we can see why he became even more afraid.
In contrast to the organic disorders discussed in the
previous chapter, which by definition have biological
causes, fear and anxiety disorders may be brought about
by learning. Accordingly, the cognitive-behavioral
model of abnormality often proves useful in understanding them.

Fourth, these disorders lead people to act in self-
defeating fashion. This puts a strain on any explanation
that starts by assuming that people are hedonists. In
other words, if we believe that people are inherently
driven to maximize pleasure and minimize pain, then
how can disorders that involve excessive fear and anxi-

ety come about through learning? People who suffer
from these problems are dominated by them.

Wayne Gretzky almost gave up a career that has
earned him boundless acclaim and fortune. Other individuals we encounter in this chapter avoid people altogether, or become housebound for decades, or are
unable to fall asleep without frightening nightmares.
The self-defeating aspect of fear and anxiety disorders
has been dubbed the *neurotic paradox* (Mowrer, 1960)
because neurotic individuals act in ways that make
their problems worse. Theorists have labored long to
make sense of the neurotic paradox. Here the psychodynamic model of abnormality is useful, because it
explicitly recognizes that people function at different
levels. What appears paradoxical on one level may be
quite sensible on another.

Finally, although fear and anxiety disorders can be
tenacious, there is help for those who suffer from them.
Indeed, some of the highest rates of cure for any psychological difficulty are for these particular problems. There
is controversy in many cases about their exact causes.
Just the same, there is a consensus that they can be
treated. Behavior therapy often proves successful, in
which the fearful individual is gradually exposed to the
situation so that he learns that his fear is unwarranted
and/or that he can cope with its consequences.

Some psychologists argue that behavior therapy
is useful to the degree that it leads an individual to
feel more in control of the frightening situation. With
his sense of efficacy bolstered, he can better function
within the given situation (Bandura, 1977, 1986).

DEFINING FEAR AND ANXIETY

I will eventually discuss how psychologists explain and
treat disorders involving fear and anxiety. First,

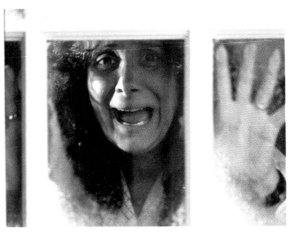

Fear is a reaction to threat, either actual or anticipated.

though, I need to be more thorough with respect to terminology (see Table 7.1). **Fear** is a complex of reactions that we show in response to some threat, either actual or anticipated (Marks, 1987).

Emotionally, we experience fear as an unpleasant feeling; we feel alarm, dread, fright, panic, and terror. If we experience fear over a prolonged period of time, we will also feel tired and overwhelmed.

Cognitively, we experience fear as specific thoughts about the dire consequences we face. If we are driving at high speed along a highway, we may worry about what will happen if another car swerves in front of us. We expect to hear squealing brakes, crunching metal, and broken glass. It is said that in moments of extreme fear our life passes before our eyes; more commonly, though, our mode of death flits through awareness.

Physiologically, we experience fear as a pounding heart, tensed muscles, a dry mouth, weakness, faintness, and the urge to urinate. These and other physiological responses (see Figure 7.1) are termed the body's **emergency reaction,** which results from the secretion of epinephrine by the adrenal glands, which in turn stimulates the sympathetic nervous system.

Behaviorally, we experience fear as a tendency either to freeze in place or to flee from what has frightened us. Other characteristic behaviors include aggression on the one hand and avoidance on the other. An individual who is afraid might show any and all of these responses, often in rapid succession.

Like fear, the term **anxiety** refers to a complex of reactions in response to a threat. Emotionally, physiologically, and behaviorally, anxiety is indistinguishable from fear. The critical difference is that we reserve the term *anxiety* for reactions in which the source of danger is unclear and/or diffuse. Thus, it differs from fear in terms of the associated cognitions. We are frightened about specific objects and situations, whereas we are anxious about life in general. Accordingly, **fear disorders** are problems characterized by expectations of specific harm, and **anxiety disorders** are problems characterized by more diffuse expectations. The distinction between fear and anxiety is not always so clear-cut, which means that it can be difficult to classify a given problem as a fear versus anxiety disorder (Marks, 1987). I choose to refer to these problems collectively as fear and anxiety disorders.

In the past, theorists regarded fear and anxiety as monolithic states, what Rachman and Hodgson (1980) termed a *lump approach*—lumping together all the manifestations of fear or anxiety and expecting them all to be either present or absent. A more sophisticated view takes the opposite approach and regards the components of fear and anxiety—their emotional, cognitive, physiological, and behavioral aspects—as potentially independent (Koksal & Power, 1990; Lang, 1969, 1970). A person can have primarily a cognitive fear, entertaining dire expectations but showing no other response. Or he can have primarily a behavioral fear. And so on.

Anxiety disorders are characterized by diffuse expectations of threat. (The Shriek *by Edvard Munch*)

TABLE 7.1

TERMINOLOGY *Several related terms prove crucial in discussing fear and anxiety disorders.*

TERM	DEFINITION
fear	a complex of reactions—emotional, cognitive, physiological, and behavioral—shown in response to threat
anxiety	a complex of reactions to danger that is unclear and/or diffuse
neurosis	a problem marked by excessive anxiety, avoidance of problems rather than confrontation, and self-defeating tendencies
stress	the reaction that takes place when a person tries to meet the demands of external events

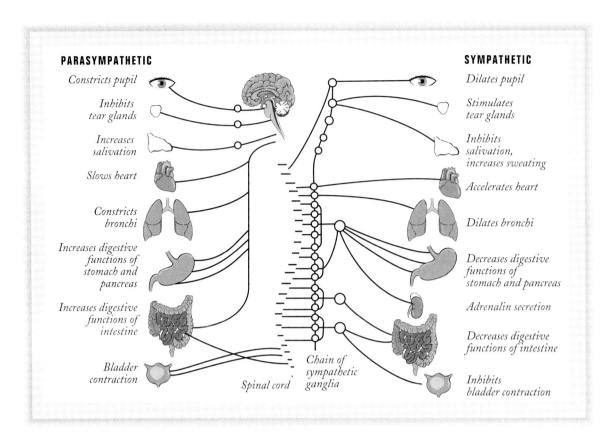

PARASYMPATHETIC

Constricts pupil

Inhibits tear glands

Increases salivation

Slows heart

Constricts bronchi

Increases digestive functions of stomach and pancreas

Increases digestive functions of intestine

Bladder contraction

Spinal cord

Chain of sympathetic ganglia

SYMPATHETIC

Dilates pupil

Stimulates tear glands

Inhibits salivation, increases sweating

Accelerates heart

Dilates bronchi

Decreases digestive functions of stomach and pancreas

Adrenalin secretion

Decreases digestive functions of intestine

Inhibits bladder contraction

FIGURE 7.1

THE BODY'S EMERGENCY REACTION   *The sympathetic nervous system produces the arousal that characterizes the body's emergency reaction. The parasympathetic nervous system counteracts arousal.*

The value of this approach, which admittedly complicates any discussion of these disorders, is that the different aspects of fear and anxiety may best be combated with different interventions. The therapist must determine exactly how an individual's disorder is constituted (Rachman, 1978).

This may be particularly important when we consider anxious individuals from different social groups. Although identifiable versions of fear and anxiety disorders exist in virtually all cultures, their specific manifestations sometimes differ; further, the emotional, cognitive, physiological, and behavioral symptoms may cohere in different ways depending on ethnicity (e.g., Beiser, Benfari, Collomb, & Ravel, 1976; Tseng et al., 1990). For example, Neal and Turner (1991) described research suggesting that anxiety disorders among urban African Americans often involve suspiciousness of others, a finding not typical among European Americans. The exact significance of this pattern is unclear, but it needs to be taken into account in diagnosis and treatment of these disorders.

Another term pertinent here is **neurotic disorder,** or *neurosis,* which refers to a psychological problem marked by excessive anxiety, avoidance of problems rather than confrontation, and self-defeating tendencies. Imagine someone who tells a would-be suitor, "Oh sure, call me—we'll go out," and then spends weeks dreading the possibility that the person will call, not answering the phone or the door. This is neurotic behavior.

The concept of neurosis has a long and complex history. Originally introduced in 1769 by William Cullen to describe problems presumably resulting from a damaged nervous system, neurosis became a favorite notion of psychoanalyst Sigmund Freud (1926), who gave it a specific theoretical meaning. He proposed that a neurosis was a psychological problem brought about by a person's attempts to keep emotional conflicts hidden from awareness. According to the generation of psychologists and psychiatrists under Freud's sway, psychological problems were regarded either as psychoses or neuroses (Chapter 2). In the former case, the attempts to keep conflicts hidden fail, and the person becomes psychotic—unable to distinguish fantasy from reality. In the latter case, the attempts are more successful, and the person goes about life, although in a less than optimal fashion.

While I am discussing difficult-to-define terms, I should mention **stress,** another notion with a long and complex history (Lazarus, 1966). It encompasses what happens when external events make demands on us. Sometimes stress refers to the external events themselves ("that place was a pressure cooker"), sometimes stress refers to our bodily response to a challenge ("I have a stress headache"), and sometimes stress refers to our emotional response ("I'm all stressed out"). It is not invariably bad; it can stimulate growth and creativity. But sometimes it is harmful, and its psychological consequences include disorders dominated by fear and anxiety—the focus of the present chapter. In other cases, stress contributes to problems such as conversion disorder and psychogenic amnesia (Chapter 8), depression (Chapter 9), physical illness (Chapter 10), sexual dysfunction (Chapter 11), and schizophrenia (Chapter 12). When stress is used to explain the occurrence of a disorder, we should try to be specific about the critical factors. Otherwise, what can result is a circular explanation.

The fear and anxiety disorders include five in particular—phobia, panic disorder, generalized anxiety disorder, obsessive-compulsive disorder, and post-traumatic stress disorder—which I now discuss in detail (see Table 7.2). These five disorders represent just one way of subdividing problems characterized by fear and anxiety (Tyrer, 1989). They all overlap, in that an individual who warrants one diagnosis is usually at increased risk for the others as well. This may represent genuine vulnerability to discrete problems, but it may also mean that contemporary diagnostic systems propose overly fine categories.

Stress refers to what happens when external events make demands on us. This air traffic controller experiences his share of stress.

Fear and anxiety disorders also overlap with depression, so much so that it proves difficult to find anxious individuals who are not at least a bit depressed, and vice versa (Breier, Charney, & Heninger, 1984; Clayton et al., 1991; Walker, Katon, Jemelka, & Roy-Byrne, 1992). Some theorists have called for a merging of anxiety and depression (Foa & Foa, 1982) or at least an explicit recognition of their considerable overlap (Kendler, Neale, Kessler, Heath, & Eaves, 1992d). Others disagree (Klerman, 1977). Regardless of how this debate ends, you should be aware that when our focus is on people with fear and anxiety disorders, as

TABLE 7.2

FEAR AND ANXIETY DISORDERS *DSM-IV describes several disorders marked by excessive fear and anxiety.*

DISORDER	CHARACTERIZATION AND TREATMENT
specific phobia	a persistent fear of a circumscribed object or situation
	helped by behavior therapy (exposure)
social phobia	a persistent fear of being in a situation where some act must be performed under the scrutiny of others
	helped by behavior therapy (exposure)
panic disorder	a problem characterized by recurrent attacks of panic: discrete periods of intense fear
	helped by behavior therapy (exposure), cognitive therapy, imipramine
agoraphobia	the fear of being in a situation from which escape is not possible; often co-occurs with panic disorder
	helped by behavior therapy (exposure), cognitive therapy, imipramine
generalized anxiety disorder	excessive and unrealistic anxiety that cuts across a variety of life domains
	helped by tranquilizers, behavior therapy, "talking" therapies
obsessive-compulsive disorder	a disorder characterized by obsessions and/or compulsions
	helped by psychosurgery, antidepressants, behavior therapy (exposure, thought stopping)
post-traumatic stress disorder	a disorder that follows the experience of a highly traumatic event, characterized by reexperiencing the event, avoiding reminders of the event, numbing of general responsiveness, and feeling anxious
	helped by talking about experiences in a supportive context

it is in this chapter, we are at the same time discussing those who are depressed (Weissman, 1988).

PHOBIA

A *phobia* refers to an exaggerated fear. DSM-IV distinguishes between phobias that involve specific stimuli in the environment versus those that involve the performance of given behaviors in the presence of others. I discuss these in turn.

SPECIFIC PHOBIA

Wayne Gretzky suffered from what DSM-IV identifies as a **specific phobia:** a persistent fear of a circumscribed object or situation. When the person with a specific phobia encounters what he fears, he shows an immediate fear response. Often the person will anticipate situations where he might encounter the object and go to great lengths to avoid them.

I once read about a woman who was afraid of feathers. She would not use a feather pillow, for example, and neither would she venture into parts of her hometown where she might encounter a bird or a feather that had dropped from one. She limited her travels out of town for the same reason. What started out as a circumscribed phobia ended up dictating how she lived.

DSM-IV tells the diagnostician not to make a diagnosis of specific phobia unless the fear interferes with a person's normal routine. An individual who lives in a landlocked region may well be greatly afraid of open bodies of water, but so long as he stays where he is, his fear is not a bona fide phobia.

Theorists have prepared long lists of names for given instances of specific phobias, but in point of fact, the vast majority of them fall into a small number of categories:

◆   blood, injured tissue, or illness

◆   animals—especially dogs, snakes, insects, and mice

◆   closed spaces *(claustrophobia)*

◆   heights *(acrophobia)*

◆   air travel

One survey of adults in the United States found that almost half of those with specific phobias feared

Among the common specific phobias is claustrophobia, the fear of enclosed spaces.

blood, injured tissue, or illness (Agras, Sylvester, & Oliveau, 1969).

Remember the discussion of how to define abnormality (Chapter 1)? The point was made that professionals and everyday people alike may disagree about the abnormality of given behaviors. In the case of specific phobias, we usually do not have as much dissent. The person with a specific phobia herself admits that her fear is irrational—far out of the bounds of reality. A woman who is afraid of spiders is afraid not only of encountering one in her bedroom but also of looking at a picture of one in a book. A spider in the flesh might be dangerous, but there is no way that a picture of a spider is dangerous.

Epidemiology   In the grand scheme of disorders, specific phobias are not among the most severe, and many people who suffer from them do not seek professional help. Accordingly, we do not know as much about their epidemiology as we would like. We can estimate, however, that mild versions of phobias are rather common in the general population of the United States—affecting perhaps 10% of all individuals (Robins et al., 1984). Severe phobias, which interfere with life to the point of keeping a person at home, afflict about 2% to 3% of the population (Boyd et al., 1990; Marks, 1986; Reich, 1986). There is a marked sex difference in specific phobias; women who warrant this diagnosis outnumber men by about two to one (Marks,

1987). Phobias also show a regular progression in age of onset (see Figure 7.2). Fear of tangible objects usually begins in early childhood. More abstract fears appear later.

Treatment   The phobias of children often disappear without treatment, whereas those of adults persist unless mental health professionals (or airplane pilots) intervene. Happily, several behavior therapy strategies are currently available for ridding people of specific phobias (Marks, 1987). These are discussed in detail later in the chapter.

SOCIAL PHOBIA

A second type of phobia is called a **social phobia:** a persistent fear of being in a situation where a person must perform some act under the scrutiny of others. The individual with a social phobia is afraid that he will act in a way that is humiliating or embarrassing. For example, he might be unable to eat in front of others, or speak, or write. He might be unable to urinate in a public bathroom. Or he might be afraid of blushing.

Social phobias give rise to an anxiety response when the situation is encountered, as well as when the person anticipates it. As you might imagine, this kind of phobia can prove highly disruptive. If and when the person does perform the feared behavior, his anxiety might well hamper his performance so much that he truly is embarrassed. This only creates further anxiety. Even though an individual with social phobia recognizes his fears as excessive, he may plan his life in such a way that he is never put in the social situations he fears.

Do not confuse a social phobia with a specific phobia. With a social phobia, the person is not afraid of the act or the situation per se. Rather, it is the possibility of anxiety, embarrassment, or humiliation *in the eyes of other people* that is feared. So, the person who is afraid to eat in public may anticipate that he will choke or spit. The person who is afraid of talking in front of others may anticipate that his voice will squeak.

Masters, Burish, Hollon, and Rimm (1987) described the social phobia of an insurance salesman in his early forties. Let me call him Mr. Cooper. He was afraid of talking to his coworkers and clients. In particular, he was afraid to return phone calls and attend sales meetings. Calling potential clients on the phone to request an appointment—obviously an important and common activity for someone who sells insurance—was the most frightening prospect of all. Mr. Cooper feared that they would reject his requests and regard him as a failure.

Epidemiology   Social phobias are diagnosed among 1% to 2% of adults in the United States, and somewhat more frequently among women than men (Reich, 1986; Schneier, Johnson, Hornig, Liebowitz, & Weissman, 1992; Weissman, 1985). By far the most common of these phobias are fear of public speaking and generic fear of any and all social situations (Pollard & Henderson, 1988). The onset of social phobias is usually during adolescence, and they can be chronic in the absence of intervention. If the phobia is severe, additional problems might develop, such as depression or substance abuse (Kushner, Sher, & Beitman, 1990).

Treatment   To the degree that a social phobia is not severe or pervasive, it can be alleviated with behavior therapy as readily as a specific phobia (Barlow, 1992; Butler, Cullington, Munby, Amies, & Gelder,

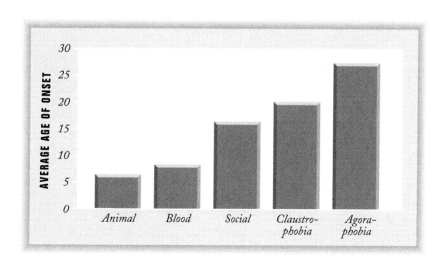

FIGURE 7.2

AVERAGE AGE OF ONSET FOR DIFFERENT PHOBIAS
Phobias about concrete objects usually appear earlier in life than more abstract phobias.
SOURCE: DATA DERIVED FROM "AGE OF ONSET IN DIFFERENT PHOBIAS," BY L.-G. OST, 1987, *Journal of Abnormal Psychology, 96,* PP. 223–229.

1984; Gelernter et al., 1991). More severe cases are more difficult to treat, as you might imagine.

PANIC DISORDER

The defining characteristic of a **panic disorder** is recurrent attacks of panic, discrete periods of intense fear and anxiety. The word "panic" comes from Pan, the Greek god of nature who would suddenly appear from nowhere to drive people mad. Panic attacks usually last for several minutes, and they are a problem not because of their duration but because of their sheer intensity.

I have already noted the various manifestations of fear and anxiety, but these fail to do justice to how extreme they become during a panic attack. These symptoms include the following:

◆ accelerated and/or fluctuating heart beat

◆ sweating

◆ trembling

◆ shortness of breath or sensation of smothering

◆ choking

◆ chest pains

◆ nausea or abdominal upset

◆ dizziness or faintness

◆ a sense of depersonalization ("this is not me that this is happening to") and/or unreality ("this is not really taking place")

◆ fear of going crazy or losing control

◆ fear of dying

◆ numbness or tingling in one's extremities

◆ flushes or chills

Not all panic attacks have all these features, to be sure, but they give you a sense of what it means to have the disorder.

DSM-IV considers four or more symptoms necessary for the diagnosis of a panic attack. An occasional panic attack is not all that unusual, and so a diagnosis of panic disorder is made only when these attacks are accompanied by a persistent concern—lasting at least 1 month—about future attacks or their consequences. Panic attacks are so distressing that people suffering from them attempt suicide much more often than those in the general population (Fawcett, 1992; Korn et al., 1992; Noyes, 1991).

The frequency of panic attacks varies greatly, from but once in a person's life to daily. These attacks occur suddenly and unexpectedly. Obviously, they are not a sign of a disorder if they occur in situations in which the person is genuinely threatened.

AGORAPHOBIA

According to DSM-IV, there are two versions of panic disorder: with and without **agoraphobia**—the fear of being in a setting from which escape is impossible. Part of this fear is focused on fear itself; individuals with agoraphobia are afraid that help may be unavailable should anxiety or panic occur. There are people with "pure" agoraphobia, without panic attacks. In the majority of cases, however, panic attacks and agoraphobia occur together. Agoraphobia is sometimes regarded as one type of phobia, but because it is usually much more severe in its consequences, and because it occurs with great frequency among those susceptible to panic attacks (Thompson, Bland, & Orn, 1989; Weissman, Leaf, Holzer, & Merikangas, 1985), DSM-IV merges it with panic disorder.

The agoraphobic individual imposes strict travel prohibitions on himself, as a rule avoiding crowded stores, bridges, public transportation, and the like. *Agora* comes from a Greek word meaning marketplace, and agoraphobia—literally fear of the crowded market—has been recognized since antiquity. At the same time, the individual with the disorder may recognize that such self-imposed prohibitions are groundless.

Again, do not confuse this fear with a specific phobia. It is not the store per se that the agoraphobic individual fears but rather the inability to escape from it should the need arise. The connection with panic disorder is therefore obvious. Agoraphobia might follow a panic attack because the person is afraid of having another panic attack. Such attacks are necessarily

The agoraphobic individual often finds public transportation frightening and may avoid using it.

difficult to predict, and they occur in no particular type of place, so the person prone to them increasingly limits his or her travel. Indeed, agoraphobic people can eventually become completely housebound.

When I worked as a psychologist at a Veterans Administration Medical Center, one of our patients was Mr. Winter, a 43-year-old man who was brought in by his family for treatment because he had not set foot out of their home in 19 years—not once. Needless to say, a person cannot manifest agoraphobia in this way without the active help of other people. Mr. Winter stayed inside for almost two decades because he did all the cooking and cleaning for his large family. Apparently no one wished to upset the status quo. Finally, several of his younger siblings married and left home, making Mr. Winter's role superfluous and his behavior upsetting to the remaining family members. They agreed that he had a problem needing treatment, and so they literally dragged him to our hospital. He was so shaken by his trip that it was several days before he could have a coherent conversation with us.

Like the other disorders so far discussed, agoraphobia exists in degrees. In milder cases, the person travels with distress but does not limit what he does. In somewhat more severe cases, the person travels at some times but not at others. He visits stores at off-hours, for example, when they are not as crowded. He may bring a companion, because this may alleviate distress. And in the most severe cases, like Mr. Winter, the person becomes housebound.

Interestingly, agoraphobia often subsides at night and when the weather is overcast (Marks, 1987). Some agoraphobic individuals can control their anxiety simply by wearing dark glasses. Perhaps fear of vast expanses is at the core of this disorder. When these are obscured, no fear is triggered.

EPIDEMIOLOGY

Panic disorder with agoraphobia is more crippling than panic disorder without. Both sorts of problems usually begin during a person's twenties, and they will persist unless there is some kind of intervention (Pollack et al., 1990). The tendency to abuse alcohol and drugs in an attempt to calm one's nerves is a possible consequence of panic disorder (Cox, Norton, Swinson, & Endler, 1990; Markowitz, Weissman, Ouellette, Lish, & Klerman, 1989). Perhaps 3% of Americans have panic disorders (Kessler et al., 1994; Reich, 1986; Weissman, 1985; Whitaker et al., 1990), with women twice as likely as men to be diagnosed (Kessler et al., 1994).

TREATMENT

Until recently, there was no satisfactory treatment for panic disorder. Now there exist several effective ways to help. Panic attacks can often be alleviated with medication—not with tranquilizers as you might expect but with **imipramine,** an antidepressant (Klein, 1964; Mavissakalian, 1990). There is currently a great deal of theoretical speculation about the biological basis of panic disorders, and they might someday be classified as discrete problems in their own right, not simply as one type of fear and anxiety disorder. Another recent treatment for panic attacks encourages the person to reattribute his bodily symptoms of panic to a more benign source than his own weakness and vulnerability (Beck & Emery, 1985; Beck, Sokol, Clark, Berchick, & Wright, 1992; Evans, Holt, & Oei, 1991).

Agoraphobia can also be helped with behavior therapy techniques in which the person is gradually exposed to the situations he fears (Marks, 1990). The long-term effectiveness of these approaches has been demonstrated and rivals that of biomedical treatment (Margraf, Barlow, Clark, & Telch, 1993). As with all treatments of these disorders, the success of behavior therapy depends on the pervasiveness of the fears.

GENERALIZED ANXIETY DISORDER

This next disorder differs from phobias because it is not linked to particular events or objects, and it differs from panic disorders because its symptoms do not occur in discrete bursts. Instead, **generalized anxiety disorder (GAD)** refers to excessive and unrealistic anxiety that cuts across a variety of life's domains: work, finances, family, friends, health, and the like. DSM-IV proposes that a person with GAD experiences anxiety on more days than not during at least a 6-month period. Further, the individual has difficulty controlling his or her worry.

Anxiety presents itself in a variety of ways. The individual may experience *restlessness,* feeling constantly on edge. He may complain of *fatigue.* He may have *difficulty with concentration.* He may have problems with *irritability.* He may show excessive *muscle tension:* trembling, twitching, and restlessness. He may experience *disturbed sleep.*

All of these different manifestations of GAD can feed into one another, so much so that we would hesitate to say which are primary and which are secondary. DSM-IV simply tells the diagnostician to count the number of symptoms and, after a given number (usually three) is exceeded, to offer a diagnosis of generalized anxiety disorder. It can be difficult to make a clean distinction between what is normal versus abnormal. Like many problems, GAD exists in degrees. The more symptoms a person displays, the greater the number of life domains in which they are shown, and the longer they last, the more likely we are to say with confidence that a person has a problem.

Some theorists fail to be convinced that GAD should be considered a specific difficulty warranting its own diagnosis (cf. Barlow, Blanchard, Vermilyea, Vermilyea, & DiNardo, 1986). Perhaps it is a personality style that contributes to other difficulties (see Nisita, Petracca, & Cassano, 1990). The majority of individuals who qualify for this diagnosis also meet diagnostic criteria for other disorders (Sanderson & Barlow, 1990).

All of us know people who are extremely anxious across a variety of situations. For example, several years ago one of my students confided that she was constantly on edge. I already knew that Ms. Gupta experienced a great deal of anxiety when taking examinations in my class. She asked constant questions before, during, and after each test. She complained that her mind went blank even when she knew the material well. Once, on a multiple-choice exam, she skipped a question early on and did not realize until the very end of the test that almost all of her intended answers were off by one question. On another exam, Ms. Gupta omitted her name and *her student number.*

What I did not know until she told me was that she fretted just as much about her friends and family, her part-time job and its demands, and what she would do after graduation. She apparently slept fitfully. When she did fall asleep, she would grind her teeth. She held herself so tensely that her neck and back always hurt. By any and all criteria, Ms. Gupta experienced generalized anxiety disorder.

EPIDEMIOLOGY

Prevalence estimates are obviously a bit arbitrary, because they depend on the specific diagnostic criteria employed and whether we wish to diagnose GAD only when other problems are not present. We can tentatively estimate that the most severe form of generalized anxiety—one meeting DSM diagnostic criteria—occurs in about 3% to 4% of American adults today, with women outnumbering men (Kessler et al., 1994; Reich, 1986; Weissman, 1985; Whitaker et al., 1990). This disorder usually begins in early adulthood, and its course is chronic.

Cross-cultural comparisons are less informative than we would like. According to some studies, anxiety is more common in modern Western societies than in less technological cultures, but other investigations disagree (Hollifield, Katon, Spain, & Pule, 1990). Hampering these comparisons is that while most cultures recognize a state akin to anxiety, its particular manifestations differ—in some cases with bodily symptoms predominating, in other cases emotional symptoms, and still other cases cognitive ones (Guthrie & Tanco, 1980). Perhaps the best I can say is that anxiety is a universal occurrence, but a person's culture dictates how it is labeled and experienced.

TREATMENT

In the contemporary Western world, GAD is frequently treated with tranquilizing medication, which necessarily reduces the symptoms of anxiety in the short run but obviously does nothing to change the external circumstances that may have given rise to them in the first place (Cassano, Perugi, Musetti, & Savino, 1990). For this reason, mental health professionals often recommend that GAD be attacked through psychological means: talking therapies and/or behavior therapy. These approaches often succeed in curbing a person's anxiety (Borkovec & Costello, 1993; Shader & Greenblatt, 1983).

OBSESSIVE-COMPULSIVE DISORDER

An **obsession** is a persistent idea, thought, impulse, or image that an individual experiences as intrusive, senseless, and disquieting. The person tries to ignore or suppress the obsession, with varying success. It is recognized by the individual as a product of his or her mind. Obsessions are not simply exaggerated versions of realistic worries.

An obsession is experienced as alien to the individual's own makeup. It is not a Top 40 song that repeats itself over and over in your mind, or a list of things to buy at the grocery store, or a prayer or mantra that you silently repeat because it brings comfort. Instead, obsessions are ugly and foreign: the thought that you might kill a friend or relative, that you have contracted a dreaded disease, or that you might blurt out a blasphemous notion at a religious service.

In my own clinical work, I once spoke to a young woman who told me of her recurrent impulse to take a butcher knife and carve out the heart of her young child while he slept. Ms. Chambers was a devoted mother, and her son was happy and healthy. But she could not rid her mind of the vivid image that she would kill him. This of course distressed her greatly, and the more she worried about her impulse, the more elaborate her obsession became and the more frequently it occurred.

An obsession is cognitive, whereas a **compulsion** is behavioral: a repetitive act carried out in a ritualistic manner in order to prevent or neutralize some dreaded consequence. Compulsions produce marked distress and interference with everyday life. The individual recognizes their excessiveness but still cannot curb them. Most compulsions involve either cleaning (to prevent contamination) or checking (to prevent disaster). These rituals can become highly elaborate and incredibly time-consuming.

Rachman and Hodgson (1980, pp. 115-116) offered these sketches of compulsive individuals they had interviewed:

> *A 28-year old patient had checking rituals precipitated by a fear of harming others. He was unable to drive his car, as this provoked intolerable thoughts and checking rituals, and he avoided crowded streets for fear of causing harm to others. He repeatedly checked razors, pins, glass, and so forth.*
>
> *A 34-year-old married woman had checking rituals precipitated by contact with other people. Looking at or talking to people, or giving them food, led to checking behavior in order to ensure that no harm came to them.*
>
> *A 36-year-old man had checking rituals focused on excrement; he engaged in prolonged and meticulous inspections of any speck of brown, particularly on his clothes and rugs.*
>
> *A 40-year-old nursery school teacher checked that all rugs and carpets were absolutely flat lest someone trip over them, and spent long periods looking for needles and pins on the floor and in furniture. She repeatedly checked to ensure that all cigarettes and matches were extinguished.*

The point is not that checking per se is problematic. If we hear a crash somewhere in the house, we should get up and see what happened. The problem is that checking rituals leave little time for anything else.

Because the same people usually experience both obsessions and compulsions, most diagnostic systems—including DSM-IV—group them together under the rubric of **obsessive-compulsive disorder** (or **OCD**). There is often a close relationship between obsessions and compulsions; the compulsion is undertaken to counteract the dangers that form the obsession.

For example, Ms. Chambers, the woman I described earlier with the impulse to carve out the heart of her child, also engaged in a ritual of hiding butcher knives around the house so that she could not find them. Then she worried that she had hidden them in places where her son could get at them and cut his fingers. She constantly kept checking to see that the knives were safe.

After performing a compulsive ritual, the person usually feels relieved. If she is prevented from performing it, she reports mounting tension. Early in the history of OCD, the person may try to resist the compulsion, but this becomes so unpleasant that later she makes no show of resistance and instead gives in readily whenever the impulse moves her. Compulsive individuals do not enjoy their rituals, so those of you who are inveterate stamp collectors, soap opera fans, or video game players can rest assured that your hobby does not qualify as psychological abnormality.

Like phobias, the content of obsessions and compulsions is quite narrow. Although in principle people could be obsessed about all manner of things, their obsessions and compulsions almost always center around themes of the following:

✦ contamination

✦ violence

✦ religious blasphemy

The latter theme—blasphemy—is not encountered today with the same frequency as 100 years ago, no doubt because we are now a much more secular society. Fear of contamination, on the other hand, has increased with the spread of modern ideas about germs, and at present it is the most common theme of obsessions (Akhtar, Wig, Varma, Pershad, & Verma, 1975).

EPIDEMIOLOGY

According to epidemiological surveys, mild forms of obsessive-compulsive disorder occur with some frequency in the general population, although they are not sufficiently disruptive to bring an individual into the mental health system (Rachman & de Silva, 1978). Severe versions of the disorder, those that take more than 1 hour per day and interfere with a person's normal routine, occur at the rate of 2% to 3% among contemporary Americans (Rasmussen & Eisen, 1992; Robins et al., 1984; Whitaker et al., 1990). The problem seems to occur equally among men and women, although Rachman and Hodgson (1980) reported that women are more apt than men to have compulsions that involve cleaning (see also Noshirvani, Kasvikis, Marks, Tsakiris, & Monteiro, 1991). The onset of the disorder is usually in adolescence or early adulthood, although it is not uncommon for it to begin during childhood. Its course is usually chronic if there is no intervention, although symptoms may wax and wane over the years.

Those with OCD are frequently depressed as well, and there is a lively debate about why this link exists. According to one view, depression makes it difficult for people to resist obsessive thoughts and compulsive acts. The depressed person presumably cannot control his own internal states (Wegner, 1989). Another theory makes the opposite argument. The tendency to ruminate about negative possibilities takes the occasional bad mood that we all experience and generalizes it into a full-blown depression (Nolen-Hoeksema, 1990). Another problem that occurs along with obsessive-compulsive disorder is abuse of alcohol, undertaken to curb anxiety.

TREATMENT

Historically, obsessions and compulsions were considered intractable (Stern, 1978). Treatment is still difficult. Tranquilizers like Valium and Librium are not that helpful. Psychosurgery brings some relief to severe cases, and antidepressant medication also helps to a degree (Marks & O'Sullivan, 1988). Behavior therapy is also somewhat successful (e.g., Foa, Kozak, Steketee, & McCarthy, 1992), although behavioral techniques are apparently more useful for curtailing compulsions than obsessions (Rachman & Hodgson, 1980).

POST-TRAUMATIC STRESS DISORDER

The last of the fear and anxiety disorders to be discussed is **post-traumatic stress disorder (PTSD).** By definition, this problem follows a highly traumatic event, one that produced fear, helplessness, or terror in the individual. DSM-IV notes that such a stressful event must include the possibility of death or serious injury. For example:

◆   military combat

◆   civilian disasters like fires or earthquakes

◆   internment in POW camps, concentration camps, or refugee camps

◆   rape or assault

◆   accidents like auto crashes

◆   highjacking and kidnapping

◆   torture

Bereavement, financial loss, and divorce—although unpleasant—are not usually regarded as the sorts of events that can produce post-traumatic stress.

Post-traumatic stress disorder follows a highly traumatic event, such as internment in a concentration camp. Shown here is the entrance to the infamous Nazi camp in Auschwitz, Poland.

Like other disorders, the diagnosis of PTSD must be culturally sensitive. The specific traumas that give rise to the disorder may differ across groups, and so too may its specific manifestations. For example, Mollica and colleagues (1992) developed a measure of PTSD suitable for use among torture victims in Southeast Asia, and it places greater emphasis on shame and disrupted social relationships than do analogous measures used in Western countries.

What defines PTSD is not simply the traumatic event and the person's immediate distress reaction but also the *reexperience of the trauma* in any of several ways. He may have recurrent and intrusive recollections of the event. Or the person might have frequent nightmares in which the traumatic event is relived. While awake, he might experience flashbacks, acting and feeling as if the event literally is happening again. These flashbacks can be triggered by some association with the event.

Here are brief examples of how individuals with PTSD reexperience the original trauma:

◆   *I once worked with a Vietnam veteran who could not escape his memories of a gruesome incident in which the head of his best friend was blown off his body, to land at my patient's feet.*

◆   *I have a friend who was raped years ago; during her waking life she goes about her business with few thoughts of the assault. With some frequency, though, she awakens at night from the same nightmare, in which the rapist again is attacking her.*

✦ *Another Vietnam veteran I knew who experienced post-traumatic stress disorder would have flashbacks whenever he smelled Vietnamese food.*

✦ *Solomon and Prager (1992) discovered that during the Persian Gulf War in 1991, when Israel was under missile attacks from Iraq, individuals who decades before survived the Nazi concentration camps were more likely than other Israelis to be distressed and feel vulnerable.*

Also part of the DSM-IV definition of PTSD is a *numbing of general responsiveness* not present prior to the trauma and a persistent *avoidance* of stimuli associated with the original trauma.

In 1980, when I was working with Vietnam veterans suffering post-traumatic stress disorder, American hostages were held captive in the United States embassy in Tehran. Unlike the rest of us, who followed the grim events in Iran with great interest, most of the veterans I knew tried not to read about it or to watch newscasts, because they became too upset. The futility of the hostage situation reminded them of the analogous futility of our country's involvement in Vietnam, and their symptoms worsened.

Post-traumatic stress disorder is classified with the other fear and anxiety disorders because *symptoms of anxiety* accompany its other manifestations. The individual is hyperalert and shows an exaggerated startle response. He feels irritable or angry. He has sleep disturbances and concentration difficulties.

EPIDEMIOLOGY

Symptoms of PTSD usually begin immediately after the stressful event, but in some cases they appear months or even years later. The epidemiology of this particular disorder is difficult to specify, and perhaps not intrinsically meaningful, because there is nothing universal about the figures for a given time and place. A general survey of adults in the United States during 1981 found the overall prevalence of post-traumatic stress disorder to be about 1%, with the most typical case being a female subjected to a physical attack and the next most typical a male wounded during the Vietnam War (Helzer, Robins, & McEvoy, 1987) (see Figure 7.3). More recent surveys yield about the same 1% prevalence estimate (Breslau & Davis, 1992; Davidson, Hughes, Blazer, & George, 1991). We know that the disorder can afflict men and women, and individuals of all ages, including children. Alcohol or drug abuse is a possible consequence.

Not everyone exposed to a traumatic event experiences symptoms of PTSD. In fact, only a minority of individuals do so, even when the event in question is a horrible one (Brom, Kleber, & Witztum, 1992; Norris, 1992). Considerable debate thus takes place as to what determines who will develop the disorder.

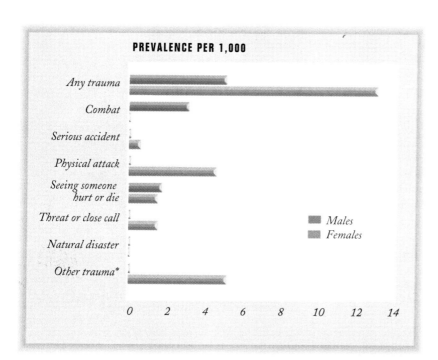

FIGURE 7.3

STRESSOR TYPE AND PTSD IN THE UNITED STATES, 1981
*The most typical case of post-traumatic stress disorder in the contemporary United States is an assaulted female. *Other traumas may include a spouse's affair, being poisoned, and having a miscarriage.*
SOURCE: DATA DERIVED FROM "POST-TRAUMATIC STRESS DISORDER IN THE GENERAL POPULATION," BY J. E. HELZER, L. N. ROBINS, AND L. McEVOY, 1987, *New England Journal of Medicine, 317*, PP. 1630–1634.

Some are of the opinion that post-traumatic stress disorder develops only among those with psychological problems prior to the trauma (Boulanger, 1986). Others argue that the particular qualities of the trauma suffice to explain the development of the disorder. In other words, we cannot say that two people have experienced the "same" trauma just because they both were assaulted or under enemy fire. Some versions of such events are more frightening than others, and perhaps the sheer intensity of the trauma and the fear response it elicits produce PTSD (Perry, Difede, Musngi, Frances, & Jacobsberg, 1992).

For example, a study of those in the area of the volcanic explosion in 1980 of Mount St. Helens found a direct relationship between the amount of exposure to the disaster and subsequent likelihood of developing PTSD (Shore, Tatum, & Vollmer, 1986). Studies of soldiers find much the same relationship between the duration and intensity of combat and the later appearance of the disorder (e.g., Buydens-Branchey, Noumair, & Branchey, 1990).

Still others suggest that it is what ensues in the aftermath of trauma, whether the person feels supported and safe, that determines the eventual outcome (Young & Erickson, 1988). This means crisis intervention following trauma should limit the development of PTSD. Similarly, perhaps the ability to find meaning in the traumatic event protects a victim against later difficulties (Frankl, 1963).

These different possibilities need not be incompatible. Whether a person develops PTSD may reflect an interaction among factors existing before, during, and after the traumatic event (Gidycz & Koss, 1991; McCranie, Hyer, Boudewyns, & Woods, 1992; Mejo, 1990; Resnick, Kilpatrick, Best, & Kramer, 1992; Rubonis & Bickman, 1991).

No definitive study of the risk factors for the disorder exists, because it would need a prospective design—studying research subjects prior to the trauma in question. Needless to say, we cannot easily predict the occurrence of highly traumatic events. One exception is an investigation by Card (1987), who followed up on a prior study of 50,000 ninth graders who in 1960 completed a battery of personality questionnaires. In 1982, 1,500 of these subjects were recontacted; 481 of them had served in Vietnam, and the researcher determined whether or not each experienced post-traumatic stress disorder following his hitch. This information was then correlated with the measures of pre-trauma personality. Only one of many measures—low self-esteem—predicted the subsequent development of PTSD, but this makes sense. The extent of disturbing experiences during combat also proved relevant.

Another exception is a study by Nolen-Hoeksema and Morrow (1991). Just 2 weeks before the 1989

Loma Prieta earthquake near San Francisco, these researchers administered questionnaires to 137 Stanford University students assessing various personality characteristics. After the quake, these students again completed questionnaires. Those who were most distressed in the aftermath of the earthquake had been depressed in the first place and had a cognitive style of ruminating about negative events. Also predicting the degree of distress after the quake was the extent to which students experienced personal danger or difficulty.

TREATMENT

Once it begins, post-traumatic stress disorder is apt to last for years, even decades (Green et al., 1990; Kluznik, Speed, Van Valkenburg, & Magraw, 1986; Kuch & Cox, 1992; Solkoff, 1992; Sutker, Winstead, Galina, & Allain, 1990). There is some agreement that individuals can be helped if they talk about their experiences in a supportive context (Marks, 1987; Murray, 1992; Solomon, Gerrity, & Muff, 1992). Support can take various forms. For example, Morris and Silove (1992) propose that South American torture victims suffering from PTSD are best served by a focus

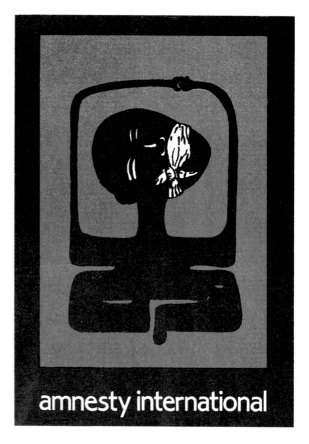

Post-traumatic stress disorder may be one of the consequences of torture.

on the trauma itself, whereas their counterparts in Southeast Asia are best helped by a focus on the consequences of the trauma.

Whatever form support takes, we can interpret its benefits in different ways. Those of a psychodynamic persuasion see support as allowing catharsis, whereas those who favor the cognitive-behavioral model see it as allowing exposure and thus extinction (cf. Brom, Kleber, & Defares, 1989).

A new treatment of PTSD that is attracting attention asks clients to make sweeping eye movements while imagining the original traumatic event (Shapiro, 1989). Fear is apparently reduced. How best to interpret this intervention is unclear, but it may be an example of the more general strategy of exposure and extinction (Dyck, 1993).

THEORETICAL PERSPECTIVES

There are a number of theoretical perspectives that have been brought to bear on the fear and anxiety disorders. Several of the popular models of abnormality introduced in Chapter 3 have much to say about the origin and treatment of these problems. Here I consider in detail the approaches that the biomedical, psychodynamic, and cognitive-behavioral models take. Because fear and anxiety are composed of different aspects, it is not surprising that all these models make a contribution to understanding and treating these disorders.

BIOMEDICAL MODEL

Those of a biomedical persuasion focus quite obviously on the biological aspects of fear and anxiety. I have already mentioned the physiological reactions that characterize them. Much attention has recently been paid to specifying just how these changes take place and what is physically wrong with individuals who have fear and anxiety disorders. Several physiological mechanisms have been described.

Physiological mechanisms   A great deal of interest has focused on the set of neurons in the body that inhibit anxiety. These neurons communicate with the neurotransmitter **GABA (gamma-amino-butyric acid).** Some believe that these neurons do not function properly in people with fear and anxiety disorders (Haefely, 1990). Anxious individuals have overly low levels of GABA activity. This means their inhibitory neurons do not sufficiently inhibit the other neurons responsible for anxiety.

The best evidence for this view of fear and anxiety is the effectiveness of a group of drugs referred to as **benzodiazepines,** which include such well known tranquilizers as Valium and Librium. Some neurons in the brain are specifically sensitive to benzodiazepines. These drugs lower the threshold for inhibitory neurons to fire, thereby combating a person's anxiety.

Different anxiety disorders respond differently to different drugs, suggesting—if the biomedical model is correct here—that there really are different sorts of anxiety with different biological bases and that these can be identified by the way they respond to various drugs (Klein, 1964). GABA is but one of the physiological mechanisms so far implicated in these disorders (Peroutka, 1990).

PET scan studies suggest that obsessive-compulsive disorder may be caused by abnormal brain characteristics, specifically overactivity in parts of the brain responsible for attention and perseveration (Baxter et al., 1987). By this view, the individual finds it difficult to resist unwanted thoughts and impulses. Further suggesting a physiological mechanism for obsessive-compulsive disorder is the tendency of people with Tourette's syndrome to have obsessive-compulsive symptoms (Pitman, Green, Jenike, & Mesulam, 1987). As noted in Chapter 6, Tourette's syndrome is caused by neurotransmitter abnormalities.

Panic can sometimes be produced by *hyperventilation*—breathing too deeply and/or quickly (McLeod & Lance, 1989). Hyperventilation results in the constriction of arteries supplying blood to the brain, which leads in turn to light-headedness, increased heart rate, dry mouth, and sweaty palms. The person might feel that he is having a heart attack, and panic follows. One simple treatment of panic disorder is therefore to instruct people how to breathe properly (Hibbert & Chan, 1989).

Additionally, researchers have shown that panic attacks can be produced among susceptible people by injecting them with **sodium lactate,** the chemical that builds up in our bodies when we exercise. When it is introduced directly into the bloodstreams of vulnerable individuals, or when they breathe a mixture of carbon dioxide and oxygen, a panic attack ensues (Woods & Charney, 1988). Similar interventions with people not prone to panic attacks have little effect. The importance of these demonstrations is their implication that a biochemical abnormality is at the basis of panic attacks, one activated by the challenge. However, the specific mechanism by which sodium lactate predisposes panic attacks is not clear, although it is possible that sensitive individuals begin to hyperventilate as sodium lactate increases, thus triggering a panic attack.

Some theorists propose that how we respond to such a biological challenge constitutes a strong diagnostic test for panic disorder (Dager, Cowley, & Dunner, 1987). Others are less convinced, observing that a response to sodium lactate is more strongly associated with a history of occasional panic *attacks* than it is with a history of full-blown panic *disorder* (McNally, 1990).

As mentioned earlier, panic attacks can be helped with the antidepressant medication imipramine, which presumably works via a different pathway than do the benzodiazepines (Klein, 1964; Mavissakalian & Perel, 1992a, 1992b). The mechanism behind this effect is not known. At one time it was believed that the benzodiazepines had no effect on panic, and imipramine no effect on non-panic anxiety, but this neat distinction cannot be maintained in light of more recent evidence (McNally, 1990).

Another example of physiological mechanisms in fear and anxiety disorders are reports that the experience of overwhelming terror can permanently alter a person's brain chemistry (Pitman, van der Kolk, Orr, & Greenberg, 1990). The effect is to make the individual more susceptible to fear and anxiety in the future, because the brain structures that trigger the body's emergency response have become overly sensitive. A related change attributed to the experience of terror is an increase in the secretion of **endorphins:** chemicals akin to opiates that blunt pain; this may explain the numbness that often accompanies post-traumatic stress disorder.

Genetic and evolutionary considerations   A related concern of biomedical theorists is placing fear and anxiety disorders in a genetic and evolutionary context. If the mechanisms responsible for these disorders are physiological, then perhaps they are the product of evolution. Biomedical theorists accordingly point to the continuity across species in their reactions to threat. This, of course, supports an evolutionary basis.

Darwin (1872/1899) theorized extensively about fear in his book *The Expression of the Emotions in Man and Animals,* arguing that the capacity to be afraid evolved because it was—usually—an adaptive response to a real threat. The tendency to freeze in place or to flee obviously helped one survive to see another day.

> Even extreme fear often acts at first as a powerful stimulant. A man or animal driven through terror to desperation, is endowed with wonderful strength, and is notoriously dangerous in the highest degree.   (Darwin, 1872/1899, p. 81)

Darwin's theorizing has been continued more recently by Plutchik (1980, 1984), who has similarly argued that fear is a biologically based response to situations characterized by threat. Fear indeed is a universal emotion, experienced and recognized in all cultures around the world.

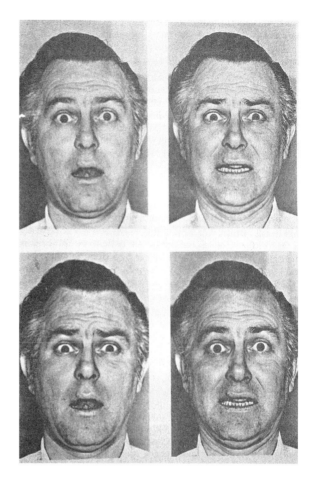

Fear is a universal emotion, experienced and recognized by people in all cultures around the world.   (Source: From P. Ekman and W. V. Friesen, *Motivation and Emotion,* Vol. 10, 1986, pp. 159-167. Reprinted by permission of W. W. Norton.)

It is not difficult to argue that fear can be adaptive. Mild levels of fear and anxiety enhance a variety of behaviors including such biologically pertinent ones as eating and sexual activity (Hinde, 1970). Learning is facilitated as well by moderate levels of arousal (Spence, 1960). However, this argument does not explain the existence of fear and anxiety disorders, which by definition are maladaptive. How do theorists explain these problems?

One possible explanation is that the predisposition to be fearful evolved in a setting where it was adaptive, but now it is displayed in another setting—the modern world—where it is not. To take the simplest case, if we live in a place where everything that makes us afraid can be successfully dealt with by freezing or by running away, then these are useful reflexes. Along these lines, Rapoport (1988, 1989) has suggested that obsessive-compulsive disorder—which often takes the form of repetitive cleaning—is derived from instincts to groom oneself and one's fellows.

According to some theorists, obsessive-compulsive disorder derives from the instinct to groom oneself and one's fellows.

Another possible explanation of the existence of these disorders is that the tendency to experience fear and anxiety is an individual difference. Some people are much more likely to be fearful than others by virtue of the makeup of their nervous system. The people who fall at the extreme end of the fearful dimension are precisely those who develop fear and anxiety disorders. Their response to threat is too highly tuned. What is advantageous for more placid individuals creates serious problems for this particular group.

Consider the following research. Mice and rats can be selectively bred for fearfulness—operationalized as the readiness to learn an avoidance response to an aversive stimulus such as electric shock (e.g., Broadhurst, 1975). An interesting aspect of these investigations is that fearful animals have fewer neural sites onto which benzodiazepines bind (Robertson, 1979). They readily acquire escape and avoidance responses, which points to the adaptive role played by fear and anxiety—but if pushed to an extreme, this capacity has its drawbacks.

Among people, the tendency to be generally nervous or not—usually termed **neuroticism** (or **trait anxiety**)—constitutes one of our basic traits, stable across time and situations (Conley, 1985; Norman, 1963). Eysenck (1990a) has studied neuroticism extensively, measuring it with a questionnaire that poses questions like the following:

1. Are you moody?

2. Do you ever experience attacks of shaking or trembling?

3. Does your mind wander while you are trying to concentrate?

4. Do you think of yourself as an irritable person?

5. Do your feelings get hurt easily?

The more a person agrees with statements such as these, the more neurotic he or she is said to be.

Neuroticism is associated with complaints of ill health (Costa & McCrae, 1980) and the poor negotiation of life's crises (Costa & McCrae, 1978). Pertinent to the present discussion, neurotic individuals are likely to suffer from fear and anxiety disorders (Jorm, 1989), although of course we should not interpret this correlation as necessarily meaning that neuroticism leads to these problems. Maybe the opposite is true; fear and anxiety disorders lead a person to be generally nervous. Or maybe there is some third factor responsible for neuroticism on the one hand and these disorders on the other.

Counting toward the possibility that neuroticism precedes fear and anxiety disorders are studies showing that neuroticism is heritable (e.g., Plomin, Chipuer, & Loehlin, 1990). This means that variation in the trait (across people) corresponds to variation in genes (again across people). The magnitude of the heritability of neuroticism is about 40%, roughly the same as for most other personality traits (Plomin, 1986). For comparison, the heritability of intelligence is about 60% (Snyderman & Rothman, 1987); neuroticism is less tied to genetic variation than is intelligence, but of the same order of magnitude.

The following question is thereby raised: What is the heritability of the various fear and anxiety disorders (Goldberg, True, Eisen, & Henderson, 1990; Stevenson, Batten, & Cherner, 1992; Wang, Crowe, & Noyes, 1992)? Research suggests that these are heritable to about the same extent as neuroticism (Andrews, Stewart, Allen, & Henderson, 1990; Marks, 1987). The highest heritability estimate is for panic disorder (Kendler, Neale, Kessler, Heath, & Eaves, 1992a, 1992b, 1992c; Torgersen, 1983).

The biggest difficulty in using the personality trait of neuroticism to explain the existence of fear and anxiety disorders is that it fails to explain why an individual develops, let us say, an obsessive-compulsive disorder rather than a generalized anxiety disorder, or vice versa (Mackinnon, Henderson, & Andrews, 1990). On the one hand, the overlap among these disorders has already been noted, and we should not expect much specificity here. But on the other hand, these problems can be distinguished by diagnosticians. Maybe the safest conclusion is that neuroticism is a contributing factor to all these disorders but not a specific cause of any one of them in particular. Eysenck (1976) would agree, proposing that the particular disorder that a person develops depends not only on his or her level of neuroticism, but also on other personality traits and specific experiences.

Biomedical treatment   The treatment that flows most readily from the biomedical perspective is pharmacological in nature, usually benzodiazepine or imipramine as discussed earlier. There is little doubt that these medications control the symptoms of both generalized anxiety disorder and panic disorder (e.g., Greenblatt & Shader, 1974). Antidepressant medications have been used with some success in treating obsessive-compulsive disorder, but there is disagreement about why these work; some believe that they are effective simply because they combat depression, thus allowing the person to control his thoughts and behaviors better (Mattick, Andrews, Hadzi-Pavlovic, & Christensen, 1990). There is less reason to think that medications like these are helpful in cases of phobia or post-traumatic stress disorder (M. J. Friedman, 1988).

Janowsky, Addario, and Risch (1987, pp. 152-153) described their pharmacological treatment of a middle-aged man who suffered from panic attacks and generalized anxiety disorder:

> *Mr. R. is a 42-year-old married White man who works as a city administrator. He has requested a consultation for treatment of his panic attacks. He describes a long history of having periods of extreme uneasiness, consisting of sweating, an ever-fearful feeling, a fast heart rate, a tight feeling in his chest, occasional hyperventilation, and a feeling of dread when confined in closed-in places, such as elevators or restaurants. Between episodes, which have occurred approximately once per week, the patient reports having felt mildly to moderately anxious, but able to function well. The patient had previously been treated for his panic attacks and anxiety with diazepam (Valium). . . .*
>
> *On the basis of the patient's history, it was decided that a trial of [imipramine] was indicated. . . . After 2 weeks . . . the patient stated that he felt slightly more relaxed. He was seen at 2-week intervals . . . and by the end of the second month of treatment was much improved, having almost no serious panic attacks. However, he also continued to avoid elevators and restaurants because he feared that he might have an attack.*

These physicians continued to prescribe Valium to Mr. R. and also referred him for behavior therapy to alleviate his fear of enclosed spaces. He progressed well, and the Valium was eventually discontinued. He continued to take imipramine to hold his panic in check.

Even when medications are effective in treating fear and anxiety disorders, there is an apparent contradiction in their typical use. If people have a disorder because of abnormal bodily processes, then the most

TABLE 7.3

POSSIBLE SIDE EFFECTS OF BENZODIAZEPINES
Though widely prescribed for fear and anxiety disorders, benzodiazepines—minor tranquilizers—are not without potential side effects.

drowsiness
lightheadedness
dry mouth
depression
nausea
constipation
blurry vision

effective way to help them is to intervene permanently to change the disordered bodily process. Medications do not do this; rather, they counteract disordered biochemistry without making any lasting changes. Said another way, Valium and imipramine do not cure anxiety disorders; by their rationale, in order to be effective, they must continue to be used (Marks & O'Sullivan, 1988). The irony is that when their short-term use is indicated, it is precisely in circumstances in which external events produce anxiety. Tranquilizers can and do help people through these rough times. But it is precisely in these circumstances as well that psychological interventions seem the most direct and beneficial in the long run.

The obvious benefit of medication is relief from the troubling—sometimes paralyzing—symptoms of fear and anxiety. The drawbacks include dietary restrictions and possible side effects (see Table 7.3), as well as the possibility of overlooking the external causes of problems. In the case of tranquilizers, we might also have to contend with dependence and abuse,[1] although mental health professionals disagree about how widespread these problems actually are (Gudex, 1991; Miller & Gold, 1991; Rifkin, 1990; Schweizer, Rickels, Case, & Greenblatt, 1990; Talley, 1990).

PSYCHODYNAMIC MODEL

Freud (1926) is well known for his theorizing about fear and anxiety disorders. He distinguished among three types of anxiety:

◆ *realistic anxiety*: a reaction to immediate and actual threat, what I have been describing as fear

---

[1] A new drug for treating anxiety disorders—**buspirone**—reportedly has fewer side effects than the benzodiazepines and does *not* lead to dependence and hence abuse (Napoliello & Domantay, 1991; Rickels, 1990; Taylor & Moon, 1991). Buspirone appears to work by targeting activity of the neurotransmitter *serotonin*, suggesting the involvement of yet another biological system in the anxiety disorders (Eison, 1990; Taylor, 1990).

◆ *neurotic anxiety*: a reaction to unacceptable impulses, typically sexual or aggressive in nature

◆ *moral anxiety*: a reaction to one's own conscience (the internalization of societal oughts and shoulds)

According to Freud, fear and anxiety disorders develop because of excessive anxiety of the neurotic or moral type and/or poor ways of dealing with it. Symptoms represent attempts to cope with anxiety when its actual sources—id impulses or superego prohibitions—are too threatening for the person to acknowledge. Thus, common to all these disorders is **repression,** the active keeping of material in the unconscious. Repression ties up psychological energy so it is not available for more productive purposes.

Freud's thinking about anxiety disorders went through several stages (Zerbe, 1990). Earlier in his career, he placed a fair amount of emphasis on constitutional (biological) factors in predisposing neurosis (Sulloway, 1979). He also acknowledged the role of actual traumatic events, such as sexual abuse, in making people susceptible to anxiety (Erdelyi, 1985). But later in his career, his emphasis was more purely intrapsychic, interpreting anxiety symptoms as displacements of unconscious fears.

In some cases, a person's anxiety is so pervasive that it is not attached to any particular situation or event. Freud termed this sort of anxiety **free-floating anxiety,** arguing that it is divorced in the person's conscious mind from given events and circumstances. There are particular sources of the anxiety, but these are too threatening to acknowledge, so the person keeps them hidden and experiences only their effects.

Symptoms as symbols   In other cases, anxiety becomes attached to particular events or circumstances. Although these are not what really worry the person, they provide clues because they bear a symbolic relationship to the actual source of distress. For example, with respect to phobias, the object or situation that a person professes to fear is not really what he fears. It somehow symbolizes his actual fear. Presumably, it is easier to deal with the symbol than the actuality.

In the well known case of Little Hans, Freud (1909a) described a young boy who was afraid of horses, not because horses posed any real threat to him, but because they were reminiscent of his father, of whom he was greatly afraid. The boy was presumably in the throes of the Oedipal conflict— *the desire to possess the opposite-sex parent sexually and the consequent fear of retaliation from the same-sex parent. What Little Hans really feared, according to Freud, was castration at the hands of his father. This was too upsetting to think about,*

because it would also require admitting his sexual desire for his mother, so Hans instead shunted his fear off to horses.

Along these lines, obsessive-compulsive disorder was interpreted by Freud (1909b) as a symbolic struggle. He suggested that a person obsesses about what he really wants to see happen. Earlier I pointed out that people tend to be obsessed about a narrow range of topics, chiefly those involving cleanliness and violence. Freud proposed that these impulses—to be messy and to be aggressive—are harbored within all people, but particularly the obsessive-compulsive individual. They stem from the anal stage of psychosexual development, during which toilet training takes place. Here the child must bend to the will of his parents, who demand that he be neat and clean. He would rather be messy, defecating when and where he wishes. He becomes extremely angry with his parents for asking that he rein in his desires.

When impulses are too strong and prohibitions too strict, what results is a **fixation,** an arresting of development so that the concerns of this early period in life continue to be the concerns of adulthood. None of this takes place at a conscious level, though, so the obsessed individual honestly believes he is concerned with being clean. The psychodynamic point, of course, is just the opposite. What the person really fears is acknowledging that the very last thing he wants to be is prim and proper.

Psychoanalytic theorists predict that obsessive-compulsive disorder is particularly apt to occur among those who possess the personality style sometimes described as obsessive (Chapter 13). These are individuals who are inordinately neat, orderly, and punctual. By psychoanalytic thought, this style reflects a fixation at the anal stage of development, and should—when the person experiences subsequent stress—give rise to a full-blown obsessive-compulsive disorder (Shapiro, 1965). The problem with this hypothesis is that the evidence contradicts it. There indeed are people who show an obsessive style (Peterson, 1992), but research shows that they are *not* at increased risk for obsessive-compulsive disorder (Rachman & Hodgson, 1980). Perhaps the resolution lies in the fact that people with an obsessive style like their personality; they find their neatness and punctuality a source of pride and satisfaction. But as you recall, those with an obsessive-compulsive disorder experience their obsessions or compulsions as alien and distasteful.

As yet another example of how psychodynamic theorists view symptoms as symbols, the person with post-traumatic stress disorder is evidencing what Freud (1920) called the *compulsion to repeat,* going back to a traumatic event over and over again to make sense of it. This tendency proved critical in the evolution of Freud's theories. Early versions of psychoanalytic theory regarded people as motivated solely to reduce tension—satisfying their instincts as quickly and thoroughly as possible. But during World War I, *battle neuroses* came to Freud's attention—what we would now call post-traumatic stress disorder—in which a person vividly relived horrible events. This did not square with the view of people as motivated to reduce tension, because here they were clearly increasing their fear and arousal.

But Freud believed some events were so traumatic that they overpowered an individual's normal capacity to reduce tension. These events would not go away until the person had come to grips with them, dissipating the excess energy these events introduced into the mind. In some cases, this happens over the course of time; the person "recovers" from the trauma. In other cases, the trauma was so great that the person's way of dealing with life events is permanently altered (Freud, 1920). This is most likely to happen when the trauma he experienced happens to coincide with lingering childhood fears, somehow underscoring his helplessness (Brenner, 1982).

For example, one of my colleagues told me of a Vietnam veteran suffering from post-traumatic stress disorder. It began when Mr. Garcia's unit was overrun by enemy soldiers. The men hid in the bushes in the hope that they would be overlooked, but some were discovered and killed on the spot. Soon thereafter, Mr. Garcia developed PTSD. It is important to know that as a child, he was present while several of his siblings were sexually abused. He struggled to remain silent and undetected, expecting to be the next victim of abuse, but he was spared. Mr. Garcia's subsequent experience in Vietnam, which would have been horrible for anyone, took on additional meaning because it was so similar to the earlier trauma he had experienced when young.

Psychodynamic treatment   In psychodynamic treatment of the fear and anxiety disorders, the therapist attempts to undo the process presumably giving rise to them (Compton, 1992a, 1992b, 1992c, 1992d). This means bringing unconscious material to light, after identifying it through dream interpretation or free association. The energy once tied up in symptoms is freed, and a catharsis occurs. Various techniques have been developed to achieve this goal (Zerbe, 1990), including the following:

✦ urging people to talk about how they feel

✦ encouraging them to develop satisfying outlets such as hobbies

✦ helping them develop insights into the causes of their anxiety

✦ making them feel more secure

✦ assisting them to feel more in control of their impulses

✦ advising them how to form mature relationships with others

Central to all these efforts is the creation of a supportive relationship between the therapist and his client.

Contemporary psychodynamic approaches to these disorders target the individual's object relations for change (e.g., L. Friedman, 1988; Settlage, 1993). Freud's emphasis on the causal role of early experiences is maintained, as well as his idea that these disorders represent immature defense mechanisms gone awry (Frayn, 1990). Less emphasis is placed on energy and drives and more on the social reality that shapes fear and anxiety (Kaplan, 1990). Some psychodynamic theorists argue for the incorporation of cognitive-behavioral concepts and treatment techniques (e.g., Windholz, 1990).

Psychodynamic therapy of the fear and anxiety disorders involves more than simply treating symptoms. Psychoanalysts acknowledge that symptoms can be removed by different interventions, but they assume that doing so does not attack the real problem. The removal of one symptom without treating the underlying problem will presumably result in the development of another, perhaps more serious symptom (Reider, 1976). This phenomenon, called *symptom substitution*, sounds plausible, but there is little evidence for it. When people's phobias are removed by behavior therapy, for example, they usually go on to live a life free of fear and anxiety (Kazdin, 1982). Symptom substitution does not typically occur.

In conclusion, the psychodynamic perspective on fear and anxiety disorders falls short of being fully satisfactory. Although highly influential in providing a vocabulary and way of thinking about these sorts of problems, the details of this approach are wrong. There is little research evidence, for example, that the specific childhood events posited by Freud typically lead to disorders. There is also little evidence that the conflicts that give rise to them are narrowly sexual or aggressive. And there is little evidence that psychodynamic therapy is as effective in treating fear and anxiety disorders as other available treatment strategies.

COGNITIVE-BEHAVIORAL MODEL

The last perspective on fear and anxiety disorders I discuss is provided by the cognitive-behavioral model.

Actually, this model provides us with several accounts of these disorders. One is strictly behavioral, emphasizing **conditioning**—simple learning of associations. Another is strictly cognitive, emphasizing illogical beliefs. And a third combines behavioral and cognitive ideas, giving us an integrated cognitive-behavioral approach to these disorders.

Behavioral approaches   Here the paradigm case of fear is provided by animal studies of classical conditioning using aversive stimuli (Mineka, 1985). When an animal is repeatedly exposed to loud noises or painful electric shocks, it comes to associate these with other stimuli in its immediate environment. It then responds to these other stimuli in their own right.

Suppose a rat is put in a box with an electrified grid as its floor. A tone sounds, and then the rat is shocked for a few seconds through the grid floor. This is repeated a number of times. Eventually the rat will show a characteristic response to the tone itself; it crouches, urinates, and defecates. Its heart rate accelerates. Its ongoing behavior is interrupted. According to theorists, the rat has learned to fear the tone through its association with the shock.

Given the opportunity, an animal will readily learn to avoid or escape from an aversive stimulus. And if there is a preceding stimulus such as a tone, it serves as a signal that the aversive stimulus is imminent. The animal will then take steps to do whatever is needed to head it off.

Such basic studies with animals have inspired a complex theoretical edifice applied to fear and anxiety disorders. Critical in this evolution was the study by Watson and Rayner (1920) of the infant Little Albert, described in Chapter 1. This case served as a persuasive demonstration that fears could be acquired in a human just as they were in an animal. Little Albert's fear of white, furry things is typically identified as a phobia. If he acquired his disorder through simple learning, then perhaps so too did people suffering other disorders.

Different disorders involving fear and anxiety reflect different variations on these basic processes of learning. Phobias of specific objects or situations reflect the simplest case of aversive conditioning. Generalized anxiety disorder presumably reflects a fear acquired in one situation that has been widely generalized to others. And so on.

The immediate objection to such explanations is how to account for the persistence of disorders. Conditioning theory suggests that most people with these difficulties do not later confront the actual stimuli that originally gave rise to their fears. Their avoidance is so successful that they do not ever again encounter whatever frightened them in the first place. Hence

they cannot learn that it is safe. But what maintains this avoidance?

One popular answer was provided by O. Hobart Mowrer (1939, 1950, 1960) in his **two process theory** of fear and avoidance. According to Mowrer, animals or people first acquire fear through classical conditioning. That is the first process. Then they learn that behaviors that avoid the original situation reduce fear. When they engage in these behaviors, avoidance is reinforced by the reduction of fear, and thus—by operant conditioning—they readily acquire these habits. That is the second process.

The paradox, if you will, of such behaviors is that animals or people never get a chance to learn anything to the contrary about the actual danger of the situation, because they always avoid it. Fear is preserved, even in situations that do not warrant it. In this way, the neurotic paradox previously described can be explained while still arguing that individuals are motivated to feel good. Applied to obsessive-compulsive disorder, for example, this theory proposes that people engage in compulsions because they reduce the anxiety associated with obsessions. Hence the rituals are reinforced and maintained over time (Rachman & Hodgson, 1980).

The practical implication of conditioning theories is that the most efficient way of combating disorders should be by exposing the individual to whatever it is that is feared and preventing escape or avoidance (Lee & Oei, 1993). Her fear should extinguish following exposure, because it is no longer associated with danger. The very first behavior therapy techniques, by the way, were deployed against phobias. All of them expose the individual—either literally or symbolically—to whatever it is she fears (e.g., Wolpe, 1958). If she is afraid of small animals, she might be sent on a tour of local pet shops. Or if he has a cleaning compulsion, he might be instructed to pick up and handle filthy items encountered on the sidewalk.

Various behavior therapy techniques that rely on exposure have been used with great success to treat fear and anxiety disorders. These include the following:

✦ **systematic desensitization:** The individual is taught to relax and then imagine objects or situations of which he is afraid, starting with mild images and moving gradually to more frightening images until these no longer elicit fear.

✦ **flooding:** The individual is exposed repeatedly to the objects or situations of which he is afraid until these elicit no fear.

✦ **modeling:** The individual watches another person successfully confront the objects or situations of which he is afraid until these elicit no fear.

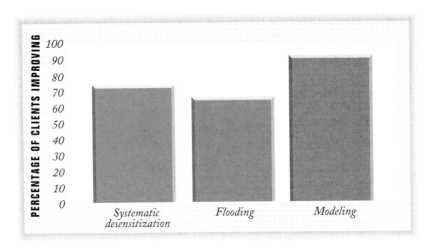

FIGURE 7.4

SUCCESS OF BEHAVIOR
THERAPY TECHNIQUES IN
TREATING SIMPLE
PHOBIAS   *Figures represent
the number of individuals
showing "marked improvement"
following treatment.*
SOURCE: DATA DERIVED FROM *Fears and
Phobias*, BY I. M. MARKS, 1969, NEW
YORK: ACADEMIC PRESS.

All are effective, particularly in reducing physiological and behavioral symptoms (see Figure 7.4).

There has been a great deal of research comparing these different approaches and trying to isolate their critical ingredients. According to Marks:

> The irreducible minimal element was found to be exposure to the discomforting stimuli. . . . When exposure was omitted from therapy, the treatment ceased to be effective. . . . This is the strongest argument for exposure's being at the core of fear reduction. In time, exposure, too, may be shown to have a variety of constit-

uents, but at present we can only guess at them. (1990, pp. 181–182)

The typical figure given for improvement is about 80% of the individuals who participate in these programs (Marks, 1990). Exposure helps those suffering from specific phobias, social phobias, panic disorder, generalized anxiety, compulsions, and post-traumatic stress disorder (Barlow, 1988).

Figure 7.5 presents a hierarchy of feared images. It was developed for the systematic desensitization of a 40-year-old male with a fear of heights dating back to his service in the army air corps during World War II (Masters, Burish, Hollon, & Rimm, 1987). He had been a navigator for a plane that flew on numerous combat missions. The fears that arose during this experience generalized to a pervasive and chronic fear of being in high places. The hierarchy is arranged in order of increasing anxiety as experienced by the client. He was taught to relax and then to work his way up the hierarchy of images, never moving on unless he felt at ease. A typical desensitization session lasts between 15 and 30 minutes. Relief usually occurs within thirty sessions (Wolpe, 1958).

Behavioral treatments of fears and phobias rely on exposure. Here a woman is being treated for her fear of heights.

Obsessive thoughts are more difficult to treat with behavioral techniques. This is not surprising because obsessions are not the overt responses against which behavior therapy is best used. One potentially useful technique is *thought stopping*, in which the individual learns to distract himself from his obsessive thoughts (Stern, 1978). After the obsessive individual fixes his obsession clearly in his mind, the therapist interrupts him by yelling "Stop!" To the degree that this interrupts the obsession, it is reinforcing. At any time and place, the client can then say "Stop!" to himself when his obsession begins.

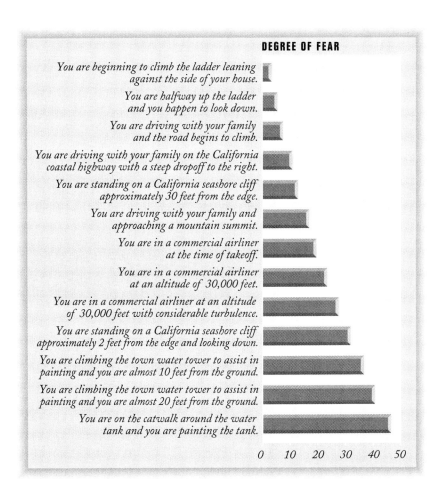

DEGREE OF FEAR

- *You are beginning to climb the ladder leaning against the side of your house.*
- *You are halfway up the ladder and you happen to look down.*
- *You are driving with your family and the road begins to climb.*
- *You are driving with your family on the California coastal highway with a steep dropoff to the right.*
- *You are standing on a California seashore cliff approximately 30 feet from the edge.*
- *You are driving with your family and approaching a mountain summit.*
- *You are in a commercial airliner at the time of takeoff.*
- *You are in a commercial airliner at an altitude of 30,000 feet.*
- *You are in a commercial airliner at an altitude of 30,000 feet with considerable turbulence.*
- *You are standing on a California seashore cliff approximately 2 feet from the edge and looking down.*
- *You are climbing the town water tower to assist in painting and you are almost 10 feet from the ground.*
- *You are climbing the town water tower to assist in painting and you are almost 20 feet from the ground.*
- *You are on the catwalk around the water tank and you are painting the tank.*

0   10   20   30   40   50

FIGURE 7.5

SYSTEMATIC DESENSITIZATION HIERARCHY   *Here is an actual hierarchy used in the systematic desensitization of a man's fear of heights (see text).* SOURCE: FROM *Behavior Therapy* (3D ED., P. 65), BY J. C. MASTERS, T. G. BURISH, S. D. HOLLON, AND D. C. RIMM, 1987, SAN DIEGO: HARCOURT BRACE JOVANOVICH.

The success of a therapy technique does not necessarily validate its theoretical rationale. While clinicians were using techniques based on conditioning with quite good success, theorists became increasingly disenchanted with the conditioning explanation of fear and anxiety disorders. Here are the sorts of concerns that were voiced (Marks, 1987):

1. TERMINOLOGY   The original conditioning explanations used terminology associated with animal learning: conditioned stimulus, unconditioned stimulus, and the like. A problem surfaces when these terms are employed outside the laboratory. When applied to actual disorders, they become metaphorical. Consider a woman who is afraid of traveling on public transportation. She can recall no traumatic incident associated with such travel. What then is the unconditioned stimulus? If we cannot identify the unconditioned stimulus, what then is the unconditioned response?

2. ABSENCE OF LEARNING   In fact, the woman in my example is rather typical in that the majority of individuals with fear and anxiety disorders can report no particular traumatic incident with which

their fear began. Although there is no question that disorders can begin with trauma, the fact remains that a fundamental premise of conditioning approaches is without consistent support. In many cases, people fear things that have never threatened them (Merckelbach, Arntz, Arrindell, & de Jong, 1992; Ollendick & King, 1991).

Consider the fear of snakes, one of the most common of the specific phobias. The vast majority of people who are afraid of snakes have never encountered one (e.g., Murray & Foote, 1979). How is it possible for them to be afraid of them? Conditioning cannot provide the answer. While it might be argued that they have repressed the memory of what originally frightened them, this takes us out of the realm of learning theories and into the realm of psychodynamic theory.

One possibility is that many of the objects and events of which people are afraid are not learned at all; people intrinsically fear them (Marks, 1987). Among most species of monkeys, for instance, writhing movements like those made by a snake frighten the animals the first time they see them (Vochteloo, Timmermans,

Duijghuisen, & Vossen, 1991). Large staring eyes are similarly frightening. So too are blood and dismembered body parts. The fear of heights is innate in many species, including people, as shown in the familiar example of a *visual cliff*, in which an infant will not crawl over a glass pane covering a steep falloff (see Figure 7.6).

3. DIFFICULTY OF CONDITIONING FEARS IN PEOPLE As it turns out, the most venerable parable of the conditioning approach—that of Little Albert—is far from typical. It is difficult to establish fears in people through conditioning. The history of psychology has seen numerous failures to replicate Watson and Rayner's original demonstration (e.g., English, 1929; Thorndike, 1935), but rarely are these failures mentioned by behavioral psychologists eager to bolster their argument about the importance of conditioning (Samelson, 1980).

Furthermore, even when fears are conditioned in people in the laboratory, they are usually quite frag-

FIGURE 7.6

VISUAL CLIFF *Children are reluctant to crawl across a transparent surface when the pattern below suggests depth. This implies that fear of heights may have an inherent basis.*

ile—that is, easily extinguished. Fear and anxiety disorders, in contrast, are highly resilient and often chronic. Remember Wayne Gretzky's fear of flying. Although his fear apparently began with a few close calls early in his career, the thousands of flights he subsequently took without encountering any danger were not sufficient to extinguish his fear.

Faced with the evidence that it is difficult to condition fears directly, theorists have argued that disorders are usually acquired vicariously, by observing others with these problems and then making them one's own through the process of *modeling* (Bandura, 1986). Repeated modeling maintains the fear.

Examples of this certainly exist. One likely reason why Wayne Gretzky continued to be afraid of flying, even when his midair mishaps ceased, was the presence of a frightened flying companion. But there is reason to be skeptical of modeling as a widespread explanation. The majority of people with phobias or obsessive-compulsive disorder, for instance, do not have a friend or family member with the same disorder (Marks, 1987). And even if there is a relative with the same sort of disorder, the details may differ. Two phobic individuals in the same family might be afraid of different situations; two obsessive-compulsive individuals might have different rituals.

4. INCUBATION It should be obvious by now that a traumatic incident can sometimes be identified that is relevant to the fear an individual displays. One of the interesting aspects of these cases is that there may be a time lag between the incident and the development of the disorder.

Marks (1987), for example, described a young man who had his leg fractured in a motorcycle accident. During his recovery, he experienced no anxiety when thinking or talking about motorcycles and in fact looked forward to riding again. But once he got back on his motorcycle, he became extremely anxious. He returned home and never rode again. His accident had something to do with his fear, but why did it take 6 months to develop?

Along these same lines, some cases of posttraumatic stress disorder do not develop immediately following the traumatic incident. It may take months or even years, when some trifling incident seems to unleash the problem. In contrast, when fear is studied as I have described among laboratory subjects, there is no lag between conditioning and the manifestation of a fear response.

5. SYMBOLISM The strong point of the psychodynamic account of fears and phobias is its recognition that these disorders have symbolic aspects.

This is one of the weak points of the conditioning approach.

Prince (1914) described the case of a woman who had a phobia of church bells. The phobia began following her mother's death from a lingering illness. The woman would go every day to church to pray for her mother's recovery, to the accompaniment of church bells. One day she happened to neglect her prayers, and by coincidence, that was the day her mother died. Shortly thereafter, she began to fear the ringing of church bells. There is no difficulty in making sense of the woman's phobia. The ringing church bells symbolized her guilt about neglecting her prayers. The point is that a conditioning model of phobias cannot readily explain this dynamic.

Behavioral theorists have tried to explain such symbols in terms of "stimulus generalization" (Marks, 1987), but this does a disservice to what is meant by a symbol as well as to what is meant by stimulus generalization. Again, we see a problem with learning terminology applied metaphorically.

6. FIT TO DIFFERENT DISORDERS The conditioning model does not do equal justice across the range of fear and anxiety disorders. Its best fit is probably to specific phobias, which is why I have used so many of these as examples. But the other disorders do not lend themselves nearly as well to a conditioning explanation. Because at least some obsessions and compulsions raise a person's anxiety, as opposed to lowering it, it is difficult to argue that these represent responses acquired because they reduce fear. And in panic disorder, although the conditioning model can explain why people come to avoid situations associated with panic attacks, it cannot explain why a person would have these attacks in the first place. They often appear with no obvious precipitant.

Seligman (1970, 1971) attempted to correct the problems of the conditioning view of fear and anxiety disorders, while still interpreting them within the context of learning theory. He took issue with the traditional assumption of animal learning theories that all responses are acquired in essentially the same way, according to the same psychological laws. This position is termed *equipotentiality* and has been a mainstay of animal learning: "Pigeon, rat, monkey, which is which? It doesn't matter. . . . Behavior shows astonishingly similar properties" (Skinner, 1956, pp. 230-231). Equipotentiality provides the rationale that allows psychologists to study rats and pigeons doing arbitrary things like running through mazes or pecking at levers and then generalizing to people.

Although equipotentiality makes the study of learning a simple and grand endeavor, it turns out to be a wrong assumption. Some things are easier to learn than other things, and what is easy or difficult depends in a sensible way on the species in question. The belated discovery that the "laws of learning" may vary with the species and with the response to be learned has made for a revolution in the psychology of learning (Seligman & Hager, 1972).

Seligman (1970, 1971) argued that there are several types of learning defined by how easily they occur. Of interest here is one of these types: **prepared learning,** which is a form of learning presumably predisposed by the evolutionary history of a species. It can be recognized by several criteria. It occurs suddenly, sometimes with but a single exposure. It can take place with wide separation in time and space between stimulus and response. It is "irrational" in that a person acknowledges that the learned association makes no sense. And it is highly resistant to extinction.

Seligman further argued that the recognition of biological constraints on learning sheds light on the fear and anxiety disorders. Fears presumably prove difficult to condition in the laboratory because researchers often use biologically irrelevant objects or situations. This may explain why fears are acquired so readily outside of the laboratory and why they adhere to such a narrow range of objects—those that were potentially hazardous in the course of evolution (Epstein, 1992). It may also explain why fear and anxiety can be so resistant to extinction. Some theorists have extended notions of preparedness to obsessive-compulsive disorder, again arguing that biologically relevant themes are at work (Rachman & Hodgson, 1980).

Laboratory investigations have tested some of the hypotheses derived from this theory. Specifically, classical conditioning should take place more readily to "natural" stimuli, such as spiders and snakes, than to "artificial" stimuli, such as electric outlets or automobiles (e.g., Ohman, Fredrikson, Hugdahl, & Rimmo, 1976). Research support for preparedness is at best mixed (e.g., McNally, 1987). However, it might still be useful in explaining fears and phobias outside the laboratory.

Cognitive approaches Another perspective within the cognitive-behavioral approach looks at the characteristic thoughts and beliefs entertained by individuals who suffer from fear and anxiety disorders. Kelly (1955) sketched an early version of this notion, regarding anxiety as the emotion that accompanies a person's realization that he does not know how to make sense of what is occurring.

The most thorough statement of the cognitive approach is by Beck and Emery (1985). According to them, at the core of all these disorders is an individual's sense of exaggerated vulnerability. He views himself as subject to dangers over which he has no control; further, he lacks the ability to ensure his own safety. These beliefs lead to the various manifestations of anxiety and also end up interfering with how he actually confronts threats. They produce disasters, which then validate the doubts—thus a vicious circle.

Cognitive theorists suggest that panic attacks stem from a person's particular way of interpreting bodily symptoms—as evidence that he is going crazy or going to die—which then magnifies these symptoms until a full-blown attack occurs (Clark, 1988). This view is even used to make sense of why biological challenges like sodium lactate produce panic attacks. The individual *expects* them to do so (Sanderson, Rapee, & Barlow, 1989). Similarly, cognitive theorists interpret the effectiveness of drug treatments as due at least in part to the person's expectations.

Helping to maintain fear and anxiety are certain core beliefs—Beck and Emery (1985) regard them as "illogical"—and styles of thinking that make it difficult for the individual to notice any evidence to the contrary. In phobias, a person's beliefs focus on certain objects and situations. In generalized anxiety disorder, the person sees himself as at risk for broader dangers: rejection or attack or disease or death.

Beck and Emery make extensive use of the notion of a cognitive **schema**—a set of organized beliefs about some topic, in this case, one's own vulnerability. A man with a social phobia, for example, presumably entertains a theory about what will happen to him in certain social situations if he behaves in particular ways. This schema about himself and the social world influences his subsequent feelings, attention, memories, and actions. Schema concepts have become popular within psychology, but they can be ambiguous and/or circular (Costello, 1992; Segal, 1988). Usually they are not measured independently of the sorts of behaviors they are invoked to explain. Relatedly, the success of cognitive therapy, although beginning to be established, has not yet been linked to changes in postulated cognitive schemas (Brewin, 1989).

Cognitive approaches usually do not grapple with the origins of anxiety-producing cognitive schemas. They can explain why these cognitive structures maintain themselves; it is the nature of a schema to resist contrary evidence. But it is another matter to explain where they originate. Usually the point is made that they are the product of socialization, but actual studies documenting the origin of anxiety-producing beliefs in specific childhood experiences have yet to be undertaken.

The cognitive approach gives rise to its own therapeutic strategy: identifying the thoughts that maintain anxiety and then trying to change them (Beck, 1991).

Thoughts can sometimes be combated through persuasion or logic, encouraging the individual to explore the presumed consequences of his or her exaggerated beliefs and see that they have little basis. Other times, thoughts are effectively challenged by encouraging the client to act differently.

Consider the 23-year-old woman treated by Cottraux and Mollard (1988) for a lifelong phobia surrounding the swallowing of food. Since infancy, this woman had been afraid to swallow. Her mother reportedly had to pinch her nose in order to make her open her mouth and eat. When the woman was 10 years of age, she choked while eating in a restaurant. Those present had to reach down her throat in order to remove the trapped food. Following this episode, she could eat only by mincing all of her food first. And while eating, she constantly checked with her fingers that no large pieces of food were caught in her mouth.

According to Cottraux and Mollard, at the core of this woman's phobia was a schema linking eating and danger. She feared choking and subsequent death. As a result, she avoided being alone because she believed that only other people could rescue her if she did begin to choke. She could not work or attend school. She could not go shopping.

In treatment, the woman's beliefs about eating and choking were identified, examined, and disputed. For example, she interpreted salivation as a sign that she was beginning to choke. A more reasonable interpretation, which she eventually accepted, was that her salivation indicated that she was eating in normal fashion. The possibility that salivation made swallowing easier had never before occurred to her until it was pointed out in therapy as an alternative to her prevailing beliefs.

Also challenged in treatment was the sweeping generalization made by the woman on the basis of the single episode of choking when she was 10. In view of all the food consumed before and after this episode, how reasonable was it for her to believe that this was a likely future occurrence? She originally responded that she was an unlucky person, hence apt to choke. Then the basis for her belief in being unlucky was disputed. Treatment worked well for this woman. She stopped mincing her food and checking her mouth while eating. She began to venture out alone, and she started to take university classes.

The effectiveness of cognitive therapy for fear and anxiety disorders is just now being evaluated, but reports so far are promising. For example, Michelson and colleagues (1990) found that panic disorder can be treated effectively in a 12-week period using cognitive therapy. The hope is that the changes brought about by these interventions will be long-lasting, because they impart to the individual skills that he or she can use to combat fear and anxiety in the future (Emmelkamp & Beens, 1991; Foa, Kozak, Steketee, & McCarthy, 1992; Oakley & Padesky, 1990; Sokol, Beck, Greenberg, Wright, & Berchick, 1989).

Cognitive-behavioral treatment   Many therapists today do not distinguish between behavioral and cognitive treatments of disorders, instead combining techniques from both strategies. As just noted, one of the effective ways to combat people's beliefs about their own lack of ability is to devise exercises that demonstrate to them that they do have the ability. Some cognitive theorists believe that such behavioral strategies as gradual exposure are effective precisely because they challenge fearful people's thoughts about their abilities to confront stressful situations (Bandura, 1977, 1986). Once beliefs are changed, then behaviors change.

Consider some of the approaches that are used to treat fear and anxiety disorders. Note how they combine behavioral and cognitive elements. For example, one version of systematic desensitization for phobias allows the fearful individual to choose how quickly or

slowly he progresses through the hierarchy of fearful images (MacDonough, Adams, & Tesser, 1973). This is more effective in eventually reducing fear than having the therapist make such decisions, presumably because it allows the client to feel more in control.

Butler, Cullington, Munby, Amies, and Gelder (1984) devised a cognitive-behavioral treatment for social phobias that combines the identification and change of irrational beliefs with relaxation and gradual exposure to feared situations. Barlow and his colleagues treat panic disorder with a cognitive-behavioral approach that includes gradually exposing individuals to the physiological symptoms of panic, training them how to breathe correctly, providing them with information about panic attacks, and correcting their exaggerated beliefs about them (Barlow, 1990, 1992; Margraf, Barlow, Clark, & Telch, 1993). All of these treatment components arguably strengthen one another, and what results is an effective strategy for alleviating what otherwise might be an intractable difficulty.

Such multiple treatments also have been created for GAD, obsessive-compulsive disorder, and PTSD (e.g., Borkovec & Mathews, 1988; Borkovec et al., 1987; Clark, Salkovskis, & Chalkey, 1985; Keane & Kaloupek, 1982). Although the general effectiveness of such cognitive-behavioral approaches is well accepted, uncertainty remains about their critical ingredients.

CONCLUSIONS

I have discussed in this section three different approaches to fear and anxiety disorders: the biomedical, the psychodynamic, and the cognitive-behavioral. None of them is complete. Yet each has its strengths.

Freud's account of fear and anxiety disorders is probably the least compelling, despite its role in early thinking about the psychological aspects of these disorders. On the more positive side, the hypothesis that early events play a role in later disorders is reasonable, although psychoanalysts are hardly alone in making this general prediction. Perhaps the major contribution of the psychodynamic approach is that symptoms have meaning to the individual; they are not simply bodily responses. They hold significance in his or her life.

Some combination of the current models is no doubt needed to explain particular disorders (see Focus on Sex Differences in Fear and Anxiety Disorders). Indeed, a biopsychosocial perspective seems most compelling. Evolution has produced physiological mechanisms like the GABA system that underlie our experience of fear and anxiety, within normal and abnormal ranges. Processes of learning influence how and why we attach these experiences to specific events and circumstances in the world. Not to be overlooked in this process of attachment is the meaning of events, at both conscious and unconscious levels.

Professor Gallagher and his controversial technique of simultaneously confronting the fear of heights, snakes, and the dark.

FOCUS ON

Sex Differences

in Fear and

Anxiety Disorders

MALES AND FEMALES DIFFER in the likelihood of experiencing several of the fear and anxiety disorders covered in this chapter: simple phobia, social phobia, panic disorder, generalized anxiety disorder, and post-traumatic stress disorder (see Figure 7.7). In each case, women are more likely to suffer from the problem than men (Bourdon, Boyd, Rae, & Burns, 1988; Cameron & Hill, 1989). Indeed, among those with fear and anxiety disorders, women are more likely than men to have a severe and chronic version (Scheibe & Albus, 1992).

Sex differences in the prevalence of psychological problems seem to be more the rule than the exception, so it is instructive to stop and consider some of the reasons why men and women might differ in the problems they apparently experience. The possibility of inadvertent bias by diagnosticians must be considered, although it seems unlikely that all documented sex differences reside solely in the eye of the beholder. What more substantive reasons can be cited for these differences in prevalence? As implied in the text, we should not expect any single explanation to suffice in all cases.

The biomedical model of abnormality suggests that the basis for sex differences in fear and anxiety is found in the biological differences between the sexes. However, there is no good evidence that biological differences between men and women directly translate themselves into the observed prevalence differences.

A somewhat more complex proposal is that the biological predisposition to be fearful may have different consequences for men and women. Men who are neurotic are more likely than their female counterparts to use drugs or alcohol to calm and/or distract themselves (e.g., Harris, Noyes, Crowe, & Chaudhry, 1983). What results is a difference in diagnosable problems. This hypothesis also accounts for why men are more apt than women to have substance abuse problems. A similar argument has been made about why women are more likely to be depressed than men: they do not resort to drugs to distract themselves from negative thoughts.

A related argument that makes no mention of substance abuse simply posits that women are more apt to ruminate about fearful possibilities than are men (Nolen-Hoeksema, 1991). In fact, research suggests that women are worried and concerned about a broader range of topics (e.g., Kessler & McLeod, 1984; Lampert & Friedman, 1992). Something about the way gender roles have developed in our society results in women being more concerned about matters than men.

Speaking of gender roles, those in the United States expect women to be passive and dependent and men to be stoic and unexpressive. Said another way, the typical female role in our society is an anxiety disorder waiting to happen (Fodor, 1974). Whether

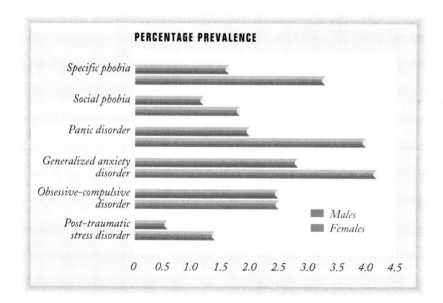

FIGURE 7.7

SEX DIFFERENCES IN THE PREVALENCE OF FEAR AND ANXIETY DISORDERS   *In general, women are more likely than men to experience fear and anxiety disorders.*

we term it being demure, modest, and feminine or passive, cautious, and fearful, we end up with women encouraged by their socialization to act in ways that are very close to being "disorders" from the DSM perspective. A prediction from this analysis is that sex differences in the prevalence of fear and anxiety disorders in our society will narrow if and when our gender roles converge.

A final point to make about sex differences as they relate to fear and anxiety disorders looks at the role of actual events in producing fear and anxiety. In our society, women are much more vulnerable to physical dangers than men. They are more likely to be charged with the care of children and hence to worry about their welfare as well. They are also more likely to be impoverished and thus forced to live and work in unsafe conditions.

Consider the crime of rape. By some estimates, perhaps 1 million women are raped every year in the United States (Beirne & Messerschmidt, 1991). This is a staggering statistic. Burgess and Holmstrom (1974) described what follows rape as the *rape trauma syndrome.* The acute phase of this syndrome lasts for several weeks following the assault, and here the victim is either excessively emotional or excessively subdued. In the long-term phase, she struggles to come to grips with the assault. She tries to avoid reminders of the crime. She may change her job or her residence. She may be highly anxious. And she may be depressed. In many ways, the rape trauma syndrome is an example of PTSD (cf. Bownes, O'Gorman, & Sayers, 1991; Dahl, 1989). More generally, any of the fear and anxiety disorders can follow in the wake of sexual assault (Girelli, Resick, Marhoefer-Dvorak, & Hutter, 1986; Kilpatrick, Veronen, & Resick, 1979).

Psychologists in recent years have increasingly recognized that the victim of sexual assault may need specific help in dealing with the ensuing fear and anxiety. Cognitive-behavioral strategies like those described in the text appear promising (e.g., Foa, Rothbaum, Riggs, & Murdock, 1991). Needless to say, the goal for us all is to change society so that sexual assaults do not occur in the first place. When women (and men) can lead safer lives than they do now, perhaps we will see a marked decrease in the prevalence of fear and anxiety disorders.

More generally, the point made earlier that fear and anxiety have different components is important to keep in mind when we try to explain these disorders and devise treatments for them. We increasingly encounter the conclusion that a combination of treatments—for instance, benzodiazepines *and* exposure—is superior to the use of just one or the other (Greist, 1992; Heimberg & Barlow, 1991; Mattick, Andrews, Hadzi-Pavlovic, & Christensen, 1990; Mavissakalian, 1990; Rickels & Schweizer, 1990).

Although much work remains to be done, fear and anxiety disorders represent a success story for psychology. Compared to just a few decades ago, we know an incredible amount about the risk factors and mechanisms that produce these disorders. We also know a great deal about how to help people who suffer from them. In subsequent chapters, I frequently mention the ideas discussed in this chapter, because excessive fear and anxiety figure in many other disorders.

Summary

DEFINING FEAR AND ANXIETY

✦ Fear refers to the emotional, cognitive, physiological, and behavioral responses we make when specifically threatened. Anxiety refers to a similar complex of responses that we make to nonspecific threats. There exist several disorders characterized by excessive fear and anxiety.

PHOBIA

✦ A specific phobia is a persistent fear of a circumscribed object or situation. A social phobia is a persistent fear of being in a situation where some act must be performed under the critical scrutiny of others.

PANIC DISORDER

✦ In panic disorder, the individual experiences recurrent attacks of panic: discrete periods of intense fear. Frequently occurring along with panic attacks is agoraphobia, the persistent fear of being in a situation from which escape is not possible.

GENERALIZED ANXIETY DISORDER

✦ Generalized anxiety disorder involves excessive and unrealistic anxiety cutting across a variety of life's domains.

OBSESSIVE-COMPULSIVE DISORDER

✦ In obsessive-compulsive disorders, people experience persistent obsessions—intrusive and disquieting ideas—or compulsions—repetitive acts carried out to prevent some dreaded consequence.

POST-TRAUMATIC STRESS DISORDER

✦ Post-traumatic stress disorder follows some traumatic event, and is marked by a repeated reexperiencing of the trauma, reduced involvement in the external world, and diverse signs of anxiety.

THEORETICAL PERSPECTIVES

✦ Several of the popular models of abnormality have a great deal to say about the origin and treatment of fear and anxiety disorders.

✦ The biomedical model attempts to specify the physiological mechanisms giving rise to fear and anxiety; a number of such mechanisms seem to exist. The biomedical model also tries to make sense of fear and anxiety disorders in terms of genetics and evolutionary theory, suggesting that these problems are extreme and perhaps outmoded versions of once adaptive reactions. Biomedical treatment relies on drugs. Tranquilizers are effective in reducing symptoms of fear and anxiety. Imipramine, an antidepressant, is useful for combating panic attacks.

✦ The psychodynamic model interprets the symptoms of fear and anxiety disorders in symbolic terms, as signs of underlying emotional conflicts that the person is unable to consciously acknowledge. This approach has the virtue of explaining why people tend to fear a narrow range of objects and situations; they have specific symbolic significance. Psychodynamic treatment aims at bringing unconscious material to light, presumably freeing the energy tied up in symptoms and making it available for other purposes.

✦ The cognitive-behavioral model provides several perspectives on fear and anxiety disorders. One perspective views them as the product of simple conditioning. This approach is persuasive in many cases, and has inspired successful treatments, but nonetheless possesses certain theoretical shortcomings. An attempt to address these theoretical difficulties while still viewing fear and anxiety disorders in terms of learning theory suggests that these disorders are the result of prepared learning, conditioning predisposed by evolution. Another perspective provided by the cognitive-behavioral model explains fear and anxiety disorders as due to exaggerated beliefs about vulnerability. Therapy attempts to change these beliefs and replace them with more benign notions.

✦ The future will probably see an integration of these approaches to explain and treat fear and anxiety disorders.

Key Terms

agoraphobia	free-floating anxiety
anxiety	GABA (gamma-amino-butyric acid)
anxiety disorder	
benzodiazepine	generalized anxiety disorder; GAD
buspirone	imipramine
compulsion	modeling
conditioning	neurotic disorder
emergency reaction	neuroticism; trait anxiety
endorphins	obsession
fear	obsessive-compulsive disorder; OCD
fear disorder	panic disorder
fixation	post-traumatic stress disorder; PTSD
flooding	

prepared learning

repression

schema

social phobia

sodium lactate

specific phobia

stress

systematic
  desensitization

two process theory

Somatoform and Dissociative Disorders

8 *In Oshkosh, Wisconsin, the local people gather at Menominee Park to pass the time. Mark, age 31, was in the park one day, where he met a 26-year-old woman who called herself Franny. As the two talked, Franny rapidly underwent several profound changes in how she behaved. Her friends told Mark that she suffered from a psychological problem:* multiple personality disorder. *The changes he witnessed were the comings and goings of the different personalities that inhabited her body. The woman's real name was Sarah.*

Several days later, Mark called Sarah and asked her out, but it was Franny who went on the date. Over a

cup of coffee, she told him about another personality, Jennifer, a 20-year-old woman who liked to dance and have a good time. Later during the date, Mark asked Jennifer to come forth. When she did, he asked her, "Can I love you?" In the backseat of his car, they began to have intercourse, when yet another personality emerged—Emily, a 6-year-old girl. Mark asked Emily to keep the activities she witnessed a secret, but Emily and Franny subsequently "told" Sarah what had happened. She called the police and told them she had been sexually assaulted.

Are you confused by this story? The events actually happened, setting the stage for one of the strangest criminal trials in recent years (Smolowe, 1990; see also Perr, 1991; Serban, 1992). Mark was tried under a Wisconsin law making it a crime to have sex with those known to be incapable of understanding their own conduct. The key issue was whether he knew that Sarah suffered from multiple personality disorder. Critical in establishing this point was the testimony of her different personalities, who were sworn in separately.

Mark was found guilty by a jury, but then a circuit judge ordered a new trial, because Mark's lawyer had not been allowed to request a psychiatric examination of Sarah. The ruling reflects the widespread skepticism that surrounds multiple personality disorder. Indeed, some critics have argued that the disorder does not exist, but is intentionally manufactured by an individual (Orne, Dinges, & Orne, 1984) and/or unintentionally created by the encouragement and interest of a therapist (Kluft, 1987, 1989; Spanos, Weekes, & Bertrand, 1985). In any event, if it could be argued that Sarah did not actually have this problem, then there would be no basis for the original charge against Mark.

The prosecution decided not to ask for a second trial, citing concerns about Sarah's condition. It was feared that the rigors of another trial would cause her to deteriorate. In fact, she reported that the number of separate personalities within her had increased from 21 to 46 in the 5 months between the original incident with Mark and his subsequent trial.

This case introduces the subject matter of the present chapter: disorders in which an individual's problems are other than they first seem. In **somatoform disorders,** the person shows symptoms such as pain, blindness, or deafness that seem to imply the presence of a physical illness or injury—yet none exists. And in **dissociative disorders,** the person shows breaks in memory, consciousness, and/or identity that seem to imply the presence of a neurological impairment—yet again none exists.

Both groups of disorders were once classified together as forms of *hysteria,* which I have already

French neurologist Jean Charcot (1825–1893) treated hysteria with hypnosis.

mentioned several times throughout the book. Hysteria in turn was considered one of the neuroses. Recent diagnostic systems have separated them in order to be more precise, but I can still make similar points about each (cf. Roy, 1982).

Somatoform and dissociative disorders are challenging for most of us to conceptualize because they are characterized by discontinuities. In the case of somatoform disorders, the discontinuity is between a person's physical malfunctioning and the underlying causes. In the case of dissociative disorders, the discontinuity is between a person's different memories or selves. Obviously, Sarah did not simply act in different ways at different times, which we all do. Instead, she claimed that her memories and her very sense of self were fragmented. Her dominant personality Sarah did not know what her fun-loving personality Jennifer was doing unless told by yet a third personality.

We expect an individual to be coherent—single and unified. The idea of a person having two or more selves is jarring. And the idea that someone is blind even though his eyes work perfectly well also strikes us as unusual. We are tempted to believe that these people are faking (Merskey, 1992).

Many of us have on occasion fabricated physical or psychological symptoms to avoid dreaded engagements. But somatoform and dissociative disorders are not the same thing. Tabloid discussions of these problems are often so exaggerated that they invite disbelief (see Jaroff, 1993), but some number of these exist. Those who genuinely experience such difficulties are *not* willfully controlling their symptoms.

Relatedly, these disorders put a great strain on our assumption of continuity between normality and abnormality. In Chapter 7, it was easy to see that fear and anxiety disorders exist in degrees, that ordinary people in their everyday lives experience mild versions of these problems. But is there a mild or mundane version of multiple personality disorder?

By definition, somatoform and dissociative disorders do not have organic causes. A man who cannot see because his visual cortex has been damaged is not showing a conversion disorder; he simply cannot see. A woman who displays different identities or shows profound problems with memory because of a neurological disease is not diagnosed with a dissociative disorder; she has a neurological problem. In Chapter 6, I argued against separating too rigidly organic and psychological etiologies, but in the case of these disorders, what makes them so interesting is precisely our ability to make this separation.

The psychodynamic model is often useful in specifying the direct causes of these disorders, because it took form in an attempt to explain them. Psychodynamic theories explicitly recognize the discontinuities within people and have no difficulty explaining why individuals may show different strands of memory and consciousness. Somatoform disorders are interpreted as the channeling of emotional conflicts into physical symptoms. These symptoms presumably bear a symbolic relationship to the conflict in question. Abse (1987) described the case of a woman who became blind in one eye after seeing a hated rival enter a room; her other eye, which was covered by the wide-brimmed hat she was wearing, was unaffected, because with it she had not seen the other woman.

Dissociative disorders are similarly seen as attempts to cope with threatening memories and impulses by segregating them from conscious life. Multiple personality disorder is a striking version of this tendency. Here rather than threatening impulses being kept completely out of consciousness, they take on an existence of their own, apart from the preexisting consciousness of the person. This way the one personality does not know what the others are doing, as you saw in the case of Sarah, who was oblivious to the sexual activities of Jennifer. As I discuss later, traumatic events may figure prominently in the past of those who develop dissociative disorders.

Anxiety is often involved in the somatoform and dissociative disorders, but not necessarily manifest anxiety as discussed in the preceding chapter. Instead, if we follow psychodynamic thinking, we can argue that the anxiety involved here is below the surface and that the symptoms we see are defenses against it. The person may consciously be quite cool, calm, and collected, precisely because his defenses are adequate to the task at hand. But as you learned in Chapter 3, the tying up of psychic energy in defenses may cost a person dearly, creating other problems in living.

Diagnosis of the somatoform and dissociative disorders is apt to be a thorny matter, precisely because we cannot rely solely on surface symptoms. Although it is straightforward to ascertain that this person is not walking or hearing or whatever, it is another thing to show that his inability is not due to organic impairment or malingering. Rather, the diagnostician must show that his problem stems from underlying psychological dynamics. By definition, the patient is not in the best position to tell her much of anything. The person with somatoform disorder truly believes he has a physical problem (Krull & Schifferdecker, 1990). And the person with amnesia cannot explain why he has lost his memory.

The possibility of confusing somatoform and dissociative disorders with other problems having actual organic etiology is a constant risk. Because the risks for overlooking actual organic impairment are considerable, we find some health professionals being conservative and opting to treat people as if they really do have a physical problem. Hypochondriacal individuals, for example, may change doctors until they find one to take their symptoms at face value. Granted the recent increase in malpractice suits in the United States, many physicians may be ever more willing to go along with the complaints of their patients, even when they appear hypochondriacal.

Any time a diagnosis is made by the *exclusion* of factors, the risk of error is increased (Chapter 2). In some number of cases, obvious mistakes *are* made. A particularly notable demonstration comes from a study by Pincus and Tucker (1978) in which individuals diagnosed with somatoform disorder at one point in time were later contacted. More than half of them were found to be suffering from actual physical ailments, including such neurological problems as Parkinson's disease and multiple sclerosis. While some of these illnesses developed independently of somatoform disorder, it seems as if many of the original diagnoses were wrong. The diagnostician mistook early signs of neurological disease for somatoform symptoms (see also Jones & Barklage, 1990; Slater & Glithero, 1965).

Striking about these disorders is that some of them have changed markedly in prevalence over the years (Shorter, 1992). Conversion disorder, the most dramatic form of somatoform disorder, was common during the 19th century. Today, the condition is rare. Perhaps education about how our bodies work and do not work has been responsible for this change. If we interpret an individual's conversion symptoms as a "solution" to an emotional problem, then the solution cannot be viable unless it is credible to his or her unconscious mind (Shorter, 1992).

Other problems, notably multiple personality disorder, have shown an apparent rise during the late

Interest in multiple personality disorder was sparked by the famous case of The Three Faces of Eve. *Joanne Woodward played Eve in the 1957 movie based on this story.*

20th century (Goff & Simms, 1993). Although this problem was first described in the 1800s, so few cases were reported during the first part of the 20th century that many experts decided the disorder was extinct, if it ever had existed. But then the famous case of "The Three Faces of Eve" surfaced in the 1950s (Thigpen & Cleckley, 1954, 1957), and thereafter additional cases were documented. Not only have the number of multiple personality cases increased, but so too has the apparent complexity of individual cases. Most of the classic cases in the 1800s had but two or three separate personalities. But today dozens of personalities can be found. Remember that Sarah had 46 different personalities at last count. What is behind such inflation?

Psychological treatments for somatoform and dissociative disorders exist. Somatoform disorders often prove highly resistant (Nemiah, 1980b), although the dissociative disorders have an impressively high rate of improvement. This includes multiple personality disorder—and illustrates an important point: We might think that the most unusual forms of psychological abnormality would prove particularly intractable, but this is not always so (Ross, 1990).

SOMATOFORM DISORDERS

Before I discuss specific somatoform disorders, I want to introduce several terms to describe conditions that might be confused with them. As already noted, a valid diagnosis of somatoform disorders can be a challenge, because they often look like something else. The diagnostician must be alert to the possibility that he may not be seeing a somatoform disorder but one of the following instead:

♦ **malingering:** intentional faking by the individual in order to achieve some specific goal

♦ **factitious disorder:** again, intentional faking of the signs of illness for no reason except medical attention; in some cases, called *Munchausen syndrome*, this takes a chronic course as the person alters medical records and tests, requests multiple operations, and the like

♦ **psychosomatic disorder:** physical basis to the symptom, even if the eventual cause of this physical basis is psychological in nature (an ulcer brought about by stress is a psychosomatic disorder because it involves actual damage to the stomach lining, whereas complaints of a stomach ache with no tissue pathology would be a somatoform disorder)

The most likely possibility other than a somatoform disorder is an actual physical illness.

An interesting example of what is known as Munchausen syndrome by proxy *was a 14-year-old in Ypsilanti, Michigan, named Katherine Stuart (Dowling, 1990). Her mother was so concerned about her daughter's health that she brought her to one doctor or another almost every other day since her birth for such complaints as heart trouble, epilepsy, back pain, dizziness, nausea, ulcer, learning disability, and weak ankles. Over the years, Katherine had been subjected to numerous X-rays, allergy tests, pelvic exams, and ultrasound tests. Physicians always found the girl to be in perfect physical health, although she and her mother reported numerous complaints and symptoms. One year, Katherine missed 62 of a possible 180 school days. Mrs. Stuart herself was retired on a disability pension because of poor health. When this case came to the attention of juvenile authorities, a county judge charged Mrs. Stuart with neglect and removed her daughter from her custody. She had previously lost two other children for the same reason. Even so, Mrs. Stuart maintained that she was a loving parent doing her best.*

Somatoform disorders sometimes co-occur with anxiety and depression. You saw in the previous chapter that anxiety includes physiological symptoms, and to the degree that these predominate, it can be difficult to say whether an individual has an anxiety disorder or a somatoform disorder (see Focus on Morita Psy-

chotherapy). Similarly, depression also includes characteristic physiological symptoms; in some forms of depression, these predominate (Chapter 9). Again, it can be difficult to decide just what is depression and what is a somatoform disorder. Some theorists are of the opinion that all of these should be classified together (e.g., Kenyon, 1976; Ladee, 1966).

DSM-IV distinguishes among several somatoform disorders (see Table 8.1). Appreciate that specific phobias concerning illnesses—also called **nosophobias**—might be classified here, although I have already mentioned them in the previous chapter. And eating disorders such as *anorexia nervosa*, in which a person has unrealistic ideas about the size and shape of her body, might also be considered a somatoform disorder.

TABLE 8.1

SOMATOFORM DISORDERS *DSM-IV describes several disorders with apparent physical symptoms that involve no physical cause.*

DISORDER	CHARACTERIZATION AND TREATMENT
conversion disorder	the alteration or loss of physical functioning that suggests a bodily cause but instead is an expression of a psychological conflict or need
	helped by supportive therapy, family therapy, physical interventions capitalizing on suggestibility
hypochondriasis	the preoccupation with having or contracting serious disease, in the absence of any medical reason
	difficult to treat; may be helped by behavior therapy
somatization disorder	the repeated concern with a variety of bodily complaints, in the absence of any medical reason
	difficult to treat; may be helped by cognitive-behavior therapy, family therapy
body dysmorphic disorder	the preoccupation with an imagined defect in the appearance of a normal-appearing person
	may be outgrown; may be helped by antidepressants, cognitive therapy
pain disorder	the preoccupation with pain in the absence of an adequate physical basis for it
	difficult to treat; may be helped by behavior therapy

CONVERSION DISORDER

A **conversion disorder** (formerly called **hysteria**) is the epitome of a somatoform disorder; here the individual shows an alteration or loss of physical functioning that suggests a bodily cause but actually is an expression of a psychological conflict or need (Mace, 1992a, 1992b). The term *conversion* is used to indicate that the psychological issue is converted into physical symptoms—from dramatic ones such as a loss of sight or a false pregnancy to more mundane ones such as nausea or constipation. In general, it appears that the more mundane symptoms predominate (Lakosina, Kostiunina, Kal'ke, & Shashkova, 1987). The brief examples presented here include only a single symptom, but different symptoms are typically present. They may show changing patterns over time. Remember my description in Chapter 1 of Anna O., the first psychoanalytic patient, who showed a complex set of symptoms.

Unlike most of the disorders it enumerates, DSM-IV goes beyond the mere description of symptoms in characterizing conversion disorder and additionally requires that the diagnostician present evidence for the involvement of psychological factors in the initiation and/or exacerbation of the apparent physical symptoms. For example, during an argument, a person may suddenly be unable to lift her arms. In this case, there is a clear and close relationship in time between an upsetting event and the development of symptoms. We assume that the paralysis is a way of keeping her from acknowledging unconscious rage.

In my own clinical work, I encountered Mr. Whitehead, a man who woke up one day unable to see. His wife brought him to the hospital, where he first was examined by eye doctors, who could find nothing wrong with his eyes. Then he was examined by neurologists, who could find nothing wrong with his central nervous system. Finally, Mr. Whitehead was examined by psychiatrists and clinical psychologists, and the nature of his problem became clear. The night before, he had fought with his wife about her physical appearance. Over the years, she had gained a great deal of weight, and he told her that she looked ugly. She countered that he was unattractive himself and that maybe they should get a divorce. The next morning, Mr. Whitehead awoke completely blind. There is an obvious connection between the conflict and the symptoms.

An additional psychological mechanism that may be involved in conversion disorder is **secondary gain.** In other words, the symptom allows the person to achieve some reward or avoid some punishment. Consider the example of a soldier whose hand becomes

Early in the 20th century, a bent back like the man's in the picture was a common conversion symptom. It is rarely encountered today.

paralyzed so that he cannot fire his gun. He does not have to enter combat, to kill or be killed. Other examples include those who might not receive attention or concern from friends and family until they develop a particular physical problem. Remember, though, that conversion disorders do *not* involve intentional faking.

Another example comes from my career as a teacher. I was at a small school where one of my students was suddenly unable to hear what I was saying to her. My colleagues who taught her had the same experience. We assumed that Ms. Goldfarb had a serious ear infection, but then her roommate told me that she had no difficulty hearing her boyfriend when she talked to him on the phone. It was only her teachers she could not hear. Apparently, she found us critical, so she quite literally turned us off. Apparently, her boyfriend was simply loving, so he continued to come through loud and clear.

Characterization   As mentioned in Chapter 6, one of the striking aspects sometimes characterizing conversion disorder is an indifference on the part of the individual to his or her physical symptoms: ***la belle indifference.*** You might think that waking up one morning to find yourself unable to see would be cause for alarm, but this is not what happens in the case of conversion disorder. Typically, it is other people who bring the person into the health care system. DSM-IV does not use *la belle indifference* as a formal symptom of the disorder, because some legitimate medical patients display considerable stoicism concerning their symptoms. However, this aspect of conversion disorder

FOCUS ON

Morita

Psychotherapy

MORITA PSYCHOTHERAPY IS an approach developed and used in Japan to treat neurotic disorders, chiefly *taijinkyofusho*, also known as anthropophobia (Chapter 2). Here the person is greatly fearful of direct interaction with others; he or she is also highly preoccupied with somatic symptoms such as blushing and what they might communicate.

In the latter part of the ninth grade I began to become self-conscious about looking people in the eye. I felt that when I entered class everyone was looking at me. My body became tense. It was awful! However, when I went walking outside of class, I didn't feel tense at all.

Gradually my excessive self-consciousness grew stronger. When I entered class I became quite tense. My movements lost their naturalness and fluidity. And I couldn't respond properly when called on in class. On top of that, even walking along outside of class became painful.

I began to be morbidly afraid of meeting anyone else's eye. I became oversensitive to people standing beside me. It was terrible! Around the end of my senior year in high school I began to be self-conscious of my facial expression. When called on in class I had the feeling that my teacher was watching my mouth. My mouth was frozen! Horrible! Even when I left the classroom my mouth felt tight, so I'd practice opening it properly in front of a mirror.   (Reynolds, 1976, p. 22)

Anthropophobia overlaps with social phobia as discussed in Chapter 7 but at the same time also resembles the various somatoform disorders discussed in the present chapter. In any event, anthropophobia and its treatment with Morita psychotherapy illustrate how psychological problems and their remedies are best understood in terms of their cultural context.

In Japan, socialization encourages in most individuals a strong desire to pursue self-fulfilling tasks (Reynolds, 1976). Socialization also encourages a heightened sensitivity to what others think and feel. These two motives may work at cross-purposes to one another. The individual desires to live life fully, to excel and to achieve, yet not at the expense of others. Wishes and desires are rarely expressed directly, because the Japanese do not want to incur the social indebtedness that would result from direct requests.

Communication instead is highly indirect, as people keep their motives to themselves.

This style of expression makes sense within a culture where people feel generally obligated to one another. Their needs are often met *without* direct requests. What we might identify in the United States as lack of assertiveness plays a different role in Japan; it is part of a tacit social contract *not* to burden others with obligations beyond those already assumed as members of a family, community, and nation.

According to Shoma Morita (1874–1938), who developed Morita psychotherapy, anthropophobia results when individuals become overly aware of what others might be thinking about them and fearful that their motives are an open book. They become preoccupied with their body and its inadvertent signals. This somatic preoccupation in turn heightens their interpersonal difficulties.

Symptom relief is not the goal of Morita psychotherapy. Instead, individuals are encouraged to accept their symptoms and get on with their lives. Symptoms may come and go; neither their presence nor their absence is a stable enough foundation for one's identity. This view is congruent with Buddhist teachings about the need to accept suffering as part of life.

Morita psychotherapy focuses on the individual's behavior. Someone is "cured" of anthropophobia to the degree that symptoms cease to interfere with accomplishments and social obligations. This emphasis on behavior is not to be confused with American behaviorism. Morita psychotherapists do not dismiss thoughts and feelings; instead, they help their clients regard thoughts and feelings in such a way that productive behavior is possible. Indeed, a Morita therapist may congratulate a client for possessing sufficient social sensitivity to be able to experience the symptoms of anthropophobia.

What are the specific techniques used in this kind of therapy? Treatment usually begins with a week of bed rest in a hospital. Except to use the toilet or to eat, individuals must stay in bed. They do not read, watch television, or interact with others. The therapist visits once a day, spending about 1 minute checking on the client. While in bed, individuals are told to think about their problems. Invariably, they become bored after several days, and their symptoms begin to seem insignificant. When allowed out of bed, they are often exhilarated. However, the Morita therapist cautions them that their relief will wane, just as their symptoms did during bed rest.

It is better not to think so much about symptoms and their relief; instead, one should work. And so the second phase of Morita psychotherapy puts clients to work around the hospital, cleaning, painting, cooking, and so on. They are told to focus on the work per se. Interactions with others are minimal. Gradually, the work load is increased.

Individuals begin to attend lectures by the therapist in which the theory of Morita psychotherapy is explained. There may be some discussion, but these meetings resemble formal education more than Western group therapy.

The chief contact between clients and therapists is in terms of a daily diary that clients keep in which they describe what they *did* (as opposed to felt or thought) during the day. Diary entries are shown to the therapist every day, and he makes comments on them in red ink. He applauds those who accept the Morita approach and admonishes those who do not.

Upon discharge, individuals often keep in touch with those at the hospital where they were treated. They receive a monthly newsletter, and they attend further lectures on Morita psychotherapy. Morita psychotherapists report that 90% of their clients are "cured" in the sense that they are able to resume activities once precluded by their problems. As noted, these individuals may or may not still experience symptoms.

We could make sense of Morita psychotherapy and its effectiveness with anthropophobia in psychodynamic terms, or existential terms, or behavioral terms, or cognitive terms. But that would miss the point. Morita psychotherapy makes sense in its own terms, as a product of a particular culture and its inherent psychological processes.

is instructive in showing why the problem is interpreted as a defense against a person's underlying and unacknowledged anxiety. At some level, he "knows" that he is not disabled in the way that he appears to be. *La belle indifference* is the result of this knowledge.

Diagnosticians are aided by the fact that these disorders mimic physical problems but often not in precise ways. A common example is called *glove anesthesia*, in which the person loses the ability to feel in his hands, in the same pattern as if he were wearing gloves. However, the nerves in the hand are not so distributed. Neurological impairment in our hands usually takes on a different pattern. Table 8.2 shows some of the other ways to distinguish conversion symptoms from actual physical ones.

Epidemiology   As noted earlier, the prevalence of conversion disorder has decreased over the last century (see Figure 8.1). Estimates place the figure at no more than 1% of the contemporary United States population (Goodwin & Guze, 1989). The disorder is more common among women than men, perhaps by two or three to one. The disorder is also more common among the less educated, which supports the idea that conversion disorder only appears when it is credible to the person experiencing it.

It usually develops abruptly, in times of crisis, and resolves itself just as quickly. However, in some people, conversion disorder takes on a more chronic course, where it produces other problems for them. They might develop a chronic sick role. Or they might de-

velop actual physical problems, depending on the nature of the original conversion symptoms. For example, people who do not move their arms or legs may experience muscular atrophy.

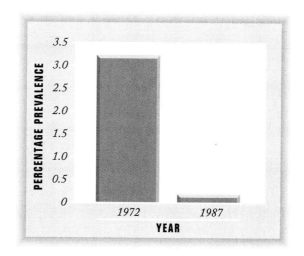

FIGURE 8.1

CONVERSION DISORDER OVER TIME   *In 1972 and 1987, a survey of residents in a town in West Bengal, India, found a marked decrease over time in the prevalence of conversion disorder.*

SOURCE: DATA DERIVED FROM "IS HYSTERIA ON THE WANE?" BY D. N. NANDI, G. BANERJEE, S. NANDI, AND P. NANDI, 1992, *British Journal of Psychiatry, 160*, PP. 87–91.

HYPOCHONDRIASIS

Another somatoform disorder is **hypochondriasis,** where the person is preoccupied with having a serious disease or greatly fears that he will develop one. Hypochondriasis goes beyond a normal and healthy concern

TABLE **8.2**

DISTINGUISHING ORGANIC FROM CONVERSION SYMPTOMS *By definition, conversion symptoms have no physical causes. So, part of the task of the diagnostician is to distinguish conversion from organic symptoms. Although this is not always possible to do with certainty, here are some procedures that may prove useful.*
SOURCE: ADAPTED FROM *HYSTERICAL CONVERSION REACTIONS,* BY M. I. WEINTRAUB, 1983, NEW YORK: SPECTRUM.

SYMPTOM	POSSIBLE DIAGNOSTIC TESTS
paralysis	in conversion disorder, the pattern of paralysis does not conform to the actual distribution of nerves; also, sudden and unexpected pressure on the muscles in question results in a protective counterresponse; also, paralysis may be evident only when certain movements—e.g., clenching a fist—are made and not others; finally, movement is observed during sleep
difficulty walking	in conversion disorder, the individual walks in a stereotyped manner—e.g., always zigzagging or grabbing furniture for support—which in actuality takes great coordination; also, the individual rarely falls
loss of smell	in conversion disorder, loss of smell is often one-sided, which is extremely rare in organic cases; also, the individual does not respond to spirits of ammonia, which is a nerve irritant as much as an olfactory stimulus
loss of taste	in conversion disorder, taste may be lost without the loss of smell (or vice versa); in organic cases, these two senses are usually lost together
blindness	in conversion disorder, the pupil responds to bright or dim light (note: this test is far from foolproof)
deafness	in conversion disorder, deafness is usually in one ear; when deafness is due to organic causes, if the "good" ear is plugged while the individual reads aloud his voice raises in pitch
seizures	in conversion disorder, what looks like a grand mal seizure (Chapter 6) occurs without loss of consciousness and without characteristic EEG patterns; also, the person is not stuporous afterwards

with well-being; in its extreme form, it exceeds the bounds of reality. According to DSM-IV, the diagnosis should be made when an individual's preoccupation with disease is at odds with medical opinion, when it results in significant distress or impairment, and when it lasts at least 6 months.

Like hysteria, hypochondriasis has a long documented history. Centuries ago, it was interpreted in somatic terms, as resulting from problems with the *hypochondrium,* a region of the upper abdomen beneath the ribs. (Contemporary anatomists no longer recognize this part of the body as a separate organ.) If hysteria was a problem with women, then hypochondriasis historically was a problem with men (Nemiah, 1980b). We can assume that earlier diagnostic schemes regarding hysteria as unique to women were able to maintain this position by diagnosing male "hysterics" as suffering from hypochondriasis.

The concerns of the hypochondriacal individual are well known. Kellner (1986, p. 3) presents the attitude of a typical patient, quoted from a 1730 treatise: "I have sent for you, doctor, to consult you about a distemper of which I am well assured I shall never be cured."

In relatively recent centuries, hypochondriasis was seen as directly caused by either neurological or environmental conditions, like heavy food or overpopulation. Eventually, it was seen as being psychological in nature, although modern opinion acknowledges that physiological characteristics may predispose or exacerbate it. For instance, those who are attuned to their own physical sensations are more likely to be hypochondriacs. Hypochondriasis often co-occurs with symptoms of anxiety and depression (Barsky, Wyshak, & Klerman, 1992), and all possible influences among these different disorders can exist (Kellner, 1986).

Characterization Those with hypochondriasis may believe they have cancer despite the contrary evidence of dozens of medical tests. Or if they are celibate, they may live in fear of contracting a sexually transmitted disease. These are not realistic concerns. Some theorists believe there is an important distinction between believing that you have a disease you do not have versus fearing that you will contract one (Kellner, 1986), although DSM-IV groups these together.

Epidemiology Hypochondriasis usually begins in the twenties, although its onset has been described at all ages (Barsky, Frank, Cleary, Wyshak, & Klerman, 1991). The disorder may be triggered by an actual illness, which presumably raises the individual's consciousness about the possibility of other maladies. The course is usually chronic if there is no intervention. The person tends not to see a psychotherapist but rather goes to various medical specialists. As noted earlier, doctor switching is common, and eventually the person may find a doctor who will minister to the apparent symptoms. A sympathetic physician can inadvertently encourage the problem (Kellner, 1986). The ordering of medical tests might not reassure the person so much as "prove" that something is truly wrong.

The prevalence of hypochondriasis is estimated to be about 1% in the contemporary United States, and the disorder occurs approximately equally among men and women. Because hypochondriacal individuals are more likely to seek help from medical doctors than from mental health professionals, this may be an underestimate. A recent study found that fully 5% of medical outpatients satisfied DSM diagnostic criteria for this disorder (Barsky, Wyshak, Klerman, & Latham, 1990).

SOMATIZATION DISORDER

In **somatization disorder,** the person repeatedly voices a variety of bodily complaints, often long-standing in nature. This disorder is sometimes called **Briquet's syndrome,** after the French physician who first described it. Those with somatization disorder frequently seek medical attention, but specific causes cannot be found for their problems. In practice, it overlaps considerably with hypochondriasis, but the abstract distinction lies in the nature of the complaints. If an individual focuses on one or two symptoms, and fears a particular disease, she is hypochondriacal. If she has a long history of complaints and fears that run the

gamut of diseases, she is suffering from somatization disorder.

Characterization Table 8.3 lists the different types of symptoms mentioned by DSM-IV that indicate somatization disorder. Diagnosis is recommended only when the individual complains about symptoms in *all* categories. Mild versions of the disorder are familiar and probably quite common. Being aware of our bodily sensations is healthy. We should all listen to what our bodies tell us; the problem occurs when the body seems to speak volumes. Then a person's life is compromised (Barsky, 1988).

Baur (1988) described the American poet Sara Teasdale (1884–1933), who early in life developed an exaggerated concern with her health. When she was but a child, her family used the pretense of her supposedly poor health as an excuse to avoid arguments over travel and vacations. At every opportunity, Teasdale was put to bed to conserve her strength. She grew into a woman who, despite her success as a poet, was beset with constant complaints of illness. She rarely left her bed. Her entire

TABLE 8.3

SYMPTOMS OF SOMATIZATION DISORDER *DSM-IV classifies the possible symptoms of somatization disorder under several general headings, requiring that a certain number of symptoms from each category be present. In each case, the symptom cannot be fully explained by a known medical condition.*
SOURCE: *DSM-IV DRAFT CRITERIA*, 1993, WASHINGTON, DC: AMERICAN PSYCHIATRIC ASSOCIATION.

at least four *pain symptoms*

> a history of pain in at least four different sites (e.g., head, abdomen, back, joints, extremities, chest, rectum) or functions (e.g., sexual intercourse, menstruation, urination)

at least two *gastrointestinal symptoms*

> a history of gastrointestinal problems other than pain (e.g., nausea, diarrhea, bloating, vomiting except when pregnant, food intolerance)

at least one *sexual symptom*

> a history of sexual or reproductive symptoms (e.g., sexual indifference, erectile or ejaculatory dysfunction, irregular menstruation)

at least one *pseudoneurological symptom*

> a history of symptoms or deficits suggesting a neurological disorder other than pain (e.g., conversion symptoms such as blindness or dissociative symptoms such as amnesia)

"May I please be excused? I have a tension headache."
Drawing by Weber; © 1972. The New Yorker Magazine, Inc.

life revolved around symptoms and their imagined consequences. At 49, she broke a vein in her hand. Thinking it meant a stroke, she committed suicide.

Epidemiology Studies disagree about the prevalence of somatization disorder, with estimates ranging from .2% to 2% among females in the United States today (Swartz, Blazer, George, & Landerman, 1986). The disorder is rarely encountered in males (Tomasson, Kent, & Coryell, 1991). It runs in families, so that as many as 20% of the first-degree female relatives of those with somatization disorder may have the disorder themselves (Arkonac & Guze, 1963). It is modestly heritable (Sigvardsson, von Knorring, Bohman, & Cloninger, 1984). And it is more likely among the less educated (Escobar, Rubio-Stipec, Canino, & Karno, 1989; Swartz, Landerman, Blazer, & George, 1989).

Somatization disorder starts early in life, as in the example of Sara Teasdale, and many theorists emphasize the role of the family in socializing the disorder. By this view, it is a lifestyle more than a discrete problem. One of its unfortunate consequences is that people may have unnecessary medical treatments, even surgery, which then add to their somatic complaints (Fink, 1992a, 1992b). Its course without intervention is chronic, and it is frequently associated with anxiety and depression (Rief, Schaefer, Hiller, & Fichter, 1992; Simon & VonKorff, 1991). Many who study somatiza-

tion disorder comment that little is known about its causes and treatments because it can be so difficult to identify in the first place.

BODY DYSMORPHIC DISORDER

Body dysmorphic disorder is defined as a preoccupation with an imagined defect in physical appearance[1] (Hollander, Neville, Frenkel, Josephson, & Liebowitz, 1992). According to DSM-IV, a person warranting this diagnosis must experience significant distress or impairment in functioning because of this preoccupation.

Like other somatoform disorders, body dysmorphic disorder may be accompanied by depression (Phillips, 1991). Treatment for depression may therefore be useful, if a person's distress about his or her appearance is a manifestation of the low self-esteem that usually characterizes depression (Chapter 9). When severe, body dysmorphic disorder leads the person to shun certain occupational and social demands, because of his or her concern with the supposed physical flaw. The problem usually persists for several years, and may foreshadow later problems. Connolly and Gipson (1978) followed up 86 individuals who had cosmetic surgery 15 years earlier; of the 86, 32 were subsequently characterized as severely neurotic and another 6 as schizophrenic.

Characterization Here is a good example of a disorder with extremely ambiguous boundaries. Is there anyone who is completely satisfied with how he or she looks? Surveys suggest that the majority of contemporary Americans are dissatisfied with some aspect of their appearance, from their size or shape to more specific details (e.g., Fitts, Gibson, Redding, & Deiter, 1989). Even celebrities such as Oprah Winfrey, Cher, Dolly Parton, and Michael Jackson have agonized over their physical appearance, to the point of making drastic changes in how they look.

In body dysmorphic disorder, however, typical concerns are greatly exaggerated. It is only when people's dissatisfaction becomes excessive and starts to interfere with their life that we should consider the diagnosis of body dysmorphic disorder. The diagnosis

American poet Sara Teasdale (1884–1933) worried about her health throughout her life.

[1] Two related problems deserve mention. In *delusional parasitosis*, individuals believe—incorrectly—that their skin is infected by parasites (Morris, 1991; Musalek, Bach, Passweg, & Jaeger, 1990; Wykoff, 1987). *Olfactory reference syndrome* refers to a person's mistaken belief that his or her body emanates a disgusting odor (Bishop, 1980; Bourgeois, 1973; Munro & Pollock, 1981). These disorders are rare and poorly understood, and there is disagreement about whether they are discrete syndromes in their own right or symptoms that characterize a variety of other disorders.

is made when no defect exists at all (Thomas, 1984) or when a person's concern is far out of proportion to the reality of some minor imperfection.

When I was in college, a friend of mine took me into her confidence and confessed that she had extremely ugly ears. I had known her for several years, and I looked at her in puzzlement. Then I realized that I had never seen her ears. She had long hair that she always braided in such a way that her ears could not be seen. And she never swam or jogged or wore headphones or did anything that would disturb how she wore her hair. She went on to tell me that she hated her appearance and worried that she would never have a normal life because of her ears. She had consulted several plastic surgeons about having her ears reshaped. None of the doctors was willing to undertake the surgery, which she interpreted as proof that her looks were beyond repair. I was at a loss for something to say, although I murmured words intended to be comforting. Touched by my concern, she moved her braids aside to give me a glimpse of . . . two perfectly normal ears. When I told her that her ears looked great, she became upset and walked away without a word. Although we continued our friendship, we never discussed her ears again. I believe that her dissatisfaction with them continued.

Epidemiology   The most common focus of body dysmorphic disorder is facial flaws: wrinkles, spots on

the skin, excessive facial hair, or the shape of the nose, mouth, jaw, or eyebrows. Less common are concerns with other parts of the body: feet, hands, or breasts.

The onset of this disorder is usually during adolescence, when our concern with physical appearance begins in earnest (Andreasen & Bardach, 1977). Because this is a recently described disorder, we know little about its prevalence and course (Munro & Stewart, 1991). It appears to afflict women more than men (Fitts, Gibson, Redding, & Deiter, 1989), which is hardly surprising granted our culture's emphasis on female beauty. Standards are so stringent that few women, particularly as they age, can attain them. Consider that almost 90% of cosmetic surgeries in this country involve women. In *The Beauty Myth*, Naomi Wolf (1991) estimates that more than 1 million American women have had breast implants, despite the considerable cost of the operation and its well documented dangers. In some number of cases, the procedure is undertaken for medical reasons (after surgery for breast cancer, for instance), but much more frequently, the motivation is simply dissatisfaction with one's appearance.

Comparisons across time and place would be fascinating, although they do not exist. We can only speculate, drawing on the frequently heard charge that those of us in the contemporary United States are far too concerned with our appearance.

Our physical appearance is associated with a variety of stereotypes; the person who is seen as beautiful is also regarded as more intelligent, socially skilled, and so on (Hatfield & Sprecher, 1986). Good-looking people tend to marry "above" what would otherwise be expected, granted their nonphysical characteristics (Elder, 1969). By implication, then, the person who is not good-looking misses out on all of this, and so there is some validity in being worried about appearance (Cialdini, 1985). The irony, of course, is that when this worry takes on a life of its own, it becomes a self-fulfilling prophecy.

PAIN DISORDER

The final somatoform disorder I discuss is **pain disorder,** a preoccupation with pain in the absence of an adequate physical basis. In some cases, the psychological basis of chronic pain is clear, because it does not mimic what is known about pain that has a physical basis; that is, it occurs in patterns at odds with the actual distribution of neurons. In other cases, there is a clear link between the pain and secondary gain. Again we can infer a psychological etiology. But there can be ambiguity as well. We can have a problem—pain—with neither a physical nor a psychological basis evident.

The majority of Americans are dissatisfied with some aspect of their appearance, but it is only when this dissatisfaction takes on excessive degrees that we speak of body dysmorphic disorder.

Characterization   Pain itself is a puzzle, and we must beware of making too clean a distinction between physiological pain and psychological pain. Prevailing opinion is that both contribute to its experience. What after all is pain? It can result from the stimulation of any sensory receptor. Interestingly, we are still not sure if our body has *particular* receptors for pain.

Pain provides a warning signal about potentially dangerous objects in the environment. Our attention is grabbed when we contact them, and this is obviously advantageous. But sometimes pain outlives its usefulness, and continues to occupy our attention after danger has passed.

A popular account of pain is **gate-control theory,** which suggests that the experience of pain is regulated by as yet undiscovered "gates" in the spinal cord (Melzack, 1973). Various factors determine whether these gates are open or closed, including psychological influences. We have all had the experience of being occupied with some other activity while we suffer an injury. Only after our attention is drawn to the injury do we even notice it. Presumably, the pain gates were closed. Perhaps some people who experience chronic pain do so because their pain gates are always open. Endorphins may render an individual insensitive to pain by closing the gates (Basbaum & Fields, 1984); the Chinese practice of acupuncture might also work this way (Chapman, Wilson, & Gehrig, 1976). And psychological tactics like hypnotism or biofeedback might also be useful in combating pain because they affect how these pain gates operate.

Kellner (1986) described Ms. H.F., a 47-year-old woman with a long history of complaints about pain. She experienced backaches, headaches, and stomach aches. There was rarely a day when she felt free of these symptoms. Her abdominal pain was particularly troublesome. It had begun 13 years before, when she was experiencing marital problems. She improved somewhat, but the symptoms became much more severe following her husband's death several years later. Several operations brought her no relief. She was prescribed tranquilizers, painkillers, and antidepressants, again with no success. Although Ms. H.F. was willing to participate in psychotherapy, this also failed to alleviate her pain.

Epidemiology   Pain disorder usually starts in the thirties or forties, and in about half the cases it follows an actual physical trauma. Chronic pain is common in general medical practice, but unambiguously identifying it as pain disorder is difficult. The prevalence of this disorder is not really known, but it appears to be more common among women than men (Verbrugge,

Acupuncture can eliminate pain, perhaps by closing the hypothesized pain gates in the spinal cord.

1980). This may simply reflect greater willingness on the part of women to acknowledge pain.

For the sake of clarity, I repeat an important point. Even though somatoform symptoms do not have organic causes, they are real to the people who experience them. Those with pain disorder hurt, despite the ostensible lack of tissue damage. It is a mistake to dismiss such problems as malingering or "just in the head."

EXPLANATIONS

Attempts to explain somatoform disorders in psychological terms began in earnest with Freud. As you know, his first patients suffered from conversion disorders, and his attempts to make psychological sense of their physical symptoms marked the beginning of psychoanalytic thinking (Chapter 1).

However, the history of this disorder dates back much earlier than Freud (Shorter, 1992). The problem was recognized by early Greek physicians, who interpreted it in physical terms. Hysteria comes from the Greek word *hysterus*, meaning *womb*, and they believed that hysteria occurred when a woman's uterus became dislodged and wandered throughout her body. It would then lodge itself in various places, and depending on the site, it would produce symptoms of one type or another.

Of necessity, hysteria was considered a woman's disease, and it was often interpreted in specifically sexual terms. It seemed to afflict, in particular, young female virgins. Hippocrates, for example, suggested that the womb wandered when it was discontented, and this might be the case in the absence of sexual relations. The obvious cure was marriage and frequent sexual intercourse (Weintraub, 1983). Other cures included prayers and the administration of foul-smelling substances to the nose to drive the uterus back to where it belonged (Mora, 1980).

In time, conversion disorder ceased to be interpreted as a wandering womb, but it continued to be seen as a disease of women, as well as linked to sexuality. Theorizing about conversion disorder focused on its presumed somatic causes until the 20th century. Perhaps the best known investigator of conversion disorders was the French neurologist Jean Charcot (1825–1893), who did much to legitimize their study and treatment. For most of his career, he believed they were the result of a congenital degeneration of the brain. However, they could be treated through hypnotism, which he similarly interpreted as having a direct effect on the nervous system. Charcot believed that only hysterics could be hypnotized, and so he used susceptibility to hypnotism as a strong diagnostic test for the disorder.

Freud was greatly influenced by Charcot, but he found himself in disagreement with several of Charcot's strongest pronouncements regarding conversion disorder. Specifically, Freud felt that psychological factors were crucially involved in its etiology. And so psychoanalytic theory began in opposition to Charcot, proposing that unconscious conflicts, often sexual in nature, gave rise to the symptoms of hysteria. Treatment via hypnotism was effective not because of its effect on the nervous system but rather because it brought unconscious material to light.

Freud originally used hypnotism in his treatment of hysterics, but then abandoned the technique. Some of his patients could not be hypnotized; in other cases, it had unanticipated effects. Specifically, Freud found that some of his female patients who were hypnotized became attracted to him. Alarmed, Freud developed techniques such as free association that accomplished the same purpose of identifying unconscious material while keeping the patient more in control.

Contemporary theorists believe that somatoform disorders have a number of contributing causes, which interact in various ways to bring about one or more problems (Kellner, 1986, 1990). These causes come from different domains—physiological, psychodynamic, cognitive, and behavioral—so we can conclude that an integrated perspective, one that draws on the explanations suggested by different models of abnormality, is the most reasonable approach. More generally, this integration needs to be contextualized in terms of the individual's larger culture, which provides ways of thinking about one's own body and its relationship to psychological factors (Fabrega, 1990). As the cultural distance between patient and diagnostician increases, there will be greater discrepancies between the interpretations each gives to specific somatic symptoms (e.g., Angel & Guarnaccia, 1989).

Physiological sensitivity   One predisposition to somatoform disorders is *physiological sensitivity*. Some people are more likely than others to be aware of their own physical sensations. Research suggests that people's thresholds for various sensations differ, including thresholds for pain. Along these lines, our tolerance for pain—the amount of aversive stimulation we can tolerate before identifying it as painful—also differs markedly. As you might imagine, those with somatoform disorders have low sensation thresholds and low pain tolerance (e.g., Bianchi, 1971).

These differences may reflect something inherent about the individual. The association between anxiety and somatoform disorders has already been noted. Some theorists believe that those with somatoform disorders experience more arousal than other people, for the same genetic reasons that people with fear and anxiety disorders do (Farber, 1981). Alternatively—or additionally—people may learn to be more sensitive versus less sensitive to their bodily sensations.

We can go a step further and speculate about cultural differences in pain tolerance (Zborowski, 1969), which seem to parallel cultural differences in the likelihood of experiencing somatoform disorders (Hes, 1958, 1968). Those who tolerate large amounts of pain without complaint—for example, those of northern European descent—tend *not* to have somatoform disorders. In other words, our culture affects how we attend to, experience, and express bodily sensations (Fabrega, 1990; Lin, Carter, & Kleinman, 1985).

Personality predispositions   Physiological sensitivity by itself is not sufficient to create somatoform disorders. The sort of *cognitive interpretation* a person places on bodily sensations is also critical (Cioffi, 1991). Some people regard a racing heart or sweaty palms as a source of alarm, which heightens their attention to them (Barsky, Wyshak, & Klerman, 1990).

People differ in their sensitivity to pain. We can presume that most football players have high thresholds for pain.

Others are quite indifferent and hence inattentive (Hitchcock & Mathews, 1992).

A pertinent personality dimension is Byrne's (1964) **repression-sensitization.** Individuals at one end, *repressors,* tend not to focus on disturbing occurrences; those at the other end, *sensitizers,* pay particular attention to them. When repressors versus sensitizers are compared on their somatic complaints, sensitizers are more likely to report such symptoms as headaches, colds, nausea, and heart palpitations (Byrne, Steinberg, & Schwartz, 1968).

Another pertinent personality dimension is **anxiety sensitivity** (Reiss & McNally, 1985). People differ here not in the degree to which they experience the symptoms of anxiety, but rather in terms of how they make sense of them. Some people believe that rapid heartbeats signal an impending heart attack; others regard them as simply annoying. Anxiety sensitivity reflects the tendency to respond to fear with fear, setting into operation a cascade of increasing anxiety and laying the ground for somatoform disorders.

Psychoanalytic theorists have long described a **histrionic personality disorder** (or **hysterical personality disorder**), a style thought to predispose somatoform disorders in general and conversion disorders in particular (Chodoff & Lyons, 1958). I discuss this style more fully in Chapter 13, but in the present context, note that the histrionic individual is dramatic and self-centered, and shows shallow and shifting emotions (Pollak, 1981). The link between this style and complaints of poor health is well established (e.g., de Leon, Saiz-Ruiz, Chinchilla, & Morales, 1987; Lilienfeld, Van Valkenburg, Larntz, & Akiskal, 1986).

Alexithymia   Some theorists suggest that somatoform disorders are apt to occur among people who have *difficulty expressing their emotions* in words. The phenomenon is called **alexithymia** (Sifenos, 1973, 1974). Alexithymic individuals seem to lack the words to express strong feelings, usually retreating into a recital of the bodily sensations that accompany emotion (Ots, 1990; Parsons & Wakeley, 1991). Those with alexithymia are at increased risk for both somatoform and psychosomatic disorders (Lesser, 1985; Taylor, Parker, Bagby, & Acklin, 1992).

Sifenos (1974, p. 153) described one of his alexithymic patients, a 50-year-old bachelor who was an engineer suffering from a peptic ulcer and several cardiac problems:

> *The patient was a passive, somewhat obese man who seemed to be totally unconcerned. . . . He admitted readily that he did not want to see a psychiatrist and disclaimed*

any psychiatric problems. . . . He claimed never to worry about his health, nor to understand people who were "hypochondriacs." During the interview, he was calm, but he looked puzzled when asked to describe his emotions. "I don't know what you mean, doctor," was his usual answer to such questions. Asked specifically whether he experienced fear, anger, or sadness, he looked perplexed. No, he had not, or he could not remember. . . . He had very few dreams and claimed not to understand what daydreaming was all about.

Relevant here is research by James Pennebaker and his colleagues, who studied individuals whose spouses recently died (Pennebaker, Hughes, & O'Heeron, 1987; Pennebaker & O'Heeron, 1984). They asked these research subjects if they had talked to another person about their grief. Some had and some had not, and among those who had not spoken to another person, the extent of their physical complaints during the subsequent year were markedly increased.

The notion of alexithymia and the research by Pennebaker's group lead to the conclusion that when people are experiencing some strong emotion, and they lack the ability and/or the opportunity to talk about it, they may end up with an increase in physical symptoms, with or without actual physical damage. A contemporary view sees these somatic symptoms as a way of communicating when other channels—like words—are unavailable. Somatoform disorders are a plea for help or attention by people who cannot otherwise ask for it.

This view has the virtue of explaining why the particular forms of somatoform disorders have changed over the years. The language has to be meaningful within a given time and place and consistent with prevailing scientific theories (Shorter, 1992). In Freud's era—Victorian Europe—bizarre physical symptoms were more credible as cries for help than they are today. We now employ vaguer and more diffuse complaints (Stefanis, Markidis, & Christodoulou, 1976).

Social influences   Supporting the communication view of the somatoform disorders are studies of the families of people with these disorders (deGruy et al., 1989; Robinson, Greene, & Walker, 1988). Communication is amiss in these families. Consider that complaints of pain are more common among those with many siblings as opposed to those with few (e.g., Gonda, 1962): What better way to get the attention of parents whose attention may be spread thin than to complain of pain? Other studies suggest that the families of hypochondriacal children and adolescents tend not to communicate their feelings in a direct fashion (e.g., Loof, 1970). Parents and children alike are silent in interviews, although they show considerable twitching, blushing, and hyperventilating.

Relatedly, somatoform disorders run through families, and while this may reflect genetic influences on physiological sensitivity, these would seem to pale in comparison to the direct socialization and modeling that occur in these families (see Edwards, Zeichner, Kuczmierczyk, & Boczkowski, 1985). Family systems theorists sometimes describe entire families as hypochondriacal, to emphasize that a preoccupation with illness permeates the family system, to such an extent that it is *the* style of the family. There are even reports of striking similarity of the particular sorts of symptoms reported by family members. For instance, all of them may complain of headaches, or fear cancer, or show similar conversion disorders (e.g., Apley, 1958).

Along these same lines is the phenomenon of **mass hysteria,** in which individuals in large groups all show the same groundless somatic complaint (e.g., Cole, Chorba, & Horan, 1990; Colligan et al., 1979; Krug, 1992; Rockne & Lemke, 1992; Small, Propper, Randolph, & Eth, 1991; Struewing & Gray, 1990). There is no question about the absence of a biological basis to the similar symptoms, as one might find in a family. Rather, through observation, people develop physical problems by suggestion alone. For example, during the 1950s, when polio was still prevalent, there were numerous localized epidemics of paralysis suggestive of polio but eventually proving not to be so (Sirois, 1974).

M. I. Weintraub speculated that those in high school marching bands are at particular risk for mass hysteria because their role mandates synchronization of movement.

Do you remember the widely reported story in 1994 of hospital employees apparently being overcome by fumes they said emitted from the body of a young woman who had just died of heart failure? Exhaustive analyses revealed no evidence of these fumes, and her family eventually had to sue to recover her body in order to bury it. I suspect that the hospital employees may have been victims of mass hysteria.

History gives us other examples, often taking place in monasteries and convents and involving frenzied twitching and dancing (Richer, 1885). A contemporary equivalent has been suggested by Weintraub (1983), who speculates that those in high school marching bands are at particular risk for mass hysteria because their role demands synchronized movement. At present, the problem is most apt to occur among adolescent females in closely knit groups (Weintraub, 1983).

Trauma   I now move to another ingredient in the etiology of the somatoform disorders: *traumatic*

events. Many of these disorders start with some bad occurrence (Escobar, Canino, Rubio-Stipec, & Bravo, 1992). In conversion disorders, a particular incident triggers symptoms in the majority of cases (House & Andrews, 1988). Hypochondriasis and somatization disorder often begin with actual illnesses, which probably serve to heighten anxiety about future illnesses. And losses in childhood such as bereavement may place a person at increased risk for somatoform disorders as an adult (Kellner, 1986). Even mass hysteria is more likely to occur among those who had earlier lost a parent to death or divorce (Small & Nicholi, 1982).

Kerry Lane Wheeler is a young man who once served time in the California prison system for robbery (Serrano, 1990). Ever since a fight in prison, he has not uttered a sound; he communicates by writing and using a form of sign language. He reports that he is unable to speak because of an injury suffered during the fight. Physicians have found no physical basis for his silence, and some have suggested that his inability to speak is a conversion disorder. If indeed this is a correct diagnosis, then the role of trauma in producing it is clear. One of the themes in Wheeler's written communications is that a prisoner should never complain or make waves. His silence guaranteed his adherence to this code.

Reinforcement   A final aspect of the etiology of somatoform disorders is the *reinforcement of symptoms.* I have noted that symptoms can bring secondary gain, allowing the person to avoid some undesired activity and/or win attention and reassurance from others. Kreitman, Sainsbury, Pearce, and Costain (1965), for example, note that the comment about a spouse, "He is good to me when I am ill," may be a tip-off that the person is hypochondriacal. At the same time, we cannot be simplistic about the role of reinforcement. Friends and family members are much more likely to be negative than positive in their response (Kreitman et al., 1965).

If we wish to search for what is reinforcing about these disorders, it might be wise to remember some of the solutions to the neurotic paradox sketched by learning theorists (Chapter 7). Perhaps somatoform disorders are rewarding because they distract the person from other concerns that are more upsetting. Perhaps they take on a life of their own because when a person recites his complaints, he stops thinking about other bad things—such as his deteriorating marriage.

An integrated view   Figure 8-2 presents a scheme for how these factors might interact in predisposing somatoform disorders. This diagram is consistent with research evidence concerning the risk factors and maintenance of conditions for these disorders. The problem with this integrated view is that it does not speak directly to why an individual develops one somatoform disorder rather than another. I can note, though, that the disorders discussed in this section seem to vary from relatively circumscribed to rela-

tively pervasive. Perhaps this dimension captures their severity. The differences among them might be more of degree than of kind (Sims, 1988). Could we argue that people develop one disorder rather than another depending on the intensity and/or chronicity of the various risk factors I have discussed?

TREATMENTS

Treatments for somatoform disorders target for change the factors that may contribute to them: physiological, emotional, behavioral, cognitive, interpersonal, and so on. Individual success varies according to how entrenched the disorder happens to be. It is ironic that psychoanalytic therapy, though developed precisely by Freud for the purpose of treating such problems, is no longer thought to be particularly effective (Nemiah, 1980b). Psychoanalysis requires that a person evidence a degree of *psychological mindedness*—the ability to think about and express one's own ideas, motives, feelings, and uncertainties—and it is precisely this psychological mindedness that is lacking in somatoform patients.

For conversion disorders, the prognosis is decent. About 50% of patients no longer have their symptoms 1 year after their first appearance (Nemiah, 1980b). For a substantial minority, though, perhaps 20%, the symptoms are unremitting even after decades. Effective treatment depends less on the symptoms and more on the individual's psychological makeup. Supportive therapy helps those who—obviously—developed their symptoms primarily in response to unmet needs. In other cases, family therapy may be useful. And in still other cases, physical interventions are used, which presumably capitalize on the suggestibility of the individual with conversion disorder.

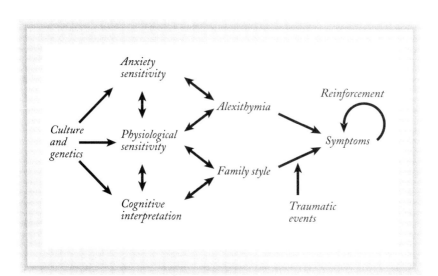

FIGURE 8.2

AN INTEGRATED MODEL OF SOMATOFORM DISORDERS
Somatoform disorders result from a combination of diverse causes.

For hypochondriasis, prognosis is poor. Long-term follow-ups find that the vast majority of hypochondriacal patients continue to report somatic complaints (Kenyon, 1964; Morrison, 1990). According to some theorists, behavior therapy that systematically attacks the different components of the disorder might be worth exploring (Stern & Fernandez, 1991; Visser & Bouman, 1992), but few such studies have yet been conducted (Warwick & Salkovskis, 1990). Prognosis is also poor for pain disorder. Note that any conclusions about treatment are muddied by the problem of accurately diagnosing this problem in the first place.

Somatization disorder similarly has a bleak picture in that a person rarely experiences complete relief of her symptoms (Nemiah, 1980b). Unnecessary medical procedures may exacerbate her physical complaints. People with this problem have many times the number of surgical procedures compared to the general population (e.g., Cohen, Robins, Purtell, Altmann, & Reid, 1953). Further, psychological help is apt to be strongly resisted.

Body dysmorphic disorders may simply be outgrown. Those that are more severe must be treated aggressively. Cognitive therapy like that described in the previous chapter can help alter the significance a person attaches to minor or nonexistent physical flaws, thereby alleviating the disorder (Rosen, Saltzberg, & Srebnik, 1989). Some studies report improvement in body dysmorphic disorder following antidepressant medication (e.g., Filteau, Pourcher, Baruch, Bouchard, & Vincent, 1992; Jenike, 1984).

In general, Morrison (1990) suggests that the therapist treat somatoform disorders by providing emotional support and encouragement when the individual ignores symptoms and decreases medication. Further, the therapist should educate him about the meaning of illness and the role it plays in his life. Therapy of this sort seems to proceed best when the aid of the individual's family can be enlisted. This approach is cognitive-behavioral in nature, because it tries to create an atmosphere in which somatic complaints are reacted to differently.

For example, Feuerstein, Labbé and Kuczmierczyk (1986) described the successful treatment of a 21-year-old male who for 15 years had experienced abdominal pain and difficulty walking. No adequate physical basis for these complaints could be found. At the time he began treatment, he was in a wheelchair, afraid to walk because of the associated pain and dizziness that his attempts caused. He was treated with a flooding procedure (Chapter 7), encouraged to walk regardless of how he felt. His pain continued, but he began to move about freely. Eventually, his pain subsided as well.

DISSOCIATIVE DISORDERS

Dissociative disorders are marked by discontinuities in memory, consciousness, and/or identity (see Table 8.4). I introduce this section by defining **dissociation**: the splitting of consciousness into discrete streams, with little or no communication between or among them. The notion dates back to the 1800s (Ellenberger, 1970). Dissociation is related to Freud's notion of the unconscious (Chapter 3) but differs critically. Dissociation and the unconscious both explain why people may have motives, thoughts, and feelings of which they are unaware—but where Freud's concept regards consciousness as unitary, dissociation is based

TABLE 8.4

DISSOCIATIVE DISORDERS *According to DSM-IV, several disorders are marked by dissociation.*

DISORDER	CHARACTERIZATION AND TREATMENT
dissociative amnesia	the sudden inability to recall personally important information following psychological trauma
	may go away without treatment; helped by recapturing memories, reducing anxiety
dissociative fugue	the loss of personal memory, travel away from home, and the establishment of a new identity following psychological trauma
	may go away without treatment; helped by recapturing memories, reducing anxiety
multiple personality disorder	the existence within the same person of two or more distinct personalities, each with its own enduring and characteristic style; these different personalities alternate in taking full control of the person's behavior
	helped by "introducing" personalities to one another, breaking down barriers of amnesia, and fusing fragmented identity
depersonalization disorder	the recurrent and distressing feeling that one is an outside observer of one's own thoughts or actions
	may go away without treatment; helped by recapturing memories, reducing anxiety

on the idea that consciousness can be split into different parts.

The Freudian theory of the mind is often captured with the metaphor of an iceberg. The part below the surface (below the conscious mind) is the unconscious mind. In contrast, the notion of dissociation sees the mind as a collection of icebergs, some in contact with others and some not (see Figure 8.3). Without acknowledgment that consciousness can be split from itself, dissociative disorders are impossible.

Actually, dissociative *disorders* are rare. However, dissociative *experiences* are relatively common, according to a survey of adults in Winnipeg by Ross, Joshi, and Currie (1990). Figure 8.4 presents their findings that a number of people report experience with discontinuities in memory, consciousness, or identity. Perhaps it is easier to understand the dissociative disorders if we think of them as dissociative experiences carried to an extreme.

DISSOCIATIVE AMNESIA

I discussed organic amnesia in Chapter 6. I also introduced **dissociative amnesia** (remember Table 6.1). It

FIGURE 8.3

DISSOCIATIVE ICEBERGS
The notion of dissociation regards consciousness as split into different parts, some in contact with one another and some not. Remember Freud's metaphor of the mind as an iceberg; in dissociation, the mind is seen as a collection of icebergs.

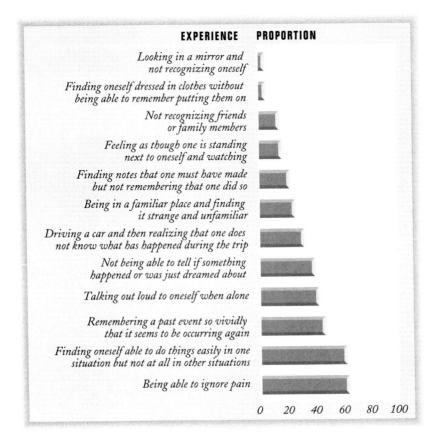

FIGURE 8.4

FREQUENCY OF DISSOCIATIVE EXPERIENCES
Dissociative disorders are rare, but dissociative experiences are not. This chart shows the proportions of everyday people in one study who reported a dissociative experience occasionally occurring to them.
SOURCE: DATA DERIVED FROM "DISSOCIATIVE EXPERIENCES IN THE GENERAL POPULATION," BY C. A. ROSS, S. JOSHI, AND R. CURRIE, 1990, *American Journal of Psychiatry, 147,* PP. 1547–1552; EXACT FIGURES PROVIDED BY COLIN A. ROSS.

"Jane Doe" was found wandering in Florida in 1980, suffering from highly generalized amnesia. Although she was later identified by her parents, she never regained her memory.

is defined by DSM-IV as the sudden inability to recall personally important information, usually of a traumatic nature. Memory loss is more extensive than can be accounted for by ordinary forgetfulness, but obviously there is a region between forgetfulness and amnesia that is difficult to judge. By definition, dissociative amnesia cannot have an organic cause. Instead, psychological factors prove relevant. It is typically observed in the immediate aftermath of severe stress, usually when life is threatened but occasionally when identity is at risk (Brna & Wilson, 1990).

Characterization   During an episode of amnesia, the person is perplexed and disoriented. When memory loss surrounds past events, the person is typically aware of his amnesia, which is different from the usual case of organic amnesia.

In my own clinical work, I once encountered a man who had no personal knowledge. Mr. Q. did not know his name, his home, or even how he managed to make it to the admitting room of our hospital. He had no identification, and even the tags on his clothing gave us no clue about his identity. We learned, when his memory returned, that his amnesia had been precipitated when

his wife of 20 years abruptly asked for a divorce. Mr. Q. was so shaken by this event, so unwilling to accept it, that he blotted out the memory of it, and of his wife, and of the last two decades of his life, and of everything that might give rise to these memories.

At some level, though, Mr. Q. retained his memories even while suffering from amnesia. The hospital in question was a Veterans Administration Medical Center, and it was located in a complex of several hospitals, each serving different populations. As we subsequently discovered, Mr. Q. was a Vietnam era veteran and had presented himself at the one institution where he was eligible for treatment.

Epidemiology   Because dissociative amnesia invariably follows in the wake of a trauma, information about its prevalence in given times and places is arbitrary, reflecting the frequency or infrequency of traumatic events. During times of military combat, dissociative amnesia is more frequent than during times of peace. The annual incidence of localized amnesia during times of peace is estimated at between 5 and 10 cases per 100,000 adults; it occurs more often among females than males (Koski & Marttila, 1990; Miller, Petersen, Metter, Millikan, & Yanagihara, 1987). When dissociative amnesia occurs among males, it is usually after military combat.

Rapid recovery is the rule, typically within a few days.[2] Often nothing needs to be done for the person's memory to return. Other times her memory can be jogged by confrontation-tranquilizing medication—such as *sodium amytal* (related to so-called truth serum)—which presumably liberates her memory by stifling the anxiety that keeps it repressed (Perry & Jacobs, 1982). Hypnotism can also speed recall (MacHovec, 1981). In any case, the person's memory usually returns all at once. Recurrence is rare.

DISSOCIATIVE FUGUE

Related to dissociative amnesia is the even more infrequently encountered disorder, **dissociative fugue.** In its classic form, people with this disorder lose their personal memory, travel away from home, and establish a new identity under which they live for varying

---

[2] An exception to this generalization currently in the public eye is people reporting memories of sexual abuse years or even decades after it originally occurred. These memories had apparently been repressed all this time, unavailable to consciousness. These recovered memories, particularly when used as the basis of criminal charges, are the subject of much controversy. Loftus (1993) surveyed these reports as well as research and theory bearing on them, reluctantly concluding that psychologists do not yet know enough to determine the accuracy of such memories.

amounts of time. If you are a student of music, you know that a *fugue* is a composition in which the same theme is repeated and interwoven by successive voices or instruments. This notion captures what often occurs in dissociative fugue. The new identity may be a variant of the previous one—a similar name is chosen; similar habits are evidenced; and so on.

Fugue is precipitated by severe stress, such as military combat, natural disasters, or interpersonal strife. Heavy alcohol use immediately before the fugue episode can be a contributing factor, as can severe conflicts in such areas as sexuality, aggression, and finances (Nemiah, 1980a).

Characterization   Unlike dissociative amnesia, the person suffering from dissociative fugue is not necessarily perplexed and confused. To the observer, she is going about her business as usual, although typically in quiet and modest fashion (Nemiah, 1980a). People with dissociative amnesia usually enter the mental health system when the police find them wandering the streets. In contrast, people with fugue are usually brought to the attention of psychiatrists or psychologists after they have recovered their memories. Little is therefore known about its treatment.

Here is a case of dissociative fugue originally reported by Pierre Janet (1859–1947). Janet was a French psychiatrist who had studied with Charcot, and who popularized the notion of dissociation (van der Kolk & van der Hart, 1989). Janet (1920) described the fugue of Mr. P., a 30-year-old railway clerk living in a small French town at the turn of the century. Ten years earlier, Mr. P. had fled from Lorraine, a part of France that had been annexed by Germany, and he harbored vague fears that the German police were continuing to search for him. Work was stressful because he was called on to do tasks for which he had little aptitude. Family quarrels were common. One day at work he was accused of stealing a small amount of money. His superiors did not take the charge seriously, but Mr. P. fretted about it for days.

Then one afternoon, after several drinks, he lost his identity and vanished. He wandered for the next 9 days, eventually turning up in Belgium. At first he had no recollection of what had ensued, but later his memory returned. He reported that he secured money and then took a series of trains to ever more distant cities, fearing that the police were after him. In Brussels, he had tried to enlist for service in the Dutch Indies, but he was turned down. His money dwindled, and he lay down in a field of snow to die. Then Mr. P. thought of his family, and his identity suddenly returned.

Perhaps the most puzzling thing about dissociative fugue is what the person is thinking about during the episode. As noted, the individual is not aware that he has lost his identity. How is this possible? We can suppose that the individual is not bothered by his lack of identity because he quite simply is not thinking about it. What defines identity after all is the continuity of your existence—the fact that you have a history. Yet much of the time you are not explicitly cognizant of it. Are you thinking of your third-grade teacher at this moment? Your first job? Who last sent you a Valentine? Of course not. You could bring these to mind, if and when you had a reason, but otherwise, your attention is elsewhere.

If we interpret dissociative fugue as motivated—an escape from stress—then the individual has all sorts of reasons *not* to pay attention to his history and instead to focus on the business at hand. Along these lines, those in a fugue state reportedly are single-minded and highly restricted in their emotions (Abse, 1987). Said another way, the part of the mind that is in control of what an individual does during a fugue episode is dissociated from the other parts of the person.

Epidemiology   The most dramatic version of fugue disorder—the assumption of an altogether new identity—is exceedingly uncommon, and there are no reliable estimates of its prevalence (Riether & Stoudemire, 1988). More commonly, people with dissociative fugue do little more than abandon their identity and travel away from their customary haunts. Fugue states are usually quite brief, lasting only a few hours or days, although there have been cases described in which the person maintains a new identity for years. When memory returns, it does so suddenly. Recurrence is uncommon.

MULTIPLE PERSONALITY DISORDER

Yet another dissociative disorder is **multiple personality disorder (MPD),** described by DSM-IV as **dissociative identity disorder.** It is defined by the following criteria:

- the presence within the same person of two or more distinct identities or personalities, each with its own enduring and characteristic style

- at least two of these identities or personalities recurrently take control of the person's behavior

- the inability to recall important personal information, above and beyond ordinary forgetfulness

Characterization   To these criteria, let me add that barriers of amnesia typically exist among the separate personalities, so that one personality may not know what happens to another personality when it is in control. In these cases, each personality has its own set of memories, social relationships, and behaviors. According to some reports, different personalities may evidence different allergies, body temperatures, eyeglass prescriptions, IQ scores, and sexual orientations (Miller, Blackburn, Scholes, White, & Mamalis, 1991; Miller & Triggiano, 1992; Putnam, 1984; Putnam, Zahn, & Post, 1990).

In other cases of MPD, there are degrees of overlap in memories and styles. Some personalities may be aware of the existence of others. You saw in the case of Sarah, described at the beginning of the chapter, that some of her personalities were capable of communicating with others.

The typical individual with this disorder is aware that there are gaps in his or her life, which occur when different personalities are in control. Transition from one personality to another usually takes place within seconds or minutes. These transitions are often triggered by stress or idiosyncratic cues. With hypnosis or tranquilizing medication, an examining psychiatrist or psychologist can elicit different personalities.

The different personalities are usually given names by the person, sometimes proper names and sometimes names with symbolic significance. DSM-III-R offered the example of a particular personality called Melody because she expressed herself chiefly through music. And I once saw a videotaped interview with a woman who had a destructive personality named Death.

The different personalities may have different relationships with each other. Putnam (1989) proposed that most of the personalities encountered in MPD can be classified into the categories shown in Table 8.5. Note that some may be allies of one another. Some may "help" others. It is at times possible to identify one personality as more mature and stable than the others. A given personality may have its own diagnosable psychological disorder (such as depression) that is not evident in the others. Other times the different personalities are rivals, trying to sabotage one another. Suicide attempts, self-mutilation, and violence frequently occur with this disorder. Many transitions between personalities take place precisely at moments of danger. One personality may put herself in a dangerous situation, and then leave to let another personality handle it.

Epidemiology   Putnam (1989) estimated that there are several thousand cases of MPD in the United States today, although this may be a conservative figure. The onset of the disorder is usually in childhood, following severe abuse, usually sexual in nature (e.g., Ross et al., 1990, 1991). Women with this problem

TABLE 8.5

TYPES OF PERSONALITIES IN MULTIPLE PERSONALITY DISORDERS *From his clinical observations, Putnam suggested that the following alternative personalities are encountered with some frequency among individuals with multiple personality disorder.*
SOURCE: ADAPTED FROM *DIAGNOSIS AND TREATMENT OF MULTIPLE PERSONALITY DISORDER,* BY F. W. PUTNAM, 1989, NEW YORK: GUILFORD.

host personality: the personality that controls the body for the greatest percentage of time; the host is typically anxious, depressed, and suffering from various somatic symptoms

child personalities: personalities of infants and children; these hold memories of earlier traumatic experiences

persecutor personalities: personalities that sabotage the individual's life; these presumably are the internalization of the individual's original abuser(s)

protector personalities: personalities that counterbalance the persecutor personalities by protecting the person's safety

memory trace personality: the personality with a complete history of the individual's life

promiscuous personalities: personalities that express forbidden impulses, often sexual

anesthetic or analgesic personalities: personalities that deny feeling pain and are activated when the body is hurt; they may be involved in the self-mutilation sometimes observed among those with multiple personality disorder

the original personality: the personality identified by the others as the one that developed just after birth, from which they split off; the original personality is typically not the host personality

outnumber men by at least three to one, probably accounted for by the marked sex difference in abuse. Although boys and girls are *both* subject to abuse, females are by far the more typical victims of sexual abuse (see Figure 8.5).

Although childhood abuse is a risk factor, the disorder may not be evident until years later, usually surfacing during the late twenties. MPD rarely goes away by itself, but with age, the disorder becomes less florid. There are some hints that it runs through families, but the significance of this is not clear granted the small number of reported cases.

This disorder is particularly troublesome because it precludes the continuity in experience, memory, and behavior that makes it possible to live as a normal person (Dell & Eisenhower, 1990). One of the best arguments against the charge that people with MPD are faking is the fact that close examination reveals their lives as anything but rewarding. Without intervention, MPD is chronic. However, at present there

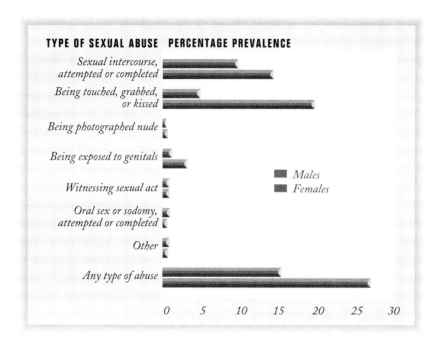

FIGURE **8.5**

PREVALENCE OF CHILDHOOD
SEXUAL ABUSE REPORTED BY
ADULTS   *In 1985, a general
survey of American adults asked
respondents about the occurrence of
different types of sexual abuse
prior to age 18.*
SOURCE: DATA DERIVED FROM "SEXUAL
ABUSE IN A NATIONAL SURVEY OF
ADULT MEN AND WOMEN," BY D.
FINKELHOR, G. HOTALING, I. A. LEWIS,
AND C. SMITH, 1990, *Child Abuse and
Neglect, 14,* PP. 19–28.

is considerable promise for treatments in which the different personalities are introduced to one another, as it were, and metaphorically fused into a single entity (Putnam, 1989). The mere introduction of dissociated selves is a critical first step toward integration.

DEPERSONALIZATION DISORDER

Most people have experienced an isolated episode in which they have felt depersonalized, like an outside observer of their own thoughts or actions. Although there is no break with reality, these people have a sense of detachment, as if they were in a dream. One or more of their senses may be numb, and they feel as if they are not in total control of their actions, including what they are saying. These feelings are unpleasant, and they usually begin suddenly and dissipate slowly over minutes or hours.

When episodes of depersonalization are recurrent and a source of marked distress to the individual, they are described as **depersonalization disorder,** which DSM-IV includes as one more type of dissociative disorder. Remember that depersonalization is a possible symptom of a panic disorder; depersonalization disorder should not be diagnosed if *other* symptoms of panic are present. And depersonalization may accompany temporal lobe epilepsy; again, the diagnostician needs to be aware of this possibility.

Characterization   The individual with this disorder often experiences the related state of **derealiza-**

tion, an alteration of perception so that the external world no longer seems real. Objects do not look right, changing size or shape. Other people seem dead or mechanical. Also co-occurring with this disorder are somatic complaints such as dizziness and a fear of going insane. Sense of time might be altered as well.

Freud (1936) described an episode of depersonalization that occurred to him when he first visited Athens in 1904 and saw the Acropolis. He could not quite believe that his presence there was real. He went on to interpret this episode as a residual from his youth, when he longed to travel and see the world, but did not because he felt oppressed by his domineering father. By disbelieving his visit to the Acropolis, Freud was presumably denying the upsetting memory of his childhood rivalry with his father.

More generally, we see here the psychodynamic interpretation of depersonalization and indeed all dissociative symptoms: attempts to protect the self against threatening memories and impulses.

Epidemiology   We know little about the epidemiology of depersonalization disorder, although it can be precipitated by stress, such as accidents or war (Noyes, Hoenk, Kuperman, & Slymen, 1977). Protracted stress is thought to be a common cause, such as that encountered in a concentration camp (Putnam,

1989). It is primarily a disorder of young people, rarely described in those over 40 years of age.

In a few case studies, this disorder has been effectively treated with behavior therapy in which the person is repeatedly exposed to situations associated with depersonalization (Sookman & Solyom, 1978). Its effectiveness implies the involvement of anxiety (Chapter 7). Other case studies attest to the effectiveness of insight-oriented treatment; the individual is encouraged to see depersonalization as an inadequate solution to problems at hand (Torch, 1987). Large-scale investigations of the treatment of depersonalization disorder have not yet been conducted.

EXPLANATIONS

Like the somatoform disorders, the dissociative disorders are best explained by noting that several risk factors exist, which probably need to combine for the disorder to develop (see Figure 8.6). Remember that dissociative experiences themselves are relatively common, whereas dissociative disorders are not, implying that the various causes must be present in unusual degrees in order for a full-blown problem to appear.

Trauma   Stressful events contribute to almost all types of dissociative disorder. In the case of amnesia and fugue, the link between trauma and disorder is obvious, because these disorders typically develop in immediate response to a troubling occurrence. Similarly, depersonalization also shows a close link to disturbing events in the immediate environment (e.g., Kahn et al., 1989).

In the case of MPD, the association between trauma and disorder has not always been so obvious. When it first began to be described in the 1800s, few psychiatrists had any inkling that trauma played a role. According to Putnam (1989), several factors conspired against this discovery. For one thing, the typical investigator encountered in his lifetime perhaps one individual with MPD, which made it difficult to discern patterns. For another thing, the abuse of children was simply not recognized as a common occurrence, and investigators had little impetus to explore it further. When it was encountered, the sexual abuse of children was referred to quaintly as seduction, and following Freud's lead, many clinicians dismissed reports of such abuse as fantasies—perhaps even unconscious wishes on the part of the victims (Masson, 1984).

We are more sophisticated today. We know that children are abused with alarming frequency (MacFarlane & Waterman, 1986). And we know that this abuse has long-term psychological consequences, increasing the risk for a variety of problems (Browne & Finkelhor, 1986). According to contemporary studies, severe abuse in childhood is present in perhaps 95% of MPD cases (Putnam, Guroff, Silberman, Barban, & Post, 1986).

This is a staggering statistic, because there are few if any other findings in psychology documenting that 95% of any group of people have shared the same experience. Do not misunderstand this result, though, because it does not mean that 95% of abused children develop MPD. Rather, it means that of those with this disorder, 95% were abused. MPD is far from a typical consequence of abuse. However, it seems all but impossible to have developed this problem without being abused.

What determines the development of MPD following abuse? One answer is in terms of the nature of the abuse. Multiple personality individuals are typically subject to multiple abuses, sexual and physical, over

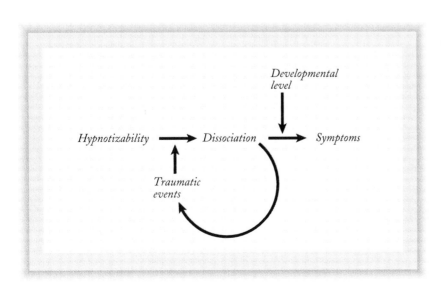

FIGURE 8.6

AN INTEGRATED MODEL OF DISSOCIATIVE DISORDERS
This diagram illustrates how dissociative disorders might develop from their contributing causes.

an extended period of time. I do not mean to trivialize any case of abuse, but there is obviously a difference between being fondled once or twice by a babysitter and being sadistically tortured over many years.

The following passage from the book Sybil, *the best-selling biography of a woman with MPD (Schreiber, 1974), is not for the squeamish. It captures how extensive and horrible abuse may be in the childhood of most of those who later develop this disorder:*

> There was still another morning ritual with which Hattie Dorsett took great pains. After placing Sybil on the kitchen table, Hattie would force into the child's vagina an array of objects that caught . . . [her] . . . fancy—a flashlight, a small empty bottle, a little silver box, the handle of a regular dinner knife, a little silver knife, a buttonhook. Sometimes the object was her finger, performing as it did when she bathed the child and scrubbed so zealously that at two and a half the child locked the door and tried to bathe herself. . . .
>
>   "You might as well get used to it," her mother, inserting one of these foreign bodies, explained to her daughter at six months. . . . "That's what men will do when you grow up. They put things in you, and they hurt you, and they push you around. . . . So I might as well prepare you." (p. 210)

Earlier in the chapter, I speculated about the apparent increase in MPD in recent decades and the inflation in the number of personalities per case (see Figure 8.7). Perhaps earlier diagnosticians simply did not recognize or fully describe the disorder when they encountered it.

But perhaps child abuse has taken an insidious turn in recent years, becoming more prevalent *and* perhaps more perverse (MacFarlane & Waterman, 1986) (see Figure 8.8). The number of discrete personalities that a person has can be predicted by the number of different traumas to which she was exposed as a child (Putnam, Guroff, Silberman, Barban, & Post, 1986).

Even among those who do not have multiple personality disorder, the extent to which dissociative experiences follow in the wake of abuse can be accounted for by the extent of the abuse. In a study of 278 female college students, Briere and Runtz (1988) found that approximately 15% of them had sexual contact with a significantly older individual prior to age 15. Women who experienced such early sexual contact tended to report more symptoms of anxiety, depression, somatization, *and* dissociation than did other women; the extent of symptoms was directly related to such variables as the number of abusers, the use of force during victimization, and the length of time over which the abuse occurred (see also Chu & Dill, 1990; Sandberg & Lynn, 1992). These are the same sorts of variables that predict the proliferation of alternative personalities among those with multiple personality disorder.

Hypnotic susceptibility   As is clear from this discussion of abuse and MPD, trauma is a necessary but not sufficient condition for dissociative disorders to develop. A second ingredient needs to be present: the ability or tendency to have dissociative experiences when exposed to stress. Related to this is a personality

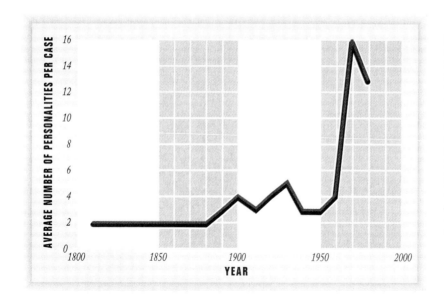

FIGURE 8.7

MULTIPLE PERSONALITY DISORDER, 1800 TO THE PRESENT   *The overall number of multiple personality case histories has increased over time, as has the average number of personalities per case.*
SOURCE: ADAPTED FROM "HAS MULTIPLE PERSONALITY DISORDER REMAINED CONSISTENT OVER TIME?" BY D. C. GOFF AND C. A. SIMMS, 1993, *Journal of Nervous and Mental Disease, 181,* FIGURE 2, P. 599. REPRINTED WITH PERMISSION.

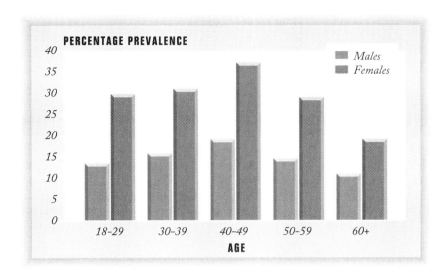

FIGURE **8.8**

CHILDHOOD SEXUAL ABUSE OVER TIME   *In the 1985 survey of the occurrence of sexual abuse prior to age 18, as illustrated in Figure 8.5, older adults were less likely to report sexual abuse during childhood, implying that the prevalence of childhood sexual abuse in the United States is increasing.*

SOURCE: DATA DERIVED FROM "SEXUAL ABUSE IN A NATIONAL SURVEY OF ADULT MEN AND WOMEN," BY D. FINKELHOR, G. HOTALING, I. A. LEWIS, AND C. SMITH, 1990, *Child Abuse and Neglect, 14,* PP. 19–28.

dimension that we can identify as susceptibility to hypnosis; by implication, *hypnotizability* predisposes dissociative disorders (Frischholz et al., 1992).

I have mentioned hypnosis throughout the chapter without giving it a formal definition. **Hypnosis** is a state of consciousness characterized by increased suggestibility. There is controversy surrounding this phenomenon (Sarbin & Coe, 1972). Is the hypnotized state altogether different from ordinary wakefulness or simply an extension of the mundane following of someone else's lead (Kihlstrom, 1985)?

We know that a person can be hypnotized by asking him to narrow his attention to what the hypnotist is saying, and then to follow his directions (Hilgard, 1977). Not everyone can be hypnotized; indeed, the ability to be hypnotized falls along a dimension as do most personality characteristics.

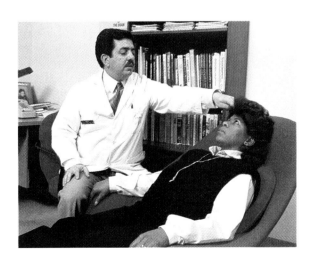

Hypnosis sometimes helps those with dissociative disorders.

Those who are susceptible to hypnotism show a variety of striking behaviors involving dissociation. Although these are exaggerated in popular presentations of hypnosis, a hypnotized person can in fact show selective forgetting (and subsequent remembering) as well as unresponsiveness to pain (Hilgard, 1973). One of the most intriguing aspects of hypnosis is the emergence, in some hypnotized people, of a part of them—a separate consciousness, according to some theorists—called the *hidden observer,* which is unavailable to the hypnotized consciousness but still aware in its own right. The hidden observer can communicate in various ways with the hypnotist, such as signaling with a finger or writing on a tablet, while the hypnotized individual is oblivious to its messages.

Numerous studies have tried to characterize hypnotic susceptibility by relating it to other personality characteristics. For our purposes, note the consistent finding that those susceptible to hypnotism are individuals who have the ability to engage freely in fantasy (Kihlstrom, 1985), which seems akin to dissociation. And note as well that those with dissociative disorders are particularly amenable to hypnotism (Putnam, 1989), which of course is why theorists link hypnotizability to these disorders (Zamansky & Bartis, 1984).

By extension, then, dissociative disorders may involve self-hypnosis; that is, the person induces a trance in herself in response to stressful circumstances (Bliss, 1980). She thereby can dissociate herself from the worst aspects of a trauma. The greater the trauma, the more elaborate the self-hypnotism, reaching its zenith in the case of MPD where altogether different personalities are created to bear the brunt of abuse.

Mechanisms of dissociation   I have proposed that the dissociative disorders are apt to occur among those who experience trauma *and* who are adept at self-hypnosis. But these notions in and of themselves fail to explain why a person develops one dissociative disorder rather than another. As with the somatoform disorders, perhaps we can argue that dissociative disorders fall along a continuum of severity that reflects the underlying degree of dissociation. If we think of dissociation as the splitting of consciousness into separate streams, the various disorders can be arrayed in terms of the degree to which there is one central stream with minor rivulets occasionally running off from it versus notably separate streams, each large and sustained.

Granted that the notion of dissociation in response to stress describes what is going on in the dissociative disorders, what can we say further about this process? If trauma and hypnotic susceptibility are *risk factors* for the dissociative disorders, then what are the *mechanisms* by which these translate themselves into the problems I have described?

One explanation is provided by psychodynamic theorists, who have long talked about **complexes**—identified as constellations of feelings and impulses that influence behavior somewhat independently of the other aspects of a person. The Oedipal dynamics are sometimes described as a complex in this sense because they supposedly play themselves out regardless of what else is going on with the person. And you have probably encountered the notion of an *inferiority complex,* introduced by Freud's associate Alfred Adler (1927) to capture a similar idea—that a bundle of thoughts and feelings about being inadequate exists in most of us, segregated in many cases from our other aspects but nevertheless influencing our actions when triggered.

Cognitive psychologists note that such psychodynamic notions of complexes are compatible with contemporary views of the mind based on experimental studies of thought and memory (e.g, Kihlstrom, 1990). What earlier theorists described anthropomorphically as complexes are nowadays referred to mechanistically as *production modules* (McClelland, Rumelhart, et al., 1986; Rumelhart, McClelland, et al., 1986), but the same idea is conveyed. According to this view, the mind is composed of different systems, each devoted to a specific task, and they carry out their business in relative independence of one another. Perhaps traumatized individuals develop a production module devoted to coping with stress.

This line of theorizing can explain the barriers of amnesia that exist between and among different states/complexes/modules. Two mechanisms may be at work here. First is simply the fact that well learned routines, cognitive or behavioral, are carried out without awareness; these are often described as **automatic processing**

(Shiffrin & Schneider, 1984). While engaged in automatic processing, the individual can do other activities.

The second mechanism may be the phenomenon of **state dependent recall,** which refers to the fact that it is easiest to recall information when in the situation in which it was originally acquired (Eich, 1980). Sometimes this state refers to a physical place. We can recall people's names if we see them again in the place where we met them, but not if we bump into them someplace else. But sometimes the state refers to our internal state—including our emotions. If we learn material while anxious, we later remember it better when anxious. In other words, our cognitive schemes can be organized along emotional dimensions. Perhaps there are schemes to which we have access only while anxious, or depressed, or terrified (Bower, 1981). Again, we can extrapolate these ideas to propose that the dissociative disorders represent an exaggeration of these normal tendencies.

Psychodynamic theorists propose that the barriers of amnesia are motivated—maintained by a censor. The view I am sketching does not propose a separate censor but rather regards censorship as inherent in the very architecture of the mind. The mind is constituted so that different memory systems tend to be segregated from one another. I am not so sure that Freud's psychoanalytic account and the more modern cognitive account are really at odds, once we consider the different languages with which they are phrased.

Those who write about consciousness have described it as a property of the mind that "emerges" granted sufficient complexity and organization of mental activity (Sperry, 1969, 1976, 1987). When a complex becomes sufficiently large and active, it can achieve its own consciousness just as any singular mind does. There is nothing contradictory about arguing that a person can have more than one consciousness. We would expect precisely this when different constellations of thoughts and feelings become segregated from one another.

Some capacity for dissociation is present in all people, because we all experience dissociation nightly when we dream. Do you see how a dream can be described as a dissociated state (Gabel, 1989)? In a dream, you are conscious of certain complex experiences, but ever so rarely are you conscious of the fact that there is another you, lying in bed having the dream. This is precisely what is meant by dissociation. In the case of dissociative disorders, these experiences are obviously more profound and disruptive.

Perhaps the mental activity of infants is dissociated, and it is only in the course of socialization that we learn to integrate our different thoughts and feelings (see Focus on Consciousness across History). This

FOCUS ON

Consciousness

across History

IN A PROVOCATIVE BOOK, Julian Jaynes (1976) argued that the very notion of consciousness is a cultural product. In other words, our ancestors thousands of years ago had no concept of consciousness. When they heard "voices" in their head, they did not identify these as aspects of their own self but rather as the visitations of gods and goddesses. It was only about 3,000 years ago, according to Jaynes, that people started to group these voices together as a unified self and label it *consciousness*.

The evidence that Jaynes used was historical, and he studied texts such as Homer's *Iliad* and *Odyssey* for mention of consciousness. Older texts made no mention of the idea. Instead, "internal" events were all attributed to gods and goddesses. Then all of a sudden consciousness made its appearance.

Consciousness serves an adaptive role. It is a way of jerking us to attention when confronted with novel or dangerous events. Our ancestors certainly had this ability; we may surmise that the capacity to pay particular attention when threatened or confronted with the unusual conferred a great selection advantage. But it is interesting that this ability was perhaps not identified by our ancestors as something for which they were responsible.

By this view, dissociation was not only in existence thousands of years ago but was the natural state of affairs for most people. When the notion of consciousness was invented, people started to have a different view of their minds and of themselves. Historians have pointed out that the modern idea of a self as a unified entity with its own unique characteristics apart from the world dates to the Middle Ages (Baumeister, 1987). Maybe this is what happened as the notion of consciousness diffused through the general population.

These ideas give us a different way of thinking about *possession*, which I discussed in Chapter 1. Perhaps what our ancestors identified as possession by spirits or devils was a form of dissociation. Nowadays we might diagnose an ostensibly possessed individual as suffering from multiple personality disorder, but

back then there was no such concept. Such occurrences might even have been common, in part because of prevailing beliefs and in part because life in those days was remarkably harsh, particularly for children (Aries, 1962). Even today, some people with MPD view one of their personalities as an evil spirit (Crabtree, 1985).

Psychiatrists from India have reported that MPD is exceedingly rare in their country because the person with these sorts of symptoms is typically diagnosed as having a *possession syndrome*—that is, the individual believes that he or she is possessed (Adityanjee, Raju, & Khandelwal, 1989). This belief is presumably much more accepted in that culture than in our own.

Before those of us in the United States feel too modern, consider Putnam's (1989) account of an individual with MPD who was hospitalized in this country. Most of the time, she was a meek and mild young woman. But at night, there emerged one of her personalities who was a profane and gruff male, who would stalk the hospital corridors cursing loudly. How did the night staff respond? They locked themselves in the nurses station and prayed, thinking that the patient was possessed. **Plus ça change, plus c'est la même chose;** *the more things change, the more they remain the same.*

Psychologist Julian Jaynes has argued that consciousness is a cultural invention, appearing in the Western world sometime during the early Greek era. (The Argonauts in the Land of the Bebrykes, *by Novios Plautios, frieze from the* Ficoroni Cist, *from Praeneste, Museo Nazionale di Villa Giulia, Rome.*)

process can be disturbed by traumatic events during childhood, as seems to happen in the dissociative disorders. It is possible that different complexes are brought to bear on the different aspects of the person's life. There is a complex for dealing with trauma and one for not (Ross & Gahan, 1988). To the degree that the nontraumatic consciousness is unaware of the traumatic complex, and vice versa, we have the makings of a dissociative disorder.

Putnam (1989) notes that the abuse that foreshadows multiple personality disorder almost always occurs at a particular time in life, between the ages of 2 and 4, which may bear on this argument. Perhaps we get the profound dissociation that characterizes MPD only when there is a disruption in the very process by which a unitary consciousness is being formed. To the previous discussion of trauma and hypnotic susceptibility as risk factors for dissociative disorders, I should add a *developmental trajectory* to the process. Maybe different disorders appear depending on when trauma originally occurs.

It is reported that those who later develop MPD often have imaginary playmates while young (Bliss, 1980). When coupled with severe trauma and hypnotic susceptibility, maybe these imaginary playmates become the different personalities. In other cases, these playmates foreshadow the development of depersonalization disorders in adults, and maybe this occurs in the absence of profound trauma in childhood (Myers, 1976).

These sorts of mechanisms seem able to account for the range of dissociative disorders, according to the proliferation and segregation of cognitive systems. At one extreme, we have dissociative amnesia and depersonalization, in which consciousness is split into only two streams. At the other extreme, we have multiple personality disorder, in which dissociation has divided consciousness into a number of substantial groups, perhaps to the extent that we cannot even identify which is the "main" consciousness.

TREATMENTS

In dissociative amnesia, dissociative fugue, and depersonalization, "treatment" may simply involve waiting until the disorders go away. Indeed, dissociative experiences in general become less common with age (see Figure 8.9). If these disorders linger or are too distressing, the process can be hurried along by breaking down barriers of amnesia and uniting dissociated states of consciousness. Often the mere recapture of a thread of memory is sufficient to make a person's consciousness unitary. Other times the process needs to be facilitated by behavioral, psychodynamic, and/ or pharmacological interventions that work against anxiety, presumably at the root of dissociation in the first case.

With multiple personality disorder, treatment is more complicated. Still, the same general principles apply. Putnam (1989) outlines several treatment strategies. First is getting the individual to accept the diagnosis, by no means simple. Next is fostering communication and cooperation between and among the various personalities. Putnam recommends creating an explicit contract with all of them not to do harm to one another or sabotage treatment. Another technique is to use a central bulletin board or notebook in which the different personalities leave messages for one an-

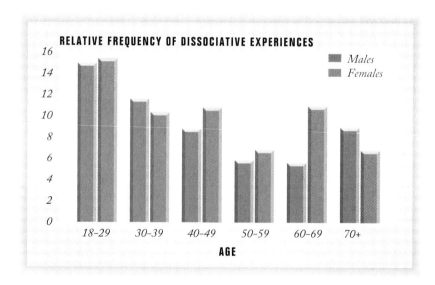

RELATIVE FREQUENCY OF DISSOCIATIVE EXPERIENCES

FIGURE 8.9

DISSOCIATIVE EXPERIENCES WITH AGE   *These figures are the relative frequencies with which dissociative experiences like those in Figure 8.4 are reported by people of different ages.*
SOURCE: DATA DERIVED FROM "DISSOCIATIVE EXPERIENCES IN THE GENERAL POPULATION," BY C. A. ROSS, S. JOSHI, AND R. CURRIE, 1990, *American Journal of Psychiatry, 147*, PP. 1547–1552.

other and record their activities. The therapist can serve as a go-between, as might those personalities who have always played this role. Then the different personalities are encouraged to engage in internal dialogues. The person is taught coping skills that do not involve switching from one personality to another. And she is taught to make the switches willfully rather than automatically in response to stress.

Other techniques that are sometimes used in the treatment of MPD are hypnotism and sodium amytal, to breach barriers of amnesia. Sometimes videotapes are made of the various personalities to show one another, although Putnam (1989) cautions that this can be highly upsetting for those personalities not yet willing or able to accept each other's existence.

Granted the role of severe abuse in the backgrounds of virtually all people with this disorder, the issue must be addressed in therapy. As you may recall from my earlier discussion of post-traumatic stress disorder, talking about the abuse in a supportive context is often useful (Chapter 7).

Therapy for multiple personality disorder can be highly complex, for all the reasons that any treatment is difficult, magnified and multiplied. One of the issues irrelevant in the treatment of other problems is whether it is ethical even to proceed with treatment in the first place. Is it right to disband a person's repertoire of personalities? The goal of therapy is to integrate or fuse fragmented selves (Kluft, 1984, 1988), but said another way, this means destroying entities qualifying as persons in their own right. Some therapists are reluctant to do this; understandably, so too are some individuals with MPD, and not all who begin therapy stick with it.

Among those who do stay with a therapy program, prognosis is good, as I earlier emphasized. The vast majority of individuals show some improvement (Coons, 1986; Kluft, 1985), although this does not necessarily mean that they evidence a total integration of all their alternative selves. More commonly, improvement means greater continuity among memories, identities, and behaviors, yet short of total unity (Putnam, 1989).

Bryant, Kessler, and Shirar (1992) described the successful treatment of Judy, a young woman with multiple personality disorder. As a child, she had experienced repeated incidents of physical and sexual abuse. She was coerced into posing for pornographic photos. As she tells her story:

> *I created an inside friend called "Little Judy"; she began to talk to me and I to her. I liked to hear her voice, and*

> *I could play with her whenever I wanted. I felt so glad she was my friend; she made me feel good in my upside-down world. We were inseparable. My secluded and lonely world was now filled with laughter and hope. I knew better than to tell anyone of my secret friend, for fear they would take her away, just as they had taken away everything else.   (pp. 2–3)*

Over time, such "inside friends" proliferated, and they became sealed off from one another. As an adult, Judy displayed full-blown MPD. She eventually entered treatment, which proceeded much as already sketched, introducing her different personalities to one another and fusing them.

> *I think anything less than integration is only a superficial bandage on a large deep wound. I believe that integration is worth the effort. Finally, after being subject to abuse, never feeling good about myself, and hiding inside all these years, I am able to experience the good things in life.   (p. 234)*

After treatment for multiple personality disorder, Judy remained a person who had been terribly abused. But she felt able to embark on a new life and consider for the first time the possibilities of a husband, friends, and a career.

I have discussed somatoform and dissociative disorders in this chapter, and I close by returning to the point made at the very beginning when these terms were introduced. Once upon a time, these disorders were seen as aspects of the same general problem. I remain convinced that they share many features in common—symptoms, causes, and treatments. Throughout the book, I have been noting the continuity between normality and abnormality, but here you see an example of continuity among different types of abnormality.

Summary

✦ In somatoform disorders, an individual shows physical symptoms such as pain, blindness, or deafness that seem to suggest the presence of an illness or injury, although none is present. In dissociative disorders, the person shows breaks in memory, consciousness, or identity that seem to suggest the presence of a neurological impairment, although again none is present. These disorders are difficult to conceptualize because they are characterized by discontinuities. Often useful in explaining them is the psychodynamic model of abnormality, which views their symptoms as attempts to cope with threatening memories and impulses.

SOMATOFORM DISORDERS

✦   Several types of somatoform disorder exist. All must be distinguished from malingering, faking, and psychosomatic disorders, as well as from actual physical illness.

✦   A conversion disorder involves the alteration or loss of physical functioning for psychological reasons: keeping a conflict out of awareness and/or achieving secondary gain.

✦   Hypochondriasis is a preoccupation with having or contracting a disease, in the absence of any good reasons for this preoccupation.

✦   Somatization disorder resembles hypochondriasis, except that the person complains about a greater variety of symptoms and fears a greater range of diseases.

✦   Body dysmorphic disorder is a preoccupation with an imagined defect in one's own appearance.

✦   Pain disorder is characterized by chronic pain in the absence of an adequate physical basis for it.

✦   The somatoform disorders probably have a number of contributing causes, including enhanced physiological sensitivity to sensations, dire interpretations of these sensations, difficulty expressing emotions in words, modeling, actual traumatic events, and reinforcement of symptoms.

✦   Treatments for the somatoform disorders take different forms, from reassurance and support to confrontation and setting limits. The more entrenched a disorder, the less responsive to treatment it is. Hypochondriasis and somatization disorder in particular resist treatment and have a chronic course.

DISSOCIATIVE DISORDERS

✦   There exist several dissociative disorders, and all can be understood in terms of the phenomenon of dissociation: the splitting of consciousness into two or more discrete streams with little or no communication between or among them.

✦   In dissociative amnesia, the person is suddenly unable to recall personally important information. Dis-

sociative amnesia occurs in the immediate aftermath of severe stress.

✦   Related to dissociative amnesia is dissociative fugue, in which a person loses his personal memory, travels away from home, and establishes a new identity under which he lives. Again, dissociative fugue occurs in response to stress.

✦   Multiple personality disorder (also called dissociative identity disorder) is a rare and fascinating problem in which different personalities exist within the same body, often unaware of one another. It is more common among women than men, and severe physical and sexual abuse during childhood is present in the vast majority of cases.

✦   Depersonalization disorder is characterized by episodes in which a person feels like an outside observer of his own thoughts and behaviors.

✦   Like somatoform disorders, dissociative disorders are brought about by the interaction of several factors, notably trauma and the capacity for self-hypnosis. Although dissociation seems bizarre, the psychological mechanisms responsible for it may be quite mundane. When one segregates thoughts and feelings from one another, these may develop their own consciousness.

✦   The dissociative disorders can all be treated by breaking down the barriers of amnesia that exist between dissociated states. Sometimes the mere passage of time accomplishes this, and other times the therapist must take steps to encourage the process. Prognosis tends to be good for the problems characterized by dissociation, including multiple personality disorder.

Key Terms

alexithymia

anxiety sensitivity

automatic processing

body dysmorphic disorder

complex

conversion disorder; hysteria

depersonalization disorder

derealization

dissociation

dissociative amnesia

dissociative disorder

dissociative fugue

factitious disorder

gate-control theory

histrionic personality
disorder; hysterical
personality disorder

hypnosis

hypochondriasis

la belle indifference

malingering

mass hysteria

Morita psychotherapy

multiple personality
disorder; MPD;
dissociative identity
disorder

nosophobia

pain disorder

psychosomatic disorders

repression-sensitization

secondary gain

somatization disorder;
Briquet's syndrome

somatoform disorder

state dependent recall

Mood Disorders

9

As school children, we all learned about *Abraham Lincoln (1809–1865), the sixteenth President of the United States. We learned that he rose from humble beginnings to become a great leader, presiding over the Civil War and the emancipation of the slaves. We learned that he was somber. But did we learn in school that Lincoln spent a great deal of his adult life seriously depressed? His contemporaries and biographers alike agree on this fact, although today's public has not assimilated it. We want to think of our leaders as energetic and confident. Lincoln in contrast was slow, fatigued, and indecisive—typical signs of deep*

depression. There is a lesson here: Greatness comes in many forms.

> *Lincoln had numerous bouts with depression. His first love was Ann Rutledge, but she died unexpectedly when he was 26 years old. He became distraught, so much so that his friends feared he would kill himself. They hid knives and razors from him. This went on for months.*
>
> *Another well documented episode in Lincoln's life occurred when he was first supposed to marry Mary Todd: He did not show up for the wedding. His friends found him wandering about, restless, desperate, and unhappy. Again, those close to him feared that he would kill himself.*
>
> *Yet another episode of depression followed the death of his son Willie. Lincoln was President at the time, and although there were critical decisions to make concerning the Civil War, instead he would spend long hours just sitting alone, mourning his son.*

Lincoln's case well illustrates some of the generalizations I can make about **mood disorders:** problems marked by alterations in mood. In *depression*, the person experiences excessive sadness and unhappiness. In *mania*, the person experiences inappropriate elation and acts in reckless fashion. Some people with mood disorders alternate between the extremes of both.

President Abraham Lincoln (1809–1865) spent a great deal of his adult life severely depressed.

Depression is one of the best examples of the continuity between normality and abnormality. It has its everyday version, the feelings of sadness and hurt that almost all of us experience when our ongoing pursuit of goals is thwarted. Normal depression causes us to pause and take stock when we are frustrated. But depression may slide ever so insidiously into a serious problem affecting all spheres of our being—emotions, thoughts, actions, physiology, and even interpersonal relationships. In its extreme, it takes a great toll on human happiness and productivity. Depressive episodes can last for months, and they can recur over the years, as they did for Abraham Lincoln. Depression can quite literally be a fatal abnormality, given its strong link with suicide. Most of those who commit suicide in our society are severely depressed as well. If their depression were to go away, so too in many cases would their desire to kill themselves.

Depression also tends to co-occur with other psychological problems, to such a degree that by some estimates the majority of depressed individuals also satisfy DSM criteria for at least one other disorder (Sanderson, Beck, & Beck, 1990). In Chapter 7, I noted that depression and anxiety tend to be present in the same people (Brady & Kendall, 1992). In Chapter 6, I mentioned that many people who develop a neurological disease also develop depression. And in Chapter 5, you saw that many of those with substance abuse problems are depressed. Epidemiologists dub this *comorbidity*: the co-occurrence of two disorders, in this case depression and virtually any other form of psychopathology (Maser & Cloninger, 1990). Depression is often encountered in the aftermath of serious physical problems as well, such as a heart attack.

Some diagnosticians distinguish between *primary mood disorders*, in which depression exists prior to other difficulties, and *secondary mood disorders*, in which mood alterations follow other problems, psychological or physical (Costello & Scott, 1991; Winokur, 1990). On the face of it, primary and secondary mood disorders may look the same, but the distinction becomes important when we try to treat them (Goodwin & Guze, 1989). We would want to do something different for a person who is just depressed than we would for a person who is depressed and schizophrenic, depressed and anorexic, or depressed and alcoholic.

Mood disorders take different forms (see Table 9.1). DSM-IV distinguishes most basically between *depressive disorder* (also called *unipolar disorder*), in which the predominant symptom is depressive episodes, and *bipolar disorder*, in which depressive and manic episodes alternate. There are cases of pure mania, but these are rare, and they are usually classified as variants of bipolar disorder (Goodwin & Guze, 1989).

Although the description of Lincoln as depressed is not controversial, some have argued more speculatively that he suffered from bipolar disorder (Fieve, 1976). What is the evidence for this? His depressive episodes were clear. Manic episodes are harder to specify, but we do know that as a young man Lincoln went through a wild phase in which he was overtalkative, bombastic, and insulting. He was involved in a number of fistfights. His excessive energy and inappropriate actions may indicate manic episodes. Along these lines, after his political career began, Lincoln continued to show bursts of prodigious energy. He gave numerous speeches in a short period of time, during an era when politicians wrote their own. His contemporaries described him as agitated and nervous during these bursts of activity; he also acted impulsively and slept little.

On the other hand, we may be reading too much between the lines in these attempts to argue that Lincoln suffered from bipolar disorder. Fistfights were common among young men on the frontier. And nonstop campaigning typifies politicians from all eras. Lincoln was never out of control, as happens in extreme forms of mania.

TABLE 9.1

MOOD DISORDERS *Although both are classified by DSM-IV as mood disorders, unipolar disorder and bipolar disorder differ in important ways.*

	UNIPOLAR DISORDER	BIPOLAR DISORDER
characterization	depressive episodes	alternating depressive and manic episodes
lifetime prevalence	20%	1%
sex ratio	females twice as likely as males to be depressed	about equal
developmental aspects	occurs across the lifespan; most common in young adulthood; variable course	rare among children; onset usually in mid-20s; may have chronic course
risk factors	heredity; stress; social loss and isolation; dependency; helplessness	heredity; stress (?)
effective treatments	antidepressants; ECT; interpersonal psychotherapy; behavior therapy; cognitive therapy	lithium; psychological counseling regarding compliance and life skills

Still, moderate versions of both mania and depression can be useful to a person. If a modicum of depression makes him stop and think, then a tad of mania helps him forge ahead and explore new possibilities. When an individual is entering a manic episode, even if it peaks in great tumult, on the way "up" he can be productive and charming.

Bipolar disorder is genetically predisposed, which lends some strength to the position that the capacity to experience extreme moods can be adaptive. The evidence is somewhat less solid that depressive disorder is genetically based, but there is still good reason to think that genetics plays at least some role here as well. Regardless, psychological and environmental factors are clearly implicated in depressive disorder.

Over the years, various classifications of the mood disorders have been proposed. The overarching issue has been whether to include unipolar and bipolar disorder together (Marneros, Deister, & Rohde, 1990). Prior to the 20th century, they were simply placed in the same category (Goodwin & Jamison, 1990). Then they were pulled apart, with depressive disorder considered a neurosis and bipolar disorder a psychosis. Now they have again been placed in the same DSM category—mood disorders—but within this general category, they are distinguished from one another.

Not too many years ago, those who suffered from mood disorders were fated to go through their lives as best they could, sometimes recovering on their own and sometimes not. Suicide was a constant threat. Now we know a great deal about the causes of mood disorder, both unipolar and bipolar, and we have effective treatments available for both.

As with the anxiety disorders, the mood disorders are profitably examined from a variety of perspectives. Most of the models of abnormality I have identified have something important to say about depression, either unipolar or bipolar or both. We should expect that an integrated perspective will someday be at hand (see Akiskal & McKinney, 1973; Billings & Moos, 1985; Monroe & Simons, 1991).

DEPRESSIVE DISORDER

In its extreme form, the sort that would alert mental health professionals, **depressive disorder** (or **unipolar disorder** or **depression**) is characterized by episodes of excessive and inappropriate sadness, loss of interest in pleasurable activities, and various other symptoms from all spheres of functioning.

SIGNS OF DEPRESSION

We would not want to say simply that a person's mood is depressed, or her thoughts, or her actions, or her physiology. Rather, it is the whole person who is depressed, and we can readily identify emotional, motivational, somatic, behavioral, and cognitive symptoms (see Table 9.2). According to DSM-IV, a depressive episode is marked by at least five major symptoms, including either a depressed mood or the loss of interest and pleasure. An episode must last at least 2 weeks.

Mood   The depressed person shows a depressed mood, although he may not use the term *depressed* to describe what he feels. Possible synonyms to which the diagnostician must be alert include *sad, blue, in the dumps,* or *empty.* Depression can also show up as an irritable or angry mood.

Anhedonia   Another characteristic sign of depression is **anhedonia:** reduced interest and/or pleasure in the pursuit of everyday activities. The depressed person is apathetic. The sort of activities that used to grab his attention—from work to play—no longer hold the same appeal. If you have ever had a depressed friend, you know that the typical response to your question "Do you want to . . .?" is no, he does not.

Weight change   People who are depressed may lose their appetite not only for activities per se but specifically for life's pleasures, like eating. The depressed person may show a significant weight loss— 5 or 10 pounds or even more within a month's time. This is not due to a deliberate diet but rather to the fact that he is simply not hungry and food holds no appeal. Alternatively, he may experience a precipitous weight gain from constant snacking, perhaps in an attempt to feel better with sweets and chocolates.

TABLE 9.2

SYMPTOMS OF A DEPRESSIVE EPISODE *Depression may show itself in all spheres of psychological functioning.*

TYPE OF SYMPTOM	EXAMPLE
emotional	depressed mood
motivational	loss of interest or pleasure in activities; fatigue or loss of energy
somatic	weight loss or gain; insomnia or hypersomnia
behavioral	psychomotor agitation or retardation
cognitive	feelings of worthlessness; excessive guilt; diminished ability to think or concentrate; recurrent thoughts of death

One sign of depression is reduced interest in the pursuit of activities once experienced as pleasurable.

pressed individuals complain that they lack energy, a symptom known as **anergia.** I think you can start to see how the various manifestations of depression can exacerbate one another. The person unable to get a good night's sleep is going to feel tired. The person who feels tired is not going to be interested in any activities, pleasurable or not. And so it goes—which means that depression can be a vicious cascade of ever more diverse and severe symptoms.

Negative cognitions   Depression affects as well how people think about themselves and the world. Depressed people have a negative view of things, particularly of their own worth and competence. Self-blame is frequent, along with excessive and inappropriate guilt. Profound hopelessness may also characterize depression. Attempts to tell these individuals that their negative beliefs are unwarranted are apt to fall on deaf ears.

Sleep disturbance   The depressed person may also experience sleep disturbances. He might evidence hypersomnia, sleeping 12 or 14 hours or more per day. Alternatively, he might evidence insomnia, typically a form known as **terminal insomnia (or early morning awakening)**: the inability to fall asleep after awakening (Gillin, Duncan, Pettigrew, Frankel, & Snyder, 1979). (Terminal refers to the fact that it occurs at the end of a person's sleep cycle.) The depressed insomniac is usually exhausted but unable to get a good night's sleep. He will awaken after several hours and start to ruminate, tossing and turning things over in his mind and being unable to drift back to sleep.

Psychomotor disturbance   Yet another way in which depression shows itself is in terms of psychomotor agitation versus retardation. Depressed people may be restless and nervous, in their thoughts and movements, or sluggish and unresponsive. In unipolar disorder, agitated depression is more common than retarded depression (Beigel & Murphy, 1971), whereas the opposite is true in bipolar disorder (Depue & Monroe, 1978). Biomedical approaches to depression focus greatly on several neurotransmitters thought to be deficient in depression. Among their other effects, these influence motor movement, so it is hardly surprising that agitation or retardation are signs of depression. Antidepressant medication is presumably effective because it regularizes these neurotransmitters, and in fact, among the first symptoms of depression to respond to this medication are the somatic ones.

Anergia   Another way in which a person might be depressed is by constantly feeling fatigued. De-

I remember once trying to cheer up a depressed friend by pointing out all her notable accomplishments. She got tears in her eyes, and said, "I could never be as nice a person as you are, to be able to remember all those things about someone else and then tell them. I don't deserve to have friends."

In recent years, several theorists have been so struck with the cognitive characteristics of depression and their tenacity in the face of contrary evidence that they have elevated these striking characteristics to a primary—causal—role in depression. Not surprisingly, therapy from this perspective is cognitive, attacking the person's beliefs and the mental processes that maintain them.

Concentration disturbance   The depressed person may also complain of an inability to concentrate or make decisions. Certainly, the indecisiveness of depressed people is notorious. They dawdle endlessly, over what to wear, what to eat, and where to go. This system is related to negative cognitions in that at least part of the problem is brought about by a tendency to second-guess everything and to dwell on the negative consequences of every act, thus inhibiting decision making.

Cognitively minded theorists assign a central role to rumination in the maintenance of this disorder (e.g., Nolen-Hoeksema, 1991; Zullow, 1984). All of us become depressed, goes the argument, but the difference between a person who develops a full-blown depressive episode versus a person who does not is that the former individual concentrates on the negative.

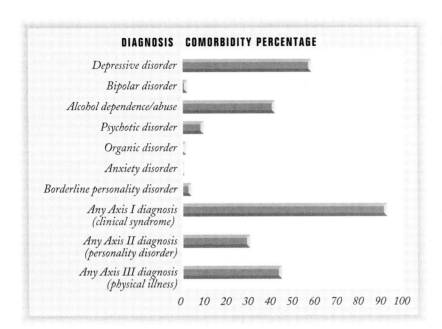

FIGURE **9.1**

COMORBIDITY OF SUICIDE
AND DSM DISORDERS
*In a random sample of suicide
victims in Finland, the vast
majority warranted a DSM
diagnosis. Almost half of these
victims were given two or more
diagnoses.*
SOURCE: DATA DERIVED FROM "MENTAL
DISORDERS AND SUICIDE," BY M. M.
HENRIKSSON ET AL., 1993, *American
Journal of Psychiatry, 150,* PP. 935–940.

Thoughts of death   Finally, DSM-IV points out
that recurrent thoughts of death and specifically suicide
may mark depression (see Figure 9.1). These thoughts
are sometimes translated into specific plans that are
then carried out.

SUICIDE AND DEPRESSION

Suicide is among the leading causes of death in the
United States (National Institute of Mental Health,
1986). In our country, perhaps 30,000 people kill
themselves each year, and for every completed suicide,
there may be ten or more uncompleted attempts. It
may occur among any and all groups, but I can offer
some generalizations about those in our society who
are most likely to take their own lives (Holinger, 1987;
Klerman, 1987).

   Children are the least likely to commit suicide.
And although suicide rates are increasing at an
alarming pace among adolescents, the absolute risk of
suicide rises steadily throughout adulthood[1] (see Figure
9.2). Thus, the elderly are the most likely to kill themselves, particularly in the face of serious physical illness.
Whites and Native Americans are more likely to kill
themselves than African Americans.

   More women attempt suicide than do men, but
among completed suicides, men outnumber women
by more than three to one. The difference lies largely

*Recurrent thoughts of death and specifically suicide may
characterize a depressive episode. (The Suicide, by K.
Kollwitz, National Gallery of Art, Rosenwald Collection,
Washington, DC)*

---

[1] This does not mean that *depression* increases with age; see
pp. 263–264.

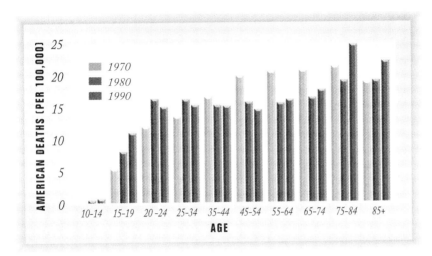

FIGURE 9.2

PREVALENCE OF SUICIDE IN THE UNITED STATES
In the United States, the risk of suicide rises steadily with age.
SOURCE: DATA DERIVED FROM *Statistical Abstract of the United States* (113TH ED.), 1993, WASHINGTON, DC: U.S. DEPARTMENT OF COMMERCE.

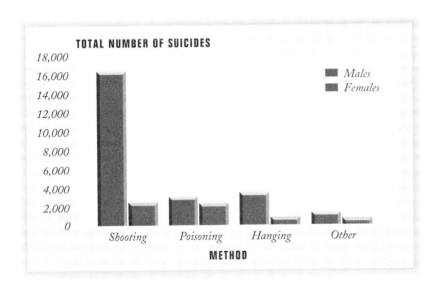

FIGURE 9.3

METHOD OF SUICIDE IN THE UNITED STATES, 1990
Men are much more likely than women to take their own lives by using a firearm.
SOURCE: DATA DERIVED FROM *Statistical Abstract of the United States* (113TH ED.), 1993, WASHINGTON, DC: U.S. DEPARTMENT OF COMMERCE.

in the chosen method (Marzuk et al., 1992). Women use less lethal means such as an overdose of sleeping pills, whereas men usually opt for more lethal methods such as hanging or shooting themselves (see Figure 9.3). Women are increasingly using more lethal means to commit suicide, which means that the sex difference in completed suicides is becoming smaller (Martinez & Cameron, 1992).

In theory, suicide attempts and completed suicides represent different motives, but in practice, there is difficulty in distinguishing the two. The point that should be emphasized is that the person who makes an unsuccessful suicide attempt is very much at risk for actual suicide; the person who eventually kills himself has made a previous attempt about half the time. If nothing else, you should think of the suicidal individual as intensely ambivalent (Shneidman, 1987).

There are drastically different rates of suicide across different societies, a point made a century ago by sociologist Emile Durkheim (1897/1951), who argued that suicide rates could be understood within a society as a function of such sociological factors as the dominant religion, societal expectations about what people should and should not do, and social stress and turmoil. Durkheim's ideas remind us that even a profoundly personal act like suicide takes place within the context of a larger society.

Along these lines, although not strictly a function of depression, it is interesting to note the recent debate over the right of elderly and ill individuals to die with dignity (Hendin & Klerman, 1993). In some cases, this means withholding heroic medical interventions that prolong life without restoring the person's health. In other cases, this means assisting the terminally ill

In his campaign of assisted suicides, Dr. Jack Kevorkian (right) has helped spark public discussion of the right of all individuals to die with dignity. He appears here with one of his patients and his attorney.

person in actually killing himself. A decade ago, these debates simply did not take place. Today they signal a change in our societal attitudes.

As mentioned already, there is a strong link in Western societies between severe depression and suicide (Jacobsson, 1988). The majority of suicides in the United States are committed by those who are extremely depressed; about 15% of those with severe depression harbor suicidal thoughts. One of the factors predicting whether depressed individuals will attempt suicide is their degree of hopelessness (Beck, Kovacs, & Weissman, 1975). And given that they are hopeless, suicide becomes more likely to the degree that they have concrete plans for carrying out their death. Alcoholism is also a contributing factor to suicide; rate of suicide among those who abuse alcohol occurs at twenty times that of the general population (Adams & Overholser, 1992; Merrill, Milner, Owens, & Vale, 1992). Table 9.3 lists some further risk factors for suicide.

Singer Kurt Cobain's suicide in 1994 received wide publicity because of the popularity of his band Nirvana (Handy, 1994). In many ways, though, his suicide was typical. At age 27, Cobain had achieved unimagined success as a songwriter and performer, yet he had long-standing problems with depression and substance abuse. His parents divorced when he was 8 years old, and he was shuttled between the homes of relatives. In high school, he was the victim of beatings from other students offended by his iconoclastic attitudes.

Cobain never seemed comfortable with the acclaim accorded him.

"None of this would have happened had he not been so famous," insists Daniel House, a friend of Cobain's. . . .

TABLE 9.3

RISK FACTORS FOR SUICIDE *What is the probability that an individual will carry out a threat of suicide? The Los Angeles Suicide Prevention Center asks for the information listed here.*
SOURCE: FROM "MODELS FOR PREDICTING SUICIDE RISK," BY R. E. LITMAN, 1974, IN *Psychological Assessment of Suicidal Risk*, C. NEURINGER (ED.), SPRINGFIELD, IL: CHARLES C. THOMAS.

1. *Age and sex:* Males and those over 50 years of age are at greater risk.
2. *Depressive symptoms:* Severely depressed people are at greater risk.
3. *Stress:* If an individual has recently experienced such stressful events as divorce or unemployment, he or she is at greater risk.
4. *Plan:* The person with a specific and highly lethal plan for suicide is at greater risk than someone with a vague and/or less lethal plan.
5. *Social support:* Those without supportive friends or family members are at greater risk.
6. *Prior suicidal behavior:* People who have made prior suicide attempts are at greater risk.
7. *Medical status:* Those with chronic illnesses are at greater risk than those without.
8. *Communication:* Risk for suicide is greater when individuals and their relatives have broken off communication and reject efforts to reestablish communication.
9. *Reaction of significant others:* Risk is greater when significant others react to crises with defensiveness, denial, punitiveness, or rejection.

The suicide of musician Kurt Cobain attracted a great deal of attention in 1994. In many ways, his was a typical suicide.

"When Nirvana started catching on, he was kind of bewildered. His music was so personal, it amazed him when people came out in droves to hear it." (Handy, 1994, p. 72)

Life was particularly stressful in the weeks before his death. Rumors swirled that Nirvana was breaking up. The band backed out of a planned tour. Cobain overdosed by swallowing fifty tranquilizers, and he slipped into a coma. Although he recovered, some suspected that this represented an unsuccessful suicide attempt. His friends and family members confronted him about his drug abuse and demanded that he clean himself up. Shortly thereafter, Kurt Cobain ended his life with a shotgun blast to the head.

What can we do about suicide? Mental health professionals and everyday people alike should be aware of the risk factors for suicide; the more present, the more aggressive the intervention should be (see Table 9.3 again). A suicidal individual can sometimes be persuaded *not* to act without talking further to someone about it. Hope should be encouraged, however possible. When suicidal wishes are entwined with depression, we should obviously help the person with his depression, in the ways available to us. A depressed person is most at risk for suicide precisely as his depression begins to lift (Pokorny, 1968). This may strike you as paradoxical, but it appears to mean that the person has regained enough resolve and energy to follow through on a plan made earlier.

Suicide hotlines are commonplace in many parts of the country, and people feeling suicidal are encour-

Suicide hotlines are now commonplace in many parts of the country, but in general, they are not effective in reducing suicide rates.

aged to call and talk to counselors. Researchers report, however, that suicide hotlines are *not* greatly effective in lowering the overall suicide rate in a given community (Bridge, Potkin, Zung, & Soldo, 1977). It seems the vast majority of callers are not in serious need of help and are using the service for something other than its intended purpose (Hirsch, 1981). Young white females may be the only group dissuaded from suicide by the use of these hotlines (Miller, Coombs, Leeper, & Barton, 1984; Stein & Lambert, 1984).

TYPES OF DEPRESSION

Like many other disorders, depression exists in degrees, falling along a continuum. DSM-IV acknowledges this fact by calling on diagnosticians to characterize depression as *mild, moderate,* or *severe,* according to the number of symptoms present, their duration, and the degree to which they disrupt social and occupational functioning. Depression can take an incredible toll on a person's well-being, not just in the obvious ways when she is incapacitated and suicidal, but also in the less obvious case of "mild" depression in which she is walking but wounded. DSM-IV uses the term **dysthymic disorder** to describe a relatively mild yet chronic form of depression.

A depressive episode is termed **melancholic depression** when it is dominated by bodily symptoms and is worse in the morning. Some believe that a melancholic depression—because of its symptoms—responds particularly well to antidepressant medications, although this is far from universally accepted (Joyce & Paykel, 1989).

Overlapping with the notion of melancholic depression is that of **endogenous depression,** a cluster of symptoms involving somatic changes, psychomotor retardation, loss of interest in life, and lack of responsiveness to the environment; the opposite is **reactive depression** (also called **exogenous depression**), which tends *not* to be characterized by these particular symptoms. The traditional position has been that endogenous depression is biological in nature—*endogenous* means *from within*—whereas reactive depression is a response to external events. The current opinion is that it is difficult to pull the etiology of depression apart in this way; biological and environmental causes probably interact to predispose most if not all cases of depression. Perhaps the reactive-endogenous distinction is one of degree, from mild to severe, more than of kind (Zimmerman, 1986).

An intriguing disorder involving mood has been dubbed **seasonal affective disorder** (or **SAD**). Moods show a regular relationship to the season, worsening in the winter and lifting in the summer (Rosenthal et al., 1984). The interpretation favored by those who

In seasonal affective disorder (SAD), depression increases during the winter.

I borrowed the lights from the psychiatrist who was doing the study and took them home for two weeks. I was supposed to sit under them . . . letting them shine on both sides of my face. She gave me a list of times to choose from so that I could fit it into my work schedule. . . . This worked for me. In general the lights gave me a tremendous sense of well-being. . . . It was something I looked forward to—the actual experience of sitting there under the lights. (p. 100)

It is not clear whether SAD should be classified with unipolar or bipolar disorder, and DSM-IV allows the qualification *seasonal pattern* to be applied to either type of mood disorder. Perhaps it finds a more ready fit with depression because the depressive episodes in SAD are usually more apparent than the manic ones (White, Lewy, Sack, Blood, & Wesche, 1990). The explosion of popular books and articles on this disorder implies that it is an exceedingly common problem (e.g., Costigan, 1985; Nadis, 1987). However, a community survey in Iceland—where people are presumably at high risk because of its northern latitude—found that only about 4% of the residents met diagnostic criteria (Magnusson & Stefansson, 1993). Seasonal affective disorder was more common among women and younger adults.

THE EPIDEMIOLOGY OF DEPRESSION

Depression is one of the most common forms of psychological abnormality. At any given moment, perhaps one in twenty Americans is in the midst of a severe depressive episode. Many more suffer from milder versions. The lifetime chances of at least one depressive episode severe enough to warrant the attention of a psychologist or psychiatrist may be as high as one in five.

Depression runs through families (Downey & Coyne, 1990). Indeed, families as a whole are depressed or not, and according to some theories, the depressions of the individual family members serve to maintain the depressions of each other (Keitner & Miller, 1990). Colds and the flu are obviously contagious, but so too are ways of feeling, including depression.

Depression exists across the lifespan. Not too long ago, theorists considered it rare among children, even nonexistent (McKnew, Cytryn, & Yahraes, 1983). But now diagnosticians recognize depression among children as common, although still not as frequent as among adults (Fleming & Offord, 1990; Keller, Lavori, Beardslee, Wunder, & Ryan, 1991).

At one time it was believed that depression became more likely as people aged. This makes sense.

study it is not that the season per se is critical but rather that decreasing and increasing amounts of sunlight determine mood swings by affecting hormones (Jacobsen & Rosenthal, 1988). The recommended treatment is phototherapy—exposing the person to very strong light for several hours a day (Rosenthal & Blehar, 1989).

Hyman (1990) interviewed a 40-year-old woman with seasonal affective disorder who benefited from phototherapy:

> *In general, when winter comes what my body wants to do is hibernate. When it's dark I want to go to bed and pull the covers over my head and sleep. I have to force myself out of the house. I find myself going to bed earlier and earlier . . . feeling more negative about life in general. Mostly it's a sense that I can't stand it one minute longer. (p. 95)*

> *I hate these feelings in winter. They disrupt the flow of my life and I resent them. . . . In November it's this tremendous feeling that I'm sliding down a dark tunnel. I know I'm going to get depressed and sad and unhappy, and there's nothing I can do about it. (p. 104)*

Depression runs in families, reflecting the roles of genetics and common life experiences, not the least of which is the presence in one's life of a depressed person.

After all, depression often begins with a loss, and as we age, losses accumulate (Kennedy, Kelman, & Thomas, 1990). We lose our loved ones to death. We lose our physical capacities. We lose our dreams. We necessarily lose our future. But as it turns out, young adults are currently at greater risk for depression than their parents or grandparents.

A survey conducted in three U.S. cities—Baltimore, St. Louis, and New Haven—questioned a randomly chosen 10,000 adults about whether they had a major depressive episode at any point in life (Robins et al., 1984). When the researchers examined these episodes as a function of age, they discovered that the younger adults were more likely to have had a major depressive episode than the older ones. Appreciate that the older adults had obviously been alive longer and hence had many more occasions to have been depressed at some point. When we adjust the figures for the amount of time the respondents had been alive, they show a tenfold difference in the likelihood of being depressed across several generations (Seligman, 1988).

If we take these findings at face value, they imply greatly increasing rates of depression in our society as young adults age (see Figure 9.4). Indeed, further epidemiological studies document this pattern in countries around the world, although to varying degrees (e.g., Cross-National Collaborative Group, 1992). Further studies are obviously needed to map

these apparent increases in the prevalence of depression into social, political, and economic changes during recent decades.

Another striking epidemiological fact concerning depression is the sex difference in its prevalence, which is evident for adults of all ages (again see Figure 9.4) and in most countries, including the United States (Weissman et al., 1993). By most estimates, there are twice as many severely depressed women as men (Nolen-Hoeksema, 1990), and some recent studies document an increasing discrepancy.

One simple explanation for this difference is that men and women differ in their willingness to report feeling sad. This may account for some of what we see, but it does not explain all of it. Reports of sadness are but one depressive symptom, and a diagnosis of depression can be made readily in the absence of this one symptom. Another answer along these lines is that men are more apt than women to turn to substance abuse and other antisocial activities when depressed. The fact of their depression may get lost—to themselves as well as to others—in the chaos that these reactions create. Women, in contrast, simply become depressed. Another possibility is that women are more likely than men to ruminate about events in their lives, exacerbating and maintaining whatever depression these events may have triggered (Nolen-Hoeksema, 1991).

There are more explanations to be found in the research literature. Those who have examined the sex difference in depression stress that no single factor ac-

Women are twice as likely to be depressed as men. The exact reasons for this difference are unknown, although most psychologists believe that it has a variety of causes.

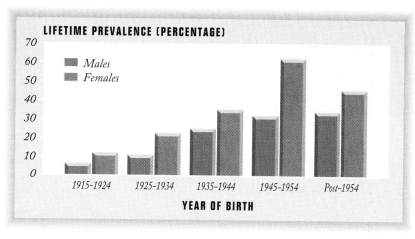

FIGURE 9.4

PREVALENCE OF DEPRESSION WITH AGE   *Diagnostic interviews were conducted with the relatives of those people with mood disorders. Because depression is moderately heritable, prevalence estimates were higher than those in the general population. But, note the clear differences in prevalence depending on sex and year of birth.*
SOURCE: DATA DERIVED FROM "CONTINUING FEMALE PREDOMINANCE IN DEPRESSIVE ILLNESS," BY A. C. LEON, G. L. KLERMAN, AND P. WICKRAMARATNE, 1993, *American Journal of Public Health, 83,* PP. 754–757.

counts for it (Nolen-Hoeksema, 1987). Consider that when boys and girls are depressed, there is no difference favoring females; if anything, little boys are somewhat more apt to be depressed. It is only with the onset of puberty that we start to see females outnumbering males. Perhaps biology is involved, because puberty marks the beginning of dramatic hormonal differences between males and females. Perhaps not. For example, although hormonal factors *may* contribute to depression (Bardwick, 1971), they do not do so to an extent that accounts for the sex difference we observe.

Some theorists wonder about the contribution of **premenstrual syndrome** (**PMS**) to depressive disorder. PMS refers to physical and psychological symptoms that occur during the late luteal phase of a woman's menstrual cycle, including fatigue, abdominal bloating, headache, irritability, anxiety, and depression; symptoms disappear after the onset of menstruation (Backstrom & Hammarback, 1991; Mortola, 1992). According to some estimates, 10% of women experience PMS (e.g., Morse, Dennerstein, Farrell, & Varnavides, 1991; Steiner, 1992), which raises the possibility that it produces the greater likelihood of women being depressed (Hurt et al., 1992).

As I mentioned in Chapter 2, discussions of PMS in terms of psychological abnormality are highly controversial. Even if we regard this avenue as worthy of exploration, research suggests that PMS makes at best a small contribution to the observed sex difference in depression (e.g., Ramcharan, Love, Fick, & Goldfien, 1992). Realize that the duration of any depressive symptoms associated with PMS is far too brief to warrant a DSM-IV diagnosis of depression. Indeed, some critics have questioned whether PMS is even a discrete syndrome (see Rodin, 1992; Tucker & Whalen, 1991; Ussher, 1992).

Regardless, if female hormones are a major cause of depression, then why are men depressed at all? Why does the sex difference persist through old age, after women have passed menopause, and hormonal differences between men and women have necessarily decreased?

Other explanations point to the fact that this is, after all, still a man's world. Women have more restricted opportunities than men and hence fewer achievements. And women may be rewarded for their passivity and emotionality, and/or thwarted in their attempts to be assertive (Peterson, Maier, & Seligman, 1993).

Another possible reason why women are more depressed than men is women's relatively greater chance of social isolation. Brown and Harris (1978), in a study of depression among women, found that several interpersonal factors were related to the existence of depression in this group:

◆ death of one's mother before the age of 11

◆ lack of an intimate relationship with a spouse or lover

◆ no job away from home

◆ three or more children at home to be taken care of

When these factors are all present, a woman is quite likely to be depressed.

Let me mention briefly what is known about differences in depression across socioeconomic class. They appear less dramatic than the ones I have discussed with regard to age and sex (e.g., Somervell, Leaf, Weissman, Blazer, & Bruce, 1989; Zung, Mac-Donald, & Zung, 1988). Some studies report that those from the lower classes have more depression than their counterparts in the middle class, which makes sense if we believe stressful life events can bring about depression. For example, depression is common among the homeless (Belcher & DiBlasio, 1990; Klein, Behnke, & Peterson, 1993; La Gory, Ritchey, & Mullis, 1990; Ritchey, La Gory, Fitzpatrick, & Mullis, 1990). What is perhaps most notable about these particular findings is that they are not more robust than they are.

Some investigators have looked at depression across cultures. Overall prevalence rates are not readily available for widespread comparisons, yet it is clear that every society recognizes something akin to depression. As you saw with fear and anxiety disorders (Chapter 7), the specific manifestations and configurations of depressive symptoms may differ across societies (Kleinman & Good, 1985). There are some hints that people in nontechnological cultures have more somatic symptoms than cognitive ones; in Western cultures, guilt is a more common complaint. Also, suicide is rather unlikely to accompany depression in nontechnological societies (Jacobsson, 1988).

Although there are not strong differences in the prevalence of depression across social classes, the disorder is quite common among the homeless.

THE COURSE OF DEPRESSION

When a person becomes severely depressed, meeting DSM criteria, his depressive episode typically lasts between 3 and 6 months, although it may be as short as a few weeks or as long as a lifetime (Goodwin & Guze, 1989). These episodes are usually self-limiting, lifting without intervention. This does not mean that they should be ignored, because 3 to 6 months is not a trivial amount of time during which to be incapacitated; further, the risk of suicide looms.

For example, rock-and-roll pioneer Del Shannon shot himself in 1990 in the midst of a severe depressive episode (Goldberg, 1990). His well known songs from the 1960s—like "Runaway"—were tales of loneliness and betrayal. He abused alcohol and tranquilizers. Shannon's first marriage ended in a painful divorce, leaving him estranged from his children. His career declined after the 1960s. He constantly voiced his unhappiness, until he took his life at age 55.

When a person does recover from depression, which occurs in 90% of the cases, there is about a 50-50 chance that she will experience another depressive episode at some point in the future (Keller, Shapiro, Lavori, & Wolfe, 1982). Risk of another episode is greatest immediately after her recovery, so the longer she stays free of depression, the greater the likelihood that she will continue to be nondepressed (e.g., Maj, Veltro, Pirozzi, Lobrace, & Magliano, 1992; Wells, Burnam, Rogers, Hays, & Camp, 1992). Recurrence is not as well understood as the initial causes of a depressive episode, but it appears as if a stable life prior to the first episode and the absence of substance abuse make for a good prognosis (e.g., Giles, Jarrett, Biggs, Guzick, & Rush, 1989; Lewinsohn, Zeiss, & Duncan, 1989; Sargeant, Bruce, Florio, & Weissman, 1990). We know that the process of recovery can be speeded by a variety of treatments, but we do not yet have enough long-term information available about the relative success of these treatments in preventing future episodes (Belsher & Costello, 1988).

Each of several models of abnormality has something important to say about the onset and treatment of depressive disorder. In the next few sections, I survey their contributions separately, and then attempt to integrate them. I begin with biomedical explanations.

BIOMEDICAL APPROACHES

You may remember from Chapter 2, in the discussion of the history of diagnostic systems, that depression (then called *melancholia*) has been one of the disorders described since ancient times. Like fear and anxiety, depression is one of the human universals, in both its normal and abnormal forms. Among the earliest theories of this disorder were those that implicated something amiss with the body.

When the ancient Greeks tried to make sense of depression, they did so in terms of the popular *humoural theory:* an account of illness that traced different diseases to imbalances among different bodily fluids, or humours (Chapter 1). The Greek physician Hippocrates (ca. 460–377 B.C.) is credited with popularizing this viewpoint (Jackson, 1986). According to Hippocrates, the body contained four basic fluids: blood, yellow bile, black bile, and phlegm. If the person's fluids were in balance, then she was healthy. When her humours were out of balance, she developed an illness in accordance with the specific imbalance. Too much black bile brought about melancholia. Indeed, the word *melancholia* means *black bile* in Greek.

The amine hypothesis   Current theories still have much to say about the biological basis of depression, focusing on the depressed person's microscopic fluids—her neurotransmitters, to use the modern term. Biomedical theorists are particularly interested in **norepinephrine** and **serotonin.** Depression presumably results from their overly low activity. Because these two neurotransmitters are examples of what are called biological amines, the theory that depression results from their insufficiency is sometimes referred to as the **amine hypothesis** (Fritze et al., 1992; Schildkraut, 1965).

Several lines of evidence support the amine hypothesis (Rothschild, 1988). First, we know that drugs that decrease the activity of these neurotransmitters—such as *reserpine,* used to treat high blood pressure—may produce depression as a side effect. Second, other drugs that increase the activity of these neurotransmitters—notably antidepressant medications such as *imipramine*—improve depression among depressed individuals and produce mania among those not initially depressed. Third, when the spinal fluid or urine of individuals is examined for byproducts of the metabolism of these neurotransmitters, we find that they are relatively low or high depending on the person's level of depression. The risk for suicide is increased in direct proportion to the dwindling of these metabolic byproducts (Asberg, Nordstrom, & Traskman-Bendz, 1986; Ricci & Wellman, 1990).

Granted that norepinephrine and serotonin are involved in depression, just what is the mechanism that leads from their low activity to the gamut of depressive symptoms, which are not simply somatic but also emotional, cognitive, and behavioral? Here we enter more speculative territory, but it is believed that these neurotransmitters, among other roles, help regulate the hypothalamus. The hypothalamus is a critical link between the nervous system and the endocrine system, particularly via the pituitary gland. It is involved in sleep, appetite, sexuality, and physical movement—exactly the domains in which depressive symptoms exist (Grahame-Smith, 1992; Jacobs, 1991).

In Chapter 2, I briefly discussed the *dexamethasone suppression test* (or *DST*), proposed by some as a strong diagnostic test for depression. You can better understand the details of this test now, because it presumably measures the degree to which hormonal rhythms are thrown out of kilter. However, as was also explained in Chapter 2, the DST is not a perfect indicator of depression, cautioning us that the amine hypothesis—which provides its rationale—probably does not tell the whole story about depression.

Neurotransmitters can directly influence mood. We know that there is a part of the brain—the **medial forebrain bundle**—involved in reward. If an electrode is implanted in the medial forebrain bundle of a rat, and the rat can push a lever to stimulate it, the rat will do so indefinitely, never pausing to eat or sleep, until it dies (Olds & Milner, 1954). This so-called *pleasure center* seems to need adequate levels of norepinephrine and serotonin to operate. Generalizing to people, we conclude that low levels of these neurotransmitters diminish our capacity for pleasure. The rest of the depressive symptoms, and notably the sad mood and loss of interest in pleasurable activities, follow. Perhaps low levels of norepinephrine and serotonin activity deaden the person's emotional capacity. Deprived of the capacity to be rewarded for what he does, he becomes ever more oblivious to his environment.

There may be several routes to deficient levels of norepinephrine and serotonin. One may be via stressful events, those that interfere with the pursuit of goals. When these events multiply, they decrease the levels of these neurotransmitters (Weiss & Simson, 1988), and the person becomes less active and less motivated to pursue future activities. I mentioned earlier the possibility that depression can be adaptive when it causes us to pause in frustrating pursuits, avoiding further failures through passivity (Suarez, Crowe, & Adams, 1978). If we live in a world surrounded by brick walls, it is adaptive to have a mechanism that leads us to stop battering our heads against the wall and wait until the bricks have been removed or softened (Rippere, 1977).

Stressful life events precede many forms of abnormality, but the link between stressful events and depression is a particularly robust one (Thoits, 1983). We know that among people with depressive episodes, some number have experienced such severe losses as the death of a child, physical illness, divorce, or unemployment (Paykel et al., 1969). Not everyone who experiences these losses becomes depressed, and not everyone who is depressed experiences these losses, but there is a substantial correlation.

A second and not incompatible biochemical route to depression may be genetic predisposition. We can presume that people's typical levels of neurotransmitter activity exist along a continuum, so that some individuals are simply operating with more versus less than others. Those who have chronically low activity are at risk for depression; for these people, an episode can be precipitated by events that are innocuous to those with more resilient systems.

Heritability of depression   Relevant to this argument about a biologically based individual difference in susceptibility to depression are studies of its heritability (Moldin, Reich, & Rice, 1991). As already mentioned, depressive disorders run through families. Can we say that the route includes genetic factors? Results here are somewhat inconsistent (McGuffin & Katz, 1989). Some but not all studies of identical versus fraternal twins find greater concordance for depression among the former than the latter, which of course is the most direct prediction concerning the heritability of the disorder (Andrews, Stewart, Allen, & Henderson, 1990; McGuffin, Katz, & Rutherford, 1991; Wierzbicki, 1987).

More consistent in support are investigations of depression among adopted children. The strategy of these studies is to start with a sample of children who have been given up by their biological parents and then raised by adoptive parents. Then their depression is ascertained, as well as that of their biological versus foster parents. Whether or not the children become depressed is better predicted by depression (or not) of their biological parents than that of their foster parents (Cadoret, 1978; von Knorring, Cloninger, Bohman, & Sigvardsson, 1983; Wender et al., 1986). A family history of the disorder is neither necessary nor sufficient, but it is a risk factor nonetheless.

Biomedical treatments   In discussing the biological approaches to depression, I must mention the development of several effective treatments. First, we have antidepressant drugs, of which several types exist (Conte & Karasu, 1992). **Tricyclics** are a class of drugs that include amitriptyline and imipramine and are manufactured under such names as Elavil and Tofranil. They alleviate depressive episodes by keeping the neurons that secrete norepinephrine and serotonin from reabsorbing them. Thus, tricyclics leave more of these neurotransmitters available to stimulate other neurons.

MAO inhibitors are a second class of antidepressants, known by such brand names as Nardil and Parnate. They are effective in treating depression because they inhibit *monamine oxidase,* the enzyme responsible for breaking down norepinephrine in the brain. Again, MAO inhibitors make neurotransmitters more available, but by a different action than the tricyclics.

Finally, **Prozac** (the brand name for **fluoxetine**) is an antidepressant that works much the same as tricyclics do, except that it is thought to target serotonin specifically, keeping more of it available by preventing its reabsorption.

The general interpretation of these drugs is what I have already described: In various ways, they affect

When first introduced, the antidepressant Prozac was greeted with much enthusiasm. Opinion is now more modest and in some quarters even skeptical.

TABLE 9.4

POSSIBLE SIDE EFFECTS OF ANTIDEPRESSANT MEDICATIONS *Each of the frequently prescribed antidepressants has potential side effects.*

tricyclics	drowsiness; dizziness; lethargy; blurred vision; weight gain; low blood pressure; dependence
MAO inhibitors	same as tricyclics; episodes of extremely high blood pressure if certain foods (cheese, aged meats, red wine, avocados) are eaten
Prozac	same as tricyclics, but perhaps less frequently; suicidal impulses (see text)

the levels of neurotransmitters in the brain, and eventually regularize disrupted biological rhythms (Blier, de Montigny, & Chaput, 1990). The person takes these drugs until their active ingredients build up to therapeutic levels in the blood, which may take several weeks (Preskorn, 1989). According to some reports, the more severe the depression, the longer it takes these drugs to work, which makes sense. A physician prescribes one drug rather than another based on anticipated or actual side effects (see Table 9.4), as well as the person's idiosyncratic response (Cole & Bodkin, 1990; Tollefson, 1991). Some people will respond to a tricyclic but not an MAO inhibitor, or vice versa. On the whole, the side effects are more risky for MAO inhibitors than for tricyclics or Prozac, so the physician will usually prescribe one of these latter drugs first. In many cases, once depression lifts, a person may continue to take antidepressants to stave off future episodes (Loonen, Peer, & Zwanikken, 1991).

Janowsky, Addario, and Risch (1987) described the pharmacological treatment of Mrs. O., a 35-year-old woman who for a decade had suffered from recurrent episodes of dissatisfaction, irritability toward her children and husband, withdrawal, lethargy, and crying. These episodes lasted from several days to several weeks. She had at one time been prescribed antidepressants by her physician father. Her symptoms lessened, but she discontinued the medication because she felt that it put her father in charge of her life. About a year later, she sought out a psychiatrist and requested another trial of antidepressants, this time "on her own terms" (p. 57).

Mrs. O. was prescribed Tofranil, a common tricyclic, and within a few weeks reported notably less irritability and lethargy. She experienced constipation and a dry mouth, among the possible side effects of this drug, but these effects were alleviated by another medication. Two

months later, Mrs. O. felt better than she had in years. Then she discontinued the Tofranil and experienced a relapse. She began taking it again, and her depression lifted once more. This time she experienced no side effects. Mrs. O. continued to take Tofranil and to be free from depressive episodes.

Prozac is the newest of the antidepressant drugs. When first on the market, it was greeted with wild enthusiasm, even gracing the cover of *Newsweek* (March 26, 1990). Many people praised its rapid operation, as well as its help in treating such difficulties as bulimia, obsessive-compulsive disorder, substance abuse, and the like. Opinions have now begun to swing the other way (Toufexis, 1990). Some have even complained that Prozac produces intense suicidal impulses in depressed individuals who did not previously have such notions, which means that it may end up worsening the condition it attempts to improve (Teicher, Glod, & Cole, 1990). These charges have resulted in ongoing lawsuits against the manufacturer of Prozac.[2] This cycle of enthusiasm followed by grave doubts is not unusual for any new treatment, pharmaceutical or otherwise, until more long-term data are collected.

Another treatment that stems from the biomedical approach is **electroconvulsive shock therapy (ECT).** This intervention has popular connotations of being barbaric, but the facts are more benign. ECT proves to be an effective and rapid treatment of depression. Carefully used, it is neither cruel nor painful. Ironically, fatalities from ECT are notably fewer than those resulting from the use of antidepressant medication (Coffey & Weiner, 1990; Greenberg & Fink, 1992).

Where did anyone ever get the idea that depression could be alleviated by passing an electric current through the brain to induce a seizure? The story is that patients suffering from schizophrenia who also had epilepsy showed a reduction of their schizophrenic symptoms in the immediate aftermath of a seizure (Kalinowsky, 1980). Physicians wondered therefore if the deliberate triggering of a seizure could bring relief to schizophrenics. Seizures were first induced by chemicals, but then it was discovered that electric current was easier to control. And so ECT was created, in 1938, as a treatment of schizophrenia. It is important to understand that it is not the shock per se but rather the induction of a convulsion that brings relief (Martin, 1989); ECT is more properly referred to as "convulsive" therapy rather than "shock" therapy (Kalinowsky, 1980).

---

[2] Whatever the eventual outcome of these suits, appreciate that only a very small proportion of Prozac users have reported such side effects (Bost & Kemp, 1992; Fava & Rosenbaum, 1991).

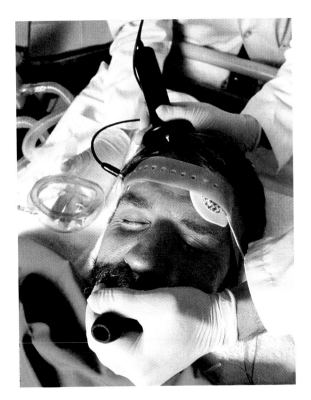

Electroconvulsive shock therapy (ECT) is an effective and rapid treatment for depression. Its drawbacks, however, include memory disruption for events during the course of treatment.

Following the extensive use of ECT, it was eventually concluded that the procedure was not useful in the treatment of schizophrenia. But because the treatment already existed, it was tried with other disorders. Controlled studies showed that ECT indeed helps those suffering from depression. Stereotypes notwithstanding, ECT is performed while the patient is hospitalized and given a sedative so that he is unconscious. In recent years, a muscle relaxant has been added as well so that the person is less likely to thrash about and get hurt during the induced seizure. Electrodes are attached to the scalp, and a current of 75 to 100 volts is passed through the brain for a fraction of a second, inducing a convulsion that lasts for about 1 minute. These shocks are given several times per week for 2 or 3 weeks.

Depression lifts in the majority of cases, perhaps 80% or 90% (Persad, 1990), even for individuals who have not responded to antidepressant medications. Some believe that ECT works particularly well for endogenous depression, but the evidence here is equivocal (Scott, 1989). It is agreed that this method works more rapidly than antidepressant medication or psychotherapy, so sometimes ECT is the choice for the depressed person who is acutely suicidal (Greenblatt,

1977). Along these lines, those who wish to shorten their recovery time may opt for this treatment rather than others.

The drawbacks of ECT include memory disruption for events during the period that shocks are given (Breggin, 1979). There is a suspicion on the part of many that long-term memories may be disrupted as well, but this has proved difficult to document. ECT nowadays is usually *unilateral*—one electrode is placed on the forehead and the other on the side of the head, so that current does not pass through the individual's language center. In years past, ECT was *bilateral*—electrodes were placed on both sides of the head. We now believe that unilateral treatment disrupts the patient's memory to a lesser degree than the traditional, bilateral approach.

No one knows exactly why ECT works (Fink, 1990). Proponents of the amine hypothesis argue that it affects levels of neurotransmitter activity in the brain (Couvreur, Ansseau, & Franck, 1989). The procedure presumably stimulates greater release of neurotrans-

Aerobic exercise may be effective in decreasing and preventing episodes of depression. One obvious explanation is that exercise alters the individual's biological makeup, but the possibility must also be considered that exercise boosts the individual's sense of control and self-esteem.

mitters and/or causes them to linger longer. Because shock has such a pervasive effect, actually pinpointing specific mechanisms may be impossible (King & Liston, 1990).

Yet another biomedical treatment of depression currently attracting a fair amount of attention is *aerobic exercise:* activity such as jogging, swimming, and cycling that raises the heart rate for an extended period of time and leads to an improved ability to bring oxygen into the blood. Experiments show that programs of dancing or running can decrease depression (e.g., McCann & Holmes, 1984) and prevent it from occurring in the wake of stressful events (Roth & Holmes, 1987). Longitudinal surveys suggest that people who exercise regularly are less likely to become depressed than their sedentary counterparts (Farmer et al., 1988).

The obvious explanation of why aerobic exercise is antidepressive is that it somehow regularizes bodily rhythms and thus combats the disorder. Perhaps increased endorphins play some role. However, such somatic explanations have not been firmly established, and perhaps aerobic exercise is beneficial not just because of a direct effect on the body but through an indirect effect on self-esteem and feelings of efficacy.

Conclusions   Biomedical approaches to depression have much to offer, but they also have several shortcomings. First, the research evidence in all cases is less than perfect. Every finding I have described is solid in that it occurs at a level greater than chance, but they do not reflect invariant "laws" of depression. Plenty of exceptions exist. Some people become depressed without stressful life events occurring. Some depressed people do not show reduced neurotransmitters. Some do not have a family history of depression. Some do not respond well to antidepressant medications. And so on. Processes besides biological ones must be at work.

Second, these findings have been stitched together from different lines of work. No researcher has simultaneously examined all the biomedical pieces in the same group of depressed individuals. It would be compelling support for the amine hypothesis if we found that people with a family history of depression were those who unambiguously evidenced faulty neurotransmitters, that these people responded most quickly and thoroughly to antidepressant medications, and so on. Alas, such studies do not yet exist.

Third, as is patently obvious, brains are complex. While it is true, for example, that stress reduces norepinephrine activity, it also does all sorts of other things to the brain. Similarly, ECT affects neurotransmitters, but it also influences other brain systems. Depression runs through families, but so do other characteristics

and difficulties. In each case, a researcher might choose to focus on the patterns consistent with the amine hypothesis, but there is no guarantee that the amines are the critical link in these studies. They may instead be mere correlates of what is crucial. In any event, I doubt that even the most ardent of the biomedical investigators of depression think these constructs tell the whole story, so I now turn to other models of abnormality.

PSYCHODYNAMIC APPROACHES

There exist several psychodynamic accounts of depression, starting with that of Karl Abraham (1911/1927). Abraham emphasized the role of early loss in the life of the depression-prone person, suggesting that she retreats in the wake of later disappointments to an earlier mode of functioning characterized by excessive dependency. Subsequent psychodynamic theories elaborated this emphasis on early loss and the resulting emotional neediness (Blatt, 1992).

Mourning and melancholia   Freud theorized about depression in his 1917 essay "Mourning and Melancholia," in which he contrasted mourning (grief) with melancholia (depression). Grief and depression share many features—sadness, somatic disruption, and impaired concentration. But grief is a normal part of everyday life, whereas depression in its extreme is not. What is the difference? According to Freud, the striking feature of depression is self-blame. As noted already, the depressed individual feels more than just sad. She also feels that she is a bad person. This is not what happens in grief.

Freud then observed that if the sorts of things that a depressed person says about herself were instead said about another person, we would not hesitate in saying that she is angry at that other person. Perhaps here is an important clue for understanding the disorder. It may be that the depressed person is angry at herself.

Where does this internalized anger originate? Freud's answer points to childhood experiences. In the course of growing up, the infant incorporates aspects of her parents into her own self-concept. Perhaps the person who is later prone to depression had parents who failed to meet her needs while she was an infant. Subconsciously, she becomes enraged at them. In her identification with her parents, she incorporates not only their laudable characteristics but also those aspects at which she is angry. What is created, therefore, is a person who is angry when her needs are not met, and she directs this anger inward. All of this takes place on an unconscious level. She does not identify her emotion as anger, and she certainly does not identify the target of her unacknowledged anger as her parents. But this anger produces the full range of symptoms—emotional, cognitive, physiological, and behavioral—that characterize depression.

Figuring in the psychodynamic view of depression is the notion of a **dependent personality disorder,** in which a person excessively relies on others for support and approval (Chapter 13). This personality style presumably represents a fixation at the oral stage, when the child is at greatest vulnerability to the processes that set her up for subsequent depression (Birtchnell, 1988; Chodoff, 1972).

Evaluating psychodynamic theories   All psychodynamic theories of depression stress conflicts about dependency and associated feelings of ambivalence (Mendelson, 1974). What is the evidence for these theories? Several lines of research bear on them, but there is a gap between the complexity of psychodynamic theorizing and the relatively broad-based predictions that have been investigated.

Let me start by considering a dependent personality style as a predisposition to depression. On the one hand, there exists a cluster of personality traits that we can identify as dependent (Peterson, 1992), and these traits characterize those with depression (Overholser, Kabakoff, & Norman, 1989). On the other hand, people's level of dependency seems to rise and fall with their level of depression, implying that dependency is more of a concomitant of depression than a cause (Hirschfeld et al., 1983, 1989; Weissman & Paykel, 1974).

What about the prediction that depressed people are apt to have experienced more disappointments in childhood than those who are not depressed? Evidence is mixed, but there is some support for this hypothesis (Orvaschel, Weissman, & Kidd, 1980). Childhood losses, particularly the loss of a parent to death or divorce, bear a relationship to adult depression; losses in the immediate past often trigger depressive episodes (Lloyd, 1980).

These findings are consistent with the psychodynamic formula. At the same time, losses may be depressing not simply because they affect a person's internal psychological functioning but also because they affect the environment in which that person lives (McLeod, 1987). Consider a young child whose father dies. Not only has she lost her father but also the standard of living that the father's presence made possible. She may as a result be exposed to more hardships; these hardships in turn might create a vulnerability to depression because her life—objectively—has become more difficult.

Actress Mariette Hartley described such childhood dynamics in her autobiography (Hartley, 1990). Her early years were extremely unhappy, which she attributed to the emotional distance of her mother, Polly. Polly's father was behaviorist John Watson (Chapter 1). Watson believed that children should be treated without sentiment, and this was exactly how he raised his own daughter. She in turn raised her daughter, Mariette, without any outward expression of physical affection.

Polly abused alcohol and made numerous suicide attempts throughout her life. Her husband, Paul, was also an alcoholic and suicidal. He could not keep a steady job. Obviously, Mariette grew up in a chaotic household. She reported a feeling of constant doom and threat. At age 14, she began to drink heavily herself and engage in sexual activity. At 18, she married an ex-convict who beat her. Ms. Hartley suffered from depressive episodes, particularly when memories of her childhood were rekindled by ongoing events. Eventually, Mariette Hartley recovered and became in reality the sunny individual she had long portrayed in her professional roles.

And what about the psychodynamic prediction that depressed people are angry? Here several studies

Early in her adult life, actress Mariette Hartley suffered from depression, due presumably to an unhappy childhood.

have been done, usually finding that those with depression express somewhat more anger than those without (e.g., Mook, Van der Ploeg, & Kleijn, 1990; Riley, Treiber, & Woods, 1989). However, this result is ambiguous because it does not address whether anger is turned inward.

Yet another prediction from this perspective is that depressed individuals think about their parents in different ways than nondepressives. Again several studies have taken a look at such notions, suggesting that those who are depressed remember their parents as unaffectionate and controlling (Gerlsma, Emmelkamp, & Arrindell, 1990). If these memories are reliable, we can imagine that these styles of parenting would create a vulnerability to depression.

The safest conclusion is that no single psychodynamic factor stands out. On the average, depressed individuals evidence many of the characteristics deemed important by the psychodynamic approach, but there is a problem in teasing these apart from the symptoms of depression. We need longitudinal studies to see if these characteristics existed prior to depressive episodes or developed alongside other manifestations of depression. Few such studies exist, and those that do are equivocal in their findings.

Interpersonal psychotherapy   However meager the support for a psychodynamic approach to the causes of depression, matters are more encouraging when it comes to treatment. A time-limited version of psychodynamic therapy called **interpersonal psychotherapy** proves effective as a treatment for the disorder (Klerman, Weissman, Rounsaville, & Chevron, 1984).

Interpersonal therapy focuses on interpersonal issues and conflicts. As you have seen, social losses and isolation are associated with depression, so the explicit attempt to address them seems reasonable. The goal of this intervention is to help the client get along better with other people. Interpersonal psychotherapy has more of a here-and-now emphasis than traditional psychoanalysis, but it agrees with the psychodynamic premise that people are depressed because of longstanding difficulties in relating to people so that their needs and wishes are met.

As part of an investigation of different treatments of depression, interpersonal therapy was conducted over a 12-week period (Elkin et al., 1989). For those patients who completed the full 12 weeks of therapy, 55% were deemed fully recovered in that their depressive symptoms fell to insignificant levels. Many other patients showed marked improvement. In comparison, 57% of patients who took tricyclics met the criteria for full recovery within 12 weeks.

Klerman and colleagues (1984) provided the case example of Ruth C., a 62-year-old woman whose depression began following her husband's death from a lingering vascular disease. As his illness progressed, he became paranoid and finally incoherent. After he died, Mrs. C. experienced unrelenting sadness, guilt about her feelings of anger during her husband's illness, a sense of inadequacy, social withdrawal, sleep difficulty, and problems concentrating. She felt hopeless about her depression, though she was not suicidal. She was hospitalized and prescribed antidepressant medication. Her depression lifted while she was in the hospital, but she relapsed upon discharge, even though she continued to take the drugs.

Then she began interpersonal psychotherapy. Her antidepressants were discontinued. Initial therapy sessions revealed that Ruth had enjoyed a satisfying relationship with her husband but that his death left her bereft of social contacts. During his illness, she had increasingly limited her interactions with others in order to take care of him. This had made her angry, feelings compounded by the fact that he was dying and thus leaving her. Ruth recognized that she needed to develop new friendships, but she was pessimistic about being able to do so. She anticipated that others would reject her, but this did not happen. When she occasionally did get together with acquaintances and coworkers, she always enjoyed herself. However, Ruth held herself in check and did not allow these casual relationships to grow.

Her therapist proposed several goals. First was to help Mrs. C. overcome her guilt concerning her husband. Apparently, her guilt led her to continue grieving: To cease mourning would somehow mean she was neglectful or uncaring. The therapist encouraged her to distinguish between realistic and unrealistic grief. Second was to help Mrs. C. resume meaningful social activities. She was embarrassed to recontact old friends because she had neglected them during her husband's illness. The therapist suggested that she simply explain to her friends the reason for her absence from their lives and see what happened. Again, Mrs. C. was encouraged to distinguish what was realistic about her fears from what was not.

In therapy sessions, her relationship with her husband was exhaustively reviewed, along with his death and her reaction to it. She eventually came to believe that much of her anger at him was understandable and did not mean she loved him any less. She completed her mourning and felt better. She resumed her old friendships and began several new ones. And she even started to do volunteer work and planned to take some college courses.

COGNITIVE-BEHAVIORAL APPROACHES

Cognitive-behavioral approaches to depression have proliferated in recent years, so we should not speak of a single approach stemming from this model but rather a family of them. The more behavioral of these approaches emphasize the role of the environment in predisposing and maintaining depression, whereas the more cognitive stress the role of thoughts and beliefs. As you would imagine, treatment from the cognitive-behavioral perspective attempts to undo the processes supposedly giving rise to depression.

Behavioral theory and treatment   According to a theory first proposed by Charles Ferster (1966, 1973) and elaborated by Peter Lewinsohn (1974), depression results when a person experiences low levels of reward, and thus is put in a position in which whole classes of learned behavior begin to be extinguished. Simply put, not getting enough goodies in the world translates into the various symptoms of depression. Imagine the dreariest bus station in which you have ever been stranded, and then try to think about having to live there forever. Your reaction? You would be depressed, and this is the premise of the **behavioral theory of depression** proposed by Ferster and Lewinsohn. Indeed, depressed people report fewer pleasant events in their lives than do nondepressives (Lewinsohn & Libet, 1972) (see Table 9.5).

The behavioral theory of depression sounds quite simple, and it is, so long as we limit our attention to environments that are truly deficient in rewards. But there are other ways of being depressed due to inadequate rewards, including the lack of abilities needed to win them. *Social skills* refer to the sorts of things that people do to achieve satisfactory interactions with others. Some people who are depressed are markedly inept at getting along with other people (Libet &

Lewinsohn, 1973). They say the wrong things, or they say them at the wrong times, or they simply say nothing at all. In any event, other people do not respond well to the interpersonal style of those who are depressed.

A related idea is that depression-prone individuals are unassertive (Heiby, 1989). This explains why women are more apt to be depressed than men; presumably, a woman cannot or does not assert her own needs and wants to the degree that the typical man does (Culkin & Perrotto, 1985; Dua & McNall, 1987; Gayton, Havu, Baird, & Ozman, 1983).

Along these lines, Coyne (1976) suggests that depression results from troubling interactions. He believes that people who are depressed exacerbate their problem by alienating those in their immediate vicinity. Studies have shown that others react to depressed individuals with anger or annoyance (e.g., Becker, 1988; Coyne, 1985). If possible, they break off their interac-

TABLE **9.5**

PLEASANT EVENTS *According to the behavioral theory of depression, when we experience too few pleasant occurrences in life—like those shown below—we are at risk for depression.*

The more depressed people are, the less likely it is that they have experienced pleasant events such as the following during the preceding month.

being in the country
going to a concert
reading a novel
hearing a lecture
going camping
laughing
playing with animals
attending a party
skiing
singing to oneself
bowling
listening to a radio show
getting a massage
sleeping late
swimming
riding a horse
looking at the moon
tending houseplants
sewing
people-watching
cooking a meal
keeping a diary
jogging
reading the newspaper
flirting

According to the behavioral theory of depression, lack of rewards in one's environment produces depression. The straightforward therapeutic recommendations that follow from behavioral theory are to enrich the depressed individual's world and to impart skills that allow rewards to be gained where and when available.

tions as quickly as possible. They may initially try to cheer up their depressed friend or overlook his complaints. But eventually, their reaction is to feel depressed themselves. Rewards have suddenly been removed from *their* social world and replaced with the black cloud of depression. Depressed people are depressing. This notion explains why whole families can be depressed.

The therapy for depression that is derived from the behavioral view takes two forms, one simple and the other more complex (Hoberman & Lewinsohn, 1985). The simple intervention is to enrich a person's world, moving him out of that dreary bus station. He is encouraged to quit a horrible job, redecorate a grubby apartment, cultivate more interesting hobbies, and/or stop pursuing futile goals. There is a widespread cliche today urging people to be good to themselves, but the simplicity of this advice does not detract from its merit. The cultivation of simple pleasures can combat depression (e.g., Fuchs & Rehm, 1977).

In its more complex form, behavioral therapy imparts to the individual skills that may be lacking, so that he is better able to navigate the social world (Bellack, Hersen, & Himmelhoch, 1981). What abilities does he lack? How can he identify and attain realistic goals? Strategies along these lines alleviate depression (Weissman, 1984). To the degree that the depressed person lives in a depressed family, the family as a whole might be included in such therapy, so that the family can learn ways of relating that break the vicious circle of depression (Spitz, 1988).

Depressed people can be highly tentative in their interactions with others, fearing rejection. One way this is manifested is through the use of vague words and expressions, particularly when one's own needs and wishes are being conveyed (Hargie, Saunders, & Dickson, 1981). Not surprisingly, other people cannot easily meet requests that are unclear. Part of social skills training is to alert the depressed individual to such conversational ploys as the following:

◆ ambiguous designations ("stuff")

◆ negative intensifiers ("not infrequently")

◆ approximations ("kind of like")

◆ bluffs ("and so on")

◆ indeterminate numbers ("a couple of")

◆ probabilistic qualifications ("are not necessarily")

Needless to say, communication can never be perfectly precise, but depressed individuals may not realize how vaguely they express themselves.

Contrast these different ways of asking a friend over the telephone if the two of you can get together to discuss your friendship:

◆ *Hello, Frank. There's some stuff I thought we could toss around at some point. I've not been real happy about the last couple of times we've seen each other. You know. We used to be a bit closer. Now it's kind of different. Not always. I'm not really not all that upset, but if it's not a bother, maybe we could make a plan to get together. Whenever. I know you're busy. You tell me what might work.*

◆ *Hello, Frank. I would like to talk to you about what happened last Thursday when we went to the baseball game. You didn't discuss your new job, even though I asked you about it three times. And you didn't mention your new girlfriend at all. I know she's important to you, and I'd like to know more about her. Just a month ago, we talked a lot about what was going on in our lives, and I miss that part of our friendship. Can you explain to me why you were so distant? Let's meet for lunch tomorrow at 12:30 and have a serious talk. I really want to talk this through. We can go to the new restaurant on the corner.*

The first conversation disguises what you feel and want. It invites nothing. In contrast, the second conversation is more direct and likely to result in a resolution of your problem.

The behavioral theory can be criticized not for what it proposes about depression but for what it leaves unsaid. The possibility that depression leads to a lack of reward rather than vice versa is not given enough consideration (Hammen, 1991). The fact that the disorder is *not* strongly associated with social class puts a strain on any theory that so greatly emphasizes the role of the environment. Plus, biological and motivational influences are not acknowledged. (Conversely, biomedical approaches such as those previously discussed can be faulted for neglecting environmental considerations.)

Learned helplessness   Another cognitive-behavioral perspective on depression starts with the possible parallel between depression and **learned helplessness:** the maladaptive passivity that may follow exposure to uncontrollable aversive events (Peterson, Maier, & Seligman, 1993). Let me give you some background by turning back the clock to an animal learning laboratory in the 1960s (Overmier & Seligman, 1967; Seligman & Maier, 1967).

A dog was held immobile in a harness, and brief bursts of electric shock were delivered to its legs

According to the theory of learned helplessness, uncontrollable events may eventually lead to depression.

through attached electrodes. The shocks came without a signal on a random schedule. Because of the harness, there was nothing the dog could do to avoid or escape them. The next day, the dog was placed in a long box with a wire floor and a low barrier in the middle. A shock was delivered through the floor of the box. If the dog jumped over the barrier, the shock was turned off. If the dog failed to make this response, then the shock stayed on for 5 seconds. The process was repeated, again and again. The typical dog placed in this box readily learns to jump the barrier and turn off the shock.

But the dog previously immobilized and given shocks did not learn to escape the shock in this new situation. Instead, it just sat there and endured the shock. Why should an animal previously exposed to shocks that it could not control later behave passively when exposed to shocks that it could control? An apparent answer might be that the dog was somehow traumatized in the original circumstance, and that it could not respond because of physical damage—but while the dog had experienced pain the previous day, it suffered no physical injury.

A cognitive interpretation of the dog's helplessness proves more compelling. Perhaps the dog learned, when immobilized in the harness and given shocks, that nothing it did mattered. Regardless of the responses it did or did not make, the shocks still came. It learned a particular expectation—that responses and outcomes have no relationship to each other—which was then carried into the second situation, where responses and outcomes were related. However, the expectation about what would happen in the future created passivity and apathy. The animal "learned" an expectation in the first situation that produced "helplessness" in the second (Maier & Seligman, 1976).

Shortly after learned helplessness was described in animals, psychologists noted the possible parallel between it and the maladaptive passivity that characterizes many human failures of adaptation, including depression (Seligman, 1974, 1975). In fact, the learned helplessness phenomenon has been demonstrated in laboratory studies with human beings. More benign events than electric shocks—usually problems that cannot be solved—are substituted, but with the identical effects on later behavior. Following experience with uncontrollability, a person becomes passive (e.g., Hiroto & Seligman, 1975).

If this phenomenon is analogous to depression, it provides a simple and efficient way to learn about the disorder. Helplessness can be produced reliably in the laboratory, whereas quite obviously depression cannot. As a laboratory model for depression, learned helplessness gives researchers a test track for possible treatments or preventions of depression (Chapter 4).

Continued studies of helplessness in people led to an interest in how a person explains the causes of an uncontrollable event (Abramson, Seligman, & Teasdale, 1978). These causes set the parameters for helplessness following uncontrollable events by determining how general the expectation of future helplessness will be. Causal explanations more likely than others to produce pervasive helplessness are those that point to internal ("it's me"), stable ("it's going to last forever"), and global ("it's going to undermine everything I do") factors. People have a characteristic way of explaining events, their **explanatory style.** If a person relies on internal, stable, and global causes, then he is at increased risk for helplessness and depression when uncontrollable events occur (Peterson & Seligman, 1984).

Both helplessness and depression are marked by passivity, sadness, cognitive impairment, loss of self-esteem, anxiety, appetite loss, sleep disruption, and neurotransmitter depletion. Both dissipate with the passage of time. Both are associated with a belief that responding is futile. And both are linked to the tendency to explain uncontrollable events with internal, stable, and global causes.

However, learned helplessness is not a perfect account of depression, for several reasons. First, the analogy encounters a problem with respect to suicidal ideation. Learned helplessness shows itself not as the wish or attempt to die, but simply as passivity. The motive to end one's own life must arise from sources other than those specified by this model.

Second, there is a problem with respect to sex differences, and how they are manifested across the lifespan. There is no good evidence that the tendency to be helpless differs for men and women. Yet following the onset of puberty, females are much more likely to be depressed than males.

Third, learned helplessness does not speak to the distinctions made within types of depression, instead treating all depressions as pretty much the same, except insofar as people use different causal explanations to explain uncontrollable events. Consider that the symptoms of helplessness sound most like those of endogenous depression, yet endogenous depression is typically regarded as biological—not psychological.

Fourth, the evidence is inconsistent concerning the claim that cognitive factors precede depression (Coyne & Gotlib, 1983). Research does not always show that beliefs in response-outcome independence and a "depressive" explanatory style are risk factors for depression. These cognitions maintain depression once it is present, but they may or may not bring about an initial depressive episode (Brewin, 1985).

Cognitive theory and treatment   One more approach is Aaron Beck's (1967, 1976) **cognitive theory of depression.** He contends that depression is not so much a disorder of mood as one of thought. According to Beck, the depressed person thinks about herself, her world, and her future in pessimistic terms. Everything is bleak and grim. Presumably, she sees things as worse than they really are. Why does she maintain this worldview? Why don't events to the contrary challenge her depressive beliefs? Beck suggests two possible answers.

First, the depressed person is prone to **automatic thoughts:** unbidden and habitual ways of thinking that continually put her down.

Suppose you are at a party, and you see an attractive person that you met a few weeks before. You might walk across the room to strike up a conversation. Then again, automatic thoughts might freeze you midstep:

◆ *He won't remember who I am.*

◆ *He's probably waiting for his girlfriend.*

◆ *I'll say something stupid.*

◆ *I look fat in this outfit.*

◆ *I hate parties.*

◆ *I'm going to die old and lonely.*

And as though automatic thoughts like these were not depressing enough, Beck argues that depression is further maintained by **errors in logic:** slipshod ways of thinking that keep self-deprecating beliefs immune to reality (Cook & Peterson, 1986). A depressed person selectively attends to bad events while overlooking good ones. Or she may overly personalize the petty

hassles of her everyday life. Waiting in a slow checkout line at the grocery store is proof positive that *she* is a loser, for picking this time to go shopping, for choosing that particular line, for believing that express checkout really means express, and so on.

This cognitive theory of depression draws our attention to the hopelessness that characterizes depressed people in general and suicidal individuals in particular (Kashani, Dandoy, & Reid, 1992). As mentioned earlier, hopelessness about the future seems to be one of the most important factors predicting whether a person will attempt suicide. Agreement with statements such as the following are associated with these suicidal impulses and actions (Beck, Weissman, Lester, & Trexler, 1974):

◆ I might as well give up because I can't make things better for myself.

◆ My future seems dark to me.

◆ All I can see ahead of me is unpleasantness rather than pleasantness.

Beck's theory gives rise to an effective treatment of depression: **cognitive therapy** (Beck, 1991; Beck, Rush, Shaw, & Emery, 1979). In this approach, the therapist works with the depressed client to challenge her negative beliefs. Beck describes this kind of therapy as "collaborative empiricism" to emphasize that the therapist and client work together (collaborate) to check the client's beliefs against the facts (empiricism).

Here is how cognitive therapy might proceed with Ms. Nakatani, a depressed college student. The first step is to identify her automatic thoughts, the habitual put-downs that flash through her mind in the course of a typical day. The therapist asks her to pay attention to these thoughts, and not just to the emotional damage they cause. She is encouraged to write them down, along with the feelings they produce. She finds that social interactions make her feel depressed and uneasy because she thinks that she is boring.

Then she is asked to challenge each automatic thought by asking what evidence she has for believing it. Ms. Nakatani might find herself hard-pressed to justify her belief that she is boring. People often seek her out to chat. They laugh at her jokes. They never walk away from her.

The therapist knows that automatic thoughts are not only elusive, they are deeply embedded; clients challenge them only with great reluctance. Recognizing the difficulty of changing such beliefs, the therapist devises an experiment to help Ms. Nakatani challenge what she believes—a behavioral approach.

"You think you're boring? Why don't you find out by calling five of your friends on the phone? Keep talking until the person ends the conversation. How long would someone spend talking to you if you were an interesting person? How long would the conversation last if you were boring?" Ms. Nakatani's maladaptive beliefs can be effectively challenged if these experiences are appropriately chosen. Then, most likely, her depression will lift.

Cognitive therapy involves weekly sessions over several months. The procedure effectively alleviates depression in more than half the cases, rivaling tricyclics in effectiveness (e.g., Rush, Beck, Kovacs, & Hollon, 1977; Stravynski & Greenberg, 1992).

However, cognitive theory and therapy have some problems (Haaga, Dyck, & Ernst, 1991). Research has not yet shown that Beck's therapy works by specifically changing how depressed people think (Brewin, 1989). Studies have not been that fine-grained. Also, the particular beliefs that characterize depression also occur in other forms of abnormality, which means that Beck's approach may be calling for more specificity than actually exists. And he has been somewhat vague about the origin of maladaptive cognitive habits.

There is reason to question one of the basic premises of the cognitive approach to depression, namely that those with depression are illogical. The other side of this coin is obviously that nondepressives are logical, seeing the world as it really is. But a great deal of research suggests the opposite. The nondepressed entertain exaggerated views of themselves and the world, placing themselves in the best possible light. Taylor

(1989) calls these *positive illusions:* beliefs that we are above average in looks, sense of humor, and popularity, that things will always work out for the better, that this is the best of all possible worlds.

The tendency of most people to hold clearly implausible beliefs of unmitigated cheerfulness is intriguing, and it may have a basis in evolution (Tiger, 1979). But it calls Beck's theory into question. We cannot contrast depressed individuals with nondepressives on the basis of the reality of their beliefs. In some circumstances, it is the depressed who end up judging themselves and their impact on the world most accurately (e.g., Alloy & Abramson, 1979; Lewinsohn, Mischel, Chaplin, & Barton, 1980). This so-called *depressive realism* may occur simply because those who are depressed are willing to entertain negative possibilities. The downside, of course, is that more positive possibilities may be overlooked.

There is another problem with Beck's theory. He uses the notion of a **depressive schema** to explain negative beliefs and the tendency to process information in ways that maintain them. As pointed out in Chapter 7, schema notions have become popular in cognitive approaches to abnormality, but if we invoke these as explanations, we must not treat them as something that only abnormal people have. *Everyone* organizes their beliefs in a particular way. Those who are depressed have negative ideas at the center of their worldview, just as the nondepressed have positive ones. We gain nothing from introducing schema notions unless we can somehow identify depression-prone individuals prior to a depressive episode by their information-processing biases. To date there is little evidence that this can be done. Beck waffles on this issue,

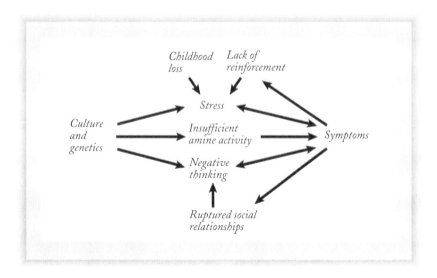

FIGURE 9.5

DIATHESIS-STRESS MODEL OF DEPRESSION   *Biological, psychological, and environmental causes combine to produce depression.*

regarding depressive schemas as "latent" when a person is not in an episode, which is merely another way of saying that there is no sign of them when she is not depressed.

CONCLUSIONS

I have criticized each theoretical approach to depression, but these criticisms do not overshadow their positive contributions. Each has much to say about possible risk factors for depression, and Figure 9.5 diagrams how these might all come to bear in bringing about a particular depressive episode. These risk factors must be placed in their social context, because you have seen how important interpersonal and societal influences on depression can be. Missing in Figure 9.5 is any sense of the weights to be placed on the different factors, or whether they intermingle differently from case to case. For example, we can regard Figure 9.5 in diathesis-stress terms (Chapter 3), but the diathesis might variously be biological or psychological or both, and perhaps it might be overridden by sufficient stressful environmental events (Monroe & Simons, 1991).

As for treatments, we now appear to be moving beyond past competition among approaches into a new era in which the possibility of combining them is being entertained and evaluated (Robinson, Berman, & Neimeyer, 1990). The conclusion seems to be that antidepressant medications *and* psychological therapy are superior to either by itself (Karasu, 1990; Lazarus, 1992; Perry, 1990a; but see Hollon, Shelton, & Loosen, 1991). Perhaps such combinations will become the preferred means of treating depressive disorder. As I pointed out earlier, depression has an alarmingly high rate of recurrence, even after successful intervention, so further attempts to devise treatments are warranted.

BIPOLAR DISORDER

One of my first therapy cases was Mr. M., a middle-aged man who was unambiguously manic. Mr. M. was brought to the hospital by the police, who had picked him up after several complaints that he was annoying adolescent females by making offensive sexual comments. He went willingly with the police, professing his genuine puzzlement why these young "babes" (his word) did not want to sleep with him.

In the hospital, Mr. M. was unable to sleep or even to sit still for more than a minute at a time. I interviewed him in a small room where I sat on a chair while he paced rapidly back and forth. I felt like I was watching a tennis match. He answered my questions with great amusement.

He reported that he was sleeping only 1 or 2 hours every night, that he had never felt so well in his life, and that he had great plans to pursue. By this point, it was obvious to me that he was manic, so I decided to take the lead, asking him if he was planning on leaving his wife or quitting his job. This question actually gave him some pause, and he said that in fact he was planning to do both of those things, even though he had been married for 30 years and employed at the same firm for 20. He was planning on moving to Hawaii right after his divorce, to take Tom Selleck's place on "Magnum, P.I." Because he was destined to become a television star, he did not need to be encumbered by a middle-aged wife. But how did I know all of this?

I explained to him that the sort of problem he appeared to have sometimes led a person to do some very risky things, to upset applecarts best left alone. Mr. M. sobered for just a minute, and he said to me that he was a bit scared of himself, and he was glad he was talking to somebody who might know that he had a problem.

Inappropriate elation is a possible sign of a manic episode.

With this example in mind, I turn to **bipolar disorder** (formerly called **manic-depression**), characterized by alternating episodes of depression and mania.

SIGNS OF MANIA

You already know what a depressive episode looks like, so here is how a diagnostician recognizes a manic episode. In many ways, **mania** consists of symptoms that are the polar opposite of those that characterize depression (see Table 9.6). According to DSM-IV, a manic episode is defined by the presence for a week or more of the following sorts of symptoms:

Mood   The manic individual typically shows an elevated and expansive mood, although he may be irritable as well. Mania is not simply feeling good; it is feeling too good. Manics are often referred to as high, because their mood has soared just as if they have taken a drug that produces euphoria. Along these lines, the manic individual might display an inflated self-esteem, perhaps to the point of grandiosity.

Sleep disturbance   He may also show a decreased need for sleep, getting by on just a couple of hours a night without feeling tired.

Talkativeness   He may be more talkative than usual, a phenomenon sometimes referred to as **pressured speech** because he seems unable to control his flow of words. It is as if he were an overinflated tire that has just sprung a leak from which the words escape.

Racing thoughts   Relatedly, the manic individual experiences his thoughts as racing, and the onlooker gets a flavor of this by trying to follow the person as he talks. He shows what is called **flight of ideas,** as one topic of conversation leads to another and another and still another, with dizzying speed, never returning to the original point of departure.

Distractibility   The manic individual is also highly distractable. He shows an increase in activity, often appearing highly agitated as he pursues dozens of activities simultaneously. Finally, he may become excessively involved in pleasurable yet foolish activities, engaging in sexual indiscretions, buying sprees, or high-risk business ventures.

TYPES OF BIPOLAR DISORDER

Bipolar disorder can be a mixed category, subsuming people who alternate between episodes of mania and depression as well as individuals who experience only mania. Although bipolar disorder is defined by the presence of manic and/or depressive episodes, this does not mean that people who meet the criteria for diagnosis are always at one extreme or the other. There may be long periods in which they are normal; indeed, episodes of normality are more likely than episodes of either depression or mania (Coryell, Keller, et al., 1989). However, some individuals pass almost immediately from one extreme to the other. The alternation between mania and depression is highly variable across individuals (see Figure 9.6). Some show a regular pattern, with either rapid or slow changes between mood extremes. Others show no pattern at all.

A mild version of a manic episode is described as **hypomania.** Here the person shows an elevated mood and an increase in energy without impaired function-

TABLE 9.6

SYMPTOMS OF A MANIC EPISODE *In many ways, the symptoms of a manic episode are the opposite of those of a depressive episode.*

TYPE OF SYMPTOM	EXAMPLE
emotional	elevated and expansive mood
motivational	excessive involvement in pleasurable yet foolish pursuits
somatic	decreased need for sleep
behavioral	increased activity; increased talkativeness
cognitive	racing thoughts; increased distractability

Because of his well documented bursts of prodigious energy and accomplishment, some have described President Theodore Roosevelt (1858–1919) as hypomanic.

FIGURE **9.6**

THE LIFE COURSE OF AN
INDIVIDUAL WITH BIPOLAR
DISORDER   *The complex
series of mood swings in bipolar
disorder can best be captured
visually, as shown here.*
SOURCE: FROM "GRAPHIC
REPRESENTATION OF THE LIFE COURSE
OF ILLNESS IN PATIENTS WITH
AFFECTIVE DISORDER," BY R. M. POST,
P. P. ROY-BYRNE, AND T. W. UHDE,
1988, *American Journal of Psychiatry, 145,*
p. 845. REPRINTED WITH PERMISSION.

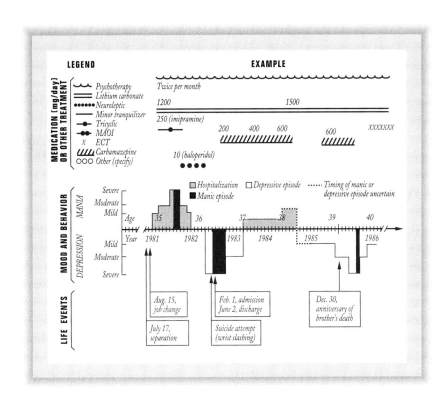

ing. Hypomania can be advantageous to individuals, and its link with achievement has long been noted (see Focus on Mania and Literary Creativity). Among the famous individuals who have been described as hypomanic are Winston Churchill and Theodore Roosevelt (Fieve, 1976). Some depressed individuals also experience hypomanic episodes. Prior to DSM-IV, these individuals were classified as unipolar depressives. The current diagnostic system includes them with those who satisfy the criteria for bipolar disorder, under the assumption that they share more in common with them than they do with unipolar depressives. **Bipolar I disorder** refers to individuals with unambiguously manic episodes, whereas **bipolar II disorder** refers to those who experience hypomanic episodes only.

A mild version of bipolar disorder is called **cyclothymic disorder,** in which the person alternates between mild depression and hypomania. Cyclothymic disorder meets the strict diagnostic criteria for neither depressive nor manic episodes.

THE EPIDEMIOLOGY AND COURSE OF BIPOLAR DISORDER

About 1% of adults suffer from bipolar disorder at some point in their life, which means that it is less common than depressive disorder. Prevalence appears

comparable across different nations (e.g., Leff, Fischer, & Bertelsen, 1976), as do symptoms (e.g., Shan-Ming, Deyi, Zhen, Jingsu, & Taylor, 1982). Bipolar disorder occurs approximately equally among males and females, another difference from depressive disorder. It cuts as well across social class and race. It runs through families. The onset of this disorder is usually during the middle twenties (Goodwin & Jamison, 1990), although it may occur during adolescence or later in life. Usually, though, bipolar disorder develops before age 30. It appears as if the bipolar individual first suffers from a manic episode, although this may simply mean that mania attracts more attention than depression. In 80% of cases, it is a manic episode rather than a depressive one that brings the individual with bipolar disorder into the mental health system (Dunner, Fleiss, & Fieve, 1976). (By the way, the pejorative term *maniac* is derived from the word *manic.*)

Without intervention, bipolar disorder is chronic, and in the typical case, the person shows ever shorter periods of normality between manic or depressive episodes. Episodes become longer and more severe.

Professional golfer Bert Yancey suffered from bipolar disorder since his college days (Sutton, 1990). Between 1966 and 1972, he won seven PGA tournaments and earned more than $500,000. But the episodes of mania

FOCUS ON

*Mania and
Literary
Creativity*

THERE IS A LONG-STANDING belief in the Western world that equates madness with genius. Remember the cult of Dionysus discussed in Chapter 5. Dionysus himself was regarded as mad and was thought to lead people—when they drank his wine—into both madness *and* creativity. Indeed, the term *genius* is derived from a Latin word meaning *spirit* or *demon*; the point is, of course, that those who soar above their peers are inspired by magical forces, which can also have a darker side.

At this juncture in your study of abnormal psychology, you know that it is incorrect to equate abnormality per se with genius. People who are severely anxious or depressed are anything but creative. However, one intriguing exception is an apparent link between mania and literary creativity (Goodwin & Jamison, 1990). The attempt to associate mania with notable accomplishment is fraught with methodological threats. The identification of "genius" can only be done from the vantage of history, which means that studies are necessarily retrospective. Investigations usually rely on material gathered for other purposes. What results in effect is a collection of case studies—provocative to be sure—but difficult to use in making causal claims.

If we look at major poets in the 20th century who warrant a diagnosis of bipolar disorder, we have no trouble identifying such individuals as Hart Crane, Robert Lowell, and Anne Sexton. But what proportion of the total number of major poets do such individuals represent? If there is a link between mania and creativity, then the number of bipolar poets should exceed the 1% prevalence rate of the disorder in the general population. Coming up with an unambiguous number is a challenge.

The cautious conclusion from such historical studies is that at least some individuals with notable accomplishments in literature suffered from bipolar disorder. This conclusion becomes more than trivial when juxtaposed with the virtual dearth of examples of creative individuals suffering from most other forms of psychological disorder. If nothing else, we know

that bipolar disorder does not preclude literary accomplishment.

Another conclusion from these historical studies is that bipolar individuals work most creatively when manic. William Blake, for instance, was described by his contemporaries as writing with boundless energy when in an ecstatic mood. To varying degrees, the same point has been made about Edgar Allen Poe, Lord Byron, Alfred Lord Tennyson, Percy Bysshe Shelley, Samuel Taylor Coleridge, and Gerard Manley Hopkins.

More systematic studies support this impression (e.g., Coryell, Endicott, et al., 1989). These investigations did not study the most famous writers in society but did have the virtues of formal diagnostic interviews and matched control groups. For example, Andreasen (1987) compared thirty participants in the prestigious University of Iowa Writer's Workshop to a group of thirty individuals who were not writers but were comparable in age, education, and sex. Among the writers, 43% met the criteria for bipolar disorder at some point in life versus only 10% of the control subjects. The writers were also much more likely to have relatives with some form of affective disorder. Most of the bipolar writers were diagnosed as bipolar II, meaning that their manic episodes were not the most severe possible.

Given that there is an association between mania and literary creativity, what are the mechanisms responsible? Some are easy to specify. The individual who is lively and energetic is going to embark on a large number of projects, some of which may one day be regarded as creative. The person who is outgoing and a risk taker is going to have intriguing life experiences.

One more mechanism is proposed by Sylvan Arieti (1976). From a psychoanalytic perspective, Arieti suggested that creativity results when a person gains access to the *primary process thought* of the id and elaborates it with the *secondary process thought* of the ego into a socially valued project. A manic individual, by this formula, has an easier time tapping into primary process thought, because his thinking is necessarily more rapid, fluid, and grandiose than that of nonmanic individuals. If his mania is not too disruptive, he then is in a position to use the "genius" that his thinking has provided. Needless to say, mania per se does not guarantee creativity or genius. If the person lacks the necessary skills to represent his thoughts visually or verbally, then there will be no creative product.

and depression became increasingly worse and more disruptive as he aged. He was no longer able to compete on the professional tour and even had difficulty in his less demanding job as a golf instructor.

Until recent decades, nothing could be done to alleviate bipolar disorder, and the only treatment was to restrain the person during his manic episodes. Today, we have effective treatment, discussed later in this chapter, which helped Yancey and helps others like him. In 1988, Bert Yancey was able to mount a modest comeback on the Senior PGA tour.

ETIOLOGY

In contrast to depressive disorder, which is profitably approached from a variety of theoretical perspectives, bipolar disorder nowadays is regarded in mainly biological terms. The evidence is quite good that bipolar disorder is a problem that is genetically predisposed and best treated with medication. The actual physiological mechanisms responsible for the disorder are not as clear, but the inference is straightforward from the very nature of the symptoms that there is something amiss in whatever regulates biological rhythms. In Chapter 6, I characterized the nervous system as a homeostasis governed by checks and balances. At least descriptively, bipolar disorder involves a particularly "rough" set of checks and balances, as if a manic state were countered by a depressive one that overshoots its mark, and vice versa.

Family studies, adoption studies, and twin studies all give us reason to believe that bipolar disorder is a heritable problem (McGuffin & Katz, 1989). For example, if one identical twin is diagnosed with bipolar disorder, the chances are 58% that the other twin will have the disorder as well; this rate of concordance is three times higher than that found among fraternal twins.

In 1987, what appeared to be a groundbreaking discovery was made when researchers studied a large number of Old Order Amish individuals in Pennsylvania (Egeland et al., 1987). This is an ideal group in which to study the heritability of bipolar disorder, not because it occurs at a greater frequency in this group—it does not—but because the Old Order Amish do not use alcohol or drugs, which might muddle the diagnosis of a mood disorder. Furthermore, they keep very good genealogical records and are a group into which few "outsiders" have married since the early 1700s when the community was founded.

Researchers took a blood sample from each member of this group, which allowed them to ascertain their genetic makeup. And, of course, each was diagnosed as bipolar or not. A striking pattern emerged. *Every*

As a closed community that avoids drug and alcohol use, the Old Order Amish are an ideal group in which to study the heritability of mood disorders.

individual diagnosed with bipolar disorder had a particular gene present on chromosome 11. No one without this gene was diagnosed with the disorder. This seemed an extremely important discovery, as important for the biomedical model of abnormality as any since the discovery of the link between syphilis and general paresis (Chapter 1).

More recent discoveries have tarnished this finding, however, suggesting the need for more caution in conducting studies into the heritability of disorders (Merikangas, Spence, & Kupfer, 1989). First, other research groups investigating different closed communities found similar evidence that particular genes were linked to bipolar disorder (Mellon, 1989), but these genes proved to be different from the one identified by the Pennsylvania research group (e.g., Baron et al., 1987). What this means is that a single gene may predispose the disorder, but not in every case. The predisposition might typically be polygenic (Faraone, Kremen, & Tsuang, 1990; Gershon, Martinez, Goldin, & Gejman, 1990; Simpson, Folstein, Meyers, & DePaulo, 1992).

Second, follow-up studies of the original Amish subjects yielded different results (Kelsoe et al., 1989). When new individuals were diagnosed and added to the sample, and the correlations between genetic makeup and diagnosis recalculated, the previously discovered relationship was no longer apparent. The preliminary reports were simply that—preliminary—and they did not hold up as the research continued.

These qualifications do not overturn the general conclusion that bipolar disorder is heritable; the family, twin, and adoption studies still exist and are unanimous in this implication. What the qualifications mean is that the specific genes responsible for bipolar disorder have yet to be identified.

TREATMENT

In the 1940s, it was discovered that **lithium**—a naturally occurring salt—was useful in controlling both manic and depressive episodes of the bipolar individual. Lithium was introduced widely in the United States during the 1970s, and it is now the treatment of choice for the disorder. It makes the highs less high and the lows less low; it literally dampens mood swings.

In order to be effective, lithium must be taken continuously, and it must attain a certain level of concentration in the blood. Then it prevents future episodes of depression and mania (O'Connell, Mayo, Flatow, Cuthbertson, & O'Brien, 1991). Lithium does not cure bipolar disorder in the sense of making it go away. Instead, the medication controls the symptoms. If and when the person stops taking it, he is likely to suffer a relapse.

Lithium is not without its drawbacks (Gitlin, Cochran, & Jamison, 1989). Side effects include thirst, frequent urination, and skin irritation. It may produce muscle tremors, which happened to golfer Bert Yancey when he first began to take lithium in 1975. His mood swings were controlled, but his golf swings were not, and so his game suffered. In overly high doses, it can damage the kidneys and liver. In establishing a therapeutic dose, a physician must be careful to prescribe just enough lithium so as not to tax the patient's body. In monitoring his patient's blood level, the physician must additionally keep track of kidney and liver functions.

Compliance with lithium is a problem, in part because of the side effects just enumerated and in part because the individual may miss the highs that a hypomanic or manic episode can provide. A person maintained on lithium may stop taking the medication when confronted with a life crisis, rationalizing that the crisis will not get him down so much if he unleashes his mania. Unfortunately, crisis and mania do not neatly cancel each other out, and usually what happens is that the person shortly faces two problems: the life crisis and a manic episode.

How does lithium work? Here there is no lack of theories, but no consensus either (Jefferson, 1989, 1990). Perhaps we can understand the mechanism for lithium only when we understand exactly what is responsible for bipolar disorder. Speculation centers mostly on neurotransmitters. Lithium may affect the permeability of neurons and thus the process by which they fire. In the case of bipolar disorder, though, the theorist must explain not only why these sometimes fire too readily but also why they sometimes do not fire readily enough (Avissar, Schreiber, Danon, & Belmaker, 1988).

Does the evidence I have surveyed for a biological etiology and treatment preclude any contribution of psychology and psychologists? I think not. Bipolar disorder may be heritable, but it is *not* inherited as a whole. The concordance for this disorder is not perfect for identical twins. Something other than genetics must determine who does or does not develop this problem. If we look into the background of those who develop bipolar disorder, we often find traumatic events (Bidzinska, 1984), so what we probably need is a diathesis-stress conception.

Psychological stress—obviously the province of psychologists—may play some role in triggering specific episodes of mania or depression. Both the initial occurrence of bipolar disorder as well as subsequent episodes may follow in the wake of stressful events (e.g., Aronson & Shukla, 1987; Chung, Langeluddecke, & Tennant, 1986; Ellicott, Hammen, Gitlin, Brown, & Jamison, 1990; Hunt, Bruce-Jones, & Silverstone, 1992). Along these lines, Swann and colleagues (1990) proposed that cases of bipolar disorder fall along a continuum of sensitivity to environmental events. Those whose disorder is more versus less sensitive to the environment may show different patterns of neurotransmitter dysfunction.

The biological treatment of bipolar disorder is not simply a matter of individuals lining up to receive lithium pills. As already noted, compliance is a problem, and it is important that those taking lithium understand why the medication is necessary (Cochran & Gitlin, 1988). Mr. M., the case example at the beginning of this section, improved greatly with lithium. As a psychologist, I did not write his prescription, monitor his blood levels, or evaluate his kidney and liver functions—but I did talk to him about compliance, about how to navigate his life crises, about how to repair the damage he had done to himself and others, and about how to recognize warning signs that another episode was threatening. Simply put, psychology should continue to have something to offer in the conceptualization and treatment of bipolar disorder (Miklowitz & Goldstein, 1990).

In this chapter, I have discussed the mood disorders—unipolar and bipolar. You saw that they are much better understood than they once were, and furthermore, that we have effective treatments for them. Let me return to one of the issues I raised in the very beginning of this chapter—whether these two mood disorders really belong together in a classification scheme. The matter will only be resolved as we learn more about the mechanisms responsible for each, and as we eventually move to an etiological classification. Both unipolar and bipolar disorder come about from an interplay of biological *and* psychological influences; their eventual mix will be the deciding factor concerning our conceptualization of the relationship between the two (Bradley, 1990).

Summary

✦ Mood disorders are problems marked by alterations in mood. In depression, the person experiences excessive and inappropriate sadness. In mania, the person experiences excessive and inappropriate elation.

DEPRESSIVE DISORDER

✦ Depressive disorder (or depression) is characterized by depressive episodes that affect all spheres of functioning: mood, thoughts, actions, and physiology.

✦ In our society, severe depression is closely linked to suicidal thoughts and attempts. More women than men attempt suicide, but more men than women succeed. The risk of suicide steadily rises as an individual ages.

✦ Depression is one of the most common types of psychological abnormality. It runs through families, is more common among young adults than older adults, and is more common among women than men.

✦ Most episodes of depression lift on their own, after 3 to 6 months, but half of the time another episode follows.

✦ Biomedical approaches to unipolar depression focus on the amine hypothesis: a theory proposing that depression results from insufficient activity of the neurotransmitters norepinephrine and serotonin. Biological treatments for depression attempt to increase their activity. Several strategies are successful, including drugs (tricyclics, MAO inhibitors, and Prozac), electroconvulsive shock therapy, and aerobic exercise.

✦ Psychodynamic approaches to unipolar disorder emphasize the role of early loss in the life of the depression-prone individual, which creates excessive dependency and emotional neediness. Research support for these theories is equivocal. Interpersonal psychotherapy is a psychodynamic treatment effective for depression. In this therapy, the focus is on interpersonal issues and conflicts.

✦ There exist several cognitive-behavioral theories of depression. The behavioral theory of depression proposes that the disorder results from insufficient rewards in the environment, either because rewards do not exist or because the person lacks the skills to win them. Therapy from this view attempts to enrich the depressed person's world and/or impart greater social skills. Learned helplessness refers to the maladaptive passivity that may follow exposure to uncontrollable aversive events. The individual who experiences uncontrollability in one situation comes to believe in his or her own helplessness, and this belief may then produce depression in other situations. According to the cognitive theory of depression, people become depressed as a result of excessively negative thinking that is maintained by erroneous logic. Cognitive therapy proceeds by challenging these negative beliefs.

✦ Biomedical, psychodynamic, and cognitive-behavioral models all contribute something to our understanding of the causes and treatments of unipolar disorder. Each by itself is probably incomplete, and the future may well see an integrated approach.

BIPOLAR DISORDER

✦ Formerly called manic-depression, bipolar disorder is characterized by an alternation of depressive and manic episodes. In many ways, a manic episode involves the opposite symptoms of a depressive episode; when manic, the individual is greatly elated, expansive, and energetic.

✦ Theorists regard bipolar disorder as very much a biological problem. It is clearly heritable, and the treatment of choice is with medication—specifically lithium, a naturally occurring salt that dampens mood swings. However, there is still a role for psychology in the conceptualization and treatment of bipolar disorder.

Key Terms

amine hypothesis
anergia
anhedonia
automatic thoughts
behavioral theory of depression
bipolar disorder; manic-depression
Bipolar I disorder
Bipolar II disorder
cognitive theory of depression
cognitive therapy
cyclothymic disorder
dependent personality disorder
depressive disorder; unipolar disorder; depression
depressive schema
dysthymic disorder
electroconvulsive shock therapy; ECT
endogenous depression
errors in logic

explanatory style
flight of ideas
hypomania
interpersonal psychotherapy
learned helplessness
lithium
mania
MAO inhibitors
medial forebrain bundle
melancholic depression
mood disorders
norepinephrine
premenstrual syndrome; PMS
pressured speech
Prozac; fluoxetine
reactive depression; exogenous depression
seasonal affective disorder; SAD
serotonin
terminal insomnia; early morning awakening
tricyclics

Mind-Body Disorders

10 *Following a successful college career in track and football, Travis Williams was drafted by the Green Bay Packers in 1967, when they were the best team in football. Williams was one of the best players on this legendary team. Nicknamed the Roadrunner, his specialty was turning a kickoff into an immediate touchdown. In his rookie year, he did this four times, setting an NFL record that remains unbroken to this day. On January 14, 1968, his rookie season ended on the highest possible note when the Packers won Super Bowl II. Travis Williams died 23 years later, at the age of only 45.*

Football player Travis Williams could outrun everything but trouble. After a brief but spectacular career as a professional football player, Williams encountered numerous difficulties and died at age 45.

My concern in this chapter is with disorders involving an interplay between mind and body. Although pinpointing the causes of Travis Williams's death is impossible, it seems plausible to suggest that the accumulation of stress and misfortune he experienced following the end of his football career contributed to his poor health and ultimately to his early death.

It was said that Williams could outrun everything but trouble (Newman, 1991). His career lasted only 4 years, and he never made more than $35,000 per year. He had a large family—eight children to support—so he never had enough money. A knee injury prematurely ended his career, and his life began to unravel. The only job he could find was working as a bouncer at a flophouse. In 1979, he broke the jaw of a man he found with his wife, and he was sentenced to a year in the county jail. Then his wife killed someone while driving intoxicated, and she was sent to the same jail. Their children were divided between the grandparents. Williams's wife became a drug abuser, and he began to drink heavily. With nowhere else to turn, he started to live on the streets, and he suffered bouts of severe depression. Then his wife died of an overdose, followed shortly by the death of his mother from colon cancer. Then his younger sister died. Then his best friend died. At age 45, Williams himself died of heart failure.

Did stress contribute to the death of Travis Williams? Probably. Did his drinking play a role? Probably. Did the lack of stable social support have anything to do with it? Probably. These all fall under the umbrella of psychology. One of the most important discoveries within recent years is that psychological

MINDS AND BODIES THROUGHOUT HISTORY

Aristotle: *Mens Sano in Corpore Sano*
Descartes: Mind-Body Dualism
Heroic Medicine and Its Alternatives
The Advent of Modern Medicine
  The waning of heroic techniques
  Germ theory
  Immune system

MINDS AND BODIES MORE RECENTLY

Franz Alexander: Psychosomatic Medicine
Hans Selye: General Adaptation Syndrome
Stressful Life Events and Hassles
The Cognitive Revolution
  Stress and coping
  Cognitive personality variables
Social Support
Behavior and Health Promotion
Psychoneuroimmunology

PARTICULAR MIND-BODY DISORDERS

Cardiovascular Diseases
  Psychological risk factors
  Psychological treatment
Cancer
  Psychological risk factors
  Psychological treatment
Gastrointestinal Disorders
  Gastroesophagal reflux
  Peptic ulcer
  Irritable bowel syndrome
Asthma
  Psychological risk factors
  Psychological treatment

FOCUS ON *Hypertension among African Americans*

FOCUS ON *Shamanism and Alternative Medicine*

factors contribute to poor health. Said more positively, psychological factors also lead to good health and longer life.

Everyone has a story to tell about a family member who "postponed" death until an important event—a birthday, an anniversary, or a holiday—took place. For example, Mark Twain was born in 1835 on the day that Halley's comet was visible in the United States. He died 75 years later on the very day that the comet returned. Throughout his life, he commented that he was waiting for its return in order to die.

That people may delay their own deaths while awaiting important occurrences is not just folklore, as a systematic study of Chinese Americans showed (Phillips & Smith, 1990). Researchers studied the death records of individuals in San Francisco's Chinatown immediately before and immediately after the Harvest Moon Festival. Deaths dipped before the festival, and peaked right afterward.

We can identify psychological *risk factors* for illness simply by ascertaining what correlates with good versus bad health. It is more difficult to specify the *mechanisms* that translate the risk factors into assaults on physical well-being. But in recent years, much progress has been made with respect to our understanding of these mechanisms.

Traditionally, psychologists have studied physical illnesses influenced by psychological factors under the rubric of **psychosomatic disorders.** Recall from Chapter 8 that somatoform disorders look like physical illnesses but do not involve any actual tissue damage. In

Research suggests that the death rate decreases before holidays, such as the Harvest Moon Festival shown here celebrated in California.

Writer Mark Twain (Samuel Clemens) was born in 1835 on the day that Halley's comet was visible; he died 75 years later on the very day the comet returned.

contrast, psychosomatic disorders are "real" physical disorders, with a demonstrable pathology of the body. Over the years, the field of psychosomatic medicine concerned itself with but a handful of disorders: ulcers, asthma, hypertension, and a few others. These diseases were identified by early psychosomatic theorists as under the sway of emotional conflicts. Now, psychologists believe that a number of diseases are influenced by psychological factors. Indeed, perhaps all diseases are, and so I do not want to limit our discussion to the classic psychosomatic disorders.

DSM-IV handles this matter by suggesting that the label **psychological factors affecting medical condition** be used whenever psychological factors act in any of the following ways:

◆ coinciding in time with the beginning or worsening of a physical illness

◆ interfering with the treatment of a medical condition

◆ creating additional health risks

◆ eliciting physiological responses that precipitate or exacerbate a medical condition

Psychological factors include clinical syndromes, symptoms such as anxiety, personality traits, coping styles, and unhealthy habits.

I can make several generalizations about these broad influences. First, the field has languished for years under too strict a distinction between what is categorized as mind and what is categorized as body. There are historical reasons for this rigid distinction, but it is still overly limiting.

Second, despite the possible relevance of psychological factors to illness, we must beware of concluding that these are the only influences or even the most important ones. We all carry with us vulnerabilities and resiliences as part of our genetic inheritance. One of the best predictors of longevity, for example, is how long our ancestors lived. Although Travis Williams was buffeted by life, perhaps early death was common in his family.

Most contemporary theorists argue that we need an explicitly broad view to grasp the factors that make good or bad health likely. No single model of abnormality is going to suffice for explaining mind-body disorders. Remember the *diathesis–stress model* introduced in Chapter 3 as an integrative approach to abnormality? It has one of its most worked-through applications with regard to the sorts of problems I discuss in this chapter. People bring a certain weakness (the diathesis) to a situation, which when coupled with environmental events (stress) results in physical illness. Similarly, the *biopsychosocial model*, also introduced in Chapter 3, works well for conceptualizing mind-body disorders.

Consider Travis Williams again. Biologically, he may have been at risk for early death because of a family predisposition to poor health. His years of drinking and living on the streets may have weakened his body's ability to fight off disease. Psychologically, the numerous losses he experienced right before his death and the severe depression from which he suffered may have taken a toll. And socially, the lack of other people in his life to provide emotional support may have been a factor, too. Further, as an African American male, Williams was at increased risk for heart disease, so perhaps part of his ethnic inheritance added to the likelihood that he would die the way he did (see Focus on Hypertension among African Americans).

A third point to make about mind-body disorders is that to implicate a psychological factor in illness is *not* to blame the person for falling ill, although we can slip quite easily into this way of thinking (Sontag, 1979, 1988). For example, a recent debate within the organ transplant community is about whether to donate kidneys to alcoholics (John et al., 1989). Many oppose doing this, for two reasons. The first is pragmatic: Alcoholics are poor risks for transplants. But the second reason is steeped in morality: Alcoholics, because they have damaged their kidneys by excessive drinking, do not "deserve" the new lease on life that a kidney transplant will give them.

A similar issue arose in early 1991 when President George Bush referred to infants born with AIDS as the "innocent" victims of this disease. Critics jumped on his comment as implying that other victims of AIDS—that is, gay men and intravenous drug users—were somehow not so innocent, because their behavior presumably caused the disease.

The problem with this kind of reasoning is the unstated assumption that psychological risk factors for illness are freely chosen. So, Travis Williams chose to play football rather than prepare for another sort of career. And he chose to get in a fight and thus be sent to jail. Most psychologists are uncomfortable with the notion of absolutely free choice, holding instead that people's decisions are determined. If we do not criticize people for "choosing" to develop chicken pox or the mumps, does it make any sense to criticize them for developing mind-body disorders?

Fourth, granted the influence of psychological factors on physical health and illness, there is still considerable disagreement about the specificity of this influence. Do certain psychological states or traits make given illnesses more or less likely, or do they simply exert a general influence on well-being? As I discuss later, theorists over the years have proposed

Are infants born with AIDS any more "innocent" than other victims of this disease?

FOCUS ON

Hypertension

among African

Americans

CARDIOVASCULAR DISEASES are the leading cause of death for all Americans, but their prevalence nonetheless varies across different groups. African Americans, for example, are at much greater risk than European Americans, males by 33% and females by 60% (U.S. Department of Health and Human Services, 1992). Examination of why this might be underscores the multiplicity of psychological influences on physical well-being (James, 1984a, 1984b).

Some theorists have pointed to biological differences between Blacks and Whites as responsible for the differential risk of heart disease, and others to dietary differences (see discussions by Eisner, 1990; Francis, 1990; Klag, Whelton, Coresh, Grim, & Kuller, 1991). But in addition to any roles played by biology or diet, psychological factors figure prominently.

As later discussed, Franz Alexander theorized that chronic anger results in hypertension, which in turn leads to a cardiovascular disease. On the average, African Americans show elevated blood pressure, and perhaps this may be the result of accumulated anger at a world filled with prejudice and discrimination. A study by Krieger (1990) supports this hypothesis. She interviewed Black and White women in California, determining their health status—specifically, their blood pressure—as well as how they responded to instances of unfair treatment based on race or gender. Among African Americans, those who reacted to unfair treatment by keeping quiet and accepting the discrimination were *four* times more likely to be hypertensive than those who reacted by speaking out and

taking some action. Among European Americans, there was no such association, perhaps because very few of them reacted to unfair treatment by quietly accepting the discrimination.

Another psychological influence on hypertension that helps explains why African Americans are at increased risk for cardiovascular diseases is a personality variable dubbed **John Henryism.** John Henry is a figure in American folklore, a black railroad worker whose job of laying track by hand was threatened when a steam hammer was introduced to do the same work. According to legend, a contest took place between John Henry and the steam hammer. John Henry won the contest, laying more track, but he died thereafter of a heart attack.

Researcher Sherman James saw in this legend a metaphor for African Americans who believe that they can control *all* events in their lives solely through hard work and determination (James, Hartnett, & Kalsbeek, 1983; James, LaCroix, Kleinbaum, & Strogatz, 1984). He created a questionnaire asking respondents the degree to which they believed in such values and then investigated the relationship of John Henryism to blood pressure among black males. Those who scored high on the John Henryism measure but were low in socioeconomic status were most likely to be hypertensive (James, Strogatz, Wing, & Ramsey, 1987). Constant striving for control over events without the resources to achieve it may take a toll on health, although third variables possibly confound this conclusion. Assuming the validity of this finding, it would seem to apply to all groups (Duijkers, Drijver, Kromhout, & James, 1988). However, it fits particularly well for contemporary African Americans (James, Keenan, Strogatz, Browning, & Garrett, 1992), who often face a very real limit to what they can attain regardless of how hard they work. Mind-body disorders such as hypertension, no less than other psychological difficulties, must be located in their societal context.

that "dependent" individuals are at risk for ulcers, "angry" people for heart disease, "hopeless" folks for cancer, and so on. There is a theoretical elegance that surrounds these formulations, but the opposite opinion is that such highly specific links usually do not exist (Friedman & Booth-Kewley, 1987).

Fifth, perhaps the deliberate encouragement of certain psychological states and behaviors can promote

health. The disciplines of *behavioral medicine* and *health psychology* have recently emerged. They try to cultivate health by psychological means. We know that behavioral risk factors for poor health, such as smoking or not exercising, can be changed, with beneficial effects on a person's health. Less clear is whether personality characteristics and emotional styles, when changed by therapy, will confer similar health benefits.

Sixth, health and illness prove difficult to define, and thus to measure and research. Different eras have given us different conceptions of what it means to be healthy or ill, and the current belief is that no single and simple definition will suffice. Rather, a number of factors count toward our judgment that an individual is ill or not, but most are neither necessary nor sufficient. These factors include general complaints about feeling ill, specific symptoms such as shortness of breath, demonstrable tissue pathology, presence of germs, longevity, and being alive or dead. Even this last factor is not without ambiguity, because there are different criteria for being alive or dead. Often these are mandated by state laws: cessation of brain waves, for example, versus cessation of cardiac function.

These possible criteria may disagree with one another. Someone might feel fine but harbor all sorts of dire germs. Someone else might be free of germs but feel poorly. Or someone might live a long but impaired life, or a short but vigorous one. One of the intriguing puzzles of modern epidemiology is why women have more illnesses than men but at the same time live longer (Verbrugge, 1989).

In the extreme, of course, we have no difficulty recognizing that someone is ill or dead. No one would argue that Travis Williams, at the end of his life, was anything but ailing. The more puzzling cases are those in between.

I next discuss the history of the relationship between minds and bodies. My hope is that you will see how theories about this relationship dictate how illness is regarded—in particular, what its causes and its treatments might be. The remainder of the chapter discusses psychological influences on mind-body disorders including cardiovascular disease, cancer, gastrointestinal disorders, and asthma.

MINDS AND BODIES THROUGHOUT HISTORY

Drastically different conceptions of *mind* and *body* have characterized different eras (see Figure 10.1). I look here at the history of Western thought, which gave rise most directly to psychiatry and clinical psychology. But the history of Eastern thought on this matter is no less fascinating, illustrating the same variety of perspectives (van Straten, 1983). The point is that the way we conceptualize the relationship between minds and bodies dictates how we explain psychological influences on physical well-being.

ARISTOTLE: *Mens Sano in Corpore Sano*

"A healthy mind in a healthy body." Early thinkers such as Aristotle (384–322 B.C.) made no firm distinction between minds and bodies. They expected that minds and bodies would show continuity, with the health of one reflecting the health of the other. Greek standards of beauty referred not merely to good looks but also to an inner beauty that was necessarily shown in physical appearance.

Recall the theory of humours, mentioned in Chapter 9 as an early account of depression. This

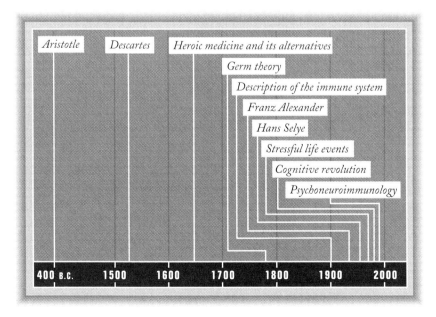

FIGURE 10.1

HISTORY OF MIND-BODY CONCEPTUALIZATIONS
Conceptualizations of the relationship between minds and bodies have changed throughout history, influencing importantly how theorists and practitioners view mind-body disorders and their possible treatments.

"A healthy mind in a healthy body."

DESCARTES: MIND-BODY DUALISM

The noted philosopher René Descartes (1596–1650) made many contributions to Western thought, including a strong stance concerning the separateness of mind and body, a position known as **mind-body dualism.** Contrast this notion with the easy interaction posited by the Greek thinkers before him. See how mind-body dualism poses for us a considerable problem in explaining (or even allowing for) the existence of mind-body disorders. If minds and bodies are separate, then there cannot even be disorders brought about by the influence of the one on the other.

Descartes was one of the first theorists to propose an account of how the body moved. As a young man in Paris, he had visited parks that had mechanized statues connected to plates in the walkways. When passersby stepped on a plate, a hydraulic mechanism forced water through pipes into the limbs of a statue, causing it to move. If mechanical beings moved about in this way, perhaps people did too. After all, the parts of the body are connected by tubes (nerves). Muscles swell when they are used. And the brain contains hollow spaces (cerebral ventricles) filled with fluid. Putting this all together, Descartes hypothesized that our bodies moved when fluid traveled from the brain through the nerves to swell the muscles and make such movement possible.

theory was also at one time the dominant account of physical health. It held that physical and emotional health were not altogether different things. When a person's bodily fluids (humours) were imbalanced, he became ill, mentally and physically. Treatment consisted of attempting to restore the balance. The earliest physicians, individuals like Hippocrates (ca. 460–377 B.C.) and Galen (129–200), routinely ministered to the whole person, treating his physical symptoms as well as his psyche.

There are two points to draw out about this early era of conceptualizing minds and bodies. First, the mutual influences of minds and bodies needed no particular explanation because they were not seen as separate. Said another way, if I were writing this textbook in ancient Greece, there would be no need for a chapter on mind-body disorders, because all problems would be seen in these terms. Second, humoural theory provided the most popular theory of illness in the Western world well into the 1800s, hypothesizing but one disease state (humoural imbalance). This view of illness was finally supplanted by germ theory, which proposed a variety of illnesses, each associated with a particular type of germ. But let us not get ahead of ourselves. I turn next to ideas proposed in the 1600s.

French philosopher René Descartes (1596–1650) popularized the position of mind-body dualism.

Descartes correctly anticipated the role of the brain in initiating movement and the importance of the nerves in making it possible. He was wrong about the mechanism of this effect—we now know that nerves work via electrical and chemical processes as opposed to hydraulic ones—but his theory is still impressive. It provided a thoroughly scientific (mechanistic) view of people and their behavior. There was just one problem with this theory: It courted disaster. In saying that our behavior had mechanical causes, Descartes was implying that people did not have free will. Because Christian doctrine is based on the assumption of free will, he was implying that these teachings were wrong. In the 17th century this was heresy and punishable by death. But Descartes solved his dilemma by proposing that the body works in a mechanical fashion, subject to causes and effects. The soul (mind) is free. The only point of contact for body and mind, according to Descartes, was the *pineal gland,* because it is one of the few structures in the brain that is not symmetric.

When psychology and psychiatry emerged in the 1800s, theorists found that scientific concepts—including causality—could be applied to the mind. This development in effect dismissed the original basis of Descartes's distinction. But by this time, altogether different disciplines had sprung up to explain bodies on the one hand (neurology, biology) and minds on the other (psychology, psychiatry). The mind-body dualism originally proposed by Descartes had become the mind-body problem, a puzzle to be explained without the means for doing so.

HEROIC MEDICINE AND ITS ALTERNATIVES

As described in Chapter 1, medical practice in the 1700s and early 1800s is referred to as **heroic medicine** (Weil, 1988). The name reflects the aggressive approach taken by orthodox physicians. Humoural theory was still popular, and thus physicians believed that an imbalance of fluids was responsible for illness. But a new twist had been added. With the advent of *materialism,* the philosophical doctrine that all living things should be explained only with reference to physical and chemical forces, physicians thought that illness was *not* self-limiting. In other words, people who fell ill could not get better on their own. To believe otherwise was to endow the body with powers that nonliving entities did not have—the doctrine of *vitalism,* which most physicians disavowed—and this was not acceptable.

If a person fell ill, the physician had to do something or else the illness would inevitably progress toward death. What was to be done? Guided by humoural theory, the doctor would try to restore the balance among his patient's fluids by using various "heroic" methods. The more extreme the better, because the physician was working against an inevitable clock.

Bleeding was a popular practice at this time. Physicians assumed that the removal of "bad" blood from a patient would restore his system to an optimal balance. This was done by removing a pint of blood, then another, still another, and so on, throughout the day and night. If you have ever donated blood, you know that a pint of blood is the maximum ever taken within a 56-day period. Draining away quarts of blood from those already ill was, of course, not the best way to bring them back to health. I described in Chapter 1 how George Washington may have died because of such treatment.

Bleeding was not the only medical practice rationalized by humoural theory. Other interventions to restore humoural balance were also popular:

> *Intestinal purging was held in high esteem, and the drug most often used to produce it was calomel (mercurous chloride). Heroic doctors gave their patients huge doses of calomel . . . until the patient began to salivate freely, a sign that the drug was working. Toxicology tests today list salivation as an early sign of mercury poisoning, one of the most dangerous forms of heavy metal poisoning. (Weil, 1988, p. 13)*

These practices look barbaric from the vantage of the 20th century, but the heroic doctors were sincere in their belief that this was the way to go about the business of restoring health. Nonetheless, spirited criticism of orthodox medical practice was common in the 1800s. Many suspected that going to a physician was actually bad for one's health, and alternative healing traditions flourished (Fuller, 1988).

Some advocated the use of traditional herbs. Others counseled individuals to improve their diets. Popular recommendations included eating food made from cereals; C. W. Post and John Harvey Kellogg were among the leaders of this movement in the United States. We of course know them today as the namesakes of giant cereal companies. Another important person was Sylvester Graham, who invented the graham cracker as a health food. Post, Kellogg, Graham, and their followers advocated bland food, and their products, at least in original form, were deliberately designed to be without taste. No wonder they later needed to add sugar to make them more appealing.

In the early 1800s, **homeopathy** developed as an alternative to traditional medicine. Here the physician

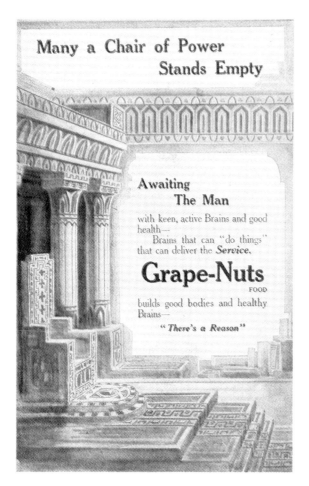

Many breakfast cereals in the United States were originally introduced as health foods, when alternatives to heroic medicine appeared in the 1800s. A healthy diet was deemed important to physical and psychological well-being.

do things to promote well-being and that the body possessed the capacity to restore itself to health. These notions allowed for the influence of psychological factors on health.

The clearest statement of how psychological factors play a role in health and illness was the *mind cure*, described already in Chapter 1. Stemming from mesmerism and popularized by Mesmer's followers, it held that people's health and illness were solely products of their mind. Even death was caused by incorrect thinking. If a person thought correctly, he or she need never die.

Phineas P. Quimby (1802–1866) was one of the most influential proponents of mind cure in the United States (Braden, 1963). He came from a modest New England family and received little formal education. In his thirties, Quimby was struck by tuberculosis. He was treated with heroic means, and his condition worsened. He gave up his job as a clockmaker and all hopes of recovery. Then while taking a carriage ride, Quimby for no good reason urged the horse to top speed. After the ride, he felt strong again, miraculously recovered from his ailments.

He started to learn about mesmerism, eventually using these techniques to heal people. Quimby concluded that the power of mesmerism and indeed of any medical treatment derived from the confidence of the patient in the healer. He took this insight one step further and argued that disease was simply an incorrect belief.

> *For an individual is to himself what he thinks he is, and he is in his belief sick. If I believe I am sick, I am sick, for my feelings are my sickness, and my sickness is my belief in my mind. Therefore . . . to cure the disease is to correct the error, destroy the cause, and the effect will cease.   (Braden, 1963, p. 56)*

Quimby healed individuals by sitting quietly with them in a room. Without speaking, he would "sense" the nature of the disease and the associated belief. He would identify these to the patient and suggest that he or she would soon feel better.

Sometimes Quimby treated individuals solely through correspondence. Here is an example:

> *The gentleman had written the good doctor [i.e., Quimby] requesting that he visit his wife. . . . She had been confined to her bed for more than a year, unable to lie on her left side or raise herself in bed. Unable to visit her in person, Quimby said he would try an experiment and asked to be informed of the results. He would, he said, begin absent treatment, continuing until the next Sunday, when between eleven and twelve o'clock he would make her walk.*
>
> *The letter was received Wednesday. That night the wife was nervous and uneasy, but on Thursday was more comfortable, turning on her left side for the first time in*

treated illness by administering minute amounts of various drugs, the smaller the better. Homeopathic cures were more effective than those of heroic medicine, if only because they had no particular effect on the ill individual. At the same time, **chiropractic medicine** developed as well, based on the manipulation of a patient's bones and joints. Also in the 1800s, the **popular health movement** took form, which urged people to take responsibility for their own health by learning more about their bodies and how to treat them.

We can contrast heroic medicine with its alternatives in terms of how it conceptualized the relationship between mind and body. Briefly, heroic medicine did not accord any special influence to the mind. Those who practiced it were thoroughly deterministic, and their target was bodily fluids. Disease was thought to have a course of its own. In contrast, the alternatives were based on a broader conception of how people fall ill. Alternative healers believed that people could *almost a year. On Sunday her husband attended church between eleven and twelve, and on his return found her up and dressed. . . . Next day she . . . breakfasted with the family and continued to improve.   (p. 67)*

Quimby attracted a large following, including Mary Baker Eddy, who founded Christian Science in 1879. To this day, Christian Scientists eschew medical care, deeming it unnecessary for the right-thinking person.

THE ADVENT OF MODERN MEDICINE

Doctors who practiced heroic medicine were not pleased about the alternatives that developed in the 1800s (Coulter, 1982). The American Medical Association (AMA) was founded in 1846 to combat rival medical traditions, particularly homeopathy. The AMA gained control of medical schools and state licensing boards. It decreed that licensed physicians should not work with other sorts of healers, and indeed, that they should not treat patients who had previously consulted other healers. Naturally, the growth of alternative healing approaches slowed down as a result.

The waning of heroic techniques   Probably more important than the AMA's political strong-arming was a change in the way medical practice was carried out. So in one sense, the alternatives did win: Heroic practices of bleeding and purging were phased out, replaced with treatments involving small doses of drugs, as the homeopaths advocated. An insidious aspect of this new medical practice was the growing use of sedating drugs—notably alcohol and opiates—to combat illness. There is no reason to think that these practices actually cured anyone, but patients left a doctor's office feeling comfortably numb.

Germ theory   Germ theory also emerged at this time, eventually replacing humoural theory as an account of illness. In its starkest form, **germ theory** proposes that illnesses are caused by microorganisms known as *germs*. Germs are necessary and sufficient conditions for illness. Every disease has its own germ, recognizable by a careful description of a patient's symptoms. Germs create problems for the individual because they interfere at the cellular level with his

Mary Baker Eddy (1821–1910) founded Christian Science in 1879. Christian Scientists believe that medical care is unnecessary for the right-thinking person. This belief is an extreme statement concerning the influence of purely psychological factors on physical health.

French scientist Louis Pasteur (1822–1895) made important contributions to germ theory, an account of illness that supplanted the long-standing humoural theory and still guides many medical interventions today.

bodily functioning. Treatments that remove the germ are effective because they put an end to this interference. Procedures that keep it from entering the body in the first place preclude illness.

As this theory became popular, medicine was re-shaped in the process (Magner, 1992). During the 1800s, diagnosis became much more important. Medical tests that fine-tuned a diagnosis were widely used, as were scientific instruments for measuring and recording bodily processes. Drugs to eradicate different germs proliferated, and the power to prescribe these drugs was eventually limited by legislative action to licensed physicians. We also saw the advent of *immunization*—giving the person a tiny amount of a germ in order to build up his resistance. Additionally, the field of *public health* began, guided by the realization that one way to combat illness was to prevent it in the first place. How? Remove the environmental sources of germs. Hygiene became not simply a matter of etiquette but of health as well.

Germ theory was popular because interventions based on it enhanced the health of the average citizen. Yet despite its practical benefits, germ theory is not strictly true. We now know that germs are an important ingredient in many illnesses, but germs per se are not always the whole story. There are some diseases—such as heart disease and many forms of cancer—in which no microorganism is responsible. See Table 10.1 for a contemporary classification of diseases, and note that only one category—*infectious diseases*—lists germs as a necessary cause.

Even if we look only at infectious diseases, germ theory is still not strictly true. Many of us most of the time are host to germs without falling ill. Other influences must conspire as well for germs to create disease. For instance, they must be present in sufficient number, and the person's body must be vulnerable to the germ at that particular time. Furthermore, germ theory disregards psychological factors. It views patients as little more than the battleground on which physicians and germs fight. What patients think or feel or do is irrelevant, so long as they are compliant (i.e., they take their medications and follow advice).

Immune system   The phenomenon of *immunity* to disease has been familiar throughout the world for centuries (Silverstein, 1989). People knew, for example, that if a person contracted smallpox during a particular epidemic, he or she would be spared during a subsequent one. And in different parts of the world, *inoculation* was part of folk medicine. A person was deliberately exposed to material from the body of an infected individual, to develop a mild case of the given disease. He later would be immune to the disease.

Understanding just how immunity and inoculation work had to wait until the 20th century, when the various parts of the **immune system** were described by researchers. The immune system was discovered

TABLE 10.1

CLASSIFICATION OF DISEASES *Here is one possible classification of diseases. For the most part this is an etiological system (see Chapter 2), but the categories suggested here are* not *mutually exclusive.*

CLASSIFICATION	DESCRIPTION	EXAMPLE
developmental birth defects	diseases resulting from prenatal or neonatal events	fetal alcohol syndrome (Chapter 14)
heritable diseases	diseases with a substantial genetic component	Huntington's chorea (Chapter 6)
metabolic diseases	diseases arising from abnormalities in the body's biochemistry	phenylketonuria
degenerative diseases	diseases associated with aging	cardiovascular and neoplastic diseases
cardiovascular diseases	diseases of the heart and/or circulatory system	hypertension, heart attack
neoplastic diseases	diseases characterized by tumors	cancer
immunological diseases	diseases of the immune system, in which it either attacks itself, is over-reactive, or is under-reactive	rheumatoid arthritis, allergies, AIDS
infectious diseases	diseases caused by infection with germs	syphilis (Chapter 6)
nutritional deficiency diseases	diseases caused by malnourishment or inappropriate diet	anemia
diseases caused by physical agents	diseases linked to mechanical, chemical, or physical causes	hernia, radiation sickness
iatrogenic diseases	diseases caused by treatment of other diseases	side effects of medications
idiopathic diseases	diseases of undetermined cause	many instances of hypertension

SOURCE: DERIVED FROM *A Survey of Human Diseases*, BY D. T. PURTILO AND R. B. PURTILO, 1989, BOSTON: LITTLE BROWN.

much later than the other major systems of the body, because it is not located in a single organ. It is not even a single entity, but rather a host of cells present throughout the body. The discovery of the immune system made it possible for theorists of a materialistic bent to explain how people could recover from illness without positing a mystical will to live.

The immune system allows our body to make a biological distinction between self and nonself. When it recognizes something as nonself, it attacks it, using several strategies. Over the years, immunologists have disagreed about the specific mechanisms of immunological defense. The current conclusion is that many ways exist to mount the defense and that the particular strategy differs from disease to disease.

The nonself, the foreign material that invades the body, is called an **antigen.** Antigens include germs, of course, which we can subdivide into bacteria, viruses, and parasites. Antigens also include cells from other individuals or species, drugs, and cancer cells that form within our own body. And in *autoimmunological diseases,* such as rheumatoid arthritis, the immune system treats its own cells as antigens.

Antigens stimulate various immunological responses. One is the production of **antibodies** by white blood cells called **B cell lymphocytes,** which originate in bone marrow (hence the B) and are then carried to the lymph nodes, spleen, and tonsils. Simply put, antibodies destroy or deactivate antigens.

Another mode of fighting off an invasion is by **T cell lymphocytes,** white blood cells that are produced in the thymus (hence the T). These fight antigens in several ways, including killing foreign cells as well as stimulating the activity of **phagocytes,** cells that literally "eat" (or engulf) foreign material (see Figure 10.2). T cells also interact with B cells, activating or deactivating them as needed.

Yet another means by which the immune system fights off antigens is with **natural killer (NK) cells,** which directly attack cancerous cells and those infected with viruses. Cancerous cells are thought to be killed via the secretion of a chemical called *interferon,* which you might recognize as the name of an experimental drug for the treatment of cancer. In administering interferon, physicians are trying to mimic the operation of NK cells.

In some cases, the body can fight off an invasion the first time an attack is mounted. In other cases, the immune system "learns" how to do this only through experience. Lymphocytes become increasingly adept at recognizing an antigen and triggering the appropriate response, which means that the immune system is self-regulating. The immune system recognizes particular antigens, designs a defense against them, and then

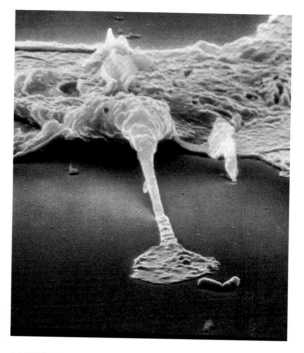

FIGURE 10.2

PHAGOCYTE AT WORK   *Among the important components of the immune system are phagocytes, which engulf invading material. Here a phagocyte reaches out to eat bacteria.*

remembers this information for future attacks. The process is nothing short of miraculous. One of the enduring concerns of immunology is detailing exactly how this recognition and memory takes place.

Because the players on the immunological team circulate in the blood, they are often studied by researchers via blood samples. (Sometimes saliva samples are used.) A robust immune response is marked by an increase in the number of these players following the introduction of a foreign material—so here you have another example of a biological challenge, in this case one used to gauge the strength of the immune response. When the response to a challenge is sluggish or nonexistent, the immune system is said to be suppressed. We thus talk of **immunosuppression.**

AIDS well illustrates this last point. AIDS is so devastating because it compromises the body's ability to fight off antigens by attacking the T cells that alert the immune system to antigen invasion. Illnesses rare in the general population become much more likely among those with AIDS because their bodies never start to defend against them in the first place.

MINDS AND BODIES MORE RECENTLY

With the advent of germ theory and the description of the immune system, researchers and theorists continued to investigate influences on health and illness. In the last few decades, these inquiries have led to a much more complex view of the matter. Germs remain important figures on the stage, but they must now share it with psychological factors such as stress, attitudes, and traits. Note the circular nature of scientific progress. It took 3,000 years for the Western world to rediscover what Aristotle had told us long ago: Minds and bodies mutually influence one another.

FRANZ ALEXANDER: PSYCHOSOMATIC MEDICINE

Leading the rediscovery of psychological factors was physician Franz Alexander (1939, 1950), who theorized within the psychodynamic tradition about the relationship between unconscious conflicts and physical illnesses. Following Freud's example, he proposed that symptoms have a symbolic relationship to conflict. He also proposed that particular biological pathways link the symptoms to the conflict. Freud did not have to specify such mechanisms when he explained hysteria. After all, hysterical symptoms have no physical basis, so there is no damage to explain. But if psychological factors have actual physical effects, these must be explained.

Suppose an individual is constantly hostile and competitive. He thereby experiences chronic excitation of the body's emergency response, the effect of which is to produce high blood pressure. High blood pressure then puts him at risk for cardiac disease.

Alexander theorized in particular about several diseases, including hypertension, ulcers, asthma, and arthritis. He specified the underlying conflict and hypothesized how it gives rise to biological processes that produce the illness in question. Alexander's pronouncements proved highly influential, satisfying both mind advocates (because they specified the symbolism of symptoms) and body advocates (because they specified physiological mechanisms). The only problem with his theorizing is that it proved to be mostly wrong (Weiner, 1977). His best evidence was striking case studies, in which a person with a given physical symptom clearly had the conflict in question.

For instance, Alexander described a young woman with colitis who experienced frequent bouts of diarrhea. These attacks occurred whenever her financial debts were brought to her attention. There is a long-standing tradition of psychodynamic theorizing that equates feces with money (consider the expression filthy rich), and so the interpretation follows that this woman was repaying her debts in a symbolic way, with diarrhea, because she could not repay them more literally (Brown, 1959). At the same time, she conveyed her annoyance that the matter had been brought up.

Case studies like these seem to confirm Alexander's theory. But they may be isolated coincidences, or they may identify the right ingredients but misplace the cause. An inability to fulfill obligations might be a result of colitis which—after all—keeps a person close to home.

Also, Alexander posited highly specific links between psychological factors and particular illnesses, and again this claim has not fared too well in the ensuing years. As noted, some theorists believe that psychological factors, including emotional conflicts, are nonspecific risk factors, making any and all illnesses more likely. Others admit some specificity, making broad distinctions between cardiac disease, for example, and cancer, but certainly not the fine distinctions that Alexander proposed.

A version of Alexander's hypothesis proposes that emotional conflicts produce physical illness for individuals in characteristic ways. Some may be susceptible to respiratory problems, others to gastrointestinal difficulties, and so on. The idea that stress and conflict affect one system of a person's body rather than another is supported by research, but an important qualification needs to be made: The system in question varies across the person's life (Vaillant, 1978). At any given time, somatic symptoms in one sphere may dominate, but these spheres change. Again, this finding argues against the fine detail of Alexander's theorizing because we would expect more stability in symptoms than is actually observed.

But Alexander is justifiably honored as the founder of the modern psychosomatic perspective (Weiner, 1977). He was right in his general thrust that emotional conflicts can take a toll on physical well-being. He relegitimized looking for the psychological basis of symptoms. And he elevated this theorizing to a new level by searching for the actual mechanisms that lead from psychological factors to physical symptoms.

HANS SELYE: GENERAL ADAPTATION SYNDROME

A telling argument for nonspecificity emerged from the research of Canadian physiologist Hans Selye (1956), who offered an influential description of how the body responds to stress. He proposed that regardless of the given type of environmental stressor, its continued presence leads to the same set of physiological reactions, which he called the **general adaptation syndrome** (see Figure 10.3). It has three stages:

- *alarm reaction:* internal resources are mobilized to restore homeostasis

- *resistance:* resources are used to fight off the effects of the stressor

- *exhaustion:* if resistance is unsuccessful, resources are eventually depleted and resistance to new stressors is reduced

The strength of Selye's general adaptation syndrome is, indeed, that it is *general*. The stressor can be a physical stimulus such as extreme cold. It can be a psychological stressor, such as difficult demands at work or an unhappy romance. Or it can be a germ.

Stress saps the individual's overall resilience, and any stressor makes one more vulnerable to the effects of any other stressor. There is no specificity hypothesized here at all. We would expect psychological problems to be risk factors for a variety of physical illnesses. We would also expect physical illnesses to be risk factors for a variety of psychological problems. These expectations are born out by the relevant research (e.g., Numan, Barklind, & Lubin, 1981).

Stressful Life Events and Hassles

One of the best known lines of research taking off from Selye's perspective is that of Thomas Holmes and Richard Rahe (1967), who specified a number of life events that require some sort of adjustment on the part of the individual to whom they occur (see Figure 10.4). The death of one's spouse, divorce, and the loss of one's job are stressful life events requiring considerable adjustment. Even "good" events such as marriage, retirement, or a new job can be seen as stressful because they involve a readjustment. When we ascertain, in a 6- or 12-month period, the number and severity of stressful events that occur to people, we find a positive correlation with the likelihood that they will develop emotional or physical problems. In other words, the greater the stress, the more likely people are to become psychologically or physically debilitated.

More specifically, researchers have shown that stress interferes with the functioning of the immune system, thus making illness more likely (Cohen & Williamson, 1991). Individuals experiencing stressful events, such as final examinations, show more immunosuppression than do their nonstressed counterparts (e.g., Glaser et al., 1985, 1992; Kiecolt-Glaser et al., 1984, 1986). They are also more likely to develop colds when exposed to respiratory viruses (Cohen, Tyrrell, & Smith, 1991).

It is not simply major life events that take a toll on well-being. Following the lead of the Holmes and Rahe (1967) approach, Kanner, Coyne, Schaefer, and Lazarus (1981) devised a measure of what they called *hassles:* minor annoyances of everyday life such as broken zippers, parking tickets, and having to feed a neighbor's pet. As these hassles accumulate, so too does the likelihood of emotional and physical problems. In their sheer number, hassles may prove more important influences on well-being than major life events (e.g., Weinberger, Hiner, & Tierney, 1987).

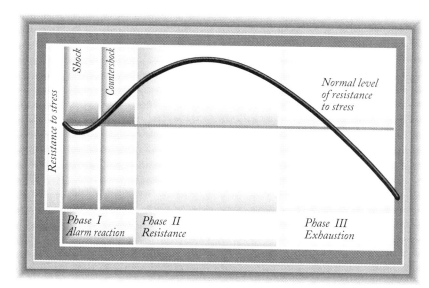

FIGURE 10.3

General Adaptation Syndrome   *According to Hans Selye, individuals respond to all instances of continued stress in the same manner. The general adaptation syndrome has three stages: alarm reaction, resistance, and—eventually—exhaustion.*

FIGURE 10.4

STRESSFUL LIFE
EVENTS   *Certain life events
cause us to experience relative
degrees of stress.*
SOURCE: DATA DERIVED FROM "THE
SOCIAL READJUSTMENT RATING SCALE,"
BY T. H. HOLMES AND R. H. RAHE,
1967, *Journal of Psychosomatic Research,*
11, PP. 213–218. USED WITH
PERMISSION.

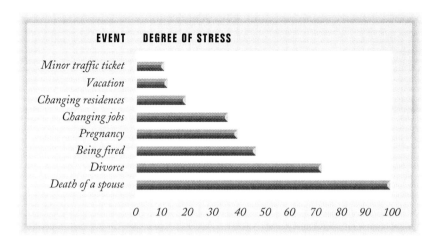

THE COGNITIVE REVOLUTION

The earliest work on stressful life events and illness was done in the early 1960s by epidemiologists like Holmes and Rahe. Their research procedure was quite simple: Determine the number of stressful events people have experienced, determine their physical health, and then calculate the correlation between the two. But psychologists also became interested in this type of research, and they looked not simply at the occurrence or nonoccurrence of stressful events but additionally at what people thought about them. This inquiry began in earnest in the middle to late 1960s, exactly as cognitive theorizing swept through psychology as a whole, in what has come to be known as the *cognitive revolution* (Gardner, 1985).

Once researchers looked at what people thought about stressful events, it became clear that taking into account particular ways of thinking about these events improved the ability to predict which events would or would not make illness more likely. "Exits" such as divorce bring more problems than do "entrances" such as beginning college. Events seen as unpredictable, uncontrollable, and/or meaningless are more likely to lead to illness and death (Mineka & Henderson, 1985). Furthermore, events associated with emotional conflict are particularly debilitating, as Alexander hypothesized years before. In some cases, these ways of thinking reflect the grim reality of the events, but in other cases, they go beyond the facts of the matter and represent a purely cognitive set of influences.

Stress and coping   The best known cognitive treatment of stress is the one introduced by Richard Lazarus (1966, 1982, 1991; Lazarus & Folkman, 1984). He argued that stressful events and their impact can be understood only in terms of how the individual perceives them. In **primary appraisal,** the individual asks what is at stake in the event. Events take on altogether different significance depending on their implications for the individual. A speeding ticket, for example, means one thing if a person is driving on a suspended driver's license, and something else if she is not. In **secondary appraisal,** the individual takes stock of the resources at her disposal for meeting the demands of the event. Can I cope with it? And how? Again, events may differ drastically depending on whether the person believes she can handle it, and how.

Problem-focused coping refers to attempts to meet the stressful event head-on and remove its effects. *Emotion-focused coping* is more indirect, referring to attempts to moderate one's own emotional response to an event that itself cannot be altered. Lazarus pointed out that no strategy of coping is invariably preferred. Different events demand different coping styles. Broken radiators tend to require problem-focused coping, whereas broken hearts usually respond best to emotion-focused coping. But the point is that the impact of a stressful event depends on how the individual appraises it.

Cognitive personality variables   Along these same lines, some researchers began to investigate cognitive personality variables—habitual ways of thinking about the events that befall us. They discovered links between these ways of thinking and subsequent illness. Suzanne Kobasa (1979), for instance, studied a personality dimension labeled **hardiness:** the ability to find meaning and challenge in the demands of life. She showed in a series of studies that hardy individuals were less likely than others to fall ill when confronted with stressful events (e.g., Kobasa, 1982; Kobasa, Maddi, & Courington, 1981; Kobasa, Maddi, & Kahn, 1982).

Michael Scheier and Charles Carver (1985, 1987) investigated a personality dimension they identified as **dispositional optimism,** defined as the expectation that good events will be plentiful in the future. They found that optimistic individuals are less likely to fall ill, that they rehabilitate themselves more quickly from illnesses, and the like (e.g., Scheier et al., 1989).

Much of my own research falls within this line of work. With my colleagues, I have investigated how an individual's **explanatory style**—which you encountered in Chapter 9 as a correlate of depression—is associated with illness (Peterson & Bossio, 1991). Explanatory style reflects how people habitually explain the causes of bad events that befall them. Some people favor an efficacious and upbeat style of explanation ("it was just one of those days"), whereas others favor sweeping and self-blaming explanations ("I'm not good at anything I do").

In a series of studies, we have found that a "depressive" explanatory style is associated with poor health, as measured in a variety of ways:

Those with a rich and supportive network of friends enjoy better health and longer lives than those who are socially estranged.

✦ symptom reports

✦ physician examinations

✦ suppressed immune system

✦ doctor visits

✦ length of survival with cancer and heart disease

Because of the association between explanatory style and depression, we have tried to show that the links between explanatory style and poor health are not simply by-products of the association of both with depression. In other words, we calculated the correlation between explanatory style and health by holding constant statistically the effects of depression. There is still a link between explanatory style and poor health, although I hasten to add that this does not rule out depression as one route between the two.

Untouched in the research so far described is just what the mechanisms might be that lead from ways of thinking to poor health. One possibility is simply that those who think in negative ways experience the world as a particularly stressful place, and so are put at risk for any and all illnesses. Other possibilities include direct consequences of negative thinking on the immune system, depression, and passivity (Lin & Peterson, 1990; Peterson, 1988; Peterson, Colvin & Lin, 1992).

SOCIAL SUPPORT

Yet another way that personality variables might affect health is through their influence on the person's social

relationships. One of the well established findings in epidemiology is that people with a rich and supportive network of friends and family enjoy better health and longer lives than their counterparts who are socially estranged (Cobb, 1976). Other people are healthy for us, psychologically and physically.

How is it that other people work their magic on us? Theorists have attacked this question by asking just what it is that people provide for one another, and they use the term **social support** to grasp the benefits that are involved. Social support includes such things as the following:

✦ emotional reassurance

✦ tangible resources such as money or shelter

✦ advice about tackling problems

✦ perspective—telling a person how he or she might see things

Any of a number of interpersonal exchanges can be classified as social support. Some are obviously relevant to our physical health. Other people can be quite helpful in our campaigns to lose weight or exercise more. But the effects of social support transcend health-specific advice, and lead us back to where we started: Others are simply good for us.

There appear to be several routes between social support and physical well-being. For example, people in supportive relationships tend to have more resilient immune systems, to be in better moods, and to experience fewer stressful events (Cohen, 1988). The other side of the coin is that ruptured social relationships can take a toll on our health. Studies suggest that unhappy marriages can adversely affect the physiology of both husbands and wives (Gottman & Levenson, 1992; Levenson & Gottman, 1983, 1985), including their immune functioning (e.g., Kiecolt-Glaser et al., 1987, 1988).

For centuries, poets have advised us that we could die of a broken heart, and this romantic assertion is backed up by solid data. Studies show that people are at increased risk for death themselves following the death of their spouse (Stroebe & Stroebe, 1987).

For example, Richard Nixon died in 1994, 10 months after the death of his wife Pat. According to Holmes and Rahe's scheme of life events, the death of a spouse is the single most stressful occurrence a person can experience, and former President Nixon's grief was well documented.

However, the widower or widow is not at continual risk. Vulnerability is increased for only about 6 to 12 months after his or her loss. During this time, the person is apt to be depressed, listless, and have a sluggish immune response (Bartrop, Luckhurst, Lazarus, Kiloh, & Penny, 1977). But if the person does not die during this period—and he or she usually does not—then health eventually rebounds.

Stroebe and Stroebe (1987) suggest that various factors can moderate the relationship between bereavement and poor health. Although death is never a pleasant event, it is easier to find meaning in some deaths

The death of a spouse is a highly stressful event that temporarily puts the surviving spouse at risk for death as well. President Richard Nixon (right), shown here at the funeral of his wife Pat, died in 1994, just 10 months after Pat's death.

than others. In these cases, the surviving spouses are not so apt to fall ill, and thus we return to research linking cognitive factors to health. Appreciate that other people who rally around bereaved individuals can buffer them against threats to their health. Again we see that other people are healthy for us.

BEHAVIOR AND HEALTH PROMOTION

The idea that behavior has something to do with physical health is a relatively new one. With the background provided in this chapter, you can see why. Past conceptions of illness left no room for behavioral factors. To be sure, people could make injuries more or less likely, depending on how they behaved, but illnesses were brought about by invading germs that overwhelmed the immune system. These are microscopic events that take place largely in isolation from behavior.

However, as epidemiological data became increasingly available in recent decades, researchers were struck by the nonrandom distribution of particular illnesses across the population as a whole. Some groups of people were more likely to develop certain illnesses than others. Part of this variation could be explained by differential exposure to germs or toxins. Syphilis was long recognized as something more likely to be experienced by sailors than other people, and so was scurvy. Theorists eventually realized that both illnesses had something to do with the lifestyle of sailors: sexual activity with someone carrying the syphilis germ and a diet deficient in vitamin C, respectively.

Throughout the 20th century, as researchers took an ever closer look at who fell ill and who did not, they discovered a set of behaviors that were related to people's general health or illness. Belloc (1973; Belloc & Breslow, 1972), for example, studied such health-conscious behaviors as these:

◆ eating breakfast

◆ not eating between meals

◆ keeping weight within normal limits

◆ sleeping 8 hours a night

◆ exercising

◆ not smoking

◆ not drinking to excess

Those who engaged in such habits were on the average healthier than those who did not. They also lived longer (see Figure 10.5). All these risk factors are behavioral in nature, which suggests that if people can be encouraged to change their behaviors, then they should live longer and better.

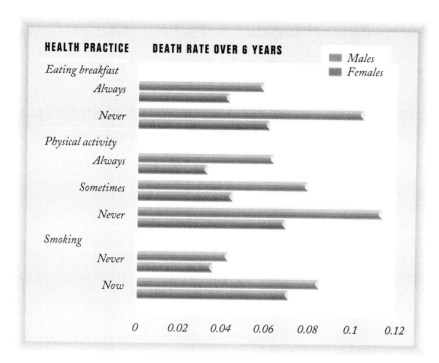

FIGURE 10.5

HEALTHY HABITS

Belloc surveyed the health practices of males and females in the United States, then followed the research participants for almost 6 years. This figure shows the proportion who died during this period as a function of selected health practices.

SOURCE: DATA DERIVED FROM "RELATIONSHIP OF HEALTH PRACTICES AND MORTALITY," BY N. B. BELLOC, 1973, *Preventive Medicine, 2,* PP. 67–81.

Such findings have proven incredibly important in the way the healing professions have approached the treatment and prevention of illness. Taylor, Denham, and Ureda (1982) took a broad look at history and described three major eras in the approach to illness and health. In the first era, up to the time when germ theory appeared, the focus was solely on *disease treatment*. People went about their lives until they fell ill; then physicians entered the picture and attempted to combat the illness. In the second era, starting with germ theory, the focus expanded to *disease prevention*. Public health workers tried to prevent germs from entering the body. Swamps that hosted malaria-carrying mosquitoes were drained; surgeons began to wash their hands before and after they operated; food was inspected and dated for freshness. What these two eras had in common is that the individual who was supposed to benefit from their approach was passive: He or she did nothing except go along with the efforts of the physician or the public health expert. Then in the third and most recent era, taking form in just the past few decades, the focus has shifted to *health promotion*. The person is called on to make an active effort to behave in a health-promoting way.

How can people be encouraged to behave in healthy ways, and not to behave in unhealthy ways? Here is where psychologists enter the picture, as experts in behavior change. They have adapted a variety of therapy techniques—particularly from the cognitive-behavioral approach—to promote health. Strategies involving relaxation or biofeedback have been

As the hazards of smoking have become known, there has been a great increase in attempts to persuade the general public not to smoke. Some people, though not all, are getting the message.

particularly popular (Goleman & Gurin, 1993). Sometimes these techniques are merged with mass communication strategies to give us broad, media-based programs to promote health (Winett, King, & Altman, 1989).

For example, the Stanford Five City Project was a community-based health promotion program that targeted more than 100,000 California residents (Farquhar,

FOCUS ON

Shamanism and

Alternative

Medicine

THE APPROACH TO HEALING represented by contemporary medical professions is but one of many to be found around the world. In a large number of cultures, including some in the contemporary United States, shamans are consulted not just by people with psychological problems but also by those with physical illnesses (Chapter 1). The work of shamans is sometimes called *faith healing*. However, this term may be unnecessarily pejorative, implying that treatment relies on "mere" suggestion and that benefits are either illusory or limited to problems without an actual biological basis—that is, limited to somatization disorders (Chapter 8).

An expanded conception of how minds and bodies are related does not regard shamanism in such a limited way (Hufford, 1993). The possibility that shamans can successfully treat physical illness should be considered. We can certainly be as skeptical of shamanism as we are of more conventional medical procedures—but not necessarily more so (Danesi & Adetunji, 1994). Many of those who seek out conventional medical treatment also rely on shamans, which if nothing else means that healers of all stripes should be aware of the practices of the others and the assumptions on which these are based (Jackson, 1993).

A related point concerns the growing popularity of so-called *alternative medicine* among patients in the United States. Alternative medicine includes techniques developed more than a century ago in the wake of heroic medicine (such as homeopathy), treatments borrowed from other cultures (such as acupuncture and herbs), strategies associated with the New Age movement (such as healing crystals), and so on. Many of these techniques are based on explicitly broad conceptions of how psychological factors can influence health and illness.

A general survey of adults in the United States, conducted in 1990, found that 34% of respondents had used at least one form of alternative medicine during the past year (Eisenberg et al., 1993). Individuals with more education and higher incomes were *more likely* than others to have sought alternative treatment. Visits to alternative healers were as common as those to primary care physicians, and out-of-pocket money spent for alternative medicine exceeded that spent for hospitalizations.

According to this survey, the majority of those receiving alternative treatment also saw conventional physicians for the same illnesses. Some call these alternative approaches *complementary medicine*, because patients do not see them as incompatible with conventional treatments. However, patients usually do not inform their physicians about their use of alternative approaches, which suggests that they fear criticism or rejection.

Shamanism and alternative medicine deserve greater attention from the scientific establishment than they have received in the past. Our understanding of mind-body disorders can only be increased by studying the different approaches to healing—when they work, when they do not, and why. In 1991, the United States Congress established the Office of Alternative Medicine as part of the National Institutes of Health, indicating that this scrutiny is beginning in earnest.

Maccoby, & Solomon, 1984). The goal of the program was to increase knowledge about health and illness, encourage healthier habits, and decrease mortality rates. A variety of strategies were employed, including informational messages delivered through television, radio, and newspapers; classes and lectures; contests; and environmental changes like labeling food in restaurants. These interventions continued for 6 years and were successful in meeting their goals. When the residents of targeted communities were compared to those of otherwise comparable towns, they showed increased knowledge of the risk factors for disease, decreased blood pressure and heart rate, decreased smoking, and decreased risk for cardiovascular disease.

A critical difference between health promotion and psychotherapy is that the typical client in therapy is hurting and has an immediate motivation to do things in order to feel better. In contrast, the ordinary citizen who is asked to promote his own health might feel perfectly fine. Health promotion messages suggest that if he makes changes in the short run, forgoing such immediate pleasures as drinking and smoking, he will benefit in the long run.

Health promotion campaigns have only checkered success at best. People may believe there is a link between behavior and health, but they see themselves as immune to these principles, incapable of a lifestyle change, or unwilling to make the necessary sacrifices.

People often desire unrealistically immediate results from their efforts. At any rate, health promotion is not simply a matter of providing information and exhortation. These campaigns must be based on sophisticated notions of why we behave and how we can change (Peterson & Stunkard, 1989).

PSYCHONEUROIMMUNOLOGY

In my previous sketch of the immune system, I rendered its operation in rather mechanical terms, and this in fact is how it was first understood—as a reflexive response to the invasion of foreign material. In the last several years, researchers have learned that the immune system is much more complex than a simple reflex (Pelletier & Herzing, 1989). It communicates with both the endocrine and nervous systems, resulting in a constant give-and-take among all of them. The point here is that because psychological factors are unambiguously involved in the nervous system and endocrine system, then if the immune system is intimately linked to these systems, it is necessarily influenced by psychological factors as well (Vollhardt, 1991).

In the past decade or two a new field has emerged, known as **psychoneuroimmunology,** which explicitly recognizes the mutual influences among psychological, neurological, and immunological factors (Ader & Cohen, 1981). It was sparked by the discovery that the body's immune response could be conditioned. In a classic experiment with rats as subjects, Ader and Cohen (1975) paired a saccharine taste with a drug that suppressed their immune functioning. This pairing was done several times. Then the taste was presented alone, and a biological challenge was mounted against the rats: Antigens were introduced into their bodies. Their immune systems responded sluggishly to the invasion. Immunosuppression did not occur when the taste was not presented.

Do you see the importance of this demonstration? On a theoretical level, it shows that psychological factors—in this case, learning—directly influence the operation of the immune system. On a practical level, it shows that certain environmental stimuli can become associated with poor immune functioning. If and when these stimuli are encountered, the individual is at increased risk for poor health. The other side of the coin, by implication, is that immune system resilience can also be conditioned (Kiecolt-Glaser & Glaser, 1992), which means that health can be boosted through an association with "healthy" stimuli.

Writer and editor Norman Cousins (1976) provided a well known example of how health might be boosted through pleasant events and experiences. While traveling, Cousins was struck by a potentially fatal disease of the connective tissue of his body. Upon returning to the United States, he was hospitalized and given little chance of survival. He responded not at all to conventional medical treatment. He decided that if he wanted to live, he needed to give his immune system a jump start. He checked out of the hospital and into a fancy hotel. He watched funny movies and reruns of "Candid Camera." He survived and went on to live a long and fulfilling life. According to Cousins, he laughed himself to recovery.

This story is a case study, of course, so we cannot say with certainty that laughter was the critical cause of his unexpected recovery. However, the example of Norman Cousins is consistent with the correlational studies already described that link optimism to better health.

Another important discovery concerning psychoneuroimmunology is that a depressed mood is associated with poor functioning of the immune system

Writer and editor Norman Cousins attributed his recovery from a potentially fatal disease to the mustering of his positive emotions.

(Schleifer, Keller, Siris, Davis, & Stein, 1985). While epidemiologists had long documented that illness and death were more likely among the depressed, the mechanism bringing this about was not understood (e.g., Kaplan & Reynolds, 1988; Parmelee, Katz, & Lawton, 1992; Silverstone, 1990). Biochemical research now suggests that among the physiological changes that accompany depression is an interference with immune functioning, perhaps brought about by an increase in *cortisol,* a hormone secreted by the adrenal glands when we are stressed (Friedman & DiMatteo, 1989).

Researchers are currently working to understand the biochemical pathways that link the nervous system, the endocrine system, and the immune system. In Chapter 6, I pointed out that the nervous system and the endocrine system each communicates within itself, by neurotransmitters and hormones, respectively. Discoveries in psychoneuroimmunology blur this distinction, because the immune system is sensitive to both neurotransmitters and hormones.

This section on psychoneuroimmunology completes my historical discussion of the relationship between the mind and the body. Remember that I began by noting that the relationship between the two has had a long and often contentious history. Perhaps with the advent of psychoneuroimmunology we have a resolution. We know that the mind and the body are in constant communication with one another along several different channels. The possibility that psychological factors can influence physical health, often doubted or theoretically precluded, has been conclusively shown. I can now proceed to detail the mechanisms in specific cases.

PARTICULAR MIND-BODY DISORDERS

In the remainder of the chapter, I discuss several mind-body disorders (see Table 10.2). No single model of abnormality suffices to explain how psychological factors influence disease or promote health. Granted the variety of diseases, we should assume that the blend of determinants will vary from disease to disease and possibly across time for a given disease.

Although I have discussed the immune system in some detail, this is but one possible pathway of psychological influence. In an ironic way, our increased understanding of the immune system makes this a less important influence on illness than it once was. At the turn of the century, the majority of Americans died from infectious diseases (Purtilo & Purtilo, 1989). But with the strides made in the treatment and prevention of these diseases, they are now much less likely

TABLE 10.2

PARTICULAR MIND-BODY DISORDERS *There are a variety of illnesses influenced by psychological factors. In many cases, these illnesses can be prevented or treated by psychological interventions.*

DISEASE	CHARACTERIZATION AND PSYCHOLOGICAL TREATMENT
cardiovascular disease	difficulty with the heart and circulatory system (e.g., coronary heart disease, myocardial infarction, arteriosclerosis, hypertension, stroke)
	helped by reducing behavioral risk factors, cultivating social support, changing Type A style
cancer	disease marked by uncontrollable growth of cells
	helped by changing behavioral risk factors, encouraging hope and will to live (perhaps), participating in group therapy (perhaps)
gastrointestinal disorder	problem with the gastrointestinal system (e.g., gastroesophagal reflux, peptic ulcer, irritable bowel syndrome)
	helped by reducing behavioral risk factors, participating in behavior therapy (e.g., relaxation, biofeedback)
asthma	interference with normal breathing that occurs when the airways leading into the lungs constrict and fill with mucus
	helped by reducing behavioral risk factors, participating in behavior therapy (e.g., anxiety reduction techniques, biofeedback, operant conditioning)

to cause death[1] (see Figure 10.6). More common today is death by heart disease or cancer, and so I begin my discussion with these illnesses.

CARDIOVASCULAR DISEASES

The *circulatory system,* so named because it circulates blood throughout the entire body, carries oxygen and nutrients to our cells, and waste material away from

---

[1] Nonetheless, infectious diseases have not been eradicated, and some—such as AIDS—are on the increase. At least two factors are relevant (Lemonick, 1994). First, people from different parts of the globe are increasingly likely to come into contact with one another and the germs that each may harbor. Second, many germs show a remarkable capacity for mutation into forms that resist conventional antibiotics.

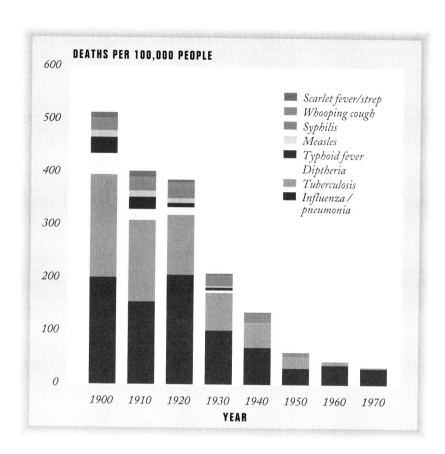

FIGURE **10.6**

DEATH BY INFECTIOUS
DISEASES IN THE UNITED
STATES   *Throughout the
20th century, deaths due to
infectious diseases have
dramatically decreased in
the United States.*
SOURCE: *Historical Statistics of the United
States,* 1976, WASHINGTON, DC: U.S.
DEPARTMENT OF COMMERCE.

them. The heart is a muscle that rhythmically contracts, sending blood away from it through the arteries and then getting it back through the veins. This system is usually quite efficient, and in a lifetime of 70 + years, a person's heart will beat more than 25 billion times, pumping the equivalent of 100 million gallons of blood through its vessels.

But things can go amiss. **Cardiovascular diseases** encompass various difficulties with the heart and circulatory system:

♦ *coronary heart disease:* blockage of the arteries that supply blood to the heart muscle

♦ *myocardial infarction (MI):* heart attack; death of part of the heart muscle due to oxygen or nutrient deprivation

♦ *arteriosclerosis:* impairment in blood supply or elasticity of blood vessels, such as blockage of the arteries by deposits of cholesterol

♦ *hypertension:* high blood pressure

♦ *cerebrovascular accident:* stroke; abnormality in the blood supply to the brain, resulting in damage to the brain

These problems frequently co-occur because they exacerbate one another. The chain of influence might start

with high blood pressure, for example, which increases the likelihood of coronary heart disease by as much as fourfold. Or it might start with arteriosclerosis. Once the arteries are clogged, blood pressure necessarily increases, because the same amount of blood must now be pumped through a smaller opening. In any case, weakness or abnormality in one part of the circulatory system may show up as damage elsewhere.

Cardiovascular diseases are currently the leading cause of death in the United States, for both men and women. Epidemiologists express how fatal a disease is in terms of its *annual mortality incidence*—how many people per 100,000 in the general population die from the disease in a given year. In 1970, cardiovascular diseases were associated with 464 deaths per 100,000, more than half of all deaths in the United States. There has, however, been a trend for the better. By 1980 the figure had fallen to 420 deaths per 100,000 (Levy & Moskowitz, 1982). By 1990, the annual mortality incidence was even lower (U.S. Department of Health and Human Services, 1992).

Psychological risk factors   Why the decrease? Most agree that our society has become more aware of the risk factors for cardiovascular diseases, particularly those that have to do with our behavior. We have worked to reduce our risk. Among the demonstrated risk factors for the various cardiovascular diseases are cigarette smoking, obesity, lack of exercise, and a diet high in saturated fats (and thus cholesterol). These risk factors exert a *synergistic* influence on one another. In other words, the risk associated with each habit multiplies when others are present.

These risk factors can be altered, although doing so is not always easy. In the long run, our society will probably find it easier to prevent people from developing health-threatening habits in the first place, through educational campaigns and the like, than to try persuading them to give up the bad habits they have already acquired.

Health psychologists interested in cardiovascular diseases have turned their attention to a personality style that appears to increase the risk of heart disease (Friedman & Rosenman, 1974). Called the **Type A coronary-prone behavior pattern** (Type A for short), this style was first described in the 1950s by two physicians, Meyer Friedman and Ray Rosenman. As usually characterized, it is marked by the following traits:

✦   strong competitiveness

✦   time urgency

✦   hostility in the face of frustration

The Type A individual fits our stereotype of the high-powered, impatient businessperson. A person with the opposite style is called Type B, exemplified by somebody we might call laid-back or mellow.

Type A (or B) style is measured with an interview or questionnaire designed for this purpose, and then individuals are followed over time to see who develops cardiovascular disease. On the whole, we can conclude that the Type A style is a risk factor. Type A individuals are approximately two to three times more likely to develop heart disease than their Type B counterparts (Rosenman et al., 1975). However, I must qualify this general conclusion.

First, when researchers take a close look at the components of the Type A pattern, they usually find that it is the hostility of Type A individuals that puts them at risk for heart disease (Matthews, 1982; Smith, 1992). The other components may be irrelevant in influencing its development.

Second, not all studies find the Type A style to be a risk factor. When this style was first described, research results seemed more uniform in linking it to cardiovascular diseases. In recent years, there have been more failures to find the link (e.g., Ragland & Brand, 1988b). This could mean several things (Miller, Turner, Tinsdale, Posavac, & Dugoni, 1991). One possibility is that researchers and/or journal editors early on may not have been interested in reporting

The Type A individual is competitive, time urgent, and hostile in the face of frustration. Basketball coach Bobby Knight vents his anger at one of his players after pulling him from the game.

"no" results. Another possibility is more intriguing: People have made use of the widespread publicity about the Type A style to assess their own risk for heart disease and to make compensatory changes elsewhere, as in their diet or frequency of exercise.

Third, some studies suggest that whereas the Type A style is a risk factor for initial heart attacks, it might also be beneficial in recovery. It seems that when a Type A individual has a heart attack, he is more likely to make a good recovery than the Type B individual who has a heart attack (Ragland & Brand, 1988a). Again, this finding admits to two interpretations. On the one hand, perhaps Type As have more severe heart attacks than Type Bs; those few who do survive are more robust than the Type Bs who survive. On the other hand, perhaps Type As can muster their resources better than Type Bs in order to recover from heart attacks.

What is the mechanism linking the Type A style to cardiovascular diseases? The critical ingredient seems to be anger at a world that thwarts what the individual wants to do. Imagine what happens when he is always angry: His bodily emergency reaction is constantly engaged, which includes an increase in heart rate and blood pressure. Eventually, this weakens the cardiovascular system, particularly when coupled with other risk factors for heart disease. This hypothesis linking anger to cardiovascular diseases through the intermediary of the body's emergency reaction is not all that different from Franz Alexander's proposition decades earlier. At least this part of his theorizing has survived the test of research.

Psychological treatment   Granted that Type A behavior is a risk factor, what is a person to do? Some Type A individuals can compensate in other areas of their lives, trying to reduce their overall likelihood of cardiovascular disease. The more direct attack, assuming that a person is willing, is to try and change the style itself. Strategies for changing Type A behavior have been developed, relying first on information about the components of the style and second on cognitive-behavioral interventions that address these components.

Mr. Labrador was a middle-aged executive who suffered a near-fatal heart attack. Because he showed a classic Type A style, he was referred upon recovery to a treatment program to change his behavior. He was given the following drills to practice (cf. Friedman & Rosenman, 1974):

♦ *go often to restaurants where you know you have to wait*

♦ *do not schedule appointments for specific times*

♦ *listen to others without interrupting*

♦ *never interfere with an individual doing a job slowly*

♦ *if you drive through a yellow light at an intersection, turn right at the next corner and drive around the block to the intersection again; go through the light only when it is green*

♦ *plan times of the day during which you do nothing*

These particular exercises targeted Mr. Labrador's time urgency by trying to slow him down. He also practiced analogous exercises designed to change his competitiveness and hostility.

Studies show that these strategies are effective in reducing the Type A style (Nakano, 1990; Nunes, Frank, & Kornfeld, 1987; Roskies et al., 1986). These changes in turn map into reduced risk for cardiovascular diseases (Friedman, 1989; Johnston, 1989; Thoreson &

Powell, 1992). We know from one study that reductions in Type A style have led to reductions in cholesterol (Gill et al., 1985). We know from another study that reductions in Type A style have led to decreased blood pressure (Bennett, Wallace, Carroll, & Smith, 1991). We know from yet other studies that the risk of recurrent cardiovascular diseases has decreased among those who receive Type A counseling (Friedman et al., 1986; Mendes de Leon, Powell, & Kaplan, 1991; Powell & Thoreson, 1988).

The Type A style raises a point about what we consider normal or abnormal. Despite the association between this way of behaving and cardiovascular diseases, at the same time it is linked to success (e.g., high salaries among workers). Perhaps we must make a decision about the relative merits of a successful life versus one free of cardiovascular disease. The rejoinder, of course, is that there are domains of life in which success is not contingent on competitiveness, time urgency, or hostility.

CANCER

Cancer is not a single disease, but rather a group of several hundred diseases, all characterized by the uncontrollable growth of cells. The body's cells are always in the process of growing, and in the normal individual this process simply keeps pace with the loss of cells, with no net gain. In cancer, certain cells keep multiplying, eventually leading to the death of normal cells. If unchecked, it leads to the death of the afflicted individual. Cancer is currently second only to cardiovascular diseases as the cause of death among citizens in the United States, accounting for more than 200 deaths per 100,000 individuals every year. Almost a million new cases of cancer are diagnosed every year. As things now stand, about 75 million Americans will develop cancer at some point in their lives.

Different cancers are usually identified by the types of cells involved (see Figure 10.7). *Leukemia* refers to cancer of the blood cells or the blood-forming organs. *Sarcoma* is cancer of the bone, muscle, or connective tissue. *Carcinoma* is cancer of the epithelial cells (cells on the inner or outer surfaces of the body, such as the lungs or skin). *Lymphoma* is cancer of the lymph system, which is critical in fighting infection.

Usually, the body is successful in detecting and disabling its own abnormal cells. But in cancer, this process is inadequate. A cell mutates in such a way that it multiplies beyond the needs of the body. The exact reason why this happens is not clear, and there may well be as many specific causes as there are types of cancer.

The abnormal cell keeps multiplying, and each new cell has the same pathological property of division.

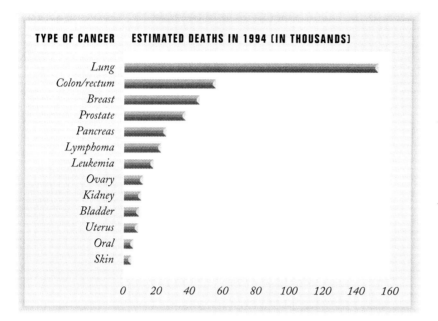

TYPE OF CANCER	ESTIMATED DEATHS IN 1994 (IN THOUSANDS)

Lung
Colon/rectum
Breast
Prostate
Pancreas
Lymphoma
Leukemia
Ovary
Kidney
Bladder
Uterus
Oral
Skin

0   20   40   60   80   100   120   140   160

FIGURE 10.7

ESTIMATED DEATHS BY
CANCER IN THE UNITED
STATES, 1994   *Cancer is one
of the leading causes of death in
the contemporary United States.
As this graph shows, lung cancer
is the most common form of fatal
cancer, although cancer may attack
almost any bodily system.*
SOURCE: DATA DERIVED FROM
"STOPPING CANCER IN ITS TRACKS," BY
J. M. NASH, 1994 (APRIL 25), *Time*,
PP. 54–61.

A **tumor,** a mass of cells, is eventually formed. Not all tumors are cancerous. The difference between a **malignant tumor** (cancerous) as opposed to a **benign tumor** (noncancerous) is the degree to which it is self-contained. Benign tumors are not necessarily innocuous because they can obstruct or press into normal tissue. Still, benign tumors obey the bodily edict not to spread unchecked. Malignant tumors are always dangerous because they are not self-contained. Cells from a cancerous tumor can spread throughout the body, forming new tumors. The spread of cancer cells is called **metastasis.** Metastasis itself is a variable process, affecting one part of the body or many.

Psychological risk factors   As already mentioned, cancer probably has many direct causes, and an even larger number of indirect ones (Levy, 1985). Among the direct influences are such behavioral factors as smoking, drinking, eating a diet rich in fat, sunbathing, and engaging in certain sexual practices. And obviously, any behavior that puts a person in contact with cancer-triggering substances such as asbestos, coal dust, or paint fumes is also a risk factor. It is highly unlikely that these behaviors alone are sufficient causes of cancer. Rather, they become important contributors when other influences are present as well.

The indirect psychological influences on cancer are more controversial, but many psychologists now accept that psychological states and traits have some influence on factors that themselves directly cause or promote cancer. Studies have linked stressful life events to the onset of various forms of cancer, although the statistical relationships involved are quite modest in size. Many people get cancer without any unusual experience with stress, and conversely, many people experience stress yet do not get cancer.

To identify why stressful events are linked to cancer, some researchers have studied the process experimentally with animal subjects, manipulating aspects of stressful experiences to see which make cancer more versus less likely. The typical procedure starts with animals bred to be susceptible to cancer. Then the researcher injects them with malignant cells. Finally, they are exposed to some experience or not. Does the experience trigger the growth of cancerous tumors in these animals? You can see that this procedure is not ethically possible with people. You can also see that it is not strictly parallel to the development of cancer among people, because the research is in effect done with sledgehammers.

Some studies like these show that stress (e.g., exposure to repeated electric shocks) results in the growth of cancerous tumors (e.g., Sklar & Anisman, 1979). At the same time, not all such studies support this conclusion. Stress sometimes results in a decreased likelihood of cancer, presumably because the immune system has been stimulated into greater activity (Sklar & Anisman, 1981). Perhaps the effect of stress on the development of cancer depends on whether the stress is acute or chronic, on the type of cancer involved, and finally on when the stress occurs in the process of tumor development (Justice, 1985). Remember the point made in Chapter 7 that stress is not necessarily harmful. If nothing else, these results show us that it might be hazardous to offer broad generalizations about the operation of the immune system as a whole (O'Leary, 1990).

Animal studies suggest that uncontrollability is a critical factor in explaining the effect of stress on cancer. Visintainer, Volpicelli, and Seligman (1982) exposed cancer-susceptible rats to uncontrollable versus controllable electric shocks, finding that the former stimulated the growth of tumors. Other studies with this same basic paradigm suggest that uncontrollability adversely affects the immune system, which may explain why cancer becomes more likely (Peterson & Bossio, 1991).

I now move from stressful events to personality dispositions. It has long been believed that certain traits are associated with the eventual onset of cancer (Sontag, 1979). In the 2nd century, for example, the Greek physician Galen proposed that melancholic (depressed) individuals were most likely to develop cancer. This opinion has been echoed throughout history: Cancer is apt to occur among those who are emotionally nonexpressive, depressed, helpless, and/or hopeless (see Gross, 1989; Jensen, 1991).

Longitudinal studies have been conducted, measuring hypothesized personality predispositions and then following subjects over time to see who develops cancer (e.g., Hahn & Petitti, 1988; Persky, Kempthorne-Rawson, & Shekelle, 1987). Numerous factors threaten the validity of such studies (Levenson & Bemis, 1991). For instance, a large number of research subjects must be included, because cancer itself is a relatively rare event. An adequate time period must be allowed for cancer to develop in the research subjects. Another threat is the possible existence of confounds. Traits might bear a statistical relationship to the subsequent development of cancer simply because they are somehow linked to environmental or occupational factors that themselves produce cancer.

Hans Eysenck (1988) discussed in detail two studies conducted by researchers in Yugoslavia. Each study followed hundreds of men and women for a full decade. At the beginning of the studies, the participants filled out questionnaires measuring such dispositions as helplessness, hopelessness, and emotional repression. These factors showed a surprisingly strong correlation with whether the individuals developed cancer at some point in the ensuing years. Indeed, personality exerted a stronger relationship on the development of cancer than did habits like smoking and drinking. This is *not* the typical finding.

The Yugoslavian studies have been criticized (Amelang, 1991; Derogatis, 1991; Fox, 1991) and in turn defended (Eysenck, 1990b, 1991). Other studies have been unsuccessful in finding any link between personality and cancer (e.g., Zonderman, Costa, &

McCrae, 1989), whereas still others support their conclusions but at much less robust levels (e.g., Schmale & Iker, 1971). Perhaps the best conclusion right now is that results are mixed but encouraging enough to warrant further research. Future studies should do more than just establish (or fail to establish) correlations across decades between traits and cancer. They should attempt to understand what might mediate any correlations that exist, because personality cannot instantly transmute itself into cancerous cells (cf. Gil, 1989; Linkins & Comstock, 1990). Is the pathway, if one exists, solely immunological as the animal research implies, or does it also loop outside the body through unhealthy habits?

Psychological treatment   Regardless, it is clear that psychologists have an important role to play in the prevention and treatment of this set of diseases. The existence of behavioral risk factors for cancer is noncontroversial, and attempts to prevent people from acquiring unhealthy habits, or help them rid themselves of them if they have already been acquired, can only be beneficial.

Another contribution that psychologists can make to cancer treatment is through the use of behavior therapy techniques to encourage patients to comply with medical treatments. Some resist because they do not believe the treatments are effective. Others become depressed or anxious or frightened upon receiving a cancer diagnosis, and thus avoid treatment altogether. Along these lines, some individuals might be reluctant to check for warning signs of cancer (e.g., breast self-examination by women) because they are afraid of what they might find. And still other patients find the side effects of conventional cancer treatment aversive—notably the nausea that accompanies chemotherapy or radiation therapy (Carey & Burish, 1988). Sustaining patients' motivation in the face of such side effects may require psychotherapeutic intervention. Further, cancer is sometimes extremely painful, and psychologists can help cancer patients reduce their pain.

Does psychological intervention play a role in altering the progression of cancer once it begins? This inquiry is even more controversial than the research that asks about the influence of personality dispositions on the onset of cancer. There are reports that a "fighting spirit" is associated with a good prognosis in cancer (Snyder, 1989).

Physician Bernie Siegel (1989) described John Florio, a patient who showed remarkable resilience in the face of cancer. Mr. Florio was a 78-year-old landscape gardener who was contemplating retirement when he developed abdominal pain. In the course of treating what seemed to be an ulcer, his doctors discovered that he had cancer of the stomach. Dr. Siegel urged him to have surgery as soon as possible. Mr. Florio demurred:

> *"You forgot something." "What did I forget?" . . . "It's springtime. I'm a landscape gardener, and I want to make the world beautiful. That way if I survive, it's a gift. If I don't, I will have left a beautiful world." (p. 9)*

Mr. Florio postponed the surgery until he was ready. He went through the operation well, but further tests showed that the cancer had spread to his lymph nodes. Dr. Siegel then suggested that he consider chemotherapy. Again Florio demurred:

> *"You forgot something." "What did I forget this time?" "It's still spring. I don't have time for that." (p. 10)*
>
> *Dr. Siegel did not see his patient again for 4 years. Then Mr. Florio made an appointment. Dr. Siegel was afraid that the appointment was related to the cancer. Not exactly: "I have a hernia from lifting boulders in my landscape business" (p. 10).*
>
> *Mr. Florio refused to be admitted to the hospital, so Dr. Siegel repaired the hernia under local anesthesia in his office. Medical tests revealed that he was free of cancer. Siegel believed that Mr. Florio's passion for his life's work kept him too busy to be sick.*

Case examples like that of John Florio suggest the hypothesis that interventions encouraging people to muster their will to survive might be helpful in combating cancer. In an exciting study, Spiegel, Bloom, Kraemer, and Gottheil (1989) showed that group therapy increased the longevity of women with severe cases of breast cancer. Research subjects were randomly assigned to one of two conditions: supportive group therapy sessions meeting once a week versus a "control" condition that did not receive group therapy. Women in both groups received comparable medical treatment. The women were followed for a 10-year period, until almost all of them had died. Those in the treatment group survived, on the average, 18 months longer than those in the comparison group. This is a meaningful difference; the study was the first methodologically sound demonstration that a psychological intervention is linked to the life expectancy of cancer patients.

But the study also raised puzzling questions. First, was it something about the experimental group that increased life, or something about the comparison group that decreased life? The design of the study did not allow these possibilities to be distinguished. In fact, the life expectancy of those in the comparison

Group therapy, like that depicted here, increases the longevity of women with severe cases of breast cancer. The exact mechanisms for the effectiveness of this intervention are not known, but research to date certainly suggests that psychotherapy may have an important role in the treatment of cancer.

group seemed to be lower than typical, implying that something inadvertent may have happened to those in the control group to reduce their life expectancy. Second, the study did not tell us why therapy was beneficial, if indeed it was. As part of the research, a battery of personality measures were administered to the subjects, but these proved unrelated to life expectancy. The mechanism here, therefore, remains a mystery. Third, the study did not show that psychotherapy cures cancer, only that it may extend the life expectancy of those with it.

Other researchers are picking up the example of Spiegel et al., conducting their own investigations of psychotherapy for cancer patients (Greer, Moorey, & Baruch, 1991; Grossarth-Maticek & Eysenck, 1991). It is too early to say just what the outcome will be, but all agree that we are entering an exciting era, not only for cancer treatment but also for clinical psychology.

GASTROINTESTINAL DISORDERS

Gastrointestinal disorders are among the most common physical complaints. The gastrointestinal system—from the mouth through the esophagus through the stomach through the small intestine and through the large intestine to the rectum—is about 30 feet long in the typical adult, and difficulties can occur at all points along the way (see Figure 10.8).

Gastroesophagal reflux   One trouble spot involves **gastroesophagal reflux,** a condition in which gastric juice moves upward from the stomach into the esophagus, where it creates the sensation we refer to

FIGURE **10.8**

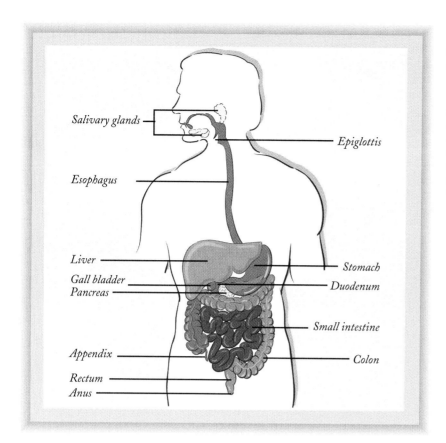

THE GASTROINTESTINAL
SYSTEM   *In the typical adult,
the gastrointestinal system is
about 30 feet long. Problems such
as reflux, ulcer, and irritable
bowel syndrome are among the
most common gastrointestinal
disorders. Stress and other
psychological factors play a role in
many of these ailments.*

Salivary glands

Epiglottis

Esophagus

Liver

Stomach

Gall bladder

Duodenum

Pancreas

Small intestine

Appendix

Colon

Rectum

Anus

as heartburn. A *sphincter*—or valve—between the stomach and esophagus is supposed to keep this from happening, but it fails occasionally for almost all of us, and frequently for some of us. Reflux is most likely to occur when a person is prone, because here she does not have the help of gravity to keep her gastric juice where it belongs.

Among the behavioral risk factors for heartburn are smoking and drinking, and the ingestion of chocolate, fruit juices, and fried foods. Pregnancy is also associated with it. The fetus creates pressure from below that may interfere with the operation of the sphincter, and so too may the hormonal changes during pregnancy.

Clinical observation links chronic stress and anxiety to reflux, although systematic studies have not yet been done (Prokop, Bradley, Burish, Anderson, & Fox, 1991). As people become anxious, their breathing changes, and they swallow air. Then they relax their sphincter in an attempt to clear the air—that is, they try to burp. But the side effect of a burp is that gastric juice might surge up the esophagus along with the trapped air.

Reflux is usually treated with antacids or by simply telling the person to elevate her head while she sleeps. But it can also be treated by advising the person to change what she eats, when she eats, and how much she eats at a given time. Biofeedback is helpful in teaching a person how to use her sphincter more effectively. She swallows a small tube that measures the pressure exerted by the sphincter, registering it on a meter that she can observe. In one study of this procedure, 7 out of 10 patients learned to increase their sphincter pressure, which in turn reduced their symptoms (Schuster, 1983).

Peptic ulcer   Another example of a gastrointestinal disorder is a **peptic ulcer,** a lesion in the stomach or duodenum (see Figure 10.8 again). "Peptic" refers to *pepsin,* thought to be the specific ingredient in digestive juices that actually creates the lesion. Perhaps as many as 10% of the American population will develop a peptic ulcer at some point in their lives. In severe cases, substantial blood is lost or an actual perforation occurs in the stomach or intestine. Approximately 10,000 deaths occur every year in the United States from peptic ulcers.

The immediate cause is simple to specify: Digestive juices secreted in the stomach or small intestine overwhelm the mucus that protects these organs from precisely this occurrence. Thus, ulcers result from too much digestive juice, insufficient mucus, or both.

Recent research implicates, at least for the vast majority of duodenal ulcers, the causal role of a specific bacterium, ***Helicobacter pylori,*** which inflames the alimentary canal and affects the secretion of digestive juices (Blaser, 1992). Antibiotics that kill this bacterium are highly effective in treating duodenal ulcers (Rauws & Tytgat, 1990). If treated individuals remain free of *Helicobacter pylori,* their ulcers do not recur (George et al., 1990).

These findings are exciting, but they do not mean that ulcers are the result solely of a bacterial infection. Consider that perhaps 90% of people who have duodenal ulcers show evidence of being infected with *Helicobacter pylori*—but that still leaves the remaining 10%, who must have a different etiology (Nensey, Schubert, Bologna, & Ma, 1991). Consider also that the link between bacterial infection and ulcers of the stomach is much less robust than for ulcers of the duodenum (Wang, 1991). Consider finally that the majority of individuals with no history of ulcers show antibodies to *Helicobacter pylori,* which means that they were previously exposed to the bacterium yet were able to fight it off (Meyer et al., 1991). Why?

Perhaps psychological influences are also important, a conclusion supported by a number of lines of research. Future work is needed to understand exactly how these psychological factors interact with biological influences such as *Helicobacter pylori.*

What are the psychological risk factors for ulcers? Stress has been implicated. For example, air traffic controllers, a group of people who experience more than the typical amount of stress, also have more than their share of peptic ulcers (Cobb & Rose, 1973).

Researchers have taken a close look at the formation of ulcers by studying their development in animals. In one of the first studies of this type, pairs of monkeys were restrained and exposed to periodic electric shocks (Brady, Porter, Conrad, & Mason, 1958). One monkey—dubbed the executive—could press a lever in order to avoid the shock, for both him and his colleague, who had no such control (see Figure 10.9). The executive eventually developed duodenal ulcers and died, whereas the other monkey—who received the physically identical shocks—showed no sign of ulcers whatsoever.

This study implies that the stress of making decisions (i.e., being an executive) increases the risk of ulcers. As it turns out, though, subsequent research showed this conclusion to be backwards (Weiss, 1971). The original executive monkey study had not randomly assigned monkeys to the executive condition. Instead, the two monkeys were both given a lever with which to control shock, and the one that learned the lever response first was designated the executive. The speed with which a monkey learns this sort of response is

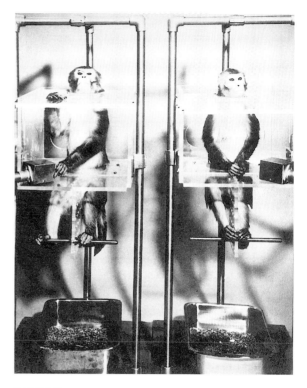

FIGURE 10.9

EXECUTIVE MONKEY   *Early studies suggested that animals able to avoid or terminate electric shock by pushing a lever (like the monkey on the left) were more likely to develop ulcers than were animals without control (like the monkey on the right). However, more recent studies show that these initial investigations were flawed by nonrandom assignment of animals to experimental conditions. When the studies are done correctly, data reveal that the* lack *of control makes ulcers more likely.*
SOURCE: WALTER REED ARMY INSTITUTE OF RESEARCH, WASHINGTON.

heritable, along with a tendency to develop duodenal ulcers.

Correctly done, this study shows that animals *deprived* of control over aversive events are the ones most likely to develop ulcers. Another contributing factor is the animal's experience with unpredictable—as opposed to predictable—aversive events, whether or not any control is possible over them (Weiss, 1970). These results are consistent with the epidemiological finding that individuals most at risk for ulcers are those in the lowest socioeconomic classes in our society. They are precisely the people we would expect to experience unpredictable and uncontrollable events (Susser, 1967).

Alexander (1950) hypothesized that ulcers were most likely to occur among those who are dependent on others and thereby unable to assert themselves. The need to be nurtured presumably leads to a chronic activation of the digestive process, as if the person were ready to be fed. This eventually leads to an ulcer.

Consistent with this formula, Grinker and Robbins (1954) described the case of a 31-year-old woman with a peptic ulcer. No one in her life met her needs for esteem and nurturance. Her father had died 2 years before her ulcer developed. She had been the least favorite of his four daughters. He was an alcoholic and verbally abusive. The patient's mother was overbearing and critical. The patient was married to a man who drank and was frequently unfaithful. Immediately before her ulcer developed, her husband had told their young daughter that the patient was a tramp; she had been pregnant before marriage, and he had been trapped into marrying her. The daughter became distant from the patient, which greatly upset her because it reminded her of the unsatisfactory relationship she had with her own mother. The woman's ulcer responded well to medical treatment, and she began psychotherapy to resolve the conflicts she experienced with her family members.

This is a good example of Alexander's theorizing about the causes of ulcers, but in general, these hypotheses have not fared as well as his proposal linking anger to cardiovascular diseases. Why? There is some evidence that people with ulcers have emotional problems but not that these problems typically revolve around dependency. And further, these emotional problems are linked as well to other diseases, including cardiovascular illness, asthma, arthritis, and migraine headaches (Friedman & Booth-Kewley, 1987).

As for the treatment of ulcers, sometimes surgery is recommended, or sometimes just a change in diet to bland foods. Today, it is most common to see ulcers treated with antibiotics, or with drugs (like *cimetidine*) that inhibit the secretion of digestive juices. In both cases, these are more effective for duodenal than gastric ulcers, and they occasionally have side effects that make them unworkable. Psychologists have therefore been busy developing psychological interventions. These are usually cognitive-behavioral in nature. People are taught to reduce their anxiety by relaxation, assertiveness training, and cognitive restructuring. Said another way, their coping skills are increased, thereby reducing some of the factors that contribute to peptic ulcers (Brooks & Richardson, 1980).

Irritable bowel syndrome   Ulcers can also occur in the large intestine (or colon), as in the disease of *colitis.* However, I complete my journey along the gas-

trointestinal system by considering a much more common affliction of the large intestine: **irritable bowel syndrome (IBS).** The diagnostic criteria include the following:

◆ abdominal pain, usually relieved by defecation

◆ disturbed defecation—that is, changes in frequency, form, or passage of one's stool

◆ bloating or feelings of a distended abdomen

◆ no evidence of organic disease

These symptoms occur at least occasionally in as many as 20% of all Americans. IBS compromises people's lives to varying degrees, depending on the frequency and severity of the symptoms. It results in more than 100,000 hospital admissions every year.

What is going on here? In the process of digestion, food is moved through our gastrointestinal system by muscular contractions. One early theory about IBS proposed that it was caused by excessive contractions of the colon. Individuals with the disorder have more contractile activity than normal comparison subjects. However, when the comparison is expanded to include patients with anxiety disorders, it becomes apparent that anxious people also have increased activity of the colon but suffer no symptoms of IBS (Latimer et al., 1981). Excessive muscular activity is thus a necessary but not sufficient cause of the syndrome.

In the absence of any unique organic influences on IBS, theorists have sought an answer in the psychological realm. "Stress" proves to be too glib an explanation, because those with the disorder report no more stressful life events than anxious comparison subjects without it (West, 1970). A more promising account is cognitive in nature. People prone to the disorder may interpret their colon activity differently from the way others do (Latimer, 1983). These interpretations in turn exacerbate the problem. Another possibility is that it is produced at least in part by reinforcement—the attention people receive when they voice complaints of illness. According to some reviews, IBS probably has no single cause but rather is a heterogeneous category for patients with complaints about moving their bowels (Sammons & Karoly, 1987).

Ms. F. was a 20-year-old woman who had experienced attacks of diarrhea and abdominal cramps since childhood (Grinker & Robbins, 1954). When she began attending college, the attacks intensified. They were worse when Ms. F. spent time with her family members, from whom she demanded much more attention than she received.

She was particularly jealous of her younger brother. She had wanted a sister, and upon the birth of her brother, she repeatedly urged her parents to take him back to the hospital and exchange him for a girl. Ms. F.'s problems with diarrhea subsided when her psychotherapist suggested she spend more time outside the home with friends. The problems vanished altogether when she married and moved away.

The traditional medical treatment for irritable bowel syndrome has been a high-fiber diet coupled with drugs that reduce bowel spasms. There is no solid evidence that this is effective. It seems more promising to treat IBS patients as individuals with psychological problems that surface in the symptoms of the disorder. One avenue is to give them drugs for their anxiety or depression. Another avenue is to undertake psychotherapy, particularly cognitive-behavioral treatments that focus on education, relaxation, and techniques of coping with stress (Blanchard, Schwarz, & Neff, 1988). Also, biofeedback concerning bowel contractions has been used with some success (Furman, 1973), as has hypnosis (Whorwell, Prior, & Faragher, 1984). Because we do not know the actual physiological processes that underlie irritable bowel syndrome, it is difficult to say just what it is about these therapy techniques that help.

ASTHMA

Asthma is an interference with normal breathing that occurs when the airways leading into the lungs constrict and fill with mucus. The lungs must therefore work harder to bring in fresh air and expel stale air. Obviously, individuals with asthma experience shortness of breath. They might also feel as if they are choking. They cough. They wheeze. Asthma attacks occur at different frequencies, and with varying degrees of severity. Perhaps 5% of Americans suffer from at least occasional asthma attacks, and another 7% of the population at one point used to suffer from them. Asthma is more common among children than adults, which means that the condition can be outgrown. However, this does not mean that it should be ignored, because in some instances, it can be fatal. In the United States, asthma accounts for approximately 17 deaths every year per 100,000 individuals.

The triggers for these attacks vary greatly. In some cases, asthma results from an extremely sensitive immune system. The body responds in an overly aggressive manner to antigens such as cigarette smoke, pollen, or dust. These attacks are an extreme version of an allergic response, and individuals prone to them are described as having *extrinsic asthma*, because the trigger is outside their body. If external triggers in the form of antigens cannot be identified, we speak of *intrinsic asthma.*

Psychological risk factors   The role of emotions in asthma has long been suspected. Theorists as far back as Hippocrates regarded it as a condition precipitated by strong emotions. And the role of expectation has been implicated as far back as 1886, when Sir James McKenzie presented an artificial rose to an asthmatic patient allergic to roses (Prokop et al., 1991). She did not know it was artificial, and she had an asthma attack. Along these lines, some sort of learning may well take place, because stimuli associated with the attacks can come to elicit them on their own.

People's habits show a reliable association with the occurrence, severity, and frequency of asthma attacks. Smoking makes it worse. So too does any behavior that brings a person into contact with allergic substances.

Ironically, attacks can be exacerbated by the medications prescribed to treat them. Drugs such as *corticosteroids*—compounds akin to hormones produced by the adrenal glands—are frequently used by asthmatics, because they reduce inflammation in the airways of the lungs. But if overused, they can produce a rebound effect by the body, as it struggles to attain a homeostasis, and the lungs become even more constricted and more filled with mucus.

An earlier generation of researchers sought to find a relationship between specific personality characteristics and asthma (see Kinsman, Dirks, & Jones, 1982). They hypothesized that people at risk for respiratory diseases tend to be dependent, aggressive, and anxious. The actual evidence linking these specific characteristics to asthma is weak (Weiner, 1977). Instead, I conclude as I have elsewhere that emotional difficulties bear a nonspecific relationship to the disorder (Friedman & Booth-Kewley, 1987).

Another line of research that was once popular focused on parents as somehow responsible for the asthma attacks of their children (Block, 1969). They were thought to precipitate and maintain asthma by being overly anxious and protective. In fact, at one time, severe asthma among children was treated by removing them from their homes. Again, research has not supported this possibility, suggesting—if anything—that parental overprotectiveness may be a *consequence* of their child having such attacks. If watching a child choking and turning colors is not enough to make a parent worried and solicitous, then what is? At some level, of course, psychological factors have something to do with asthma. As already described, expectations, classical conditioning, habits, and emotional difficulties are involved. Contemporary opinion holds that asthma results from a physiological predisposition that is exacerbated by psychological factors (Prokop et al., 1991).

Billy was a youngster referred to treatment because of severe asthma (Grinker & Robbins, 1954). He was small for his age and socially withdrawn. He had wheezing attacks almost every evening, and it was common for his mother to sit up all night with him. Billy was allergic to a variety of common items such as feathers; coming into contact with them would cause an asthma attack. Attacks were also precipitated by his mother making plans to leave the house. When she went into the hospital to give birth to the family's new baby, Billy suffered almost constantly from asthma until her return. His father had little to do with him, blaming his wife for producing the attacks. Billy was not helped by medication. Some reduction in the frequency of his asthma attacks occurred during psychotherapy aimed at improving his peer skills, but this might simply have reflected the passage of time and Billy's physical maturation.

Asthma attacks are often treated with biomedical means, but psychological interventions play an important role as well.

Psychological treatment   The pharmacological treatment of this condition is far from foolproof, and corticosteroids can have rather severe side effects. Psychological interventions have therefore been gaining attention. It appears that strategies for reducing anxiety, such as systematic desensitization, reduce the frequency and severity of asthma attacks (Creer, 1991; Lehrer, Sargunaraj, & Hochron, 1992). Part of what occurs during an attack is that the person becomes afraid, and the physiological symptoms of anxiety make her attack worse. Biofeedback has also been used with some success, as the person learns to control her breathing and in particular the constriction of the airways of her lungs (e.g., Vachon & Rich, 1976). Finally, operant conditioning techniques in which children are rewarded for not having to be hospitalized for asthma attacks reduces the frequency of such hospitalizations (e.g., Dahl, Gustafsson, & Melin, 1990; Kotses, Lewis, & Creer, 1990).

In this chapter, I have discussed how psychological factors influence physical health, as well as how psychological interventions can prevent illness or aid in recovery. My focus has been on the quantity of life—how long people live and the degree to which they are free of disease. But there is more to life than simply its quantity. The quality of life—how people live for as long or as short a time as they do—is surely as important, and some psychologists interested in health have urged the field to focus on how psychology adds to the quality of life (Seeman, 1989).

Living well is sometimes referred to as *wellness,* and the concept cannot be defined merely by longevity or freedom from disease. It involves satisfactory relationships with family members and friends, a fulfilling career, and a zest for the ongoing process of life. A person need not choose between quantity and quality of life, because the influences on one are often the same for the other. When we discuss mind-body influences, we should not make the absence of disorders our sole criterion of health. In an intriguing book titled *Worried Sick,* Arthur Barsky (1988) expressed his alarm at the recent trend in the United States to pursue "health" in a grim and unrealistic fashion, trying to avoid each and every symptom and illness. To live in this way, Barsky tells us, is not to live at all. Everyone must find a meaning or purpose to life, and longevity and freedom from illness seem terribly poor candidates.

Summary

✦ Psychosomatic disorders are physical illnesses influenced by psychological factors. Recent years have seen an explosion of knowledge about the psychological risk factors for illness as well as the mechanisms that lead from these factors to physical well-being.

MINDS AND BODIES THROUGHOUT HISTORY

✦ A view across history shows that the relationship between mind and body has been conceived in drastically different ways. Early Greek thinkers like Hippocrates posited great continuity between the psychological and the physical, expecting each to influence the other. In contrast, French philosopher Descartes proposed that minds and bodies represented altogether different realms; minds were free, whereas bodies were determined. This mind-body dualism persisted into the 20th century, although eventually scientists came to regard both mind and body as subject to causes.

✦ Medical practice reflected mind-body dualism. In the 19th century, physicians treated illnesses in heroic fashion designed to restore balance among bodily humours. Psychological factors were not part of the picture. Alternatives to orthodox medicine acknowledged the importance of psychological influences on illness, although these were short-lived with the growth of modern medicine, spurred by the proposal of germ theory and the description of the immune system. Again, these allowed no role for psychological influences on physical well-being.

MINDS AND BODIES MORE RECENTLY

✦ The 20th century saw psychological factors put back into the health and illness equation. Franz Alexander theorized within the psychodynamic tradition about the possible link between emotional conflicts and illness. Hans Selye introduced an influential view of how all organisms, including people, respond to stress. Susceptibility to illness was one of the consequences of poor coping with stress. Subsequent researchers showed that psychological factors influence the nature and extent of stress that people experience. Cognitive factors are particularly important. Finally, the new field of psychoneuroimmunology took form, based on the explicit recognition that the nervous system, endocrine system, and immune system are in constant communication with one another.

PARTICULAR MIND-BODY DISORDERS

✦ The leading cause of death in the United States today is cardiovascular disease, which has among its risk factors habits such as smoking and the Type A personality style (competitiveness, time urgency, and especially hostility). These risk factors can be modified psychologically.

✦ The second leading cause of death today is cancer, a family of diseases characterized by the uncontrollable growth of cells. Again, cancer has obvious behavioral risk factors such as smoking and drinking, as well as any behavior that brings a person into contact with cancer-triggering substances. Experimental studies with animals suggest that uncontrollable aversive events influence the growth of cancer cells. More controversial is whether personality factors influence the onset and/or progression of cancer. There is some evidence that people who are depressed and hopeless are at risk for cancer, whereas those with a "fighting spirit" are more likely to recover. Other studies have not found these links, so work here continues.

✦ Gastrointestinal disorders include gastroesophageal reflux (heartburn), peptic ulcer (a lesion in the stomach or duodenum), and irritable bowel syndrome (disturbances in defecation). Given behaviors may exacerbate all of these disorders. The role of stress and emotional conflict is less clear, although it does appear as if peptic ulcers are made more likely by uncontrollable, unpredictable aversive events. Behavior therapy can help the gastrointestinal disorders.

✦ Asthma refers to a constriction of the airways to the lungs, resulting in hampered breathing. Classical conditioning, expectancies, and stress contribute to asthma. Research has *not* supported earlier hypotheses explaining asthma in terms of a dependent personality style or an overly protective family. Behavior therapy can be used to help alleviate the severity and frequency of asthma attacks.

Key Terms

antibodies	B cell lymphocytes
antigen	benign tumor
asthma	cancer

cardiovascular diseases

chiropractic medicine

dispositional optimism

explanatory style

gastroesophagal reflux

gastrointestinal disorders

general adaptation
    syndrome

germ theory

hardiness

Helicobacter pylori

heroic medicine

homeopathy

immune system

immunosuppression

irritable bowel
    syndrome; IBS

John Henryism

malignant tumor

metastasis

mind-body dualism

natural killer (NK) cells

peptic ulcer

phagocytes

popular health
    movement

primary appraisal

psychological factors
    affecting medical
    condition

psychoneuroimmunology

psychosomatic disorders

secondary appraisal

social support

T cell lymphocytes

tumor

Type A coronary-prone
    behavior pattern

Sexual Disorders

11

MR. X. WAS A 31-YEAR-OLD MALE who was sexually turned on by breasts (Kremer & den Daas, 1990). Touching and stroking them was a critical part of his sexual activity. So what? Many men are excited by breasts. The "so what" is the fact that he was turned on by his *own* breasts. He even wished that they looked and felt more like a woman's breasts, because this might enhance his sexual arousal. Mr. X. was married, and his wife fully supported his decision to seek medical help for his problem. He undertook treatment, not to rid himself of this unusual desire but rather to bring it to reality. He

found a physician who would administer female hormones to stimulate the growth of his breasts. When they increased to the size of an average woman's, Mr. X was satisfied, and his hormone treatments were discontinued. His new and improved breasts became even more of a sexual focus than before; merely touching them produced an erection and eventual orgasm.

Mr. X.'s interest in his own breasts and the medical treatment he received may strike you as unusual, but one of the lessons evident from any discussion of human sexuality is that there are few universals. Granted a sufficiently close look, perhaps everyone's sexual practices appear idiosyncratic, which is to say unusual to everyone else.

With this case as my springboard, I begin this chapter, which concerns itself with psychological problems surrounding sexuality. DSM-IV divides sexual problems into several categories (see Table 11.1). **Sexual dysfunctions** refer to sexual inabilities: problems in moving from desire to excitement to sexual activity to orgasm. Sexual dysfunctions are problems with the mechanics of sex, although sex is never just mechanical.

While some individuals have difficulties with sexual performance, for others it is the nature of their sexual activities that is deemed abnormal. DSM-IV uses the term **paraphilia** to describe the recurring intense desire to have sexual activity with an inappropriate individual or in an inappropriate fashion. To warrant a DSM-IV diagnosis of paraphilia, a person must either have acted on this sexual desire or have

TABLE 11.1

Types of Sexual Disorders *DSM-IV describes several disorders entailing sexuality.*

Disorder	Characterization and Treatment
sexual dysfunction	sexual inability; a problem with sexual desire, excitement, activity, and/or orgasm
	helped by sex therapy
paraphilia	preferred or exclusive sexual activity with an inappropriate individual or in an inappropriate fashion
	treated biomedically or behaviorally
transsexualism	disorder of adults in which their experiences of themselves as males or females is at odds with their anatomical sex
	helped by gender reassignment surgery

experienced marked distress because of it. Sexual activity with prepubescent children or nonconsenting adults is one example.

Is Mr. X.'s interest in breasts a paraphilia? Maybe yes, maybe no. He had orgasms only when his breasts were stimulated, but he and his wife by their own report enjoyed a satisfying sexual relationship. In contrast, many unusual sexual practices interfere with a person's relationships with others. Consider a man who is turned on only by shoes or garters. Because he is apt to be indifferent to the women who wear them, how can a meaningful human relationship then ensue?

A third problem involving sexuality is **gender identity disorder** (often called **transsexualism** among adults), in which people's experience of themselves as male or female is at odds with their anatomical sex. An individual might feel like a man trapped in a woman's body or a woman trapped in a man's body. Cases of transsexualism are rare, but they have attracted a great deal of attention, because they are contrary to the way we think things are "supposed" to be. We expect people's gender identity to be congruent with their anatomy.

Mr. X. was *not* a transsexual, despite his wish to have female breasts. He experienced himself as male, and he was not dissatisfied with his genitals. Indeed, the appearance of his breasts was not the issue so much as how they responded to stimulation.

Here are several general points about sexual disorders. First, we must locate these problems in their time and place. People in all cultures have had strong notions about sexuality, but these vary across cultures. If you are not yet convinced that there is an ambiguous distinction between what is considered normal and abnormal behavior, you need look no further than sexual disorders for an excellent example. In some cultures, sex with animals is an important religious ritual (Traub-Werner, 1986). In our society, this is condemned.

What is considered normal and abnormal also changes within a given society. Only a few decades ago, in the United States, masturbation was considered harmful (Comfort, 1967; Hare, 1962). It was thought to cause fits and fevers, blindness, acne, and decay of the spinal cord. Nowadays, if not quite giving its blessing to masturbation, psychology has moved it out of the "hazardous to one's health" category. Along these same lines, homosexuality was once considered to be a psychological disorder; now it is viewed as an alternative approach to sexuality (see Chapter 2).

A second and related point is that when I discuss sexual disorders, I cannot help but stray into legal and moral arenas (Ames & Houston, 1990). Many of the problems from which people suffer are simply that: problems. Talking to oneself or feeling excessively sad

is abnormal, but few legal codes consider these actions against the law, and few moral teachings would brand them as evil. Not so with sexuality. Law and religion invariably have much to say about sexual activities. Sometimes their statements agree with psychological designations of abnormality, but sometimes they do not. Transsexualism, for example, is not illegal in our society. It is seen as abnormal, however, and some regard it as immoral. Sex with children, for another example, is widely considered to be abnormal, immoral, and illegal. Rape, as yet another example, is not included in DSM-IV as abnormal, but it is illegal and immoral.

A third thing to emphasize about sexuality and sexual disorders is that we must bring to bear all the models of abnormality that concern contemporary psychologists. Sexual disorders are mind-body problems, like the difficulties discussed in the last chapter. Sexual activity, normal or abnormal, represents an entwining of psychological and biological factors. Sorting these out is a vexing concern for those who try to understand sexual disorders.

This is not an idle issue, because attempts to help people with their sexual disorders are necessarily based on our theories about what causes them in the first place. DSM-IV, for instance, calls on the diagnostician to distinguish between sexual dysfunctions in which organic causes play a primary role and those in which they do not. A host of physical conditions can produce sexual difficulties; for example, circulatory problems resulting from diabetes may lead to impotence. We treat these differently from the ostensibly identical difficulties that have their origins solely in the psychological realm, such as excessive anxiety resulting from sexually related trauma (Kaplan, 1974). Nonetheless, all of this rests on a fine distinction between what is biological and what is psychological. Although we have cases in which one clearly overshadows the other, in many instances of sexual difficulty, both biological and psychological determinants work together (Halvorsen & Metz, 1992a; Krause et al., 1991; Schover, Friedman, Weiler, Heiman, & LoPiccolo, 1982).

A fourth idea to keep in mind when discussing sexual disorders is the need to qualify many statements by referring to men or to women. Men and women experience sexuality differently, and therefore the sorts of problems they encounter tend to be different as well. Certain sexual dysfunctions, such as impaired desire, are more common among women than men. Paraphilias are overwhelmingly more common among men than women. And transsexualism is several times more likely among biological males than biological females.

These differences between men and women are striking, and they call for an explanation. Again, there

We must qualify many statements about sexuality by referring to men or women.

is controversy whether we should use biological factors to account for them or whether we should invoke learning and culture. Perhaps the middle ground is best, regarding male-female differences as due to some combination of nature *and* nurture.

A final point about sexual disorders: DSM-IV, for better or for worse, puts its focus on the individual. Problems are located within individual men and women. This is not the only way to regard sexual problems, and it might not even be the best way. Perhaps they should be regarded as inherently the problem of the sexual pair. By this view, individuals do not have sexual problems, only couples do. While premature ejaculation is something that a male does, it is a problem for both him and his partner if it produces less than satisfactory sexual relations between them.

As a way of providing a context for my discussion of problems in the here and now, an overview of the history of sexuality in the Western world follows. History teaches us that social and cultural values shape prevailing conceptualizations of sexuality and its disor-

ders. In some cases they have exacerbated problems or even created them. After providing you with this historical background, I move to sexual dysfunctions, paraphilias, and transsexualism.

A HISTORY OF SEXUALITY

I can start the history of sexuality at virtually any point once life appeared on the planet, because sexual reproduction followed shortly thereafter. But let me start with the earliest groups of human beings and note that for them sexuality was a phenomenon of great significance. It was interpreted in magical terms, seen as a way of communicating directly with the forces of nature. In many past societies, sexual activity was an explicit part of religious worship (e.g., Manniche, 1987). For example, those who worshipped the god of wine—Dionysus—would get intoxicated and dance around a giant phallus (Chapter 5). Then they would engage in a frenzy of sexual activity with one another.

Human sexuality has never been something that people do with their genitals alone—and to repeat, it has always been imbued with significance. Why? One obvious reason is that sexuality is responsible for the next generation, for creating life, and this was as magical to our distant ancestors as it is to us today. Another obvious reason is that sexual activity provides intense pleasure. Other pleasurable experiences are often compared to an orgasm, but we rarely hear an orgasm compared to anything else. In our society, as well as in many others, sexual activity is a way of showing affection for another person. Sexuality is part of our very identity. People engage in sexual activity for many reasons, some of them important and some of them profound.

Among its many roles, sexual activity is a way of showing affection for another person.

FIGURE 11.1

RECENT HISTORY OF SEXUALITY *Sexuality has always been a topic of great social importance, and during the 20th century it has been subjected to scientific study. This time line shows some of the relatively recent societal events and scientific contributions that have shaped contemporary beliefs about sexuality.*

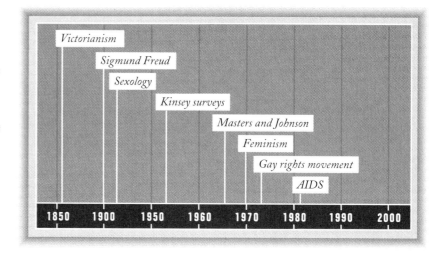

EARLY CHRISTIANITY

Christianity has been one of the most important influences in the history of the Western world. This religion has affected not just the rise and fall of nations but also people's attitudes toward sexuality (e.g., Fuchs, 1983; Phipps, 1970). Many of the attitudes held by the very early Christians have survived until the present day.[1] How many of these specific beliefs sound familiar to you?

✦ Sexuality is a powerful force that at the same time is to be mistrusted.

✦ The most respected states are virginity and celibacy.

✦ The epitome of temptation is lust.

✦ Particularly evil are homosexuality, contraception, and sexual activity outside marriage.

These attitudes were exactly those of the earliest Christians, almost 2,000 years ago. Humankind's "original sin," as the Bible relates in the Book of Genesis, is sexual.

As Christianity spread throughout the Western world, its beliefs and teachings pervaded all of the emerging social institutions, eventually affecting education, business, government, and even the military. Brought along with this influence were specific attitudes toward sexuality (see Figure 11.1).

Original sin, as related in the Genesis account of Adam and Eve and shown here in the Sistine Chapel, involved sexuality.

VICTORIANISM

The influence of Christian beliefs about sexuality is no better illustrated than in the 19th century, when sexuality became cloaked in a mass of restrictions we now refer to as **Victorianism,** after the long-reigning Queen Victoria (1819–1901) of England. The central tenet of Victorianism, insofar as sexuality was concerned, was that sexual drives, feelings, and activities should be repressed and denied (Gay, 1984). These beliefs take the mistrust of the early Christians even further. It is one thing to say that sexuality should be mistrusted; it is another thing to say that sexuality does not exist.

According to the Victorians, the "ideal" woman experienced no sexual feelings (Barret-Ducrocq,

---

[1] Christianity is not alone in its endorsement of these attitudes. Judaism also endorses many of these beliefs, and a variety of other religions—Western and Eastern—urge temperance and restraint in sexual activities.

The Victorian era takes its name from the long-reigning Queen Victoria (1819–1901) of England. An important aspect of Victorian culture was the denial of sexuality.

tion. Medical practice was affected as well. Gynecology as a medical specialty did not exist. Nor did obstetrics; male doctors had nothing to do with the process of birth. Men and women routinely wore *chastity belts*, mechanical devices to prevent sexual arousal and/or intercourse.

Masturbation was regarded as a plague on society (Money, Prakasam, & Joshi, 1991). Chronic masturbation was believed to be a cause of insanity, a belief expressed in medical textbooks well into the 20th century. Parents were greatly worried if their children persisted in its practice. A boy who could not be dissuaded by threats and punishments was sometimes castrated. A like-minded girl might have her clitoris removed to deaden her capacity for pleasure. Female genital mutilation is a cultural practice still common in parts of the contemporary world, notably Africa (see Barker-Benfield, 1975; Koso-Thomas, 1987; Lightfoot-Klein, 1989; Walker, 1993).

For all the effort that went into the denial of sexuality, the Victorians merely drove it underground (Marcus, 1966). This era saw the flourishing of child abuse, prostitution, sexually transmitted diseases, and pornography.

1991). However, she could be corrupted by outside influences, such as men, who did experience sexual feelings if they were reminded of sex. The trick was to keep sex out of the minds of Victorian men. Aspects of Victorianism seem comic from today's vantage. Animals in zoos wore trousers, lest men see their genitals and be reminded that they too had them. Pianos had little skirts around their legs, lest men be reminded that women had ankles. Women wore huge bustles and massive petticoats to obscure their bodies. When Victorians ate chicken, they referred to the breast as a neck, because it was too risqué to call a chicken breast by that name. Not only were chickens denied breasts, so too were women. Women had bosoms, not breasts. And women had limbs, not legs.

Other aspects of Victorianism were not simply silly. The widespread attempt to deny sexuality had serious implications (Davenport-Hines, 1990; Fout, 1992). Classic writings—including the Bible and the sonnets of Shakespeare—were rewritten to remove any reference to sexuality. Medical journals containing pictures of sexual organs were restricted in their circula-

In the Victorian era, women wore huge bustles and massive petticoats to obscure the fact that they had bodies beneath their skirts.

Gay (1984) described Frederick Hankey, a wealthy young man in Victorian England, who collected pornography and made a good living selling books and pictures to others. He frequented brothels that specialized in young girls who could be beaten and otherwise maltreated. According to Hankey, he killed a number of these prostitutes and collected their skin. His favorite activity was supposedly watching a public execution through a brothel window while having sex.

Even by today's standards, Hankey's reported behavior is horrifying—illegal, immoral, and abnormal. It reminds us that sexuality did not cease to exist during Victorian times, regardless of the expressed societal codes. Here you see an issue that still splits our society today. Does the repression of sexuality in one place in society result in its showing up in another place, perhaps with more serious consequences than in the first?

SIGMUND FREUD

It was during the Victorian era that Freud began to theorize. You have learned that Freud's theories about the importance of human sexuality were met with surprise and resistance from those around him. With what you now know about the Victorian era, you can understand that the opposition to Freud's theories went beyond mere quibbling. In proposing his psychoanalytic theory, Freud was broaching a topic that officially did not exist (see Masson, 1986).

The details of psychoanalytic theory were even more unthinkable. Rather than regarding sexuality as evil, Freud regarded it as primal. Rather than denying people's sexual identities, he proposed that all people, including children, were inherently sexual creatures. Freud brought human sexuality out of the dark closet to which the Victorians had banished it. Other forces conspired as well. The Industrial Revolution brought an increasing number of people to cities, which provided greater anonymity and thus fostered sexual activity. The end of World War I and growing economic prosperity brought a giddiness to much of the Western world, as well as a more openly hedonistic tone. The "Roaring Twenties" were not simply about beaded dresses, dance fads, and cheap gin; they were also about sexuality, as people in Europe and the United States became more liberal in their sexual attitudes and behaviors.

HUMAN SEXUALITY RESEARCH

Freud legitimized a scientific look at sexuality. The field of **sexology** developed, devoted to the scientific study of sex (Walling, 1904). Different researchers documented the range of sexual practices within Western society and around the world (e.g., Ellis, 1901–1914). To this day, one of the primary contributions of sexuality research is providing information (Brecher, 1969). Once investigators were permitted to acknowledge sexuality, they discovered many people engaged in practices unimagined by others.

Alfred Kinsey   Alfred Kinsey, a biologist at Indiana University, was the first to undertake large-scale studies of "normal" human sexuality in the United States. In the 1940s and 1950s, Kinsey and his colleagues interviewed thousands of everyday Americans about their sexual practices. The *Kinsey reports*, as the published results of these surveys came to be known, provided information heretofore unknown about who did what with whom, when, how often, and under what circumstances (Kinsey, Pomeroy, & Martin, 1948; Kinsey, Pomeroy, Martin, & Gebhard, 1953).

The importance of the Kinsey reports cannot be overestimated. They showed a much greater range of sexual behavior than existed in society's stated codes. When I teach about paraphilias, I mention various ways that people can be turned on: with leather and lace, whips and chains, peeping and being peeped. The majority of my students seem reluctant to recognize that such practices exist. However, somebody must be doing these things: Kinsey's surveys and others attest to the frequency of ostensibly "unusual" sexual activities.

If anything, the prevalence of some sexual practices is underestimated by surveys. The representativeness of a researcher's sample and the validity of subjects' responses are problems that plague this sort of research. People attach great significance to sexuality, and in our society this significance may revolve around sin and/or guilt. If a researcher knocks on your door or phones you and wishes to speak to you about your sexual practices, some of which you yourself regard with great ambivalence, would you be willing to participate in this survey? And if you did participate, would you be candid?

There is no definitive answer to just how biased sexuality surveys are, because we obviously have no way of comparing those who respond with those who do not, and we usually have no way of independently verifying what people report. Therefore, we should not put much stock in particular estimates—12% versus 17% versus 23%—for a particular sexual activity. Instead, we should view the results of surveys as useful in two general ways: first for documenting the range of sexual activities in which people engage, and second for showing broad changes over time. Figure 11.2, for instance, contrasts Kinsey's data and more recent data regarding women's sexual behavior.

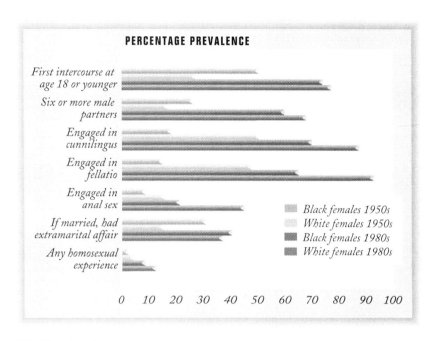

FIGURE 11.2

WOMEN'S SEXUAL BEHAVIOR IN THE UNITED STATES, 1950S AND 1980S
A study in the 1980s surveyed women in the United States about their sexual behavior, then compared the findings with those from the Kinsey surveys of the 1950s. The research data indicate that U.S. women are engaging in first intercourse at a younger age and are more varied in their sexual activity.
SOURCES: DATA DERIVED FROM *Sexual Behavior in the Human Female,* BY A. C. KINSEY, W. D. POMEROY, C. E. MARTIN, AND P. H. GEBHARD, 1953, PHILADELPHIA: SAUNDERS; "KINSEY REVISITED, PART I," BY G. E. WYATT, S. D. PETERS, AND D. GUTHRIE, 1988, *Archives of Sexual Behavior, 17,* PP. 201–239; "KINSEY REVISITED, PART II," BY G. E. WYATT, S. D. PETERS, AND D. GUTHRIE, 1988, *Archives of Sexual Behavior, 17,* PP. 289–332. USED WITH PERMISSION.

With regard to changes in behavior, we can say that since the 1940s and 1950s, people in the United States have been increasingly more likely to have sex prior to marriage and to do so at ever earlier ages (Wyatt, Peters, & Guthrie, 1988a, 1988b). In and out of marriage, people have also become more varied in what they do. There have also been changes in people's attitudes about sexual practices: Over the decades Americans have become more liberal about sexual matters—that is, more accepting of homosexuality, contraception, abortion, and premarital sex (Katcha-dourian, 1989).

In the 1960s and 1970s, sexual practices and atti-tudes seemed to reach a critical level of liberalness, in an era referred to as the *sexual revolution.* In retrospect, this label is hyperbole. Still, people became more liberal about sexual matters, and the widespread availability of birth control pills on the one hand and legalized abortion on the other made it possible for people to separate procreation from recreation, if they so desired.

Although it may be an overstatement to term it a revolution, in the 1960s and 1970s, American society saw a liberalization of sexual attitudes and behaviors. This photo shows a "love-in" held in Los Angeles in the 1960s.

William Masters and Virginia Johnson   Part of the increasingly liberal attitude of society toward sexuality was an even greater willingness to study it scientifically, and along with Kinsey, the giant figures in sexuality research include William Masters and Virginia Johnson (1966). Their initial contribution was to bring human sexual activity into the laboratory. Where Kinsey asked people about sexuality, Masters and Johnson observed them under controlled conditions. They watched their volunteer subjects become aroused and experience orgasm. The subjects were hooked up to recording devices that traced the physiological changes associated with the sexual response.

Masters and Johnson's initial research was important for the basic information it provided. Not until 1966, when their landmark book *Human Sexual Response* was published, had there been a detailed account of just what happens to our bodies when we engage in sex. Some of their findings were at odds with conventional wisdom—but conventional wisdom was wrong. Freud, for example, had popularized the notion that "mature" women experienced orgasm through stimulation of the vagina. "Immature" women in contrast responded to stimulation of the clitoris. Masters and Johnson (1966) showed that vaginas are rather insensitive to erotic stimulation and that clitoral orgasm is the typical orgasm.

The later work of Masters and Johnson (1970) is equally important. They followed their investigation of sexual response with a study of how the sexual response can go awry—what I described earlier as sexual dysfunction. In addition, they devised a strategy for helping people rid themselves of sexual dysfunc-tions. Their approach to **sex therapy** has been widely used and in many cases effective. I describe sex therapy in more detail later in the chapter.

FEMINISM

Another important historical development was the growth of *feminism* in the 1970s and thereafter. Feminism concerns itself not only with political and economic matters but also sexual issues. Feminists observe that sexuality often involves power. Susan Brownmiller (1975) wrote an important book, *Against Our Will*, in which she analyzed rape not narrowly as a sexual act but as a crime of violence and a way that men assert control over women.

During the recent ethnic strife in Bosnia, there were widespread reports of soldiers raping all the females they captured, apparently under the directions of their leaders who saw this as a way of further subjugating communities (P. Lewis, 1993). Rape is always a horrible crime but particularly for Muslim women like those in Bosnia, who may find themselves ostracized following their victimization. A further consequence may be the abandonment of the babies conceived during the rapes. In any event, systematic rapes by invading armies have been common throughout history (Brownmiller, 1975).

Feminist discussions raised the consciousness of the entire society about rape. The crime is now much more likely to be reported than in years past, though most believe that rape is still one of the least frequently reported crimes (see Figure 11.3).

FIGURE 11.3

RAPES REPORTED TO THE POLICE IN THE UNITED STATES, 1960–1990   *In recent decades, the number of rapes reported to the police in the United States has steadily increased. Most agree, however, that these figures represent but a fraction of the number of rapes that actually occur.*
SOURCES: *Historical Statistics of the United States*, 1976, WASHINGTON, DC: U.S. DEPARTMENT OF COMMERCE; *Statistical Abstract of the United States*, 1993, WASHINGTON, DC: U.S. DEPARTMENT OF COMMERCE.

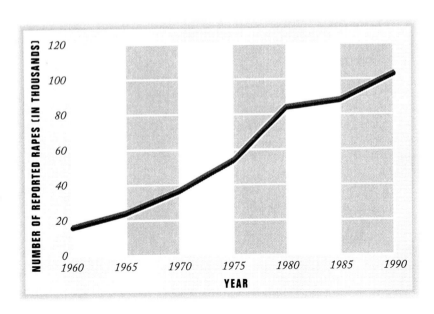

Anita Hill is shown here in 1991, testifying about sexual harassment before the Senate Judiciary Committee hearings on Supreme Court nominee Clarence Thomas.

nists and their opponents differ over just how such fulfillment should be achieved—in or out of traditional marriage—but they agree that it should occur.

GAY RIGHTS MOVEMENT

Yet another important social event influencing our attitudes toward sexuality has been the *gay rights movement.* The official beginning of this movement is often placed on the night of June 29, 1969, when the gay customers of the Stonewall Inn in New York's Greenwich Village fought back against a police raid. This event served as a catalyst only because more general changes in society were already taking place. Throughout much of the 20th century, homosexuality per se was considered a mental disorder (Bayer, 1987). This judgment was weakened by studies showing that societies other than our own differed greatly in their acceptance of homosexuality (Ford & Beach, 1951). Also, studies within our own society showed that gay men and lesbians did not differ from heterosexuals on measures of psychological adjustment and well-being (e.g., Hooker, 1957; see also Kehoe, 1986).

The gay rights movement articulated the position that gay men and lesbians had problems only to the degree that they were a persecuted minority (see Miranda & Storms, 1989). Part of this persecution was the tendency of mental health professionals to regard a homosexual orientation as abnormal. As recently as the 1970s, the American Psychiatric Association considered it a clinical syndrome. But following intensive political pressure from gay rights activists, this position was modified in DSM-III (American

The idea that sexual bantering and "flirtation" might better be seen as harassment was ushered in by the feminist movement. That the sexual revolution was more for the benefit of men than women was also suggested. Why were birth control pills developed for women rather than men? There is nothing inherent in female physiology to make it easier to interrupt than male physiology. In fact, it may be just the opposite. But whether intentionally or not, our society has placed much of the responsibility for birth control solely on women.

It is impossible to characterize all feminists with regard to specific attitudes toward sexuality. Regardless, feminism has effectively challenged many of the double standards concerning male and female sexuality. Even conservative thinkers such as Maribel Morgan (1973), author of *The Total Woman,* argue that the sexual fulfillment of women is important. Femi-

The gay rights movement is based on the premise that those with a homosexual orientation are a persecuted minority.

Psychiatric Association, 1980). DSM-III proposed that only *ego-dystonic homosexuality* was a problem: a homosexual orientation about which someone feels upset. This was obviously a compromise that does not say much, because *any* activity about which we feel badly is potentially problematic. DSM-III-R let this category go altogether, and it did not reappear in DSM-IV.

Homosexuality is no longer considered a psychological disorder but rather one approach to sexuality out of many (Garnets, Hancock, Cochran, Goodchilds, & Peplau, 1991). It demands an explanation, to be sure, but no more than heterosexuality. As I discuss later in this chapter, psychology lacks a good theory concerning *any* sexual orientation.

Two well publicized studies have recently suggested some biological basis to a homosexual orientation, and the larger implications of these results have been the subject of much discussion (see Henry, 1993). In the first of these studies, LeVay (1991) compared the size of the anterior hypothalamus of the brain of heterosexual and gay men. He found a twofold difference favoring heterosexual men in the volume of one of the cell groups thought to regulate male sexual behavior. Does this show a biological basis to male homosexuality? Perhaps, but further research is needed. Consider that this research can only be done via autopsy, after death, and that LeVay's gay research subjects were all men who had died of AIDS. One of the possible consequences of AIDS is brain atrophy (e.g., Sonnerborg et al., 1990), which means that LeVay's investigation may have been confounded.

In a second study, Hamer, Hu, Magnuson, Hu, and Pattatucci (1993) found that male homosexuality is heritable, specifically, through the mother. In other words, these researchers found that gay men had a higher proportion of gay male relatives on the mother's side than is found in the general population. When Hamer and colleagues compared the DNA of pairs of gay brothers, 33 out of 40 shared genetic material in the same area of the X chromosome. The X chromosome is contributed by one's mother, and while the Hamer group did *not* identify a gay gene, these findings are consistent with their family study. Unanswered of course is the mechanism by which genetics and brain structure may influence sexual orientation, homosexual or otherwise.

AIDS

The story I have been telling about the history of sexual activity is one of people becoming increasingly tolerant of sexuality. But in 1981, open sexual expression encountered a roadblock when the first case of AIDS was diagnosed in the United States. As you well know, AIDS is a grave public issue (see Figure 11.4). At this writing, it is an inevitably fatal disease that spreads when the virus responsible for it is transmitted via bodily fluids from one person to another. In addition to the sharing of drug needles and the transfusion of infected blood, a common mode of transmission is sexual.

When first identified in the United States, AIDS occurred overwhelmingly among gay men, and others managed to distance themselves from it. Eventually it became clear that vulnerability to AIDS through sexual activity has nothing to do with sexual *orientation* but rather with sexual *practices*, including intercourse with a person infected with the virus.

It is interesting to examine our society's reaction to AIDS from the vantage of the history of sexuality.

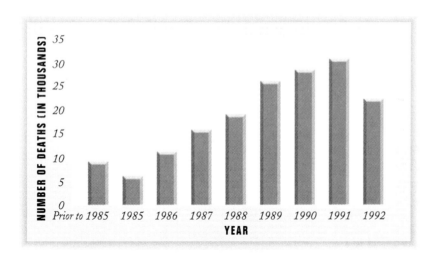

FIGURE 11.4

DEATHS BY AIDS IN THE UNITED STATES *Since its initial diagnosis in 1981, AIDS has taken the lives of many thousands of Americans.*
SOURCE: *Statistical Abstract of the United States,* 1993, WASHINGTON, DC: U.S. DEPARTMENT OF COMMERCE.

For all its movement toward liberal attitudes, our society is still not completely open and tolerant about sexuality. If we were as liberal as we claim to be, we would not have seen AIDS regarded as solely a gay problem. We would not have seen objections to public discussion of AIDS prevention. We would not have seen resistance to the advertising of latex condoms. Even today, when information about AIDS is available, it is usually offered in highly abstract fashion. We hear about safe sex and not sharing bodily fluids, but this information seems to have come out of the Victorian era, because it is so sanitized.

By some reports, people's sexual activity has changed because of the threat of AIDS and other sexually transmitted diseases (e.g., Lau et al., 1992; Mays, Albee, & Schneider, 1989; Murstein, Chalpin, Heard, & Vyse, 1989). People are less liberal than during the immediately preceding generation, but sexual activity has not changed so drastically that the sexual transmission of AIDS has ceased (Roffman, Gillmore, Gilchrist, Mathias, & Krueger, 1990).

In an ironic way, our cultural legacy equating sex with sin and guilt is responsible for the continued spread of sexual diseases. Sex is too basic an impulse to expect most people to refrain from sexual activity altogether, so what we hope is that people will conduct themselves in a responsible way. But our ambivalence about sexual matters precludes our being thoughtful. We have sex only when we are drunk. We have sex without taking appropriate precautions. We have sex without talking to our partners. And so it goes.

SEXUAL FUNCTION AND DYSFUNCTION

I start this discussion of sexual function and dysfunction by considering the role of hormones in sexual activity. Then I describe what happens as an individual moves without difficulty through the process of sexual excitement to orgasm, relying on Masters and Johnson's (1966) work. Keep in mind that difficulties can take place at any step along the way. After this description of people's nonproblematic sexual response, I describe the various ways that problems can arise. I close this section with a description of sex therapy, which of course is intended to help people remedy their problems.

HORMONES

Males and females have characteristic sex hormones: **testosterone** in males and **estrogen** and **progestin** in females. Their role in normal and abnormal sexuality

is a complex one.[2] These sex hormones must be present in optimal amounts at appropriate times for normal physical development to occur, particularly the growth of the testes or ovaries, genitals, and secondary sexual characteristics (Money & Ehrhardt, 1972). Sex hormones trigger the onset of puberty and regulate the complex bodily changes that make reproduction possible.

The role of sex hormones in the purely physiological aspects of sexual development is noncontroversial. Less agreed upon is just what role these hormones play in sexual behavior. Among lower animals, sexual activity is closely tied to circulating hormone levels (Beach, 1971). Bulls or stallions that have been castrated show no interest in sexual activity. They also become more tame, illustrating a link between testosterone and aggression present in many species. Female animals similarly show an interest in sex, or not, depending on the presence of estrogen and/or progestin in their systems.

But among people, these generalizations are not so accurate, although neither are they completely off base (Katchadourian, 1989). Males who lose their testicles through injury or disease *before* puberty develop little sexual interest, but if this occurs *after* puberty, sexual desire and activity sometimes remain for years in the absence of testosterone. Men suffering from naturally occurring low levels of testosterone might experience little sexual desire, a condition that can be remedied by hormone injections. But such individuals, even without hormone treatments, can have erections and orgasms. Among adult males with no testosterone deficiency, levels of testosterone apparently have no relationship to their sexual interest or activity.

Some researchers have attempted to document an increase in sexual desire or activity by females around the time of ovulation—when conception is most likely because of hormonally controlled changes—but results are equivocal (Bancroft, 1983). The level of female hormones bears no clear relationship to the intensity of sexual desire or the frequency of sexual activity. Studies of sexual activity before and after menopause—when levels of certain female hormones drastically decrease—are similarly unclear in their implications (Masters & Johnson, 1970). On the average, women after menopause are less likely to have intercourse frequently, but this may well have something to do with their partners, or it might reflect the fact that the

---

[2] Indeed, it is an oversimplification to identify the sex hormones as I have just done. Testosterone is produced by the testes of the male, to be sure, but it is also produced in the adrenal glands of both men and women, as well as in the ovaries. Also, estrogen and progestin are not single hormones but rather classes of hormones, of which several exist in each case.

physical changes accompanying menopause sometimes make the physical act of intercourse less pleasant than it once was. In any case, there is great variation in women's sexual activity after menopause, with some reporting greater sexual activity and increased pleasure (Woodruff-Pak, 1988).

Studies of women with hormonal difficulties paint a similarly complex picture (Dennerstein, Burrows, Wood, & Hyman, 1980). Sometimes low levels of female hormone are associated with decreased sexual desire; sometimes low levels of *male* hormone—which occurs when a woman's adrenal glands do not function—are associated with decreased sexual desire. And sometimes not. Along these lines, the use of birth control pills, which work by influencing a woman's hormones, bears no clear relationship to sexual activity (e.g., Wielandt & Hansen, 1989).

What about the effects of hormones on *sexual orientation?* There has been a long search for hormonal influences in this area. According to some theorists, if a male has too little testosterone, he is inclined to be gay; if a female has too little estrogen or progestin—or too much testosterone—she is similarly inclined to be a lesbian (Money, 1980). The stereotypes of gay men as effeminate and lesbians as masculine reflect this kind of thinking. But the sum total of this research has been nil. Hormones in and of themselves do not dictate sexual orientation (Dancey, 1990).

The bottom line is that hormones are involved in human sexual activity, but they are but one ingredient, with psychological factors being another. Human sexuality is a symbolic activity as well as a physiological one, so you should not be surprised by the complex interplay of its determinants or the fact that research results are so frequently unclear.

Human Sexual Response

Masters and Johnson (1966) describe the human sexual response in terms of four stages that people pass through as they become sexually turned on (see Figure 11.5). A preliminary stage—initial *desire* for sexual activity—should be added to their list, because desire of course sets the stage for what ensues (Kaplan, 1974).

Following desire, the first stage of sexual response as described by Masters and Johnson is *excitement,* physiological arousal in response to internal or external stimuli. Human beings are sexually responsive to an incredible variety of stimuli. Touch is the most obvious source of arousal, particularly when one's erotic zones—the genitals, mouth, ears, buttocks, inner thighs, soles of the feet, and toes—are stimulated. But we also respond sexually to specific smells, tastes, and visual cues. Our own thoughts and images can also be arousing.

During sexual excitement, breathing quickens, as does heart rate. Muscular tension and blood flow to the genitals increase. A male's penis becomes erect. A female's clitoris swells, and the walls of her vagina moisten. Excitement is not simply physiological, though, because our thinking is affected as well. Attention turns to the sexual task at hand, and we become increasingly oblivious to other matters. When we are sexually excited, we attempt to exert some control over the process, pacing the rate of arousal as we wish. When our excitement increases, it typically does so unevenly, and it can be interrupted altogether. External events can be distracting. Internal annoyances in the form of anxiety or guilt can also derail the process.

The second stage of sexual response is called *plateau,* and here physiological arousal peaks. Hearts pound, breathing becomes heavy, and nostrils flare. Attention is so focused on arousal that all other matters fade into the corners of perception. The sense of pain is blunted. Allergies temporarily subside. Bleeding from cuts decreases. The genitals show their most obvious arousal during the plateau phase. A male's penis becomes most erect, and its color changes. His erection is now stable, and he can briefly turn his attention away from sexual activity without losing his erection. His testes increase in size and are lifted up within the scrotum. During this phase, a few drops of clear fluid are usually secreted from his penis. A female's vagina continues to swell; it lengthens and expands. Lubrication continues, although it actually slows down when plateau is reached. Her vagina darkens in color, reflecting its increasing congestion with blood. Also during this stage, the outer third of her vagina swells, narrowing the vaginal opening. Her external labia also swell. During excitement, her clitoris increases in size, but during the plateau phase, it decreases.

The third stage of the human sexual response is *orgasm,* which occurs when the sexually aroused person continues to be stimulated. During orgasm, the accumulated tension of all this sexual excitement is released. The person experiences orgasm as intense pleasure. Some have even described it as an altered state of consciousness. Though lasting but seconds, an orgasm is one of the most pleasurable experiences a human being can have.

Among males, the feelings of orgasm tend to accompany the physiological act of ejaculation, which starts as a sense that it is imminent and unstoppable, and then gives way to contractions of the penis and ejaculation.

Among females, orgasm begins with a feeling of momentary suspension. The tension and tingling in her clitoris reach a peak and spread through her vagina and her entire pelvic region. Then she experiences

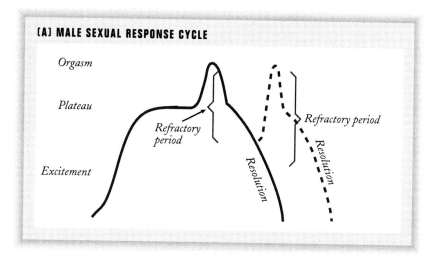

(A) MALE SEXUAL RESPONSE CYCLE

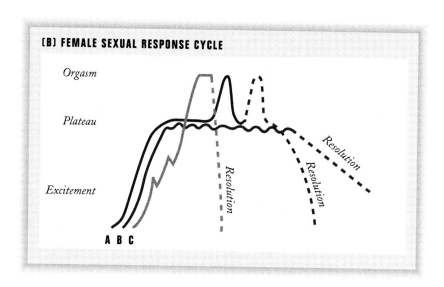

(B) FEMALE SEXUAL RESPONSE CYCLE

FIGURE 11.5

HUMAN SEXUAL RESPONSE   *Masters and Johnson described the sexual response cycles of males (a) and females (b) in terms of four stages: excitement, plateau, orgasm, and resolution.*
SOURCE: *Human Sexual Response* (P. 5), BY W. H. MASTERS AND V. E. JOHNSON, 1966, BOSTON: LITTLE, BROWN. USED WITH PERMISSION.

warmth spreading through her entire body, culminating in rhythmic sensations in her pelvis.

Male and female orgasm obviously "look" different to the outside observer, because females do not have such a noticeable event as ejaculation. However, men and women seem to experience orgasm in much the same way. In a study that bears on this matter, both sexes were asked to describe in writing their feelings during orgasm (Vance & Wagner, 1976). Their descriptions were edited to remove any reference to particular body parts that would identify the writers as males or females, and then these descriptions were shown to male and female readers. The readers were asked to decide, based on each written description, if the individual who had provided it was a male or a female. They could not make the distinction.

Still, I can point to several differences between the orgasms of males and females. Although both experience muscle contractions during orgasm, and although these occur at the same rate—every 0.8 seconds—they typically last longer among women (10 to 30 seconds) than among men (5 to 10 seconds). Also, women's orgasms are more variable in a subjective sense, whereas men's orgasms are more apt to follow the same script every time. The significance of the variability of women's orgasms is not clear (Darling, Davidson, & Conway-Welch, 1990).

The fourth stage of the human sexual response is *resolution.* It follows orgasm and is characterized by an immediate relaxation of muscular tension. Heart rate and respiration gradually return to normal. Males usually enter a refractory period, during which time another orgasm is impossible. Women are more capable of having a series of orgasms in rapid succession before entering the resolution stage. Women's greater capacity for multiple orgasms is one notable difference between men and women in terms of their sexual response (Darling, Davidson, & Jennings, 1991). It should be pointed out, though, that some men experience multiple orgasms, and some women do not (Katchadourian, 1989).

SEXUAL DYSFUNCTIONS

While we have no difficulty defining *sexual dysfunction* as a difficulty experienced during sexual response, there is more controversy in cataloging the different ways that sexual expression and experience can go awry (Schover et al., 1982). Masters and Johnson (1970) favor a description of problems in terms of the sexual couple, but DSM-IV instead "locates" sexual problems in individual men or women. Further, this diagnostic manual organizes problems temporally, identifying given difficulties in terms of when they occur in the course of sexual response.

Sexual desire disorders   The following problems are identified with the stage of initial excitement:

♦   **hypoactive sexual desire disorder:** persistent lack of sexual fantasies and lack of desire for sexual activity

♦   **sexual aversion disorder:** persistent aversion or avoidance of genital sexual contact with a partner

These disorders overlap, and they can co-occur in the same person (see Ponticas, 1992). The distinction is that in the case of hypoactive sexual desire disorder, the person simply experiences no desire, entertains no fantasies about sex, and initiates no sexual activity, whereas in the case of sexual aversion disorder, the person does have a response to the thought of sexual activity, and it is a negative one.

Rosen and Leiblum (1989) described James and Diane O'Neil, a couple in their mid-forties. They had been married for 4 years, during which time their sexual relationship had become increasingly distant. The major problem was that James had little interest in any form of intimate or sexual contact with his wife. Prior to their marriage, the O'Neils had enjoyed a passionate courtship, but matters changed dramatically following their honeymoon. They visited Ireland, where James had been born and raised. He was embarrassed by Diane on their trip to his native country, seeing her as a "crude Yankee" and wanting nothing to do with her sexually. In the ensuing years, James's lack of sexual desire resulted in numerous quarrels, and he withdrew into his work. The couple was considering a divorce at the time they *entered sex therapy, which proved to be successful when the therapist identified and helped the couple understand their cultural differences.*

Sexual desire disorders can be difficult to diagnose. The diagnostician must take into account situations in the person's life before making a diagnosis. What is clear is that all people some of the time experience little desire or even negative reactions to sexuality (Alexander, 1993; Shahar, Lederer, & Herz, 1991). It is also clear that some people all of the time have these reactions. The diagnostic problem is what to do with the more numerous cases in between. Estimates of the prevalence of these problems differ greatly; Figure 11.6 summarizes results from recent surveys. There is some agreement that disorders of desire are more common among women than men, which is not surprising. The consequences for sexual activity are different for women than for men, and greater caution on the part of women is certainly to be expected. Plus, women more so than men still bear the historical legacy linking sexuality with sin and public disgrace.

Sexual arousal disorders   The next set of disorders identified by DSM-IV involve a person's failure to attain or sustain sexual arousal, assuming that desire is present and that stimulation is appropriate. There

Everyone occasionally experiences periods of little sexual desire.

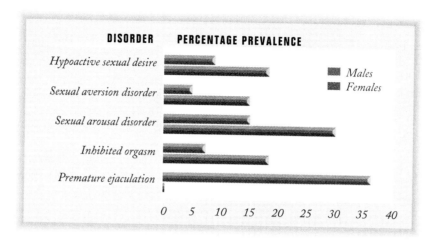

FIGURE 11.6

PREVALENCE OF SEXUAL DYSFUNCTIONS   *These estimates are medians based on surveys of American adults. Considerable variation exists from survey to survey, due in part to differences in how questions were posed. What is clear, however, is that many sexual dysfunctions are quite common among both males and females.*
SOURCES: DATA DERIVED FROM "FREQUENCY OF SEXUAL DYSFUNCTION IN 'NORMAL' COUPLES," BY E. FRANK, C. ANDERSON, AND D. RUBINSTEIN, 1978, *New England Journal of Medicine, 299*, PP. 111–115; "THE EPIDEMIOLOGY OF THE DSM-III PSYCHOSEXUAL DYSFUNCTIONS," BY S. G. NATHAN, 1986, *Journal of Sex and Marital Therapy, 12*, PP. 267–281; "INCIDENCE AND PREVALENCE OF THE SEXUAL DYSFUNCTIONS," BY I. P. SPECTOR AND M. P. CAREY, 1990, *Archives of Sexual Behavior, 19*, PP. 389–408.

are two sexual arousal disorders, one for females and the other for males:

+ **female sexual arousal disorder:** persistent failure to attain or maintain the lubrication-swelling response of sexual excitement until sexual activity is complete, and/or a persistent lack of a sense of excitement or pleasure during sexual activity

+ **male erectile disorder:** persistent failure to attain or maintain an adequate erection until completion of sexual activity

These diagnoses are also difficult to make. Most people, some of the time, experience a lack of arousal, so the diagnosis hinges on what "persistent" means.

Consider this example of male erectile disorder:

Mr. M. is a fast-talking, high-energy, 50-year-old, never-married sports car enthusiast. He has lived in life's fast lane, flying jet planes, gambling, drinking, and palling around with the guys. He also is very attached to his 85-year-old mother, whom he visits daily in a nursing home. Mr. M. says that his mother has never considered any woman he dated good enough for him to marry.

When he recently became engaged to a 48-year-old divorced mother of two, he developed impotence. He has not told his mother about the engagement and is concerned because his fiancée does not approve of his sports cars, thrice-weekly poker games, or male friends. Mr. M. says he's ready to settle down and give up his bachelor life. (Althof, 1989, p. 253)

The issue addressed in Mr. M.'s therapy was of course whether he really was ready to settle down. As he decreased the number of visits to his mother and expressed to his fiancée his desire to maintain his male friendships, his ability to have an erection returned.

Refer again to Figure 11.6, which includes estimates of the frequencies of sexual arousal disorders. Again, notice that women seem more likely than men to warrant this sort of diagnosis.

Orgasm disorders   DSM-IV specifies several difficulties that occur during the orgasm phase of sexual response—that is, when desire and arousal are present but something is amiss with orgasm:

+ **female orgasmic disorder** (or **inhibited female orgasm**): persistent delay or absence of orgasm by a woman following a normal sexual excitement phase

+ **male orgasmic disorder** (or **inhibited male orgasm**): persistent delay or absence of orgasm by a male following a normal sexual excitement phase

+ **premature ejaculation**: persistent ejaculation with minimal sexual stimulation and before the person wishes it

In each case, DSM-IV calls on the diagnostician to take into account such factors as the individual's age and sexual experience, as well as the sort of sexual stimulation he or she receives. Is it adequate in focus, intensity, and duration? An alternative definition of premature ejaculation, suggested by Masters and Johnson (1970), is that it is an orgasm by the male prior to the satisfaction of his partner. Once more, refer to Figure 11.6 for some estimates of the prevalence of orgasm disorders among contemporary Americans.

Heiman and Grafton-Becker (1989) described Carole, a 61-year-old woman who was not able to have an orgasm. She had been married for 34 years, but her husband had refused to be intimate with her for several decades. Carole had affairs with other men, and she became aroused during their lovemaking. However, in recent years, she never had an orgasm. She sought treatment for this problem. A critical event in her life occurred when she was forcibly raped at age 46. The rapist was arrested and subsequently sent to prison. However, he had recently been paroled and had raped another woman, also named Carole, whom he then murdered. Carole testified at the trial, which rekindled memories of the earlier assault against her. Her therapist urged her to explore the emotional associations she had to orgasm, and many of them filled her with fear. The therapist also began a version of Masters and Johnson's sex therapy program, and Carole began to have occasional orgasms. However, she terminated therapy when her current lover asked her to make a more serious commitment to him.

Sexual pain disorders   Finally, DSM-IV notes two other sexual dysfunctions. Both involve pain during sexual response, which obviously interferes with enjoyment, if not preventing it altogether. In **dyspareunia,** the person experiences recurrent pain in the genitals before, during, or after sexual activity. In **vaginismus,** a female experiences recurrent spasms of the vagina that make intercourse difficult or impossible.

For example, Mr. and Mrs. K. were a married couple in their mid-twenties (Leiblum, Pervin, & Campbell, *1989). Mrs. K. feared penetration because she experienced extreme spasms of her vagina. The couple had never had intercourse during their 4 years of marriage. However, they were otherwise sexually active, and Mrs. K. regularly experienced orgasms through manual and oral stimulation. She had been molested as a child, and she regarded her genitals as particularly fragile and vulnerable. Mr. K. in turn was greatly concerned about hurting her during intercourse. When they decided they wanted a child, they sought treatment. Sex therapy proved successful for them, and an important ingredient was instructing them about what happened during intercourse and what did not. They began to have intercourse regularly, and Mrs. K. became pregnant. Although Mr. K. was somewhat hesitant, they continued to have intercourse during her pregnancy, after she reassured him that no harm would come to her because of it.*

The sexual pain disorders appear more common among women than men. As many as 15% of all women experience occasional pain during sexual activity, and 2% to 3% experience it chronically (Kolodny, Masters, Johnson, & Biggs, 1979).

Causes of sexual dysfunctions   What causes sexual dysfunctions? The immediate answer is that something interferes with the process by which a person moves through the stages of sexual response. Anxiety is a frequently cited culprit, although we must be careful about glibly offering this as an explanation (Norton & Jehu, 1984). After all, the sexual response involves arousal, by definition, and mild tension enhances sexual desire, not interferes with it. We must delve deeper into the meaning of anxiety, and we can expect to find guilt, shame, confusion, ambivalence, and/or fears inculcated by cultural and religious values as well as specific socialization within the family (Kaplan, 1974). The person might be insecure about his or her own sexual appeal or performance, which creates and then exacerbates problems. It is unsurprising that different sexual dysfunctions frequently co-occur in the same individual (Donahey & Carroll, 1993; Segraves & Segraves, 1991). Previous sexual trauma may also contribute to sexual dysfunction.

A person who has had a heart attack might fear that sexual excitement will produce another one. An individual who has had surgery might feel disfigured and incomplete. Legal and illegal drugs can produce sexual problems (Brock & Lue, 1993). Many people with sexual dysfunctions also suffer from other psychological problems, from fear and anxiety disorders to depression to schizophrenia (Fagan, Schmidt, Wise, & Derogatis, 1988; Meisler & Carey, 1991; Safir & Almagor, 1991; Schreiner-Engel & Schiavi, 1986).

Furthermore, sexual dysfunction can result from problems in a relationship, such as inequalities, insecurities, and disagreements (Barbach, 1990; Zilbergeld, 1992).

Sometimes sexual dysfunctions are caused simply by ignorance. People may not know what to do to satisfy themselves or their sexual partners. Or the knowledge they possess fails to get translated into action. For this reason, contemporary sex therapy stresses education on the one hand and communication between partners on the other.

Sexual dysfunctions range from being highly general to showing situational specificity—occurring with one sexual partner but not another, or during masturbation but not intercourse, or vice versa.

For example, Arthur T. was a 55-year-old chief executive officer in a large firm whose marriage ended following his prolonged affair with another woman (Rosen & Leiblum, 1989). Throughout his marriage, Mr. T. had never experienced sexual desire for his wife, and they rarely had intercourse. With other women, he experienced strong desire, and he enjoyed intercourse with them. Mr. T.'s sexual desire disorder can be described as situational because it only occurred with his wife.

Sexual dysfunctions also vary in terms of being present throughout the individual's sexual life (in which case they are termed *lifelong*), or whether they developed after a period of satisfactory sexual response (in which case they are called *acquired*). The case of Carole, described earlier, exemplifies an acquired sexual dysfunction.

Whatever their initial cause, sexual dysfunctions can be a vicious circle. The individual experiences less than satisfactory sexual activity on one occasion and then worries that it might happen again. If the worry is sufficiently distracting, continued problems are almost guaranteed. Sexual response becomes an observed performance as the person watches himself or herself behave, rather than simply behaving. This scrutiny is apt to be inhibiting.

Kaplan (1974) described a married couple whose deteriorating sexual relationship exemplifies this vicious circle. When first married, their sexual relationship was satisfactory, but then the wife happened to complain that intercourse sometimes did not last long enough for her to have an orgasm. The husband apparently harbored a great deal of unacknowledged ambivalence about sex, and once his performance had been criticized, he became progressively less interested. She then became increasingly dissatisfied. Eventually, he was unable to achieve

an erection at all. Both the wife and the husband then began to feel guilty about acting selfishly, and their marriage as a whole suffered.

The different models of abnormality have each been applied to sexual dysfunctions in the ways that you would expect. Biomedical approaches focus on their physiological aspects. One biomedical treatment for male erectile disorder is a *penile implant*, a plastic prosthesis inserted into the penis to make it erect (e.g., Tiefer, Pedersen, & Melman, 1988). Another treatment is an external *vacuum device* that creates an erection via suction (e.g., van Thillo & Delaere, 1992). Yet another biomedical treatment consists of *drugs* that facilitate erections (e.g., Morley, 1993). These strategies prove satisfactory for a number of men and their sexual partners, though not always (Montorsi, Guazzoni, Bergamaschi, & Rigatti, 1993).

Psychodynamic theorists look for deep-seated conflicts that might be at the base of problems (Mehler, 1992). The cognitive-behavioral model predictably looks at sexual dysfunctions in terms of bad habits produced by classical conditioning and/or irrational thoughts that create and maintain anxiety. The family systems model locates sexual problems in the context of the relationship in which they occur, stressing that satisfactory sexual expression is not likely to happen when the relationship is otherwise problematic. Those of a more sociocultural persuasion trace sexual dysfunctions to larger societal attitudes that aggrandize sexual activity as well as snicker about it. The media all too infrequently link sexuality to love and tenderness, rarely suggesting that sexuality might involve something other than multiple orgasms, night and day, in any and all circumstances. The media can also be blamed for associating sexuality with violence and exploitation. Granted these stereotypes, we are understandably confused about sexuality and its expression.

SEX THERAPY

Some suggest that there are no sexual problems per se, that these are simply symptoms of other difficulties. Others regard sexual dysfunctions as circumscribed. Doubtlessly, each perspective is right some of the time (Catalan, Hawton, & Day, 1990). Sex therapists have had success in a number of cases treating sexual dysfunctions in their own right. This need not mean that they developed as discrete problems. Given the importance of sexuality, it follows that people's more general problems with anxiety or depression, fed by poor self-esteem, could only be helped if their sexual life improved.

Several approaches to sex therapy exist, including insight-oriented approaches (e.g., Ravart & Cote, 1992) and those based on the family systems model (e.g., Leiblum & Rosen, 1991). The most widely used approach to sex therapy today is that developed by Masters and Johnson (1970), which is the focus here. Its essential aspects are as follows (Halvorsen & Metz, 1992b):

1. Sexual dysfunctions are circumscribed problems. In other words, treatment focuses on sexual problems per se, not on broader, deeper, or hidden matters.

2. Emphasis is on the treatment of couples, because both people are affected by a sexual dysfunction. The most effective solution lies in the joint efforts of the involved individuals.

3. The sex therapy program is intensive yet also time-limited. It takes place daily over a period of several weeks. Individuals are given "homework" assignments to complete outside the therapy session, and completion of these is critical to the eventual success.

4. Couples are educated about the basic workings of their bodies. They are given material to read as well as exercises to carry out that enhance their own recognition of feelings and sensations.

5. The couple is encouraged to communicate with one another about what they want and what they do not want. Perhaps for the first time in their sexual relationship, partners tell one another what they find pleasurable.

Within the context of these general guidelines, Masters and Johnson instruct the couple to carry out specific exercises, which vary depending on the specific sexual dysfunction.

A technique with wide applicability is **sensate focus,** which encourages the couple to stop paying attention to worries and stress—often about sexual performance—and instead focus on their own sensual pleasure. Individuals are told to stroke and touch one another in ways that are pleasurable. They are told to focus on the sensation of touching another person and the enjoyment they feel in so doing. They are reminded that sexual intercourse is not the goal of this sort of behavior; their own pleasure is.

Here is a representative exercise using sensate focus:

> *I'd like you both to get ready for bed—to take your clothes off, shower, and relax. I want you [the woman] to lie on*

Virginia Johnson and William Masters pioneered the scientific study of human sexual response and developed the most widely used approach to sex therapy.

> *your belly. Then you [the man] caress her back as gently and sensitively as you can. Move your hands very slowly. . . . Concentrate only on how it feels to touch her body and skin.*
>
> *In the meantime, I want you [the woman] to focus your attention on the sensations you feel when he caresses you. Try not to let your mind wander. Don't think about anything else, don't worry about whether he's getting tired, or whether he is enjoying it—or anything. Be "selfish" and just concentrate on your sensations; let yourself feel everything.   (Kaplan, 1974, p. 209)*

Masters and Johnson advise couples *not* to attempt intercourse while practicing sensate focus, under the assumption that attempted intercourse will heighten anxiety and thus will work at cross-purposes. Once the notion of pleasure has been added to the couple's sexual repertoire, matters can take their own course.

How successful is the Masters and Johnson approach to sex therapy? They cite extremely high rates of improvement, with 80% to 90% of the couples they treat reporting successful results (cf. Hawton, Catalan, & Fagg, 1991, 1992). Some critics who have scrutinized the therapy outcome studies suspect these figures are too high, reflecting a selection bias into therapy of people whose sexual dysfunctions are highly circumscribed (Cole, 1985). Along these lines, some individuals—for various reasons—are unwilling to begin or complete sex therapy (see Hawton, Catalan, & Fagg, 1992; Huws, 1992; Simpson & Ramberg, 1992). It is also not clear from their reports just how Masters and Johnson define successful treatment. Little is known about the recurrence of sexual dysfunctions following sex therapy (McCarthy, 1993). As usually practiced, it can be criticized as well for neglecting cultural differences in how individuals regard sexuality (Lavee, 1991) and larger issues in the relationship of the sexually interacting couple (Metz & Dwyer, 1993).

However, these criticisms do not overshadow the value of sex therapy. All agree that the Masters and Johnson approach is a far improvement over those of a previous generation of therapists, who tried to treat sexual dysfunctions by talking to clients rather than instructing couples in how to go about solving their problems (Halvorsen & Metz, 1992b; Marks, 1981).

PARAPHILIAS

My discussion of sexual response was deliberately general, because I did not specify just what it was people find sexually exciting. To speak about a *paraphilia*—persistent sexual activity with an inappropriate individual or in an inappropriate fashion—I have to introduce terminology concerning such details. Our **sexual object** is the person or thing we find sexually arousing. Our **sexual aim** is what we wish to do with the sexual object. Taken together, sexual object and sexual aim are referred to as **sexual orientation.**

Sexual orientation is often described in quite broad terms. We speak of individuals as being heterosexual or homosexual, for example, but virtually no one's sexual orientation is accurately described by these terms (Stoller, 1985). You can be sexually turned on by men rather than women, but some men are nonetheless more appealing than others, because of their appearance, or age, or ethnicity, or status, or habits, or any of a million other features that render sexual orientation more than a simple either-or categorization. A paraphilia seems highly specific, but no more so than many sexual orientations become when we examine them closely.

DSM-IV proposes that a paraphilia is a recurrent pattern of becoming sexually aroused by one of the following:

✦ nonhuman objects

✦ suffering or humiliation of oneself or another person

✦ children or nonconsenting individuals

Rather than enumerating the possible examples of a paraphilia in order to define it, Money (1984, p. 165) suggests that it is simply a recurrent sexual response to "an unusual or unacceptable stimulus." This makes the role of social judgment in identifying a paraphilia quite clear, because somebody must decide what is unusual or unacceptable.

The vast majority of those with paraphilias are men. This does not mean that they are never described in women, because such cases indeed exist (e.g., Foerster, Foerster, & Roth, 1976; Grob, 1985; Raphling, 1989). Still, more than 95% occur among men.

An individual with a paraphilia shows great consistency in his interest. At the same time, people with one paraphilia often have others (Abel & Osborn, 1992; Bradford, Boulet, & Pawlak, 1992; Fedora et al., 1992). These individuals may also have other problems (Fagan et al., 1991). In particular, they tend to be socially estranged. This is obvious, given that a paraphilia may draw a person away from satisfying relationships with others. Perhaps half of the men with paraphilias are married, and their sexual relationships with their wives, unless they happen to be collaborators in the paraphilias, usually suffer.

Among the paraphilias is exhibitionism: displaying one's genitals to unwilling strangers.

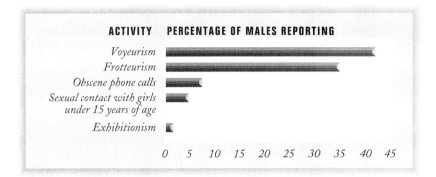

FIGURE 11.7

PREVALENCE OF PARAPHILIAC
ACTIVITY   *A survey of male
college students suggests that
paraphiliac acts are quite common.*
SOURCE: DATA DERIVED FROM
"PATTERNS OF SEXUAL AROUSAL AND
HISTORY IN A 'NORMAL' SAMPLE OF
YOUNG MEN," BY T. L. TEMPLEMAN
AND R. D. STINNETT, 1991, *Archives of
Sexual Behavior, 20,* PP. 137–150.

Individuals with paraphilias are often characterized as immature (Cohen, Seghorn, & Calmas, 1969).
Some, notably those who molest children, are rather
rigid and prudish in their other sexual activities (Overholser & Beck, 1986). Interestingly, sexual dysfunctions can be common among those with paraphilias
(Moser, 1992; Trojan, 1991). It is difficult to determine if they are inherently linked to having a paraphilia
or if they stem from the stigma associated with such
a sexual interest.

EPIDEMIOLOGY

It is perhaps even more difficult to estimate the prevalence of paraphilias. Much of what we know about
them comes from people who have been arrested for
a crime that involves their particular sexual interest.
In these cases, what we have are paraphiliac acts, which
may or may not conform to the definition of a paraphilia. DSM-IV distinguishes between the occasional
sexual act that is unusual and the persistent preference
for such acts (see Figure 11.7).

It is not even clear how to go about counting the
number of people who have one paraphilia or another.
One strategy, clever but not foolproof, is to estimate
the popularity of a given sexual activity from the volume of the pornography business devoted to it. If we
wish to know the popularity of sex with animals versus
sex with amputees, for example, we would visit an
"adult" bookstore and see what is for sale (e.g., Dietz
& Evans, 1982; Lebegue, 1985). This strategy, at best,
only tells us the relative prevalence of these particular
interests, not their overall rates of occurrence.

Many discussions of paraphilia center on such
illegal activities as these:

✦ *pedophilia:* sexual activity with a prepubescent
child

✦ *voyeurism:* sexual pleasure from looking at unsus-
pecting others who are disrobing, nude, or engaged in sexual activity

✦ *exhibitionism:* sexual pleasure from displaying
one's genitals to unwilling strangers

✦ *frotteurism:* sexual pleasure from rubbing up
against and/or touching nonconsenting individuals

✦ *zoophilia:* sexual activity with an animal

✦ *necrophilia:* sexual activity with a corpse

*For example, entertainer Paul Reubens (a.k.a. Pee-wee
Herman) came to the public's attention June 26, 1991,
when he was arrested in Florida for indecent exposure
(Wilkinson, 1991). Undercover police officers at the
South Trail XXX, a pornographic theater, reported that
Reubens took his penis out of his pants and stroked it
while watching a film. It is unclear whether this was*

*In 1991, actor Paul Reubens (a.k.a. Pee-wee Herman) was
arrested for indecent exposure in an "adult" theater. The
arrest and ensuing publicity in effect ended his career.*

a common activity on Reubens's part, but as of this writing his career as an actor has essentially ended because of this arrest.

A more notorious example of illegal sexual activities is provided by serial killer Jeffrey Dahmer, convicted in 1992 of the murders of fifteen young men in Milwaukee (e.g., Toufexis, 1992). Dahmer would pick up his victims, ostensibly for a consensual sexual encounter, and then drug them. While they were unconscious but still alive, he would attempt to perform lobotomies on them, drilling holes in their head in order to create mindless companions under his complete control. When his experiments failed, he would kill them. He had sex with their corpses and sometimes kept parts of their bodies. When they arrested him, police officers found a severed head in his refrigerator as well as a heart Dahmer planned to eat later. He had also preserved the penis of one of his victims in formaldehyde. In 1994, Dahmer was killed by a fellow prisoner.

Other paraphilias are not illegal in their own right but still draw attention because they involve injury to self or others:

♦ *sexual sadism:* sexual pleasure from inflicting pain or humiliation on another

♦ *sexual masochism:* sexual pleasure from being hurt or humiliated by another

Or consider *transvestism*, which refers to an individual deriving sexual pleasure from dressing and acting like a member of the opposite sex. This is illegal in some parts of the country but not others. Regardless, the transvestite might find himself the subject of physical attacks by others who are affronted by what he is doing.

And then there are *fetishes*, which refer to sexual pleasure from activity with nonliving objects, such as shoes or underwear. A fetish in and of itself is not illegal, but it can lead a person into trouble if he, for example, steals the objects that turn him on.

Serial killer Jeffrey Dahmer reportedly had sex with the corpses of some of his victims, an example of necrophilia, one of the more unusual paraphilias.

A transvestite like this man, "Billy Boy," derives sexual pleasure from dressing and acting like a member of the opposite sex.

A "new" sexual activity attracting interest involves hanging oneself or otherwise depriving oneself of oxygen while masturbating: *asphyxiophilia* (Gowitt & Hanzlick, 1992; Money, Hingsburger, & Wainwright, 1991). Presumably, asphyxiation enhances orgasm; it also proves fatal in some cases.

If I continue to enumerate different paraphilias, it will begin to look like a laundry list of Latin words (Money, 1984). Instead, I turn to how psychologists have explained paraphilias.

CONCEPTIONS OF PARAPHILIAS

The conceptualization of unusual sexual orientations across time reflects the general historical trends in the explanation of abnormality. Until the 20th century, when the term *paraphilia* was introduced by sexologists, these sorts of sexual practices were usually called *perversions* (Money & Lamacz, 1989). To call somebody a pervert, even today, is to capture its historical connotations of immorality. A pervert was considered a heretic and perhaps even a witch.

The legal system on the whole simply borrowed religious judgments about right and wrong with respect to sexuality. The person who in 17th-century colonial America was guilty of sodomy, adultery, zoophilia, and/or rape was subject to the death penalty. Under "sodomy" were classified such practices as oral sex, anal sex, and homosexual activity. These were often referred to as crimes against nature—meaning a violation of church teachings that the exclusive purpose of sexual activity is to procreate. The only sexual activity that was *not* a perversion was male-female genital intercourse. The couple in question was to be married, and the male was to be in the superior position during intercourse.

If nothing else, this view of sexuality kept explanations simple. Heterosexual intercourse within marriage was in accord with God's plan, and thus it did not need an explanation. Anything else was an abomination, readily explained as a moral lapse—as a sin or a crime or both.

Biomedical explanations and treatments   In the 1800s, perversion was rescued, as it were, from moral and legal realms by physicians, who did not change its definition but provided a new rationale for why it was bad: perversion led to *degeneracy* (Chamberlin & Gilman, 1985). It was a disease that sapped the vitality of the mind and body. What was the mechanism by which this happened? Via the loss of semen, presumably the most valued of all the bodily fluids (Tissot, 1832). The perversions used up semen for no good purpose, as did masturbation, and thus they were to

be avoided. This account is very male-centered, because only men have semen to use or misuse. However, this theory by implication also applied to women, dismissing them as weak and inferior to men, physically and mentally, because they have no semen at all (Money, 1985).

To this day, biomedical theorists search for biological accounts of sexual orientation in general and the paraphilias in particular. One interesting twist uses the theory of evolution as an explanation. Theorists argue that paraphilias can be advantageous among a population of individuals with finite resources (e.g., Weinrich, 1987). Paraphilias benefit the group as a whole because some of its members channel their sexual energy into outlets that do not produce children. Children who are born receive a greater share of resources, and eventually everyone triumphs. By this view, then, paraphilias should be heritable, which is not as paradoxical as it sounds if we remember that modern evolutionary theory draws our attention to the survival not of individuals but genes.

Unusual sexual orientations run through families (Gaffney, Lurie, & Berlin, 1984), but this of course does not prove that these orientations are heritable. We would be most convinced by twin and adoption studies that yielded heritability estimates, but these have not been conducted.

Even if paraphilias are heritable, a full biomedical explanation would require that we specify the mechanism. Here researchers have been unsuccessful in finding physiological differences between those with "normal" versus "abnormal" sexual orientations. Brain structure and function have been examined, as have hormone levels, temperament, physique, and the like, all with little to show for the effort.

A biological theory still popular suggests that men with paraphilias are *oversexed*. Their sex drive is too high, presumably because they have too much testosterone. The argument then follows that they are chronically aroused and hence their sexual activity is readily and indiscriminately attached to all manner of objects and aims, some of which are objectionable.

Counting against this theory is that those with a paraphilia often have sexual dysfunctions (Trojan, 1991). There also is no good evidence that men with paraphilias have unusually high levels of testosterone (Buhrich, Theile, Yaw, & Crawford, 1979). Nonetheless, the idea that a paraphilia represents hypersexuality has given rise to interventions that attempt to reduce the sex drive. Usually this is undertaken by the authorities when the person's sexual activities endanger others, as in the case of child abuse or rape. The perpetrator might be castrated or have surgery to remove part of his hypothalamus (Schmidt & Schorsch, 1981). As you remember from Chapter 6, the hypothalamus is involved in the regulation of drives, including the sexual drive.

The consequences of these procedures have been studied in Europe, where they have occasionally been undertaken for convicted rapists and child molesters (Rieber & Sigusch, 1979). On the whole, sex drive and sexual activity are reduced, but by no means is this a universal effect (Heim, 1981).

A less irreversible strategy embodying the same assumption is the use of drugs that lower the sex drive (Money, 1970, 1987). Depo-Provera is the trade name of the best known of these drugs, called **antiandrogens.** These drugs affect the pituitary gland so that the secretion of male sex hormones is inhibited. Depo-Provera is injected into a man's muscles once or twice per week, which is sufficient for it to reduce the level of testosterone in his body and thus his sexual interest, arousal, and activity (Menghini & Ernst, 1991). If and when the drugs are curtailed, his sexual interest and activity return.

Robert was a 22-year-old janitor with a history of chronic exhibitionism, dating to age 11 (Wincze, 1989). At that age, he learned that exposing his genitals was a quick means of achieving sexual satisfaction without encumbering himself with a relationship that he did not feel capable of achieving. He exposed himself to attractive women about four times a day. Although he was repeatedly arrested, Robert persisted in his exhibitionism. He also masturbated frequently, by his report as often as fifteen times per day. He described himself as unattractive, unhandy, and unathletic.

Exhibitionism provided not only a source of sexual gratification to Robert but also a way to reduce the feelings of anxiety he frequently experienced. Faced with a jail term, he consented to be administered Depo-Provera. For the first time in a decade, Robert experienced relief from his sexual urges. However, he then went to trial, was found guilty, and was incarcerated for 8 months. He was not allowed to continue Depo-Provera in prison, and immediately upon release, he exposed himself again and was arrested yet again. This time he was allowed to resume the medication, and he took it over a number of years, during which time he did not once expose himself. Robert was an unusually successful case, perhaps because he was highly compliant and viewed himself as having a problem that needed help.

None of these procedures—castration, surgery, or antiandrogens—is specific in its effects to paraphiliac activity. Paraphiliac activity is reduced because all sexual activity is reduced (Berlin & Meinecke, 1981).

These strategies, whatever their success, raise ethical questions (Melella, Travin, & Cullen, 1989). Castration and brain surgery are irreversible, and seem to belong in the cruel and unusual punishment category that most of us profess to abhor. The effects of Depo-Provera are reversible, but there are potentially serious side effects such as weight gain and hypertension. While many of us may not be ethically bothered when aggressive steps are taken against individuals who themselves victimize others, the fear remains that these interventions might someday be used to decrease the sexual interest and activity of those whose sexual orientations are merely eccentric.

Psychodynamic explanations and treatments   As you would expect from a perspective that assigns great importance to sexuality, the psychodynamic approach has much to say about paraphilias (Sandler, 1989). Remember that this perspective sees all people as inherently sexual. At birth, children possess a highly generalized sexuality termed **polymorphous perversity:** They can and do derive sexual gratification through stimulation of a variety of body parts. Therefore, psychodynamic explanations do not have to account for sexual interest in the first place, or even for an attachment to unusual objects or situations. All they need to account for is why an unusual sexual orientation is to be found to the exclusion of a more conventional one.

Freud saw the process of psychosexual development, if allowed to run a "normal" course, as culminating in a heterosexual orientation with genital intercourse as the preferred and exclusive mode of sexual activity. If a person successfully passed through the psychosexual stages, this eventuality was guaranteed. If, however, there was a disruption along the way, he might develop an alternative sexual orientation.

According to Freud, the paraphilias represented severe disruptions in psychosexual development (see Limentani, 1991). He thought they resulted from events during the Oedipal stage and the child's discovery that his mother did not have a penis. (Freud posited a belief among young children, or at least boys, that everyone had a penis, Mom included.) Although all little boys presumably make this discovery, it is more shocking to some than to others, Freud hypothesized, and it leads them to fear that they may lose their own penises, castrated at the hands of vengeful fathers who do not approve of the sexual desires they harbor toward their mothers.

Depending on the paraphilia in question, the resulting sexual orientation denies the possibility of castration. For example, a boy might become a transvestite because in so doing he assures himself, unconsciously, that mother really does have a penis, because under his dress he too possesses one. And if his mother has a penis, then there is no reason to fear that he will ever be castrated.

This formulation requires that specific childhood events occur for particular paraphilias to develop, but research fails to bear out this prediction (e.g., Condron & Nutter, 1988; Hillbrand, Foster, & Hirt, 1990). Among exhibitionists, for example, or sadists, we cannot find the particular emotional conflicts and stresses that psychodynamic explanations propose. People with paraphilias may well have their share of emotional problems as adults, but these might be a consequence of having a stigmatized sexual orientation. Psychodynamic treatment of the paraphilias tries to bring insight to the paraphiliac by revealing unconscious memories and conflicts from long ago that have given rise to unusual sexual orientation. However, such insight-oriented therapy rarely works.

The waning of traditional approaches   As the 20th century unfolded, there was a growing recognition that biomedical and psychodynamic perspectives by themselves were incomplete. Research like Kinsey's surveys showed that many sexual practices considered deviant were in fact widespread in even the most staid communities. Furthermore, surveys showed that the boundaries around most sexual orientations were quite indefinite. Among American males, for example, Kinsey, Pomeroy, and Martin (1948) found that about 65% were exclusively heterosexual, whereas about 5% of males were exclusively gay. But what about the 30% who fell into neither extreme category? Thousands of years of Western tradition held that individuals were either heterosexuals or perverts, which does not allow for the middle ground that many people occupy.

Along these same lines, cross-cultural studies documented an incredible variety of sexual practices around the world (see Focus on Sexuality among Sambian Males). Every culture has its own ideas about normal and abnormal sexuality, and these codes often vary dramatically. We must think about sexual orientation not simply as a moral or biological matter, but additionally—and importantly—as dictated by learning and culture.

Behavioral explanations and treatments   In keeping with the growing popularity of behaviorism, theories were proposed that all sexual orientations, including paraphilias, were determined by conditioning (e.g., Marks, 1972; Storms, 1981). Presumably, people can learn to associate sexual arousal with all manner of stimuli. The sexual orientation that we develop reflects the idiosyncrasies of our sexual history, particularly around the time of puberty, when sexual impulses become particularly strong and salient, and

orgasm begins to be regularly experienced. If we first experience orgasm in regard to members of our own sex who have green eyes, then such individuals become our sexual object. If we first experience orgasm in the context of a fight or argument, then it becomes our sexual aim to experience arousal in response to pain or anger. These initial learning experiences are elaborated through fantasy and strengthened through masturbation.

The problem with these simple theories of sexual orientation is that they are too simple. Of course our experiences with sexual arousal and orgasm influence our subsequent sexual activity. And of course early experiences are often more important than later ones, as Freud himself proposed. But there are some critical gaps in the conditioning account of sexual orientation.

For starters, many people develop much of their sexual orientation prior to actual sexual experience culminating in orgasm. It seems as if our sexual orientation leads us into certain experiences rather than others, so that these experiences strengthen our orientation rather than creating it out of thin air. The counter to this argument is that conditioning can occur vicariously, through the process of modeling. But stop and judge whether this is likely (cf. Gottman, 1989). At least in the contemporary United States, few of us as children or adolescents ever observe sexual activity by others that culminates in orgasm. So just what is modeled for us? The media are filled with provocative scenes and messages, to be sure, but do these create sexual orientations or simply direct and strengthen them?

There are additional problems with behavioral accounts. Contrary to the idea that conditioning is all that matters in creating sexual orientations, people have certain sexual experiences that do not result in a sexual orientation. Furthermore, sexual orientations, once established, prove highly resistant to change; new ones typically do not develop. If they were simply a matter of conditioning, we would observe extinction in some cases and counterconditioning in others.

Behavior therapists have reported some success in changing paraphiliac orientations, but it is far from a simple procedure (Johnston, Hudson, & Marshall, 1992). The undesirable sexual response, such as arousal to prepubescent children, must be removed. This can be done by pairing pictures of young children with aversive stimuli, either electric shock or mental images of disapproval from friends and family members. Then a desirable response must be created, say by pairing pictures of adults with sexual pleasure (Schwartz & Masters, 1983).

How successful are these procedures? There is disagreement about how to interpret the research literature (see Blair & Langon, 1971). Most investigations

FOCUS ON

Sexuality among

Sambian Males

SEVERAL TIMES IN THIS chapter, I mentioned the importance of cross-cultural studies of sexuality. A striking example is an anthropological investigation by Stoller and Herdt (1985). They described the sexual practices of the Sambia people, an isolated tribe in the Eastern Highlands region of Papua New Guinea. Virtually all adult men among the Sambia can be described as heterosexual, desiring sexual activity—and specifically genital intercourse—only with adult women. But their route to this sexual orientation is quite different from what those of us in the United States might expect.

Until the age of about 7, Sambian boys spend most of their time with their mothers and other female members of the tribe. The men of the tribe have little to do with their sons. But then the boys are taken from their mothers by the men to begin the process that will transform them into adult males—warriors, husbands, and fathers. The men explain the secret of being a male among the Sambia: Each boy must drink as much semen as possible, because semen defines a male. The boys are told that males do not produce semen themselves, and so they must obtain it from other males, who have taken it from a preceding generation.

The young boys are told to perform fellatio on the cohort of adolescent males, sucking their penises and swallowing the ejaculated semen. This goes on for several years, until the younger boys become adolescents themselves and take on the associated role. At this point, they cease performing fellatio themselves; not to refrain would be seen as grievously wrong, because it would mean stealing semen that by right was to be given to the younger generation. According to Stoller and Herdt (1985), the younger boys do not report that performing fellatio on another male is arousing. However, having fellatio performed on oneself is acknowledged as highly pleasurable, despite the fact that it depletes one of semen. During this entire period, the young males have nothing to do with women.

But when the adolescent male ends his teenage years, he takes a wife. His behavior now becomes heterosexual. He no longer participates in oral sex with other males. Indeed, homosexuality is viewed with great scorn among the Sambia, so much so that the practice is almost unknown among them.

According to the account of sexual orientation championed by conditioning theorists, none of this is possible.

> From the start of their erotic lives and for the years of their peak orgasmic capacity, these young men are propelled into intense, obligatory, praiseworthy, powerfully gratifying homoerotism. At the same time as males are positively reinforced, females are negatively reinforced. . . . Yet the youths, when marriage approaches, start to create, without deprogramming, powerfully erotic heterosexual daydreams. And they will desire women the rest of their lives, without ever forgetting the homoerotic joys. . . . Probably, if Sambia society allowed adult married men to be homoerotic, some, as in our society, would be bisexual. But most would not; they love their lust for women. And it is that lust—with its depth and breadth—that the behavioristic account says should not be there. (Stoller & Herdt, 1985, p. 401)

The study does not tell us what creates the sexual orientation of adult Sambia men. But it does make clear that conditioning is inadequate as an explanation. If nothing else, our understanding of sexual orientation must start by placing the individual in his or her cultural context.

The development of sexual orientation among Sambian males challenges Western conditioning theories.

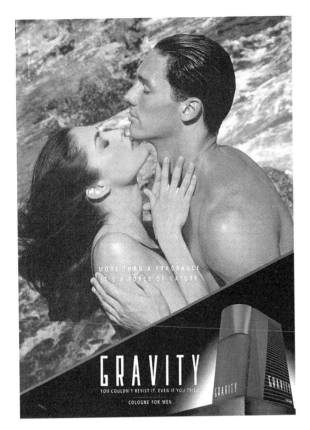

The media are filled with sexually provocative scenes and messages that influence our conceptions of sexuality and our sexual behavior.

are case studies, which means that we cannot generalize from them (e.g., McNally & Lukach, 1991; Moergen, Merkel, & Brown, 1990). Clients have frequently been convicted criminals whose treatment has been court-ordered. Such individuals have a great incentive to see treatment through to its intended conclusion, or at least to report that they have. My sense is that paraphiliac orientations can be changed with behavior therapy for some individuals but most readily in those cases where the rudiments of an "acceptable" orientation are already in place (cf. Schwartz & Masters, 1984).

For example, Mr. D. was a 31-year-old engineer with a history of exhibitionism dating to age 20 (Daitzman & Cox, 1980). He exposed himself to women and masturbated to orgasm about every 6 months, usually when he was experiencing stress at work. He had been arrested four times. His marriage was in jeopardy, although Mr. D. reported that he and his wife had a satisfying sexual relationship. He sought treatment because of the legal and personal difficulties his periodic exhibitionism created.

*He was treated with an **aversive conditioning** procedure. With his therapist, he created a hierarchy of ten mental images in increasing order of their association with exhibitionism. He was asked to imagine these scenes and envision vomiting. Valeric acid, a foul-smelling organic chemical, was placed under his nose during these sessions. Also part of therapy was the creation of a hierarchy of "appropriate" sexual images involving his wife, which were paired with relaxation.*

Both Mr. D. and his wife participated willingly in his treatment, and she helped him practice the scenes at home. Mr. D. was followed for 18 months after the end of formal treatment, during which time he experienced no impulses to exhibit himself. His relationship with his wife greatly improved, and their marriage was preserved. Several years later, he exposed himself again after drinking heavily at a party. Mr. D. resumed treatment.

Prepared learning   Sexual orientations are not infinite. They tend to be attached to a rather narrow range of people, things, and situations. Simple behavioral accounts cannot explain this selectivity. Suppose a boy has a satisfying sexual encounter with a girl in the back seat of a car. He later seeks out this girl or others like her, or he focuses on the perfume she wore or her particular style of undergarments. But he does not develop an orientation to the road atlas that was on the seat, or to the empty soda cans that were on the floor. Sexual orientation does not extend to such things.

The same point was made in Chapter 7 about the selectivity of phobias on the one hand and obsessive-compulsive disorders on the other. Theorists have explained these in terms of *prepared learning,* suggesting that people are "prepared" by their evolutionary history to attach fear to certain stimuli more than to others. A similar argument can be made about sexual orientation, that the sorts of conditioning that take place during sexual encounters show selectivity as well. We are "prepared" to have certain sexual orientations rather than others. At the same time, within the ranges provided by this preparedness, there is great variety.

Prepared learning is not simple conditioning, because it brings our evolutionary history into the picture (Epstein, 1975). An account of sexual orientation in terms of preparedness makes most sense when we are talking about rather simple stimuli. Among people's fetishes, two types predominate: the *tactile* ("touchy-feely") ones, like leather, lace, and rubber items, which have specific textures reminiscent of human skin or hair; and the *olfactory-gustatory* ("smelly-tasty") ones, like perfume, sweaty underwear, urine, or feces. We can readily identify these as involving biologically potent stimuli. The weakness of this account is that mechanisms are not specified, and it makes no room for the larger cultural context that clearly shapes sexual orientation.

Conclusions

Where does this leave us? Paraphilias are problems difficult to define, occurring among an unknown number of individuals, for poorly understood reasons, and proving resistant to available strategies for change. In a way, this set of conclusions is not surprising. If nothing else, we know that paraphilias represent one form of sexual orientation, and we do not have a theory that satisfactorily accounts for the development and change of sexual orientation per se, much less for its specific instances. The best we can say is that sexual orientation develops from an interplay among biological, psychological, and cultural factors (Wise, 1985), which leads us to the biopsychosocial model. But this integrative model remains simply a slogan until its details are filled in, and theorists have just begun to do this with regard to the development of sexual orientation.

John Money (1986, 1988) has made an intriguing start along these lines, drawing a parallel between the development of sexual orientation and the development of language. After centuries of wrangling about the nature-nurture issue as it applies to language, most linguists today accept that language results from a biological readiness to acquire a language by abstracting its grammatical principles from the specific examples to which a child is exposed. Money suggests that everyone is similarly predisposed to have a sexual orientation, yet it is shaped by specific experiences. This is not a conditioning account of sexuality, because a sexual orientation is more than just conditioned associations between stimuli and responses. Rather, Money posits the sexual equivalent of the grammar of a language in what he calls a **lovemap,** which depicts "the idealized lover, the idealized love affair, and the idealized program of . . . activity with that lover" (Money & Lamacz, 1989, p. 43).

The important point in this analogy is that we do not directly learn grammar by being exposed to sentences; rather, we infer it from the language we hear, then use this grammar to create and comprehend future sentences, any number of which will be unique to our experience. Most of us cannot articulate the rules of grammar we use so effortlessly in understanding and producing language. Relatedly, the lovemap is the grammar for our subsequent sexual activity. We abstract its parameters from our various experiences though it need not be—and probably is not—encountered in its entirety during these early experiences. We most likely cannot specify just what our lovemaps look

According to John Money, we abstract the "grammar" for our subsequent sexual activity from early experiences.

like, but we use them in our sexual activity just as readily as we use grammar in speaking.

The lovemap notion explains why so many different influences on sexuality appear to be present, yet with none carrying the entire burden of accounting for it. In keeping with the analogy, language works this way as well. Money's theory explains not just sexual orientation but also sexual response, and why the former is more difficult to change than the latter. When we call on people to change their sexual orientation, we in effect are asking them to speak a different language, and this is a problem for anyone once the critical period for acquisition has passed. Sexual dysfunctions respond better to treatment because we are merely calling on people to speak more fluently.

But Money's lovemap itself is just a map, not a full-blown theory. Maybe it is only the promise of a map because it is obviously incomplete, failing to grapple with the motivational and emotional aspects of sexuality (Bergner, 1988). Money has published some case studies in which he has tried to articulate individual lovemaps, and he has made several efforts to trace their development over time. But future research is needed to see if this perspective represents a genuine integration of the various influences on sexual orientation. We need to know exactly how different factors contribute to an individual's lovemap, why men and women apparently develop different ones, and how they might change in adulthood. Finally, we need to know the role played by a person's family and culture. We need to know if it is profitable to describe an individual as sexually multilingual, incoherent, or mute.

TRANSSEXUALISM

To discuss transsexualism, I must first distinguish between **gender identity**—whether the self is experienced as a male or female—and anatomical sex. For the majority of people, these are concordant. Most people with penises and testes experience themselves as males; most with vaginas and ovaries experience themselves as females. But there are some individuals whose gender identities are at odds with their anatomical sex. They have a *gender identity disorder.*

CHARACTERIZATION

Gender identity disorder is rare, although it can occur among children, adolescents, and adults. *Transsexualism* is the label usually applied to this disorder among adults.[3] DSM-IV provides the following criteria for diagnosing this condition:

✦ a strong and persistent cross-gender identification, shown for example by the stated desire to be the other sex, frequently "passing" as the other sex, or the stated wish to live and be treated as the other sex

✦ persistent psychological discomfort and sense of inappropriateness about the sex to which one has been assigned, which may include the desire to be rid of one's primary and secondary sexual characteristics, and to acquire those of the opposite sex

Transsexualism is not to be confused with *transvestism*, in which an individual dresses like the opposite sex but has no desire to be rid of his or her genitals. To complicate matters, there are transsexual transvestites—individuals who meet the definitions of both transsexualism *and* transvestism (Blanchard, Clemmensen, & Steiner, 1987). The point is that the two are defined differently (Buhrich & McConaghy, 1977; Pomeroy, 1975).

Transsexualism is also not to be confused with homosexuality, because it is independent of sexual orientation. Transsexuals may have any of a number of possible sexual orientations: heterosexual, homosexual, bisexual, asexual, whatever (see Tsoi, 1990, 1992).

Geri Lisa Fritz is a 41-year-old baseball player who came to public attention after trying out for the all-

woman *Colorado Silver Bullets team (White, 1994). She went through 5 weeks of tryouts with the team, but was cut just short of making the final roster, because at 5 feet 11 inches and 260 pounds she was judged not fit enough to play professional sports. After being cut, Fritz revealed to the press that she was born a man. A year before, she had legally changed her name from Jerry to Geri Lisa and had begun hormone therapy to encourage female characteristics. Fritz suffers from a gender identity disorder and hopes eventually to have a sex-change operation. She had previously played professional baseball as a male but did not tell the team about her history during the tryout. To their credit, team officials did not make much of her eventual revelation:*

> *"I don't know if it's fair for anybody to offer stereotypes as to who looks like a man and who looks like a woman," coach Tommy Jones says. . . . "You take people for face value unless you have a reason to believe otherwise." (p. 2c)*

When I first introduced the idea of transsexualism in the beginning of the chapter, I made the point that this disorder challenges the way we think about gender and sexuality. Consider a transsexual whose gender identity is that of a female and whose genitals are those of a male. This person is turned on by men and engages in sexual activity with them. What is this person's sexual orientation? She would regard herself as a heterosexual, and so might we, because there is no good reason to give biology precedence over psychology in defining sexual orientation. Still, to the outside observer who knows nothing about her transsexualism, she seems to be a gay man.

Transsexualism occurs in about one of every 30,000 biological males, and one of every 100,000 biological females. Its onset is very early in life, invariably preceded by a gender identity disorder of childhood. (The converse is not true. Although at increased risk for sexual difficulties, the typical child with a gender identity disturbance does *not* become a transsexual adult.) For as long as they can remember, transsexuals felt that something was amiss with the body in which they found themselves. They are often anxious or depressed. There is not a single report of the disorder going away once it is present.

The causes of transsexualism remain a mystery, although speculation has centered on biological causes on the one hand versus environmental causes on the other. Some theorists argue that something went wrong during prenatal development for individuals who eventually become transsexuals; perhaps the hormones to which they were exposed changed them (Pauly, 1974). But among adults who are transsexuals,

---

[3] A more precise usage of these terms reserves *transsexualism* to describe the problem of an adult with gender identity disorder who wishes to be rid of the genitals with which he or she was born (Bradley et al., 1991).

there is no reliable difference in their physiology that supports this speculation (e.g., Gooren, 1990).

Children who will become transsexuals act differently from other children, showing exaggeratedly "masculine" or "feminine" characteristics, as the case may be, tempting some theorists to suggest that modes of child-rearing that encourage the behavior of the opposite sex may contribute to the disorder (Green, 1987). However, this possibly confuses cause with effect; it may well be that acting like a "tomboy" or a "sissy" is simply the early manifestation of transsexualism rather than its cause.

TREATMENT

The only successful treatment developed to date for transsexualism is to refashion the transsexual's genitals, changing them from male to female (or vice versa). **Gender reassignment surgery,** as this practice is called, strikes many as even more unusual than transsexualism itself, and it has been a controversial procedure since originally devised in the 1950s. Indeed, some hospitals in the United States that used to perform this procedure no longer do so. It usually follows a period of hormone treatments that encourage male or female secondary sexual characteristics.

In the case of male-to-female reassignment, the individual's testicles are surgically removed, and an artificial vagina is created, lined with the skin of the penis. Because males and females have the same sorts of nerves in their genitals, this procedure creates a sexually responsive vagina. In the case of female-to-male reassignment, things are a bit more complicated, but in effect, the vagina is turned inside out to fashion a penis that is sexually responsive in the sense that its stimulation can lead to orgasm. However, surgery to date has not been able to route blood vessels through the new penis so that it can become erect. The new penis of course does not ejaculate.

Perhaps two thirds of the individuals report improved adjustment following surgery, although this conclusion must be qualified by saying that a comparison group of transsexuals *not* undertaking surgery is typically unavailable (Abramowitz, 1986; but see Mate-Kole, Freschi, & Robin, 1990). Perhaps transsexuals, whether or not they have surgery, adjust better as they age, so surgery may not be the critical factor (Meyer & Reter, 1979). Female-to-male surgery results in more successful psychological adjustment than does male-to-female surgery. This is intriguing, because male-to-female operations are surgically simpler, with fewer medical complications such as infection.

Do not overlook the practical problems that ensue from gender reassignment surgery. The individual typically has a name change and obtains a new driver's

In the early 1950s, Christine Jorgensen had a well publicized sex-change operation, which brought transsexualism and its surgical treatment into general awareness.

license, new voter registration, new credit cards, even a new birth certificate. The paper history of a person becomes discontinuous. The individual's gender is now at odds with his or her chromosomes, which matters when chromosome tests are used to identify whether someone is a male or a female, as in sports competitions. The larger society does not easily accommodate any of this, which takes its toll on postoperative transsexuals.

In some cases, surgery and its aftermath lead to a particularly bad outcome. The person becomes psychotic, attempts suicide, or requests another surgery to return his or her original genitals. Researchers need to study which transsexuals fare well after surgery and which do not (e.g., Blanchard, Steiner, Clemmensen, & Dickey, 1989; Calanca, 1991). Some psychologists believe that individuals who are at risk for a poor adjustment following surgery should be treated instead with psychotherapy, not to remove their transsexualism but to help them come to grips with it without a surgical "cure" (e.g., Kirkpatrick & Friedmann, 1976).

In this chapter, you encountered three sorts of problems revolving around sexuality: sexual dysfunctions, paraphilias, and transsexualism. Sexual dysfunctions are problems with sexual response, and can be readily understood as vicious circles into which any of us may blunder. Paraphilias are a special case of sexual orientation. These exemplify the familiar notion of continuity between normality and abnormality. Transsexualism seems a striking exception to this principle. Does anything in the mundane lives of most people correspond to transsexualism?

I think there are parallels, which may be less than obvious because they do not involve our genitals. Remember the great significance we attach to sexuality, and how it pervades our very identities. Remember as well the body dysmorphic disorder discussed in Chapter 8, a preoccupation with a "flaw" in appearance. Might transsexualism be an extreme version of such a disorder?

And might gender reassignment surgery be a dramatic version of such practices as coloring our hair or reshaping our noses? Is it any more unusual—in principle—than dieting to change our shape or lifting weights to do the same? Countless women in the United States have surgery every year to change the size of their breasts. Countless men combat baldness every year with toupees, hair transplants, or hormone treatments. How is gender reassignment surgery different? If the primary answer is that it is different because it involves genitals, then the case for continuity has been made.

Summary

◆ Sexual disorders encompass sexual dysfunctions, which are problems with desire, excitement, activity, and/or orgasm; paraphilias, which refer to sexual activity with inappropriate individuals or in inappropriate circumstances; and transsexualism, which involves an individual's gender identity not being consistent with his or her anatomical sex. To understand problems with sexuality, we must understand sexuality itself and the great significance placed on sexuality by all societies.

A HISTORY OF SEXUALITY

◆ A view across history and around the world reveals great diversity in how sexuality is regarded. However, virtually all societies have strong codes about what is abnormal, illegal, and immoral.

◆ The modern Western world has inherited many of its particular attitudes toward sexuality from early Christian teachings that linked sexuality to sin and guilt. In the Victorian era, this ambivalent attitude toward sexuality resulted in widespread attempts to repress and deny its existence.

◆ Starting with the theories of Freud, the 20th century saw sexuality regarded in an increasingly liberal and tolerant way. Part of this increased acceptance of sexuality was a willingness to study it scientifically. Kinsey undertook extensive surveys of "normal" sexual practices in the United States, and his results were important because of the variety they demonstrated within our society. Masters and Johnson studied sexual

activity in the laboratory, providing the first good description of the physiological processes involved in the human sexual response.

◆ More recent influences on sexuality include the sexual revolution, feminism, the gay rights movement, and AIDS.

SEXUAL FUNCTION AND DYSFUNCTION

◆ For both males and females, sexual response can be described as proceeding through four stages: excitement, plateau, orgasm, and resolution. Difficulties can occur at any of these stages, and DSM-IV describes sexual dysfunctions that involve problems with initial desire, continued activity, and/or the achievement of orgasm.

◆ Sexual dysfunctions can have a variety of physical and psychological causes. Useful in a number of cases for treating sexual dysfunctions with psychological causes is sex therapy as developed by Masters and Johnson. This approach stresses information and communication, and it tries to get the couple to associate sexual activity with pleasure as opposed to anxiety.

PARAPHILIAS

◆ Sexual orientation refers to what an individual finds sexually arousing and what he or she wants to do during sexual activity. Paraphilias well illustrate the fuzzy boundaries of abnormality because some sexual orientations are deemed by society to be unusual and/ or objectionable. In some cases, as when they involve the infliction of pain on unwilling or nonconsenting individuals, the objection is clear. In other cases, there is much more ambiguity.

◆ The overall prevalence of paraphilias is unknown, because of the secretive nature of such activities. These unusual sexual orientations are highly stable; they are found almost exclusively among males; they are sometimes associated with other psychological problems; their causes are largely unknown; and they are difficult to change with available therapy techniques.

◆ We will understand paraphilias better once we have available a general theory of how sexual orientation originates and changes.

TRANSSEXUALISM

◆ Transsexualism is a rare problem, although it attracts our attention because it challenges the way we think about gender and sex. The causes of transsexualism are not known, although when it exists, this problem has been present throughout the individual's life. The only available treatment is a surgical one: changing people's genitals from male to female, or vice versa, in order to match their gender identity. This procedure appears successful in two thirds of the cases, although critics have raised questions about this conclusion.

Key Terms

antiandrogens

dyspareunia

estrogen

female orgasmic disorder; inhibited female orgasm

female sexual arousal disorder

gender identity

gender identity disorder

gender reassignment surgery

hypoactive sexual desire disorder

lovemap

male erectile disorder

male orgasmic disorder; inhibited male orgasm

paraphilia

polymorphous perversity

premature ejaculation

progestin

sensate focus

sexology

sex therapy

sexual aim

sexual aversion disorder

sexual dysfunctions

sexual object

sexual orientation

testosterone

transsexualism

vaginismus

Victorianism

Schizophrenic Disorders

12

SOMETIME IN THE 1930S, HENRY AND Gertrude met. *At first, Gertrude did not much care for Henry, but after an ambivalent courtship in which he threatened suicide if she stopped seeing him, they married. They had little to say to one another, nor did they have friends in common. Henry drank heavily, and soon found himself without work. Gertrude, on the other hand, worked as a practical nurse to support them both. Neither of them wanted children, but after being married for 3 years, Gertrude became pregnant. Her doctor said she would have twins, but she instead had quadruplets: four identical*

352

Researchers interested in schizophrenia have for decades studied the Genain sisters: identical quadruplets who all developed schizophrenia.

girls weighing a total of 15 pounds. When first born, Nora, Iris, Myra, and Hester were sickly and difficult to feed. However, after 6 weeks in the hospital, they all went home in good condition. As you might imagine, Henry and Gertrude were not ideally suited for the task of raising children. They had a bad marriage; they had little money; and Henry was—to be blunt—an unemployed alcoholic.

Then as now, the birth of quadruplets fascinated other people, and a steady stream of visitors came to see the little girls. Henry began to charge each visitor 25 cents to peek at his daughters. At the same time, he and his wife feared kidnappers, and so they locked and double-locked their doors and windows. Suspicion and fear filled their household.

Henry and Gertrude regarded their daughters as one person split by unusual happenstance into four bodies. None of the four girls was ever treated as whole or healthy or adequate. They were never allowed to play with other children. Gertrude took a dislike to Hester, the youngest and smallest of the quadruplets, claiming she was just like Henry. At age 3, Hester started to masturbate, which intensified her mother's dislike of her, because now Gertrude felt her daughter was oversexed.

Henry began to make illegal moonshine in the basement of their house. He had a series of not-too-secret affairs, and he contracted a sexually transmitted disease. Once when drunk, he shot at his wife with a pistol, thinking she was an intruder.

When the girls turned 5, they started school. They worked hard and were average students. But their classmates teased them and called them dumb. Henry and Gertrude insisted that Nora and Myra—the older two *girls—were gifted, whereas the other two lagged far behind. Teachers felt that all four of the girls were over-protected and restricted by their parents.*

At about age 6, the girls were given dancing and singing lessons because Henry and Gertrude wanted them to be entertainers. They had some talent, and made a little money during the next few years performing, but their planned career never went very far.

Their parents continued to battle, and essentially turned all of the household chores over to the girls. Gertrude continued to worry about Hester's masturbation, particularly when she found Hester and Iris, at age 12, stimulating one another. She took both of them to a doctor who removed part of the clitoris of each girl, so as to deaden any pleasurable sensations. But both girls continued to masturbate, breaking the stitches following their surgeries. Gertrude then tied their hands to the bed when they went to sleep.

Henry was also interested in the sexuality of his daughters, and he insisted on watching them dress and undress. Sex was discussed only as a dangerous topic, and the sisters were forbidden to have anything to do with boys. However, Henry fondled their breasts and buttocks.

Obviously, this is not a typical way to grow up. It is not surprising, then, that the daughters began to develop problems. Hester was the first, becoming irritable and depressed while still in high school. Then her behavior became bizarre. She "confessed" to her mother that she had a long series of sexual affairs dating back to elementary school. Rather than recognizing all of this as a frank psychotic episode, Henry and Gertrude decided that their daughter was mentally retarded—from too much masturbation, they concluded. Hester was removed from school and kept at home, heavily sedated with drugs.

Shortly thereafter, Nora and Iris began to experience a host of physical symptoms: allergies, stomach spasms, menstrual irregularities, and fainting spells. They were able to finish high school, however, as did Myra.

All of the sisters except Hester went to work, where they performed poorly at best. Over the next few years, each had a psychotic episode, as had Hester several years earlier. All four were eventually diagnosed with schizophrenia. Because their parents were unable to pay the resulting medical bills, the National Institute of Mental Health entered the picture, offering to provide free treatment in return for the opportunity to study the girls.[1] Numerous studies were carried out (Buchsbaum, 1984; Buchsbaum et al., 1984; Mirsky & Quinn, 1988; Rosenthal, 1963), and investigations of the quadruplets continue to this day.

---

[1] In case you did not notice, the names of the four daughters start with the same initials as the National Institute of Mental Health (NIMH); these are not their real names, but this is how they are always identified in the NIMH-sponsored reports.

Schizophrenia may well be the prototype of psychological abnormality. Sometimes described as a thought disorder, it is characterized by patently false perceptions and beliefs, a disorganized style of thinking, and neglect of the basics of living. None would disagree that schizophrenia is a label attached to unusual and problematic ways of behaving, such as those displayed by Nora, Iris, Myra, and Hester. However, consensus about the fact of abnormality does not mean the same thing as consensus about how to conceptualize it.

Schizophrenia theory and research have been marked by constant skirmishes among advocates of different models of abnormality. Holding down one end of these debates were those seeing schizophrenia as a discrete disease of the nervous system (e.g., Kety, 1974). On the other end were theorists stressing the experiential, environmental, and/or sociocultural influences on this way of behaving (e.g., Boyle, 1990; Goffman, 1961; Laing, 1967; Sarbin & Mancuso, 1980; Scheff, 1966; Szasz, 1961). These individuals took strong issue with the characterization of schizophrenia as an illness.

Emerging from such controversies was the conclusion that we must examine schizophrenia from a number of vantage points, including biological *and* environmental perspectives (Rosenthal & Kety, 1968). The task of the theorist is to articulate the possible causes and treatments of this problem in ways that do justice to its complexity (Goldstein, 1988; Mirsky & Duncan, 1986).

Schizophrenia may not be sensibly described as a single problem, but rather as a group of problems. An individual who warrants a diagnosis of schizophrenia according to one of the current systems, such as DSM-IV, may share little in common with other "schizophrenic" individuals. The heterogeneity of schizophrenia has probably contributed to the controversy surrounding how best to conceive it. Perhaps any of a number of theorists have been correct in their conclusions about a subset of schizophrenic individuals. Some explicitly recognize the heterogeneity of the disorder by referring to **schizophrenia spectrum disorders,** which include not only schizophrenia but also similar problems, in particular personality disorders characterized by odd behavior (Chapter 13).

Schizophrenia is relatively rare, diagnosed in perhaps 1% of adults. However, because it can be so severe and chronic, it represents a considerable problem, not just to the individuals who carry the diagnosis, but also to society as a whole. Schizophrenia may be the most common psychological problem of the homeless (Doutney, Buhrich, Virgona, Cohen, & Daniels, 1985; Koegel, Burnam, & Farr, 1988; Susser, Struening, & Conover, 1989).

In part because of deinstitutionalization (Chapter 15), severe psychological problems, including schizophrenia, are more likely to be found among the homeless.

In the early part of the 20th century, Swiss psychiatrist Eugen Bleuler (1857–1939) coined the term schizophrenia, from the Greek schiz (split) and phren (mind), to emphasize the split between thought and emotion that characterizes this disorder.

The reality of schizophrenia is often grim, but there are numerous myths and misunderstandings that surround it that make schizophrenia seem even worse than it actually is (Bernheim & Lewine, 1979) (see Table 12.1). Myth number one is that schizophrenic individuals have a split (i.e., multiple) personality. You

TABLE 12.1

MYTHS ABOUT SCHIZOPHRENIA *Although schizophrenia is a severe disorder, there exist numerous myths about the problem that make it seem even worse than it is, including those listed here.*
SOURCE: *SCHIZOPHRENIA*, BY K. F. BERNHEIM AND R. R. J. LEWINE, 1979, NEW YORK: NORTON.

1. Schizophrenic individuals have a split personality.
2. Schizophrenic individuals are dangerous.
3. Schizophrenic individuals are constantly out of control.
4. Schizophrenia is a progressive condition.
5. Schizophrenia is biologically inevitable.

know from Chapter 8 that multiple personality disorder is a dissociative disorder, something altogether different from schizophrenia. The misunderstanding probably results from the word root *schiz*, which means *split*. But the split in schizophrenia is not within an individual's personality but rather between his thoughts and emotions. Those with the disorder sometimes show a marked inconsistency between what they think and what they feel. This led Swiss psychiatrist Eugen Bleuler (1911/1950) to coin the term *schizophrenia* to capture what he saw as the most salient symptom of the disorder.

Myth number two is that schizophrenic individuals are dangerous. To be sure, these individuals might hurt someone else, but in terms of the sheer statistics, they are not particularly dangerous (e.g., Chuang, Williams, & Dalby, 1987). Schizophrenic individuals are sometimes highly agitated. While their behavior might frighten others, it is usually they who are more frightened than the onlookers. Contributing to the perception of them as dangerous are newspaper headlines that every so often mention former mental patients committing crimes.[2] Whether or not a given headline is strictly true, it is always misleading because the information tends to stick in our heads. We are less likely to remember the many more crimes committed by perfectly "sane" individuals. In other words, we are prey to a cognitive illusion, a strong association between schizophrenia and danger that does not exist (Kahneman & Tversky, 1973).

Myth number three holds that those with the disorder are constantly out of control. When a person is having what is known as a *psychotic episode*, his grasp of reality is in fact tenuous. His thoughts, feelings, and actions have a life of their own, independent of the external world. But schizophrenia is not a constant psychotic episode. Schizophrenic individuals may have such episodes, but only some of the time. We have the notion that people diagnosed with the disorder are constantly out of control because this is how they are usually discussed. The fact is that the most bizarre symptoms come and go; other aspects can be more chronic.

Myth number four is that schizophrenia is a progressive condition, inevitably worsening until a person dies. This too is an incorrect notion, originating in the theoretical pronouncements of 19th century psychiatrists like Emil Kraepelin. What we nowadays call schizophrenia, they dubbed *dementia praecox*, Latin for precocious (or premature) dementia (Morel, 1852). By definition at that time, dementia was progressive, so it followed that schizophrenia was also progressive. This idea was irrefutable—to the extent that an individual who "recovered" from schizophrenia was rediagnosed. He or she could not have had schizophrenia in the first place, because someone with it can only worsen and die. Eventually psychiatrists and psychologists realized that the disorder shows a highly variable course (Ram, Bromet, Eaton, Pato, & Schwartz, 1992). Some individuals show an insidious decline. Others make a full recovery. And still others cycle over their lives, in and out of the diagnostic category.

Myth number five is that schizophrenia is biologically inevitable. It has long been recognized that the disorder runs in families, an impression bolstered by modern twin, family, and adoption studies. But we now know that schizophrenia per se is not an inherited disease in the way that Huntington's chorea is. Instead, it is a heritable problem, meaning that the likelihood

of having this difficulty has something to do with genes, but not to the exclusion of environmental determinants. Said another way, individuals with schizophrenic relatives do not have a biological time bomb ticking away in their genes. They may have a biological *predisposition* to develop the problem granted particular circumstances, but this is not the same as a biological *predestination*.

SYMPTOMS, SUBTYPES, AND OTHER PSYCHOTIC SYNDROMES

In this section, I cover the diagnostic approach of DSM-IV, which specifies criteria not just for schizophrenia per se but also for several subtypes. Also discussed are psychological disorders that share with schizophrenia prominent psychotic symptoms (see Table 12.2). The relationship of these syndromes to schizophrenia is a topic of great interest.

SCHIZOPHRENIA

To diagnose schizophrenia, DSM-IV tells us to look for the following: (a) psychotic symptoms lasting at least 1 month; (b) a marked deterioration in such areas as work, social relations, and self-care; and (c) signs of some sort of disturbance for at least 6 months. If these criteria are met, then a general diagnosis of schizophrenia is made.

TABLE 12.2

SCHIZOPHRENIA AND OTHER PSYCHOTIC SYNDROMES
Several disorders described in DSM-IV, including schizophrenia, involve prominent psychotic symptoms.

DISORDER	CHARACTERIZATION
schizophrenia	false sensations, perceptions, and beliefs; disorganized style of thinking; neglect of the basics of living
schizophreniform disorder	schizophrenic-like symptoms that last for less than 6 months
schizoaffective disorder	symptoms of a depressive or manic episode and a psychotic episode
delusional disorder	persistent, nonbizarre delusion, not due to any other type of psychological abnormality, such as schizophrenia

---

[2] Some epidemiological studies find that those with schizophrenia are more likely to be arrested than individuals in the general population (e.g., Hodgins, 1992). However, a detailed look at these arrests suggests that people with schizophrenia are more frequently apprehended following crimes than perpetrators in general, which obviously confounds the use of "arrests" as a measure of crime (Robertson, 1988). In any event, the crimes for which schizophrenic individuals are arrested are typically of minor severity (Lindquist & Allebeck, 1990).

Psychotic symptoms   Psychotic symptoms include **delusions:** patently false beliefs. These are not merely quaint or eccentric ideas but rather notions to which virtually no one in an individual's specific culture would grant any credence. In our society, an example of a delusion might be that Vanna White is sending you secret messages when she turns the cards on "Wheel of Fortune." Or the CIA has planted a radio transmitter in your brain. Or Princess Diana is hiding in your broom closet.

Although delusions characterize schizophrenia around the world, their content often represents culture-specific influences. Diagnosticians who work with clients from different social groups must be alert to how delusions may manifest themselves. For example, Tateyama and colleagues (1993) compared schizophrenic delusions in Japan and Germany. Delusions about self-aggrandizement, world destruction, and physical injuries were equally common in both countries, but German patients were more likely to report delusions involving sin, guilt, and religion, whereas Japanese patients were more likely to report delusions about other people slandering them. These differences seem to reflect the importance of Christianity in Germany versus the importance of group orientation in Japan.

Psychotic symptoms also include **hallucinations:** sensory experiences that no one else confirms or supports. While everyone's sensory experiences are private, for most of us, most of the time, they are not idiosyncratic. They have *intersubjective reality*—that is, others agree that they are legitimate sensations. When a woman says that she stopped her car at the intersection because the light was red, the other people in her car would agree that this was a "real" experience. A hallucination has no such intersubjective reality, which is why it is regarded as psychotic.

The most common type of schizophrenic hallucination is auditory. Schizophrenic individuals hear voices, and these invariably are unpleasant. They may be accusatory, telling the person he is evil or inept. Or they may be commands to do something dangerous.

A schizophrenic individual with whom I worked as a clinician had been a cook, and his job was to stir a giant vat of scalding hot soup. For weeks he heard voices commanding him to drown himself in the soup, and one day he gave way to the command. He did not drown, but he severely burned himself.

Another sign of a psychotic episode is disorganized speech. That schizophrenic individuals speak differently from others has been of great interest to mental health professionals, who have sought clues

Psychotic symptoms include disturbances in thinking and perception, as shown in this sketch by an artist diagnosed with schizophrenia. Note the staring eye, which suggests a paranoid preoccupation.

in their language about the psychological processes involved in the disorder (Wrobel, 1990). Theorists have introduced colorful terms to capture the peculiar nature of schizophrenic speech. **Word salad** is one such metaphor, to convey the idea that a schizophrenic individual's words may come out as a tumble, as if they had been tossed in the same way as the ingredients of a salad. **Clang associations** are another characteristic of schizophrenic speech; the person strings together words that rhyme but otherwise show no apparent link.

A similar idea is conveyed by the notion of **loose associations:** wispy and difficult to follow transitions from one topic to another.

Dear . . .

I wasn't thinking too well when I was speaking to you but I do believe you were the postman whom I spent the night with. It is still Dr. David . . . in my heart. Am sick because of the screw driver. Please no hard feelings. . . . I would not harm you.

Sincere regards . . .   (Lehmann, 1980, p. 1160)

Along these same lines, schizophrenic individuals sometimes coin their own words, and such **neologisms** are very difficult for the listener to understand, even when they mean something to the speaker.

> *A schizophrenic woman who had been hospitalized for several years kept repeating, in an otherwise quite rational conversation, the word "polamolalittersjitterstittersleelita." Her psychiatrist asked her to spell it out, and she then proceeded to explain to him the meaning of the various components, which she insisted were to be used as one word. "Polamolalitters" was intended to recall the disease poliomyelitis. . . . The component "litters" stood for untidiness and messiness, the way she felt inside. (Lehmann, 1980, p. 1161)*

Yet another possible way to be labeled psychotic is with **catatonic behavior:** grossly inappropriate bodily movements or postures. A person who is being catatonic unflinchingly holds the same position for hours. He is stuporous, oblivious to the environment. He is

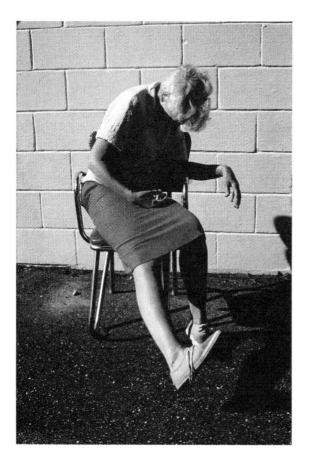

One possible symptom of schizophrenia is catatonic behavior: grossly inappropriate bodily movements or postures.

mute. Or he is inattentive to all instructions or attempts to move him. Alternatively, he may engage in frenetic movement, again with no obvious relationship to what is occurring around him.

Finally, a psychotic episode may be evident in **negative symptoms** that involve deficits. A schizophrenic individual might display **flat affect**: no evident emotion whatsoever. She might be unable to experience pleasure, a state termed **anhedonia.** She might behave listlessly.

Deteriorated functioning   The second DSM-IV criterion for schizophrenia is deteriorated functioning. In extreme cases, what this means is clear.

> *One individual I knew had some years earlier wandered off into a snowstorm, neglecting to put on his shoes or even socks. His legs froze, necessitating amputation of both of them above the knee. He was then fitted with artificial limbs. He could move around quite well, but he often neglected to take care of what remained of his legs, particularly during his psychotic episodes. Minor scratches and scrapes, inevitable when an individual wears artificial limbs, would become massively infected, requiring hospitalization. On several occasions, further amputation was required because his wounds were so badly infected.*

Suicide is relatively common among schizophrenic individuals (Gottesman, 1991). When a person is psychotic, it is difficult to say that his suicide reflects a sincere desire to die. Regardless, mortality rates for those with this disorder greatly exceed those found in the general population (Black & Fisher, 1992).

Duration of at least 6 months   The final substantive criterion suggested by DSM-IV for diagnosing schizophrenia is that problems, including the aforementioned symptoms, exist for at least 6 months. The individual is not expected to be acutely psychotic for this entire period. Instead, his or her psychotic episode is preceded by a deterioration of functioning and/or followed by lingering signs of peculiarity, such as social withdrawal, inappropriate affect, digressive speech, and a lack of initiative.

SCHIZOPHRENIA SUBTYPES

DSM-IV follows a long-standing practice in distinguishing among a number of schizophrenia subtypes (see Figure 12.1). In each case, an individual meets the generic criteria for schizophrenia, plus additional

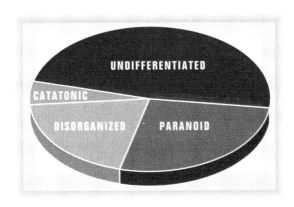

FIGURE 12.1

RELATIVE PREVALENCE OF DSM SCHIZOPHRENIA
SUBTYPES AMONG HOSPITALIZED INDIVIDUALS
*DSM-IV distinguishes several subtypes of schizophrenia. The
most common—undifferentiated schizophrenia—is an
explicitly miscellaneous category.*
SOURCE: DATA DERIVED FROM "A FAMILY STUDY OF THE SUBTYPES OF
SCHIZOPHRENIA," BY K. S. KENDLER, A. M. GRUENBERG, AND M. T.
TSUANG, 1988, *American Journal of Psychiatry, 145,* PP. 57–62.

ones. Although the subtypes sound quite distinct in
the abstract, in practice it can be difficult to identify
them. Perhaps in DSM-V or beyond, we will no longer
encounter this particular subclassification (Kay, 1990).

Catatonic subtype   In **catatonic schizophrenia,**
the schizophrenic individual alternates between
different manifestations of catatonia, from stupor to
agitation and back. Mutism is common. One of the
intriguing features of this kind of behavior is the occasional phenomenon of **waxy flexibility,** which refers
to the fact that the limbs of the schizophrenic individual can be moved ever so slowly into a particular position, which will then be maintained, sometimes for
hours.

Catatonic behavior implies that at least some
forms of schizophrenia may involve biology. It is virtually impossible for most of us to maintain the same
position for minutes at a time, much less hours. Perhaps something special about the catatonic individual's
nervous system allows this sort of motionlessness. Current biological speculation centers on neurotransmitters as an important influence on schizophrenia.
Among their many roles in the body, neurotransmitters
moderate our motor movement.

Catatonic schizophrenia was apparently common
some decades ago, but it is rarely encountered today
(Curran & Marengo, 1990). Just why this subtype
has all but vanished is not clear, but it might reflect
the growing use of antipsychotic medications to treat

schizophrenia. These medications are thought to work
by targeting neurotransmitters, and perhaps catatonic
behavior is the most immediately affected symptom.

Disorganized subtype   In **disorganized schizophrenia,** the central features are incoherence, loose
associations, and inappropriate affect. There are no
systematized delusions or hallucinations. This subtype
was once called *hebephrenic schizophrenia,* to convey the
immaturity of the individual warranting the diagnosis.
(*Hebe* means *youth,* and is the basic word root of
heebie-jeebies, a previous generation's term for fits of
giggling.)

An individual with disorganized schizophrenia
behaves in a notably disorganized fashion, showing
little interest in his social environment. He typically
acts inconsistently with the demands and expectations
of a given situation, smiling and grimacing. This kind
of schizophrenic individual typically has a particularly
severe thought disorder, and his prognosis is poor
(Fenton & McGlashan, 1991; Gross & Huber, 1985;
Jonsson & Jonsson, 1992). Like catatonic schizophrenia, this subtype is no longer as frequently encountered
as it once was. Again, the reason might be that antipsychotic medications effectively treat the most salient
symptoms, thus precluding the blatant versions of
this subtype.

Paranoid subtype   **Paranoid schizophrenia**
meets the general diagnostic criteria for schizophrenia,
and the paranoid individual additionally experiences
prominent and systematized delusions. Alternatively,
auditory hallucinations centering on a single theme
may mark this subtype. The paranoid themes tend to
be limited in number. The person might aggrandize
himself, believing that he is the son of God, or the

*Artist Martin Ramirez was diagnosed in 1935 with
paranoid schizophrenia. Once institutionalized, he made
hundreds of highly patterned and abstract drawings dealing
with themes from his past.*

czar of Russia, or some other important person. He might be extremely jealous. He might believe that he is being persecuted, for example, by the FBI, the PLO, or the like.

In 1989, a 22-year-old man named Kenneth Noid was arrested for walking into a Domino's Pizza shop in Georgia with a .357 Magnum and taking two employees hostage (Time, 1989). Noid apparently believed that the Domino's advertising campaign urging consumers to "avoid the Noid" who maliciously turned pizzas cold was directed at him! His hostages escaped without harm, and Kenneth Noid eventually surrendered to police, leaving us with a memorable example of paranoia.

Traditional psychoanalytic thinking proposes that paranoia is a *projection,* a turning out of one's own hostile feelings. Aggrandizing oneself presumably helps with this defense by boosting self-esteem. If you are going to be persecuted, holding some all-powerful international organization responsible reinforces delusions of importance.

The paranoid individual shows none of the bizarre motor behavior of the catatonic subtype, and none of the incoherence of the disorganized subtype. He may, however, be highly anxious, angry, and argumentative. The person who warrants this diagnosis tends to function better than schizophrenic individuals in general (Fenton & McGlashan, 1991), unless he begins to act on his paranoid beliefs. Then he courts obvious trouble.

Undifferentiated subtype   Next is **undifferentiated schizophrenia,** the diagnosis reserved for schizophrenic individuals who cannot be described clearly as catatonic, disorganized, or paranoid. They either fall short of all these other subtypes, or they fall into more than one of the categories.

For example, Bernheim and Lewine (1979) described the case of Mary, a 37-year-old woman hospitalized off and on over a number of years. Prior to each hospitalization, Mary would become agitated and would find it difficult to organize her thoughts. She would talk out loud to herself, rock back and forth in her chair, and ignore other people. Sometimes she would wander the streets. Notice that none of the defining symptoms for the other subtypes of schizophrenia predominates, which is why Mary is best described as having undifferentiated schizophrenia.

Undifferentiated schizophrenia is a miscellaneous category, yet it is probably the most frequently used subdiagnosis (Lehmann, 1980). When a miscellaneous diagnosis is the rule rather than the exception, we have reason to doubt the coverage of the diagnostic system being employed.

Residual subtype   DSM-IV includes one more subtype of schizophrenia, based on the course of the disorder rather than on the symptoms per se. Someone with **residual schizophrenia** at one time met the diagnostic criteria for schizophrenia and at the present time shows mild signs of some schizophrenic symptoms; e.g., blunted emotions, social withdrawal, eccentricity, and/or somewhat illogical thinking. She does not experience hallucinations and delusions, or at least they are not prominent.

This can be a controversial diagnosis. Why? Because it seems to presuppose that schizophrenia is a medical illness. Only illnesses have residual symptoms. A severe case of the flu that lingers as a sore throat can sensibly be called residual. But once we describe schizophrenia this way, we do not allow it to be anything other than a discrete illness. In contrast, if we view schizophrenia differently, then milder signs of this problem are simply that—milder signs—and not a separate problem in their own right.

PROCESS VERSUS REACTIVE SCHIZOPHRENIA

Of the many distinctions made among cases of schizophrenia, one of the most useful pertains to the initial onset of the problem (Garmezy, 1970). When schizophrenic symptoms come over a person gradually, with no obvious precipitant, what ensues is called **process schizophrenia.** Presumably, the problem developed because of some internal process unfolding.

Neil was a young man who had a happy and uneventful childhood (Blakely, 1991). Once a teenager, Neil occasionally experienced bursts of rage and expressed unrealistic fears about the intentions of others. His family dismissed these as signs of an adolescent phase. However, he slowly became more disturbed and more disturbing:

> *"He would rush into the house and jump into a bathtub of cold water, believing that was the only thing that would save him from dying," [his mother] remembers. "One Christmas Eve I stayed up all night in a freezing house—he'd turned off the furnace because he thought it was spewing poisonous gas into the air." Another time, Neil raced from his bedroom as though 40 devils were chasing him and ran, stark naked, out the front door. (p. 50)*

Neil was eventually diagnosed as suffering from schizophrenia, a problem still with him more than a decade later.

When schizophrenic symptoms occur suddenly, in response to some stressful event in the environment, we refer to it as **reactive schizophrenia.** The thinking here is that this type of schizophrenia is a reaction to external occurrences.

Janowsky, Addario, and Risch (1987) described the case of Mr. G., a 32-year-old man who was a successful lawyer. He was married and had two young children. His life was happy and fulfilling until the day he came home unexpectedly to find his wife in bed with his best friend. Mr. G.'s initial reaction was anger and depression, but a few days later he began to speak about "fusing with God, dispensing peace on Earth, and a need to fight the 'giant conspiracy'" (p. 1). He heard voices calling his name and chanting the word love *over and over. This psychotic episode was clearly a reactive one, and Mr. G. was admitted to a hospital for treatment.*

When first proposed by Bleuler (1924/1976), the process-reactive distinction was treated as a typology: purely biological cases of schizophrenia on the one hand versus maladaptive responses to stress on the other. This distinction is now regarded as identifying endpoints on a continuum, with many schizophrenic individuals some place in between. The distinction, however conceptualized, has remained because it bears a good relationship to prognosis (Garmezy, 1970). Those at the process end of the continuum tend not to fare as well as those at the reactive end. Said another way, sudden schizophrenic episodes in response to stressful events resolve themselves more quickly and fully than do cases of schizophrenia that occur slowly and insidiously (Herron, 1979). In the case of Mr. G., this is exactly what happened. With treatment, his symptoms decreased. He and his wife began marital therapy, and he did not experience another psychotic episode.

Positive versus Negative Symptoms

Another proposed distinction among schizophrenic symptoms classifies flagrant signs of psychosis—such as hallucinations, delusions, and disordered thinking—as **positive symptoms** (Crow, 1980; McGlashan & Fenton, 1992). Flat affect and anhedonia, as men-

Artist Adolf Wölfli suffered from a series of schizophrenic episodes. His paintings usually focused on themes from his childhood, in which he depicted himself as an idealized figure known as "Saint Adolf."

tioned earlier in this chapter, are classified as *negative symptoms* (Andreasen, 1982). The terms *positive* and *negative* refer to ways of behaving that represent excesses (the positive symptoms) versus deficits (the negative symptoms). As you remember from Chapter 6, the analogous distinction is made between positive and negative symptoms of organic disorders. Not all agree that the symptoms of schizophrenia can be so readily classified, arguing instead that negative symptoms are better conceptualized as signs of a particularly severe and/or chronic problem (see Lindenmayer, Kay, & Friedman, 1986; Marneros, Deister, & Rohde, 1992; Peralta, de Leon, & Cuesta, 1992).

Among those theorists and researchers who think the distinction is valid, we find some intriguing hypotheses (Crow, 1985). First, we have a new typology of schizophrenia: categories characterized by (a) positive symptoms, (b) negative symptoms, and (c) both positive and negative symptoms. Second, biomedical theorists propose that positive and negative symptoms may have different biological causes, specifically problems with brain function versus brain structure, respectively (Crow, 1982). And third, positive and negative symptoms might therefore require different treatments. Antipsychotic medication usually alleviates only positive symptoms, which means that only some schizophrenic individuals should be given such medication.

Note that these possible distinctions among types of schizophrenia and schizophrenic symptoms overlap. Process schizophrenia often includes negative symptoms, catatonic behavior, and marked disorganization. Particularly when it develops early in life, this constellation has a poor prognosis.

SCHIZOPHRENIFORM DISORDER

When a person displays schizophrenic-like symptoms for at least 1 month, but for less than 6 months, she may be given the diagnosis of **schizophreniform disorder,** which means—literally—having the appearance or form of schizophrenia. The relationship of this disorder to full-blown schizophrenia is an issue of debate (Hoff, Riordan, O'Donnell, Morris, & DeLisi, 1992; Marengo, Harrow, & Westermeyer, 1991). Obviously, if an individual diagnosed with schizophreniform disorder manifests symptoms for more than 6 months, then the diagnosis is changed to schizophrenia. But in some ways, this particular disorder seems to be distinct from schizophrenia, having—for one thing—a better prognosis (Coryell & Tsuang, 1986). At any rate, DSM-IV suggests that the most confident diagnosis is made when a person's problems are resolved in less than 6 months. Otherwise, the diagnosis should be considered provisional, because if symptoms continue for more than 6 months, the diagnosis must be changed to schizophrenia.

SCHIZOAFFECTIVE DISORDER

DSM-IV tells the diagnostician *not* to make the diagnosis of schizophrenia if a mood disorder seems to be present, because the symptoms of unipolar disorder and particularly bipolar disorder overlap with the substantive symptoms of schizophrenia. A manic individual is often described as psychotic and may show the same disordered speech and thought as a schizophrenic individual. Sometimes it proves difficult to decide with certainty that a person has a mood disorder or schizophrenia, however, and this is when the diagnosis of **schizoaffective disorder** comes into play. Here the individual satisfies the criteria for a depressive or manic episode as well as the criteria for a psychotic episode.

Family studies suggest that those with schizoaffective disorder are related to those with schizophrenia *and* those with mood disorders, which suggests that it may be a literal combination of the two (see Coryell & Zimmerman, 1988; Gershon et al., 1982, 1988; Maj, Starace, & Pirozzi, 1991; Tsuang, 1991). Other studies find that those with this disorder respond better to antipsychotic drugs than to antidepressants and/or lithium, suggesting that schizoaffective disorder belongs with schizophrenia (Stephens, 1978). Still other studies show just the opposite: Schizoaffective individuals respond better to lithium than to antipsychotic medications, leading of course to a different conclusion (Goodnick & Meltzer, 1984).

This disorder is rare, and we do not know much about it. It may well be just a miscellaneous category reflecting the deficiencies of our diagnostic system more than a discrete entity in its own right (Levitt & Tsuang, 1988).

DELUSIONAL DISORDER

Delusional disorder (also called **paranoid disorder**) is a problem marked by a persistent, nonbizarre delusion not due to any other type of psychological abnormality. Although distinct from schizophrenia, delusional disorders may provide insight into the cognitive dynamics of delusions in cases unencumbered by hallucinations or deteriorated functioning.

What emerges clearly is that delusions are used as defenses. The common precipitants of delusional disorders are such life stresses as physical disability or emigration to a new culture (e.g., Eitinger & Grunfeld, 1966). We can surmise that these occurrences threaten the individual, and in order to cope, he or she resorts to delusional beliefs. We can further recognize delusional beliefs as *displacements,* attempts to deflect anxiety from the real sources of concern. Similar processes might be at work in schizophrenia. Perhaps we need to look at delusions less as primary symptoms and more as attempts to cope with its more basic manifestations.

A handful of themes capture common delusions:

+ *erotomanic:* the person believes that he or she is loved by another, who does not have these feelings and may even be a total stranger

+ *grandiose:* the person believes that he has a fabulous but unrecognized talent, or along these same lines, that he has made a great discovery, such as how to make gasoline out of water

+ *jealous:* the person is convinced, in the absence of any evidence, that her spouse or lover is unfaithful; she takes great lengths to intervene in the imagined infidelity

+ *somatic:* the person believes that a foul odor is being emitted from the skin, mouth, rectum, or vagina, that he or she is infected with insects or parasites, and/or that parts of the body are misshapen and/or malfunctioning

+ *persecutory:* the person believes that he or she is being conspired against, poisoned, maligned, or harassed

These beliefs are not simply entertained as idle thoughts. Typically, the delusional individual will act on them and thereby create all sorts of problems for herself and others.

Delusional disorders come to the public's attention when someone becomes obsessed with a celebrity and begins to stalk the individual, sometimes with tragic consequences (e.g., De Becker, 1990; People Weekly, 1992; Toufexis, 1989):

> *In 1989, actress Rebecca Schaeffer was shot to death by a young man who regarded himself as a fan.*
>
> *In 1988, a man showed up at Universal Studios and killed two security guards after they refused to let him see actor Michael Landon.*
>
> *In 1982, actress Theresa Saldana was stabbed by a supposed fan. The man was apprehended and imprisoned, and he has repeatedly threatened to kill her when he gets out of jail.*
>
> *A fan of skater Katarina Witt mailed her hundreds of marriage proposals, obscene letters, and nude photos of himself. He even sent death threats. He would come to her door at 3 A.M. Once he masturbated on her doorstep. He was eventually sentenced to prison.*
>
> *A fan of talk show host David Letterman refers to herself as Mrs. Letterman and has repeatedly broken into his Connecticut home.*
>
> *A woman who calls herself Billie Jean Jackson presents herself as Michael Jackson's wife; she was sentenced to jail for violating a court order to stay away from his home.*
>
> *A young woman has written actor Michael J. Fox more than 6,000 threatening letters, urging him to divorce his wife. The woman signs the letters "Your No. 1 Fan."*

Talk show host David Letterman has been stalked by a woman who refers to herself as Mrs. Letterman and has repeatedly broken into his Connecticut home. Celebrity stalkers may suffer from delusional disorder.

Delusional disorders, particularly in their earliest stages, can be difficult to distinguish from paranoid schizophrenia. In fact, they might simply be milder versions of this more severe problem. Or—depending on their particular content—they might be versions of somatoform disorders or personality disorders.

EPIDEMIOLOGY

Whatever the ambiguity in defining schizophrenia and distinguishing it from related psychological problems, I can still offer some conclusions about its epidemiology (Wyatt, Alexander, Egan, & Kirch, 1988). First, it occurs at about the rate of 1% throughout the world. Differences from country to country might reveal more about the stringency of the diagnostic criteria being employed than about the actual prevalence of the problem (Sartorius et al., 1986; but see Focus on Schizophrenia across History).

The apparent constancy of this rate is potentially important in light of theories that point to environmental events as causes. If stress were the primary cause of schizophrenia, its prevalence should rise and fall across time and place according to the occurrence of stressful events. This is not the case, although—as I will discuss—stressful events can trigger a schizophrenic episode. For example, rates of the disorder did not show an increase in Europe during World War I or World War II, nor in the United States during the Great Depression of the 1930s (e.g., Dohan, 1966; Slater, 1943; Wagner, 1946). Perhaps most surprisingly, it did not erupt among the inmates of the Nazi death camps (e.g., Eitinger, 1967). These intriguing statistics tell us that stress per se cannot bear the sole explanatory load.

Second, schizophrenia seems to occur at about the same rate among men and women, although some recent studies show that men are more likely to be diagnosed with schizophrenia than women (e.g., Iacono & Beiser, 1992; Thara & Rajkumar, 1992).

THE STANDARD HISTORIES OF abnormality assume that schizophrenia has always been present. What was called "madness" in centuries past is what we nowadays identify as schizophrenia. However, an intriguing counterargument can be mounted against this account (Torrey, 1988b). Perhaps schizophrenia is a relatively new arrival on the historical scene. If so, then the generally accepted explanations of this disorder are incomplete.

Although acknowledging that his evidence is not definitive, Torrey (1988b) nonetheless makes a case for the historical recency of schizophrenia. According to his research, there are many descriptions of madness throughout history, from the Bible to the writings of Hippocrates to the plays of Shakespeare, but none contains a clear description of the syndrome of schizophrenia. To be sure, individual symptoms are described, but never in the specific constellation that characterizes it. For example, there are *no* cases of madness to be found in which auditory hallucinations are present in the absence of visual hallucinations.

Readily recognizable descriptions of schizophrenia suddenly appeared in the 17th century. In the 1800s, there was an explosion of such descriptions, first in Europe and then in the United States. Writers in the 1800s frequently commented that "madness" was on an obvious increase.

Is it possible that schizophrenia as we know it first occurred in the 17th century, and then increased in prevalence during the ensuing years? The skeptic might argue that it existed all along but was only noticed with the advent of psychiatric hospitals. Along these lines, prior to hospitals, schizophrenic individuals may have perished so quickly that the prevalence of the problem was necessarily low. Indeed, because life expectancy in general was so low in centuries past, most of those predisposed to develop schizophrenia may not have lived long enough to do so.

But let us momentarily suspend this skepticism, because these sorts of arguments are themselves not definitive. Assume that schizophrenia did not exist before the 17th century. Why and how did it then appear? Two possibilities can be cited, one environmental and the other biological. They are not incompatible.

The environmental hypothesis proposes that schizophrenia is a disorder of urbanization (Torrey & Bowler, 1990). As large numbers of people began to live in cities, the associated stresses produced reactions in some residents that we came to identify as schizophrenia. The biological hypothesis proposes that schizophrenia is caused by a virus that appeared for the first time in the 17th century and was spread through the close contact of city life.

The possibility that this disorder is caused by a virus has intrigued some modern researchers (Torrey, 1988a, 1991). No such virus has yet been discovered, and I must emphasize that most schizophrenia researchers choose to look elsewhere for the causes of the disorder (Gottesman, 1991). Still, there are several indirect lines of evidence hinting that a *schizovirus* may exist (King & Cooper, 1989).

First, studies have found antibodies in the blood of schizophrenic individuals not found in the blood of those without the disorder (Galinowski et al., 1992). Second, among those with schizophrenia in the United States and Europe, there is an increased 10% likelihood that they were born during late winter months. This epidemiological finding implies that prenatal events more common during the middle of winter—like viral infection—somehow increase the later risk of schizophrenia (Torrey, Torrey, & Peterson, 1977). Third, some epidemiological studies show that the prevalence of schizophrenia apparently varies across time and place, as would be expected if a viral infection were at work (Torrey, 1987). Fourth, studies of identical twins *discordant* for schizophrenia (i.e., pairs of twins in which one has schizophrenia and the other does not) replicate many of the findings concerning neurological correlates of schizophrenia (Bracha, Torrey, Bigelow, Lohr, & Linington, 1991; Goldberg et al., 1990). In other words, schizophrenic twins are neurologically different from their nonschizophrenic counterparts, even though they are genetically identical. What this implies is that these biological bases might be acquired.

The possible existence of a schizovirus does not invalidate research identifying other risk factors. Granted the complexity of the immune system and its influence by neurological and psychological factors, a viral risk factor for schizophrenia can be readily added to existing theories. What is exciting practically about these ideas is that new ways to treat and perhaps prevent schizophrenia may someday be devised. What is exciting conceptually is that even a disorder often cited as the epitome of a "mental illness" needs to be placed in a historical context.

Just what to make of these findings is unclear. Do they represent a long present but overlooked sex difference in prevalence or some new aspect of schizophrenia?

It is generally agreed that the average age of onset differs for men versus women (Tien & Eaton, 1992). Men are typically diagnosed with schizophrenia before the age of 25, and women typically after this age. Also, the prognosis for females seems better than for males (Munk-Jorgensen & Mortensen, 1992). In any event, we need to investigate such sex differences further (Hambrecht, Maurer, Hafner, & Sartorius, 1992; Rector & Seeman, 1992; Shtasel, Gur, Gallacher, Heimberg, & Gur, 1992; Wahl & Hunter, 1992).

Third, schizophrenia runs in families. By any and all of the strategies for inferring heritability, it proves heritable. I discuss these findings in detail when I turn to the biological basis of schizophrenia. But for now, note that the likelihood of being diagnosed with schizophrenia increases to the degree that an individual has various blood relatives who warrant this diagnosis. The closer the relationship, the more likely two individuals are to be concordant.

Fourth, at least in the United States, this disorder is more likely to occur among members of the lower class than among their middle- or upper-class counterparts (see Figure 12.2). Skeptics raise the possibility that this pattern reflects, at least in part, differences across social classes in the seeking of early treatment and/or the receiving of particular diagnoses (e.g., Adebimpe, 1994). In any event, the reported relationship between social class and schizophrenia appears particularly strong in large cities; there is little relationship between them in smaller towns (Clausen & Kohn, 1959).

Assuming there is a link between social class and schizophrenia, what is the causal direction? We could argue that a lower socioeconomic status, because of its attendant stress, is more likely to precipitate a psychotic episode. Or we could argue that schizophrenic individuals, because of the occupational disruption that results, drift toward the lower class as their earning power diminishes. Longitudinal research, in which the same individuals are followed over time, supports both interpretations (see Goldberg & Morrison, 1963). People already in the lower class are more apt to develop schizophrenia than people in higher social classes (Lewis, David, Andreasson, & Allebeck, 1992); and those who develop schizophrenia at some point in their life are more apt to suffer a loss in socioeconomic status than those who never develop it (Borga, Widerlov, Stefansson, & Cullberg, 1992).

Fifth, schizophrenia tends to be a disorder first encountered during young adulthood (Eaton et al., 1992). Although it is theoretically possible and occasionally observed among children, the diagnosis is usually not made until after puberty. People are rarely diagnosed with schizophrenia for the first time after age 45.

A longitudinal study of some 2,000 schizophrenic individuals suggests further that the disorder takes its most severe form during early adulthood (Bleuler, 1978). This is surprising granted the earlier opinion that schizophrenia was necessarily a progressive condition. It appears that for most schizophrenic individuals, symptoms become no worse after 5 years from the initial onset. On the average, people improve.

In this study, 20% made a good recovery, showing no further symptoms and entering into a normal social and occupational life, a figure reported by other researchers as well (e.g., Breier, Schreiber, Dyer, & Pickar, 1991; Carone, Harrow, & Westermeyer, 1991). On the negative side, about 40% of those diagnosed with the disorder showed recurring psychotic episodes. What about the remaining individuals? As noted, on the average, their symptoms improved, but this is not to say that they are fully rid of problematic ways of behaving (see Figure 12.3). Although no longer psychotic, these individuals were apathetic, anhedonic, and inactive. According to critics of the mental health system, at least some of this diminishment is due not just to

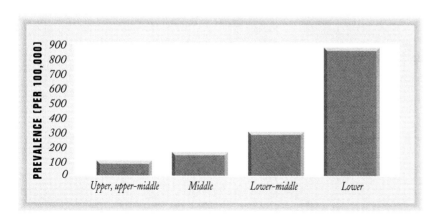

FIGURE 12.2

SCHIZOPHRENIA AND SOCIAL CLASS   *In the United States, schizophrenia is more likely to be diagnosed among those from the lower socioeconomic class.*

SOURCE: DATA DERIVED FROM *Social Class and Mental Illness*, BY A. B. HOLLINGSHEAD AND F. C. REDLICH, 1958, NEW YORK: WILEY.

About 10% of those with schizophrenia are permanently institutionalized. (Psychopathic Ward, *lithograph by R. Riggs, Philadelphia Museum of Art*)

schizophrenia itself but also to prolonged institutionalization.

Once they recognized that the prognosis of schizophrenia was variable, researchers attempted to identify factors that could predict good versus poor outcome, as operationalized by rehospitalization and/or recurrence of psychotic episodes. Among the factors linked with a favorable outcome is good social adjustment prior to the initial psychotic episode (e.g., Erickson, Beiser, Iacono, Fleming, & Lin, 1989). In particular, schizophrenic individuals who are married fare better than those who are not (Jonsson & Jonsson, 1992).

CAUSES

We know a fair amount about the various risk factors for schizophrenia—the variables that make a subsequent diagnosis of schizophrenia more or less likely. Both biological and environmental risk factors exist. However, a full explanation of its causes must account for *how* these risk factors translate themselves into the disorder. We know much less about mechanisms, although not for any lack of effort by theorists.

Two problems have plagued our understanding of the causes of schizophrenia. First, most researchers have proceeded from the vantage of but a single model of abnormality, ignoring the possibility that this disorder has a variety of entwined determinants not captured by any single perspective. Second, because schizophrenia is such a heterogeneous category, it may well be that different instances have different etiologies (Kety, 1980).

BIOLOGICAL RISK FACTORS

An impressive amount of evidence points to biology as playing an important role in schizophrenia. I begin my discussion by looking specifically at one of the findings already mentioned: the tendency of schizophrenia to run in families.

Genetics   Figure 12.4 shows that the closer the biological relatedness of two individuals, the more likely they are to be concordant for schizophrenia. This conclusion is supported by some of the most elegant procedures we have for estimating heritability. For example, in a study of identical twins raised apart—in different environments—the overall concordance of

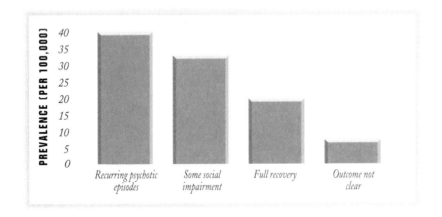

FIGURE 12.3

OUTCOMES OF SCHIZOPHRENIA   *In a longitudinal study of schizophrenia, Bleuler described these outcomes. Note the considerable variation.*
SOURCE: DATA DERIVED FROM *The Schizophrenic Disorders*, BY M. BLEULER, 1978, NEW HAVEN, CT: YALE UNIVERSITY PRESS.

How many of the problems associated with schizophrenia are
the result of prolonged institutionalization? (Etching by
A. Tardieu, depicting a patient at Charenton Hospital; from
Des Maladies Mentales by J. E. Esquirol, Philadelphia
Museum of Art)

schizophrenia was about the same figure found in studies of identical twins raised together (Gottesman &
Shields, 1972).

A different study compared the offspring of
schizophrenic and nonschizophrenic mothers, all of
whom had been placed in foster homes within a few
days of being born (Heston, 1966). These children
were followed for years, and the researcher ascertained
whether or not they developed schizophrenia. *Only* the
offspring of the schizophrenic mothers were eventually
diagnosed with it. The prevalence among the adopted
individuals was essentially the same figure as that
among offspring raised by their own schizophrenic
mothers (see also Kety, 1988).

Still another study looked at the offspring of nonschizophrenic mothers who were adopted by a parent
who subsequently developed schizophrenia (Wender,
Rosenthal, Kety, Schulsinger, & Welner, 1973). This
is a strong test of the hypothesis that this disorder is
produced by a stressful environment. Being raised by
a schizophrenic parent is obviously a highly stressful
experience (Anthony & Cohler, 1987), and if we
wanted to argue further that the disorder can be produced by such processes as modeling and identification, then the children raised by schizophrenic parents
should be at greatly increased risk for subsequent schizophrenia themselves. But the intriguing finding from
this study is that children with a nonschizophrenic
biological parent did *not* have an elevated chance of
developing the disorder themselves, even when raised
by a schizophrenic parent.

The research so far described looks at schizophrenia in either-or terms: a person either meets the diagnostic criteria or not. When researchers look at it in
continuous terms, as a host of behaviors that people

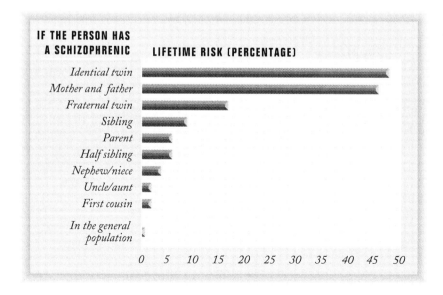

FIGURE 12.4

**LIFETIME RISK OF
SCHIZOPHRENIA**   *The
chance that a person will be
diagnosed with schizophrenia at
some point in life varies according
to whether he or she has relatives
with this problem.*
SOURCE: DATA DERIVED FROM
Schizophrenia Genesis, BY I. I.
GOTTESMAN, 1991, NEW YORK:
FREEMAN. USED WITH PERMISSION.

can display in degrees of more versus less, the same sort of conclusion follows. "Mild" versions of schizophrenia, those short of DSM criteria, are more likely to occur among the relatives of schizophrenic individuals than among those without this disorder (Mirsky & Duncan, 1986).

Although the risk of schizophrenia is increased by every schizophrenic relative an individual has, the chances are never 100%. A child of two schizophrenic parents has less than a 50% chance of being diagnosed with the disorder at some point in his life. Furthermore, if his identical twin is diagnosed, he still has less than a 50% chance of developing the problem. Genetics are a clear risk factor for schizophrenia but not the whole picture.

Studies like these do not tell us which genes might confer the added risk for schizophrenia. In the 1980s, an exciting report described a specific genetic anomaly in the only two members of a large family who were diagnosed with schizophrenia (Bassett, McGillivray, Jones, & Pantzar, 1988). However, subsequent studies did not confirm these anomalies in other families; the original report might have been a fluke. The search for specific genes continues (e.g., Hallmayer et al., 1992; Macciardi et al., 1992; Nanko et al., 1992; Owen, Craufurd, & St. Clair, 1990).

A final gap in what we know about genetics and schizophrenia is that the mechanism leading from a genetic risk factor to its manifestations has not yet been specified. Obviously, without knowing what the genes might be, we have no way of saying how they code for biological structures and functions that in turn predispose schizophrenia.

Neurological abnormalities   A number of studies suggest that there is something amiss in the nervous system of schizophrenic individuals. Investigations of young children at risk for schizophrenia—by virtue of having schizophrenic relatives—show that a variety of their neuropsychological systems are immature or out of synchrony with one another (Fish, 1984). These children have difficulty standing or sitting unaided. They are clumsy and awkward. They have difficulty following moving objects with their eyes, or reaching out and grasping them. And they cannot readily transfer objects from one hand to another.

These findings are worthy of note, implying as they do that a genetic predisposition to schizophrenia may be evident in specific perceptual and motor skills early in life. However, these findings at the same time are more of a tickle than an answer to the causes of schizophrenia. Neurological abnormalities are not evident in all at-risk children. They by and large resolve themselves early on, so that the adolescent or adult who is to develop schizophrenia shows few if any

of them. Finally, the relationship of these childhood abnormalities to the substantive adult symptoms is not clear, although biomedical theorists favor an interpretation that points to a difficulty in integrating neurological systems. This deficit, if it exists, would explain the neurological abnormalities observed among high-risk infants as well as the psychotic symptoms observed among schizophrenic adults.

Neurological studies of adults with schizophrenia similarly provide numerous hints yet no definitive answer (Casanova & Kleinman, 1990). The simplest summary is that many studies point to abnormalities in the nervous system of schizophrenic individuals, but the particular problem differs from sample to sample, and in no case does a single anomaly cut across all those who are diagnosed.

Some studies find that some of those with schizophrenia have abnormally enlarged cerebral ventricles, the hollow spaces in the brain (Bornstein, Schwarzkopf, Olson, & Nasrallah, 1992; Holsenbeck et al., 1992; Raz & Raz, 1990; Van Horn & McManus, 1992). Other studies link this anomaly to the negative symptoms of schizophrenia but not to the positive ones (Andreasen, Olsen, Dennert, & Smith, 1982). However, findings from still other investigations provide a much less clear picture of the physiological correlates of positive versus negative symptoms (Moscarelli, Cesana, Ciussani, Novati, & Cazzullo, 1989; Wilms et al., 1992).

Additionally, some studies imply that the rate of metabolic activity in the frontal cortex of schizophrenic individuals is abnormally low (see Figure 12.5); still others fail to support this finding (Buchsbaum et al., 1990; Budinger, 1992; Sedvall, 1992). Along these lines, investigation after investigation has found something abnormal in those diagnosed with schizophrenia, including EEG patterns, cortical size, neural density, blood flow to the brain, and so on; study after study has also failed to find the same effect (see Mirsky & Duncan, 1986).

Dopamine   Perhaps the most attention to biological factors in schizophrenia has centered on the role of the neurotransmitter *dopamine*. According to the **dopamine hypothesis,** schizophrenia is caused by abnormalities in parts of the brain sensitive to dopamine (Goldstein & Deutch, 1992). Different versions of the dopamine hypothesis exist, variously suggesting that the disorder is linked with an overabundance of the neurotransmitter, an increased number of dopamine-sensitive receptors, an enhanced sensitivity of these receptors, and/or an asynchrony of different dopamine systems in the brain. Regardless, several lines of evidence point to excessive dopamine activity in schizophrenic individuals.

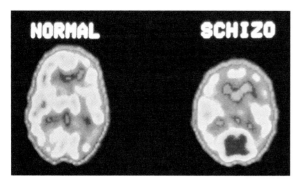

FIGURE 12.5

PET Scan of Schizophrenic Brain   *Metabolic activity may be abnormal in the brain of a schizophrenic individual.*

First, drugs that increase the amount of dopamine in the brain sometimes produce a state that is indistinguishable from schizophrenia (Lieberman, Kinon, & Loebel, 1990). Among the effects of chronic amphetamine use is an increase in the levels of dopamine. An amphetamine-induced psychosis presents itself clinically as something that looks a great deal like an acute schizophrenic episode (Connell, 1958). As the amphetamine is reduced, the dopamine is reduced, and the person returns to normal.

Second, drugs that decrease dopamine activity in the brain reduce the severity and extent of schizophrenic symptoms, particularly positive symptoms (Kleinman et al., 1984). The antipsychotic medications, to be discussed shortly, all share an effect on the amount of dopamine activity in the brain.

Third, an intriguing relationship exists between schizophrenia and Parkinson's disease, suggesting that in some ways they are biochemical opposites (Seeman & Niznik, 1990). Because Parkinson's disease is unambiguously neurological, and because it is immediately caused by *too little* dopamine activity in the brain, the inference follows that schizophrenia has something to do with *too much* dopamine activity.

Drugs used to treat Parkinson's disease work by increasing levels of dopamine activity. If given in excess amounts, the side effect in a Parkinsonian individual is a syndrome that looks like schizophrenia. Conversely, drugs used to treat schizophrenia work by decreasing the levels of dopamine activity. If given in excess amounts, the side effect in a schizophrenic individual is a syndrome that looks like Parkinson's disease. The physician must therefore be careful in prescribing medications for one disorder versus the other so as not to overshoot the dosage and end up producing something that is like the opposite (Davidson et al., 1987). Because such overshooting is rather common, it is customary to administer counteracting drugs. The coun-

teracting drug for one is essentially the drug used to treat the other, and vice versa.

Fourth, the most direct evidence for the role of dopamine in schizophrenia comes from autopsies of the brains of schizophrenic individuals. Some studies have found an excess of dopamine-sensitive receptors (e.g., Pearce, Seeman, Jellinger, & Tourtellotte, 1990). This seems to happen in particular when the individual in question displays prominent positive symptoms (but see Breier et al., 1987; Farde et al., 1990; Sarai, Matsunaga, & Kimura, 1990). Again, we encounter a link between dopamine and positive symptoms. A potential ambiguity in these autopsy findings is that the prolonged use of antipsychotic medication can result in precisely this excess (Snyder, 1981). In other words, the autopsy findings might reflect a by-product of the drug treatment for schizophrenia, not a preexisting condition of the person.

For the time being, we can conclude that available evidence supports some form of the dopamine hypothesis. Excess dopamine activity is characteristic of some schizophrenic individuals, particularly those with positive symptoms. Decreases in this activity are linked with improvement, increases with greater deterioration. Yet there are inadequacies in this hypothesis. It does not apply to all cases or all symptoms of schizophrenia, which was the original hope when it was formulated. Further, the relation between dopamine and the other biological factors implicated in schizophrenia is not known. Presumably, if the dopamine hypothesis is viable, what is heritable about schizophrenia is a tendency toward increased dopamine activity, but this has not been shown, in large part because of the difficulty of studying microscopic neurological processes (Lee & Seeman, 1980). Finally, the mechanism leading from excess dopamine to the specific symptoms has not yet been explicitly spelled out (but see Cohen & Servan-Schreiber, 1992).

ENVIRONMENTAL RISK FACTORS

At this point, we cannot dismiss the role of biology in schizophrenia. Nonetheless, we are also aware that biology has yet to reveal the full answer. It might never provide the whole answer, at least so long as we describe schizophrenia in such broad terms. The day may come when some subset of what we now call schizophrenia will be sufficiently explained with a narrowly biological etiology, but as for the whole of schizophrenia, we will likely need to look additionally at the environment to understand its causes.

Stress   Longitudinal studies suggest that schizophrenic individuals have more than their share of stressful life events, both early in life as well as immediately prior to the development of schizophrenic symptoms (Malla, Cortese, Shaw, & Ginsberg, 1990; Nuechterlein et al., 1992; Steinberg & Durell, 1968). For example, the loss of a job or a divorce may immediately foreshadow a schizophrenic episode. (Remember Mr. G., described earlier, and the precipitation of psychosis by his wife's affair.) Relapses are also predicted by the occurrence of stressful life events.

Studies of stress and schizophrenia yield results that are not particularly robust, nor is there any clue as to exactly what type of life event is specifically associated with its development. Perhaps no specific link exists (Dohrenwend, Shrout, Link, & Skodol, 1987). Furthermore, stressful life events foreshadow *many* forms of psychopathology. Stress per se may be a better explanation of schizophreniform and delusional disorders than it is of full-blown schizophrenia.

Family interaction   Perhaps the best case for environmental risk factors has to do with the patterns of communication within the family. According to this view, the family of the individual who will develop schizophrenia communicates in a contradictory and/or bizarre way. The child is necessarily confused. Because he cannot leave the situation, and because he or she lacks the cognitive wherewithal to demand clarification, he retreats into schizophrenia (Bateson, Jackson, Haley, & Weakland, 1956).

Theorists who attribute the origins of schizophrenia to disordered family interaction point to highly idiosyncratic beliefs in the family of the schizophrenic individual (Lidz, 1975). Ideas about reality that are not accepted outside the family may have great currency within it. For instance, think back to the identical quadruplets described earlier in the chapter. In their family, puritanical beliefs were combined with sexual abuse; Nora, Iris, Myra, and Hester were never encouraged to think of themselves as whole people; Henry and Gertrude were in a constant struggle with one another, using the children as tools in their fights. This was an unusual family, to be sure.

How have these hypotheses about family interaction fared? On the one hand, research has failed to bear out the specifics of such predictions (Angermeyer, 1978; Jacobs, 1986). And the difficulty in identifying cause and effect remains. However, we can tentatively say that the families of schizophrenic individuals, even prior to the schizophrenic episode, are sometimes unusual (Goldstein, 1988). Parents can be domineering. They can be cold as well as overprotective. The child's own needs may be subordinated to those of the parent, suggesting to theorists such as Ronald Laing (1959) that the child never develops a complete sense of self. At the same time, appreciate that the correlation between unusual family styles and subsequent schizo-

Some theorists have proposed that the course of schizophrenia is influenced by family interaction.

phrenia among offspring is quite modest in magnitude. Most individuals diagnosed with schizophrenia come from mundane families.

The clearest role of the family in schizophrenia comes from investigations of the prognosis of the disorder (Leff & Vaughn, 1985). A schizophrenic individual's *subsequent* improvement or not is related to the degree to which the family is emotionally overinvolved and excessively critical. This characteristic, termed **expressed emotion (EE),** is ascertained through family interviews and observations. The greater a family's EE, the worse the prognosis for a schizophrenic family member, a finding shown in more than a dozen different studies (Parker & Hadzi-Pavlovic, 1990). For those in families with high EE, the chance of relapse is greater than 50%, in contrast to a relapse rate of 10% for those in low EE families. Unusual for psychological research of this type, the basic finding has been replicated in several countries, including Australia, Brazil, Czechoslovakia, Italy, and Spain (e.g., Bertrando et al., 1992; Martins, de Lemos, & Bebbington, 1992; Montero, Gomez-Beneyto, Ruiz, Puche, & Adam, 1992; Mozny & Votypkova, 1992; Vaughan et al., 1992).

The studies of EE and relapse have been criticized because the families that are high versus low in expressed emotion may well differ in additional ways that influence relapse. Said another way, these are correlational studies, and confounds might threaten findings. But some of the studies have controlled statistically for obvious confounds such as the disorder's severity.

Also strengthening the conclusion that EE is critical are further studies with more refined designs. First,

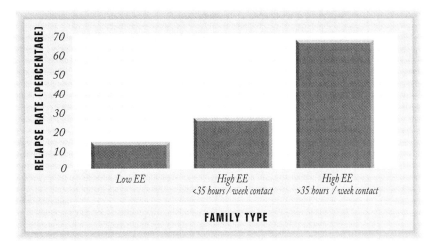

FIGURE 12.6

EXPRESSED EMOTION AND RELAPSE IN SCHIZOPHRENIA   *Researchers studied 128 individuals in Great Britain following their discharge from a hospital after a schizophrenic episode. All were discharged home, and the expressed emotion (EE) of their families was ascertained. During a 6-month period, relapse rate (i.e., return to the hospital) was highest for those individuals in high EE families who spent a great deal of time at home in face-to-face contact with other family members.*
SOURCE: DATA DERIVED FROM "THE INFLUENCE OF FAMILY AND SOCIAL FACTORS ON THE COURSE OF PSYCHIATRIC ILLNESS," BY C. VAUGHN AND J. P. LEFF, 1976, *British Journal of Psychiatry, 129,* PP. 125–137.

EE has a deleterious effect on schizophrenic individuals discharged from the hospital when they spend a great deal of time with their families but not when contact is more limited (Vaughn & Leff, 1976) (see Figure 12.6). Second, interventions that reduce a family's EE decrease the chance of relapse among schizophrenic family members (Kuipers, Birchwood, & McCreadie, 1992).

We should not blame the family for relapse, however. An earlier generation of theorists pointed an accusing finger at the mothers of those with schizophrenia, even giving them a particular name: *schizophrenogenic mothers*—mothers who produce schizophrenia in their children (Fromm-Reichmann, 1948). This is insidious, revealing a misunderstanding of psychological findings (see Neill, 1990).

AN INTEGRATED CONCEPTION

Taken together, research results implicate both biological and environmental variables as contributing factors to schizophrenia. Each line of evidence can be second-guessed, and failure to replicate particular findings seems quite common in this line of work. Part of the problem stems from the difficulty in diagnosing schizophrenia in the first place, and another part lies in the fact that it is often an extreme form of abnormality; as a result, the schizophrenic individual is not an ideal research subject. But if we accept research findings at face value, we can see that they are not incompatible. The fact that no class of variables is overwhelmingly implicated by itself with regard to schizophrenia suggests that the disorder is multiply determined. A likely strategy for its explanation, therefore, is to ask how we might integrate the biological and environmental risk factors.

Diathesis-stress   One possible approach is with the *diathesis-stress model.* By this view, an individual brings a constitutional predisposition to develop schizophrenia to the events in his life. The predisposition might be genetic and/or the result of subtle illnesses or injuries early in life. In either case, the predisposition is a tendency to produce excess dopamine in the wake of stress (see Figure 12.7). Excess dopamine produces the range of symptoms that we label schizophrenic. So, under stressful circumstances, the vulnerable person develops the disorder. It does not develop if the person carries no predisposition. And it does not develop in the absence of stress.

What are the psychological effects of excessive dopamine activity? Neurons with dopamine receptors tend to be concentrated in some parts of the brain rather than others, which means that the dopamine

FIGURE **12.7**

AN INTEGRATED MODEL OF
SCHIZOPHRENIA
*Contemporary theorists agree that
schizophrenia involves a complex
etiology that includes both
biological and environmental
risk factors.*

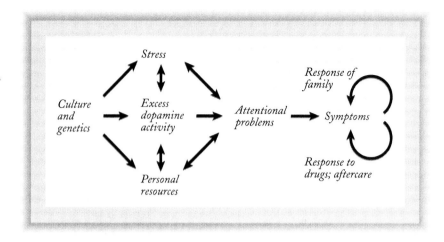

hypothesis refers not simply to a neurotransmitter but also to specific places in the brain, namely those involved in arousal and reinforcement: the midbrain and hypothalamus (Carlson, 1986). If schizophrenia involves overactivity of the dopamine system, individuals with schizophrenia should be overly sensitive to environmental stimuli (Braff & Geyer, 1990). If casual thoughts and actions are reinforced, they increase in frequency. Experiences run amok as trivial thoughts and sensations take on great importance. People become unable to concentrate on what is important, because everything seems to be (Cohen & Servan-Schreiber, 1993).

The role of attention   A great deal of research over the years has looked at the role of attention in schizophrenia (Erlenmeyer-Kimling & Cornblatt, 1992). Theorists usually liken attention to a filter, a presumed mechanism that allows us to sort out stimuli into those that are processed and those that are not (Broadbent, 1958). Most of us can exercise at least some control over attention. In a crowded room, we listen to the person with whom we are talking but not to other people. On a crowded highway, we attend to the cars about us but not to the billboards along the way.

At times, some stimuli demand our attention, even if we are not anticipating them. They become salient because they are intense, important, intriguing, or dangerous. Our attention is jerked away from our ongoing activity and onto those stimuli. And our attention can be jerked again onto yet other stimuli that are just as intense, important, and so on.

Suppose schizophrenic individuals find *all* stimuli equally demanding. Their attentional filters are not doing their job, because they let in too much information (Feldon & Weiner, 1992). Research supports this

characterization, because schizophrenic individuals often perform poorly at laboratory tasks that require them to pay attention to some stimuli but not to others (Shakow, 1963). Along these same lines are findings that those diagnosed with schizophrenia think in overinclusive terms (Saccuzzo & Braff, 1986). They abstract concepts from both relevant and irrelevant information. This might reflect the same deficit in filtering information.

If schizophrenic individuals have a problem with how they think and perceive caused by too much incoming information, then the symptoms of schizophrenia start to make sense. Hallucinations and delusions might be strong versions of the daydreams that most of us have no difficulty tuning out or dismissing. Those with schizophrenia usually hear voices, for example, when there is background noise: traffic, the wind, the roar of the ocean. They have some raw material for the sensation of hearing, but they overinterpret what they hear. Their disorganized speech might be the result of constant intrusions of thoughts and sensations. As a result of all of this, they are bound to be overwhelmed, anxious, depressed, or confused.

An individual once hospitalized with schizophrenia provided the following description of her thinking during this period of her life:

> *What I do want to explain, if I can, is the* **exaggerated state of awareness** *in which I lived before, during and after my acute illness. At first it was as if parts of my brain "awoke" which had been dormant, and I became interested in a wide assortment of people, events, places and ideas which normally would make no impression on me. . . . The walk of a stranger in the street could be a "sign" to me which I must interpret. Every face in the*

windows of a passing streetcar would be engraved on my mind, all of them concentrating on me and trying to pass me some sort of message. . . . A hodge-podge of unrelated stimuli were distracting me from things which should have had my undivided attention.   (MacDonald, 1960, p. 218)

This description nicely illustrates the problems with attention that characterize schizophrenia.

An integrated model linking excess dopamine activity to the psychological characteristics of schizophrenia is consistent with most of the evidence we have about risk factors, but many details need to be added. What is the constitutional predisposition to schizophrenia? A family history seems to be an indicator, but it is an imperfect one. How does this predisposition interact with environmental events to produce schizophrenia? Why does this disorder take on such diverse forms? How are negative symptoms explained?

TREATMENTS

The story of treatments for schizophrenia parallels the search for its causes. The same sorts of controversies have ensued. None would argue that antipsychotic medications, introduced widely in the 1950s, have been helpful in the alleviation and control of some schizophrenic symptoms. We might even say that they revolutionized the treatment of this disorder (Andreasen, 1984). However, the treatment picture is not fully captured by a biomedical approach. Positive

symptoms are usually better controlled than negative ones. Medications do not cure schizophrenia in the way that penicillin cures pneumonia. Finally, these medications can have terrible side effects for some individuals, so much so that they cannot and will not continue to take them.

Medication is simply one weapon in the armory of the therapist who treats schizophrenia; it needs to be supplemented by psychologically based treatments, including the creation of a more benign and supportive setting for the recovering individual. The practical problem, though, is that medication is easy to prescribe and relatively inexpensive. Psychological therapy and social engineering are time-consuming and expensive, and providing the full range of therapeutic options for schizophrenic individuals does not appear to be where society is investing its resources.

In the middle 1950s, perhaps 600,000 individuals in the United States were patients in psychiatric wards and hospitals. By the early 1970s, this figure was cut virtually in half; and by the late 1970s, it was cut in half yet again, even though the overall population of the United States was increasing (Witkin, 1981) (see Figure 12.8). But this does not mean that all these former patients lived happily ever after. Many were warehoused, sent to cheap boarding homes little better than their hospitals. Many wound up on the streets. Many wound up back in hospitals, for short but recurrent stays, in the phenomenon sometimes referred to as *revolving door psychiatry*. But it is unfair to lay the blame for all of this at the feet of psychiatrists; it is our society as a whole that has chosen, however unwittingly, *not* to provide the continued care needed to help schizophrenic individuals rejoin the world (Chapter 15).

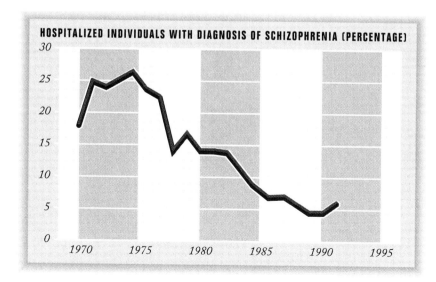

FIGURE 12.8

HOSPITALIZATIONS OVER TIME *Both the absolute number and the proportion of individuals hospitalized with a diagnosis of schizophrenia have decreased over time. Discharge records from six psychiatric hospitals in North America showed clear evidence of this trend.*

SOURCE: DATA DERIVED FROM "SHIFTS IN DIAGNOSTIC FREQUENCIES OF SCHIZOPHRENIA AND MAJOR AFFECTIVE DISORDERS AT SIX NORTH AMERICAN PSYCHIATRIC HOSPITALS, 1972–1988," BY A. L. STOLL ET AL., 1993, *American Journal of Psychiatry, 150,* PP. 1668–1673.

In the 1800s, schizophrenic patients were treated in a variety of ways, including placing them in a "circulating chair" and spinning them around.

EARLY BIOMEDICAL APPROACHES

The various medical treatments appearing throughout history have all been used with schizophrenia. In fact, they were often tried first with schizophrenic individuals, because it has long been considered the most serious of the disorders. We saw this in the case of convulsive therapies, now used with success to treat unipolar depression.

Instructive along these lines are **lobotomies.** There are actually several forms of lobotomy, but all refer to a surgical procedure in which nerve fibers connecting the frontal lobes of the brain to the thalamus are severed. *Great and Desperate Cures,* by psychologist Elliot Valenstein (1986), is a history of this procedure, at one time a highly popular biomedical treatment for schizophrenia. The point of the title is that desperate problems demand desperate solutions. Schizophrenia is a frightening disorder, and an individual in the midst of a psychotic episode perfectly exemplifies what we mean by abnormality, in all of its aspects.

The operation was pioneered in 1935 by a Portugese neurologist named Eges Moniz, who interpreted the procedure as a way of decreasing the influence of negative emotions (presumably housed in the thalamus) on thinking (presumably housed in the frontal lobes). Moniz performed the operation on a single patient, entering the brain through the top of his skull. The patient apparently improved after the operation, and so Moniz published his results to great fanfare. In 1949, he received the Nobel Prize for medicine.

Different physicians elaborated on the original strategy, coming up with different methods for entering the skull and severing neural fibers. Two American doctors, Walter Freeman and James Watts, devised the simplest alternative, entering the brain through the eye socket, after pushing the eye aside (see Figure 12.9).

In retrospect, perhaps the most amazing thing about lobotomies is that they did not do more damage. Some patients survived the procedure and even improved. Little skepticism was initially expressed about the effectiveness of the procedure as a treatment of schizophrenia (and depression). Freeman and Watts toured the country, and personally performed thousands of lobotomies. They wrote a popular book on

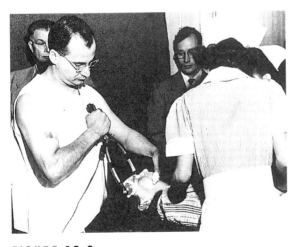
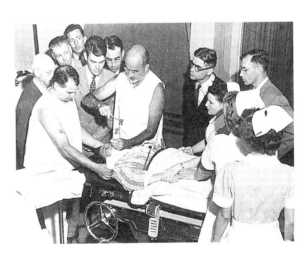

FIGURE 12.9

TRANSORBITAL LOBOTOMY   *Lobotomies were at one time widely used as a treatment for schizophrenia. In one typical procedure, the individual would first be anesthetized with ECT (shown on left) and then be lobotomized by having the brain entered through the eye socket (shown on right).*

the subject (Freeman & Watts, 1942). By the 1950s, tens of thousands of lobotomies had been performed in this country alone.

Criticism began to surface in the mid-1950s. Systematic looks at how people fared in its aftermath showed that, on the average, they were worse off than before. Patients became apathetic and withdrawn. They developed seizure disorders. Some became hyperactive. They had trouble learning. As many as 20% died (Moser, 1969). We now recognize these varied effects as associated with brain damage, which after all was what lobotomies created.

With the introduction of drug treatments for schizophrenia in the 1950s, there was a marked drop in the number of lobotomies performed. The procedure is occasionally carried out today, usually for intractable epilepsy, pain, or obsessive-compulsive disorder (Mindus & Jenike, 1992). Psychosurgery has become more refined because of technological advances that allow more discrete lesions to be made by the surgeon, yet the approach is still highly controversial (Diering & Bell, 1991). Valenstein's general point remains. Desperate problems demand desperate cures. When our backs are against the wall, we will seize any apparent solution to a pressing problem.

Drug treatment for schizophrenia often helps control flagrant psychotic symptoms but not social estrangement.

CHLORPROMAZINE

As early as the 16th century, physicians knew that extracts from a plant called *Rauwolfia* (dogbane) had a calming effect on highly agitated individuals (Arieti, 1974). In the 1950s, researchers isolated the critical ingredient of this plant, an alkaloid given the name *reserpine*. When administered to psychotic individuals, reserpine had a beneficial effect. Shortly thereafter, another researcher discovered how to create a synthetic drug that had the same calming effect as reserpine yet worked faster and had fewer side effects. This drug, **chlorpromazine,** has become the most popular treatment of schizophrenia. Chlorpromazine is sometimes described as a *phenothiazine,* or a *neuroleptic,* or a *major tranquilizer;* for our purposes, these are all synonyms. One version or another is manufactured under a variety of trade names, with Thorazine probably the most popular.[3]

Chlorpromazine is not a barbiturate or minor tranquilizer; in proper doses, it sedates a person without putting him or her to sleep. It reduces anxiety, but more importantly, it decreases the severity and frequency of the positive symptoms of schizophrenia. The drug presumably works by binding to dopamine

receptors in the brain, preventing dopamine itself from doing so. Thus, excessive dopamine activity is reduced.

For many schizophrenic individuals, chlorpromazine controls their acute psychotic episodes. If they continue to take the medicine, it reduces the likelihood of future episodes. As noted earlier, these drugs do not seem to have much effect on negative symptoms. But even if chlorpromazine only somewhat helps some schizophrenic individuals, it still represents an incredible improvement over previously available treatments.

John M. was a 28-year-old man with a long history of schizophrenia (Janowsky, Addario, & Risch, 1987). He experienced accusatory auditory hallucinations. He believed that the FBI followed him and that people whispered about him, calling him a homosexual. Mr. M. lived at best a checkered existence, in and out of hospitals. However, when he was prescribed Haldol, one of the major tranquilizers, his symptoms decreased, and he was able to obtain and keep a job. He did not like to take Haldol, and whenever he discontinued his medication, he experienced a severe relapse within several weeks. His family and his therapist urged him to stay on the medication, but Mr. M. did not wish to regard himself as having a problem. The medication was proof to him that he did, so he was reluctant to take it. He was switched to another major tranquilizer administered by injection every 2 weeks. This proved much more satisfactory, and Mr. M.'s condition stabilized. He was able to do a good job at work and stay out of the hospital.

---

[3] There are other drugs used to treat schizophrenia that are chemically different than chlorpromazine. *Halperidol*, better known by its trade name Haldol, is an example. Much of what is said in this chapter about chlorpromazine applies to antipsychotic drugs like Haldol as well.

The benefits of the major tranquilizers are qualified by the occasional side effects that sometimes make them even less desirable than the condition they help treat (see Table 12.3). Many of these side effects are only temporary, however, and many can be removed or reduced by decreasing the dose.

Among the most common side effects are **extrapyramidal symptoms,** which resemble the movement disturbances that characterize Parkinson's disease. The person's facial muscles may become immobile, so that her expression seems glum and unhappy. Her extremities may tremble, and she may experience muscle spasms. She might salivate uncontrollably. Her gait can slow, and she may walk in a shuffling manner. She may be unable to sit still, always bouncing her legs up and down. And she might have an uncontrollable urge to pace. Extrapyramidal symptoms can be controlled with medications used to treat Parkinson's disease.

A very serious side effect of chlorpromazine, which occurs among a minority of individuals, usually older ones, is **tardive dyskinesia:** involuntary movements of the lips, tongue, and face (Casey, 1990). These movements can be highly embarrassing for the schizophrenic individual as well as distracting to others. Tardive dyskinesia seems to appear when neuroleptics are reduced or discontinued, which creates an obvious dilemma when curtailing the dosage is necessary to remedy other side effects that have developed. Tardive dyskinesia is not reversible once it appears. A caveat is in order, though, and that is that this condition might be produced at least in part by whatever brings about schizophrenia in the first place (Awouters, Niemegeers, & Janssen, 1990). Long before the advent of chlorpromazine, tardive dyskinesia was observed among some older individuals with schizophrenia (Kraepelin, 1913/1971).

CLOZAPINE

A newly introduced drug—**clozapine**—has attracted attention because its use apparently does not lead to tardive dyskinesia (Stephens, 1990). Furthermore, this drug seems effective for schizophrenic individuals who do not respond to typical neuroleptics (Fitton & Heel, 1990). Clozapine reduces not only the positive symptoms of schizophrenia but also the negative ones.

Like any medication, clozapine has side effects (Safferman, Lieberman, Kane, Szymanski, & Kinon, 1991). Weight gain is reported among many who use the drug (Leadbetter et al., 1992). The threshold for seizures may be lowered (Jann, 1991). And a potentially fatal reduction in the number of white blood cells occurs in about 1% to 2% of individuals who use clozapine (Ogle & Miller, 1991). For this reason, blood must be monitored on a weekly basis. Clozapine thus ends up as an expensive treatment. Over a year, the prescription may cost $4,000 and the blood monitoring an additional $9,000 (Wallis & Willwerth, 1992). Nonetheless, for a number of schizophrenic individuals, clozapine represents a vast improvement over chlorpromazine.

TABLE 12.3

POSSIBLE SIDE EFFECTS OF MAJOR TRANQUILIZERS
Although the major tranquilizers control many of the symptoms of schizophrenia, these drugs are not without the possibility of serious side effects, including those listed here.

extrapyramidal symptoms
tardive dyskinesia
dry mouth and throat
drowsiness and oversedation
depression
weight gain
constipation
blurry vision
susceptibility to sunburn
menstrual difficulties (among women)
impotence (among men)
jaundice
hypotension (i.e., low blood pressure)
racing and irregular heartbeat

Kevin Buchberger provides a dramatic example of how clozapine can help an individual with schizophrenia (Wallis & Willwerth, 1992). At age 33, he had spent a decade suffering from recurrent psychotic episodes. He was haunted by a spirit that took the form of a golden beam of light. Buchberger believed that the spirit had previously haunted an executed murderer. In his own words, "It tormented me, but I never knew what it wanted" (p. 53). Conventional neuroleptics brought him no relief, and he literally lost 10 years of his life wrestling with his symptoms. However, he responded extremely well to clozapine. His symptoms ceased, and he was able for the first time to take a job. Kevin Buchberger also established relationships with others and began to do volunteer work, counseling other individuals with schizophrenia.

Just why clozapine works so well is not clear (Lidsky & Banerjee, 1992; Meltzer, 1991). Like chlorpromazine, it reduces dopamine activity. But it also appears to affect the activity of several other neurotransmitters, including **serotonin** (Meltzer & Gudelsky, 1992). Unfortunately, the role of serotonin in schizophrenia is not known. As you remember, serotonin has been implicated in depression (Chapter 9), so perhaps it is involved in the emotional aspects of schizophrenia. If so, then the effectiveness of this particular drug for negative symptoms makes sense.

PSYCHOLOGICAL TREATMENTS

Many schizophrenic individuals do not comply with drug treatment (Buchanan, 1992; Mulaik, 1992). As noted, one reason is the side effects. Another reason is failure of typical neuroleptics to touch the negative symptoms. At least in part, the flagrant hallucinations and delusions distract the person from his chronic emptiness and social isolation. To ask him to give up such psychotic symptoms with nothing to replace them is to ask a great deal.

Drug treatment needs to be supplemented with psychological therapies (Falloon, 1992). Part of this psychological intervention should be supportive and educational, to help a person understand why medication is helpful and also to appreciate what the medication cannot do. But psychotherapy for schizophrenia may also be more substantial (Kessler, 1990; Zahniser, Coursey, & Hershberger, 1991). To date, though, there is no consensus about which psychological approaches are most useful. What we have instead are numerous suggested strategies derived from a variety of models of abnormality.

For example, *psychodynamic approaches* have been used to treat schizophrenia (e.g., Fromm-Reichmann, 1948; Rosen, 1947). If a good rapport can be established—and this can be difficult—then improvement sometimes occurs (see Coursey, 1989; Robbins, 1992; White, 1989). The practical problem with such approaches is that they are time-consuming and expensive. So few systematic outcome studies have been conducted that it is impossible to offer any general conclusions about the success of psychodynamic treatment (see Cullberg, 1991; Wasylenki, 1992). Some theorists regard psychodynamic treatment, when not accompanied with medication, as potentially harmful to schizophrenic individuals.

Behavior therapy has been used with good effect to target specific behaviors that create problems for the schizophrenic individual (Benton & Schroeder, 1990; Tarrier, 1991; Tarrier & Barrowclough, 1990).

A woman with schizophrenia constantly hoarded towels in the hospital where she was staying (Ayllon, 1963). This habit greatly annoyed the hospital staff as well as her fellow patients. Using a strategy called **stimulus** *satiation, the hospital staff began to give her towel after towel, turning her preferred habit into an odious one through constant repetition. Note that this intervention did not "cure" the woman of her schizophrenia, but it made her less disruptive, and the long-term hope was that this would start to chip away at the social isolation that often accompanies the disorder.*

Sometimes behavior therapy is carried out on an entire hospital ward. In a **token economy,** patients earn tokens from staff members for desirable behaviors such as staying awake, making eye contact, initiating conversation, keeping clean, and so on (Kazdin, 1977). They lose tokens for negative behaviors. Tokens can be used to "purchase" desired commodities—cigarettes, candy, weekend passes, and movie tickets. Token economies embody the behaviorist view of the world, except that the system of prevailing rewards and punishments is made highly explicit.

Cognitive therapy has been suggested as a strategy for treating some of the cognitive dysfunctions that characterize schizophrenia (Spring & Ravdin, 1992). The therapist helps the schizophrenic person articulate what he is thinking and evaluate it against the evidence. Changes need to occur not just in the content of thinking but in the processes involved, like attention, abstraction, and concept formation. Studies to date imply that cognitive therapy leads to modest improvements in how schizophrenic individuals think, but unfortunately, this approach does not normalize schizophrenic thought (Brenner, Hodel, Roder, & Corrigan, 1992).

Family therapy for those with schizophrenia stems from the assumption that dynamics within the family are critical to the maintenance of schizophrenia (Anderson, Reiss, & Hogarty, 1986; Beels, 1975; Goldstein, 1986; McFarlane, 1983). The majority of schizophrenic individuals in the United States today live with their families, so any strategy that can reduce emotional overinvolvement and criticism is bound to help (Berkowitz, Shavit, & Leff, 1990).

In *group therapy*, individuals with schizophrenia meet together once or twice a week with a therapist to discuss common problems and devise solutions (Wilson, Diamond, & Factor, 1990). Outcome studies attest to the effectiveness of such group therapy; imparted are interpersonal skills and techniques for coping with the diverse problems associated with the disorder (Beeber, 1991; Douglas & Mueser, 1990; Eckman et al., 1992; Kanas, 1991).

A large part of my own clinical work some years ago consisted of coordinating such groups for schizophrenic individuals following their discharge from the hospital.

The typical group included eight to ten members. We met weekly over a period of months. Group membership was not fixed; participants came and went. My goal was to facilitate interaction among these individuals, fostering the social skills and contacts they would need to get along in the larger world. Our discussions would often center on the stigma they carried with them as former mental patients.

Sometimes family and group approaches are combined in *psychoeducational programs,* in which individuals with schizophrenia and their family members meet with therapists who provide information about the disorder and practical advice about social skills, coping, physical fitness, nutrition, health care services, and the like (e.g., Kane, DiMartino, & Jimenez, 1990). The goal of these programs is to help not only diagnosed individuals but also those who live with them.

The most ambitious adjunct to drug treatment is **milieu therapy:** a total treatment system designed to facilitate improvement of schizophrenic individuals (Almond, 1975). This can be done within a psychiatric hospital or other settings like halfway houses or day treatment centers (Artiss, 1962). Different mental health professionals work as a coordinated team so that therapy in effect takes place over the entire day.

For example, in a hospital, the ward as a whole is thought of as a community where the patients live. They are expected to participate in the life of the community, attending activities and participating in meetings. A patient government may be created, with elected officers who work with the staff to make decisions that affect the nature of life on the ward. In the hospital where I once worked, the patients decided to ban caffeinated coffee from the ward coffee pot; they felt it was not healthy for their doctors and nurses to be so jittery all of the time.

The 1975 movie One Flew over the Cuckoo's Nest, *based on Ken Kesey's novel of the same title, depicts the dehumanizing aspects of institutionalization.*

Milieu therapy can include a token economy. Patients earn privileges by participating appropriately in various activities, staying out of bed during the day, and refraining from bizarre behavior (cf. Kahn & White, 1989). These privileges might take the form of being able to leave the ward and the hospital for weekends, making phone calls, having visitors, seeing movies, and the like. This aspect of milieu therapy tries to mimic on a small-scale a larger society where certain ways of behaving have certain consequences (Gunderson, 1980). "Craziness" does not result in rewards, something which patients quickly realize (see Cohen & Khan, 1990).

This kind of therapy may look heavy-handed, and it is. When I first began to work on a ward with milieu therapy, I did not like the system at all because it exaggerated the conformity that plagues the outer world. But as I came to learn more about schizophrenia, I saw the point. The goal of a milieu system is to give the person the self-control that her problem denies her, so that she can retreat from the larger world if and when she wants to, not because she has no other response available.

Milieu therapy is a total treatment system, usually within a setting where the schizophrenic individual lives, such as a psychiatric hospital. In effect, therapy takes place over the entire day, involving virtually every aspect of daily living.

How should we conceptualize schizophrenia? It is a problem that involves the entire person, as a biological, psychological, and social being. The most reasonable way to help the schizophrenic individual is by recognizing all these facets of the problem. Drug therapy coupled with support and information, placed in a setting that encourages less troubled behavior, seems to be the way to proceed.

Summary

✦ Schizophrenia is a severe form of abnormality, characterized by psychotic episodes and deteriorated functioning evident for at least 6 months. This disorder has also proved controversial, as theorists over the years have debated how to conceptualize it—as a discrete illness or as a biopsychosocial problem.

SYMPTOMS, SUBTYPES, AND OTHER PSYCHOTIC SYNDROMES

✦ DSM-IV specifies several subtypes of schizophrenia: catatonic, disorganized, paranoid, undifferentiated, and residual. Perhaps more useful is the distinction between reactive versus process schizophrenia, which reflects how rapidly or slowly symptoms develop, respectively, and is related to good versus bad prognosis, again respectively. Another potentially useful distinction is between cases of schizophrenia in which positive symptoms such as hallucinations and delusions predominate versus those in which negative symptoms such as flat affect and social withdrawal predominate. These instances may have different etiologies and respond to different treatments.

✦ Several other disorders appear similar to schizophrenia. In schizophreniform disorder, schizophrenic-like symptoms are present, but for less than 6 months. In schizoaffective disorder, the individual shows signs of both schizophrenia and mood disorder. A delusional disorder revolves around a firmly held false belief.

EPIDEMIOLOGY

✦ The prevalence of schizophrenia is about 1% in cultures around the world. It seems to occur equally among men and women, although recent surveys challenge this conclusion. Schizophrenia is more common among the lower socioeconomic class, but only in large cities. It is primarily a problem of young adulthood, and shows a variety of outcomes, from total recovery to chronic institutionalization.

CAUSES

✦ Evidence suggests that schizophrenia has both biological and environmental causes. In biological terms, it is a heritable disorder associated with various neurological abnormalities. Theoretical attention has centered on the role of excessive activity of neurons sensitive to dopamine. In environmental terms, schizophrenic episodes may be foreshadowed and triggered by stressful events. A family style of excessive emotional involvement and criticism bodes poorly for the long-term prognosis of the schizophrenic individual.

✦ A full explanation of the causes of schizophrenia needs to encompass both biological and environmental factors, which appear to entwine in some way to bring it about, perhaps by creating problems with how a person attends to stimuli.

TREATMENTS

✦ Chlorpromazine is a drug that controls the positive symptoms of schizophrenia. However, it does not affect the negative symptoms, and it may have a host of highly undesirable side effects. More promising as a treatment is clozapine, which effectively treats both positive and negative symptoms.

✦ Drug treatment of schizophrenia needs to be supplemented with psychological therapy, which can include psychodynamic treatment, behavior therapy, cognitive therapy, family therapy, group therapy, and milieu therapy.

Key Terms

anhedonia	neologism
catatonic behavior	paranoid schizophrenia
catatonic schizophrenia	positive symptoms (of schizophrenia)
chlorpromazine	
clang association	process schizophrenia
clozapine	reactive schizophrenia
delusion	residual schizophrenia
delusional disorder; paranoid disorder	schizoaffective disorder
	schizophrenia
disorganized schizophrenia	schizophrenia spectrum disorders
dopamine hypothesis	schizophreniform disorder
expressed emotion; EE	serotonin
extrapyramidal symptoms	tardive dyskinesia
flat affect	token economy
hallucination	undifferentiated schizophrenia
lobotomy	waxy flexibility
loose association	word salad
milieu therapy	
negative symptoms (of schizophrenia)	

Personality Disorders

13 Many people today still recognize the name of Sarah Bernhardt (1844–1923), and we know that she was one of the first internationally acclaimed actresses. Much more lost to history were Bernhardt's personal idiosyncrasies, which were numerous and followed with great interest by her contemporaries (Time-Life Books, 1992). According to one of her managers, "If there's anything more remarkable than watching Sarah act, it's watching her live" (p. 74).

For example, Bernhardt was obsessed with death and fascinated by violence. She kept a satin coffin in

Throughout her life, actress Sarah Bernhardt (1844–1923) behaved in markedly eccentric ways.

her room and was often photographed in it. She treated her lovers roughly, pushing one from a second-story window and horsewhipping another. Although she publicly opposed capital punishment, on several occasions she secretly arranged to witness an execution. When in Chicago, she made a point to visit the stockyards and watch the slaughter of cattle.

Bernhardt at the same time was an animal lover, and she collected in particular big cats. Lions, pumas, cheetahs, and ocelots had the free run of her many homes. She also kept a pet alligator from Louisiana, named Ali-Gaga, who unfortunately liked to eat the other pets in the household. Bernhardt sometimes appeared in public adorned with a live chameleon. She also loved chinchillas, but in this case only when they were in the form of fur coats, which she wore all the time, even in summer.

When Sarah Bernhardt died (at age 78), 30,000 people attended her funeral in Paris. Her mausoleum was marked with but a single word: **Bernhardt**. As much now as then, that was all that could be said about a life that defied any simple summary.

Sarah Bernhardt was not just famous but also eccentric. Parallels between her and certain contemporary celebrities are obvious. In this chapter, I discuss a variety of unusual individuals. In some cases, eccentricity is charming (Weeks, 1988). But in other cases, peculiar people are frightening to others and socially estranged.

How can we distinguish eccentricity from disordered personality?

Drawing the line between mere eccentricity and its more insidious versions is an obviously difficult judgment to make. DSM-IV attempts to handle the matter by identifying certain **personality disorders:** constellations of inflexible and maladaptive styles of behaving. The diagnosis of a personality disorder should be made only if these styles are pervasive (surfacing in a wide range of life's domains) and stable (persisting throughout much of adult life).

As you may recall from Chapter 2, personality disorders are coded on Axis II of DSM-IV, and are distinguished from the clinical syndromes on Axis I. Because personality disorders might predispose or exacerbate given clinical syndromes, a therapist should have this information available (Nestadt, Romanoski, Samuels, Folstein, & McHugh, 1992). Furthermore, those with personality disorders seem to respond poorly to most forms of therapy, so again this information is useful (e.g., Reich & Green, 1991; Shea et al., 1990). As described by DSM-IV, these disorders also constitute problems in their own right because they interfere with people's adaptation, particularly to the social world, and because they may be the source of significant personal distress.

As with other psychological abnormalities, we cannot speak of personality disorders without referring to the individual's social context. Although not wholly in the eye of the beholder, these disorders reside at least partly there. DSM-IV in effect suggests that eccentricity becomes a disorder when other people cease being amused by a person's extreme style.

Did Sarah Bernhardt have a personality disorder? She seems to be a strong candidate. Although beloved by many, she was feared by some. Her romantic relationships were tempestuous. Her preoccupation with death and violence hint strongly that she was not always happy.

As noted in Chapter 2, DSM personality disorders prove extremely difficult to diagnose reliably (Mellsop, Varghese, Joshua, & Hicks, 1982). This is hardly surprising granted the inherent problem we confront in defining them. Perhaps diagnosticians should approach these disorders as Masters and Johnson approach sexual dysfunctions (Chapter 11)—by locating them not within individuals but within interacting social groups (Leary, 1957).

Understand that I am *not* arguing against the notion of personality disorders; they capture something important about abnormality. Some people certainly have problems by virtue of their habitual ways of acting. They do not get along well with other people. They are never quite satisfied with themselves. They fail to make the most of their human potential. These are not acute problems like a depressive episode or a bout with amnesia. Instead, they are chronic and pervasive problems. By including personality disorders, DSM-IV extends its coverage beyond acute difficulties marked by a handful of prominent symptoms.

The particular personality disorders that DSM-IV identifies are somewhat arbitrary, both for what is included as well as for what is not (Tyrer, 1988). There is a historical reason for this. Over the last century, literally hundreds of personality disorders have been described, inspired in a variety of ways—clinical observations, theoretical predictions, and empirical investigations (Millon, 1981). To create DSM-III and its successors, the American Psychiatric Association commissioned several committees to reduce these many personality disorders to a small number of the most useful ones. What ensued was an obvious compromise (Pincus, Frances, Davis, First, & Widiger, 1992), not an overall vision of what it means to have a dysfunctional personality (Millon, 1990b). So, DSM-IV includes only ten personality disorders, and these are the focus of this chapter (see Table 13.1).

As I discuss the particular personality disorders, keep in mind that theoretical and research interest has varied greatly from disorder to disorder. In some cases, we know a fair amount. In other cases, I can only

Few people exist at the extreme of any personality characteristic.

TABLE 13.1

DSM-IV PERSONALITY DISORDERS *DSM-IV describes ten different personality disorders.*

DISORDER	CHARACTERIZATION AND TREATMENT
paranoid	pervasive yet unwarranted belief that others intend harm perhaps helped by neuroleptics
schizoid	indifference to others and a restricted range of emotional expression no available treatment
schizotypal	peculiarities in thoughts, actions, and appearance perhaps helped by neuroleptics
antisocial	irresponsible behavior toward others no available treatment
borderline	instability in mood, relationships, and self-image perhaps helped by cognitive therapy, behavior therapy
histrionic	excessive emotionality and attention-seeking perhaps helped by supportive therapy, behavior therapy
narcissistic	grandiosity about the self, hypersensitivity to what others think, and lack of empathy perhaps helped by cognitive therapy, behavior therapy
avoidant	social discomfort, fear of evaluation, and timidity perhaps helped by cognitive therapy, social skills training
dependent	dependence on and submissiveness to others perhaps helped by behavior therapy (e.g., social skills training, assertiveness training, systematic desensitization), cognitive therapy
obsessive-compulsive	perfectionism and inflexibility perhaps helped by behavior therapy (e.g., systematic desensitization, flooding, response prevention)

define the disorder and give a brief example, because we know so little.

PERSONALITY TYPOLOGIES

Although the formal notion of personality disorder has been proposed only within the last century (Tyrer & Ferguson, 1988), the roots go back many thousands of years, to the very beginning of what we recognize as theorizing about personality (Jastrow, 1915). The first such personality theories were *typologies:* catalogs of various types of people.

Although character types are excellent illustrations, most psychologists today no longer accept them as a useful theory of personality. They are too simple; the majority of people fall somewhere between suggested categories. For every person who perfectly represents the ideal of a coward, let us say, and for every person who perfectly does not, there are a vast number of individuals who represent neither extreme—they are somewhat cowardly, some of the time, in some situations. Typologies fall short because they do not acknowledge the continuity of virtually all personality characteristics.

Clinicians like Freud were the first to study personality from a scientific perspective, and they did so

in order to understand the problems of specific individuals. It makes sense that typologies of disordered personalities have been popular, because clinicians encounter such extreme examples of behavior that they can readily believe they are seeing unambiguous "types" of problems. However, personality psychology is now a much more comprehensive field, applying to both normal and abnormal individuals (Peterson, 1992). The future should bring an ever more sophisticated view of these disorders as problems are examined from the vantage of contemporary theories (e.g., Trull, 1992; Widiger & Trull, 1992). For the time being, however, DSM-IV still uses a typology to describe personality disorders.

THE ODD PERSONALITY DISORDERS

DSM-IV separates its various personality disorders into three groups, which can be respectively characterized as *odd, dramatic,* and *timid.* I begin by covering the odd personality styles. Interest in these disorders stems from their possible relationship to severe clinical syndromes, specifically schizophrenia (Chapter 12).

PARANOID PERSONALITY DISORDER

The central feature of an individual with the **paranoid personality disorder** is a pervasive yet unwarranted belief that other people intend harm. This often takes the form of expecting to be exploited. Sometimes paranoia revolves around extreme jealousy. Those with a paranoid personality disorder read malicious intent into innocuous comments. They are overly sensitive to criticism. They are argumentative and unforgiving. Not surprisingly, granted their vigilant and suspicious style, these individuals keep their distance from others.

Siever and Kendler (1986) provide a brief description of a 36-year-old man who readily fits the diagnosis of paranoid personality disorder. The man was an engineer who worked in a large office with a number of other engineers. He felt that his fellow workers conspired to give him the most difficult assignments and further thwarted his efforts by deliberately removing crucial information from files. Other people found him tense, aloof, and angry. He had changed jobs four times in 6 years, always because he felt his coworkers were out to get him. He was unmarried and had no friends. He entered the mental health system unwillingly, at the urging of his supervisor at work.

Epidemiology   This disorder is not frequently diagnosed. Although many of us sometimes feel that others oppose our will and wishes, no more than 1% of adults believe this consistently enough to warrant the diagnosis of paranoid personality disorder (Kendler & Gruenberg, 1982). It appears that the problem is more common among males than females (Millon, 1986b). For that matter, a sex difference in prevalence is found for most of the specific personality disorders

(see Focus on Sex Differences in Personality Disorders).

Explanation   Psychodynamic theorists explain paranoia with the defense mechanism of *projection* (Colby, 1977). Paranoid individuals harbor unacknowledged sexual and aggressive impulses toward others. They defend against these impulses by reversing the direction of the malice.

In my own clinical work, I once encountered a young man who was haunted by the belief that his wife was having affairs behind his back, with any and all possible men. He reached for his wallet and said, "Let me show you a picture of my wife," but I told him that I would rather hear more about what he had to say. I was being truthful, but I also did not want to run the risk that he might think I was interested in his wife. After several sessions in which we talked about his wife's supposed extramarital affairs, I simply asked him to tell me about his affairs. A sheepish grin came over his face, and he said, "I try not to think about those." Perhaps imagining his wife having affairs helped him put his own out of mind.

Theories linking paranoia to projection may have a ring of truth to them, as you can see in this case, but they have not been systematically tested, so their status remains unclear (Bornstein, Scanlon, & Beardslee, 1989; Heilbrun & Cassidy, 1985).

In Chapter 12, you encountered a form of schizophrenia characterized by paranoid beliefs. What is the relationship between paranoid personality disorder and paranoid schizophrenia? The individual with a paranoid personality disorder is not flagrantly psychotic; except for her beliefs about the motives of others, she has a grasp on the world. And her behavior does not deteriorate to the point that she neglects the basics of self-care. But according to some studies, the paranoid individual bears a family resemblance to the schizophrenic individual, literally as well as metaphorically (e.g., Kendler & Gruenberg, 1982). So, this personality disorder is more apt to be diagnosed among the biological relatives of schizophrenics than among "normal" comparison subjects. This perhaps hints at a biological basis to the disorder—but an environmental interpretation is of course also possible. Perhaps growing up in the vicinity of an unpredictable, frightening individual (the schizophrenic relative) is sufficient to make anyone generally frightened and suspicious (Cupalova & Vachutkova, 1989).

Paranoid personality disorder may well slide into psychotic versions of paranoia as the person's beliefs move from suspicions to firmly held convictions. A longitudinal investigation of those diagnosed with this disorder early in life would shed light on the question of how these individuals compare to schizophrenics. Do they become more suspicious under stress? Are they eventually diagnosed as schizophrenic?

Treatment   Not much is known about the treatment of this disorder (Adler, 1990). It is virtually a given that such individuals do not fare well in therapy, because they are bound to be as suspicious of the therapist as they are of other individuals (Bullard, 1960). Furthermore, they tend not to have much insight into the possibility that their suspicions stem from factors within themselves as opposed to what other people are actually doing. According to Ellison and Adler (1990), the neuroleptics used to treat positive symptoms of schizophrenia sometimes help reduce the suspicion of those with paranoid personality disorder.

SCHIZOID PERSONALITY DISORDER

Individuals with **schizoid personality disorder** show a widespread indifference to other people and a restricted range of emotional experience and expression. Neither praise nor criticism moves them. Those who warrant this description have few friends or confidants. They maintain some connection with their relatives, but even these encounters tend to be cool and aloof. Schizoid individuals have no sense of humor. They lack social skills, yet do not speak or act in a bizarre way. Rather, it is their lack of engagement with others that makes them seem odd.

Those with this disorder prefer solitary work and hobbies (Millon, 1981). If their work requires interaction with others, they are apt to perform poorly. If the work can be done in isolation, though, they often perform very well. These individuals apparently have little sexual interest. Men who warrant this diagnosis almost never date or marry. Women might marry but only after a passive courtship.

Consider Millon and Millon's (1974) description of Margaret. A young college student, she did well in her classes, to which she devoted much of her time. Margaret avoided parties and other aspects of the college social scene. She occasionally went on a date but never enjoyed doing so. She had few friends, although this did not bother her in the least. She rarely experienced dismay or joy or anger or any strong emotion. She expressed puzzlement that other people seemed to get so "excited" about matters she found silly. More generally, Margaret had little insight into other people and how she related to them.

Epidemiology   Little is known about the epidemiology of schizoid personality disorder. Those with the diagnosis apparently are not unhappy with their

lot in life, and I chose the double negative deliberately, because they are neither happy nor unhappy about most things. They simply do not experience strong emotions. In its extreme, this is not a common problem. According to the estimates that are available, this diagnosis can be made of no more than 1% of contemporary adults (Casey, 1988). As with paranoid personality disorder, it seems as if more men than women have this problem (Millon, 1986b).

Explanation   Speculation about the origins of this style center on biological contributions on the one hand versus unusual child rearing on the other. Perhaps schizoid individuals lack the biological apparatus to experience strong emotions; they are *anhedonic,* receiving no pleasure from sensual or intellectual means. Millon (1981) describes the schizoid individual as suffering from affective anemia. Anhedonia characterizes several disorders besides this one, including schizophrenia, and it may result from biological anomalies in the brain, specifically the *limbic system,* involved in the expression of emotions. Some theorists believe that schizoid individuals share the same biological predisposition to oddness as schizophrenics.

Another suggestion is that a schizoid style stems from a person's experiences in early childhood; for whatever reason she was unable to form a secure attachment with her mother or father (cf. Bowlby, 1969). Within the first year of life, the typical child forms a strong emotional bond with her primary caretaker, showing great distress when separated and relief upon being reunited (Ainsworth & Wittig, 1969). But a small number of infants show indifference to the comings and goings of their caretakers. An inconsistent, critical, and/or rejecting style of parenting may be at the root of this indifference (Ainsworth, 1973, 1989). Regardless, once it has been established, this style can persist throughout life (Hazan & Shaver, 1987). In the case of the schizoid individual, perhaps the original style of relating was none at all, because no bond was ever established in infancy (Millon, 1981). Her style of attachment is best characterized as *de*tachment.

Treatment   Treatment of this disorder remains a puzzle because so few people who warrant the diagnosis enter the mental health system. The biological link with schizophrenia perhaps implies that antipsychotic medication is worth exploring, but as you recall from Chapter 12, such drugs are usually more effective in controlling flagrant psychotic symptoms as opposed to oddness per se.

SCHIZOTYPAL PERSONALITY DISORDER

The notion of **schizotypal personality disorder** emerged in the 1950s from studies of individuals who were biologically related to schizophrenics yet not

FOCUS ON

Sex Differences in

Personality

Disorders

VARIOUS PSYCHOLOGICAL disorders show a sex difference in prevalence. To explain these, theorists sometimes point to biological differences, sometimes to lifestyle differences. Another possibility is that sex differences represent a bias imposed by diagnosticians, a tendency to identify a problem more readily among men than among women, or vice versa.

The issue of sex differences and their explanation have attracted a great deal of attention with respect to personality disorders (see Figure 13.1). Most of the disorders have a sex difference (Reich, 1987), and the possibility of diagnostic bias is quite real granted the difficulties encountered in defining and recognizing these problems. The more ambiguous a situation, the more likely we are to impose a bias on its interpretation.

One way to investigate possible bias is by creating a written description of an individual's psychological complaints and presenting different versions of this description to diagnosticians, varying *only* the reported sex of the individual. If different diagnoses are made for males and females, then their sex must be influencing the process, because everything else has been held constant. Studies using this sort of procedure show that the sex of an individual can influence the diagnosis of specific personality disorders (Adler, Drake, & Teague, 1990; Ford & Widiger, 1989; Warner, 1978). All else being equal, women are more likely to be diagnosed with a personality disorder that occurs more commonly among women, such as histrionic disorder, and men are more likely to be diagnosed with a personality disorder that occurs more commonly among men, such as antisocial disorder.

Such demonstrations are obviously important in making diagnosticians sensitive to the assumptions they may unwittingly bring to their task. However, they do not allow us to estimate the degree to which biases influence actual diagnoses of real men and women (Kass, Spitzer, & Williams, 1983; Williams & Spitzer, 1983). And they do not support the argument that diagnoses of personality disorders are *entirely* the result of bias. After all, such diagnoses do not occur in the absence of symptoms.

A broader view of diagnostic bias looks not at the use of specific criteria but at the criteria themselves. These might embody a sex bias, which means that even

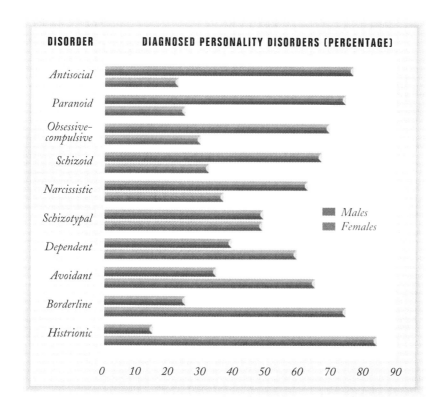

FIGURE **13.1**

SEX DIFFERENCES IN DIAGNOSED PERSONALITY DISORDERS   *Almost all the personality disorders described in DSM-IV show a sex difference in diagnosed prevalence.*
SOURCES: DATA DERIVED FROM *Diagnostic and Statistical Manual of Mental Disorders* (4TH EDITION), 1994, WASHINGTON, DC: AMERICAN PSYCHIATRIC ASSOCIATION; "PREVALENCE AND STABILITY OF THE DSM-III-R PERSONALITY DISORDERS IN A COMMUNITY-BASED SURVEY OF ADOLESCENTS," BY D. P. BERNSTEIN ET AL., 1993, *American Journal of Psychiatry, 150,* PP. 1237–1243; "SEX DISTRIBUTION OF DSM-III PERSONALITY DISORDERS IN PSYCHIATRIC OUTPATIENTS," BY J. H. REICH, 1987, *American Journal of Psychiatry, 144,* PP. 485–488.

if a diagnostician objectively employs them, systematic errors still result (Kaplan, 1983a, 1983b). Think about the different personality disorders and the symptoms that count toward their diagnosis. Many of these symptoms are stereotypically feminine or masculine (Sprock, Blashfield, & Smith, 1990), with the effect of making many of the disorders themselves stereotypically feminine or masculine (Rienzi & Scrams, 1991). It is therefore unsurprising that "feminine" personality disorders like the histrionic and dependent styles are diagnosed more frequently among women and that "masculine" personality disorders like the antisocial and narcissistic styles are diagnosed more frequently among men.

Said another way, at least some of the DSM-IV personality disorders look like exaggerated versions of gender roles widespread in our society (Nuckolls, 1992). "Feminine" personality disorders involve excessive emotionality and dependence, whereas "masculine" disorders involve excessive assertiveness and independence. Is it reasonable to regard cultural categories as abnormal? Is it reasonable to diagnose and treat an individual who is following a societal mandate? If norms for male and female behavior result in distress, perhaps the norms themselves should be reevaluated.

themselves psychotic (Rado, 1956). Those satisfying these criteria tend to be uncomfortable around others, deficient at social relationships, and peculiar in thoughts, actions, and appearance. For instance, one example of a peculiar thought would be a belief in the occult that is not endorsed by one's subculture.

Individuals with schizotypal personality disorder tend to have bizarre fantasies or preoccupations. They are unkempt, or they prefer to dress in strange clothing. They can be digressive or vague when they speak, and they use words differently from others. They may talk to themselves. And they experience great anxiety around people, especially those who are unfamiliar to them.

Weeks (1988) described the case of Bill, a young man whose parents raised him in a joyless and authoritarian way. They were never spontaneous with him. Instead, strings were attached to every show of affection. Even as a boy, Bill was unwilling to speak to his parents about his insecurities, because he was afraid they would be used against him.

He proved to be a markedly inconsistent student, sometimes excelling at science projects but just as often staring out the classroom windows. He had numerous arguments with his teachers, and he fought frequently with his classmates. In elementary school, he would spend his lunch hour walking around the playground backwards. At age 13, Bill made a public vow of celibacy and founded his own "anti-sex league." He began to believe in flying saucers. He joined a group that demanded acts of vandalism and desecration from its members.

By the time Bill reached college, he was a loner except for his involvement in extreme political movements. He became an anarchist and spent time in jail after participating in a protest in which he pointed a plastic pistol at the mayor's head. He completed his college studies in jail, subsisting on a self-imposed diet of bread and beans. He received a degree in peace studies, while also becoming an expert in chemical weapons.

Does Bill have a schizotypal personality disorder? I am not sure, but he is certainly an unusual person. Is there a danger here in pathologizing what might be quite innocent, someone marching to a different drummer? Possibly—which is one reason why personality disorders are so controversial. A diagnostic label might encourage us to dismiss individuals as disturbed who are merely eccentric or ahead of their time. History is certainly filled with unusual individuals who have nonetheless made important contributions.

The counter to this point is that DSM-IV does not call for this diagnosis solely on the basis of peculiarity of behavior. The diagnostician is additionally told to look for social impairment. Granted the nature of the social world and its pervasive press toward conformity, we can argue that peculiarity almost *guarantees* social or occupational impairment as others react negatively to the individual. These are no longer independent diagnostic criteria, and impairment might not be an inherent aspect of peculiar behavior so much as an effect given a less than tolerant world.

Epidemiology   Whatever its potential for misuse, the diagnosis of schizotypal personality disorder is infrequently made. General population surveys suggest that it occurs in about 1% of adults (e.g., Kendler, Gruenberg, & Strauss, 1981), and about equally among men and women. It is more common among those already in the mental health system, particularly those who are hospitalized (Mellsop, Varghese, Joshua, & Hicks, 1982).

Explanation   Remember that the notion of this disorder emerged from studies of the relatives of schizophrenics (Spitzer, Endicott, & Gibbon, 1979). This was a theoretically motivated quest, an attempt to find some of the factors that predisposed schizophrenia. Presumably, the characteristics of the schizotypal individual might hint at whatever makes schizophrenia more likely for some than for others.

Theoretical explanations of schizotypal personality disorder therefore have usually taken place in the context of its presumed relationship with schizophrenia. Not surprisingly, granted how the diagnostic criteria were devised, subsequent studies have found that schizophrenic individuals have more than their expected share of schizotypal relatives (Kendler, Gruenberg, & Strauss, 1981; Kendler, Masterson, Ungaro, & Davis, 1984) and that schizotypal individuals have more than their share of schizophrenic relatives (Battaglia et al., 1991; Lenzenweger & Loranger, 1989; Siever et al., 1990) (see Figure 13.2).

Psychologist Paul Meehl (1962, 1989, 1990) has theorized extensively about what schizotypal and schizophrenic individuals have in common, and he suggests that the problem involves a central neurological deficit in paying attention and integrating thoughts. Although these deficits are merely hypothesized, not

yet located in a specific part of the brain, it is still possible to deduce many schizotypal symptoms from them. Consider that people unable to integrate their thoughts will think in a way that others find idiosyncratic. Their unusual thoughts will translate into unusual habits and ways of relating to other people. According to Meehl, what determines whether individuals are schizotypal versus schizophrenic is the stressfulness of the setting in which they find themselves. High stress, because it makes more demands on cognitive skills, produces schizophrenia, whereas low stress leaves the person with schizotypal personality disorder (Fenton & McGlashan, 1989).

Treatment   The treatment of this personality disorder has not been systematically investigated (Mehlum et al., 1991), but if the speculation about its relationship to schizophrenia proves valid, steps should be taken to keep the schizotypal individual out of stressful situations that make his or her peculiarity more dysfunctional than it already is. This means that the schizotypal individual needs to be identified as early as possible, perhaps in childhood. However, this disorder has not been described long enough for anyone to know with certainty that it is stable across decades.

Some attempts have been made to prescribe for schizotypal individuals the sorts of medications that are used to control the more flagrant symptoms of schizophrenia. Neuroleptics appear effective to the de-

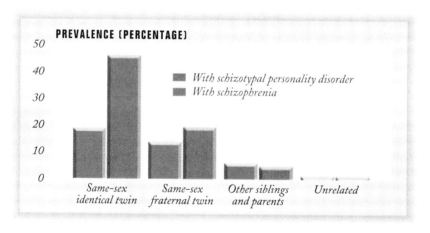

FIGURE 13.2

Schizotypal Personality Disorder and Schizophrenia among Relatives of Those with Schizophrenia   *Schizotypal personality disorder is of interest because of its presumed relationship to schizophrenia. As this graph shows, schizophrenic individuals have more than their share of close relatives with schizotypal personality disorder.*

Source: Data derived from "'True' Schizotypal Personality Disorder," by S. Torgersen, S. Onstad, I. Skre, J. Edvardsen, and E. Kringlen, 1993, *American Journal of Psychiatry, 150,* pp. 1661–1667.

gree that the schizotypal individual shows prominent delusions and hallucinations (Stone, 1983). These drugs do *not* change more "routine" peculiarities nor the social awkwardness and anxiety that characterize this personality style.

THE DRAMATIC PERSONALITY DISORDERS

The second group of DSM-IV personality disorders are those marked by dramatic, emotional, and/or erratic behavior. These disorders clearly illustrate the social consequences of a dysfunctional personality style because other people cannot help but react, usually in negative fashion, to such strikingly unusual ways of behaving. Perhaps the dramatic nature of these disorders explains why they seem to receive so much attention from mental health professionals.

ANTISOCIAL PERSONALITY DISORDER

With the aptly named **antisocial personality disorder,** there is a long-standing pattern of behaving irresponsibly to others. The person who warrants this diagnosis lies, steals, and vandalizes as a child. He initiates fights, plays hooky from school, runs away from home, and is physically cruel to others.

Continued into adulthood, the antisocial individual fails to honor his financial obligations. He has a checkered work history. He may shirk his duties as a parent. Almost invariably, he is incapable of sustaining relationships with family members or friends. Relationships that do exist for him are brief, distant, shallow, and marked by the callousness that colors his behavior in general. The antisocial individual does not express remorse for his activities (Cleckley, 1976). He feels justified about hurting or mistreating others.

Antisocial personality disorder comes to our attention most notably when the individual involved is a habitual criminal, such as Gary Gilmore, whose story was told by Norman Mailer (1979) in The Executioner's Song *and more recently by his brother Mikal Gilmore (1994) in* Shot in the Heart. *Gilmore was a drifter who had been in and out of trouble his entire life. He began to use drugs when he was 10 years old. He was a tattoo artist by trade, and he would tattoo obscene words onto the skin of customers he disliked, in places where they could not see what he was doing. On parole from prison, Gilmore carried out a series of senseless murders. Arrested and convicted, he himself asked to be executed, and his self-proclaimed "right to die" attracted much media attention, in part because capital punishment had not been exercised in the United States for 10 years. Gary Gilmore was indeed executed on January 17, 1977.*

Although antisocial personality disorder is not synonymous with criminal activity, some habitual criminals like murderer Gary Gilmore warrant the diagnosis. This photo shows Gilmore in 1976. His story was told by Norman Mailer in The Executioner's Song *and by his brother, Mikal Gilmore, in* Shot in the Heart.

Criminal activity is not synonymous with this disorder. Any number of criminals carry out their illegal activities for reasons that have nothing to do with being antisocial. Many of them are what we call *socialized,* meaning that their activities are coordinated with others to whom they have an allegiance. Antisocial personality disorder is something different—a lack of concern for the feelings and desires of other people.[1] Gary Gilmore was a loner, and that stamps him as antisocial more than his murder spree alone.

Epidemiology   About 3% to 4% of American males meet the criteria for antisocial personality disorder, as opposed to only 1% of females, indicating a marked sex difference in this personality style (Robins

[1] At least some antisocial individuals are portrayed in the media as charming, even charismatic. Consider the descriptions of mass murderer Charles Manson that stressed the loyalty of his followers. These portrayals misrepresent antisocial personality disorder. To be sure, Manson had several followers, but they were hardly typical human beings swayed by his charm. Those with this disorder are far from charismatic. If anything, they are just the opposite, because their personality style invariably turns people off.

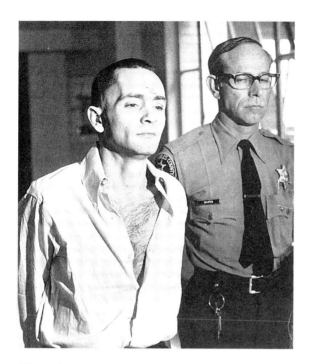

The media sometimes portray antisocial individuals like Charles Manson as charismatic, but these depictions are usually misrepresentations.

et al., 1984). It runs through families, and it shows a strong link with alcohol and drug abuse. Antisocial personality disorder tends as well to be most common among the lower class, which may reflect in part diagnostic biases. In any event, this disorder is usually diagnosed among those under the age of 40. Although highly stable through adolescence and early adulthood

(e.g., Mannuzza et al., 1991), the style nonetheless seems to reduce in prevalence and intensity after middle age.

Explanation   Theorists of a biomedical persuasion try to specify the physiological mechanisms that might produce the salient characteristics of the antisocial style (Millon, 1981). They point to the tendency of antisocial activity to run in families as possible evidence for its heritability. Twin studies have been conducted for criminal activity in general (e.g., Dalgaard & Kringlen, 1976), as well as this personality disorder in particular (e.g., Grove et al., 1990), and they show a moderate degree of heritability.

Adoption studies point to the same conclusion (see Figure 13.3). In several investigations, the criminal record of adopted children was compared to that of their biological versus adoptive parents, and again the evidence is in favor of biological similarity—although it is by no means an invariant relationship (e.g., Hutchings & Mednick, 1974; Schulsinger, 1972).

Granted its heritability, what might be the biological underpinnings of antisocial personality disorder? One theory suggests that those with this disorder are chronically underaroused (Lykken, 1957). In other words, their nervous systems do not respond with the same vigor to threat and stress as do the nervous systems of other individuals. What this means is that the person with antisocial personality disorder tends not to experience the physiological symptoms of fear and anxiety. Presumably, in the absence of these feelings, impulsivity and lack of remorse develop (Raine, Venables, & Williams, 1990). When impulsivity and lack of remorse are

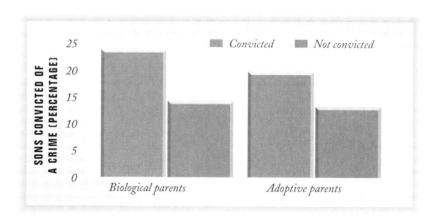

FIGURE 13.3

HERITABILITY OF CRIMINALITY   *A study of 15,000 men adopted in Denmark between 1924 and 1946 determined whether or not they or their parents—biological or adoptive—had ever been convicted of a crime. The findings suggest that criminal activity is heritable.*

SOURCE: DATA DERIVED FROM "GENETIC INFLUENCES IN CRIMINAL CONVICTIONS," BY S. A. MEDNICK, W. F. GABRIELLI, AND B. HUTCHINGS, 1984, *Science, 224*, PP. 891–894.

coupled with the appropriate environmental circumstances, antisocial personality disorder may result.

Part of the evidence for this hypothesis is the presence of abnormal electroencephalogram (EEG) patterns (Chapter 6). Researchers describe EEG patterns as "normal" or not, according to how typical they are. Although the exact form of abnormality might differ, studies show that those with antisocial personality disorder have three times the likelihood of having an abnormal EEG pattern than the general population—about 50% versus 15% (e.g., Fishbein, Herning, Pickworth, & Haertzen, 1989; Sayed, Lewis, & Brittain, 1969). Among these abnormal patterns is one associated with low arousal of the cortex.

This biomedical explanation slides into a cognitive-behavioral one when we ask how low levels of arousal affect behavior. The answer usually focuses on learning, and studies suggest that those with this disorder are deficient at laboratory tasks that involve learning to avoid punishment, such as an electric shock (Scerbo et al., 1990). Although those with this disorder can readily learn other sorts of tasks, they have trouble with avoidance tasks. Perhaps their failure to be aroused makes this type of learning difficult. For the rest of us, the anticipation of punishment is sufficient to keep us on the straight and narrow. Those with antisocial personality disorder may not have the equipment to learn this sort of association.

Schachter and Latané (1964) compared the performance of antisocial with nonantisocial individuals on avoidance learning under different experimental circumstances. They injected research subjects with adrenalin, which *increased* their arousal. This manipulation brought the avoidance learning of the antisocial subjects up to "normal" levels, at least as long as the adrenalin rush lasted.

In a related investigation of avoidance learning, Schachter and Latané (1964) injected subjects with chlorpromazine, which *decreased* their arousal. When antisocial individuals were asked to score their own performance, they cheated more if they had been given chlorpromazine as opposed to an inert substance. Again, the interpretation is that whatever arousal the antisocial individuals experienced in the first place was reduced by the drug, with further deleterious effects on their behavior.

These demonstrations have some practical implications. They suggest that one way to reduce antisocial acts among those with underaroused nervous systems is through the use of stimulants. As I discuss in Chapter 14, children who are hyperactive or have attention deficits can be helped by stimulants as well. These childhood disorders may in some cases be the forerunner of antisocial personality disorder in adulthood, and the success of this kind of intervention is not as surprising as it first sounds.

Another implication is that tranquilizers—obviously the opposite of stimulants—will *not* reduce antisocial acts; if anything, they should increase them. The antisocial individual is often a substance abuser. If the abused drug is alcohol or another sedating substance, then we can predict that this will only exacerbate whatever antisocial tendencies he had in the first place (Luthar, Anton, Merikangas, & Rounsaville, 1992). Steele and Josephs (1990) argue that alcohol has this effect on all individuals, reducing their awareness of the consequences of their acts and thus leading them—granted other predispositions and provocations—into antisocial activities.

The status of these implications is unknown. No one has systematically explored them, perhaps because of the ethical issues they raise. Researchers have not conducted further experimental investigations like those of Schachter and Latané (1964). Again, ethical concerns may be the reason.

Psychodynamic and sociocultural theorists look not within the person to explain the lack of conscience but rather at the circumstances of his upbringing. Something went wrong during his early development to prevent his superego—which internalizes the oughts and shoulds of society—from emerging (Fenichel, 1945). Along these lines, the behavior of the antisocial individual can be described as childlike. We excuse impulsivity and moral transgressions among children because, after all, they are children. But when an adult acts in the same way, we are more disturbed by these actions, and we deem them antisocial. Those who grew up to be antisocial had parents who failed to satisfy early needs, presumably because they were rejecting or neglectful, abusive or inconsistent (Cadoret & Stewart, 1991; Pollock et al., 1990).

Research shows a link between inadequate child rearing and later diagnosis of antisocial personality disorder (e.g., Patterson, DeBaryshe, & Ramsey, 1989; Roff, 1974). But we must ask about cause and effect. It might be that the early antisocial tendencies of the child created a bad style of parenting, rather than vice versa. Or the operative factor might be the biological mechanism already discussed, which shows itself on the one hand in poor parenting and on the other in antisocial acts by the child, with no direct link between the two. Needless to say, the eventual conclusion will probably be that nature and nurture interact to produce this disorder (Cadoret, Troughton, Bagford, & Woodworth, 1990).

Treatment   Whatever the causes of this disorder, I do not have much to say about its effective treatment (Adler, 1990; Gerstley et al., 1989; Quality Assurance Project, 1991a). My earlier comments about the role of stimulants in reducing antisocial behavior are speculative. Even if a person's arousal is increased, antisocial

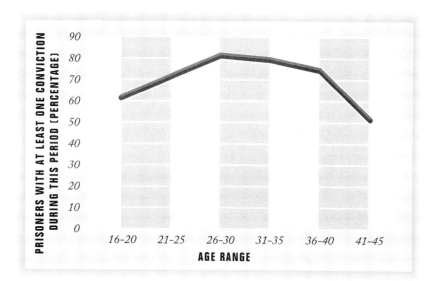

FIGURE **13.4**

ANTISOCIAL ACTS WANING
WITH AGE   *In a study of
male prisoners diagnosed with
antisocial personality disorder,
criminal convictions became less
likely as the prisoners aged.*
SOURCE: DATA DERIVED FROM "MALE
PSYCHOPATHS AND THEIR CRIMINAL
CAREERS," BY R. D. HARE, L. M.
MCPHERSON, AND A. E. FORTH, 1988,
*Journal of Consulting and Clinical
Psychology,* 56, PP. 710–714.

acts may have become so habitual after many years
that merely providing arousal later on does not change
what he does. You must also remember that people
with personality disorders do not respond well to psychotherapy. This is certainly the case with antisocial
individuals, because they tend to lie.

So much of therapy outcome research rests on the
report of the individual that he is or is not improving
(Chapter 4). More so than most other troubled individuals, antisocial individuals will often exaggerate their
improvement, telling stories about how they have seen
the error of their ways. All of this is rewarding to the
therapist, who wants to believe that change is taking
place, but the good reports tend not to reflect changes
in actual behavior. The only positive thing I have to say
about antisocial acts is that they decrease with age (Arboleda-Florez & Holley, 1991) (see Figure 13.4).

BORDERLINE PERSONALITY DISORDER

Another dysfunctional style classified as dramatic and
erratic is the **borderline personality disorder.** As described in DSM-IV, this disorder involves marked instability in a person's moods, relationships, impulses,
and self-image that greatly exaggerate the fluctuations
virtually all of us show across time. The borderline style
begins in early adulthood and presents itself in a variety
of domains. The individual who warrants this diagnosis
makes frantic efforts to avoid feeling abandoned. She
may act impulsively and in self-damaging fashion. She
requires high maintenance from her friends and family.
She needs constant attention to soothe her moods and
stroke her insecurities. She ends up baffling and exhausting others as well as herself.

*Marilyn Monroe, shown here with Arthur Miller, displayed
some of the instability that characterizes borderline personality
disorder.*

Theoretical interest in borderline personality disorder is great, particularly among psychodynamic theorists intrigued by the instability that marks the problem (Goldstein, 1989). These theorists try to explain what might have gone wrong during early childhood, at the very time that an individual's identity is being created, to produce such swings. According to some, the borderline style is increasing in today's society, which gives rise to questions about the factors that might be responsible for it (Cushman, 1990; Stone, 1986).

Goldstein (1985) described the case of Ms. W., a young woman who exemplified most of the central features of borderline personality disorder. She was a recent college graduate, unmarried, and working as a librarian at a local university. She came into therapy complaining of fluctuating moods, explosive rage at work, dangerous activities such as shoplifting, drug abuse, and alcohol binges, and profound dissatisfaction with her job, her social life, and even her very self. To the casual onlooker, Ms. W. seemed to be a fully functioning person, with a great deal going for her. She was intelligent, a college graduate, and employed in a secure job. She had what looked like a good relationship with a young man with whom she spent a great deal of time and shared many interests.

Yet Ms. W. felt that something was missing. Her job was not exciting. She had no female friends, and she did not really care for her boyfriend. She was just going through the motions with him, which had been her romantic pattern since adolescence: to get involved with one man at a time, for a period of several months, but then to move on to another. She never experienced any deep feelings for them, instead using them only to ward off her boredom or anxiety. She said she felt guilty about using men, but she had never broken off a relationship for this reason. Rather, Ms. W. ended one relationship only after she had entered a new one that looked more exciting.

Epidemiology   About 3% to 5% of individuals can be described as having a borderline personality disorder (Widiger & Frances, 1986). The diagnosis is made more frequently among women than men (Millon, 1986b). Although few family studies have been conducted, it appears that the borderline style runs through families (Links, Steiner, & Huxley, 1988). The prognosis is not good. Borderline personality disorder can be highly stable (see Lofgren, Bemporad, King, Lindem, & O'Driscoll, 1991), making borderline individuals notoriously difficult to treat in therapy.

Explanation   As already mentioned, interest in this disorder has been widespread among psychodynamic theorists. Descriptively, I can say that borderline individuals do not have a fully integrated sense of

self—although their self is not as split as in multiple personality disorder. Recall that despite its name, MPD is not considered a personality disorder (Chapter 8); still, there may be some overlap between it and the borderline style.

Theorists concern themselves in particular with **object relations**: the mental representations people have of themselves and others (Greenberg & Mitchell, 1983). Object relations obviously develop over time, as the child internalizes her experiences. Parents are critical here, because the child's formation of her own identity is the result of how her parents treat her. If they are consistent, warm, and nurturant, then that will be the identity that takes form in the young child. But if they are inconsistent, alternating between harshness and indulgence, then that is how she will experience the world and eventually herself. The adult borderline individual is presumably living out her childhood experiences by using the lessons she learned there (Mahler, 1971). If mother and father are alternatively good and evil, all in the same guise, then so too is the world, and most insidiously, so too is the self.

Research has not taken a fine-grained look at all the processes hypothesized by object relations theories, but we can conclude that some disruption during childhood is typical (Westen, 1989, 1990b). One or more negative styles of child rearing may be present, and profound abuse, both physical and sexual, figures into the early lives of many borderline individuals (e.g., Byrne, Velamoor, Cernovsky, Cortese, & Losztyn, 1990; Ogata et al., 1990; Shearer, Peters, Quaytman, & Ogden, 1990; Westen, Ludolph, Misle, Ruffins, & Block, 1990). Again, this suggests some link to multiple personality disorder, in which early abuse is also prominent. Overwhelming early loss, such as the loss of a parent to death or divorce, also appears to be a risk factor for borderline personality disorder (Ludolph et al., 1990).

The case of Ms. W., the young librarian described earlier, supports this general formulation. She was one of seven children, and she grew up constantly vying with her siblings for her father's attention. He apparently favored her because she was the most attractive of his daughters, but he presented a highly inconsistent image to her, to which she responded with inconsistency of her own. She either idealized him or wanted nothing to do with him. Ms. W. was not physically brutalized by her parents, but her mother and father constantly fought and threatened one another with divorce. She saw her siblings only as rivals, never as people in their own right. Tragically, she never learned to see herself as a person either, or at least as an integrated one. According to the object relations theorists, her difficulties stem from these deficient object relations.

Several investigators have searched for biological correlates of borderline personality disorder (Burgess, 1992; Lahmeyer, Reynolds, Kupfer, & King, 1989; Lucas, Gardner, Cowdry, & Pickar, 1989). For some time, their interest centered on how borderline individuals respond to the dexamethasone suppression test, once thought to be a strong diagnostic test for unipolar depression (Chapter 9). So, went the reasoning, if they respond the same way on this test as depressives, then maybe this personality disorder is a variant of depression. Because the test is no longer regarded as specific to any given diagnostic category, however, the basis for this hypothesis vanished (Korzekwa, Steiner, Links, & Eppel, 1991).

Another view of this disorder is that it is not a syndrome in its own right but rather a symptom present in a variety of psychological problems. This explains first its frequency and second its co-occurrence with various anxiety and mood disorders. Theoretical and research interest in borderline personality disorder remains high (Zanarini, Gunderson, Frankenburg, & Chauncey, 1990).

Treatment   Treatment is a puzzle. Although psychodynamic theorists are responsible for the interest in this problematic style, at the same time they admit that traditional insight-oriented therapy is not apt to be successful with borderline individuals, precisely because they cannot achieve insight (Aronson, 1989a; Higgitt & Fonagy, 1992). They lack the cognitive abilities—the appropriate object relations, as it were—to turn their attention to the self and regulate how they think and feel. As you can imagine, dropout rates from therapy are high (Gunderson et al., 1989). Issues of transference and countertransference frequently occur, as clients split the therapist just as they split other people in their lives (Cohen & Sherwood, 1989).

More promising, perhaps, are cognitive techniques such as those developed by Aaron Beck, in which the borderline individual is explicitly taught to identify troublesome thoughts and feelings, and then to bring them under control (Beck, Freeman, et al., 1990; Fleming & Pretzer, 1990). This strategy is not incompatible with object relations theories (Westen, 1991). It almost follows from them, because what they do in effect is teach the adult individual what most children learn while growing up.

Alice was a 34-year-old woman diagnosed with borderline personality disorder (Freeman, 1988). She experienced chronic feelings of depression and emptiness dating back to her childhood. Her mother believed that the world was a vicious place, and so she tried to prepare Alice for its cruelty by slapping her across the face on a daily basis.

Alice eventually accepted the slaps without crying; then her mother would hit her harder in order to make her more emotionally responsive. Alice grew up thinking that she was a bad person. She had few friends. She hung closely to those friends she did have, always fearing that they were on the verge of abandoning her. She had been married for 15 years, but she did not trust her husband to stay with her. As a result, she was passive with him and never expressed any dissatisfaction, even when it was legitimate to do so.

Cognitive therapy with Alice targeted for change her feelings of depression and emptiness. Automatic thoughts linked to abandonment were associated with these feelings, so Alice was encouraged to articulate these thoughts and evaluate them against the evidence. Her husband's steadfastness over the years of their marriage provided a strong argument against her belief that he was on the verge of leaving. So too did his willingness to become involved in couples therapy. Therapy did not eradicate Alice's distress, but her depression decreased, and her relationship with her husband improved. As long as she continued to monitor her automatic thoughts, she was able to get along better in the world and was less a victim of her feelings than she had been before treatment began.

Also promising are behavioral techniques that target for change specific problematic behaviors such as self-injurious actions. For example, Linehan and her colleagues developed an approach they call *dialectical behavior therapy* based on the assumption that individuals with borderline personality disorder have not learned how to regulate their emotions. Treatment proceeds by formulating a hierarchy of goals and trying to achieve each with suitable behavioral strategies (Linehan, 1987; Linehan, Armstrong, Suarez, Allmon, & Heard, 1991).

HISTRIONIC PERSONALITY DISORDER

You encountered the **histrionic personality disorder** in Chapter 8, where it was also identified as **hysterical personality disorder,** presumably predisposing conversion disorder.[2] According to DSM-IV, the histrionic individual is excessively emotional and attention-seeking. This diagnosis is made only when there has been a long-standing, pervasive pattern of behaving this way.

Histrionic individuals constantly seek reassurance, approval, or praise from others. They express themselves with great exaggeration, in ways most of us

[2] Some theorists distinguish between *hysterical* and *histrionic* personality disorders, treating the latter as a more severely disturbed version of the former (e.g., Kernberg, 1986). For our purposes, I treat these terms as synonymous (cf. Millon, 1981).

would deem inappropriate. I know a few people, for example, who throw their arms around even their most casual acquaintances whenever they see them. Similarly, they are prone to temper tantrums over the tiniest disappointment or provocation. A broken zipper or a letter delayed by the postal service brings a reaction that others would reserve for a fatal illness.

This personality disorder is diagnosed much more frequently in women than men, and some argue that the diagnostic criteria are biased so as to guarantee this. DSM-IV proposes that one of the signs of a histrionic style is being inappropriately seductive in appearance or behavior. Our society routinely describes women as seductive, but rarely men, even when they act in a flamboyantly sexual way. Along these lines, another suggested manifestation of this personality disorder is overconcern with physical appearance—again the sort of description that we do not apply to men.

Some theorists therefore recommend a more balanced set of diagnostic criteria for this disorder (Kernberg, 1986). For men, we should look for exaggerated

Among males, a histrionic style is marked by exaggerated patterns of masculinity.

patterns of masculinity: excessive independence, promiscuity, an attitude of dominance over women, and sulking when aspirations cannot be fulfilled. Psychodynamic theorists at one time spoke of a *phallic character,* an individual supposedly fixated at the phallic stage of development (Reich, 1949). A more contemporary version of this style is what Mosher and Sirkin (1984) identify as a *macho personality orientation.*

The more equal opportunity symptoms of a histrionic style as described by DSM-IV include being uncomfortable when he or she is not the center of attention. The person demonstrates a rapidly shifting and shallow expression of feelings and an extreme self-centeredness that shows itself in the inability to tolerate the slightest delay of gratification.

One of my casual acquaintances seems to exemplify this style of behaving. He can never wait to talk when we encounter one another. Regardless of what I might be doing, even if it is talking to somebody else, he intrudes. When I ask him how he is doing, he recites numerous complaints about his life: ailing relatives, frustrations at work, unhappy romances, and the like. Virtually all of us have such problems, but for him they are earth-shattering. He wants to be reassured that things will be all right, yet he is never relieved by my statements that they will be.

Epidemiology   As already mentioned, histrionic personality disorder is diagnosed more frequently in women than men, and overall, surveys estimate its prevalence to be about 2% (Nestadt et al., 1990). Furthermore, the disorder seems to run in families.

Explanation   In my discussion of this style in Chapter 8, I pointed out that a predisposition to anxiety might contribute to it. The constant seeking of reassurance represents an attempt to reduce feelings of trepidation. This idea does not provide a full picture, though, and so we must look to other possible influences on the development of this personality disorder. We already know that psychodynamic theorists hypothesize fixations at the phallic stage of development. More generally, they point to unconscious conflicts about sexuality (Fenichel, 1945). According to classic psychoanalytic formulations, a histrionic style stems from fear of castration (among men) and penis envy (among women). It is an elaborate defense against these thoughts. Related to this line of reasoning are clinical impressions that histrionic individuals come from disturbed families, where fathers alternate between seductiveness and harshness, and where mothers are domineering (Kernberg, 1986).

Treatment   Biomedical treatments of this style do not exist (Ellison & Adler, 1990), and attempts at change fall into the psychotherapeutic arena. Histrionic individuals are poorly suited for classical psychoanalysis because of its emphasis on insight (Adler, 1990). Rather, therapy needs to be supportive on the one hand and behavioral on the other, instructing the person explicitly in how she can get along better in the world (Beck, Freeman, et al., 1990). Unfortunately, not enough research has been conducted to say that any of these interventions are successful (Quality Assurance Project, 1991b).

NARCISSISTIC PERSONALITY DISORDER

Another dramatic style that overlaps considerably with the one just described is the **narcissistic personality disorder.** In Greek mythology, Narcissus was the Greek shepherd who fell in love with his own reflection in a pond. He lingered over it for so long that he eventually turned into a daffodil that still bears his name. His other legacy is less pleasant: a personality style marked by a pervasive grandiosity about the self, need for admiration, and a lack of empathy. Narcissistic individuals are their own best friends, to the exclusion of befriending anyone else.

Millon and Millon (1974) provide an example of a narcissistic individual in their description of Steven, a young man whose wife insisted that he enter therapy because he was selfish and preoccupied with his job and his hobbies. Steven was gentle and good-humored, but he contributed nothing to the marriage except his income. To his wife fell all household responsibilities. He spent all of his spare time painting, which he regarded as a means of self-fulfillment. He had few friends. He recognized himself as socially isolated but attributed this to his obvious talent and intelligence. In any event, he readily acknowledged that he preferred his own company to that of others.

Epidemiology   According to surveys, narcissistic personality disorder is diagnosed in about 1% of adults, more so in men than women (Millon, 1986b). Some have argued that narcissism, in both its normal and abnormal versions, is much more common in today's world than in centuries past (Lasch, 1978). This claim is difficult to verify, but our contemporary cultural values in fact encourage people to aggrandize themselves, to be overly concerned with what others think, yet—at the same time—not to worry too much about them except insofar as their opinions carry consequences. "So," goes the joke, "I've talked enough about myself. What do *you* have to say about me?" I have

"Is there someone else, Narcissus?"

Drawing by Charles Addams; © 1974 The New Yorker Magazine, Inc.

elsewhere mentioned the individualistic emphasis of our society, and so perhaps the rise of this personality disorder—if it is on the upswing—is to be expected.

Markus and Kitayama (1991) support this reasoning with their more general discussion of how culture influences people's sense of self. In contrast to individuals in societies that assume a fundamental interdependence between self and others, many of us in the contemporary United States strive to maintain our independence from other people and to express our own unique characteristics. At their extremes, these tendencies may result in problems such as narcissistic personality disorder.

Along these lines, recall the positive illusions discussed in Chapter 9, the absence of which characterize depression (Taylor, 1989). At least in today's society, a positive view of the self—even when at odds with the facts—is associated with health and happiness, success and achievement, probably because it encourages coping and perseverance (Peterson, Maier, & Seligman, 1993). But the narcissistic personality disorder shows that a positive illusion can be taken too far, even in a world like our own (Peterson & Bossio, 1991). If an individual's sense of self is overly positive, so much so that it is impossible to sustain it in view of contrary evidence from the world, then brittleness results.

Explanation   This personality disorder has long interested psychologists, particularly those of a psychodynamic orientation (Freud, 1914). In their formulations, we find the most thorough discussions of what might bring about this style of behaving (e.g., Kernberg, 1975; Kohut, 1971, 1977; Rosenfeld, 1964). Most agree that narcissism represents a fixation in the way a person maintains self-esteem. The desire to feel good about oneself is deeply ingrained in human nature, but the way in which this is achieved usually shows a developmental trajectory. Children maintain their sense of self by being at the center of their world; as Piaget (1928, 1929) and other child psychologists have argued, children can only be egocentric. But with age, people usually come to satisfy their own needs to feel positively about themselves by achieving stable relationships with others. This development never takes place for the narcissistic individual, presumably because of faulty family dynamics encountered early in life.

The evidence bearing on these proposals is difficult to evaluate, because object relations theorists tend to cite only isolated clinical cases in support of their etiological theories (Joubert, 1992). More systematic research into narcissism has been conducted with questionnaires administered to large samples of research subjects (Raskin & Hall, 1979, 1981). Participants are presented with narcissistic statements such as these:

✦ I like to be the center of attention.

✦ I am a special person.

✦ I am never satisfied unless I have everything I want.

Those who agree tend also to be dominant and exhibitionistic (Emmons, 1984). Narcissism measured in this way also correlates with extreme mood swings (Emmons, 1987), which supports the psychodynamic notion that the surface satisfaction of the narcissistic individual masks a deeper insecurity.

In contrast to psychodynamic formulations, Millon (1981) sees narcissistic personality disorder as a product of social learning. It is produced in a child by parents who view their child as more special than he or she really is. Early experience with being pampered and spoiled creates an individual who feels entitled to special treatment throughout his or her life.

Treatment   Attempts to treat this personality disorder have typically been psychodynamic, but we are

The public role of Madonna is that of a highly exhibitionistic individual.

left with no sense of the usefulness of such strategies (Aronson, 1989b; Glasser, 1992). Object relations theorists disagree about psychodynamic therapy for those with this disorder. Kernberg (1975) believes that narcissism can be directly treated with psychoanalysis, whereas Kohut (1971, 1977) thinks that psychoanalysis is of limited use; the therapist must first attack the narcissism by empathizing deeply with the narcissistic individual and communicating this understanding. This presumably shows him that other people are capable of understanding, and removes the fixation that has produced his narcissism in the first place.

Millon (1981) observes that narcissistic individuals typically do not seek out therapy. Only a painful blow sends them reeling into a therapist's office. When this happens, perhaps cognitive-behavior therapy can be undertaken to help narcissistic clients articulate how they see themselves and what they want from others (Beck, Freeman, et al., 1990). The goal of such therapy is not to replace an inflated sense of self with a diminished one so much as to provide individuals with a more complex view of self. This view should incorporate good and bad aspects and include respect for other people in their own right. Only then can she or he ever strengthen the sense of self. Said in these terms, the cognitive approach sounds fully consistent with the notions of the object-relations theorists.

THE TIMID PERSONALITY DISORDERS

The third cluster of personality disorders described by DSM-IV includes problems marked chiefly by fearfulness and anxiety. Not surprisingly, these personality styles bear a relationship to various disorders involving fear and anxiety like those discussed in Chapter 7.

AVOIDANT PERSONALITY DISORDER

An individual who experiences widespread and long-standing social discomfort, hypersensitivity to evaluation, and feelings of inadequacy has an **avoidant personality disorder.** The major consequence of this style of behaving is the avoidance of social or occupational activities that involve contact with others. Those with this personality disorder try to stay in the corner at work or at parties. They are typically tongue-tied, always expecting to say something foolish. They are highly anxious around others, and one of the things they are most anxious about is looking anxious. So, we have a vicious circle: The avoidant personality style leads to the avoidance of others, which only strengthens the original style.

Social phobia, discussed in Chapter 7, can accompany this personality disorder, as can depression. Almost by definition, those with this disorder have no close friends or confidantes. They occasionally spend time with their relatives, but that is about it.

James was a bookkeeper who described himself as shy, fearful, and quiet (Millon & Millon, 1974). He was unmarried and lived with his mother, herself an anxious and insecure individual. In his late twenties, James had not dated since high school. He had not attended a single party during the past 5 years. He did well at his job, because he was conscientious. However, he associated with no one. He ate lunch alone and never took a coffee break with his fellow workers. His life took a turn for the worse when some new workers began to tease him. Although he wanted to be accepted by these individuals, he feared rejection and thus did not try to enter into their kidding. The teasing worsened, and James became so anxious about it that he began to make a number of errors. His anxiety increased, and he started to stay home from work.

Epidemiology   Avoidant personality disorder is a relatively new diagnosis, so we know little about its

epidemiology. Prior to DSM-III, problems of this sort were classified across the range of other personality disorders, from schizoid to narcissistic. Overlap certainly exists. About 1% of contemporary adults warrant the diagnosis (Zimmerman & Coryell, 1989), and it is more frequently encountered in women than men (Millon, 1986b).

Explanation   What causes the avoidant pattern? Although definitive studies have not yet been done, we expect that there is at least some biological component to this disorder, because timidity is heritable (Buss & Plomin, 1975, 1984). It appears to be an extreme version of shyness, a frequently investigated personality trait that appears to reflect biologically based predispositions to be introverted and anxious (Daniels & Plomin, 1985).

Besides a constitutional predisposition, some theorists have pointed to a history of devaluation and rejection (Millon, 1981, 1986b). The child who is belittled and criticized may come to associate other people with pain rather than pleasure. He becomes passive. The child's family might be the culprit here (Arbel & Stravynski, 1991), but his peer group can also play a damaging role.

Whatever the initial causes, the avoidant personality style perpetuates itself, because the person never puts himself in a position to challenge his negative associations with social interactions. In fact, the anxiety he experiences may produce bad interactions, so even when he tests reality, it confirms his worst fears.

Treatment   Therapy has to proceed carefully, because the avoidant individual is bound to be anxious with the therapist. Revealing deep fears is apt to be quite painful, so the therapist must work diligently to establish trust. Cognitive-behavior therapy is somewhat successful in treating some of the problems associated with this personality disorder (e.g., Alden, 1989; Heimberg & Barlow, 1991). The person is encouraged to think differently about himself and the world, and then gather information that supports these notions. As you would suspect, social skills training is an important part of such therapy (Stravynski, Lesage, Marcouiller, & Elie, 1989).

DEPENDENT PERSONALITY DISORDER

Another style characterized by excessive timidity is the **dependent personality disorder,** in which the individual displays a widespread and long-standing pattern of being dependent on and submissive to others. He or she cannot make everyday decisions without a great deal of advice and reassurance. Often, the dependent person simply opts to be completely passive, letting others decide everything from the mundane—what socks to wear in the morning—to the profound—where to go to school, whom to marry, and what career to pursue. Going hand in hand with this dependent style is difficulty in initiating projects and doing things on one's own. This is not the same thing as procrastination. Rather, the operative factor is the individual's discomfort and helplessness about being alone. Often, the dependent person will go to great lengths to avoid being socially isolated. He or she holds on to relationships and is devastated when they end. A great deal of time is spent worrying about being abandoned.

It follows that if an individual is this dependent on the advice and presence of others, he is also highly sensitive to their criticism and disapproval. All of this sensitivity translates into a willingness to go along with what other people suggest, even if these suggestions conflict with his personal tastes or values. "You want to go to a steak place for dinner? That's okay, even though I'm a vegetarian. I'll have a baked potato." The dependent person will do almost anything to help other people, perhaps as a way of assuring himself that he is liked and thus not at risk for rejection.

Up to a point, relying on other people is the very business of life. You saw in the discussions of antisocial and schizoid disorders what happens when somebody is unmoved by what others think. But excessive neediness is just as problematic. A highly dependent person is paralyzed at work if the job requires independent thinking or unilateral action. And in his social life, he tends to have but a handful of friends, to whom he literally clings.

Mr. G. was a middle-aged man whose extreme dependency was long-standing (Millon & Millon, 1974). As a child, he was regarded by his parents as highly fragile. He was pampered and overprotected, never allowed to exert himself or to take on any responsibilities. His parents arranged a marriage for him, and he went to work for his brothers-in-law. Mr. G. functioned mainly as a helper, running errands, buying cigarettes, and the like. He was teased at work but did not seem to mind because most of the teasing was good-natured. After 15 years, he lost his job when the factory where he worked closed. Then he just stayed at home, hoping that something would happen.

Epidemiology   Dependent personality disorder is diagnosed more frequently than many of the other personality disorders, at the rate of about 2% to 3% among contemporary adults (Casey, 1988). The diagnosis is made more often for women than for men (Millon, 1986b). Again, I raise the question as to whether this implies something inherent about fe-

males, something about the way women are socialized in our society, and/or something about the biases that diagnosticians bring to this personality disorder.

Explanation   A previous generation of theorists described dependent people as shiftless, weak-willed, or inadequate (Esman, 1986). But these are simply labels that do not tell us *why* an individual might act this way. Psychodynamic theorists provide one such answer by suggesting that dependent individuals are fixated at the oral stage of psychosexual development (Abraham, 1927). Because of excessive frustrations or indulgences very early in life, they have adopted a style in which some other person—presumably a representation of their parents—will always be there to care for them and give them everything they need. Infants take this stance without reflection, but adults suspect that things might not always correspond to their desires. The other characteristics of dependency thus emerge: fear of being alone, submissiveness, and inability to take any initiative. These strategies maintain the dependent person's basic wish and hope that she will always be nurtured.

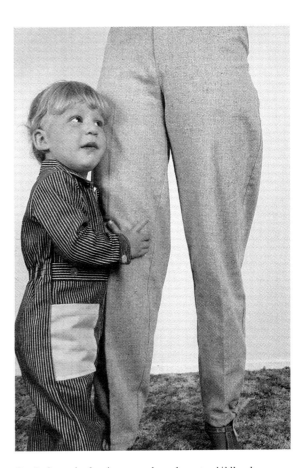

Psychodynamic theorists trace dependency to childhood experiences.

Psychodynamic theorists interpret the submissiveness of dependent individuals as a *reaction formation:* a disguise of how they really feel, which is rage at the individual to whom they are being so nice, for past injustices or the possibility of future ones. That dependent personality disorder co-occurs with depression is consistent—in psychodynamic eyes—with the hypothesis that the dependent individual is in actuality hiding anger. Remember Freud's proposal that depression represents anger turned inward.

What is the evidence for this formulation? Psychodynamic theorists present case studies in support of the notion that this personality disorder is associated with childhood problems surrounding separation from parents. But systematic studies have not yet been carried out. As I noted in Chapter 9, the co-occurrence of depression and dependency might well reflect dependency that follows from depression, rather than vice versa.

Among the few factors reliably implicated in dependency is a protracted illness during childhood (American Psychiatric Association, 1987). This may set into operation the sort of psychodynamics hypothesized to produce dependency. Alternatively or additionally, a childhood illness might lead parents to worry about their child and cater to her more than they do their other children. A dependent style results, not because the child has unmet oral needs, but because she is rewarded for being passive and submissive (Millon, 1981). The problem, of course, is when she grows up and takes with her these habits from the sickroom.

Treatment   As noted several times, therapy with people who have personality disorders is difficult because they play out their styles in therapy, just as they do everywhere else. Working with the dependent individual, the therapist can be fooled into thinking that things are going well, as the client appears to go along with every therapeutic suggestion and reports great success in an attempt to please the therapist (Millon, 1981). The reality may not be so simple, because the goal of therapy must be to reduce the person's dependence.

Cognitive-behavioral strategies are probably the most useful. People can be taught social skills and assertiveness, and to challenge automatic thoughts about abandonment. Through systematic desensitization, they can also learn that being alone need not be associated with feelings of anxiety and helplessness. Presumably, if dependent individuals try out a new style, it should pay off enough that they will continue it. Outcome studies to date support the tentative success of such strategies in leading people to be less dependent (e.g., Turkat & Carlson, 1984).

OBSESSIVE-COMPULSIVE PERSONALITY DISORDER

The person with an **obsessive-compulsive personality disorder** is perfectionistic and inflexible. This demanding style can result in certain accomplishments and achievements in life, but it is included among personality disorders because perfectionism carried to an extreme virtually guarantees that an individual never sees her projects as good enough. Hence, they might never be finished because she attends endlessly to every trivial detail.

This style shows itself interpersonally as a stubborn demand that other people do things the way that the obsessive-compulsive individual wishes. "There are two points of view here," we can imagine her saying, "the wrong one and mine." DSM-IV further characterizes this sort of individual as overly conscientious, moralistic, and scrupulous. She judges others as well as herself harshly. Those with an obsessive-compulsive style take pleasure—so to speak—in rules and routines, prizing their work over emotions and other people. They are not expressive, and they distrust and disapprove of emotional displays in others. Not surprisingly, others see them as stiff or stilted.

Oldham and Frosch (1986) provide the following description of a young man who well exemplifies the essentials of obsessive-compulsive personality disorder:

> The oldest of four siblings, he remembered his father as a stranger and his mother as distant and demanding. Warmth and closeness were lacking, and he learned to seek approval by excelling at school, although he felt little satisfaction with the honors he earned. After years of stalling, beset with doubts, he married for fear of losing his fianceé. He was neither affectionate nor demonstrative; the marriage failed as his wife despaired that she could never be sure that he loved her. Indecisiveness, doubt, and inhibitions haunted him; he was a poor judge of other people.... He could experience affection and aggression when alone, yet these feelings evaporated in the presence of the person toward whom he had the feelings. (p. 246)

Epidemiology   According to community surveys, this disorder occurs in perhaps 2% to 3% of contemporary Americans (Casey, 1988). It is more frequently diagnosed among men than women, and it seems to run in families. Some interesting speculation, not yet supported by appropriate data, holds that cultures that value work, punctuality, and orderliness have more than their share of those with an obsessive-compulsive personality disorder (Millon, 1981).

Explanation   In decades past, theorists believed that obsessive-compulsive personality disorder predisposed obsessive-compulsive disorder, as discussed in Chapter 7. But remember the conclusion that the personality style proves largely independent of the anxiety disorder (Pollak, 1987). There is a critical difference between the two. The person with an obsessive-compulsive personality likes his obsessive routines, whereas the person with obsessive-compulsive disorder finds his repetitive thoughts and impulses alien and disconcerting.

The effect of this overlap in terminology is redundancy in theorizing and research, and so we do not know too much about the etiology of this particular personality disorder. Traditionally, theories have been highly similar to those proposed for the anxiety disorder, but these are now seen as much less pertinent than they once were thought to be (Millon, 1981).

In looking elsewhere for explanations, some theorists have been struck by the fact that this personality style involves anhedonia, as pointed out earlier for the schizoid style (Millon, 1981). Perhaps the inability to feel pleasure is a biological predisposition. Of course, it must be coupled with other factors, and recent attention has looked at the family style of obsessive-compulsive individuals. Maybe perfectionistic and inflexible parents end up producing children who are just the same, through modeling on the one hand and explicit reward and punishment on the other (Lidz, 1971).

Treatment   Because of the long-standing psychodynamic interest in obsessions and compulsions, insight-oriented therapy is frequently recommended for obsessive-compulsive personality disorder. However, as is by now familiar, other than isolated case studies, we are left with no way to evaluate the success of these endeavors (Oldham & Frosch, 1986).

Behavioral techniques such as systematic desensitization, flooding, and/or response prevention—useful in treating anxiety disorders—have also been used with this personality disorder, with some success in the short run (Ricciardi et al., 1992; Steketee, Foa, & Grayson, 1982). Their long-term effectiveness has yet to be evaluated.

CONCLUSIONS

Personality disorders are most compelling when we focus on striking examples. When we delve into matters of cause and treatment, our understanding starts to slip away. To conclude this chapter, I would like to lead us out of this state of affairs by suggesting that the culprit here is the assumption that the best way to understand these disorders is via a typology that ignores the social setting. As noted earlier, contemporary personality psychologists have by and large abandoned the search for typologies of personalities per se, so what reason is there to think that a typology of disordered personalities is appropriate?

Once we stop assuming that there are discrete types of people, then many of the apparent puzzles about personality disorders vanish as well:

1. **WHY IS IT SO DIFFICULT TO DIAGNOSE PERSONALITY DISORDERS RELIABLY?**   Because diagnosticians are using an either-or system to describe clearly continuous phenomena. Diagnosing a personality disorder is like diagnosing extraversion or shyness. We can identify people at one extreme or the other, but there is no discrete break that occurs as we leave normal territory and enter the abnormal. In keeping with this argument, diagnostic reliability improves with the use of a structured interview or a validated questionnaire that specifies quantitative criteria and explicit cutoff values (Ferguson & Tyrer, 1988; Reich, 1989; Standage, 1989).

2. **WHY DO PERSONALITY DISORDERS TAKEN AS A WHOLE SEEM SO WIDESPREAD IN THE GENERAL POPULATION?**   By one report they are diagnosed in more than 11% of adults (Reich, Yates, & Nduaguba, 1989), and by another in more than 15% (Zimmerman & Coryell, 1989) (see Figure 13.5). The answer is that we are talking about personality traits that are widely distributed in the general population.

3. **WHY DO MANY PERSONALITY DISORDERS SEEM MOST PREVALENT IN EARLY ADULTHOOD?** The fact that they then taper off through the rest of adulthood contradicts the view of these disorders as present throughout life (Reich, Nduaguba, & Yates, 1988). The resolution is again to appreciate the social context in which disordered personality is displayed. Young adults face important transitions not encountered in middle age, and it may well be that these are unsettling experiences.

4. **AND WHY DO PEOPLE SO FREQUENTLY SEEM TO HAVE MORE THAN ONE PERSONALITY DISORDER?** Because the criteria used to describe them are imprecise and overlapping (Blashfield & Breen, 1989; Nurnberg et al., 1991; Oldham et al., 1992). When you hear that a person has two (or three or four) personality disorders, you should not assume that they have more troubles than someone with but one personality disorder. Having two is not like having mumps *and* chicken pox simultaneously. Rather, many personality disorders are defined by similar symptoms, which makes multiple diagnoses almost inevitable (e.g., Herbert, Hope, & Bellack, 1992; Kavoussi & Siever, 1992; Schneier, Spitzer, Gibbon, Fyer, & Liebowitz, 1991). The creators of DSM-IV attempted to minimize the overlapping of criteria, and future studies will reveal if this reduces multiple diagnoses.

FIGURE **13.5**

PREVALENCE OF
PERSONALITY DISORDERS
*According to epidemiological
surveys, personality disorders are
widespread among the adult
population in the United States.*

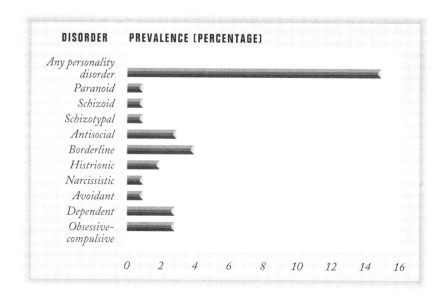

| DISORDER | PREVALENCE (PERCENTAGE) |

(Bar chart showing prevalence percentages for: Any personality disorder, Paranoid, Schizoid, Schizotypal, Antisocial, Borderline, Histrionic, Narcissistic, Avoidant, Dependent, Obsessive-compulsive. Horizontal axis ranges from 0 to 16, marked at 0, 2, 4, 6, 8, 10, 12, 14, 16.)

Another questionable assumption tucked into the notion of personality disorders is that these styles have a biological basis (McGuffin & Thapar, 1992; Siever & Davis, 1991; Stein, 1992). If we assume that personality types are discrete categories, then we almost have to link them with underlying biological characteristics, some of which indeed exist in either-or fashion (Peterson, 1992). The practical problem with this assumption is that it has directed the attention of researchers inward, to look at genetics, brain structure and function, and the endocrine system, rather than outward, to look at the social context from which personality emerges.

At the same time, I am not saying that biology has nothing to do with personality, because researchers have provided clear heritability estimates for certain styles of behaving—termed **temperament**—such as activity level, fearfulness, and the like (Peterson, 1992). But most theorists regard temperament as simply a style that is not identical to the whole of what we mean by personality. The DSM-IV personality disorders are not described in terms of temperament, nor should they be, because an active (or passive) temperament is neither adaptive nor maladaptive. It depends on how it is channeled and on the settings in which people find themselves.

Thomas and Chess (1977) give the example of an outgoing child who fearlessly explores her world. In a benign setting, like a small town, she finds all sorts of wonders that a more passive child will not. She might develop a lifelong passion for traveling, or researching, or getting to know others. But the same child in a more hazardous setting, like a rough city, may be propelled by her style into dangerous activities and interests. Maybe she grows

up tough or jaded or not at all. What is the point? We cannot speak of personality styles as functional or dysfunctional by describing them in solely biological terms.

DSM-IV assumes that personality disorders predispose clinical syndromes. At one level, this is true. When we develop acute problems, we necessarily do so in accordance with our more general personality. And some people are more likely to develop certain problems than others, again by virtue of their more general style of personality. But in most cases there is little evidence that a personality disorder is a bad seed waiting to erupt in moments of stress into a clinical syndrome (Widiger & Shea, 1991).

Instead, a personality disorder might contribute to other difficulties because of how it leads an individ-

How temperament influences personality depends on the setting in which individuals find themselves.

ual to behave, and the sorts of reactions it elicits from others. Further, a so-called personality disorder might not be a predisposition to a clinical syndrome so much as a milder version of it (Loranger et al., 1991). The clinical syndrome and the personality disorder may be the same way of behaving, to different degrees, and not two separate problems with a causal link between them.

Where does this leave us? As noted, we should not dispense altogether with the notion that some people make trouble for themselves by virtue of their personality style. This is a reasonable idea that should be included in any discussion of the psychology of abnormality. I suggest instead that we should stop viewing these styles as falling into discrete categories. The alternative is dimensional classification: describing problematic personality styles along quantitative dimensions. People develop troubles to the degree that they occupy extreme positions on these dimensions.

Such criticisms of the DSM approach to personality disorders have been widely voiced, even by those responsible for the American Psychiatric Association's diagnostic manual (Task Force on DSM-IV, 1991). Theorists have thus attempted to identify the dimensions along which such disorders are most sensibly described. One strategy here is to ascertain which Axis II diagnoses co-occur (and which do not), and then see what underlying dimensions organize such a clustering (Millon, 1990a). If you are familiar with the statistical technique of *factor analysis*, you see this as a variant of the procedure, which tries to identify a simpler and presumably underlying set of dimensions responsible for a larger set of correlations among variables (in this case, personality disorder diagnoses).

In several such studies, three dimensions were identified, corresponding to the three clusters of personality disorders: odd, dramatic, and timid (Bell & Jackson, 1992; Zimmerman & Coryell, 1990). Note, however, that these are dimensions, not categories. A given person could be high, medium, or low with respect to any of these. Thus, a person's personality style is captured by a profile of quantitative scores, not a diagnostic category.

Another strategy is to arrive at these dimensions on an a priori theoretical basis. Millon (1990b), for example, proposed that any individual's personality can be described in terms of the reinforcements that characterize his or her life (see Figure 13.6). Different patterns prevail, defined by combinations of different dimensions. One important dimension is the degree to which people seek primarily positive reinforcement versus primarily negative reinforcement. That is, where do individuals fall in the tendency to pursue pleasure versus avoid pain? A second dimension is defined by where people find the source of their reinforcements—within themselves versus within others. A third dimension is the activity versus passivity with which people pursue reinforcements.

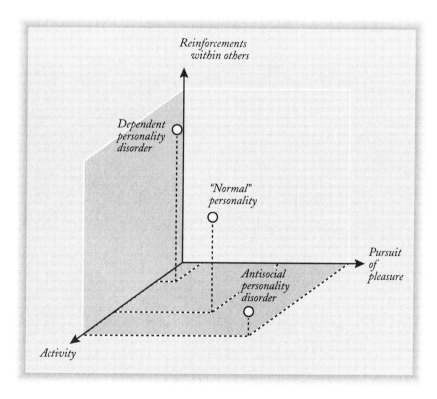

FIGURE **13.6**

DIMENSIONS OF REINFORCEMENT   *Millon hypothesizes that both normal and abnormal personality can be described along dimensions that reflect characteristic reinforcements. A person may seek primarily positive reinforcement (versus negative reinforcement), may find these reinforcements within other people (versus the self), and may pursue these actively (versus passively). This graph shows where antisocial personality and dependent personality disorders would be found in this scheme. For comparison, the placement of a "normal" (i.e., average) personality is also depicted.*
SOURCE: DATA DERIVED FROM *Toward a New Personology*, BY T. MILLON, 1990, NEW YORK: WILEY.

According to Millon (1990b), these three dimensions can be used to characterize personality in general and personality disorders in particular. For example, the antisocial personality disorder can be described as an extreme style of pursuing positive reinforcement by actively becoming independent of other people. Conversely, the dependent personality disorder represents an extreme style of attaining negative reinforcement by passively becoming subordinate to others.

Millon's (1990b) scheme explicitly recognizes that personality disorders are continuous with styles of normal personality. People with personality disorders exaggerate the sorts of approaches to reinforcement that characterize people in general. Further, Millon suggests that some of these disorders are combinations of extreme versions of still others, which helps explain the overlap among them. In Millon's scheme, the paranoid personality disorder is an extreme version of the antisocial, narcissistic, and obsessive-compulsive disorders. The borderline personality disorder is thought to be an extreme version of the histrionic and dependent disorders. Finally, the schizotypal personality disorder is hypothesized as an extreme version of the avoidant and schizoid disorders.

Granted that we can identify such dimensions of dysfunction, what do we do with them? Remember that it is difficult to speak of characteristics per se as functional or dysfunctional until we locate them in their particular contexts, so we should couple our description of people's personalities with a description of their habitual settings. Given where they work and live, do their styles get them into trouble? If so, we can attempt to change their styles, to change their settings, or both. We can look at the DSM-IV personality disorders as difficult styles across a variety of settings, but our understanding would be sharpened if we tried to specify just where the schizoid, or antisocial, or dependent person lived.

This is a familiar idea within the field of personality psychology; it is termed **interactionism:** Personality traits and settings interact to determine what people do (Nisbett & Ross, 1991). My overall conclusion about personality disorders is that theorists interested in them should follow the lead of the interactionists (Endler & Edwards, 1988).

Interactionism can be a sophisticated notion because traits and situations do not simply combine in a mechanical way to influence what a person does. Rather, people and their environments mutually influence one another, which then changes the causal mix. We know that given environments influence people. Remember the childhood experiences that foreshadow such personality disorders as the schizoid style, or the borderline style, or the dependent style.

What about the idea that people can influence situations? Psychologist David Buss (1987) describes three kinds of influences. In what he calls *evocation,* the person unintentionally acts so as to elicit a given response from his environment. The paranoid individual, for instance, constantly tests others, conveying his profound mistrust. The consequence? People forever tested and questioned eventually tire of the process and start to harbor ill feelings toward the individual. A paranoid style exacerbates itself, not because there is some latent entity lurking within the person, but rather because there is a vicious cycle that involves behavior (Cantor, 1990).

In what Buss calls *manipulation,* people intentionally deploy tactics to alter the world in which they live. The tactics they choose are influenced by their traits, to be sure, but the consequences of these tactics change the person. Consider a dependent style, which might start with an attempt to curry favor with others. The person may end up being constantly exploited by others.

Finally, Buss identifies a third sort of influence he calls *selection,* in which a person chooses to enter or avoid given settings—which obviously will or will not influence his subsequent actions. Antisocial individuals, for example, might be drawn to the fast lane, perhaps because it promises more stimulation than the sidewalk. Once there, they are shaped in such a way that their lifestyle becomes faster and faster. Or con-

Wilderness programs like Outward Bound may change a person's way of behaving, but these changes are apt to be temporary when the person returns to his or her typical way of life.

sider the schizoid individual who does not seek out the company of other people. He fails to develop social skills, which further bar him from social settings.

All of these examples show how interactionism can explain the stability of the so-called personality disorders, not because the person has an invariant trait to be dysfunctional, but because his habits influence his settings, which in turn strengthen his habits. The good news from this vantage is that we can also push against these vicious circles, breaking a person out of them by altering his environment.

Reid (1986) reports that wilderness programs like Outward Bound are more effective in altering personality disorders, at least in the short run, than conventional psychotherapy or medication. This is not surprising, because for most of us, the wilderness represents a highly unusual setting. The problem is when the person returns from the wild, because he may well come back to the settings that reinforced his dysfunctional style in the first place. Lifestyle changes are not vacations; they have to be permanent.

In this chapter, I discussed personality disorders. The DSM approach to these disorders has received a great deal of criticism. This criticism reflects mainly the complexity of the subject matter. "Personality" admits to many theoretical treatments, none of which is unanimously accepted (Peterson, 1992). The goal of viewing disorders in biopsychosocial terms thus becomes even more difficult to attain in the particular case of personality disorders.

Summary

✦ Personality disorders are inflexible and maladaptive styles of behaving; they may exacerbate clinical syndromes as well as constitute problems in their own right.

PERSONALITY TYPOLOGIES

✦ DSM-IV specifies ten different personality disorders, and this particular list can be criticized both for what it includes and for what it excludes. Also subject to criticism is the DSM-IV assumption that people's personalities can be described in terms of discrete categories. Nonetheless, the general idea of a personality disorder adds something useful to our understanding of abnormality.

THE ODD PERSONALITY DISORDERS

✦ DSM-IV personality disorders fall into three groups. The first group consists of personality styles that can be characterized as odd. A person with a paranoid personality disorder displays a pervasive belief

that other people intend to harm him. A person with a schizoid personality disorder shows widespread indifference to other people and a restricted range of emotional experience and expression. A person with a schizotypal personality disorder tends to be peculiar in thoughts, actions, and appearance.

THE DRAMATIC PERSONALITY DISORDERS

✦ The second group of DSM-IV personality disorders involves personality styles that are dramatic, emotional, and/or erratic. Those with antisocial personality disorder show long-standing patterns of behaving irresponsibly toward others. Borderline personality disorder refers to a style marked by instability in mood, relationships, and self-image. Histrionic personality disorder is an emotional and attention-seeking style. Those diagnosed with a narcissistic personality disorder are grandiose about the self, hypersensitive to what others think, and lacking in empathy.

THE TIMID PERSONALITY DISORDERS

✦ The third group of DSM-IV personality disorders are marked by fearfulness and anxiety. Social discomfort, fear of evaluation, and timidity characterize the avoidant personality disorder. An individual who is excessively dependent on and submissive to others has a dependent personality disorder. An obsessive-compulsive personality disorder refers to a perfectionistic and inflexible style of behaving.

CONCLUSIONS

✦ In contrast to the DSM-IV approach, many contemporary theorists believe that problematic personality styles should be viewed on the one hand in terms of continuous dimensions of behaving and on the other hand in terms of their social context.

Key Terms

antisocial personality disorder
avoidant personality disorder
borderline personality disorder
dependent personality disorder
histrionic personality disorder; hysterical personality disorder
interactionism

narcissistic personality disorder
object relations
obsessive-compulsive personality disorder
paranoid personality disorder
personality disorder
schizoid personality disorder
schizotypal personality disorder
temperament

Disorders of Childhood and Adolescence

14

AT AGE 14, WENDY WAS 5 FEET 3 inches tall and weighed 110 pounds (Leon & Dinklage, 1989). Although her weight was typical for a female of her height and age, she thought she was fat and began to diet. In the next 2 years, she dropped to 78 pounds. She stopped having menstrual periods. She still felt fat. Wendy became increasingly preoccupied with food, planning exactly what she would eat and when, and she avoided situations where she might be pressured to eat more than she wished. On a typical day, she consumed an egg, part of a slice of bread, a single carrot stick, and some diet soda.

In addition to restricting her calories, Wendy also worked hard to burn off the calories that she did consume. She exercised every day, swimming laps in the family pool. She did this regardless of the weather. Even when it was thundering outside, she would sneak out of the house to swim.

Wendy's parents were obviously aware of what she was doing. Her dieting led to a number of family fights. She tried to avoid sitting down at the table with her parents and older brothers. If they did insist that she join them, she toyed with her food, cutting it into ever smaller pieces, but never actually eating it. Before she became a teenager, Wendy had been highly obedient, complying with all of her parents' wishes and demands. They were therefore confused by her stubbornness surrounding her weight. They did not know what to do, particularly when she insisted that she felt fine about herself. The evidence suggested otherwise. Once an excellent student, Wendy's grades began to fall as her preoccupation with dieting continued. She also lost her friends.

Her parents finally insisted that she go to the family pediatrician, but the physician was unsuccessful in helping her to gain weight. She refused to eat more food, dropped more weight, and ended up weighing only 68 pounds. At this point, over her strong objections, she was hospitalized for treatment.

Wendy's problem is all too familiar. Called *anorexia nervosa*, it is an eating disorder that usually develops during adolescence. Anorexia nervosa can be fatal, because the person's weight drops below the level needed to sustain life.

The present chapter concerns itself with disorders that first become evident during early development (see Table 14.1). What does it mean to take a developmental perspective on people's problems? We must locate a person in his or her life course. This is a relatively new approach within the psychology of abnormality, which is usually interested in the problems of adults at single points in time. But all people are in the process of developing—changing, if you wish—and the problems they encounter can take on different forms and require different treatments depending on where they find themselves in development.

Differences among people of various ages reflect not just developmental contrasts but also what are known as **cohort differences.** By virtue of being born into a given group at a given time and place (a cohort), people carry certain characteristics with them throughout life. Contrast those born during the Great Depression with those born during the affluent postwar years. These groups of people will always be different from one another, not just because of their ages, but because they grew up subject to different historical influences.

TABLE 14.1

DISORDERS OF INFANCY, CHILDHOOD, OR ADOLESCENCE *A variety of psychological problems first occur in the context of early development.*

DISORDER	CHARACTERIZATION AND TREATMENT
mental retardation	a problem first evident during childhood in which an individual displays below average intellectual functioning *and* impaired ability to meet the demands of everyday life
	helped by education, behavior therapy, and skill-specific interventions
learning disorder	difficulty in acquiring or performing a specific skill relevant to learning
	helped by skill-specific interventions
autism	a pervasive developmental disorder characterized by gross impairment in social interaction and communication
	helped by fenfluramine and behavior therapy
attention-deficit/ hyperactivity disorder	a disorder marked by high activity level and inability to pay attention
	helped by stimulants and behavior therapy
conduct disorder	a disorder in which a child is socially disruptive and upsetting to others
	helped by behavior therapy
separation anxiety disorder	anxiety disorder of childhood characterized by excessive anxiety about being separated from a caretaker (i.e., parent) and/or familiar surroundings
	helped by behavior therapy and cognitive therapy
obesity	the excess accumulation of body fat, conventionally defined as some percentage—like 20%—in excess weight over what is considered average for a person of a given sex, age, and height
	helped by behavior therapy that entails lifestyle change
anorexia nervosa	an eating disorder characterized by the refusal to maintain minimal body weight
	helped by behavior therapy and family therapy
bulimia nervosa	an eating disorder that involves ingesting large amounts of high-calorie food in a short amount of time, feeling out of control while doing so, and then ridding oneself of these calories
	helped by antidepressants, behavior therapy, and cognitive therapy

A full developmental perspective requires highly detailed statements about people that take into account all spheres of development.

In Chapter 9, I discussed dramatic differences across the generations in terms of the prevalence of depression. These are cohort differences, and while their exact interpretation is not clear, they remind us not to ignore a person's particular place in history.

A full developmental perspective on the psychology of abnormality would require highly detailed statements about people and their problems that take into account where they are in all spheres of their development—physical, cognitive, social, and so on—as well as the relevant historical and cultural influences. Such a perspective is an ideal that does not exist in psychology today. Much of what we know about abnormality concerns the problems of generic adults, even though there is no such thing as a generic adult.

The disorders that specifically characterize children and adolescents have been the subject of intensive study in recent years (Ollendick & Hersen, 1989). Other disorders are profitably viewed in developmental terms as well, but detailed scrutiny has yet to take place. Suffice it to say that all disorders have a characteristic developmental trajectory (see Focus on Developmental Psychopathology).

To begin this discussion of child and adolescent disorders, here are some general points. First, these problems can be difficult to understand. No psychological disorder leaps off the page to be perfectly grasped, of course, but those of childhood and adolescence can be particularly elusive. Human development has a jagged edge. The different spheres of development are not perfectly synchronized, and the diagnostician always faces the problem of deciding what represents a genuine problem versus a developmental lag.

The 2-year-old who occasionally wets his bed is doing what many 2-year-olds do. The 12-year-old who occasionally wets his bed has a disorder. But at what age do we draw the line between "normal" and "abnormal" bed-wetting? Probably in no particular place.

Second, children and adolescents cannot readily communicate their problems. They are not as articulate as adults, and so they might have considerable difficulty phrasing what bothers them. Relatedly, children do not seek treatment for their own psychological problems. A depressed adult, for example, can readily say that she experiences a depressed mood and can ask a mental health professional for help. A depressed child, in contrast, may not be able to say that he is depressed or that he needs treatment.

The problems of children and adolescents are thus filtered through the observations of adults, typically their parents and teachers. This introduces a level of complexity. A child or adolescent with a problem is someone who is a problem to an adult, for whatever reason. This is not to say that adults are intolerant, simply that the problems faced by young people are tied up in their relationships with significant adults. An important implication here is that a child in treatment is rarely the only client; so too are the adults involved with him.

Third, in focusing on the disorders of children and adolescents, we must take into account such social institutions as the family and school. Consider developmental disturbances that involve problems with intellectual abilities. A person who has trouble reading or writing may not attract much attention as an adult, but for a child or adolescent who must go to school, illiteracy cannot be sidestepped.

Historically, child and adolescent disorders have been explained by generalizing "down" from our familiar models of abnormality: the psychodynamic, the cognitive-behavioral, and the biomedical. But this generalization should not be automatic, because children and adolescents are not scaled-down versions of adults, psychologically or biologically.

DSM-IV approaches developmental disorders by specifying a large and diverse category of problems

Disorders of childhood and adolescence can only be understood in terms of social institutions like school.

"YOU JUST TOLD ME TO BEHAVE. YOU DIDN'T TELL ME WHO TO BEHAVE **LIKE**!"

"Dennis the Menace," by Hank Ketcham, January 26, 1994. © *1994, North America Syndicate.*

FOCUS ON

Developmental

Psychopathology

DEVELOPMENTAL PSYCHO-**pathology** concerns itself with psychological problems in their developmental context (Achenbach, 1974; Cicchetti, 1984; Garber, 1984; Kazdin, 1989; Rutter, 1988; Sroufe & Rutter, 1984). Emerging from a combination of the fields of developmental psychology and psychopathology, it stands in contrast to the more traditional models of abnormality, that focus on the problems of generic adults. Developmental psychopathology adds a time trajectory to explanations. Different problems take place at different periods of development, or they have different manifestations depending on where they occur in the life span. They require different treatments in accordance with the individual's developmental level. Children, for example, may need therapies that approach their problems indirectly, as through play activities (e.g., Doverty, 1992; J. M. Lewis, 1993).

Developmental psychopathologists usually adhere to a biopsychosocial conception of problems. They regard the biological, psychological, and social aspects of problems as bidirectionally influencing one another. This perspective is termed *transactional,* to emphasize the constant give-and-take between the various influences on behavior, normal and abnormal. As in family systems theories, the same factors can be simultaneous causes and effects. For example, a child's actions influence the way her parents treat her, and this treatment in turn shapes her further actions.

Developmental psychopathology has been applied most frequently to the problems of children, and the present chapter provides quite a few examples of how this perspective has been brought to bear on childhood disorders. But all the disorders covered earlier in the book have salient developmental issues.

Substance abuse (Chapter 5)   Once the exclusive province of adults, substance abuse is now encountered increasingly among adolescents and even children. We can assume that early onset of substance abuse, if unchecked, foreshadows even more severe consequences. Researchers have begun to map out the manner in which children progress from one drug to another—from cigarettes and alcohol to marijuana to cocaine

(Yu & Williford, 1992). Many mental health professionals agree that prevention of substance abuse is a more profitable strategy than treatment after problems develop, and interventions must obviously be geared to the individual's developmental level. Messages that make sense to adolescents may have no effect on children, and vice versa.

Organic disorders (Chapter 6)   Many organic disorders occur to older adults. For example, Alzheimer's disease and strokes typically occur only among older individuals. At the same time, the antecedents of many of these disorders lie earlier in life, in genetics and/or family practices that encourage given habits. When organic disorders occur among children, they can have different prognoses than the "identical" problems for adults. A child with brain damage, for instance, is much more likely to make a satisfactory recovery than is an adult, because the child's nervous system is more malleable.

Fear and anxiety disorders (Chapter 7)   These disorders may look much the same in children as adults, but even so, there are some important differences. For example, small children tend to be afraid of tangible objects, whereas adults are more likely to be afraid of abstract entities. Children are frequently the victims of violence, either at home or in their community, which may predispose post-traumatic stress disorder (Garbarino, 1992). More generally, the roots of many fear and anxiety disorders stretch to childhood. The differential socialization of males versus females may help account for the sex differences observed in the prevalence of these disorders.

Somatoform and dissociative disorders (Chapter 8) One of the ingredients of somatoform disorders is a family style that encourages individuals to focus on bodily complaints. This might explain the chronicity of these problems; somaticizing can become part of the child's very identity and mode of coping with stressful situations. And early trauma plays a role in many dissociative disorders. Indeed, I speculated in Chapter 8 that the timing of trauma during early development might account for the particular dissociative disorder that actually develops.

Mood disorders (Chapter 9)   Theorists at one time believed that children did not become depressed. Now it is recognized that depression can and does occur even among the very young. Purely somatic symptoms of depression are less common among children than adults. Instead, a sad mood predominates. And a child is much less able to articulate his or her depressive symptoms. Depressed youngsters, in fact, are often viewed as model children, because they are so quiet and compliant (McKnew, Cytryn, & Yahraes, 1983).

Bipolar disorder is unusual among children, but some cases have been described (e.g., Davis, 1979; Isaac, 1991; Weinberg & Brumback, 1976). Its existence among adolescents is better documented (Goodwin & Jamison, 1990). Mania in children cannot be recognized as it is among adults, and the diagnostician must be alert to the ways that individuals of different ages show inflated self-esteem and reckless activity. Interestingly, the age of onset of bipolar disorder bears no consistent relationship to its eventual severity or course. Whether biomedical treatments such as lithium are suitable for children with bipolar disorder is not clear (e.g., Bertagnoli & Borchardt, 1990; Carr, Dorrington, Schrader, & Wale, 1983).

Mind-body disorders (Chapter 10)   Psychological influences on physical health obviously occur at all points in life, but many of these influences have their beginnings in childhood. Consider healthy habits such as exercising, sleeping soundly, and eating well. These are learned early in life. Parents and teachers who wish to encourage physically healthy habits among children must be aware that children's conceptions of health and illness differ dramatically from those of adults (Peterson & Bossio, 1991). Children cannot be provided a "health" rationale for behavior change, because they do not understand how their bodies work or how illness comes about. Indeed, among children a sense of vulnerability to illness is *negatively* associated with preventive health behavior, like brushing their teeth

(Kalnins & Love, 1982). In other words, children who are ill or believe themselves at risk for illness are less likely to behave in healthy ways.

Sexual disorders (Chapter 11)   You saw in the discussion of sexuality and its disorders that problems can originate early in life. Gender identity disorder is an obvious example. More generally, as young people in our society become sexually active at increasingly early ages, we must be ever more attentive to the messages they receive about healthy sexual expression.

Schizophrenia (Chapter 12)   Childhood schizophrenia was at one time regarded as much the same disorder as schizophrenia among adults. However, critical differences are now recognized (Green, Padron-Gayol, Hardesty, & Bassiri, 1992; Rutter & Lockyer, 1967; Werry, 1992). Children who warrant this diagnosis are less likely than their adult counterparts to have prominent delusions and hallucinations. They are much more likely to be males than females. They are not more likely to come from the lower class. And they usually do not grow up to be schizophrenic adults.

Personality disorders (Chapter 13)   Personality disorders are occasionally described among children, although DSM-IV is explicit that these are problems of adults (e.g., Beren, 1992; Cohen, 1991). Nonetheless, you saw in my discussion of the origins of personality disorders that theorists are unanimous that early experiences are critical risk factors. Even the alternative conception of personality disorders that I offered, which stressed the role of transactions between the person and his or her situation, looked to early experiences. The more frequently these occur, the more entrenched the subsequent personality disorder is apt to be.

descriptively titled "Disorders Usually First Diagnosed in Infancy, Childhood, or Adolescence." Eating disorders are grouped together in their own category by DSM-IV, but they often begin during adolescence and thus merit discussion along with these other problems. Some developmental disorders are extremely common, others quite rare (see Figure 14.1). I discuss many of these in the present chapter, starting with mental retardation.

MENTAL RETARDATION

Jamie was a 5-year-old girl referred to a psychologist by her preschool teacher (M. T. Erickson, 1987). Although Jamie was older than all her classmates, she lacked many of their social and intellectual skills. She did not interact with her classmates at all. According to her parents, she did not start to walk until she was 2, and she spoke her first words only when she was 3. While pregnant with

FIGURE 14.1

LIFETIME PREVALENCE OF CHILDHOOD AND ADOLESCENT DISORDERS   *The disorders of childhood and adolescence show a wide range in diagnosed prevalence.*

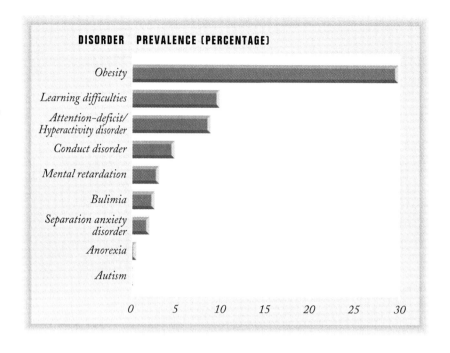

Jamie, her mother had tried to induce an abortion. Her attempt failed, but she bled intermittently throughout the rest of her pregnancy. Jamie was born prematurely, after a difficult delivery. She did not leave the hospital for a month. Her parents had no experience with young children and did not find anything unusual about their young daughter. However, the psychologist tentatively diagnosed Jamie as mentally retarded.

Mental retardation refers to a problem first evident during childhood in which an individual displays below average intellectual functioning *and* an impaired ability to meet the demands of everyday life—self-care, communication, home living, and so on. As you may recall, DSM-IV describes mental retardation on Axis II (Chapter 2). It exists in different forms and degrees, encompassing both physical and mental difficulties:

> Retarded individuals vary widely in intellectual ability, from the profoundly retarded who may possess no speech and no testable IQ, and who must live vegetative lives under continual medical supervision, to the mildly retarded, many of whom appear to have perfectly normal intellectual ability until confronted by tasks of mathematics or reading. Some retarded individuals also have disabling physical handicaps, but many have none. Some have severe emotional problems, but others are remarkably well adjusted. Some will require protective care throughout their lives, but others will be able to live independently as adults.   (Edgerton, 1979, pp. 2–3)

The fact that some individuals have limited intellectual abilities has long been recognized (Deitz &

Repp, 1989). Written references to those with mental retardation go back to at least 1500 B.C. Often their lot in life included inhumane treatment at the hands of "normal" individuals. In Greek and Roman society, for example, they were often exterminated—killed outright or abandoned by their families and left to die. In the Middle Ages, they were used as slaves to physicians or kept for the amusement of the nobility. Henry II of England (1133–1189) offered what has been described as the first working definition of mental retardation when he designated "natural fools" as wards of the king. Interestingly, this royal decree distinguished between the mentally retarded and the mentally ill; only the former were accorded the king's protection.

In the 1800s, theorists began to discuss mental retardation in terms of biological theories. Darwinian thinking provided a scientific rationale for regarding those with retardation as unfit, and it was recommended that such individuals not be allowed to have children. Forced sterilization was common, a practice that still persists today (Dowben & Heartwell, 1979; Krais, 1989).

In the 20th century, particularly during the last few decades, we have seen a raising of consciousness concerning mental retardation. Still, considerable controversy remains concerning how to define it and how to prevent or treat it. There is agreement that mental retardation involves low intelligence, but the best way to measure this important aspect of retardation remains unclear.

In the Middle Ages, those with mental retardation were sometimes kept for the amusement of the nobility.

INTELLIGENCE TESTING

Since Alfred Binet developed the modern intelligence test at the turn of the century, discussions of mental retardation have been entwined with issues of intelligence testing, itself a highly controversial field (Gould, 1981). As described in Chapter 2, Binet was asked to identify children who could profit from traditional education. He devised the strategy of asking children to perform a series of tasks highly similar to the tasks they would be called on to do in school: offering definitions, reasoning, manipulating symbols, and the like. These tasks were arranged in order of difficulty, and children were tested to see how far they could proceed before they reached their limit.

Binet described an individual's performance relative to that of other children the same age. There was an average performance associated with 8-year-olds, 10-year-olds, and so on. The child who achieved the average performance for a given age was said to have the corresponding *mental age*. The child's actual age—his *chronological age*—of course could be younger, older, or the same.

William Stern (1914) later added the refinement of dividing a child's mental age by his or her chronological age, then multiplying the resulting number by 100 to yield what we now refer to as **intelligence quotient** or **IQ.** Higher IQ scores indicate that the child can perform at a level older than his age. Lower scores indicate performance typical of a younger child. Necessarily, the average

child's IQ is 100, because this means that his mental age is the same as his chronological age.

IQ scores tend to be distributed in a bell curve, and nowadays we define IQ in terms of where a person falls along this distribution of scores. Although we glibly speak of people above a certain IQ as gifted, and others below a given cutoff as mentally retarded, appreciate that these are arbitrary designations.

IQ tests were soon developed suitable for group administration, and there was widespread interest in testing all children, a practice that continues to this day. Tests were used to designate some children as retarded and thus to remove them from traditional classrooms. Binet's original intent was to identify children who could profit from education, not those who could not, but his tests have sometimes taken on a life of their own.

Many psychologists now believe that such tests do not measure innate ability to learn so much as the degree to which a student can meet the demands of traditional classrooms (Peterson, 1991a). "Intelligence" tests are skewed toward certain forms of intelligence rather than others. Many current theorists regard intelligence as plural—as a *set* of skills that may vary independently of one another—rather than as a monolithic characteristic that people possess to varying degrees (e.g., Gardner, 1983). Furthermore, intelligence tests might not be fair to individuals from backgrounds other than those where the tests were devised. Minorities and the poor may end up scoring low because they approach the world in ways different from other students.

Most mental health professionals, including the authors of DSM-IV, have stopped using such tests as the only criterion of retardation (Reber, 1992). Following court challenges, it is now illegal to use intelligence tests as the sole basis of placement in classes for the mentally retarded (Deitz & Repp, 1989). However, IQ scores are still used to designate various levels (see Figure 14.2). The lower an individual's IQ, the lower the possible intellectual attainment and the greater the disruption in life. The more severe the level of retardation, the fewer people fall into the category, which is to be expected granted the characteristic distribution of IQ scores.

In the United States, about 3% of children are mentally retarded (Edgerton, 1979). Among these children, about two thirds are males. This sex difference favoring males is apparent not just for mental retardation but also for many other childhood disorders, including learning disorders (see Figure 14.3). The nervous system of males develops more slowly than does that of females, making it more vulnerable to illness or injury; perhaps this explains the sex differences (Kolb & Whishaw, 1990).

FIGURE **14.2**

LEVELS OF MENTAL RETARDATION   *Although IQ scores are no longer used as the sole criterion for diagnosing mental retardation, they are used to designate levels of retardation, as this figure shows.*

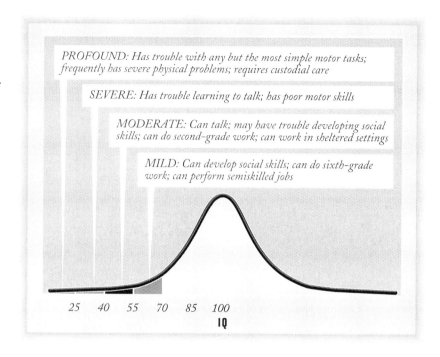

PROFOUND: Has trouble with any but the most simple motor tasks; frequently has severe physical problems; requires custodial care

SEVERE: Has trouble learning to talk; has poor motor skills

MODERATE: Can talk; may have trouble developing social skills; can do second-grade work; can work in sheltered settings

MILD: Can develop social skills; can do sixth-grade work; can perform semiskilled jobs

25   40   55   70   85   100

IQ

FIGURE **14.3**

SEX DIFFERENCES IN PREVALENCE OF CHILDHOOD AND ADOLESCENT DISORDERS   *Almost all the disorders of childhood and adolescence show a sex difference in diagnosed prevalence.*

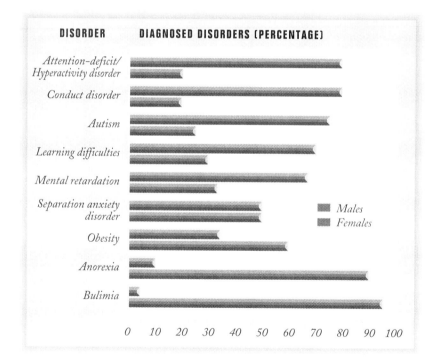

DISORDER   **DIAGNOSED DISORDERS (PERCENTAGE)**

Attention-deficit/ Hyperactivity disorder

Conduct disorder

Autism

Learning difficulties

Mental retardation

Separation anxiety disorder

Obesity

Anorexia

Bulimia

■ *Males*
■ *Females*

0   10   20   30   40   50   60   70   80   90   100

ORGANIC RETARDATION

When mental retardation is linked to a specific illness, injury, or physiological abnormality, it is termed **organic retardation.** A wide variety of factors can be responsible for organic retardation, from illnesses and injuries of the mother during pregnancy to brain trauma to malnutrition to metabolic disorders. The retardation created by such assaults ranges from mild to severe, and much of what I said in Chapter 6 about organic brain disorders applies here. Organic retardation fits our definition of an organic disorder, as the special case in which deficits are intellectual in nature.

About 1 of every 2,000 children born in the United States shows some form of fetal alcohol syndrome, which includes distinctive facial features and mental retardation.

Drugs and alcohol   A growing problem that results in mental retardation among children is the use of drugs or alcohol during pregnancy.[1] These can have profound effects on both the physical and intellectual development of the child, as is now widely recognized.

Fetal alcohol syndrome refers to a complex of characteristics seen among children born to alcoholic mothers: small size, heart and limb defects, distinctive facial features (e.g., widely spaced eyes, a flat nose, and a deep upper lip), mental retardation, and various learning disabilities. At one time, it was believed that a pregnant woman had to consume vast amounts of alcohol during pregnancy for this to occur, but we now know that even moderate drinking during pregnancy has the potential to harm the developing fetus. Its liver is not effective in breaking down alcohol, which means that even small amounts of alcohol consumed by the pregnant woman can linger in the body of the fetus and do damage (Overholser, 1990).

About one of every 2,000 children born in the United States today shows some version of fetal alcohol syndrome (Abel & Sokol, 1991). The long-term consequences of this problem are not clear, because we have only recently begun to study it. But it appears grim, because the physical damage is irreversible. If we as-

sume that a person's nervous system sets the parameters for his or her behavior, the child with fetal alcohol syndrome will carry this challenge throughout life (Spohr & Steinhausen, 1984).

A number of psychoactive drugs ingested during pregnancy, including nicotine, can also harm the developing fetus. But let me consider one particular example that is capturing public interest: children born to mothers addicted to crack cocaine. These **crack babies** come into the world not only addicted to the drug and hence going through withdrawal but also with a variety of physical and intellectual problems. Crack babies have profound difficulties in learning, perhaps because the brain mechanisms that underlie attention are damaged specifically by this drug.

> *At a therapy center in New York City, the saddest child brought in one morning is three-year-old Felicia, a small bundle of bones in a pink dress, whose plastic hearing aids keep falling off, tangling with her gold earrings. She is deaf, and doctors are not sure how much she can see. She functions at the capacity of a four-month-old. Like a rag doll, she can neither sit nor stand by herself; her trunk is too weak and her legs are too stiff. A therapist massages and bends the little girl's legs, trying to make her relax. Next year her foster mother will put Felicia in a special school full time in hopes that the child can at least learn how to feed herself.   (Toufexis, 1991, p. 56)*

Down syndrome   Genetic anomalies might also lead to organic retardation (see Table 14.2). The best known and most common is **Down syndrome**, which is caused by the presence of an extra set of genes on the 21st chromosome (Holtzman & Epstein, 1992).

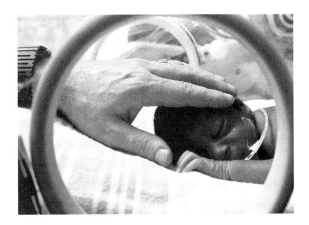

Children born to mothers addicted to crack cocaine come into the world physically dependent on the drug and thus go through withdrawal from the moment of birth. They also evidence a variety of physical and intellectual problems.

---

[1] Although a great deal of attention is paid to the hazards to the fetus of alcohol and drug use by pregnant women, the possibility needs to be considered as well that substance abuse by males can be dangerous because of effects on sperm (Obe & Ristow, 1979).

TABLE 14.2

TYPES OF MENTAL RETARDATION WITH A GENETIC BASIS *Several hundred forms of mental retardation are genetically influenced. Besides Down syndrome, some of the better known examples include those listed here.*
SOURCE: DERIVED FROM "MENTAL RETARDATION," BY L. CYTRYN AND R. S. LOURIE, 1980. IN H. I. KAPLAN, A. M. FREEDMAN, AND B. J. SADOCK (EDS.), COMPREHENSIVE TEXTBOOK OF PSYCHIATRY (VOL. 3), BALTIMORE: WILLIAMS & WILKINS.

SYNDROME	CHARACTERIZATION
trisomy 13 syndrome	facial abnormalities and seizures, caused by anomaly of chromosome 13
trisomy 18 syndrome	cardiac abnormalities and short stature, caused by anomaly of chromosome 18
trisomy 22 syndrome	growth retardation and congenital heart disease, anomaly of chromosome 22
Klinefelter's syndrome	in males only; atrophy of testes, caused by anomaly of sex chromosomes (XXY)
Turner's syndrome	in females only; small stature and webbed neck, caused by anomaly of sex chromosomes (X); mental retardation in only a minority of individuals
phenylketonuria	vomiting, seizures, and musty odor, caused by metabolic disorder, transmitted by a recessive gene
Tay-Sachs disease	progressive mental deterioration and loss of visual function, transmitted by a recessive gene

Children with this genetic makeup may share a number of features, including the following:

◆ epicanthic folds at the inside corners of the eyes

◆ slanting eyes

◆ a broad-bridged nose

◆ short, broad hands

◆ sparse, fine hair

◆ dry skin

About 25% of those with organic retardation have Down syndrome. Most of these children have IQs that place them in the severely to moderately retarded range. Males outnumber females (Verma & Huq, 1987). Life expectancy at present is only 35 to 40 years on the average (see Figure 14.4), in part because those with Down syndrome may have congenital heart disease (Baird & Sadovnick, 1987, 1988; Thase, 1982). Down syndrome is more likely to occur among the children of older mothers (Gaulden, 1992). By some estimates, children with this syndrome are six times more likely to be born to mothers over age 35 than to those under (e.g., Hansen, 1986). However, a study in 1994 found that the number of Down syndrome births to older women in the United States was decreasing, presumably due to prenatal diagnosis and selective abortion (Henry & Levy, 1994).

There is considerable variation in the ability of those with Down syndrome to meet the demands of everyday life. Language difficulties exist, and few can live completely on their own as adults. However, they

FIGURE 14.4

DOWN SYNDROME LIFE EXPECTANCY *Although life expectancy for those with Down syndrome has increased in recent years, it is still less than that of the general population.*
SOURCE: GRAPH ADAPTED FROM "LIFE EXPECTANCY IN DOWN SYNDROME ADULTS," BY P. A. BAIRD AND A. D. SADOVNICK, 1988, *Lancet, 8624,* P. 1355. USED WITH PERMISSION.

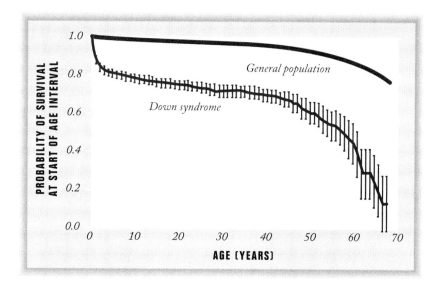

typically form good relationships with others and can live quite well with some supervision from a relative, friend, or other caretaker.

In recent years, we have seen a revision in what is expected of a child born with Down syndrome. The prognosis was once considered extremely bleak, and parents were advised to institutionalize their child. As it turns out, institutionalization is debilitating in its own right. Those individuals put into special institutions fare much worse—physically, intellectually, and socially—than those raised by their own family. Presumably, the family provides a more stimulating and supportive environment in which the child can develop. We have an important reminder that retardation, even with a clear physical cause, can be treated. Down syndrome is not curable, but the person can cope with it in better or worse ways. Nowadays, parents send their children with Down syndrome to school, where they learn to read and write. This was unheard of just a generation ago (Sloper, Cunningham, Turner, & Knussen, 1990).

Actor Christopher Burke, known for his work on the television show "Life Goes On," has Down syndrome. Just a generation ago, such an accomplishment by someone with Down syndrome was inconceivable.

SOCIOCULTURAL RETARDATION

When an individual's mental retardation cannot be traced specifically to physical causes, it is termed **sociocultural retardation.** Perhaps 75% of the mentally retarded fit this designation (Edgerton, 1979). Presumably, the causes of this form of retardation reside in social disadvantage. Those with sociocultural retardation tend to come from the lower class and/or minority groups, though not invariably. Many poor children show superior intelligence, and many rich children do not.

Individuals with sociocultural retardation typically do not come to anyone's attention until they enter school, because their chief problem is meeting the demands of the typical classroom. Once they leave school, we know little about what happens to them; we assume they go on to lead their lives in satisfactory fashion.

These facts bother some theorists, who suggest that we use the term *6-hour retardation* to describe children with low IQs whose only evident difficulty in adaptation is poor school performance. Granted what IQ scores are best suited to predict (i.e., classroom grades), there is considerable circularity, because we know from the start that these children will not do particularly well at a typical school. But what does the label add besides the risk of reifying something better thought of as a behavior?

Social disadvantage can take a toll on intellectual attainment.

Granted that there is more to sociocultural retardation than just a label placed on one group by another, what brings it about? There is a consensus that the immediate environments of those who live in poverty are not intellectually stimulating. These children are not exposed to books or educational television, and their parents' attention is elsewhere.

At the same time, we must not overlook the possible role played by biological factors in what looks like sociocultural retardation. Intelligence is heritable, and early stimulation is necessary for normal development of the brain and nervous system. Those at a social disadvantage may have poor diets, they may lack appropriate medical care, and they may be exposed to environmental toxins. Subtle biological disruptions may result that limit intellectual attainment. Accordingly, we should not treat organic retardation and sociocultural retardation as rigidly distinct categories.

THE MECHANISMS OF MENTAL RETARDATION

We have a good understanding of the risk factors for mental retardation: biological insult in the case of organic retardation and social disadvantage in the case of sociocultural retardation. But given these risk factors—and certainly these are not invariant causes—what actually produces the low intellectual attainment and failure of adaptation that define mental retardation? Researchers have barely scratched the surface, although cognitive psychologists have begun to administer to retarded individuals the same sorts of tasks used for years to map out the processes that underlie "normal" thinking and problem solving (Brooks & McCauley, 1984). Some differences have emerged that represent a first step toward specifying the actual mechanisms of retardation.

Studies show that mentally retarded individuals have specific difficulties with *attention* (e.g., Nettelbeck, Hirons, & Wilson, 1984). Consider that many of the cognitive tasks we face in life demand that we pay attention to some stimuli but not to others. Complex objects have many stimulus characteristics, some of which are relevant and some of which are not. In laboratory experiments, retarded individuals tend to pay attention to the color or position of objects, which creates a problem if these prove irrelevant to the task at hand. Perhaps even more debilitating is the fact that those with retardation have difficulty changing their mental set—that is, switching attention from one dimension to another. Instead, they persevere on a given dimension, even if it proves irrelevant.

Other studies suggest that mentally retarded individuals have problems with their *short-term memory* (e.g., Whiteley, Zaparniuk, & Asmundson, 1987). They cannot hold new information in their mind as

long as can other individuals. A simple example is reading a telephone number out of a phone book, then walking across the room to dial. Most of us can do this with no difficulty, so long as we are not interrupted on our way to the phone. But the retarded cannot. This is but a single example, and mental retardation involves much more than not remembering phone numbers. Imagine not being able to hold *any* sort of information like this in your mind. Interestingly, among those with mental retardation, there apparently is no corresponding problem with respect to long-term memory. Once committed to permanent memory, information is as accessible to the retarded as to the nonretarded. The problem seems to lie in getting it there in the first place.

There is some debate whether this deficit in short-term memory represents a problem with the strategies that the mentally retarded use (or fail to use) versus structural problems with the brain. We know, for example, that people can increase the span and content of short-term memory by rehearsing information (saying the phone number over and over), by chunking the items of information into meaningful wholes ("2-18 is my birthday"), and so on. Perhaps the retarded do not have these strategies available to them.

Yet other studies show that mentally retarded individuals do not *process information as quickly* as do the nonretarded (e.g., Nugent & Mosley, 1987). Even the simplest of tasks, such as recognizing information flashed on a screen, takes the mentally retarded notably longer (Kail, 1992). To some theorists, this implies that there are structural problems with their brains. But it may derive from attentional problems as well, or incorrect strategies as just sketched.

I have discussed rather molecular mechanisms that may underlie mental retardation. Also implicated are problems with *meta-cognition:* people knowing what they know and being able to apply this knowledge deliberately to solve problems. Studies of expert problem solvers in various domains show that they differ from novices by virtue of their familiarity with what it takes to solve a certain problem (Chi, Feltovich, & Glaser, 1981). They can recognize that a problem is of a certain sort requiring a certain solution. They can also recognize when a possible solution is failing and hence when it is time to switch gears and try something else. And they know how to evaluate their own solutions as correct or not. All of us have domains of life in which our meta-cognition is not well developed, and so we blunder along. But if meta-cognition is a general difficulty for those with mental retardation, imagine how life might be (Ellis, Woodley-Zanthos, Dulaney, & Palmer, 1989).

Whatever purely cognitive problems might exist, they are compounded by the individual's emotional reaction to what he or she perceives as failure. Remember the *learned helplessness* phenomenon described in Chapter 9? When people encounter events they cannot control, they respond by becoming passive and listless, depressed and inattentive. Some investigators have applied helplessness ideas to mental retardation (e.g., DeVellis & McCauley, 1979; Weisz, 1979). They find that those with retardation perform well on tasks until they reach one they cannot solve; then they are inordinately disrupted, becoming passive and demoralized. They cannot succeed at subsequent problems that they could have solved perfectly well had they not encountered the unsolvable one along the way.

Adding to the plight of the mentally retarded is the social stigma that is associated with retardation, and the rudeness—deliberate or inadvertent—of "normal" people. The retarded are severely restricted in what they are allowed to do. Little wonder that mental retardation is sometimes associated with depression, anxiety, and substance abuse (e.g., Einfeld, 1992; Vitiello & Behar, 1992; Vitiello, Spreat, & Behar, 1989). The mentally retarded are, after all, people, and they respond in a human way to the roadblocks placed in their way, by fate or by society, exactly as everyone else would: with frustration and anger, which may eventually give rise to other problems.

TREATMENT OF MENTAL RETARDATION

Our conception of the cause of mental retardation affects how we approach its solution. There are two general strategies. According to the first, mental retardation reflects a permanent defect in the brain. According to the other, it represents a developmental delay, so that mentally retarded individuals attain their intellectual development at a slower pace than others. Using the former approach, we would try to help the individual compensate for her particular deficits, as you saw for the organic disorders in Chapter 6. With the second strategy, we would put the person in a setting that will allow her intellectual development to proceed.

Neither approach suggests that we should leave the person alone, yet this was often the plight of those with mental retardation. Matters began to change in the United States in the 1960s, with new legislation requiring that all handicapped children—including those with mental retardation—be given a free public education *in the least restrictive environment.* This meant that to the degree possible, those with mental retardation would be educated at the same schools as other children, and often in the same classroom, in a practice called **mainstreaming.**

The overall effectiveness of mainstreaming is not clear, and different programs produce different results.

In the best of worlds, both the child with mental retardation and the child without would benefit from their interaction, intellectually and otherwise. This does not always happen, but do we blame mainstreaming for this or the way it is carried out?

More specifically, interventions to help the retarded usually employ behavior therapy techniques on the one hand and cognitive approaches on the other. Consider the first. A target behavior to be increased or decreased is specified, an appropriate reinforcer or punisher is chosen, and the behavior therapist presents the reinforcer or punisher contingently on the behavior in question (Matson & Coe, 1992; Reid, Phillips, & Green, 1991; Vollmer & Iwata, 1992).

Among the behaviors that might be targeted in behavior therapy are self-injurious actions, which can be common among those with severe mental retardation (Matson, 1989). Some individuals bang their heads against the wall or floor, slap their own faces, or pinch themselves. The significance of these actions is unclear, but they present a danger nonetheless. Behavior therapy helps to reduce their frequency (e.g., Lucero, Frieman, Spoering, & Fehrenbacher, 1976).

In other cases, while the individual does not pose a physical danger to himself, he engages in such actions as spinning about or rocking, which take his attention away from appropriate activities. Behavior therapy can reduce these behaviors as well, although generalization of benefits to other settings may be limited (Schmid, 1986).

Along the same lines, behavior therapy can be used to impart social skills and self-care abilities, which may also be lacking among those with severe mental retardation. Individuals who can use a toilet correctly, for example, get along easier in our world than those who cannot. Those who can feed and dress themselves can live at home without disrupting the household, and thus reap further benefits. Again, research shows that these interventions are successful (Casteles & Glass, 1986).

Cognitive interventions have been designed based on the specific information deficits documented among those with mental retardation, as described earlier. Strategies for improving attention, problem solving, and short-term memory have been taught to those with mental retardation (e.g., Crawford & Siegel, 1982; Dorry & Zeaman, 1975). Although further research is needed, the results so far are promising. Children taught these strategies make greater strides in school than those who are not (Ross & Ross, 1973).

In an ideal world, mental retardation would be headed off at the pass. Certainly in those cases of organic retardation where the specific cause is known, we can prevent it. Signs in bars warn against the dangers of pregnant women drinking alcohol. And the

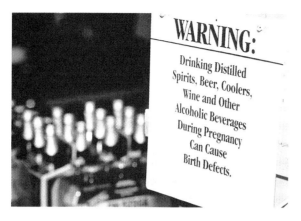

Organic retardation, like that associated with fetal alcohol syndrome, can sometimes be prevented by behavioral change.

widespread publicity about crack babies might—we can only hope—reduce that source of retardation as well.

In the case of sociocultural retardation, prevention takes the form of programs that try to identify children at risk for failure in school, then impart the sorts of skills that will help them succeed in traditional school settings. Some programs provide stimulation to very young infants and parent training to their mothers and fathers (e.g., Field, Widmayer, Stringer, & Ignatoff, 1980; Widmayer & Field, 1981). Other programs attempt to meet the nutritional needs of young children (e.g., Casto & Mastropieri, 1986; Guralnick, 1988). Research suggests that such programs, at least in the short run, boost intellectual attainment.

The best known prevention program in the United States is Head Start, where children are given preschool instruction focusing on cognitive and social

Programs like Head Start give preschool children instruction that focuses on cognitive and social skills.

skills. In addition, their medical and nutritional needs are ascertained and met. This program and others like it have been controversial (see Locurto, 1991; Schweinhart & Weikart, 1989, 1991; Spitz, 1991, 1993). However, some studies have shown that they achieve at least partial success (see Figure 14.5); those who participate do better in school than those who do not (Zigler, 1975, 1985; Zigler & Weikart, 1993). At the same time, Head Start does not completely close the gap (Lee, Brooks-Gunn, Schnur, & Liaw, 1990). This makes sense. It is not enough merely to give a child a head start if the rest of the race is to be run against the wind.

LEARNING DIFFICULTIES

As pointed out, mental retardation refers to pervasive intellectual problems. In contrast, other disorders appearing early in life may involve more circumscribed problems, difficulties encountered with acquiring or performing a specific skill—reading, speaking, or moving. These problems usually surface when the child enters the school system, and they are typically treated by special education teachers rather than mental health professionals.

DSM-IV describes problems with reading, writing, and arithmetic as **learning disorders,** for obvious reasons, but other developmental problems can be grouped with them as well. Indeed, the exact classification of learning difficulties is a subject of debate (Baker & Cantwell, 1989). This is hardly surprising. These problems are tied to a given time and place, and we should expect their definition to change. To use a forced example, a person living in a nonliterate society is never going to have a problem with reading or writing. As new ways of acquiring and using information develop, then new problems might occur as well.

Table 14.3 (see page 422) lists some of the learning difficulties recognized in DSM-IV, as well as a sketch of what the problems involve. Perhaps as many as 10% of all children in the United States today have one or more of these problems (Baker & Cantwell, 1989). In virtually every case, boys are more likely to have these problems than girls. These disorders can be chronic, and their existence among adults is increasingly recognized (Felsenfeld, Broen, & McGue, 1992; Gajar, 1992; White, 1992).

In third grade, 9-year-old Jeff showed a great deal of trouble reading and spelling (M. T. Erickson, 1987). His infancy and earlier childhood had been uneventful. When he began elementary school, Jeff showed no difficulty with the approach to reading taken by his teachers,

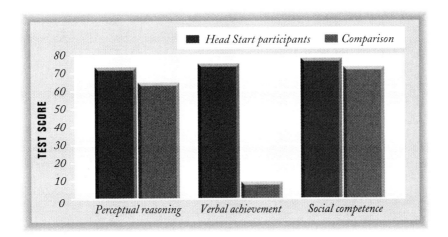

FIGURE 14.5

THE EFFECTS OF HEAD START   *Researchers compared 333 disadvantaged children who participated in Head Start programs in New Jersey and Oregon to 204 children without such preschool experience. Clear differences emerged showing that Head Start is intellectually and socially advantageous for participants. (Note: The data shown here were transformed to be comparable across the different tests.)*
SOURCE: DATA DERIVED FROM "ARE HEAD START EFFECTS SUSTAINED?" BY V. E. LEE, J. BROOKS-GUNN, E. SCHNUR, AND F. LIAW, 1990, *Child Development, 61*, PP. 495–507. USED WITH PERMISSION.

which stressed phonics. His third-grade teacher took a different approach, stressing words and sentences, and Jeff was unable to master even the basics. He became frustrated and refused to participate in his reading group. On several occasions, he tore up his spelling papers. His parents were unaware of his problems with reading and spelling until the third-grade teacher brought them to their attention. His mother, an avid reader, was highly upset. His father did not think reading was important and expressed little concern about Jeff's apparent learning difficulties.

Mental retardation does not preclude the diagnosis of a specific learning difficulty. The diagnostician must make the judgment—granted the individual's overall intellectual level—whether there is a lag or deficit in the acquisition of a specific ability. Consider a person who has an IQ of 60. Given appropriate schooling, he should be able to read. If he cannot learn to read, then he warrants a diagnosis of reading disorder.

ETIOLOGY

What causes these disorders? No shortage of hypotheses exists. At one time, it was believed that they were brought about by specific lesions in the part of the brain responsible for the skill in question. Certainly

this is a reasonable hypothesis because many adults who have trouble speaking or writing or reading have such lesions. However, subsequent research has been unable to locate these hypothesized lesions among children with learning difficulties (Baker & Cantwell, 1989).

A more subtle version of this hypothesis proposes that the child with a learning disorder has **minimal brain damage (MBD),** either caused prenatally or influenced genetically. These children often show what are called "soft" signs of neurological problems—irregular EEG patterns, difficulties in coordinating movement, and mixed patterns of dominance of eyes, hands, and/or feet (e.g., Marosi et al., 1992). Again, this hypothesis has not fared well because no "hard" signs of neurological difficulty have been consistently documented among those with learning disorders. Still, at least some learning difficulties are heritable, which points to a biological etiology, undiscovered though it may be (Lewis & Thompson, 1992; Tallal, Townsend, Curtiss, & Wulfeck, 1991).

Other explanations specify problems with more psychological functions, such as perception, attention, imagery, and the like. Still others suggest that environmental factors such as large family size or poverty put children at risk for learning problems. And one intriguing theory suggests that learning problems result from the way we socialize boys versus girls (McGuiness, 1985). Boys are encouraged to engage in

TABLE 14.3

TYPES OF LEARNING DIFFICULTIES *DSM-IV describes the following disorders that can make learning difficult. As noted in the text, other ways of classifying these problems exist. Indeed, DSM-IV labels only the first three as learning disorders.*

DISORDER	CHARACTERIZATION
reading disorder*	impairment in the development of skills at recognizing words and comprehending written text
written expression disorder*	impairment in the development of skills at writing (spelling, punctuating, using grammar, organizing, and so on)
mathematics disorder*	impairment in the development of skills at arithmetic (understanding mathematical concepts, decoding word problems, counting, calculating, and so on)
motor skills disorder	impairment in the development of skills at coordinating the body
expressive language disorder	impairment in the development of skills at communicating with speech (choosing words, acquiring vocabulary) and in general acquiring speech slowly or incorrectly
phonological disorder	impairment in the development of skills at pronouncing sounds and words correctly
stuttering	disturbance in the fluency and time patterning of speech

Considered a learning disorder by DSM-IV.

gross motor activity (e.g., running and jumping), whereas girls are encouraged to pursue fine motor activity (e.g., sewing). According to this line of theorizing, skill at fine motor activity facilitates language development. We therefore can make sense of why girls are unlikely to develop learning problems, because so many of them involve language. It may well be that there is no single etiology of learning difficulties, but that several factors—from genetics to socialization—entwine to bring them about. The mix may change from disorder to disorder and from child to child.

Learning difficulties have consequences far beyond narrowly intellectual ones. The child who falls behind in school because he cannot speak or read as well as his peers is apt to become frustrated and disappointed. His parents might panic. His classmates might tease or ostracize him. His teachers might ignore him. All of this sets the stage for emotional or conduct difficulties later in life, which occur at greater than chance rates among those once diagnosed with learning problems (Faigel, Doak, Howard, & Sigel, 1992; Fristad, Topolosky, Weller, & Weller, 1992; Schachter, Pless, & Bruck, 1991; Wright-Strawderman & Watson, 1992). Part of placing disorders in a developmental context is appreciating that problems do not develop in a vacuum. That learning disabilities during childhood are risk factors for other disorders later in life is a good example of the developmental approach to abnormality.

TREATMENT

What can we do about these disorders? Parents hope that they will be outgrown, that they represent a lag rather than a deficit; nevertheless, specific instruction in the skill in question speeds the process along (Wilson & Sindelar, 1991). Explicit attention to metacognition may also prove beneficial, because the child with a learning difficulty might not be aware of just how to go about using these skills to master a given task (Montague, 1992).

AUTISM

Another disorder that involves problems with intellectual abilities is **autism,** which DSM-IV calls **autistic disorder.** Autism is considered a pervasive developmental disorder, which means that it is characterized by a widespread impairment in social interaction and communication. The autistic individual also shows a highly restricted repertoire of activities and interests.

Although it has been described only since 1943, autism has intrigued a number of theorists, and recent history reveals a variety of perspectives on the disorder. For example, the term *autism* itself reflects the impression of early theorists that the individual with the disorder was preoccupied with his or her own inner fantasies, preferring these to external reality (e.g., Bettelheim, 1967). Along these lines, autism was often grouped with childhood schizophrenia, because of the hallucinations and delusions thought to characterize both disorders. Current opinion is that autism is different from schizophrenia, and indeed that the central problem is not an overly rich mental life but instead a profound impairment in communication. Theorizing about causes has changed as well, from an earlier emphasis on poor parenting to a current belief in biological etiologies.

These autistic children do not interact with one another, showing one of the defining characteristics of the disorder.

In the movie Rain Man, *Dustin Hoffman portrayed a character with autism. His character had certain extraordinary abilities sometimes occurring among those with this disorder.*

Autism was first described when Leo Kanner (1943) published a paper describing eleven children from his clinical practice who seemed qualitatively different from other children. Chief among the characteristics of this group was their inability to develop or maintain relationships with other children or adults. Kanner also noted that those with autism had problems acquiring speech, and if they did speak at all, they evidenced such bizarre tendencies as **echolalia**—echoing back to another whatever was said, rather than responding to it—and **pronominal reversal**—substituting *you* for *I.*

Kanner hypothesized that autistic children had normal or above-normal intelligence. Testing the IQ of such a child is obviously difficult, and so his conclusion was based on the fact that the autistic child typically possesses a good rote memory and may be skilled at solving puzzles. It is no longer believed that autism is characterized by normal intelligence. Most have below average intelligence. When testing is possible, only 20% of autistic children have IQs that place them within the normal range (Ritvo & Freeman, 1978).

Kanner was also struck by the fact that some of the children he described possessed certain skills that stood out against their otherwise deficient abilities. These *islands of excellence* often included a special talent at mathematical calculation or music or mechanics.

Thanks to the 1988 movie *Rain Man,* we are all familiar with the gifts that the autistic may have (see Treffert, 1989). Yet these abilities do not define autism. The majority of autistic children have no such talents. Of course, those who do challenge the way we think about intelligence as a singular entity (Kehrer, 1992).

Kanner's characterization of autism is elaborated by DSM-IV. To warrant a diagnosis, a child must show symptoms from each of three general groups. First, impaired social interaction with others shows itself as problems with nonverbal communication, emotional expression, and peer relationships. Second, problems with language can show up as delayed language acquisition, inability to sustain a conversation, or stereotyped use of language. Finally, restricted and repetitive patterns of behavior are evidenced as adherence to specific nonfunctional routines or rituals, limited interests, and stereotyped movements, e.g., spinning or head-banging.

A teacher reported that each morning he would read a list of 10 activities for the day printed on the board. One morning, he erased the last three items. Daniel, an autistic child, became terrified and screeched perseveratively for the remainder of the morning, "Where's 8, 9, 10?" As soon as the three items were returned to the board, Daniel became friendly and cooperative. (Goldfarb, 1980, p. 2532)

By definition, autism must have its onset during infancy or early childhood—before the child turns 3 years old. It is rare, occurring in only 3 to 5 per 10,000 children (Schreibman & Charlop, 1989). It is more common among boys than girls, by a factor of three or four to one. At one time, autism was thought to be more prevalent among the upper classes as opposed to the lower classes, but this theory has not held up. It probably reflected a bias in diagnosis: Lower-class children with autistic symptoms were labeled retarded, whereas upper-class children were labeled autistic. It also appears to run in families, with a concordance as high as 36% reported among identical twins; further, if one identical twin is autistic, 82% of the time his or her twin shows some form of cognitive impairment as well (Folstein & Rutter, 1977).

ETIOLOGY

Like many disorders, autism occurs in degrees, but in its most extreme form, where many of the diagnostic criteria are satisfied, what we have is a bizarre child. Parents are understandably confused and frightened by their autistic offspring. You can imagine how they felt when early explanations of autism centered on their role in producing the disorder in their children. Psychodynamic theorists in particular proposed that parents were rejecting, obsessive, aloof, and emotionally cold (Hobson, 1990). The phrase *refrigerator mother* was coined to describe the sort of parent who produced autism in her child (Bettelheim, 1967).

This sort of theorizing is now recognized as insidious, blaming the parents of an autistic child for something they quite literally had nothing to do with. Consider the anguish of having a child who is socially absent, coupled with reading or hearing that *you* made him this way. In some cases of autism, the salient symptoms do not show themselves for some months, which only adds to the devastation experienced by parents who thought they were raising a normal child.

These early theorists were not intentionally malicious, of course, but they were guilty of confusing cause with effect. Having a child who is autistic exerts an influence on the parent, and what may seem like aloofness may be a reaction to the child's tantrums and bizarre behavior (Rimland, 1964; Rutter, 1968). Well controlled studies of the parents of autistic children find that they do *not* differ in their personalities or interaction styles from the parents of other children (Schreibman & Charlop, 1989).

Explanations of autism today center on biological etiologies (Courchesne, 1991; Folstein & Piven, 1991; Fotheringham, 1991; Schreibman & Charlop, 1989; Smalley, 1991). We should have suspected this all along, granted the substantial sex difference, the presence of the disorder from birth, and its heritability. Other evidence buttresses the conclusion that biological factors are importantly involved in the etiology of the disorder. Autistic children tend to have a history of complications during birth. Some possess a sex chromosome defect. Others have more than their share of neurological abnormalities such as epilepsy (e.g., Ritvo et al., 1990).

More specific attention has focused on the neurotransmitter **serotonin,** which you have already encountered in our discussion of depression. The level of serotonin in the blood usually changes across the life span, starting out at relatively high levels and then tapering off throughout childhood and stabilizing in adulthood. Among a subset of autistic individuals—maybe 30% to 40%—this tapering off does not occur, suggesting that their nervous system fails to mature in a normal fashion. Some researchers have found that higher serotonin levels among autistic individuals are linked to lower intellectual functioning (Cook et al., 1990).

TREATMENT

The practical implication of these results is that perhaps we can intervene with procedures that lower the level of serotonin. **Fenfluramine** is an amphetamine that does precisely this, and it sometimes—though not always—leads to an improvement among autistic children's symptoms (Stubbs, Budden, Jackson, Terdal, & Ritvo, 1986). However, not all children show a good response, and the drug can have dangerous side effects (Varley & Holm, 1990). Work continues on how to treat autism biomedically (du Verglas, Banks, & Guyer, 1988).

In the meantime, behavioral treatments are the most widely used form of intervention. Following the pioneering demonstrations of Ivar Lovaas (1987; Lovaas, Schreibman, & Koegel, 1974; Lovaas & Smith, 1989), operant conditioning techniques have been used to bring the child's behavior into more acceptable ranges, by punishing bizarre and self-destructive behavior. Some strides toward helping the child acquire language have also been made through behavior therapy, although the process is necessarily painstaking, proceeding one sound, one word, and one sentence at a time. In no way does operant conditioning "cure" autism in the sense of making it go away altogether. But it helps. Children show gains in intelligence, language, and social functioning (Kamps et al.,

1992; Koegel, Koegel, Hurley, & Frea, 1992). Some number are even able to be mainstreamed into regular classrooms. Prognosis is apparently best for those with higher IQs.

Despite the promise of these interventions—drug therapy and behavior therapy—the outcome at present for those with autism is not encouraging. Current estimates are that the majority are not able to live on their own as adults, requiring instead at least some supervision (Gillberg, 1991; Wolf & Goldberg, 1986). Even in the best of cases, the individual with autism is apt to be quite socially impaired. We know that institutionalization is associated with the worst prognosis, but unfortunately not all families have the resources needed to raise their autistic child at home, particularly as the child becomes older and more difficult to control.

A striking exception to the bleak prognosis of autism is Sean Barron, who was diagnosed with autism at age 5 (Hubbard, 1992). As a youngster, he showed virtually all of the defining symptoms. For the first 4 months of his life, he cried almost constantly, and he was not comforted when his mother or father picked him up. At age 1, he was impossible for his parents to control. He hated to be touched. He made no eye contact with anyone. He developed bizarre rituals. He would pick at the carpet in the family living room for hours at a time. He would run up to cars in the street and stare at their speedometer needles. He began to speak, and memorized the call letters for hundreds of radio stations. He would ask everyone he met which stations they listened to. He memorized the dialogue for countless episodes of "Gilligan's Island."

Against the advice of almost everyone, Sean's parents sent him to public school, and he did rather well in most of his subjects. As Sean looks back on this experience, he believes the structure provided by school was helpful. Despite his success in school, he remained socially isolated. He had no friends. An apparent turning point came when he was a teenager, and the family was watching a television movie about an autistic boy. He turned to his parents and asked them, "I'm autistic, too, aren't I?" (p. 86). Sean began to work harder to control his rituals, and he began to make friends. He attended college and graduated with a degree in early childhood education. As of this writing, Sean is in his thirties. He has a satisfying job and is living a full life.

Just why Sean recovered so completely from autism is not clear. Some mental health professionals who have heard about this unusual outcome have speculated that the original diagnosis was wrong (Hubbard, 1992). Perhaps it is more reasonable to take his story at face value, recognizing that there are important exceptions to even the most sound generalizations.

ATTENTION-DEFICIT/HYPERACTIVITY DISORDER

Hyperactive is part of our everyday vocabulary. Much more frequently than not, the label is applied to a boy in grade school (Whalen, 1989). He is impulsive, always acting before thinking. He is in constant trouble with his peers and his teachers. He has difficulty staying focused on one task at a time. He shifts quickly from one activity to another, leaving a trail of unfinished business. He has a high activity level, and he demands attention, sensation, and gratification.

Janowsky, Addario, and Risch (1987, p. 226) described the following case of a young boy who is hyperactive:

> *The patient is a 9-year-old boy who is brought . . . for evaluation. His mother is extremely concerned by his progressive inability to function appropriately in the classroom. His teachers have told her that the patient is unable to control his level of motor activity. He is said to have trouble concentrating and is "fidgety." The patient's mother states that he has always been a restless child, and that while her other children were able to routinely nap or focus on single activities, the patient was easily distracted, unable to complete tasks, and always calling for attention. The mother further states that the patient has always been a difficult child to manage . . . having continued discipline problems, running into the street in spite of continued warnings, and climbing trees in the neighborhood in spite of her admonitions.*

Hyperactivity has been studied for years. It has gone by various names: *hyperkinesis, hyperkinetic impulse disorder,* and *minimal brain dysfunction,* among others (Hassler, 1992). DSM-IV uses the term **attention-deficit/hyperactivity disorder (ADHD)** to capture the idea that such a child's difficulty involves not just his activity level but also his ability to pay attention. As recently as DSM-III, diagnosticians separated such problems into those in which overactivity predominated and those in which attention deficits predominated. But in theory as well as in practice, this proves unwieldy (Quay, 1986; Rutter & Shaffer, 1980). DSM-IV directs the diagnostician to make the distinction if possible but allows a "combined" designation for use in other cases.

Hyperactive behavior is often associated with attentional problems.

According to DSM-IV, a child is diagnosed as having ADHD if for at least 6 months he shows signs of either inattention or impulsivity. Onset of these problems must be by age 7, and they must be apparent in at least two situations, for example at school *and* at home. Inattention is recognized by such signs as failure to be concerned with the details of activities; difficulty in sustaining work or play; not listening to what is said; and losing materials necessary for activities. Impulsivity is evidenced by fidgeting with one's hands or feet; not being able to remain seated when required to do so; blurting out answers to questions before they are completed; and difficulty waiting in line or taking turns in games or group situations. Attention-deficit/hyperactivity disorder is not diagnosed if the child has autism.

As discussed earlier, manifestations of a particular problem change across the life span, even within the childhood years. In the case of ADHD, infants show poor regulation of patterns of activity, eating, and sleeping (Ross & Ross, 1982). Toddlers with ADHD show signs of gross overactivity, running, jumping, and climbing incessantly (Hartsough & Lambert, 1985). A somewhat older child with ADHD does not show this overall flurry of movement but instead is fidgety and restless and may have poor peer relationships (Pelham & Bender, 1982).

The correctly diagnosed ADHD child is not simply active. There is more to the problem than this, no matter how exhausting an active child can be for a teacher or parent. Additionally, his problems with attention mean that he is apt to do quite poorly in school and indeed in any domain of life in which instruction is given (Semrud-Clikeman et al., 1992; Whalen, 1989). He also tends to do poorly in establishing friendships, which means that he is a lonely and isolated child. Other emotional difficulties—such as depression—may also accompany this disorder (Biederman, Newcorn, & Sprich, 1991).

Attention-deficit/hyperactivity disorder is a prevalent problem nowadays, usually regarded as the most common psychological difficulty of childhood (Weiss, 1985). Epidemiological studies estimate that between 3% and 15% of children in the United States may warrant the diagnosis, with some studies providing estimates as high as 24% (Whalen, 1989). At the same time, we must be cautious about these estimates because they are usually based on surveys of parents or teachers who use rating scales to indicate the frequency of the ADHD behaviors described earlier. These rating scales might overestimate what is really going on.

There is no disagreement, however, that boys are three to six times more likely to be hyperactive than girls. When we employ a particularly stringent definition, the sex difference becomes even more pronounced (Whalen, 1989). Among the most severe instances of ADHD, boys are ten times more likely to be represented than girls.

Some studies indicate that ADHD children are more likely to be found among those in the lower classes than in the upper classes; other studies find no such relationship (Whalen, 1989). Part of the problem in discerning a clear link between social class and ADHD is that ADHD in turn is associated with conduct disorder (to be discussed shortly), which in turn is also associated with membership in the lower classes (Abikoff & Klein, 1992; Hinshaw, 1992; Shaywitz & Shaywitz, 1991). Less confounded is research linking ADHD to family adversity, such as parental divorce, overcrowdedness, parental emotional difficulties, and the like (McGee, Williams, & Silva, 1984). But these links are not unique to this disorder.

The long-term prognosis for a child diagnosed with attention-deficit/hyperactivity disorder varies (Klein & Mannuzza, 1991; Lie, 1992). About half the children who at one time warrant this label seem to "outgrow" the problem altogether by the time they are young adults, with no evidence of psychological or social difficulties. This suggests that ADHD is sometimes a developmental lag that resolves itself in time. But it may also mean that those who overcome the problem have had special experiences or support. Research has tended to focus on the pathology associated with this disorder, so we know little about the success stories (Whalen, 1989).

The other half of children with ADHD continue to have problems into their adult years (Bellak & Black, 1992; Mannuzza et al., 1991). They might develop substance abuse problems. They may end up in trouble with the law. And they tend to earn lower incomes than would otherwise be expected. Are these consequences the direct result of the problems associated with ADHD, or are they the result of the difficulties into which ADHD may lead a child? Or are they really due to the conduct disorders that—as just noted—sometimes accompany ADHD?

ETIOLOGY

What causes attention-deficit/hyperactivity disorder? There is no absolute consensus, although I can bring some order to theorizing by splitting it into hypotheses that emphasize inherent biology versus those that emphasize toxins versus those that emphasize the social environment. Such perspectives need not be mutually exclusive, and this disorder might be brought about by some combination of them all (e.g., Rapoport & Quinn, 1975).

On the biological side, studies have found that ADHD runs through families, particularly through blood relations, implying some basis in genetics (Biederman et al., 1992; Biederman, Faraone, Keenan, & Tsuang, 1991). Other studies have found that ADHD in children is correlated with such heritable problems in their biological parents as alcoholism, depression, and antisocial behavior. A preponderance of such problems is *not* found among the adoptive parents of hyperactive children. Further supporting the heritability of the disorder are findings from twin studies showing that activity level is heritable (e.g., Buss & Plomin, 1975, 1984). If we regard ADHD as involving an extreme activity level, then we can argue that it is in part heritable. Recent twin studies in which the children were formally diagnosed with ADHD support this conclusion (Gross-Tsur, Shalev, & Amir, 1991; Stevenson, 1992).

Assuming that there is some basis in genetics, what might be the actual physiological mechanism? Speculation over the years has focused on the possibility that ADHD children have deficits in their central nervous system that lead to underarousal, perhaps because of abnormally low levels of the neurotransmitters *dopamine* and *norepinephrine* (Levy, 1991). In a review of the relevant research literature, Whalen characterized the hypothesis as scientifically appealing, but the support for it is frail at best: "Contradictory evidence is the rule rather than the exception" (1989, p. 149).

Although studies have found various physiological differences between ADHD children and others, these differences do not neatly map into the nature and extent of symptoms, as you would think they should if physiology were the actual mechanism. It is also possible to concede that these differences exist in physiology, but then argue that they are the consequence of ADHD rather than the cause. Children with this disorder live a stressful life, and stress affects a variety of biological systems.

Other explanations of attention-deficit/hyperactivity disorder emphasize the role of toxins. These include environmental lead, which is found in products from paint to toy soldiers to metal food containers and is also discharged into the atmosphere when leaded gasoline is burned. According to one estimate, the amount of lead in the atmosphere today is 2,000 times the level it was prior to the Industrial Revolution (Marshall, 1983). The potential relevance to hyperactivity is that lead is a neurotoxin, even in rather low blood concentrations. Research results linking lead to the specific symptoms of ADHD have been contradictory, but there is agreement that excess lead is associated with small but reliable decrements in measured IQ.

Along these lines, recent years have seen the coming and going of a number of hypotheses proposing that hyperactivity is caused by food additives, food dyes, and/or excess sugar consumption (Gans, 1991). We thus treat the problem by changing the child's diet. In some cases, wildly enthusiastic claims have been made, as in the case of the *Feingold diet*, which suggests that as many as half the children with ADHD can be helped if they eat foods without additives (Feingold, 1976). The problem with these claims is that the relevant studies are flawed; the child's parents and teachers are aware of the intervention and its intended effect. When the diet is varied without telling the adults, results are not so encouraging.

Whalen (1989) suggests that additives or excess sugar may play an occasional role in exacerbating the disorder. Perhaps 5% of hyperactive children show oversensitivity to such substances, and obviously they are helped by changes in their diet. However, at present there seems to be no reason to think that even in these cases food additives bear the entire burden. And there is no basis for recommending that the diets of all hyperactive children be limited.

Finally, there are purely social explanations of hyperactivity. It is frequently proposed that hyperactivity is caused by poor parenting, social disadvantage, and/or bad teaching (Haddad & Garralda, 1992), but the research is inconclusive. Correlational studies have shown a link between family stress and ADHD, but the direction of causality is not clear. A more sophisticated view suggests that we look at the joint effect of child and setting to understand why problems might ensue that are labeled ADHD. A child with an active and restless temperament raised by rigid and staid parents no doubt will chafe more than the same child with more tolerant and flexible parents. Conversely, the rigid and staid parents will probably have no difficulty with a placid child. The same point can be made about match and mismatch between a child's style and that of a particular classroom teacher.

Treatment

Treatments of attention-deficit/hyperactivity disorder show the same variety as its explanations. Consistent with the underarousal hypothesis is the finding that ADHD children are often helped with stimulants (Brown, 1991; Whalen & Henker, 1991). Perhaps 60% to 90% of them show at least some improvement when given **Ritalin** or **Dexedrine.** Presumably, stimulants like these enhance the child's neurological arousal. So far, it has proved difficult to find physiological differences between children who do and do not respond to this medication. Furthermore, the stimulants used to treat this disorder may have side effects such as insomnia, listlessness, and temporarily stunted growth.

The hyperactive 9-year-old boy described earlier was treated with a stimulant (Janowsky, Addario, & Risch, 1987). The medication was successful in reducing his motor activity. He became less of a discipline problem at home, and his grades at school improved markedly. However, the boy also developed considerable trouble sleeping and showed a worrisome weight loss due to decreased appetite. He continued to take the medication, but his mother was concerned with the possible long-term effects. The standard procedure in such cases is first to decrease the dosage of the stimulant to the bare minimum needed to maintain improvement and second to discontinue medication periodically to see if it is still necessary.

Some psychologists worry that the medications give the wrong message to children, namely that their problem with attention and conduct—and perhaps all other problems they may encounter in their lives—have only physiological causes and can be remedied solely with drugs. This of course is a message that any medication can convey, and is hardly a reason to recommend against drugs. Still, remember that we are dealing with children. A young child may not be able to

distinguish problems with physical causes from those without, or to recognize that problems have multiple causes. Whalen (1989) described children who excuse their own misbehavior by pointing out quite explicitly that they cannot help themselves, because after all they are hyperactive.

Studies suggest that behavior therapy techniques can decrease problematic aspects of ADHD (e.g., Anastopoulos, DuPaul, & Barkley, 1991; Erhardt & Baker, 1990; Fehlings, Roberts, Humphries, & Dawe, 1991; Horn et al., 1991; Whalen & Henker, 1991). A target behavior is chosen, and reinforcers or punishers are used to increase or decrease it accordingly. The child's parents are often involved in this form of treatment, which in effect teaches them to be behavior therapists.

To unravel the mysteries of this developmental disorder, we need longitudinal studies that start with children before they have a problem, following them for a sufficient amount of time to see who develops ADHD and who does not, and among those with the disorder, who improves and who does not. This type of research is starting to be done (Klein & Mannuzza, 1991). For example, Jacobvitz and Sroufe (1987) found that very young children with intrusive and overstimulating parents were later apt to be overactive as toddlers and hyperactive when entering kindergarten. These researchers believe that the infant learns during the first year of life to regulate his or her arousal and attention; if this process is interrupted (e.g., by given parental styles), a cascade of processes are set into effect that put the infant at risk for attention-deficit/hyperactivity disorder.

CONDUCT DISORDER

Like children with ADHD, those with **conduct disorder** are socially disruptive and upsetting to others. Although the two problems may occur in the same children, they have distinct meanings (Hinshaw, 1987). Conduct disordered children violate the rights of others and the norms of what is appropriate for those their age. They are frequently violent. They can be cruel not only to people but to animals as well. And they have been known to set fires or otherwise destroy the property of others. Stealing is also common. These children obviously show little concern for others, and they express scant remorse for their deeds. Children who warrant the diagnosis of conduct disorder are frequently truant from school. They may begin to use drugs and alcohol much earlier than their peers, and they tend to engage in sexual activity at an earlier age.

Mo, a thirteen-year-old boy, was referred by juvenile court because he had been caught stealing a television set. His previous contacts with the court involved truancy from school.

Mo was the third of seven children. His father deserted the home when Mo was two years old and has not been home since that time. The younger children were fathered by a man with whom his mother currently lives. Mo does not get along with this man, who has physically abused him on several occasions while drunk. His older brothers are currently in a juvenile training school for car theft. . . .

Mo freely admitted that he hates school and is looking forward to dropping out and getting a job, and moving away from his family. When asked what kind of job he would get, he responded that he didn't know but that "something would turn up." Mo's enjoyment seems to revolve around his friends. . . . He and an older boy were assigned the job of stealing a television to furnish the group's club room. Mo would not identify the other boy, who had escaped, or other members of his group.   (M. T. Erickson, 1987, p. 230)

If this description sounds like a childhood version of antisocial personality disorder discussed in Chapter 13, it is no coincidence. Almost 40% of the children with conduct disorder end up as adults diagnosed with antisocial personality disorder (Robins, 1970). Some problem in adulthood is almost guaranteed, particularly substance abuse.

About 5% of children in the United States warrant this diagnosis, with boys outnumbering girls perhaps by as much as four to one (Baum, 1989). Half the children with this disorder are hyperactive as well,

Conduct disorder among children may be a forerunner of antisocial personality disorder among adults.

which makes it difficult to point definitely to which is the actual problem for these children (Shaywitz & Shaywitz, 1991). But there is some agreement that conduct disorder has a much worse outcome. These children are frequently depressed (Puig-Antich, 1982), particularly boys.

ETIOLOGY

There is good reason to posit some role of biology in conduct disorder. Antisocial activity in general is heritable. Children with conduct disorder are found in some studies to show the same autonomic underarousal that characterizes adults with antisocial personality disorder (Baum, 1989). In other words, children with conduct disorder do not experience the same degree of anxiety and fear as do other children, and this may be the raw material from which their disruptive activities result.

The existence of biological influences does not preclude the role of the environment, and other studies show that this disorder is most apt to result among children whose parents are "maladjusted, inconsistent, arbitrary, and prone to explosive expressions of anger" (Baum, 1989, p. 182). Their mothers are more likely to be depressed or anxious than women in general. Their fathers show a variety of problems as well, including criminality, alcoholism, desertion, and sexual promiscuity. The direction of causality is not clear in these correlations. Indeed, we should expect mutual influences among all these factors, with their effects cascading over time (Patterson, DeBaryshe, & Ramsey, 1989). For example, the presence in a family of a conduct disordered child might influence the degree of parental problems (Olson, 1992), which in turn affect the child, putting him at increased risk for behavioral difficulties (e.g., Barkley & Cunningham, 1979). Consider that parents of conduct disordered children issue a large number of commands and criticisms (Forehand, King, Peed, & Yoder, 1975; Frick et al., 1992). Moreover, these commands, when compared to those of parents of other children, tend to be vague or impossible for the child to comply with (Forehand, Wells, & Sturgis, 1978).

TREATMENT

When parents are taught more effective ways of dealing with their children—such as issuing commands that are direct and possible to follow—their disruptive behavior is reduced (Baum & Forehand, 1981). The degree of antisocial conduct is able to be influenced by this *parent training* (Graziano & Diament, 1992).

For instance, in the parent training program of psychologist Gerald Patterson (1974), parents are taught to reward their child's desirable behaviors, ignore some undesirable behaviors, and punish other undesirable behaviors.

Research attests to the effectiveness of this program (e.g., Bank, Marlowe, Reid, Patterson, & Weinrott, 1991). However, the most severe forms of conduct disorder prove quite intractable (e.g., Keller et al., 1992). Early identification and intervention might be the most beneficial strategy in combating this disorder, before it leads to self-fulfilling prophecies (Beitchman, Inglis, & Schachter, 1992; Zigler, Taussig, & Black, 1992).

SEPARATION ANXIETY DISORDER

The fear and anxiety diagnoses specified by DSM-IV can be applied "downward" to children: phobia, obsessive-compulsive disorder, panic disorder, posttraumatic stress disorder, and generalized anxiety disorder. There is one exception—because it occurs in its most obvious form only among children. When a child shows excessive anxiety about being separated from her caretaker (i.e., parent) and/or familiar surroundings, she is said to have a **separation anxiety disorder.** It is normal for children to experience some discomfort when separated from those to whom they are attached; this occurs once an emotional bond is formed with a major caretaker, typically in the first year of life.

Separation anxiety disorder is more than just this normal discomfort. According to DSM-IV, it can be recognized by unrealistic worry that harm will occur to the caretaker, reluctance to go to school because this means being separated from the caretaker, reluctance to be alone in the house, temper tantrums when faced with separation from the caretaker, and so on.

This disorder should be distinguished from a phobia that revolves around school. School phobia is somewhat common among school-age children, but it involves a fear of school per se (Kennedy, 1965). In separation anxiety disorder, the child avoids school but not because she is afraid of it. Rather, school represents separation from her caretaker. Separation anxiety disorder is a more serious problem in that children who experience it almost always have another disorder as well (Last, 1989). Studies suggest that separation anxiety disorder in childhood foreshadows various anxiety disorders in adulthood (Chapter 7), in particular panic disorder (Ayuso, Alfonso, & Rivera, 1989).

Separation anxiety disorder may follow a move to a new school or neighborhood.

Maria was an 8-year-old girl who was greatly afraid of being apart from her father. Ever since she began to attend elementary school, Maria had expressed a constant fear that some mishap would occur to her father and that he would die. Although a good student, she became increasingly reluctant to go to school. When at home, she insisted on being in the same room as her father. At night, she would usually crawl into bed with him. Her parents were having marital problems, and Maria's separation anxiety often figured in quarrels between them. Her father and mother had very little time alone to themselves, and a divorce seemed likely. Treatment of Maria's family as a whole was undertaken, with good success.

At present, we have little information about the epidemiology of this disorder; a recent study estimated that about 2% of children meet the diagnostic criteria set forth by DSM (Bowen, Offord, & Boyle, 1990). Last (1989) reported that the sex distribution is approximately equal, and that the majority of children referred for treatment come from the lower classes.

Separation anxiety disorder often has a sudden onset, coincidental with an actual stressor, such as moving to a new school or neighborhood, or the death of a family member. It may also begin after a lingering illness. Some speculate that it is most likely to occur during periods of transition—into grade school, into middle school, and the like (Last, 1989). The child who experiences the problem at one transition may reexperience it again when faced with another.

ETIOLOGY

Explanations of separation anxiety disorder parallel the sorts of explanations you encountered in Chapter 7 when I discussed fear and anxiety disorders among adults. Biomedical theories emphasize the heritability of anxiety disorders. Supporting this notion is the finding that the mothers of children with separation anxiety disorders are quite likely to have a history of anxiety disorders themselves (Harris, Noyes, Crowe, & Chaudhry, 1983).

Of course, this finding does not uniquely support a biomedical explanation. Psychoanalytic explanations point to something deficient in the parent-child interaction that shows itself as separation anxiety disorder on the part of the child and some neurosis or another on the part of the parent (Estes, Haylett, & Johnson, 1956). Cognitive-behavioral explanations propose that the child learns to fear separation from her caretaker, perhaps because of parental comments about leaving and never coming back (Garvey & Hegreves, 1966). Again, this perspective predicts emotional disturbance on both sides of the parent-child bond.

TREATMENT

Some success has been reported in treating children with this disorder. Behavioral techniques that involve gradually exposing the child to separations from her caretaker are useful (Last, 1989). Cognitive interventions may be undertaken as well that help the child identify and dismiss any irrational beliefs that might fuel anxiety upon separation.

EATING DISORDERS

There are several disorders that involve eating—too much, too little, or too unusual.[2] The onset of these disorders is often during childhood, but they can and do occur across the life span. Not only do they repre-

sent a psychological problem, but additionally each of the eating disorders carries with it the risk of physical problems, in some cases even death.

I cannot speak about eating and eating disorders without mentioning biology on the one hand and the larger culture on the other. Obviously, eating is necessary for our physical survival, and any disruption in our normal eating pattern takes a toll. That people tend to find high-calorie food particularly tasty is no coincidence; this reflects the operation of evolution. Throughout the history of our species, high-calorie food was scarce, and our ancestors who were especially motivated to seek it out lived longer than their counterparts who did not. "Sweetness" is a property of food that signifies a high concentration of sugar, in the good old days a sign that the food would be good for us.

But the 20th century has played a massive trick on many of us in the United States, scattering about the landscape 7-Elevens filled with Wing-Dings, Chips Ahoy! cookies, and Haagen-Dasz ice cream—substances with all the cues of 4 million years of evolution telling us to ingest them in as large a quantity as possible with few of the benefits that these cues used to signal. Any of us with a sweet tooth know the frustration of being unable to resist one more bite of a candy bar. Does calling our impulse an evolutionary imperative rather than a moral weakness help us resist it any better? Probably not, but the explanation is more reasonable.

Our culture influences our eating not just by making food available or not, but also by mandating what is or is not desirable to eat. Every culture has its own *cuisine,* preferred and familiar styles of serving food, as well as prohibitions about what should not be eaten. Sometimes these prohibitions are based in religion; Jews and Moslems do not eat pork, for example. Other times these prohibitions reflect health considerations; American colonists in the 1700s avoided tomatoes, in keeping with their belief that they caused syphilis. In some segments of contemporary society, we see trends toward "healthy" food and eating styles.

Another influence of culture on our eating has to do with what is considered attractive or unattractive in terms of body build. Some cultures consider plumpness attractive, a sign of happiness or prosperity. Other cultures, in particular our own right now, have a standard that emphasizes just the opposite: extreme leanness. Again, it is no coincidence that anorexia nervosa—an eating disorder marked by general emaciation—is apparently on the upswing in our society. Cultural standards of course are not the sole determinant of whether an individual has an eating disorder, but they are certainly an important ingredient among the mix of risk factors (McCarthy, 1990; Raphael & Lacey, 1992).

---

[2] Let me note in passing two rare eating disorders, usually encountered among children as opposed to adults. *Pica* is the persistent eating of nonnutritive substances such as dirt, plaster, paint, string, or animal feces. *Rumination* is the regurgitation without nausea of already-swallowed food, followed by chewing and reswallowing it. Both pica and rumination pose obvious physical dangers to the child. Indeed, they can be fatal.

OBESITY

Obesity is the excess accumulation of body fat. It is conveniently defined as a percentage—like 20%—in excess weight over what is considered average for a person of a given sex, age, and height, but this is far from a foolproof definition. It is more accepted in research circles to measure the thickness of the skin in the triceps area (i.e., the back of the upper arm), which reflects the amount of fat tissue beneath the skin. This measurement gauges more directly how much fat a person has in his body, avoiding the problems associated with simple height and weight figures (Seltzer & Mayer, 1965). A cutoff is usually specified, like 1 standard deviation greater than the mean, above which the individual is considered obese.

Obesity—however it is defined—is not an either-or phenomenon. It is continuous because its criteria are continuous. And the risks associated with it, both psychological and physical, increase directly with its criteria. Where do we stop being plump and start being obese? In no particular place, although we can recognize without difficulty the extreme cases.

I am reminded of Walter Hudson, who received a great deal of publicity some years ago in his attempts to lose weight (e.g., Plummer, 1987). He was a 42-year-old man who weighed in excess of 1,200 pounds! His waist measured 103 inches, almost 9 feet around.

Walter Hudson is shown here venturing outside for the first time in 18 years after losing almost 700 pounds.

Who are the obese? I can offer some very good generalizations about groups of people in our society more likely than others to be obese, including recent immigrants, those in the lower class, individuals older than 50 years of age, and women. If we start to combine these categories, speaking for example about lower-class females who are recent immigrants and older than 50, the typical individual in this group is obese. By most estimates, obesity is relatively common in affluent countries. In the United States, more than 20% of adults today are obese (Kuczmarski, 1992; Rand & Kuldau, 1990), making it among the most common problems we face (see Figure 14.6).

Obesity shows great stability across the life span. Overweight infants are at risk for becoming overweight children; overweight children are at risk for becoming overweight adolescents; and so on. Part of this stability may reflect the role of genetics; obesity is heritable (e.g., Stunkard et al., 1986). Another part may reflect early nutritional habits. During infancy, overeating proliferates the number of fat cells. This proliferation is permanent, and if an individual's body tissue is composed of a relatively large number of fat cells, it is easier to gain weight later in life. Appreciate that weight gain or loss in adulthood does not involve the addition or loss of fat cells, but rather a change in the size of these cells.

The physical health consequences of obesity are well documented and need little elaboration. Being overweight puts people at risk for a variety of illnesses, notably heart disease. These health consequences may be worse for men than for women, because the sexes tend to gain weight in different ways. Women often gain weight in their hips and legs, whereas men often gain weight in their abdomens. The male pattern of weight gain, whether shown by a male or a female, is associated with health problems and early death to a greater extent than is the female pattern of weight gain (Bjorntorp, 1992; Pi-Sunyer, 1991). But remember, both patterns represent health risks.

Although *not* included in DSM-IV as a mental disorder, obesity is associated with psychological problems. Those who are overweight usually do not feel good about themselves. They disparage their body and more generally their own worth and attractiveness.

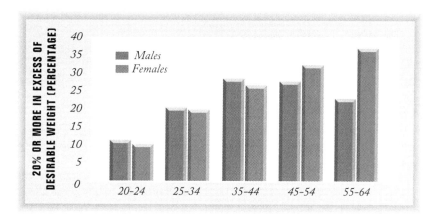

FIGURE 14.6

PREVALENCE OF OBESITY IN THE UNITED STATES   *In the United States, the likelihood of obesity increases with age, particularly for females. Obese males, because of their typical pattern of weight gain, are at greater risk for early death than are obese females.*
SOURCE: DATA DERIVED FROM "DESCRIPTIVE EPIDEMIOLOGY OF BODY WEIGHT AND WEIGHT CHANGE IN U.S. ADULTS," BY D. F. WILLIAMSON, 1993, *Annals of Internal Medicine, 119*, PP. 646–649. USED WITH PERMISSION.

Obesity has diverse causes, among them a genetic predisposition.

Others can certainly help them out with this. In our society, there is a considerable stigma associated with being overweight, and those who are obese have fewer friends and social contacts. Once I was in a grocery store, waiting in the checkout line behind several people, including one who was heavy. I heard someone loudly comment, "Look at all the food that fat person is buying!" Not surprisingly, obesity tends to co-occur with anxiety disorders and depression.

Etiology   Why are some people obese? There is a short answer to this question: They consume more calories than they expend. But the longer answer, which tries to grapple with why some people consume more calories than they expend, has numerous qualifications. There are different types of obesity, with different risk factors and mechanisms. The best I can do at present is specify some of the factors that contribute to obesity in at least some individuals.

I have already mentioned that obesity is heritable, which means that genetic risk factors are at work. One biological mechanism is an abnormally high *set-point,* an example of physiological homeostasis. Some people may simply be constituted to maintain a higher than average weight. Their bodies resist attempts to lose weight by maintaining their "obese" homeostasis. Indeed, some extremely heavy people do not eat more than their thinner counterparts; their bodies instead use the calories much more efficiently (Spitzer & Rodin, 1981). There has been other recently announced research linking a specific gene to a person's sense of being "full." The research indicates that this gene is defective in some obese people.

As already mentioned, eating habits early in life influence later obesity by determining the number of fat cells in an individual's body. Children's styles of eating are influenced by processes of modeling. People might come to eat in response to environmental and emotional cues that have little to do with hunger (Leon & Dinklage, 1989). Children learn, by observing their parents, that people eat when they are happy (or sad), when they are bored, or when they are trying to make a good impression (Hammer, 1992). The notion that "food is love" is so widespread in our culture that it is virtually unheard of to have a social gathering that does not revolve around food. These habits, established early in life, determine our subsequent weight just as readily as do more purely biological influences.

Other contributors to being obese include a sedentary lifestyle. Studies show that the obese are much less active than other people (Mayer, 1965). Perhaps being inactive is the real culprit, not the sheer amount of food consumed.

Treatment   There is no shortage of treatments for this disorder, from biomedical to psychological (e.g., Bray, 1992; Brownell & Wadden, 1992; Kral, 1992; Phinney, 1992; Silverstone, 1992). Weight loss books are among the most popular in the self-help genre. They have been for years, suggesting that there are no shortcuts to weight loss.

I can offer several generalizations about the treatment of obesity:

✦ Prevention is much more effective than treatment; in other words, the most effective way not to be obese as an adult is to have avoided being obese at earlier points in life.

✦ Many forms of weight loss, from diets and fasts to individual psychotherapy to behavior therapy to family therapy to exercise programs, work in the short run in the sense that people lose weight.

✦ Many forms of weight loss fail in the long run in the sense that people tend to gain back the weight they have lost.

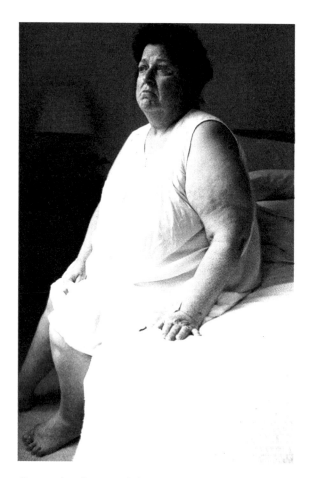

Because they disparage their own appearance, those who are overweight may be depressed.

Weight loss books are highly popular in the United States, but the only guaranteed way to lose weight and keep it off is for the individual to make a permanent lifestyle change, decreasing the intake of calories and/or increasing their expenditure.

People cannot maintain weight loss if they go back to the style of life that led them to gain weight in the first place. This sounds commonsensical, but it is obviously a message that the general public does not want to hear. Crash diets are popular because they promise that a few weeks of deprivation will permanently solve a weight problem. Weight loss just does not work this way, and a person's weight tends to be highly stable across time.

The only way to keep weight off once it has been lost is to literally change one's lifestyle, eating less and/or exercising more for the rest of one's days (Wing, 1992). This conclusion follows from studies of interventions that do work in the long run, strategies that teach people to approach eating in a self-consciously moderate way (e.g., Epstein, Wing, Koeske, & Valoski, 1987).

ANOREXIA NERVOSA

I started this chapter with the description of Wendy, the teenager who suffered from the eating disorder of **anorexia nervosa,** which I can now define more formally as the refusal to maintain a minimal body weight, an intense fear of gaining weight, and a distorted perception of one's own body weight, size, or shape. Among females, cessation of menstruation is one more diagnostic criterion.

The word *anorexia* literally means no appetite, but this is a misnomer, because loss of appetite in anorexia nervosa is unusual. Those who have it experience pangs of hunger, but they resist them (Garfinkel, 1974). Rather, it is extreme loss of weight that is salient, brought about by the deliberate restriction of what is consumed. Conventionally, a body weight of 85% or less of what is expected for someone of a given sex, age, and build is used as a guideline in defining the presence of anorexia, but this is an arbitrary cutoff. Like obesity and so many other disorders, anorexia nervosa exists in degrees, and there is no particular place where we divide individuals neatly into two groups, those with and those without the problem.

Anorexia can be life-threatening. A minimal body weight is needed to maintain life, and on the way to death by starvation, the anorexic individual may seriously affect her bodily metabolism, so that other physical problems arise as well (Comerci, 1990). By current estimates, fatality rates from this disorder are between 3% and 21% (Crisp, Callender, Halek, & Hsu, 1992; Leon & Dinklage, 1989). Part and parcel of anorexia is the individual's resistance to treatment; she does not believe anything is wrong with her, and so she does not take steps to solve the problem, because that would mean acknowledging its existence.

Singer Karen Carpenter, shown here in 1980 with her brother Richard, died of heart failure due to anorexia nervosa.

Those with anorexia may be highly anxious, and they may sleep only 3 or 4 four hours per night (Halmi et al., 1991). Sometimes their excess activity becomes ritualized, as they carry out steps to burn off the calories that they do consume. You saw this in the case of Wendy, who was driven to exercise vigorously every day. Also accompanying anorexia nervosa are symptoms of depression, although it is important to distinguish the appetite loss and weight loss that may be depressive symptoms from anorexia in its own right (Toner, Garfinkel, & Garner, 1986).

This eating disorder afflicts mainly adolescent females. Among females 12 to 18 years old, between .1% and 1% warrant the diagnosis. It is more common among middle- and upper-class females than among those from the lower class, perhaps reflecting the greater pressure toward thinness found in the middle and upper classes.

Anorexia nervosa shows no single course. As noted, some number of individuals actually die. Others show an intermittent course. And if there is any good news about anorexia, the typical case is a young woman who suffers from a single episode, regains weight, and does not again encounter the problem (American Psychiatric Association, 1987).

The opinion is invariably offered that anorexia nervosa is increasing in our society. Although it is difficult to compare incidence rates across time, anorexia has apparently increased in Western societies during just the past few decades (e.g., Lucas, Beard, O'Fallon, & Kurland, 1991; Willi & Grossman, 1983), exactly as standards for female beauty have changed to emphasize slenderness (see Garner, Garfinkel, Schwartz, & Thompson, 1980).

At the same time, it is also clear that anorexia is not just a disorder of our time and place. It was described as early as the 1600s (Morton, 1694), and in an intriguing book, Rudolph Bell (1985) pointed out how the deliberate restriction of food was common in the Middle Ages among Italian women later regarded as saints by the Catholic Church. Apparently, thinness and denial of appetite were seen as proof of holiness, so you have another example of how societal standards—in this case, regarding piety—influence an individual's style of eating.

Etiology   There are abundant explanations of anorexia nervosa but no clear consensus about its causes. Perhaps we need an integrated account that draws on physiological, psychodynamic, cognitive-behavioral, and sociocultural explanations (Nagel & Jones, 1992a, 1992b). Following are some of the ingredients that we might include.

Some theorists speculate that anorexia nervosa results from endocrine problems. Disturbances in the body are a consequence of the weight loss that characterizes the disorder, but some argue that these changes may sometimes precede the weight loss. For example, cessation of menstruation follows weight loss, but in almost 40% of anorexic females, menstruation stops *before* any significant weight loss occurs (e.g., Halmi, Goldberg, Eckert, Casper, & Davis, 1977). And menstruation does not invariably return when weight is regained (e.g., Falk & Halmi, 1982). The observation has also been made that anorexia is not equivalent in its physical manifestation to starvation, as might happen during a famine. People starved against their will do not become agitated, nor do they become sleepless. Perhaps these findings point to a physiological basis to the disorder.

Psychodynamic theorists speculate that anorexia nervosa involves conflicts about sexuality, independence, and most generally maturity (Bruch, 1978; Mahowald, 1992). For reasons that stretch back to deficient parenting during early childhood, the potential anorexic individual is unable to cope with the demands of the world, which may change greatly as she is poised at the beginning of adolescence. She "copes" as

it were by seizing control not over the external world but rather over her weight.

Cognitive-behavioral theorists observe that this eating disorder can develop among those who have come to associate weight gain and eating with negative consequences—say, fighting around the dinner table. Furthermore, the distorted view of the body might be interpreted in terms of irrational beliefs inculcated during childhood concerning food and weight.

Theorists who stress the role of family interaction argue that anorexia should be examined in the context of the family. The anorexic child is a "symptom" of more pervasive problems of relating to one another within the family (Lundholm & Waters, 1991). Minuchin, Rosman, and Baker (1978) suggested that these family problems are compounded by a family style of valuing loyalty and denying conflict. The child desires autonomy but is caught in a conflict because of these values. With no other avenue available, she seizes control over her own eating, with anorexia as a result. Family therapy attempts to shift these struggles to a more benign terrain.

In an intriguing study, Crisp, Harding, and McGuinness (1974) found that parents became *more* anxious and depressed as their anorexic child regained her normal weight. This is exactly the prediction that family systems theorists would make who see anorexia as a way of defusing family conflict and unhappiness.

Treatment   As already noted, therapy is often resisted by those with anorexia nervosa. When the condition becomes life threatening, involuntary treatment may be needed. The first step is to stabilize the individual's physical condition. If she will not eat on her own, she can be given IVs or fed through a tube. Obviously, these are far from desirable forms of treatment, and sometimes "deals" can be made not to use them if the individual agrees to eat on her own.

A variety of treatments have been tried, although we do not yet know how to help anorexic individuals in a consistent way. Nowadays, behavior therapy programs that attempt to modify eating patterns receive a great deal of attention. Also widely used are family therapy approaches that modify communication and interaction within a family. Studies show that about 40% of individuals in treatment recover fully, and another 30% improve (e.g., Crisp et al., 1991; Garfinkel & Garner, 1982; Hsu, 1980). For many, however, eating-related problems remain for years (Hsu, Crisp, & Callender, 1992; Kennedy & Garfinkel, 1992). It is not clear what factors predict those most likely to improve, although one rule of thumb is that a person's level of functioning before the problem developed is associated with how well she will do afterwards (Leon & Dinklage, 1989).

BULIMIA NERVOSA

The last eating disorder I discuss is **bulimia nervosa,** which refers to ingesting large amounts of high-calorie food in a short amount of time *(binging),* feeling out of control while doing so, and then ridding oneself of this food through vomiting, laxatives, diuretics, starvation, strenuous exercise, and the like *(purging).* Unlike obesity and anorexia, which are defined in part by weight, the bulimic individual may appear quite normal to the onlooker.

Many of us have had the occasion to eat much too much; holiday meals like Thanksgiving can only be described as a binge. We respond to this binge by cutting back on our eating for the next few days. These are bulimic behaviors, but they do not add up to bulimia because they are infrequent. DSM-IV says that bulimia should be diagnosed only when the individual binges at least twice a week for at least 3 months. Some individuals do this much more frequently—binging and purging daily—and they may do so over a period of years.

Binging and purging are the most salient symptoms of bulimia, but they are not the only ones. They are typically carried out in secret, and the bulimic individual experiences great shame over her behavior. Particularly while binging, she feels out of control. Her eating is not pleasurable so much as compelled (Heatherton & Baumeister, 1991). The bulimic individual is usually overconcerned with her body shape and weight. Depression also frequently accompanies this problem.

Tennis player Carling Bassett-Seguso suffered from bulimia while a teenager. She was playing on the professional circuit with considerable success, but then she began to gain weight.

> *"At 15, I wasn't heavy by any means," she says, "but I . . . went from 111 to 126. At 14, 15, 16, your body starts to mature, you start to put on puppy fat. You want to look good all the time. You start feeling pressure. . . ."*
>
> *Another player, an older woman she will not identify, showed the 16-year-old how to put her fingers down her throat and instantly rid herself of all those calories. Soon, she says, the habit had taken her captive. "It becomes part of your life, like smoking," says Bassett. "Or it's like being an alcoholic. It's so easy to get into and so hard to get out of. I hated myself that I couldn't stop." (Neill & Sider, 1992, p. 98)*

Bassett-Seguso would throw up as often as ten times a day. She married another tennis player, Robert Seguso, and at first kept her problem hidden from him. Then came an incident in which she passed out, brought on

in part by metabolic irregularities caused by her constant purging. This proved to be a turning point for her. She told her husband about her bulimia and began to take control of the problem. Becoming pregnant also helped her confront her disorder, because she was concerned for the welfare of her unborn child.

The demographics of bulimia are similar to those of anorexia, in that both disorders are typically encountered among females from the middle and upper classes. However, the typical bulimic individual is a woman in her twenties. Bulimia is a somewhat more common problem than anorexia, occurring among about 5% of college-age women. Reports in the popular media that this disorder is rampant on college campuses have been exaggerated. Bulimic behaviors—occasional binging and purging—have been confused with the disorder itself (Schotte & Stunkard, 1987).

Whatever its frequency, bulimia carries with it serious problems. Not as life-threatening as anorexia, this eating disorder nonetheless leads to electrolyte imbalance and dehydration (Comerci, 1990). These in turn can lead to cardiac problems and even death. If a person vomits frequently, the enamel of her teeth

Tennis player Carling Bassett-Seguso struggled with bulimia, at one point throwing up ten times a day.

can erode. And occasionally, the stomach or esophagus ruptures, again due to excessive vomiting. The psychological consequences of bulimia have already been noted: depression and isolation. Binging and purging can be quite time-consuming, thus interfering with other activities.

Etiology   I can say as little definitively about the causes of bulimia as I could about the causes of anorexia. Again, we probably need to specify some combination of factors. It has been suggested that those with bulimia have a deficiency in serotonin, and are thus impelled to eat food containing *tryptophan,* a precursor of this neurotransmitter (e.g., Goldbloom & Garfinkel, 1990). Whether or not bulimia originates in a physiological problem, it certainly can be maintained as one, because the description of binging and purging is reminiscent of the vicious circle that characterizes drug intoxication and withdrawal. Bulimia may start out as strategic—a deliberate attempt to alter weight or shape. In some cases, the strategic use of bulimic behaviors never escalates into a problem. But in other cases it does, perhaps when individuals lack a sense of autonomy and self-control (cf. Strauss & Ryan, 1987).

Actress and fitness icon Jane Fonda reportedly suffered from bulimia for years.

Treatment   To treat bulimia nowadays, therapists often use antidepressant medication (Walsh, 1991), to combat the depression that accompanies the disorder. This is effective in a number of cases, implying that bulimia is secondary to depression (Walsh, Hadigan, Devlin, Gladis, & Roose, 1991). Other treatment strategies include behavior therapy and cognitive therapy, to help the person identify the circumstances and thoughts that make binging more likely and then to challenge or avoid them in the future (Agras, 1991; Fairburn & Hay, 1992). Again, such interventions appear to be helpful in a number of cases (Fairburn et al., 1991; Hartmann, Herzog, & Drinkmann, 1992). At the same time, the risk of relapse is great (Herzog, Keller, Lavori, & Sacks, 1991).

In this chapter, I discussed disorders that occur in the course of development, particularly during childhood and adolescence. The psychology of abnormality will someday locate all problems in their developmental context, because people's lives obviously unfold over time. So too do their problems.

Summary

✦ The psychology of abnormality increasingly recognizes that people's problems should be described in the context of development, specifying where people find themselves in the life course. To date, this developmental perspective has been brought to bear most fully on the particular problems of children and adolescents, and so these are the focus of this chapter.

MENTAL RETARDATION

✦ Mental retardation refers to a problem first evident during childhood in which an individual displays below average intellectual functioning and an impaired ability to meet the demands of everyday life.

✦ In organic retardation, the problem is clearly linked to a specific illness, injury, or physiological abnormality. For example, use of alcohol or drugs by pregnant women may result in mental retardation among their offspring. For another example, Down syndrome is a form of organic retardation caused by an extra set of genes.

✦ In sociocultural retardation, the problem is not linked to a biological cause; it is instead considered the result of social disadvantage.

✦ The psychological mechanisms of mental retardation include difficulties with attention, short-term memory, rapid information processing, and meta-cognition.

✦ Treatment of mental retardation involves prevention when possible and remediation through specific instruction.

LEARNING DIFFICULTIES

✦ Learning disabilities are circumscribed difficulties with acquiring or performing a specific skill such as reading or speaking.

AUTISM

✦ Autism is a profound disturbance in social interaction and communication, apparently due to biological causes, perhaps abnormally high levels of serotonin.

ATTENTION-DEFICIT/HYPERACTIVITY DISORDER

✦ Children with attention-deficit/hyperactivity disorder (ADHD) display a high activity level coupled with an inability to sustain attention. The causes of ADHD are not clear, but hypotheses have suggested neurological problems, environmental toxins, and social disadvantage. Some children with ADHD can be helped with stimulants, others with behavior therapy.

CONDUCT DISORDER

✦ Conduct disorder is marked by a child's consistent violation of the rights of others. It appears to be the forerunner of antisocial personality disorder among adults, and is explained in much the same way: by a combination of biological and social influences. In some cases, conduct disorder can be alleviated through behavior therapy, but the most severe forms often prove quite intractable.

SEPARATION ANXIETY DISORDER

✦ Children may experience the same fear and anxiety disorders encountered among adults, but DSM-IV additionally specifies a problem unique to children: separation anxiety disorder.

EATING DISORDERS

✦ Obesity is the accumulation of excess body fat. Quite common in the United States today, obesity has many causes, several of which date to childhood. Obesity is relatively easy to treat in the short run, yet quite difficult in the long run.

✦ Anorexia is the refusal to maintain a minimal body weight. Most common among adolescent females, this disorder may be fatal in as many as 21% of the cases. Its causes are the subject of debate, and consistently effective treatments have not yet been devised. Currently favored strategies are behavior therapy and family therapy.

✦ In bulimia, an individual ingests large amounts of high-calorie food and then rids herself of it, often through vomiting. Bulimia is most common among young adult females, and it often co-occurs with depression. The causes of bulimia are as poorly understood as those of anorexia. Antidepressant medication, behavior therapy, and cognitive therapy have all been used with some success to treat it.

Key Terms

anorexia nervosa

attention-deficit/
  hyperactivity disorder;
  ADHD

autism; autistic disorder

bulimia nervosa

cohort differences

conduct disorder

crack baby

developmental
  psychopathology

Dexedrine

Down syndrome

echolalia

fenfluramine

fetal alcohol syndrome

intelligence quotient; IQ

learning disorders

mainstreaming

mental retardation

minimal brain damage;
  MBD

obesity

organic retardation

pronominal reversal

Ritalin

separation anxiety
  disorder

serotonin

sociocultural retardation

Abnormality in a Community and Legal Context

15

As I HAVE REITERATED THROUGHOUT the text, we cannot discuss abnormality without placing it in its social context. The very identification of abnormality is a social judgment, and social conditions can be risk factors or buffering factors for virtually all disorders. When we turn our attention to treatment and prevention, the social context is just as important. Treatment involves a social relationship between clients and therapists, and prevention can only take place when society as a whole decides to allocate resources to this purpose. In this final chapter, I focus on two more aspects

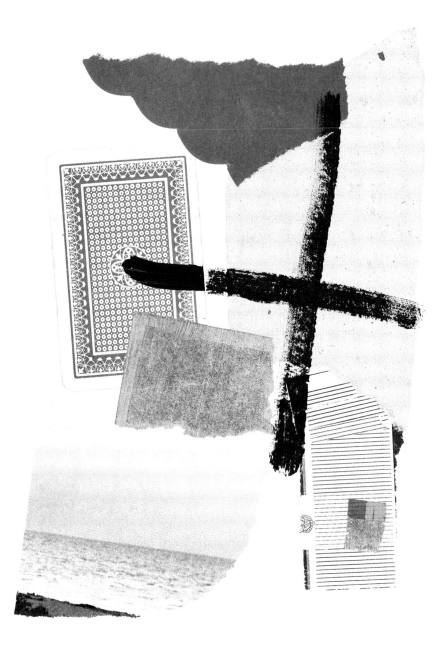

of the social context of psychological problems: the community mental health movement and the legal system.

THE COMMUNITY MENTAL HEALTH MOVEMENT

In the United States, large-scale prevention of psychological abnormality has been linked in recent decades to the *community mental health movement*. This movement does not include all attempts at prevention, and it is not identical with community psychology (Chapter 3). Still, a review of its history is instructive (Bloom, 1984) (see Figure 15.1).

HISTORY

The idea that psychological problems can be prevented or limited is nothing new. At least one of the rationales for any sort of treatment is that people's problems will be less severe if they are in therapy than if not. Nonetheless, the impetus for the community mental health movement in the United States was discontent with the way that traditional mental health professionals went about their business. Bloom (1984) described a number of criticisms that led to the search for a better alternative.

First, traditional mental health professionals are concerned with individuals to the exclusion of the community in which they find themselves. Most of the models of abnormality focus on processes—biochemical, emotional, behavioral, and cognitive—within an individual, giving insufficient attention to the fact that these processes do not exist in isolation from outer influences, notably the person's community.

Second, the traditional emphasis has been not only on the individual but also on a specific sort of individual: the person who shows up at the therapist's office. Those who do not do so are more likely to be the very young, the very old, the poor, and ethnic minorities. Yet, the people in these groups often have more than their share of difficulties. Relatedly, the typical emphasis of mental health professionals has been on long-term therapy, which—because it is expensive in both time and money—presents a further blockade to serving the greatest number of people who might benefit from these services.

Third, mental health professionals have tended to focus on the treatment of problems, not their prevention. Even more conspicuously, there has been an emphasis solely on psychopathology. Virtually no attention has been paid to what it might mean to enhance psychological well-being—to promote mental health, as it were. Along these lines, traditional mental

FIGURE **15.1**

HISTORY OF COMMUNITY
MENTAL HEALTH
MOVEMENT   *Since its
beginning, the community mental
health movement has had a
checkered history.*

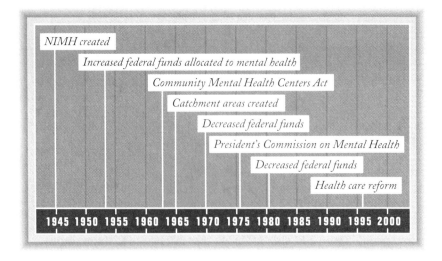

health professionals have been reactive, rather than proactive, responding to problems as they present themselves rather than anticipating just what sorts of services a given community might need and how these might best be developed. When problems such as substance abuse increase suddenly, the mental health system can become overwhelmed.

Fourth, as a result of the aforementioned emphases, mainstream mental health services have not been integrated within other institutions in society: schools, businesses, social welfare agencies, and the like. These might well provide vehicles for delivering help as well as being the ingredients in a useful coalition for ministering to the well-being of whole communities.

With these criticisms widely recognized, several historical factors came together in the 1950s, setting the stage for the emergence of the community mental health movement in the 1960s. For one, in the 1950s drug treatment of psychological abnormality rapidly increased. In particular, the availability of the major tranquilizers, used to treat the flagrant psychotic symptoms of schizophrenia, had the practical effect of speeding up patient discharge from psychiatric hospitals. Furthermore, in many cases, new admissions decreased. As mentioned in Chapter 12, the introduction of major tranquilizers was followed by a 75% reduction in the number of patients hospitalized with psychiatric diagnoses.

Another historical factor emerging in the 1950s was the creation of the **therapeutic community.** Individuals in hospitals were treated less as medical patients, who simply waited for recovery on a ward, and more as members of a community, composed of patients and staff, who worked together in democratic fashion to regulate patient behavior, privileges, and eventually discharge (Jones, 1968). Again, this ap-

peared to speed up the discharge process, and more importantly, it sent a clear message: Regarding hospitalized individuals as members of a community is a sensible strategy. Why not continue the same policy once patients are out of the hospital?

A final historical influence started out as an administrative decision with regard to how to run state hospitals: decentralization. Traditionally, state psychiatric hospitals were very large, and patients were sent to them from throughout the state. Once in the hospital, they were housed according to their prescribed

Historically, many patients in psychiatric hospitals found themselves on back wards where they received little if any treatment.

treatment—with shock, with drugs, or not at all. Those on "back wards" were accorded little treatment, allocated few resources, and had about them a pervading sense of despair. In most state hospitals, patients languished in these wards, where they remained for decades, or even life.

In an attempt to change this state of affairs, patients began to be housed according to their home communities, regardless of their diagnosis or treatment. Patients with differing severity of problems were placed together—in effect with their neighbors. Again, this underscored the plausibility of regarding patients as members of a community. And staff members had reasons to become familiar with particular neighborhoods, those from which their patients came and to which many would return.

These factors led to an increased interest in preventing problems by interventions at the community level (Chapter 3). One of the drawbacks of all this was the tendency on the part of some to regard any and all hospitalizations as bad, which helped fuel the massive deinstitutionalization that occurred in more recent years, dumping many individuals on the street without giving them the resources to care for themselves. The federal government had not been involved in mental health services until shortly after World War II. The National Institute of Mental Health (NIMH) was created in 1946 by an act of Congress and was charged with the "improvement of the mental health of the people of the United States" (United States Congress, 1946, p. 1). Part of this mandate included helping states determine how to most effectively prevent, diagnose, and treat psychological problems.

Some teeth were put into this latter charge in the 1950s when Congress appropriated money for NIMH to funnel to state mental hospitals, to fund demonstration projects, which were then written up to serve as examples for other hospitals. This culminated in 1961 with a report and recommendations that even more funds be allocated to mental health (Joint Commission on Mental Illness and Health, 1961). The commission in charge of this report recommended the creation of more (but smaller) hospitals, emphasizing the treatment of acute conditions. (The implication was that people would not stay long in these hospitals.) The commission also recommended that money be spent on public education about psychological problems.

When this report reached President John Kennedy's desk, he enthusiastically endorsed it. Kennedy had a sister with mental retardation, and his family had a long-standing interest in mental health services. Part of Kennedy's presidential agenda was creating a national mental health program. In a dramatic message to Congress, Kennedy called for the identification of

On October 31, 1963, President John Kennedy (1917–1963) signed the Community Mental Health Centers Act into law.

the causes of psychological abnormality and their eradication:

> Prevention is far more desirable for all concerned. It is far more economical and it is far more likely to be successful. Prevention will require both selected specific programs directed especially at known causes, and the general strengthening of our fundamental community, social welfare, and educational programs which can do much to eliminate or correct the harsh environmental conditions which often are associated with mental retardation and mental illness.   (Kennedy, 1963, p. 2)

Particularly notable about this message, according to Bloom (1984), is not only that it was the first time an American President had ever delivered such a message about psychological problems, but also that it focused on prevention.

Congress went on in 1963 to pass the Community Mental Health Centers Act (United States Congress, 1963), and Kennedy signed the bill into law just 1 month before his death. An additional bill was passed in 1965, subdividing the country into about 1,500 so-called *catchment areas*, each encompassing 75,000 to 200,000 individuals (United States Congress, 1965). These catchment areas were evaluated in terms of their need for improved mental health services, and federal funds were allocated accordingly. The plan was for the federal funding to be decreased every year, replaced by nonfederal funds.

By law, the community mental health centers in each catchment area were to provide the following services:

✦ inpatient care

✦ outpatient care

+ emergency services

+ partial hospitalization

+ consultation and education

All of these should be familiar to you except **partial hospitalization,** which refers to care for those who do not need round-the-clock hospitalization, yet need more care than provided in weekly or monthly visits. For example, one common implementation of partial hospitalization is a *day hospital,* where patients arrive in the morning for activities and therapy and leave for home in the late afternoon.

The eventual plan was that community mental health centers would provide as well diagnosis, rehabilitation, precare, aftercare, training, research, and evaluation. All residents within a given catchment area were to be eligible to receive services, regardless of their ability to pay. This was truly a comprehensive plan for mental health.

However, the community mental health movement was embroiled in political conflict, even during its earliest planning. The American Medical Association lobbied against the initial bill (Bartemeier, 1963). Then, as the United States became involved in the Vietnam War, and later as inflation began to grow, there was less interest from Presidents Richard Nixon and Gerald Ford to support the sorts of social programs that the community mental health centers represented.

The movement had a brief reprieve during the presidency of Jimmy Carter, who brought with him into the White House a commitment to mental health, dating back to his days as Georgia's governor. Once elected President, Carter created the President's Com-

mission on Mental Health to take stock of the needs of the United States with regard to mental health and to decide how these might best be met. The commission produced a report with more than 100 specific recommendations, many of which called for revigorization of the community mental health program as originally envisioned (President's Commission on Mental Health, 1978). It further recommended that the National Institute of Mental Health establish within itself a center for prevention.

Further changes took place during the Carter years. There was a massive shift from inpatient to outpatient treatment. From 1970 to 1980, outpatient care increased fourfold. The number of hospital beds devoted to psychiatric patients dwindled (see Figure 15.2). By 1980, half the people in the United States were within reach of community mental health centers.

In 1980, Ronald Reagan was elected President following a campaign waged largely around economic issues. He proposed and implemented a number of plans that curbed inflation by cutting federal funding, particularly of social programs, and allowed states greater latitude in how they dealt with their social problems. What money there was available to states was provided through *block grants,* a lump sum not earmarked for specific purposes. Traditionally, federal money given to the states would be designated for particular purposes. Reagan put an end to this procedure, in effect saving a great deal of money, because the block grants invariably totaled less than the categorical grants previously awarded. During the Reagan and Bush presidencies, there was massive reduction in the funding of community mental health programs. We will have to wait and see how the present and future administrations will deal with mental health issues.

FIGURE 15.2

THE EFFECTS OF DEINSTITUTIONALIZATION
The deinstitutionalization movement has led to a marked decrease in the number of patients in psychiatric hospitals in the United States.
SOURCE: DATA DERIVED FROM "THE DEMOGRAPHY OF DEINSTITUTIONALIZATION," BY H. H. GOLDMAN, 1983. IN L. L. BACHRACH (ED.), *Deinstitutionalization,* SAN FRANCISCO: JOSSEY-BASS.

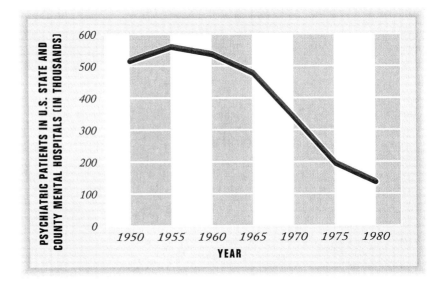

EVALUATION

The goal of prevention inherent in the community mental health movement in the United States has not been met. Why? First, it embraced the medical model. In a way this is understandable, because the field of public health provided the original inspiration, and mental health throughout the 20th century has been the province of biologically oriented physicians. But many psychologically caused problems can be readily prevented, by providing information on the one hand and reducing stressful life events on the other. The physicians running the community mental health centers have not necessarily thought in these terms. When they have tried to do so, they lose their unique expertise (Kubie, 1968).

Another practical problem with this movement concerns who is supposed to pay for it. It is unfair to blame the Republican administrations of Nixon, Ford, Reagan, and Bush for withholding funds from these centers, because part of the original plan was to gradually reduce federal funding. Obviously, not enough thought went into just where the compensating funds would come from. We know that states have been unwilling or unable to pick up the slack, and there is no reason to think that less urgent federal budget slashing would have changed matters much.

Finally, we can quarrel with the premise that the best way to treat and prevent abnormality is in the context of the community. Clearly, we need to take into account a person's social setting, but a geographically defined "community" is simply one rendering (cf. Sanders, 1966). Only some people live (in the psychological sense) in such a community. Other people conceptualize their social environment differently, and perhaps their numbers are increasing. Do all people befriend their neighbors? Do they work in the same neighborhood where they live? Do they get as concerned about local politics as national events? Not all people in a given locale interact with one another. A psychologically meaningful community might not exist for many individuals.

Another criticism of community-based treatment is that it may not make much sense to close down state psychiatric hospitals, if the alternative is sending the person back to the setting that contributed to his or her problem in the first place. The original rationale for state hospitals was that individuals would benefit from time away from their stressful community. Along these lines, large psychiatric hospitals may well have better facilities than local general hospitals, precisely because they are large and have a special interest in psychological abnormality. None of this excuses the way state psychiatric hospitals sometimes have erred, but perhaps the plan of closing

them down altogether rather than reforming them was hasty and extreme.

But they were closed, in extremely large numbers, in the deinstitutionalization movement. It is somewhat difficult to evaluate deinstitutionalization, given all the other events that have transpired while mental hospitals emptied out during the 1960s and 1970s. The hope was that those previously on chronic wards in state mental hospitals would receive community-based outpatient care. Indeed, community-based outpatient care increased greatly. However, there is a troubling fact about all of this. The people who left the state mental hospitals were *not* the same people served by the new community mental health centers. For example, consider that 60% of patients discharged from state hospitals were over 55 years of age, whereas only 5% of the patients seen at community mental health centers were of this age (Chu & Trotter, 1974). Many people were overlooked in the shuffle of deinstitutionalization (Martin, 1990).

Some years ago, a friend told me that one of his relatives had been hospitalized repeatedly during her adult life for bipolar disorder. As sometimes occurs, her manic episodes became more severe over time, and her behavior more hazardous. Lithium proved somewhat effective in controlling her manic episodes, but she would not stay on the medication. A relapse would occur shortly after each release from the hospital. Her last hospitalization was in a distant state where she happened to be visiting. My friend was in contact via the telephone with his relative's psychiatrist and pleaded with him not to release the individual until a family member could come to the state and see her.

However, the hospital policy—shaped by the deinstitutionalization movement—mandated discharge once an acute psychotic episode was resolved. The relative was given an appointment at an outpatient clinic and released from the hospital. I must add that the relative wished to leave. In any event, she never kept her appointment. She was not seen for 6 months, and then her body was found in a river. The investigating police officers never determined whether her death was a suicide, an accident, or a murder.

As this example illustrates, people discharged from state mental hospitals during deinstitutionalization showed an alarmingly high death rate (Goplerud, 1979). In retrospect, this is not surprising. We know that massive disruptions in an individual's life are associated with increased illness and death. We also know that some number of the individuals discharged from these hospitals wound up on the streets. The exact number is unclear, because the homeless are of necessity a difficult population to enumerate (Dennis,

Buckner, Lipton, & Levine, 1991). Certainly not all of the homeless today are former psychiatric patients.

But a history of severe psychological problems, coupled with the deinstitutionalization movement, is one direct route into homelessness. In one study, for instance, researchers discovered that fully 35% of patients discharged from a state mental hospital were homeless within 3 months (Belcher & Toomey, 1988). Once homeless, even those in the best of health are at increased risk for all manner of other problems (Fischer & Breakey, 1991). The community mental health centers were supposed to protect against this possibility. If discharged patients receive aftercare, they do better than if not. But discharged patients tend not to make use of aftercare programs, even when they are available, which means that the community mental health centers have somehow failed to reach out to those people in their catchment areas who most need help (Searight & Handal, 1988).

Along these lines, one of the goals of the community mental health program is to provide services to underserved ethnic minorities. Sue, Fujino, Hu, Takeuchi, and Zane (1991) studied the utilization of outpatient services provided by the Los Angeles County Department of Mental Health between 1983 and 1988. They concluded that African Americans and European Americans were making much more adequate use of these services than were Asian Americans or Mexican Americans. Individuals in these latter two groups did not enter the community mental health system in numbers that would be expected given the makeup of the larger population of Los Angeles. One apparently critical factor in explaining the underutilization of available services was whether potential clients spoke English. Also relevant was whether potential clients and therapists were from the same ethnic group. The obvious implication is that programs would be more effective if their staffs were as linguistically and ethnically diverse as the communities they try to serve.

In sum, it is difficult to explain the outcome of the community mental health movement in the United States. Did it fail because of insufficient funding, because of how it was carried out, or because the entire idea was wrong-headed (Lamb & Talbott, 1986)? Consider the possibility that some psychological disorder is inevitable. Perhaps envisioning a society with no problems is utopian. Indeed, prevention attempts in European countries, though differing in details, have encountered the same difficulties as the community mental health program in the United States (Neumann, 1991; Rowland, Zeelan, & Waismann, 1992; Uffing, Ceha, & Saenger, 1992).

Nonetheless, the rate of many problems rises and falls with social conditions, so these can be sensibly targeted for change. You know from my discussion in Chapter 3 that specific programs of prevention have often been successful. In its intended scope, the community mental health movement was radical, but perhaps not radical enough, because the larger society in which it was embedded did not change sufficiently (Neighbors, 1987).

Bernard Bloom (1984), one of the important figures in community psychology, offered a balanced evaluation of the movement. It succeeded with respect to three goals: returning mental health services to the community, providing short-term services to community residents, and providing indirect services through consultation to mental health facilities. It failed in meeting all of the mental health needs of the community, in involving the community as a whole in planning and evaluating the centers, in preventing problems in the first place, and in reducing community stresses. Put another way, this movement did its best work in the most traditional areas of clinical service. Failure became more likely as the clinician moved further from what he or she was trained to do.

Bloom offered the further opinion that while the battle may have been lost, the war was won. The community mental health movement was part of other trends present in the 1960s and 1970s that changed our society forever. Like the civil rights and the voting rights movements, the community mental health movement highlighted inequalities within society and our shared obligation to do what we can to eradicate these inequalities. Today there is little debate about whether society should do something about poverty, disability, malnutrition, illiteracy, and discrimination. The debate has shifted to details of how and how much. This represents a true revolution over previous societal attitudes. The goal of prevention has become an important one for the United States, no matter how ambivalently or tentatively the goal itself is carried out.

PSYCHOLOGY AS A PROFESSION

Our society is governed by complex rules and laws, created, interpreted, and enforced by institutions long predating the formal existence of psychology as a discipline. As psychology developed in the United States throughout the 20th century, it grew into a self-conscious profession represented by several large national organizations, notably the American Psychological Association (APA) (Hilgard, 1987). The APA attempts to promote psychology as a profession, and part of this involves the need to protect the reputation of the field by encouraging psychologists to act in an ethical (and legal) way.

To this end, the APA has proposed ethical principles and a code of conduct for psychologists[1] (American Psychological Association, 1992). Put forth are six broad principles:

♦ Psychologists strive to maintain high standards of competence.

♦ Psychologists seek to promote integrity in their science, teaching, and practice.

♦ Psychologists uphold professional standards of conduct, making clear their roles and obligations, accepting responsibility for their actions, and adapting their methods to the needs of different groups.

♦ Psychologists accord appropriate respect to the fundamental rights, dignity, and worth of all people.

♦ Psychologists contribute to the welfare of those with whom they interact professionally.

♦ Psychologists are aware of their responsibilities to the community and society in which they work and live.

These principles are made concrete by detailed guidelines about how psychologists should conduct their professional activities (research, teaching, diagnosis, treatment, and so on). For example, a psychologist who undertakes assessment must use only current tests and explain the results to clients in ways they can understand.

In the practice of psychotherapy, a psychologist must make clear to his or her clients before therapy begins such matters as the intended nature and course of therapy, the fees, and the limits on confidentiality. Clients must also give their consent to be treated. Sexual intimacies with clients are strictly forbidden, despite popular movies that make this seem like an accepted practice. More generally, *dual relationships* between psychologists and their clients should be avoided because of the inherent conflict of interest involved. Psychologists should not see their own students or research assistants in therapy; they should not enter into business partnerships with clients; and so on.

Psychologists are no more immune to charges of malpractice and fraud than professionals in any other field. Although relatively few psychotherapists are sued (Dorken, 1990), when this does happen, claims are usually made with regard to breach of confidentiality, inappropriate treatment, failure to anticipate suicide,

and sexual impropriety (Conte & Karasu, 1990). The APA's code of conduct can be used by both psychologists and the general public to judge these difficult matters. Although the code of conduct is not a legal document in its own right, it can and does inform legal proceedings.[2] Courts and other public bodies often rely on the APA's code to help them evaluate the conduct of individual psychologists.

Another function of the APA is to evaluate graduate training programs in clinical psychology against standards developed by the organization. It also evaluates internships in diagnosis, assessment, and psychotherapy. In many states, completion of an APA-approved graduate program and internship is required for licensure as a practicing psychologist.

The APA also takes public stances on issues that affect psychology as a profession, such as federal funding of research, prescription privileges, insurance reimbursement for psychotherapy, and national health care. The APA actively lobbies with regard to these issues in Washington, D.C. On public concerns to which psychological theory and research bear, the organization also offers advice. So, recent years have seen the APA take positions with respect to the equal rights amendment, abortion, gun control, homelessness, and gay rights. Usually, its stance is a politically liberal one. Not all psychologists approve of the APA's involvement in social and political issues, preferring instead that the organization concern itself narrowly with the promotion of research and training.[3] However, the rationale for APA's involvement is that this is the best way in a complex society like our own to promote and protect psychology as a profession.

PSYCHOLOGISTS AS EXPERT WITNESSES

Psychology often interacts with the legal system, especially with regard to issues of diagnosis and treatment (but see Focus on Psychological Testimony in Court). So far we have assumed that treatment follows a simple agreement between a client and a therapist to work together on a given problem. This is often the case. But sometimes the client and the therapist are in conflict. Fees may be disputed, or the client may feel exploited or mistreated. Here the legal system might be called on to help adjudicate the disagreement. Other

---

[1] Other professions that work with psychologically troubled individuals have comparable codes of ethics.

[2] In some states, the APA code of conduct is formally included in licensure statutes and thus its principles are part of law.

[3] In the late 1980s, a rival professional organization—the American Psychological Society (or APS)—was created to promote the strictly scientific goals of psychology. At least in part, the impetus for the APS was disenchantment with the extremely broad social agenda of the APA.

FOCUS ON

Psychological

Testimony in

Court

ALTHOUGH MOST PSYCHOLO-gists who serve as expert witnesses testify about diagnostic and treatment issues, there are several other areas that deserve mention. For example, psychological research about the validity of eyewitness testimony has been introduced in the courts, as well as research about the sorts of group processes that occur in juries which might affect their verdicts (see Loftus & Monahan, 1980; Monahan & Walker, 1988). Also, research pertaining to stereotypes has been introduced in cases concerning alleged gender discrimination (Fiske, Bersoff, Borgida, Deaux, & Heilman, 1991). Psychologists may consult with lawyers about choosing potential jurors and developing the most persuasive case to present to them (Cutler, 1990; Patterson, 1986; Vore, 1989).

Psychologists may also be asked to testify in child custody and visitation suits (Herman, 1990), as well as in disputed adoptions and placements in foster care (Carrieri, 1991). Remember the massive media coverage of the Woody Allen–Mia Farrow custody dispute, the struggle over Baby Jessica, and the desire by Kimberly Mays *not* to be visited by her biological parents.[4] In each of these cases, psychological testimony was heard.

In cases involving children, one important consideration proposed by law is *the best interests of the child* (Maccoby & Mnookin, 1992). Most jurisdictions identify this as the overriding concern in placing a child; what will benefit the son or daughter takes precedence over what will benefit the father or mother. This principle is consistent with the general tenor of the legal system in the United States, which affords special protection to minors because they are not able to fend for themselves. Details differ from jurisdiction to jurisdiction, however, about just what constitutes the best-interests of the child. Guidelines usually mentioned include emotional bonds between the parties involved and the child, the capacity and disposition of the par-

ties involved to raise and nurture the child, the length of time the child has lived with the parties involved, and the preference of the child, if the child is able to express a preference.

One more area in which psychologists are increasingly being called on as expert witnesses is in cases involving alleged sexual abuse of children (Berliner & Loftus, 1992). There have been a number of well publicized examples in recent years in which the testimony of the children proved very difficult to evaluate. What can the court make of memories that are incomplete, inconsistent, and traumatic (Chapter 8)? Should a young child be subjected to harsh cross-examination? Must he or she face the accused? There are no simple answers, of course, but psychologists whose expertise includes young children exposed to trauma have a unique contribution to make in such cases (Eth, 1988; Myers, 1993; Yates, 1987).

In many court decisions involving children, the "best interests of the child" are given priority. Although psychological testimony was heard, the court decision returning Baby Jessica to her birth parents was based on a different criterion.

---

[4] At the time of this writing, though, Ms. Mays changed her mind and is now living with her biological parents. This, too, may change.

Psychologists may testify in court as expert witnesses.

times the client is in conflict with society, as when he or she is accused of committing a crime, and then the therapist might be called on to help resolve matters. Again, the legal system oversees the details of this process.

When psychologists testify in court about psychological topics, they often do so as an *expert witness,* which means that the court recognizes them as especially knowledgeable in the case being considered (Brodsky, 1991). Because they are designated as experts, they can include in their testimony ideas from the research literature. Even if an expert has not conducted a given study herself, she can still testify about it. The court will not consider what she says as hearsay evidence (Loftus, 1991).

It is unlikely that psychology and the legal system will stop trafficking with each other in the foreseeable future. But realize that there are inherent tensions between these two approaches to human conduct (Morris, 1982). Psychology is a scientific discipline based on the assumption of **determinism**—what people do has causes. It is best equipped to offer generalizations about people per se, and individual cases may or may not fit these conclusions. The legal system, in contrast, is based on the assumption of **free will**—what people do represents their own choice, unless there are extenuating circumstances.

Furthermore, the legal system is concerned with individual cases, not people in general. The statistical significance of "results" on which psychological research puts so much weight is not a criterion that makes any sense in a court of law.

Finally, the legal system relies on advocacy. The prosecution and defense both try to make the strongest possible arguments. Justice is served by the interplay. The scientific ideal calls for much more even-handedness on the part of individuals. But when psychologists testify as expert witnesses, they necessarily do so as advocates. As a result, when on opposite sides of a case, they often disagree with one another. The general public may view this disagreement cynically, seeing psychologists and other mental health professionals as arbitrary or even mercenary. Appreciate, though, that the legal system demands advocacy. Witnesses on opposite sides of a case should be expected to disagree.

These contrasting ideas—determinism versus free will, generalities versus individual cases, scientific even-handedness versus legal advocacy—can create a discrepancy between what psychologists do best and what those who ask the psychologists to appear in court want them to do. It is not surprising that the role of psychology vis-à-vis the legal system is controversial and in constant flux (Coleman, 1984; Havard, 1992).

The rest of this chapter presents a snapshot of the relationship between psychology and the legal system as it currently exists in the United States with respect to abnormality (see Focus on the Legal Context of Abnormality in China). I organize this material, somewhat arbitrarily, into issues that concern the rights of those with disorders and issues that pertain to abnormality and crime.

THE RIGHTS OF THOSE WITH DISORDERS

People with problems do not cease being citizens because they are anxious or depressed or schizophrenic. At one time they were denied equal protection under the law, but matters have changed in recent decades (Sehdev, 1976; Weiner, 1981). Here is what an individual with a problem can expect in a legal sense when embarking (or not) on treatment.

INVOLUNTARY COMMITMENT

You read earlier in this chapter of the trend in recent decades to decrease the number of individuals in hospitals for treatment of psychological problems. This does not mean that hospitals have been closed completely. Some large number of people are still patients in psychiatric hospitals under the assumption that this is the best way to help them with their particular problem.

The majority of people hospitalized for psychological problems—about 75%—have been voluntarily admitted (Monahan & Shah, 1989). That is to say, they have given their consent to be treated there.[5] Once in the hospital, however, they do not always get to leave as readily as they arrived. The staff might decide that their condition does not allow them to be

---

[5] There is some question whether everyone who gives "voluntary" consent to be hospitalized understands exactly what this consent involves.

FOCUS ON

The Legal Context of Abnormality in China

THE MATERIAL DISCUSSED IN this chapter pertains to the relationship between psychology and the legal system in the United States. This qualification is important, because widely differing relationships exist between psychology and legal systems around the world. The United States system, like the British one from which it is derived, concerns itself greatly with the protection of individual rights, and hence we see much attention to how this is played out with respect to a person with a psychological problem.

Contrast this concern with what we see in China, a country much more concerned than the United States with the common welfare of the state. The presumption of innocence before a trial is much less explicit in China than in the United States. The purpose of a trial in China seems to be to allow the defendant to confess guilt and express remorse. From the vantage of the United States, such trials look staged, but this of course is the point within Chinese society.

In any event, China has long considered the relationship between people with psychological disorders and the law, with written records on the matter dating back more than 2,000 years (Liu, 1981). I draw on Veronica Pearson's (1992) survey of Chinese legal rulings and practices, based on her visit in the late 1980s to psychiatric hospitals in Guangzhou, Beijing, and Shashi.

A striking aspect of China, at least in contrast to the United States, is that involuntary commitments to psychiatric hospitals are almost nonexistent. Indeed, there are no equivalents in China of commitment laws. Does this therefore mean that all admissions to psychiatric hospitals are voluntary? Not exactly. In many cases, the individual is simply not asked what she wants. Other people—usually family members but also friends and fellow workers—have the legal and moral responsibility to commit the person if they find themselves unable to take responsibility for the consequences of what she does. They do so by making an application to the court. The person goes along with the process because there is no other option available to her.

Once hospitalized, psychiatric patients in China have no generally agreed-upon rights. Civil liberties are unilaterally suspended. There is no right to treatment, and in fact, many hospitals are merely custodial. When treatment is undertaken, consent of the patient is not needed, even for hazardous procedures like psychosurgery.

According to Pearson (1992), political dissidents in China are *not* sent to psychiatric hospitals, as they were in the former Soviet Union. She comments that China has other ways of dealing with dissidents. Hospital beds in China are too scarce and expensive to be used for this purpose.

Like the United States, China recognizes the notion of diminished responsibility in excusing criminal activity.[6] Two criteria must be met. First, the offender must have been suffering from a disorder at the time the crime was committed. Second, this disorder must be of such severity that the individual lost the capacity to distinguish right from wrong or to control behavior.

What differs from practice in the United States is that the assessment of insanity is carried out by a panel of individuals who submit a written report to the court. Usually the request for an examination originates from the police (as opposed to the defense attorney in the United States). The panel interviews the accused, his family, and those at his *danwei* (place of work). No one is allowed to refuse an interview. Although the written report submitted to the court is not binding, its recommendation is followed more than 90% of the time. In the typical case leading to a judgment of insanity, the crime in question is rape or attempted rape. We encounter the insanity plea most frequently in the United States in cases of homicide.

Although this has been but a brief overview of the relationship in China between abnormality and the legal system, notice its congruence with other aspects of Chinese culture that value the maintenance of social order. At least with regard to psychological abnormality, there seems to be little call within China for the sorts of individual rights that are so important to those of us in the United States. You have a final reminder about the importance of putting people and their actions in a particular context. In this case, the legal context of abnormality must itself be located within its cultural context.

---

[6] However, China has long allowed the equivalent of a guilty but mentally ill verdict.

discharged, in which case their status is converted into what is known as **involuntary commitment.** The remaining 25% of psychiatric patients come directly into hospitals against their will, again as involuntarily committed individuals.

How does all of this occur? Procedures differ from state to state, but to sketch the process, it begins when somebody—a police officer, a mental health professional, or perhaps a friend, family member, or fellow worker—makes a complaint to the police or the court that the individual in question poses a danger. If this allegation is taken seriously, then the police take the person to a clinic or physician for an examination.

If an emergency situation seems to be present, the court can order the person to be hospitalized for further observation. Depending on the state, the length of these emergency hospitalizations varies from a single day to several weeks. In some states, a hearing must be held to see if further hospitalization is justified.

Holding people in a psychiatric hospital against their will is in direct conflict with our society's cherished notion of freedom of movement. As such, this procedure is not undertaken glibly. It is a formalized process carried out under the supervision of the legal system, and one of two general criteria must be docu-

mented if people are to be involuntarily committed: They must pose a danger to themselves, or a danger to others.

Danger to the self   A person can be involuntarily committed if he suffers some psychological disability—which means that he needs treatment, that he is somehow dangerous to himself, and/or that he is in no position to take care of himself. Some suggest that involuntary commitment by this criterion be guided by the **thank-you test:** Will the involuntarily committed individual, once recovered from whatever problem he suffers, thank those who carried out the commitment?

The conditions for psychological disability are easiest to recognize when they exist in the extreme. Repeated suicide attempts constitute good evidence that an individual poses a danger to herself. Her failure to feed or clothe herself when it is possible to do so similarly constitutes good evidence that she cannot take care of herself. But the cautions I have often raised about recognizing abnormality apply here as well. Problems ensue when the criteria for involuntary commitment are not so clearly met.

In 1987, Joyce Brown came to the nation's attention when she argued that she had a right to live on the streets of New York. Here she is shown lecturing at Harvard Law School, following her release from the hospital to which she had been involuntarily committed.

A well known example of how fuzzy involuntary commitment can be is the case of Joyce Brown, who came to our nation's attention in 1987, when Mayor Edward Koch of New York City ordered a campaign to remove "severely mentally ill homeless people" from the streets of Manhattan and take them to facilities where they would receive care (Hornblower, 1987). Among the very first people picked up in this campaign was Joyce Brown, a woman in her forties who had been living in the streets for at least a year. She defecated in her clothing or on the sidewalk. She begged for money from passersby, but sometimes she threw the money away or set it on fire.

She was picked up by the authorities and taken to Bellevue Hospital, where she was diagnosed as suffering from chronic schizophrenia. But she was angry about what had happened to her. She felt that her right to live on the streets, no matter how strange it might look to others, had been violated. She contacted the New York Civil Liberties Union. They agreed with her.

At a court hearing to review her involuntary commitment, Ms. Brown told her story. To many who heard her, she came off as eccentric but lucid. The authorities presented little evidence that she had ever been harmful to herself. However, they defended her involuntary commitment on the grounds of decency, saying that they were trying to intervene before something bad happened to her. As it eventually turned out, the court ruled in favor of her involuntary commitment. She stayed in Bellevue for several months, and then was discharged. Joyce Brown went back to living on the streets.

Danger to others   The second criterion used to justify involuntary commitment is whether the individual constitutes a danger to society—that is, to other people (Monahan, 1992). Again, in the extreme, we can recognize this quite easily. Repeated attempts to hurt others constitute good evidence that the person is harmful. But as I have said before, matters are not always so clear-cut. The justification for involuntary commitment is not past evidence of dangerousness but a judgment that the person will be dangerous in the future.

There is good reason to believe that psychologists cannot predict future dangerousness with any sort of accuracy (Kress, 1979). In a well known study, 967 involuntarily committed patients were released following a court order about the inappropriateness of the hospitals where they resided (Steadman & Keveles, 1972; Steadman, Vanderwyst, & Ribner, 1978). Researchers followed up on these individuals, none of whom had been judged to be free of the condition that had justified their original hospitalization. In the 4 years following their release, only 2.7% of these individuals later behaved in such a way as to wind up in jail or another hospital. Further, the researchers were unable to discover any factor that successfully distinguished the handful of those who did act dangerously from those who did not.

Thus, the vast majority of those deemed "criminally insane" did not act in a criminal or insane fashion, and it proved impossible to predict the small minority who did. These findings call into question the very idea that the judgment of future dangerousness to others constitutes a reasonable criterion for involuntary commitment. Some suggest that the criterion be modified to mean dangerousness not for the indefinite future but for some relatively brief and specified time. This might well improve our ability to predict this kind of behavior (McNiel & Binder, 1987; Rofman, Askinazi, & Fant, 1980). Along these lines, Brouillette and Paris (1991) suggested that decisions to commit

people because of presumed dangerousness take into account how serious their problems are and how readily they can be treated. Another possibility to consider is that psychologists try to judge the relative risk of dangerousness in the future rather than attempting to predict specific instances of violent behavior (Litwack, Kirschner, & Wack, 1993). Risk assessment then becomes one of several factors to weigh in decisions about involuntary commitment.

Some have called for tossing out this criterion altogether, especially if it means that people can be confined because they are merely suspected of being dangerous. I should point out that this is not something typically done in our society, even when we can say with confidence that individuals will likely be dangerous in the future. Others have argued that involuntary commitment is justified if the person merely disturbs other people. This has been one of the stated rationales for removing homeless people from the streets: not because they are dangerous to themselves but because they *bother* everyone else. Much as we would all like to be protected from what bothers us, society should consider if this is a reasonable way to proceed.

Evaluation   According to the research conducted, once a person begins the process of involuntary commitment, the odds are very good that it will continue on to its end, with the person being sent to a hospital (e.g., Mahler & Co, 1984). The legal system is involved, to be sure, but judges are reluctant to disagree with "experts" about the advisability of involuntary commitment.

Lower-class males, ethnic minorities, and those without homes are much more likely to be committed (e.g., Dunn & Fahy, 1990; Lindsey & Paul, 1989; Lindsey, Paul, & Mariotto, 1989; Owens, Harrison, & Boot, 1991; Pipe, Bhat, Matthews, & Hampstead, 1991; Riecher, Rossler, Loffler, & Fatkenheuer, 1991) (see Figure 15.3). Also, involuntary commitment is more likely to be undertaken because of a presumed

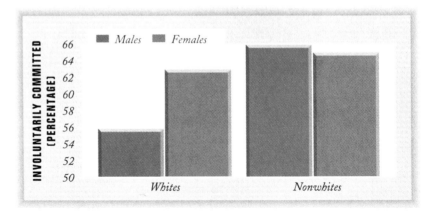

FIGURE **15.3**

INCIDENCE OF INVOLUNTARY COMMITMENT
Researchers determined what happened to individuals brought to a New York City hospital. Whether patients were admitted involuntarily depended on their race and gender.
SOURCE: DATA DERIVED FROM "RACE DIFFERENCES IN INVOLUNTARY HOSPITALIZATIONS," BY S. ROSENFIELD, 1984, *Journal of Health and Social Behavior, 25,* PP. 14–23.

danger to others as opposed to the self (Segal, Watson, Goldfinger, & Averbuck, 1988), yet the objectionable acts are usually harmless (Rubin & Mills, 1983).

Taken together, these findings suggest to some critics that the process is doing something more than seeing to it that troubled individuals are being helped. These critics view involuntary commitment as a means of social control by which those who are in power clamp down on those who are not. Back at the height of the Cold War between the United States and the former Soviet Union, we in this country frequently heard about how psychiatry and psychology were used as tools of political repression in that country (e.g, Fireside, 1979). Dissidents were branded mentally ill and sent against their will to prison hospitals.

Is the possibility too remote that something like this goes on in the United States? A mental health professional can serve the political needs of the state without consciously acknowledging that he or she is actually suppressing alternative ways of thinking or acting. The individual can quite sincerely carry out an involuntary commitment that nonetheless looks to an outsider like political suppression.

A more satisfactory alternative to involuntary commitment as it is currently carried out may involve committing individuals to treatment as outpatients (Scheid-Cook, 1987). The individual is legally required to undergo treatment, yet without the massive readjustment that hospitalization involves. We would expect that the stigma associated with being hospitalized is also substantially reduced. Research to date suggests that this alternative is a promising one. In one study, for instance, Hiday and Scheid-Cook (1989) found that patients involuntarily committed to outpatient treatment fared better than comparable patients undergoing involuntary inpatient treatment. Notably, they were more likely to utilize aftercare services following their treatment.

THE RIGHTS OF HOSPITALIZED PATIENTS

Granted that some individuals find themselves hospitalized, voluntarily or involuntarily, what can they expect? Historically, once under care for psychological problems, an individual abdicated any and all of her rights. Things are different now, and here are a few of the modern ideas and guarantees that psychiatric patients have (Knobel, 1974; Weiner, 1981).

First, those who are hospitalized as mental patients are still guaranteed certain civil rights, such as the right to manage their personal and financial affairs, vote, marry, divorce, or make a will. At the same time, these rights can be abridged if a patient is judged incompetent to handle such matters. Then the court will appoint a guardian to look after the patient. The extreme cases of incompetence are easy to recognize.

What rights are accorded mental patients?

More middling ones are fuzzy (Gutheil & Bursztajn, 1986; Ochroch, 1990). And there are different sorts of incompetence, such as the ability to make short-term decisions versus long-term ones (Culver & Gert, 1990).

Second, mental patients are entitled to a certain amount of space in their physical environment. Sleeping quarters must be arranged so that they have some privacy. Enough toilets should be available so that no more than eight patients share any given one. And patients can wear their own clothing. Again, these rights can be abridged if the person's particular problem warrants it. A suicidal individual would probably be given much less privacy than other patients, and she would probably not be allowed to wear a belt, because she could use it to hang herself.

Third, patients are allowed to work while hospitalized, but they cannot be compelled to do so because this would amount to involuntary servitude. This is not always a clear-cut issue. You have seen that the trend on some wards is to run them as communities; this usually involves having patients do some work on the ward. Work like this can be beneficial to all. So where do we draw the line? Courts have ruled that a patient can be required to work if the work is therapeutic. Does scrubbing the floor constitute therapeutic work? For the sake of argument, I suggest that cleaning your living quarters is a more legitimate way to act "sane" than making knotty pine knickknacks. Others might disagree.

It is sometimes suggested that patients should not be engaged in work that makes money for the hospital in question, although again this issue treads murky waters. When does saving money become making money? A patient scrubbing a floor means that a hospital employee does not have to do it. Is this making money, or saving it, or what?

Fourth, the involuntarily committed patient is entitled to the least restrictive environment that can be provided. In other words, a judgment is made whether he is served better in the hospital or out of it, and if in it, whether he is better served on a locked ward or an open one. Should he be restricted to the grounds or given free access to leave them? And so on. Whatever the decision, it should always go in the direction of the least restriction.

But even this clear directive can be difficult to apply in the concrete. Consider the use of *physical restraints* in psychiatric hospitals. Patients who are highly agitated or violent might quite literally be tied down, strapped by their arms and legs onto a bed. On the face of it, this looks like a "cruel and unusual" practice that some would like to see banished altogether. The alternative—presumably less restrictive—is to administer tranquilizing medication to the agitated or violent patient. But is drugging a person into a stupor really less restrictive than tying her down? Does it help her to learn to control her impulses? Is it really less cruel?

Fifth, people who are involuntarily committed have the right to receive treatment. This may sound strange; why else would an individual be in a psychiatric hospital in the first place? But remember that involuntarily committed people are sent away because they are dangerous to themselves or others. This need not have anything to do with treatment. However, court decisions have affirmed that a person committed against his will *must* be treated; otherwise the hospitalization is simply internment. The law does not require that treatments be guaranteed to work, which you know from Chapter 4 can prove difficult. But the staff must make a good faith effort to provide what in their professional estimation is appropriate treatment. An important benefit of this requirement has been mandating a certain number of professional staff members for hospitals of given sizes, a decision sparked by a 1971 lawsuit in Alabama in response to a patient-to-doctor ratio of 2,000 to 1 in state psychiatric hospitals!

Sixth, on the other side of the coin is the patient's right to refuse treatment (McGough & Carmichael, 1977). For purely medical conditions, people have the right to refuse to take medications or have surgery or receive blood transfusions. Some of us regard their decisions as regretful, but their right to do so is widely recognized. But what about people with psychological problems (Draper & Dawson, 1990)? Are they in a similar position to refuse treatment, even if they have been involuntarily committed? Not necessarily (Lebegue & Clark, 1981). There are circumstances in which a mental patient can be forced to undergo treatment: (a) when judged incompetent, (b) when judged a danger to self or others, or (c) when refusal is too costly for the community.

There are certain instances, however, when the patient can refuse. Psychiatric patients can refuse treatment when it violates their religious beliefs. For instance, Christian Scientists do not believe in taking medications and cannot be compelled to do so. The other reason a psychiatric patient can refuse a given treatment is when there is a less obtrusive treatment available that is arguably as effective. In the treatment of depression, antidepressants and cognitive therapy are viable alternatives to electroconvulsive shock, and so a patient can refuse shock treatment. In point of fact, the vast majority of patients who refuse treatment eventually receive it (Appelbaum, 1988; Hoge, Gutheil, & Kaplan, 1987), suggesting that this "right" cannot be exercised indefinitely against the contrary wishes of therapists.

What we see with regard to the rights of those with disorders is similar to the rights of everyone else, although more starkly drawn: a balancing act between the rights of the individual and the rights of society. Mental patients can get squeezed because there is a great deal of power invested in mental health professionals, and after all, they are the ones who make the relevant judgments here, to which the legal system often defers.

CONFIDENTIALITY AND THE THERAPIST'S DUTY TO WARN

Pulitzer Prize winner Anne Sexton was in psychotherapy for 5 years in the early 1960s for a variety of problems including substance abuse, depression, and suicide attempts. She eventually took her own life. In an unprecedented action, her psychiatrist made available to a writer 300 hours of tapes of his psychotherapy sessions with Sexton to be used in a biography of the poet (Hubbard, Mathison, Healy, & Fine, 1991). According to the psychiatrist, she gave him permission to use the tapes as he saw fit, and Sexton's daughter, who is her literary executor, approved of what he did. However, many mental health professionals regard this as a serious breach of confidentiality. "It's important for every patient to know that regardless of how famous they [sic] get, we're

The case of Pulitzer Prize winner Anne Sexton raises important questions about confidentiality in therapy. After her death by suicide, her therapist made available to a biographer tapes of his psychotherapy sessions with her.

With important exceptions, the client in therapy can expect that the things he or she says will be held in confidence.

not going to give away their confidences when they die" *(p. 63), commented a member of the American Psychiatric Association's ethics committee.*

Does a client in therapy have the right to regard everything he says a privileged communication? This is a protection that is afforded to those who enter into professional relationships with lawyers or members of the clergy. By and large, it is recognized that the client in therapy has the right to expect that the things he or she says will be held in confidence. Treatment of psychological problems rests importantly on confidentiality because it allows the most appropriate client-therapist relationship to develop.

In recent years, several exceptions to confidentiality have surfaced.[7] One is when there is a reason to suspect that child abuse has taken place. Then there

is a legally mandated requirement to report this suspicion to the authorities (e.g., Guyer, 1990). This requirement reflects the particular horror with which our society regards child abuse. But let me pose some rhetorical questions. Is child abuse more heinous than stealing nuclear secrets, or importing tons of cocaine, or doing insider trading on the stock market? And why should a lawyer be able to keep information confidential but not a psychotherapist?

How does this get played out in therapy? The therapist is required to explain the limits on confidentiality, but this can make a client reluctant to speak and might derail effective treatment. If the therapist says nothing, what happens if the topic arises? The client should be reported to the authorities, but suppose the suspicion then proves groundless?

A second important exception to confidentiality has to do with the therapist's **duty to warn** somebody that a client has made specific threats against his or her life. This dates from a famous instance, the Tarasoff case.

A man in therapy at the University of California Counseling Center repeatedly voiced his intentions to kill Tatiana Tarasoff, a woman with whom he had become romantically obsessed (Stone, 1976). She spurned his advances, and the client confided to his therapist that he planned to kill her. The therapist went to the campus police, who questioned the client who said he was just expressing his fantasies. The therapist was reprimanded for breaking confidentiality, and he was told to shred all of the information he had from therapy sessions in which these "fantasies" had been expressed. Two months later, the client stabbed Tarasoff to death. Her parents successfully sued the university, arguing that the therapist employed at the counseling center had a duty to warn their daughter.

---

[7] Among other difficult areas concerning confidentiality are how the therapist should respond to court subpoenas, the need to publicly document diagnosis and treatment for insurance reimbursement, the status of shared personal information in group therapy sessions, and the possibility that the police and/or a collection agency might need to be contacted if therapy bills are not paid.

What resulted from this tragic event was a court rule explaining when a therapist has the duty to warn somebody about threats. The situation has to involve a specific person, and the client must be judged dangerous. "I hate men" leads to no duty to warn; "I'm going to poison my husband" is a different matter. Further, the therapist must warn the actual person who is in danger, not simply tell the police or some proxy with no special relationship to the potential victim.

Again, whatever good is served by this rule is balanced by some thorny questions about how to proceed with therapy granted this exception to confidentiality. I am not wise enough to know exactly how such matters should be resolved, but I draw your attention to what is still evolving as a legal and psychotherapeutic issue (cf. Kermani & Drob, 1987).

ABNORMALITY AND CRIME

A different sort of concern takes place when a person with a psychological problem finds himself accused of a crime. The legal systems in the United States and most places around the world recognize that certain psychological problems make it impossible to treat an accused individual in the same manner as an individual without such problems (Maeder, 1985). A person may have committed a crime because of his problem, in which case it makes no sense to find him guilty. Or if a defendant is flagrantly psychotic, it is impossible for him to participate in a defense of the charge. Suppose a person develops a problem after the trial, which makes it difficult to punish him. I now consider these issues in more detail.

INSANITY PLEA

Insanity is not a psychological term but a legal one. Being insane is not equivalent to suffering from a DSM-IV disorder or indeed from any particular problem specified in current diagnostic systems. A psychologist or psychiatrist who testifies in court is not called on to say that a person has a psychological problem, but rather to say that the defendant fits the criteria of insanity as specified by the law. The mental health professional's task would be much easier if insanity were unambiguously defined in terms of particular diagnoses and not others (cf. Ciccone, 1992; Lewis, 1990; Reichlin, Bloom, & Williams, 1993). Instead, a person may be deemed insane in the absence of a DSM-IV diagnosis or sane in the presence of one.

The general idea behind an insanity plea is easy to grasp. According to the legal system's notions of right and wrong, people are responsible for their actions unless there is a reason for them not to be. This means that people are *not* held accountable for the crimes that they commit if there is an extenuating circumstance: Something must counter the argument that they freely undertook the crime in question. Being a minor is one such reason. Being intoxicated is another.[8] Being hit on the head might also be an extenuating circumstance, and having a psychological problem that interferes with a person's ability to be responsible is yet another. Here we have the basis for the **insanity plea**: a defense against an accusation on the grounds that the individual was suffering from a psychological problem at the time the crime was committed.

Different states use different criteria for describing insanity, and they have changed over time (Simon & Aaronson, 1988). These criteria are discussed shortly. The practical import of this variation is that identical individuals acting in the identical way may be treated differently according to where they happen to be. They might find themselves acquitted in one locality by reason of insanity, and being held responsible for their crime in another. Similarly, the same individual will have been handled quite differently over the years. The theoretical point is that the various ways insanity can be defined are less than ideal, otherwise a consensus would have emerged long ago.

The insanity plea becomes even more complex in practice when the defendant suffers from multiple personality disorder. Although some experts are skeptical about the very existence of this disorder (see Chapter 8), recent years have seen an increase in the number of insanity pleas made on its basis (Scott, 1994). Consider the difficult questions this raises. Can different personalities be given different verdicts depending on their degree of participation in the crime in question? What happens if one personality meets the criteria for insanity and another does not? How can a group of personalities be punished for the acts of one or a few?

For example, James Carlson was charged in Arizona with rape. He claimed to be suffering from multiple personality disorder and that only some of his eleven different personalities knew anything about the assault. Each was sworn in separately. His plea was unsuccessful, as it turned out, and all of him was found guilty. In an earlier case, accused rapist Billy Milligan—who also experienced multiple personality disorder—was found not guilty by reason of insanity.

---

[8] Although our society punishes people under some circumstances for being intoxicated—for underage drinking, public drunkenness, drunk driving, and so on—any further crimes they commit while intoxicated are regarded differently, usually as less serious offenses. Thus, if an individual kills someone else while intoxicated, he is likely to be charged with manslaughter rather than murder.

The case of John Hinckley, Jr., shown here flanked by Secret Service agents, sparked widespread discussion of the insanity plea after he shot Ronald Reagan and James Brady.

Many people react very strongly to the notion of the insanity plea, feeling it is simply a way for somebody to get away with criminal conduct. Perhaps some do not understand its intent, which is not to subvert the legal system but rather to maintain its basic premise that only those fully responsible for their acts can be held accountable for them.

This controversy swirled in particular with regard to the case of John Hinckley, Jr., the young man who shot President Reagan, wounding him and three others, including James Brady, the President's press secretary, after whom the Brady Bill for gun control is named. Hinckley was immediately arrested and about 2 years later brought to trial, where he pleaded not guilty by reason of insanity.

Here is what was going on in Hinckley's life prior to the shooting of President Reagan (Caplan, 1984). He was a withdrawn young man, in and out of therapy for various problems. He had developed a fascination with the movie Taxi Driver. *Perhaps he identified with the main character, a taxi driver who was going nowhere in his life until he intervened to rescue a child prostitute (played by actress Jodie Foster) from her pimp, and was acclaimed as a hero. Hinckley fell in love with Jodie Foster and sent her countless letters, poems, and presents, none of which she ever acknowledged. He believed that she needed to be rescued. He thought that if she would fall in love with him, he could rescue her. He further decided that if he were to undertake a great historic deed, then this would sway her to him, as happened after a fashion in the movie. So he shot the President.*

Both the defense and the prosecution presented testimony from mental health experts. There was never an

issue that Hinckley had shot at President Reagan. The attack was documented by a television news camera. The issue was whether he was responsible for what he had done at the time that he did it. Whatever criteria are used to judge insanity, they apply to the moment of the criminal act, which means that in court, the person's state of mind must be reconstructed after the fact.

The prosecution alleged that Hinckley was sane— that is, responsible for his actions—because the sorts of things he did, like drifting about and becoming infatuated with a movie and an actress, were not beyond the pale of many young men in this country. He was pictured as troubled, suffering from mild depression and several personality disorders, but not to the extent that these problems precluded responsibility for his actions. The prosecution further presented Hinckley as immature and a seeker of fame, but still culpable.

The defense presented experts who testified to the contrary, arguing that his problems were much more serious, to the point that they precluded responsibility for his actions. One expert testified that Hinckley's MMPI scores indicated severe psychopathology. Another expert testified that he was suffering from both depression and schizophrenia. Yet another expert argued that Hinckley showed some of the brain anomalies that sometimes characterize schizophrenia (Chapter 12); you know that this is far from a foolproof index, but the evidence was allowed in court.

The defense prevailed, and Hinckley was acquitted by reason of insanity, and sent to a hospital for treatment. Legally, he could have been released from the hospital after 50 days, a fact that no doubt fueled the controversy that then erupted. (In point of fact, Hinckley was not released that soon. At this writing, he is still there. It is perhaps ironic that he would have been eligible for parole from jail long ago had he been found guilty.) People could not understand how a person could shoot the President and then have a chance to walk away free. They had seen the crime on television and expected "justice" to prevail. In point of fact, justice did, but the everyday person's notion of what this means is probably a bit more of the eye-for-an-eye variety than one based on abstract notions of intent and responsibility.

M'Naghten rule   In the contemporary United States, there are three basic rules for determining insanity, introduced at different points in time (see Table 15.1). All still have their adherents, with each prevailing at least someplace in the United States by decree of the appropriate state legislature.

The first of these rules dates to the 1840s, when Daniel M'Naghten attempted to murder the British Prime Minister. As it turned out, he mistakenly shot the secretary of the Prime Minister, but a murder had still been

TABLE 15.1

CRITERIA FOR INSANITY PLEAS *Depending on the jurisdiction, different criteria are used in the United States to determine insanity.*

RULE	CHARACTERIZATION
M'Naghten	At the time of the crime did the person suffer from a problem so that he did not know what he was doing, or did not know that what he was doing was wrong?
Durham	Did the crime result from a mental disease or defect?
American Law Institute	Did the crime result from a mental disease or defect of the person so that he lacked substantial capacity either to appreciate the wrongfulness of his conduct or to conform his conduct to the requirements of law?

committed. In examining the accused, the authorities discovered that M'Naghten heard the voice of God telling him to kill the Prime Minister. Because he suffered from delusions and hallucinations—not the intent to do evil— he was acquitted and sent to an insane asylum, where he lived out the rest of his life.

The decision outraged many people in England, who wanted to see what looked like willful murder be severely punished. Queen Victoria in particular was upset and demanded that a more stringent test of insanity be devised. This test came to be known as the **M'Naghten rule,** and it proposes that the accused can plead insanity only if at the time of the crime he suffered from a defect of reason so that he did not know what he was doing, or did not know that what he was doing was wrong. Applied to Hinckley (or M'Naghten, for that matter), the case would have to be made that either he did not know that he had shot at anyone, or that he did not know shooting someone was wrong.

Recall Jeffrey Dahmer, whose unusual sexual activities were described in Chapter 11. Dahmer killed a number of individuals, and he pleaded not guilty by reason of insanity. However, this plea did not succeed, because the *prosecution was able to argue that he knew what he did was wrong. For example, in the aftermath of the murders, Dahmer took steps to hide the evidence. He once was questioned by the police following the complaints of neighbors that a naked boy was trying to escape from his apartment. Dahmer explained this incident away. So, the conclusion followed that he was not insane while committing his crimes.*

The M'Naghten rule is stringent, as originally intended, and some critics think it is too narrow. It does not allow for the possibility that people may know their action to be wrong yet be unable to resist doing it. In some jurisdictions, this rule is supplemented with an additional consideration allowing the insanity defense if criminal acts were the product of an *irresistable impulse.*

The M'Naghten rule for determining insanity takes its name from the case of Daniel M'Naghten, who in the 1840s attempted to murder the British Prime Minister after he heard the voice of God telling him to do so.

Durham rule   The second major approach to defining insanity is also named after an individual accused of a criminal act.

In 1951, Monte Durham of Washington, D.C., was charged with breaking into a house. He pleaded insanity, but the judge disallowed the plea on the grounds that the M'Naghten rule was not satisfied. Durham was convicted. However, he won an appeal on the grounds that the M'Naghten rule was outmoded because it focused too narrowly on knowledge of right or wrong, and that modern conceptions of psychology recognized that this knowledge was but one of many influences on behavior.

The **Durham rule** embodies this argument, proposing that the insanity plea is justified in cases where the act in question resulted from a *mental disease* or *mental defect.* It is broader than the M'Naghten rule, but it is no easier to apply in the concrete. The definition of mental disease or defect is not a clear one, and it can be overinterpreted. Also, attributing the causes of given behaviors to given aspects of people, specifically to their problematic selves or their nonproblematic selves, is difficult if not meaningless. People behave, not parts of people. Still, the Durham rule has its adherents.

ALI rule   The third rule used to judge insanity is called the **American Law Institute (ALI) rule.** It was proposed by a group that was opposed to both the M'Naghten and Durham rules. The gist of the ALI rule is as follows:

> A person is not responsible for criminal conduct if at the time of such conduct as a result of mental disease or defect he lacks substantial capacity either to appreciate the criminality (wrongfulness) of his conduct or to conform his conduct to the requirements of law.   (American Law Institute, 1962, p. 66)

The ALI rule has subsequently been elaborated and now defines mental disease or defect as a condition that affects thoughts or emotions in such a way that "behavior controls" are impaired—that is, the person cannot control what he or she does (Weiner, 1985). Also, courts have made it clear that the burden of proof for establishing insanity lies with the defense.

The ALI rule explicitly states that we cannot argue for the existence of a mental defect if the only evidence is repeated criminal activity. This gets around the problem that surrounds certain horrible crimes, like those committed by Jeffrey Dahmer, in which we automatically assume that the person who did such things

must be insane. The ALI rule says no, at least not in the technical sense of being excused from a crime on the grounds that virtually no one else would have done it.

This rule is favored by its adherents over the previous ones for determining insanity because it is more flexible. The ALI rule gives the jury or judge latitude to determine whether the term *appreciate* is to be used narrowly to refer to knowledge of wrongfulness as in the M'Naghten rule, or more broadly as in the irresistable impulse corollary. The phrase *substantial capacity* makes it explicit that the influence of mental disease or defect is not to be regarded as an either-or effect but rather something that exists in degrees. This rule does not completely solve all the problems of the previous ones, and critics still point to the fact that applying it requires specific knowledge of technicalities, both psychological and legal. Even so, it is now widely used in the United States.

Guilty but mentally ill?   In the wake of cases like John Hinckley's, there have been calls for a **guilty but mentally ill (GBMI) verdict,** which tries to have it both ways. In other words, we must determine first if a person is sane or insane, then if he or she is guilty or innocent of the criminal act. It is possible for a number of combinations to exist, including insanity *and* guilt, from which this proposed verdict takes its name. An individual who is found guilty of a crime is sentenced for the crime, whether or not that individual is judged to be insane.

As I have been trying to make clear in this section, the GBMI verdict seems a contradiction of terms. If a person is insane, he is not responsible for his actions; how then can he be punished? The GBMI verdict has considerable emotional appeal because it satisfies the public's (mistaken) belief that criminals and their lawyers frequently take advantage of the insanity plea. But the GBMI verdict is unlikely to see wide adoption.

Perhaps more likely in the future is the striking of the insanity plea altogether, as several states have already done. This seems problematic to me, for reasons already explained, but the U.S. Supreme Court has not forbidden states to remove the option represented by the insanity plea.

I have so far touched only upon definitions of insanity and how these have evolved over time. But what about the actual use of the insanity plea? It might be instructive for you to stop and estimate how many trials in the United States involve insanity pleas.

Fewer than 1% of cases in the United States see a defendant offering an insanity plea (Steadman, 1980). In these, only about 25% of the defendants are actually acquitted by virtue of their plea (see Figure

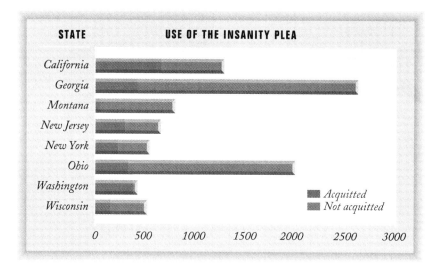

FIGURE 15.4

USE OF THE INSANITY PLEA   *Researchers studied almost 1 million court cases in eight different states, locating 8,953 insanity pleas. This graph shows the number of these cases resulting in acquittal or not.*
SOURCE: DATA DERIVED FROM "THE VOLUME AND CHARACTERISTICS OF INSANITY DEFENSE PLEAS," BY L. A. CALLAHAN, H. J. STEADMAN, M. A. MCGREEVY, AND P. C. ROBBINS, 1991, *Bulletin of the American Academy of Psychiatry and the Law, 19,* PP. 389–393.

15.4); they almost always have a history of psychological problems and warrant a DSM diagnosis, usually schizophrenia (Callahan, Steadman, McGreevy, & Robbins, 1991).

Be that as it may, the insanity plea deserves special attention because it underscores important issues concerning responsibility and abnormality (Szasz, 1963). It sits at the intersection between psychology and the legal system. If an altogether happy resolution seems not to exist, do not be dismayed. As emphasized, psychology on the one hand and the legal system on the other represent very different ways to make sense of what people do. Perhaps it is amazing that they share any common ground at all.

COMPETENCE TO STAND TRIAL

In terms of the sheer numbers of people involved, many more accused individuals in the United States are affected by another psychological/legal decision: whether they are judged **competent to stand trial** (Bacon, 1969). Here there is a question whether the person can understand legal proceedings and is able to contribute to her own defense. As you know from reading thus far, any of a number of psychological problems—from head injury to severe depression to schizophrenia—might make it impossible for a person to stand trial until the problem is resolved.

Competence to stand trial is not a defense against the accusation; it is not a judgment about the person's responsibility for the act in question. Rather, it is a here-and-now judgment, one that is necessary lest trials become something other than the delivery of justice.[9] While waiting to become competent, the person is typically kept at a mental hospital. Bail is not granted. More than 90% of the patients deemed incompetent eventually are judged competent and complete the trial process (Pendleton, 1980).

The actual decision that a person is incompetent to stand trial is the result of an interview much like the one described in Chapter 2 for deciding if an individual has a problem. Focus is on the person's orientation to the present reality—whether she understands the charges against her, how courts work, and so on. A thorny issue emerges here concerning the use of involuntary treatment to establish an individual's competence to stand trial. Some argue that this violates the constitutionally guaranteed right not to bear witness against oneself.

In the past, the judgment of incompetence to stand trial led to a bizarre state of affairs in which defendants might be judged incompetent and then

---

[9] The guiding principle is that defendants should not be tried in absence. Usually this means physical absence, but the point can be extended to include psychological absence as well.

kept in a mental hospital far longer than they would have been incarcerated in jail had they gone to trial and been found guilty (McGarry & Bendt, 1969). Various cases have been documented in which individuals were judged incompetent to stand trial for rather trivial crimes and then were institutionalized for literally decades. In 1972, the Supreme Court made this possibility less likely by ruling that a person cannot be confined indefinitely.

The case in question was a mentally retarded man named Theon Jackson who could neither speak nor hear. He was charged with several robberies—totaling $9 in cash—and then found incompetent to stand trial. Although the maximum sentence he could have received had he gone to trial was 60 days, after more than 3 years he was still hospitalized, no closer to being judged competent than he was when the process began. The Court unanimously agreed that Jackson should be freed, because in effect he was serving a life sentence.

An interesting issue is whether a person judged incompetent to stand trial is in a position to refuse treatment. You have seen that under some circumstances an individual can be allowed to do so. However, the details of these rules make it extremely unlikely that a person already judged incompetent will be allowed to opt out of treatment, because incompetence is one of the exceptions to this right to refuse treatment.

COMPETENCE TO BE PUNISHED

A final area where psychology and the legal system come into contact with one another has to do with the individual who is accused and convicted of a crime, and then—on the verge of punishment—develops a severe psychological problem. At least in principle, this person is deemed incompetent to be punished. The grounds are that the person does not appreciate what is being done to him; hence, this constitutes cruel and unusual treatment.

One way around this problem is probably less satisfactory than first meets the eye. There are so-called *forensic hospitals* for such individuals. The stated rationale is that these facilities exist for treatment, but they still are in effect prisons (Adler, 1980) and are often housed within prison walls. In any event, there is agreement that a large number of incarcerated individuals—perhaps as many as 25%—experience serious psychological disorders (e.g., Steadman, Fabisiak, Dvoskin, & Holohean, 1987).

Another complex matter is what to do when a person has been sentenced to death, but then becomes

A convicted individual who develops severe psychological problems may be deemed incompetent to be punished until the problems resolve. But what happens when the individual has been sentenced to death?

severely troubled (Small & Otto, 1991). In 1986, the Supreme Court ruled that such a person cannot be executed until his problem resolves itself.

In the case of a death row prisoner named Gary Alverod, therapists made a plea that their work could only proceed if his sentence were commuted to life imprisonment (Radelet & Barnard, 1988).

The counterargument, which I find somewhat strained, is that the individual sentenced to death is best served when he is able to participate fully in appeals of his sentence; thus, treatment should be aggressively pursued even when the individual faces capital punishment. Similar issues—perhaps to an even greater degree—arise when a prisoner is mentally retarded (Baroff, 1991).

The psychology of abnormality makes contact with larger social systems, including the community and the legal system. It behooves anyone involved in one of these fields to know something about the others. More generally, the point with which this textbook began—that abnormality must be placed in its social context—is underscored by the discussion in this chapter.

Thank you and good night.

Summary

✦ Abnormality must be located in its social context, and this includes the community and the legal system.

THE COMMUNITY MENTAL HEALTH MOVEMENT

✦ The community mental health movement began with great expectations in the 1960s. One of its goals was to shift the care of people with psychological problems from large state hospitals to smaller clinics in the community. More profoundly, community mental health centers were charged as well with preventing problems from occurring in the first place.

✦ Although the number of patients in psychiatric hospitals in the United States decreased dramatically in the 1970s and 1980s, so too did the number of homeless individuals with psychological problems. Said another way, community mental health centers did not take over from state psychiatric hospitals. The important goal of prevention was largely neglected by the community mental health movement. In recent years, the movement has been moribund. The reasons are subject to debate. Some point to insufficient federal funding, others to the less than efficient way many community mental health centers were run.

PSYCHOLOGY AS A PROFESSION

✦ The American Psychological Association is a national organization that promotes psychology as a profession. To this end, it maintains a code of conduct, evaluates graduate training programs and internships, and takes public stances on issues affecting psychology.

PSYCHOLOGISTS AS EXPERT WITNESSES

✦ Although psychology and the legal system have frequent contact, they embody different ways of understanding human conduct. Psychology assumes that be-

havior has causes; it attempts to offer generalizations about people per se. The legal system, in contrast, assumes that behavior is freely chosen unless there exist extenuating circumstances; it attempts to render decisions about individual persons. Also, the legal system is based on advocacy, whereas psychology as a science is called on to be more even-handed in its explanations and use of evidence.

THE RIGHTS OF THOSE WITH DISORDERS

✦ About 25% of admissions to psychiatric hospitals are involuntary, carried out over the individual's objections. The process of involuntary commitment is done under the supervision of the legal system. It requires that an individual be judged dangerous to the self and/or others. These judgments are far from foolproof, and involuntary commitment is thus controversial.

✦ In recent decades, various rights of psychiatric patients have been recognized. Individuals in hospitals are guaranteed such civil rights as voting and making a will. They have the right to receive treatment as well as the right to refuse it. They are entitled to the least restrictive environment that can be provided. However, these rights can be abridged if exercising them is thought to work against the patient's good.

✦ What clients tell their therapists is usually confidential. Exceptions include child abuse and specific threats against another person. Then the therapist is required to break confidentiality.

ABNORMALITY AND CRIME

✦ A person with a psychological problem who is accused of a crime may plead not guilty by reason of insanity. Insanity is a legal term, not a psychological one, and different criteria for judging insanity have been proposed. Despite the great interest that the insanity plea stimulates, it occurs in only a small fraction of criminal cases.

✦ Much more common is a person being deemed incompetent to stand trial because of a current psychological problem that makes it impossible for him to understand or participate in legal proceedings. Most individuals judged incompetent eventually stand trial.

✦ A person may also be judged incompetent to be punished, which means that by virtue of a psychological problem, he does not understand his sentence. Instead of being sent to a prison, he instead goes to a forensic hospital for treatment; the distinction may exist more in principle than in practice.

Key Terms

American Law Institute
  (ALI) rule

competent to stand trial

determinism

Durham rule

duty to warn

free will

guilty but mentally ill
  (GBMI) verdict

insanity plea

involuntary commitment

M'Naghten rule

partial hospitalization

thank-you test

therapeutic community

GLOSSARY*

acetylcholine neurotransmitter linked to Alzheimer's disease (6)

addiction physical dependence on a psychoactive drug, shown by tolerance and withdrawal (5)

addictive personality hypothesized set of traits that lead people to overindulge their appetites when anxious (5)

agoraphobia fear of being in a situation from which escape is not possible (7)

AIDS dementia complex intellectual impairment caused directly by the AIDS virus (6)

alcoholic according to the biomedical model of abnormality, individual with the disease of alcoholism; more generally, an alcohol abuser (5)

Alcoholics Anonymous; AA self-help group for recovering alcohol abusers (5)

alcoholism according to the biomedical model of abnormality, disease that leads people to abuse alcohol (5)

alexithymia inability to express emotions in words (8)

Alzheimer's disease a progressive neurological disease characterized by forgetfulness, confusion, and loss of ability to care for oneself (6)

American Law Institute (ALI) rule a rule for judging an insanity plea: Did the crime in question result from a mental disease or defect of the person so that he lacked substantial capacity either to appreciate the wrongfulness of his conduct or to conform his conduct to the requirements of law? (15)

amine hypothesis theory that depression results from an insufficiency of norepinephrine and serotonin (9)

amnestic syndrome; organic amnesia memory impairment due to an organic cause (6)

amphetamine synthetic stimulant such as Benzedrine (5)

amphetamine psychosis psychotic state characterizing acute amphetamine intoxication (5)

analogue research investigation of abnormality in the laboratory by creating phenomena analogous to disorders (4)

analysand the recipient of psychoanalytic therapy (3)

anergia lack of energy (9)

anhedonia reduced interest and pleasure in the pursuit of everyday activities (9, 12)

anorexia nervosa eating disorder characterized by refusal to maintain minimal body weight (14)

Antabuse *see* disulfiram

antagonists chemicals that block the effects of psychoactive drugs (5)

antiandrogens drugs such as Depo-Provera that affect the pituitary gland so that the secretion of male sex hormones is inhibited (11)

antibodies substances that destroy or deactivate antigens (10)

antigen any foreign material that invades the body and triggers the immune system (10)

antisocial personality disorder personality disorder involving a long-standing pattern of behaving irresponsibly to others (13)

anxiety complex of reactions to a danger that is unclear and/or diffuse (7)

anxiety disorder problem characterized by diffuse expectations of harm (7)

anxiety sensitivity personality dimension reflecting the degree to which symptoms of anxiety are regarded as threatening (8)

aphasia problem stemming from brain damage and involving inability to express and/or comprehend speech or writing (6)

assessment process of gathering information about a given person in order to make a diagnosis (2)

asthma interference with normal breathing that occurs when the airways leading into the lungs constrict and fill with mucus (10)

attention-deficit/hyperactivity disorder; ADHD disorder marked by high activity level and inability to pay attention (14)

aura (preceding a migraine) warning sign that a person is about to have a migraine headache (6)

aura (preceding a seizure) warning sign that a person is about to have a grand mal seizure (6)

autism; autistic disorder pervasive developmental disorder characterized by gross impairment in social interaction and communication (14)

automatic processing the carrying out of well learned routines, cognitive or behavioral, without awareness (8)

automatic thoughts unbidden and habitual ways of thinking (9)

autonomic nervous system the part of the nervous system that controls heart, lungs, and digestive organs (6)

avoidant personality disorder personality disorder involving widespread and long-standing social discomfort, fear of evaluation, and timidity (13)

Bacchus *see* Dionysus

barbiturates synthetic depressants such as phenobarbital, prescribed to aid sleep (5)

---

*Parenthetical numbers indicate the chapter(s) where terms appear in text.

465

B cell lymphocytes   white blood cells, produced in bone marrow, that secrete antibodies (10)

behavior therapy   therapy techniques based on principles of learning (1, 3)

behavioral assessment   assessment tradition in which the diagnostician attempts to describe people and their problems in terms of actual behavior and the situations in which it occurs (2)

behavioral theory of depression   an explanation of depression proposing that it results from low levels of reward (9)

behaviorism   approach to psychology concerned with overt behavior and processes of learning (1)

Bender Gestalt Test   test developed by Lauretta Bender for measuring brain damage (2)

benign tumor   self-contained tumor, not composed of cancerous cells (10)

benzodiazepine   tranquilizer such as Valium or Librium used to treat anxiety (7)

biofeedback   operant conditioning therapy technique that helps a person learn to control abnormal bodily responses (6)

biomedical model   approach to abnormality that assumes people are physical systems (3)

biomedical therapy   treatment that intervenes biologically (3)

biopsychosocial model   perspective on abnormality that acknowledges the role played by biological, psychological, and social factors (3)

bipolar disorder; manic-depression   mood disorder characterized by the alternation of episodes of depression and mania (9)

Bipolar I disorder   bipolar disorder characterized by unambiguous manic episodes (9)

Bipolar II disorder   bipolar disorder characterized by hypomanic but not manic episodes (9)

blood alcohol content; BAC   percentage of alcohol circulating in the blood (5)

body dysmorphic disorder   preoccupation with an imagined defect in the appearance of a normal-appearing person (8)

borderline personality disorder   personality disorder characterized by instability in mood, relationships, and self-image (13)

Briquet's syndrome   *see* somatization disorder

bulimia nervosa   eating disorder that involves ingesting large amounts of high-calorie food in a short amount of time, feeling out of control while doing so, and then ridding oneself of these calories (14)

buspirone   antianxiety drug that works by targeting serotonin (7)

caffeine   stimulant found in coffee, tea, and chocolate (5)

cancer   a group of diseases characterized by uncontrollable growth of cells (10)

cardiovascular diseases   diseases of the heart and circulatory system (10)

case study   intensive investigation of a single individual (4)

CAT scan; computerized axial tomography   device for making three-dimensional X-ray pictures of the brain (2)

catatonic behavior   grossly inappropriate bodily movement or posture (12)

catatonic schizophrenia   subtype of schizophrenia characterized by prominent catatonic behavior (12)

catharsis   the beneficial effects of speaking about long repressed conflicts (1)

central nervous system   the brain and spinal cord (6)

cerebral cortex   the very outer layer of the brain (6)

cerebral hemispheres   the two symmetric structures that comprise the cerebral cortex (6)

chiropractic medicine   treatment of illness by manipulating bones and joints (10)

chlorpromazine   drug frequently used to treat schizophrenia (12)

clang association   characteristic of schizophrenic speech: stringing together rhyming words not otherwise associated (12)

classical conditioning   process by which people learn to associate particular emotional reactions to previously neutral stimuli (3)

client   recipient of psychotherapy (3)

client-centered therapy   humanistic treatment devised by Carl Rogers (3)

clinical psychologist   therapist with advanced training in psychology (3)

clinical syndrome   an acute problem that brings a person into treatment (2)

clozapine   drug used to treat both positive and negative symptoms of schizophrenia (12)

cocaine   stimulant derived from the leaves of the coca plant (5)

codependency   relationship between substance abuser and another person, in which substance abuse is maintained because of the tacit aid and encouragement of the other person (5)

cognitive assessment   assessment tradition in which the diagnostician attempts to describe people and their problems in terms of the contents and styles of thinking that create or maintain difficulties (2)

cognitive-behavior therapy   approach to therapy that combines behavioral and cognitive techniques (3)

cognitive-behavioral model   approach to abnormality that assumes people are information-processing systems (3)

cognitive disorder   DSM-IV term for a problem involving an alteration in consciousness or cognition to which biological factors contribute (6)

cognitive theory of depression   explanation of depression proposing that it results from thinking negatively about the self, the world, and the future (9)

cognitive therapy   approach to therapy that targets thoughts and beliefs for change (3, 9)

cohort differences   psychological differences among groups of people born at different times and places (14)

coma   complete loss of consciousness and responsiveness to environmental stimuli (6)

community psychology   the application of psychological knowledge in community settings to prevent problems (3)

competent to stand trial   the judgment that an individual can understand legal proceedings and contribute to his own defense (15)

complex   constellation of feelings and impulses that influence behavior somewhat independently of the other aspects of a person (8)

compulsion   repetitive act intentionally carried out in a stereotyped manner in order to prevent or neutralize some dreaded consequence (7)

computerized axial tomography   *see* CAT scan

conditioning   the learning of simple associations (7)

conduct disorder   disorder in which a child is socially disruptive and upsetting to others (14)

confabulation   symptom of Korsakoff's syndrome: the filling in of memory gaps with imaginary events (6)

confound   an unmeasured variable responsible for the apparent relationship between two other variables (4)

containment   *see* secondary prevention

controlled drinking   therapeutic approach to alcohol abuse, in which the abuser is taught to drink in moderation (5)

conversion disorder; hysteria   alteration or loss of physical functioning that suggests a bodily cause but instead is an expression of a psychological conflict or need (8)

coprolalia   symptom of Tourette's syndrome: the involuntary blurting out of obscene words (6)

correlation coefficient   quantitative measure of the degree to which two variables show a linear relationship (4)

correlational investigation   study of the relationship between two variables in a sample of research subjects (4)

couples therapy; marital therapy   treatment of a couple as a unit (3)

crack   potent and inexpensive form of cocaine produced by free-basing (5)

crack baby   baby born to a mother addicted to crack cocaine (14)

crisis intervention   strategy of secondary prevention that helps people resolve life crises (3)

cross-cultural psychopathology   the field that investigates problems in their cultural context (1)

cross-tolerance   tolerance to a psychoactive drug due to the repeated use of another psychoactive drug (5)

culture-bound syndrome   disorder occurring only within a specific culture (2)

curanderas   individuals in Mexican-American communities who heal mental and physical distress (1)

cyclothymic disorder   a moderate version of bipolar disorder, in which the person alternates between mild depression and hypomania (9)

defense mechanism   strategy deployed by the ego that protects the person from unpleasant realities (3)

delirium   global impairment of thinking marked in particular by inability to pay attention (6)

delirium tremens; DTs   extreme form of withdrawal from alcohol, characterized by sweating, shaking, irritability, seizures, hallucinations, confusion, and disorientation (5, 6)

delusion   a patently false belief (12)

delusional disorder; paranoid disorder   a type of abnormality marked by a persistent, nonbizarre delusion, not due to any other type of psychological abnormality, such as schizophrenia (12)

dementia   global impairment of cognitive functioning marked in particular by problems with memory (6)

demonology   the assumption that people can be "taken over" by a spirit or deity, which causes them to act in unusual ways (1)

dependent personality disorder   personality disorder in which the individual shows a widespread and long-standing pattern of being dependent on and submissive to others (9, 13)

depersonalization disorder   recurrent and distressing feeling that one is an outside observer of one's own thoughts or actions (8)

depressants   psychoactive drugs that reduce awareness of external stimuli and slow down bodily functions (5)

depression   *see* depressive disorder

depressive disorder; unipolar disorder; depression   mood disorder characterized by episodes of excessive and inappropriate sadness as well as a variety of other symptoms (9)

depressive schema   constellation of negative beliefs and tendencies to process information in ways that maintain these beliefs, thought to cause depression (9)

derealization   alteration of perception so that the external world no longer seems real (8)

determinism   philosophical assumption that what people do has causes (15)

detoxification   letting a psychoactive drug clear the user's body (5)

developmental psychopathology   the field that studies disorders in their developmental context (14)

Dexedrine   stimulant used to treat ADHD (14)

diagnosis   placing people in categories according to the problems they have (2)

diagnostic interview   interview with an individual with the goal of diagnosing his or her problem (2)

diathesis-stress model   model of abnormality that views problems as resulting from a preexisting state of the person (the diathesis) coupled with an environmental event (the stress) (3)

dimensional classification   description of people's problems along continuous dimensions, in "how much" terms rather than "either-or" terms (2)

Dionysus; Bacchus   Greek god of wine (5)

disorganized schizophrenia   subtype of schizophrenia characterized by incoherence, loose associations, and inappropriate affect, without systematized delusions or hallucinations (12)

dispositional optimism   the general expectation that good events will be plentiful in the future (10)

dissociation   a splitting of consciousness into two or more discrete streams, with little or no communication between or among them (8)

dissociative amnesia   sudden inability to recall personally important information following psychological trauma (6, 8)

dissociative disorder   type of abnormality characterized by breaks in memory, consciousness, and/or identity without a physical cause (8)

dissociative fugue   loss of personal memory, travel away from home, and establishment of a new identity following psychological trauma (8)

dissociative identity disorder   *see* multiple personality disorder

disulfiram; Antabuse   drug that results in severe nausea and feelings of impending death when combined with even a single drink (5)

dopamine   neurotransmitter linked to schizophrenia and Parkinson's disease (6)

dopamine hypothesis   theory that schizophrenia is caused by excess activity of the neurotransmitter dopamine (12)

double-blind design   research design in which participants—both patients and therapists—are kept in the dark as to who is given a placebo and who is given the experimental treatment (4)

Down syndrome   common form of organic retardation, caused by the presence of an extra set of genes on the 21st chromosome (14)

DSM-IV; *Diagnostic and Statistical Manual of Mental Disorders, Fourth Edition*   diagnostic system published in 1994 by the American Psychiatric Association that is widely used in the United States (2)

Durham rule   a rule for judging an insanity plea: Did the crime in question result from the person's mental disease or mental defect? (15)

duty to warn   therapist's obligation to warn people that a client has made specific threats against their life (15)

dyspareunia   recurrent pain in the genitals before, during, or after sexual activity (11)

dysthymic disorder   mild yet chronic form of depression (9)

early morning awakening   *see* terminal insomnia

echolalia   symptom of autism: echoing back whatever is said, rather than responding to it (14)

eclectic therapist   therapist who subscribes to no specific approach to treatment but rather tries to take something useful from all treatments (3)

ego   mental structure that takes into account external reality (3)

ego psychologists   theorists who propose theories similar to Freud's but who place more emphasis on the ego as an active—not reactive—entity (3)

electroconvulsive shock therapy; ECT   treatment for depression in which a brief electric current is passed through the brain of an individual in order to induce a convulsion (9)

emergency reaction   response of the body to threat (7)

endocrine system   set of glands that secrete hormones (6)

endogenous depression   form of unipolar disorder characterized by somatic symptoms, psychomotor retardation, loss of interest in life, and lack of responsiveness to the environment (9)

endorphins   opiates produced by the brain, which play an important role in the body's attempt to relieve pain (5, 7)

epilepsy   neurological disorder characterized by seizures (6)

errors in logic   slipshod ways of thinking that keep negative beliefs immune to reality (9)

estrogen   a class of female sex hormones (11)

ethnic group   collection of individuals who share the same culture and regard themselves as belonging to the same involuntary group (5)

ethyl alcohol   active ingredient in all alcoholic beverages (5)

etiology   factors that have led up to a problem (2)

excitation   process by which one neuron causes another neuron to fire (6)

existentialism   doctrine that a person's experience is primary, that existence precedes essence (1, 3)

exogenous depression   *see* reactive depression

exorcism   procedure for inducing a demon to leave a body it has possessed (1)

experiment   investigation in which certain events are deliberately manipulated and the effects of these manipulations on other events are measured (4)

experimental psychopathology   investigation of abnormality through experimentation (4)

explanatory style a person's characteristic way of explaining the causes of events (9, 10)

expressed emotion; EE degree to which family members are emotionally overinvolved and excessively critical of one another (12)

extrapyramidal symptoms common side effects of antipsychotic medication, akin to the movement disturbances that characterize Parkinson's disease (12)

factitious disorder faking the signs of illness for no reason except to receive medical attention (8)

family assessment assessment tradition in which the diagnostician attempts to describe people and their problems in the context of their marriage or family (2)

family resemblance set of attributes that tend to cut across examples of a concept (1)

family systems model approach to abnormality that takes the position that all problems reflect disturbances in the family (3)

family therapy treatment of a family as a whole (3)

fear complex of reactions—emotional, cognitive, physiological, and behavioral—shown in response to threat (7)

fear disorder problem characterized by expectations of specific harm (7)

female orgasmic disorder; inhibited female orgasm persistent delay or absence of orgasm in a woman following normal sexual excitement and sexual activity judged "adequate" to produce orgasm (11)

female sexual arousal disorder persistent failure to attain or maintain the lubrication-swelling of sexual excitement until sexual activity is complete and/or a persistant lack of a sense of excitement or pleasure during sexual activity (11)

feminist therapy intervention informed by feminist philosophy (3)

fenfluramine an amphetamine that reduces the level of serotonin in the blood, used as a treatment for autism (14)

fetal alcohol syndrome complex of characteristics seen among children born to alcoholic mothers: small size, heart and limb defects, distinctive facial features, and mental retardation (14)

fixation in psychoanalytic theory, failure to resolve a particular stage of psychosexual development, so that the concerns of that stage show up in adult personality (3, 7)

flat affect lack of expressed emotion (12)

flight of ideas symptom of mania in which the person changes the topic of conversation from one to another to still another with great rapidity (9)

flooding behavior therapy technique for treating fear and anxiety in which the individual is exposed repeatedly to the objects or situations of which he or she is afraid (7)

fluoxetine *see* Prozac

focal seizure; partial seizure seizure that disrupts the functioning of only part of the brain (6)

forebrain top layer of the brain (6)

free association Freud's technique for unearthing unconscious conflicts; the person says whatever comes to mind without censorship (1)

free-floating anxiety anxiety divorced from given events and circumstances (7)

free will philosophical assumption that what people do represents their own choice (15)

frontal lobes brain structures located at the very front of the cortex and involved in the ability to plan ahead and anticipate the consequences of acts (6)

functional disorder problem resulting from abnormal experience imposed on normal brain structure and function (6)

GABA (gamma-amino-butyric acid) neurotransmitter involved in anxiety (7)

gastroesophagal reflux passage of gastric juice upward from the stomach into the esophagus, where it creates a burning sensation (10)

gastrointestinal disorders problems of the gastrointestinal system (10)

gate-control theory an account of pain suggesting that its experience is regulated by as yet undiscovered "gates" in the spinal cord (8)

gender identity whether the self is experienced as male or female (11)

gender identity disorder disorder characterized by a discrepancy between gender identity and anatomical sex (11)

gender reassignment surgery surgical treatment for transsexualism, in which male or female genitals are respectively refashioned into female or male genitals (11)

general adaptation syndrome description of the stages involved in an organism's general reaction to any stressor: mobilization of resources, attempts to fight off the effects of the stressor, and—if resistance is unsuccessful—the depletion of resources and reduction of resilience to new stressors (10)

general paresis progressive paralysis and loss of intellectual ability caused by untreated syphilis (1, 6)

generalized anxiety disorder; GAD excessive and unrealistic anxiety that cuts across a variety of life domains (7)

generalized convulsive epilepsy *see* grand mal epilepsy

generalized nonconvulsive epilepsy *see* petit mal epilepsy

generalized seizure seizure that disrupts the functioning of the entire brain (6)

germ theory hypothesis that germs are necessary and sufficient causes of illness (1, 10)

gestalt therapy humanistic-existential treatment devised by Frederick (Fritz) Perls (3)

grand mal epilepsy; generalized convulsive epilepsy   form of epilepsy marked by highly dramatic, generalized seizures lasting several minutes (6)

group therapy   treatment of a group of people not related by blood or marriage (3)

guilty but mentally ill (GBMI) verdict   a controversial court verdict that allows a person to be judged both insane and guilty of a crime (15)

hallucination   sensory experience that no one else confirms or supports (12)

hallucinogens   psychedelics that produce hallucinations (5)

Halstead-Reitan Neuropsychological Battery   a well known set of neuropsychological tests (2)

hardiness   ability to find meaning and challenge in the demands of life (10)

hashish   psychoactive drug derived from resin that exudes from the hemp plant (5)

Helicobacter pylori   bacterium that causes duodenal ulcers (10)

helping alliance   relationship between the therapist and client in which they see each other as working toward the same goal (4)

heritability   degree to which variation in behavior across people has a basis in variation in genes (3)

heroic medicine   term used to describe medical practice during the 1700s and 1800s, when "heroic" interventions like bleeding and purging were routinely undertaken to cure disease (1, 10)

heroin   narcotic derived from morphine (5)

hindbrain   bottom layer of the brain (6)

hippocampus   structure of the forebrain thought to be involved in processing memories (6)

histrionic personality disorder; hysterical personality disorder   personality disorder marked by excessive emotionality and attention-seeking (8, 13)

homeopathy   treatment of illness by administering minute amounts of various drugs (10)

humanism   doctrine that the needs and values of human beings take precedence over material things (1, 3)

humoural theory   age-old account of illness that traces different diseases to imbalances among different bodily fluids—or humours (1)

Huntington's chorea   progressive neurological disease caused by a single dominant gene and characterized by bizarre movements and dementia (6)

hypnosis   state of consciousness characterized by increased suggestibility (8)

hypoactive sexual desire disorder   persistent lack of desire for sexual activity (11)

hypochondriasis   preoccupation with having or contracting serious disease, in the absence of any medical reason (8)

hypomania   subdued version of a manic episode, in which the person shows an elevated mood and an increase in energy without any impairment in functioning (9)

hypothalamus   brain structure that links the nervous system and the endocrine system (6)

hysteria   *see* conversion disorder

hysterical personality disorder   *see* histrionic personality disorder

id   mental structure containing irrational and emotional impulses (3)

identified patient   according to the family systems approach, person who shows family problems most blatantly (3)

imipramine   antidepressant used to treat panic (7)

immune system   the body's defense against foreign material, such as germs (6, 10)

immunosuppression   sluggish or nonexistent response of the immune system to an antigen (10)

incidence   rate of new cases of a disorder in a given period of time for a population (3)

inhalants   volatile substances such as glue, paint, and gasoline whose fumes can be inhaled to produce intoxication (5)

inhibited female orgasm   *see* female orgasmic disorder

inhibited male orgasm   *see* male orgasmic disorder

inhibition   the process by which one neuron causes another neuron not to fire (6)

insanity plea   defense against an accusation on the grounds that the individual suffered from a psychological problem at the time the crime was committed (15)

insight   bringing of conflicts and motives into awareness (3)

intelligence quotient; IQ   numerical estimate of intelligence derived from an intelligence test; traditionally, the quotient of mental age to chronological age, multiplied by 100 (2, 14)

interactionism   the position that people's personality traits and their settings interact to determine what they do (13)

International Classification of Diseases; ICD   World Health Organization's diagnostic system of medical and psychological problems (2)

interpersonal psychotherapy   a therapy for depression that focuses on interpersonal issues and conflicts in order to help the individual get along better with other people (9)

intoxication   alteration in consciousness following ingestion of a psychoactive drug (5, 6)

involuntary commitment   admission to a psychiatric hospital against an individual's will (15)

irritable bowel syndrome; IBS   problem of the large intestine characterized by abdominal pain, disturbed defecation, and bloating or feelings of a distended abdomen (10)

John Henryism personality variable reflecting the degree to which a person believes that all events in life can be controlled solely through hard work and determination (10)

kappa statistic used to measure the degree of agreement between diagnosticians, correcting for chance (2)

Korsakoff's syndrome a form of memory loss accompanying severe alcoholism, and caused by thiamine deficiency (6)

la belle indifference in conversion disorder, lack of concern on the part of the individual regarding his or her physical symptoms (8)

learned helplessness maladaptive passivity that may follow exposure to uncontrollable aversive events (9)

learning disorders difficulties encountered with acquiring or performing a specific skill relevant to reading, writing, and arithmetic (14)

lithium naturally occurring salt that controls both manic and depressive episodes of the bipolar individual (9)

lobotomy surgical procedure in which nerve fibers connecting the frontal lobes of the brain to the thalamus are severed, formerly used to treat schizophrenia (12)

longitudinal design study that follows research participants over time (4)

loose association difficult to follow transition between two topics (12)

lovemap hypothesized biological and psychological entity that functions as the "grammar" of sexual activity (11)

LSD (lysergic acid diethylamide) potent synthetic hallucinogen (5)

Luria-Nebraska Neuropsychological Battery a well known set of neuropsychological tests (2)

magic special arts thought to liberate the immaterial forces of nature; magic includes certain words or spells, substances, and symbols (1)

magnetic resonance imaging; MRI imaging technique relying on magnetism to ascertain neurological structure and function (2)

mainstreaming the practice of educating those with mental retardation in the same schools as other children, and often in the same classrooms (14)

male erectile disorder persistent failure to attain or maintain an erection until sexual activity is complete and/or a persistent lack of a sense of excitement or pleasure during sexual activity (11)

male orgasmic disorder; inhibited male orgasm persistent delay or absence of orgasm in a man following normal sexual excitement and sexual activity judged "adequate" to produce orgasm (11)

malignant tumor tumor comprising cancerous cells (10)

malingering intentional faking of physical symptoms in order to achieve some specific goal (8)

mania enhanced mood and inappropriate sense of well-being (9)

manic-depression *see* bipolar disorder

MAO inhibitors class of antidepressant medication that presumably works by inhibiting monamine oxidase, the enzyme responsible for breaking down norepinephrine (9)

marijuana psychoactive drug derived from the leaves and flowers of the hemp plant (5)

marital therapy *see* couples therapy

mass hysteria individuals in a large group all showing the same groundless somatic complaint (8)

matching models specification of which therapies work best for which problems (4)

mechanism process by which risk factors translate into disorders (3)

medial forebrain bundle the part of the brain involved in reward (9)

medical model explanation of abnormality in terms of bodily injuries, illnesses, and/or defects (1)

medicine man *see* shaman

melancholic depression form of unipolar disorder dominated by bodily symptoms that are most severe in the morning (9)

mental retardation problem first evident during childhood in which an individual displays below average intellectual functioning and impaired ability to meet demands of everyday life (14)

mental status exam part of a diagnostic interview, in which the diagnostician attempts to guage an individual's present psychological state (2)

mescaline hallucinogen derived from the peyote cactus (5)

mesmerism techniques for redistributing animal magnetism, known today as hypnotism (1)

meta-analysis statistical technique that combines quantitatively the results of separate experimental studies (4)

metastasis the spread of cancer cells throughout the body (10)

methadone synthetic narcotic often used in substitution therapy (5)

methaqualone synthetic depressant similar in its effects to barbiturates (5)

midbrain middle layer of the brain (6)

midrange theory explanation of abnormality that does not attempt to be generally applicable (3)

migraine recurrent headache marked by throbbing and pulsating pain and usually accompanied by other characteristic symptoms (6)

milieu therapy the organization of a total treatment system to facilitate improvement of individuals (12)

mind-body dualism philosophical doctrine that minds and bodies are separate realms with little or no influence on one another (10)

mind cure a popular movement in the 1800s based on the premise that all human ills, including mental and physical distress, could be eradicated if people simply thought in the correct way (1)

minimal brain damage; MBD subtle neurological damage once thought to be the cause of learning disorders (14)

Minnesota Multiphasic Personality Inventory; MMPI a well known personality inventory used to aid diagnosis (2)

M'Naghten rule a rule for judging an insanity plea: At the time of the crime did the person suffer from a problem so that he did not know what he was doing, or did not know that what he was doing was wrong? (15)

modeling process by which people learn new behaviors by watching others perform them (3, 7)

mood disorders problems marked by alterations in mood (9)

moral treatment reforms occurring in the 1800s based on the idea that people with psychological abnormality should be treated in a moral and humane fashion (1)

Morita psychotherapy Japanese treatment for anthropophobia (8)

morphine narcotic derived from opium (5)

multiaxial classification description of people and their problems in several simultaneous ways (2)

multi-infarct (MI) dementia; vascular dementia form of dementia caused by multiple strokes occurring over time (6)

multiple personality disorder; MPD; dissociative identity disorder existence within the same person of two or more distinct personalities—each with its own enduring and characteristic style—that alternate in taking full control of the person's behavior (8)

multiple regression correlational procedure that ascertains the associations between a set of variables and another variable in a sample of research subjects (4)

multiple sclerosis; MS progressive neurological disease in which myelin deteriorates (6)

myelin white, fatty substance that covers and protects some neurons, allowing them to send their messages more rapidly (6)

myth of mental illness term popularized by Thomas Szasz, who argued that psychological abnormality is *not* an illness but instead a problem in living (1)

narcissistic personality disorder a personality disorder characterized by a pervasive grandiosity about the self, hypersensitivity to what others think, and a lack of empathy (13)

narcotics; opiates; opioids opium and its derivatives, such as morphine and heroin (5)

natural killer (NK) cells cells that directly kill cells infected with viruses as well as cancerous cells (10)

negative symptoms (of schizophrenia) flat affect, anhedonia, and social withdrawal (12)

neo-Freudians theorists who follow Freud and are influenced by him, but who stress psychological and social determinants of behavior more than biological determinants (1, 3)

neologism a coined word (12)

nervous system the brain and network of nerve cells throughout the entire body (6)

neurology subfield of medicine concerned with diseases and disorders of the nervous system (1)

neuron an individual nerve cell (6)

neuropsychological assessment assessment tradition in which the diagnostician attempts to describe people and their problems in terms of the brain and nervous system (2)

neurotic disorder problem marked by excessive anxiety, avoidance of problems rather than confrontation, and self-defeating tendencies (2, 7)

neuroticism; trait anxiety tendency to be generally nervous or not (7)

neurotransmitter chemical secreted by one neuron that affects another neuron (3, 6)

nicotine stimulant found in tobacco (5)

nonspecific factor ingredient in successful therapy characterizing no given approach to therapy (4)

norepinephrine neurotransmitter linked to depression (6, 9)

nosophobia simple phobia concerning illness (8)

obesity excess accumulation of body fat, conventionally defined as some percentage—like 20%—in excess weight over what is considered average for a person of a given sex, age, and height (14)

object relations mental representations people have of themselves and others (3, 13)

objective test diagnostic procedure in which test scores are assigned according to explicit rules (2)

obsession persistent idea, thought, impulse, or image that the individual experiences as intrusive, senseless, and disquieting (7)

obsessive-compulsive disorder; OCD disorder characterized by obsessions and/or compulsions (7)

obsessive-compulsive personality disorder personality disorder characterized by perfectionism and inflexibility (13)

operant conditioning process by which people learn to associate responses with their consequences (3)

operational definition concrete measure of an abstract concept (1, 4)

opiates *see* narcotics

opioids *see* narcotics

opium psychoactive drug derived from the juice of the poppy (5)

organic amnesia   *see* amnestic syndrome

organic disorder   psychological problem caused by physical injury, illness, or defect (6)

organic personality syndrome   lasting change in personality following neurological damage (6)

organic retardation   mental retardation clearly linked to a specific illness, injury, or physiological abnormality (14)

organic syndrome   cluster of symptoms caused by neurological damage or dysfunction (6)

Ortgeist   intellectual spirit of a particular culture (4)

outcome research   investigation of the effectiveness of treatment (4)

overdetermined behavior   psychoanalytic assumption that even the most simple action has numerous causes (3)

pain disorder   preoccupation with pain in the absence of an adequate physical basis for it (8)

panic disorder   problem characterized by recurrent attacks of panic: discrete periods of intense fear (7)

paradoxical intervention   family therapy technique in which the therapist communicates the message "don't change" in such a way that in resisting the intervention, the family indeed changes (3)

paranoid disorder   *see* delusional disorder

paranoid personality disorder   personality disorder marked by the pervasive yet unwarranted belief that other people intend to do one harm (13)

paranoid schizophrenia   subtype of schizophrenia characterized by prominent and systematized delusions, or frequent auditory hallucinations centering on the same theme (12)

paraphilia   preferred or exclusive sexual activity with an inappropriate individual or in an inappropriate fashion (11)

parasympathetic nervous system   the part of the autonomic nervous system that counteracts arousal (6)

Parkinson's disease   progressive neurological disease characterized by a tremor, rigid muscles, and an expressionless face (6)

partial hospitalization   provision of care to a person who does not need round-the-clock hospitalization, yet needs more care than weekly or monthly visits to a therapist (15)

partial seizure   *see* focal seizure

patient   recipient of biomedical therapy (3)

peptic ulcer   lesion in the stomach or duodenum (10)

peripheral nervous system   the part of the nervous system that links the central nervous system to the muscles, glands, and sensory organs (6)

personality disorder   inflexible and maladaptive style of behaving (2, 13)

personality inventory   a set of objective tests that attempts to measure the range of important individual differences (2)

personological assessment   assessment tradition in which the diagnostician attempts to describe people and their problems in rich and complex ways (2)

PET scan; positron emission tomography   device for revealing patterns of metabolic activity in the brain (2)

petit mal epilepsy; generalized nonconvulsive epilepsy   form of epilepsy marked by generalized seizures lasting only several seconds (6)

phagocytes   cells that literally "eat" (or engulf) foreign material (10)

phencyclidine; PCP   synthetic hallucinogen originally used as a surgical anesthetic and analgesic (5)

phenomenology   description of an individual's conscious experience in terms that are meaningful for that individual (1, 3)

pituitary gland   the so-called master gland, which influences the secretions of many other glands (6)

placebo effect   benefit due to expectations on the part of the therapist and/or the person with the problem (4)

polygraph   the so-called lie detector; a device for measuring emotional arousal (2)

polymorphous perversity   Freud's term for the highly generalized sexuality of young children, who presumably can and do receive sexual arousal through the stimulation of many bodily parts (11)

polysubstance dependence   use by a person of more than one drug at a time (5)

popular health movement   18th-century social movement urging people to take responsibility for their own health by learning more about their bodies and how to treat them (10)

population   the larger group to which results of a research investigation are intended to apply (4)

positive symptoms (of schizophrenia)   flagrant signs of psychosis, such as hallucinations, delusions, and disordered thinking (12)

positron emission tomography   *see* PET scan

post-traumatic stress disorder; PTSD   disorder that follows the experience of a highly traumatic event, characterized by reexperiencing the event, avoiding reminders of the event, numbing of general responsiveness, and feeling anxious (7)

premature ejaculation   persistent ejaculation with minimal sexual stimulation and before the person wishes it (11)

premenstrual syndrome; PMS   physical and psychological symptoms that occur during the late luteal phase of a woman's menstrual cycle (9)

prepared learning   learning predisposed by the evolutionary history of a species (7)

pressured speech   symptom of mania in which the person is unable to control his flow of words (9)

prevalence   percentage of people in a population who have a disorder at a particular time (3)

primary appraisal   the individual's assessment of what is at stake when a stressful event occurs (10)

primary prevention   preventive intervention intended to eliminate the basic causes of problems (3)

process schizophrenia   type of schizophrenia in which symptoms come over a person gradually, with no obvious precipitant (12)

progestin   a class of female sex hormones (11)

prognosis   the likely outcome of a problem (2)

projective test   diagnostic procedure that asks clients to respond to ambiguous stimuli (2)

pronominal reversal   symptom of autism: substituting *you* for *I* (14)

Prozac; fluoxetine   antidepressant medication that presumably works by keeping the neurons that secrete serotonin from reabsorbing it (9)

psilocybin   hallucinogen derived from a particular species of mushroom (5)

psychedelics   psychoactive drugs touted by their users as "consciousness-expanding" (5)

psychiatrist   therapist with training in medicine (3)

psychoactive drugs   chemicals that affect brain activity and thereby the nature of consciousness (5)

psychoanalysis   Freud's theory and therapy that stress the importance of unconscious conflicts in causing problems (1)

psychoanalyst   therapist with training in a given field— say clinical psychology or psychiatry—and additional education at a special institute that teaches psychoanalysis (3)

psychoanalytic model   approach to abnormality proposed by Sigmund Freud that assumes people are energy systems (3)

psychodynamic theories   group of theories proposed by those who followed Freud and were concerned with explaining the workings of the mind (3)

psychological factors affecting medical condition   DSM-IV term used to describe psychological factors coinciding in time with the beginning or worsening of a physical illness (10)

psychometric assessment   assessment tradition in which the diagnostician attempts to describe people and their problems along carefully defined dimensions using standardized questionnaires (2)

psychomotor epilepsy   *see* temporal-lobe epilepsy

psychoneuroimmunology   field that studies the interrelations among psychological factors, the nervous system, and the immune system (6, 10)

psychophysiological assessment   assessment tradition in which the diagnostician attempts to describe people and their problems in terms of physical systems (2)

psychosexual stages   according to Freud, stages through which children pass during development, defined by the part of the body that provides gratification of the sexual instinct (3)

psychosomatic disorders   physical illnesses influenced by psychological factors (8, 10)

psychotherapy   treatment that intervenes psychologically (3)

psychotic disorder   problem in which the person's ability to test reality is impaired (2)

reactive depression; exogenous depression   form of unipolar disorder *not* characterized by the symptoms that mark endogenous depression (9)

reactive schizophrenia   type of schizophrenia in which symptoms occur suddenly to a person, in response to some stressful event in the environment (12)

real relationship   aspects of client-therapist interaction that reflect the facts of their practical existence in the real world (4)

reciprocal determinism   Albert Bandura's idea that people and the environment mutually influence each other (3)

reframing intervention   family therapy intervention in which the therapist encourages a more benign interpretation of what is going on in the family (3)

rehabilitation   therapy that helps the individual compensate for loss of certain abilities by development of new ones (6)

relapse prevention   attempt to prevent a return to drug abuse following treatment (5)

reliability   degree to which an operationalization yields the same results on different occasions (4)

reliability (of a diagnostic system)   degree to which different diagnosticians arrive at the same diagnosis for an individual (2)

repression   the active keeping of material in the unconscious (7)

repression-sensitization   personality dimension reflecting a person's habitual response to disturbing occurrences; repressors tend to ignore these, whereas sensitizers tend to pay particular attention to them (8)

research design   overall structure of a research investigation and its elements (4)

research diagnostic criteria   explicit rules to be used in diagnosing patients for inclusion (and exclusion) in research studies (2, 4)

residual schizophrenia   subtype of schizophrenia used to describe individuals who at one time met the diagnostic criteria for schizophrenia but at the present time no longer do—continuing, however, to evidence mild signs of some schizophrenic symptoms (12)

risk factor   event or characteristic that makes a specific disorder more likely (3)

Ritalin   stimulant used to treat ADHD (14)

Rorschach Inkblot Test   well known projective test consisting of a series of symmetric inkblots (2)

sample   the individuals actually studied in a research investigation (4)

schema   organized set of beliefs about some subject (3, 7)

schizoaffective disorder   type of abnormality in which the individual satisfies the criteria for a depressive or manic episode as well as the criteria for a psychotic episode (12)

schizoid personality disorder   personality disorder marked by widespread indifference to other people and restricted range of emotional experience and expression (13)

schizophrenia   type of abnormality characterized by false sensations, perceptions, and beliefs, a disorganized style of thinking, and neglect of the basics of living (12)

schizophrenia spectrum disorders   the range of disorders that appear related to schizophrenia (12)

schizophreniform disorder   type of abnormality characterized by schizophrenic-like symptoms that last for less than 6 months (12)

schizotypal personality disorder   personality disorder characterized by peculiarities in thoughts, actions, and appearance (13)

scientific model   deliberately simplified version of some phenomenon created to facilitate scientific theorizing and research (3)

seasonal affective disorder; SAD   form of mood disorder in which moods show a regular relationship to the season, worsening in winter and lifting in summer (9)

secondary appraisal   the individual's assessment of the resources at her disposal for meeting demands of a stressful event (10)

secondary gain   achievement of reward or avoidance of punishment because of a symptom (8)

secondary prevention; containment   preventive intervention intended to control problems before they become more serious (3)

seizure   uncontrolled and disorganized firing of a large number of neurons in the brain (6)

self-actualization   according to humanistic psychologists, inherent tendency of people to make the most of their potential (3)

sensate focus   sex therapy technique that encourages the couple to stop paying attention to worries and stress—often about sexual performance—and instead focus on sensual pleasure (11)

separation anxiety disorder   anxiety disorder of childhood characterized by excessive anxiety about being separated from a caretaker (i.e., parent) and/or familiar surroundings (14)

serotonin   neurotransmitter hypothesized to be involved in depression, some cases of autism, and perhaps schizophrenia (6, 9, 12, 14)

sex therapy   psychotherapy for sexual dysfunction (11)

sexology   scientific study of sex (11)

sexual aim   what an individual wishes to do with the sexual object (11)

sexual aversion disorder   persistent aversion or avoidance of sexual contact with a partner (11)

sexual dysfunctions   sexual inabilities: problems with sexual desire, excitement, activity, and/or orgasm (11)

sexual object   the person or thing that an individual finds sexually arousing (11)

sexual orientation   an individual's sexual object and sexual aim (11)

shaman; witch doctor; medicine man   an individual sensitive to the immaterial forces found in nature and well versed in the arts of magic (1)

social phobia   persistent fear of being in a situation where some act must be performed under the scrutiny of others (7)

social support   supportive relationships with other people (3, 10)

sociocultural model   approach to abnormality that emphasizes the larger societal and cultural context in which abnormality occurs (3)

sociocultural retardation   mental retardation that cannot be traced specifically to physical causes (14)

sodium lactate   chemical that builds up in the body during exercise, which can precipitate a panic attack among those vulnerable to them (7)

somatic nervous system   the part of the nervous system that controls the skeletal muscles and sense organs (6)

somatization disorder; Briquet's syndrome   repeated concern with a variety of bodily complaints, in the absence of any medical reason (8)

somatoform disorder   type of abnormality characterized by physical symptoms such as pain, blindness, or deafness without a physical cause (8)

specific phobia   persistent fear of a circumscribed object or situation (7)

spontaneous recovery; spontaneous remission   improvement without professional intervention (4)

Stanford-Binet Intelligence Scale   a well known intelligence test, based on Terman's translation of Alfred Binet's original test (2)

state dependent recall   tendency to remember information better when in the state during which it was originally learned (8)

statistical significance   whether results of a research investigation are unlikely to have occurred by chance (4)

stimulants   psychoactive drugs that stimulate the nervous system (5)

stress   reaction that takes place when a person tries to meet demands of external events (7)

stroke   bursting or blocking of an artery that supplies blood to the forebrain (6)

strong diagnostic test   simple procedure that unambiguously identifies an individual as having a certain problem or not (2)

substance abuse   symptoms indicating circumscribed impairment and distress due to drug use (5)

substance dependence   symptoms indicating severe impairment and distress due to drug use (5)

substance-induced cognitive disorders   demonstrable impairments of the brain and nervous system brought about by use of psychoactive drugs (5)

substance-related disorders   behavioral problems associated with use of psychoactive substances (5)

substitution therapy   treatment of narcotic abuse by substituting a longer-lasting opiate that is more gradual in its effects than heroin or morphine (5)

superego   mental structure that has internalized society's dictates (3)

sympathetic nervous system   the part of the autonomic nervous system that produces arousal (6)

syndrome   pattern of symptoms presumably reflecting an underlying cause (2)

systematic desensitization   behavior therapy technique for treating fear and anxiety in which the individual is taught to relax and then imagine objects or situations of which he or she is afraid, starting with mild images and moving gradually to more severe images (7)

tardive dyskinesia   possible side effect of antipsychotic medication: involuntary movements of the lips, tongue, and face (12)

T cell lymphocytes   white blood cells produced in the thymus that fight antigens in several ways, including killing foreign cells and stimulating activity of phagocytes (10)

temperament   biologically based styles of behaving; e.g., a person's activity level (13)

temporal-lobe epilepsy; psychomotor epilepsy   form of epilepsy marked by focal seizures lasting several minutes (6)

terminal insomnia; early morning awakening   inability to fall asleep after awakening (9)

tertiary prevention   preventive intervention intended to prevent relapse of problems (3)

testosterone   male sex hormone (11)

thank-you test   a suggested criterion for involuntary commitment: Will the involuntarily committed individual, once recovered from whatever problem he or she suffers, thank those who carried out the commitment? (15)

THC (delta-9-tetrahydrocannabinol)   active ingredient in marijuana (5)

Thematic Apperception Test; TAT   well known projective test consisting of a series of ambiguous pictures (2)

therapeutic community   treatment strategy in which hospital patients live together in democratic fashion and work with staff members to regulate their own behavior, privileges, and eventual discharge (15)

therapy manual   an explicit description of what a therapist should do in particular sessions (4)

tic   an abrupt, rapid, and repetitive movement (6)

token economy   behavior therapy carried out on an entire hospital ward, in which patients earn tokens for desirable behaviors and lose them for negative behaviors—with the tokens then exchanged for commodities (12)

tolerance   need to take more and more of a psychoactive drug in order to produce the same effect (5)

Tourette's syndrome   neurological condition characterized by multiple tics (6)

trait anxiety   *see* neuroticism

tranquilizers   synthetic depressants such as Valium and Librium, widely prescribed for anxiety disorders (5)

transsexualism   gender identity disorder among adults (11)

trephination   Stone Age practice of drilling holes in the skull, perhaps to allow evil spirits to escape (1)

tricyclics   a class of antidepressant medication that presumably works by keeping the neurons that secrete the neurotransmitter norepinephrine and serotonin from reabsorbing them (9)

tumor   a mass of cells (10)

two process theory   Mowrer's theory of avoidance learning, in which an individual first learns through classical conditioning to fear certain stimuli, and then learns through operant conditioning to avoid these stimuli (7)

Type A coronary-prone behavior pattern   style of behaving linked to cardiovascular disease and characterized by strong competitiveness, time urgency, and hostility in the face of frustration (10)

unconscious   according to Freud, mental activity kept from awareness because it is threatening (3)

undifferentiated schizophrenia   subtype of schizophrenia used to describe individuals who cannot be diagnosed clearly as catatonic, disorganized, or paranoid (12)

unipolar disorder   *see* depressive disorder

vaginismus   spasms of the vagina that make intercourse difficult or impossible (11)

validity   degree to which an operationalization captures the concept it purports to measure (4)

validity (of a diagnostic system)   degree to which a diagnostic system identifies coherent problems (2)

vascular dementia   *see* multi-infarct dementia

Victorianism   19th-century historical period characterized by widespread denial and repression of sexuality (11)

waxy flexibility   when the limbs of a catatonic individual can be moved slowly into a particular position, which is then maintained, sometimes for hours (12)

Wechsler Adult Intelligence Scale; WAIS well known intelligence test for adults, based on David Wechsler's original scale (2)

Wechsler Intelligence Scale for Children; WISC well known intelligence test for children, based on David Wechsler's original scale (2)

Wechsler Preschool and Primary Scale of Intelligence; WPPSI well known intelligence test for extremely young children, based on David Wechsler's original scale (2)

witch doctor *see* shaman

witches people, usually women, who supposedly make a pact with the devil and are thereby granted special powers (1)

withdrawal alteration in consciousness following cessation or reduction of psychoactive drug use (5, 6)

word salad metaphor describing schizophrenic speech, used to convey the idea that a schizophrenic's words may come out as a tumble (12)

Zeitgeist intellectual spirit of a particular historical era (4)

Abel, E. L., & Sokol, R. J. (1991). A revised conservative estimate of the incidence of FAS and its economic impact. *Alcoholism, Clinical and Experimental Research, 15*, 514–524.

Abel, G. G., & Osborn, C. (1992). The paraphilias: The extent and nature of sexually deviant and criminal behavior. *Psychiatric Clinics of North America, 15*, 675–687.

Abikoff, H., & Klein, R. G. (1992). Attention-deficit hyperactivity and conduct disorder: Comorbidity and implications for treatment. *Journal of Consulting and Clinical Psychology, 60*, 881–892.

Abraham, K. (1911/1927). Notes on the psycho-analytic investigation and treatment of manic-depressive insanity and allied conditions. In *Selected papers on psychoanalysis.* London: Hogarth Press.

Abraham, K. (1927). *Selected papers on psychoanalysis.* London: Hogarth Press.

Abramowitz, S. (1986). Psychosocial outcomes of sex reassignment surgery. *Journal of Consulting and Clinical Psychology, 54*, 183–189.

Abramson, L. Y., Metalsky, G. I., & Alloy, L. B. (1989). Hopelessness depression: A theory-based subtype of depression. *Psychological Review, 96*, 358–372.

Abramson, L. Y., Seligman, M. E. P., & Teasdale, J. D. (1978). Learned helplessness in humans: Critique and reformulation. *Journal of Abnormal Psychology, 87*, 49–74.

Abse, D. W. (1987). *Hysteria and related mental disorders: An approach to psychological medicine.* Bristol, England: Wright.

Achenbach, T. M. (1974). *Developmental psychopathology.* New York: Wiley.

Achenbach, T. M. (1986). Developmental perspectives on psychotherapy and behavior change. In S. L. Garfield & A. E. Bergin (Eds.), *Handbook of psychotherapy and behavior change* (3rd ed.). New York: Wiley.

Acklin, M. W., McDowell, C. J., & Orndoff, S. (1992). Statistical power and the Rorschach: 1975-1991. *Journal of Personality Assessment, 59*, 366–379.

Adams, D. M., & Overholser, J. C. (1992). Suicidal behavior and history of substance abuse. *American Journal of Drug and Alcohol Abuse, 18*, 343–354.

Adams, H. E., Feuerstein, M., & Fowler, J. L. (1980). Migraine headache: Review of parameters, etiology, and intervention. *Psychological Bulletin, 87*, 217–237.

Adams, R. D. (1969). The anatomy of memory mechanisms in the human brain. In G. A. Talland & N. C. Waugh (Eds.), *The pathology of memory.* New York: Academic Press.

Adebimpe, V. R. (1994). Race, racism, and epidemiological surveys. *Hospital and Community Psychiatry, 45*, 27–31.

Ader, R., & Cohen, N. (1975). Behaviorally conditioned immunosuppression. *Psychosomatic Medicine, 37*, 333–340.

Ader, R., & Cohen, N. (1981). Conditioned immunopharmacological responses. In R. Ader (Ed.), *Psychoneuroimmunology.* New York: Academic Press.

Adityanjee, Raju, G. S., & Khandelwal, S. K. (1989). Current status of multiple personality disorder in India. *American Journal of Psychiatry, 146*, 1607–1610.

Adler, A. (1927). *The practice and theory of individual psychology.* New York: Harcourt, Brace, & World.

Adler, D. A. (1990). Personality disorders: Treatment of the nonpsychotic chronic patient. *New Directions for Mental Health Services, 47*, 3–15.

Adler, D. A., Drake, R. E., & Teague, G. B. (1990). Clinicians' practices in personality assessment: Does gender influence the use of DSM-III Axis II? *Comprehensive Psychiatry, 31*, 125–133.

Adler, G. (1980). Correctional (prison) psychiatry. In H. I. Kaplan, A. M. Freedman, & B. J. Sadock (Eds.), *Comprehensive textbook of psychiatry* (Vol. 3, 3rd ed.). Baltimore: Williams & Wilkins.

Agras, W. S. (1991). Nonpharmacologic treatments of bulimia nervosa. *Journal of Clinical Psychiatry, 52*, 29–33.

Agras, W. S., Sylvester, D., & Oliveau, D. (1969). The epidemiology of common fears and phobias. *Comprehensive Psychiatry, 10*, 151–156.

Ainsworth, M. D. S. (1973). The development of infant-mother attachment. In B. M. Caldwell & H. N. Ricciuti (Eds.), *Review of child development research* (Vol. 3). Chicago: University of Chicago Press.

Ainsworth, M. D. S. (1989). Attachments beyond infancy. *American Psychologist, 44*, 709–716.

Ainsworth, M. D. S., & Wittig, B. A. (1969). Attachment and exploratory behavior of one-year-olds in a strange situation. In B. M. Foss (Ed.), *Determinants of infant behavior* (Vol. 4). London: Methuen.

Akhtar, S. (1988). Four culture-bound psychiatric syndromes in India. *International Journal of Social Psychiatry, 34*, 70–74.

Akhtar, S., Wig, N. N., Varma, V. K., Pershad, D., & Verma, S. K. (1975). Phenomenological analysis of symptoms in obsessive-compulsive neurosis. *British Journal of Psychiatry, 127*, 342–348.

Akiskal, H. S., & McKinney, W. T. (1973). Depressive disorders: Toward a unified hypothesis. *Science, 182*, 20–29.

Akutsu, P. D., Sue, S., Zane, N. W. S., & Nakamura, C. Y. (1989). Ethnic differences in alcohol consumption among Asians and Caucasians in the United States: An investigation of cultural and physiological factors. *Journal of Studies on Alcohol, 50*, 261–267.

Albee, G. W. (1982). Preventing psychopathology and promoting human potential. *American Psychologist, 37*, 1043–1050.

Albert, M. L., & Helm-Estabrooks, N. (1988a). Diagnosis and treatment of aphasia. Part I. *JAMA, 259*, 1043–1047.

Albert, M. L., & Helm-Estabrooks, N. (1988b). Diagnosis and treatment of aphasia. Part II. *JAMA, 259,* 1205–1210.

Alden, L. E. (1988). Behavioral self-management controlled-drinking strategies in a context of secondary prevention. *Journal of Consulting and Clinical Psychology, 56,* 280–286.

Alden, L. E. (1989). Short-term structured treatment for avoidant personality disorder. *Journal of Consulting and Clinical Psychology, 57,* 756–764.

Alexander, B. (1993). Disorders of sexual desire: Diagnosis and treatment of decreased libido. *American Family Physician, 47,* 832–838.

Alexander, F. (1939). Emotional factors in essential hypertension. *Psychosomatic Medicine, 1,* 139–152.

Alexander, F. (1950). *Psychosomatic medicine: Its principles and applications.* New York: Norton.

Allen, D. L. (1992, November). Hurricane Andrew, a reporter's dispatch: The story of three families. *Psychology Today,* 38–41 + .

Alloy, L. B., & Abramson, L. Y. (1979). Judgment of contingency in depressed and nondepressed college students: Sadder but wiser? *Journal of Experimental Psychology: General, 108,* 441–487.

Almond, R. (1975). Issues in milieu treatment. *Schizophrenia Bulletin, 1,* 12–26.

Althof, S. E. (1989). Psychogenic impotence: Treatment of men and couples. In S. R. Leiblum & R. C. Rosen (Eds.), *Principles and practice of sex therapy: Update for the 1990s.* New York: Guilford.

Amelang, M. (1991). Tales from Crvenka and Heidelberg: What about the empirical basis? *Psychological Inquiry, 2,* 233–236.

American Law Institute. (1962). *Model penal code: Proposed official draft.* Philadelphia: Author.

American Medical Association. (1935). *Standard classified nomenclature of disease.* Chicago: Author.

American Psychiatric Association. (1952). *Diagnostic and statistical manual of mental disorders.* Washington, DC: Author.

American Psychiatric Association. (1968). *Diagnostic and statistical manual of mental disorders* (2nd ed.). Washington, DC: Author.

American Psychiatric Association. (1980). *Diagnostic and statistical manual of mental disorders* (3rd ed.). Washington, DC: Author.

American Psychiatric Association. (1987). *Diagnostic and statistical manual of mental disorders* (3rd ed., Rev.). Washington, DC: Author.

American Psychiatric Association. (1993). *DSM-IV draft criteria.* Washington, DC: Author.

American Psychiatric Association. (1994). *Diagnostic and statistical manual of mental disorders* (4th ed.). Washington, DC: Author.

American Psychiatric Association Task Force on Laboratory Tests in Psychiatry. (1987). The dexamethasone suppression test: An overview of its current status in psychiatry. *American Journal of Psychiatry, 144,* 1253–1262.

American Psychological Association. (1992). Ethical principles of psychologists and code of conduct. *American Psychologist, 47,* 1597–1611.

American Public Health Association. (1962). *Mental disorders: A guide to control methods.* New York: Author.

Ames, M. A., & Houston, D. A. (1990). Legal, social, and biological definitions of pedophilia. *Archives of Sexual Behavior, 19,* 333–342.

Anastasi, A. (1982). *Psychological testing* (5th ed.). New York: Macmillan.

Anastopoulos, A. D., DuPaul, G. J., & Barkley, R. A. (1991). Stimulant medication and parent training therapies for attention deficit-hyperactivity disorder. *Journal of Learning Disabilities, 24,* 210–218.

Anderson, A., & Gordon, R. (1978). Witchcraft and the status of women: The case of England. *British Journal of Sociology, 29,* 171–184.

Anderson, C. M., Reiss, D. J., & Hogarty, G. E. (1986). *Schizophrenia and the family: A practitioner's guide to psychoeducation and management.* New York: Guilford.

Anderson, H. R., Dick, B., Macnair, R. S., Palmer, J. C., & Ramsey, J. D. (1982). An investigation of 140 deaths associated with volatile substance abuse in the United Kingdom (1971–1981). *Human Toxicology, 1,* 207–221.

Andreasen, N. C. (1982). Negative symptoms in schizophrenia: Definition and reliability. *Archives of General Psychiatry, 39,* 784–788.

Andreasen, N. C. (1984). *The broken brain: The biological revolution in psychiatry.* New York: Harper & Row.

Andreasen, N. C. (1987). Creativity and mental illness: Prevalence rates in writers and their first-degree relatives. *American Journal of Psychiatry, 144,* 1288–1292.

Andreasen, N. C., & Bardach, J. (1977). Dysmorphophobia: Symptom or disease? *American Journal of Psychiatry, 134,* 673–676.

Andreasen, N. C., Carson, R., Diksic, M., Evans, A., Farde, L., Gjedde, A., Hakim, A., Lal, S., Nair, N., Sedvall, G., Tune, L., & Wong, D. (1988). Workshop on schizophrenia, PET, and dopamine D2 receptors in the human neostriatum. *Schizophrenia Bulletin, 14,* 471–484.

Andreasen, N. C., & Grove, W. M. (1982). The classification of depression: Traditional versus mathematical approaches. *American Journal of Psychiatry, 139,* 45–52.

Andreasen, N. C., Olsen, S. A., Dennert, J. W., & Smith, M. R. (1982). Ventricular enlargement in schizophrenia: Relationship to positive and negative symptoms. *American Journal of Psychiatry, 139,* 297–302.

Andrews, G., Stewart, G., Allen, R., & Henderson, A. S. (1990). The genetics of six neurotic disorders: A twin study. *Journal of Affective Disorders, 19,* 23–29.

Angel, R., & Guarnaccia, P. J. (1989). Mind, body, and culture: Somatization among Hispanics. *Social Science and Medicine, 28,* 1229–1238.

Angermeyer, M. (1978). Twenty years double bind: Attempt at a critical review. *Psychiatrische Praxis, 5,* 106–117.

Annoyed with the Noid. (1989, February 13). *Time,* 63.

Antebi, D., & Bird, J. (1992). The facilitation and evocation of seizures. *British Journal of Psychiatry, 160,* 154–164.

Anthony, E. J., & Cohler, B. J. (Eds.) (1987). *The invulnerable child.* New York: Guilford.

Apley, J. (1958). A common denominator in the recurrent pains of childhood. *Proceedings of the Royal Society of Medicine, 51,* 1023–1024.

Appelbaum, P. S. (1988). The right to refuse treatment with antipsychotic medications: Retrospect and prospect. *American Journal of Psychiatry, 145,* 413–419.

Arbel, N., & Stravynski, A. (1991). A retrospective study of separation in the development of adult avoidant personality disorder. *Acta Psychiatrica Scandinavica, 83,* 174–178.

Arboleda-Florez, J., & Holley, H. L. (1991). Antisocial burnout: An exploratory study. *Bulletin of the American Academy of Psychiatry and the Law, 19,* 173–183.

Aries, P. (1962). *Centuries of childhood: A social history of family life.* New York: Vintage.

Arieti, S. (1974). *Interpretation of schizophrenia* (2nd ed.). New York: Basic Books.

Arieti, S. (1976). *Creativity: The magic synthesis.* New York: Basic Books.

Arkonac, O., & Guze, S. B. (1963). A family study of hysteria. *New England Journal of Medicine, 268,* 239–242.

Aronson, T. A. (1989a). A critical review of psychotherapeutic treatments of the borderline personality: Historical trends and future directions. *Journal of Nervous and Mental Disease, 177,* 511–528.

Aronson, T. A. (1989b). Paranoia and narcissism in psychoanalytic theory: Contributions of self psychology to the theory and therapy of the paranoid disorders. *Psychoanalytic Review, 76,* 329–351.

Aronson, T. A., & Shukla, S. (1987). Life events and relapse in bipolar disorder: The impact of a catastrophic event. *Acta Psychiatrica Scandinavica, 75,* 571–576.

Artiss, K. L. (1962). *Milieu therapy in schizophrenia.* New York: Grune & Stratton.

Asberg, M., Nordstrom, P., & Traskman-Bendz, L. (1986). Cerebrospinal fluid in depressives: An overview. *Annals of the New York Academy of Sciences, 487,* 243–255.

Ash, P. (1949). The reliability of psychiatric diagnosis. *Journal of Abnormal and Social Psychology, 44,* 272–276.

Asher, R., & Brissett, D. (1988). Codependency: A view from women married to alcoholics. *International Journal of the Addictions, 23,* 331–350.

Aubuchon, P., Haber, J. D., & Adams, H. E. (1985). Can migraine headaches be modified by operant pain techniques? *Journal of Behavior Therapy and Experimental Psychiatry, 16,* 261–263.

Avissar, S., Schreiber, G., Danon, A., & Belmaker, R. H. (1988). Lithium inhibits adrenergic and cholinergic increases in GTP binding in rat cortex. *Nature, 331,* 440–442.

Awouters, F., Niemegeers, C. J., & Janssen, P. A. (1990). "Tardive" dyskinesia: Etiological and therapeutic aspects. *Pharmacopsychiatry, 23,* 33–37.

Ayllon, T. (1963). Intensive treatment of psychotic behavior by stimulus satiation and food reinforcement. *Behaviour Research and Therapy, 1,* 53–61.

Ayuso, J. L., Alfonso, S., & Rivera, A. (1989). Childhood separation anxiety and panic disorder: A comparative study. *Progress in Neuro-Psychopharmacology and Biological Psychiatry, 13,* 665–671.

Bachman, D. L., Wolf, P. A., Linn, R. T., Knoefel, J. E., Cobb, J. L., Belanger, A. J., White, L. R., & D'Agostino, R. B. (1993). Incidence of dementia and probable Alzheimer's disease in a general population: The Framingham Study. *Neurology, 43,* 515–519.

Backman, M. E. (1989). *The psychology of the physically ill patient: A clinician's guide.* New York: Plenum.

Backstrom, T., & Hammarback, S. (1991). Premenstrual syndrome—psychiatric or gynaecological disorder? *Annals of Medicine, 23,* 625–633.

Bacon, D. L. (1969). Incompetency to stand trial: Commitment to an inclusive test. *Southern California Law Review, 42,* 444.

Baird, P. A., & Sadovnick, A. D. (1987). Life expectancy in Down syndrome. *Journal of Pediatrics, 110,* 849–854.

Baird, P. A., & Sadovnick, A. D. (1988). Life expectancy in Down syndrome adults. *Lancet, 8624,* 1354–1356.

Baker, L., & Cantwell, D. P. (1989). Specific language and learning disorders. In T. H. Ollendick & M. Hersen (Eds.), *Handbook of child psychopathology* (2nd ed.). New York: Plenum.

Baldwin, B. A. (1979). Crisis intervention: An overview of theory and practice. *Counseling Psychologist, 8,* 43–52.

Ball, J., Corty, E., Bond, H., Myers, C., & Tommasello, A. (1988). The reduction of intravenous heroin use, non-opiate abuse, and crime during methadone maintenance treatment: Further findings. *NIDA Research Monographs, 81,* 224–230.

Bancroft, J. (1983). *Human sexuality and its problems.* Edinburgh, Scotland: Churchill-Livingstone.

Bandura, A. (1969). *Principles of behavior modification.* New York: Holt, Rinehart, & Winston.

Bandura, A. (1977). Self-efficacy: Toward a unifying theory of behavioral change. *Psychological Review, 84,* 191–215.

Bandura, A. (1986). *Social foundations of thought and action.* Englewood Cliffs, NJ: Prentice-Hall.

Bank, L., Marlowe, J. H., Reid, J. B., Patterson, G. R., & Weinrott, M. R. (1991). A comparative evaluation of parent-training interventions for families of chronic delinquents. *Journal of Abnormal Child Psychology, 19,* 15–33.

Barbach, L. G. (1990). *For yourself: The fulfillment of female sexuality.* New York: Anchor Books.

Barbeau, A. (1980). Cholinergic treatment in the Tourette syndrome. *New England Journal of Medicine, 302,* 1310–1311.

Bardwick, J. M. (1971). *The psychology of women: A study of bio-cultural conflicts.* New York: Harper & Row.

Barker, R., & Larner, A. (1992). Substance P and multiple sclerosis. *Medical Hypotheses, 37,* 40–43.

Barker-Benfield, B. (1975). Sexual surgery in late-nineteenth-century America. *International Journal of Health Services, 5,* 279–288.

Barkley, R. A., & Cunningham, C. E. (1979). The effect of methylphenidate on the mother-child interactions of hyperactive young children. *Archives of General Psychiatry, 36,* 201–208.

Barlow, D. H. (Ed.). (1981). *Behavioral assessment of adult disorders.* New York: Guilford.

Barlow, D. H. (1988). *Anxiety and its disorders.* New York: Guilford.

Barlow, D. H. (1990). Long-term outcome for patients with panic disorder treated with cognitive-behavioral therapy. *Journal of Clinical Psychiatry, 51,* 17–23.

Barlow, D. H. (1992). Cognitive-behavioral approaches to panic disorder and social phobia. *Bulletin of the Menninger Clinic, 56,* 14–28.

Barlow, D. H., Blanchard, E. B., Vermilyea, J. A., Vermilyea, B. B., & DiNardo, P. A. (1986). Generalized anxiety and generalized anxiety disorder: Description and reconceptualization. *American Journal of Psychiatry, 143,* 40–44.

Baroff, G. S. (1991). Establishing mental retardation in capital cases: A potential matter of life and death. *Mental Retardation, 29,* 343–349.

Baron, M., Risch, N., Hamburger, R., Mandel, B., Kushner, S., Newman, M., Drumer, D., & Belmaker, R. H. (1987). Genetic linkage between X-chromosome markers and bipolar affective illnesses. *Nature, 326,* 289–292.

Barret-Ducrocq, F. (1991). *Love in the time of Victoria: Sexuality, class, and gender in nineteenth-century London.* New York: Verso.

Barsky, A. J. (1988). *Worried sick: Our troubled quest for wellness.* Boston: Little, Brown.

Barsky, A. J., Frank, C. B., Cleary, P. D., Wyshak, G., & Klerman, G. L. (1991). The relation between hypochondriasis and age. *American Journal of Psychiatry, 148,* 923–928.

Barsky, A. J., Wyshak, G., & Klerman, G. L. (1990). The somatosensory amplification scale and its relationship to hypochondriasis. *Journal of Psychiatric Research, 24,* 323–334.

Barsky, A. J., Wyshak, G., & Klerman, G. L. (1992). Psychiatric comorbidity in DSM-III-R hypochondriasis. *Archives of General Psychiatry, 49,* 101–108.

Barsky, A. J., Wyshak, G., Klerman, G. L., & Latham, K. S. (1990). The prevalence of hypochondriasis in medical outpatients. *Social Psychiatry and Psychiatric Epidemiology, 25,* 89–94.

Bartemeier, L. (1963). *Hearings before the Subcommittee on Health of the Committee on Labor and Public Welfare, U.S. Senate, March 5, 6, 7.* Washington, DC: U.S. Government Printing Office.

Bartrop, R. W., Luckhurst, E., Lazarus, L., Kiloh, L. G., & Penny, R. (1977). Depressed lymphocyte function after bereavement. *Lancet, 97,* 834–836.

Basbaum, A. I., & Fields, H. L. (1984). Endogenous pain control systems: Brainstem spinal pathways and endorphin circuitry. *Annual Review of Neuroscience, 7,* 309–338.

Bassett, A. S., McGillivray, B. C., Jones, B. D., & Pantzar, J. T. (1988). Partial trisomy chromosome 5 cosegregating with schizophrenia. *Lancet, 108,* 799–801.

Bateson, G., Jackson, D. D., Haley, J., & Weakland, J. (1956). Toward a theory of schizophrenia. *Behavioral Science, 1,* 251–264.

Battaglia, M., Gasperini, M., Sciuto, G., Scherillo, P., Diaferia, G., & Bellodi, L. (1991). Psychiatric disorders in the families of schizotypal subjects. *Schizophrenia Bulletin, 17,* 659–668.

Baum, C. G. (1989). Conduct disorders. In T. H. Ollendick & M. Hersen (Eds.), *Handbook of child psychopathology* (2nd ed.). New York: Plenum.

Baum, C. G., & Forehand, R. L. (1981). Long-term follow-up assessment of parent training by use of multiple outcome measures. *Behavior Therapy, 12,* 643–652.

Baumeister, R. F. (1987). How the self became a problem: A psychological review of historical research. *Journal of Personality and Social Psychology, 52,* 163–176.

Baur, S. (1988). *Hypochondria: Woeful imaginings.* Berkeley: University of California Press.

Baxter, L. R., Phelps, M. E., Mazziotta, J. C., Guze, B. H., Schwartz, J. M., & Selin, C. E. (1987). Local cerebral glucose metabolic rates in obsessive-compulsive disorder: A comparison with rates in unipolar depression and normal controls. *Archives of General Psychiatry, 44,* 211–218.

Bayer, R. (1987). *Homosexuality and American psychiatry: The politics of diagnosis.* Princeton: Princeton University Press.

Beach, F. A. (1971). Hormonal factors controlling the differentiation, development, and display of copulatory behavior in the ramstergig and related species. In E. Tobach, L. R. Aronson, & E. Shaw (Eds.), *The biopsychology of development.* New York: Academic Press.

Bear, D. M., & Fedio, P. (1977). Quantitative analysis of interictal behavior in temporal lobe epilepsy. *Archives of Neurology, 34,* 454–467.

Beattie, M. (1987). *Codependent no more.* New York: Harper/Hazelden.

Beck, A. T. (1962). Reliability of psychiatric diagnosis: A critique of systematic studies. *American Journal of Psychiatry, 119,* 210–216.

Beck, A. T. (1967). *Depression: Clinical, experimental, and theoretical aspects.* New York: Hoeber.

Beck, A. T. (1976). *Cognitive therapy and the emotional disorders.* New York: International Universities Press.

Beck, A. T. (1991). Cognitive therapy: A 30-year retrospective. *American Psychologist, 46,* 368–375.

Beck, A. T., & Emery, G. (1985). *Anxiety disorders and phobias: A cognitive perspective.* New York: Basic Books.

Beck, A. T., Freeman, A., & Associates. (1990). *Cognitive therapy of personality disorders.* New York: Guilford.

Beck, A. T., Kovacs, M., & Weissman, A. (1975). Hopelessness and suicidal behavior: An overview. *JAMA, 234,* 1146–1149.

Beck, A. T., Rush, A. J., Shaw, B. F., & Emery, G. (1979). *Cognitive therapy of depression.* New York: Guilford.

Beck, A. T., Sokol, L., Clark, D. A., Berchick, R. J., & Wright, F. (1992). A crossover study of focused cognitive therapy for panic disorder. *American Journal of Psychiatry, 149,* 778–783.

Beck, A. T., Weissman, A., Lester, D., & Trexler, L. (1974). The measurement of pessimism: The hopelessness scale. *Journal of Consulting and Clinical Psychology, 42,* 861–865.

Becker, R. E. (1988). Interpersonal interaction and depression. *Behavior Therapist, 11,* 115–118.

Beebe, D. K., & Walley, E. (1991). Substance abuse: The designer drugs. *American Family Physician, 43,* 1689–1698.

Beeber, A. R. (1991). Psychotherapy with schizophrenics in team groups: A systems model. *American Journal of Psychotherapy, 45,* 78–86.

Beels, C. C. (1975). Family and social management of schizophrenia. *Schizophrenia Bulletin, 1,* 97–118.

Beigel, A., & Murphy, D. L. (1971). Unipolar and bipolar affective illness. *Archives of General Psychiatry, 24,* 215–220.

Beirne, P., & Messerschmidt, J. (1991). *Criminology.* San Diego: Harcourt Brace Jovanovich.

Beiser, M., Benfari, R. C., Collomb, H., & Ravel, J. L. (1976). Measuring psychoneurotic behavior in cross-cultural surveys. *Journal of Nervous and Mental Disease, 163,* 10–123.

Beitchman, J. H., Inglis, A., & Schachter, D. (1992). Child psychiatry and early intervention: IV. The externalizing disorders. *Canadian Journal of Psychiatry, 37,* 245–249.

Belcher, J. R., & DiBlasio, F. A. (1990). The needs of depressed homeless persons: Designing appropriate services. *Community Mental Health Journal, 26,* 255–266.

Belcher, J. R., & Toomey, B. G. (1988). Relationship between the deinstitutionalization model, psychiatric disability, and homelessness. *Health and Social Work, 13,* 145–153.

Bell, R. C., & Jackson, H. J. (1992). The structure of personality disorders in DSM-III. *Acta Psychiatrica Scandinavica, 85,* 279–287.

Bell, R. M. (1985). *Holy anorexia.* Chicago: University of Chicago Press.

Bellack, A. S., & Hersen, M. (Eds.). (1985). *Dictionary of behavior therapy techniques.* New York: Pergamon.

Bellack, A. S., Hersen, M., & Himmelhoch, J. (1981). Social skills training compared with pharmacotherapy and psychotherapy in the treatment of unipolar depression. *American Journal of Psychiatry, 138,* 1562–1567.

Bellak, L., & Black, R. B. (1992). Attention-deficit hyperactivity disorder in adults. *Clinical Therapeutics, 14,* 138–147.

Belloc, N. B. (1973). Relationship of health practices and mortality. *Preventive Medicine, 2,* 67–81.

Belloc, N. B., & Breslow, L. (1972). Relationship of physical health status and family practices. *Preventive Medicine, 1,* 409–421.

Belsher, G., & Costello, C. G. (1988). Relapse after recovery from unipolar depression: A critical review. *Psychological Bulletin, 104,* 84–96.

Belsky, J. (1988). The "effects" of infant day care reconsidered. *Early Childhood Research Quarterly, 3,* 235–272.

Bender, L. (1938). A visual motor gestalt test and its clinical use. *American Orthopsychiatric Association Research Monograph* (No. 3).

Bennett, D. A., & Evans, D. A. (1992). Alzheimer's disease. *Disease-A-Month, 38,* 1–64.

Bennett, P., Wallace, L., Carroll, D., & Smith, N. (1991). Treating Type A behaviours and mild hypertension in middle-aged men. *Journal of Psychosomatic Research, 35,* 209–223.

Bennion, L. J., & Li, T. K. (1976). Alcohol metabolism in American Indians and whites: Lack of racial differences in metabolic rate and liver alcohol dehydrogenase. *New England Journal of Medicine, 294,* 9–13.

Benton, M. K., & Schroeder, H. E. (1990). Social skills training with schizophrenics: A meta-analytic evaluation. *Journal of Consulting and Clinical Psychology, 58,* 741–747.

Beren, P. (1992). Narcissistic disorders in children. *Psychoanalytic Study of the Child, 47,* 265–278.

Bergner, R. M. (1988). Money's "lovemap" account of the paraphilias: A critique and reformulation. *American Journal of Psychotherapy, 42,* 254–262.

Berkowitz, R., Shavit, N., & Leff, J. P. (1990). Educating relatives of schizophrenic patients. *Social Psychiatry and Psychiatric Epidemiology, 25,* 216–220.

Berlin, F. S., & Meinecke, C. F. (1981). Treatment of sex offenders with antiandrogenic medication: Conceptualization, review of treatment modalities, and preliminary findings. *American Journal of Psychiatry, 138,* 601–607.

Berliner, L., & Loftus, E. F. (1992). Sexual abuse accusations: Desperately seeking reconciliation. *Journal of Interpersonal Violence, 7,* 570–578.

Bernheim, K. F., & Lewine, R. R. J. (1979). *Schizophrenia.* New York: Norton.

Bernstein, D. P., Cohen, P., Velez, C. N., Schwab-Stone, M., Siever, L. J., & Shinsato, L. (1993). Prevalence and stability of the DSM-III-R personality disorders in a community-based survey of adolescents. *American Journal of Psychiatry, 150,* 1237–1243.

Bertagnoli, M. W., & Borchardt, C. M. (1990). A review of ECT for children and adolescents. *Journal of the American Academy of Child and Adolescent Psychiatry, 29,* 302–307.

Bertrando, P., Beltz, J., Bressi, C., Clerici, M., Farma, T., Invernizzi, G., & Cazzullo, C. L. (1992). Expressed emotion and schizophrenia in Italy: A study of an urban population. *British Journal of Psychiatry, 161,* 223–229.

Betancourt, H., & Lopez, S. R. (1993). The study of culture, ethnicity, and race in American psychology. *American Psychologist, 48,* 619–637.

Bettelheim, B. (1967). *The empty fortress.* New York: Free Press.

Beutler, L. E., Crago, M., & Arizmendi, T. G. (1986). Research on therapist variables in psychotherapy. In S. L. Garfield & A. E. Bergin (Eds.), *Handbook of psychotherapy and behavior change* (3rd ed.). New York: Wiley.

Bianchi, G. N. (1971). Origins of disease phobia. *Australian and New Zealand Journal of Psychiatry, 5,* 241–257.

Bidzinska, E. J. (1984). Stress factors in affective diseases. *British Journal of Psychiatry, 144,* 161–166.

Biederman, J., Faraone, S. V., Keenan, K., Benjamin, J., Krifcher, B., Moore, C., Sprich-Buckminister, S., Ugaglia, K., Jellinek, M. S., Steingard, R., Spencer, T., Norman, D., Kolodny, R. C., Kraus, I., Perrin, J., Keller, M. B., & Tsuang, M. T. (1992). Further evidence for family-genetic risk factors in attention deficit hyperactivity disorder: Patterns of comorbidity in probands and relatives psychiatrically and pediatrically referred samples. *Archives of General Psychiatry, 49,* 728–738.

Biederman, J., Faraone, S. V., Keenan, K., & Tsuang, M. T. (1991). Evidence of familial association between attention deficit disorder and major affective disorders. *Archives of General Psychiatry, 48,* 633–642.

Biederman, J., Newcorn, J., & Sprich, S. (1991). Comorbidity of attention deficit hyperactivity disorder with conduct, depressive, anxiety, and other disorders. *American Journal of Psychiatry, 148,* 564–577.

Bigelow, H. J. (1850). Dr. Harlow's case of recovery from the passage of an iron bar through the head. *American Journal of Medical Science, 20,* 13–22.

Billings, A. G., & Moos, R. H. (1985). Psychosocial stressors, coping, and depression. In E. E. Beckham & W. R. Leber (Eds.), *Handbook of depression: Treatment, assessment, and research.* Homewood, IL: Dorsey.

Binet, A., & Simon, T. (1913). *A method of measuring the development of the intelligence of young children* (3rd ed.). Chicago: Chicago Medical Book.

Bird, S. J. (1985). Presymptomatic testing for Huntington's disease. *JAMA, 253,* 3286–3291.

Birtchnell, J. (1988). Defining dependence. *British Journal of Medical Psychology, 61,* 111–123.

Bishop, E. R. (1980). An olfactory reference syndrome: Monosymptomatic hypochondriasis. *Journal of Clinical Psychiatry, 41,* 57–59.

Bjorntorp, P. (1992). Abdominal fat distribution and disease: An overview of epidemiological data. *Annals of Medicine, 24,* 15–18.

Black, D. R., Gleser, L. J., & Kooyers, K. J. (1990). A meta-analytic evaluation of couples weight-loss programs. *Health Psychology, 9,* 330–347.

Black, D. W., & Fisher, R. (1992). Mortality in DSM-III-R schizophrenia. *Schizophrenia Research, 7,* 109–116.

Blair, C. D., & Langon, R. I. (1971). Exhibitionism: Etiology and treatment. *Psychological Bulletin, 89,* 439–463.

Blakely, M. K. (1991, June). Dangerous to himself or others. *Lear's Magazine,* pp. 46–51, 95–96.

Blanchard, E. B. (1992). Psychological treatment of benign headache disorders. *Journal of Consulting and Clinical Psychology, 60,* 537–551.

Blanchard, E. B., Schwarz, S. P., & Neff, D. F. (1988). Two-year follow-up of behavioral treatment of irritable bowel syndrome. *Behavior Therapy, 19,* 67–73.

Blanchard, R., Clemmensen, L. H., & Steiner, B. W. (1987). Heterosexual and homosexual gender dysphoria. *Archives of Sexual Behavior, 16,* 139–152.

Blanchard, R., Steiner, B. W., Clemmensen, L. H., & Dickey, R. (1989). Prediction of regrets in postoperative transsexuals. *Canadian Journal of Psychiatry, 34,* 43–45.

Blaser, M. J. (1992). Hypotheses on the pathogenesis and natural history of *Helicobacter pylori*-induced inflammation. *Gastroenterology, 102,* 720–727.

Blashfield, R. K. (1984). *The classification of psychopathology: Neo-Kraepelinian and quantitative approaches.* New York: Plenum.

Blashfield, R. K., & Breen, M. J. (1989). Face validity of the DSM-III-R personality disorders. *American Journal of Psychiatry, 146,* 1575–1579.

Blatt, S. J. (1992). The differential effect of psychotherapy and psychoanalysis with anaclitic and introjective patients: The Menninger Psychotherapy Research Project revisited. *Journal of the American Psychoanalytic Association, 40,* 691–724.

Blau, J. N. (1992). Migraine triggers: Practice and theory. *Pathologie Biologie, 40,* 367–372.

Bleach, G., & Claiborn, W. L. (1974). Initial evaluation of hot-line telephone crisis centers. *Community Mental Health Journal, 10,* 387–394.

Bleuler, E. (1911/1950). *Dementia praecox or the group of schizophrenias.* New York: International Universities Press.

Bleuler, E. (1924/1976). *Textbook of psychiatry.* New York: Arno Press.

Bleuler, M. (1978). *The schizophrenic disorders: Long-term patient and family studies.* New Haven, CT: Yale University Press.

Blier, P., de Montigny, C., & Chaput, Y. (1990). A role for the serotonin system in the mechanism of action of antidepressant treatments: Preclinical evidence. *Journal of Clinical Psychiatry, 51,* 14–20.

Bliss, E. L. (1980). Multiple personalities: Report of fourteen cases with implications for schizophrenia and hysteria. *Archives of General Psychiatry, 37,* 1388–1397.

Block, J. (1969). Parents of schizophrenic, neurotic, and asthmatic and congenitally ill children. *Archives of General Psychiatry, 20,* 659.

Bloom, B. L. (1984). *Community mental health: A general introduction* (2nd ed.). Monterey, CA: Brooks/Cole.

Blume, S. B. (1984). *The disease concept of alcoholism today.* Minneapolis: Johnson Institute.

Bordin, E. S. (1979). The generalizability of the psychoanalytic concept of the working alliance. *Psychotherapy: Theory, Research, and Practice, 16,* 252–260.

Borga, P., Widerlov, B., Stefansson, C. G., & Cullberg, J. (1992). Social conditions in a total population with long-term functional psychosis in three different areas of Stockholm county. *Acta Psychiatrica Scandinavica, 85,* 465–473.

Boring, E. G. (1950). *A history of experimental psychology* (2nd ed.). New York: Appleton-Century-Crofts.

Borkovec, T. D., & Costello, E. (1993). Efficacy of applied relaxation and cognitive-behavioral therapy in the treatment of generalized anxiety disorder. *Journal of Consulting and Clinical Psychology, 61,* 611–619.

Borkovec, T. D., & Mathews, A. M. (1988). Treatment of nonphobic anxiety disorders: A comparison of nondirective, cognitive, and coping desensitization therapy. *Journal of Consulting and Clinical Psychology, 56,* 877–884.

Borkovec, T. D., Mathews, A. M., Chambers, A., Ebrahimi, S., Lytle, R., & Nelson, R. (1987). The effects of relaxation training with cognitive or nondirective therapy and the role of relaxation induced anxiety in the treatment of generalized anxiety disorder. *Journal of Consulting and Clinical Psychology, 55,* 883–888.

Bornstein, R. A., Schwarzkopf, S. B., Olson, S. C., & Nasrallah, H. A. (1992). Third-ventricle enlargement and neuropsychological deficit in schizophrenia. *Biological Psychiatry, 31,* 954–961.

Bornstein, R. F., Scanlon, M. A., & Beardslee, L. A. (1989). The psychodynamics of paranoia: Anality, projection, and suspiciousness. *Journal of Social Behavior and Personality, 4,* 275–284.

Bost, R. O., & Kemp, P. M. (1992). A possible association between fluoxetine use and suicide. *Journal of Analytical Toxicology, 16,* 142–145.

Boswell, D. L., & Litwin, W. J. (1992). Limited prescription privileges for psychologists: A 1-year follow up. *Professional Psychology: Research and Practice, 23,* 108–113.

Boulanger, G. (1986). Predisposition to post-traumatic stress disorder. In C. Kadushin & G. Boulanger (Eds.), *The Vietnam veteran defined: Fact and fiction.* Hillsdale, NJ: Erlbaum.

Bourdon, K. H., Boyd, J. H., Rae, D. S., & Burns, B. J. (1988). Gender differences in phobias: Results of the ECA community survey. *Journal of Anxiety Disorders, 2,* 227–241.

Bourgeois, M. (1973). Autodysomophobia and the olfactory reference syndrome: Seven case histories. *Annales Medico-Psychologiques, 2,* 353–376.

Bowen, M. (1989). Frontal lobe function. *Brain Injury, 3,* 109–128.

Bowen, R. C., Offord, D. R., & Boyle, M. H. (1990). The prevalence of overanxious disorder and separation anxiety disorder: Results from the Ontario Child Health Study. *Journal of the American Academy of Child and Adolescent Psychiatry, 29,* 753–758.

Bower, G. H. (1981). Mood and memory. *American Psychologist, 36,* 129–148.

Bowlby, J. (1969). *Attachment and loss: Vol. 1. Attachment.* New York: Basic Books.

Bownes, I. T., O'Gorman, E. C., & Sayers, A. (1991). Assault characteristics and posttraumatic stress disorder in rape victims. *Acta Psychiatrica Scandinavica, 83,* 27–30.

Boyd, J. H., Rae, D. S., Thompson, J. W., Burns, B. J., Bourdon, K. H., Locke, B. Z., & Regier, D. A. (1990). Phobia: Prevalence and risk factors. *Social Psychiatry and Psychiatric Epidemiology, 25,* 314–323.

Boyd, J. H., Weissman, M. M., Thompson, W. D., & Myers, J. K. (1983). Different definitions of alcoholism, I: Impact of seven different definitions on prevalence rates in a community survey. *American Journal of Psychiatry, 140,* 1309–1313.

Boyle, M. (1990). *Schizophrenia: A scientific delusion.* London: Routledge.

Boyle, P. (1993). The hazards of passive- and active-smoking. *New England Journal of Medicine, 328,* 1708–1709.

Boyle, R. H., & Ames, W. (1983, April 11). Too many punches, too little concern. *Sports Illustrated,* 44–67.

Bracha, H. S., Torrey, E. F., Bigelow, L. B., Lohr, J. B., & Linington, B. B. (1991). Subtle signs of prenatal maldevelopment of the hand ectoderm in schizophrenia: A preliminary monozygotic twin study. *Biological Psychiatry, 30,* 719–725.

Braden, C. S. (1963). *Spirits in rebellion: The rise and development of new thought.* Dallas: Southern Methodist University Press.

Bradford, J. M., Boulet, J., & Pawlak, A. (1992). The paraphilias: A multiplicity of deviant behaviours. *Canadian Journal of Psychiatry, 37,* 104–108.

Bradley, S. J. (1990). Affect regulation and psychopathology: Bridging the mind-body gap. *Canadian Journal of Psychiatry, 35,* 540–547.

Bradley, S. J., Blanchard, R., Coates, S., Green, R., Levine, S. B., Meyer-Bahlburg, H. F., Pauly, I. B., & Zucker, K. J. (1991). Interim report of the DSM-IV Subcommittee on Gender Identity Disorders. *Archives of Sexual Behavior, 20,* 333–343.

Brady, E. U., & Kendall, P. C. (1992). Comorbidity of anxiety and depression in children and adolescents. *Psychological Bulletin, 111,* 244–245.

Brady, J. V., Porter, R. W., Conrad, D. G., & Mason, J. W. (1958). Avoidance behavior and the development of gastroduodenal ulcers. *Journal of the Experimental Analysis of Behavior, 1,* 69–72.

Braff, D. L., & Geyer, M. A. (1990). Sensorimotor gating and schizophrenia: Human and animal model studies. *Archives of General Psychiatry, 47,* 181–188.

Brandt, J., Celentano, D., Stewart, W., Linet, M., & Folstein, M. F. (1990). Personality and emotional disorder in a community sample of migraine headache sufferers. *American Journal of Psychiatry, 147,* 303–308.

Brandt, J., Quaid, K. A., & Folstein, S. E. (1989). Presymptomatic DNA testing for Huntington's disease. *Journal of Neuropsychiatry and Clinical Neurosciences, 1,* 195–197.

Bray, G. A. (1992). Drug treatment of obesity. *American Journal of Clinical Nutrition, 55,* 538–544.

Brayne, C., Day, N., & Gill, C. (1992). Methodological issues in screening for dementia. *Neuroepidemiology, 11,* 88–93.

Brecher, E. M. (1969). *The sex researchers.* Boston: Little, Brown.

Breggin, P. R. (1979). *Electroshock: Its brain-disabling effects.* New York: Springer.

Breier, A., Charney, D. S., & Heninger, G. R. (1984). Major depression in patients with agoraphobia and panic disorder. *Archives of General Psychiatry, 41,* 1129–1135.

Breier, A., Schreiber, J. L., Dyer, J., & Pickar, D. (1991). National Institute of Mental Health longitudinal study of chronic schizophrenia: Prognosis and predictors of outcome. *Archives of General Psychiatry, 48,* 239–246.

Breier, A., Wolkowitz, O. M., Doran, A. R., Roy, A., Boronow, J., Hommer, D. W., & Pickar, D. (1987). Neuroleptic responsivity of negative and positive symptoms in schizophrenia. *American Journal of Psychiatry, 144,* 1549–1555.

Brenner, C. (1982). *The mind in conflict.* New York: International Universities Press.

Brenner, H. D., Hodel, B., Roder, V., & Corrigan, P. (1992). Treatment of cognitive dysfunctions and behavioral deficits in schizophrenia. *Schizophrenia Bulletin, 18,* 21–26.

Breslau, N., & Davis, G. C. (1992). Posttraumatic stress disorder in an urban population of young adults: Risk factors for chronicity. *American Journal of Psychiatry, 149,* 671–675.

Breslau, N., Kilbey, M. M., & Andreski, P. (1993a). Nicotine dependence and major depression: New evidence from a prospective investigation. *Archives of General Psychiatry, 50,* 31–35.

Breslau, N., Kilbey, M. M., & Andreski, P. (1993b). Vulnerability to psychopathology in nicotine-dependent smokers: An epidemiologic study of young adults. *American Journal of Psychiatry, 150,* 941–946.

Breu, G. (1990, November 5). For a family facing incurable Huntington's disease, finding out is better than the dread of suspicion. *People Weekly,* 133–140.

Breuer, J., & Freud, S. (1895). Studies on hysteria. *Standard edition* (Vol. 2). London: Hogarth.

Brew, B. J. (1992). Medical management of AIDS patients: Central and peripheral nervous system abnormalities. *Medical Clinics of North America, 76,* 63–81.

Brewin, C. R. (1985). Depression and causal attributions: What is their relation? *Psychological Bulletin, 98,* 297–309.

Brewin, C. R. (1989). Cognitive change processes in psychotherapy. *Psychological Review, 96,* 379–394.

Bridge, T. P., & Ingraham, L. J. (1990). Central nervous system effects of human immunodeficiency virus type 1. *Annual Review of Medicine, 41,* 159–168.

Bridge, T. P., Potkin, S. G., Zung, W. W., & Soldo, B. J. (1977). Suicide prevention centers: Ecological study of effectiveness. *Journal of Nervous and Mental Disease, 164,* 18–24.

Briere, J., & Runtz, M. (1988). Symptomatology associated with childhood sexual victimization in a nonclinical adult sample. *Child Abuse and Neglect, 12,* 51–59.

Brna, T. G., & Wilson, C. C. (1990). Psychogenic amnesia. *American Family Physician, 41,* 229–234.

Broadbent, D. E. (1958). *Perception and communication.* London: Pergamon.

Broadhurst, P. L. (1975). The Maudsley reactive and nonreactives strains of rats: A survey. *Behavior Genetics, 5,* 299–319.

Brock, G. B., & Lue, T. F. (1993). Drug-induced male sexual dysfunction: An update. *Drug Safety, 8,* 414–426.

Brodsky, S. L. (1991). *Testifying in court: Guidelines and maxims for the expert witness.* Washington, DC: American Psychological Association.

Brom, D., Kleber, R. J., & Defares, P. B. (1989). Brief psychotherapy for post-traumatic stress disorders. *Journal of Consulting and Clinical Psychology, 57,* 607–612.

Brom, D., Kleber, R. J., & Witztum, E. (1992). The prevalence of posttraumatic psychopathology in the general and the clinical population. *Israel Journal of Psychiatry and Related Sciences, 28,* 53–63.

Bromberg, W. (1975). *From shaman to psychotherapist: A history of the treatment of mental illness.* Chicago: Regnery.

Brooks, D. N. (1984). Head injury and the family. In D. N. Brooks (Ed.), *Closed head injury: Psychological, social, and family consequences.* Oxford: Oxford University Press.

Brooks, G. R., & Richardson, F. C. (1980). Emotional skills training: A treatment program for duodenal ulcer. *Behavior Therapy, 11,* 198–207.

Brooks, P. H., & McCauley, C. (1984). Cognitive research in mental retardation. *American Journal of Mental Deficiency, 88,* 479–486.

Brouillette, M. J., & Paris, J. (1991). The dangerousness criterion for civil commitment: The problem and a possible solution. *Canadian Journal of Psychiatry, 36,* 285–289.

Brown, C. S. (1991). Treatment of attention deficit hyperactivity disorder: A critical review. *DICP, 25,* 1207–1213.

Brown, G. W., & Harris, T. O. (1978). *Social origins of depression.* New York: Free Press.

Brown, J. A. C. (1964). *Freud and the post-Freudians.* New York: Penguin.

Brown, L. S. (1992). A feminist critique of the personality disorders. In L. S. Brown & M. Ballou (Eds.), *Personality and psychopathology: Feminist reappraisals.* New York: Guilford.

Brown, N. O. (1959). *Life against death.* Middletown, CT: Wesleyan University Press.

Brown, S. A., Goldman, M. S., Inn, A., & Anderson, L. (1980). Expectations of reinforcement from alcohol: Their domain and relation to drinking patterns. *Journal of Consulting and Clinical Psychology, 48,* 419–426.

Brown, S. D. (1980). Coping skills training: An evaluation of a psychoeducational program in a community mental health setting. *Journal of Community Psychology, 8,* 314–322.

Browne, A., & Finkelhor, D. (1986). Impact of child sexual abuse: A review of the research. *Psychological Bulletin, 99,* 66–77.

Brownell, K. D., & Wadden, T. A. (1992). Etiology and treatment of obesity: Understanding a serious, prevalent, and refractory disorder. *Journal of Consulting and Clinical Psychology, 60,* 505–517.

Brownmiller, S. (1975). *Against our will: Men, women, and rape.* New York: Simon & Schuster.

Bruch, H. (1978). *The golden cage: The enigma of anorexia nervosa.* Cambridge: Harvard University Press.

Bruvold, W. H. (1993). A meta-analysis of adolescent smoking prevention programs. *American Journal of Public Health, 83,* 872–880.

Bryant, D., Kessler, J., & Shirar, L. (1992). *The family inside: Working with the multiple.* New York: Norton.

Buchanan, A. (1992). A two-year prospective study of treatment compliance in patients with schizophrenia. *Psychological Medicine, 22,* 787–797.

Buchsbaum, M. S. (1984, August). The Genain quadruplets. *Psychology Today,* 46–51.

Buchsbaum, M. S., Mirsky, A. F., DeLisi, L. E., Morihisa, J., Karson, C. N., Mendelson, W. B., King, A. C., Johnson, J., & Kessler, R. (1984). The Genain quadruplets: Electrophysiological, positron emission, and X-ray tomographic studies. *Psychiatry Research, 13,* 95–108.

Buchsbaum, M. S., Nuechterlein, K. H., Haier, R. J., Wu, J., Sicotte, N., Hazlett, E., Asarnow, R., Potkin, S., & Guich, S. (1990). Glucose metabolic rate in normals and schizophrenics during the Continuous Performance Test assessed by positron emission tomography. *British Journal of Psychiatry, 156,* 216–227.

Buckley, H. B. (1992). Syphilis: A review and update of this "new" infection of the '90s. *Nurse Practitioner, 25,* 29–32.

Budinger, T. F. (1992). Critical review of PET, SPECT, and neuroreceptor studies in schizophrenia. *Journal of Neural Transmission (Supplementum), 36,* 3–12.

Buhrich, N., & McConaghy, N. (1977). The discrete syndromes of transvestism and transsexualism. *Archives of Sexual Behavior, 6,* 483–495.

Buhrich, N., Theile, H., Yaw, A., & Crawford, A. (1979). Plasma testosterone, serum FSH, and serum LH levels in transvestism. *Archives of Sexual Behavior, 8,* 49–53.

Bullard, D. M. (1960). Psychotherapy of paranoid patients. *Archives of General Psychiatry, 2,* 137–141.

Burgess, A. W., & Holmstrom, L. L. (1974). *Rape: Victims of crisis.* Bowie, MD: Brady.

Burgess, J. W. (1992). Neurocognitive impairment in dramatic personalities: Histrionic, narcissistic, borderline, and antisocial disorders. *Psychiatry Research, 42,* 283–290.

Burstein, A. G. (1989). *Rorschach's test: Scoring and interpretation.* New York: Hemisphere.

Bursten, B. (1979). Psychiatry and the rhetoric of models. *American Journal of Psychiatry, 136,* 661–666.

Buss, A. H., & Plomin, R. (1975). *A temperament theory of personality.* New York: Wiley.

Buss, A. H., & Plomin, R. (1984). *Temperament: Early developing personality traits.* Hillsdale, NJ: Erlbaum.

Buss, D. M. (1987). Selection, evocation, and manipulation. *Journal of Personality and Social Psychology, 53,* 1214–1221.

Butcher, J. N., Dahlstrom, W. G., Graham, J. R., Tellegen, A., & Kaemmer, B. (1989). *Manual for the restandardized Minnesota Multiphasic Personality Inventory: MMPI-2. An interpretative and administrative guide.* Minneapolis: University of Minnesota Press.

Butler, G., Cullington, A., Munby, M., Amies, P., & Gelder, M. (1984). Exposure and anxiety management in the treatment of social phobia. *Journal of Consulting and Clinical Psychology, 52,* 642–650.

Buydens-Branchey, L., Noumair, D., & Branchey, M. (1990). Duration and intensity of combat exposure and post-traumatic stress disorder in Vietnam veterans. *Journal of Nervous and Mental Disease, 178,* 582–587.

Byck, R. (Ed.). (1975). *Cocaine papers by Sigmund Freud.* New York: Stonehill.

Byrne, C. P., Velamoor, V. R., Cernovsky, Z. Z., Cortese, L., & Losztyn, S. (1990). A comparison of borderline and schizophrenic patients for childhood life events and parent-child relationships. *Canadian Journal of Psychiatry, 35,* 590–595.

Byrne, D. (1964). Repression-sensitization as a dimension of personality. In B. A. Maher (Ed.), *Progress in experimental personality research* (Vol. 1). New York: Academic Press.

Byrne, D., Steinberg, M. A., & Schwartz, M. S. (1968). Relationship between repression-sensitization and physical illness. *Journal of Abnormal Psychology, 73,* 154–155.

Cadoret, R. J. (1978). Evidence for genetic inheritance of primary affective disorder in adoptees. *American Journal of Psychiatry, 135,* 463–466.

Cadoret, R. J. (1986). Epidemiology of antisocial personality. In W. H. Reid et al. (Eds.), *Unmasking the psychopath: Antisocial personality and related syndromes.* New York: Norton.

Cadoret, R. J., & Stewart, M. A. (1991). An adoption study of attention deficit/hyperactivity/aggression and their relationship to adult antisocial personality. *Comprehensive Psychiatry, 32,* 73–82.

Cadoret, R. J., Troughton, E., Bagford, J., & Woodworth, G. (1990). Genetic and environmental factors in adoptee antisocial personality. *European Archives of Psychiatry and Neurological Sciences, 239,* 231–240.

Cahalan, D. (1978). Implications of American drinking practices for prevention and treatment of alcoholism. In G. A. Marlatt & P. E. Nathan (Eds.), *Behavioral approaches to alcoholism.* New Brunswick, NJ: Rutgers Center of Alcohol Studies.

Calanca, A. (1991). The transsexual after sex change: Evolution and prognosis. *Helvetica Chirurgica Acta, 58,* 257–260.

Callahan, L. A., Steadman, H. J., McGreevy, M. A., & Robbins, P. C. (1991). The volume and characteristics of insanity defense pleas: An eight-state study. *Bulletin of the American Academy of Psychiatry and the Law, 19,* 389–393.

Cameron, O. G., & Hill, E. M. (1989). Women and anxiety. *Psychiatric Clinics of North America, 12,* 175–186.

Campbell, D. T., & Fiske, D. W. (1959). Convergent and discriminant validation by the multitrait-multimethod matrix. *Psychological Bulletin, 56,* 81–105.

Canino, I. A., & Spurlock, J. (1994). *Culturally diverse children and adolescents: Assessment, diagnosis, and treatment.* New York: Guilford.

Canter, A. (1985). The Bender-Gestalt Test. In C. S. Newmark (Ed.), *Major psychological assessment instruments.* Boston: Allyn & Bacon.

Cantor, N. (1990). From thought to behavior: "Having" and "doing" in the study of personality and cognition. *American Psychologist, 45,* 735–750.

Cantor, N., Smith, E. E., French, R. deS., & Mezzich, J. (1980). Psychiatric diagnosis as prototype categorization. *Journal of Abnormal Psychology, 89,* 181–193.

Caplan, L. (1984). *The insanity defense and the trial of John W. Hinckley, Jr.* Boston: Godine.

Caramazza, A. (1988). Some aspects of language processing through the analysis of acquired aphasia: The lexical system. *Annual Review of Neuroscience, 11,* 395–421.

Card, J. J. (1987). Epidemiology of PTSD in a national cohort of Vietnam veterans. *Journal of Clinical Psychology, 43,* 6–17.

Carey, M. P., & Burish, T. G. (1988). Etiology and treatment of psychological side effects associated with cancer chemotherapy: A critical review and discussion. *Psychological Bulletin, 104,* 307–325.

Carlson, N. R. (1986). *Physiology of behavior* (3rd ed.). Boston: Allyn & Bacon.

Carnegie, D. (1936). *How to win friends and influence people.* New York: Simon & Schuster.

Carone, B. J., Harrow, M., & Westermeyer, J. F. (1991). Posthospital course and outcome in schizophrenia. *Archives of General Psychiatry, 48,* 247–253.

Carr, J. E., & Tan, E. K. (1976). In search of the true amok: Amok as viewed within the Malay culture. *American Journal of Psychiatry, 133,* 1295–1299.

Carr, V., Dorrington, C., Schrader, G., & Wale, J. (1983). The use of ECT for mania in childhood bipolar disorder. *British Journal of Psychiatry, 143,* 411–415.

Carrieri, J. R. (1991). *Child custody, foster care, and adoptions.* New York: Lexington.

Carroll, B. J., Curtis, G. C., & Mendels, J. (1976a). Neuroendocrine regulation in depression. I. Limbic system-adrenocortical dysfunction. *Archives of General Psychiatry, 33,* 1039–1044.

Carroll, B. J., Curtis, G. C., & Mendels, J. (1976b). Neuroendocrine regulation in depression. II. Discrimination of depressed from nondepressed patients. *Archives of General Psychiatry, 33,* 1051–1058.

Carson, R. C. (1991). Dilemmas in the pathway of DSM-IV. *Journal of Abnormal Psychology, 100,* 302–307.

Carty, R. C., & Breault, G. C. (1967). Gheel: A comprehensive community mental health program. *Perspectives in Psychiatric Care, 5,* 281–285.

Casanova, M. F., & Kleinman, J. E. (1990). The neuropathology of schizophrenia: A critical assessment of research methodologies. *Biological Psychiatry, 27,* 353–362.

Casey, D. E. (1990). Tardive dyskinesia. *Western Journal of Medicine, 153,* 535–541.

Casey, P. (1988). The epidemiology of personality disorder. In P. Tyrer (Ed.), *Personality disorders: Diagnosis, management, and course.* London: Wright.

Cassano, G. B., Perugi, G., Musetti, L., & Savino, M. (1990). Drug treatment of anxiety disorders. In N. Sartorius, V. Andreoli, G. Cassano, L. Eisenberg, P. Kielholz, P. Pancheri, & G. Racagni (Eds.), *Anxiety: Psychobiological and clinical perspectives.* New York: Hemisphere.

Casteles, E. E., & Glass, C. R. (1986). Training in social and interpersonal problem-solving skills for mildly and moderately retarded adults. *American Journal of Mental Deficiency, 91,* 35–42.

Casto, G., & Mastropieri, M. (1986). The efficacy of early intervention programs. *Exceptional Children, 52,* 417–424.

Catalan, J., Hawton, K., & Day, A. (1990). Couples referred to a sexual dysfunction clinic: Psychological and physical morbidity. *British Journal of Psychiatry, 156,* 61–67.

Cermak, T. L. (1986). *Diagnosing and treating co-dependence.* Minneapolis: Johnson Institute.

Chadda, R. K., & Ahuja, N. (1990). Dhat syndrome: A sex neurosis of the Indian subcontinent. *British Journal of Psychiatry, 156,* 577–579.

Chalmers, E. M. (1991). Volatile substance abuse. *Medical Journal of Australia, 154,* 269–274.

Chamberlin, J. E., & Gilman, S. L. (1985). *Degeneration: The dark side of progress.* New York: Columbia University Press.

Chandler, P. W. (1970). *American criminal trials* (Vol. 1). New York: AMS Press.

Chapman, C. R., Wilson, M. E., & Gehrig, J. D. (1976). Comparative effects of acupuncture and transcutaneous stimulation of the perception of painful dental stimuli. *Pain, 2,* 265–283.

Chen, C. S. (1968). A study of the alcohol-tolerance effect and an introduction of a new behavioral technique. *Psychopharmacologia, 12,* 433–440.

Chesler, P. (1972). *Women and madness.* New York: Doubleday.

Cheung, Y. W. (1989). Making sense of ethnicity and drug use: A review and suggestions for future research. *Sociology of Pharmacology, 3,* 55–82.

Chi, I., Lubben, J. E., & Kitano, H. H. L. (1989). Differences in drinking behavior among three Asian-American groups. *Journal of Studies on Alcohol, 50,* 15–23.

Chi, M. T. H., Feltovich, P. J., & Glaser, R. (1981). Categorization and representation of physics problems by experts and novices. *Cognitive Science, 5,* 121–152.

Chodoff, P. (1972). The depressive personality. *Archives of General Psychiatry, 27,* 666–667.

Chodoff, P., & Lyons, H. (1958). Hysteria, the hysterical personality, and "hysterical" conversion. *American Journal of Psychiatry, 114,* 734–740.

Chodorow, N. (1989). *Feminism and psychoanalytic theory.* New Haven, CT: Yale University Press.

Chou, T. (1992). Wake up and smell the coffee: Caffeine, coffee, and the medical consequences. *Western Journal of Medicine, 157,* 544–553.

Chowdhury, A. N. (1991). Penis-root perception of koro patients. *Acta Psychiatrica Scandinavica, 84,* 12–13.

Chu, F. D., & Trotter, S. (1974). *The madness establishment.* New York: Grossman.

Chu, J. A., & Dill, D. L. (1990). Dissociative symptoms in relation to childhood physical and sexual abuse. *American Journal of Psychiatry, 147,* 887–892.

Chuang, H. T., Devins, G. M., Hunsley, J., & Gill, M. J. (1989). Psychosocial distress and well-being among gay and bisexual men with human immunodeficiency virus infection. *American Journal of Psychiatry, 146,* 876–880.

Chuang, H. T., Williams, R., & Dalby, J. T. (1987). Criminal behaviour among schizophrenics. *Canadian Journal of Psychiatry, 32,* 255–258.

Chung, R. K., Langeluddecke, P., & Tennant, C. (1986). Threatening life events in the onset of schizophrenia, schizophreniform psychosis, and hypomania. *British Journal of Psychiatry, 148,* 680–685.

Cialdini, R. B. (1985). *Influence: Science and practice.* Glenview, IL: Scott, Foresman.

Cicchetti, D. (1984). The emergence of developmental psychopathology. *Child Development, 55,* 1–7.

Ciccone, J. R. (1992). Murder, insanity, and medical expert witnesses. *Archives of Neurology, 49,* 608–611.

Cioffi, D. (1991). Beyond attentional strategies: Cognitive-perceptual model of somatic interpretation. *Psychological Bulletin, 109,* 25–41.

Claridge, G. (1978). Animal models of schizophrenia: The case for LSD-25. *Schizophrenia Bulletin, 4,* 186–209.

Clark, D. M. (1988). A cognitive model of panic attacks. In S. Rachman & J. D. Maser (Eds.), *Panic: Psychological perspectives.* Hillsdale, NJ: Erlbaum.

Clark, D. M., Salkovskis, P. M., & Chalkey, A. J. (1985). Respiratory control as a treatment for panic attacks. *Journal of Behavior Therapy and Experimental Psychiatry, 16,* 23–30.

Clark, L. A., & Watson, D. (1991). Tripartite model of anxiety and depression: Psychometric evidence and taxonomic implications. *Journal of Abnormal Psychology, 100,* 316–336.

Clark, R. E. (1948). The relationship of schizophrenia to occupational income and occupational prestige. *American Sociological Review, 13,* 325–330.

Clarke, J. (1972). *The life and times of George III.* London: Weidenfeld & Nicolson.

Clausen, J. A., & Kohn, M. L. (1959). Relation of schizophrenia to the social structure of a small city. In B. Pasamanick (Ed.), *Epidemiology of mental disorder.* Washington, DC: AAAS.

Clayton, P. J., Grove, W. M., Coryell, W., Keller, M., Hirschfeld, R., & Fawcett, J. (1991). Follow-up and family study of anxious depression. *American Journal of Psychiatry, 148,* 1512–1517.

Clayton, R. R. (1986). Multiple drug use: Epidemiology, correlates, and consequences. In M. Galanter (Ed.), *Recent developments in alcoholism* (Vol. 4). New York: Plenum.

Cleckley, H. (1976). *The mask of sanity* (5th ed.). St. Louis: Mosby.

Cloninger, C. R. (1987). Neurogenetic adaptive mechanisms in alcoholism. *Science, 236,* 410–416.

Cobb, S. (1976). Social support as a moderator of life stress. *Psychosomatic Medicine, 38,* 300–314.

Cobb, S., & Rose, R. M. (1973). Hypertension, peptic ulcer, and diabetes in air traffic controllers. *JAMA, 224,* 489–492.

Cochran, S. D., & Gitlin, M. J. (1988). Attitudinal correlates of lithium compliance in bipolar affective disorders. *Journal of Nervous and Mental Disease, 176,* 457–464.

Cochrane, R., & Bal, S. (1990). The drinking habits of Sikh, Hindu, Muslim, and white men in the West Midlands: A community survey. *British Journal of Addiction, 85,* 756–769.

Coffey, C. E., & Weiner, R. D. (1990). Electroconvulsive therapy: An update. *Hospital and Community Psychiatry, 41,* 515–521.

Cohen, C. P., & Sherwood, V. R. (1989). Becoming a constant object for the borderline patient. *Bulletin of the Menninger Clinic, 53,* 287–299.

Cohen, D. J., Riddle, M. A., & Leckman, J. F. (1992). Pharmacotherapy of Tourette's syndrome and associated disorders. *Psychiatric Clinics of North America, 15,* 109–129.

Cohen, J. A. (1960). A coefficient of agreement for nominal scales. *Educational and Psychological Measurement, 20,* 37–46.

Cohen, J. D., & Servan-Schreiber, D. (1992). Context, cortex, and dopamine: A connectionist approach to behavior and biology in schizophrenia. *Psychological Review, 99,* 45–77.

Cohen, J. D., & Servan-Schreiber, D. (1993). A theory of dopamine function and its role in cognitive deficits in schizophrenia. *Schizophrenia Bulletin, 19,* 85–104.

Cohen, M. E., Robins, E., Purtell, J. J., Altmann, M. W., & Reid, D. E. (1953). Excessive surgery in hysteria. *JAMA, 151,* 977–986.

Cohen, M. L., Seghorn, T., & Calmas, W. (1969). Sociometric study of the sex offender. *Journal of Abnormal Psychology, 74,* 249–255.

Cohen, M. M., & Shiloh, Y. (1977–1978). Genetic toxicology of lysergic acid diethylamide (LSD-25). *Mutation Research, 47,* 183–209.

Cohen, S. (1988). Psychosocial models of the role of social support in the etiology of physical disease. *Health Psychology, 7,* 269–297.

Cohen, S., & Khan, A. (1990). Antipsychotic effect of milieu in the acute treatment of schizophrenia. *General Hospital Psychiatry, 12,* 248–251.

Cohen, S., & Syme, S. L. (1985). *Social support and health.* Orlando, FL: Academic Press.

Cohen, S., Tyrrell, D. A., & Smith, A. P. (1991). Psychological stress and susceptibility to the common cold. *New England Journal of Medicine, 325,* 606–612.

Cohen, S., & Williamson, G. M. (1991). Stress and infectious disease in humans. *Psychological Bulletin, 109,* 5–24.

Cohen, Y. (1991). Grandiosity in children with narcissistic and borderline disorders: A comparative analysis. *Psychoanalytic Study of the Child, 46,* 307–324.

Colby, K. M. (1977). Appraisal of four psychological theories of paranoid phenomena. *Journal of Abnormal Psychology, 86,* 54–59.

Cole, J. O., & Bodkin, J. A. (1990). Antidepressant drug side effects. *Journal of Clinical Psychiatry, 51,* 21–26.

Cole, N. (1985). Sex therapy: A critical appraisal. *British Journal of Psychiatry, 147,* 337–351.

Cole, T. B., Chorba, T. L., & Horan, J. M. (1990). Patterns of transmission of epidemic hysteria in a school. *Epidemiology, 1,* 212–218.

Coleman, L. (1984). *The reign of error: Psychiatry, authority, and law.* Boston: Beacon.

Coleman, R. J. (1992). Current drug therapy for Parkinson's disease: A review. *Drugs and Aging, 2,* 112–124.

Colligan, M. J., Urtes, M. A., Wisseman, C., Rosensteel, R. E., Anania, T. L., & Hornung, R. W. (1979). An investigation of apparent mass psychogenic illness in an electronics plant. *Journal of Behavioral Medicine, 2,* 297–309.

Colohan, A. R., & Oyesiku, N. M. (1992). Moderate head trauma: An overview. *Journal of Neurotrauma, 9,* 259–264.

Comerci, G. D. (1990). Medical complications of anorexia nervosa and bulimia nervosa. *Medical Clinics of North America, 74,* 1293–1310.

Comfort, A. (1967). *The anxiety makers.* New York: Delta.

Compton, A. (1992a). The psychoanalytic view of phobias. Part I: Freud's theories of phobias and anxiety. *Psychoanalytic Quarterly, 61,* 206–229.

Compton, A. (1992b). The psychoanalytic view of phobias. Part II: Infantile phobias. *Psychoanalytic Quarterly, 61,* 230–253.

Compton, A. (1992c). The psychoanalytic view of phobias. Part III: Agoraphobia and other phobias of adults. *Psychoanalytic Quarterly, 61*, 400–425.

Compton, A. (1992d). The psychoanalytic view of phobias. Part IV: General theory of phobias and anxiety. *Psychoanalytic Quarterly, 61*, 426–446.

Condron, M. K., & Nutter, D. E. (1988). A preliminary examination of the pornography experience of sex offenders, paraphiliacs, sexual dysfunction patients, and controls based on Meese Commission recommendations. *Journal of Sex and Marital Therapy, 14*, 285–298.

Conger, J. J. (1951). The effects of alcohol on conflict behavior in the albino rat. *Quarterly Journal of Studies on Alcohol, 12*, 1–29.

Conger, J. J. (1956). Reinforcement theory and the dynamics of alcoholism. *Quarterly Journal on Studies on Alcohol, 13*, 296–305.

Conley, J. J. (1985). Longitudinal stability of personality traits: A multitrait-multimethod-multioccasion analysis. *Journal of Personality and Social Psychology, 49*, 1266–1282.

Connell, P. H. (1958). *Amphetamine psychosis.* London: Chapman & Hall.

Connolly, F. H., & Gipson, M. (1978). Dysmorphophobia: A long-term study. *British Journal of Psychiatry, 132*, 568–570.

Conte, H. R., & Karasu, T. B. (1990). Malpractice in psychotherapy: An overview. *American Journal of Psychotherapy, 44*, 232–246.

Conte, H. R., & Karasu, T. B. (1992). A review of treatment studies of minor depression: 1980–1991. *American Journal of Psychotherapy, 46*, 58–74.

Cook, E. H., Leventhal, B. L., Heller, W., Metz, J., Wainwright, M., & Freedman, D. X. (1990). Autistic children and their first-degree relatives: Relationships between serotonin and norepinephrine levels and intelligence. *Journal of Neuropsychiatry and Clinical Neuroscience, 2*, 268–274.

Cook, M. L., & Peterson, C. (1986). Depressive irrationality. *Cognitive Therapy and Research, 10*, 293–298.

Cookerly, J. R. (1980). Does marital therapy do any lasting good? *Journal of Marital and Family Therapy, 6*, 393–397.

Coons, P. M. (1986). Treatment progress in 20 patients with multiple personality disorder. *Journal of Nervous and Mental Disease, 174*, 715–721.

Cooper, M. L., Russell, M., Skinner, J. B., & Windle, M. (1992). Development and validation of a three-dimensional measure of drinking motives. *Psychological Assessment, 4*, 123–132.

Coren, S. (Ed.). (1990). *Left-handedness: Behavioral implications and anomalies.* New York: Elsevier.

Coren, S. (1992). *The left-hander syndrome: The causes and consequences of left-handedness.* New York: Free Press.

Coren, S., & Halpern, D. F. (1991). Left-handedness: A marker for decreased survival fitness. *Psychological Bulletin, 109*, 90–106.

Coryell, W., Endicott, J., Keller, M., Andreasen, N., Grove, W., Hirschfeld, R. M., & Scheftner, W. (1989). Bipolar affective disorder and high achievement: A familial association. *American Journal of Psychiatry, 146*, 983–988.

Coryell, W., Keller, M., Endicott, J., Andreasen, N., Clayton, P., & Hirschfeld, R. (1989). Bipolar II illness: Course and outcome over a five-year period. *Psychological Medicine, 19*, 129–141.

Coryell, W., & Tsuang, M. T. (1986). Outcome after 40 years in DSM-III schizophreniform disorder. *Archives of General Psychiatry, 43*, 324–328.

Coryell, W., & Zimmerman, M. (1988). The heritability of schizophrenia and schizoaffective disorder: A family study. *Archives of General Psychiatry, 45*, 323–327.

Costa, P. T., & McCrae, R. R. (1978). Objective personality assessments. In M. Storandt, I. C. Siegler, & M. F. Elias (Eds.), *The clinical psychology of aging.* New York: Plenum.

Costa, P. T., & McCrae, R. R. (1980). Somatic complaints in males as a function of age and neuroticism: A longitudinal analysis. *Journal of Behavioral Medicine, 3*, 245–257.

Costello, C. G. (1992). Problems in recent tests of two cognitive theories of panic. *Behaviour Research and Therapy, 30*, 1–5.

Costello, C. G., & Scott, C. B. (1991). Primary and secondary depression: A review. *Canadian Journal of Psychiatry, 36*, 210–217.

Costigan, K. (1985, May 20). Cabin fever. *Forbes, 234+.*

Cotton, N. (1979). The family incidence of alcoholism: A review. *Journal of Studies on Alcohol, 40*, 89–116.

Cottraux, J., & Mollard, E. (1988). Cognitive therapy of phobias. In C. Perris, I. M. Blackburn, & H. Perris (Eds.), *Cognitive psychotherapy: Theory and practice.* Berlin: Springer-Verlag.

Coulter, H. L. (1982). *Divided legacy: The conflict between homeopathy and the American Medical Association.* Berkeley, CA: North Atlantic Books.

Courchesne, E. (1991). Neuroanatomic imaging in autism. *Pediatrics, 87*, 781–790.

Coursey, R. D. (1989). Psychotherapy with persons suffering from schizophrenia: The need for a new agenda. *Schizophrenia Bulletin, 15*, 349–353.

Cousins, N. (1976). Anatomy of an illness (as perceived by the patient). *New England Journal of Medicine, 295*, 1458–1463.

Couvreur, V., Ansseau, M., & Franck, G. (1989). Electroconvulsive therapy and its mechanism of action. *Acta Psychiatrica Belgica, 89*, 96–109.

Cox, B. J., Norton, G. R., Swinson, R. P., & Endler, N. S. (1990). Substance abuse and panic-related anxiety: A critical review. *Behaviour Research and Therapy, 28*, 385–393.

Cox, G. L., & Merkel, W. T. (1989). A qualitative review of psychosocial treatments for bulimia. *Journal of Nervous and Mental Disease, 177*, 77–84.

Cox, W. M. (1985). Personality correlates of substance abuse. In M. Galizio & S. A. Maisto (Eds.), *Determinants of substance abuse: Biological, psychological, and environmental factors.* New York: Plenum.

Coyne, J. C. (1976). Toward an interactional description of depression. *Psychiatry, 39*, 28–40.

Coyne, J. C. (1985). Studying depressed persons' interactions with strangers and spouses. *Journal of Abnormal Psychology, 94*, 231–232.

Coyne, J. C., & Gotlib, I. H. (1983). The role of cognition in depression: A critical appraisal. *Psychological Bulletin, 94,* 472–505.

Crabtree, A. (1985). *Multiple man: Explorations in possession and multiple personality.* New York: Praeger.

Craik, F. I. M., & Lockhart, R. S. (1972). Levels of processing: A framework for memory research. *Journal of Verbal Learning and Verbal Behavior, 11,* 671–684.

Craske, M. G., & Barlow, D. H. (1991). Contributions of cognitive psychology to assessment and treatment of anxiety. In P. R. Martin (Ed.), *Handbook of behavior therapy and psychological science.* New York: Pergamon.

Craufurd, D. I., & Harris, R. (1986). Ethics of predictive testing for Huntington's chorea: The need for more information. *British Medical Journal, 293,* 249–251.

Crawford, K. A., & Siegel, P. S. (1982). Improving the visual discrimination of mentally retarded children: A training strategy. *American Journal of Mental Deficiency, 87,* 294–301.

Creer, T. L. (1991). The application of behavioral procedures to childhood asthma: Current and future perspectives. *Patient Education and Counseling, 17,* 9–22.

Crisp, A. H., Callender, J. S., Halek, C., & Hsu, L. K. (1992). Long-term mortality in anorexia nervosa: A 20-year follow-up of the St. George's and Aberdeen cohorts. *British Journal of Psychiatry, 161,* 104–107.

Crisp, A. H., Harding, B., & McGuinness, B. (1974). Anorexia nervosa. Psychoneurotic characteristics of parents: Relationship to prognosis. *Journal of Psychosomatic Research, 18,* 167–173.

Crisp, A. H., Norton, K., Gowers, S., Halek, C., Bowyer, C., Yeldham, D., Levett, G., & Bhat, A. (1991). A controlled study of the effect of therapies aimed at adolescent and family psychopathology in anorexia nervosa. *British Journal of Psychiatry, 159,* 325–333.

Cross-National Collaborative Group. (1992). The changing rate of major depression: Cross-national comparisons. *JAMA, 268,* 3098–3105.

Crow, T. J. (1980). Positive and negative schizophrenia symptoms and the role of dopamine. *British Journal of Psychiatry, 137,* 383–386.

Crow, T. J. (1982). Two dimensions of pathology in schizophrenia: Dopaminergic and non-dopaminergic. *Psychopharmacology Bulletin, 18,* 22–29.

Crow, T. J. (1985). The two syndrome concept: Origins and current status. *Schizophrenia Bulletin, 11,* 471–486.

Crow, T. J., Cross, A. J., Cooper, S. J., Deakin, J. F. W., Ferrier, I. N., Johnson, J. A., Joseph, M. H., Owen, F., Poulter, M., Lofthouse, R., Corsellis, J. A. N., Chambers, D. R., Blessed, G., Perry, E. K., Perry, R. H., & Tomlinson, B. E. (1984). Neurotransmitter receptors and monoamine metabolites in the brains of patients with Alzheimer-type dementia, and depression, and suicides. *Neuropharmacology, 23,* 1561–1569.

Culkin, J., & Perrotto, R. S. (1985). Assertiveness factors and depression in a sample of college women. *Psychological Reports, 57,* 1015–1020.

Cullberg, J. (1991). Recovered versus nonrecovered schizophrenic patients among those who have had intensive psychotherapy. *Acta Psychiatrica Scandinavica, 84,* 242–245.

Cullen, W. (1769/1816). *A synopsis of nosology.* Philadelphia: William Fry.

Culver, C. M., & Gert, B. (1990). The inadequacy of incompetence. *Milbank Quarterly, 68,* 619–643.

Cummings, J. L. (1992). Depression and Parkinson's disease: A review. *American Journal of Psychiatry, 149,* 443–454.

Cupalova, R., & Vachutkova, M. (1989). The influence of paranoic parents on the education of children. *Acta Universitatis Palackianae Olomucensis Facultatis Medicae, 122,* 383–386.

Curran, V., & Marengo, J. T. (1990). Psychological assessment of catatonic schizophrenia. *Journal of Personality Assessment, 55,* 432–444.

Cushman, P. (1990). Why the self is empty: Toward a historically situated psychology. *American Psychologist, 45,* 599–611.

Cutler, B. L. (1990). The status of scientific jury selection in psychology and law. *Forensic Reports, 3,* 227–232.

Cytryn, L., & Lourie, R. S. (1980). Mental retardation. In H. I. Kaplan, A. M. Freedman, & B. J. Sadock (Eds.), *Comprehensive textbook of psychiatry* (Vol. 3, 3rd ed.). Baltimore: Williams & Wilkins.

Dager, S. R., Cowley, D. S., & Dunner, D. L. (1987). Biological markers in panic states: Lactate-induced panic and mitral valve prolapse. *Biological Psychiatry, 22,* 339–359.

Dahl, J. A., Gustafsson, D., & Melin, L. (1990). Effects of a behavioral treatment program on children with asthma. *Journal of Asthma, 27,* 41–46.

Dahl, J. A., Melin, L., & Leissner, P. (1988). Effects of a behavioral intervention on epileptic seizure behavior and paroxysmal activity: A systematic replication of three cases of children with intractable epilepsy. *Epilepsia, 29,* 172–183.

Dahl, S. (1989). Acute responses to rape. *Acta Psychiatrica Scandinavica (Supplementum), 355,* 56–62.

Dahlstrom, W. G., Lachar, D., & Dahlstrom, L. E. (1986). *MMPI patterns of American minorities.* Minneapolis: University of Minnesota Press.

Daitzman, R. J., & Cox, D. J. (1980). An extended case report: The nuts and bolts of treating an exhibitionist. In D. J. Cox & R. J. Daitzman (Eds.), *Exhibitionism: Description, assessment, and treatment.* New York: Guilford.

Dale, A. J. D. (1980). Organic mental disorders associated with infections. In H. I. Kaplan, A. M. Freedman, & B. J. Sadock (Eds.), *Comprehensive textbook of psychiatry* (Vol. 2, 3rd ed.). Baltimore: Williams & Wilkins.

Dalgaard, O. S., & Kringlen, E. (1976). A Norwegian twin study of criminality. *British Journal of Criminology, 16,* 213-232.

Dana, R. H. (1985). Thematic Apperception Test (TAT). In C. S. Newmark (Ed.), *Major psychological assessment instruments.* Boston: Allyn & Bacon.

Dancey, C. P. (1990). Sexual orientation in women: An investigation of hormonal and personality variables. *Biological Psychology, 30,* 251–264.

Danesi, M. A., & Adetunji, J. B. (1994). Use of alternative medicine by patients with epilepsy: A survey of 265 epileptic patients in a developing country. *Epilepsia, 35,* 344–351.

Daniels, D., & Plomin, R. (1985). Origins of individual differences in infant shyness. *Developmental Psychology, 21,* 118–121.

Darling, C. A., Davidson, J. K., & Conway-Welch, C. (1990). Female ejaculation: Perceived origins, the Grafenberg spot/area, and sexual responsiveness. *Archives of Sexual Behavior, 19,* 29–47.

Darling, C. A., Davidson, J. K., & Jennings, D. A. (1991). The female sexual response revisited: Understanding the multiorgasmic experience in women. *Archives of Sexual Behavior, 20,* 527–540.

Darling, M. R., & Arendorf, T. M. (1992). Review of the effects of cannabis smoking on oral health. *International Dental Journal, 42,* 19–22.

Darwin, C. R. (1872/1899). *The expression of the emotions in man and animals.* New York: Appleton.

Davenport-Hines, R. P. T. (1990). *Sex, death, and punishment: Attitudes to sex and sexuality in Britain since the Renaissance.* London: Collins.

Davidson, J. R., Hughes, D., Blazer, D. G., & George, L. K. (1991). Post-traumatic stress disorder in the community: An epidemiological study. *Psychological Medicine, 21,* 713–721.

Davidson, M., Keefe, R. S., Mohs, R. C., Siever, L. J., Losonczy, M. F., Horvath, T. B., & Davis, K. L. (1987). L-dopa challenge and relapse in schizophrenia. *American Journal of Psychiatry, 144,* 934–938.

Davis, R. E. (1979). Manic-depressive variant syndrome of childhood: A preliminary report. *American Journal of Psychiatry, 136,* 702–706.

De Becker, G. (1990, February 12). In his words. *People Weekly,* 103–106.

deGruy, F. V., Dickinson, P., Dickinson, L., Mullins, H. C., Baker, W., & Blackmon, D. (1989). The families of patients with somatization disorder. *Family Medicine, 21,* 438–442.

Deitz, D. E. D., & Repp, A. C. (1989). Mental retardation. In T. H. Ollendick & M. Hersen (Eds.), *Handbook of child psychopathology* (2nd ed.). New York: Plenum.

de Leon, J., Saiz-Ruiz, J., Chinchilla, A., & Morales, P. (1987). Why do some psychiatric patients somatize? *Acta Psychiatrica Scandinavica, 76,* 203–209.

Dell, P. F., & Eisenhower, J. W. (1990). Adolescent multiple personality disorder: A preliminary study of eleven cases. *Journal of the American Academy of Child and Adolescent Psychiatry, 29,* 359–366.

Dennerstein, L., Burrows, G. D., Wood, C., & Hyman, G. (1980). Hormones and sexuality: Effect of estrogen and progestogen. *Obstetrics and Gynecology, 56,* 316–322.

Dennis, D. L., Buckner, J. C., Lipton, F. R., & Levine, I. S. (1991). A decade of research and services for homeless mentally ill persons: Where do we stand? *American Psychologist, 46,* 1129–1138.

Dent, J. Y. (1941). *Anxiety and its treatment: With special reference to alcoholism.* London: John Murray.

Depue, R. A., & Monroe, S. M. (1978). Learned helplessness in the perspective of the depressive disorders: Conceptual and definitional issues. *Journal of Abnormal Psychology, 87,* 3–20.

Derogatis, L. R. (1991). Personality, stress, disease, and bias in epidemiological research. *Psychological Inquiry, 2,* 238–242.

Des Jarlais, D. C., Friedman, S. R., Novick, D. M., Sotheran, J. L., Thomas, P., Yancovitz, S. R., Mildvan, D., Weber, J., Kreek, M. J., & Maslansky, R. (1989). HIV-1 infection among intravenous drug users in Manhattan, New York City, from 1977 through 1987. *JAMA, 261,* 1008–1012.

DeVellis, R. F., & McCauley, C. (1979). Perception of noncontingency and mental retardation. *Journal of Autism and Developmental Disorders, 9,* 261–270.

Devins, G. M., & Seland, T. P. (1987). Emotional impact of multiple sclerosis: Recent findings and suggestions for future research. *Psychological Bulletin, 101,* 363–375.

DeWitt, K. N. (1978). The effectiveness of family therapy: A review of outcome research. *Archives of General Psychiatry, 35,* 549–561.

Diering, S. L., & Bell, W. O. (1991). Functional neurosurgery for psychiatric disorders: A historical perspective. *Stereotactic and Functional Neurosurgery, 57,* 175–194.

Dietz, P. E., & Evans, B. (1982). Pornographic imagery and prevalence of paraphilia. *American Journal of Psychiatry, 139,* 1493–1495.

Dinwiddie, S. H., Zorumski, C. F., & Rubin, E. H. (1987). Psychiatric correlates of chronic solvent abuse. *Journal of Clinical Psychiatry, 48,* 334–337.

Dobson, K. S. (1985). The relationship between anxiety and depression. *Clinical Psychology Review, 5,* 307–324.

Dohan, F. C. (1966). Wartime changes in hospital admissions for schizophrenia. *Acta Psychiatrica Scandinavica, 42,* 1–23.

Dohrenwend, B. P., Shrout, P. E., Link, B. G., & Skodol, A. E. (1987). Social and psychosocial risk factors for episodes of schizophrenia. In H. Hafner, W. F. Gattaz, & W. Janzarik (Eds.), *Search for the causes of schizophrenia.* Berlin: Springer-Verlag.

Dohrenwend, B. S., & Dohrenwend, B. P. (Eds.). (1974). *Stressful life events: Their nature and effects.* New York: Wiley.

Dohrenwend, B. S., & Dohrenwend, B. P. (Eds.). (1981). *Stressful life events and their contexts.* New York: Neale Watson.

Dollard, J., & Miller, N. E. (1950). *Personality and psychotherapy: An analysis in terms of learning, thinking, and culture.* New York: McGraw-Hill.

Donahey, K. M., & Carroll, R. A. (1993). Gender differences in factors associated with hypoactive sexual desire. *Journal of Sex and Marital Therapy, 19,* 25–40.

Dorken, H. (1990). Malpractice claims experiences of psychologists: Policy issues, cost comparisons with psychiatrists, and prescription privilege implications. *Professional Psychology: Research and Practice, 21,* 150–152.

Dorry, G. W., & Zeaman, D. (1975). Teaching a simple reading vocabulary to retarded children: Effectiveness of fading and nonfading procedures. *American Journal of Mental Deficiency, 799,* 711–716.

Douglas, M. S., & Mueser, K. T. (1990). Teaching conflict resolution skills to the chronically mentally ill: Social skills training groups for briefly hospitalized patients. *Behavior Modification, 14,* 519–547.

Douglas, W. O. (1974). *Go east, young man.* New York: Random House.

Doutney, C. P., Buhrich, N., Virgona, A., Cohen, A., & Daniels, P. (1985). The prevalence of schizophrenia in a refuge for homeless men. *Australian and New Zealand Journal of Psychiatry, 19,* 233–238.

Doverty, N. (1992). Therapeutic use of play in hospital. *British Journal of Nursing, 1,* 77, 79–81.

Dowben, C., & Heartwell, S. F. (1979). Legal implications of sterilization of the mentally retarded. *American Journal of Diseases of Children, 133,* 697–699.

Dowling, C. (1990, March 18). Case of child abuse or just mother's love? *Detroit Free Press,* pp. 1, 4.

Dowling, G. P., McDonough, E. T., & Bost, R. O. (1987). "Eve" and "Ecstasy": A report of five deaths associated with MDEA and MDMA. *JAMA, 257,* 1615–1617.

Downey, G., & Coyne, J. C. (1990). Children of depressed parents: An integrative review. *Psychological Bulletin, 108,* 50–76.

Draper, R. J., & Dawson, D. (1990). Competence to consent to treatment: A guide for the psychiatrist. *Canadian Journal of Psychiatry, 35,* 285–289.

Dua, J. K., & McNall, H. M. (1987). Assertiveness in men and women seeking counselling and not seeking counselling. *Behaviour Change, 4,* 14–19.

Duffy, J. (1979). *The healers: A history of American medicine.* Urbana: University of Illinois Press.

Duijkers, T. J., Drijver, M., Kromhout, D., & James, S. A. (1988). "John Henryism" and blood pressure in a Dutch population. *Psychosomatic Medicine, 50,* 353–359.

Dunn, J., & Fahy, T. A. (1990). Police admissions to a psychiatric hospital: Demographic and clinical differences between ethnic groups. *British Journal of Psychiatry, 156,* 373–378.

Dunner, D. L., Fleiss, J. L., & Fieve, R. R. (1976). The course of development of mania in patients with recurrent depression. *American Journal of Psychiatry, 133,* 905–908.

Durkheim, E. (1897/1951). *Suicide.* New York: Free Press.

du Verglas, G., Banks, S. R., & Guyer, K. E. (1988). Clinical effects of fenfluramine on children with autism: A review of the research. *Journal of Autism and Developmental Disorders, 18,* 297–308.

Dyck, M. J. (1993). A proposal for a conditioning model of eye movement desensitization treatment for posttraumatic stress disorder. *Journal of Behavior Therapy and Experimental Psychiatry, 24,* 201–210.

Eaton, W. W., Bilker, W., Haro, J. M., Herrman, H., Mortensen, P. B., Freeman, H., & Burgess, P. (1992). Long-term course of hospitalization for schizophrenia: Part II. Change with passage of time. *Schizophrenia Bulletin, 18,* 229–241.

Eckman, T. A., Wirshing, W. C., Marder, S. R., Liberman, R. P., Johnston-Cronk, K., Zimmerman, K., & Mintz, J. (1992). Technique for training schizophrenic patients in illness self-management: A controlled trial. *American Journal of Psychiatry, 149,* 1549–1555.

Edgerton, R. E. (1979). *Mental retardation.* Cambridge: Harvard University Press.

Edwards, G. (1986). The alcohol dependence syndrome: A concept as stimulus to enquiry. *British Journal of Addiction, 81,* 171–183.

Edwards, G., & Gross, M. M. (1976). Alcohol dependence: Provisional description of a clinical syndrome. *British Medical Journal, 1,* 1058–1061.

Edwards, G., Hawker, A., Hensman, C., Peto, J., & Williamson, V. (1973). Alcoholics known or unknown to agencies: Epidemiological studies in a London suburb. *British Journal of Psychiatry, 123,* 169–183.

Edwards, P. W., Zeichner, A., Kuczmierczyk, A. R., & Boczkowski, J. (1985). Familial pain models: The relationship between family history of pain and current pain experience. *Pain, 21,* 379–384.

Efron, R. (1957). Conditioned inhibition of uncinate fits. *Brain, 80,* 561–566.

Egan, V. (1992). Neuropsychological aspects of HIV infection. *AIDS Care, 4,* 3–10.

Egeland, J. A., Gerhard, D. S., Pauls, D. L., Sussex, J. N., Kidd, K. K., Allen, C. R., Hostetter, A. M., & Housman, D. E. (1987). Bipolar affective disorders linked to DNA markers on chromosome II. *Nature, 325,* 783–787.

Eich, J. E. (1980). The cue-dependent nature of state dependent retrieval. *Memory and Cognition, 8,* 157–173.

Einfeld, S. L. (1992). Clinical assessment of psychiatric symptoms in mentally retarded individuals. *Australian and New Zealand Journal of Psychiatry, 26,* 48–63.

Eisner, G. M. (1990). Hypertension: Racial differences. *American Journal of Kidney Diseases, 16,* 35–40.

Eisenberg, D. M., Kessler, R. C., Foster, C., Norlock, F. E., Calkins, D. R., & Delbanco, T. L. (1993). Unconventional medicine in the United States: Prevalence, costs, and patterns of use. *New England Journal of Medicine, 328,* 246–252.

Eison, M. S. (1990). Serotonin: A common neurobiologic substrate in anxiety and depression. *Journal of Clinical Psychopharmacology, 10,* 26–30.

Eitinger, L. (1967). Schizophrenia among concentration camp survivors. *International Journal of Psychiatry, 3,* 403–406.

Eitinger, L., & Grunfeld, B. (1966). Psychoses among refugees in Norway. *Acta Psychiatrica Scandinavica, 42,* 315–328.

Elder, G. H. (1969). Appearance and education in marriage mobility. *American Sociological Review, 34,* 519–533.

Elkin, I., Shea, T., Watkins, J. T., Imber, S. D., Sotsky, S. M., Collins, J. F., Glass, D. R., Pilkonis, P. A., Leber, W. R., Docherty, J. P., Fiester, S. J., & Parloff, M. B. (1989). National Institute of Mental Health treatment of depression collaborative research program. *Archives of General Psychiatry, 46,* 971–982.

Ellenberger, H. F. (1970). *The discovery of the unconscious: The history and evolution of dynamic psychiatry.* New York: Basic Books.

Ellertsen, B., Troland, K., & Klove, H. (1987). MMPI profiles in migraine before and after biofeedback treatment. *Cephalalgia, 7,* 101–108.

Ellicott, A., Hammen, C., Gitlin, M., Brown, G., & Jamison, K. (1990). Life events and the course of bipolar disorder. *American Journal of Psychiatry, 147,* 1194–1198.

Ellis, A. (1962). *Reason and emotion in psychotherapy.* New York: Stuart.

Ellis, H. (1901–1914). *Studies in the psychology of sex* (6 vols.). Philadelphia: Davis.

Ellis, N. R., Woodley-Zanthos, P., Dulaney, C. L., & Palmer, R. L. (1989). Automatic-effortful processing and cognitive inertia in persons with mental retardation. *American Journal of Mental Retardation, 93,* 412–423.

Ellison, J. M., & Adler, D. A. (1990). A strategy for the pharmacotherapy of personality disorders. *New Directions for Mental Health Services, 47,* 43–63.

Emerick, R. E. (1991). The politics of psychiatric self-help: Political factions, interactional support, and group longevity in a social movement. *Social Science and Medicine, 32,* 1121–1128.

Emmelkamp, P. M., & Beens, H. (1991). Cognitive therapy with obsessive-compulsive disorder: A comparative evaluation. *Behaviour Research and Therapy, 29,* 293–300.

Emmons, R. A. (1984). Factor analysis and construct validity of the Narcissistic Personality Inventory. *Journal of Personality Assessment, 48,* 291–300.

Emmons, R. A. (1987). Narcissism: Theory and measurement. *Journal of Personality and Social Psychology, 52,* 11–17.

Endicott, J., & Spitzer, R. L. (1978). A diagnostic interview: The Schedule for Affective Disorders and Schizophrenia. *Archives of General Psychiatry, 35,* 837–844.

Endler, S., & Edwards, J. M. (1988). Personality disorders from an interactional perspective. *Journal of Personality Disorders, 2,* 326–333.

Engel, G. L. (1980). The clinical application of the biopsychosocial model. *American Journal of Psychiatry, 137,* 535–544.

English, H. B. (1929). Three cases of the "conditioned fear response." *Journal of Abnormal and Social Psychology, 34,* 221–225.

Enns, C. Z. (1993). Twenty years of feminist counseling and therapy: From naming biases to implementing multifaceted practice. *Counseling Psychologist, 21,* 3–87.

Epstein, A. W. (1975). The fetish object: Phylogenetic considerations. *Archives of Sexual Behavior, 4,* 303–308.

Epstein, A. W. (1992). Common human phobias. *Journal of the Louisiana State Medical Society, 144,* 329–330.

Epstein, L. H., Wing, R. R., Koeske, R., & Valoski, A. (1987). Long-term effects of family-based treatment of childhood obesity. *Journal of Consulting and Clinical Psychology, 55,* 91–95.

Erdelyi, M. H. (1985). *Psychoanalysis: Freud's cognitive psychology.* New York: Freeman.

Erhardt, D., & Baker, B. L. (1990). The effects of behavioral parent training on families with young hyperactive children. *Journal of Behavior Therapy and Experimental Psychiatry, 21,* 121–132.

Erickson, D. H., Beiser, M., Iacono, W. G., Fleming, J. A., & Lin, T. Y. (1989). The role of social relationships in the course of first-episode schizophrenia and affective psychosis. *American Journal of Psychiatry, 146,* 1456–1461.

Erickson, M. T. (1987). *Behavior disorders of children and adolescents.* Englewood Cliffs, NJ: Prentice-Hall.

Erickson, R. C. (1987). The question of casualties in inpatient small group psychotherapy. *Small Group Behavior, 18,* 443–458.

Ericson, R. V. (1975). *Criminal reactions: The labelling perspective.* Farnborough, England: Saxon House.

Erikson, E. H. (1950). *Childhood and society.* New York: Norton.

Erikson, E. H. (1963). *Childhood and society* (2nd ed.). New York: Norton.

Erlenmeyer-Kimling, L., & Cornblatt, B. A. (1992). A summary of attentional findings in the New York High-Risk Project. *Journal of Psychiatric Research, 26,* 405–426.

Escobar, J. I., Canino, G., Rubio-Stipec, M., & Bravo, M. (1992). Somatic symptoms after a natural disaster: A prospective study. *American Journal of Psychiatry, 149,* 965–967.

Escobar, J. I., Rubio-Stipec, M., Canino, G., & Karno, M. (1989). Somatic symptom index (SSI): A new and abridged somatization construct: Prevalence and epidemiological correlates in two large community samples. *Journal of Nervous and Mental Disease, 177,* 140–146.

Esman, A. H. (1986). Dependent and passive-aggressive personality disorders. In A. M. Cooper, A. J. Frances, & M. H. Sacks (Eds.), *The personality disorders and neuroses.* New York: Basic Books.

Estes, H. R., Haylett, C. H., & Johnson, E. M. (1956). Separation anxiety. *American Journal of Psychotherapy, 10,* 682–695.

Eth, S. (1988). The child victim as witness in sexual abuse proceedings. *Psychiatry, 51,* 221–232.

Evans, L., Holt, C., & Oei, T. P. (1991). Long term follow-up of agoraphobics treated by brief intensive group cognitive behavioural therapy. *Australian and New Zealand Journal of Psychiatry, 25,* 343–349.

Exner, J. E. (1974). *The Rorschach: A comprehensive system* (Vol. 1). New York: Wiley.

Exner, J. E. (1978). *The Rorschach: A comprehensive system* (Vol. 2). New York: Wiley.

Exner, J. E., & Wylie, J. R. (1977). Some Rorschach data concerning suicide. *Journal of Personality Assessment, 41,* 339–348.

Eysenck, H. J. (1952). The effects of psychotherapy: An evaluation. *Journal of Consulting Psychology, 16,* 319–324.

Eysenck, H. J. (1976). *Sex and personality.* Austin: University of Texas Press.

Eysenck, H. J. (1986). A critique of contemporary classification and diagnosis. In T. Millon & G. L. Klerman (Eds.), *Contemporary directions in psychopathology: Toward the DSM-IV.* New York: Guilford.

Eysenck, H. J. (1988). Personality and stress as causal factors in cancer and coronary heart disease. In M. P. Janisse (Ed.), *Individual differences, stress, and health psychology.* New York: Springer-Verlag.

Eysenck, H. J. (1990a). Genetic and environmental contributions to individual differences: The three major dimensions of personality. *Journal of Personality, 58,* 245–261.

Eysenck, H. J. (1990b). The prediction of death from cancer by means of personality/stress questionnaire: Too good to be true? *Perceptual and Motor Skills, 71,* 216–218.

Eysenck, H. J. (1991). Reply to criticisms of the Grossarth-Maticek studies. *Psychological Inquiry, 2,* 297–323.

Fabrega, H. (1990). The concept of somatization as a cultural and historical product of Western medicine. *Psychosomatic Medicine, 52,* 653–672.

Fagan, P. J., Schmidt, C. W., Wise, T. N., & Derogatis, L. R. (1988). Sexual dysfunction and dual psychiatric diagnoses. *Comprehensive Psychiatry, 29,* 278–284.

Fagan, P. J., Wise, T. N., Schmidt, C. W., Ponticas, Y., Marshall, R. D., & Costa, P. T. (1991). A comparison of five-factor personality dimensions in males with sexual dysfunction and males with paraphilia. *Journal of Personality Assessment, 57,* 434–448.

Faigel, H. C., Doak, E., Howard, S. D., & Sigel, M. L. (1992). Emotional disorders in learning disabled adolescents. *Child Psychiatry and Human Development, 23,* 31–40.

Fairburn, C. G. (1988). The current status of the psychological treatments for bulimia nervosa. *Journal of Psychosomatic Research, 32,* 635–645.

Fairburn, C. G., & Hay, P. J. (1992). The treatment of bulimia nervosa. *Annals of Medicine, 24,* 297–302.

Fairburn, C. G., Jones, R., Peveler, R. C., Carr, S. J., Solomon, R. A., O'Connor, M. E., Burton, J., & Hope, R. A. (1991). Three psychological treatments for bulimia nervosa: A comparative trial. *Archives of General Psychiatry, 48,* 463–469.

Fairweather, G. W. (1979). Experimental development and dissemination of an alternative to psychiatric hospitalization: Scientific methods for social change. In R. F. Munoz, L. R. Snowden, & J. G. Kelly (Eds.), *Social and psychological research in community settings.* San Francisco: Jossey-Bass.

Fairweather, G. W., Sanders, D. H., Cressler, D. L., & Maynard, H. (1969). *Community life for the mentally ill.* Chicago: Alpine.

Falk, J. R., & Halmi, K. A. (1982). Amenorrhea in anorexia nervosa: Examination of the critical body weight hypothesis. *Biological Psychiatry, 17,* 799–806.

Falloon, I. R. (1992). Psychotherapy of schizophrenia. *British Journal of Hospital Medicine, 48,* 164–170.

Faraone, S. V., Kremen, W. S., & Tsuang, M. T. (1990). Genetic transmission of major affective disorders: Quantitative models and linkage analyses. *Psychological Bulletin, 108,* 109–127.

Farber, S. L. (1981). *Identical twins reared apart: A reanalysis.* New York: Basic Books.

Farde, L., Wiesel, F. A., Stone-Elander, S., Halldin, C., Nordstrom, A. L., Hall, H., & Sedvall, G. (1990). D2 dopamine receptors in neuroleptic-naive schizophrenic patients: A positron emission tomography study with [11c]raclopride. *Archives of General Psychiatry, 47,* 213–219.

Farmer, M. E., Locke, B. Z., Moscicki, E. K., Dannenberg, A. L., Larson, L. S., & Radloff, L. S. (1988). Physical activity and depressive symptoms: The NHANES I epidemiologic follow-up study. *American Journal of Epidemiology, 128,* 1340–1351.

Farquhar, J. W., Maccoby, N., & Solomon, D. (1984). Community applications of behavioral medicine. In W. D. Gentry (Ed.), *Handbook of behavioral medicine.* New York: Guilford.

Farrer, L. A. (1986). Suicide and attempted suicide in Huntington's disease: Implications for preclinical testing of persons at risk. *American Journal of Medical Genetics, 24,* 305–311.

Fava, M., & Rosenbaum, J. F. (1991). Suicidality and fluoxetine: Is there a relationship? *Journal of Clinical Psychiatry, 52,* 108–111.

Fawcett, J. (1992). Suicide risk factors in depressive disorders and in panic disorders. *Journal of Clinical Psychiatry, 53,* 9–13.

Fedora, O., Reddon, J. R., Morrison, J. W., Fedora, S. K., Pascoe, H., & Yeudall, L. T. (1992). Sadism and other paraphilias in normal controls and aggressive and nonaggressive sex offenders. *Archives of Sexual Behavior, 21,* 1–15.

Fehlings, D. L., Roberts, W., Humphries, T., & Dawe, G. (1991). Attention deficit hyperactivity disorder: Does cognitive behavioral therapy improve home behavior? *Journal of Developmental and Behavioral Pediatrics, 12,* 223–228.

Feighner, J. P., Robins, E., Guze, S. B., Woodruff, R. A., Winokur, G., & Munoz, R. (1972). Diagnostic criteria for use in psychiatric research. *Archives of General Psychiatry, 26,* 57–63.

Feingold, B. F. (1976). Hyperkinesis and learning disabilities linked to the ingestion of artificial food colors and flavors. *Journal of Learning Disabilities, 9,* 551–559.

Feldon, J., & Weiner, I. (1992). From an animal model of an attentional deficit towards new insights into the pathophysiology of schizophrenia. *Journal of Psychiatic Research, 26,* 345–366.

Felsenfeld, S., Broen, P. A., & McGue, M. (1992). A 28-year follow-up of adults with a history of moderate phonological disorder: Linguistic and personality results. *Journal of Speech and Hearing Research, 35,* 1114–1125.

Fenichel, O. (1945). *The psychoanalytic theory of neurosis.* New York: Norton.

Fenton, W. S., & McGlashan, T. H. (1989). Risk of schizophrenia in character disordered patients. *American Journal of Psychiatry, 146,* 1280–1284.

Fenton, W. S., & McGlashan, T. H. (1991). Natural history of schizophrenia subtypes: I. Longitudinal study of paranoid, hebephrenic, and undifferentiated schizophrenia. *Archives of General Psychiatry, 48,* 969–977.

Fentress, D. W., Masek, B. J., Mehegan, J. E., & Benson, H. (1986). Biofeedback and relaxation-response training in the treatment of pediatric migraine. *Developmental Medicine and Child Neurology, 28,* 139–146.

Ferguson, B., & Tyrer, B. (1988). Classifying personality disorder. In P. Tyrer (Ed.), *Personality disorders: Diagnosis, management, and course.* London: Wright.

Ferguson, M. (1980). *The Aquarian conspiracy: Personal and social transformation in the 1980s.* Los Angeles: Tarcher.

Ferster, C. B. (1966). Animal behavior and mental illness. *Psychological Record, 16,* 345–356.

Ferster, C. B. (1973). A functional analysis of depression. *American Psychologist, 28,* 857–870.

Festinger, L. (1957). *A theory of cognitive dissonance.* Evanston, IL: Row, Peterson.

Feuerstein, M., Labbé, E. E., & Kuczmierczyk, A. R. (1986). *Health psychology: A psychobiological perspective.* New York: Plenum.

Fiedler, F. E. (1950). A comparison of therapeutic relationships in psychoanalytic, non-directive, and Adlerian therapy. *Journal of Consulting Psychology, 14,* 436–445.

Fiedler, F. E. (1951). Factor analysis of psychoanalytic, non-directive, and Adlerian therapeutic relationships. *Journal of Consulting Psychology, 15,* 32–38.

Field, T. M., Widmayer, S. M., Stringer, S., & Ignatoff, E. (1980). Teenage, lower-class, black mothers and their preterm infants: An intervention and developmental follow-up. *Child Development, 51,* 426–436.

Fieve, R. R. (1976). *Moodswing: The third revolution in psychiatry.* New York: Bantam.

Filsinger, E. (1983). *Marriage and family assessment.* Beverly Hills, CA: Sage.

Filteau, M. J., Pourcher, E., Baruch, P., Bouchard, R. H., & Vincent, P. (1992). Dysmorphophobia (body dysmorphic disorder). *Canadian Journal of Psychiatry, 37,* 503–509.

Fink, M. (1990). How does convulsive therapy work? *Neuropsychopharmacology, 3,* 73–82.

Fink, P. (1992a). Surgery and medical treatment in persistent somatizing patients. *Journal of Psychosomatic Research, 36,* 439–447.

Fink, P. (1992b). The use of hospitalizations by persistent somatizing patients. *Psychological Medicine, 22,* 173–180.

Finkelhor, D., Hotaling, G., Lewis, I. A., & Smith, C. (1990). Sexual abuse in a national survey of adult men and women: Prevalence, characteristics, and risk factors. *Child Abuse and Neglect, 14,* 19–28.

Finn, P. R., Zeitouni, N. C., & Pihl, R. O. (1990). Effects of alcohol on psychophysiological hyperactivity to non-aversive and aversive stimuli in men at high risk for alcoholism. *Journal of Abnormal Psychology, 99,* 79–85.

Fiore, M. C. (1992). Trends in cigarette smoking in the United States: The epidemiology of tobacco use. *Medical Clinics of North America, 76,* 289–303.

Fireside, H. (1979). *Soviet psychoprisons.* New York: Norton.

Fischer, P. J., & Breakey, W. R. (1991). The epidemiology of alcohol, drug, and mental disorders among homeless persons. *American Psychologist, 46,* 1115–1128.

Fish, B. (1984). Characteristics and sequelae of the neurointegrative disorder in infants at risk for schizophrenia: 1952–1982. In N. F. Watt, E. J. Anthony, L. C. Wynne, & J. E. Rolf (Eds.), *Children at risk for schizophrenia: A longitudinal perspective.* Cambridge: Cambridge University Press.

Fishbein, D. H., Herning, R. I., Pickworth, W. B., & Haertzen, C. A. (1989). EEG and brainstem auditory evoked response potentials in adult male drug abusers with self-reported histories of aggressive behavior. *Biological Psychiatry, 26,* 595–611.

Fisher, E., & Thompson, J. K. (1994). A comparative evaluation of cognitive-behavioral therapy (CBT) versus exercise therapy (ET) for the treatment of body image disturbance. *Behavior Modification, 18,* 171–185.

Fiske, S. T., Bersoff, D. N., Borgida, E., Deaux, K., & Heilman, M. E. (1991). Social science research on trial: The use of sex stereotyping research in *Price Waterhouse v. Hopkins. American Psychologist, 46,* 1058–1069.

Fitton, A., & Heel, R. C. (1990). Clozapine: A review of its pharmacological properties and therapeutic use in schizophrenia. *Drugs, 40,* 722–747.

Fitts, S. N., Gibson, P., Redding, C. A., & Deiter, P. J. (1989). Body dysmorphic disorder: Implications for its validity as a DSM-III-R clinical syndrome. *Psychological Reports, 64,* 655–658.

Flasher, L. V., & Maisto, S. A. (1984). A review of theory and research on drinking patterns among Jews. *Journal of Nervous and Mental Disease, 172,* 596–603.

Fleming, B., & Pretzer, J. L. (1990). Cognitive-behavioral approaches to personality disorders. *Progress in Behavior Modification, 25,* 119–151.

Fleming, J. E., & Offord, D. R. (1990). Epidemiology of childhood depressive disorders: A critical review. *Journal of the American Academy of Child and Adolescent Psychiatry, 29,* 571–580.

Flinn, D., & Bazzell, W. (1983). Psychiatric aspects of abnormal movement disorders. *Brain Research Bulletin, 11,* 153–161.

Flynn, B. S., Worden, J. K., Secker-Walker, R. H., Badger, G. J., Geller, B. M., & Costanza, M. C. (1992). Prevention of cigarette smoking through mass media intervention and school programs. *American Journal of Public Health, 82,* 827–834.

Foa, E. B., & Emmelkamp, P. M. G. (Eds.). (1983). *Failures in behavior therapy.* New York: Wiley.

Foa, E. B., & Foa, U. G. (1982). Differentiating depression and anxiety: Is it possible? Is it useful? *Psychopharmacology Bulletin, 18,* 62–68.

Foa, E. B., Kozak, M. J., Steketee, G. S., & McCarthy, P. R. (1992). Treatment of depressive and obsessive-compulsive symptoms in OCD by imipramine and behaviour therapy. *British Journal of Clinical Psychology, 31,* 279–292.

Foa, E. B., Rothbaum, B. O., Riggs, D. S., & Murdock, T. B. (1991). Treatment of posttraumatic stress disorder in rape victims: A comparison between cognitive-behavioral procedures and counseling. *Journal of Consulting and Clinical Psychology, 59,* 715–723.

Fodor, I. S. (1974). The phobic syndrome in women: Implications for treatment. In V. Franks & V. Burtle (Eds.), *Women in therapy: New psychotherapies for a changing society.* New York: Brunner/Mazel.

Foerster, K., Foerster, G., & Roth, E. (1976). Necrophilia in a 17 year old girl. *Schweizer Archiv fur Neurologie, Neurochirugie und Psychiatrie, 119,* 97–107.

Fogelson, D. L., Nuechterlein, K. H., Asarnow, R. F., Subotnik, K. L., & Talovic, S. A. (1991). Interrater reliability of the Structured Clinical Interview for DSM-III-R, Axis II: Schizophrenia spectrum and affective spectrum disorders. *Psychiatry Research, 39,* 55–63.

Folstein, M. F., Bassett, S. S., Anthony, J. C., Romanoski, A. J., & Nestadt, G. R. (1991). Dementia: Case ascertainment in a community survey. *Journal of Gerontology, 46,* 132–138.

Folstein, S. E., & Piven, J. (1991). Etiology of autism: Genetic influences. *Pediatrics, 87,* 767–773.

Folstein, S. E., & Rutter, M. (1977). Infantile autism: A genetic study of 21 twin pairs. *Journal of Child Psychology and Psychiatry, 18,* 297–321.

Forastiere, F., Corbo, G. M., Michelozzi, P., Pistelli, R., Agabiti, N., Brancato, G., Ciappi, G., & Perucci, C. A. (1992). Effects of environment and passive smoking on the respiratory health of children. *International Journal of Epidemiology, 21,* 66–73.

Ford, C. S., & Beach, F. A. (1951). *Patterns of sexual behavior.* New York: Harper & Row.

Ford, M. R., & Widiger, T. A. (1989). Sex bias in the diagnosis of histrionic and antisocial personality disorders. *Journal of Consulting and Clinical Psychology, 57,* 301–305.

Forehand, R. L., King, H. E., Peed, S., & Yoder, P. (1975). Mother-child interactions: Comparisons of a non-compliant clinic group and a non-clinic group. *Behaviour Research and Therapy, 13,* 79–84.

Forehand, R. L., Wells, K., & Sturgis, E. (1978). Predictors of child noncompliant behavior in the home. *Journal of Consulting and Clinical Psychology, 46,* 179.

Fotheringham, J. B. (1991). Autism: Its primary psychological and neurological deficit. *Canadian Journal of Psychiatry, 36,* 686–692.

Foucault, M. (1965). *Madness and civilization: A history of insanity in the age of reason.* New York: Random House.

Fout, J. C. (Ed.). (1992). *Forbidden history: The state, society, and the regulation of sexuality in modern Europe.* Chicago: University of Chicago Press.

Fox, B. H. (1991). Quandaries created by unlikely numbers in some of Grossarth-Maticek's studies. *Psychological Inquiry, 2,* 242–247.

Frances, A. (1982). Categorical and dimensional systems of personality diagnosis: A comparison. *Comprehensive Psychiatry, 23,* 516–527.

Francis, C. K. (1990). Hypertension and cardiac disease in minorities. *American Journal of Medicine, 88,* 3–8.

Francis, J., Martin, D., & Kapoor, W. N. (1990). A prospective study of delirium in hospitalized elderly. *JAMA, 263,* 1097–1101.

Frank, E., Anderson, C., & Rubinstein, D. (1978). Frequency of sexual dysfunction in "normal" couples. *New England Journal of Medicine, 299,* 111–115.

Frank, J. D. (1974). *Persuasion and healing* (Rev. ed.). New York: Schocken Books.

Frank, J. D. (1978). *Psychotherapy and the human predicament: A psychosocial approach.* New York: Schocken Books.

Frankl, V. E. (1963). *Man's search for meaning: An introduction to logotherapy.* New York: Washington Square Press.

Frankl, V. E. (1975). Paradoxical intention and dereflection. *Psychotherapy: Theory, Research, and Practice, 12,* 226–237.

Frayn, D. H. (1990). Regressive transferences—A manifestation of primitive personality organization. *American Journal of Psychotherapy, 44,* 50–60.

Frazer, J. G. (1922). *The golden bough: A study in magic and religion.* New York: Macmillan.

Fredman, N., & Sherman, R. (1987). *Handbook of measurements for marriage and family therapy.* New York: Brunner/Mazel.

Freedman, A. M. (1980). Opiate dependence. In H. I. Kaplan, A. M. Freedman, & B. J. Sadock (Eds.), *Comprehensive textbook of psychiatry* (Vol. 2, 3rd ed.). Baltimore: Williams & Wilkins.

Freeman, A. (1988). Cognitive therapy of personality disorders: General treatment considerations. In C. Perris, I. M. Blackburn, & H. Perris (Eds.), *Cognitive psychotherapy: Theory and practice.* Berlin: Springer-Verlag.

Freeman, W., & Watts, J. W. (1942). *Psychosurgery.* Springfield, IL: Charles C Thomas.

Freud, A. (1937). *The ego and the mechanisms of defense.* London: Hogarth.

Freud, S. (1900). The interpretation of dreams. *Standard edition* (Vol. 4). London: Hogarth.

Freud, S. (1909a). Analysis of a phobia in a five-year-old boy. *Standard edition* (Vol. 10). London: Hogarth.

Freud, S. (1909b). Notes upon a case of obsessional neurosis. *Standard edition* (Vol. 10). London: Hogarth.

Freud, S. (1911). Psycho-analytic notes on an autobiographical account of a case of paranoia (dementia paranoides). *Standard edition* (Vol. 12). London: Hogarth.

Freud, S. (1914). On narcissism. *Standard edition* (Vol. 14). London: Hogarth.

Freud, S. (1917). Mourning and melancholia. *Standard edition* (Vol. 14). London: Hogarth.

Freud, S. (1920). Beyond the pleasure principle. *Standard edition* (Vol. 18). London: Hogarth.

Freud, S. (1926). Inhibitions, symptoms, and anxiety. *Standard edition* (Vol. 20). London: Hogarth.

Freud, S. (1930). Civilization and its discontents. *Standard edition* (Vol. 21). London: Hogarth.

Freud, S. (1936). A disturbance of memory on the acropolis. *Standard edition* (Vol. 22). London: Hogarth.

Freud, S. (1950). Project for a scientific psychology. *Standard edition* (Vol. 1). London: Hogarth.

Frick, P. J., Lahey, B. B., Loeber, R., Stouthamer-Loeber, M., Christ, M. A., & Hanson, K. (1992). Familial risk factors to oppositional defiant disorder and conduct disorder: Parental psychopathology and maternal parenting. *Journal of Consulting and Clinical Psychology, 60,* 49–55.

Fried, D., Crits-Christoph, P., & Luborsky, L. (1992). The first empirical demonstration of transference in psychotherapy. *Journal of Nervous and Mental Disease, 180,* 326–331.

Friedman, H. S., & Booth-Kewley, S. (1987). The "disease-prone personality": A meta-analytic view of the construct. *American Psychologist, 42,* 539–555.

Friedman, H. S., & DiMatteo, M. R. (1989). *Health psychology.* Englewood Cliffs, NJ: Prentice-Hall.

Friedman, L. (1988). The clinical popularity of object relations concepts. *Psychoanalytic Quarterly, 57,* 667–691.

Friedman, M. (1989). Type A behavior: Its diagnosis, cardiovascular relation, and the effect of its modification on recurrence of coronary artery disease. *American Journal of Cardiology, 64,* 12–19.

Friedman, M., & Rosenman, R. H. (1974). *Type A behavior and your heart.* New York: Knopf.

Friedman, M., Thoresen, C. E., Gill, J. J., Ulmer, D., Powell, L. H., Price, V. A., Brown, B., Thompson, L., Rabin, D. D., Breall, W. S., Bourg, E., Levy, R., & Dixon, T. (1986). Alteration of Type A behavior and its effect on cardiac recurrences in post myocardial infarction patients: Summary results of the recurrent coronary prevention project. *American Heart Journal, 112,* 653–665.

Friedman, M. J. (1988). Toward rational pharmacotherapy for posttraumatic stress disorder: An interim report. *American Journal of Psychiatry, 145,* 281–285.

Frischholz, E. J., Braun, B. G., Sachs, R. G., Schwartz, D. R., Lewis, J., Shaeffer, D., Westergaard, C., & Pasquotto, J. (1992). Construct validity of the Dissociative Experiences Scale: II. Its relationship to hypnotizability. *American Journal of Clinical Hypnosis, 35,* 145–152.

Fristad, M. A., Topolosky, S., Weller, E. B., & Weller, R. A. (1992). Depression and learning disabilities in children. *Journal of Affective Disorders, 26,* 53–58.

Fritze, J., Deckert, J., Lanczik, M., Strik, W., Struck, M., & Wodarz, N. (1992). Status of the amine hypothesis in depressive disorders. *Nervenarzt, 63,* 3–13.

Fromm, E. (1947). *Man for himself.* New York: Rinehart.

Fromm-Reichmann, F. (1948). Notes on the development of treatments of schizophrenics by psychoanalytic psychotherapy. *Psychiatry, 2,* 263–273.

Fuchs, C. Z., & Rehm, L. P. (1977). A self-control behavior therapy program for depression. *Journal of Consulting and Clinical Psychology, 45,* 206–215.

Fuchs, E. (1983). *Sexual desire and love: Origins and history of the Christian ethic of sexuality and marriage.* New York: Seabury.

Fuller, R. C. (1988). *Alternative medicine and American religious life.* New York: Oxford.

Furman, S. (1973). Intestinal biofeedback in functional diarrhea: A preliminary report. *Journal of Behavior Therapy and Experimental Psychiatry, 4,* 317–321.

Gabel, S. (1989). Dreams as a possible reflection of a dissociated self-monitoring system. *Journal of Nervous and Mental Disease, 177,* 560–568.

Gaffney, G. R., Lurie, S. F., & Berlin, F. S. (1984). Is there family transmission of pedophilia? *Journal of Nervous and Mental Disease, 172,* 546–548.

Gajar, A. (1992). Adults with learning disabilities: Current and future research priorities. *Journal of Learning Disabilities, 25,* 507–519.

Galinowski, A., Barbouche, R., Truffinet, P., Louzir, H., Poirier, M. F., Bouvet, O., Loo, H., & Avrameas, S. (1992). Natural autoantibodies in schizophrenia. *Acta Psychiatrica Scandinavica, 85,* 240–242.

Gallup, G. (1972). *The sophisticated poll watcher's guide.* Princeton, NJ: Princeton Opinion Press.

Gambill, J. D., & Kornetsky, C. (1976). Effects of chronic *d*-amphetamine on social behavior of the rat: Implications for an animal model of paranoid schizophrenia. *Psychopharmacology, 50,* 215–223.

Gannon, M., & Murphy, D. (1992). Psychiatric disorders in Parkinson's disease. *British Journal of Hospital Medicine, 47,* 663–666.

Gans, D. A. (1991). Sucrose and delinquent behavior: Coincidence or consequence? *Critical Reviews in Food Science and Nutrition, 30,* 23–48.

Gara, M. A., Rosenberg, S., & Goldberg, L. (1992). DSM-III-R as a taxonomy: A cluster analysis of diagnoses and symptoms. *Journal of Nervous and Mental Disease, 180,* 11–19.

Garbarino, J. (1992). *Children in danger: Coping with the consequences of community violence.* San Francisco: Jossey-Bass.

Garber, J. (1984). Classification of childhood psychopathology: A developmental perspective. *Child Development, 55,* 30–48.

Gardner, H. (1983). *Frames of mind: The theory of multiple intelligences.* New York: Basic Books.

Gardner, H. (1985). *The mind's new science: A history of the cognitive revolution.* New York: Basic Books.

Garfield, S. L. (1986). Research on client variables in psychotherapy. In S. L. Garfield & A. E. Bergin (Eds.), *Handbook of psychotherapy and behavior change* (3rd ed.). New York: Wiley.

Garfield, S. L., & Bergin, A. E. (1986). Introduction and historical overview. In S. L. Garfield & A. E. Bergin (Eds.), *Handbook of psychotherapy and behavior change* (3rd ed.). New York: Wiley.

Garfinkel, P. E. (1974). Perception of hunger and satiety in anorexia nervosa. *Psychological Medicine, 4,* 309–315.

Garfinkel, P. E., & Garner, D. M. (1982). *Anorexia nervosa: A multidimensional perspective.* New York: Brunner/Mazel.

Garmezy, N. (1970). Process and reactive schizophrenia: Some conceptions and issues. *Schizophrenia Bulletin, 1,* 30–74.

Garner, D. M., Garfinkel, P. E., Schwartz, D., & Thompson, M. (1980). Cultural expectations of thinness in women. *Psychological Reports, 47,* 483–491.

Garnets, L., Hancock, K. A., Cochran, S. D., Goodchilds, J., & Peplau, L. A. (1991). Issues in psychotherapy with lesbians and gay men: A survey of psychologists. *American Psychologist, 46,* 964–972.

Garvey, A. J., Bliss, R. E., Hitchcock, J. L., Heinold, J. W., & Rosner, B. (1992). Predictors of smoking relapse among self-quitters: A report from the Normative Aging Study. *Addictive Behaviors, 17,* 367–377.

Garvey, W., & Hegreves, S. R. (1966). Desensitization techniques in the treatment of school phobia. *American Journal of Orthopsychiatry, 36,* 147–152.

Gaulden, M. E. (1992). Maternal age effect: The enigma of Down syndrome and other trisomic conditions. *Mutation Research, 296,* 69–88.

Gay, P. (1984). *The bourgeois experience: Victoria to Freud: Vol. 1. The education of the senses.* New York: Oxford.

Gay, P. (1988). *Freud: A life for our time.* New York: Norton.

Gayton, W. F., Havu, G., Baird, J. G., & Ozman, K. (1983). Psychological androgyny and assertiveness in females. *Psychological Reports, 52,* 283–285.

Gelernter, C. S., Uhde, T. W., Cimbolic, P., Arnkoff, D. B., Vittone, B. J., Tancer, M. E., & Bartko, J. J. (1991). Cognitive-behavioral and pharmacological treatments of social phobia: A controlled study. *Archives of General Psychiatry, 48,* 938–945.

George, L. L., Borody, T. J., Andrews, P., Devine, M., Moore-Jones, D., Walton, M., & Brandl, S. (1990). Cure of duodenal ulcer after eradication of *Helicobacter pylori. Medical Journal of Australia, 153,* 145–149.

Gerlsma, C., Emmelkamp, P. M., & Arrindell, W. A. (1990). Anxiety, depression, and perception of early parenting: A meta-analysis. *Clinical Psychology Review, 10,* 251–277.

Gershon, E. S., DeLisi, L. E., Hamovit, J., Nurnberger, J. I., Maxwell, M. E., Schreiber, J., Dauphinais, D., Dingman, C. W., & Guroff, J. J. (1988). A controlled family study of chronic psychoses: Schizophrenia and schizoaffective disorder. *Archives of General Psychiatry, 45,* 328–336.

Gershon, E. S., Hamovit, J., Guroff, J. J., Dibble, E., Leckman, J. F., Sceery, W., Targum, S. D., Nurnberger, J. I., Goldin, L. R., & Bunney, W. E. (1982). A family study of schizoaffective, bipolar I, bipolar II, unipolar, and normal control probands. *Archives of General Psychiatry, 39,* 1157–1167.

Gershon, E. S., Martinez, M., Goldin, L. R., & Gejman, P. V. (1990). Genetic mapping of common diseases: The challenges of manic-depressive illness and schizophrenia. *Trends in Genetics, 6,* 282–287.

Gerstley, L., McLellan, A. T., Alterman, A. I., Woody, G. E., Luborsky, L., & Prout, M. (1989). Ability to form an alliance with the therapist: A possible marker of prognosis for patients with antisocial personality disorder. *American Journal of Psychiatry, 146,* 508–512.

Gidycz, C. A., & Koss, M. P. (1991). Predictors of long-term sexual assault trauma among a national sample of victimized college women. *Violence and Victims, 6,* 175–190.

Gil, T. E. (1989). Psychological etiology to cancer: Truth or myth? *Israel Journal of Psychiatry and Related Sciences, 26,* 164–185.

Gilberstadt, H., & Duker, J. (1965). *A handbook for clinical and actuarial MMPI interpretation.* Philadelphia: W. B. Saunders.

Gilbert, L. A. (1980). Feminist therapy. In A. Brodsky & R. T. Hare-Mustin (Eds.), *Women and psychotherapy.* New York: Guilford.

Giles, D. E., Jarrett, R. B., Biggs, M. M., Guzick, D. S., & Rush, A. J. (1989). Clinical predictors of recurrence in depression. *American Journal of Psychiatry, 146,* 764–767.

Gill, J. J., Price, V. A., Friedman, M., Thoresen, C. E., Powell, L. H., Ulmer, D., Brown, B., & Drews, F. R. (1985). Reduction in Type A behavior in healthy middle-aged American military officers. *American Heart Journal, 110,* 503–514.

Gillberg, C. (1991). Outcome in autism and autistic-like conditions. *Journal of the American Academy of Child and Adolescent Psychiatry, 30,* 479–482.

Gillham, R. A. (1990). Refractory epilepsy: An evaluation of psychological methods in outpatient management. *Epilepsia, 31,* 427–432.

Gillin, J. C., Duncan, W., Pettigrew, K. D., Frankel, B. L., & Snyder, F. (1979). Successful separation of depressed, normal, and insomniac subjects by EEG sleep data. *Archives of General Psychiatry, 36,* 85–90.

Gillum, R. F. (1979). Pathophysiology of hypertension in blacks and whites: A review of the basis of racial blood pressure differences. *Hypertension, 1,* 468–475.

Gilmore, M. (1994). *Shot in the heart.* New York: Doubleday.

Girelli, S. A., Resick, P. A., Marhoefer-Dvorak, S., & Hutter, C. K. (1986). Subjective distress and violence during rape: Their effects on long-term fear. *Violence and Victims, 1,* 35–46.

Gitlin, M. J., Cochran, S. D., & Jamison, K. R. (1989). Maintenance lithium treatment: Side effects and compliance. *Journal of Clinical Psychiatry, 50,* 127–131.

Glaser, R., Kiecolt-Glaser, J. K., Bonneau, R. H., Malarkey, W., Kennedy, S., & Hughes, J. (1992). Stress-induced modulation of the immune response to recombinant hepatitis B vaccine. *Psychosomatic Medicine, 54,* 22–29.

Glaser, R., Kiecolt-Glaser, J. K., Stout, J. C., Tarr, K. L., Speicher, C. E., & Holliday, J. E. (1985). Stress-related impairments in cellular immunity. *Psychiatry Research, 16,* 233–239.

Glass, L. L., Kirsch, M. A., & Parris, F. N. (1977). Psychiatric disturbances associated with Erhard Seminars Training: I. A report of cases. *American Journal of Psychiatry, 134,* 245–247.

Glasser, M. (1992). Problems in the psychoanalysis of certain narcissistic disorders. *International Journal of Psycho-Analysis, 73,* 493–503.

Glassman, A. H. (1993). Cigarette smoking: Implications for psychiatric illness. *American Journal of Psychiatry, 150,* 546–553.

Goff, D. C., & Simms, C. A. (1993). Has multiple personality disorder remained consistent over time? A comparison of past and recent cases. *Journal of Nervous and Mental Disease, 181,* 595–600.

Goffman, E. (1961). *Asylums.* Garden City, NY: Anchor.

Goldberg, E. M., & Morrison, S. L. (1963). Schizophrenia and social class. *British Journal of Psychiatry, 109,* 785–802.

Goldberg, J., True, W. R., Eisen, S. A., & Henderson, W. G. (1990). A twin study of the effects of the Vietnam War on posttraumatic stress disorder. *JAMA, 263,* 1227–1232.

Goldberg, M. (1990, March 22). Del Shannon: 1934–1990. *Rolling Stone, 20,* 124.

Goldberg, T. E., Ragland, J. D., Torrey, E. F., Gold, J. M., Bigelow, L. B., & Weinberger, D. R. (1990).

Neuropsychological assessment of monozygotic twins discordant for schizophrenia. *Archives of General Psychiatry, 47,* 1066–1072.

Goldbloom, D. S., & Garfinkel, P. E. (1990). The serotonin hypothesis of bulimia nervosa: Theory and evidence. *Canadian Journal of Psychiatry, 35,* 741–744.

Golden, C. J., Hammeke, T., & Purisch, A. (1980). *The Luria-Nebraska neuropsychological battery manual* (Revised). Los Angeles: Western Psychological Services.

Goldfarb, W. (1980). Pervasive developmental disorders of childhood. In H. I. Kaplan, A. M. Freedman, & B. J. Sadock (Eds.), *Comprehensive textbook of psychiatry* (Vol. 3, 3rd ed.). Baltimore: Williams & Wilkins.

Goldman, H. H. (1983). The demography of deinstitutionalization. In L. L. Bachrach (Ed.), *Deinstitutionalization.* San Francisco: Jossey-Bass.

Goldman, H. H., Skodol, A. E., & Lave, T. R. (1992). Revising Axis V for DSM-IV: A review of measures of social functioning. *American Journal of Psychiatry, 149,* 1148–1156.

Goldman, M. S., Brown, S. A., & Christiansen, B. A. (1987). Expectancy theory: Thinking about drinking. In H. T. Blane & K. E. Leonard (Eds.), *Psychological theories of drinking and alcoholism.* New York: Guilford.

Goldner, V. (1985). Feminism and family therapy. *Family Process, 24,* 31–47.

Goldstein, K. (1944). The mental changes due to frontal lobe damage. *Journal of Psychology, 17,* 187–208.

Goldstein, M. (1990). The decade of the brain: An era of promise for neurosurgery and a call to action. *Journal of Neurosurgery, 73,* 1–2.

Goldstein, M., & Deutch, A. Y. (1992). Dopaminergic mechanisms in the pathogenesis of schizophrenia. *FASEB Journal, 6,* 2413–2421.

Goldstein, M. J. (1988). The family and psychopathology. *Annual Review of Psychology, 39,* 283–299.

Goldstein, M. Z. (Ed.). (1986). *Family involvement in the treatment of schizophrenia.* Washington, DC: American Psychiatric Press.

Goldstein, W. N. (1985). *An introduction to the borderline conditions.* Northvale, NJ: Aronson.

Goldstein, W. N. (1989). Update on psychodynamic thinking regarding the diagnosis of the borderline patient. *American Journal of Psychotherapy, 43,* 321–342.

Goleman, D., & Gurin, J. (Eds.). (1993). *Mind/body medicine: How to use your mind for better health.* Yonkers, NY: Consumer Reports Books.

Gomez, J., & Rodriguez, A. (1989). An evaluation of the results of a drug sample analysis. *Bulletin on Narcotics, 41,* 121–126.

Gonda, T. A. (1962). The relation between complaints of persistent pain and family size. *Journal of Neurology, Neurosurgery, and Psychiatry, 25,* 277–281.

Gonzalez, J. P., & Brogden, R. N. (1988). Naltrexone: A review of its pharmacodynamic and pharmacokinetic properties and therapeutic efficacy in the management of opioid dependence. *Drugs, 35,* 192–213.

Goodnick, P. J., & Meltzer, H. Y. (1984). Treatment of schizoaffective disorders. *Schizophrenia Bulletin, 10,* 30–48.

Goodrich, T. J., Rampage, C., Ellman, B., & Halstead, K. (1988). *Feminist family therapy.* New York: Norton.

Goodwin, D. W. (1970). The alcoholism of F. Scott Fitzgerald. *JAMA, 212,* 86–90.

Goodwin, D. W. (1979). Alcoholism and heredity: A review and hypothesis. *Archives of General Psychiatry, 36,* 57–61.

Goodwin, D. W., & Guze, S. B. (1989). *Psychiatric diagnosis* (4th ed.). New York: Oxford.

Goodwin, D. W., Schulsinger, F., Knop, P., Mednick, S., & Guze, S. B. (1977). Alcoholism and depression in adopted-out daughters of alcoholics. *Archives of General Psychiatry, 34,* 751–755.

Goodwin, D. W., Schulsinger, F., Moller, N., Hermansen, L., Winokur, G., & Guze, S. B. (1974). Drinking problems in adopted and nonadopted sons of alcoholics. *Archives of General Psychiatry, 31,* 164–169.

Goodwin, F. K., & Jamison, K. R. (1990). *Manic-depressive illness.* New York: Oxford.

Gooren, L. (1990). The endocrinology of transsexualism: A review and commentary. *Psychoneuroendocrinology, 15,* 3–14.

Goplerud, E. N. (1979). Unexpected consequences of deinstitutionalization of the mentally disabled elderly. *American Journal of Community Psychology, 7,* 315–328.

Gorsky, R. D., Schwartz, E., & Dennis, D. (1988). The mortality, morbidity, and economic costs of alcohol abuse in New Hampshire. *Preventive Medicine, 17,* 736–745.

Gottesman, I. I. (1991). *Schizophrenia genesis: The origins of madness.* New York: Freeman.

Gottesman, I. I., & Shields, J. (1972). *Schizophrenia and genetics: A twin study vantage point.* New York: Academic Press.

Gottman, J. M., & Levenson, R. W. (1992). Marital processes predictive of later dissolution. Behavior, physiology, and health. *Journal of Personality and Social Psychology, 63,* 221–233.

Gottman, J. S. (1989). Children of gay and lesbian parents. *Marriage and Family Review, 14,* 177–196.

Gould, S. J. (1981). *The mismeasure of man.* New York: Norton.

Gowitt, G. T., & Hanzlick, R. L. (1992). Atypical autoerotic deaths. *American Journal of Forensic Medicine and Pathology, 13,* 115–119.

Grady, D., & Ernster, V. (1992). Does cigarette smoking make you ugly and old? *American Journal of Epidemiology, 135,* 839–842.

Grafman, J. (1984). Memory assessment and remediation. In B. A. Edelstein & E. T. Couture (Eds.), *Behavioral assessment and rehabilitation of the traumatically brain-damaged.* New York: Plenum.

Graham, J. R. (1990). *MMPI-2: Assessing personality and psychopathology.* New York: Oxford.

Grahame-Smith, D. G. (1992). Serotonin in affective disorders. *International Clinical Psychopharmacology, 6,* 5–13.

Graziano, A. M., & Diament, D. M. (1992). Parent behavioral training: An examination of the paradigm. *Behavior Modification, 16,* 3–38.

Greaves, G. B. (1980). An existential theory of drug dependence. In D. J. Lettieri, M. Sayers, & H. W. Pearson (Eds.), *Theories on drug abuse: Selected contemporary perspectives.* Rockville, MD: NIDA Research Monograph Series.

Greden, J. F. (1980). Caffeine and tobacco dependence. In H. I. Kaplan, A. M. Freedman, & B. J. Sadock (Eds.), *Comprehensive textbook of psychiatry* (Vol. 2, 3rd ed.). Baltimore: Williams & Wilkins.

Green, B. L., Lindy, J. D., Grace, M. C., Gleser, G. C., Leonard, A. C., Korol, M., & Winget, C. (1990). Buffalo Creek survivors in the second decade: Stability of stress symptoms. *American Journal of Orthopsychiatry, 60,* 43–54.

Green, M. F., Satz, P., Smith, C., & Nelson, L. (1989). Is there atypical handedness in schizophrenia? *Journal of Abnormal Psychology, 98,* 57–61.

Green, R. (1987). *The "sissy boy syndrome" and the development of homosexuality.* New Haven, CT: Yale University Press.

Green, W. H., Padron-Gayol, M., Hardesty, A. S., & Bassiri, M. (1992). Schizophrenia with childhood onset: A phenomenological study of 38 cases. *Journal of the American Academy of Child and Adolescent Psychiatry, 31,* 968–976.

Greenberg, J. R., & Mitchell, S. A. (1983). *Object relations in psychoanalytic theory.* Cambridge: Harvard University Press.

Greenberg, L., & Fink, M. (1992). The use of electroconvulsive therapy in geriatric patients. *Clinics in Geriatric Medicine, 8,* 349–354.

Greenblatt, D. J., & Shader, R. I. (1974). *Benzodiazepines in clinical practice.* New York: Raven.

Greenblatt, M. (1977). Efficacy of ECT in affective and schizophrenic illness. *American Journal of Psychiatry, 134,* 1001–1005.

Greer, S., Moorey, S., & Baruch, J. (1991). Evaluation of adjuvant psychological therapy for clinically referred cancer patients. *British Journal of Cancer, 63,* 257–260.

Greist, J. H. (1992). An integrated approach to treatment of obsessive-compulsive disorder. *Journal of Clinical Psychiatry, 53,* 38–41.

Gretzky, W. (1990). *Wayne Gretzky: An autobiography.* New York: HarperCollins.

Grinker, R. R., & Robbins, F. P. (1954). *Psychosomatic case book.* New York: Blakiston.

Grinspoon, L., & Bakalar, J. B. (1980). Drug dependence: Nonnarcotic agents. In H. I. Kaplan, A. M. Freedman, & B. J. Sadock (Eds.), *Comprehensive textbook of psychiatry* (Vol. 2, 3rd ed.). Baltimore: Williams & Wilkins.

Grob, C. S. (1985). Female exhibitionism. *Journal of Nervous and Mental Disease, 173,* 253–256.

Grob, G. N. (1991). Origins of DSM-I: A study in appearance and reality. *American Journal of Psychiatry, 148,* 421–431.

Gross, G., & Huber, G. (1985). Psychopathology of basic stages of schizophrenia in view of formal thought disturbances. *Psychopathology, 18,* 115–125.

Gross, J. (1989). Emotional expression in cancer onset and progression. *Social Science and Medicine, 28,* 1239–1248.

Gross-Tsur, V., Shalev, R. S., & Amir, N. (1991). Attention deficit disorder: Association with familial-genetic factors. *Pediatric Neurology, 7,* 258–261.

Grossarth-Maticek, R., & Eysenck, H. J. (1991). Creative novation behaviour therapy as a prophylactic treatment for cancer and coronary heart disease: Part I—Description of treatment. *Behaviour Research and Therapy, 29,* 1–16.

Grossman, H. Y., Mostofsky, D. I., & Harrison, R. H. (1986). Psychological aspects of Gilles de la Tourette syndrome. *Journal of Clinical Psychology, 42,* 228–235.

Grove, W. M., & Andreasen, N. C. (1986). Multivariate statistical analysis in psychopathology. In T. Millon & G. L. Klerman (Eds.), *Contemporary directions in psychopathology: Toward the DSM-IV.* New York: Guilford.

Grove, W. M., Eckert, E. D., Heston, L., Bouchard, T. J., Segal, N., & Lykken, D. T. (1990). Heritability of substance abuse and antisocial behavior: A study of monozygotic twins reared apart. *Biological Psychiatry, 27,* 1293–1304.

Gruenberg, E. M. (1980). Epidemiology. In H. I. Kaplan, A. M. Freedman, & B. J. Sadock (Eds.), *Comprehensive textbook of psychiatry* (Vol. 1, 3rd ed.). Baltimore: Williams & Wilkins.

Gruetzner, H. (1988). *Alzheimer's: A caregiver's guide and sourcebook.* New York: Wiley.

Gudex, C. (1991). Adverse effects of benzodiazepines. *Social Science and Medicine, 33,* 587–596.

Gunderson, J. G. (1980). A reevaluation of milieu therapy for nonchronic schizophrenic patients. *Schizophrenia Bulletin, 6,* 64–69.

Gunderson, J. G., Frank, A. F., Ronningstam, E. F., Wachter, S., Lynch, V. J., & Wolf, P. J. (1989). Early discontinuance of borderline patients from psychotherapy. *Journal of Nervous and Mental Disease, 177,* 38–42.

Guralnick, M. (1988). Efficacy research in early childhood programs. In S. Odom & M. Karnes (Eds.), *Early intervention for infants and children with handicaps.* Baltimore: Brooks.

Gurman, A. S., Kniskern, D. P., & Pinsof, W. M. (1986). Research on marital and family therapies. In S. L. Garfield & A. E. Bergin (Eds.), *Handbook of psychotherapy and behavior change* (3rd ed.). New York: Wiley.

Gusella, J. F., Tanzi, R. E., Anderson, M. A., Hobbs, W., Gibbons, K., Raschtchian, R., Gilliam, T. C., Wallace, M. R., Wexler, N. S., & Conneally, P. M. (1984). DNA markers for nervous system diseases. *Science, 225,* 1320–1326.

Gusella, J. F., Wexler, N. S., Conneally, P. M., Naylor, S. L., Anderson, M. A., Tanzi, R. E., Watkins, P. C., Ottina, K., Wallace, M. R., Sakaguchi, A. Y., Young, A. B., Shoulson, I., Bonilla, E., & Martin, J. B. (1983). A polymorphic DNA marker genetically linked to Huntington's disease. *Nature, 306,* 234–238.

Gutheil, T. G., & Bursztajn, H. J. (1986). Clinicians' guidelines for assessing and presenting subtle forms of patient incompetence in legal settings. *American Journal of Psychiatry, 143,* 1020–1023.

Guthrie, G. M., & Tanco, P. P. (1980). Alienation. In H. C. Triandis & J. G. Draguns (Eds.), *Handbook of cross-cultural psychology: Psychopathology* (Vol. 6). Boston: Allyn & Bacon.

Guyer, M. J. (1990). Child psychiatry and legal liability: Implications of recent case law. *Journal of the American Academy of Child and Adolescent Psychiatry, 29*, 958–962.

Haaga, D. A., Dyck, M. J., & Ernst, D. (1991). Empirical status of cognitive theory of depression. *Psychological Bulletin, 110*, 215–236.

Haddad, P. M., & Garralda, M. E. (1992). Hyperkinetic syndrome and disruptive early experiences. *British Journal of Psychiatry, 161*, 700–703.

Haefely, W. E. (1990). The GABA_A-benzodiazepine receptor complex and anxiety. In N. Sartorius, V. Andreoli, G. Cassano, L. Eisenberg, P. Kielholz, P. Pancheri, & G. Racagni (Eds.), *Anxiety: Psychobiological and clinical perspectives.* New York: Hemisphere.

Hahn, R. C., & Petitti, D. B. (1988). Minnesota Multiphasic Personality Inventory-rated depression and the incidence of breast cancer. *Cancer, 61*, 845–848.

Haley, J. (1973). *Uncommon therapy: The psychiatric techniques of Milton H. Erickson, M. D.* New York: Norton.

Haley, J. (1976). *Problem solving therapy.* San Francisco: Jossey-Bass.

Haley, J. (1987). *Problem-solving therapy* (2nd ed.). San Francisco: Jossey-Bass.

Hallmayer, J., Maier, W., Ackenheil, M., Ertl, M. A., Schmidt, S., Minges, J., Lichtermann, D., & Wildenauer, D. (1992). Evidence against linkage of schizophrenia to chromosome 5q11-q13 markers in systematically ascertained families. *Biological Psychiatry, 31*, 83–94.

Halmi, K. A., Eckert, E., Marchi, P., Sampugnaro, V., Apple, R., & Cohen, J. (1991). Comorbidity of psychiatric diagnoses in anorexia nervosa. *Archives of General Psychiatry, 48*, 712–718.

Halmi, K. A., Goldberg, S. C., Eckert, E., Casper, R., & Davis, J. M. (1977). Pretreatment evaluation in anorexia nervosa. In R. A. Vigersky (Ed.), *Anorexia nervosa.* New York: Raven Press.

Halvorsen, J. G., & Metz, M. E. (1992a). Sexual dysfunction, Part I: Classification, etiology, and pathogenesis. *Journal of the American Board of Family Practice, 5*, 51–61.

Halvorsen, J. G., & Metz, M. E. (1992b). Sexual dysfunction, Part II: Diagnosis, management, and prognosis. *Journal of the American Board of Family Practice, 5*, 177–192.

Hambrecht, M., Maurer, K., Hafner, H., & Sartorius, N. (1992). Transnational stability of gender differences in schizophrenia? An analysis based on the WHO study on determinants of outcome of severe mental disorders. *European Archives of Psychiatry and Clinical Neuroscience, 242*, 6–12.

Hamer, D. H., Hu, S., Magnuson, V. L., Hu, N., & Pattatucci, A. M. L. (1993). A linkage between DNA markers on the X chromosome and male sexual orientation. *Science, 261*, 321–327.

Hammen, C. (1991). Generation of stress in the course of unipolar depression. *Journal of Abnormal Psychology, 100*, 555–561.

Hammer, L. D. (1992). The development of eating behavior in childhood. *Pediatric Clinics of North America, 39*, 379–394.

Handy, B. (1994, April 18). Never mind. *Time*, 70–72.

Hansell, A. G. (1990). *The effects on children of a father's severe closed head injury.* Unpublished doctoral dissertation, University of Michigan, Ann Arbor.

Hansen, J. P. (1986). Older maternal age and pregnancy outcome: A review of the literature. *Obstetrical and Gynecological Survey, 41*, 726–742.

Hardie, R. J. (1989). Problems and unanswered questions concerning levodopa treatment in Parkinson's disease. *Acta Neurologica Scandinavica, 126*, 77–82.

Hare, E. H. (1962). Masturbatory insanity: The history of an idea. *Journal of Mental Science, 452*, 2–25.

Hare, R. D., McPherson, L. M., & Forth, A. E. (1988). Male psychopaths and their criminal careers. *Journal of Consulting and Clinical Psychology, 56*, 710–714.

Hargie, O., Saunders, C., & Dickson, D. (1981). *Social skills in interpersonal communication.* London: Croom Helm.

Harper, P. S. (1992). The epidemiology of Huntington's disease. *Human Genetics, 89*, 365–376.

Harris, E. L., Noyes, R., Crowe, R. R., & Chaudhry, D. R. (1983). Family study of agoraphobia: Report of a pilot study. *Archives of General Psychiatry, 40*, 1061–1064.

Harrison, L. D. (1992). Trends in illicit drug use in the United States: Conflicting results from national surveys. *International Journal of the Addictions, 27*, 817–847.

Harrison, P. A. (1989). Women in treatment: Changing over time. *International Journal of the Addictions, 24*, 655–673.

Hartley, M. (1990). *Breaking the silence.* New York: Putnam's Sons.

Hartmann, A., Herzog, T., & Drinkmann, A. (1992). Psychotherapy of bulimia nervosa: What is effective? A meta-analysis. *Journal of Psychosomatic Research, 36*, 159–167.

Hartmann, H. (1939). *Ego psychology and the problem of adaptation.* New York: International Universities Press.

Hartsough, C. S., & Lambert, N. M. (1985). Medical factors in hyperactive and normal children: Prenatal, developmental, and health history findings. *American Journal of Orthopsychiatry, 55*, 190–201.

Hassler, F. (1992). The hyperkinetic child: A historical review. *Acta Paedopsychiatrica, 55*, 147–149.

Hatfield, A. B. (1991). The National Alliance for the Mentally Ill: A decade later. *Community Mental Health Journal, 27*, 95–103.

Hatfield, E., & Sprecher, S. (1986). *Mirror, mirror: The importance of looks in everyday life.* Albany, NY: SUNY Press.

Hathaway, S. R., & McKinley, J. C. (1943). *The Minnesota Multiphasic Personality Inventory.* Minneapolis: University of Minnesota Press.

Havard, J. D. (1992). Expert scientific evidence under the adversarial system: A travesty of justice? *Journal of the Forensic Science Society, 32*, 225–235.

Hawton, K., Catalan, J., & Fagg, J. (1991). Low sexual desire: Sex therapy results and prognostic factors. *Behaviour Research and Therapy, 29*, 217–224.

Hawton, K., Catalan, J., & Fagg, J. (1992). Sex therapy for erectile dysfunction: Characteristics of couples, treatment outcome, and prognostic factors. *Archives of Sexual Behavior, 21*, 161–175.

Hazan, C., & Shaver, P. (1987). Romantic love conceptualized as an attachment process. *Journal of Personality and Social Psychology, 52*, 511–524.

Hazelrigg, M. D., Cooper, H. M., & Borduin, C. M. (1987). Evaluating the effectiveness of family therapies: An integrative review and analysis. *Psychological Bulletin, 101*, 428–442.

Healy, D., & Williams, J. M. G. (1988). Dysrhythmia, dysphoria, and depression. The interaction of learned helplessness and circadian dysrhythmia in the pathogenesis of depression. *Psychological Bulletin, 103*, 163–178.

Heath, D. B. (1984). Cross-cultural studies of alcohol use. In M. Galanter (Ed.), *Recent developments in alcoholism* (Vol. 2). New York: Plenum.

Heath, D. B. (1990–1991). Uses and misuses of the concept of ethnicity in alcohol studies: An essay in deconstruction. *International Journal of the Addictions, 25*, 607–628.

Heather, N., Robertson, I., MacPherson, B., & Allsop, S. (1987). Effectiveness of a controlled drinking self-help manual: One-year follow-up results. *British Journal of Clinical Psychology, 26*, 279–287.

Heatherton, T. F., & Baumeister, R. F. (1991). Binge eating as escape from self-awareness. *Psychological Bulletin, 110*, 86–108.

Heiby, E. M. (1989). Multiple skill deficits in depression. *Behaviour Change, 6*, 76–84.

Heider, F. (1958). *The psychology of interpersonal relations.* New York: Wiley.

Heilbrun, A. B., & Cassidy, J. C. (1985). Toward an explanation of defensive projection in normals: The role of social cognition. *Journal of Social and Clinical Psychology, 3*, 190–200.

Heim, N. (1981). Sexual behavior of castrated sex offenders. *Archives of Sexual Behavior, 10*, 11–19.

Heiman, J. R., & Grafton-Becker, V. (1989). Orgasmic disorders in women. In S. R. Leiblum & R. C. Rosen (Eds.), *Principles and practice of sex therapy: Update for the 1990s.* New York: Guilford.

Heimberg, R. G., & Barlow, D. H. (1991). New developments in cognitive-behavioral therapy for social phobia. *Journal of Clinical Psychiatry, 52*, 21–30.

Helms, J. E. (1992). Why is there no study of cultural equivalence in standardized cognitive ability testing? *American Psychologist, 47*, 1083–1101.

Helzer, J. E., Canino, G. J., Yeh, E. K., Bland, R. C., Lee, C. K., Hwu, H. G., & Newman, S. (1990). Alcoholism—North America and Asia. A comparison of population surveys with the Diagnostic Interview Schedule. *Archives of General Psychiatry, 47*, 313–319.

Helzer, J. E., Robins, L. N., & McEvoy, L. (1987). Posttraumatic stress disorder in the general population: Findings of the epidemiologic catchment area survey. *New England Journal of Medicine, 317*, 1630–1634.

Helzer, J. E., Robins, L. N., Taibelson, M., Woodruff, R. A., Reich, T., & Wish, E. D. (1977). Reliability of psychiatric diagnosis: I. A methodological review. *Archives of General Psychiatry, 34*, 129–133.

Hendin, H., & Klerman, G. L. (1993). Physician-assisted suicide: The dangers of legalization. *American Journal of Psychiatry, 150*, 143–145.

Henriksson, M. M., Aro, H. M., Marttunen, M. J., Heikkinen, M. E., Isometsa, E. T., Kuoppasalmi, K. I., & Lonnqvist, J. K. (1993). Mental disorders and suicide. *American Journal of Psychiatry, 150*, 935–940.

Henry, T., & Levy, D. (1994, August 26). Little change in Down syndrome births. *USA Today*, p. 7D.

Henry, W. A. (1993, July 26). Born gay? *Time*, 36–39.

Herbert, J. D., Hope, D. A., & Bellack, A. S. (1992). Validity of the distinction between generalized social phobia and avoidant personality disorder. *Journal of Abnormal Psychology, 101*, 332–339.

Herman, S. P. (1990). Special issues in child custody evaluations. *Journal of the American Academy of Child and Adolescent Psychiatry, 29*, 969–974.

Hermann, B., & Whitman, S. (1992). Psychopathology in epilepsy: The role of psychology in altering paradigms of research, treatment, and prevention. *American Psychologist, 47*, 1134–1138.

Herron, W. G. (1979). The current state of process-reactive schizophrenia. *Journal of Psychology, 101*, 157–168.

Herzog, D. B., Keller, M. B., Lavori, P. W., & Sacks, N. R. (1991). The course and outcome of bulimia nervosa. *Journal of Clinical Psychiatry, 52*, 4–8.

Hes, J. P. (1958). Hypochondriasis in oriental Jewish immigrants: A preliminary report. *International Journal of Social Psychiatry, 4*, 18–23.

Hes, J. P. (1968). Hypochondriacal complaints in Jewish psychiatric patients. *Israel Annals of Psychiatry and Related Disciplines, 6*, 134–142.

Heston, L. L. (1966). Psychiatric disorders in foster home reared children of schizophrenic mothers. *British Journal of Psychiatry, 112*, 819–825.

Hibbert, G. A., & Chan, M. (1989). Respiratory control: Its contribution to the treatment of panic attacks: A controlled study. *British Journal of Psychiatry, 154*, 232–236.

Hiday, V. A., & Scheid-Cook, T. L. (1989). A follow-up of chronic patients committed to outpatient treatment. *Hospital and Community Psychiatry, 40*, 52–59.

Higgitt, A., & Fonagy, P. (1992). Psychotherapy in borderline and narcissistic personality disorder. *British Journal of Psychiatry, 161*, 23–43.

Hilgard, E. R. (1973). A neodissociation interpretation of pain reduction in hypnosis. *Psychological Review, 80*, 396–411.

Hilgard, E. R. (1977). *Divided consciousness: Multiple controls in human thought and action.* New York: Wiley.

Hilgard, E. R. (1987). *Psychology in America: A historical survey.* San Diego: Harcourt Brace Jovanovich.

Hillbrand, M., Foster, H., & Hirt, M. (1990). Rapists and child molesters: Psychometric comparisons. *Archives of Sexual Behavior, 19*, 65–71.

Hinde, R. A. (1970). *Animal behavior: A synthesis of ethology and comparative psychology* (2nd ed.). New York: McGraw-Hill.

Hinshaw, S. P. (1987). On the distinction between attentional deficits/hyperactivity and conduct/aggression disorders in child psychopathology. *Psychological Bulletin, 101,* 443–463.

Hinshaw, S. P. (1992). Academic underachievement, attention deficits, and aggression: Comorbidity and implications for intervention. *Journal of Consulting and Clinical Psychology, 60,* 893–903.

Hiroto, D. S., & Seligman, M. E. P. (1975). Generality of learned helplessness in man. *Journal of Personality and Social Psychology, 31,* 311–327.

Hirsch, S. (1981). A critique of volunteer-staffed suicide prevention centres. *Canadian Journal of Psychiatry, 26,* 406–410.

Hirschfeld, R. M. A., Klerman, G. L., Clayton, P. J., Keller, M. B., McDonald-Scott, P., & Larkin, B. H. (1983). Assessing personality: Effects of the depressive state on trait measurement. *American Journal of Psychiatry, 140,* 695–699.

Hirschfeld, R. M. A., Klerman, G. L., Lavori, P., Keller, M. B., Griffith, P., & Coryell, W. (1989). Premorbid personality assessments of first onset of major depression. *Archives of General Psychiatry, 46,* 345–350.

Hitchcock, P. B., & Mathews, A. (1992). Interpretation of bodily symptoms in hypochondriasis. *Behaviour Research and Therapy, 30,* 223–234.

Hoberman, H. M., & Lewinsohn, P. M. (1985). The behavioral treatment of depression. In E. E. Beckham & W. R. Leber (Eds.), *Handbook of depression: Treatment, assessment, and research.* Homewood, IL: Dorsey.

Hobson, R. P. (1990). On psychoanalytic approaches to autism. *American Journal of Orthopsychiatry, 60,* 324–336.

Hodges, K. (1993). Structured interviews for assessing children. *Journal of Child Psychology and Psychiatry and Allied Disciplines, 34,* 49–68.

Hodgins, S. (1992). Mental disorder, intellectual deficiency, and crime: Evidence from a birth cohort. *Archives of General Psychiatry, 49,* 476–483.

Hodgson, R. J., & Rankin, H. J. (1982). Cue exposure and relapse prevention. In W. M. Hay & P. E. Nathan (Eds.), *Clinical case studies in the behavioral treatment of alcoholism.* New York: Plenum.

Hodiamont, P. (1991). How normal are anxiety and fear? *International Journal of Social Psychiatry, 37,* 43–50.

Hoff, A. L., Riordan, H., O'Donnell, D. W., Morris, L., & DeLisi, L. E. (1992). Neuropsychological functioning of first-episode schizophreniform patients. *American Journal of Psychiatry, 149,* 898–903.

Hofmann, A. (1968). Psychotomimetic agents. In A. Burger (Ed.), *Drugs affecting the central nervous system* (Vol. 2). New York: Marcel Dekker.

Hoge, S. K., Gutheil, T. G., & Kaplan, E. (1987). The right to refuse treatment under Rogers v. Commissioner: Preliminary empirical findings and comparisons. *Bulletin of the American Academy of Psychiatry and the Law, 15,* 163–169.

Hohenshil, T. H. (1992). DSM-IV progress report. *Journal of Counseling and Development, 71,* 249–251.

Holden, C. (1989). "Ice Age" in Hawaii. *Science, 246,* 889.

Holinger, P. C. (1987). *Violent deaths in the United States: An epidemiological study of suicide, homicide, and accidents.* New York: Guilford.

Hollander, E., Neville, D., Frenkel, M., Josephson, S., & Liebowitz, M. R. (1992). Body dysmorphic disorder: Diagnostic issues and related disorders. *Psychosomatics, 33,* 156–165.

Hollifield, M., Katon, W., Spain, D., & Pule, L. (1990). Anxiety and depression in a village in Lesotho, Africa: A comparison with the United States. *British Journal of Psychiatry, 156,* 343–350.

Hollingshead, A. B., & Redlich, F. C. (1958). *Social class and mental illness: A community study.* New York: Wiley.

Hollon, S. D., & Shelton, M. (1991). Contributions of cognitive psychology to assessment and treatment of depression. In P. R. Martin (Ed.), *Handbook of behavior therapy and psychological science.* New York: Pergamon.

Hollon, S. D., Shelton, R. C., & Loosen, P. T. (1991). Cognitive therapy and pharmacotherapy for depression. *Journal of Consulting and Clinical Psychology, 59,* 88–99.

Holmes, T. H., & Rahe, R. H. (1967). The social readjustment rating scale. *Journal of Psychosomatic Research, 11,* 213–218.

Holsenbeck, L. S., Davidson, L. M., Hostetter, R. E., Casanova, M. F., Taylor, D. O., Kelley, C. T., Perrotta, C., Borison, R. L., & Diamond, B. (1992). Ventricle-to-brain ratio and symptoms at the onset of first-break schizophrenia. *Schizophrenia Bulletin, 18,* 427–435.

Holtzman, D. M., & Epstein, C. J. (1992). The molecular genetics of Down syndrome. *Molecular Genetic Medicine, 2,* 105–120.

Hooker, E. (1957). The adjustment of the male overt homosexual. *Journal of Projective Techniques, 21,* 18–31.

Horn, W. F., Ialongo, N. S., Pascoe, J. M., Greenberg, G., Packard, T., Lopez, M., Wagner, A., & Puttler, L. (1991). Additive effects of psychostimulants, parent training, and self-control therapy with ADHD children. *Journal of the American Academy of Child and Adolescent Psychiatry, 30,* 233–240.

Hornblower, M. (1987, November 23). Down and out—but determined. Does a mentally disturbed woman have the right to be homeless? *Time,* 29.

Horney, K. (1937). *Neurotic personality of our times.* New York: Norton.

Horton, A. D., & Retzlaff, P. D. (1991). Family assessment: Toward DSM-III-R relevancy. *Journal of Clinical Psychology, 47,* 94–100.

Horvath, A. O., & Greenberg, L. S. (1989). Development and validation of the Working Alliance Inventory. *Journal of Counseling Psychology, 36,* 223–233.

House, A. O., & Andrews, H. B. (1988). Life events and difficulties preceding the onset of functional dysphonia. *Journal of Psychosomatic Research, 32,* 311–319.

Howard, G., Evans, G. W., Toole, J. F., Tell, G., Rose, L. A., Espeland, M., & Truscott, B. L. (1990). Characteristics of stroke victims associated with early cardiovascular mortality in their children. *Journal of Clinical Epidemiology, 43,* 49–54.

Hsu, L. K., Crisp, A. H., & Callender, J. S. (1992). Psychiatric diagnoses in recovered and unrecovered anorectics 22 years after onset of illness: A pilot study. *Comprehensive Psychiatry, 33,* 123–127.

Hsu, L. K. G. (1980). Outcome of anorexia nervosa. *Archives of General Psychiatry, 37,* 1041–1046.

Hubbard, K. (1992, March 23). Winning the war within. *People Weekly,* 81–87.

Hubbard, K., Mathison, D., Healy, L. S., & Fine, A. (1991, August 26). Poetic justice? *People Weekly,* 62–64.

Hubel, D. H. (1979). The brain. *Scientific American, 241,* 45–53.

Hufford, D. J. (1993). Epistemologies in religious healing. *Journal of Medicine and Philosophy, 18,* 175–194.

Hugdahl, K., Satz, P., Mitrushina, M., & Miller, E. N. (1993). Left-handedness and old age: Do left-handers die earlier? *Neuropsychologia, 31,* 325–333.

Hughes, G. V., & Boland, F. J. (1992). The effects of caffeine and nicotine consumption on mood and somatic variables in a penitentiary inmate population. *Addictive Behaviors, 17,* 447–457.

Hughes, J. R., Gulliver, S. B., Fenwick, J. W., Valliere, W. A., Cruser, K., Pepper, S., Shea, P., Solomon, L. J., & Flynn, B. S. (1992). Smoking cessation among self-quitters. *Health Psychology, 11,* 331–334.

Hughes, J. R., Oliveto, A. H., Helzer, J. E., Higgins, S. T., & Bickel, W. K. (1992). Should caffeine abuse, dependence, or withdrawal be added to DSM-IV and ICD-10? *American Journal of Psychiatry, 149,* 33–40.

Hundley, T. (1992, July 19). Qat's this? It's Yemen's choice chew. *Chicago Tribune,* pp. 17, 22.

Hunt, N., Bruce-Jones, W., & Silverstone, T. (1992). Life events and relapse in bipolar affective disorder. *Journal of Affective Disorders, 25,* 13–20.

Hurt, S. W., Schnurr, P. P., Severino, S. K., Freeman, E. W., Gise, L. H., Rivera-Tovar, A., & Steege, J. F. (1992). Late luteal phase dysphoric disorder in 670 women evaluated for premenstrual complaints. *American Journal of Psychiatry, 149,* 525–530.

Hutchings, B., & Mednick, S. A. (1974). Registered criminality in the adoptive and biological parents of registered male criminal adoptees. In R. R. Fieve, D. Rosenthal, & H. Brill (Eds.), *Genetic research in psychiatry.* Baltimore: Johns Hopkins University Press.

Huws, R. (1992). Non-attendances at a marital and sexual difficulties clinic: A controlled intervention study. *International Journal of Social Psychiatry, 38,* 304–308.

Huxley, A. (1954). *The doors of perception.* New York: Harper & Row.

Hyland, J. M. (1991). Integrating psychotherapy and pharmacotherapy. *Bulletin of the Menninger Clinic, 55,* 205–215.

Hyman, J. W. (1990). *The light book.* Los Angeles: Tarcher.

Iacono, W. G., & Beiser, M. (1992). Are males more likely than females to develop schizophrenia? *American Journal of Psychiatry, 149,* 1070–1074.

Isaac, G. (1991). Bipolar disorder in prepubertal children in a special educational setting: Is it rare? *Journal of Clinical Psychiatry, 52,* 165–168.

Isajiw, W. (1974). Definitions of ethnicity. *Ethnicity, 1,* 111–124.

Itkonen, J., Schnoll, S., & Glassroth, J. (1984). Pulmonary dysfunction in "freebase" cocaine abusers. *Archives of Internal Medicine, 144,* 2195–2197.

Jackson, L. E. (1993). Understanding, eliciting, and negotiating clients' multicultural health beliefs. *Nurse Practitioner, 18,* 30–43.

Jackson, S. W. (1986). *Melancholia and depression from Hippocratic times to modern times.* New Haven, CT: Yale University Press.

Jacobs, B. L. (1991). Serotonin and behavior: Emphasis on motor control. *Journal of Clinical Psychiatry, 52,* 17–23.

Jacobs, T. (Ed.). (1986). *Family interaction and psychopathology: Theories, methods, and findings.* New York: Plenum.

Jacobsen, F. M., & Rosenthal, N. E. (1988). Seasonal affective disorder and the use of light as an antidepressant. In F. Flach (Ed.), *Affective disorders.* New York: Norton.

Jacobson, N. S., & Bussod, N. (1983). Marital and family therapy. In M. Hersen, A. E. Kazdin, & A. S. Bellack (Eds.), *The clinical psychology handbook.* New York: Pergamon.

Jacobson, N. S., Holtzworth-Munroe, A., & Schmaling, K. B. (1989). Marital therapy and spouse involvement in the treatment of depression, agoraphobia, and alcoholism. *Journal of Consulting and Clinical Psychology, 57,* 5–10.

Jacobsson, L. (1988). On the picture of depression and suicide in traditional societies. *Acta Psychiatrica Scandinavica (Supplementum), 344,* 55–63.

Jacobvitz, D., & Sroufe, L. A., (1987). The early caregiver-child relationship and attention-deficit disorder with hyperactivity in kindergarten: A prospective study. *Child Development, 58,* 1496–1504.

Jagger, J. (1992). Prevention of brain trauma by legislation, regulation, and improved technology: A focus on motor vehicles. *Journal of Neurotrauma, 9,* 313–316.

James, S. A. (1984a). Coronary heart disease in black Americans: Suggestions for research on psychosocial factors. *American Heart Journal, 108,* 833–838.

James, S. A. (1984b). Socioeconomic influences on coronary heart disease in black populations. *American Heart Journal, 108,* 669–672.

James, S. A., Hartnett, S. A., & Kalsbeek, W. D. (1983). John Henryism and blood pressure differences among black men. *Journal of Behavioral Medicine, 6,* 259–278.

James, S. A., Keenan, N. L., Strogatz, D. S., Browning, S. R., & Garrett, J. M. (1992). Socioeconomic status, John Henryism, and blood pressure in black adults: The Pitt County Study. *American Journal of Epidemiology, 135,* 59–67.

James, S. A., LaCroix, A. Z., Kleinbaum, D. G., & Strogatz, D. S. (1984). John Henryism and blood pressure differences among black men: II. The role of occupational stressors. *Journal of Behavioral Medicine, 7,* 259–275.

James, S. A., Strogatz, D. S., Wing, S. B., & Ramsey, D. L. (1987). Socioeconomic status, John Henryism, and hypertension in blacks and whites. *American Journal of Epidemiology, 126,* 664–673.

James, W. (1890). *Principles of psychology* (2 vols.). New York: Holt.

Jampala, V. C., Zimmerman, M., Sierles, F. S., & Taylor, M. A. (1992). Consumers' attitudes toward DSM-III and DSM-III-R: A 1989 survey of psychiatric educators, researchers, practitioners, and senior residents. *Comprehensive Psychiatry, 33,* 180–185.

Janet, P. (1920). *The major symptoms of hysteria.* New York: Macmillan.

Janiger, O., & Dobkin de Rios, M. (1989). LSD and creativity. *Journal of Psychoactive Drugs, 21,* 129–134.

Jann, M. W. (1991). Clozapine. *Pharmacotherapy, 11,* 179–195.

Janowsky, D. S., Addario, D., & Risch, S. C. (1987). *Psychopharmacology case studies* (2nd ed.). New York: Plenum.

Jaroff, L. (1993, November 29). Lies of the mind. *Time,* 52–59.

Jarvis, M. J., Raw, M., Russell, M. A., & Feyerabend, C. (1982). Randomized controlled trial of nicotine chewing-gum. *British Medical Journal, 285,* 537–540.

Jastrow, J. (1915). The antecedents of the study of character and temperament. *The Popular Science Monthly, 86,* 590–613.

Jaynes, J. (1976). *The origins of consciousness in the breakdown of the bicameral mind.* Boston: Houghton Mifflin.

Jefferson, J. W. (1989). Lithium: A therapeutic magic wand. *Journal of Clinical Psychiatry, 50,* 81–86.

Jefferson, J. W. (1990). Lithium: The present and the future. *Journal of Clinical Psychiatry, 51,* 17–19.

Jellinek, E. M. (1947). Recent trends in alcoholism and in alcohol consumption. *Quarterly Journal of Studies in Alcohol, 8,* 1–42.

Jellinek, E. M. (1960). *The disease concept of alcoholism.* Highland Park, NJ: Hillhouse Press.

Jenike, M. A. (1984). A case report of successful treatment of dysmorphophobia with tranylcypromine. *American Journal of Psychiatry, 141,* 1463–1464.

Jenkins, J. O., & Hunter, K. C. (1983). Minorities. In M. Hersen, A. E. Kazdin, & A. S. Bellack (Eds.), *The clinical psychology handbook.* New York: Pergamon.

Jensen, A. B. (1991). Psychosocial factors in breast cancer and their possible impact upon prognosis. *Cancer Treatment Reviews, 18,* 191–210.

Jerison, H. J. (1973). *Evolution of the brain and intelligence.* New York: Academic Press.

Jessor, R., Chase, J. D., & Donovan, J. E. (1980). Psychosocial correlates of marijuana use and problem drinking in a national sample of adolescents. *American Journal of Public Health, 70,* 604–613.

Jilek, W. G., & Jilek-Aall, L. (1985). The metamorphosis of "culture-bound" syndromes. *Social Science and Medicine, 21,* 205–210.

John, D., Callender, C. O., Flores, J., Toussaint, R. M., Yeager, C., Bond, O., & Gear, J. C. (1989). Renal transplantation in substance abusers revisited: The Howard University Hospital experience. *Transplantation Proceedings, 21,* 1422–1424.

Johnson, B., Greenwalt, J., & Hauser, S. (1990, June 25). A vital woman chooses death. *People Weekly,* 40–43.

Johnson, H. (1989). *Vintage: The story of wine.* New York: Simon & Schuster.

Johnson, R. C. (1989). The flushing response and alcohol use. In D. Spiegler, D. Tate, S. Aitken, & C. Christian (Eds.), *Alcohol use among U.S. ethnic minorities.* Rockville, MD: National Institute on Alcohol Abuse and Alcoholism Research.

Johnson, R. E., Stevens, V. J., Hollis, J. F., & Woodson, G. T. (1992). Nicotine chewing gum use in the outpatient case setting. *Journal of Family Practice, 34,* 61–65.

Johnston, D. W. (1989). Prevention of cardiovascular disease by psychological methods. *British Journal of Psychiatry, 154,* 183–194.

Johnston, P., Hudson, S. M., & Marshall, W. L. (1992). The effects of masturbatory reconditioning with nonfamilial child molesters. *Behaviour Research and Therapy, 30,* 559–561.

Joint Commission on Mental Illness and Health. (1961). *Action for mental health.* New York: Basic Books.

Jones, J. B., & Barklage, N. E. (1990). Conversion disorder: Camouflage for brain lesions in two cases. *Archives of Internal Medicine, 150,* 1343–1345.

Jones, M. (1968). *Social psychiatry in practice: The idea of a therapeutic community.* New York: Penguin.

Jones, M. C. (1924). A laboratory study of fear: The case of Peter. *Journal of Genetic Psychology, 31,* 308–315.

Jonsson, S. A., & Jonsson, H. (1992). Outcome in untreated schizophrenia: A search for symptoms and traits with prognostic meaning in patients admitted to a mental hospital in the preneuroleptic era. *Acta Psychiatrica Scandinavica, 85,* 313–320.

Jorm, A. F. (1989). Modifiability of trait anxiety and neuroticism: A meta-analysis of the literature. *Australian and New Zealand Journal of Psychiatry, 23,* 21–29.

Joseph, R. (1986). Confabulation and delusional denial: Frontal lobe and lateralized influences. *Journal of Clinical Psychology, 42,* 507–520.

Joubert, C. E. (1992). Antecedents of narcissism and psychological reactance as indicated by college students' retrospective reports of their parents' behaviors. *Psychological Reports, 70,* 1111–1115.

Joyce, P. R., & Paykel, E. S. (1989). Predictions of drug response in depression. *Archives of General Psychiatry, 46,* 89–99.

Judd, L. L. (1990). The decade of the brain: Prospects and challenges for NIMH. *Neuropsychopharmacology, 3,* 309–310.

Jung, C. G. (1924). *Psychological types.* New York: Random House.

Justice, A. (1985). Review of the effects of stress on cancer in laboratory animals: Importance of time of stress application and types of tumor. *Psychological Bulletin, 98,* 108–138.

Kaas, J. H. (1987). The organization of neocortex in mammals: Implications for theories of brain function. *Annual Review of Psychology, 38,* 129–151.

Kahn, A., Van de Merckt, C., Rebuffat, E., Mozin, M. J., Sottiaux, M., & Blum, D. (1989). Sleep problems in healthy preadolescents. *Pediatrics, 84,* 542–546.

Kahn, E. M., & White, E. M. (1989). Adapting milieu approaches to acute inpatient care for schizophrenic patients. *Hospital and Community Psychiatry, 40,* 609–614.

Kahneman, D., & Tversky, A. (1973). On the psychology of prediction. *Psychological Review, 80,* 237–251.

Kail, R. (1992). General slowing of information-processing by persons with mental retardation. *American Journal of Mental Retardation, 97,* 333–341.

Kalant, O. J. (1966). *The amphetamines: Toxicity and addiction.* Toronto: University of Toronto Press.

Kalinowsky, L. B. (1980). Convulsive therapies. In H. I. Kaplan, A. M. Freedman, & B. J. Sadock (Eds.), *Comprehensive textbook of psychiatry* (Vol. 3, 3rd ed.). Baltimore: Williams & Wilkins.

Kalnins, I., & Love, R. (1982). Children's concepts of health and illness—and implications for health education: An overview. *Health Education Quarterly, 9,* 104–115.

Kamps, D. M., Leonard, B. R., Vernon, S., Dugan, E. P., Delquadri, J. C., Gershon, B., Wade, L., & Folk, L. (1992). Teaching social skills to students with autism to increase peer interaction in an integrated first-grade classroom. *Journal of Applied Behavior Analysis, 25,* 281–288.

Kanas, N. (1991). Group therapy with schizophrenic patients: A short-term homogeneous approach. *International Journal of Group Psychotherapy, 41,* 33–48.

Kandel, D. B. (1991). The social demography of drug use. *Milbank Quarterly, 69,* 365–414.

Kane, C. F., DiMartino, E., & Jimenez, M. (1990). A comparison of short-term psychoeducational and support groups for relatives coping with chronic schizophrenia. *Archives of Psychiatric Nursing, 4,* 343–353.

Kanner, A. D., Coyne, J. C., Schaefer, C., & Lazarus, R. S. (1981). Comparison of two modes of stress measurement: Daily hassles and uplifts versus major life events. *Journal of Behavioral Medicine, 4,* 1–39.

Kanner, L. (1943). Autistic disturbances of affective contact. *Nervous Child, 2,* 217–250.

Kaplan, D. M. (1990). Some theoretical and technical aspects of gender and social reality in clinical psychoanalysis. *Psychoanalytic Study of the Child, 45,* 3–24.

Kaplan, G. A., & Reynolds, P. (1988). Depression and cancer mortality and morbidity: Prospective evidence from the Alameda County Study. *Journal of Behavioral Medicine, 11,* 1–13.

Kaplan, H. S. (1974). *The new sex therapy.* New York: Brunner/Mazel.

Kaplan, M. (1983a). A woman's view of DSM-III. *American Psychologist, 38,* 786–792.

Kaplan, M. (1983b). The issue of sex bias in DSM-III: Comments on the articles by Spitzer, Williams, and Kass. *American Psychologist, 38,* 802–803.

Kaplan, R. F., Cooney, N. L., Baker, L. H., Gillespie, R. A., Meyer, R. E., & Pomerlau, O. F. (1985). Reactivity to alcohol-related cues: Physiological and subjective responses in alcoholics and non-problem drinkers. *Journal of Studies on Alcohol, 46,* 267–272.

Karasu, T. B. (1990). Toward a clinical model of psychotherapy for depression. I. Systematic comparison of three psychotherapies. *American Journal of Psychiatry, 147,* 133–147.

Kashani, J. H., Dandoy, A. C., & Reid, J. C. (1992). Hopelessness in children and adolescents: An overview. *Acta Paedopsychiatrica, 55,* 33–39.

Kass, F., Spitzer, R. L., & Williams, J. B. (1983). An empirical study of the issue of sex bias in the diagnostic criteria of DSM-III Axis II Personality Disorders. *American Psychologist, 38,* 799–801.

Katchadourian, H. A. (1989). *Fundamentals of human sexuality* (5th ed.). Fort Worth, TX: Holt, Rinehart, & Winston.

Kaufman, D. M., & Solomon, S. (1992). Migraine visual auras: A medical update for the psychiatrist. *General Hospital Psychiatry, 14,* 162–170.

Kaufman, E. (1985). Family systems and family therapy of substance abuse: An overview of two decades of research and clinical experience. *International Journal of the Addictions, 20,* 897–916.

Kaufman, M. (1971). *Homeopathy in America: The rise and fall of a medical heresy.* Baltimore: Johns Hopkins University Press.

Kaul, T. J., & Bednar, R. L. (1986). Experiential group research: Results, questions, and suggestions. In S. L. Garfield & A. E. Bergin (Eds.), *Handbook of psychotherapy and behavior change* (3rd ed.). New York: Wiley.

Kavoussi, R. J., & Siever, L. J. (1992). Overlap between borderline and schizotypal personality disorders. *Comprehensive Psychiatry, 33,* 7–12.

Kay, S. R. (1990). Significance of the positive-negative distinction in schizophrenia. *Schizophrenia Bulletin, 16,* 635–652.

Kazdin, A. E. (1977). *The token economy.* New York: Plenum.

Kazdin, A. E. (1982). Symptom substitution, generalization, and response covariation: Implications for psychotherapy outcome. *Psychological Bulletin, 91,* 349–365.

Kazdin, A. E. (1989). Developmental psychopathology: Current research, issues, and directions. *American Psychologist, 44,* 180–187.

Keane, T. M., & Kaloupek, D. (1982). Imaginal flooding in the treatment of a post-traumatic stress disorder. *Journal of Consulting and Clinical Psychology, 50,* 138–140.

Kehoe, M. (1986). A portrait of the older lesbian. *Journal of Homosexuality, 12,* 157–161.

Kehrer, H. E. (1992). Savant capabilities of autistic persons. *Acta Paedopsychiatrica, 55,* 151–155.

Keitner, G. I., & Miller, I. W. (1990). Family functioning and major depression: An overview. *American Journal of Psychiatry, 147,* 1128–1137.

Keller, M. (1970). The great Jewish drink mystery. *British Journal of Addiction, 64,* 289–296.

Keller, M. (1976). The disease concept of alcoholism revisited. *Journal of Studies on Alcohol, 37,* 1694–1717.

Keller, M. B., Lavori, P. W., Beardslee, W. R., Wunder, J., & Ryan, N. (1991). Depression in children and adolescents: New data on "undertreatment" and a literature review on the efficacy of available treatments. *Journal of Affective Disorders, 21,* 163–171.

Keller, M. B., Lavori, P. W., Beardslee, W. R., Wunder, J., Schwartz, C. E., Roth, J., & Biederman, J. (1992). The disruptive behavioral disorder in children and adolescents. *Journal of the American Academy of Child and Adolescent Psychiatry, 31,* 204–209.

Keller, M. B., Shapiro, R. W., Lavori, P. W., & Wolfe, N. (1982). Recovery in major depressive disorder. *Archives of General Psychiatry, 39,* 905–910.

Kellner, R. (1986). *Somatization and hypochondriasis.* New York: Praeger.

Kellner, R. (1990). Somatization: Theories and research. *Journal of Nervous and Mental Disease, 178,* 150–160.

Kelly, G. A. (1955). *The psychology of personal constructs.* New York: Norton.

Kelsoe, J. R., Ginns, E. I., Egeland, J. A., Gerhard, D. S., Goldstein, A. M., Bale, S. J., Pauls, D. L., Long, R. T., Kidd, K. K., Conte, G., Housman, D. E., & Paul, S. M. (1989). Re-evaluation of the linkage relationship between chromosome 11p loci and the gene for bipolar affective disorder in the Old Order Amish. *Nature, 342,* 238–243.

Kemp, S. (1985). Modern myth and medieval madness: Views of mental illness in the European Middle Ages and Renaissance. *New England Journal of Psychology, 14,* 1–8.

Kemp, S. (1990). *Medieval psychology.* New York: Greenwood.

Kendall, P. C., & Hollon, S. D. (Eds.). (1981). *Assessment strategies for cognitive-behavioral intervention.* New York: Academic Press.

Kendell, R. E. (1975). *The role of diagnosis in psychiatry.* London: Blackwell.

Kendell, R. E. (1991). Relationship between the DSM-IV and the ICD-10. *Journal of Abnormal Psychology, 100,* 297–301.

Kendler, K. S., & Gruenberg, A. M. (1982). Genetic relationship between personality disorder and the "schizophrenic spectrum" disorders. *American Journal of Psychiatry, 139,* 1185–1186.

Kendler, K. S., Gruenberg, A. M., & Strauss, J. S. (1981). An independent analysis of the Copenhagen sample of the Danish adoption study of schizophrenia: II. The relationship between schizotypal personality disorder and schizophrenia. *Archives of General Psychiatry, 38,* 982–987.

Kendler, K. S., Gruenberg, A. M., & Tsuang, M. T. (1988). A family study of the subtypes of schizophrenia. *American Journal of Psychiatry, 145,* 57–62.

Kendler, K. S., Heath, A. C., Neale, M. C., Kessler, R. C., & Eaves, L. J. (1992). A population-based twin study of alcoholism in women. *JAMA, 268,* 1877–1882.

Kendler, K. S., Masterson, C. C., Ungaro, R., & Davis, K. L. (1984). A family history study of schizophrenia-related personality disorders. *American Journal of Psychiatry, 141,* 424–427.

Kendler, K. S., Neale, M. C., Kessler, R. C., Heath, A. C., & Eaves, L. J. (1992a). Childhood parental loss and adult psychopathology in women: A twin study perspective. *Archives of General Psychiatry, 49,* 109–116.

Kendler, K. S., Neale, M. C., Kessler, R. C., Heath, A. C., & Eaves, L. J. (1992b). Generalized anxiety disorder in women: A population-based twin study. *Archives of General Psychiatry, 49,* 267–272.

Kendler, K. S., Neale, M. C., Kessler, R. C., Heath, A. C., & Eaves, L. J. (1992c). Major depression and generalized anxiety disorder: Same genes, (partly) different environments? *Archives of General Psychiatry, 49,* 716–722.

Kendler, K. S., Neale, M. C., Kessler, R. C., Heath, A. C., & Eaves, L. J. (1992d). The genetic epidemiology of phobias in women: The interrelationships of agoraphobia, social phobia, situational phobia, and simple phobia. *Archives of General Psychiatry, 49,* 273–281.

Kennedy, G. J., Kelman, H. R., & Thomas, C. (1990). The emergence of depressive symptoms in late life: The importance of declining health and increasing disability. *Journal of Community Health, 15,* 93–104.

Kennedy, J. F. (1963). *Message from the President of the United States relative to mental illness and mental retardation.* Washington, DC: U.S. Government Printing Office.

Kennedy, S. H., & Garfinkel, P. E. (1992). Advances in diagnosis and treatment of anorexia nervosa and bulimia nervosa. *Canadian Journal of Psychiatry, 37,* 309–315.

Kennedy, W. A. (1965). School phobia: Rapid treatment of 50 cases. *Journal of Abnormal Psychology, 70,* 285–289.

Kenny, D. A. (1979). *Correlation and causality.* New York: Wiley.

Kenny, M. G. (1978). Latah: The symbolism of a putative mental disorder. *Culture, Medicine, and Psychiatry, 2,* 209–231.

Kenyon, F. E. (1964). Hypochondriasis: A clinical study. *British Journal of Psychiatry, 110,* 478–488.

Kenyon, F. E. (1976). Hypochondriacal states. *British Journal of Psychiatry, 129,* 1–4.

Kermani, E. J., & Drob, S. L. (1987). Tarasoff decision: A decade later dilemma still faces psychotherapists. *American Journal of Psychotherapy, 41,* 271–285.

Kernberg, O. F. (1975). *Borderline conditions and pathological narcissism.* New York: Jason Aronson.

Kernberg, O. F. (1986). Narcissistic personality disorder. In A. M. Cooper, A. J. Frances, & M. H. Sacks (Eds.), *The personality disorders and neuroses.* New York: Basic Books.

Kessler, R. C. (1979). A strategy for studying differential vulnerability to the psychological consequences of stress. *Journal of Health and Social Behavior, 20,* 100–108.

Kessler, R. C., McGonagle, K. A., Zhao, S., Nelson, C. B., Hughes, M., Eshleman, S., Wittchen, H.-U., & Kendler, K. S. (1994). Lifetime and 12-month prevalence of DSM-III-R psychiatric diagnoses in the United States. *Archives of General Psychiatry, 51,* 8–19.

Kessler, R. C., & McLeod, J. D. (1984). Sex differences in vulnerability to undesirable life events. *American Sociological Review, 49,* 620–631.

Kessler, R. J. (1990). Models of disease and the diagnosis of schizophrenia. *Psychiatry, 53,* 140–147.

Kety, S. S. (1974). From rationalization to reason. *American Journal of Psychiatry, 131,* 957–963.

Kety, S. S. (1980). The syndrome of schizophrenia: Unresolved questions and opportunities for research. *British Journal of Psychiatry, 136,* 421–436.

Kety, S. S. (1988). Schizophrenic illness in the families of schizophrenic adoptees: Findings from the Danish national sample. *Schizophrenia Bulletin, 14,* 217–222.

Khantzian, E. J. (1980). An ego/self theory of substance dependence: A contemporary psychoanalytic perspective. In D. J. Lettieri, M. Sayers, & H. W. Pearson (Eds.), *Theories on drug abuse: Selected contemporary perspectives.* Rockville, MD: NIDA Research Monograph Series.

Kiecolt-Glaser, J. K., Fisher, L. D., Ogrocki, P., Stout, J. C., Speicher, C. E., & Glaser, R. (1987). Marital quality, marital disruption, and immune function. *Psychosomatic Medicine, 49,* 13–34.

Kiecolt-Glaser, J. K., Garner, W., Speicher, C. E., Penn, G. M., Holliday, J. E., & Glaser, R. (1984). Psychosocial modifiers of immunocompetence in medical students. *Psychosomatic Medicine, 46,* 7–14.

Kiecolt-Glaser, J. K., & Glaser, R. (1992). Psychoneuroimmunology: Can psychological interventions modulate immunity? *Journal of Consulting and Clinical Psychology, 60,* 569–575.

Kiecolt-Glaser, J. K., Glaser, R., Strain, E. C., Stout, J. C., Tarr, K. L., Holliday, J. E., & Speicher, C. E. (1986). Modulation of cellular immunity in medical students. *Journal of Behavioral Medicine, 9,* 5–21.

Kiecolt-Glaser, J. K., Kennedy, S., Malkoff, S., Fisher, L., Speicher, C. E., & Glaser, R. (1988). Marital discord and immunity in males. *Psychosomatic Medicine, 50,* 213–229.

Kihlstrom, J. F. (1985). Hypnosis. *Annual Review of Psychology, 36,* 385–418.

Kihlstrom, J. F. (1990). The psychological unconscious. In L. A. Pervin (Ed.), *Handbook of personality: Theory and research.* New York: Guilford.

Kilpatrick, D. G., Veronen, L. J., & Resick, P. A. (1979). The aftermath of rape: Recent empirical findings. *American Journal of Orthopsychiatry, 49,* 658–669.

Kimble, D. P. (1990). Functional effects of neural grafting in the mammalian central nervous system. *Psychological Bulletin, 108,* 462–479.

King, B. H., & Liston, E. H. (1990). Proposals for the mechanism of action of convulsive therapy: A synthesis. *Biological Psychiatry, 27,* 76–94.

King, D. J., & Cooper, S. J. (1989). Viruses, immunity, and mental disorder. *British Journal of Psychiatry, 154,* 1–7.

King, G. S., Smialek, J. E., & Troutman, W. G. (1985). Sudden death in adolescents resulting from the inhalation of typewriter correction fluid. *JAMA, 253,* 1604–1606.

Kinsey, A. C., Pomeroy, W. D., & Martin, C. E. (1948). *Sexual behavior in the human male.* Philadelphia: Saunders.

Kinsey, A. C., Pomeroy, W. D., Martin, C. E., & Gebhard, P. H. (1953). *Sexual behavior in the human female.* Philadelphia: Saunders.

Kinsman, R. A., Dirks, J. F., & Jones, N. F. (1982). Psychomaintenance of chronic physical illness: Clinical assessment of personal styles affecting medical management. In T. Millon, C. Green, & R. Meagher (Eds.), *Handbook of clinical health psychology.* New York: Plenum.

Kirkpatrick, M., & Friedmann, C. T. (1976). Treatment of requests for sex-change surgery with psychotherapy. *American Journal of Psychiatry, 133,* 1194–1196.

Klag, M. J., Whelton, P. K., Coresh, J., Grim, C. E., & Kuller, L. H. (1991). The association of skin color with blood pressure in U.S. blacks with low socioeconomic status. *JAMA, 265,* 599–602.

Klee, H. (1992). Social factors implicated when drug users share injecting equipment. *International Conference on AIDS, 8,* 215.

Klein, D. F. (1964). Delineation of two drug-responsive anxiety syndromes. *Psychopharmacologia, 5,* 397–408.

Klein, M. E., Behnke, S. H., & Peterson, C. (1993). Depressive symptoms among sheltered homeless mothers. *The Community Psychologist, 26,* 24–26.

Klein, R. G., & Mannuzza, S. (1991). Long-term outcome of hyperactive children: A review. *Journal of the American Academy of Child and Adolescent Psychiatry, 30,* 383–387.

Kleinman, A. (1977). Depression, somatization, and the "new cross-cultural psychiatry." *Social Science and Medicine, 11,* 3–10.

Kleinman, A., & Good, B. (Eds.). (1985). *Culture and depression.* Berkeley: University of California Press.

Kleinman, J. E., Karson, C. N., Weinberger, D. R., Freed, W. J., Berman, K. F., & Wyatt, R. J. (1984). Eye-blinking and cerebral ventricular size in chronic schizophrenic patients. *American Journal of Psychiatry, 141,* 1430–1432.

Klerman, G. L. (1977). Anxiety and depression. In G. D. Burrows (Ed.), *Handbook of studies on depression.* Amsterdam: Elsevier.

Klerman, G. L. (1987). Clinical epidemiology of suicide. *Journal of Clinical Psychiatry, 48,* 33–38.

Klerman, G. L. (1990). The psychiatric patient's right to effective treatment: Implications of *Osheroff v. Chestnut Lodge. American Journal of Psychiatry, 147,* 409–418.

Klerman, G. L., Weissman, M. M., Rounsaville, B. J., & Chevron, E. S. (1984). *Interpersonal psychotherapy of depression.* New York: Basic Books.

Kluft, R. P. (1984). Treatment of multiple personality disorder: A study of 33 cases. *Psychiatric Clinics of North America, 7,* 9–29.

Kluft, R. P. (1985). The treatment of multiple personality disorder (MPD): Current concepts. In F. F. Flach (Ed.), *Directions in psychiatry.* New York: Hatherleigh.

Kluft, R. P. (1987). The simulation and dissimulation of multiple personality disorder. *American Journal of Clinical Hypnosis, 30,* 104–118.

Kluft, R. P. (1988). The postunification treatment of multiple personality disorder: First findings. *American Journal of Psychotherapy, 42,* 212–228.

Kluft, R. P. (1989). Iatrogenic creation of new alter personalities. *Dissociation: Progress in the Dissociative Disorders, 2,* 83–91.

Kluznik, J. C., Speed, N., Van Valkenburg, C., & Magraw, R. (1986). Forty-year follow-up of United States prisoners of war. *American Journal of Psychiatry, 143,* 1443–1446.

Knapp, M. J., Knopman, D. S., Soloman, P. R., & Pendlebury, W. H. (1994). A 30-week randomized controlled trial of high-dose tacrine in patients with Alzhemier's disease. *Journal of the American Medical Association, 271,* 985–991.

Knobel, M. (1974). The rights of the mentally ill: Towards a review of the concept of psychiatry and the psychiatrist. *Mental Health and Society, 1,* 228–245.

Kobasa, S. C. (1979). Stressful life events, personality, and health: An inquiry into hardiness. *Journal of Personality and Social Psychology, 37,* 1–11.

Kobasa, S. C. (1982). Commitment and coping in stress resistance among lawyers. *Journal of Personality and Social Psychology, 42,* 707–717.

Kobasa, S. C., Maddi, S. R., & Courington, S. (1981). Personality and constitution as mediators in the stress-illness relationship. *Journal of Health and Social Behavior, 22,* 368–378.

Kobasa, S. C., Maddi, S. R., & Kahn, S. (1982). Hardiness and health: A prospective study. *Journal of Personality and Social Psychology, 42,* 168–177.

Koegel, L. K., Koegel, R. L., Hurley, C., & Frea, W. D. (1992). Improving social skills and disruptive behavior in children with autism through self-management. *Journal of Applied Behavior Analysis, 25,* 341–353.

Koegel, P., Burnam, M. A., & Farr, R. K. (1988). The prevalence of specific psychiatric disorders among homeless individuals in the inner city of Los Angeles. *Archives of General Psychiatry, 45,* 1085–1092.

Kohut, H. (1971). *The analysis of the self.* New York: International Universities Press.

Kohut, H. (1977). *The restoration of the self.* New York: International Universities Press.

Koksal, F., & Power, K. G. (1990). Four Systems Anxiety Questionnaire (FSAQ): A self-report measure of somatic, cognitive, behavioral, and feeling components. *Journal of Personality Assessment, 54,* 534–545.

Kolata, G. (1986). Genetic screening raises questions for employers and insurers. *Science, 232,* 317–319.

Kolb, B., & Whishaw, I. Q. (1990). *Fundamentals of human neuropsychology* (3rd ed.). New York: Freeman.

Kolb, L. (1962). *Drug addiction: A medical problem.* Springfield, IL: Charles C Thomas.

Koller, W. C. (1992). How accurately can Parkinson's disease be diagnosed? *Neurology, 42,* 6–16.

Kolodny, R. C., Masters, W. H., Johnson, V. E., & Biggs, M. A. (1979). *Textbook of human sexuality for nurses.* Boston: Little, Brown.

Korchin, S. J., & Schuldberg, D. (1981). The future of clinical assessment. *American Psychologist, 36,* 1147–1158.

Korn, M. L., Kotler, M., Molcho, A., Botsis, A. J., Grosz, D., Chen, C., Plutchik, R., Brown, S. L., & van Praag,

H. M. (1992). Suicide and violence associated with panic attacks. *Biological Psychiatry, 31,* 607–612.

Korzekwa, M., Steiner, M., Links, P., & Eppel, A. (1991). The dexamethasone suppression test in borderlines: Is it useful? *Canadian Journal of Psychiatry, 36,* 26–28.

Koski, K. J., & Marttila, R. J. (1990). Transient global amnesia: Incidence in an urban population. *Acta Neurologica Scandinavica, 81,* 358–360.

Koso-Thomas, O. (1987). *Circumcision of women: A strategy for eradication.* London: Zed Books.

Kosten, T. R., Morgan, C., & Kleber, H. D. (1991). Treatment of heroin addicts using buprenorphine. *American Journal of Drug and Alcohol Abuse, 17,* 119–128.

Kotses, H., Lewis, P., & Creer, T. L. (1990). Environmental control of asthma self-management. *Journal of Asthma, 27,* 375–384.

Kozel, N. J. (1990). Epidemiology of drug abuse in the United States: A summary of methods and findings. *Bulletin of the Pan American Health Organization, 24,* 53–62.

Kraemer, H., & Sprenger, J. (1486). *Malleus maleficarum.* Lyons.

Kraepelin, E. (1899). *Psychiatrie: Ein lehrbuch fur studirende und Aerzte.* Leipzig: Verlag von Johann Ambrosius Barth.

Kraepelin, E. (1913/1971). *Dementia praecox and paraphrenia.* Huntington, NY: Krieger.

Krais, W. A. (1989). The incompetent developmentally disabled person's right of self-determination: Right-to-die, sterilization, and institutionalization. *American Journal of Law and Medicine, 15,* 333–361.

Kral, J. G. (1992). Overview of surgical techniques for treating obesity. *American Journal of Clinical Nutrition, 55,* 552–555.

Kraus, A. S., & Forbes, W. F. (1992). Aluminum, fluoride, and the prevention of Alzheimer's disease. *Canadian Journal of Public Health, 83,* 97–100.

Krause, J., Herth, T., Maier, W., Steiger, A., Schoneich, S., & Benkert, O. (1991). An interdisciplinary study towards a multiaxial classification of male sexual dysfunction. *Acta Psychiatrica Scandinavica, 84,* 130–136.

Kreitman, N., Sainsbury, P., Pearce, K., & Costain, W. R. (1965). Hypochondriasis and depression in outpatients at a general hospital. *British Journal of Psychiatry, 111,* 607–615.

Kremer, J., & den Daas, H. P. (1990). Case report: A man with breast dysphoria. *Archives of Sexual Behavior, 19,* 179–181.

Kress, F. (1979). Evalutions of dangerousness. *Schizophrenia Bulletin, 5,* 211–217.

Krieger, N. (1990). Racial and gender discrimination: Risk factors for high blood pressure. *Social Science and Medicine, 30,* 1273–1281.

Krishtalka, L. (1989). *Dinosaur plots and other intrigues in natural history.* New York: Morrow.

Krug, S. E. (1992). Mass illness at an intermediate school: Toxic fumes or epidemic hysteria? *Pediatric Emergency Care, 8,* 280–282.

Krull, F. (1990). The problem of integrating biological and psychodynamic views in psychotherapeutic training of physicians. *Psychotherapy and Psychosomatics, 53,* 115–118.

Krull, F., & Schifferdecker, M. (1990). Inpatient treatment of conversion disorder: A clinical investigation of outcome. *Psychotherapy and Psychosomatics, 53,* 161–165.

Kubie, L. S. (1968). Pitfalls of community psychiatry. *Archives of General Psychiatry, 18,* 257–266.

Kuch, K., & Cox, B. J. (1992). Symptoms of PTSD in 124 survivors of the Holocaust. *American Journal of Psychiatry, 149,* 337–340.

Kuczmarski, R. J. (1992). Prevalence of overweight and weight gain in the United States. *American Journal of Clinical Nutrition, 55,* 495–502.

Kufferle, B. (1988). Group dynamics as an emotional turmoil precipitating psychotic manifestations. *Psychopathology, 21,* 111–115.

Kuipers, L., Birchwood, M., & McCreadie, R. G. (1992). Psychosocial family intervention in schizophrenia: A review of empirical studies. *British Journal of Psychiatry, 160,* 272–275.

Kushner, M. G., Sher, K. J., & Beitman, B. D. (1990). The relation between alcohol problems and anxiety disorders. *American Journal of Psychiatry, 147,* 685–695.

Lacks, P. (1984). *Bender Gestalt screening for brain dysfunction.* New York: Wiley.

Ladee, G. A. (1966). *Hypochondriacal syndromes.* New York: Elsevier.

La Gory, M., Ritchey, F. J., & Mullis, J. (1990). Depression among the homeless. *Journal of Health and Social Behavior, 31,* 87–102.

Lahmeyer, H. W., Reynolds, C. F., Kupfer, D. J., & King, R. (1989). Biologic markers in borderline personality disorder: A review. *Journal of Clinical Psychiatry, 50,* 217—225.

Laing, R. D. (1959). *The divided self.* London: Tavistok.

Laing, R. D. (1967). *The politics of experience.* New York: Pantheon.

Lakier, J. B. (1992). Smoking and cardiovascular disease. *American Journal of Medicine, 93,* 8–12.

Lakosina, N. D., Kostiunina, Z. G., Kal'ke, A. R., & Shashkova, N. G. (1987). Pathomorphosis of hysterical neurosis. *Zhurnal Nevropatologi I Psiyhiatrii, 87,* 1684–1688.

Lam, D. H. (1991). Psychosocial family intervention in schizophrenia: A review of empirical studies. *Psychological Medicine, 21,* 423–441.

Lam, R. W., Bloch, M., Jones, B. D., Marcus, A. M., Fox, S., Amman, W., & Hayden, M. R. (1988). Psychiatric morbidity associated with early clinical diagnosis of Huntington disease in a predictive testing program. *Journal of Clinical Psychiatry, 49,* 444–447.

Lamb, H. R., & Talbott, J. A. (1986). The homeless mentally ill: The perspective of the American Psychiatric Association. *JAMA, 256,* 498–501.

Lampert, A., & Friedman, A. (1992). Sex differences in vulnerability and maladjustment as a function of parental investment: An evolutionary approach. *Social Biology, 39,* 65–81.

Lang, A. R., Goeckner, D. J., Adesso, V. J., & Marlatt, G. A. (1975). The effects of alcohol on aggression in male social drinkers. *Journal of Abnormal Psychology, 84,* 508–518.

Lang, C. J. (1992). Multi-infarct and Alzheimer's dementia—problems of differential diagnosis. *Acta Histochemica (Supplementband), 42,* 13–18.

Lang, P. J. (1969). The mechanics of desensitization and the laboratory study of fear. In C. Franks (Ed.), *Behavior therapy: Appraisal and status.* New York: McGraw-Hill.

Lang, P. J. (1970). Stimulus control, response control, and the desensitization of fear. In D. J. Levis (Ed.), *Learning approaches to therapeutic behavior.* Chicago: Aldine.

Lasch, C. (1978). *The culture of narcissism: American life in an age of diminishing expectations.* New York: Norton.

Last, C. G. (1989). Anxiety disorders. In T. H. Ollendick & M. Hersen (Eds.), *Handbook of child psychopathology* (2nd ed.). New York: Plenum.

Latimer, P. R. (1983). *Functional gatrointestinal disorders: A behavioral medicine approach.* New York: Springer.

Latimer, P. R., Sarna, S., Campbell, D., Latimer, M., Waterfall, W., & Daniel, E. E. (1981). Colonic motor and myoelectrical activity: A comparative study of normal subjects, psychoneurotic patients, and patients with irritable bowel syndrome. *Gastroenterology, 80,* 893–901.

Lau, R. K., Jenkins, P., Caun, K., Forster, S. M., Weber, J. N., McManus, T. J., Harris, J. R., Jeffries, D. J., & Pinching, A. J. (1992). Trends in sexual behaviour in a cohort of homosexual men: A 7 year prospective study. *International Journal of STD and AIDS, 3,* 267–272.

Lauer, K., & Firnhaber, W. (1992). Epidemiologic aspects of multiple sclerosis. *Versicherungsmedizin, 44,* 125–130.

Lavee, Y. (1991). Western and non-western human sexuality: Implications for clinical practice. *Journal of Sex and Marital Therapy, 17,* 203–213.

Lazarus, A. A. (1992). The multimodal approach to the treatment of minor depression. *American Journal of Psychotherapy, 46,* 50–57.

Lazarus, R. S. (1966). *Psychological stress and the coping process.* New York: McGraw-Hill.

Lazarus, R. S. (1982). Thoughts on the relations between emotion and cognition. *American Psychologist, 37,* 1019–1024.

Lazarus, R. S. (1991). *Emotion and adaptation.* New York: Oxford University Press.

Lazarus, R. S., & Folkman, S. (1984). *Stress, appraisal, and coping.* New York: Springer.

Lazerson, J. (1992). Feminism and group psychotherapy: An ethical responsibility. *International Journal of Group Psychotherapy, 42,* 523–546.

Leadbetter, R., Shutty, M., Pavalonis, D., Vieweg, V., Higgins, P., & Downs, M. (1992). Clozapine-induced weight gain: Prevalence and clinical relevance. *American Journal of Psychiatry, 149,* 68–72.

Leary, T. (1957). *Interpersonal diagnosis of personality.* New York: Ronald Press.

Leary, T. (1964). The religious experience: Its production and interpretation. *Psychedelic Review, 1,* 324–346.

Lebegue, B. J. (1985). Paraphilias in pornography: A study

of perversions inherent in title. *Australian Journal of Sex, Marriage, and Family, 6*, 33–36.

Lebegue, B. J., & Clark, L. D. (1981). Incompetence to refuse treatment: A necessary condition for civil commitment. *American Journal of Psychiatry, 138*, 1075–1077.

Lechner, H., & Bertha, G. (1991). Multi-infarct dementia. *Journal of Neural Transmission, 33*, 49–52.

Lechtenberg, R. (1982). *The psychiatrist's guide to diseases of the nervous system.* New York: Wiley.

Lee, N. K., & Oei, T. P. (1993). Exposure and response prevention in anxiety disorders: Implications for treatment and relapse prevention in problem drinkers. *Clinical Psychology Review, 13*, 619–632.

Lee, T., & Seeman, P. (1980). Elevation of brain neuroleptic/dopamine receptors in schizophrenia. *American Journal of Psychiatry, 137*, 191–197.

Lee, V. E., Brooks-Gunn, J., Schnur, E., & Liaw, F. (1990). Are Head Start effects sustained? A longitudinal follow-up comparison of disadvantaged children attending Head Start, no preschool, and other preschool programs. *Child Development, 61*, 495–507.

Leff, J., Fischer, M., & Bertelsen, A. (1976). A cross-national epidemiological study of mania. *British Journal of Psychiatry, 129*, 428–442.

Leff, J., & Vaughn, C. (1985). *Expressed emotion in families: Its significance for mental illness.* New York: Guilford.

Lehmann, H. E. (1980). Schizophrenia: Clinical features. In H. I. Kaplan, A. M. Freedman, & B. J. Sadock (Eds.), *Comprehensive textbook of psychiatry* (Vol. 2, 3rd ed.). Baltimore: Williams & Wilkins.

Lehrer, P. M., Sargunaraj, D., & Hochron, S. (1992). Psychological approaches to the treatment of asthma. *Journal of Consulting and Clinical Psychology, 60*, 639–643.

Leiblum, S. R., Pervin, L. A., & Campbell, E. H. (1989). The treatment of vaginismus: Success and failure. In S. R. Leiblum & R. C. Rosen (Eds.), *Principles and practice of sex therapy: Update for the 1990s.* New York: Guilford.

Leiblum, S. R., & Rosen, R. C. (1991). Couples therapy for erectile disorders: Conceptual and clinical considerations. *Journal of Sex and Marital Therapy, 17*, 147–159.

Leigh, B. C. (1989). In search of the seven dwarves: Issues of measurement and meaning in alcohol expectancy research. *Psychological Bulletin, 105*, 361–373.

Leigh, B. C., & Stacy, A. W. (1991). On the scope of alcohol expectancy research: Remaining issues of measurement and meaning. *Psychological Bulletin, 110*, 147–154.

Lemonick, M. D. (1994, September 12). The killers all around. *Time*, 62–69.

Lenneberg, E. H. (1967). *Biological foundations of language.* New York: Wiley.

Lenzenweger, M. F., & Loranger, A. W. (1989). Detection of familial schizophrenia using a psychometric measure of schizotypy. *Archives of General Psychiatry, 46*, 902–907.

Leon, A. C., Klerman, G. L., & Wickramaratne, P. (1993). Continuing female predominance in depressive illness. *American Journal of Public Health, 83*, 754–757.

Leon, G. R., & Dinklage, D. (1989). Obesity and anorexia nervosa. In T. H. Ollendick & M. Hersen (Eds.),

Handbook of child psychopathology (2nd ed.). New York: Plenum.

Lesmes, G. R., & Donofrio, K. H. (1992). Passive smoking: The medical and economic issues. *American Journal of Medicine, 93*, 38–42.

Lesser, I. M. (1985). Current concepts in psychiatry: Alexithymia. *New England Journal of Medicine, 312*, 690–692.

Lettieri, D. J., Sayers, M., & Pearson, H. W. (Eds.). (1980). *Theories of drug abuse: Selected contemporary perspectives.* Rockville, MD: NIDA Research Monograph Series.

LeVay, S. (1991). A difference in hypothalamic structure between heterosexual and homosexual men. *Science, 253*, 1034–1037.

Levenson, J. L., & Bemis, C. (1991). The role of psychological factors in cancer onset and progression. *Psychosomatics, 32*, 124–132.

Levenson, R. W., & Gottman, J. M. (1983). Marital interaction: Physiological linkage and affective exchange. *Journal of Personality and Social Psychology, 45*, 587–597.

Levenson, R. W., & Gottman, J. M. (1985). Physiological and affective predictors of change in relationship satisfaction. *Journal of Personality and Social Psychology, 49*, 85–94.

Levine, H. G. (1984). The alcohol problem in America: From temperance to alcoholism. *British Journal of Addiction, 79*, 109–119.

Levitan, R. D., Blouin, A. G., Navarro, J. R., & Hill, J. (1991). Validity of the computerized DIS for diagnosing psychiatric inpatients. *Canadian Journal of Psychiatry, 36*, 728–731.

Levitt, J. J., & Tsuang, M. T. (1988). The heterogeneity of schizoaffective disorder: Implications for treatment. *American Journal of Psychiatry, 145*, 926–936.

Levy, F. (1991). The dopamine theory of attention deficit hyperactivity disorder (ADHD). *Australian and New Zealand Journal of Psychiatry, 25*, 277–283.

Levy, R. I., & Moskowitz, J. (1982). Cardiovascular research: Decades of progress, a decade of promise. *Science, 217*, 121–129.

Levy, S. M. (1985). *Behavior and cancer.* San Francisco: Jossey-Bass.

Lewinsohn, P. M. (1974). A behavioral approach to depression. In R. J. Friedman & M. M. Katz (Eds.), *The psychology of depression: Contemporary theory and research.* Washington, DC: Winston-Wiley.

Lewinsohn, P. M., & Libet, J. (1972). Pleasant events, activity schedules, and depressions. *Journal of Abnormal Psychology, 79*, 291–295.

Lewinsohn, P. M., Mischel, W., Chaplin, W., & Barton, R. (1980). Social competence and depression: The role of illusory self-perceptions. *Journal of Abnormal Psychology, 89*, 203–212.

Lewinsohn, P. M., Zeiss, A. M., & Duncan, E. M. (1989). Probability of relapse after recovery from an episode of depression. *Journal of Abnormal Psychology, 98*, 107–116.

Lewis, B. A., & Thompson, L. A. (1992). A study of developmental speech and language disorders in twins. *Journal of Speech and Hearing Research, 35*, 1086–1094.

Lewis, G., David, A., Andreasson, S., & Allebeck, P. (1992). Schizophrenia and city life. *Lancet, 340*, 137–140.

Lewis, J. M. (1993). Childhood play in normality, pathology, and therapy. *American Journal of Orthopsychiatry, 63,* 6–15.

Lewis, J. W. (1990). Premenstrual syndrome as a criminal defense. *Archives of Sexual Behavior, 19,* 425–441.

Lewis, P. (1993, October 20). Rape was weapon of Serbs, U.N. says. *New York Times,* p. A-1.

Lezak, M. D. (1976). *Neuropsychological assessment.* New York: Oxford.

Lezak, M. D. (1978). Living with the characteristically altered brain injured patient. *Journal of Clinical Psychiatry, 39,* 592–598.

Libet, J., & Lewinsohn, P. M. (1973). The concept of social skill with special reference to the behavior of depressed persons. *Journal of Consulting and Clinical Psychology, 40,* 304–312.

Lichtenstein, E., Harris, D. E., Birchler, G. R., Wahl, J. M., & Schmahl, D. P. (1973). Comparison of rapid smoking, warm, smoky air, and attention placebo in the modification of smoking behavior. *Journal of Consulting and Clinical Psychology, 40,* 92–98.

Lidsky, T. I., & Banerjee, S. P. (1992). Clozapine's mechanisms of action: Non-dopaminergic activity rather than anatomical selectivity. *Neuroscience Letters, 139,* 100–103.

Lidz, T. (1971). Family studies and changing concepts of personality development. *Canadian Journal of Psychiatry, 24,* 621–631.

Lidz, T. (1975). *The origin and treatment of schizophrenic disorders.* London: Hutchinson.

Lie, N. (1992). Follow-ups of children with attention deficit hyperactivity disorder (ADHD): Review of the literature. *Acta Psychiatrica Scandinavica, 368,* 1–40.

Lieberman, J. A., Kinon, B. J., & Loebel, A. D. (1990). Dopaminergic mechanisms in idiopathic and drug-induced psychoses. *Schizophrenia Bulletin, 16,* 97–110.

Liem, R., & Liem, J. (1978). Social class and mental illness reconsidered: The role of economic stress and social support. *Journal of Health and Social Behavior, 19,* 139–156.

Lightfoot-Klein, H. (1989). *Prisoners of ritual: An odyssey into female genital circumcision in Africa.* New York: Haworth Press.

Lilienfeld, S. O., Van Valkenburg, C., Larntz, K., & Akiskal, H. S. (1986). The relationship of histrionic personality disorder to antisocial personality and somatization disorders. *American Journal of Psychiatry, 143,* 718–722.

Limentani, A. (1991). Neglected fathers in the aetiology and treatment of sexual deviations. *International Journal of Psycho-analysis, 72,* 573–584.

Lin, E. H., Carter, W. B., & Kleinman, A. M. (1985). An exploration of somatization among Asian refugees and immigrants in primary care. *American Journal of Public Health, 75,* 1080–1084.

Lin, E. H., & Peterson, C. (1990). Pessimistic explanatory style and response to illness. *Behaviour Research and Therapy, 28,* 243–248.

Lindemann, E. (1944). Symptomatology and management of acute grief. *American Journal of Psychiatry, 101,* 141–148.

Lindenmayer, J. P., Kay, S. R., & Friedman, C. (1986). Negative and positive schizophrenic syndromes after the acute phase: A prospective follow-up. *Comprehensive Psychiatry, 27,* 276–286.

Lindquist, P., & Allebeck, P. (1990). Schizophrenia and crime: A longitudinal follow-up of 644 schizophrenics in Stockholm. *British Journal of Psychiatry, 157,* 345–350.

Lindsey, K. P., & Paul, G. L. (1989). Involuntary commitments to public mental health institutions: Issues involving the overrepresentation of blacks and assessment of relevant functioning. *Psychological Bulletin, 106,* 171–183.

Lindsey, K. P., Paul, G. L., & Mariotto, M. J. (1989). Urban psychiatric commitments: Disability and dangerous behavior of black and white recent admissions. *Hospital and Community Psychiatry, 40,* 286–294.

Linehan, M. M. (1987). Dialectical behavior therapy for borderline personality disorder. *Bulletin of the Menninger Clinic, 51,* 261–276.

Linehan, M. M., Armstrong, H. E., Suarez, A., Allmon, D., & Heard, H. L. (1991). Cognitive-behavioral treatment of chronically parasuicidal borderline patients. *Archives of General Psychiatry, 48,* 1060–1064.

Linkins, R. W., & Comstock, G. W. (1990). Depressed mood and development of cancer. *American Journal of Epidemiology, 132,* 962–972.

Links, P. S., Steiner, M., & Huxley, G. (1988). The occurrence of borderline personality disorder in the families of borderline patients. *Journal of Personality Disorders, 2,* 14–20.

Lipsey, M. W., & Wilson, D. B. (1993). The efficacy of psychological, educational, and behavioral treatment: Confirmation from meta-analysis. *American Psychologist, 48,* 1181–1209.

Litman, R. E. (1974). Models for predicting suicide risk. In C. Neuringer (Ed.), *Psychological assessment of suicidal risk.* Springfield, IL: Charles C Thomas.

Little, S. C., & McAvoy, M. (1952). Electroencephalographic studies in alcoholism. *Quarterly Journal of Studies on Alcohol, 13,* 9–15.

Littlewood, R. (1990). From categories to contexts: A decade of the "new cross-cultural psychiatry." *British Journal of Psychiatry, 156,* 308–327.

Litwack, T. R., Kirschner, S. M., & Wack, R. C. (1993). The assessment of dangerousness and predictions of violence: Recent research and future prospects. *Psychiatric Quarterly, 64,* 245–273.

Liu, X. (1981). Psychiatry in traditional Chinese medicine. *British Journal of Psychiatry, 137,* 429–433.

Lloyd, C. (1980). Life events and depressive disorder reviewed: I. Events as predisposing factors. II. Events as precipitation factors. *Archives of General Psychiatry, 37,* 529–548.

Locurto, C. (1991). Beyond IQ in preschool programs? *Intelligence, 15,* 295–312.

Loewenthal, K. M., & Goldblatt, V. (1993). Family size and depressive symptoms in orthodox Jewish women. *Journal of Psychiatric Research, 27,* 3–10.

Lofgren, D. P., Bemporad, J., King, J., Lindem, K., & O'Driscoll, G. (1991). A prospective follow-up study of so-called borderline children. *American Journal of Psychiatry, 148,* 1541–1547.

Loftus, E. F. (1991). Resolving legal questions with psychological data. *American Psychologist, 46,* 1046–1048.

Loftus, E. F. (1993). The reality of repressed memories. *American Psychologist, 48,* 518–537.

Loftus, E. F., & Monahan, J. (1980). Trial by data: Psychological research as legal evidence. *American Psychologist, 35,* 270–283.

Lohr, J. B., & Flynn, K. (1992). Smoking and schizophrenia. *Schizophrenia Research, 8,* 93–102.

Long, N., Chamberlain, K., & Vincent, C. (1994). Effect of the Gulf War on reactivation of adverse combat-related memories in Vietnam veterans. *Journal of Clinical Psychology, 50,* 138–144.

Loof, D. H. (1970). Psychophysiologic and conversion reactions in children: Selective incidence in verbal and nonverbal families. *Journal of the American Academy of Child Psychiatry, 9,* 318–331.

Loonen, A. J., Peer, P. G., & Zwanikken, G. J. (1991). Continuation and maintenance therapy with antidepressive agents: Meta-analysis of research. *Pharmaceutisch Weekblad, 13,* 167–175.

Lopez, S., Glover, K. P., Holland, D., Johnson, M. J., Kain, C. D., Kanel, K., Mellins, C. A., & Rhyne, M. C. (1989). Development of culturally sensitive psychotherapists. *Professional Psychology: Research and Practice, 20,* 369–376.

Lopez, S., & Nunez, J. A. (1987). Cultural factors considered in selected diagnostic criteria and interview schedules. *Journal of Abnormal Psychology, 96,* 270–272.

Loranger, A. W., Lenzenweger, M. F., Gartner, A. F., Susman, V. L., Herzig, J., Zammit, G. K., Gartner, J. D., Abrams, R. C., & Young, R. C. (1991). Trait-state artifacts and the diagnosis of personality disorders. *Archives of General Psychiatry, 48,* 720–728.

Lovaas, O. I. (1987). Behavioral treatment and normal educational intellectual functioning in young autistic children. *Journal of Consulting and Clinical Psychology, 55,* 3–9.

Lovaas, O. I., Schreibman, L., & Koegel, R. L. (1974). A behavior modification approach to the treatment of autistic children. *Journal of Autism and Childhood Schizophrenia, 4,* 111–129.

Lovaas, O. I., & Smith, T. (1989). A comprehensive behavioral theory of autistic children: Paradigm for research and treatment. *Journal of Behavior Therapy and Experimental Psychiatry, 20,* 17–29.

Luborsky, L. (1964). A psychoanalytic research on momentary forgetting during free association. *Bulletin of the Philadelphia Association for Psychoanalysis, 14,* 119–137.

Luborsky, L. (1983). Two helping alliance methods for predicting outcomes of psychotherapy: A counting signs vs. a global rating method. *Journal of Nervous and Mental Disease, 171,* 480–491.

Luborsky, L. (1984). *Principles of psychoanalytic psychotherapy.* New York: Basic Books.

Luborsky, L. (1985). "Further thoughts on the anti-demoralization hypothesis of psychotherapeutic effectiveness": Commentary. *Integrative Psychiatry, 3,* 24–25.

Luborsky, L., Crits-Christoph, P., & Mellon, J. (1986). Advent of objective measures of the transference concept. *Journal of Consulting and Clinical Psychology, 54,* 39–47.

Luborsky, L., & DeRubeis, R. J. (1984). The use of psychotherapy treatment manuals—a small revolution in psychotherapy research style. *Clinical Psychology Review, 4,* 5–14.

Luborsky, L., & Spence, D. P. (1978). Quantitative research on psychoanalytic therapy. In S. L. Garfield & A. E. Bergin (Eds.), *Handbook of psychotherapy and behavior change* (2nd ed.). New York: Wiley.

Lucas, A. R., Beard, C. M., O'Fallon, W. M., & Kurland, L. T. (1991). 50-year trends in the incidence of anorexia nervosa in Rochester, Minnesota: A population-based study. *American Journal of Psychiatry, 148,* 917–922.

Lucas, P. B., Gardner, D. L., Cowdry, R. W., & Pickar, D. (1989). Cerebral structure in borderline personality disorder. *Psychiatry Research, 27,* 111–115.

Lucero, W. J., Frieman, J., Spoering, K., & Fehrenbacher, J. (1976). Comparison of three procedures in reducing self-injurious behavior. *American Journal of Mental Deficiency, 80,* 548–554.

Ludolph, P. S., Westen, D., Misle, B., Jackson, A., Wixom, J., & Wiss, F. C. (1990). The borderline diagnosis in adolescents: Symptoms and developmental history. *American Journal of Psychology, 147,* 470–476.

Lukoff, D., Lu, F., & Turner, R. (1992). Toward a more culturally sensitive DSM-IV: Psychoreligious and psychospiritual problems. *Journal of Nervous and Mental Disease, 180,* 673–682.

Lundholm, J. K., & Waters, J. E. (1991). Dysfunctional family system: Relationships to disordered eating behaviors among university women. *Journal of Substance Abuse, 3,* 97–106.

Luthar, S. S., Anton, S. F., Merikangas, K. R., & Rounsaville, B. J. (1992). Vulnerability to substance abuse and psychopathology among siblings of opioid abusers. *Journal of Nervous and Mental Disease, 180,* 153–161.

Lykken, D. T. (1957). A study of anxiety in the sociopathic personality. *Journal of Abnormal and Social Psychology, 55,* 6–10.

Macciardi, F., Kennedy, J. L., Ruocco, L., Giuffra, L., Carrera, P., Marino, C., Rinaldi, V., Smeraldi, E., & Ferrari, M. (1992). A genetic linkage study of schizophrenia to chromosome 5 markers in a northern Italian population. *Biological Psychiatry, 31,* 720–728.

Maccoby, E. E., & Mnookin, R. H. (1992). *Dividing the child: Social and legal dilemmas of custody.* Cambridge: Harvard University Press.

MacDonald, N. (1960). Living with schizophrenia. *Canadian Medical Association Journal, 82,* 218–221.

MacDonough, T. S., Adams, H. E., & Tesser, A. (1973). The effects of choice in systematic desensitization. *Psychological Record, 23,* 397–404.

Mace, C. J. (1992a). Hysterical conversion. I: A history. *British Journal of Psychiatry, 161,* 369–377.

Mace, C. J. (1992b). Hysterical conversion. II: A critique. *British Journal of Psychiatry, 161,* 378–389.

MacFarlane, K., & Waterman, J. (1986). *Sexual abuse of young children: Evaluation and treatment.* New York: Guilford.

MacHovec, F. J. (1981). Hypnosis to facilitate recall in psychogenic amnesia and fugue states: Treatment variables. *American Journal of Clinical Hypnosis, 24,* 7–13.

Mackinnon, A. J., Henderson, A. S., & Andrews, G. (1990). Genetic and environmental determinants of the lability of trait neuroticism and the symptoms of anxiety and depression. *Psychological Medicine, 20,* 581–590.

MacKinnon, R. A. (1980a). Psychiatric history and mental status exam. In H. I. Kaplan, A. M. Freedman, & B. J. Sadock (Eds.), *Comprehensive textbook of psychiatry* (Vol. 1, 3rd ed.). Baltimore: Williams & Wilkins.

MacKinnon, R. A. (1980b). Psychiatric interview. In H. I. Kaplan, A. M. Freedman, & B. J. Sadock (Eds.), *Comprehensive textbook of psychiatry* (Vol. 1, 3rd ed.). Baltimore: Williams & Wilkins.

Maeder, T. (1985). *Crime and madness: The origins and evolution of the insanity defense.* New York: Harper & Row.

Magner, L. N. (1992). *A history of medicine.* New York: Marcel Dekker.

Magnusson, A., & Stefansson, J. G. (1993). Prevalence of seasonal affective disorder in Iceland. *Archives of General Psychiatry, 50,* 941–946.

Maher, B. A., & Maher, W. B. (1979). Psychopathology. In E. Hearst (Ed.), *The first century of experimental psychology.* Hillsdale, NJ: Erlbaum.

Mahler, H., & Co, B. T. (1984). Who are the "committed?" Update. *Journal of Nervous and Mental Disease, 172,* 189–196.

Mahler, M. E. (1992). Behavioral manifestations associated with multiple sclerosis. *Psychiatric Clinics of North America, 15,* 425–438.

Mahler, M. S. (1971). A study of the separation-individuation process and its possible application to borderline phenomena in the psychoanalytic situation. *The Psychoanalytic Study of the Child, 26,* 403–424.

Mahoney, M. J. (1974). *Cognition and behavior modification.* Cambridge, MA: Ballinger.

Mahowald, M. B. (1992). To be or not be a woman: Anorexia nervosa, normative gender roles, and feminism. *Journal of Medicine and Philosophy, 17,* 233–251.

Maier, S. F., & Seligman, M. E. P. (1976). Learned helplessness: Theory and evidence. *Journal of Experimental Psychology: General, 105,* 3–46.

Mailer, N. (1979). *The executioner's song.* Boston: Little, Brown.

Maj, M., Starace, F., & Pirozzi, R. (1991). A family study of DSM-III-R schizoaffective disorder, depressive type, compared with schizophrenia and psychotic and nonpsychotic major depression. *American Journal of Psychiatry, 148,* 612–616.

Maj, M., Veltro, F., Pirozzi, R., Lobrace, S., & Magliano, L. (1992). Pattern of recurrence of illness after recovery from an episode of major depression: A prospective study. *American Journal of Psychiatry, 149,* 795–800.

Malla, A. K., Cortese, L., Shaw, T. S., & Ginsberg, B. (1990). Life events and relapse in schizophrenia: A one year prospective study. *Social Psychiatry and Psychiatric Epidemiology, 25,* 221–224.

Manniche, L. (1987). *Sexual life in ancient Egypt.* London: KPI.

Mannuzza, S., Klein, R. G., Bonagura, N., Malloy, P., Giampino, T. L., & Addalli, K. A. (1991). Hyperactive boys almost grown up. V. Replications of psychiatric status. *Archives of General Psychiatry, 48,* 77–83.

Manschreck, T. C., Laughery, J. A., Weisstein, C. C., Allen, D., Humblestone, B., Neville, M., Podlewski, H., & Mitra, N. (1988). Characteristics of freebase cocaine psychosis. *Yale Journal of Biology and Medicine, 61,* 115–122.

Mantle, M. (1994, April 18). Time in a bottle. *Sports Illustrated,* 66–77.

Marcus, S. (1966). *The other Victorians.* New York: Basic Books.

Mardones, R. J. (1951). On the relationship between deficiency of B vitamins and alcohol intake in rats. *Quarterly Journal of Studies on Alcohol, 12,* 563–575.

Marengo, J. T., Harrow, M., & Westermeyer, J. F. (1991). Early longitudinal course of acute-chronic and paranoid-undifferentiated schizophrenia subtypes and schizophreniform disorder. *Journal of Abnormal Psychology, 100,* 600–603.

Margraf, J., Barlow, D. H., Clark, D. M., & Telch, M. J. (1993). Psychological treatment of panic: Work in progress on outcome, active ingredients, and follow-up. *Behaviour Research and Therapy, 31,* 1–8.

Markowitz, J. S., Weissman, M. M., Ouellette, R., Lish, J. D., & Klerman, G. L. (1989). Quality of life in panic disorder. *Archives of General Psychiatry, 46,* 984–992.

Marks, I. M. (1969). *Fears and phobias.* New York: Academic Press.

Marks, I. M. (1972). Phylogenesis and learning in the acquisition of fetishism. *Danish Medical Bulletin, 9,* 307–310.

Marks, I. M. (1981). Review of behavioral psychotherapy. II. Sexual disorders. *American Journal of Psychiatry, 138,* 750-756.

Marks, I. M. (1986). Epidemiology of anxiety. *Social Psychiatry, 21,* 167–171.

Marks, I. M. (1987). *Fears, phobias, and rituals.* New York: Oxford.

Marks, I. M. (1990). Behavioral therapy of anxiety states. In N. Sartorius, V. Andreoli, G. Cassano, L. Eisenberg, P. Kielholz, P. Pancheri, & G. Racagni (Eds.), *Anxiety: Psychobiological and clinical perspectives.* New York: Hemisphere.

Marks, I. M., & O'Sullivan, G. (1988). Drugs and psychological treatments for agoraphobia/panic and obsessive-compulsive disorders: A review. *British Journal of Psychiatry, 153,* 650–658.

Markus, H. R., & Kitayama, S. (1991). Culture and the self: Implications for cognition, emotion, and motivation. *Psychological Review, 98,* 224–253.

Marlatt, G. A. (1983). The controlled drinking controversy: A commentary. *American Psychologist, 38,* 1097–1110.

Marlatt, G. A., Baer, J. S., Donovan, D. M., & Kivlahan, D. R. (1988). Addictive behaviors: Etiology and treatment. *Annual Review of Psychology, 39,* 223–252.

Marlatt, G. A., Demming, B., & Reid, J. B. (1973). Loss

of control drinking in alcoholics: An experimental analogue. *Journal of Abnormal Psychology, 81,* 233–241.

Marlatt, G. A., & Gordon, J. R. (Eds.). (1985). *Relapse prevention.* New York: Guilford.

Marmor, J. (1975). The nature of the psychotherapeutic process revisited. *Canadian Psychiatric Association Journal, 20,* 557–565.

Marneros, A., Deister, A., & Rohde, A. (1990). The concept of distinct but voluminous groups of bipolar and unipolar diseases. III. Bipolar and unipolar comparison. *European Archives of Psychiatry and Clinical Neuroscience, 240,* 90–95.

Marneros, A., Deister, A., & Rohde, A. (1992). Validity of the negative/positive dichotomy for schizophrenic disorders under long-term conditions. *Schizophrenia Research, 7,* 117–123.

Marosi, E., Harmony, T., Sanchez, L., Becker, J., Bernal, J., Reyes, A., Diaz de Leon, A. E., Rodriguez, M., & Fernandez, T. (1992). Maturation of the coherence of EEG activity in normal and learning-disabled children. *Electroencephalography and Clinical Neurophysiology, 83,* 350–357.

Marsella, A. J. (1980). Depressive experience and disorder across cultures. In H. C. Triandis & J. G. Draguns (Eds.), *Handbook of cross-cultural psychology: Psychopathology* (Vol. 6). Boston: Allyn & Bacon.

Marsella, A. J. (1988). Cross-cultural research on severe mental disorders: Issues and findings. *Acta Psychiatrica Scandinavica (Supplementum), 344,* 7–22.

Marshall, E. (1983). EPA faults classic lead poisoning study. *Science, 222,* 906–907.

Martin, B. A. (1989). Electroconvulsive therapy for depression in general psychiatric practice. *Psychiatric Journal of the University of Ottawa, 14,* 413–417.

Martin, M. A. (1990). The homeless mentally ill and community-based care: Changing a mindset. *Community Mental Health Journal, 26,* 435–447.

Martinez, A. P., & Cameron, J. M. (1992). Trends in suicide (1983-1987). *Medicine, Science, and the Law, 32,* 289–295.

Martinez, C., & Martin, H. W. (1966). Folk diseases among urban Mexican-Americans. *JAMA, 196,* 161–164.

Martins, C., de Lemos, A. I., & Bebbington, P. E. (1992). A Portugese/Brazilian study of expressed emotion. *Social Psychiatry and Psychiatric Epidemiology, 27,* 129–134.

Marzuk, P. M., Leon, A. C., Tardiff, K., Morgan, E. B., Stajic, M., & Mann, J. J. (1992). The effect of access to lethal methods of injury on suicide rates. *Archives of General Psychiatry, 49,* 451–458.

Maser, J. D., & Cloninger, C. R. (Eds.). (1990). *Comorbidity of mood and anxiety disorders.* Washington, DC: American Psychiatric Press.

Maser, J. D., Kaelber, C., & Weise, R. E. (1991). International use and attitudes toward DSM-III and DSM-III-R: Growing consensus in psychiatric classification. *Journal of Abnormal Psychology, 100,* 271–279.

Maser, J. D., & Seligman, M. E. P. (Eds.). (1977). *Psychopathology: Experimental models.* San Francisco: Freeman.

Masling, J. M., & Bornstein, R. F. (1993). *Empirical studies of psychoanalytic theories: Vol. 4. Psychoanalytic perspectives on psychopathology.* Washington, DC: American Psychological Association.

Maslow, A. H. (1966). *The psychology of science: A reconnaissance.* New York: Harper & Row.

Maslow, A. H. (1970). *Motivation and personality* (2nd ed.). New York: Harper & Row.

Mason, D. W., Charlton, H. M., Jones, A., Parry, D. M., & Simmonds, S. J. (1985). Immunology of allograft rejection in mammals. In A. Bjorklund & U. Stenevi (Eds.), *Neural grafting in the mammalian CNS.* Amsterdam: Elsevier.

Masserman, J. H., & Carmichael, H. T. (1938). Diagnosis and prognosis in psychiatry: With a follow-up study of the results of short term general hospital therapy in psychiatric cases. *Journal of Mental Science, 84,* 893–946.

Masson, J. M. (1984). *The assault on truth: Freud's suppression of the seduction theory.* New York: Farrar, Straus, & Giroux.

Masson, J. M. (1986). *A dark science: Women, sexuality, and psychiatry in the nineteenth century.* New York: Farrar, Straus, & Giroux.

Masters, J. C., Burish, T. G., Hollon, S. D., & Rimm, D. C. (1987). *Behavior therapy: Techniques and empirical findings* (3rd ed.). San Diego, CA: Harcourt Brace Jovanovich.

Masters, W. H., & Johnson, V. E. (1966). *Human sexual response.* Boston: Little, Brown.

Masters, W. H., & Johnson, V. E. (1970). *Human sexual inadequacy.* Boston: Little, Brown.

Matarazzo, J. D. (1980). Psychological assessment of intelligence. In H. I. Kaplan, A. M. Freedman, & B. J. Sadock (Eds.), *Comprehensive textbook of psychiatry* (Vol. 1, 3rd ed.). Baltimore: Williams & Wilkins.

Matarazzo, J. D. (1983). The reliability of psychiatric and psychological diagnosis. *Clinical Psychology Review, 3,* 103–145.

Mate-Kole, C., Freschi, M., & Robin, A. (1990). A controlled study of psychological and social change after surgical gender reassignment in selected male transsexuals. *British Journal of Psychiatry, 157,* 261–264.

Matson, J. L. (1989). Self-injury and stereotypes. In T. H. Ollendick & M. Hersen (Eds.), *Handbook of child psychopathology* (2nd ed.). New York: Plenum.

Matson, J. L., & Coe, D. A. (1992). Applied behavior analysis: Its impact on the treatment of mentally retarded emotionally disturbed people. *Research in Developmental Disabilities, 13,* 171–189.

Matthews, K. A. (1982). Psychological perspectives on the Type A behavior pattern. *Psychological Bulletin, 91,* 293–323.

Matthysse, S. (1977). The role of dopamine in schizophrenia. In E. Usdin, D. A. Hamburg, & J. D. Barkus (Eds.), *Neuroregulators and psychiatric disorders.* New York: Oxford.

Mattick, R. P., Andrews, G., Hadzi-Pavlovic, D., & Christensen, H. (1990). Treatment of panic and agoraphobia: An integrative review. *Journal of Nervous and Mental Disease, 178,* 567–576.

Mavissakalian, M. (1990). Sequential combination of imipramine and self-directed exposure in the treatment of panic exposure with agoraphobia. *Journal of Clinical Psychiatry, 51,* 184–188.

Mavissakalian, M., & Perel, J. M. (1992a). Clinical experiments in maintenance and discontinuation of imipramine therapy in panic disorder with agoraphobia. *Archives of General Psychiatry, 49,* 318–323.

Mavissakalian, M., & Perel, J. M. (1992b). Protective effects of imipramine maintenance treatment in panic disorder with agoraphobia. *American Journal of Psychiatry, 149,* 1053–1057.

Mayer, J. (1965). Inactivity as a major factor in adolescent obesity. *Annals of the New York Academy of Sciences, 131,* 502–506.

Mays, V. M., Albee, G. W., & Schneider, S. F. (Eds.). (1989). *Primary prevention of AIDS: Psychological approaches.* Newbury Park, CA: Sage.

McAllister, T. W. (1992). Neuropsychiatric sequelae of head injuries. *Psychiatric Clinics of North America, 15,* 395–413.

McBride, D. C., Inciardi, J. A., Chitwood, D. D., & McCoy, C. B. (1992). Crack use and correlates of use in a national population of street heroin users. *Journal of Psychoactive Drugs, 24,* 411–416.

McCann, I. L., & Holmes, D. S. (1984). Influence of aerobic exercise on depression. *Journal of Personality and Social Psychology, 46,* 1142–1147.

McCarthy, B. W. (1993). Relapse prevention strategies and techniques in sex therapy. *Journal of Sex and Marital Therapy, 19,* 142–146.

McCarthy, M. (1990). The thin ideal, depression, and eating disorders in women. *Behaviour Research and Therapy, 28,* 205–215.

McClelland, D. C. (1989). Motivational factors in health and disease. *American Psychologist, 44,* 675–683.

McClelland, J. L., Rumelhart, D. E., & The PDP Research Group. (1986). *Parallel distributed processing: Explorations in the microstructure of cognition: Vol. 2. Psychological and biological models.* Cambridge: MIT Press.

McCrady, B. S., Noel, N. E., Abrams, D. B., Stout, R. L., Nelson, H. F., & Hay, W. M. (1986). Comparative effectiveness of three types of spouse involvement in outpatient behavioral alcoholism treatment. *Journal of Studies on Alcohol, 47,* 459–467.

McCranie, E. W., Hyer, L. A., Boudewyns, P. A., & Woods, M. G. (1992). Negative parenting behavior, combat exposure, and PTSD symptom severity: A person-event interaction model. *Journal of Nervous and Mental Disease, 180,* 431–438.

McFadden, J. (1988). Guilt is soluble in alcohol: An ego analytic view. In S. Peele (Ed.), *Visions of addiction: Major contemporary perspectives on addiction and alcoholism.* Lexington, MA: Lexington Books.

McFarlane, W. R. (Ed.). (1983). *Family therapy in schizophrenia.* New York: Guilford.

McGarry, A. L., & Bendt, R. H. (1969). Criminal vs. civil commitment of psychotic offenders: A seven year follow-up. *American Journal of Psychiatry, 125,* 1387–1394.

McGee, R., Williams, S., & Silva, P. A. (1984). Background characteristics of aggressive, hyperactive, and aggressive-hyperactive boys. *Journal of the American Academy of Child Psychiatry, 23,* 280–284.

McGlashan, T. H., & Fenton, W. S. (1992). The positive-negative distinction in schizophrenia: Review of natural history validators. *Archives of General Psychiatry, 49,* 63–72.

McGlynn, S. M. (1990). Behavioral approaches to neuropsychological rehabilitation. *Psychological Bulletin, 108,* 420–441.

McGough, L. S., & Carmichael, W. C. (1977). The right to treatment and the right to refuse treatment. *American Journal of Orthopsychiatry, 47,* 307–320.

McGue, M., Pickens, R. W., & Svikis, D. S. (1992). Sex and age effects on the inheritance of alcohol problems: A twin study. *Journal of Abnormal Psychology, 101,* 3–17.

McGuffin, P., & Katz, R. (1989). The genetics of depression and manic-depressive disorder. *British Journal of Psychiatry, 155,* 294–304.

McGuffin, P., Katz, R., & Rutherford, J. (1991). Nature, nurture, and depression: A twin study. *Psychological Medicine, 21,* 329–335.

McGuffin, P., & Thapar, A. (1992). The genetics of personality disorder. *British Journal of Psychiatry, 160,* 12–23.

McGuiness, D. (1985). *When children don't learn.* New York: Basic Books.

McKenna, J. P., & Cox, J. L. (1992). Transdermal nicotine replacement and smoking cessation. *American Family Physician, 45,* 2595–2602.

McKinney, W. T. (1988). *Models of mental disorders: A new comparative psychiatry.* New York: Plenum.

McKnew, D. H., Cytryn, L., & Yahraes, H. C. (1983). *Why isn't Johnny crying? Coping with depression in children.* New York: Norton.

McLellan, A. T., Luborsky, L., Woody, G. E., O'Brien, C. P., & Druley, K. A. (1983). Predicting response to alcohol and drug abuse treatments: Role of psychiatric severity. *Archives of General Psychiatry, 40,* 620–625.

McLeod, J. D. (1987). *Childhood parental loss and adult depression.* Unpublished doctoral dissertation, University of Michigan, Ann Arbor.

McLeod, J. G., & Lance, J. W. (1989). *Introductory neurology* (2nd ed.). Melbourne: Blackwell.

McLin, W. M. (1992). Introduction to issues in psychology and epilepsy. *American Psychologist, 47,* 1124–1125.

McNally, R. J. (1987). Preparedness and phobias: A review. *Psychological Bulletin, 101,* 283–303.

McNally, R. J. (1990). Psychological approaches to panic disorder: A review. *Psychological Bulletin, 108,* 403–419.

McNally, R. J., & Lukach, B. M. (1991). Behavioral treatment of zoophilic exhibitionism. *Journal of Behavior Therapy and Experimental Psychiatry, 22,* 281–284.

McNeal, E. T., & Cimbolic, P. (1986). Antidepressants and biochemical theories of depression. *Psychological Bulletin, 99,* 361–374.

McNiel, D. E., & Binder, R. L. (1987). Predictive validity of judgments of dangerousness in emergency civil commitment. *American Journal of Psychiatry, 144,* 197–200.

Mead, M. (1928). *Coming of age in Samoa.* New York: Morrow.

Mednick, S. A., Gabrielli, W. F., & Hutchings, B. (1984). Genetic influences in criminal convictions: Evidence from an adoption cohort. *Science, 224,* 891–894.

Mee, C. L. (1990, February). How a mysterious disease laid low Europe's masses. *Smithsonian*, 66–79.

Meehl, P. E. (1954). *Clinical versus statistical prediction*. Minneapolis: University of Minnesota Press.

Meehl, P. E. (1957). When shall we use our heads instead of the formula? *Journal of Counseling Psychology, 4*, 268–273.

Meehl, P. E. (1962). Schizotaxia, schizotypy, schizophrenia. *American Psychologist, 17*, 827–838.

Meehl, P. E. (1989). Schizotaxia revisited. *Archives of General Psychiatry, 46*, 935–944.

Meehl, P. E. (1990). Toward an integrated theory of schizotaxia, schizotypy, and schizophrenia. *Journal of Personality Disorders, 4*, 1–99.

Mehler, J. A. (1992). Love and male impotence. *International Journal of Psycho-Analysis, 73*, 467–480.

Mehlum, L., Friis, S., Irion, T., Johns, S., Karterud, S., Vaglum, P., & Vaglum, S. (1991). Personality disorders 2–5 years after treatment: A prospective follow-up study. *Acta Psychiatrica Scandinavica, 84*, 72–77.

Meichenbaum, D. (1977). *Cognitive behavior-modification: An integrative approach*. New York: Plenum.

Meisler, A. W., & Carey, M. P. (1991). Depressed affect and male sexual arousal. *Archives of Sexual Behavior, 20*, 541–554.

Mejo, S. L. (1990). Post-traumatic stress disorder: An overview of three etiological variables, and psychopharmacologic treatment. *Nurse Practitioner, 15*, 41–45.

Melamed, E. (1988). Brain grafting may reverse loss of responsiveness to levodopa therapy in Parkinson's disease. *Clinical Neuropharmacology, 11*, 77–82.

Melella, J. T., Travin, S., & Cullen, K. (1989). Legal and ethical issues in the use of antiandrogens in treating sex offenders. *Bulletin of the American Academy of Psychiatry and the Law, 17*, 223–232.

Mellon, C. D. (1989). Genetic linkage studies in bipolar disorder: A review. *Psychiatric Developments, 7*, 143–158.

Mellsop, G., Varghese, F., Joshua, S., & Hicks, A. (1982). The reliability of Axis II of DSM-III. *American Journal of Psychiatry, 139*, 1360–1361.

Meltzer, H. Y. (1991). The mechanism of action of novel antipsychotic drugs. *Schizophrenia Bulletin, 17*, 263–287.

Meltzer, H. Y., & Gudelsky, G. A. (1992). Dopaminergic and serotonergic effects of clozapine: Implications for a unique clinical profile. *Arzneimittel-forschung, 42*, 268–272.

Melzack, R. (1973). *The puzzle of pain*. London: Penguin.

Mendelson, M. (1974). *Psychoanalytic concepts of depression* (2nd ed.). New York: Halsted Press.

Mendes de Leon, C. F., Powell, L. H., & Kaplan, B. H. (1991). Change in coronary-prone behaviors in the Recurrent Coronary Prevention Project. *Psychosomatic Medicine, 53*, 407–419.

Menghini, P., & Ernst, K. (1991). Anti-androgen treatment in a retrospective evaluation of 19 sex offenders. *Nervenarzt, 62*, 303–307.

Menninger, K. (1963). *The vital balance: The life process in mental health and illness*. New York: Viking.

Merckelbach, H., Arntz, A., Arrindell, W. A., & de Jong, P. J. (1992). Pathways to spider phobia. *Behaviour Research and Therapy, 30*, 543–546.

Merikangas, K. R., Risch, N. J., Merikangas, J. R., Weissman, M. M., & Kidd, K. K. (1988). Migraine and depression: Association and family transmission. *Journal of Psychiatric Research, 22*, 119–129.

Merikangas, K. R., Spence, M. A., & Kupfer, D. J. (1989). Linkage studies of bipolar disorder: Methodologic and analytic issues. *Archives of General Psychiatry, 46*, 1137–1141.

Merluzzi, T. V., Glass, C. R., & Genest, M. (1981). *Cognitive assessment*. New York: Guilford.

Merrill, J., Milner, G., Owens, J., & Vale, A. (1992). Alcohol and attempted suicide. *British Journal of Addiction, 87*, 83–89.

Merry, J. (1966). The "loss of control" myth. *Lancet, 1*, 1267–1268.

Merskey, H. (1992). The manufacture of personalities: The production of multiple personality disorder. *British Journal of Psychiatry, 160*, 327–340.

Metz, M. E., & Dwyer, S. M. (1993). Relationship conflict management patterns among sex dysfunction, sex offender, and satisfied couples. *Journal of Sex and Marital Therapy, 19*, 104–122.

Meyer, B., Werth, B., Beglinger, C., Dill, S., Drewe, J., Vischer, W. A., Eggers, R. H., Bauer, F. E., & Stalder, G. A. (1991). *Helicobacter pylori* infection in healthy people: A dynamic process? *Gut, 32*, 347–350.

Meyer, D. (1980). *The positive thinkers*. New York: Pantheon Books.

Meyer, J. K., & Reter, D. J. (1979). Sex reassignment: Follow-up. *Archives of General Psychiatry, 36*, 1010–1015.

Mezzich, J. E., Fabrega, H., & Kleinman, A. (1992). Cultural validity and DSM-IV. *Journal of Nervous and Mental Disease, 180*, 4.

Mezzich, J. E., Fabrega, H., Mezzich, A. C., & Coffman, G. A. (1985). International experience with DSM-III. *Journal of Nervous and Mental Disease, 173*, 738–741.

Mezzich, J. E., & Solomon, H. (1980). *Taxonomy and behavioral science*. New York: Academic Press.

Michelson, L., Marchione, K., Greenwald, M., Glanz, L., Testa, S., & Marchione, N. (1990). Panic disorder: Cognitive-behavioral treatment. *Behaviour Research and Therapy, 28*, 141–151.

Mikhail, A. R. (1973). Exotic syndromes: A review. *Foreign Psychiatry, 2*, 55–84.

Miklowitz, D. J., & Goldstein, M. J. (1990). Behavioral family treatment for patients with bipolar affective disorder. *Behavior Modification, 14*, 457–489.

Miller, H. L., Coombs, D. W., Leeper, J. D., & Barton, S. N. (1984). An analysis of the effects of suicide prevention facilities on suicide rates in the United States. *American Journal of Public Health, 74*, 340–343.

Miller, J. W., Petersen, R. C., Metter, E. J., Millikan, C. H., & Yanagihara, T. (1987). Transient global amnesia: Clinical characteristics and prognosis. *Neurology, 37*, 733–737.

Miller, N. S., & Gold, M. S. (1991). Benzodiazepines: A major problem. Introduction. *Journal of Substance Abuse Treatment, 8,* 3–7.

Miller, S. D., Blackburn, T., Scholes, G., White, G. L., & Mamalis, N. (1991). Optical differences in multiple personality disorder: A second look. *Journal of Nervous and Mental Disease, 179,* 132–135.

Miller, S. D., & Triggiano, P. J. (1992). The psychophysiological investigation of multiple personality disorder: Review and update. *American Journal of Clinical Hypnosis, 35,* 47–61.

Miller, T. Q., Turner, C. W., Tindale, R. S., Posavac, E. J., & Dugoni, B. L. (1991). Reasons for the trend toward null findings in research on Type A behavior. *Psychological Bulletin, 110,* 469–485.

Miller, W. R., & Hester, R. K. (1986). The effectiveness of alcohol treatment: What research reveals. In W. R. Miller & N. Heather (Eds.), *Treating addictive behaviors: Processes of change.* New York: Plenum.

Miller, W. R., Leckman, A. L., Delaney, H. D., & Tinkcom, M. (1992). Long-term follow-up of behavioral self-control training. *Journal of Studies on Alcohol, 53,* 249–261.

Millon, T. (1981). *Disorders of personality.* New York: Wiley.

Millon, T. (1986a). A theoretical derivation of pathological personalities. In T. Millon & G. L. Klerman (Eds.), *Contemporary directions in psychopathology: Toward the DSM-IV.* New York: Guilford.

Millon, T. (1986b). The avoidant personality. In A. M. Cooper, A. J. Frances, & M. H. Sacks (Eds.), *The personality disorders and neuroses.* New York: Basic Books.

Millon, T. (1990a). The disorders of personality. In L. A. Pervin (Ed.), *Handbook of personality: Theory and research.* New York: Guilford.

Millon, T. (1990b). *Toward a new personology.* New York: Wiley.

Millon, T., & Millon, R. (1974). *Abnormal behavior and personality: A biosocial learning approach.* Philadelphia: Saunders.

Mindus, P., & Jenike, M. A. (1992). Neurological treatment of malignant obsessive-compulsive disorder. *Psychiatric Clinics of North America, 15,* 921–938.

Mineka, S. (1985). Animal models of anxiety-based disorders: Their usefulness and limitations. In A. H. Tuma & J. D. Maser (Eds.), *Anxiety and the anxiety disorders.* Hillsdale, NJ: Erlbaum.

Mineka, S., & Henderson, R. W. (1985). Controllability and predictability in acquired motivation. *Annual Review of Psychology, 36,* 495–529.

Minuchin, S. (1974). *Families and family therapy.* Cambridge: Harvard University Press.

Minuchin, S., Rosman, B. L., & Baker, L. (1978). *Psychosomatic families.* Cambridge: Harvard University Press.

Miranda, J., & Storms, M. D. (1989). Psychological adjustment of lesbians and gay men. *Journal of Counseling and Development, 68,* 41–45.

Mirsky, A. F., & Duncan, C. C. (1986). Etiology and expression of schizophrenia: Neurobiological and psychosocial factors. *Annual Review of Psychology, 37,* 291–319.

Mirsky, A. F., & Quinn, O. W. (1988). The Genain quadruplets. *Schizophrenia Bulletin, 14,* 595–612.

Mischel, W., Ebbesen, E. B., & Zeiss, A. R. (1973). Selective attention to the self: Situational and dispositional determinants. *Journal of Personality and Social Psychology, 27,* 129–142.

Moergen, S. A., Merkel, W. T., & Brown, S. (1990). The use of covert sensitization and social skills training in the treatment of an obscene telephone caller. *Journal of Behavior Therapy and Experimental Psychiatry, 21,* 269–275.

Moldin, S. O., Reich, T., & Rice, J. P. (1991). Current perspectives on the genetics of unipolar depression. *Behavior Genetics, 21,* 211–242.

Molgaard, C. A., Stanford, E. P., Morton, D. J., Ryden, L. A., Schubert, K. R., & Golbeck, A. L. (1990). Epidemiology of head trauma and neurocognitive impairment in a multi-ethnic population. *Neuroepidemiology, 9,* 233–242.

Mollica, R. F., Caspi-Yavin, Y., Bollini, P., Truong, T., Tor, S., & Lavelle, J. (1992). The Harvard Trauma Questionnaire: Validating a cross-cultural instrument for measuring torture, trauma, and posttraumatic stress disorder in Indochinese refugees. *Journal of Nervous and Mental Disease, 180,* 111–116.

Monahan, D. J., Greene, V. L., & Coleman, P. D. (1992). Caregiver support groups: Factors affecting use of services. *Social Work, 37,* 254–260.

Monahan, J. (1992). Mental disorder and violent behavior: Perceptions and evidence. *American Psychologist, 47,* 511–521.

Monahan, J., & Shah, S. A. (1989). Dangerousness and commitment of the mentally disordered in the United States. *Schizophrenia Bulletin, 15,* 541–553.

Monahan, J., & Walker, L. (1988). Social science research in law: A new paradigm. *American Psychologist, 43,* 465–472.

Monahan, L. H. (1977). Diagnosis and expectation for change: An inverse relationship? *Journal of Nervous and Mental Disease, 164,* 214–217.

Money, J. (1970). Use of an androgen-depleting hormone in the treatment of sex offenders. *Journal of Sex Research, 6,* 165–172.

Money, J. (1980). Genetic and chromosomal aspects of homosexual etiology. In J. L. Marmour (Ed.), *Homosexual behavior.* New York: Basic Books.

Money, J. (1984). Paraphilias: Phenomenology and classification. *American Journal of Psychotherapy, 38,* 164–179.

Money, J. (1985). *The destroying angel: Sex, fitness, and food in the legacy of degeneracy theory, Graham crackers, Kellogg's corn flakes, and American health industry.* Buffalo, NY: Prometheus.

Money, J. (1986). *Lovemaps: Clinical concepts of sexual/erotic health and pathology, paraphilia, and gender transposition in childhood, adolescence, and maturity.* New York: Irvington.

Money, J. (1987). Treatment guidelines: Antiandrogen and counseling of paraphiliac sex offenders. *Journal of Sex and Marital Therapy, 13,* 219–223.

Money, J. (1988). *Gay, straight, and in-between: The sexology of erotic orientation.* New York: Oxford.

Money, J., & Ehrhardt, A. A. (1972). *Man and woman, boy and girl.* Baltimore: Johns Hopkins University Press.

Money, J., Hingsburger, D., & Wainwright, G. (1991). *The breathless orgasm: A lovemap biography of asphyxiophilia.* Buffalo, NY: Prometheus.

Money, J., & Lamacz, M. (1989). *Vandalized lovemaps: Paraphilic outcome of seven cases in pediatric sexology.* Buffalo, NY: Prometheus.

Money, J., Prakasam, K. S., & Joshi, V. N. (1991). Semen-conservation doctrine from ancient Ayurvedic to modern sexological theory. *American Journal of Psychotherapy, 45,* 9–13.

Monroe, S. M., & Simons, A. D. (1991). Diathesis-stress theories in the context of life stress research: Implications for the depressive disorders. *Psychological Bulletin, 110,* 406–425.

Montague, M. (1992). The effects of cognitive and metacognitive strategy instruction on the mathematical problem solving of middle school students with learning disabilities. *Journal of Learning Disabilities, 25,* 230–248.

Montero, I., Gomez-Beneyto, M., Ruiz, I., Puche, E., & Adam, A. (1992). The influence of family expressed emotion on the course of schizophrenia in a sample of Spanish patients: A two-year follow-up study. *British Journal of Psychiatry, 161,* 217–222.

Montorsi, F., Guazzoni, G., Bergamaschi, F., & Rigatti, P. (1993). Patient-partner satisfaction with semirigid penile prostheses for Peyronie's disease: A 5-year followup study. *Journal of Urology, 150,* 1819–1821.

Mook, D. G. (1987). *Motivation: The organization of action.* New York: Norton.

Mook, J., Van der Ploeg, H. M., & Kleijn, W. C. (1990). Anxiety, anger, and depression: Relationships at the trait level. *Anxiety Research, 3,* 17–31.

Moos, R. H., & Billings, A. G. (1982). Children of alcoholics during the recovery process: Alcoholic and matched control families. *Addictive Behaviors, 7,* 155–163.

Mora, G. (1980). Historical and theoretical trends in psychiatry. In H. I. Kaplan, A. M. Freedman, & B. J. Sadock (Eds.), *Comprehensive textbook of psychiatry* (Vol. 1, 3rd ed.). Baltimore: Williams & Wilkins.

Morel, B. A. (1852). *Traite des maladies mentales.* Paris: Masson.

Morelli, R. A., Bronzino, J. D., & Goethe, J. W. (1987). Expert systems in psychiatry: A review. *Journal of Medical Systems, 11,* 157–168.

Moreno, H. R., & Plant, R. T. (1993). A prototype decision support system for differential diagnosis of psychotic, mood, and organic mental disorders. *Medical Decision Making, 13,* 43–48.

Morgan, C. D., & Murray, H. A. (1935). A method for investigating fantasies. *Archives of Neurology and Psychiatry, 34,* 289–306.

Morgan, M. (1973). *The total woman.* New York: Basic Books.

Morley, J. E. (1993). Management of impotence: Diagnostic considerations and therapeutic options. *Postgraduate Medicine, 93,* 65–67, 71–72.

Morris, M. (1991). Delusional infestation. *British Journal of Psychiatry, 159,* 83–87.

Morris, N. (1982). *Madness and the criminal law.* Chicago: University of Chicago Press.

Morris, P., & Silove, D. (1992). Cultural influences in psychotherapy with refugee survivors of torture and trauma. *Hospital and Community Psychiatry, 43,* 820–824.

Morrison, J. (1990). Managing somatization disorder. *Disease-A-Month, 36,* 537–591.

Morse, C. A., Dennerstein, L., Farrell, E., & Varnavides, K. (1991). A comparison of hormone therapy, coping skills training, and relaxation for the relief of premenstrual syndromes. *Journal of Behavioral Medicine, 14,* 469–489.

Mortola, J. F. (1992). Issues in the diagnosis and research of premenstrual syndrome. *Clinical Obstetrics and Gynecology, 35,* 587–598.

Morton, R. (1694). *Phthisiologica—or a treatise of consumptions.* London.

Moscarelli, M., Cesana, B. M., Ciussani, S., Novati, N. C., & Cazzullo, C. L. (1989). Ventricle-brain ratio and alogia in 19 young patients with chronic negative and positive schizophrenia. *American Journal of Psychiatry, 146,* 257–258.

Moser, C. (1992). Lust, lack of desire, and paraphilias: Some thoughts and possible connections. *Journal of Sex and Marital Therapy, 18,* 65–69.

Moser, H. M. (1969). A ten-year follow-up of lobotomy patients. *Hospital and Community Psychiatry, 20,* 381.

Mosher, D. L., & Sirkin, M. (1984). Measuring a macho personality constellation. *Journal of Research in Personality, 18,* 150–163.

Mowrer, O. H. (1939). A stimulus-response theory of anxiety. *Psychological Review, 46,* 553–565.

Mowrer, O. H. (1950). *Learning theory and personality dynamics.* New York: Ronald Press.

Mowrer, O. H. (1960). *Learning theory and behavior.* New York: Wiley.

Mozny, P., & Votypkova, P. (1992). Expressed emotion, relapse rate, and utilization of psychiatric inpatient care in schizophrenia: A study from Czechoslovakia. *Social Psychiatry and Psychiatric Epidemiology, 27,* 174–179.

Mulaik, J. S. (1992). Noncompliance with medication regimens in severely and persistently mentally ill schizophrenic patients. *Issues in Mental Health Nursing, 13,* 219–237.

Mulry, J. T. (1987). Codependency: A family addiction. *American Family Physician, 35,* 215–219.

Munk-Jorgensen, P., & Mortensen, P. B. (1992). Social outcome in schizophrenia: A 13-year follow-up. *Social Psychiatry and Psychiatric Epidemiology, 27,* 129–134.

Munoz, R. F., Snowden, L. R., & Kelly, J. G. (Eds.). (1979). *Social and psychological research in community settings.* San Francisco: Jossey-Bass.

Munro, A., & Pollock, B. (1981). Monosymptomatic psychoses which progress to schizophrenia. *Journal of Clinical Psychiatry, 42,* 474–476.

Munro, A., & Stewart, M. (1991). Body dysmorphic disorder and the DSM-IV: The demise of dysmorphophobia. *Canadian Journal of Psychiatry, 36,* 91–96.

Murray, E., & Foote, F. (1979). The origins of fear of snakes. *Behaviour Research and Therapy, 17,* 489–493.

Murray, J. B. (1992). Posttraumatic stress disorder: A review. *Genetic, Social, and General Psychology Monographs, 118,* 313–338.

Murray, R. M., Clifford, C. A., & Gurling, H. M. D. (1983). Twin and adoption studies: How good is the evidence for a genetic role? In M. Galanter (Ed.), *Recent developments in alcoholism* (Vol. 1). New York: Plenum.

Murstein, B. I., Chalpin, M. J., Heard, K. V., & Vyse, S. A. (1989). Sexual behavior, drugs, and relationship patterns on a college campus over thirteen years. *Adolescence, 24,* 125–139.

Musalek, M., Bach, M., Passweg, V., & Jaeger, S. (1990). The position of delusional parasitosis in psychiatric nosology and classification. *Psychopathology, 23,* 115–124.

Muskin, P. R. (1990). The combined use of psychotherapy and pharmacotherapy in the medical setting. *Psychiatric Clinics of North America, 13,* 341–353.

Myers, J. E. (1993). Expert testimony regarding child sexual abuse. *Child Abuse and Neglect, 17,* 175–185.

Myers, M. G., & Brown, S. A. (1990). Coping responses and relapse among adolescent substance abusers. *Journal of Substance Abuse, 2,* 177–189.

Myers, W. A. (1976). Imaginary companions, fantasy twins, mirror dreams, and depersonalization. *Psychoanalytic Quarterly, 45,* 503–524.

Nadelmann, E. A. (1989). Drug prohibition in the United States: Costs, consequences, and alternatives. *Science, 245,* 939–947.

Nadis, S. (1987, November/December). Cure for the winter blues. *Technology Review,* 12–13.

Nagel, K. L., & Jones, K. H. (1992a). Predisposition factors in anorexia nervosa. *Adolescence, 27,* 381–386.

Nagel, K. L., & Jones, K. H. (1992b). Sociological factors in the development of eating disorders. *Adolescence, 27,* 107–113.

Nakano, K. (1990). Effects of two self-control procedures on modifying Type A behavior. *Journal of Clinical Psychology, 46,* 652–657.

Nandi, D. N., Banerjee, G., Nandi, S., & Nandi, P. (1992). Is hysteria on the wane? A community survey in West Bengal, India. *British Journal of Psychiatry, 160,* 87–91.

Nanko, S., Gill, M., Owen, M., Takazawa, N., Moridairi, J., & Kazamatsuri, H. (1992). Linkage study of schizophrenia with markers on chromosome 11 in two Japanese pedigrees. *Japanese Journal of Psychiatry and Neurology, 46,* 155–159.

Napoliello, M. J., & Domantay, A. G. (1991). Buspirone: A worldwide update. *British Journal of Psychiatry Supplement, 12,* 40–44.

Nash, J. M. (1990, September 17). Tracking down killer genes. *Time,* 11–14.

Nash, J. M. (1994, April 25). Stopping cancer in its tracks. *Time,* 54–61.

Nathan, P. E. (1988). The addictive personality is the behavior of the addict. *Journal of Consulting and Clinical Psychology, 56,* 183–188.

Nathan, P. E. (1990). Integration of biological and psychological research on alcoholism. *Alcoholism: Clinical and Experimental Research, 14,* 368–374.

Nathan, S. G. (1986). The epidemiology of the DSM-III psychosexual dysfunctions. *Journal of Sex and Marital Therapy, 12,* 267–281.

National Institute of Mental Health. (1986). *Useful information on suicide.* Rockville, MD: U.S. Department of Health and Human Services.

National Institute on Drug Abuse. (1986). *Capsules: Overview of the 1985 household survey on drug abuse.* Rockville, MD: Author.

National Institute on Drug Abuse. (1991). *National household survey on drug abuse: Population estimates 1990.* Rockville, MD: Author.

Neal, A. M., & Turner, S. M. (1991). Anxiety disorders research with African Americans: Current status. *Psychological Bulletin, 109,* 400–410.

Nee, L. E., Caine, E. D., Polinsky, R. J., Eldridge, R., & Ebert, M. H. (1980). Gilles de la Tourette syndrome: Clinical and family study of 50 cases. *Annals of Neurology, 7,* 41–49.

Neighbors, H. W. (1987). Improving the mental health of black Americans: Lessons from the community mental health movement. *Milbank Quarterly, 65,* 348–380.

Neill, J. (1990). Whatever became of the schizophrenogenic mother? *American Journal of Psychotherapy, 44,* 499–505.

Neill, J. R. (1987). "More than medical significance": LSD and American psychiatry 1953 to 1966. *Journal of Psychoactive Drugs, 19,* 39–45.

Neill, M., & Sider, D. (1992, January 20). On the rebound. *People Weekly,* 97–98.

Neisworth, J. T., Madle, R. A., & Goecke, K. K. (1975). "Errorless" elimination of separation anxiety: A case study. *Journal of Behavior Therapy and Experimental Psychiatry, 6,* 79–82.

Neki, J. S., Joinet, B., Ndosi, N., & Kilonzo, G. (1986). Witchcraft and psychotherapy. *British Journal of Psychiatry, 149,* 145–155.

Nelkin, D., & Tancredi, L. (1989). *Dangerous diagnostics.* New York: Basic Books.

Nelson, L. D., Satz, P., Green, M., & Cicchetti, D. (1993). Re-examining handedness in schizophrenia: Now you see it, now you don't. *Journal of Experimental Clinical Neuropsychology, 15,* 149–158.

Nemiah, J. C. (1980a). Dissociative disorders (hysterical neurosis, dissociative type). In H. I. Kaplan, A. M. Freedman, & B. J. Sadock (Eds.), *Comprehensive textbook of psychiatry* (Vol. 2, 3rd ed.). Baltimore: Williams & Wilkins.

Nemiah, J. C. (1980b). Somatoform disorders. In H. I. Kaplan, A. M. Freedman, & B. J. Sadock (Eds.), *Comprehensive textbook of psychiatry* (Vol. 2, 3rd ed.). Baltimore: Williams & Wilkins.

Nensey, Y. M., Schubert, T. T., Bologna, S. D., & Ma, C. K. (1991). *Helicobacter pylori*-negative duodenal ulcer. *American Journal of Medicine, 91,* 15–18.

Nestadt, G. R., Romanoski, A. J., Chahal, R., Merchant, A., Folstein, M. F., Gruenberg, E. M., & McHugh, P. R. (1990). An epidemiological study of histrionic personality disorder. *Psychological Medicine, 20,* 413–422.

Nestadt, G. R., Romanoski, A. J., Samuels, J. F., Folstein, M. F., & McHugh, P. R. (1992). The relationship between personality and DSM-III Axis I disorders in the population: Results from an epidemiological survey. *American Journal of Psychiatry, 149,* 1228–1233.

Nettelbeck, T., Hirons, A., & Wilson, C. (1984). Mental retardation, inspection time, and central attentional impairment. *American Journal of Mental Deficiency, 89,* 91–98.

Neugebauer, R. (1979). Medieval and early modern theories of mental illness. *Archives of General Psychiatry, 36,* 477–483.

Neumann, J. (1991). Psychiatry in Europe today: Mental health status, policies, and practices. *American Journal of Psychiatry, 148,* 1386–1389.

Newlin, D. B., & Thomson, J. B. (1990). Alcohol challenge with sons of alcoholics: A critical review and analysis. *Psychological Bulletin, 108,* 383–402.

Newman, B. (1991, March 11). The last return. *Sports Illustrated,* 38–42.

Niemiec, D. (1991, June 3). A square peg in a round hole. *Detroit Free Press,* pp. 1, 9.

Nierenberg, A. A., & Feinstein, A. R. (1988). How to evaluate a diagnostic marker test: Lessons from the rise and fall of the dexamethasone suppression test. *JAMA, 259,* 1699–1702.

Nisbett, R. E., & Ross, L. (1980). *Human inference: Strategies and shortcomings of social judgment.* Englewood Cliffs, NJ: Prentice-Hall.

Nisbett, R. E., & Ross, L. (1991). *The person and the situation.* New York: McGraw-Hill.

Nisita, C., Petracca, A., & Cassano, G. B. (1990). Generalized anxiety disorder: An independent nosologic entity? In N. Sartorius, V. Andreoli, G. Cassano, L. Eisenberg, P. Kielholz, P. Pancheri, & G. Racagni (Eds.), *Anxiety: Psychobiological and clinical perspectives.* New York: Hemisphere.

Nolen-Hoeksema, S. (1987). Sex differences in unipolar depression: Theory and evidence. *Psychological Bulletin, 101,* 259–282.

Nolen-Hoeksema, S. (1990). *Sex differences in depression.* Stanford, CA: Stanford University Press.

Nolen-Hoeksema, S. (1991). Responses to depression and their effects on the duration of depressive episodes. *Journal of Abnormal Psychology, 100,* 569–582.

Nolen-Hoeksema, S., & Morrow, J. (1991). A prospective study of depression and posttraumatic stress symptoms after a natural disaster: The 1989 Loma Prieta earthquake. *Journal of Personality and Social Psychology, 61,* 115–121.

Norman, W. T. (1963). Toward an adequate taxonomy of personality attributes: Replicated factor structure in peer nomination personality ratings. *Journal of Abnormal and Social Psychology, 66,* 574–583.

Norris, F. H. (1992). Epidemiology of trauma: Frequency and impact of different potentially traumatic events on different demographic groups. *Journal of Consulting and Clinical Psychology, 60,* 409–418.

Norton, G. R., & Jehu, D. (1984). The role of anxiety in sexual dysfunctions: A review. *Archives of Sexual Behavior, 13,* 165–183.

Norwood, R. (1985). *Women who love too much.* New York: Pocket Books.

Noshirvani, H. F., Kasvikis, Y., Marks, I. M., Tsakiris, F., & Monteiro, W. O. (1991). Genetic-divergent aetiological factors in obsessive-compulsive disorder. *British Journal of Psychiatry, 158,* 260–263.

Novelly, R. A. (1992). The debt of neuropsychology to the epilepsies. *American Psychologist, 47,* 1126–1129.

Noyes, R. (1991). Suicide and panic disorder: A review. *Journal of Affective Disorders, 22,* 1–11.

Noyes, R., Hoenk, P. R., Kuperman, S., & Slymen, D. J. (1977). Depersonalization in accident victims and psychiatric patients. *Journal of Nervous and Mental Disease, 164,* 401–407.

Nuckolls, C. W. (1992). Toward a cultural history of the personality disorders. *Social Science and Medicine, 35,* 37–47.

Nuechterlein, K. H., Dawson, M. E., Gitlin, M., Ventura, J., Goldstein, M. J., Snyder, K. S., Yee, C. M., & Mintz, J. (1992). Developmental processes in schizophrenic disorders: Longitudinal studies of vulnerability and stress. *Schizophrenia Bulletin, 18,* 387–425.

Nugent, P. M., & Mosley, J. L. (1987). Mentally retarded and nonretarded individuals' attention allocation and capacity. *American Journal of Mental Deficiency, 91,* 598–605.

Numan, I. M., Barklind, K. S., & Lubin, B. (1981). Correlates of depression in chronic dialysis patients: Morbidity and mortality. *Research in Nursing and Health, 4,* 295–297.

Nunes, E. V., Frank, K. A., & Kornfeld, D. S. (1987). Psychologic treatment for the Type A behavior pattern and for coronary heart disease: A meta-analysis of the literature. *Psychosomatic Medicine, 49,* 159–173.

Nurnberg, H. G., Raskin, M., Levine, P. E., Pollack, S., Siegel, O., & Prince, R. (1991). The comorbidity of borderline personality disorder and other DSM-III-R Axis II personality disorders. *American Journal of Psychiatry, 148,* 1371–1377.

Nussbaum, M., Treves, T. A., & Korczyn, A. D. (1992). DSM-III criteria for primary degenerative dementia and multi-infarct dementia. *Alzheimer Disease and Associated Disorders, 6,* 111–118.

Oakley, M. E., & Padesky, C. A. (1990). Cognitive therapy for anxiety disorders. *Progress in Behavior Modification, 25,* 11–46.

Obe, G., & Ristow, H. (1979). Mutagenic, cancerogenic, and teratogenic effects of alcohol. *Mutation Research, 65,* 229–259.

Ochroch, R. (1990). Legal and psychological competency: Issues in clinical assessment of the elderly. *Forensic Reports, 3,* 91–105.

O'Connell, R. A., Mayo, J. A., Flatow, L., Cuthbertson, B., & O'Brien, B. E. (1991). Outcome of bipolar disorder on long-term treatment with lithium. *British Journal of Psychiatry, 159,* 123–129.

O'Farrell, T. J. (1989). Marital and family therapy in alcoholism treatment. *Journal of Substance Abuse Treatment, 6,* 23–29.

Office of Ethnic Minority Affairs. (1993). Guidelines for the providers of psychological services to ethnic, linguistic, and culturally diverse populations. *American Psychologist, 48,* 45–48.

Ogata, S. N., Silk, K. R., Goodrich, S., Lohr, N. E., Westen, D., & Hill, E. M. (1990). Childhood sexual and physical abuse in adult patients with borderline personality disorder. *American Journal of Psychiatry, 147,* 1008–1013.

Ogborne, A. C. (1989). Some limitations of Alcoholics Anonymous. *Recent Developments in Alcoholism, 7,* 55–65.

Ogle, M. R., & Miller, M. J. (1991). Clozapine: A novel antipsychotic with a controversial introduction. *Indiana Medicine, 84,* 606–610.

Öhman, A., Fredrikson, M., Hugdahl, K., & Rimmo, P. A. (1976). The premise of equipotentiality in human classical conditioning: Conditioned electrodermal responses to potentially phobic stimuli. *Journal of Experimental Psychology: General, 105,* 313–337.

Oldham, J. M., & Frosch, W. A. (1986). Compulsive personality disorder. In A. M. Cooper, A. J. Frances, & M. H. Sacks (Eds.), *The personality disorders and neuroses.* New York: Basic Books.

Oldham, J. M., Skodol, A. E., Kellman, H. D., Hyler, S. E., Rosnick, L., & Davies, M. (1992). Diagnosis of DSM-III-R personality disorders by two structured interviews: Patterns of comorbidity. *American Journal of Psychiatry, 149,* 213–220.

Olds, J., & Milner, P. (1954). Positive reinforcement produced by electrical stimulation of septal area and other regions of rat brain. *Journal of Comparative and Physiological Psychology, 47,* 419–427.

O'Leary, A. (1990). Stress, emotion, and human immune function. *Psychological Bulletin, 108,* 363–382.

O'Leary, K. D., & Borkovec, T. D. (1978). Conceptual, methodological, and ethical problems of placebo groups in psychotherapy research. *American Psychologist, 33,* 821–830.

Oliver, J. S., & Watson, J. M. (1977). Abuse of solvents "for kicks": A review of 50 cases. *Lancet, 1,* 84–86.

Ollendick, T. H. (1986). Behavior therapy with children and adolescents. In S. L. Garfield & A. E. Bergin (Eds.), *Handbook of psychotherapy and behavior change* (3rd ed.). New York: Wiley.

Ollendick, T. H., & Hersen, M. (Eds.). (1989). *Handbook of child psychopathology* (2nd ed.). New York: Plenum.

Ollendick, T. H., & King, N. J. (1991). Origins of childhood fears: An evaluation of Rachman's theory of fear acquisition. *Behaviour Research and Therapy, 29,* 117–123.

Olson, D. H., Portner, J., & Lavee, Y. (1985). *FACES III.* St Paul: Family Social Science, University of Minnesota.

Olson, S. L. (1992). Development of conduct problems and peer rejection in preschool children: A social systems analysis. *Journal of Abnormal Child Psychology, 20,* 327–350.

O'Malley, P. M., Bachman, J. G., & Johnston, L. D. (1988). Period, age, and cohort effects on substance abuse among young Americans: A decade of change. *American Journal of Public Health, 78,* 1315–1321.

On thin ice. (1992, March 30). *People Weekly,* 77.

Orford, J. (1985). *Excessive appetites: A psychological view of addictions.* Chichester, England: Wiley.

Orlinsky, D. E., & Howard, K. I. (1986). Process and outcome in psychotherapy. In S. L. Garfield & A. E. Bergin (Eds.), *Handbook of psychotherapy and behavior change* (3rd ed.). New York: Wiley.

Orne, M. T., Dinges, D. F., & Orne, E. C. (1984). On the differential diagnosis of multiple personality in the forensic context. *International Journal of Clinical and Experimental Hypnosis, 32,* 118–169.

Ornstein, R. E., & Thompson, R. (1984). *The amazing brain.* Boston: Houghton Mifflin.

Orvaschel, H., Weissman, M. M., & Kidd, K. K. (1980). Children and depression: The children of depressed parents; the childhood of depressed patients; depression in children. *Journal of Affective Disorders, 2,* 1–16.

Ost, L.-G. (1987). Age of onset in different phobias. *Journal of Abnormal Psychology, 96,* 223–229.

Ots, T. (1990). The angry liver, the anxious heart, and the melancholy spleen: The phenomenology of perceptions in Chinese culture. *Culture, Medicine, and Psychiatry, 14,* 21–58.

Overholser, J. C. (1990). Fetal alcohol syndrome: A review of the disorder. *Journal of Contemporary Psychotherapy, 20,* 163–176.

Overholser, J. C., & Beck, S. (1986). Multimethod assessment of rapists, child molesters, and three control groups on behavioral and psychological measures. *Journal of Consulting and Clinical Psychology, 54,* 682–687.

Overholser, J. C., Kabakoff, R., & Norman, W. H. (1989). The assessment of personality characteristics in depressed and dependent psychiatric inpatients. *Journal of Personality Assessment, 53,* 40–50.

Overmier, J. B., & Seligman, M. E. P. (1967). Effects of inescapable shock upon subsequent escape and avoidance learning. *Journal of Comparative and Physiological Psychology, 63,* 23–33.

Owen, F., Crow, T. J., & Poulter, M. (1987). Central dopaminergic mechanisms in schizophrenia. *Acta Psychiatrica Belgica, 87,* 552–565.

Owen, M., Craufurd, D., & St. Clair, D. (1990). Localisation of a susceptibility locus for schizophrenia on chromosome 5. *British Journal of Psychiatry, 157,* 123–127.

Owens, D., Harrison, G., & Boot, D. (1991). Ethnic factors in voluntary and compulsory admissions. *Psychological Medicine, 21,* 185–196.

Panksepp, J. (1986). The neurochemistry of behavior. *Annual Review of Psychology, 37,* 77–107.

Panting, A., & Merry, P. (1972). The long-term rehabilitation of severe head injuries with particular reference to the need for social and medical support for the patient's family. *Rehabilitation, 82,* 33–37.

Paris, J. (1992). Dhat: The semen loss anxiety syndrome. *Transcultural Psychiatric Research Review, 29,* 109–118.

Parker, G., & Hadzi-Pavlovic, D. (1990). Expressed emotion as a predictor of schizophrenic relapse: An analysis of aggregated data. *Psychological Medicine, 20,* 961–965.

Parmelee, P. A., Katz, I. R., & Lawton, M. P. (1992). Depression and mortality among institutionalized aged. *Journal of Gerontology, 47,* 3–10.

Parsons, C. D., & Wakeley, P. (1991). Idioms of distress: Somatic responses to distress in everyday life. *Culture, Medicine, and Psychiatry, 15,* 111–132.

Patterson, A. H. (1986). Scientific jury selection: The need for a case specific approach. *Social Action and the Law, 11,* 105–109.

Patterson, C. H. (1986). *Theories of counseling and psychotherapy* (4th ed.). New York: Harper & Row.

Patterson, G. R. (1974). Interventions for boys with conduct problems: Multiple settings, treatments, and criteria. *Journal of Consulting and Clinical Psychology, 42,* 471–481.

Patterson, G. R., DeBaryshe, B. D., & Ramsey, E. (1989). A developmental perspective on antisocial behavior. *American Psychologist, 44,* 329–335.

Paty, D. W., & Li, D. K. (1993). Interferon beta-1b is effective in relapsing-remitting multiple sclerosis: II. MRI analysis results of a multicenter, randomized, double-blind, placebo-controlled trial. *Neurology, 43,* 662–667.

Paul, G. L., & Lentz, R. J. (1977). *Psychosocial treatment of chronic mental patients: Milieu versus social learning programs.* Cambridge: Harvard University Press.

Pauly, I. B. (1974). Female transsexualism: Parts I & II. *Archives of Sexual Behavior, 3,* 487–507, 509–526.

Paykel, E. S., Myers, J. K., Dienelt, M. N., Klerman, G. L., Lindenthal, J. J., & Pepper, M. P. (1969). Life events and depression: A controlled study. *Archives of General Psychiatry, 21,* 753–760.

Pearce, R. K., Seeman, P., Jellinger, K., & Tourtellotte, W. W. (1990). Dopamine uptake sites and dopamine receptors in Parkinson's disease and schizophrenia. *European Neurology, 30,* 9–14.

Pearlson, G. D., Ross, C. A., Lohr, W. D., Rovner, B. W., Chase, G. A., & Folstein, M. F. (1990). Association between family history of affective disorder and the depressive syndrome of Alzheimer's disease. *American Journal of Psychiatry, 147,* 452–456.

Pearson, V. (1992). Law, rights, and psychiatry in the People's Republic of China. *International Journal of Law and Psychiatry, 15,* 409–423.

Pedersen, W. (1991). Mental health, sensation seeking, and drug use patterns: A longitudinal study. *British Journal of Addiction, 86,* 195–204.

Peele, S. (1987). Why do controlled-drinking outcomes vary by investigator, by country, and by era? Cultural conceptions of relapse and remission in alcoholism. *Drugs and Alcohol Dependence, 20,* 173–201.

Peele, S. (Ed.). (1988). *Visions of addiction: Major contemporary perspectives on addiction and alcoholism.* Lexington, MA: Lexington Books.

Peele, S. (1989). *Diseasing of America: Addiction treatment out of control.* Lexington, MA: Lexington Books.

Pelham, W., & Bender, M. E. (1982). Peer relationships in hyperactive children: Description and treatment. In K. D. Gadow & I. Bailer (Eds.), *Advances in learning and behavioral disabilities: A research annual.* Greenwich, CT: JAI Press.

Pelletier, K. R., & Herzing, D. L. (1989). Psychoneuroimmunology: Toward a mindbody model. *Advances, 5*(1), 27–56.

Pendery, M. L., Maltzman, I. M., & West, L. J. (1982). Controlled drinking by alcoholics? New findings and a reevaluation of a major affirmative study. *Science, 217,* 169–175.

Pendleton, L. (1980). Treatment of persons found incompetent to stand trial. *American Journal of Psychiatry, 137,* 1098–1100.

Pennebaker, J. W., Hughes, C. F., & O'Heeron, R. C. (1987). The psychophysiology of confession: Linking inhibitory and psychosomatic processes. *Journal of Personality and Social Psychology, 52,* 781–793.

Pennebaker, J. W., & O'Heeron, R. C. (1984). Confiding in others and illness rate among spouses of suicide and accidental-death victims. *Journal of Abnormal Psychology, 93,* 473–476.

Peralta, V., de Leon, J., & Cuesta, M. J. (1992). Are there more than two syndromes in schizophrenia? A critique of the positive-negative dichotomy. *British Journal of Psychiatry, 161,* 335–343.

Perls, F. S. (1969a). *Gestalt therapy verbatim.* Lafayette, CA: Real People Press.

Perls, F. S. (1969b). *In and out of the garbage pail.* Lafayette, CA: Real People Press.

Peroutka, S. J. (1990). Non-GABAergic mechanisms of anxiety. In N. Sartorius, V. Andreoli, G. Cassano, L. Eisenberg, P. Kielholz, P. Pancheri, & G. Racagni (Eds.), *Anxiety: Psychobiological and clinical perspectives.* New York: Hemisphere.

Perr, I. N. (1991). Crime and multiple personality disorder: A case history and discussion. *Bulletin of the American Academy of Psychiatry and the Law, 19,* 203–214.

Perris, C. (1968). The course of depressive psychosis. *Acta Psychiatrica Scandinavica, 44,* 238–248.

Perry, J. C., & Jacobs, D. (1982). Overview: Clinical applications of the amytal interview in psychiatric emergency settings. *American Journal of Psychiatry, 139,* 552–559.

Perry, S., Difede, J., Musngi, G., Frances, A. J., & Jacobsberg, L. (1992). Predictors of posttraumatic stress disorder after burn injury. *American Journal of Psychiatry, 149,* 931–935.

Perry, S. W. (1990a). Combining antidepressants and psychotherapy: Rationale and strategies. *Journal of Clinical Psychiatry, 51,* 16–20.

Perry, S. W. (1990b). Organic mental disorders caused by HIV: Update on early diagnosis and treatment. *American Journal of Psychiatry, 147,* 696–710.

Persad, E. (1990). Electroconvulsive therapy in depression. *Canadian Journal of Psychiatry, 35,* 175–182.

Persky, V. W., Kempthorne-Rawson, J., & Shekelle, R. B. (1987). Personality and risk of cancer: 20-year follow-up of the Western Electric Study. *Psychosomatic Medicine, 49,* 435–449.

Peterson, C. (1983). Clouds and silver linings: Depressive symptoms and attributions about ostensibly good and bad events. *Cognitive Therapy and Research, 7,* 575–578.

Peterson, C. (1988). Explanatory style as a risk factor for illness. *Cognitive Therapy and Research, 12,* 117–130.

Peterson, C. (1991a). *Introduction to psychology.* New York: HarperCollins.

Peterson, C. (1991b). Psychotherapy as a social process. In P. R. Martin (Ed.), *Handbook of behavior therapy and psychological science: An integrative approach.* New York: Pergamon.

Peterson, C. (1992). *Personality* (2nd ed.). San Diego, CA: Harcourt Brace Jovanovich.

Peterson, C., & Bossio, L. M. (1991). *Health and optimism.* New York: Free Press.

Peterson, C., Colvin, D., & Lin, E. H. (1992). Explanatory style and helplessness. *Social Behavior and Personality, 20,* 1–14.

Peterson, C., Maier, S. F., & Seligman, M. E. P. (1993). *Learned helplessness: A theory for the age of personal control.* New York: Oxford.

Peterson, C., & Seligman, M. E. P. (1984). Causal explanations as a risk factor for depression: Theory and evidence. *Psychological Review, 91,* 347–374.

Peterson, C., & Seligman, M. E. P. (1985). The learned helplessness model of depression: Current status of theory and research. In E. E. Beckham & W. R. Leber (Eds.), *Handbook of depression: Treatment, assessment, and research.* Homewood, IL: Dorsey.

Peterson, C., & Stunkard, A. J. (1989). Personal control and health promotion. *Social Science and Medicine, 28,* 819–828.

Phillips, D. P., & Smith, D. G. (1990). Postponement of death until symbolically meaningful occasions. *JAMA, 263,* 1947–1951.

Phillips, E. L. (1978). *The social skills basis of psychopathology: Alternatives to abnormal psychology.* New York: Grune & Stratton.

Phillips, K. A. (1991). Body dysmorphic disorder: The distress of imagined ugliness. *American Journal of Psychiatry, 148,* 1138–1149.

Phinney, S. (1992). Exercise in the treatment of obesity. *Journal of the Florida Medical Association, 79,* 400–402.

Phipps, W. E. (1970). *Was Jesus married? The distortion of sexuality in the Christian tradition.* New York: Harper & Row.

Piaget, J. (1928). *Judgment and reasoning in the child.* New York: Harcourt, Brace.

Piaget, J. (1929). *The child's conception of the world.* New York: Harcourt, Brace.

Pincus, H. A., Frances, A., Davis, W. W., First, M. B., & Widiger, T. A. (1992). DSM-IV and new diagnostic categories: Holding the line on proliferation. *American Journal of Psychiatry, 149,* 112–117.

Pincus, J. H., & Tucker, G. J. (1978). *Behavioral neurology* (2nd ed.). New York: Oxford.

Pipe, R., Bhat, A., Matthews, B., & Hampstead, J. (1991). Section 136 and African/Afro-Caribbean minorities. *International Journal of Social Psychiatry, 37,* 14–23.

Pi-Sunyer, F. X. (1991). Health implications of obesity. *American Journal of Clinical Nutrition, 53,* 1595–1603.

Pitman, R. K., Green, R. C., Jenike, M. A., & Mesulam, M. M. (1987). Clinical comparison of Tourette's disorder and obsessive-compulsive disorder. *American Journal of Psychiatry, 144,* 1166–1171.

Pitman, R. K., van der Kolk, B. A., Orr, S. P., & Greenberg, M. S. (1990). Naloxone-reversible analgesic response to combat-related stimuli in posttraumatic stress disorder: A pilot study. *Archives of General Psychiatry, 47,* 541–544.

Plomin, R. (1986). Behavioral genetic methods. *Journal of Personality, 54,* 226–261.

Plomin, R., Chipuer, H. M., & Loehlin, J. C. (1990). Behavioral genetics and personality. In L. A. Pervin (Ed.), *Handbook of personality: Theory and research.* New York: Guilford.

Plummer, W. (1987, October 26). After 27 years in his bedroom, 1,200 lb. Walter Hudson decides to take a load off. *People Weekly,* 60–61.

Plutchik, R. (1980). *Emotion: A psychoevolutionary synthesis.* New York: Harper & Row.

Plutchik, R. (1984). Emotions: A general psychoevolutionary theory. In K. R. Scherer & P. Ekman (Eds.), *Approaches to emotion.* Hillsdale, NJ: Erlbaum.

Podmore, F. (1963). *From Mesmer to Christian Science: A short history of mental healing.* New Hyde Park, NY: University Books.

Pokorny, A. D. (1968). Myths about suicide. In H. L. P. Resnik (Ed.), *Suicidal behaviors.* Boston: Little, Brown.

Pollack, M. H., Otto, M. W., Rosenbaum, J. F., Sachs, G. S., O'Neil, C., Asher, R., & Meltzer-Brody, S. (1990). Longitudinal course of panic disorder: Findings from the Massachusetts General Hospital Naturalistic Study. *Journal of Clinical Psychiatry, 51,* 12–16.

Pollak, J. M. (1981). Hysterical personality: An appraisal in light of empirical research. *Genetic Psychology Monographs, 104,* 71–105.

Pollak, J. M. (1987). Relationship of obsessive-compulsive personality to obsessive-compulsive disorder: A review of the literature. *Journal of Psychology, 121,* 137–148.

Pollard, C. A., & Henderson, J. G. (1988). Four types of social phobia in a community sample. *Journal of Nervous and Mental Disease, 176,* 440–445.

Pollock, V. E., Briere, J., Scheider, L., Knop, J., Mednick, S. A., & Goodwin, D. W. (1990). Childhood antecedents of antisocial behavior: Parental alcoholism and physical abusiveness. *American Journal of Psychiatry, 147,* 1290–1293.

Pomerleau, O. F. (1992). Nicotine and the central nervous system: Biobehavioral effects of cigarette smoking. *American Journal of Medicine, 93,* 2–7.

Pomeroy, W. (1975). The diagnosis and treatment of transvestites and transsexuals. *Journal of Sex and Marital Therapy, 1,* 215–224.

Ponticas, Y. (1992). Sexual aversion versus hypoactive sexual desire: A diagnostic challenge. *Psychiatric Medicine, 10,* 273–281.

Post, R. M., Roy-Byrne, P. P., & Uhde, T. W. (1988). Graphic representation of the life course of illness in patients with affective disorder. *American Journal of Psychiatry, 145,* 844–848.

Post, S. G. (1992). DSM-III-R and religion. *Social Science and Medicine, 35,* 81–90.

Powell, L. H., & Thoreson, C. E. (1988). Effects of Type A behavioral counseling and severity of prior acute myocardial infarction on survival. *American Journal of Cardiology, 62,* 1159–1163.

President's Commission on Mental Health. (1978). *Report to the President* (Vol. 1). Washington, DC: U.S. Government Printing Office.

Preskorn, S. H. (1989). Tricyclic antidepressants: The whys and hows of therapeutic drug monitoring. *Journal of Clinical Psychiatry, 50,* 34–42.

Prigatano, G. P. (1992). Personality disturbances associated with traumatic brain injury. *Journal of Consulting and Clinical Psychology, 60,* 360–368.

Prince, M. (1914). *The unconscious: The fundamentals of human personality, normal and abnormal.* New York: Macmillan.

Prince, R., & Tcheng-Laroche, F. (1987). Culture-bound syndromes and international disease classifications. *Culture, Medicine, and Psychiatry, 11,* 3–19.

Prokop, C. K., Bradley, L. A., Burish, T. G., Anderson, K. O., & Fox, J. E. (1991). *Health psychology: Clinical methods and research.* New York: Macmillan.

Puig-Antich, J. (1982). Major depression and conduct disorder in prepuberty. *Journal of the American Academy of Child Psychiatry, 21,* 118–128.

Purtilo, D. T., & Purtilo, R. B. (1989). *A survey of human diseases* (2nd ed.). Boston: Little, Brown.

Putnam, F. W. (1984). The psychophysiologic investigation of multiple personality disorder: A review. *Psychiatric Clinics of North America, 7,* 31–39.

Putnam, F. W. (1989). *Diagnosis and treatment of multiple personality disorder.* New York: Guilford.

Putnam, F. W., Guroff, J. J., Silberman, E. K., Barban, L., & Post, R. M. (1986). The clinical phenomenology of multiple personality disorder: Review of 100 recent cases. *Journal of Clinical Psychiatry, 47,* 285–293.

Putnam, F. W., Zahn, T. P., & Post, R. M. (1990). Differential autonomic nervous system activity in multiple personality disorder. *Psychiatry Research, 31,* 251–260.

Quaid, K. A., & Morris, M. (1993). Reluctance to undergo predictive testing: The case of Huntington disease. *American Journal of Medical Genetics, 45,* 41–45.

Quality Assurance Project. (1991a). Treatment outline for antisocial personality disorder. *Australian and New Zealand Journal of Psychiatry, 25,* 541–547.

Quality Assurance Project. (1991b). Treatment outlines for borderline, narcissistic, and histrionic personality disorders. *Australian and New Zealand Journal of Psychiatry, 25,* 392–403.

Quay, H. C. (1986). A critical analysis of DSM-III as a taxonomy of psychopathology in childhood and adolescence. In T. Millon & G. L. Klerman (Eds.), *Contemporary directions in psychopathology: Toward the DSM-IV.* New York: Guilford.

Rabins, P. V., & Folstein, M. F. (1982). Delirium and dementia: Diagnostic criteria and fatality rates. *British Journal of Psychiatry, 140,* 149–153.

Rachman, S. J. (1978). *Fear and courage.* San Francisco: Freeman.

Rachman, S. J., & de Silva, P. (1978). Abnormal and normal obsessions. *Behaviour Research and Therapy, 16,* 233–248.

Rachman, S. J., & Hodgson, R. J. (1980). *Obsessions and compulsions.* Englewood Cliffs, NJ: Prentice-Hall.

Radelet, M. L., & Barnard, G. W. (1988). Treating those found incompetent for execution: Ethical chaos with only one solution. *Bulletin of the American Academy of Psychiatry and the Law, 16,* 297–308.

Rado, S. (1926). The psychic effects of intoxicants. *The International Journal of Psychoanalysis, 7,* 396–413.

Rado, S. (1933). The psychoanalysis of pharmacothymia (drug addiction). *Psychoanalytic Quarterly, 2,* 1–23.

Rado, S. (1956). *Psychoanalysis and behavior.* New York: Grune & Stratton.

Ragland, D. R., & Brand, R. J. (1988a). Coronary heart disease mortality in the Western Collaborative Group Study: Follow-up experience of 22 years. *American Journal of Epidemiology, 127,* 462–475.

Ragland, D. R., & Brand, R. J. (1988b). Type A behavior and mortality from coronary heart disease. *The New England Journal of Medicine, 318,* 65–69.

Raimy, V. (1976). *Misunderstandings of the self: Cognitive psychotherapy and the misconception hypothesis.* San Francisco: Jossey-Bass.

Raine, A., Venables, P. H., & Williams, M. (1990). Relationships between central and autonomic measures of arousal at age 15 years and criminality at age 24 years. *Archives of General Psychiatry, 47,* 1003–1007.

Rajput, A. H. (1992). Frequency and cause of Parkinson's disease. *Canadian Journal of Neurological Sciences, 19,* 103–107.

Ram, R., Bromet, E. J., Eaton, W. W., Pato, C., & Schwartz, J. E. (1992). The natural course of schizophrenia: A review of first-admission studies. *Schizophrenia Bulletin, 18,* 185–207.

Ramani, V., & Gumnit, R. J. (1982). Management of hysterical seizures in epileptic patients. *Archives of Neurology, 39,* 78–81.

Ramcharan, S., Love, E. J., Fick, G. H., & Goldfien, A. (1992). The epidemiology of premenstrual symptoms in a population-based sample of 2650 urban women: Attributable risk and risk factors. *Journal of Clinical Epidemiology, 45,* 377–392.

Rand, C. S., & Kuldau, J. M. (1990). The epidemiology of obesity and self-defined weight problems in the general population: Gender, race, age, and social class. *International Journal of Eating Disorders, 9,* 329–343.

Randolph, T. G. (1956). The descriptive features of food addiction: Addictive eating and drinking. *Quarterly Journal of Studies on Alcohol, 17,* 198–224.

Rapaport, D. (1959). The structure of psychoanalytic theory: A systematizing attempt. In S. Koch (Ed.), *Psychology: A study of a science* (Vol. 1, pp. 55-183). New York: McGraw-Hill.

Raphael, F. J., & Lacey, J. H. (1992). Sociocultural aspects of eating disorders. *Annals of Medicine, 24,* 293–296.

Raphling, D. L. (1989). Fetishism in a woman. *Journal of the American Psychoanalytic Association, 37,* 465–491.

Rapoport, A. M. (1992). The diagnosis of migraine and tension-type headache, then and now. *Neurology, 42,* 11–15.

Rapoport, J. L. (1988). The neurobiology of obsessive-compulsive disorder. *JAMA, 260,* 2888–2890.

Rapoport, J. L. (1989). *The boy who couldn't stop washing.* New York: Dutton.

Rapoport, J. L., & Quinn, P. O. (1975). Minor physical anomalies (stigmata) and early developmental deviation: Major biologic subgroups of "hyperactive children." *International Journal of Mental Health, 4,* 29–44.

Raskin, R. N., & Hall, C. J. (1979). A narcissistic personality inventory. *Psychological Reports, 45,* 590.

Raskin, R. N., & Hall, C. J. (1981). The Narcissistic Personality Inventory: Alternate form reliability and further evidence of construct validity. *Journal of Personality Assessment, 45,* 159–162.

Rasmussen, S. A., & Eisen, J. L. (1992). The epidemiology and differential diagnosis of obsessive compulsive disorder. *Journal of Clinical Psychiatry, 53,* 4–10.

Ratcliffe, B. E. (1973). MDA. *PharmChem Newsletter, 2*(5), 1.

Rauws, E. A., & Tytgat, G. N. (1990). Cure of duodenal ulcer associated with eradication of *Helicobacter pylori. Lancet, 335,* 1233–1235.

Ravart, M., & Cote, H. (1992). Sexoanalysis: A new insight-oriented treatment approach for sexual disorders. *Journal of Sex and Marital Therapy, 18,* 128–140.

Ray, W. J., Cole, H. W., & Raczynski, J. M. (1983). Psychophysiological assessment. In M. Hersen, A. E. Kazdin, & A. S. Bellack (Eds.), *The clinical psychology handbook.* New York: Pergamon.

Raz, S., & Raz, N. (1990). Structural brain abnormalities in the major psychoses: A quantitative review of the evidence from computerized imaging. *Psychological Bulletin, 108,* 93–108.

Reber, M. (1992). Mental retardation. *Psychiatric Clinics of North America, 15,* 511–522.

Rector, N. A., & Seeman, M. V. (1992). Auditory hallucinations in women and men. *Schizophrenia Research, 7,* 233–236.

Reich, J. H. (1986). The epidemiology of anxiety. *Journal of Nervous and Mental Disease, 174,* 129–136.

Reich, J. H. (1987). Sex distribution of DSM-III personality disorders in psychiatric outpatients. *American Journal of Psychiatry, 144,* 485–488.

Reich, J. H. (1989). Update on instruments to measure DSM-III and DSM-III-R personality disorders. *Journal of Nervous and Mental Disease, 177,* 366–370.

Reich, J. H., & Green, A. I. (1991). Effect of personality disorders on outcome of treatment. *Journal of Nervous and Mental Disease, 179,* 74–82.

Reich, J. H., Nduaguba, M., & Yates, W. (1988). Age and sex distribution of DSM-III personality cluster traits in a community population. *Comprehensive Psychiatry, 29,* 298–303.

Reich, J. H., Yates, W., & Nduaguba, M. (1989). Prevalence of DSM-III personality disorders in the community. *Social Psychiatry and Psychiatric Epidemiology, 24,* 12–16.

Reich, W. (1949). *Character analysis.* New York: Farrar, Straus, & Young.

Reichlin, S. M., Bloom, J. D., & Williams, M. H. (1993). Excluding personality disorders from the insanity defense—a follow-up study. *Bulletin of the American Academy of Psychiatry and the Law, 21,* 91–100.

Reid, D. H., Phillips, J. F., & Green, C. W. (1991). Teaching persons with profound multiple handicaps: A review of the effects of behavioral research. *Journal of Applied Behavior Analysis, 24,* 319–336.

Reid, W. H. (1986). Antisocial personality. In A. M. Cooper, A. J. Frances, & M. H. Sacks (Eds.), *The personality disorders and neuroses.* New York: Basic Books.

Reider, N. (1976). Symptom substitution. *Bulletin of the Menninger Clinic, 40,* 629–640.

Reilly, R. (1989, December 18). Masters of the '80s. *Sports Illustrated,* 44–49.

Reilly, R. (1993, November 15). Quest for perfection. *Sports Illustrated,* 80–84.

Reiss, S., & McNally, R. J. (1985). Expectancy model of fear. In S. Reiss & R. R. Bootzin (Eds.), *Theoretical issues in behavior therapy.* New York: Academic Press.

Reitan, R. M., & Wolfson, D. (1985). *The Halstead-Reitan Neuropsychological Test Battery: Theory and clinical interpretation.* Tucson, AZ: Neuropsychology Press.

Resnick, H. S., Kilpatrick, D. G., Best, C. L., & Kramer, T. L. (1992). Vulnerability-stress factors in development of posttraumatic stress disorder. *Journal of Nervous and Mental Disease, 180,* 424–430.

Reynolds, D. K. (1976). *Morita psychotherapy.* Berkeley: University of California Press.

Reynolds, G. P. (1989). Beyond the dopamine hypothesis: The neurochemical pathology of schizophrenia. *British Journal of Psychiatry, 155,* 305–316.

Ricci, L. C., & Wellman, M. M. (1990). Monoamines: Biochemical markers of suicide? *Journal of Clinical Psychology, 46,* 106–116.

Ricciardi, J. N., Baer, L., Jenike, M. A., Fischer, S. C., Sholtz, D., & Buttolph, M. L. (1992). Changes in DSM-III-R Axis II diagnoses following treatment of obsessive-compulsive disorder. *American Journal of Psychiatry, 149,* 829–831.

Richer, P. (1885). *Études cliniques sur la grande hystérie.* Paris: Delahaye et Lecrosnier.

Rickels, K. (1990). Buspirone in clinical practice. *Journal of Clinical Psychiatry, 51,* 51–54.

Rickels, K., & Schweizer, E. (1990). The clinical course and long-term management of generalized anxiety disorder. *Journal of Clinical Psychopharmacology, 10,* 101–110.

Rieber, I., & Sigusch, V. (1979). Psychosurgery on sex offenders and sexual "deviants" in West Germany. *Archives of Sexual Behavior, 8,* 523–527.

Riecher, A., Rossler, W., Loffler, W., & Fatkenheuer, B. (1991). Factors influencing compulsory admission of psychiatric patients. *Psychological Medicine, 21,* 197–208.

Rief, W., Schaefer, S., Hiller, W., & Fichter, M. M. (1992). Lifetime diagnoses in patients with somatoform disorders: Which came first? *European Archives of Psychiatry and Clinical Neuroscience, 241,* 236–240.

Rienzi, B. M., & Scrams, D. J. (1991). Gender stereotypes for paranoid, antisocial, compulsive, dependent, and histrionic personality disorders. *Psychological Disorders, 69,* 976–978.

Riether, A. M., & Stoudemire, A. (1988). Psychogenic fugue states: A review. *Southern Medical Journal, 81,* 568–571.

Rifkin, A. (1990). Benzodiazepines for anxiety disorders: Are the concerns justified? *Postgraduate Medicine, 87,* 209–219.

Riley, D. M., Sobell, L. C., Leo, G. I., Sobell, M. B., & Klajner, E. (1987). Behavioral treatment of alcohol problems: A review and a comparison of behavioral and nonbehavioral studies. In W. M. Cox (Ed.), *Treatment and prevention of alcohol problems: A resource manual.* New York: Academic Press.

Riley, W. T., Treiber, F. A., & Woods, M. G. (1989). Anger and hostility in depression. *Journal of Nervous and Mental Disease, 177,* 668–674.

Rimland, B. (1964). *Infantile autism.* New York: Appleton-Century-Crofts.

Rippere, V. (1977). Comments on Seligman's theory of helplessness. *Behaviour Research and Therapy, 15,* 207–209.

Ritchey, F. J., La Gory, M., Fitzpatrick, K. M., & Mullis, J. (1990). A comparison of homeless, community-wide, and selected distressed samples on the CES-Depression Scale. *American Journal of Public Health, 80,* 1384–1386.

Ritvo, E. R., & Freeman, B. J. (1978). National Society for Autistic Children definition of the syndrome of autism. *Journal of Autism and Childhood Schizophrenia, 8,* 162–167.

Ritvo, E. R., Mason-Brothers, A., Freeman, B. J., Pingree, C., Jenson, W. R., McMahon, W. M., Peterson, P. B., Jorde, L. B., Mo, A., & Ritvo, A. (1990). The UCLA–University of Utah epidemiologic survey of autism: The etiologic role of rare diseases. *American Journal of Psychiatry, 147,* 1614–1621.

Robbins, M. (1992). Psychoanalysis and biological approaches to mental illness: Schizophrenia. *Journal of the American Psychoanalytic Association, 40,* 425–454.

Robertson, D. R., & George, C. F. (1990). Drug therapy for Parkinson's disease in the elderly. *British Medical Bulletin, 46,* 124–146.

Robertson, G. (1988). Arrest patterns among mentally disordered offenders. *British Journal of Psychiatry, 153,* 313–316.

Robertson, H. A. (1979). Benzodiazepine receptors in "emotional" and "nonemotional" mice: Comparison of four strains. *European Journal of Pharmacology, 56,* 163.

Robins, L. N. (1970). The adult development of the antisocial child. *Seminars in Psychiatry, 2,* 420–434.

Robins, L. N., & Helzer, J. E. (1986). Diagnosis and clinical assessment: The current state of psychiatric diagnosis. *Annual Review of Psychology, 37,* 409–432.

Robins, L. N., Helzer, J. E., Weissman, M. M., Orvaschel, H., Gruenberg, E., Burke, J. D., & Regier, D. A. (1984). Lifetime prevalence of specific psychiatric disorders in three sites. *Archives of General Psychiatry, 41,* 949–958.

Robins, L. N., & Przybeck, T. R. (1985). *Age of onset of drug use as a factor in drug and other disorders.* Rockville, MD: NIDA Research Monograph Series.

Robinson, D. P., Greene, J. W., & Walker, L. S. (1988). Functional somatic complaints in adolescents: Relationship to negative life events, self-concept, and family characteristics. *Journal of Pediatrics, 113,* 588–593.

Robinson, L. A., Berman, J. S., & Neimeyer, R. A. (1990). Psychotherapy for the treatment of depression: A comprehensive review of controlled outcome research. *Psychological Bulletin, 108,* 30–49.

Roca-Bennasar, M., Garcia-Mas, A., Llaneras, N., & Blat, J. (1991). Kraepelin: An expert system for the diagnosis of obsessive-compulsive disorders. *European Psychiatry, 6,* 171–175.

Rockne, R. M., & Lemke, T. (1992). Casualties from a junior-senior high school during the Persian Gulf War: Toxic poisoning or mass hysteria? *Journal of Developmental and Behavioral Pediatrics, 13,* 339–342.

Rodin, M. (1992). The social construction of premenstrual syndrome. *Social Science and Medicine, 35,* 49–56.

Roff, M. (1974). Childhood antecedents of adult neurosis, severe bad conduct, and psychological health. In D. Ricks, A. Thomas, & M. Roff (Eds.), *Life history research in psychopathology* (Vol. 3). Minneapolis: University of Minnesota Press.

Roffman, R. A., Gillmore, M. R., Gilchrist, L. D., Mathias, S. A., & Krueger, L. (1990). Continuing unsafe sex: Assessing the need for AIDS prevention counseling. *Public Health Reports, 105,* 202–208.

Rofman, E. S., Askinazi, C., & Fant, E. (1980). The prediction of dangerous behavior in emergency civil commitment. *American Journal of Psychiatry, 137,* 1061–1064.

Rogers, C. R. (1942). *Counseling and psychotherapy: Newer concepts in practice.* Boston: Houghton Mifflin.

Rogers, C. R. (1951). *Client-centered therapy: Its current practice, implications, and theory.* Boston: Houghton Mifflin.

Rogers, C. R. (1961). *On becoming a person.* Boston: Houghton Mifflin.

Rogers, C. R., Gendlin, G. T., Kiesler, D. V., & Truax, C. B. (1967). *The therapeutic relationship and its impact: A study of psychotherapy with schizophrenics.* Madison: University of Wisconsin Press.

Rogler, L. H. (1989). The meaning of culturally sensitive research in mental health. *American Journal of Psychiatry, 146,* 296–303.

Roman, P. M. (1988). Biological features of women's alcohol use: A review. *Public Health Reports, 103,* 628–637.

Rootes, L. E., & Aanes, D. L. (1992). A conceptual framework for understanding self-help groups. *Hospital and Community Psychiatry, 43,* 379–381.

Rorschach, H. (1942). *Psychodiagnostics: A diagnostic test based on perception.* Berne: Huber.

Rosch, E., & Mervis, C. B. (1975). Family resemblances: Studies in the internal structure of categories. *Cognitive Psychology, 7,* 573–605.

Rosen, J. (1947). The treatment of schizophrenic psychosis by direct analytic therapy. *Psychiatric Quarterly, 21,* 3–37.

Rosen, J. C., Saltzberg, E., & Srebnik, D. (1989). Cognitive behavior therapy for negative body image. *Behavior Therapy, 20,* 393–404.

Rosen, R. C., & Leiblum, S. R. (1989). Assessment and treatment of desire disorders. In S. R. Leiblum & R. C. Rosen (Eds.), *Principles and practice of sex therapy: Update for the 1990s.* New York: Guilford.

Rosenbaum, M. (1984). Anna O. (Bertha Pappenheim): Her history. In M. Rosenbaum & M. Muroff (Eds.), *Anna O.: Fourteen contemporary interpretations.* New York: Free Press.

Rosenblatt, P. C., Walsh, R. P., & Jackson, D. A. (1976). *Grief and mourning in cross-cultural perspective.* New Haven, CT: HRAF Press.

Rosenfeld, H. (1964). On the psychopathology of narcissism: A clinical approach. *International Journal of Psychoanalysis, 45,* 332–337.

Rosenfield, S. (1984). Race differences in involuntary hospitalizations: Psychiatric vs. labelling perspectives. *Journal of Health and Social Behavior, 25,* 14–23.

Rosenhan, D. L. (1973). On being sane in insane places. *Science, 179,* 250–258.

Rosenhan, D. L., & Seligman, M. E. P. (1984). *Abnormal psychology.* New York: Norton.

Rosenman, R. H., Brand, R. J., Jenkins, D., Friedman, M., Straus, R., & Wurm, M. (1975). Coronary heart disease in the Western Collaborative Study Group: Final follow-up experience at 8½ years. *JAMA, 233,* 872–877.

Rosenthal, D. (Ed.). (1963). *The Genain quadruplets.* New York: Basic Books.

Rosenthal, D. (1970). *Genetic theory and abnormal behavior.* New York: McGraw-Hill.

Rosenthal, D., & Kety, S. S. (Eds.). (1968). *The transmission of schizophrenia.* Oxford: Pergamon.

Rosenthal, N. E., & Blehar, M. C. (Eds.). (1989). *Seasonal affective disorders and phototherapy.* New York: Guilford.

Rosenthal, N. E., Sack, D. H., Gillin, J. C., Lewy, A. J., Goodwin, F. K., Davenport, Y., Mueller, P. S., Newsome, D. A., & Wehr, T. A. (1984). Seasonal affective disorder: A description of the syndrome and preliminary findings with light therapy. *Archives of General Psychiatry, 41,* 72–80.

Roskies, E., Seraganian, P., Oseasohn, R., Hanley, J. A., Collu, R., Martin, N., & Smilga, C. (1986). The Montreal Type A Intervention Project: Major findings. *Health Psychology, 5,* 45–69.

Ross, C. A. (1990). Twelve cognitive errors about multiple personality disorder. *American Journal of Psychotherapy, 44,* 348–356.

Ross, C. A., & Gahan, P. (1988). Cognitive analysis of multiple personality disorder. *American Journal of Psychotherapy, 42,* 229–239.

Ross, C. A., Joshi, S., & Currie, R. (1990). Dissociative experiences in the general population. *American Journal of Psychiatry, 147,* 1547–1552.

Ross, C. A., Miller, S. D., Bjornson, L., Reagor, P., Fraser, G. A., & Anderson, G. (1991). Abuse histories in 102 cases of multiple personality disorder. *Canadian Journal of Psychiatry, 36,* 97–101.

Ross, C. A., Miller, S. D., Reagor, P., Bjornson, L., Fraser, G. A., & Anderson, G. (1990). Structured interview data on 102 cases of multiple personality disorder from four centers. *American Journal of Psychiatry, 147,* 596–601.

Ross, D. M., & Ross, S. A. (1973). Storage and utilization of previously formulated mediators in educable mentally retarded children. *Journal of Educational Psychology, 65,* 205–210.

Ross, D. M., & Ross, S. A. (1982). *Hyperactivity: Current issues, research, and theory.* New York: Wiley.

Roth, D. L., & Holmes, D. S. (1987). Influence of aerobic exercise training and relaxation training on physical and psychological health following stressful life events. *Psychosomatic Medicine, 49,* 355–365.

Rothschild, A. J. (1988). Biology of depression. *Medical Clinics of North America, 72,* 765–790.

Rowland, L. A., Zeelan, J., & Waismann, L. C. (1992). Patterns of service for the long-term mentally ill in Europe. *British Journal of Clinical Psychology, 31,* 405–417.

Roy, A. (1982). *Hysteria.* Chichester, England: Wiley.

Rozin, P. (1984). Disorders of the nervous system. In D. L. Rosenhan & M. E. P. Seligman, *Abnormal psychology.* New York: Norton.

Rubin, L. C., & Mills, M. J. (1983). Behavioral precipitants to civil commitment. *American Journal of Psychiatry, 140,* 603–606.

Rubonis, A. V., & Bickman, L. (1991). Psychological impairment in the wake of disaster: The disaster-psychopathology relationship. *Psychological Bulletin, 109,* 384–399.

Rudick, R. A., Goodkin, D. E., & Ransohoff, R. M. (1992). Pharmacotherapy of multiple sclerosis: Current status. *Cleveland Clinic Journal of Medicine, 59,* 267–277.

Rumelhart, D. E., McClelland, J. L., & The PDP Research Group. (1986). *Parallel distributed processing: Explorations in the microstructure of cognition: Vol. 1. Foundations.* Cambridge: MIT Press.

Rundle, B. (1990). *Wittgenstein and contemporary philosophy of language.* Oxford: Blackwell.

Runyan, W. M. (1981). Why did van Gogh cut off his ear? The problem of alternative explanations in psychobiography. *Journal of Personality and Social Psychology, 40,* 1070–1077.

Rush, A. J., Beck, A. T., Kovacs, M., & Hollon, S. D. (1977). Comparative efficacy of cognitive therapy and imipramine in the treatment of depressed outpatients. *Cognitive Therapy and Research, 1,* 17–37.

Ruttenber, A. J. (1991). Stalking the elusive designer drugs: Techniques for monitoring new problems in drug abuse. *Journal of Addictive Diseases, 11,* 71–87.

Rutter, M. (1968). Concepts of autism: A review of research. *Journal of Child Psychology and Psychiatry, 9,* 1–25.

Rutter, M. (1988). Epidemiological approaches to developmental psychopathology. *Archives of General Psychiatry, 45,* 486–495.

Rutter, M., & Lockyer, L. (1967). A five to fifteen year follow-up of infantile psychosis. *British Journal of Psychiatry, 113,* 1168–1182.

Rutter, M., & Shaffer, D. (1980). DSM-III: A step forward or a step backward in terms of the classification of child psychiatric disorders? *Journal of the American Academy of Child Psychiatry, 19,* 371–394.

Ryle, A. (1982). *Psychotherapy: A cognitive interpretation of theory and practice.* London: Academic Press.

Saccuzzo, D. P., & Braff, D. L. (1986). Information processing abnormalities: Trait- and state-dependent components. *Schizophrenia Bulletin, 12,* 447–459.

Sacks, O. (1974). *Awakenings.* New York: Vintage.

Sacks, O. (1985a). *Migraine: Understanding a common disorder.* Berkeley: University of California Press.

Sacks, O. (1985b). *The man who mistook his wife for a hat.* New York: Simon & Schuster.

Safferman, A., Lieberman, J. A., Kane, J. M., Szymanski, S., & Kinon, B. (1991). Update on the clinical efficacy and side effects of clozapine. *Schizophrenia Bulletin, 17,* 247–261.

Safir, M. P., & Almagor, M. (1991). Psychopathology associated with sexual dysfunction. *Journal of Clinical Psychology, 47,* 17–27.

Samelson, F. (1980). J. B. Watson's Little Albert, Cyril Burt's twins, and the need for a critical science. *American Psychologist, 35,* 619–625.

Sammons, M. T., & Karoly, P. (1987). Psychosocial variables in irritable bowel syndrome: A review and proposal. *Clinical Psychology Review, 7,* 187–204.

Sandberg, D. A., & Lynn, S. J. (1992). Dissociative experiences, psychopathology, and adjustment, and child and adolescent maltreatment in female college students. *Journal of Abnormal Psychology, 101,* 717–723.

Sanders, I. T. (1966). *The community: An introduction to a social system* (2nd ed.). New York: Ronald Press.

Sanderson, W. C., & Barlow, D. H. (1990). A description of patients diagnosed with DSM-III-R generalized anxiety disorder. *Journal of Nervous and Mental Disease, 178,* 588–591.

Sanderson, W. C., Beck, A. T., & Beck, J. (1990). Syndrome comorbidity in patients with major depression or dysthymia: Prevalence and temporal relationships. *American Journal of Psychiatry, 147,* 1025–1028.

Sanderson, W. C., Rapee, R. M., & Barlow, D. H. (1989). The influence of an illusion of control on panic attacks induced via inhalation of 5.5% carbon dioxide-enriched air. *Archives of General Psychiatry, 46,* 157–162.

Sandler, J. (Ed.). (1989). *Dimensions of psychoanalysis.* London: Karnac.

Sanguinetti, M., & Catanzaro, M. (1987). A comparison of discharge teaching on the consequences of brain injury. *Journal of Neuroscience Nursing, 19,* 271–275.

Sarai, M., Matsunaga, H., & Kimura, S. (1990). Elevated plasma dopamine concentrations in unmedicated acute schizophrenics. *Japanese Journal of Psychiatry and Neurology, 44,* 557–562.

Sarbin, T. R., & Coe, W. C. (1972). *Hypnosis: A social psychological analysis of influence communication.* New York: Holt, Rinehart, & Winston.

Sarbin, T. R., & Mancuso, J. C. (1980). *Schizophrenia: Medical diagnosis or moral verdict?* New York: Pergamon.

Sargeant, J. K., Bruce, M. L., Florio, L. P., & Weissman, M. M. (1990). Factors associated with 1-year outcome of major depression in the community. *Archives of General Psychiatry, 47,* 519–526.

Sartorius, N., Jablensky, A., Korten, A., Ernberg, G., Anker, M., Cooper, J. E., & Day, R. (1986). Early manifestations and first-contact incidence of schizophrenia in different cultures. *Psychological Medicine, 16,* 909–928.

Saunders, J. B. (1989). The efficacy of treatment for drinking problems. *International Review of Psychiatry, 1,* 121–137.

Sayed, Z. A., Lewis, S. A., & Brittain, R. P. (1969). An electroencephalographic and psychiatric study of thirty-two insane murderers. *British Journal of Psychiatry, 115,* 415–424.

Scerbo, A., Raine, A., O'Brien, M., Chan, C. J., Rhee, C., & Smiley, N. (1990). Reward dominance and passive avoidance learning in adolescent psychopaths. *Journal of Abnormal Child Psychology, 18,* 451–463.

Schachter, D. C., Pless, I. B., & Bruck, M. (1991). The prevalence and correlates of behaviour problems in learning disabled children. *Canadian Journal of Psychiatry, 36,* 323–331.

Schachter, S. (1982). Recidivism and self-cure of smoking and obesity. *American Psychologist, 37,* 436–444.

Schachter, S., & Latané, B. T. (1964). Crime, cognition, and the autonomic nervous system. In D. Levine (Ed.), *Nebraska symposium on motivation.* Lincoln: University of Nebraska Press.

Schact, T., & Nathan, P. E. (1977). But is it good for psychology? Appraisal and status of the DSM-III. *American Psychologist, 32,* 1017–1025.

Scheff, T. J. (1966). *Being mentally ill: A sociological theory.* Chicago: Aldine.

Scheibe, G., & Albus, M. (1992). Age at onset, precipitating events, sex distribution, and co-occurrence of anxiety disorders. *Psychopathology, 25,* 11–18.

Scheid-Cook, T. L. (1987). Commitment of the mentally ill to outpatient treatment. *Community Mental Health Journal, 23,* 173–182.

Scheier, M. F., & Carver, C. S. (1985). Optimism, coping, and health: Assessment and implications of generalized outcome expectancies. *Health Psychology, 4,* 219–247.

Scheier, M. F., & Carver, C. S. (1987). Dispositional optimism and physical well-being: The influence of generalized outcome expectancies on health. *Journal of Personality, 55,* 169–210.

Scheier, M. F., Matthews, K. A., Owens, J. F., Magovern, G. J., Lefebvre, R. C., Abbott, R. A., & Carver, C. S. (1989). Dispositional optimism and recovery from coronary artery bypass surgery: The beneficial effects on physical and psychological well-being. *Journal of Personality and Social Psychology, 57,* 1024–1040.

Schildkraut, J. J. (1965). The catecholamine hypothesis of affective disorders: A review of supporting evidence. *American Journal of Psychiatry, 122,* 509–522.

Schleifer, S. J., Keller, S. E., Siris, S. G., Davis, K. L., & Stein, M. (1985). Depression and immunity. *Archives of General Psychiatry, 42,* 129–133.

Schmale, A. H., & Iker, H. P. (1971). Hopelessness as a predictor of cervical cancer. *Social Science and Medicine, 5,* 95–100.

Schmid, T. L. (1986). Reducing inappropriate behavior of mentally retarded children through interpolated reinforcement. *American Journal of Mental Deficiency, 91,* 286–293.

Schmidt, F. L. (1992). What do data really mean? Research findings, meta-analysis, and cumulative knowledge in psychology. *American Psychologist, 47,* 1173–1181.

Schmidt, G., & Schorsch, E. (1981). Psychosurgery of sexually deviant patients: Review and analysis of new empirical findings. *Archives of Sexual Behavior, 10,* 301–323.

Schmidt, K., Hill, L., & Guthrie, G. (1977). Running amok. *International Journal of Social Psychiatry, 23,* 264–274.

Schneier, F. R., Johnson, J., Hornig, C. D., Liebowitz, M. R., & Weissman, M. M. (1992). Social phobia: Comorbidity and morbidity in an epidemiologic sample. *Archives of General Psychiatry, 49,* 282–288.

Schneier, F. R., Spitzer, R. L., Gibbon, M., Fyer, A. J., & Liebowitz, M. R. (1991). The relationship of social phobia subtypes and avoidant personality disorder. *Comprehensive Psychiatry, 32,* 496–502.

Schoenman, T. J. (1982). Criticisms of the psychopathological interpretation of witch hunts: A review. *American Journal of Psychiatry, 139,* 1028–1032.

Schoenman, T. J. (1984). The mentally ill witch in textbooks of abnormal psychology: Current status and implications of a fallacy. *Professional Psychology: Research and Practice, 15,* 299–314.

Schooler, N. R. (1986). The efficacy of antipsychotic drugs and family therapies in the maintenance treatment of schizophrenia. *Journal of Clinical Psychopharmacology, 6,* 11–19.

Schotte, D., & Stunkard, A. J. (1987). Bulimia vs bulimic behaviors on a college campus. *JAMA, 258,* 1213–1215.

Schou, M. (1988). Lithium treatment of manic-depressive illness: Past, present, and future perspectives. *JAMA, 259,* 1834–1836.

Schover, L. R., Friedman, J. M., Weiler, S. J., Heiman, J. R., & LoPiccolo, J. (1982). Multiaxial problem-oriented system for sexual dysfunctions: An alternative to DSM-III. *Archives of General Psychiatry, 39,* 614–619.

Schreiber, F. R. (1974). *Sybil.* New York: Warner.

Schreibman, L., & Charlop, M. H. (1989). Infantile autism. In T. H. Ollendick & M. Hersen (Eds.), *Handbook of child psychopathology* (2nd ed.). New York: Plenum.

Schreiner-Engel, P., & Schiavi, R. C. (1986). Lifetime psychopathology in individuals with low sexual desire. *Journal of Nervous and Mental Disease, 174,* 646–651.

Schreter, R. K. (1993). Ten trends in managed care and their impact on the biopsychosocial model. *Hospital and Community Psychiatry, 44,* 325–327.

Schubert, M. A., & Borkman, T. J. (1991). An organizational typology for self-help groups. *American Journal of Community Psychology, 19,* 769–787.

Schuler, K., & Tinger, G. (1991). Computer-based psychiatric diagnostics: The expert system and training program DSM-III-X. *European Review of Applied Psychology, 41,* 319–322.

Schulman, E. A., & Silberstein, S. D. (1992). Symptomatic and prophylactic treatment of migraine and tension-type headache. *Neurology, 42,* 16–21.

Schulsinger, F. (1972). Psychopathy, heredity, and environment. *International Journal of Mental Health, 1,* 190–206.

Schumaker, J. F. (Ed.). (1991). *Human suggestibility: Advances in theory, research, and application.* New York: Routledge.

Schuster, M. M. (1983). Irritable bowel syndrome: Applications of psychophysiological methods to treatment. In R. Holzl & W. E. Whitehead (Eds.), *Psychophysiology of the gastrointestinal tract: Experimental and clinical applications.* New York: Plenum.

Schwartz, B. (1984). *Psychology of learning and behavior* (2nd ed.). New York: Norton.

Schwartz, M. F., & Masters, W. H. (1983). Conceptual factors in the treatment of paraphilias: A preliminary report. *Journal of Sex and Marital Therapy, 9,* 3–18.

Schwartz, M. F., & Masters, W. H. (1984). The Masters and Johnson treatment program for dissatisfied homosexual men. *American Journal of Psychiatry, 141,* 173–181.

Schweinhart, L. J., & Weikart, D. P. (1989). The High/Scope Perry Preschool study: Implications for early childhood care and education. *Prevention in Human Services, 7,* 109–132.

Schweinhart, L. J., & Weikart, D. P. (1991). "Beyond IQ in preschool programs?": Response. *Intelligence, 15,* 313–315.

Schweizer, E., Rickels, K., Case, W. G., & Greenblatt, D. J. (1990). Long-term therapeutic use of benzodiazepines. II. Effects of gradual taper. *Archives of General Psychiatry, 47,* 908–915.

Schwyzer, R. U. (1992). Multiple sclerosis: Prevention of serious illness—vision of a desired future for newly ascertained patients. *Medical Hypotheses, 37,* 115–118.

Scott, A. I. (1989). Which depressed patients will respond to electroconvulsive therapy? The search for biological predictors of recovery. *British Journal of Psychiatry, 154,* 8–17.

Scott, J. (1994, May 9). Multiple-personality cases perplex legal system. *New York Times,* pp. A1, B10.

Scott, J. P., Roberto, K. A., & Hutton, J. T. (1986). Families of Alzheimer's victims: Family support to the caregivers. *Journal of the American Geriatrics Society, 34,* 348–354.

Scott, W. A. (1958). Research definitions of mental health and mental illness. *Psychological Bulletin, 55,* 1–45.

Searight, H. R., & Handal, P. J. (1988). The paradox of psychiatric deinstitutionalization: Historical perspective and policy implications. *Journal of Health and Human Resources Administration, 11,* 249–266.

Sedvall, G. (1992). The current status of PET scanning with respect to schizophrenia. *Neuropsychopharmacology, 7,* 41–54.

Seeman, J. (1989). Toward a model of positive health. *American Psychologist, 44,* 1099–1109.

Seeman, P., & Niznik, H. B. (1990). Dopamine receptors and transporters in Parkinson's disease and schizophrenia. *FASEB Journal, 4,* 2737–2744.

Segal, S. P., Watson, M. A., Goldfinger, S. M., & Averbuck, D. S. (1988). Civil commitment in the psychiatric emergency room. II. Mental disorder indicators and three dangerousness criteria. *Archives of General Psychiatry, 45,* 753–758.

Segal, Z. V. (1988). Appraisal of the self-schema construct in cognitive models of depression. *Psychological Bulletin, 103,* 147–162.

Segraves, K. B., & Segraves, R. T. (1991). Hypoactive sexual desire disorder: Prevalence and comorbidity in 906 subjects. *Journal of Sex and Marital Therapy, 17,* 55–58.

Sehdev, H. S. (1976). Patients' rights or patients' neglect: The impact of the patients' rights movement on delivery systems. *American Journal of Orthopsychiatry, 46,* 660–668.

Seidenberg, M., & Berent, S. (1992). Childhood epilepsy and the role of psychology. *American Psychologist, 47,* 1130–1133.

Selden, B. S., Clark, R. F., & Curry, S. C. (1990). Marijuana. *Emergency Medicine Clinics of North America, 8,* 527–539.

Seligman, M. E. P. (1970). On the generality of the laws of learning. *Psychological Review, 77,* 406–418.

Seligman, M. E. P. (1971). Phobias and preparedness. *Behavior Therapy, 2,* 307–321.

Seligman, M. E. P. (1974). Depression and learned helplessness. In R. J. Friedman & M. M. Katz (Eds.), *The psychology of depression: Contemporary theory and research.* Washington, DC: Winston.

Seligman, M. E. P. (1975). *Helplessness: On depression, development, and death.* San Francisco: Freeman.

Seligman, M. E. P. (1988). *Why is there so much depression today? The waxing of the individual and the waning of the commons.* Invited lecture at the annual convention of the American Psychological Association, Atlanta.

Seligman, M. E. P., & Hager, J. (Eds.). (1972). *Biological boundaries of learning.* New York: Appleton-Century-Crofts.

Seligman, M. E. P., & Maier, S. F. (1967). Failure to escape traumatic shock. *Journal of Experimental Psychology, 74,* 1–9.

Seltzer, C. C., & Mayer, J. (1965). A simple criterion of obesity. *Postgraduate Medicine, 38,* 101–107.

Selye, H. (1956). *The stress of life.* New York: McGraw-Hill.

Semrud-Clikeman, M., Biederman, J., Sprich-Buckminster, S., Lehman, B. K., Faraone, S. V., & Norman, D. (1992). Comorbidity between ADDH and learning disability: A review and report in a clinically referred sample. *Journal of the American Academy of Child and Adolescent Psychiatry, 31,* 439–448.

Serban, G. (1992). Multiple personality: An issue for forensic psychiatry. *American Journal of Psychotherapy, 46,* 269–280.

Serrano, R. (1990, September 17). Silence of ex-con baffles San Diego family, officials. *Los Angeles Times,* pp. 1–3.

Setterberg, S. R., Ernst, M., Rao, U., Campbell, M., Carlson, G. A., Shaffer, D. A., & Staghezza, B. M. (1991). Child psychiatrists' views of DSM-III-R: A survey of usage and opinions. *Journal of the American Academy of Child and Adolescent Psychiatry, 30,* 652–658.

Settlage, C. F. (1993). Therapeutic process and developmental process in the restructuring of object and self constancy. *Journal of the American Psychoanalytic Association, 41,* 473–492.

Shader, R. I., & Greenblatt, D. J. (1983). Some current treatment options for symptoms of anxiety. *Journal of Clinical Psychiatry, 44,* 21–29.

Shahar, E., Lederer, J., & Herz, M. J. (1991). The use of a self-report questionnaire to assess the frequency of sexual dysfunction in family practice clinics. *Family Practice, 8,* 206–212.

Shakow, D. (1963). Psychological deficit in schizophrenia. *Behavioral Science, 8,* 275–305.

Shan-Ming, Y., Deyi, C., Zhen, C. Y., Jingsu, J., & Taylor, M. A. (1982). Prevalence and characteristics of mania in Chinese inpatients: A prospective study. *American Journal of Psychiatry, 139,* 1150–1153.

Shapiro, A. K., Shapiro, E., & Wayne, H. (1973). Treatment of Tourette's syndrome with haloperidol: Review of 34 cases. *Archives of General Psychiatry, 28,* 92–97.

Shapiro, D. (1965). *Neurotic styles.* New York: Basic Books.

Shapiro, F. (1989). Eye movement desensitization: A new treatment for post-traumatic stress disorder. *Journal of Behavior Therapy and Experimental Psychiatry, 20,* 211–217.

Shaywitz, B. A., & Shaywitz, S. E. (1991). Comorbidity: A critical issue in attention deficit disorder. *Journal of Child Neurology, 6,* 13–22.

Shea, M. T., Pilkonis, P. A., Beckham, E., Collins, J. F., Elkin, I., Sotsky, S. M., & Docherty, J. P. (1990). Personality disorders and treatment outcome in the NIMH Treatment of Depression Collaborative Research Program. *American Journal of Psychiatry, 147,* 711–718.

Shearer, S. L., Peters, C. P., Quaytman, M. S., & Ogden, R. L. (1990). Frequency and correlates of childhood sexual and physical abuse histories in adult female borderline inpatients. *American Journal of Psychiatry, 147,* 214–216.

Shedler, J., & Block, J. (1990). Adolescent drug use and psychological health: A longitudinal inquiry. *American Psychologist, 45,* 612–630.

Shedler, J., Mayman, M., & Manis, M. (1993). The *illusion* of mental health. *American Psychologist, 48,* 1117–1131.

Sheehan, D. V. (1984). Delineation of anxiety and phobic disorders responsive to monoamine oxidase inhibitors: Implications for classification. *Journal of Clinical Psychiatry, 45,* 29–36.

Shephard, R. A. (1986). Neurotransmitters, anxiety, and benzodiazepines: A behavioral review. *Neuroscience and Biobehavioral Reviews, 10,* 449–461.

Shepherd, M., & Sartorius, M. (Eds.). (1989). *Non-specific aspects of treatment.* Toronto: Huber.

Sher, K. J. (1987). Stress response dampening. In H. T. Blane & K. E. Leonard (Eds.), *Psychological theories of drinking and alcoholism.* New York: Guilford.

Sher, K. J. (1991). *Children of alcoholics: A critical appraisal of theory and research.* Chicago: University of Chicago Press.

Shiffrin, R. W., & Schneider, W. (1984). Automatic and controlled processing revisited. *Psychological Review, 91,* 269–276.

Shinn, M. (1987). Expanding community psychology's domain. *American Journal of Community Psychology, 15,* 555–574.

Shneidman, E. S. (1987). A psychological approach to suicide. In G. R. VandenBos & B. K. Bryant (Eds.), *Cataclysms, crises, and catastrophes: Psychology in action.* Washington, DC: American Psychological Association.

Sholevar, G. P., & Perkel, R. (1990). Family systems intervention and physical illness. *General Hospital Psychiatry, 12,* 363–372.

Shore, J. H., Tatum, E. L., & Vollmer, W. M. (1986). Psychiatric reactions to disaster: The Mount St. Helens experience. *American Journal of Psychiatry, 143,* 590–595.

Shorter, E. (1992). *From paralysis to fatigue: A history of psychosomatic illness in the modern era.* New York: Free Press.

Shtasel, D. L., Gur, R. E., Gallacher, F., Heimberg, C., & Gur, R. C. (1992). Gender differences in the clinical expression of schizophrenia. *Schizophrenia Research, 7,* 225–231.

Shure, M. B., & Spivack, G. (1988). Interpersonal cognitive problem solving. In R. H. Price, E. L. Cowen, R. P. Lorion, & J. Ramos-McKay (Eds.), *Fourteen ounces of prevention: A casebook for practitioners.* Washington, DC: American Psychological Association.

Siddall, J. W., & Keogh, N. J. (1993). Utility of computer interpretive reports based on counselors' ratings of the Diagnostic Inventory of Personality and Symptoms. *Psychological Reports, 72,* 347–350.

Siegel, B. S. (1989). *Peace, love, and healing.* New York: Harper & Row.

Siegel, J. H., Rivkind, A. I., Dalal, S., & Goodarzi, S. (1990). Early physiologic predictors of injury severity and death in blunt multiple trauma. *Archives of Surgery, 125,* 498–508.

Siever, L. J., & Davis, K. L. (1991). A psychobiological perspective on the personality disorders. *American Journal of Psychiatry, 148,* 1647–1658.

Siever, L. J., & Kendler, K. S. (1986). Schizoid/schizotypal/paranoid personality disorders. In A. M. Cooper, A. J. Frances, & M. H. Sacks (Eds.), *The personality disorders and neuroses.* New York: Basic Books.

Siever, L. J., Silverman, J. M., Horvath, T. B., Klar, H., Coccaro, E., Keefe, R. S., Pinkham, L., Rinaldi, P., Mohs, R. C., & Davis, K. L. (1990). Increased morbid risk for schizophrenia-related disorders in relatives of schizotypal personality disordered patients. *Archives of General Psychiatry, 47,* 634–640.

Sifenos, P. E. (1973). The prevalence of alexithymic characteristics in psychosomatic patients. *Psychotherapy and Psychosomatics, 22,* 255–262.

Sifenos, P. E. (1974). A reconsideration of psychodynamic mechanisms in psychosomatic symptom formation in view of recent clinical observations. *Psychotherapy and Psychosomatics, 24,* 151–155.

Sigvardsson, S., von Knorring, A. L., Bohman, M., & Cloninger, C. R. (1984). An adoption study of somatoform disorders: I. The relationship of somaticization to psychiatric disability. *Archives of General Psychiatry, 41,* 853–859.

Silberstein, S. D. (1992). Advances in understanding the pathophysiology of headache. *Neurology, 42,* 6–10.

Silbert, D. (1992). *Object relations of sexually abused women.* Unpublished doctoral dissertation, University of Michigan, Ann Arbor.

Silverman, K., Evans, S. M., Strain, E. C., & Griffiths, R. R. (1992). Withdrawal syndrome after the double-blind cessation of caffeine consumption. *New England Journal of Medicine, 327,* 1109–1114.

Silverman, R. J., & Peterson, C. (1993). Explanatory style of schizophrenic and depressed outpatients. *Cognitive Therapy and Research, 17,* 457–470.

Silverstein, A. M. (1989). *A history of immunology.* San Diego, CA: Academic Press.

Silverstone, P. H. (1990). Depression increases mortality and morbidity in acute life-threatening medical illness. *Journal of Psychosomatic Research, 34,* 651–657.

Silverstone, T. (1992). Appetite suppressants: A review. *Drugs, 43,* 820–836.

Simon, G. E., & VonKorff, M. (1991). Somatization and psychiatric disorder in the NIMH Epidemiologic Catchment Area Study. *American Journal of Psychiatry, 148,* 1494–1500.

Simon, R. J., & Aaronson, D. E. (1988). *The insanity defense: A critical assessment of law and policy in the post-Hinckley era.* New York: Praeger.

Simpson, S. G., Folstein, S. E., Meyers, D. A., & DePaulo, J. R. (1992). Assessment of lineality in bipolar I linkage studies. *American Journal of Psychiatry, 149,* 1660–1665.

Simpson, W. S., & Ramberg, J. A. (1992). The influence of religion on sexuality: Implications for sex therapy. *Bulletin of the Menninger Clinic, 56,* 511–523.

Sims, A. C. (1988). Toward the unification of body image disorders. *British Journal of Psychiatry Supplement, 2,* 51–55.

Sirois, F. (1974). Epidemic hysteria. *Acta Psychiatrica Scandinavica (Supplementum), 252,* 1–46.

Skinner, B. F. (1956). A case history in scientific method. *American Psychologist, 11,* 221–233.

Skinner, B. F. (1986). What is wrong with daily life in the western world? *American Psychologist, 41,* 568–574.

Sklar, L. S., & Anisman, H. (1979). Stress and coping factors influence tumor growth. *Science, 205,* 513–515.

Sklar, L. S., & Anisman, H. (1981). Stress and cancer. *Psychological Bulletin, 89,* 369–406.

Skre, I., Onstad, S., Torgersen, S., & Kringlen, E. (1991). High interrater reliability for the Structured Clinical Interview for DSM-III-R Axis I (SCID-I). *Acta Psychiatrica Scandinavica, 84,* 167–173.

Slade, P. D., & Russell, G. F. M. (1973). Awareness of body dimensions in anorexia nervosa: Cross-sectional and longitudinal studies. *Psychological Medicine, 3,* 188–189.

Slater, E. (1943). The neurotic constitution: A statistical study of two thousand neurotic soldiers. *Journal of Neurology and Psychiatry, 6,* 1–16.

Slater, E., & Glithero, E. (1965). A follow-up of patients diagnosed as suffering from "hysteria." *Journal of Psychosomatic Research, 9,* 9–13.

Sloper, P., Cunningham, C., Turner, S., & Knussen, C. (1990). Factors related to the academic attainments of children with Down's syndrome. *British Journal of Educational Psychology, 60,* 284–298.

Smaldino, A. (Ed.). (1991). *Psychoanalytic approaches to addiction.* New York: Brunner/Mazel.

Small, G. W., & Nicholi, A. M. (1982). Mass hysteria among schoolchildren: Early loss as a predisposing factor. *Archives of General Psychiatry, 39,* 721–724.

Small, G. W., Propper, M. W., Randolph, E. T., & Eth, S. (1991). Mass hysteria among student performers: Social relationship as a symptom predicator. *American Journal of Psychiatry, 148,* 1200–1205.

Small, M. A., & Otto, R. K. (1991). Evaluations of competency to be executed: Legal contours and implications for assessment. *Criminal Justice and Behavior, 18,* 146–158.

Smalley, S. L. (1991). Genetic influences in autism. *Psychiatric Clinics in North America, 14,* 125–139.

Smart, R. G., & Adlaf, E. M. (1986). Patterns of drug use among adolescents: The past decade. *Social Science and Medicine, 23,* 717–719.

Smart, R. G., Mann, R. E., & Anglin, L. (1989). Decreases in alcohol problems and increased Alcoholics Anonymous membership. *British Journal of the Addictions, 84,* 507–513.

Smith, C. J., Sears, S. B., Walker, J. C., & DeLuca, P. O. (1992). Environmental tobacco smoke: Current assessment and future directions. *Toxicologic Pathology, 20,* 289–303.

Smith, M. L., & Glass, G. V. (1977). The meta-analysis of psychotherapy outcome studies. *American Psychologist, 32,* 752–760.

Smith, M. L., Glass, G. V., & Miller, T. I. (1980). *The benefits of psychotherapy.* Baltimore: Johns Hopkins University Press.

Smith, T. W. (1992). Hostility and health: Current status of a psychosomatic hypothesis. *Health Psychology, 11,* 139–150.

Smits, L. (1980). *Getting off: An anthropological analysis of heroin users.* Amsterdam: Anthropologisch-Sociologisch Centrum.

Smolowe, J. (1990, November 12). The 21 faces of Sarah. *Time,* 87.

Smolowe, J. (1993, July 26). Choose your poison. *Time,* 56–57.

Snyder, J. J. (1989). *Health psychology and behavioral medicine.* Englewood Cliffs, NJ: Prentice-Hall.

Snyder, S. H. (1974). *Madness and the brain.* New York: McGraw-Hill.

Snyder, S. H. (1981). Dopamine receptors, neuroleptics, and schizophrenia. *American Journal of Psychiatry, 138,* 460–464.

Snyderman, M., & Rothman, S. (1987). Survey of expert opinion in intelligence and aptitude testing. *American Psychologist, 42,* 137–144.

Sobell, M. B., & Sobell, L. C. (1973). Individualized behavior therapy for alcoholics. *Behavior Therapy, 4,* 49–72.

Sobell, M. B., & Sobell, L. C. (1976). Second-year treatment outcome of alcoholics treated by individualized behavior therapy: Results. *Behaviour Research and Therapy, 14,* 195–215.

Sobell, M. B., & Sobell, L. C. (1978). *Behavioral treatment of alcohol problems: Individualized therapy and controlled drinking.* New York: Plenum.

Sochurek, H. (1987). Medicine's new vision. *National Geographic, 171,* 2–41.

Sokol, L., Beck, A. T., Greenberg, R. L., Wright, F. D., & Berchick, R. J. (1989). Cognitive therapy of panic disorder: A nonpharmacological alternative. *Journal of Nervous and Mental Disease, 177,* 711–716.

Solkoff, N. (1992). Children of survivors of the Nazi Holocaust: A critical review of the literature. *American Journal of Orthopsychiatry, 62,* 342–358.

Solomon, S. D., Gerrity, E. T., & Muff, A. M. (1992). Efficacy of treatments for posttraumatic stress disorder: An empirical review. *JAMA, 268,* 633–638.

Solomon, Z., & Prager, E. (1992). Elderly Israeli Holocaust survivors during the Persian Gulf War: A study of psychological distress. *American Journal of Psychiatry, 149,* 1707–1710.

Somervell, P. D., Leaf, P. J., Weissman, M. M., Blazer, D. G., & Bruce, M. L. (1989). The prevalence of major depression in black and white adults in five United States communities. *American Journal of Epidemiology, 130,* 725–735.

Sonnerborg, A., Saaf, J., Alexius, B., Strannegard, O., Wahlud, L. O., & Wetterberg, L. (1990). Quantitative detection of brain aberrations in human immunodeficiency virus type-1 infected individuals by magnetic resonance imaging. *Journal of Infectious Diseases, 162,* 1245–1251.

Sontag, S. (1979). *Illness as metaphor.* New York: Vintage Books.

Sontag, S. (1988). *AIDS and its metaphors.* New York: Farrar, Straus, & Giroux.

Sookman, D., & Solyom, L. (1978). Severe depersonalization treated by behavior therapy. *American Journal of Psychiatry, 135,* 1543–1545.

Sournia, J.-C. (1990). *A history of alcoholism.* Oxford: Basil Blackwell.

Spanos, N. P. (1978). Witchcraft in histories of psychiatry: A critical analysis and an alternative conceptualization. *Psychological Bulletin, 85,* 417–439.

Spanos, N. P., Weekes, J. R., & Bertrand, L. D. (1985). Multiple personality: A social psychological perspective. *Journal of Abnormal Psychology, 94,* 362–376.

Spector, I. P., & Carey, M. P. (1990). Incidence and prevalence of the sexual dysfunctions: A critical review of the empirical literature. *Archives of Sexual Behavior, 19,* 389–408.

Spence, K. W. (1960). *Behavior theory and learning.* Englewood Cliffs, NJ: Prentice-Hall.

Sperry, R. W. (1969). A modified concept of consciousness. *Psychological Review, 76,* 532–536.

Sperry, R. W. (1976). Changing concepts of consciousness and free will. *Perspectives in Biology and Medicine, 20,* 9–19.

Sperry, R. W. (1987). Structure and significance of the consciousness revolution. *Journal of Mind and Behavior, 8,* 37–65.

Spiegel, D., Bloom, J. R., Kraemer, H. C., & Gottheil, E. (1989). Effect of psychosocial treatment on survival of patients with metastatic breast cancer. *Lancet, 109,* 888–891.

Spitz, H. H. (1991). "Beyond IQ in preschool programs?": Comment. *Intelligence, 15,* 327–333.

Spitz, H. H. (1993). Were children randomly assigned in the Perry Preschool Project? *American Psychologist, 48,* 915.

Spitz, H. I. (1988). Family and marital therapy in the treatment of depression. In F. Flach (Ed.), *Affective disorders.* New York: Norton.

Spitzer, L., & Rodin, J. (1981). Human eating behavior: A critical review of studies in normal weight and overweight individuals. *Appetite, 2,* 293–329.

Spitzer, R. L. (1975). On pseudoscience in science, logic in remission, and psychiatric diagnosis. *Journal of Abnormal Psychology, 84,* 442–452.

Spitzer, R. L., Endicott, J., & Gibbon, M. (1979). Crossing the border into borderline personality and borderline schizophrenia: The development of criteria. *Archives of General Psychiatry, 36,* 17–24.

Spitzer, R. L., Forman, J. B. W., & Nee, J. (1979). DSM-III field trials: I. Initial interrater diagnostic reliability. *American Journal of Psychiatry, 136,* 815–817.

Spitzer, R. L., & Williams, J. B. (1980). Classification of mental disorders and DSM-III. In H. I. Kaplan, A. M. Freedman, & B. J. Sadock (Eds.), *Comprehensive textbook of psychiatry* (Vol. 1, 3rd ed.). Baltimore: Williams & Wilkins.

Spohr, H. L., & Steinhausen, H. C. (1984). Clinical, psychopathological, and developmental aspects in children with the fetal alcohol syndrome: A four-year follow-up study. *CIBA Foundation Symposium, 105,* 197–217.

Spring, B. J., & Ravdin, L. (1992). Cognitive remediation in schizophrenia: Should we attempt it? *Schizophrenia Bulletin, 18,* 15–20.

Springer, S. P., & Deutsch, G. (1985). *Left brain, right brain* (Rev. ed.). New York: Freeman.

Sprock, J., Blashfield, R. K., & Smith, B. (1990). Gender weighting of DSM-III-R personality disorder criteria. *American Journal of Psychiatry, 147,* 586–590.

Sroufe, L. A., & Rutter, M. (1984). The domain of developmental psychopathology. *Child Development, 55,* 17–29.

Stambrook, M., Moore, A. D., Peters, L. C., Deviaene, C., & Hawryluk, G. A. (1990). Effects of mild, moderate, and severe closed head injury on long-term vocational status. *Brain Injury, 4,* 183–190.

Standage, K. (1989). Structured interviews and the diagnosis of personality disorders. *Canadian Journal of Psychiatry, 34,* 906–912.

Stanton, M. D. (1981). Strategic approaches to family therapy. In A. S. Gurman & D. P. Kniskern (Eds.), *Handbook of family therapy.* New York: Brunner/Mazel.

Starek, J. E., & Keating, C. F. (1991). Self-deception and its relationship to success in competition. *Basic and Applied Social Psychology, 12,* 145–155.

Starker, S. (1989). *Oracle at the supermarket: The American preoccupation with self-help books.* New Brunswick, NJ: Transaction Publishers.

Stavric, B. (1992). An update on research with coffee/caffeine (1989-1990). *Food and Chemical Toxicology, 30,* 533–555.

Steadman, H. J. (1980). Insanity acquittals in New York State, 1965-1978. *American Journal of Psychiatry, 137,* 321–326.

Steadman, H. J., Fabisiak, S., Dvoskin, J., & Holohean, E. J. (1987). A survey of mental disability among state prison inmates. *Hospital and Community Psychiatry, 38,* 1086–1090.

Steadman, H. J., & Keveles, C. (1972). The community adjustment and criminal activity of the Baxtrom patients: 1966-1970. *American Journal of Psychiatry, 129,* 304–310.

Steadman, H. J., Vanderwyst, D., & Ribner, S. (1978). Comparing arrest rates of mental patients and criminal offenders. *American Journal of Psychiatry, 135,* 1218–1220.

Steele, C. M., & Josephs, R. A. (1990). Alcohol myopia: Its prized and dangerous effects. *American Psychologist, 45,* 921–933.

Steele, C. M., & Southwick, L. (1985). Alcohol and social behavior I: The psychology of drunken excess. *Journal of Personality and Social Psychology, 48,* 18–34.

Steenland, K. (1992). Passive smoking and the risk of heart disease. *JAMA, 267,* 94–99.

Stefanis, C., Markidis, M., & Christodoulou, G. (1976). Observations on the evolution of the hysterical symptomatology. *British Journal of Psychiatry, 128,* 269–275.

Stein, D. M., & Lambert, M. J. (1984). Telephone counseling and crisis intervention: A review. *American Journal of Community Psychology, 12,* 101–126.

Stein, G. (1992). Drug treatment of the personality disorders. *British Journal of Psychiatry, 161,* 167–184.

Steinberg, H., & Durell, J. (1968). A stressful situation as a precipitant of schizophrenic symptoms. *British Journal of Psychiatry, 114,* 1097–1105.

Steiner, M. (1992). Female-specific mood disorders. *Clinical Obstetrics and Gynecology, 35,* 599–611.

Steinglass, P. (1981). The alcoholic family at home: Patterns of interaction in wet, dry, and transitional phases of alcoholism. *Archives of General Psychiatry, 38,* 337–354.

Steinglass, P. (1985). Family systems approaches to alcoholism. *Journal of Substance Abuse Treatment, 2,* 161–167.

Steinglass, P. (1987). Psychoeducational family therapy for schizophrenia: A review essay. *Psychiatry, 50,* 14–23.

Steketee, G., Foa, E. B., & Grayson, J. B. (1982). Recent advances in the behavioral treatment of obsessive-compulsives. *Archives of General Psychiatry, 39,* 1365–1371.

Stephens, J. H. (1978). Long-term prognosis and follow up in schizophrenia. *Schizophrenia Bulletin, 4,* 25–47.

Stephens, P. (1990). A review of clozapine: An antipsychotic for treatment-resistant schizophrenia. *Comprehensive Psychiatry, 31,* 315–326.

Stern, R., & Fernandez, M. (1991). Group cognitive and behavioural treatment for hypochondriasis. *BMJ, 303,* 1229–1231.

Stern, R. S. (1978). Obsessive thoughts: The problem of therapy. *British Journal of Psychiatry, 133,* 200–205.

Stern, W. (1914). *The psychological methods of testing intelligence.* Baltimore: Warwick & York.

Stern, Y., Marder, K., Tang, M. X., & Mayeux, R. (1993). Antecedent clinical features associated with dementia in Parkinson's disease. *Neurology, 43,* 1690–1692.

Sternbach, G. L., & Varon, J. (1992). "Designer drugs": Recognizing and managing their toxic effects. *Postgraduate Medicine, 91,* 169–171, 175–176.

Sternberg, R. J., & Salter, W. (1982). Conceptions of intelligence. In R. J. Sternberg (Ed.), *Handbook of human intelligence.* Cambridge: Cambridge University Press.

Stevenson, J. (1992). Evidence for a genetic etiology in hyperactivity in children. *Behavior Genetics, 22,* 337–344.

Stevenson, J., Batten, N., & Cherner, M. (1992). Fears and fearfulness in children and adolescents: A genetic analysis of twin data. *Journal of Child Psychology and Psychiatry and Allied Disciplines, 33,* 977–985.

Stoll, A. L., Tohen, M., Baldessarini, R. J., Goodwin, D. C., Stein, S., Katz, S., Geenens, D., Swinson, R. P., Goethe, J. W., & McGlashan, T. (1993). Shifts in diagnostic frequencies of schizophrenia and major affective disorders at six North American psychiatric hospitals, 1972–1988. *American Journal of Psychiatry, 150,* 1668–1673.

Stoller, R. J. (1985). *Observing the erotic imagination.* New Haven, CT: Yale University Press.

Stoller, R. J., & Herdt, G. H. (1985). Theories of origins of male homosexuality: A cross-cultural look. *Archives of General Psychiatry, 42,* 399–404.

Stone, A. A. (1976). The Tarasoff decisions: Suing psychotherapists to safeguard society. *Harvard Law Review, 90,* 358–378.

Stone, M. H. (1983). Psychotherapy with schizotypal borderline patients. *Journal of the American Academy of Psychoanalysis, 11,* 87–111.

Stone, M. H. (1986). Borderline personality disorder. In A. M. Cooper, A. J. Frances, & M. H. Sacks (Eds.), *The personality disorders and neuroses.* New York: Basic Books.

Storms, M. D. (1981). A theory of erotic orientation development. *Psychological Review, 88,* 340–353.

Strauss, J., & Ryan, R. M. (1987). Autonomy disturbance in subtypes of anorexia nervosa. *Journal of Abnormal Psychology, 96,* 254–258.

Stravynski, A., & Greenberg, D. (1992). The psychological management of depression. *Acta Psychiatrica Scandinavica, 85,* 407–414.

Stravynski, A., Lesage, A., Marcouiller, M., & Elie, R. (1989). A test of the therapeutic mechanism in social skills training with avoidant personality disorder. *Journal of Nervous and Mental Disease, 177,* 739–744.

Stravynski, A., & Shahar, A. (1983). The treatment of social dysfunction in nonpsychotic outpatients: A review. *Journal of Nervous and Mental Disease, 171,* 721–728.

Stroebe, W., & Stroebe, M. S. (1987). *Bereavement and health: The psychological and physical consequences of partner loss.* Cambridge: Cambridge University Press.

Struewing, J. P., & Gray, G. C. (1990). An epidemic of respiratory complaints exacerbated by mass psychogenic illness in a military recruit hospital. *American Journal of Epidemiology, 132,* 1120–1129.

Strupp, H. H., & Hadley, S. W. (1979). Specific vs. nonspecific factors in psychotherapy. *Archives of General Psychiatry, 36,* 1125–1136.

Strupp, H. H., Hadley, S. W., & Gomes-Schwartz, B. (1977). *Psychotherapy for better or worse: An analysis of the problem of negative effects.* New York: Jason Aronson.

Stubbs, E. G., Budden, S. S., Jackson, R. H., Terdal, L. G., & Ritvo, E. R. (1986). Effects of fenfluramine on eight outpatients with the syndrome of autism. *Developmental Medicine and Child Neurology, 28,* 229–235.

Stunkard, A. J., Sorensen, T. I., Hanis, C., Teasdale, T. W., Chakraborty, R., Schull, W. J., & Schulsinger, F. (1986). An adoption study of human obesity. *New England Journal of Medicine, 314,* 193–198.

Stuss, D. T., Alexander, M. P., Lieberman, A., & Levine, H. (1978). An extraordinary form of confabulation. *Neurology, 28,* 1166–1172.

Suarez, Y., Crowe, M. J., & Adams, H. E. (1978). Depression: Avoidance learning and physiological correlates in clinical and analog populations. *Behaviour Research and Therapy, 16,* 21–31.

Sue, D. W., & Sue, D. (1990). *Counseling the culturally different* (2nd ed.). New York: Wiley.

Sue, S., Fujino, D. C., Hu, L., Takeuchi, D. T., & Zane, N. W. S. (1991). Community mental health services for ethnic minority groups: A test of the cultural responsiveness hypothesis. *Journal of Consulting and Clinical Psychology, 59,* 533–540.

Sue, S., & Zane, N. (1987). The role of culture and cultural techniques in psychotherapy: A critique and reformulation. *American Psychologist, 42,* 37–45.

Sullivan, H. S. (1947). *Conceptions of modern psychiatry.* Washington, DC: William Alanson White Psychiatric Foundation.

Sulloway, F. J. (1979). *Freud, biologist of the mind.* New York: Basic Books.

Sulzbacher, S., Wong, B., McKeen, J., Glock, J., & MacDonald, B. (1981). Long term therapeutic effects of a three month intensive growth group. *Journal of Clinical Psychiatry, 42,* 148–153.

Sundberg, N. D., Taplin, J. R., & Tyler, L. E. (1983). *Introduction to clinical psychology.* Englewood Cliffs, NJ: Prentice-Hall.

Surrey, J. L. (1990). Mother-blaming and clinical theory. *Women and Therapy, 10,* 83–87.

Susser, E., Struening, E. L., & Conover, S. (1989). Psychiatric problems in homeless men: Lifetime psychosis, substance use, and current distress in new arrivals at New York City shelters. *Archives of General Psychiatry, 46,* 845–850.

Susser, M. (1967). Causes of peptic ulcer: A selective epidemiological review. *Journal of Chronic Disabilities, 20,* 435–456.

Sutker, P. B., Winstead, D. K., Galina, Z. H., & Allain, A. N. (1990). Assessment of long-term psychosocial sequelae among POW survivors of the Korean conflict. *Journal of Personality Assessment, 54,* 170–180.

Sutton, S. (1990, March 12). A fight to master more than Augusta. *Sporting News,* p. 45.

Suwaki, H., Yamasaki, M., Horii, S., Watanebe, T., Kazunaga, H., & Fujimoto, A. (1992). A study of longitudinal patterns of substance abuse with special reference to multiple use problems. *Japanese Journal of Alcohol Studies, 27,* 284–296.

Swann, A. C., Secunda, S. K., Stokes, P. E., Croughan, J., Davis, J. M., Koslow, S. H., & Maas, J. W. (1990). Stress, depression, and mania: Relationship between perceived role of stressful events and clinical and biochemical characteristics. *Acta Psychiatrica Scandinavica, 81,* 389–397.

Swartz, M., Blazer, D. G., George, L. K., & Landerman, R. (1986). Somatization disorder in a community population. *American Journal of Psychiatry, 143,* 1403–1408.

Swartz, M., Landerman, R., Blazer, D. G., & George, L. K. (1989). Somatization symptoms in the community: A rural/urban comparison. *Psychosomatics, 30,* 44–53.

Swift, E. M. (1982, December 27). Greatness confirmed. *Sports Illustrated,* 40–48.

Swindle, R. W., Cronkite, R. C., & Moos, R. H. (1989). Life stressors, social resources, coping, and the 4-year course of unipolar depression. *Journal of Abnormal Psychology, 98,* 468–477.

Szasz, T. S. (1961). *The myth of mental illness.* New York: Hoeber.

Szasz, T. S. (1963). *Law, liberty, and psychiatry: An inquiry into the social uses of mental health practices.* New York: Macmillan.

Tallal, P., Townsend, J., Curtiss, S., & Wulfeck, B. (1991). Phenotypic profiles of language-impaired children based on genetic/family history. *Brain and Language, 41,* 81–95.

Talley, J. H. (1990). But what if a patient gets hooked? Fallacies about long-term use of benzodiazepines. *Postgraduate Medicine, 87,* 187–203.

Tallman, J. F., & Gallager, D. W. (1985). The GABAergic system: A locus of benzodiazepine action. *Annual Review of Neuroscience, 8,* 21–44.

Tan, E. K., & Carr, J. E. (1977). Psychiatric sequelae of Amok. *Culture, Medicine, and Psychiatry, 1,* 59–67.

Tan, S. Y., & Bruni, J. (1986). Cognitive-behavioral therapy with adult patients with epilepsy: A controlled outcome study. *Epilepsia, 27,* 225–233.

Tarrier, N. (1991). Behavioural psychotherapy and schizophrenia: The past, the present, and the future. *Behavioural Psychotherapy, 19,* 121–130.

Tarrier, N., & Barrowclough, C. (1990). Family interventions for schizophrenia. *Behavior Modification, 14,* 408–440.

Tashkin, D. P. (1990). Pulmonary complications of smoked substance abuse. *Western Medical Journal, 152,* 525–530.

Task Force on DSM-IV. (1991). *DSM-IV options book: Work in progress.* Washington, DC: American Psychiatric Association.

Tateyama, M., Asai, M., Kamisada, M., Hashimoto, M., Bartels, M., & Heimann, H. (1993). Comparison of schizophrenic delusions between Japan and Germany. *Psychopathology, 26,* 151–158.

Taylor, D. P. (1990). Serotonin agents in anxiety. *Annals of the New York Academy of Sciences, 600,* 545–556.

Taylor, D. P., & Moon, S. L. (1991). Buspirone and related compounds as alternative anxiolytics. *Neuropeptides, 19,* 15–19.

Taylor, G. J., Parker, J. D., Bagby, R. M., & Acklin, M. W. (1992). Alexithymia and somatic complaints in psychiatric out-patients. *Journal of Psychosomatic Research, 36,* 417–424.

Taylor, R. B., Denham, J. R., & Ureda, J. W. (1982). *Health promotion: Principles and clinical applications.* Norwalk, CT: Appleton-Century-Crofts.

Taylor, S. E. (1981). The interface of cognitive and social psychology. In J. Harvey (Ed.), *Cognition, social behavior, and the environment.* Hillsdale, NJ: Erlbaum.

Taylor, S. E. (1989). *Positive illusions.* New York: Basic Books.

Teicher, M. H., Glod, C., & Cole, J. O. (1990). Emergence of intense suicidal preoccupation during fluoxetine treatment. *American Journal of Psychiatry, 147,* 207–210.

Temerlin, M. K. (1968). Suggestion effects in psychiatric diagnosis. *Journal of Nervous and Mental Disease, 147,* 349–353.

Templeman, T. L., & Stinnett, R. D. (1991). Patterns of sexual arousal and history in a "normal" sample of young men. *Archives of Sexual Behavior, 20,* 137–150.

Tennov, D. (1973). Feminism, psychotherapy, and professionalism. *Journal of Contemporary Psychotherapy, 5,* 107–111.

Terman, L. M. (1916). *The measurement of intelligence.* Boston: Houghton Mifflin.

Terrenoire, G. (1992). Huntington's disease and the ethics of genetic prediction. *Journal of Medical Ethics, 18,* 79–85.

Tettenborn, B., & Kramer, G. (1992). Total patient care in epilepsy. *Epilepsia, 33,* 28–32.

Thara, R., & Rajkumar, S. (1992). Gender differences in schizophrenia: Results of a follow-up study from India. *Schizophrenia Research, 7,* 65–70.

Thase, M. E. (1982). Longevity and mortality in Down's syndrome. *Journal of Mental Deficiency Research, 26,* 177–192.

Thigpen, C. H., & Cleckley, H. (1954). A case of multiple personality. *Journal of Abnormal and Social Psychology, 49,* 135–151.

Thigpen, C. H., & Cleckley, H. (1957). *The three faces of Eve.* New York: McGraw-Hill.

Thoits, P. A. (1983). Dimensions of life events that influence psychological distress: An evaluation and synthesis of the literature. In H. Kaplan (Ed.), *Psychological stress: Trends in theory and research.* New York: Academic Press.

Thomas, A., & Chess, S. (1977). *Temperament and development.* New York: Brunner/Mazel.

Thomas, C. S. (1984). Dysmorphophobia: A question of definition. *British Journal of Psychiatry, 144,* 513–516.

Thomas, E. L., & Robinson, H. A. (1972). *Improving reading in every class: A sourcebook for teachers.* Boston: Allyn & Bacon.

Thompson, A. H., Bland, R. C., & Orn, H. T. (1989). Relationship and chronology of depression, agoraphobia, and panic disorder in the general population. *Journal of Nervous and Mental Disease, 177,* 456–463.

Thoreson, C. E., & Powell, L. H. (1992). Type A behavior pattern: New perspectives on theory, assessment, and intervention. *Journal of Consulting and Clinical Psychology, 60,* 595–604.

Thorndike, E. L. (1935). *The psychology of wants, interests, and attitudes.* London: Appleton-Century.

Thorndike, R. L., Hagan, E., & Sattler, J. (1986). *Stanford-Binet* (4th ed.). Chicago: Riverside.

Tichenor, V., & Hill, C. E. (1989). A comparison of six measures of working alliance. *Psychotherapy, 26,* 195–199.

Tiefer, L., Pedersen, B., & Melman, A. (1988). Psychosocial follow-up on penile prosthesis implant patients and partners. *Journal of Sex and Marital Therapy, 14,* 184–201.

Tien, A. Y., & Eaton, W. W. (1992). Psychopathologic precursors and sociodemographic risk factors for the schizophrenia syndrome. *Archives of General Psychiatry, 49,* 37–46.

Tiger, L. (1979). *Optimism: The biology of hope.* New York: Simon & Schuster.

Tillitski, C. J. (1990). A meta-analysis of estimated effect sizes for group versus individual control treatments. *International Journal of Group Psychotherapy, 40,* 215–224.

Time-Life Books. (1992). *Odd and eccentric people.* Alexandria, VA: Author.

Tintera, J. W., & Lovell, H. W. (1949). Endocrine treatment of alcoholism. *Geriatrics, 4,* 274–280.

Tiret, L., Hausherr, E., Thicoipe, M., Garros, B., Maurette, P., Castel, J. P., & Hatton, F. (1990). The epidemiology of head trauma in Aquitaine (France), 1986: A community-based study of hospital admissions and deaths. *International Journal of Epidemiology, 19,* 133–140.

Tissot, S. A. (1832). *A treatise on the diseases produced by onanism.* New York.

Tobler, N. (1986). Meta-analysis of 143 adolescent drug prevention programs: Quantitative outcome results of program participants compared to a control or comparison group. *Journal of Drug Issues, 16,* 537–568.

Tollefson, G. D. (1991). Antidepressant treatment and side effect considerations. *Journal of Clinical Psychiatry, 52,* 4–13.

Tomasson, K., Kent, D., & Coryell, W. (1991). Somatization and conversion disorders: Comorbidity and demographics at presentation. *Acta Psychiatrica Scandinavica, 84,* 288–293.

Tomkins, S. S. (1947). *The Thematic Apperception Test: The theory and technique of interpretation.* New York: Grune & Stratton.

Toneatto, A., Sobell, L. C., & Sobell, M. B. (1992). Gender issues in the treatment of abusers of alcohol, nicotine, and other drugs. *Journal of Substance Abuse, 4,* 209–218.

Toner, B. B., Garfinkel, P. E., & Garner, D. M. (1986). Long-term follow-up of anorexia nervosa. *Psychosomatic Medicine, 48,* 520–529.

Torch, E. M. (1987). The psychotherapeutic treatment of depersonalization disorder. *Hillside Journal of Clinical Psychiatry, 9,* 133–151.

Torgersen, S. (1983). Genetic factors in anxiety disorders. *Archives of General Psychiatry, 40,* 1085–1089.

Torgersen, S., Onstad, S., Skre, I., Edvardsen, J., & Kringlen, E. (1993). "True" schizotypal personality disorder: A study of co-twins and relatives of schizophrenic probands. *American Journal of Psychiatry, 150,* 1661–1667.

Torrey, E. F. (1986). *Witchdoctors and psychiatrists: The common roots of psychotherapy and its future.* Northvale, NJ: Aronson.

Torrey, E. F. (1987). Prevalence studies in schizophrenia. *British Journal of Psychiatry, 150,* 598–608.

Torrey, E. F. (1988a). Stalking the schizovirus. *Schizophrenia Bulletin, 14,* 223–229.

Torrey, E. F. (1988b). *Surviving schizophrenia: A family manual.* New York: Harper & Row.

Torrey, E. F. (1991). A viral-anatomical explanation of schizophrenia. *Schizophrenia Bulletin, 17,* 15–18.

Torrey, E. F., & Bowler, A. (1990). Geographical distribution of insanity in America: Evidence for an urban factor. *Schizophrenia Bulletin, 16,* 591–604.

Torrey, E. F., Torrey, B. B., & Peterson, M. R. (1977). Seasonality of schizophrenic births in the United States. *Archives of General Psychiatry, 34,* 1065–1070.

Toufexis, A. (1989, July 31). A fatal obsession with the stars. *Time,* 43–44.

Toufexis, A. (1990, July 30). Warnings about a miracle drug. *Time,* 54.

Toufexis, A. (1991, May 13). Innocent victims. *Time,* 56–60.

Toufexis, A. (1992, February 3). Do mad acts a madman make? *Time,* 17.

Traub-Werner, D. (1986). The place and value of bestiality in perversions. *Journal of the American Psychoanalytic Association, 34,* 975–992.

Treadway, D. C. (1985). Learning their dance: Changing some steps. In A. S. Gurman (Ed.), *Casebook of marital therapy.* New York: Guilford.

Treffert, D. A. (1989). *Extraordinary people: Understanding "idiot savants."* New York: Harper & Row.

Triandis, H. C., & Draguns, J. G. (Eds.). (1980). *Handbook of cross-cultural psychology: Psychopathology* (Vol. 6). Boston: Allyn & Bacon.

Trojan, O. (1991). Ethical and legal aspects of imposed sexological treatment. *Medicine and Law, 10,* 493–500.

Trull, T. J. (1992). DSM-III-R personality disorders and the five-factor model of personality: An empirical comparison. *Journal of Abnormal Psychology, 101,* 553–560.

Tseng, W. S., Asai, M., Liu, L. Q., Wibulswasdi, P., Suryani, L. K., Wen, J. K., Brennan, J., & Heiby, E. (1990). Multi-cultural study of minor psychiatric disorders in Asia: Symptom manifestations. *International Journal of Social Psychiatry, 36,* 252–264.

Tseng, W. S., Mo, K. M., Hsu, J., Li, L. S., Ou, L. W., Chen, G. Q., & Jiang, D. W. (1988). A sociocultural study of koro epidemics in Guangdong, China. *American Journal of Psychiatry, 145,* 1538–1543.

Tseng, W. S., Mo, K. M., Li, L. S., Chen, G. Q., Ou, L. W., & Zheng, H. B. (1992). Koro epidemics in Guangdong, China: A questionnaire study. *Journal of Nervous and Mental Disease, 180,* 117–123.

Tsoi, W. F. (1990). Developmental profile of 200 male and 100 female transsexuals in Singapore. *Archives of Sexual Behavior, 19,* 595–605.

Tsoi, W. F. (1992). Male and female transsexuals: A comparison. *Singapore Medical Journal, 33,* 182–185.

Tsuang, M. T. (1991). Morbidity risks of schizophrenia and affective disorders among first-degree relatives of patients with schizoaffective disorders. *British Journal of Psychiatry, 158,* 165–170.

Tucker, J. S., & Whalen, R. E. (1991). Premenstrual syndrome. *International Journal of Psychiatry in Medicine, 21,* 311–341.

Tuomisto, J., & Mannisto, P. (1985). Neurotransmitter regulation of anterior pituitary hormones. *Pharmacological Reviews, 37,* 249–332.

Turkat, I. D., & Carlson, C. R. (1984). Data-based versus symptomatic formulation of treatment: The case of a dependent personality. *Journal of Behavior Therapy and Experimental Psychiatry, 15,* 153–160.

Turner, E. L. B. (1992). *Experiencing ritual: A new interpretation of African healing.* Philadelphia: University of Pennsylvania Press.

Turner, J. A., & Chapman, C. R. (1982). Psychological interventions for chronic pain: A critical review. I. Relaxation training and biofeedback. *Pain, 12,* 1–21.

Twain, M. (1885/1961). *The adventures of Huckleberry Finn.* New York: Harcourt, Brace, & World.

Tyrer, P. (1988). What's wrong with DSM-III personality disorders? *Journal of Personality Disorders, 2,* 281–291.

Tyrer, P. (1989). *Classification of neuroses.* Chichester, England: Wiley.

Tyrer, P., & Ferguson, B. (1988). Development of the concept of abnormal personality. In P. Tyrer (Ed.), *Personality disorders: Diagnosis, management, and course.* London: Wright.

Tyson, G. M., & Range, L. M. (1987). Gestalt dialogues as a treatment for mild depression: Time works just as well. *Journal of Clinical Psychology, 43,* 227–231.

Uffing, H. T., Ceha, M. M., & Saenger, G. H. (1992). The development of deinstitutionalization in Europe. *Psychiatric Quarterly, 63,* 265–278.

United States Congress. (1946). The National Mental Health Act, P.L. 79-487. Washington, DC: U.S. Government Printing Office.

United States Congress. (1963). Mental Retardation Facilities and Community Mental Health Centers Construction Act of 1963, P.L. 88-164. Washington, DC: U.S. Government Printing Office.

United States Congress. (1965). Mental Retardation Facilities and Community Mental Health Centers Construction Act of 1965, P.L. 89-105. Washington, DC: U.S. Government Printing Office.

United States Department of Commerce. (1976). *Historical statistics of the United States: Colonial times to 1970.* Washington, DC: Author.

United States Department of Commerce. (1993). *Statistical abstract of the United States* (113th ed.). Washington, DC: Author.

United States Department of Health and Human Services. (1992). *Health United States 1991.* Hyattsville, MD: Author.

Urban, H. B. (1983). Phenomenological-humanistic approaches. In M. Hersen, A. E. Kazdin, & A. S. Bellack (Eds.), *The clinical psychology handbook.* New York: Pergamon.

Ussher, J. M. (1992). Research and theory related to female reproduction: Implications for clinical psychology. *British Journal of Clinical Psychology, 31,* 129–151.

Vachon, L., & Rich, E. S. (1976). Visceral learning in asthma. *Psychosomatic Medicine, 38,* 122–130.

Vaillant, G. E. (1977). *Adaptation to life.* Boston: Little, Brown.

Vaillant, G. E. (1978). Natural history of male psychological health: IV. What kinds of men do not get psychosomatic illness? *Psychosomatic Medicine, 40,* 420–431.

Vaillant, G. E. (1983). *The natural history of alcoholism.* Cambridge: Harvard University Press.

Vaillant, G. E. (1984). The disadvantages of DSM-III outweigh its advantages. *American Journal of Psychiatry, 141,* 542–545.

Valenstein, E. S. (1986). *Great and desperate cures.* New York: Basic Books.

Vance, E. B., & Wagner, N. N. (1976). Written descriptions of orgasms: A study of sex differences. *Archives of Sexual Behavior, 5,* 87–98.

van der Kolk, B. A., & van der Hart, O. (1989). Pierre Janet and the breakdown of adaptation in psychological trauma. *American Journal of Psychiatry, 146,* 1530–1540.

Van Horn, J. D., & McManus, I. C. (1992). Ventricular enlargement in schizophrenia: A meta-analysis of studies of the ventricle:brain ratio (VBR). *British Journal of Psychiatry, 160,* 687–697.

van Straten, N. H. (1983). *Concepts of health, disease, and vitality in traditional Chinese society: A psychological interpretation.* Wiesbaden: Steiner.

van Thillo, E. L., & Delaere, K. P. (1992). The vacuum erection device: A noninvasive treatment for impotence. *Acta Urologica Belgica, 60,* 9–13.

Varley, C. K., & Holm, V. A. (1990). A two-year follow-up of autistic children treated with fenfluramine. *Journal of the American Academy of Child and Adolescent Psychiatry, 29,* 137–140.

Vasile, R. G., Samson, J. A., Bemporad, J., Bloomingdale, K. L., Creasey, D., Fenton, B. T., Gudeman, J. E., & Schildkraut, J. J. (1987). A biopsychosocial approach to treating patients with affective disorders. *American Journal of Psychiatry, 144,* 341–344.

Vaughan, K., Doyle, M., McGonaghy, N., Blaszczynski, A., Fox, A., & Tarrier, N. (1992). The relationship between relative's expressed emotion and shizophrenic relapse: An Australian replication. *Social Psychiatry and Psychiatric Epidemiology, 27,* 10–15.

Vaughn, C., & Leff, J. P. (1976). The influence of family and social factors on the course of psychiatric illness. *British Journal of Psychiatry, 129,* 125–137.

Velasco-Suarez, M., Bautista Martinez, J., Garcia Oliveros, R., & Weinstein, P. R. (1992). Archaeological origins of cranial surgery: Trephination in Mexico. *Neurosurgery, 31,* 313–318.

Verbrugge, L. M. (1980). Sex differences in complaints and diagnoses. *Journal of Behavioral Medicine, 3,* 327–355.

Verbrugge, L. M. (1989). Recent, present, and future health of American adults. *Annual Review of Public Health, 10,* 333–361.

Verma, R. S., & Huq, A. (1987). Sex ratio of children with trisomy 21 or Down syndrome. *Cytobios, 51,* 145–148.

Visintainer, M., Volpicelli, J. R., & Seligman, M. E. P. (1982). Tumor rejection in rats after inescapable or escapable shock. *Science, 216,* 437–439.

Visser, S., & Bouman, T. K. (1992). Cognitive-behavioural approaches in the treatment of hypochondriasis: Six single case cross-over studies. *Behaviour Research and Therapy, 30,* 301–306.

Vitiello, B., & Behar, D. (1992). Mental retardation and psychiatric illness. *Hospital and Community Psychiatry, 43,* 494–499.

Vitiello, B., Spreat, S., & Behar, D. (1989). Obsessive-compulsive disorder in mentally retarded patients. *Journal of Nervous and Mental Disease, 177,* 232–236.

Vochteloo, J. D., Timmermans, P. J., Duijghuisen, J. A., & Vossen, J. M. (1991). Responses to novelty in phobic and non-phobic cynomolgus monkeys: The role of subject characteristics and object features. *Behaviour Research and Therapy, 29,* 531–538.

Vollhardt, L. T. (1991). Psychoneuroimmunology: A literature review. *American Journal of Orthopsychiatry, 61,* 35–47.

Vollmer, T. R., & Iwata, B. A. (1992). Differential reinforcement as treatment for behavior disorders: Procedural and functional variations. *Research in Developmental Disabilities, 13,* 393–417.

von Knorring, A. L., Cloninger, C. R., Bohman, M., & Sigvardsson, S. (1983). An adoption study of depressive disorders and substance abuse. *Archives of General Psychiatry, 40,* 943–950.

Vore, D. A. (1989). Psychological consultation for systematic jury selection. *American Journal of Forensic Psychology, 7,* 21–36.

Wachtel, P. (1977). *Psychoanalysis and behavior therapy: Toward an integration.* New York: Basic Books.

Wagner, P. S. (1946). Psychiatric activities during the Normandy offensive June 20–August 20, 1944. *Psychiatry, 9,* 341–364.

Wahl, O. F., & Hunter, J. (1992). Are gender effects being neglected in schizophrenia research? *Schizophrenia Bulletin, 18,* 313–318.

Walker, A. (1993). *Warrior marks: Female genital mutilation and the sexual blinding of women.* New York: Harcourt Brace.

Walker, E. A., Katon, W. J., Jemelka, R. P., & Roy-Byrne, P. P. (1992). Comorbidity of gastrointestinal complaints, depression, and anxiety in the Epidemiological Catchment Area (ECA) Study. *American Journal of Medicine, 92,* 26–30.

Walling, W. H. (Ed.). (1904). *Sexology.* Philadelphia: Puritan.

Wallis, C., & Willwerth, J. (1992, July 6). Schizophrenia: A new drug brings patients back to life. *Time,* 52–57.

Walsh, B. T. (1991). Psychopharmacologic treatment of bulimia nervosa. *Journal of Clinical Psychiatry, 52,* 34–38.

Walsh, B. T., Hadigan, C. M., Devlin, M. J., Gladis, M., & Roose, S. P. (1991). Long-term outcome of antidepressant treatment for bulimia nervosa. *American Journal of Psychiatry, 148,* 1206–1212.

Wang, K. K. (1991). The role of *Helicobacter pylori* in gastroduodenal disease. *Comprehensive Therapy, 17,* 35–38.

Wang, Z. W., Crowe, R. R., & Noyes, R. (1992). Adrenergic receptor genes as candidate genes for panic disorder: A linkage study. *American Journal of Psychiatry, 149,* 470–474.

Ward, C. H., Beck, A. T., Mendelson, M., Mock, J. E., & Erbaugh, J. K. (1962). The psychiatric nomenclature. *Archives of General Psychiatry, 7,* 198–205.

Warner, R. (1978). The diagnosis of antisocial and hysterical personality disorders: An example of sex bias. *Journal of Nervous and Mental Disease, 166,* 839–845.

Warwick, H. M., & Salkovskis, P. M. (1990). Hypochondriasis. *Behaviour Research and Therapy, 28,* 105–117.

Warzecha, G. (1991). The challenge to psychological assessment from modern computer technology. *European Review of Applied Psychology, 41,* 213–220.

Wasylenki, D. A. (1992). Psychotherapy of schizophrenia revisited. *Hospital and Community Psychiatry, 43,* 123–127.

Watson, J. B. (1913). Psychology as the behaviorist views it. *Psychological Review, 20,* 158–177.

Watson, J. B. (1930). *Behaviorism* (Rev. ed.). New York: Norton.

Watson, J. B., & Rayner, R. (1920). Conditioned emotional reactions. *Journal of Experimental Psychology, 3,* 1–14.

Watson, J. M. (1986). *Solvent abuse: The adolescent epidemic?* London: Croom Helm.

Wechsler, D. (1939). *The measurement of adult intelligence.* Baltimore: Williams & Wilkins.

Wechsler, D. (1981). *Manual for the Wechsler Adult Intelligence Scale—Revised.* New York: Psychological Corporation.

Weeks, D. J. (1988). *Eccentrics: The scientific investigation.* London: Stirling University Press.

Wegner, D. M. (1989). *White bears and other unwanted thoughts.* New York: Penguin.

Weil, A. (1972). *The natural mind: A new way of looking at drugs and the higher consciousness.* Boston: Houghton Mifflin.

Weil, A. (1988). *Health and healing* (Rev. ed.). Boston: Houghton Mifflin.

Weinberg, W. A., & Brumback, R. A. (1976). Mania in childhood: Case studies and literature review. *American Journal of Diseases of Children, 130,* 380–385.

Weinberger, M., Hiner, S. L., & Tierney, W. M. (1987). In support of hassles as a measure of stress in predicting health outcomes. *Journal of Behavioral Medicine, 10,* 19–31.

Weiner, B. A. (1981). Decade of litigation has led to redefinition of patients' rights. *Hospitals, 55,* 67–70.

Weiner, B. A. (1985). Mental disability and the criminal law. In S. J. Brakel, J. Parry, & B. A. Weiner (Eds.), *The mentally disabled and the law.* Chicago: American Bar Foundation.

Weiner, H. (1977). *Psychobiology and human disease.* New York: Elsevier.

Weinrich, J. D. (1987). *Sexual landscapes: Why we are what we are, why we love whom we love.* New York: Charles Scribner's Sons.

Weintraub, M. I. (1983). *Hysterical conversion reactions.* New York: Spectrum.

Weisberg, L., Strub, R. L., & Garcia, C. A. (1989). *Essentials of clinical neurology* (2nd ed.). Rockville, MD: Aspen.

Weiss, G. (1985). Hyperactivity: Overview and new directions. *Psychiatric Clinics of North America, 8,* 737–753.

Weiss, J. M. (1970). Somatic effects of predictable and unpredictable shock. *Psychosomatic Medicine, 32,* 397–409.

Weiss, J. M. (1971). Effects of coping behavior in different warning signaled conditions on stress pathology in rats. *Journal of Comparative and Physiological Psychology, 77,* 1–13.

Weiss, J. M., & Simson, P. E. (1988). Neurochemical and electrophysiological events underlying stress-induced depression in an animal model. *Advances in Experimental Medicine and Biology, 245,* 425–440.

Weiss, R. D., & Mirin, S. M. (1990). Psychological and pharmacological treatment strategies in cocaine dependence. *Annals of Clinical Psychiatry, 2,* 239–243.

Weissman, M. M. (1984). The psychological treatment of depression: An update of clinical trials. In J. B. Williams & R. L. Spitzer (Eds.), *Psychotherapy research: Where are we and where should we go?* New York: Guilford.

Weissman, M. M. (1985). The epidemiology of anxiety disorders: Rates, risks, and familial patterns. In H. Tuma & J. Maser (Eds.), *Anxiety and anxiety disorders.* Hillsdale, NJ: Erlbaum.

Weissman, M. M. (1988). The epidemiology of anxiety disorders: Rates, risks, and familial patterns. *Journal of Psychiatric Research, 22,* 99–114.

Weissman, M. M., Bland, R., Joyce, R. R., Newman, S., Wells, J. E., & Wittchen, H. U. (1993). Sex differences in rates of depression: Cross-national perspectives. *Journal of Affective Disorders, 29,* 77–84.

Weissman, M. M., Leaf, P. J., Holzer, C. E., & Merikangas, K. R. (1985). The epidemiology of anxiety disorders. *Psychopharmacology Bulletin, 21,* 538–541.

Weissman, M. M., & Paykel, E. S. (1974). *The depressed woman: A study of social relationships.* Chicago: University of Chicago Press.

Weisz, J. R. (1979). Perceived control and learned helplessness among retarded and nonretarded children: A developmental analysis. *Developmental Psychology, 15,* 311–319.

Wells, K. B., Burnam, M. A., Rogers, W., Hays, R., & Camp, P. (1992). The course of depression in adult outpatients: Results from the Medical Outcomes Study. *Archives of General Psychiatry, 49,* 788–794.

Wender, P. H., Kety, S. S., Rosenthal, D., Schulsinger, F., Ortmann, J., & Lunde, I. (1986). Psychiatric disorders in the biological and adoptive families of adopted individuals with affective disorders. *Archives of General Psychiatry, 43,* 923–929.

Wender, P. H., Rosenthal, D., Kety, S. S., Schulsinger, F., & Welner, J. (1973). Social class and psychopathology in adoptees: A natural experimental method for separating the role of genetic and experiential factors. *Archives of General Psychiatry, 28,* 318–325.

Werry, J. S. (1992). Child and adolescent (early onset) schizophrenia: A review in light of DSM-III-R. *Journal of Autism and Developmental Disorders, 22,* 601–624.

West, K. L. (1970). MMPI correlates of ulcerative colitis. *Journal of Clinical Psychology, 26,* 214–219.

Westen, D. (1989). Are "primitive" object relations really preoedipal? *American Journal of Orthopsychiatry, 59,* 331–345.

Westen, D. (1990a). Psychoanalytic approaches to personality. In L. Pervin (Ed.), *Handbook of personality theory and research.* New York: Guilford.

Westen, D. (1990b). Towards a revised theory of borderline object relations: Contributions of empirical research. *International Journal of Psychoanalysis, 71,* 661–693.

Westen, D. (1991). Cognitive-behavioral interventions in the psychoanalytic psychotherapy of borderline personality disorders. *Clinical Psychology Review, 11,* 211–230.

Westen, D., Ludolph, P., Misle, B., Ruffins, S., & Block, J. (1990). Physical and sexual abuse in adolescent girls with borderline personality disorder. *American Journal of Orthopsychiatry, 60,* 55–66.

Westermeyer, J. (1985). Psychiatric diagnosis across cultural boundaries. *American Journal of Psychiatry, 142,* 798–805.

Westermeyer, J. (1987). The psychiatrist and solvent-inhalant abuse: Recognition, assessment, and treatment. *American Journal of Psychiatry, 144,* 903–907.

Whalen, C. K. (1989). Attention deficit and hyperactivity disorders. In T. H. Ollendick & M. Hersen (Eds.), *Handbook of child psychopathology* (2nd ed.). New York: Plenum.

Whalen, C. K., & Henker, B. (1991). Therapies for hyperactive children: Comparisons, combinations, and compromises. *Journal of Consulting and Clinical Psychology, 59,* 126–137.

Whitaker, A., Johnson, J., Shaffer, D., Rapoport, J. L., Kalikow, K., Walsh, B. T., Davies, M., Braiman, S., & Dolinsky, A. (1990). Uncommon troubles in young people: Prevalence estimates of selected psychiatric disorders in a nonreferred adolescent population. *Archives of General Psychiatry, 47,* 487–496.

White, C. (1994, April 13). Former player kept secret from teammates. *USA Today,* 2c.

White, D. M., Lewy, A. J., Sack, R. L., Blood, M. L., & Wesche, D. L. (1990). Is winter depression a bipolar disorder? *Comprehensive Psychiatry, 31,* 196–204.

White, R. S. (1989). Psychotherapy with schizophrenic patients. *American Journal of Psychiatry, 146,* 1353–1354.

White, R. W. (1959). Motivation reconsidered: The concept of competence. *Psychological Review, 66,* 297–333.

White, W. J. (1992). The postschool adjustment of persons with learning disabilities: Current and future research priorities. *Journal of Learning Disabilities, 25,* 507–519.

Whiteley, J. H., Zaparniuk, J., & Asmundson, G. J. (1987). Mentally retarded adolescents' breadth of attention and short-term memory processes during matching-to-sample discriminations. *American Journal of Mental Deficiency, 92,* 207–212.

Whitlock, F. A. (1981). Some observations on the meaning of confabulation. *British Journal of Medical Psychology, 54,* 213–218.

Whorwell, P. J., Prior, A., & Faragher, E. B. (1984). Controlled trial of hypnotherapy in the treatment of severe refractory irritable bowel syndrome. *Lancet, 3,* 1232–1234.

Widiger, T. A., & Frances, A. J. (1986). Diagnostic criteria for borderline and schizotypal personality disorders. *Journal of Abnormal Psychology, 95,* 43–51.

Widiger, T. A., & Frances, A. J. (1987). Interviews and inventories for the measurement of personality disorders. *Clinical Psychology Review, 7,* 49–75.

Widiger, T. A., & Shea, T. (1991). Differentiation of Axis I and Axis II disorders. *Journal of Abnormal Psychology, 100,* 399–406.

Widiger, T. A., & Trull, T. J. (1992). Personality and psychopathology: An application of the five-factor model. *Journal of Personality, 60,* 363–393.

Widmayer, S. M., & Field, T. M. (1981). Effects of Brazelton demonstrations for mothers on the development of preterm infants. *Pediatrics, 67,* 711–714.

Wielandt, H., & Hansen, U. M. (1989). Sexual behavior, contraception, and unintended pregnancy among young females. *Acta Obstetricia et Gynecologica Scandinavica, 68,* 255–259.

Wierzbicki, M. (1987). Similarity of monozygotic and dizygotic child twins in level and ability of subclinically depressed mood. *American Journal of Orthopsychiatry, 57,* 33–40.

Wikler, A. (1973). Dynamics of drug dependence: Implications of a conditioning theory for research and treatment. In S. Fisher & A. M. Freedman (Eds.), *Opiate addiction: Origins and treatment.* Washington, DC: Winston.

Wilkinson, P. (1991, October 3). Who killed Pee-wee? *Rolling Stone,* 36–42, 140.

Wille, R. (1981). Ten year follow-up of a representative sample of London heroin addicts: Clinic attendance, abstinence, and mortality. *British Journal of Addiction, 76,* 259–266.

Willi, J., & Grossman, S. (1983). Epidemiology of anorexia nervosa in a defined region. *American Journal of Psychiatry, 140,* 564–567.

Williams, J. B., Gibbon, M., First, M. B., Spitzer, R. L., Davies, M., Borus, J., Howes, M. J., Kane, J., Pope, H. G., Rounsaville, B. J., & Wittchen, H. U. (1992). The Structured Clinical Interview for DSM-III-R (SCID): II. Multisite test-retest reliability. *Archives of General Psychiatry, 49,* 630–636.

Williams, J. B., & Spitzer, R. L. (1983). The issue of sex bias in DSM-III: A critique of "A woman's view of DSM-III" by Marcie Kaplan. *American Psychologist, 38,* 793–798.

Williamson, D. F. (1993). Descriptive epidemiology of body weight and weight change in U.S. adults. *Annals of Internal Medicine, 119,* 646–649.

Willwerth, J. (1994, April 25). The man from outer space. *Time,* 74–75.

Wilms, G., Van Ongeval, C., Baert, A. L., Claus, A., Bollen, J., De Cuyper, H., Eneman, M., Malfroid, M., Peuskens, J., & Heylen, S. (1992). Ventricular enlargement, clinical correlates, and treatment outcome in chronic schizophrenic inpatients. *Acta Psychiatrica Scandinavica, 85,* 306–312.

Wilson, C. L., & Sindelar, P. T. (1991). Direct instruction in math word problems: Students with learning disabilities. *Exceptional Children, 57,* 512–519.

Wilson, G. T., & Abrams, D. (1977). Effects of alcohol on social anxiety and physiological arousal: Cognitive versus pharmacological processes. *Cognitive Therapy and Research, 1,* 195–210.

Wilson, G. T., & Lawson, D. M. (1976). Expectancies, alcohol, and sexual arousal in male social drinkers. *Journal of Abnormal Psychology, 87,* 358–367.

Wilson, M. (1993). DSM-III and the transformation of American psychiatry: A history. *American Journal of Psychiatry, 150,* 399–410.

Wilson, W. H., Diamond, R. J., & Factor, R. M. (1990). Group treatment for individuals with schizophrenia. *Community Mental Health Journal, 26,* 361–372.

Wincze, J. P. (1989). Assessment and treatment of atypical sexual behavior. In S. R. Leiblum & R. C. Rosen (Eds.), *Principles and practice of sex therapy: Update for the 1990s.* New York: Guilford.

Windholz, G. (1990). Pavlov, psychoanalysis, and neuroses. *Pavlovian Journal of Biological Sciences, 25,* 48–53.

Winegar, N. (1993). Managed mental health care: Implications for administrators and managers of community-based agencies. *Families in Society, 74,* 171–177.

Winett, R. A., King, A. C., & Altman, D. G. (1989). *Health psychology and public health: An integrative approach.* Elmsford, NY: Pergamon.

Wing, R. R. (1992). Behavioral treatments of severe obesity. *American Journal of Clinical Nutrition, 55,* 545–551.

Winokur, G. (1990). The concept of secondary depression and its relationship to comorbidity. *Psychiatric Clinics of North America, 13,* 567–583.

Wise, T. N. (1985). Fetishism—Etiology and treatment: A review from multiple perspectives. *Comprehensive Psychiatry, 26,* 249–257.

Witkin, M. J. (1981). *Provisional patient movement and selective administrative data, state and county mental hospitals, by state: United States, 1977.* Washington, DC: NIMH.

Wittgenstein, L. (1953). *Philosophical investigations.* New York: Macmillan.

Wolf, L., & Goldberg, B. (1986). Autistic children grow up: An eight to twenty-four year follow-up study. *Canadian Journal of Psychiatry, 31,* 550–556.

Wolf, N. (1991). *The beauty myth.* New York: Morrow.

Wolpe, J. (1958). *Psychotherapy by reciprocal inhibition.* Stanford, CA: Stanford University Press.

Woodrow, K. M. (1974). Gilles de la Tourette's disease—A review. *American Journal of Psychiatry, 131,* 1000–1003.

Woodruff-Pak, D. (1988). *Psychology and aging.* Englewood Cliffs, NJ: Prentice-Hall.

Woods, S. W., & Charney, D. S. (1988). Applications of the pharmacologic challenge strategy in panic disorders research. *Journal of Anxiety Disorders, 2,* 31–49.

Woodward, B. (1985). *Wired: The short life and fast times of John Belushi.* New York: Pocket Books.

Woody, G. E., McLellan, A. T., Luborsky, L., & O'Brien, C. P. (1987). Twelve-month follow-up of psychotherapy for opiate dependence. *American Journal of Psychiatry, 144,* 590–596.

World Health Organization. (1990). *International classification of diseases and related health problems* (10th rev.). Geneva: Author.

Wright-Strawderman, C., & Watson, B. L. (1992). The prevalence of depressive symptoms in children with learning disabilities. *Journal of Learning Disabilities, 25,* 258–264.

Wrobel, J. (1990). *Language and schizophrenia.* Philadelphia: Benjamins.

Wyatt, G. E., Peters, S. D., & Guthrie, D. (1988a). Kinsey revisited, Part I: Comparisons of the sexual socialization and sexual behavior of white women over 33 years. *Archives of Sexual Behavior, 17,* 201–239.

Wyatt, G. E., Peters, S. D., & Guthrie, D. (1988b). Kinsey revisited, Part II: Comparisons of the sexual socialization and sexual behavior of black women over 33 years. *Archives of Sexual Behavior, 17,* 289–332.

Wyatt, R. J., Alexander, R. C., Egan, M. F., & Kirch, D. G. (1988). Schizophrenia, just the facts: What do we know, how well do we know it? *Schizophrenia Research, 1,* 3–18.

Wyckoff, J. (1975). *Franz Anton Mesmer: Between god and devil.* Englewood Cliffs, NJ: Prentice-Hall.

Wykoff, R. F. (1987). Delusions of parasitosis: A review. *Reviews of Infectious Diseases, 9,* 433–437.

Yalom, I. D. (1970). *The theory and practice of group psychotherapy.* New York: Basic Books.

Yalom, I. D. (1975). *The theory and practice of group psychotherapy* (2nd ed.). New York: Basic Books.

Yalom, I. D. (1985). *The theory and practice of group psychotherapy* (3rd ed.). New York: Basic Books.

Yates, A. (1987). Should young children testify in cases of sexual abuse? *American Journal of Psychiatry, 144,* 476–480.

Yeung, P. P., & Greenwald, S. (1992). Jewish Americans and mental health: Results of the NIMH Epidemiologic Catchment Area Study. *Social Psychiatry and Psychiatric Epidemiology, 27,* 292–297.

Yoken, C., & Berman, J. S. (1987). Third-party payment and the outcome of psychotherapy. *Journal of Consulting and Clinical Psychology, 55,* 571–576.

Young, M. B., & Erickson, C. A. (1988). Cultural impediments to recovery: PTSD in contemporary America. *Journal of Traumatic Stress Studies, 43,* 431–443.

Young T. J. (1991). Native American drinking: A neglected subject of study and research. *Journal of Drug Education, 21,* 65–72.

Yu, J., & Williford, W. R. (1992). The age of alcohol onset and alcohol, cigarette, and marijuana use patterns: An analysis of drug use progression of young adults in New York State. *International Journal of the Addictions, 27,* 1313–1323.

Zahniser, J. H., Coursey, R. D., & Hershberger, K. (1991). Individual psychotherapy with schizophrenic outpatients in the public mental health system. *Hospital and Community Psychiatry, 42,* 906–913.

Zajonc, R. B. (1984). On the primacy of affect. *American Psychologist, 39,* 117–123.

Zamansky, H. S., & Bartis, S. P. (1984). Hypnosis as dissociation: Methodological considerations and preliminary findings. *American Journal of Clinical Hypnosis, 26,* 246–251.

Zanarini, M. C., Gunderson, J. G., Frankenburg, F. R., & Chauncey, D. L. (1990). Discriminating borderline personality disorder from other Axis II disorders. *American Journal of Psychiatry, 147,* 161–167.

Zarb, J. M. (1992). *Cognitive-behavioral assessment and therapy with adolescents.* New York: Brunner/Mazel.

Zborowski, M. (1969). *People in pain.* San Francisco: Jossey-Bass.

Zencius, A., Wesolowski, M. D., & Burke, W. H. (1990). A comparison of four memory strategies with traumatically brain-injured clients. *Brain Injury, 4,* 33–38.

Zerbe, K. J. (1990). Through the storm: Psychoanalytic theory in the psychotherapy of the anxiety disorders. *Bulletin of the Menninger Clinic, 54,* 171–183.

Zigler, E. F. (1975). Has it really been demonstrated that compensatory education is without value? *American Psychologist, 30,* 935–937.

Zigler, E. F. (1985). Assessing Head Start at 20: An invited commentary. *American Journal of Orthopsychiatry, 55,* 603–609.

Zigler, E. F., & Frank, M. (Eds.). (1988). *The parental leave crisis.* New Haven, CT: Yale University Press.

Zigler, E. F., Taussig, C., & Black, K. (1992). Early childhood intervention: A promising preventative for juvenile delinquency. *American Psychologist, 47,* 997–1006.

Zigler, E. F., & Weikart, D. P. (1993). "Were children randomly assigned in the Perry Preschool Project?": Reply. *American Psychologist, 48,* 915–916.

Zilbergeld, B. (1992). *The new male sexuality.* New York: Bantam.

Zilboorg, G., & Henry, G. W. (1941). *A history of medical psychology.* New York: Norton.

Zimmerman, I. L., & Woo-Sam, J. M. (1973). *Clinical interpretation of the Wechsler Adult Intelligence Scale.* New York: Grune & Stratton.

Zimmerman, M. (1986). Melancholic subtyping: A qualitative or quantitative distinction? *American Journal of Psychiatry, 143,* 98–100.

Zimmerman, M. (1988). Why are we rushing to publish DSM-IV? *Archives of General Psychiatry, 45,* 1135–1138.

Zimmerman, M., & Coryell, W. H. (1989). DSM-III personality disorder diagnoses in a nonpatient sample: Demographic correlates and comorbidity. *Archives of General Psychiatry, 46,* 682–689.

Zimmerman, M., & Coryell, W. H. (1990). DSM-III personality disorder dimensions. *Journal of Nervous and Mental Disease, 178,* 686–692.

Zimmerman, M., Jampala, V. C., Sierles, F. S., & Taylor, M. A. (1991). DSM-IV: A nosology sold before its time? *American Journal of Psychiatry, 148,* 463–467.

Zonderman, A. B., Costa, P. T., & McCrae, R. R. (1989). Depression as a risk factor for cancer morbidity and mortality in a nationally representative sample. *JAMA, 262,* 1191–1195.

Zucker, R. A. (1987). The four alcoholisms: A developmental account of the etiologic process. In P. C. Rivers (Ed.), *Nebraska symposium on motivation* (Vol. 34). Lincoln: University of Nebraska Press.

Zucker, R. A., & Gomberg, E. S. L. (1986). Etiology of alcoholism reconsidered: The case for a biopsychosocial process. *American Psychologist, 41,* 783–805.

Zuckerman, M. (1979). *Sensation seeking: Beyond the optimal level of arousal.* New York: Wiley.

Zuckerman, M. (1990). Some dubious premises in research and theory on racial differences. *American Psychologist, 45,* 1297–1303.

Zuk, G. H. (1971). *Family therapy: A triadic-based approach.* New York: Behavioral Publications.

Zullow, H. M. (1984). *The interaction of rumination and explanatory style in depression.* Unpublished master's thesis, University of Pennsylvania, Philadelphia.

Zung, W. W., MacDonald, J., & Zung, E. M. (1988). Prevalence of clinically significant depressive symptoms in black and white patients in family practice settings. *American Journal of Psychiatry, 145,* 882–883.

CREDITS AND ACKNOWLEDGMENTS

LITERARY ACKNOWLEDGMENTS

Alcoholics Anonymous The twelve steps are reprinted with permission of Alcoholics Anonymous World Services, Inc. Permission to reprint does not mean that AA has reviewed or approved the contents of this publication, nor that AA agrees with the views expressed herein. AA is a program of recovery from alcoholism *only*—use of the Twelve Steps in connection with programs and activities which are patterned after AA, but which address other problems, does not imply otherwise.

American Psychiatric Association DSM-III-R and DSM-IV materials reprinted courtesy of the American Psychiatric Association.

G. Mellsop, F. Varghese, S. Joshua, & A. Hicks. (1982). The reliability of Axis II of DSM-III. *American Journal of Psychiatry, 139*, 1360–1361. Copyright 1982 by the American Psychiatric Association. Reprinted by permission.

American Psychological Association American Psychological Association. (1992). Ethical principles of psychologists and code of conduct. *American Psychologist, 47*, 1597–1611. Copyright 1992 by the American Psychological Association. Adapted by permission.

Office of Ethnic Minority Affairs. (1993). Guidelines for the providers of psychological services to ethnic, linguistic, and culturally diverse populations. *American Psychologist, 48*, 45–48. Copyright 1993 by the American Psychological Association. Adapted by permission.

C. Peterson, M. E. P. Seligman, & G. E. Vaillant. (1988). Pessimistic explanatory style is a risk factor for physical illness: A thirty-five year longitudinal study. *Journal of Personality and Social Psychology, 55*, 23–27. Copyright 1988 by the American Psychological Association. Reprinted by permission.

W. H. Freeman and Company From *Schizophrenia Genesis: The Origins of Madness* by Irving I. Gottesman. Copyright © 1991 by Irving I. Gottesman. Reprinted with permission of W. H. Freeman and Company.

PHOTO CREDITS

Chapter 1
3 Bob Daemmrich/Image Works
4 Mark Richards/PhotoEdit
6 David Young-Wolff/PhotoEdit
7 Felicia Martinez/PhotoEdit
10 Reuters/Bettmann
11 W. Resin Malecki/PhotoEdit
14 Rare Book and Manuscripts Division, The New York Public Library, Astor, Lenox and Tilden Foundations
15 Stock Montage
17 Peter Menzel/Stock, Boston
18 (top)   The Bettmann Archive
18 (bottom)   Culver Pictures
20 Culver Pictures
22 Prints and Photographs Collection, History of Medicine Division, National Library of Medicine

24 Culver Pictures
25 Culver Pictures
26 Culver Pictures
28 (top)   Culver Pictures
28 (bottom)   The Bettmann Archive
29 (top)   Stock Montage
29 (bottom)   The Bettmann Archive

Chapter 2
35 Culver Pictures
37 Deni McIntyre/Photo Researchers
38 SmithKline Beecham
40 (top)   Detroit Free Press
40 (bottom)   The Bettmann Archive
49 (left)   Merritt Vincent/PhotoEdit
49 (right)   D. & I. MacDonald/Picture Cube
54 (bottom)   Will & Deni McIntyre/Photo Researchers
55 Stephen Collins/Photo Researchers
58 Bob Daemmrich/Stock, Boston
59 Bob Daemmrich/Image Works
60 Brian Seed/Tony Stone Images
62 National Institutes of Health/Science Source/Photo Researchers
63 Bob Daemmrich/Stock, Boston

Chapter 3
71 Paul Meredith/Tony Stone Images
76 (top)   Bernsau/Image Works
76 (bottom)   Lea Merrim/Monkmeyer
78 R. Sidney/Image Works
79 The Bettmann Archive
84 The Bettmann Archive
85 Skjold/PhotoEdit
87 Ruszniewski, Vandystadt/Photo Researchers
90 John Ficara/Woodfin Camp & Associates
93 National Mental Health Association
94 The Bettmann Archive

Chapter 4
102 Bob Daemmrich/Tony Stone Images
104 Reuters/Bettmann Newsphotos
105 J. Sohm/Image Works
106 Courtauld Institute Galleries, London
113 Bill Pierce/Rainbow
115 Reproduced from "Lectures on the Diseases of the Nervous System" by J. M. Charcot, 1879
120 Billy Barnes/Stock, Boston

Chapter 5
125 The Bettmann Archive
127 Bob Daemmrich/Stock, Boston
128 Studio Koppermann
129 UPI/Bettmann Newsphotos
130 UPI/Bettmann Newsphotos
131 (top)   Bob Daemmrich/Image Works
131 (bottom)   Tony Freeman/PhotoEdit
132 David Wells/Image Works
133 Robert Brenner/PhotoEdit

NAME INDEX

Martinez, A. P., 260
Martinez, C., 16
Martinez, M., 283
Martins, C., 370
Marttila, R. J., 241
Marzuk, P. M., 260
Masek, B. J., 187
Maser, J. D., 43, 113, 256
Masling, J. M., 78
Maslow, A. H., 83–84
Mason, D. W., 176
Mason, J. W., 314
Masserman, J. H., 42
Masson, J. M., 245, 326
Masters, J. C., 197, 212–213
Masters, W. H., 324, 328, 331–334, 336,
        338–339, 344, 346, 382
Masterson, C. C., 388
Mastropieri, M., 420
Matarazzo, J. D., 51, 59
Mate-Kole, C., 349
Mathews, A., 217, 236
Mathias, S. A., 331
Mathison, D., 454
Matson, J. L., 419
Matsunaga, H., 369
Matthews, B., 452
Matthews, K. A., 308
Matthysse, S., 71
Mattick, R. P., 208, 219
Maurer, K., 365
Mavissakalian, M., 199, 206, 219
Mayer, J., 432, 434
Mayeux, R., 175
Mayman, M., 8
Maynard, H., 95
Mayo, J. A., 284
Mays, K., 448
Mays, V. M., 331
McAllister, T. W., 179
McAvoy, M., 130
McBride, D. C., 147
McCann, I. L., 271
McCarthy, B. W., 339
McCarthy, M., 47, 431
McCarthy, P. R., 202, 217
McCauley, C., 418–419
McClelland, D. C., 55
McClelland, J. L., 248
McConaghy, N., 348
McCoy, C. B., 147
McCrady, B. S., 142
McCrae, R. R., 207, 311
McCranie, E. W., 204
McCreadie, R. G., 371
McDonough, E. T., 153
McDowell, C. J., 55
McEvoy, L., 203
McFadden, J., 131
McFarlane, W. R., 377
McGarry, A. L., 461
McGee, R., 426
McGillivray, B. C., 368
McGlashan, T. H., 359–361, 388
McGlynn, S. M., 179
McGonagle, K. A., 6, 52

McGough, L. S., 454
McGreevy, M. A., 460
McGue, M., 139, 420
McGuffin, P., 268, 283, 402
McGuiness, D., 421
McGuinness, B., 436
McHugh, P. R., 382
McKeen, J., 86
McKenna, J. P., 152
McKenzie, Sir J., 316
McKinley, J. C., 56
McKinney, W. T., 113, 257
McKnew, D. H., 263, 411
McLellan, A. T., 121, 150
McLeod, Jane D., 109, 218, 272
McLeod, J. G., 180, 205
McLin, W. M., 185
McManus, I. C., 368
McNall, H. M., 274
McNally, R. J., 206, 215, 236, 346
McNeal, E. T., 71
McNiel, D. E., 452
McPherson, L. M., 392
Mead, M., 25
Mednick, S., 139, 390
Mee, C. L., 14
Meehl, P. E., 56, 388
Mehegan, J. E., 187
Mehler, J. A., 337
Mehlum, L., 388
Meichenbaum, D., 26, 83
Meinecke, C. F., 343
Meisler, A. W., 336
Mejo, S. L., 204
Melamed, E., 176
Melella, J. T., 343
Melin, L., 185, 317
Mellon, C. D., 283
Mellon, J., 121
Mellsop, G., 42, 47, 382, 388
Melman, A., 337
Meltzer, H. Y., 362, 376–377
Melzack, R., 234
Mendels, J., 49
Mendelson, M., 42, 272
Mendes de Leon, C. F., 309
Menghini, P., 343
Menninger, K., 34
Merckelbach, H., 213
Merikangas, J. R., 186
Merikangas, K. R., 186, 198, 283, 391
Merkel, W. T., 89, 346
Merluzzi, T. V., 60
Merrill, J., 261
Merry, J., 141
Merry, P., 173
Merskey, H., 224
Mervis, C. B., 9
Mesmer, F. A., 21–23, 294
Messerschmidt, J., 219
Mesulam, M. M., 205
Metalsky, G. I., 48
Metter, E. J., 241
Metz, M. E., 322, 338–339
Meyer, B., 314
Meyer, D., 23

Meyer, J. K., 349
Meyers, D. A., 283
Mezzich, A. C., 43
Mezzich, J., 10, 43, 48, 53
Michelson, L., 216
Mikhail, A. R., 46
Miklowitz, D. J., 89, 284
Miller, A., 392
Miller, E. N., 168
Miller, H. L., 262
Miller, I. W., 263
Miller, J. W., 241
Miller, M. J., 376
Miller, Neal E., 83
Miller, Norman S., 208
Miller, S. D., 243
Miller, Thomas I., 118–119
Miller, Todd Q., 308
Miller, W. R., 133, 145
Millichap, J. G., 187
Milligan, B., 456
Millikan, C. H., 241
Millon, R., 385, 396, 398–399
Millon, T., 42, 382, 384–385, 390, 393–
        394, 396–401, 403–404
Mills, H., 28
Mills, M. J., 453
Milner, G., 261
Milner, P., 267
Mindus, P., 375
Mineka, S., 211, 300
Minuchin, S., 87, 436
Miranda, J., 329
Mirin, S. M., 70
Mirsky, A. F., 354, 368
Mischel, W., 81, 278
Misle, B., 393
Mitchell, S. A., 79, 393
Mitrushina, M., 168
M'Naghten, D., 457–458
Mnookin, R. H., 448
Mock, J. E., 42
Moergen, S. A., 346
Moldin, S. O., 268
Molgaard, C. A., 167
Mollard, E., 216
Mollica, R. F., 202
Monahan, D. J., 95
Monahan, J., 448–449, 452
Monahan, L. H., 42
Money, J., 325, 331–332, 339, 342–343,
        347
Moniz, E., 374
Monroe, M., 392
Monroe, S. M., 92, 257–258, 279
Montague, M., 422
Monteiro, W. O., 201
Montero, I., 370
Montorsi, F., 337
Mook, D. G., 11
Mook, J., 273
Moon, S. L., 208
Moore, A. D., 179
Moorey, S., 312
Moos, R. H., 109, 143, 257
Mora, G., 21, 27, 235